Maudsley and Burn's Land Law: Cases and Materials

D0718810

Maudsley and Burn's

Land Law:

Cases and Materials

by E. H. Burn
B.C.L., M.A.
Barrister and Honorary Bencher of Lincoln's Inn;
Professor of Law in the City University;
Emeritus Student of Christ Church, Oxford

Eighth Edition

OXFORD
UNIVERSITY PRESS

OXFORD
UNIVERSITY PRESS

Great Clarendon Street, Oxford OX2 6DP

Oxford University Press is a department of the University of Oxford.
It furthers the University's objective of excellence in research, scholarship,
and education by publishing worldwide in

Oxford New York

Auckland Bangkok Buenos Aires Cape Town Chennai
Dar es Salaam Delhi Hong Kong Istanbul Karachi Kolkata
Kuala Lumpur Madrid Melbourne Mexico City Mumbai Nairobi
São Paulo Shanghai Taipei Tokyo Toronto

Oxford is a registered trade mark of Oxford University Press
in the UK and in certain other countries

Published in the United States
by Oxford University Press Inc., New York

© Oxford University Press 2004

British Library Cataloguing in Publication Data
Data available

Library of Congress Cataloging in Publication Data
Data available

ISBN 0 406 97137 4

10 9 8 7 6 5 4 3 2 1

Typeset in New Baskerville
by Doyle & Co, Colchester

Printed in Great Britain
on acid-free paper by
The Bath Press, Bath

Preface to the Eighth Edition

On 13 October 2003 the Land Registration Act 2002 and the Land Registration Rules 2003 came into force, and superseded the Land Registration Act and Rules of 1925. This has necessitated the rewriting of chapter 2 on Registered Land and the more detailed integration of the new legislation into each chapter of this edition. English land law has been very fortunate in three of those responsible for its legislative development and for the commentaries on it. They have in each of three centuries been one and the same person. In the nineteenth century Edward Wolstenholme for the Conveyancing Act of 1881 and the Settled Land Act of 1882; in the twentieth Sir Benjamin Cherry for the 1925 legislation; and in the twenty-first Charles Harpum for the Land Registration Act 2002.

Since the last edition there have been significant developments in judge-made law. Extracts from twenty-five cases have been added in this new edition. The House of Lords has refined in detail the rule in *Barclays Bank plc v O'Brien* in mortgages, and the concept of adverse possession in limitation of actions; developed the contractual nature of a lease; and explained the characteristics of a tenancy at will and the meaning of 'as of right' in the acquisition of an easement by prescription.

The Court of Appeal has applied the law of proprietary estoppel and constructive trusts where the parties have failed to satisfy the formalities of section 2 of the Law of Property (Miscellaneous) Provisions Act 1989; and four times considered the establishment of the equity in proprietary estoppel and the form of relief; followed *Re Ellenborough Park* where a similar easement was created by prescription; distinguished *Phipps v Pears* where the adjacent tenements were not bonded together; twice continued the disapproval, begun by Sir Frederick Pollock in 1903, of the doctrine of a clog on the equity of redemption; and revisited sections 78 and 79 of the Law of Property Act 1925 (the important decision of *Great Nicholson (South) Ltd v McAllister* arrived too late for substantial inclusion in the text and appears in various footnotes only).

There have also been important decisions at first instance; on the relationship between previous cases on section 30 of the Law of Property Act 1925 and sections 14 and 15 of the Trusts of Land and Appointment of Trustees Act 1996; on the rare creation of an easement by reservation based on the common intention of the parties; on the effect of an increase in user of an easement of drainage on the dominant tenement created by prescription; on the duties of a mortgagee and a receiver on the sale of mortgaged property; and on the tripartite relationship between landlord, tenant and squatter in the context of limitation of actions in registered land.

The activities of the Law Commission continue unabated. In addition to the Consultative Document and Report on Land Registration for the Twenty-First Century (both Joint Reports with Her Majesty's Land Registry), Reports have been published on Renting Homes, and Towards a Compulsory Purchase Code; and a Consultation Paper on Termination of Tenancies for Tenant Default. The Land Registry has also published a Consultation Paper on E-Conveyancing. A Consultation Paper is promised for later in 2004 on Easements and Analogous Rights and Land Obligations.

I would particularly like to thank Marilyn Kennedy-McGregor, Barrister of Gray's Inn and Lincoln's Inn, and John Cartwright, Solicitor and Student of Christ Church, Oxford (who revised the Index) for their valuable comments and advice.

Finally, I wish to thank the publishers for undertaking the compilation of the Tables of Cases, Statutes and Statutory Instruments, and for their ready and expert help at all times. In particular, I would like to thank Isabel Isaacson, my commissioning editor at LexisNexis UK, who has encouraged me over so many years, and Juliet and Jonathan Doyle for master-minding the production of this edition.

This edition purports to state the law as it was on 1 July 2004, but more recent developments have been incorporated where space permitted.

2 September 2004   E.H.B.

Contents

List of Abbreviations

Statutes and Rules

AEA	Administration of Estates Act
AJA	Administration of Justice Act
CTTA	Capital Transfer Tax Act
FA	Finance Act
IHTA	Inheritance Tax Act
LCA	Land Charges Act
LLCA	Local Land Charges Act
LPA	Law of Property Act
LP(A)A	Law of Property (Amendment) Act
LRA	Land Registration Act
LRR	Land Registration Rule
MHA	Matrimonial Homes Act
PAA	Perpetuities & Accumulations Act
SI	Statutory Instrument
SLA	Settled Land Act
TA	Trustee Act
TCPA	Town and Country Planning Act
TLATA	Trusts of Land and Appointment of Trustees Act

Journals

Anglo-Am	Anglo-American Law Review
ASCL	Annual Survey of Commonwealth Law
Aust LJ	Australian Law Journal
CLJ	Cambridge Law Journal
CLP	Current Legal Problems
CLY	Current Law Year Book
Conv	Conveyancer
Conv (NS)	Conveyancer (New Series)
Conv Prec	Precedents for the Conveyancer
Cornell LQ	Cornell Law Quarterly
EG	Estates Gazette
HLR	Harvard Law Review
JPL	Journal of Planning and Property Law
	Journal of Planning and Environmental Law
L&TR	Landlord and Tenant Review
LJ News	Law Journal Newspaper
LQR	Law Quarterly Review
LS	Legal Studies
LSG	Law Society's Gazette
LT	Law Times
Mich LR	Michigan Law Review
MLR	Modern Law Review
NILQ	Northern Ireland Law Quarterly
NLJ	New Law Journal
OJLS	Oxford Journal of Legal Studies
SJ	Solicitor's Journal
U of WALR	University of Western Australia Law Review
Yale LJ	Yale Law Journal

Books

C & B	Cheshire and Burn, The Modern Law of Real Property (16th edn, 2000)
Emmet	Emmet and Farrand on Title
Gale	Gale on Easements (17th edn, 1997)
Gray	Elements of Land Law (3rd edn, 2001)
H & B	Harpum and Bignell, Registered Land – The New Law. A Guide to the Land Registration Act 2002
H & M	Hanbury and Martin, Modern Equity (16th edn, 2001)
Holdsworth	A History of English Law
M & B	Maudsley and Burn, Trusts and Trustees: Cases and Materials (6th edn, 2002)
M & W	Megarry and Wade, The Law of Real Property (6th edn, 2000)
MM	Megary, Manual of the Law of Real Property (8th edn, 2002)
R & R	Ruoff and Roper, The Law and Practice of Registered Conveyancing (1991 edn) looseleaf, (2004 edn) looseleaf
	Annotated Land Registration Act 2002
Smith	Property Law (2nd edn, 2003)
Snell	Equity (30th edn, 2000)
W & C	Wolstenholme and Cherry, Conveyancing Statutes (13th edn, 1972)
W & H	Whitehouse and Hassall, Trusts of Land, Trustee Delegation and the Trustee Act 2000: A Practical Guide (2nd edn, 2001)

Acknowledgments

The permissions which were granted to reproduce extracts from the following publications are gratefully acknowledged.

Law Reports
All England Reports
Commonwealth Law Reports
Estates Gazette Case Summaries
Estates Gazette Law Reports
Family Law Reports
Incorporated Council of Law Reporting
Property and Compensation Reports
Times Law Reports

Textbooks and Treatises
Abbey and Richards, *Blackstone's Guide to the Land Registration Act 2002* (2002, Oxford University Press).
Cheshire and Burn, *The Modern Law of Real Property* (16th edn, 2002, LexisNexis UK)
Gale on Easements (17th edn 1997, Sweet & Maxwell).
Getzler, ed., *Rationalizing Property, Equity and Trusts: Essays in Honour of Edward Burn* (2003, LexisNexis UK).
Hanbury and Martin, *Modern Equity* (16th edn, 2001, Sweet & Maxwell).
Harpum and Bignell, *Registered Land: The New Law. A Guide to the Land Registration Act* (2002, Jordans).
Maitland, *Lectures on Equity* (revised 1936, Cambridge University Press).
Maudsley, *The Modern Rule of Perpetuities* (1979, Butterworths).
Maudsley and Burn, *Trusts and Trustees: Cases and Materials* (8th edn, 2004, LexisNexis UK).
Megarry and Wade, *The Law of Real Property* (6th edn, 2000, Sweet & Maxwell).
Morris and Leach, *The Rule Against Perpetuities* (2nd edn 1962, Sweet & Maxwell)
Preston and Newsom, *Restrictive Covenants Affecting Freehold Land* (9th edn, 1998, Sweet & Maxwell).
Snell's Equity (30th edn, 2000, Sweet & Maxwell)
Tee, ed., *Land Law Issues, Debates, Policy* (2002, Willan Publishing).
Whitehouse and Hassall, *Trusts of Land, Trustee Delegation and the Trustee Act* (2nd edn, 2001, LexisNexis UK).

Journals
Cambridge Law Journal
Conveyancer and Property Lawyer
Law Quarterly Review
Modern Law Review
New Law Journal
Oxford Journal of Legal Studies
Solicitors Journal

Reports
Central Statistical Office Social Trends
Director General of Fair Trading
Law Commission Consultation Documents
Law Commission Reports
Law Reform Committee Reports

Table of Statutes

Page references printed in **bold** type indicate where the Act is set out in part or in full.

Table of Statutory Instruments

Page references printed in **bold** type indicate where the Statutory Instrument is set out in part or in full.

Table of Cases

Page references printed in **bold** type indicate where the case is set out in part or in full.

A

B

M

Q

R

S

W

Part One. Basic Concepts

1. Introductory Topics

I. Estates and Interests in Land

A. Introduction

I. FREEHOLD AND LEASEHOLD ESTATES

The theory of the common law is that all land is held of the King who is the supreme feudal lord. Subjects may hold directly of the King or of other subjects superior to themselves. Those who hold directly of the King are tenants in chief. Intermediate holders between the King and the tenants in actual possession are mesne lords.[1]

A holder of land is entitled to a number of legal rights in respect of his land-holding, and these legal rights are 'crystallised into one thing'.[2] This is the tenant's 'estate'. To ascertain his rights, it is necessary to decide what estate he owns and to know what rights and duties the law attaches to that type of estate.

Freehold estates, i.e. the estates held by freehold tenure, are those which were in use in the feudal system. In medieval times that system was the basis of the social, military and economic structure of the state; and the holding of freehold land was itself the basis of social position, wealth and power.[3] It was essential for the security of the state and of the social structure that the ownership of freehold estates should be protected; and it is not surprising that the land law was the first of the fields of private law to be undertaken by the King's Court.[4]

The freehold estates are the fee simple, fee tail, life estate and estate pur autre vie. They are freehold because they were recognised by the feudal order, because persons holding such estates in possession were recognised as standing upon a rung in the feudal ladder, and because the remedies available in the King's Court were available to the owner of such an estate and gave a claimant specific recovery. Such estates are 'real property' or 'realty', and are contrasted with the terms of years, a leasehold estate, whose owners were never on the feudal ladder; they could not protect themselves by the same actions as the freeholder; their estate as personal property, or 'personalty', passed on intestacy with chattels. A convenient way of distinguishing between freeholds and leaseholds is to note that freeholds are always of indefinite duration, leaseholds for a fixed period or such as can be made certain. But this is just a label; it does not help to understand the basic gulf between the two, which was so obvious to the medieval lawyer.

Something will be said here of the freehold estates; leaseholds will be considered in a later chapter. But a further sub-division must be introduced here because of the treatment of estates by the 1925 legislation. This is the distinction between legal estates and equitable interests. Pursuant to the Legislature's insistence upon the legal estate being the basis of conveyancing with beneficial interests kept off the title, the 1925 legislation permits two estates only to exist as legal estates, one freehold and one leasehold, all other interests being capable of existing in equity only.

II. CONVEYANCING

A knowledge of the estates and interests recognised at law and in equity is necessary to an understanding of conveyancing; that is, the practice of creating and transferring estates and interests in land. The owner of an estate may transfer

---

[1]   Under LRA 2002, s. 79 Her Majesty may grant an estate in fee simple absolute in possession out of demesne land to Herself, thus enabling such land to be registered: p. 114, post. For the abolition of feudal tenure in Scotland, see Abolition of Feudal Tenures etc (Scotland) Act 2000, which comes into force on 28 November 2004.

[2]   Hargreaves, *Introduction to Land Law* (4th edn, 1963), p. 46.

[3]   In Victorian times, see the conversation between Major Grantly and his father, Archdeacon Grantly, in the *Last Chronicle of Barset*, by Anthony Trollope (1867), chapter 58: 'I wonder people are so fond of land', said the Major. 'It is a comfortable feeling to know that you stand on your own ground. Land is about the only thing that can't fly away. And then, you see, land gives so much more than the rent. It gives position and influence and political power.'

[4]   Maitland, *Forms of Action at Common Law*, pp. 20, et seq.

it to another, as on the sale of a house, or create a series of smaller interests out of it, as on the creation of a lease; or create other rights which are recognised at law or in equity, but which are not estates in land, such as a licence or a restrictive covenant. Details of the practice of conveyancing are beyond our present scope; but it is material to say here that there are two quite separate and distinctive methods of conveyancing in operation in England and Wales at the present day; that relating to unregistered land and that relating to registered land. The former is the development of techniques which reach back to medieval times. The system in essence is one whereby the estate owner proves his title to land by showing from deeds and documents in his possession that he derives his title lawfully from some person or persons who have been in peaceful possession for a long period of time. In the nature of things, the title to his estate can never be proved absolutely, for there may have been an interference with the rights of the true owner many years back. However, with the assistance of the Limitation Acts,[5] proof of title during the last fifteen years is, for practical purposes, sufficient; and a purchaser is required to trace the title back to a good root of title at least fifteen years old.[6] On completion of the purchase, the deeds are handed over to the purchaser, and he will make title in a similar manner when he decides to sell.

A much more satisfactory system of proof of title is that of registration of the title in a central registry. The change involves the recording of all interests in land which need to be placed on the register. In England and Wales, a system of registration of title, introduced in 1862,[7] was superseded by more comprehensive legislation in 1925,[8] which was substantially revised by the Land Registration Act 2002. The compulsory change to the registered system is triggered by a number of specified events, for example, where unregistered land is sold; subsequent conveyancing of the land is then based on the title so registered. There is also provision for voluntary registration of title. The system is explained in Chapter 2.

At the present time the transition from unregistered to registered conveyancing continues. Compulsory registration of title was finally extended to the whole of England and Wales as from 1 November 1990. It is, however, still necessary to understand the unregistered system, and to distinguish between the doctrines applicable to the two. In the discussions which follow, the two systems will be compared wherever possible.

B. Legal Estates

I.   THE FEE SIMPLE ABSOLUTE IN POSSESSION [9]

Challis, *Law of Real Property* (3rd edn, 1911), p. 218

'A *fee simple* is the most extensive in *quantum*, and the most absolute in respect to the rights which it confers, of all estates known to the law. It confers, and since the beginning of legal history it always has conferred, the lawful right to exercise over, upon, and in respect to, the land, every act of ownership which can enter

---

[5]   See p. 206, post.
[6]   LPA 1969, s. 23, p. 80, post.
[7]   Land Registry Act 1862, repealed by LRA 2002, s. 135, Sch. 13.
[8]   LRA 1925, p. 102, post.
[9]   C & B, pp. 165–183; Gray, pp. 293–318; M & W, paras. 3.005, 3.041–3.077; MM, pp. 40–45; Smith, pp. 35–41.

into the imagination, including the right to commit unlimited waste; and, for all practical purposes of ownership, it differs from the absolute dominion of a chattel, in nothing except the physical indestructibility of its subject.'

The rights of a fee simple owner are, however, limited by the rights of his neighbour and by statute, in particular by the Town and Country Planning Acts [10] and the Rent Acts. [11]

A fee simple may be absolute, [12] determinable, subject to a condition [13] or base. [14]

(a)   Definition

LAW OF PROPERTY ACT 1925

1. Legal estates and equitable interests. —(1) The only estates in land which are capable of subsisting or of being conveyed or created at law are —
    (*a*)   An estate in fee simple absolute in possession;
    (*b*)   A term of years absolute. [15]
(2) The only interests or charges in or over land which are capable of subsisting or of being conveyed or created at law are —
    (*a*)   An easement, [16] right, or privilege in or over land for an interest equivalent to an estate in fee simple absolute in possession or a term of years absolute;
    (*b*)   A rentcharge [17] in possession issuing out of or charged on land being either perpetual or for a term of years absolute;
    (*c*)   A charge by way of legal mortgage; [18]
    (*d*)   [19] … and any other similar charge on land which is not created by an instrument; [20]
    (*e*)   Rights of entry exercisable over or in respect of a legal term of years absolute, or annexed, for any purpose, to a legal rentcharge.

---

[10]   P. 1012, post.

[11]   P. 472, post.

[12]   A fee simple may also be (*a*) a 'flying freehold', where 'a man may have an inheritance in an upper chamber though the lower buildings and soil be in another': Co Litt 48b; Lincoln's Inn Act 1860 which regulates flying freeholds in New Square, Lincoln's Inn. See the claim to a 'subterranean flying freehold' of a cellar in *Grigsby v Melville* [1974] 1 WLR 80 at 83, [1973] 3 All ER 455 at 458; (*b*) a 'movable fee', where 'the fee itself is a continuing estate, but it is an estate in land which from time to time changes its position': *Baxendale v Instow Parish Council* [1982] Ch 14 at 20, [1981] 2 All ER 620 at 625 per MEGARRY V-C (foreshore capable of being granted as it might be from time to time); *Welden v Bridgewater* (1592) Moore KB 302, Cro Eliz 421 (lot meadows, where two or more have a fee simple in a measured part of a meadow, but the precise part owned is determined by lots at specified times). See [1982] Conv 208 (R. E. Annand).

[13]   P. 23, post.

[14]   P. 115, post.

[15]   See pp. 431 et seq., post.

[16]   See pp. 690 et seq., post.

[17]   See LP (Entailed Interests) A 1932; s. 2. The Rentcharges Act 1977 is phasing out certain kinds of rentcharge: C & B, pp. 450–451, 704–715; Gray, pp. 537–539; M & W, paras. 4.048–4.051, 18.005, 18.014–18.039; MM, pp.407–413.

[18]   See pp. 793 et seq., post.

[19]   As amended by Finance Act 1963, s. 73, Sch. 14, Part VI, and Tithe Act 1936, s. 48, Sch. 9.

[20]   E.g. tithe redemption annuity (which replaced tithe rentcharge in 1936. See M & W, para. 18.009). This was itself extinguished as from 2 October 1977: FA 1977, s. 56.

(3) All other estates, interests, and charges in or over land take effect as equitable interests.

(4) The estates, interests, and charges which under this section are authorised to subsist or to be conveyed or created at law are (when subsisting or conveyed or created at law) in this Act referred to as 'legal estates', and have the same incidents as legal estates subsisting at the commencement of this Act; and the owner of a legal estate is referred to as 'an estate owner' and his legal estate is referred to as his estate.

(5) A legal estate may subsist concurrently with or subject to any other legal estate in the same land in like manner as it could have done before the commencement of this Act.

(6) A legal estate is not capable of subsisting or of being created in an undivided share in land [1] or of being held by an infant.

7. Saving of certain legal estates and statutory powers. —(1) A fee simple which, by virtue of the Lands Clauses Acts, or any similar statute, [2] is liable to be divested, [3] is for the purposes of this Act a fee simple absolute, [4] and remains liable to be divested as if this Act had not been passed, [and a fee simple subject to a legal or equitable right of entry or re-entry is for the purposes of this Act a fee simple absolute]. [5]

---

[1] See pp. 200 et seq., post.

[2] *Tithe Redemption Commission v Runcorn UDC* [1954] Ch 383, [1954] 1 All ER 653 (highway vested in the local highway authority; Local Government Act 1929 held to be 'a similar statute' within LPA 1925, s. 7(1)).

[3] These Acts provide that land granted for certain public purposes shall revert to the grantor, his successors or some other person, if the purpose fails or is not carried out.

[4] As amended by Reverter of Sites Act 1987, which excludes from s. 7(1) the School Sites Acts, the Literary and Scientific Institutions Act 1854 and the Places of Worship Sites Act 1873. The right of reverter in those cases is replaced by a trust of land. Where, for example, a school site ceases to be used for purposes for which it was originally granted, the charitable trustees continue to hold the legal estate on a trust of land for the revertee: s. 1 (as amended by TLATA 1996, s. 5; Sch 2, para. 6); *Habermehl v A-G* [1996] EGCS 148 *Fraser v Canterbury Diocesan Board of Finance* [2001] Ch 669 (claim statute-barred); *Bath and Wells Diocesan Board of Finance v Jenkinson* [2002] 3 WLR 202, [2002] 4 All ER 245. They may apply to the Charity Commissioners to have the interests of the revertee extinguished: s. 2. A revertee in some circumstances may be entitled to compensation: s. 2(4). For the difficulties caused by the original s. 7(1), see Law Commission Report on Rights of Reverter 1981 (Law Com No 111, Cmnd 8410). The Act departs in a significant number of respects from the Report's recommendations. See Current Law Statutes Annotated (J. Hill); [1987] Conv 408 (D. Evans).

[5] The words in square brackets were added by LP (A) A 1926 Sch., and the intention of the Legislature appears to have been to include as legal estates certain holdings, common in the North of England, where a fee simple is purchased in return for a perpetual rentcharge upon the land. But the enactment is, in its terms, wider than this, and appears to include a grant to A in fee simple subject to a right of entry in the grantor on the happening of some event, such as, for example, A's marrying outside a certain religious persuasion. One would have expected a fee simple subject to such a condition to have been an equitable interest, and for such a grant to have created a settlement. Indeed SLA 1925, s. 1(1)(ii)(b) provides that a grant of a fee simple ... subject to an executory limitation over on the happening of some event shall create a settlement; it would be strange if the distinction were to depend upon the difference between an executory gift over and the right of the grantor to re-enter and terminate for breach of condition. It is tempting to suggest that the words of the amendment are wider than the Legislature intended; how they will be construed is not known. C & B, p. 168; M & W, para. 4.041– 4.042; [1985] Conv 311. Since 1996 base and determinable fees take effect behind a trust of land: TLATA 1996, s. 25(1), Sch. 3, para. 2.

(2) A fee simple vested in a corporation which is liable to determine by reason of the dissolution of the corporation is, for the purposes of this Act, a fee simple absolute. [6]

205. General definitions. —(1) (xix) 'Possession' includes receipt of rents and profits or the right to receive the same, if any.

In **District Bank Ltd v Webb** [1958] 1 WLR 148, [1958] 1 All ER 126, [7] the question was whether an estoppel was raised against vendors by reason of a recital that they were 'seised in unencumbered fee simple in possession upon trust for sale,' when the property was subject to a lease. DANCKWERTS J held that the representation was not sufficiently unambiguous to create an estoppel, and added at 150, at 127:

'Secondly, the words "in possession" are relied upon, but I do not think that "in possession" means vacant possession. It seems to me that the meaning is "fee simple in possession" as opposed to "fee simple in reversion" and there again it seems to me impossible for the bank to rely upon such representation in the recital to cause the vendors to be bound by any estoppel.'

(b) Creation [8]

LAW OF PROPERTY ACT 1925

60. Abolition of technicalities in regard to conveyances and deeds.— (1) A conveyance of freehold land to any person without words of limitation, or any equivalent expression, shall pass to the grantee the fee simple or other the whole interest which the grantor had power to convey in such land, unless a contrary intention appears in the conveyance. [9]

(2) A conveyance of freehold land to a corporation sole by his corporate designation without the word 'successors' shall pass to the corporation the fee simple or other the whole interest which the grantor had power to convey in such land, unless a contrary intention appears in the conveyance.

(4) The foregoing provisions of this section apply only to conveyances and deeds executed after the commencement of this Act:

Provided that in a deed executed after the thirty-first day of December, eighteen hundred and eighty-one, [10] it is sufficient —
    (a) In the limitation of an estate in fee simple, to use the words 'in fee simple,' without the word 'heirs'.

---

[6]   As to whether the lands of a corporation upon its dissolution reverted to the donor or escheated to the lord, see Co Litt 13b; Gray, *Rule against Perpetuities* (4th edn), ss. 44–52; Challis, *Law of Real Property* (3rd edn), pp. 35–36, 467–468; *Hastings Corpn v Letton* [1908] 1 KB 378; *Re Woking UDC (Basingstoke Canal) Act 1911* [1914] 1 Ch 300; *Re Sir Thomas Spencer Wells* [1933] Ch 29; (1933) 49 LQR 240; (1934) 50 LQR 33 (F. E. Farrer); (1935) 51 LQR 347 (M. W. Hughes), 361 (F. E. Farrer).
[7]   See also *Re Morgan* (1883) 24 ChD 114 at 116.
[8]   C & B, pp. 168–172; Gray, p. 304; M & W, paras. 3.026–3.032; MM, pp. 37–39; Smith, p. 37.
[9]   A similar rule applies to devises: Wills Act 1837, s. 28.
[10]   The Conveyancing Act 1881 came into force on 1 January 1882.

205. General definitions.—(1) In this Act unless the context otherwise requires, the following expressions have the meanings hereby assigned to them respectively, that is to say: —

(ii) 'Conveyance' includes a mortgage, charge, lease, assent, vesting declaration, vesting instrument, disclaimer, release and every other assurance of property or of an interest therein by any instrument, except a will. ...

(c) Alienability [11]

RE BROWN
[1954] Ch 39, [1953] 2 All ER 1342 (ChD, HARMAN J)

The testator devised freehold properties in trust for his wife for life, and after her death, on his youngest son attaining 21, for all the sons then living in equal shares as tenants in common. Clause 6 of the will provided that if any son should allow his share to be vested in any person other than one of the brothers, that share should be held on discretionary trusts for the son and his wife and children. The question, on one son wishing to sell outside the family, was whether the restriction upon alienation was good.

Held. No.

HARMAN J: This is a point on which it appears that the authorities give no certain guide, and the various editors of Jarman on Wills give it up, as textbook writers, therein more fortunate than judges, are entitled to do with the bland statement that the law is uncertain.

The point is a very narrow one, and it is whether a restriction on alienation appended to an absolute devise of real estate is good or no. The instinct of any equity lawyer is, to start with, to say that all restraints on absolute interests which tend to negative the rights attached to those interests are abhorred by the law and disallowed. That is a general rule cited by Jarman (8th edn, vol. 2, p. 1477): 'A power of alienation is necessarily and inseparably incidental to an estate in fee.'

The view at the outset is that anything which seeks to deprive the feoffee (so to call him) of his rights is void, but there is no doubt that some degree of restriction may be put upon him ...

As I have said, the instinct of any Chancery lawyer is to say that this is a restriction quite inconsistent with an absolute interest in real estate (or in proceeds of sale, for that matter) and that the restriction is not good. Mr Thompson, [12] however, has been able to persuade me that there is a great deal to be said for the view that a restriction of this sort may be good, if it do not amount to a total restriction. He starts with Coke upon Littleton (11th edn., Part 1, book 3, section 360), where the translation is as follows: 'Also if a feoffment be made upon this condition, that the feoffee shall not alien the land to any, this condition is void because when a man is enfeoffed of lands or tenements, he hath power to alien them to any person by the law: For if such a condition should be good, then the condition should oust him of all the power which the law gives him, which should be against reason; and therefore such a condition is void.' That is to say,

---

[11]   C & B, pp. 367–368; M & W, paras. 3.071–3.072; MM, p. 43; (1917) 33 LQR 11 (E. Jenks); (1917) 33 LQR 236, 342 (C. Sweet); (1954) 70 LQR 15 (R.E.M.). A life interest may be made determinable upon the happening of various events, including alienation. This is the basis of protective trusts: *Brandon v Robinson* (1811) 18 Ves 429; *Rochford v Hackman* (1852) 9 Hare 475; H & M, p. 191.

[12]   Counsel for infants interested under the discretionary trusts.

it is repugnant to the gift. The passage following (section 361) is in these terms: 'But if the condition be such that the feoffee shall not alien to such a one, naming his name, or to any of his heirs, or of the issues of such a one, etc. or the like, which conditions do not take away all power of alienation from the feoffee, etc., then such condition is good.' That merely says that you may point out a certain person (or, I suppose, persons) and prohibit alienation to him or them: quaere as to how many persons may you extend that prohibition? According to two cases to which I shall refer in a moment, you may extend it to all the world except a certain class of people; but that seems to me to be a very curious way to read the doctrine of Coke, which, after all, merely says that you may exclude A or B from the world of people to whom it is permissible to alienate.

The earliest case to which I was referred is a decision of the Court of King's Bench, where the judgment was given by Lord Ellenborough CJ, *Doe* d. *Gill v Pearson* (1805) 6 East 172. The gift in that case was of a piece of land to 'my daughters ... Ann and Hannah, their heirs and assigns for ever, as tenants in common, and not as joint tenants; *upon this special proviso and condition*, that in case my said daughters Ann and Hannah Collett, or either of them, shall have no lawful issue, that then and in such case they or she having no lawful issue as aforesaid shall have no power to dispose of her share in the said estates so above given to them except to her sister or sisters, or to their children.' The exception was confined to sisters and the children of sisters, which is a narrow enough class, although one does not know exactly how many there were in the class. There were five daughters ... the whole court, the Court of King's Bench, decided apparently that the condition not to alienate except to a class consisting of four sisters and their children was good.

That case was considered in *Attwater v Attwater* (1853) 18 Beav 330, where Sir John Romilly MR refused to follow the Court of King's Bench, and merely said that, notwithstanding *Doe* d. *Gill v Pearson*, he held the opposite. The limitation in *Attwater v Attwater* was: 'I bequeath to *Gay Thomas Attwater*, jun., eldest son of my niece, the family estate at *Charlton, Wilts.*, to become his property on attaining the age of 25 years, with an injunction never to sell it out of the family; but, if sold at all, it must be to one of his brothers hereafter named.' He had three brothers. Sir John Romilly declined to hold that condition good; in his judgment he said: 'It is obvious, that if the introduction of one person's name, as the only person to whom the property may be sold, renders such a proviso valid, a restraint on alienation may be created, as complete and perfect as if no person whatever was named; inasmuch as the name of the person who alone is permitted to purchase, might be so selected, as to render it reasonably certain that he would not buy the property, and that the property could not be aliened at all. It appears to me also, that this is the true construction of the words used by the testator; it is, in truth, an injunction never to sell the hereditaments devised at all. ... It is not, in my opinion, desirable to impose fresh fetters on the enjoyment of property, and it appears to me, that this proviso is distinctly at variance with the rules laid down by Lord Coke, and which have always been considered and treated as good law. I am of opinion, therefore, that this clause is merely inoperative.'

That is a decision on a limitation exactly in pari materia to the one before me. I should feel no difficulty about following it, rather than *Doe* d. *Gill v Pearson* (1805) 6 East 173, but for the fact that in *Re Macleay* (1875) LR 20 Eq 186, the great authority of Sir George Jessel appears to be on the other side. In that case the devise was 'to my brother J. on the condition that he never sells out of the family'. The limitation was not, therefore, to named persons, it was 'out of the family'. Sir George Jessel said at 187: ... 'It has been suggested, however, that it is void as being repugnant to the quality of the estate, that is to say, that you cannot restrict the right of an owner in fee of alienating in any way in which he may think fit. If that were the law, the condition would be plainly void. But, with the exception of one authority, a case decided by my immediate predecessor, I am not aware that the law has ever been laid down in that way.' Sir George Jessel then discussed the point in Coke on Littleton, *Muschamp v Bluet* (1617) J Bridg 132, *Attwater v Attwater* (1853) 18 Beav 330 and *Jacobs v Brett* (1875) LR 20 Eq 1. He decided at 189: 'So that, according to the old books, Sheppard's Touchstone being to the same effect, the test is whether the condition takes away the whole power of alienation substantially: it is a question of substance, and not of mere form.' ... He came to the conclusion that the words were not sufficiently restrictive to be in substance an absolute bar. His reason was that 'the family' was a larger term than 'sister or sisters, or their children' and that the only restriction was to sell and not to dispose, which might include leases or mortgages. He came to the conclusion that the limitation in that case was a good one.

That decision, therefore, inclines to the view for which Mr. Thompson has argued. In *Re Rosher* (1884) 26 ChD 801, however, Pearson J felt it necessary to make an elaborate attack upon Sir George Jessel's decision in *Re Macleay* (1875) LR 20 Eq 186. Although the decision in *Re Rosher* was, as a matter of construction that the restriction was in effect an absolute one, Pearson J delivered a long judgment explaining why he could not agree that *Re Macleay* was well decided. The restriction in *Re Rosher* was that if the testator's 'son, his heirs or devisees' wished to sell over a certain period, property worth £15,000 had to be offered to the testator's wife during her lifetime at a price of £3,000; and the judge held that that meant in effect that it could not be sold at all, because nobody would give away property worth £15,000 for £3,000. Although *Re Rosher*, qua its decision, is not of much help, it shows that in the view of Pearson J, *Re Macleay* was wrongly decided.

I need take the law no further. I have to choose one way or the other ...

It is most pertinent to remember, as Mr. Armstrong[13] has also pointed out to me, that the class to whom it is permissible to alienate begins with three for any one share and that the prohibition goes on not only during the joint lives of all the brothers, but during the lives of the survivors and survivor of them, and therefore a period will be reached when there are two, and then only one, and at last no person to whom any alienation is allowed. If none it is plainly bad. If it is only one, that in substance, as in *Muschamp v Bluet*, is equivalent to none. If one be bad, are two good? It seems to me that a class of this sort, which is bound to be a diminishing class, brings it about, in substance, that this is a general prohibition on alienation. It would be an extraordinary thing if no-one could postulate of any one of these brothers that he would or would not during his lifetime be able to dispose of his own share; and that it must depend on whether he outlives two of his brothers. In my view, this is the kind of restriction which the law views, or should view, with dislike. It is exactly the same kind of condition as in *Attwater v Attwater*, and I think that I should be at liberty to follow that decision were it necessary for me to do so, but I do not think that I need follow any case in this region, because the cases are inconsistent with one another, and I am entitled to take my own view. It is pertinent that a number of persons, as in this clause, is in essence different from a class consisting, for instance, as Sir George Jessel's did in *Re Macleay*, of members of the family, which he said was a large indeterminate class of people and might, of course, increase as time went on;

13   Counsel for the sons.

whereas, if alienation be restricted to three or four or five persons such as brothers, the class is bound to diminish as death takes its toll of the members. I hold therefore, that the restriction in clause 6 of the will is an attempt to fetter the natural qualities of the interest given, and is accordingly void and can be disregarded.[14]

II. THE TERM OF YEARS ABSOLUTE [15]

LAW OF PROPERTY ACT 1925

1. Legal estates and equitable interests. —(1) p. 6, ante.

C. Equitable Interests

LAW OF PROPERTY ACT 1925

1. Legal estates and equitable interests. —(3) All other estates, interests, and charges in or over land take effect as equitable interests.

(7) Every power of appointment over, or power to convey or charge land or any interest therein, whether created by a statute or other instrument or implied by law, and whether created before or after the commencement of this Act (not being a power vested in a legal mortgagee or an estate owner in right of his estate and exercisable by him or by another person in his name and on his behalf), operates only in equity.

(8) Estates, interests, and charges in or over land which are not legal estates are in this Act referred to as 'equitable interests,' and powers which by this Act are to operate in equity only are in this Act referred to as 'equitable powers.'

4. Creation and disposition of equitable interests.—(1) Interests in land validly created or arising after the commencement of this Act, which are not capable of subsisting as legal estates, shall take effect as equitable interests, and, save as otherwise expressly provided by statute, interests in land which under the Statute of Uses or otherwise could before the commencement of this Act have been created as legal interests, shall be capable of being created as equitable interests:

Provided that, after the commencement of this Act (and save as hereinafter expressly enacted), an equitable interest in land shall only be capable of being validly created in any case in which an equivalent equitable interest in property real or personal could have been validly created before such commencement.[16]

---

[14] Cf. *Caldy Manor Estate Ltd v Farrell* [1974] 1 WLR 1303, [1974] 3 All ER 753. A fee simple determinable (whether on alienation or for any other reason) is settled land under SLA 1925, s. 1(1)(ii)(c) (as amended by TLATA 1996, s. 25(1), Sch. 3, para. 2(2)), and the land thus becomes alienable by the tenant for life (p. 326, post). Any term which would operate to restrict the tenant for life's freedom of alienation is void: SLA 1925, s. 106, p. 345, post. See also on sterilisation of land, *Overseas & Commercial Developments Ltd v Cox* [2002] All ER (D) 253 (Apr).

[15] Chap. 8, p. 431, post.

[16] See the discussion in *National Provincial Bank Ltd v Ainsworth* [1965] AC 1175, [1965] 2 All ER 472, on the question of interests capable of existing as proprietary rights; p. 135, post.

I. ENTAILED INTERESTS [17]

(a) Phasing Out

The entailed interest has long been used as an essential part of a strict settlement. Land was settled, usually on marriage, to the eldest son for life, with remainder to his son in tail. That entailed interest was limited so that, if the son died without issue, an entailed interest was given to the second son and so on. It became an anachronism, mainly because of taxation, and as from 1 January 1997 the Trusts of Land and Appointment of Trustees Act 1996 prevents any attempt to create a new entailed interest. Existing interests are not affected.

TRUSTS OF LAND AND APPOINTMENT OF TRUSTEES ACT 1996

SCHEDULE 1

5.—(1) Where a person purports by an instrument coming into operation after the commencement of this Act to grant to another person an entailed interest in real or personal property, the instrument—
- (a) is not effective to grant an entailed interest, but
- (b) operates instead as a declaration that the property is held in trust absolutely for the person to whom an entailed interest in the property was purportedly granted. [18]

(2) Where a person purports by an instrument coming into operation after the commencement of this Act to declare himself a tenant in tail of real or personal property, the instrument is not effective to create an entailed interest.

(b) Creation [19]

The sections of the Law of Property Act 1925 on the creation of entailed interests before 1997 were repealed by the Trusts of Land and Appointment of Trustees Act 1996, section 25(2), Schedule 4.

LAW OF PROPERTY ACT 1925

60. Abolition of technicalities in regard to conveyances and deeds.—(4) The foregoing provisions of this section [20] apply only to conveyances and deeds executed after the commencement of this Act:

Provided that in a deed executed after the thirty-first day of December, eighteen hundred and eighty-one, [1] it is sufficient —
- (b) In the limitation of an estate tail, to use the words 'in tail' without the words 'heirs of the body', [2] and

---

[17]   C & B, Chapter 12; M & W, paras. 3.078–3.091; MM, pp. 32, 39, 45–47; Biancalana, *The Fee Tail and the Common Recovery in Mediaeval England 1176–1502* (2001).
[18]   See [2000] Conv 445 at 465–473 (E.B. Histed).
[19]   C & B, pp. 273–280; M & W, paras. 3.033–3.038; MM, pp. 32, 39; Smith, pp. 41–42.
[20]   See p. 8, ante.
[1]   The Conveyancing Act 1881 came into force on 1 January 1882.
[2]   Note that the words 'heirs of the body' remain sufficient. The technical common law required that an estate tail be created by the use of the word 'heirs' plus words of procreation: 'heirs of the body' was the most common formula. The Conveyancing Act 1881 provided the alternative.

(*c*) In the limitation of an estate in tail male or in tail female, to use the words 'in tail male' or 'in tail female,' as the case requires, without the words 'heirs male of the body,' or 'heirs female of the body.'

130. Creation of entailed interests in real and personal property.—(1) An interest in tail or in tail male or in tail female or in tail special (in this Act referred to as 'an entailed interest') may be created by way of trust in any property, real or personal, [3] but only by the like expressions as those by which before the commencement of this Act a similar estate tail could have been created by deed (not being an executory instrument) in freehold land, and with the like results, including the right to bar the entail either absolutely or so as to create an interest equivalent to a base fee, and accordingly all statutory provisions relating to estates tail in real property shall apply to entailed interests in personal property.

Personal estate so entailed (not being chattels settled as heirlooms) may be invested, applied, and otherwise dealt with as if the same were capital money or securities representing capital money arising under the Settled Land Act, 1925, from land settled on the like trusts.

(2) Expressions contained in an instrument coming into operation after the commencement of this Act, which, in a will, or executory instrument coming into operation before such commencement, would have created an entailed interest in freehold land, [4] but would not have been effectual for that purpose in a deed not being an executory instrument, shall (save as provided by the next succeeding section) operate in equity, in regard to property real or personal, to create absolute, fee simple or other interests corresponding to those which, if the property affected had been personal estate, would have been created therein by similar expressions before the commencement of this Act. [5]

(3) Where personal estate (including the proceeds of sale of land directed to be sold and chattels directed to be held as heirlooms) is, after the commencement of this Act, directed to be enjoyed or held with, or upon trusts corresponding to trusts affecting, land in which, either before or after the commencement of this Act an entailed interest has been created, and is subsisting, such direction shall be deemed sufficient to create a corresponding entailed interest in such personal estate.

(c) Rule in Shelley's Case [6]

LAW OF PROPERTY ACT 1925

131. Abolition of the rule in Shelley's case. —Where by any instrument coming into operation after the commencement of this Act an interest in any property is expressed to be given to the heir or heirs or issue or any particular heir or any class of the heirs or issue of any person in words which, but for this section (and

---

[3] Before 1926 an estate tail could not be created in personalty; and not, therefore, in an interest under a trust for sale.

[4] Before 1926 an entail could be created in a will or executory instrument without the use of the formal words required for creation of a fee tail by deed. In a will or executory instrument informal words were sufficient if the intention was clear. C & B, p. 279.

[5] For the effect of this provision, see (1938) 6 CLJ 67 (S. J. Bailey); (1947) 9 CLJ 46 (R. E. Megarry); 185 (S. J. Bailey); 190 (J. H. C. Morris); *Re Crossley's Settlement Trusts* [1955] Ch 627, [1955] 2 All ER 801; C & B, pp. 279–280; M & W, para. 3.038.

[6] C & B, pp. 280–292, Challis, *Law of Real Property* (3rd edn, 1911), pp. 152–167. The rule still applies to an instrument coming into operation before 1926: *Re Routledge* [1942] Ch 457, [1942] 2 All ER 418 (testator died in 1874); *Re Williams* [1952] Ch 828, [1952] 2 All ER 502 (testator died in 1921).

paragraph 5 of Schedule 1 to the Trusts of Land and Appointment of Trustees Act 1996) [7] would, under the rule of law known as the Rule in Shelley's case, have operated to give to that person an interest in fee simple or an entailed interest, such words shall operate in equity as words of purchase and not of limitation, and shall be construed and have effect accordingly, and in the case of an interest in any property expressed to be given to an heir or heirs or any particular heir or class of heirs, the same person or persons shall take as would in the case of freehold land have answered that description under the general law in force before the commencement of this Act.

(d) Barring an Entail [8]

1. INTER VIVOS

FINES AND RECOVERIES ACT 1833

1. Meaning of certain words and expressions. —'estate' shall extend to an estate in equity as well as at law … ; 'base fee' shall mean exclusively that estate in fee simple into which an estate tail is converted where the issue in tail are barred, but persons claiming estates by way of remainder or otherwise are not barred; …

15. Power, after 31st Dec. 1833, to dispose of entailed lands in fee simple or for a less estate, saving the rights of certain persons. — … After the thirty-first day of December one thousand eight hundred and thirty-three every actual tenant in tail, whether in possession, remainder, contingency or otherwise, shall have full power to dispose of for an estate in fee simple absolute or for any less estate the lands entailed, as against all persons claiming the lands entailed by force of any estate tail which shall be vested in or might be claimed by … the person making the disposition, at the time of his making the same, and also as against all persons … whose estates are to take effect after the determination or in defeasance of any estate tail; [9] saving always the rights of all persons in respect of estates prior to the estate tail in respect of which such disposition shall be made, and the rights of all other persons, except those against whom such disposition is by this Act authorized to be made.

19. Power, after 31st Dec. 1833, to enlarge base fees; saving the rights of certain persons.— … After the thirty-first day of December one thousand eight hundred and thirty-three, in every case in which an estate tail in any lands shall have been barred and converted into a base fee, either before or on or after that day, the person who, if such estate tail had not been barred, would have been actual tenant in tail of the same lands, shall have full power to dispose of such lands as against all persons, … whose estates are to take effect after the

---

[7]   As inserted by TLATA 1996, s. 25(1), Sch. 3, para. 4(14).

[8]   C & B, pp. 283–288; M & W, paras. 3.088–3.091; MM, pp. 46–47. See the correspondence in the Times in 1995 (18 and 25 November, and 3 December) on the Bennet entail in Jane Austen's *Pride and Prejudice*. See also [2003] Conv 187 (A. Samuels). See also the sheer delight with which judge and counsel greeted the creation of a base fee in Cyril Hare's *He should have died hereafter* (1958), pp. 110–113.

[9]   *Re St Albans' Will Trust* [1963] Ch 365, [1962] 2 All ER 402, where a disentailing assurance was held good under this section when executed by the heir presumptive (contingent upon the Duke dying without issue) with the consent of the protector of the settlement, on the ground that he was a 'tenant in tail in contingency'. But it was held in *Re Midleton's Will Trusts* [1969] 1 Ch 600, [1967] 2 All ER 834 that such a person did not have a contingent interest, but a mere expectancy.

determination or in defeasance of the base fee into which the estate tail shall have been converted, so as to enlarge the base fee into a fee simple absolute; saving always the rights of all persons in respect of estates prior to the estate tail which shall have been converted into a base fee, and the rights of all other persons, except those against whom such disposition is by this Act authorized to be made. [10]

22. The owner of the first existing estate under a settlement, prior to an estate tail under the same settlement, to be the protector of the settlement. — ... If, at the time when there shall be a tenant in tail of lands under a settlement, there shall be subsisting in the same lands or any of them, under the same settlement, any estate for years determinable on the dropping of a life or lives, or any greater estate (not being an estate for years), prior to the estate tail, then the person who shall be the owner of the prior estate, or the first of such prior estates if more than one then subsisting under the same settlement, or who would have been so if no absolute disposition thereof had been made, (the first of such prior estates, if more than one, being for all the purposes of this Act deemed the prior estate), shall be the protector of the settlement so far as regards the lands in which such prior estate shall be subsisting, and shall for all the purposes of this Act be deemed the owner of such prior estate. [11]

34. Where there is a protector, his consent requisite to enable an actual tenant in tail to create a larger estate than a base fee. —Provided always, ... that if at the time when any person, actual tenant in tail of lands under a settlement, but not entitled to the remainder or reversion in fee immediately expectant on the determination of his estate tail, shall be desirous of making under this Act a disposition of the lands entailed, there shall be a protector of such settlement, then and in every such case the consent of such protector shall be requisite to enable such actual tenant in tail to dispose of the lands entailed to the full extent to which he is herein-before authorized to dispose of the same; but such actual tenant in tail may, without such consent, make a disposition under this Act of the lands entailed, which shall be good against all persons who, by force of any estate tail which shall be vested in or might be claimed by, or which but for some previous act or default would have been vested in or might have been claimed by, the person making the disposition at the time of his making the same, shall claim the lands entailed.

35. Where a base fee, and a protector, his consent requisite to the exercising of a power of disposition. — Provided always, ... that where an estate tail shall have been converted into a base fee, in such case, so long as there shall be a protector of the settlement by which the estate tail was created, the consent of such protector shall be requisite to enable the person who would have been

---

[10] If the tenant in tail is not in possession, the interests of the remaindermen are only affected if the entail is barred with the consent of the protector of the settlement: ss. 22, 34, infra.

[11] Section 32 allowed a settlor to appoint not more than three persons to act as protector of the settlement in lieu of the person described in s. 22. This power of appointing a special protector has been abolished for settlements made after 1925: LPA 1925, 7th Sch., repealing s. 32 Fines and Recoveries Act 1833.

   If there is no protector under s. 22, the Court may be protector (s. 33); or the tenant in tail in remainder may disentail without consent: *Re Darnley's Will Trusts* [1970] 1 WLR 405, [1970] 1 All ER 319.

tenant of the estate tail if the same had not been barred to exercise, as to the lands in respect of which there shall be such protector, the power of disposition herein-before contained.

2. BY WILL

LAW OF PROPERTY ACT 1925

176. Power for tenant in tail in possession to dispose of property by specific devise or bequest. —(1) A tenant in tail of full age [12] shall have power to dispose by will, by means of a devise or bequest referring specifically [13] either to the property or to the instrument under which it was acquired or to entailed property generally —

(a) of all property of which he is tenant in tail in possession at his death; and

(b) of money (including the proceeds of property directed to be sold) subject to be invested in the purchase of property, of which if it had been so invested he would have been tenant in tail in possession at his death;

in like manner as if, after barring the entail, he had been tenant in fee-simple or absolute owner thereof for an equitable interest at his death, but, subject to and in default of any such disposition by will, such property shall devolve in the same manner as if this section had not been passed.

(2) This section applies to entailed interests authorised to be created by this Act as well as to estates tail created before the commencement of this Act, but does not extend to a tenant in tail who is by statute restrained from barring or defeating his estate tail, whether the land or property in respect whereof he is so restrained was purchased with money provided by Parliament in consideration of public services or not, or to a tenant in tail after possibility of issue extinct, and does not render any interest which is not disposed of by the will of the tenant in tail liable for his debts or other liabilities.

(3) In this section 'tenant in tail' includes an owner of a base fee in possession who has power to enlarge the base fee into a fee-simple without the concurrence of any other person.

(4) This section only applies to wills executed after the commencement of this Act, or confirmed or republished by codicil executed after such commencement.

(e) Descent

LAW OF PROPERTY ACT 1925

130. Entailed interests in real and personal property. [14] —(4) In default of and subject to the execution of a disentailing assurance or the exercise of the testamentary power conferred by this Act, an entailed interest (to the extent of the property affected) shall devolve as an equitable interest, from time to time, upon the persons who would have been successively entitled thereto as the heirs

---

[12] See Family Law Reform Act 1969, s. 1, p. 341, n. 1, post.

[13] See *Acheson v Russell* [1951] Ch 67, [1950] 2 All ER 572, where the action was held to apply to a will which said: 'All my other estate and interest in the family property at' K.H. It was clear from the context that entailed interests were intended to be included: (1950) 66 LQR 449 (R. E. Megarry).

[14] As amended by TLATA 1996, s. 25(2), Sch. 4.

of the body (either generally or of a particular class) of the tenant in tail or other person, or as tenant by the curtesy, if the entailed interest had, before the commencement of this Act, been limited in respect of freehold land governed by the general law in force immediately before such commencement, and such law had remained unaffected.

II. LIFE INTERESTS [15]

(a) Creation

A life interest may be created by the use of any words showing an intention to create a life interest. [16] As explained above, [17] the rule now is that a conveyance executed after 1925 passes to the grantee the whole interest which the grantor had power to convey, unless a contrary intention appears in the conveyance. For conveyances executed before 1926, the rule was that, in a conveyance inter vivos, [18] a life estate only was conveyed unless the correct technical words for the conveyance of a greater estate were used. [19]

The significance of the grant of a life interest was much increased since the coming into operation of the Settled Land Act 1882, under which a tenant for life [20] enjoyed powers which extended far beyond his beneficial life interest. The crucial question in a grant of land therefore is not whether a claimant may enjoy the land for his life, but whether before 1997 he had the powers of a tenant for life under the Settled Land Act 1925, [1] or after 1996 the powers delegated to him by the trustees of land under the Trusts of Land and Appointment of Trustees Act 1996. [2]

(b) Waste[3]

A limited owner may not use land to the prejudice of those entitled in reversion or remainder. The remedy is by action for damages or an injunction. There are four forms of waste.

1. PERMISSIVE

In **Woodhouse v Walker** (1880) 5 QBD 404, a devise to a tenant for life provided that she should keep the premises in repair. She failed to do so, and after her death the remainderman brought an action against her executor under a statute of William IV [4] which gives an action against the executor of a deceased person

---

[15]   C & B, pp. 93, 291–299; Gray, pp. 815–818; M & W, paras. 3.007, 3.093–3.114; MM, pp. 47–52.
[16]   See also LPA 1925, s. 149(6), p. 455, post, and p. 8, ante.
[17]   See p. 8, ante; LPA 1925, s. 60(1).
[18]   Wills Act 1837, ss. 28, 34, reversed this rule with regard to wills.
[19]   Litt 1; Co Litt 20a; Conveyancing Act 1881, s. 51; LPA 1925, s. 60(4) and pp. 8, 13, ante.
[20]   Now defined by SLA 1925, ss. 19, 20; p. 339, post.
[1]   See pp. 341 et seq., post; and for the problems which arise where the court seeks to protect a tenant for life: *Bannister v Bannister* [1948] 2 All ER 133 p. 615, post; *Binions v Evans* [1972] Ch 359, [1972] 2 All ER 70, p. 617, post; *Dodsworth v Dodsworth* (1973) 228 EG 1115, p. 671, post; *Ivory v Palmer* [1975] ICR 340; *Griffiths v Williams* (1977) 248 EG 947, p. 673, post; *Ungurian v Lesnoff* [1990] Ch 206; *Costello v Costello* (1994) 70 P & CR 297.
[2]   TLATA 1996, ss. 6, 8 and 9, pp. 271–275 post.
[3]   C & B, pp. 295–299; Gray, pp. 69–70; M & W, paras. 3.098–3.103; MM, pp. 48–52; Smith, pp. 42–43; (1950) 13 Conv (NS) 278 (M. E. Bathurst).
[4]   Civil Procedure Act 1833.

in respect of wrongs committed by the testator to another in relation to his property. In upholding the action, LUSH J said at 406:

'This action is brought to recover out of her personal estate the expenses he has so incurred. It is remarkable that no direct authority is to be found for a case which must, we should suppose, have frequently occurred, and that we have to go back to first principles in order to find a solution of the question raised.

Before the statutes of Marlbridge [5] (52 Hen 3) and of Gloucester (6 Edw 1, c. 5) an action for waste lay against a tenant in dower and tenant by the curtesy, but none against a tenant for life or years. The reason was, as stated by Coke in 2 Inst 300, "for that the law created their estates and interests, therefore the law gave against them a remedy: but tenant for life or years came in by demise and lease of the owner of the land, & c., and therefore he might in his demise have provided against the doing of waste by his lessee, and if he did not, it was his negligence and default."

Here it is plainly implied that, where the grantor in his grant provides against the doing of waste, the grantee will be liable for waste in like manner as a tenant in dower or by curtesy was liable, and this is in perfect accordance with legal principle as expressed by the maxims, "Qui sentit commodum, sentire debet et onus et transit terra cum onere": Co Litt 231a and see per Holroyd J in *Burnett v Lynch* (1826) 5 B & C 589 at 607. The first of these maxims has a very wide application in our law. See Broom's Maxims.

The statute of Marlbridge, c. 23, extended the common law liability by ordaining that "fermors during their term shall not make waste, sale nor exile of house, woods or men, nor of anything belonging to the tenements that they have to ferm without special licence had by writing of covenant making mention that they may do it, which if they do and thereof be convict they shall yield full damage and shall be punished by amerciament grievously."

The term "fermors" here, says Coke, 2 Inst 145, comprehended all who held by lease for life or lives, or for years by deed or without deed, and the words "do or make waste" in legal understanding in this place (as well as in the statute of Gloucester) includes as well permissive waste which is "waste by reason of omission or not doing, as for want of reparation, as waste by reason of commission, as to cut down timber trees or prostrate houses and the like: for he that suffereth a house to decay which he ought to repair doth the waste."

The "special licence" mentioned in the statute of Marlbridge is commonly expressed by the well-known phrase "without impeachment of waste."

The statute of Gloucester gives, as a more stringent remedy, a writ of waste under which the tenant was liable to forfeiture of the thing wasted and treble damages.

The right of action against a tenant for life belongs to the owner in fee of the immediate reversion.

In course of time an action on the case founded on the statute of Westminster 2, came to be substituted for the writ of waste, as being a more simple and practical remedy, and the writ of waste having fallen into disuse was ultimately abolished by 3 & 4 Wm 4, c. 27, s. 36. But the rights and liabilities of the parties remained as before, the remedy only being changed: *Bacon v Smith* (1841) 1 QB 345. It is not necessary in this case to enter into the question whether an action on the case for permissive waste can be maintained against a tenant for life or years,

---

[5] 'I prefer Marlborough to Marlberge, to say nothing to Marlbridge which is an idiotism' (F. W. Maitland in a letter to H. A. L. Fisher, 7 July 1893, quoted in *Letters of Frederick William Maitland*, ed. C. H. S. Fifoot, p. 122).

upon whom no express duty to repair is imposed by the instrument which creates the estate. The modern authorities, or rather the dicta upon this point, appear to be strangely in conflict with the ancient reading of the statutes. [6] See notes to *Greene v Cole* (1672) 2 Wms Saund 252.

We think it must be held, upon the principle before mentioned, that in this case the tenant for life was liable at common law, and that the plaintiff as immediate reversioner had a right of action, and probably might have obtained an injunction against her for the permitted waste, if he had made such an application in her lifetime. The right of action which at common law would have died with the person is continued by 3 & 4 Wm 4, c. 42, s. 2, against the executor.'

2. VOLUNTARY

In **Dashwood v Magniac** [1891] 3 Ch 306, a testator gave to his widow an equitable life tenancy[7] in the West Wycombe estate, which was situated partly in Buckinghamshire and partly in Oxfordshire, the devise requiring her to keep the estate in repair and entitling her to fell timber (not being ornamental timber) necessary for such repairs.

The estate contained beech trees which were timber in Buckinghamshire, though not in Oxfordshire. The widow cut and sold a large number of these trees to furniture manufacturers in High Wycombe and the proceeds of the sale were treated as her income.

On the widow's death, the remainderman brought this action for (inter alia) voluntary waste. The defendants relied on a local usage which would permit a limited owner to cut beech trees (even though they were 'timber') and to treat the proceeds as income; and on the fact that the testator had so treated the beech trees during his lifetime.

The Court of Appeal (LINDLEY and BOWEN LJJ, KAY LJ dissenting) affirmed CHITTY J in holding that, by reason of the local usage, the widow had not committed waste.

LINDLEY LJ said at 351: 'Laying aside all custom, whether ancient or modern, this action would fail, for the tenant for life would have done nothing wrong; she cut beech in the ordinary course of good forestry, and, apart from custom, that was not waste.

As regards the beech woods in *Oxfordshire*, where beech trees are not timber, this is admitted to be true. But as regards the beech woods in *Buckinghamshire*, where beech is timber, the case is said to be different. The testator made no distinction between his estates in the one county and those in the other; he gave the rents and profits of both alike to Lady *Dashwood* for life, with power to cut timber for repairs; but yet it is contended that, although she was entitled to cut and sell beech trees in those parts of the estates which were in *Oxfordshire*, she was not entitled to do the same with beech trees on those parts of the estates which were in *Buckinghamshire*. Such a conclusion would, I think, startle the

---

[6]   KAY J held in *Re Cartwright* (1889) 41 ChD 532 that, in the absence of express provisions, a tenant for life was not liable for permissive waste. *Warren v Keen* [1954] 1 QB 15, [1953] 2 All ER 1118 contains a dictum of DENNING LJ that a weekly tenant is not liable for permissive waste. A tenant for years is liable for permissive waste: *Dayani v Bromley London Borough Council* [1999] 3 EGLR 144 (contains a detailed analysis referring to authorities from the tenth century).

[7]   The estate was given to her for 100 years if she should so long live. After 1925, such leases, if granted at a rent or a fine, became leases for 90 years. If no rent or fine is payable, an equitable life interest is given: LPA 1925, s. 149(6), p. 455, post.

testator, and would be to defeat, and not carry out, his intentions as expressed in his will.

It is contended by the Appellants that, beech being timber by custom in *Buckinghamshire*, cutting it, even in the ordinary course of good forestry, is necessarily waste and actionable.

… If it is said that there cannot be a custom to commit waste, the answer is that there may be a usage which renders that not waste as between persons claiming under a particular instrument framed with reference to the usage which would be waste as between other persons. …

The ordinary law of waste is, therefore, I think, not applicable as between the persons claiming under the will with which we have to deal. In other words the cutting of beech woods according to the usage was not waste in the contemplation of this testator; and, it not being waste, the Plaintiffs cannot claim the proceeds of their sale. …'

KAY LJ (dissenting) said at 371: 'The custom or usage relied on in the present case is one which would entirely alter the ordinary common law of waste as applicable to this estate, and would enable the tenant for years, who is made impeachable of waste, to commit waste, notwithstanding the infirmity of her estate in that respect. It seems to me that, to produce that effect, it must be at least proved that from time immemorial such a limited owner, though impeachable of waste, has been accustomed to exercise the right so claimed.

In this case there is not the slightest evidence that any limited owner who was impeachable of waste ever attempted to exercise any such right, and the usage for the owners of the fee simple, or for limited owners who were not impeachable of waste, to manage the woods in the way which is complained of, cannot, as it seems to me, possibly justify a limited owner, who is impeachable of waste, in doing the same.' [8]

3. AMELIORATING

In **Doherty v Allman** (1878) 3 App Cas 709, a tenant for a long term of years had covenanted in the lease to 'uphold, support, maintain and keep the demised premises … in good order, repair and condition'. The premises which had been used as a corn store, and then for military purposes, fell into disrepair. The lessee decided to convert the store premises into dwelling houses, which would greatly increase their value. The question was whether he could be restrained on the grounds that he would be in breach of contract or would be committing waste.

The House of Lords (Lord CAIRNS LC, Lords O'HAGAN, BLACKBURN and GORDON) refused an injunction on either ground. [9] Lord O'HAGAN said at 724:

'Now we have, I think, established for the purposes of this decision the principles in this case by which we ought to abide. In the case of *Mollineux v Powell* (1730) 3 P Wms 268, n., which contains perhaps the clearest dictum we have upon the matter, two conditions as to the exercise of jurisdiction in cases of waste

---

[8]   Larch is not timber. A tenant for life does not therefore commit waste by felling a plantation of larch when ripe for felling; he is entitled to the proceeds of sale and is under no obligation to replace it at his own expense: *Re Harker's Will Trusts* [1938] Ch 323, [1938] 1 All ER 145.

[9]   There is, however, technically an act of waste for which an action for damages would lie at law. But, no damage being suffered, no damages would be recoverable. See *Mancetter Developments Ltd v Garmanson Ltd* [1986] QB 1212, [1986] 1 All ER 449 (tenant who, in removing trade fixtures, failed to make good holes left behind in landlord's brickwork, held liable in damages for voluntary waste); p. 101, n. 20.

have been very clearly pointed out, and one at least of those conditions is expressly recognised afterwards in the Irish case of *Coppinger v Gubbins* (1846) 3 Jo & Lat 411. Those conditions are that the waste with which a Court of Equity, or your Lordships acting as a Court of Equity, ought to interfere, should be not ameliorating waste, nor trivial waste. It must be waste of an injurious character— it must be waste of not only an injurious character, but of a substantially injurious character, and if either the waste be really ameliorating waste—that is a proceeding which results in benefit and not in injury—the Court of Equity, and your Lordships acting as a Court of Equity, ought not to interfere to prevent it. I think that is perfectly well established. On the other hand, if the waste be so small as to be indifferent to the one party or the other—if it be, as has been said by a great authority in our law, such a thing as twelvepence worth of waste, a Court of Equity, and your Lordships acting as a Court of Equity, ought not to interfere on account of the triviality of the matter. Now, in my view of the case, those principles decide the question so far as this portion of it is concerned; for it appears to me that we have here established to the full satisfaction of your Lordships, by a series of authorities to which I shall not refer, that the waste, to be of any sort of effect with a view to an injunction, must be a waste resulting in substantial damage.'

4. EQUITABLE

LAW OF PROPERTY ACT 1925

135. Equitable waste. — An equitable interest for life without impeachment of waste does not confer upon the tenant for life any right to commit waste of the description known as equitable waste, unless an intention to confer such right expressly appears by the instrument creating such equitable interest.

VANE v LORD BARNARD
(1716) 2 Vern 738 (Earl COWPER LC)

The Defendant on the Marriage of the Plaintiff his eldest Son with the Daughter of *Morgan Randyll,* and 10,000*l* Portion settled (*inter alia*) *Raby Castle* on himself for Life, without Impeachment of Waste Remainder to his Son for Life, and to his first and other Sons in Tail Male.

The Defendant the Lord *Barnard* having taken some Displeasure against his son, got *two Hundred* Workmen together, and of a sudden, in a few Days, stript the Castle of the Lead, Iron, Glass, Doors, and Boards, & c. to the value of 3,000*l.*

The Court upon filing the Bill, granted an Injunction to stay Committing of Waste, in pulling down the Castle; and now, upon the Hearing of the Cause, decreed, not only the Injunction to continue, but that the Castle should be repaired, and put into the same Condition it was in, in *August* 1714, and for that Purpose a Commission was to issue to ascertain what ought to be repaired, and a Master to see it done at the Expense and Charge of the Defendant the Lord *Barnard*; and decreed the Plaintiff his Costs.

In **Turner v Wright** (1860) 2 De GF & J 234, Lord CAMPBELL LC held that an owner in fee simple subject to an executory limitation over was liable for equitable waste. He said at 243:

'Equitable waste is that which a prudent man would not do in the management of his own property. This Court may interfere where a man unconscientiously exercises a legal right to the prejudice of another—and an act may in some sense be regarded as unconscientious if it be contrary to the dictates of prudence and reason, although the actor, from his peculiar frame of mind, does the act without any malicious motive. The prevention of acts amounting to equitable waste may well be considered as in furtherance of the intention of the testator, who, no doubt, wished that the property should come to the devisee over in the condition in which he, the testator, left it at his death; the first taker having had the reasonable enjoyment of it, and having managed it as a man of ordinary prudence would manage such property were it absolutely his own.'

III. DETERMINABLE INTERESTS AND INTERESTS SUBJECT TO A CONDITION

There is a basic difference between determinable interests and interests subject to a condition. The former is a grant of something less than the interest specified; the latter is a grant of the interest subject to a liability to be cut down. To give land to trustees so long as it is used for Church purposes is a grant less than a fee simple. To give land to trustees in fee simple subject to a condition that the fee simple shall terminate if the land is not used for Church purposes is a fee simple subject to a condition. The difference is that between an eleven inch ruler and a foot ruler subject to the last inch being cut off. Whether or not a grant is one or the other is a matter of construction, and is thus reduced to a matter of words. There are many difficulties and fine distinctions, but these are unavoidable; the interests are similar, but different, and the line between the two must be drawn somewhere. [10]

In **Re Bowen** [1893] 2 Ch 491, STIRLING J said at 495:
'The question which I have to decide, therefore, appears to me to reduce itself to one of the construction of the testator's will—*i.e.*, whether the testator has given the property to charity, in perpetuity, subject to an executory gift in favour of the residuary legatee, or whether he has given it for a limited period, leaving the undisposed of interest to fall into residue.'

In **Re Sharp's Settlement Trusts** [1973] Ch 331 at 340, [1972] 3 All ER 151 at 156, PENNYCUICK V-C referred to: 'the extremely artificial distinction between a "determinable fee" and a "fee simple on condition." For explanation of these expressions see *Megarry and Wade, The Law of Real Property*, 3rd edn (1966) p. 75 et seq. and in particular the statement at p. 77:
"The question is whether the words limit the utmost time of continuance of the estate, or whether they mark an event which, if it takes place in the course of that time, will defeat an estate already granted; in the first case the words take effect as a limitation, in the second as a condition. A limitation marks the bounds or compass of the estate, a condition defeats the estate before it attains its boundary."
The distinction has been described in an Irish case as "little short of disgraceful to our jurisprudence": see the quotation in *Megarry and Wade* at p. 78. I am bound to say that according to modern ideas this criticism appeals to me. However, the distinction is well established and must be accepted so far as it is comprehensible.'

---

[10] For the differences between a determinable fee and a fee subject to a condition, see C & B, pp. 359–367; M & W, paras. 3.060–3.077; MM, pp. 41–45.

II. Registration and Notice

A. The Doctrine of the Bona Fide Purchaser of a Legal Estate for Value Without Notice [11]

The recognition of the use, and later of the trust, [12] has given to English law a unique form of duality of ownership. The feoffees to uses (later the trustees) own a legal estate which, like other forms of legal ownership, is valid against all the world. They obtain, however, no personal benefit from their legal ownership, for they must hold the land and all the income from it for the benefit of the beneficiaries.

The interest of the beneficiaries has its origin in the willingness of the Chancellor to give relief in a situation in which the owner of the legal estate had undertaken to hold his legal estate to the use of another. The conscience of the feoffee to uses was affected and the Chancellor compelled him to observe his obligation. So long as the original parties to the arrangement remained, the position is comparatively simple; but complications arise where the legal or equitable ownership changes. A change of legal ownership raises the question whether the use is enforceable against a person other than the original feoffee; a change of equitable ownership raises the question of the form of equitable ownership which the Chancellor will recognise. In general, equity followed the law and recognised in equity estates corresponding to those which were recognised at law. But that is another story; here, we are concerned with the question of enforcement of equitable interests against persons other than the original feoffee.

The use was based upon conscience. If a feoffee to uses transferred to a purchaser with notice, the purchaser was bound as being a party to the fraud; if he had no notice, the use was 'transferred' to him. A donee was bound, notice or no notice; for, without consideration being given, the original use was not changed. A use was however only binding on persons claiming through the original feoffee; and a disseisor therefore took free. [13] With the rise of the trust, however, this technicality disappeared; and an interest under a trust is now valid against all the world with the exception of a bona fide purchaser [14] of the legal estate for value [15] without notice actual, constructive [16] or imputed. [17]

---

[11]   C & B, pp. 59–66; Gray, pp. 79–91; M & W, paras. 5.005–5.025; MM, pp. 58–63; Smith, pp. 204–210; H & M, pp. 34–40; Snell, paras. 4.08–4.32; Maitland, pp. 106–116.

[12]   Holdsworth, vol. 4, pp. 407–480 and Simpson, *A History of the Land Law*, (2nd edn. 1986) pp. 173–207.

[13]   Simpson, pp. 179–181.

[14]   As to the meaning of 'purchaser', see C & B, pp. 59, 169, n. 20; M & W, paras. 3.034, 5.008; MM, p. 59.

[15]   M & W, para. 3.023. 'It means any consideration in money, money's worth ... or marriage. "Money's worth" extends to all forms of non-monetary consideration in the sense used in the law of contract, but it also includes the satisfaction of an existing debt. "Marriage", however, extends only to a future marriage: an ante-nuptial agreement ... is deemed to have been made for value as regards both the spouses and the issue of the marriage; but a promise made in respect of a past marriage ... is not.'

[16]   See *Macmillan Inc v Bishopsgate Investment Trust plc (No 3)* [1995] 1 WLR 978, [1995] 3 All ER 747, where MILLETT J said at 1000, at 769: 'In English law notice ... includes not only actual notice (including "wilful blindness" or "contrived ignorance", where the purchaser deliberately abstains from an inquiry in order to avoid learning the truth) but also constructive notice, that is to say notice of such facts as he would have discovered if he had taken proper measures to investigate them'.

[17]   In the case of those interests and charges which are registrable under the LCA 1972, registration constitutes notice: LCA 1972, ss. 2, 4, pp. 31–33, 37, post. For the meaning of imputed notice, see LPA 1925, s. 199 (1) (ii) and p. 46, n. 10, post.

It may be helpful to add three comments upon the application of this doctrine in modern law. First, in respect of rights and interests which are registrable as land charges under the Land Charges Act 1972,[18] registration constitutes notice. Thus, a purchaser takes subject to registered land charges whether he knows about them or not; and, conversely, he takes free from unregistered (but registrable) land charges even if he knows about them.[19]

Secondly, where there are successive beneficial interests in land, a trust of land exists; the trustees have power to sell the fee simple, and the equitable interests are 'overreached', that is, transferred from the land to the purchase money. Thus, the purchaser takes the land free of the equitable interests, although he knows that some exist; and, after the sale, the equitable interests exist in a fund of money whose value is equivalent to the land. A similar result is reached where land is held under a strict settlement. In other situations the doctrine may still apply. The pattern of the 1925 legislation was that all interests in land, other than the fee simple absolute in possession and the term of years absolute[20] should be either registrable or overreachable.[1] Situations have arisen to destroy the tidiness of this pattern, and in these cases the old doctrine will apply.[2] An understanding of the doctrine is essential to an appreciation of the relationship between law and equity.

Thirdly, the doctrine of the purchaser for value of the legal estate without notice is relevant only to *un*registered land ie where the title to land is derived from title deeds relating to a previous transaction. The concept of the duality of ownership, legal and equitable, developed in that context. Where a totally new system of registration of *title* to and of certain *interests* in land is introduced, wholly different concepts apply. It will be seen from Chapter 2 that such a system was made available in 1925 by the Land Registration Act, and since 1990 has been made compulsory for all dealings with land in England and Wales. The essence of a system of registration of title is that the Register controls and that any person dealing with the land will be safe in relying on the Register. The basic division

---

The doctrine of constructive notice applies differently with personalty. A transferee cannot disregard equitable interests of which he is aware or which present themselves to his notice: *Nelson v Larholt* [1948] 1 KB 339, [1947] 2 All ER 751: but, as there are no title deeds to chattels, there is no duty to examine the title: *Joseph v Lyons* (1884) 15 QBD 280 (pledgee under no obligation to search register of bills of sale, and not bound by a bill of sale assigning after-acquired property); H & M, p. 36.

Similarly with negotiable instruments; a holder may be 'in due course' without having taken steps to examine the title of the transferor: *London Joint Stock Bank v Simmons* [1892] AC 201.

[18]   See pp 29–34, post. LCA 1972 consolidates LCA 1925 (apart from local land charges) and other enactments relating to the registration of land charges. It does not make any substantive alterations.

[19]   Pp. 45–49, post.

[20]   LPA 1925, s. 1, p. 6, ante.

[1]   See RUSSELL LJ in *Shiloh Spinners Ltd v Harding* [1972] Ch 326 at 340–341, [1971] 2 All ER 307 at 313.

[2]   I.e. (1) where an interest is not registrable, e.g. restrictive covenant entered into before 1926; LCA 1972, s. 2(5), Class D (ii); *Shiloh Spinners Ltd v Harding* [1973] AC 691, [1973] 1 All ER 90 (equitable right of re-entry on breach of covenant), p. 34, post; *ER Ives Investment Ltd v High* [1967] 2 QB 379, [1967] 1 All ER 504 (estoppel licence), p. 665, post; *Poster v Slough Estates Ltd* [1969] 1 Ch 495, [1968] 3 All ER 257 (right of entry to remove fixtures at end of lease).

(2) where an interest is not overreachable, e.g. *Caunce v Caunce* [1969] 1 WLR 286, [1969] 1 All ER 722; (1974) 38 Conv (NS) 226 (capital money paid to only one trustee), p. 311, post; *Kingsnorth Finance Co Ltd v Tizard* [1986] 1 WLR 783, [1986] 2 All ER 54, p. 156, post.

is thus between estates and interests which appear on the Register and those which do not, rather than between legal estates and equitable interests. [3] But it will be seen that some cases do seem to allow this old distinction to penetrate the registered land system, and cause confusion in its administration. [4]

The Land Registration Act 1925 was reformed and replaced by the Land Registration Act 2002, which came into force on 13 October 2003.

I. THE DOCTRINE

PILCHER v RAWLINS
(1872) 7 Ch App 259 (Lord HATHERLEY LC, JAMES and MELLISH LJJ)

In 1851 the trustees of Jeremiah Pilcher's settlement advanced the funds to Rawlins on the security of land including the 'Whitchurch' property, which was conveyed by Rawlins to the trustees in a deed which noticed the trusts.

In 1856 W. H. Pilcher, the surviving trustee of the settlement, reconveyed the Whitchurch property to Rawlins, who repaid only part of the loan. Rawlins, with W. H. Pilcher's connivance, mortgaged that property to Stockwell and Lamb, showing only the title deeds prior to the 1851 mortgage and thus appearing as unincumbered owner in fee simple.

Stockwell and Lamb thus received the legal estate, not under the title deeds which showed that Rawlins had a good title prior to 1851, but through the 1851 mortgage and later reconveyance also. The complete deeds thus disclosed the trusts. There was no way in which Stockwell and Lamb could have discovered the missing deeds, or learned of their contents. The question was whether the fact that the title deeds disclosed the trusts constituted constructive notice.

Held. Stockwell and Lamb took free from the trusts as bona fide purchasers of the legal estate for value without notice.

JAMES LJ: I propose simply to apply myself to the case of a purchaser for valuable consideration, without notice, obtaining, upon the occasion of his purchase, and by means of his purchase deed, some legal estate, some legal right, some legal advantage; and, according to my view of the established law of this Court, such a purchaser's plea of a purchase for valuable consideration without notice is an absolute, unqualified, unanswerable defence, and an unanswerable plea to the jurisdiction of this Court. Such a purchaser, when he has once put in that plea, may be interrogated and tested to any extent as to the valuable consideration which he has given in order to shew the *bona fides* or *mala fides* of his purchase,

---

3   *Williams & Glyn's Bank Ltd v Boland* [1981] AC 487 at 503, [1980] 2 All ER 408 at 412, where LORD WILBERFORCE said: 'The registered system is designed to free the purchaser from the hazards of notice – real or constructive ... The only kind of notice recognised is by entry on the register'; *Parkash v Irani Finance Ltd* [1970] Ch 101 at 109, [1969] 1 All ER 930 at 933, where PLOWMAN J found a plaintiff's reliance on the doctrine 'a little surprising, since one of the essential features of registration of title is to substitute a system of registration of rights for the doctrine of notice.' See also CROSS J in *National Provincial Bank Ltd v Hastings Car Mart Ltd* [1964] Ch 9 at 16, [1963] 2 All ER 204 at 208; *Miles v Bull (No 2)* [1969] 3 All ER 1585; *Lloyds Bank plc v Carrick* [1996] 4 All ER 630; C&B p. 100.

4   *Barclays Bank Ltd v Taylor* [1974] Ch 137, [1973] 1 All ER 752; *Peffer v Rigg* [1977] 1 WLR 285, [1978] 3 All ER 745, p. 176, post; *Lyus v Prowsa Developments Ltd* [1982] 1 WLR 1044, [1982] 2 All ER 953, p. 176, post. *Lloyds Bank plc v Rosset* [1989] Ch 350, [1988] 3 All ER 915, at 404, at 925, per PURCHAS LJ; *Abbey National Building Society v Cann* [1989] 2 FLR 265, at 278, per RALPH GIBSON and WOOLF LJJ. See also *Hodgson v Marks* [1971] Ch 892, [1971] 2 All ER 684; *Williams & Glyn's Bank Ltd v Boland,* supra, p. 136, post; [1996] Conv 34 (J. Howell).

For the relevance of notice under LRA 1925 and LRA 2002, see p. 164, post.

and also the presence or the absence of notice; but when once he has gone through that ordeal, and has satisfied the terms of the plea of purchase for valuable consideration without notice, then, according to my judgment, this Court has no jurisdiction whatever to do anything more than to let him depart in possession of that legal estate, that legal right, that legal advantage, which he has obtained, whatever it may be. In such a case a purchaser is entitled to hold that which, without breach of duty, he has had conveyed to him.

In the case of *Carter v Carter* (1857) 3 K & J 617, which was decided by the present Lord Chancellor, and which was followed by the Master of the Rolls in this case, and with which I am bound to say I am unable to agree, an exception from that rule was, under the circumstances, supposed to exist.

It is very clearly expressed in a few lines of the judgment in that case: 'But here the purchaser taking the conveyance under one will, supposed by all parties to be really the last will of the testator, finds himself driven to rely upon another and a second will containing on the face of it all the trusts which the testator has created;'—and that circumstance is supposed to create the exception. To my mind there are to that supposition two short and conclusive answers—the one a matter of principle, and the other a matter of fact. My view of the principle is, that when once you have arrived at the conclusion that the purchaser is a purchaser for valuable consideration without notice, the Court has no right to ask him, and has no right to put him to contest the question, how he is going to defend himself, or what he is going to rely on. He may say, honestly and justly, 'I am not going to tell you. I have got the deeds; I defend them, and you will never be able to make me produce them, and you will never be able to produce secondary evidence of them. I am not obliged to produce them at all; probably before you get halfway through your action of ejectment you will find a *jus tertii* which you will not dispose of; the estate is in the hands of a legal tenant to whom I have let it, and no one can determine that tenancy without notice, and no one can give that notice but myself; I will not give that notice, and no Court has any power to compel me to give it. I have a right to rely, as every person defending his position has, on the weakness of the title of the person who is seeking to displace me.' That seems to be exactly the position of such a purchaser as this.
...

I am therefore of opinion that whatever may be the accident by which a purchaser has obtained a good legal title, and in respect of which he has paid his money and is in possession of the property, he is entitled to the benefit of that accident, just as a purchaser would be entitled to avail himself of the possession so acquired, without any reference to the rights of the persons who may be otherwise interested. ...

The decision in the case of *Carter v Carter* (1857) 3 K & J 617, which has been so much referred to, is a decision which I have considered for some years, and I have more than once thought it right to express my views of that case. I differ in some respects in my views from those of the Lord Chancellor with regard to that case, but I say that the right of a person without notice is absolute and unqualified, when once he has made it out.

In **Wilkes v Spooner** [1911] 2 KB 473, Spooner, the lessee of two premises, No. 137 and No. 170, in High St., East Ham, assigned the lease of No. 170 to the plaintiff and covenanted, in effect, not to compete with the plaintiff's business of general butcher. Spooner then surrendered the lease of No. 137 to the landlord with a view to terminating the restrictive covenant. The landlord knew nothing of the covenant; he accepted the surrender and granted a new lease to Spooner's son, who did. The son opened a business in competition with the plaintiff, who sued to restrain this breach of the covenant. The Court of Appeal (VAUGHAN WILLIAMS, FLETCHER MOULTON and FARWELL LJJ, reversing SCRUTTON J) held that the restrictive covenant was not binding. The landlord was a bona fide purchaser for value without notice; and the covenant, once destroyed, did not revive on the passing of the land to the son. VAUGHAN WILLIAMS LJ said at 483:

'I think that this appeal must be allowed. This case has been very well argued, but really, when certain conclusions of fact are arrived at, there is very little left to argue. It cannot seriously be disputed that the proposition which I quoted from Ashburner's Principles of Equity, p. 75, is good law. It is as follows: "A purchaser for valuable consideration without notice can give a good title to a purchaser from him with notice. The only exception is that a trustee who has sold property in breach of trust, or a person who has acquired property by fraud, cannot protect himself by purchasing it from a bona fide purchaser for value without notice." The learned author cites as authorities for that proposition the cases *Sweet v Southcote* (1786) 2 Bro CC 66, and *Re Stapleford Colliery Co, Barrow's Case* (1880) 14 ChD 432.'

II. CONSTRUCTIVE NOTICE

In **Midland Bank Ltd v Farmpride Hatcheries Ltd** (1980) 260 EG 493, the bank lent money in 1971 to the company to enable it to expand its chicken hatchery business. The loan was secured by a mortgage on a 'well-preserved 16th century mansion at Mundford, in Norfolk, together with two cottages and hatcheries and other outbuildings. Under a service agreement with the company in 1968, Mr Willey had been given a licence for himself and his family to live rent free on the premises for 20 years. Mr Willey and his wife were the sole shareholders and the only directors of the company. The licence was never disclosed to nor discovered by the bank when it was negotiating the mortgage with Mr Willey, who was acting as the company's agent. The bank's negotiator, Mr Timbers, was aware that the family was living in the house.

The company defaulted on the mortgage repayment, and the bank brought an action for possession. Mr Willey claimed that his licence was binding on the bank because it had taken the mortgage with constructive notice.[5] The Court of Appeal held that the bank was entitled to possession.

SHAW LJ said at 497: 'In my judgment Mr Willey set up a smoke-screen designed to hide even the possible existence of some interest in himself which could derogate from the interest of the company ostensibly conferred by the mortgage. To change the metaphor, he deliberately put Mr Timbers off the scent and the bank accepted the mortgage as a consequence. They would not have done so but for Mr Willey's subtle but positive indication that he had communicated all that had to be told which could be relevant to the bank's consideration of the company's application.

[5]   The issues of the binding effect of a licence on a third party (p. 609, post), and of the lifting of the veil of corporate personality were not raised. See (1982) 132 NLJ 68 (H. W. Wilkinson); [1982] Conv 67 (R. E. Annand); (1982) 79 LSG 464 (H. Lowless and J. Alder). On constructive notice generally, see *Northern Bank Ltd v Henry* [1981] IR 1, p. 311, n. 4, post.

This being so, I am of the opinion that Mr Willey is estopped from setting up any facts which would go to show that he held an interest which overrides or stands in priority to their interest as mortgagees from the company. [6]

And OLIVER LJ said at 498: 'Now of course, an agent who negotiates a sale or mortgage on his principal's behalf does not thereby make any representation that his principal has an indefeasible title to the property offered for sale or as security. As to that the purchaser or mortgagee must satisfy himself by making the usual enquiries before he completes. But in negotiating on his principal's behalf he does, in my judgment, at least represent that he has his principal's authority to offer the property free from any undisclosed adverse interest of his own. I would therefore be prepared to hold that the purchaser or mortgagee dealing with such an agent can reasonably assume that if the agent with whom he is dealing has himself an interest adverse to the title which he offers on his principal's behalf, he will disclose it. It was in my judgment reasonable for Mr Timbers not to make enquiry about an adverse interest of the negotiating agent which that agent's own reticence entitled him to assume did not exist and he did not, therefore, have constructive notice of it.' [7]

B. Registration of Land Charges

I. UNREGISTERED LAND [88]

(a) Registration Constitutes Actual Notice

LAW OF PROPERTY ACT 1925

198. Registration under the Land Charges Act, 1925, to be notice. —(1) The registration of any instrument or matter in any register, kept under the Land Charges Act 1972 or any local land charges register [9] shall be deemed to constitute actual notice of such instrument or matter, and of the fact of such registration, to all persons and for all purposes connected with the land affected, as from the date of registration or other prescribed date and so long as the registration continues in force.

---

[6]   Cf. in registered land, the proviso to LRA 1925, s. 70(1)(g); p. 131, post. See now LRA 2002, Sched 3, para. 2, p. 163, post; H & B, para. 2.47.

[7]   *Hervey v Smith* (1856) 22 Beav 299 (purchaser of house held to have constructive notice of equitable easement to use two chimneys for the passage of smoke from the mere fact of there being fourteen chimney pots on top of the chimney stack and only twelve flues in the house); *Kingsnorth Finance Co Ltd v Tizard* [1986] 1 WLR 783, [1986] 2 All ER 54, p. 156, post (mortgagee held to have constructive notice of mortgagor's wife's equitable interest in matrimonial home due to (a) his agent's inspection at a time prearranged with the mortgagor (b) his failure to make further inquiries after his agent (i) found evidence of occupation by twin 15 year old children of the mortgagor and (ii) was informed by the mortgagor, who had described himself as single on the mortgage application form, that he was separated from his wife who was residing nearby). The decision is criticised in [1986] Conv 283 (M. P. Thompson); (1986) 136 NLJ 771 (P. Luxton); [1986] All ER Rev 181 (P. J. Clarke); *Abbey National plc v Tufts* [1999] EGCS 24 (bank had no constructive notice of wife's credit status where bankrupt husband applied for loan on her behalf).

[8]   C & B, pp. 97–98, 108–110, 824–835; Gray, pp. 1086–1114; M & W, paras. 5.085–5.137; MM, pp. 93–108; Barnsley, *Conveyancing Law and Practice* (4th edn 1996), pp. 383–407; Report of the Committee on Land Charges 1956 (Cmd. 9825); [1956] CLJ 216 (H. W. R. Wade); Law Commission Report on Land Charges Affecting Unregistered Land 1969 (Law Com. No. 18, HC 125).

[9]   As amended by LLCA 1975, s. 17 (2), Sch. 1.

(2) This section operates without prejudice to the provisions of this Act respecting the making of further advances by a mortgagee,[10] and applies only to instruments and matters required or authorised to be registered in any such register.[11]

LAW OF PROPERTY ACT 1969

24. Contracts for purchase of land affected by land charge, etc. — (1) Where under a contract for the sale or other disposition of any estate or interest in land the title to which is not registered under the Land Registration Act 2002[12] ... any question arises whether the purchaser had knowledge, at the time of entering into the contract, of a registered land charge, that question shall be determined by reference to his actual knowledge and without regard to the provisions of section 198 of the Law of Property Act 1925 ...

(b) What Interests are Registrable

LAND CHARGES ACT 1972[13]

1. The registers and the index. —(1) The registrar shall continue to keep at the registry[14] in the prescribed manner the following registers, namely –

    (*a*) a register of land charges;
    (*b*) a register of pending actions;
    (*c*) a register of writs and orders affecting land;
    (*d*) a register of deeds of arrangement affecting land;
    (*e*) a register of annuities,[15]

and shall also continue to keep there an index whereby all entries made in any of those registers can readily be traced.

(6) Subject to the provisions of this Act, registration may be vacated pursuant to an order of the court.[16]

---

[10]   See p. 918, post.
[11]   As amended by LLCA 1975, s. 17 (2), Sch. 1.
[12]   As amended by LRA 2002, s. 133, Sch. 11, para. 9.
[13]   See also Land Charges Rules 1974 (SI 1974 No. 1286); 1994 (SI 1994 No. 287); 1995 (SI 1995 No. 287); Land Charges Fees Rules 1990; Fees (Amendment) Rules 1994 (SI 1994 No. 286); Land Charges (Amendment) Rules 1990 (SI 1990 No. 485); Land Charges (Amendment) Rules 1995 (SI 1995 No. 1355).
[14]   In Plymouth. In 2002–03 the combined total of applications dealt with by the Land Charges and Agricultural Credits Department was 5,895,686, representing an increase of 10.7% over the total for 2001–02. This was due mainly to a continuing increase in the number of insolvency search applications: Land Registry Annual Report 2002–03, pp. 48–49.
[15]   Sch. 1. No entries have been possible in this register since 1925.
[16]   This is wider than the corresponding LCA 1925, s. 10 (8): *Calgary and Edmonton Land Co Ltd v Dobinson* [1974] Ch 102 at 109, [1974] 1 All ER 484 at 490, per MEGARRY J. See also *Heywood v BDC Properties Ltd* [1963] 1 WLR 975, [1963] 2 All ER 1063; *Heywood v BDC Properties Ltd (No 2)* [1964] 1 WLR 971, [1964] 2 All ER 702; *Georgiades v Edward Wolfe & Co Ltd* [1965] Ch 487, [1964] 3 All ER 433; *Taylor v Taylor* [1968] 1 WLR 378, [1968] 1 All ER 843; *Rawlplug Co Ltd v Kamvale Properties Ltd* (1968) 20 P & CR 32; *Boobyer v Thornville Properties Ltd* (1968) 19 P & CR 768; *Re Longlands Farm* [1968] 3 All ER 552; *Thomas v Rose* [1968] 1 WLR 1797, [1968] 3 All ER 765 (all discussed in (1968) 118 New LJ 1167 (S. M. Cretney) pointing out that a charge can be registered without any proof of its validity, the function of the Registry being purely ministerial; but the registration of such a charge might in practice make the land unsaleable); *Hooker v Wyle* [1974] 1 WLR 235, [1973] 3 All ER 707; *Jones v Morgan* (1973) 231 EG 1167; *Mens v Wilson* (1973) 231 EG 843; *Haslemere Estates Ltd v Baker* [1982] 1 WLR 1109, [1982] 3 All ER 525; [1983] Conv 69 (J.E.M.).

(7) In this section 'index' includes any device or combination of devices serving the purpose of an index.

2. The register of land charges.—(1) If a charge on or obligation affecting land falls into one of the classes described in this section, it may be registered in the register of land charges as a land charge of that class. [17]

(2) A Class A land charge is —

   (*a*) a rent or annuity or principal money payable by instalments or otherwise, with or without interest, which is not a charge created by deed but is a charge upon land (other than a rate) created pursuant to the application of some person under the provisions of any Act of Parliament, for securing to any person either the money spent by him or the costs, charges and expenses incurred by him under such Act, or the money advanced by him for repaying the money spent or the costs, charges and expenses incurred by another person under the authority of an Act of Parliament, [18] or

   (*b*) a rent or annuity or principal money payable as mentioned in paragraph (*a*) above which is not a charge created by deed but is a charge upon land (other than a rate) created pursuant to the application of some person under any of the enactments mentioned in Schedule 2 to this Act. [19]

(3) A Class B land charge is a charge on land (not being a local land charge) [20] of any of the kinds described in paragraph (*a*) of subsection (2) above, created otherwise than pursuant to the application of any person. [1]

Cf. the position in registered land: (a) LRA 1925, ss. 56 (3), 82, p.180, post; *Rawlplug Co Ltd v Kamvale Properties Ltd*, supra; *Calgary and Edmonton Land Co Ltd v Discount Bank (Overseas) Ltd* [1971] 1 WLR 81, [1971] 1 All ER 551; *Clearbrook Property Holdings Ltd v Vernier* [1974] 1 WLR 243, [1973] 3 All ER 614; *Tiverton Estates Ltd v Wearwell Ltd* [1975] Ch 146 at 161, 171, [1974] 1 All ER 209 at 219, 228; *Lester v Burgess* (1973) 26 P & CR 536 (a useful analysis of the jurisdiction by GOULDING J); *Price Bros (Somerford) Ltd v J Kelly Homes (Stoke-on-Trent) Ltd* [1975] 1 WLR 1512, [1975] 3 All ER 369; *Calgary and Edmonton Land Co Ltd v Dobinson*, supra; *Norman v Hardy* [1974] 1 WLR 1048, [1974] 1 All ER 1170; (1974) 38 Conv (NS) 208 (F. R. Crane); *Northern Development (Holdings) Ltd v UDT Securities Ltd* [1976] 1 WLR 1230, [1977] 1 All ER 747; (1976) 41 Conv (NS) 173 (F. R. Crane); *Sowerby v Sowerby* (1982) 44 P & CR 192; *Alpenstow Ltd v Regalian Properties plc* [1985] 1 WLR 721, [1985] 2 All ER 545; *Hynes v Vaughan* (1985) 50 P & CR 444; *Chancery Lane Developments Ltd v Wades Departmental Stores Ltd* (1986) 53 P & CR 306; *Tucker v Hutchinson* (1987) 54 P & CR 106; *Carlton v Halestrap* (1988) 4 BCC 538; *Woolf Project Management Ltd v Woodtrek Ltd* (1987) 56 P & CR 134; *Cabra Estates plc v Glendower Investments Ltd* [1992] EGCS 137; *Willies-Williams v National Trust* (1993) 65 P & CR 359; *Clowes Developments (UK) Ltd v Mulchinock* [1998] 1 WLR 42 (caution removable in landowner giving undertaking in damages to purchaser); *Bhullar v McArdle* [1999] EGCS 84 (caution may be amended or varied).

(b) LRA 2002, ss. 35, 36. For the liability of a solicitor in negligence for failing to ensure that a notice under Matrimonial Homes Act 1967 (now Family Law Act 1996) was cancelled, see *Holmes v Kennard & Son* (1984) 49 P & Cr 202, p. 315, n. 13, post.

[17] For the date of effective registration and priority notices, see LCA 1972, s. 11; (1977) 74 LSG 136 (P. Freedman).

[18] E.g. a statutory charge under the Improvement of Land Act 1864.

[19] E.g. Landlord and Tenant Act 1927, s. 12, Sch. 1, para. 7 (charge in respect of improvements to business premises).

[20] As amended by LLCA 1975, s. 19, Sch 2.

[1] E.g. a charge on property recovered or preserved for an assisted person arising under the Legal Aid Act 1988, s. 16.

(4) A Class C land charge is any of the following (not being a local land charge),[2] namely —
- (i)   a puisne mortgage,[3]
- (ii) a limited owner's charge,[4]
- (iii) a general equitable charge,[5]
- (iv) an estate contract,[6]

and for this purpose —
- (i)   a puisne[7] mortgage is a legal mortgage which is not protected by a deposit of documents relating to the legal estate affected;
- (ii) a limited owner's charge is an equitable charge acquired by a tenant for life or statutory owner under the Inheritance Tax Act 1984 or under any other statute by reason of the discharge by him of any inheritance tax[8] or other liabilities and to which special priority is given by the statute;
- (iii) a general equitable charge is any equitable charge which —
- (*a*)   is not secured by a deposit of documents relating to the legal estate affected; and
- (*b*)   does not arise or affect an interest arising under a trust of land[9] or a settlement; and
- (*c*)   is not a charge given by way of indemnity against rents equitably apportioned or charged exclusively on land in exoneration of other land and against the breach or non-observance of covenants or conditions; and
- (*d*)   is not included in any other class of land charge;
- (iv) an estate contract is a contract by an estate owner or by a person entitled at the date of the contract to have a legal estate conveyed to him to convey or create a legal estate, including a contract conferring either expressly or by statutory implication a valid option to purchase,[10] a right of preemption[11] or any other like right.

(5) A Class D land charge is any of the following (not being a local land charge)[12] namely —
- (i)   an Inland Revenue charge;
- (ii) a restrictive covenant;[13]

---

[2]   As amended by LLCA 1975, s. 17(1)(*b*).
[3]   P. 915, post.
[4]   P. 338, post.
[5]   This does not include mortgages of equitable interests which are treated separately; p. 916, post.
[6]   P. 84, post.
[7]   Puisne is derived from the old French *puis* (after) *né* (born); hence a later or subsequent mortgage.
[8]   As amended by FA 1975, s. 52, Sch. 12, para. 18; IHTA 1984, s. 276, Sch. 8, para. 3(1)(*a*). See IHTA 1984, ss. 237, 238.
[9]   As amended by TLATA 1996, s. 25(1), Sch. 3, para. 12(2).
[10] *Beesly v Hallwood Estates Ltd* [1960] 1 WLR 549, [1960] 2 All ER 314; *Taylors Fashions Ltd v Liverpool Victoria Trustees Co Ltd* [1982] QB 133n, [1981] 1 All ER 897, p. 627, post (option to renew, contained in lease, held registrable as option to purchase); approved in *Phillips v Mobil Oil Co Ltd* [1989] 1 WLR 888, [1989] 3 All ER 97; [1990] Conv 168, 250 (J. Howell); [1989] All ER Rev 193 (P. H. Pettit).
[11] *Pritchard v Briggs* [1980] Ch 338, [1980] 1 All ER 294, p. 93, post; (1980) 39 CLJ 35 (C. Harpum); Barnsley, *Land Options* (2nd edn 1992), chap. 7.
[12] As amended by LLCA 1975, s. 17(1)(*b*).
[13] P. 938, post.

(iii) an equitable easement, [14]

and for this purpose —

(i)   an Inland Revenue charge is a charge on land, being a charge acquired by the Board under the Inheritance Tax Act 1984; [15]

(ii) a restrictive covenant is a covenant or agreement (other than a covenant or agreement between a lessor and a lessee) restrictive of the user of land and entered into on or after 1st January 1926;

(iii) an equitable easement is an easement, right or privilege over or affecting land created or arising on or after 1st January 1926, and being merely an equitable interest.

(6) A Class E land charge is an annuity created before 1st January 1926 and not registered in the register of annuities.

(7) A Class F land charge is a charge affecting any land by virtue of Part IV of the Family Law Act 1996. [16]

(8) A charge or obligation created before 1st January 1926 can only be registered as a Class B land charge or a Class C land charge if it is acquired under a conveyance made on or after that date.

3. Registration of land charges. —(1) A land charge shall be registered in the name of the estate owner [17] whose estate is intended to be affected. [18]

(1A) Where a person has died and a land charge created before his death would apart from his death have been registered in his name, it shall be so registered notwithstanding his death. [19]

(2) A land charge registered before 1st January 1926 under any enactment replaced by the Land Charges Act 1925 in the name of a person other than the estate owner may remain so registered until it is registered in the name of the estate owner in the prescribed manner.

(3) A puisne mortgage created before 1st January 1926 may be registered as a land charge before any transfer of the mortgage is made.

———————

Land Registry Annual Report and Accounts 2002–03, p. 49. [20]

The types of application to the Land Charges Department in 2002–03 were as follows:

14   P. 711, post.
15   As amended by FA 1975, s. 52, Sch. 12, para. 18; IHTA 1984, s. 276, Sch. 8, para. 3(1)(*b*).
16   As amended by Family Law Act 1996, s. 27, Sch 8, para. 47 (replacing MHA 1983), pp. 312–315, post.
17   P. 44, post. The name of the estate owner means the name as disclosed by the conveyance: *Standard Property Investment plc v British Plastics Federation* (1985) 53 P & CR 25; [1987] Conv 135 (J.E.A.). A person entitled to have the legal estate conveyed to him is not an estate owner: *Barrett v Hilton Developments Ltd* [1975] Ch 237, [1974] 3 All ER 944; *Property Discount Corpn Ltd v Lyon Group Ltd* [1981] 1 WLR 300, [1981] 1 All ER 379.
18   On the mechanics of the register see *Oak Co-operative Building Society v Blackburn* [1968] Ch 730 at 741, [1968] 2 All ER 117 at 121, per RUSSELL LJ.
19   Inserted by LP (Miscellaneous Provisions) Act 1994, s. 15(2). See Law Commission Report: Title on Death 1989 (Law Com No. 184, Cm 777), paras. 2–2 to 2–9; [1995] Conv 476 (L. Clements).
20   The Report for 1995–1996 was the last to give a breakdown of new registrations. The most numerous classes were C(i) (puisne mortgages); C(iv) (estate contracts); and D(ii) (restrictive covenants).

Type of application	Number of applications or names	% variation compared with 2001–02
New Registrations rectifications and renewals	97,205	+1.1%
Cancellations	49,088	–5.0%
Official Searches		
i) Full Searches	1,023,302	–6.4%
ii) Searches limited to insolvency	4,581,525	+16.3%
Total Searches	5,604,827	+11.4%
Office Copies	134,537	+1.3%
Total	5,885,657	+10.8%

In **Shiloh Spinners Ltd v Harding** [1973] AC 691, [1973] 1 All ER 90,[1] the respondents were assignees of part of leasehold premises which was subject to covenants. The appellants had the right to re-enter and retake the premises in the event of breach. The respondents were aware of this all the time, and, in breach of covenant, they demolished the premises, and argued that the right of entry was void against them because it was not registered.

The House of Lords held that the right of entry was not registrable, and was enforceable against purchasers with notice. Lord WILBERFORCE said at 718, at 96:

'The right of entry, it is said, is unenforceable against the respondent, although he took with actual notice of it, because it was not registered as a charge under the Land Charges Act 1925. There is no doubt that if it was capable of registration under that Act, it is unenforceable if not registered: the appellants deny that it was so capable either (i) because it was a legal right, not an equitable right, or (ii) because, if equitable, it does not fall within any of the classes or descriptions of charges registration of which is required.

[His Lordship held that the right of entry was equitable and continued:]

So I pass, as did the Court of Appeal, to the Land Charges Act 1925. The original contention of the respondents was that the equitable right of entry was capable of registration under Class D(iii) of the Act. In the Court of Appeal an alternative contention was raised, apparently at the court's suggestion, that it might come within Class C(iv). In my opinion this is unmaintainable. Class C(iv) embraces:

"Any contract by an estate owner or by a person entitled at the date of the contract to have a legal estate conveyed to him to convey or create a legal estate, including a contract conferring either expressly or by statutory implication a valid

[1]   (1973) 32 CLJ 218 (P. B. Fairest).

option of purchase, a right of pre-emption or any other like right (in this Act referred to as 'an estate contract')."

The only words capable of including a right of entry are "any other like right", but, in my opinion, no relevant likeness can be found. An option or right of pre-emption eventuates in a contract for sale at a price; this is inherent in "purchase" and "pre-emption"; the right of entry is penal in character and involves the revesting of the lease, in the event of default, in a previous owner. There is no similarity in law or fact between these situations. [2]

Class D(iii) reads:

"A charge or obligation affecting land of any of the following kinds, namely:— ... (iii) Any easement right or privilege over or affecting land created or arising after the commencement of this Act, and being merely an equitable interest (in this Act referred to as an 'equitable easement')."

The argument for inclusion in this class falls into two parts. First it is said that a right of entry falls fairly within the description, or at least that, if the words do not appear to include it, they are sufficiently open in meaning to admit it. Secondly it is said that the provisions of the Law of Property Act as to "overreaching" [3] compel the conclusion that a right of entry must fall under some class or sub-class of the Land Charges Act, and since this is the only one whose words can admit it, they should be so interpreted as to do so. Thus the argument depends for its success upon a combination of ambiguity, or openness of Class D(iii) with compelling consideration brought about in the overreaching provisions. In my opinion it fails under both limbs: Class D(iii) cannot be interpreted so as to admit equitable rights of entry, and no conclusive, compelling, or even clear conclusions can be drawn from the overreaching provisions which can influence the interpretation of Class D(iii).

Dealing with Class D(iii), I reject at once the suggestion that any help (by way of enlarging the content of this class) can be derived either from the introductory words, for they limit themselves to the "following kinds," or from the words "and being merely an equitable interest," for these are limiting, not enlarging, words. I leave out of account the label at the end—though I should think it surprising if so expert a draftsman had attached that particular label if the class included a right of entry. To include a right of entry in the description of "equitable easement" offends a sense both of elegance and accuracy. That leaves "easement right or privilege over or affecting land." If this were the only place where the expression occurred in the legislation, I should find it difficult to attribute to "right" a meaning so different in quality from easement and privilege as to include a right of entry. The difference between a right to use or draw profit from another man's land, and a right to take his land altogether away, is one of quality, not of degree. ... I do not further elaborate this point because a reading of their judgments leaves little doubt that the Lords Justices would

---

[2]   But a proviso in a lease requiring a lessee, who wishes to assign, first to offer a surrender of the lease to the lessor is registrable as an estate contract: *Bocardo SA v S and M Hotels Ltd* [1980] 1 WLR 17, [1979] 3 All ER 737; *Adler v Upper Grosvenor Street Investment Ltd* [1957] 1 WLR 227, [1957] 1 All ER 229; (1957) 73 LQR 157 (R. E. M.); *Creer v P and O Lines of Australia Pty Ltd* (1971) 45 ALJR 697; (1972) 88 LQR 317. This surrender proviso was doubted by CA in *Greene v Church Comrs for England* [1974] Ch 467, [1974] 3 All ER 609. On registrability, see LCA 1972, s. 2(4); *Greene v Church Comrs for England*, supra. For the position of business tenancies under Landlord and Tenant Act 1954, Part II, see *Allnatt London Properties Ltd v Newton* [1981] 2 All ER 290; [1980] Conv 418 (C. G. Blake); (1983) 127 SJ 855 (C. Coombe).

[3]   P. 293, post.

themselves have read Class D(iii) as I can only read it but for the influence of the overreaching argument.

So I turn to the latter. This, in my opinion, only becomes compelling if one first accepts the conclusion that all equitable claims relating to land are either registrable under the Land Charges Act, or capable of being over-reached under section 2 of the Law of Property Act; i.e., are capable by use of the appropriate mechanism of being transferred to the proceeds of sale of the land they affect. If this dilemma could be made good, then there could be an argument for forcing, within the limits of the possible, an equitable right of entry into one of the registrable classes, since it is obviously not suitable for overreaching. But the dilemma cannot be made good. What may be over-reached is any "equitable interest or power affecting that estate": yet "equitable interest" (for powers do not enter into the debate) is a word of most uncertain content. The searcher after a definition has to be satisfied with section 1(8) "Estates, interests, and charges in or over land which are not legal estates are in this Act referred to as 'equitable interests' "—a tautology rather than a definition. There is certainly nothing exhaustive about the expression "equitable interests";—just as certainly it has no clear boundaries. The debate whether such rights as equity, over the centuries, has conferred against the holder of the legal estate are truly proprietary in character, or merely rights in personam, or a hybrid between the two, may have lost some of its vitality in the statutory context but the question inevitably rises to mind whether the "curtain" or "overreaching" provisions of the 1925 legislation extend to what are still conveniently called "equities" or "mere equities," such as rights to rectification, or to set aside a conveyance. There is good authority, which I do not presume to doubt, for a sharp distinction between the two—I instance Lord Upjohn in *National Provincial Bank Ltd v Ainsworth* [1965] AC 1175 at 1238, [1965] 2 All ER 472 at 488 and *Snell's Principles of Equity*, 25th edn. (1960) p. 38. I am impressed by the decision in *E R Ives Investment Ltd v High* [1967] 2 QB 379, [1967] 1 All ER 504, p. 665, *post*, in which the Court of Appeal held that a right by estoppel—producing an effect similar to an easement—was not registrable under Class D(iii). Lord Denning MR referred to the right as subsisting only in equity. Danckwerts LJ thought it was an equity created by estoppel or a proprietary estoppel: plainly this was not an equitable interest capable of being overreached, yet no member of the court considered that the right—so like an easement—could be brought within Class D(iii). The conclusion followed, and the court accepted it, that whether it was binding on a purchaser depended on notice. All this seems to show that there may well be rights, of an equitable character, outside the provisions as to registration and which are incapable of being overreached.

That equitable rights of entry should be among them is not in principle unacceptable. First, rights of entry, before 1925, were not considered to confer an interest in the land. They were described as bare possibilities (*Challis's Real Property*, 3rd edn. (1911), p. 76) so that it is not anomalous that equitable rights of entry should not be treated as equitable interests. Secondly, it is important that section 10 of the Land Charges Act 1925 [4] should be given a plain and ordinary interpretation. It is a section which involves day to day operation by solicitors doing conveyancing work: they should be able to take decisions and advise their clients upon a straight-forward interpretation of the registration classes, not upon one depending upon a sophisticated, not

---

[4]   Now LCA 1972, s. 2.

to say disputable, analysis of other statutes. Thirdly, the consequence of equitable rights of entry not being registrable is that they are subject to the doctrine of notice, preserved by section 199 of the Law of Property Act. This may not give complete protection, but neither is it demonstrable that it is likely to be less effective than the present system of registration against names. I am therefore of opinion that Class D(iii) should be given its plain prima facie meaning and that so read it does not comprise equitable rights of entry. It follows that non-registration does not make the appellants' right unenforceable in this case.

The consequence is that the appellants' claim to re-enter must succeed unless the respondent can and should be relieved in equity against the appellants' legal right.'

[Relief against forfeiture was refused.] [5]

(c) Effect of Non-Registration

LAND CHARGES ACT 1972

4. Effect of land charges and protection of purchasers.[6]— (5) A land charge of Class B and a land charge of Class C (other than an estate contract) created or arising on or after 1st January 1926 shall be void as against a purchaser of the land charged with it, or of any interest in such land, unless the land charge is registered in the appropriate register before the completion of the purchase.

(6) An estate contract and a land charge of Class D created or entered into on or after 1st January 1926 shall be void as against a purchaser for money or money's worth [7] (or, in the case of an Inland Revenue charge, a purchaser within the meaning of the Inheritance Tax Act 1984) [8] of a legal estate in the land charged with it, unless the land charge is registered in the appropriate register before the completion of the purchase.

(7) After the expiration of one year from the first conveyance occurring on or after 1st January 1926 of a land charge of Class B or Class C created before that date the person entitled to the land charge shall not be able to enforce or recover the land charge or any part of it as against a purchaser of the land charged with it, or of any interest in the land, unless the land charge is registered in the appropriate register before the completion of the purchase.

(8) A land charge of Class F shall be void as against a purchaser of the land charged with it, or of any interest in such land, unless the land charge is registered in the appropriate register before the completion of the purchase.

17. Interpretation. — (1) In this Act, unless the context otherwise requires,— 'purchaser' means any person (including a mortgagee or lessee) who, for valuable consideration, takes any interest in land or in a charge on land, and 'purchase' has a corresponding meaning.

---

[5]   P. 557, n. 7, post.
[6]   Sub-ss. (1)–(4) contain provisions relating to land charges Class A.
[7]   *Midland Bank Trust Co Ltd v Green* [1981] AC 513, [1981] 1 All ER 153, infra. *Lloyds Bank plc v Carrick* [1996] 4 All ER 630 p. 50, n. 4, post.
[8]   As amended by FA 1975 s. 52, Sch. 12; IHTA 1984, s. 276, Sch. 8, para. 3(2).

MIDLAND BANK TRUST CO LTD v GREEN
[1981] AC 513 [1981] 1 All ER 153
(HL, Lords WILBERFORCE, EDMUND-DAVIES, FRASER OF TULLYBELTON, RUSSELL OF KILLOWEN and BRIDGE OF HARWICH)[9]

In 1961 a father (Walter) granted to his son (Geoffrey) a 10 year option to purchase Gravel Hill Farm, Thornton-le-Moor, Lincolnshire, of which the son was his tenant. The option was not registered under LCA 1925. In 1967 the father, wishing to deprive the son of his option, conveyed the farm, then worth about £40,000, to the mother (Evelyne) for £500. When the son discovered this, he registered the option and purported to exercise it.

The son's executors claimed that the option was binding on the mother's estate.

Held (reversing CA, and restoring OLIVER J). Option void. The mother was a 'purchaser of a legal estate for money or money's worth' under LCA 1925, ss 13(2) and 20(8). [10]

LORD WILBERFORCE: This option was, in legal terms, an estate contract and so a legal charge, class C, within the meaning of the Land Charges Act 1925. The correct and statutory method for protection of such an option is by means of entering it in the Register of Land Charges maintained under the Act. If so registered, the option would have been enforceable, not only (contractually) against Walter, but against any purchaser of the farm.

The option was not registered, a failure which inevitably called in question the responsibility of Geoffrey's solicitor. To anticipate, Geoffrey in fact brought proceedings against his solicitor which have been settled for a considerable sum, payable if the present appeal succeeds. ...

[His Lordship read LCA 1925, ss. 13 (2), 20 (8) and continued:]

Thus the case appears to be a plain one. The 'estate contract,' which by definition includes an option of purchase, was entered into after January 1, 1926; Evelyne took an interest (in fee simple) in the land 'for valuable consideration'—so was a 'purchaser': she was a purchaser for money—namely £500: the option was not registered before the completion of the purchase. It is therefore void as against her.

In my opinion this appearance is also the reality. The case is plain: the Act is clear and definite. Intended as it was to provide a simple and understandable system for the protection of title to land, it should not be read down or glossed: to do so would destroy the usefulness of the Act. Any temptation to remould the Act to meet the facts of the present case, on the supposition that it is a hard one and that justice requires it, is, for me at least, removed by the consideration that the Act itself provides a simple and effective protection for persons in Geoffrey's position—viz.—by registration.

The respondents submitted two arguments as to the interpretation of section 13(2): the one sought to introduce into it a requirement that the purchaser

[9] The 'Green Saga', which 'bids fair to rival in time and money the story of *Jarndyce v Jarndyce*' (see [1980] Ch 590 at 622, [1979] 3 All ER 28 at 32, per LORD DENNING MR), continues. For the liability of the solicitor for failing to advise the son to register the option and for failing to register it, see *Midland Bank Trust Co Ltd v Hett, Stubbs and Kemp* [1979] Ch 384, [1978] 3 All ER 571; and for conspiracy between husband and wife, see *Midland Bank Trust Co Ltd v Green (No 3)* [1982] Ch 529, [1981] 3 All ER 744. For a full review of all three cases by Sir Peter OLIVER, who tried them at first instance, see *The Green Saga* (1983) Child & Co Oxford Lecture. See also [1981] CLJ 213 (C. Harpum); (1981) 97 LQR 518 (B. Green).

[10] Now LCA 1972, ss. 4(6) and 17(1), as amended by TLATA 1996, s. 25(2), Sch. 4.

should be 'in good faith'; the other related to the words 'in money or money's worth.'

The argument as to good faith fell into three parts: first, that 'good faith' was something required of a 'purchaser' before 1926; secondly, that this requirement was preserved by the 1925 legislation and in particular by section 13(2) of the Land Charges Act 1925. If these points could be made good, it would then have to be decided whether the purchaser (Evelyne) was in 'good faith' on the facts of the case.

My Lords, the character in the law known as the bona fide (good faith) purchaser for value without notice was the creation of equity. In order to affect a purchaser for value of a legal estate with some equity or equitable interest, equity fastened upon his conscience and the composite expression was used to epitomise the circumstances in which equity would or rather would not do so. I think that it would generally be true to say that the words 'in good faith' related to the existence of notice. Equity, in other words, required not only absence of notice, but genuine and honest absence of notice. As the law developed, this requirement became crystallised in the doctrine of constructive notice which assumed a statutory form in the Conveyancing Act 1882, section 3. But, and so far I would be willing to accompany the respondents, it would be a mistake to suppose that the requirement of good faith extended only to the matter of notice, or that when notice came to be regulated by statute, the requirement of good faith became obsolete. Equity still retained its interest in and power over the purchaser's conscience. The classic judgment of James LJ in *Pilcher v Rawlins* (1872) 7 Ch App 259 at 269, p. 26, ante, is clear authority that it did: good faith there is stated as a separate test which may have to be passed even though absence of notice is proved. And there are references in cases subsequent to 1882 which confirm the proposition that honesty or bona fides remained something which might be inquired into (see *Berwick & Co v Price* [1905] 1 Ch 632 at 639; *Taylor v London and County Banking Co* [1901] 2 Ch 231 at 256; *Oliver v Hinton* [1899] 2 Ch 264 at 273).

But did this requirement, or test, pass into the property legislation of 1925?

My Lords, I do not think it safe to seek the answer to this question by means of a general assertion that the property legislation of 1922–25 was not intended to alter the law, or not intended to alter it in a particular field, such as that relating to purchases of legal estates. All the Acts of 1925, and their precursors, were drafted with the utmost care, and their wording, certainly where this is apparently clear, has to be accorded firm respect. As was pointed out in *Grey v IRC* [1960] AC 1, [1959] 3 All ER 603, the Acts of 1922–24 effected massive changes in the law affecting property and the House, in consequence, was persuaded to give to a plain word ('disposition') its plain meaning, and not to narrow it by reference to its antecedents. Certainly that case should firmly discourage us from muddying clear waters. I accept that there is merit in looking at the corpus as a whole in order to produce if possible a consistent scheme. But there are limits to the possibilities of this process: for example it cannot eliminate the difference between registered and unregistered land, or the respective charges on them.

As to the requirement of 'good faith' we are faced with a situation of some perplexity. The expression 'good faith,' appears in the Law of Property Act 1925 definition of 'purchaser' ('a purchaser in good faith for valuable consideration'), section 205(1)(xxi); in the Settled Land Act 1925, section 117(1)(xxi) (ditto); in the Administration of Estates Act 1925, section 55(1)(xviii) (' "Purchaser" means a lessee, mortgagee or other person who in good faith acquires an interest in property for valuable consideration') and in the Land Registration Act 1925, section 3(xxi) which does not however, as the other Acts do, include a reference to nominal consideration. So there is certainly some indication of an intention to carry the concept of 'good faith' into much of the 1925 code. What then do we find in the Land Charges Act 1925? We were taken along a scholarly peregrination through the numerous Acts antecedent to the final codification and consolidation in 1925—the Land Charges Registration and Searches Act 1888, the Law of Property Act 1922, particularly Schedule 7, the Law of Property (Amendment) Act 1924 as well as the Yorkshire and Middlesex Deeds Registration Acts. But I think, with genuine respect for an interesting argument, that such solution as there is of the problem under consideration must be sought in the terms of the various Acts of 1925 themselves. So far as concerns the Land Charges Act 1925, the definition of 'purchaser' quoted above does not mention 'good faith' at all. 'Good faith' did not appear in the original Act of 1888, nor in the extension made to that Act by the Act of 1922, Schedule 7, nor in the Act of 1924, Schedule 6. It should be a secure assumption that the definition of 'purchaser for value' which is found in section 4 of the Act of 1888 (… 'person who for valuable consideration takes any interest in land') together with the limitation which is now the proviso to section 13(2) of the Act of 1925, introduced in 1922, was intended to be carried forward into the Act of 1925. The expression 'good faith' appears nowhere in the antecedents. To write the word in, from the examples of contemporaneous Acts, would be bold. It becomes impossible when it is seen that the words appear in section 3(1) and in section 7(1), in each case in a proviso very similar, in structure, to the relevant proviso in section 13(2). If canons of constructions have any validity at all, they must lead to the conclusion that the omission in section 13(2) was deliberate.

My Lords, I recognise that the inquiring mind may put the question: why should there be an omission of the requirement of good faith in this particular context? I do not think there should be much doubt about the answer. Addition of a requirement that the purchaser should be in good faith would bring with it the necessity of inquiring into the purchaser's motives and state of mind. The present case is a good example of the difficulties which would exist. If the position was simply that the purchaser had notice of the option, and decided nevertheless to buy the land, relying on the absence of notification, nobody could contend that she would be lacking in good faith. She would merely be taking advantage of a situation, which the law has provided, and the addition of a profit motive could not create an absence of good faith. But suppose, and this is the respondents' argument, the purchaser's motive is to defeat the option, does this make any difference? Any advantage to oneself seems necessarily to involve a disadvantage for another: to make the validity of the purchase depend upon which aspect of the transaction was prevalent in the purchaser's mind seems to create distinctions equally difficult to analyse in law as to establish in fact: avarice and malice may be distinct sins, but in human conduct they are liable to be intertwined. The problem becomes even more acute if one supposes a mixture of motives. Suppose—and this may not be far from the truth—that the purchaser's motives were in part to take the farm from Geoffrey, and in part to distribute it between Geoffrey and his brothers and sisters, but not at all to obtain any benefit for herself, is this acting in 'good faith': or not? Should family feeling be denied a protection afforded to simple greed? To eliminate the necessity for inquiries of this kind may well have been part of the legislative intention. Certainly there is here no argument for departing—violently—from the wording of the Act.

Before leaving this part of the case, I must comment on *Re Monolithic Building Co* [1915] 1 Ch 643, which was discussed in the Court of Appeal. That was a case arising under section 93 of the Companies (Consolidation) Act 1908 which made an unregistered mortgage void against any creditor of the company. The defendant Jenkins was a managing director of the company, and clearly had notice of the first unregistered mortgage: he himself subsequently took and registered a mortgage debenture and claimed priority over the registered mortgage. It was held by the Court of Appeal, first that this was not a case of fraud: 'It is not fraud to take advantage of legal rights, the existence of which may be taken to be known to both parties' (per Lord Cozens-Hardy MR, at 663), secondly that section 93 of the Act was clear in its terms, should be applied according to its plain meaning, and should not be weakened by infusion of equitable doctrines applied by the courts during the 19th century. The judgment of Lord Cozens-Hardy MR contains a valuable critique of the well known cases of *Le Neve v Le Neve* (1747) 3 Atk 646 and *Greaves v Tofield* (1880) 14 ChD 563 which, arising under the Middlesex Registry Act 1708 and other enactments, had led the judges to import equitable doctrines into cases of priority arising under those Acts, and establishes that the principles of those cases should not be applied to modern Acts of Parliament.

My Lords, I fail to see how this authority can be invoked in support of the respondents' argument, or of the judgments of the majority of the Court of Appeal. So far from supporting them, it is strongly the other way. It disposes, for the future, of the old arguments based, ultimately, upon *Le Neve v Le Neve* for reading equitable doctrines (as to notice, etc.) into modern Acts of Parliament: it makes it clear that it is not 'fraud' to rely on legal rights conferred by Act of Parliament: it confirms the validity of interpreting clear enactments as to registration and priority according to their tenor.

The judgement of Philimore LJ in *Re Monolithic Building Co* [1915] 1 Ch 643 at 669, 670 does indeed contain a passage which appears to favour application of the principle of *Le Neve v Le Neve* and to make a distinction between a transaction designed to obtain an advantage, and one designed to defeat a prior (unregistered) interest. But, as I have explained, this distinction is unreal and unworkable: this whole passage is impossible to reconcile with the views of the other members of the Court of Appeal in the case, and I respectfully consider that it is not good law.

My Lords, I can deal more shortly with the respondents' second argument. It relates to the consideration for the purchase. The argument is that the protection of section 13(2) of the Land Charges Act 1925 does not extend to a purchaser who has provided only a nominal consideration and that £500 is nominal. A variation of this was the argument accepted by the Court of Appeal that the consideration must be 'adequate'—an expression of transparent difficulty. The answer to both contentions lies in the language of the subsection. The word 'purchaser,' by definition (section 20(8)), means one who provides valuable consideration—a term of art which precludes any inquiry as to adequacy. This definition is, of course, subject to the context. Section 13(2), proviso, requires money or money's worth to be provided: the purpose of this being to exclude the consideration of marriage. There is nothing here which suggests, or admits of, the introduction of a further requirement that the money must not be nominal.

The argument for this requirement is based upon the Law of Property Act 1925 which, in section 205(1)(xxi) defining 'purchaser' provides that 'valuable consideration' includes marriage but does not include a 'nominal consideration in money.' The Land Charges Act 1925 contains no definition of 'valuable consideration,' so it is said to be necessary to have resort to the Law of Property

Act definition: thus 'nominal consideration in money' is excluded. An indication that this is intended is said to be provided by section 199(1)(i). I cannot accept this. The fallacy lies in supposing that the Acts—either of them— set out to define 'valuable consideration'; they do not: they define 'purchaser,' and they define the word differently (see the first part of the argument). 'Valuable consideration' requires no definition: it is an expression denoting an advantage conferred or detriment suffered. What each Act does is, for its own purposes, to exclude some things from this general expression: the Law of Property Act includes marriage but not a nominal sum in money; the Land Charges Act excludes marriage but allows 'money or money's worth.' There is no coincidence between these two; no link by reference or necessary logic between them. Section 199(1)(i) by referring to the Land Charges Act 1925, necessarily incorporates—for the purposes for this provision—the definition of 'purchaser' in the latter Act, for it is only against such a 'purchaser' that an instrument is void under that Act. It cannot be read as incorporating the Law of Property Act definition into the Land Charges Act. As I have pointed out the land charges legislation has contained its own definition since 1888, carried through, with the addition of the reference to 'money or money's worth' into 1925. To exclude a nominal sum of money from section 13(2) of the Land Charges Act would be to rewrite the section.

This conclusion makes it unnecessary to determine whether £500 is a nominal sum of money or not. But I must say that for my part I should have great difficulty in so holding. 'Nominal consideration' and a 'nominal sum' in the law appear to me, as terms of art, to refer to a sum or consideration which can be mentioned as consideration but is not necessarily paid. To equate 'nominal' with 'inadequate' or even 'grossly inadequate' would embark the law upon inquiries which I cannot think were contemplated by Parliament.

I would allow the appeal.

(d) Registers in Existence before 1926

LAND CHARGES ACT 1972

5. The register of pending actions. —(1) There may be registered in the register of pending actions —

(*a*)   a pending land action; [11]

(*b*)   a petition in bankruptcy filed on or after 1st January 1926.

(4) The registrar shall forthwith enter the particulars in the register, in the name of the estate owner or other person whose estate or interest is intended to be affected.

---

[11]   Defined in LCA 1972, s. 17 (1) as 'any action or proceeding in court relating to land or any interest in or charge on land.' See *Calgary and Edmonton Land Co Ltd v Dobinson* [1974] Ch 102, [1974] 1 All ER 484; *Whittingham v Whittingham* [1979] Fam 9, [1978] 3 All ER 805; *Greenhi Builders Ltd v Allen* [1979] 1 WLR 156, [1978] 3 All ER 1163; *Selim Ltd v Bickenhall Engineering Ltd* [1981] 1 WLR 1318, [1981] 3 All ER 210; *Regan & Blackburn Ltd v Rogers* [1985] 1 WLR 870, [1985] 2 All ER 180; *Sowerby v Sowerby* (1982) 44 P & CR 192; *Haslemere Estates Ltd v Baker* [1982] 1 WLR 1109, [1982] 3 All ER 525; [1983] Conv 69 (J. E. M.); *Perez-Adamson v Perez Rivas* [1987] Fam 89, [1987] 3 All ER 20; [1987] Conv 58 (J. E. Martin); *Kemmis v Kemmis* [1988] 1 WLR 1307; and generally (1986) 136 NLJ 157 (H. W. Wilkinson); *Willies-Williams v National Trust* (1993) 65 P & CR 359.

(4A) Where a person has died and a pending land action would apart from his death have been registered in his name, it shall be so registered notwithstanding his death. [12]

(7) A pending land action shall not bind a purchaser without express notice of it unless it is for the time being registered under this section.

(8) A petition in bankruptcy shall not bind a purchaser of a legal estate in good faith, for money or money's worth, unless it is for the time being registered under this section. [13]

(10) The court, if it thinks fit, may, upon the determination of the proceedings, or during the pendency of the proceedings if satisfied that they are not prosecuted in good faith, make an order vacating a registration under this section, and direct the party on whose behalf it was made to pay all or any of the costs and expenses occasioned by the registration and by its vacation. [14]

6. The register of writs and orders affecting land. —(1) There may be registered in the register of writs and orders affecting land —

    (*a*) any writ or order affecting land [15] issued or made by any court for the purpose of enforcing a judgment or recognisance; [16]

    (*b*) any order appointing a receiver [17] or sequestrator of land;

    (*c*) any bankruptcy order, whether or not the bankrupt's estate is known to include land; [18]

    (*d*) any access order under the Access to Neighbouring Land Act 1992. [19]

(1A) No writ or order affecting an interest under a trust of land may be registered under subsection (1) above. [20]

(4) Except as provided by subsection (5) below and by section 37(5) of the Supreme Court Act 1981 [1] and section 107(3) of the County Courts Act 1984 (which make special provision as to receiving orders in respect of land of judgment debtors) every such writ and order as is mentioned in subsection (1) above, and every delivery in execution or other proceeding taken pursuant to any such writ or order, or in obedience to any such writ or order, shall be void as against a purchaser of the land unless the writ or order is for the time being registered under this section.

(5) Subject to subsection (6) below, the title of a trustee in bankruptcy shall be void as against a purchaser of a legal estate in good faith for money or money's worth, unless the bankruptcy order is for the time being registered under this section. [2]

---

[12]   As inserted by LP (Miscellaneous Provisions) Act 1994, s. 15(3).

[13]   As amended by Insolvency Act 1985, s. 235, Sch. 8, para. 21 (2), and Sch. 10.

[14]   *Calgary and Edmonton Land Co Ltd v Discount Bank (Overseas) Ltd* [1971] 1 WLR 81, [1971] 1 All ER 551; *Norman v Hardy* [1974] 1 WLR 1048, [1974] 1 All ER 1170; *Northern Development (Holdings) Ltd v UDT Securities Ltd* [1976] 1 WLR 1230, [1977] 1 All ER 747. Cf LCA 1972, s. 1(6), p. 33, ante.

[15]   *Perry v Phoenix Assurance plc* [1988] 1 WLR 940, [1988] 3 All ER 60, p. 801, post.

[16]   E.g. an order charging the land of a judgment debtor with the payment of the money due: Charging Orders Act 1979, p. 799, post. See *Stockler v Fourways Estates Ltd* [1984] 1 WLR 25, [1983] 3 All ER 501 (Mareva injunction prohibiting a party from disposing of his assets held not registrable.)

[17]   *Clayhope Properties Ltd v Evans* [1986] 1 WLR 1223, [1986] 2 All ER 795 (receivership order made against landlord for specific performance of repairing covenants held registrable). In registered land, this is registrable as a restriction under LRA 2002, s. 87(2), and as a caution under LRA 1925, s. 54.

[18]   As amended by Insolvency Act 1985, s. 235, Sch. 8, para. 21(3), and Sch. 10.

[19]   As inserted by Access to Neighbouring Land Act 1992, s. 5(1), p. 713, post.

[20]   As inserted by TLATA 1996, s. 25(1), Sch. 3, para. 12(3).

[1]   As amended by Supreme Court Act 1981, s. 15(2), Sch. 5.

[2]   As amended by County Courts Act 1984, s. 148(1), Sch. 2, para. 18.

(6) Where a petition in bankruptcy has been registered under section 5 above, the title of the trustee in bankruptcy shall be void as against a purchaser of a legal estate in good faith for money or money's worth claiming under a conveyance made after the date of registration, unless at the date of the conveyance either the registration of the petition is in force or a receiving order on the petition is registered under this section.

7. The register of deeds of arrangement affecting land. —(1) A deed of arrangement affecting land may be registered in the register of deeds of arrangement affecting land, in the name of the debtor, on the application of a trustee of the deed or a creditor assenting to or taking the benefit of the deed.

(2) Every deed of arrangement shall be void as against a purchaser of any land comprised in it or affected by it unless it is for the time being registered under this section.

8. Expiry and renewal of registrations. —A registration under section 5, section 6 or section 7 of this Act shall cease to have effect at the end of the period of five years from the date on which it is made, but may be renewed from time to time and, if so renewed, shall have effect for five years from the date of renewal.

(e) Registration Against Estate Owners Prior to Root of Title

Since the system of registration of land charges provides for the registration of charges against the name of the estate owner, a purchaser can only search against those persons whom he knows to have been estate owners. He will find their names from the deeds. But if the number of years between 1926, when the Register of Land Charges began, and the date of the purchaser is greater than 15 years, which is the statutory period of search, [3] then it is possible that persons may have been estate owners since 1925 without the purchaser knowing about them. He would then be bound by land charges registered against their names without having any way of searching against them. This hazard began in 1956, 30 years (then the statutory period of search [4]) after registration began.

When, as will be seen, [5] the statutory period of search was reduced in 1969 to 15 years, the purchaser's risk greatly increased, and some protection was needed.

LAW OF PROPERTY ACT 1969

25. Compensation in certain cases for loss due to undisclosed land charges. — (1) Where a purchaser of any estate or interest in land under a disposition to which this section applies has suffered loss by reason that the estate or interest is affected by a registered land charge, then if —

    (*a*) the date of completion was after the commencement of this Act; and

    (*b*) on that date the purchaser had no actual knowledge of the charge; and

    (*c*) the charge was registered against the name of an owner of an estate in the land who was not as owner of any such estate a party to any transaction, or concerned in any event, comprised in the relevant title;

the purchaser shall be entitled to compensation for the loss. [6]

---

[3]   P. 5, ante; p. 80, post.

[4]   LPA 1925, s. 44(1).

[5]   LPA 1969, s. 23, p. 80, post.

[6]   Payable by the Chief Land Registrar out of public funds.

(2) For the purposes of subsection (1)(*b*) above, the question whether any person had actual knowledge of a charge shall be determined without regard to the provisions of section 198 of the Law of Property Act 1925 (under which registration under the Land Charges Act 1925 or any enactment replaced by it is deemed to constitute actual notice). [7]

(9) This section applies to the following dispositions, that is to say —

    (*a*) any sale or exchange and, subject to the following provisions of this subsection, any mortgage of an estate or interest in land;

    (*b*) any grant of a lease for a term of years derived out of a leasehold interest;

    (*c*) any compulsory purchase, by whatever procedure, of land; and

    (*d*) any conveyance of a fee simple in land under Part I of the Leasehold Reform Act 1967;

but does not apply to the grant of a term of years derived out of the freehold or the mortgage of such a term by the lessee; and references in this section to a purchaser shall be construed accordingly.

(10) In this section —

'relevant title' means —

    (*a*) in relation to a disposition made under a contract, the title which the purchaser was, apart from any acceptance by him (by agreement or otherwise) of a shorter or an imperfect title, entitled to require; or

    (*b*) in relation to any other disposition, [8] the title which he would have been entitled to require if the disposition had been made under a contract to which section 44(1) of the Law of Property Act 1925 [9] applied and that contract had been made on the date of completion.

(11) For the purposes of this section any knowledge acquired in the course of a transaction by a person who is acting therein as counsel, or as solicitor or other agent, for another shall be treated as the knowledge of that other.

(f) Actual and Constructive Notice

LAW OF PROPERTY ACT 1925

199. Restrictions on constructive notice. —(1) A purchaser shall not be prejudicially affected by notice of —

    (i) any instrument or matter capable of registration under the provisions of the Land Charges Act, 1925, or any enactment which it replaces, which is void or not enforceable as against him under that Act or enactment, by reason of the non-registration thereof;

    (ii) any other instrument or matter or any fact or thing unless —

    (*a*) it is within his own knowledge, or would have come to his knowledge if such inquiries and inspections had been made as ought reasonably to have been made by him; or

    (*b*) in the same transaction with respect to which a question of notice to the purchaser arises, it has come to the knowledge of his counsel, as such, or of his solicitor or other agent, as such, or would have come to the knowledge of his solicitor or other agent, as such, if such inquiries

---

[7] P. 29, ante.

[8] E.g. compulsory purchase or acquisition under Leasehold Reform Act 1967.

[9] P. 80, post.

and inspections had been made as ought reasonably to have been made by the solicitor or other agent. [10]

In **Hollington Bros Ltd v Rhodes** [1951] 2 TLR 691, [1951] 2 All ER 578n, the plaintiffs purported to take an unsealed 7 year underlease from the defendants at a rent of £612 a year. They went into possession and paid rent, but did not register the informal lease as a land charge. The defendants then sold the legal reversion to Daymar Estates Ltd 'subject to and with the benefit of such tenancies as may affect the premises'. On the same day Daymar Estates Ltd served half a year's notice to quit on the plaintiffs, contending that Daymar Estates Ltd were not bound by the equitable lease but only by the legal tenancy from year to year. The plaintiffs agreed to take a new lease from Daymar Estates Ltd at a premium and an increased rent and sued the defendants for the difference between their old rent and the new payments.

HARMAN J held that there was no concluded agreement between the plaintiffs and the defendants, and so the plaintiffs failed. He then considered what the position would have been had there been a contract. He referred to the pre-1926 law and quoted FARWELL J in *Hunt v Luck* [1901] 1 Ch 45 at 51: [11]

'(1) A tenant's occupation is notice of all that tenant's rights, but not of his lessor's title or rights; (2) actual knowledge that the rents are paid by the tenants to some person whose receipt is inconsistent with the title of the vendor is notice of that person's rights.'

HARMAN J continued at 695, at 579:

'After 1925, however, by virtue of section 10 of the Land Charges Act 1925, [12] this contract came within Class C(iv) as a charge on or obligation affecting land, and therefore might be registered as a land charge in the Registry of Land Charges. Accordingly, by virtue of section 13(2), [13] this being a land charge of Class C is void "against a purchaser of the land charged therewith, or of any interest in such land, unless the land charge is registered in the appropriate register before the completion of the purchase." Moreover, by section 199 of the Law of Property Act 1925, a purchaser is not to be prejudicially affected by notice of any instrument or matter capable of registration under the Land Charges Act 1925, which is void against him by reason of non-registration. This land charge was not registered, and accordingly it is said that it was void against Daymar Estates, Limited, notwithstanding their notice or knowledge, and, moreover, that there was no duty lying on the plaintiffs to register the contract in order to prevent this result. This has been held to be so by Wynn Parry J in *Wright v Dean* [1948] Ch 686, [1948] 2 All ER 415 where he said that it could not be urged that there

---

[10]   This re-enacts Conveyancing Act 1882, s. 3. See also *Sharpe v Foy* (1868) 4 Ch App 35; *Re Cousins* (1886) 31 ChD 671; *Kingsnorth Finance Co Ltd v Tizard* [1986] 1 WLR 783, [1986] 2 All ER 54; *Halifax Mortgage Services Ltd v Stepsky* [1996] Ch 207, [1996] 2 All ER 277 (notice not imputed to client where solicitor was under duty to another client not to communicate the information); *Woolwich plc v Gomm* (2000) 79 P&CR 61 (imputed notice under LPA 1925, s. 199(i)(ii)(b); standard is objective and does not depend on particular instructions given by building society to its solicitor).

[11]   Approved by CA [1902] 1 Ch 428 at 432. The principle is preserved by LPA 1925, s. 14: *City of London Building Society v Flegg* [1988] AC 54 at 80, [1987] 3 All ER 435 at 445, per LORD OLIVER OF AYLMERTON; p. 316, post.

[12]   Now LCA 1972, s. 2, p. 31, ante.

[13]   Now LCA 1972, s. 4 (6). An estate contract is void only against a purchaser for money or money's worth of the legal estate.

was any such duty on the plaintiff. I propose to follow that decision, although I may observe in passing that there is in section 200(4) of the Law of Property Act 1925, a reference to "the obligation to register a land charge in respect of ... any estate contract."

The defendants' answer to this point was that in fact Daymar Estates, Limited, did not contract to obtain, and did not by the assignment get, any estate in the land expressed to override the plaintiffs' rights, and that consequently they took subject to those rights which are expressly mentioned, and that the land which they purchased was in fact only an interest in the land subject to the rights of the plaintiffs in it. This argument seemed to me attractive because it appears at first glance wrong that a purchaser, who knows perfectly well of rights subject to which he is expressed to take, should be able to ignore them. It was, moreover, pointed out that *Wright v Dean* was distinguishable in this respect because there the option which was overridden by the conveyance was not mentioned in it, nor did the purchaser take expressly subject to it. It seems to me, however, that this argument cannot prevail having regard to the words in section 13(2) of the Land Charges Act 1925 which I have quoted, coupled with the definition of "land" in the Act. The fact is that it was the policy of the framers of the 1925 legislation to get rid of equitable rights of this sort unless registered. ...

Finally, as under section 13 of the Land Charges Act 1925 ... an unregistered estate contract is void, and under section 199 of the Law of Property Act 1925, the purchaser is not to be prejudicially affected by it, I do not see how that which is void and which is not to prejudice the purchaser can be validated by some equitable doctrine.' [14]

In **Smith v Jones** [1954] 1 WLR 1089, [1954] 2 All ER 823, the defendant Jones purchased, at an auction, a farm which the plaintiff, to Jones' knowledge, occupied as a tenant.

Disputes arose between the plaintiff and defendant as to the liability for certain repairs, and eventually the plaintiff brought this action claiming that his tenancy agreement should be rectified so as to make the defendant liable for structural repairs.

The defendant contended that, even if a case for rectification could be established against the original lessor, he, as a bona fide purchaser for value, was not bound by the equity to rectify. UPJOHN J held that there was no equity for rectification; and even if there had been, the defendant would have taken free of it. On the second point, he said at 1091, at 827:

'Lastly, Mr Arnold for the plaintiff argued that as the plaintiff was in actual occupation as tenant, the defendant was affected with notice of all his rights and all his equities, including an equity to rectify. On the view I have formed of the facts and law as to rectification, this point does not strictly arise, but as it has been fully argued, I think that I ought to express my views thereon.

In *Barnhart v Greenshields* (1853) 9 Moo PCC 18, where the law is clearly and compendiously stated, the judgment of the Privy Council was delivered by Mr Pemberton Leigh, afterwards Lord Kingsdown, who said at 32: "With respect

[14]   *Markfaith Investment Ltd v Chiap Hua Flashlights Ltd* [1991] 2 AC 43 ('indistinguishable from the decision of Harman J in *Hollington Bros Ltd v Rhodes*', per Lord TEMPLEMAN). See also *Lyus v Prowsa Developments Ltd* [1982] 1 WLR 1044, [1982] 2 All ER 953, p. 176, post, where a sale expressly subject to an estate contract gave rise to a constructive trust; *Ashburn Anstalt v Arnold* [1989] Ch 1, [1988] 2 All ER 147, p. 612, post, per Fox LJ, at 25, at 164.

to the effect of possession merely, we take the law to be, that if there be a tenant in possession of land, a purchaser is bound by all the equities which the tenant could enforce against the vendor, and that the equity of the tenant extends not only to interests connected with his tenancy, as in *Taylor v Stibbert* (1794) 2 Ves 437, but also to interests under collateral agreements, as in *Daniels v Davison* (1809) 16 Ves 249, *Allen v Anthony* (1816) 1 Mer 282, the principle being the same in both classes of cases; namely, that the possession of the tenant is notice that he has some interest in the land, and that a purchaser having notice of that fact, is bound, according to the ordinary rule, either to inquire what that interest is, or to give effect to it, whatever it may be."

Then a little later on he cited the language of Lord Eldon in *Allen v Anthony* at 284: "It is so far settled as not to be disputed, that a person purchasing, where there is a tenant in possession, if he neglects to inquire into the title, must take, subject to such rights as the tenant may have."

On the other hand, Mr. Arnold has not produced any case which goes so far as to say that an equity of rectification is an equity which is enforceable against a purchaser. In my judgment it would be extending the doctrine of notice and the obligation to make inquiry far too much if the doctrine was intended to cover an equity of rectification. Of course the purchaser is bound by the rights of the tenant in occupation—that is quite clear. He is not entitled to assume—as was argued in the earlier cases, notably, I think, *Taylor v Stibbert*—that the tenant is in possession from year to year. He must look at the agreement and he is bound by the agreement, and if, as in *Daniels v Davidson*, the tenant not only has a tenancy agreement but an option to purchase, he is also bound by that.

But, in my judgment, a purchaser is not only entitled but bound to assume, when he is looking at the agreement under which the tenant holds, that that agreement correctly states the relationship between the tenant and the landlord; and he is not bound to assume or to ask or make inquiry whether the tenant has any rights to rectify that contract.

Barnhart v Greenshields (1853) 9 Moo PCC 18 was followed in the Court of Appeal by the well-known case of *Hunt v Luck* [1902] 1 Ch 428, where the principle was again stated, but as Cozens-Hardy LJ pointed out in argument, and Vaughan Williams LJ pointed out at the beginning of his judgment, the real question for determination was the true construction of the Conveyancing Act 1882; Farwell J, who heard the case at first instance [1901] 1 Ch 45, having dealt with the matter without reference to the statutory enactment. I have no doubt that that was because he treated the Act as merely declaratory of the existing law; but it is after all a matter of construction of the Act, although I have already expressed an opinion as though the matter rested solely upon decided cases.

The relevant section which re-enacts exactly, so far as relevant, the provisions of the Conveyancing Act 1882, is to be found in s. 199(1) of the Law of Property Act 1925 [His Lordship read sub-ss. (i) and (ii) (*a*) and continued]:

The question which I have to answer is this: What inspection and inquiries ought reasonably to have been made by the defendant of the tenant before the sale, so far as relevant to this question? I think the only relevant inquiry that he would have made would have been this: "May I see your tenancy agreement? I want to see whether it corresponds with the copy agreement I have seen in the auction rooms." That is the document which governed the rights of the parties.

He ought to have asked whether he had seen a correct copy, but he was under no obligation, in my view, to proceed further and say: "Does that correctly represent your rights?" In fact, if he had asked that question, the answer honestly but erroneously given would have been "Yes". Still less was he bound to take the tenant step by step through the document and ask how the tenant interpreted its provisions. He could not be so bound, and it would be most unwise for any intending purchaser to do so.

In my judgment the defendant is entitled and bound to rely on the terms of the document, and the document speaks for itself. Accordingly, had I come to a contrary conclusion upon the claim for rectification, I should have found that this action was barred by the plea of bona fide purchaser of value without notice. In the circumstances, I must dismiss the action.' [15]

In **McCarthy & Stone Ltd v Julian S Hodge & Co Ltd** [1971] 1 WLR 1547, [1971] 2 All ER 973, the plaintiffs, who were engaged in building work on the premises of Cityfield Properties Ltd, obtained on 17 February 1964 an option to purchase. On 14 March 1964, Cityfield Properties Ltd created an equitable mortgage by deposit of title deeds [16] with the defendant bank. On 13 April 1964, the bank registered the equitable mortgage under the Companies Act 1948, s. 95. [17]

On 27 September 1965 the plaintiffs registered their option as an estate contract. On 21 June 1967, Cityfield Properties Ltd were in liquidation.

One question was whether the plaintiffs' estate contract had priority over the bank's equitable mortgage. FOSTER J held that it had. The Land Charges Act 1925, s. 13(2) (now Land Charges Act 1972, s. 4(6)) did not apply, because the bank was not a purchaser for value of a legal estate. The bank was only an *equitable* mortgagee, and the priority as between the plaintiffs and the bank depended on the time of creation, in accordance with the equitable principle *Qui potior est tempore, potior est jure*. The option was created before the mortgage and therefore the bank took subject to it. [18]

II REGISTERED LAND

The Land Charges Act 1972 is not applicable where the title to land is registered. [19] Interests or charges which are registrable against the name of the estate owner under the Land Charges Act 1972 in the case of unregistered land must be protected in the case of registered land by the entry of a notice on the register of title to the land itself.

The principles of notice work differently in the two systems. An interest or charge which is not registrable under the Land Charges Act 1972 may be enforceable under the old doctrine of notice in the case of unregistered land; but in the case of registered land, it must either be protected by an entry on the register or take effect as an overriding interest. [20] There is theoretically no room

---

[15]   For registered land, see *Nurdin & Peacock plc v Ramsden & Co Ltd* [1999] 1 EGLR 119, p. 130, n.12, post.
[16]   P. 798, post.
[17]   Now Companies Act 1985, s. 396, p. 57, post.
[18]   At 1555, at 980; [1972A] CLJ 34 (P. B. Fairest), where the point is made that if the plaintiffs' interest had been a land charge in a different category within Class C (e.g. a puisne mortgage), the bank would not have been bound. An unregistered puisne mortgage is void against a purchaser for value of any interest in the land. See also (1976) CLP 25 (D. J. Hayton).
[19]   LCA 1972, s. 14.
[20]   LRA 1925, s. 70(1), p. 129, post; LRA 2002, Sch. 3, para. 2, p.162, post. Rights such as those in p. 25, n. 2, ante may be protected by an entry under LRA 1925, ss. 49(1) (*f*) (notice), 54(1) (caution), or 58(1) (restriction), pp. 165–168, post or under LRA 2002, Pt. 4 by a notice or a restriction.

in the registered system for a residual category of third party rights whose enforceability depends on the old doctrine of notice.[1]

On the other hand there is no place in the unregistered system for the safety net provision of an overriding interest under Schedule 3, paragraph 2 of the Land Registration Act 2002 or under section 70(1)(g) of the Land Registration Act 1925. Under those paragraphs, as we shall see, the rights of persons in actual occupation are protected even if the occupant has not registered them.[2] In the case of unregistered land, however, the Draconian solution is adopted whereby the failure to register a registrable interest under the Land Charges Act 1925 renders it void against a purchaser, even though he is in bad faith or actually knows,[3] and even though the holder of the right is in possession.[4] This vital difference between the two systems may well have been due to an error on the part of the draftsmen of the 1925 legislation.

[1982] Conv 213 (M. Friend and J. Newton), pp. 215–217

'It is as well to quote section 14 of the Law of Property Act 1925 in full: "14. This part of this Act shall not prejudicially affect the interest of any person in possession or in actual occupation of land to which he may be entitled in right of such possession or occupation."

The crucial words are, *This part of this Act*, for this makes it clear that it is only Part I of the Act (i.e. the first 39 sections) which are relevant. ...

The root of the problem may be traced back to the Law of Property Act 1922,[5] most of whose provisions were repealed before they ever came into force, where this particular provision originally appeared as section 33, and where it made a good deal more sense than it makes as it stands in the 1925 Act which replaced it. Part I of the Law of Property Act 1922 dealt with the "Assimilation and amendment of the law of real and personal estate." In particular, section 10 dealt with undivided shares (by reference to Schedule 3 to the act); section 11 dealt with dispositions on trust for sale (by reference to Schedule 4); and section 14 dealt with land charges (by reference to Schedule 7). The various schedules to

---

[1]   P. 24, ante.

[2]   Pp. 130, 162, post; *Williams & Glyn's Bank Ltd v Boland* [1981] AC 487, [1980] 2 All ER 408, p. 124, post.

[3]   *Midland Bank Trust Co Ltd v Green* [1981] AC 513, [1981] 1 All ER 153, p. 38, ante; *Hollington Bros Ltd v Rhodes* [1951] 2 TLR 691, [1951] 2 All ER 578n, p. 46, ante; *Markfaith Investment Ltd v Chiap Hua Flashlights Ltd* [1991] 2 AC 43. These cases would have been decided differently in registered land. As to whether such a purchaser might be bound by a constructive trust, see (1981) 97 LQR at pp. 521–522 (B. Green); p. 175, post.

[4]   The purchaser may nevertheless be bound by an unregistered registrable charge under LCA 1925 (a) by estoppel: *Taylors Fashions Ltd v Liverpool Victoria Trustees Co Ltd* [1982] QB 133n, [1981] 1 All ER 897, p. 627, post, (b) by failure to plead the non-registration when sued: *Balchin v Buckle* (1982) Times, 1 June ('One would have thought that the purchaser could waive its effect and agree to be bound by the covenant (Class D (ii)). If he chose, whether from incompetence of his own or his legal advisers or from gentlemanly consideration for the rights or convenience of others, to be bound by the covenant or not to raise the point that it was void, there was no reason why the court should raise the point for him' per STEPHENSON LJ). But he is not bound by a bare trust 'which is merely an equitable consequence of a specifically enforceable contract of sale': *Lloyds Bank plc v Carrick* [1996] 4 All ER 630; (1996) 112 LQR 549 (P. Ferguson); [1996] Conv 295 (M. P. Thompson); [1997] CLJ 32 (M. Oldham); [1996] All ER Rev 257 (P. J. Clarke); p. 64, post.

[5]   This idea is not new. The writers wish to acknowledge the views expressed by Mr Charles Harpum of Downing College, Cambridge, and by Mr David Ibbetson in (1977) 41 Conv (NS) 415, 419, n. 31.

the 1922 Act contained provisions broadly similar to those contained in the main body of the 1925 Act. Moreover, paragraph 1(1) (*f*) of Schedule 7 introduced a new category of land charge, namely: "(*f*) Any contract, by an estate owner or by a person entitled to have a legal estate conveyed to him, to convey a legal estate (including a contract conferring a valid option of purchase, a right of pre-emption and any other like right) entered into after the commencement of this Act ..."

In other words, the idea behind this provision seems to have been that estate contracts (e.g. contracts to convey a legal estate, agreements for a lease, etc.) should have been registrable as land charges, but that a person who did not so protect his interest and who was in possession or actual occupation, and who was entitled to such land in right of his possession or occupation should not thereby be prejudiced. This idea seems to be an extension of the rule in *Hunt v Luck*.[6] Had section 33 of the 1922 Act found an appropriate context in the 1925 legislation many of the present problems could have been avoided. If the section had been re-enacted in the Land Charges Act 1925, the enforceability of unregistered estate contracts in registered and unregistered conveyancing would have been identical: this would also have accorded with the general scheme of the 1925 legislation, which must surely have been to ensure that there should be no differences of substantive law between registered and unregistered conveyancing. The absence of section 33 of the 1922 Act from the Land Charges Act 1925 may be regarded as merely an error in the final stages of drafting; the consequences for property law, however, were serious. One such consequence was the decision in *Hollington Bros Ltd v Rhodes*[7] to the effect that a purchaser (as defined[8]) takes free from an unregistered estate contract where the title to the land is unregistered, even though the holder of the estate contract is in possession of the land.

This is clearly anomalous. There can be no doubt that the Law of Property Act 1922, s. 33 (as replaced by the Law of Property Act 1925, s. 14) was designed to have the same effect in unregistered conveyancing as the Land Registration Act 1925, s. 70(1) (*g*) has for registered land.[8a] The Land Registration Act 1925, s. 70(1) (*g*) refers to "the rights of every person in actual occupation of the land or in receipt of the rents and profits thereof. ..." The Law of Property Act 1925, s. 14 refers to "... the interest of any person in possession or in actual occupation of land. ..." The definition of "possession" in the Law of Property Act 1925, s. 205(1)(xix) includes "the receipt of rents and profits"; in other words, both the Law of Property Act 1925, s. 14 and the Land Registration Act 1925, s. 70(1) (*g*) were designed to protect the rights of those in actual or constructive possession of land. Yet as the law now stands, the protection afforded to such persons is radically different, depending on whether the title to the land is registered or not. There is no good reason, legal or historical for an arbitrary distinction of this sort; the fact that the law now requires it to be made suggests a need for legislative reform.'[9]

6   [1901] 1 Ch 45.
7   [1951] 2 All ER 578n, p. 46, ante.
8   LCA 1925, ss. 13(2), 20(8); and cf. LCA 1972, ss. 4(6), 17(1).
8a Now LRA 2002, Schs. 1 and 3.
9   See M & W, para. 5.121; MM, p. 88, which adds the point that the Lords and Commons Joint Committee had erroneously certified that the consolidation of LPA 1922 and LP(A)A 1924 into the various 1925 Acts made no change in the law. See LORD OLIVER OF AYLMERTON in *City of London Building Society v Flegg* [1988] AC 54, [1987] 3 All ER 435 at 80, at 445, where he says: 'The ambit of section 14 is a matter which has puzzled conveyancers ever since the Law of Property Act was enacted. ... What section 14 does not do, on any analysis, is to enlarge or add to whatever interest it is that the occupant has in right of his occupation.' He then agreed with Wolstenholme and Cherry (13th edn), vol i. p. 69, that s. 14 was designed to preserve the principle of *Hunt v Luck* [1902] 1 Ch 428; p. 46, ante; *Lloyds Bank plc v Carrick* [1996] 4 All ER 630 at 642.

C. Other Registers

I. LOCAL LAND CHARGES [10]

Registers are maintained under the Local Land Charges Act 1975 by all district councils in England and Wales, and also by London boroughs and the Common Council of the City of London. [11] Only those land charges which would not normally be disclosed by an inspection of the property or the title deeds have been made registrable. The register relates to both unregistered and registered land. [12]

LAW OF PROPERTY ACT 1925

198. Registration under the Land Charges Act, 1925, to be notice. —p. 29, ante.

LOCAL LAND CHARGES ACT 1975

1. Local land charges. —(1) A charge or other matter affecting land is a local land charge if it falls within any of the following descriptions and is not one of the matters set out in section 2 below: —

(*a*) any charge acquired either before or after the commencement of this Act by a local authority, water authority or new town development corporation under the Public Health Acts 1936 and 1937, the Public Health Act 1961 or the Highways Act 1980 (or any Act repealed by that Act), [13] or any similar charge acquired by a local authority under any other Act, whether passed before or after this Act, being a charge that is binding on successive owners of the land affected;

(*b*) any prohibition of or restriction on the use of land —

(i) imposed by a local authority on or after 1st January 1926 (including any prohibition or restriction embodied in any condition attached to a consent, approval or licence granted by a local authority on or after that date), or

(ii) enforceable by a local authority under any covenant or agreement made with them on or after that date,

being a prohibition or restriction binding on successive owners of the land affected;

---

[10] LLC Rules 1977 (SI 1977 No. 985); LLC(A) Rules 1978 (SI 1978 No. 1638); 1982 (SI 1982 No. 461); 1983 (SI 1983 No. 1591); 1986 (SI 1986 No. 129); 1987 (SI 1987 No. 389); 1990 (SI 1990 No. 485); 1992 (SI 1992 No. 194); 1995 (SI 1995 No. 260); 2003 LLC(A) Rules (SI 2003 No. 2502). On searches for and information on contaminated land, see Tromans and Clarke, *Contaminated Land* (2000); (2001) 145 SJ 827. The Act came into force on 1 August 1977 and replaces LCA 1925, s. 15 and other sections set out in LCA 1972, s. 18, Sch. 4. See Law Commission Report on Local Land Charges 1974 (Law Com No. 62 HC 71); Garner, *Local Land Charges* (12th edn), which has a useful table of all local land charges arranged alphabetically (pp. 189–202). For other registers maintained by local authorities, see Garner, *Local Land Charges*, chap. 10. See generally Silverman, *Conveyancing Handbook* (10th edn), chap B10. For local authority search forms, see CON Parts 1 and 2; (2002) 152 NLJ 1022; and for searches in commercial conveyancing (2001) 151 NLJ 1346 (A. Boulton).

[11] LLCA 1975, s. 3(1). This includes the Inner Temple and the Middle Temple, s. 3(4).

[12] See LRA 2002, Sch. 1, para. 6; Sch. 3, para. 6, pp. 159, 163, post. LRA 1925, s 70(1)(*i*), p. 132, post.

[13] As amended by Highways Act 1980, s. 343(2), Sch. 24, para. 26.

(*c*) any prohibition of or restriction on the use of land—
  (i) imposed by a Minister of the Crown or government department on or after the date of the commencement of this Act (including any prohibition or restriction embodied in any condition attached to a consent, approval or licence granted by such a Minister or department on or after that date), or
  (ii) enforceable by such a Minister or department under any covenant or agreement made with him or them on or after that date,
    being a prohibition or restriction binding on successive owners of the land affected;
(*d*) any positive obligation affecting land enforceable by a Minister of the Crown, government department or local authority under any covenant or agreement made with him or them on or after the date of the commencement of this Act and binding on successive owners of the land affected;
(*e*) any charge or other matter which is expressly made a local land charge by any statutory provision not contained in this section.

(2) For the purposes of subsection (1)(*a*) above, any sum which is recoverable from successive owners or occupiers of the land in respect of which the sum is recoverable shall be treated as a charge, whether the sum is expressed to be a charge on the land or not.

2. Matters which are not local land charges. —The following matters are not local land charges: —
(*a*) a prohibition or restriction enforceable under a covenant or agreement made between a lessor and a lessee;
(*b*) a positive obligation enforceable under a covenant or agreement made between a lessor and a lessee;
(*c*) a prohibition or restriction enforceable by a Minister of the Crown, government department or local authority under any covenant or agreement, being a prohibition or restriction binding on successive owners of the land affected by reason of the fact that the covenant or agreement is made for the benefit of land of the Minister, government department or local authority;
(*d*) a prohibition or restriction embodied in any bye-laws;
(*e*) a condition or limitation subject to which planning permission was granted at any time before the commencement of this Act or was or is (at any time) deemed to be granted under any statutory provision relating to town and country planning, whether by a Minister of the Crown, government department or local authority;
(*f*) a prohibition or restriction embodied in a scheme under the Town and Country Planning Act 1932 or any enactment repealed by that Act;
(*g*) a prohibition or restriction enforceable under a forestry dedication covenant entered into pursuant to section 5 of the Forestry Act 1967;
(*h*) a prohibition or restriction affecting the whole of any of the following areas: —
  (i) England, Wales or England and Wales;
  (ii) England, or England and Wales, with the exception of, or of any part of, Greater London;
  (iii) Greater London.

5. Registration.—(1) Subject to subsection (6) below, where the originating authority as respects a local land charge are the registering authority, it shall be their duty to register it in the appropriate local land charges register.

(2) Subject to subsection (6) below, where the originating authority as respects a local land charge are not the registering authority, it shall be the duty of the originating authority to apply to the registering authority for its registration in the appropriate local land charges register and upon any such application being made it shall be the duty of the registering authority to register the charge accordingly.

(3) The registration in a local land charges register of a local land charge, or any matter which when registered becomes a local land charge, shall be carried out by reference to the land affected or such part of it as is situated in the area for which the register is kept.

(4) In this Act, 'the originating authority', as respects a local land charge, means the Minister of the Crown, government department, local authority or other person by whom the charge is brought into existence or by whom, on its coming into existence, the charge is enforceable; [14] ...

(5) The registration of a local land charge may be cancelled pursuant to an order of the court.

(6) Where a charge or other matter is registrable in a local land charges register and before the commencement of this Act was also registrable in a register kept under the Land Charges Act 1972, then, if before the commencement of this Act it was registered in a register kept under that Act, there shall be no duty to register it, or to apply for its registration, under this Act and section 10 below shall not apply in relation to it.

10. Compensation for non-registration or defective official search certificate. —(1) Failure to register a local land charge in the appropriate local land charges register shall not affect the enforceability of the charge but where a person has purchased any land affected by a local land charge, then —

(*a*) in a case where a material personal search [15] of the appropriate local land charges register was made in respect of the land in question before the relevant time, if at the time of the search the charge was in existence but not registered in that register; or

(*aa*)in a case where the appropriate local land charges register is kept otherwise than in documentary form and a material personal search of that register was made in respect of the land in question before the relevant time, if the entitlement to search in that register conferred by section 8 above was not satisfied as mentioned in subsection (1A) of that section; or [16]

(*b*) in a case where a material official search [17] of the appropriate local land charges register was made in respect of the land in question before the relevant time, if the charge was in existence at the time of the search but (whether registered or not) was not shown by the official search certificate as registered in that register,

---

[14]   In the case of charges under the Highways Act 1980, s. 224, the originating authority is the street works authority for the street concerned.
[15]   S. 8.
[16]   As added by Local Government (Miscellaneous Provisions) Act 1982, s. 34.
[17]   S. 9.

the purchaser shall (subject to section 11(1) below[18]) be entitled to compensation for any loss suffered by him in consequence. [19]

(3) For the purposes of this section —

(*a*) a person purchases land where, for valuable consideration, he acquires any interest in land or the proceeds of sale of land, and this includes cases where he acquires as lessee or mortgagee and shall be treated as including cases where an interest is conveyed or assigned at his direction to another person;

(*b*) the relevant time —

(i) where the acquisition of the interest in question was preceded by a contract for its acquisition, other than a qualified liability contract, is the time when that contract was made;

(ii) in any other case, is the time when the purchaser acquired the interest in question or, if he acquired it under a disposition which took effect only when registered under the Land Registration Act 1925, the time when that disposition was made;

and for the purposes of sub-paragraph (i) above, a qualified liability contract is a contract containing a term the effect of which is to make the liability of the purchaser dependent upon, or avoidable by reference to, the outcome of a search for local land charges affecting the land to be purchased.

(*c*) a personal search is material if, but only if —

(i) it is made after the commencement of this Act, and

(ii) it is made by or on behalf of the purchaser or, before the relevant time, the purchaser or his agent has knowledge of the result of it;

(*d*) an official search is material if, but only if —

(i) it is made after the commencement of this Act, and

(ii) it is requisitioned by or on behalf of the purchaser or, before the relevant time, the purchaser or his agent has knowledge of the contents of the official search certificate.

(4) Any compensation for loss under this section shall be paid by the registering authority in whose area the land affected is situated; and where the purchaser has incurred expenditure for the purpose of obtaining compensation under this section, the amount of the compensation shall include the amount of the expenditure reasonably incurred by him for that purpose (so far as that expenditure would not otherwise fall to be treated as loss for which he is entitled to compensation under this section).

(7) In the case of an action to recover compensation under this section the cause of action shall be deemed for the purposes of the Limitation Act 1939[20] to accrue at the time when the local land charge comes to the notice of the purchaser; and for the purposes of this subsection the question when the charge came to his notice shall be determined without regard to the provisions of section 198 of the Law of Property Act 1925[1] (under which registration under certain enactments is deemed to constitute actual notice).

---

[18] S. 11 (1) deals with the position of mortgagees in respect of a claim.

[19] The valuation date for the correct assessment of compensation is the date of the compensation assessment hearing: *Alcoa Minerals of Jamaica Inc v Broderick* [2002] 1 AC 371; *Pound v Ashford Borough Council* [2004] 1 P & CR 12 (criteria for awarding compensation).

[20] P. 219, post.

[1] P. 29, ante.

LOCAL LAND CHARGES RULES 1977

3. Parts of the Register. —The register shall continue to be divided into parts, for the registration of different types of charge, as follows:

Part 1, for general financial charges;[2]

Part 2, for specific financial charges;

Part 3, for planning charges;

Part 4, for charges not registrable in another part of the register ('miscellaneous charges');[3]

Part 5, for charges falling within section 8(4) of the Agriculture (Miscellaneous Provisions) Act 1941 ('fenland ways maintenance charges');

Part 6, for charges falling within section 8(4) or 52(8) of the Land Compensation Act 1973 ('land compensation charges');

Part 7, for charges falling within section 1(4) or 9 of the New Towns Act 1965 ('new towns charges');[4]

Part 8, for charges falling within section 33 of the Civil Aviation Act 1949, section 21 of the Civil Aviation Act 1968 or section 16(2) of the Civil Aviation Act 1971 ('civil aviation charges');[5]

Part 9, for charges falling within section 11(1) or 16(6) of the Opencast Coal Act 1958 ('opencast coal charges');

Part 10, for charges falling within section 54(6) of the Town and Country Planning Act 1971 ('listed buildings charges');

Part 11, for charges falling within section 2(4) of the Rights of Light Act 1959 ('light obstruction notices');[6]

Part 12, for charges falling within section 31(4) of the Land Drainage Act 1976 ('drainage scheme charges').

II. COMPANIES

A register is maintained by the Registrar of Companies under the Companies Act 1985 of land charges created by a company for securing money.[7]

LAND CHARGES ACT 1972

3. Registration of land charges.—(7) In the case of a land charge for securing money created by a company before 1st January 1970 or so created at any time as a floating charge, registration under Part XII, or Chapter III of Part XXIII, of the Companies Act 1985 (or corresponding earlier enactments)[8] shall be sufficient in place of registration under this Act, and shall have effect as if the land charge had been registered under this Act.[9]

---

2   LLCA 1975, s. 6.

3   This includes a variety of prohibitions of and restrictions on the user or mode of user of land or buildings, other than planning charges.

4   Now New Towns Act 1981, ss 1 (5), 12.

5   Now Civil Aviation Act 1982, s. 55 (1).

6   P. 780.

7   Records are microfilmed and can be inspected at Crown Way, Maindy, Cardiff and Companies House, City Road, London. A company must also keep a register of charges at its registered office: Companies Act 1985, ss. 406–409. See generally McCormack, *Registration of Company Charges* (1994); Gough, *Company Charges* (2nd edn, 1995); *Buckley on the Companies Acts*; *Gore-Brown on Companies*, paras. 18–11 to 18–39; Palmer, *Company Law*, paras. 13.301–13.337.

8   As substituted by Companies Act 1989, s. 107, Sch 16, para 1.

9   *Property Discount Corpn Ltd v Lyon Group Ltd* [1981] 1 WLR 300, [1981] 1 All ER 379 (registration in companies register held sufficient, even though it was not in name of estate owner as required by LCA 1972, s. 3 (1), p. 33, ante); [1982] Conv 43 (D. M. Hare and T. Flanagan).

(8) The corresponding earlier enactments referred to in subsection (7) above are section 93 of the Companies (Consolidation) Act 1908, section 79 of the Companies Act 1929, section 95 of the Companies Act 1948 and sections 395 to 398 of the Companies Act 1985 as originally enacted.

COMPANIES ACT 1985

395. Introductory provisions.—(1) The purpose of this Part is to secure the registration of charges on a company's property. [10]

(2) In this Part —

'charge' means any form of security interest (fixed or floating) over property, other than an interest arising by operation of law; and

'property', in the context of what is the subject of a charge, includes future property.

(3) It is immaterial for the purposes of this Part where the property subject to a charge is situated.

396. Charges requiring registration.—(1) The charges requiring registration under this Part are —

(*a*) a charge on land or any interest in land, other than —

(i) in England and Wales, a charge for rent or any other periodical sum issuing out of the land, ... [11]

(*b*) a charge on goods or any interest in goods, other than a charge under which the chargee is entitled to possession either of the goods or of a document of title to them;

(*c*) a charge on intangible movable property ... of any of the following descriptions —

(i) goodwill,

(ii) intellectual property,

(iii) book debts (whether book debts of the company or assigned to the company), [12]

(iv) uncalled share capital of the company or calls made but not paid;

(*d*) a charge for securing an issue of debentures; or

(*e*) a floating charge on the whole or part of the company's property.

(2) The descriptions of charge mentioned in subsection (1) shall be construed as follows —

(*a*) a charge on a debenture forming part of an issue or series shall not be treated as falling within paragraph (*a*) or (*b*) by reason of the fact that

---

[10] Part XII (Registration of Company Charges), inserted by Companies Act 1989, s. 93. See the Diamond Report *A Review of Security Interests in Property* (1989); Law Commission Consultation Paper on Registration of Security Interests: Company Charges and Property other than Land 2002 (Law Com No. 164); (2002) 152 NLJ 1353, 1389 (S. Young); (2004) 19 International Banking and Financial Law 88 (R. Calman). On the registration of charges on property of overseas companies, see Companies Act 1989, s. 105, Sch 15, inserting a new Part XIII in the 1985 Act.

[11] *Re Molton Finance Ltd* [1968] Ch 325, [1967] 3 All ER 843 (equitable sub-mortgage); *Re Wallis & Simmonds (Builders) Ltd* [1974] 1 WLR 391, [1974] 1 All ER 561 (equitable charge by deposit of title deeds).

[12] *Re Peachdart Ltd* [1984] Ch 131, [1983] 3 All ER 204; *E Pfeiffer Weinkellerei-Weineinkauf GmbH & Co v Arbuthnot Factors Ltd* [1988] 1 WLR 150 (title reservation clause); *Re Brightlife Ltd* [1987] Ch 200, [1986] 3 All ER 673 (company's credit in its bank account held not a book debt owed to it).

the debenture is secured by a charge on land or goods (or on an interest in land or goods);

(*b*)   in paragraph (*b*) 'goods' means any tangible movable property ... other than money;

(*c*)   a charge is not excluded from paragraph (*b*) because the chargee is entitled to take possession in case of default or on the occurrence of some other event;

(*d*)   in paragraph (*c*)(ii) 'intellectual property' means —

(i)   any patent, trade mark, service mark, registered design, copyright or design right, or

(ii)   any licence under or in respect of any such right;

(*e*)   a debenture which is part of an issue or series shall not be treated as a book debt for the purposes of paragraph (*c*)(iii);

(*f*)   the deposit by way of security of a negotiable instrument given to secure the payment of book debts shall not be treated for the purposes of paragraph (*c*)(iii) as a charge on book debts;

(*g*)   a shipowner's lien on subfreights shall not be treated as a charge on book debts for the purposes of paragraph (*c*)(iii) or as a floating charge for the purposes of paragraph (*e*). [13]

(3) Whether a charge is one requiring registration under this Part shall be determined —

(*a*)   in the case of a charge created by a company, as at the date the charge is created, and

(*b*)   in the case of a charge over property acquired by a company, as at the date of the acquisition.

397. The companies charges register.—(1) The registrar shall keep for each company a register, in such form as he thinks fit, of charges on property of the company. [14]

398. Company's duty to deliver particulars of charge for registration. [15]—(1) It is the duty of a company which creates a charge or acquires property subject to a charge —

(*a*)   to deliver the prescribed particulars of the charge, in the prescribed form, to the registrar for registration, and

(*b*)   to do so within 21 days after the date of the charge's creation or, as the case may be, the date of the acquisition;

but particulars of a charge may be delivered for registration by any person interested in the charge.

399. Effect of failure to deliver particulars for registration—(1) Where a charge is created by a company and no prescribed particulars in the prescribed form are delivered for registration within the period of 21 days after the date of the charge's creation, the charge is void against —

(*a*)   an administrator or liquidator of the company, and

(*b*)   any person who for value acquires an interest in or right over property subject to the charge,

---

[13]   Reversing *Re Welsh Irish Ferries Ltd* [1986] Ch 471.

[14]   Inserted by Companies Act 1989, s. 94. A company must also keep a register of charges at its registered office: Companies Act 1985, ss. 406–409. For liability in negligence of solicitors for failing to register a charge under Companies Act 1948, s. 95 (now Companies Act 1985, s. 395), see *Re Foster* [1986] BCLC 307.

[15]   Inserted by Companies Act 1989, s. 95.

where the relevant event occurs after the creation of the charge, whether before or after the end of the 21 day period.

This is subject to section 400 (late delivery of particulars).

(2) In this Part 'the relevant event' means —

(*a*)   in relation to the voidness of a charge as against an administrator or liquidator, the beginning of the insolvency proceedings, and

(*b*)   in relation to the voidness of a charge as against a person acquiring an interest in or right over property subject to a charge, the acquisition of that interest or right;

and references to 'a relevant event' shall be construed accordingly.

(3) Where a relevant event occurs on the same day as the charge is created, it shall be presumed to have occurred after the charge is created unless the contrary is proved.

III. AGRICULTURAL CHARGES

AGRICULTURAL CREDITS ACT 1928 [16]

5. Agricultural charges on farming stock and assets. —(1) It shall be lawful for a farmer as defined by this Act by instrument in writing to create in favour of a bank as so defined a charge (hereinafter referred to as an agricultural charge) on all or any of the farming stock and other agricultural assets belonging to him as security for sums advanced or to be advanced to him or paid or to be paid on his behalf under any guarantee by the bank and interest, commission and charges thereon.

9. Registration of agricultural charges. —(1) Every agricultural charge shall be registered under this Act within seven clear days after the execution thereof, and, if not so registered, shall be void as against any person other than the farmer:

Provided that the High Court on proof that omission to register within such time as aforesaid was accidental or due to inadvertence may extend the time for registration on such terms as the Court thinks fit.

(2) The Land Registrar shall keep at the Land Registry a register of agricultural charges in such form and containing such particulars as may be prescribed.

(8) Registration of an agricultural charge under this section shall be deemed to constitute actual notice of the charge, and of the fact of such registration, to all persons and for all purposes connected with the property comprised in the charge, as from the date of registration or other prescribed date, and so long as the registration continues in force:

Provided that, where an agricultural charge created in favour of a bank is expressly made for securing a current account or other further advances, the bank, in relation to the making of further advances under the charge, shall not be deemed to have notice of another agricultural charge by reason only that it is so registered if it was not so registered at the time when the first-mentioned charge was created or when the last search (if any) by or on behalf of the bank was made, whichever last happened.

---

[16]   Agricultural Credits Regulations 1928 (S R & O 1928 No. 667); Agricultural Credits Fees Order 1985 (SI 1985 No. 372). In 2002–03 there were 1,761 new registrations, 1,676 cancellations and rectifications and 6,592 searches: Land Registry Annual Report and Accounts 2002–03, p. 49. The register is kept at the Land Registry at Plymouth.

IV. COMMONS AND TOWN AND VILLAGE GREENS [17]

COMMONS REGISTRATION ACT 1965

1. [18] **Registration of commons and town or village greens and ownership of and rights over them.** —(1) There shall be registered, in accordance with the provisions of this Act and subject to the exceptions mentioned therein [19]

(a) land in England or Wales which is common land [20] or a town or village green;

(b) rights of common over such land; and

(c) persons claiming to be or found to be owners of such land or becoming the owners thereof by virtue of this Act;

and no rights of common over land which is capable of being registered under this Act shall be registered in the register of title. [1]

(2) After the end of such period, not being less than three years from the commencement of this Act, as the Minister may by order determine [2] —

(a) no land capable of being registered under this Act shall be deemed to be common land or a town or village green unless it is so registered; and

(b) no rights of common shall be exercisable over any such land unless they are registered either under this Act or in the register of title. [3]

2. Registration authorities.—(1) The registration authority for the purposes of this Act shall be —

(a) in relation to any land situated in any county, any council of that county, [4] or, if the county is a metropolitan county, the council of the metropolitan district in which the land is situated; and

[17]   C & B, pp. 620–622; M & W, paras. 18.179–18.184; Mubhi and M, p. 442. See generally Gadsden on *Commons and Greens* (2004); Oswald, *Common Land* (1989), Denyer-Green, *Law of Commons, Towns and Village Greens*; Williams, *Rights of Common* (1880); Harris and Ryan, *Outline of the Law Relating to Common Land and Public Access to the Countryside* (1967); Clayden, *Our Common Land* (1985); [1977] JPL 352 (R. Vane); Report of Royal Commission on Common Land, 1955–1958 (Cmnd 462); (1972) 122 NLJ 1127 (V. Chapman). Decisions of the Commons Commissioners are reported in Campbell, *Decisions of the Commons Commissioners* (1972), in Current Law and in the Annual Reports of Commons, Open Spaces and Footpaths Preservation Society. See (1973) 117 SJ 537; (1974) 118 SJ 434 (I. Campbell). The office is at Golden Cross House, Duncannon Street, London. The decisions are all recorded in 78 bound volumes, in one volume or sometimes two volumes, for each county in England and Wales. The period covered is from 1965 to 1990. Most matters were determined by 1990, though any later decisions are all recorded: [1997] Conv 248 (A. Samuels).

[18]   Commons Registration (General) Regulations 1966 (SI 1996 No. 1471), as amended by SI 1968 No. 989; SI 1980 No. 1195; SI 1982 Nos. 209, 210; SI 1989 No. 2167; SI 2003 No. 994; SI 2003 No. 2260.

[19]   The Act does not apply to the New Forest, Epping Forest or to any land exempted by an order of the Secretary of State, s. 11: Commons Registration (Exempted Land) Regulations 1965 (SI 1965 No. 2001).

[20]   There are some 1½ million acres of common land.

[1]   As amended by LRA 2002 s. 133, Sch. 11, para. 7(2). For the relationship of registration under the Land Registration Acts and the Commons Registration Act, see (2002) 146 NLJ 634 (E.F. Cousins).

[2]   31 July 1970. Commons Registration (Time Limits) Order 1966 (SI 1966 No. 1470), as amended by Commons Registration (Time Limits) (Amendment) Order 1970 (SI 1970 No. 383). Applications for registration had to be made before 3 January 1970. For registration where land becomes common land or a town or village green after 2 January 1970, see Commons Registration (New Land) Regulations 1969 (SI 1969 No. 1843); *R (on the application of Whitmey) v Commons Commissioners* [2004] 32 EG 62 (CS).

[3]   As amended by LRA 2002, s. 133, Sch. 11, para. 7(2). See *Central Electricity Generating Board v Clwyd County Council* [1976] 1 WLR 151, [1976] 1 All ER 251; *Re Turnworth Down, Dorset* [1978] Ch 251, [1977] 2 All ER 105 (rights of common not registered by closing date held to be extinguished).

[4]   As amended by Local Government Act 1972, s. 272(1), Sch. 30.

(*b*) in relation to any land situated in Greater London, the council of the London borough in which the land is situated ...[5]

3. The registers.—(1) For the purposes of registering such land as is mentioned in section 1(1) of this Act and rights of common over and ownership of such land every registration authority shall maintain —

(*a*) a register of common land; and

(*b*) a register of town or village greens;

and regulations under this Act may require or authorise a registration authority to note on those registers such other information as may be prescribed.

(2) Any register maintained under this Act shall be open to inspection by the public at all reasonable times.

22. Interpretation. —(1) In this Act, unless the context otherwise requires, — 'common land' means —

(*a*) land subject to rights of common (as defined in this Act) whether those rights are exercisable at all times or only during limited periods;

(*b*) waste land of a manor not subject to rights of common;[6]

but does not include a town or village green or any land which forms part of a highway;

'rights of common' includes cattlegates or beastgates[7] (by whatever name known)[8] and rights of sole or several vesture[209] or herbage or of sole or several pasture, but does not include rights held for a term of years or from year to year;

'town or village green' means land which has been allotted by or under any Act for the exercise or recreation of the inhabitants of any locality or on which the inhabitants of any locality have a customary right[10] to indulge in lawful sports and pastimes or which falls within subsection (1A) of this section.[11]

---

[5] As amended by Local Government Act 1985, s. 16, Sch. 8, para. 10(6).

[6] *Re Britford Common* [1977] 1 WLR 39, [1977] 1 All ER 532; *Re Yateley Common, Hampshire* [1977] 1 WLR 840, [1977] 1 All ER 505; *Re Chewton Common* [1977] 1 WLR 1242, [1977] 3 All ER 509; *Baxendale v Instow Parish Council* [1982] Ch 14, [1981] 2 All ER 620; *Hampshire County Council v Milburn* [1991] 1 AC 325, [1990] 2 All ER 257 (waste land of a manor held by HL to mean 'waste land now or formerly of a manor' or 'waste land of manorial origin'); *Lewis v Mid Glamorgan County Council* [1995] 1 WLR 313, [1995] 1 All ER 760; [1995] Conv 500 (H. W. Wilkinson).

[7] Cattlegate or beastgate, sometimes called *stinted pasture*, is a right to pasture a fixed number of beasts on the land of another, generally for a part of the year only. See e.g. *Rigg v Earl of Lonsdale* (1857) 1 H & N 923; *Brackenbank Lodge Ltd v Peart* [1996] EGCS 134.

[8] *Ministry of Defence v Wiltshire County Council* [1995] 4 All ER 931 (delineated on map).

[9] The right of sole vesture, *vestura terrae*, is not merely to graze cattle, but to take away the product of the land, such as grass, corn, underwood, turf, peat, and so forth.

[10] Unaccompanied local children, picnicking, fishing in a pond, collecting bullrushes and picking mushrooms; local children, accompanied by adults, playing, picking blackberries, and studying fish and plant life; local adults picnicking, taking dogs for walks, and fishing in the pond held to amount to pastimes indulged in as of right: *Re White Lane Pond, Four Dales and Clay Pits, Thorne and Stainforth, South Yorkshire* [1984] CLY 287; cf. *Re River Don and its Banks* [1984] CLY 284, where it was held that walking with or without dogs along the banks of the River was not indulging; *Re Foreshore, East Bank of River Ouse, Nabum, Selby District, North Yorkshire* [1989] CLY 276 (pastime of idling by a river held to be customary right, which may be proved by walking, fishing and picnicking on the foreshore as of right by usage); *R v Oxfordshire County Council* [2000] 1 AC 335, [1999] 3 All ER 385 (sports and pastimes is a composite phrase in order to avoid arguments about whether an activity is a sport or a pastime: and includes 'informal recreation such as dogwalking and playing with children': per Lord HOFFMANN at 357, at 397; [1999] All ER Rev 223 (P.J. Clarke); *R v Buckinghamshire County Council* [2004] 1 EGLR 69 (agricultural use incompatible with use as of right for recreation).

[11] As amended by Countryside and Rights of Way Act 2000, s. 98(1), (2).

(1A) Land falls within this subsection if it is land on which for not less than twenty years[11a] a significant number of the inhabitants of any locality, or of any neighbourhood within a locality, have indulged in lawful sports and pastimes as of right,[11b] and either—

    (a)   continue to do so, or

    (b)   have ceased to do so for not more than such period as may be prescribed, or determined in accordance with prescribed provisions. [12]

10. Effect of registration. —The registration under this Act of any land as common land or as a town or village green, or of any rights of common over any such land, shall be conclusive evidence of the matters registered, as at the date of registration, except where the registration is provisional only.

Registration under the Act may be final or provisional. It is final if no objection was lodged before August 1972; [13] and final registration is conclusive evidence of the matters registered at the date of registration. [14] If there is any

11a   See *Oxfordshire County Council v Oxford City Council* [2004] EWHC 12 (Ch), [2004] 2 WLR 1291, [2004] 1 EGLR 105 (any period of 20 years suffices).

11b   *R v Oxfordshire County Council* [2000] 1 AC 335, [1999] 3 All ER 385 (user as of right reflects common law concept of nec vi nec clam nec precario, and does not require subjective belief in the existence of the right); *R (on the application of Beresford) v Sunderland City Council* [2003] UKHL 60, [2004] 1 AC 889 (claim to user as of right not defeated by licence or permission inferred from circumstances; mowing the grass and providing benches).

12   As inserted by Countryside and Rights of Way Act 2000, s. 98(1), (3). See Vehicular Access Across Common and Other Land (England) Regulations 2002: (2002) EG 154 (P. Hayes and R. Herbert).

13   Commons Registration (Objections and Maps) Regulations 1968 (SI 1968 No. 989), as amended by SI 1970 No. 384; *Smith v East Sussex County Council* (1977) 76 LGR 332.

14   Commons Registration Act 1965, s. 10; *New Windsor Corpn v Mellor*, supra at 392, at 51, per Lord DENNING MR; *Cooke v Amey Gravel Co Ltd* [1972] 1 WLR 1310, [1972] 3 All ER 579 (provisional registration is itself no evidence of the existence of the right registered); *Corpus Christi College Oxford v Gloucestershire County Council* [1983] QB 360, [1982] 3 All ER 995 (registration conclusive even where entry on register was wrong); *R v Mid-Sussex District Council, ex p Ridd* [1993] EGCS 183; *R v Norfolk County Council, ex p Perry* (1996) 74 P & CR 1 (power to amend under s. 13 only exercisable if land ceased to be village green after date of registration).

    For rectification of the register, see Common Land (Rectification of Registers) Act 1989, under which land may be removed from the register if it can be shown that at all times since 5 August 1945 the land has included or has been ancillary to a dwellinghouse; Common Land (Rectification of Registers) Regulations 1990 (SI 1990 No. 311); Guidance Note (Chief Commons Commissioners) 30 September 1990 (set out in [1990] Conv 463); [1989] Conv 384 (A. Samuels); *Re 1–4 White Row Cottages, Bewerley* [1991] 3 WLR 229, [1991] 4 All ER 50 (dwellinghouse held to include an unoccupied house or one which had become derelict and unfit for human habitation); *Cresstock Investments Ltd v Commons Comr* [1992] 1 WLR 1088, [1993] 1 All ER 213 (uncultivated woodland ancillary to dwelling house); cf *Re Land at Freshfields* (1993) 66 P & CR 9 (pasture land not ancillary); *Storey v Commons Comr* (1993) 66 P & CR 206 (derelict orchard ancillary to Settrington House), even though enjoyed by more than one house before present ownership); *Land at Mooredge Farm* [1994] NPC 65 nine acres of rough land not a garden); *Re Fox Barn* [1994] EGCS 149.

15   Ibid., ss. 4–7; Commons Commissioners Regulations 1971 (SI 1971 No. 1727); Commons Registration (Second Period References) Regulations 1973 (SI 1973 No. 815). The onus of establishing the validity of the registration is on the person making the registration; *Re Sutton Common Wimborne* [1982] 1 WLR 647, [1982] 2 All ER 376; *Re West Anstey Common, North Devon* [1985] Ch 329, [1985] 1 All ER 618; *Re Newton Fell, Newton in Bowland* [1988] CLY 285.

    When deciding whether to confirm a provisional registration, the Commissioner should consider not only the situation as it was at the date of registration, but also events occurring since that date; *Re Merthyr Mawr Common* [1989] 1 WLR 1014, [1989] 3 All ER 451. See also *Dynevor v Richardson* [1995] Ch 173, [1995] 1 All ER 109 (provisional registration prevents time running for purposes of lost modern grant, even when registration subsequently rejected).

such objection, the registration is provisional, and only becomes final if it is confirmed after a hearing before a Commons Commissioner. [15] There is a right of appeal from his decision by a person aggrieved to the High Court on a point of law. [16]

After July 1970, no land capable of being registered under the Act is to be deemed to be common land unless it is so registered, and no rights of common shall be exercisable over any such land unless they are either registered under the Act or have been previously registered under the Land Registration Act 1925. [17] Thus not only are unregistered rights existing before that date extinguished, but there can be no future acquisition of rights over registered commons. [18] New commons may, however, arise, for example, by grant or by prescription, and be registered. [19] In this case the land does not cease to be common land nor do the rights of common cease to be exercisable, if not registered.

The Commons Registration Act 'is ill-drafted and has given rise to many difficulties.' [20]

QUESTIONS

1.   Why is no provision made in unregistered land for the registration of equitable beneficial interests?
2.   Francis David Blackburn entered into a contract to sell a house to a purchaser who registered the contract as an estate contract against the name of Frank David Blackburn, which was the name in which Francis David Blackburn carried on business as an estate agent. Is the registration valid:
     (*a*)   against a mortgagee who does not search?

[16]   Commons Registration Act 1965, s. 18. See *Wilkes v Gee* [1973] 1 WLR 742, [1973] 2 All ER 1214; *R v Chief Commons Comr, ex p Constable* (1977) 37 P & CR 67; *Re Tillmire Common, Heslington* [1982] 2 All ER 615.
[17]   Ibid., s. 1(2); SI 1970 No. 383. Applications for registration had to be made before 3 January 1970. For registration where land becomes common land or a town or village green after 2 January 1970, see Commons Registration (New Land) Regulations 1969 (SI 1969 No. 1843); *Central Electricity Generating Board v Clwyd County Council* [1976] 1 WLR 151, [1976] 1 All ER 251 (right of common not registered by closing date held to be extinguished); *Re Turnworth Down, Dorset* [1978] Ch 251, [1977] 2 All ER 105; *Howse v Newbury District Council* (1998) 77 P & CR 231 (Greenham Common). For the liability of a solicitor who failed to search the register, see *G and K Ladenbau (UK) Ltd v Crawley and De Reya* [1978] 1 WLR 266, [1978] 1 All ER 682.
         For rights of the public over commons and waste lands, see LPA 1925, s. 193; *Mienes v Stone* (1985) CO 1217/84, noted 1985 Conv (J. R. Montgomery); *R v Secretary of State for the Environment, ex p Billson* [1999] QB 374, [1998] 2 All ER 587. See also National Parks and Access to the Countryside Act 1949, ss. 59–83; Countryside Act 1968, ss. 6, 9; *R v Doncaster Metropolitan Borough Council, ex p Braim* (1986) 85 LGR 233 (Doncaster Common "best known as the site of the St. Leger" held to be an open space within LGA 1972, s. 123(2A); [1988] Conv 369 (J. Hill); Countryside and Rights of Way Act 2000, Part I, which gives to the general public a right of access on foot to open countryside for the purpose of open-air recreation. As to whether this is compatible with the Human Rights Act 1998, see Rook, *Property Law and Human Rights*, pp. 211–219.
[18]   Ibid., s. 13(*b*); SI 1969 No. 1843, reg. 3(2).
[19]   SI 1969 No. 1843, reg. 3(1), and note 5 on p. 11.
[20]   *Corpus Christi College Oxford v Gloucestershire County Council*, supra, at 370, at 1002, per Lord DENNING MR. In 1978 the Department of the Environment issued a consultative document and in 1986 the Countryside Commission published the Report of the Common Land Forum. This contains recommendations for the amendment of the Act. See Appendices C and D for a detailed and critical summary of the present law and practice; [1985] Conv 24 (A. Samuels) which contains a bibliography; (1987) 151 LG Rev 24; (1990) 29 LSG 17 (P. Reeves).

(*b*) against a mortgagee who searches against the name of Francis David Blackburn and receives a nil certificate?

(*c*) against a mortgagee who searches against the name of Francis Davis Blackburn and receives a nil certificate?

See *Oak Co-Operative Building Society v Blackburn* [1967] Ch 1169, [1967] 2 All ER 340; revsd [1968] Ch 730, [1968] 2 All ER 117; LCA 1972, s. 10(4); *Du Sautoy v Symes* [1967] Ch 1146, [1967] 1 All ER 25; (1968) 84 LQR 303 (P.V.B.); *Diligent Finance Co Ltd v Alleyne* (1972) 23 P & CR 346; Ruoff, *Searching Without Tears* (1974), chaps. 9, 10, 11. As to errors in searches in respect of registered titles, under LRA 1925, s. 83(3), see p. 181, post, *Parkash v Irani Finance Ltd* [1970] Ch 101, [1969] 1 All ER 930; *Clark v Chief Land Registrar* [1994] Ch 370; *Hurrill v Cooper* [2003] 2 All ER 1145; *Prestige Properties Ltd v Scottish Provident Institution* [2003] Ch 1. As to such errors under LRA 2002, see s. 103 Sch. 8, para. 1(1)(c), p 196, post.

Of what significance would be the fact that the erroneous entry or certificate was due to the negligence of a clerk in the Land Registry?

See *Ministry of Housing and Local Government v Sharp* [1970] 2 QB 223, [1970] 1 All ER 1009; *Coats Patons (Retail) Ltd v Birmingham Corpn* (1971) 69 LGR 356; LCA 1972, s. 10.

3.   Is a decision that an equitable right or interest is registrable likely to improve or reduce its prospects of being enforceable against third parties?

See *ER Ives Investment Ltd v High* [1967] 2 QB 379, [1967] 1 All ER 504, p. 665, post; *Shiloh Spinners Ltd v Harding* [1973] AC 691, [1973] 1 All ER 90, p. 34, ante.

4.   Consider how the registration of a non-existent land charge can prejudicially affect a land owner. Should the Land Registrar be required to find a prima facie case for registration before adding a charge to the register?

See MEGARRY J in *Thomas v Rose* [1968] 1 WLR 1797 at 1805, [1968] 3 All ER 765 at 769, and *Rawlplug Co Ltd v Kamvale Properties Ltd* (1969) 20 P & CR 32 at 39; (1968) 118 NLJ 1167; and BRIGHTMAN J in *Jones v Morgan* (1973) 231 EG 1167; p. 32, n. 10, ante.

Consider this in the context of the Family Law Act 1996 (formerly Matrimonial Homes Act 1983); see MEGARRY J in *Miles v Bull* [1969] 1 QB 258 at 261, [1968] 3 All ER 632 at 634; *Wroth v Tyler* [1974] Ch 30, [1973] 1 All ER 897, p. 312, post.

5.   Could/should the Land Charges Act 1925 have established a better system of registration than that of registration against the name of the estate owner? Report of the Committee on Land Charges (the Roxburgh Committee) 1956 (Cmd. 9825); Report on Land Charges Affecting Unregistered Land 1969 (Law Com. No. 18, HC 125); LPA 1969, s. 25, p. 44, ante.

6.   Consider

(i)   the moral and other difficulties which are raised by allowing a purchaser with notice to ignore an equitable interest of which he is aware;

(ii) the legal difficulties of allowing the Register to be overridden by the doctrine of constructive notice;

(iii) the absurdity of putting a purchaser with his eyes shut in a better position than one with his eyes open.

7.   Read *Lloyds Bank plc v Carrick* [1996] 4 All ER 630, and the articles on p. 50, n. 4, ante and

(a)   Analyse the interrelationship between estate contracts, constructive trusts, the Land Charges Act 1972, and proprietary estoppel.

(b)   Consider whether, and if so, why, Mrs Carrick might have won if

(i)   the case had been one of registered land; (LRA 1925, s. 70(1) *(g)*, p. 130, post).

(ii)   Mrs Carrick's agreement had been a contractual nullity under the Law of Property (Miscellaneous Provisions) Act 1989, s. 2, p. 67, post.

(c)   Do you sympathise with Mrs Carrick or with Lloyds Bank plc?

D. Mere Equities [1]

In unregistered land, a mere equity (rescission for misrepresentation, or undue influence, rectification for mistake, the rights to consolidation or to reopen a foreclosure, and, perhaps, an equitable right of entry), as opposed to an equitable interest, is not binding on a bona fide purchaser of an equitable interest for value without notice.

In **Phillips v Phillips** (1861) 4 De GF & J 208, Lord WESTBURY when speaking of the occasions on which the ordinary rules of priority in point of time among claimants in equity would be disturbed by the doctrine of the bona fide purchaser, said at 218:

'Thirdly, where there are circumstances that give rise to an equity as distinguished from an equitable estate—as for example, an equity to set aside a deed for fraud, or to correct it for mistake—and the purchaser under the instrument maintains the plea of purchaser for valuable consideration without notice, the court will not interfere.' [2]

In registered land, section 116(b) of the Land Registration Act 2002 provides that a mere equity has effect from the time it arises as an interest capable of binding successors in title; and comes within the priority rules of the Act. [3]

III. Creation and Transfer of Estates and Interests

A. Legal Estates. Contract and Conveyance

I. CONTRACT [4]

A contract usually precedes the conveyance which in unregistered land effects the transfer of the legal estate to a purchaser; and a contract also usually precedes a transfer in registered land. In practice such contracts are generally in standard form. The Standard Conditions of Sale (3rd edn 1995) and the Standard Commercial Property Conditions (1st edn, 1999) [5] are standard forms of contract

---

[1]   [1995] CLJ 160–161 (H. W. R. Wade); (1955) Conv (NS) 346 (F. R. Crane); Snell, para. 2.05;M & W, paras. 5.012–5.013; (1976) 40 Conv (NS) 209 (A. R. Everton); Chambers, *Resulting Trusts* (1997), chap. 7.

[2]   For an analysis of the rule in *Phillips v Phillips*, see (2002) 118 LQR 296 (D. O'Sullivan).

[3]   Pp. 686, post.

[4]   C & B, chap. 6; Gray, chap. 9; M & W, chap. 12; MM, pp. 147–157; Barnsley, *Conveyancing Law and Practice* (4th edn, 1996), chaps. 5 and 6; Farrand, *Contract and Conveyance* (4th edn, 1983), chaps. 2 and 3; Silverman, *Law Society's Conveyancing Handbook* (2003); Kenny, *Conveyancing Practice*.

[5]   These are reproduced in *Emmet on Title*, vol. iii, pp. 443–460/2, together with Law Society's Explanatory Notes thereon; Silverman, *Standard Conditions of Sale* (6th edn, 1998). For a discussion of the original Conditions, see [1980] Conv 179 (J.E. Adams). See also National Conveyancing Protocol of the Law Society (4th edn); *Emmet on Title*, Notes and Recommendations, pp. 461–535, which sets out the steps to be taken by solicitors acting for the vendor and purchaser in domestic conveyancing.

containing a set of general conditions of sale. They are usually employed with such alterations as the parties may make for the purpose of the particular transaction. [6]

A contract for the sale or other disposition of land must comply with the general rules of the law of contract. Thus, it must be a final and complete agreement between the parties on its essential terms, [7] i.e. the parties, the property, the consideration and the interest to be granted. It is usual to make a preliminary agreement 'subject to contract', the effect of which is that, until a formal contract has been concluded, there is no contract and either party can withdraw from the negotiations with impunity. [8]

Further, a contract for the sale or other disposition of an interest in land must comply with the formalities required by statute. Before 27 September 1989 a valid contract for the sale or other disposition of land was only enforceable by action, if there was a sufficient memorandum in writing that complied with section 40 of the Law of Property Act 1925, or, failing that, if there was a sufficient act of part performance by the party seeking to enforce the contract.

This was superseded by section 2 of the Law of Property (Miscellaneous Provisions) Act 1989, under which there can be *no* contract unless it is in writing signed by or on behalf of both parties. The doctrine of part performance ceases to exist because there can be no oral contract to be partly performed. If, however, the formalities are not complied with, the facts may nevertheless give rise to proprietary estoppel or a constructive trust.

(a) Formalities Before 27 September 1989

LAW OF PROPERTY ACT 1925

40. Contracts for sale, &c., of land to be in writing. —(1) No action may be brought upon any contract for the sale or other disposition of land or any interest in land, unless the agreement upon which such action is brought, or some memorandum or note thereof, is in writing, and signed by the party to be charged or by some other person thereunto by him lawfully authorised.

(2) This section applies to contracts whether made before or after the commencement of this Act and does not affect the law relating to part performance, or sales by the court.

46. Forms of contracts and conditions of sale. —The Lord Chancellor may from time to time prescribe and publish forms of contracts and conditions of sale of land, and the forms so prescribed[9] shall, subject to any modification, or any stipulation or intention to the contrary, expressed in the correspondence, apply to contracts by correspondence, [10] and may, but only

---

[6]   See Investment Property Forum: *'Readiness For Sale': The Code of Practice for Streamlining Commercial Property Transactions* (1996).

[7]   See, e.g., *Fletcher v Davies* (1980) 257 EG 1149 (flat in Inner Temple).

[8]   *Chillingworth v Esche* [1924] 1 Ch 97; *Alpenstow Ltd v Regalian Properties plc* [1985] 1 WLR 721, [1985] 2 All ER 545 (words 'subject to contract' meaningless); *Westway Homes Ltd v Moores* [1991] 2 EGLR 193 (notice served by grantee of option to purchase headed 'subject to contract' held to be surplusage and of no effect); *Prudential Assurance Co Ltd v Mount Eden Ltd* [1997] 1 EGLR 37 (subject to licence). For the continued use of 'subject to contract' after 26 September 1989, see C & B, pp. 113–114. On lock-out agreements, see p. 75, post.

[9]   S R & O 1925 No. 779.

[10]   *Stearn v Twitchell* [1985] 1 All ER 631 (contract arising out of acceptance by single letter of oral offer to buy or sell land held not to be contract by correspondence). This section was not repealed by the LP (Miscellaneous Provisions) Act 1989. It may have been overlooked or left on the statute book out of abundance of caution: *Commission for the New Towns v Cooper (Great Britain) Ltd* [1995] Ch 259 at 287, [1995] 2 All ER 929 at 953, per STUART-SMITH LJ.

by express reference thereto, be made to apply to any other cases for which the forms are made available.

(b) Formalities after 26 September 1989

LAW OF PROPERTY (MISCELLANEOUS PROVISIONS) ACT 1989 [11]

2. Contracts of sale etc. of land to be made by signed writing —(1) A contract [12] for the sale or other disposition of an interest [13] in land can only be made in writing and only by incorporating all [14] the terms which the parties have expressly agreed in one document or, where contracts are exchanged, in each.

(2) The terms may be incorporated in a document either by being set out in it or by reference to some other document.

(3) The document incorporating [15] the terms or, where contracts are exchanged, [16] one of the documents incorporating them (but not necessarily the same one) must be signed [17] by or on behalf of each party to the contract. [18]

(4) Where a contract for the sale or other disposition of an interest in land [19] satisfies the conditions of this section by reason only of the rectification of one

---

[11] This was based on Law Commission Report on Formalities for Contracts of Sale etc of Land 1987 (Law Com No. 164, HC 2); [1987] Conv 313; [1987] Conv 71. For the changes, see *Emmet on Title*, para. 2.037; and generally, (1989) 105 LQR 555 (R. E. Annand); [1989] Conv 431 (P. H. Pettit); (1990) 10 LS 325 (L. Bentley and P. Coughlan). On options to purchase and s. 2, see *Spiro v Glencrown Properties Ltd* [1991] Ch 537, [1991] 1 All ER 600, p. 89, post. On rights of pre-emption and s. 2, see *Bircham & Co Nominees (No 2) Ltd v Worrell Holdings* Ltd (2001) 82 P & CR 437. On mutual wills and s. 2, see *Healey v Brown* [2002] 19 EG 147; *Birch v Curtis* [2002] 26 EGCS 129. See also Requirements of Writing (Scotland) Act 1995, which has not followed the English formalities.

[12] *Tootal Clothing Ltd v Guinea Properties Ltd* (1992) 64 P & CR 452 (agreement supplemental to a contract, which had been duly carried out and therefore no longer executory, held outside s. 2); [1993] Conv 89 (P. Luther); (1993) 109 LQR 191 (D. Wilde); *Record v Bell* [1991] 1 WLR 853, [1991] 4 All ER 471 (collateral contract of warranty of title held outside s. 2); (1992) 108 LQR 217 (R. J. Smith); [1991] CLJ 399 (C. Harpum); [1991] Conv 471 (M. Harwood); [1991] All ER Rev 201 (P. J. Clarke); *Pitt v PHH Asset Management Ltd* [1994] 1 WLR 327, [1993] 4 All ER 961 (lock-out agreement held outside s. 2); *Lotteryking Ltd v AMEC Properties Ltd* [1995] 2 EGLR 13 (collateral agreement to remedy defects held outside s. 2); *United Bank of Kuwait v Sahib* [1997] Ch 107, [1997] 3 All ER 215 (equitable mortgage by deposit of title deeds within s. 2), p. 798 post; *Grossman v Hooper* [2001] 2 EGLR 82 (dicta criticising collateral contract test).

[13] *Singh v Briggs* (1995) 71 P & CR 120 (s. 2 applied to executory contract for sale when vendor did not at the time have an interest in land but proposed to acquire it in order to complete sale).

[14] *Enfield London Borough Council v Arajah* [1996] 2 EGLR 21 (agreement for new lease which did not contain all, but only main terms, and was signed only by two out of three lessees held no contract).

[15] *Firstpost Homes Ltd v Johnson* [1995] 1 WLR 1567, [1995] 4 All ER 355 (letter signed by vendor and accompanying plan signed by vendor and purchaser held to be two separate documents, requiring letter to be signed by purchaser as well).

[16] *Commission for the New Towns v Cooper (Great Britain) Ltd*, supra (exchange of correspondence concerning oral agreement for sale of land held not to satisfy s. 2); *De Serville v Underwood* [2001] NPC 82; cf. *Hooper v Sherman* [1994] NPC 153 (where CA adopted a less restrictive view); [1995] CLJ 502 (A. J. Oakley); [1995] Conv 319 (M. P. Thompson).

[17] *Firstpost Homes Ltd v Johnson*, supra (typing in letter of plaintiff's own name held not to constitute a signature; decisions on signatures for the purposes of LPA 1925, s. 40 not followed).

[18] *RG Kensington Management Co Ltd v Hutchinson IDH Ltd* [2003] 2 P&CR 195 (contract to be signed by 'each party to the contract'; not by 'each party to the prospective conveyance on transfer', per NEUBERGER J at 206.

[19] *Jelson Ltd v Derby County Council* [1999] 3 EGLR 91 (planning agreement under TCPA 1990, s. 106 by a developer to transfer an affordable housing site to a Housing Association held to be within s. 2); [2000] Conv 4 (P.H.K.). Cf. *Joyce v Rigolli* [2004] EWCA Civ 79, [2004] 1 P & CR DG 22 (oral boundary agreement involving trivial exchange of land not a disposition within s. 2; [2004] Conv 226 (M.P. Thompson); cf. in unregistered land *Neilson v Poole* (1969) 20 P & CR 909 (boundary agreement not an estate contract under LCA 1972 (Class C (iv)) where its purpose was to clarify an unclear boundary).

or more documents in pursuance of an order of a court, [20] the contract shall come into being, or be deemed to have come into being, at such time as may be specified in the order.

(5) This section does not apply in relation to —

(a) a contract to grant such a lease as is mentioned in section 54(2) of the Law of Property Act 1925 (short leases);

(b) a contract made in the course of a public auction; or

(c) a contract regulated under the Financial Services Act 1986; [1]

and nothing in this section affects the creation or operation of resulting, implied or constructive trusts.

(6) In this section —

'disposition' has the same meaning as in the Law of Property Act 1925;

'interest in land' means any estate, interest or charge in or over land. [2]

(7) Nothing in this section shall apply in relation to contracts made before this section comes into force.

(8) Section 40 of the Law of Property Act 1925 (which is superseded by this section) shall cease to have effect. [3]

In **McCausland v Duncan Lawrie Ltd** [1997] 1 WLR 38, [1996] 4 All ER 995, [4] the plaintiff purchasers made a written contract on 26 January 1995 to purchase 1 Beechmore Road, London, from the defendants (the Bank) for £210,000. The contract satisfied the requirements of section 2 of the Law of Property (Miscellaneous) Provisions Act 1989, and set 26 March as the date for completion. However 26 March was a Sunday, and the vendors' solicitors wrote to the plaintiffs' solicitors suggesting the earlier date of 24 March. This was agreed to in writing. On 24 March the purchasers failed to complete and the vendors served a notice to complete which expired on 7 April. The purchasers were not ready to complete but offered to do so on 10 April. The vendors then purported to rescind the contract. The purchasers sought specific performance and damages for repudiation. They argued that there had been no valid variation of the completion date, and therefore no valid rescission of the contract.

In holding that it was necessary to satisfy the requirements of section 2 when varying a material term of an existing contract, NEILL LJ said at 44, at 1001: 'The principle of construction that Parliament is not to be intended to have amended the law "by a sidewind" is of importance when one is construing a consolidation Act. But, as Peter Gibson LJ explained in *Firstpost Homes Ltd v Johnson* [1995] 1 WLR 1567, 1571, [1995] 4 All ER 355, section 2 of the Act of 1989 was intended to effect a major change in the law. PETER GIBSON LJ said:

"Section 2 brought about a markedly different regime from that which obtained hitherto. Whereas under section 40 contracts which did not comply with its requirements were not void but were merely unenforceable by action,

[20] *Wright v Robert Leonard (Development)* [1994] EGCS 69 (rectification of contract for sale of house and chattels, otherwise caught by s. 2); *Commission for New Towns v Cooper (Great Britain) Ltd*, supra.

[1] Otherwise some forms of investment which include interests in land would be within s. 2.

[2] As amended by TLATA 1996, s. 25(2), Sch. 4.

[3] For a suggestion that part performance has not been abolished but may survive as an equitable doctrine, see *Singh v Beggs*, supra at 122, per NEILL LJ; [1997] Conv 293 (S.J. A. Swann). See also New Zealand doubts on the English formalities: New Zealand Proposed Property Act; [1994] Conv 428 at 430 (H. W. Wilkinson).

[4] [1996] Conv 366 (M. P. Thompson); (1992) 147 NLJ 219 (H. W. Wilkinson).

contracts which do not comply with section 2 are ineffective: a contract for the sale of an interest in land can only be made in writing and in conformity with the other provisions of section 2. Whereas an oral contract was allowed and enforceable provided that it was evidenced in writing and the memorandum or the note thereof was signed by or on behalf of the party against whom it was sought to be enforced, oral contracts are now of no effect and all contracts must be signed by or on behalf of all the parties. Whereas the contract or the memorandum or note evidencing the contract previously could be contained in more than one document, only one document is now allowed, save where contracts are exchanged, although reference to another document may be permitted in the circumstances laid down in subsections (2) and (3). Whereas the memorandum or note needed for section 40 did not have to contain every term of the contract, all the terms must now be contained in the document in question. Whereas the doctrine of part performance allowed certain contracts otherwise unenforceable to be enforced, that doctrine now has no application."

It seems to me to be clear that Parliament intended to introduce new and strict requirements as to the formalities to be observed for the creation of a valid disposition of an interest in land. As Stuart-Smith LJ noted in *Commission for the New Towns v Cooper (Great Britain) Ltd* [1995] Ch 259, 287c, [1995] 2 All ER 929, 952, the section enacted by Parliament was materially different from that drafted by the Law Commission. Under section 2 all the terms of the contract have to be incorporated in the signed document.

What then is the contract on which the bank seeks to rely? It was said by counsel for the bank that the bank relied on the contract dated 26 January which was created in a form which complied with section 2 and that this contract was later varied in a manner which would have been recognised by the common law and by the courts of equity. In my judgment, however, counsel for the plaintiffs was correct when he submitted that the formalities prescribed by section 2 have to be applied to the contract as varied. This was not a case where the agreement between the parties was concluded by an exchange of contracts. The only document signed by both parties was the contract dated 26 January 1995.

The law in this regard is made plain in the speech of Lord Parmoor in *Morris v Baron & Co* [1918] AC 1, 39 where he referred with approval to the following passage in the judgment of Shearman J in *Williams v Moss' Empires Ltd* [1915] 3 KB 242, 246–247:

"The principle ... is where there is alleged to have been a variation of a written contract by a new parol contract, which incorporates some of the terms in the old contract, the new contract must be looked at in its entirety, and if the terms of the new contract when thus considered are such that by reason of the Statute of Frauds it cannot be given in evidence unless in writing, then being an unenforceable contract it cannot operate to effect a variation of the original contract. ... whenever parties vary a material term [5] of an existing contract they are in effect entering into a new contract, the terms of which must be looked at in their entirety, and if the new contract is one which is required to be in writing but is not in writing, then it must be wholly disregarded and the parties are relegated to their rights under the original contract."

---

[5] 'There is no doubt that in this case the term was material in that respect as it advanced the contractual date for completion and therefore the time when either party might make time of the essence by the service of a notice to complete. But it does not follow that section 2 must be observed in order to secure the variation of a term which is immaterial.' (per MORRITT LJ at 49, at 1006).

In *Morris v Baron & Co* the House of Lords was concerned with a contract for the sale of goods which was required by section 4 of the Sale of Goods Act 1893 to be evidenced in writing. It seems to me, however, that the principle approved by Lord Parmoor is directly applicable in this case. Furthermore, there are other passages in the speeches in *Morris v Baron & Co* which show that if a contract is required to be in writing variations which are not in writing cannot be relied upon: see Lord Finlay LC, at p. 12, and Viscount Haldane, at p. 16. Lord Atkinson explained the matter, at p. 31:

"The foundation, I think, on which that rule rests is that after the agreed variation the contract of the parties is not the original contract which had been reduced into writing, but that contract as varied, that of this latter in its entirety there is no written evidence, and it therefore cannot in its entirety be enforced ..."

In these circumstances I would allow the appeal and reinstate the statement of claim. The matter should proceed to trial if the parties cannot reach some agreement. If the action does proceed the bank will be able to raise the defence of estoppel if so advised.' [6]

(c) Estoppel and Constructive Trust

Where a contract does not comply with section 2 of the Act, the facts may nevertheless give rise to proprietary estoppel or to a constructive trust.

In **Yaxley v Gotts** [2000] Ch 162, [2000] 1 All ER 711, [7] the plaintiff and second defendant (Brownie Gotts) informally agreed that the latter would purchase a house which the plaintiff would convert into flats. The plaintiff would own the ground floor and would act as the second defendant's managing agent for the four flats in the rest of the house. The house was in fact purchased by the first defendant, the second defendant's son (Alan Gotts), but the plaintiff assumed that the father had bought it. The plaintiff converted the property and acted as managing agent for two and a half years. The plaintiff and father fell out. The son refused to allow the plaintiff to manage the flats and denied that the plaintiff had any interest in the ground floor. The plaintiff commenced proceedings against the defendants. The trial judge held that the plaintiff was entitled to a leasehold interest in the ground floor by virtue of proprietary estoppel. On appeal, the defendants argued that the oral agreement between the plaintiff and the father was void by virtue of section 2 of the Law of Property (Miscellaneous Provisions) Act 1989, which requires contracts of sale of land to be in writing, and that it could not be made effective by the doctrine of proprietary estoppel.

In holding that, if there was an oral agreement between the parties, the plaintiff was entitled to a leasehold interest under a constructive trust which was expressly saved by section 2 (5) of the 1989 Act, ROBERT WALKER LJ said at 172, at 717:

---

6   Cf. *Target Holdings Ltd v Priestley* (1999) 79 P&CR 305 (agreement to vary mortgage held to be outside s. 2); [1999] Conv 414 (M.P. Thompson).

7   (2000) CLJ 23 (L. Tee); (2000) 116 LQR 11 (R.J. Smith); (2000) 63 MLR 912 (I. Moore); [2000] Conv 245 (M. Thompson); [2000] All ER Rev 242 (P.J. Clarke);' Goff & Jones, *Law of Restitution* (6th edn), chap 21.

The public policy principle

Mr Allston has not contended that the doctrine of part performance, as such, has survived the repeal of section 40 of the Law of Property Act 1925 and its replacement by section 2 of the Act of 1989. It is clear that it has not survived. But he has contended that a comparable equitable doctrine can and in this case should operate despite section 2, that is the species of equitable estoppel, generally referred as proprietary estoppel, on which the judge relied. Mr Allston has also (although only after some prompting by the court) asserted the existence of a constructive trust and has relied on the exception at the end of section 2(5).

Mr Laurence, appearing with Miss Davies for the defendants (neither appeared below), did not go so far as to contend that no form of estoppel could operate in relation to an oral or documentary consensus not amounting to a contract because of non-compliance with section 2. Nor did he submit that a plaintiff was in such a situation unable to obtain any restitutionary remedy: on the contrary, the defendants' notice of appeal concedes that Mr Yaxley is entitled to claim on a quantum meruit basis. But the defendants rely on the general principle, stated in *Halsbury's Laws of England*, 4th ed. reissue, vol. 16 (1992), pp. 849–850, para 962:

"The doctrine of estoppel may not be invoked to render valid a transaction which the legislature has, on grounds of general public policy, enacted . . . is to be invalid."

The defendants also contend that the saving at the end of section 2(5) has a narrower effect than may at first appear.

Recent cases on section 2 and estoppel

The diligence of counsel has produced five cases, decided in the course of the last three years, in which this court has made some reference to estoppel in connection with section 2 of the Act of 1989. However none of them has decided or even discussed at length the points which the defendants take in relation to proprietary estoppel and section 2(5). I can therefore refer to them fairly briefly and I do so in chronological order.

United Bank of Kuwait Plc. v. Sahib [1997] Ch. 107, [1996] 3 All ER 215, p. 798 post, is an important decision on the effect of a deposit of a land certificate unaccompanied by any document satisfying section 2. Peter Gibson LJ noted, at pp. 139–140, at pp. 223–224 that the old law as to the creation of an equitable mortgage by deposit of deeds had been akin to part performance, and was therefore equally inconsistent with the philosophy of the Act of 1989. He noted, at p. 141, at p. 225 that the Law Commission's Report on Transfer of Land: Formalities for Contracts of Sale etc. of Land (1987) (Law Com. No. 164) had contemplated that equitable remedies such as promissory estoppel and proprietary estoppel might be available to do justice in cases where section 2 had not been complied with. But Peter Gibson LJ did not find it necessary to consider the point further because the claimant bank could not on any view have been bound by any estoppel. Phillips LJ agreed, and at p. 144 at p. 227, and saw no reason to extend the list of exceptions in section 2(5).

[His Lordship referred to *McCausland v Duncan Lawrie Ltd* [1997] 1 WLR 38, p. 68 ante, and continued:]

Godden v Merthyr Tydfil Housing Association [1997] NPC 1; Court of Appeal (Civil Division) Transcript No. 370 of 1997, was another appeal (this time unsuccessful) against a striking-out order. This court rejected an argument based on estoppel by convention which Simon Brown LJ regarded as impossible (a view with which I respectfully agree). The case is of interest mainly for the citation of the passage in *Halsbury's Laws of England*, 4th ed. reissue, vol. 16, pp. 849–850, para 962, stating the public policy principle. That passage was, it seems, pointed out by Sir John Balcombe in the course of argument; Simon Brown LJ saw it as a "central objection to this whole line of argument"—but not, it is to be noted, in a context in which proprietary estoppel was being relied on.

Barely a month later *Godden* was cited, in what Peter Gibson LJ called a "somewhat garbled version," in *Bankers Trust Co. v Namdar* (unreported), 14 February 1997; Court of Appeal (Civil Division) Transcript No. 349 of 1997, pp. 19–20. Peter Gibson LJ referred to the view of Morritt LJ in *McCausland v Duncan Lawrie Ltd* [1997] 1 WLR 38, 50, [1996] 4 All ER 995, 1003, that estoppel may be available. He also referred to the Law Commission's report (Law Com. No. 164), para 5.4–5.5, and to *Cheshire and Burn's Modern Law of Real Property*, 15th ed. (1994), p. 124. Peter Gibson LJ did not accept that estoppel could have no relevance. But as the consequence was that this court decided not to allow the appellant to take a new point, the matter was not further investigated.

Finally, in *King v Jackson* [1998] 1 EGLR 30 this court took account of an oral agreement to surrender an assured shorthold tenancy, relied on by the landlord, in assessing damages for unlawful eviction under sections 27 and 28 of the Housing Act 1988. Morritt LJ gave the leading judgment but did not find it necessary to refer to any of the authorities just mentioned.

I have no hesitation in agreeing with what I take to be the views of Peter Gibson LJ, Neill LJ, and Morritt LJ, that the doctrine of estoppel may operate to modify (and sometimes perhaps even counteract) the effect of section 2 of the Act of 1989. The circumstances in which section 2 has to be complied with are so various, and the scope of the doctrine of estoppel is so flexible, that any general assertion of section 2 as a "no-go area" for estoppel would be unsustainable. Nevertheless the impact of the public policy principle to which Sir John Balcombe drew attention in *Godden v Merthyr Tydfil Housing Association* does call for serious consideration. It is not concerned with illegality (some confusion may have arisen from the inadequate report or note shown to this court in *Bankers Trust Co v Namdar*) but with what Viscount Radcliffe in *Kok Hoong v Leong Cheong Kweng Mines Ltd* [1964] AC 993, 1016, [1964] 1 All ER 300, 308, called a principle of general social policy,

> "to ask whether the law that confronts the estoppel can be seen to represent a social policy to which the court must give effect in the interests of the public generally or some section of the public, despite any rules of evidence as between themselves that the parties may have created by their conduct or otherwise."

In this case that principle must of course be applied consistently with the terms in which section 2 of the Act of 1989 has been enacted, including the saving at the end of section 2(5).

Parliament's requirement that any contract for the disposition of an interest in land must be made in a particular documentary form, and will otherwise be void, does not have such an obviously social aim as statutory provisions relating to contracts by or with moneylenders, infants, or protected tenants. Nevertheless it can be seen as embodying Parliament's conclusion, in the general public interest, that the need for certainty as to the formation of contracts of this type must in general outweigh the disappointment of those who make informal bargains in ignorance of the statutory requirement. If an estoppel would have the effect of enforcing a void contract and subverting Parliament's purpose it may have to yield to the statutory law which confronts it, except so far as the statute's saving for a constructive trust provides a means of reconciliation of the apparent conflict. …

Proprietary estoppel and constructive trusts

At a high level of generality, there is much common ground between the doctrines of proprietary estoppel and the constructive trust, just as there is between proprietary estoppel and part performance. All are concerned with equity's intervention to provide relief against unconscionable conduct, whether as between neighbouring landowners, or vendor and purchaser, or relatives who make informal arrangements for sharing a home, or a fiduciary and the beneficiary or client to whom he owes a fiduciary obligation. The overlap between estoppel and part performance has been thoroughly examined in the defendants' written submissions, with a survey of authorities from *Gregory v Mighell* (1811) 18 Ves. 328 to *Take Harvest Ltd v Liu* [1993] AC 552, [1993] 2 All ER 459.

The overlap between estoppel and the constructive trust was less fully covered in counsel's submissions but seems to me to be of central importance to the determination of this appeal. Plainly there are large areas where the two concepts do not overlap: when a landowner stands by while his neighbour mistakenly builds on the former's land the situation is far removed (except for the element of unconscionable conduct) from that of a fiduciary who derives an improper advantage from his client. But in the area of joint enterprise for the acquisition of land (which may be, but is not necessarily, the matrimonial home) the two concepts coincide.

[His Lordship referred to *Gissing v Gissing* [1971] AC 886, 905, [1970] 2 All ER 780, 790; *Lloyds Bank Plc v Rosset* [1991] 1 AC 107, 132, [1990] 1 All ER 1111, 1118 and *Grant v Edwards* [1986] Ch 638, 656, [1986] 2 All ER 426, 438 and continued:]

In this case the judge did not make any finding as to the existence of a constructive trust. He was not asked to do so, because it was not then seen as an issue in the case. But on the findings of fact which the judge did make it was not disputed that a proprietary estoppel arose, and that the appropriate remedy was the grant to Mr Yaxley, in satisfaction of his equitable entitlement, of a long leasehold interest, rent free, of the ground floor of the property. Those findings do in my judgment equally provide the basis for the conclusion that Mr Yaxley was entitled to such an interest under a constructive trust. The oral bargain which the judge found to have been made between Mr Yaxley and Mr Brownie Gotts, and to have been adopted by Mr Alan Gotts, was definite enough to meet the test stated by Lord Bridge in *Lloyds Bank Plc v Rosset*, supra, …

To recapitulate briefly: the species of constructive trust based on "common intention" is established by what Lord Bridge in *Lloyds Bank Plc v Rosset*, called an "agreement, arrangement or understanding" actually reached between the parties, and relied on and acted on by the claimant. A constructive trust of that sort is closely akin to, if not indistinguishable from, proprietary estoppel. See *Birmingham Midshires Mortgage Services Ltd v Sabherwal* (1999) 80 P & CR 256, p. 320, post. Equity enforces it because it would be unconscionable for the other party to disregard the claimant's rights. Section 2(5) expressly saves the creation and operation of a constructive trust.'

CLARKE LJ said at 181, at 726:

'3. Proprietary estoppel and the Law Commission

The Act of 1989 expressly refers to resulting, implied or constructive trusts but it does not expressly refer to proprietary estoppel, in so far as its principles are different from those relating to constructive trusts. The Act neither expressly saves the operation of the doctrine of proprietary estoppel nor expressly provides that it should have no application. Whether the principles of proprietary (or indeed other classes of estoppel) can be invoked will no doubt depend upon the principle which Robert Walker LJ has quoted from *Halsbury's Laws of England*, 4th ed. reissue, vol. 16, pp. 849–850, para 962, namely that the doctrine of estoppel may not be invoked to render valid a transaction which the legislature, on grounds of general public policy, has enacted is to be invalid or void.

It seems to me that in considering whether a particular estoppel relied upon would offend the public policy behind a statute it is necessary to consider the mischief at which the statute is directed. Where a statute has been enacted as a result of the recommendations of the Law Commission, it is, as I see it, both appropriate and permissible for the court to consider those recommendations in order to help to identify both the mischief which the Act is designed to cure and the public policy underlying it. Indeed, although I agree with Robert Walker LJ that they cannot be conclusive as to how a particular provision should be construed, I entirely agree with Beldam LJ that the policy behind section 2 of the Act of 1989 can clearly be seen from the Law Commission Report to which he refers. In my opinion the contents of that report will be of the greatest assistance in deciding whether or not the principles of particular types of estoppel should be held to be contrary to the public policy underlying the Act. In this regard it seems to me that the answer is likely to depend upon the facts of the particular case. So, for example, an attempt to apply the principles of estoppel by convention is likely to fail, as in *Godden v Merthyr Tydfil Housing Association* [1997] NPC 1; Court of Appeal (Civil Division) Transcript No. 370 of 1997, whereas an attempt to apply the principles of proprietary estoppel might well succeed, depending upon the facts of the particular case.'

BELDAM LJ said at 193, at 736:

'For my part I cannot see that there is any reason to qualify the plain words of section 2(5). They were included to preserve the equitable remedies to which the Commission had referred. I do not think it inherent in a social policy of simplifying conveyancing by requiring the certainty of a written document that unconscionable conduct or equitable fraud should be allowed to prevail.

In my view the provision that nothing in section 2 of the Act of 1989 is to affect the creation or operation of resulting, implied or constructive trusts effectively excludes from the operation of the section cases in which an interest in land might equally well be claimed by relying on constructive trust or proprietary estoppel.'[8]

---

[8]   *Shah v Shah* [2001] 3 WLR 1, [2001] 4 All ER 138 (estoppel applied in relation to s. 1 of the 1989 Act where deed not signed in presence of witnesses); [2001] Conv 441 (P.H.K.). Cf. *Actionstrength Ltd v International Glass Engineering IN.GL.EN.SpA* [2003] 2 WLR 1060, [2003] 2 All ER 615 (no estoppel where creditor acted to its detriment on faith of guarantor's oral promise; held unenforceable as failing to comply with Statute of Frauds 1677, s. 4: 'It would wholly frustrate the continued operation of section 4 in relation to contracts of guarantee if an oral promise were to be treated, without more, as somehow carrying in itself a representation that the promise would be treated as enforceable', per Lord WALKER OF GESTINGTHORPE); [2003] CLJ 551 (E. Cooke); *James v Evans* [2000] 3 EGLR 1 (no estoppel).

Proprietary estoppel will not succeed if the party relying on it does not come to equity with clean hands: *Gonthier v Orange Contract Scaffolding Ltd* [2003] EWCA 873 (documents falsified).

(d) Subject to Contract

It is unlikely that an estoppel or constructive trust will arise where the negotiations are subject to contract.

———————

In **A-G of Hong Kong v Humphreys Estate (Queen's Gardens) Ltd** [1987] AC 114, [1987] 2 All ER 387 A, as representatives of the Government of Hong Kong, reached an agreement in principle, subject to contract, with B, that, in exchange for 83 flats from B, A would grant a Crown lease of Government property for development by B. A spent some money on the flats and moved civil servants into them; and B did some work on the property. B then withdrew from the agreement. The Privy Council held that there was no estoppel to prevent B withdrawing from the agreement. B had shown that, to A's knowledge, it had retained the right to resile from the agreement, and A had failed to prove that B had created or encouraged A to expect that there would be no withdrawal. Lord TEMPLEMAN said at 127, at 395:

'In the present case the government acted in the hope that a voluntary agreement in principle expressly made "subject to contract" and therefore not binding would eventually be followed by the achievement of legal relationships in the form of grants and transfers of property. It is possible but unlikely that in circumstances at present unforeseeable a party to negotiations set out in a document expressed to be "subject to contract" would be able to satisfy the court that the parties had subsequently agreed to convert the document into a contract or that some form of estoppel had arisen to prevent both parties from refusing to proceed with the transactions envisaged by the document. But in the present case the government chose to begin and elected to continue on terms that either party might suffer a change of mind and withdraw.'

———————

In **Edwin Shirley Productions Ltd v Workspace Management Ltd** [2001] 2 EGLR 16, LAWRENCE COLLINS J said at para 50:

'I am satisfied that it will be virtually impossible to establish at trial that the negotiations were anything other than subject to contract, and that no case has been made for what Lord Templeman said in *Attorney-General of Hong Kong* would be the unlikely and unforeseeable circumstances that would allow reliance upon an estoppel to overcome the subject to contract character of their negotiations. The rationale is quite simply that proprietary estoppel and constructive trust require: (a) detrimental reliance; and (b) unconscionable conduct. Since the parties must be taken to know that a party who has agreed terms subject to contract is free to withdraw, there can be no question of reliance (particularly by a commercial enterprise involved in property transactions) or of unconscionable conduct.'[9]

(e) Law Reform

LORD WOOLF MR in the EG Millennium Issue said at p. 70:

'Even though you can now arrange a 'lock-out' if you are sufficiently knowledgeable to do so, that only provides partial compensation. Much more extensive protection is needed. It should be automatic that, once you have made

---

[9] *Gonthier v Orange Contract Scaffolding Ltd* [2003] EWCA Civ 873; (2003) Commercial Leases 773; *Secretary of State for Transport v Christos* [2003] NPC 96; [2001] Conv 447, [2003] Conv 360 (J.E.A.); *Secretary of State for Transport v Christos* [2004] 1 P & CR 228.

an offer to purchase, you can be released from the transaction only in restricted circumstances; likewise if you have accepted an offer to purchase, subject to contract. If you withdraw, without cause, you should be liable to pay compensation on a basis that recognises that the loss that you have caused to the other party is not confined to financial loss.' [10]

(f) Contracts (Right of Third Parties) Act 1999

The Contracts (Rights of Third Parties) Act 1999 has provided an exception to the doctrine of privity of contract. [11] Under the Act, which only applies to contracts entered into on and after 11 May 2000, [12] a third party may be able to enforce in his own right a term of the contract and obtain the remedies that would have been available to him in an action for breach of contract if he had been a party to the contract. [13] As far as land law is concerned, it is relevant in the area of the passing of the benefit of positive and restrictive covenants; [14] and may also be useful in enabling a licensor and a purchaser from him to include a term in their contract which will enable the licensee for enforce his licence against the purchaser. [15]

CONTRACTS (RIGHTS OF THIRD PARTIES) ACT 1999

1. Rights of third party to enforce contractual term (1) Subject to the provisions of this Act, a person who is not a party to a contract (a 'third party') may in his own right enforce a term of the contract if—

(a) the contract expressly provides that he may, or

(b) subject to subsection (2), the term purports to confer a benefit on him.

(2) Subsection (1)(b) does not apply if on a proper construction of the contract it appears that the parties did not intend the term to be enforceable by the third party.

(3) The third party must be expressly identified in the contract by name, as a member of a class or as answering a particular description but need not be in existence when the contract is entered into.

(4) This section does not confer a right on a third party to enforce a term of a contract otherwise than subject to and in accordance with any other relevant terms of the contract.

[10]   See Law Commission Conveyancing Standing Committee's suggestion of a standard form of Pre-Contract Deposit Agreement, which would go some way towards deterring gazumping. It was called a paper-tiger: (1987) Times, 17 January, and was abandoned: [1988] Conv 79. See also the Committee's House Selling the Scottish Way for England and Wales (1987). Both are reproduced in *Emmet on Title* Notes and Recommendations, pp. 311–316, 351–364. See also the DETR Consultation Paper: The key to easier buying and selling (1998) advocating a seller's pack to be provided by a person marketing a property; Home Bill 2001; [1999] Conv 81 (J.E.A.). (2000) EG 18 March, p. 132 (G. Murphy); (2001) 151 NLJ 59 (F. Bennion); [2003] Conv 263. See generally Barnsley, *Conveyancing Law and Practice* (4th edn), pp. 216–219.

[11]   On the Act generally, see *Emmet on Title*, para 2.131–2.135, 19.003A; Blundell Lectures 25th Anniversary Series 2000; The Contracts (Rights of Third Parties) Act 1999 and Its Implications for Property Transactions (A. Burrows and C. Harpum); (1999) 143 SJ 1082 (S. Bright and P.J.G. Williams); [2001] CLJ 353 (N. Andrews); (2004) 120 LQR 292 (R. Stevens); Treitel, *The Law of Contract* (11th edn), pp. 651–666. Cheshire, Fifoot and Furmston, *Law of Contract* (14th edn), pp. 512–516; Conv Prec 16–28, 19–16, 19–17.

[12]   The Act will apply to contracts entered into after 11 November 1999, if the contract expressly so provides s. 10(3).

[13]   S. 1(5).

[14]   Pp. 950 post.

[15]   *Nisshin Shipping Co Ltd v Cleaves & Co Ltd* [2003] EWHC 2602 (Comm); 153 NLJ 1705.

(5) For the purpose of exercising his right to enforce a term of the contract, there shall be available to the third party any remedy that would have been available to him in an action for breach of contract if he had been a party to the contract (and the rules relating to damages, injunctions, specific performance and other relief shall apply accordingly).

(6) Where a term of a contract excludes or limits liability in relation to any matter references in this Act to the third party enforcing the term shall be construed as references to his availing himself of the exclusion or limitation.

(7) In this Act, in relation to a term of a contract which is enforceable by a third party—

'the promisor' means the party to the contract against whom the term is enforceable by the third party, and 'the promisee' means the party to the contract by whom the term is enforceable against the promisor.[16]

QUESTIONS

1   What is the position if the formalities of section 2 of the Law of Property (Miscellaneous Provisions) Act 1989 are not observed? How far will equitable doctrines, such as estoppel and constructive trust, be used to render an oral agreement enforceable?

2.   How can a purchaser prevent gazumping by a vendor? Consider

    (a) A lock-out agreement: *Walford v Miles* [1992] 2 AC 128 at 139, [1992] 1 All ER 453 at 461; cf. *Pitt v PHH Asset Management Ltd* [1994] 1 WLR 327; [1993] CLJ 392 (C. MacMillan); [1994] Conv 58 (M. P. Thompson); C & B, p. 115. On the remedy (injunction or damages), see *Tye v House* [1997] 2 EGLR 171. For a precedent, see Conv Prec, paras, 8311–8313. On compensation for pre-contractual expenditure in the absence of a lock-out agreement, see *Regalian plc v London Docklands Development Corpn* [1995] 1 WLR 212, [1995] 1 All ER 1005; [1995] Conv 135 (M. P. Thompson); [1995] CLJ 243 (G. Virgo).

    (b) An option to purchase; p. 89, post.

II. CONVEYANCE

(a) Unregistered Land

1. REQUIREMENT OF DEED [17]

LAW OF PROPERTY ACT 1925

51. Lands lie in grant only. —(1) All lands and all interests therein lie in grant and are incapable of being conveyed by livery or livery and seisin, or by feoffment, or by bargain and sale,[18] and a conveyance of an interest in land may operate to pass the possession or right to possession thereof, without actual entry, but subject to all prior rights thereto.

52. Conveyances to be by deed. —(1) All conveyances of land or of any interest therein are void for the purpose of conveying or creating a legal estate unless made by deed.

    (2) This section does not apply to —

---

[16]   The parties may contract out of the Act. For subsequent variation or a rescission of the contract, see s. 2. On clauses to deal with aspects of the Act, see Conv. Prec. 19–B9.

[17]   C & B, pp. 400–403, 839–858; Gray, pp. 305–310; M & W, paras. 14.029–14.038; MM, pp. 158–186. S. 54(1) follows Statute of Frauds, s. 1; and s. 52(1) follows Real Property Act 1845, s. 3.

[18]   For these old methods of conveyancing, see Holdsworth, vol. 3, pp. 217–246; vol. 7, pp. 356–362.

(*a*) assents by a personal representative, [19]

(*b*) disclaimers made in accordance with sections 178 to 180 or sections 315 to 319 of the Insolvency Act 1986, [20] or not required to be evidenced in writing;

(*c*) surrenders by operation of law, including surrenders which may, by law, be effected without writing;

(*d*) leases or tenancies or other assurances not required by law to be made in writing;

(*e*) receipts other than those falling within section 115 below; [1]

(*f*) vesting orders of the court or other competent authority;

(*g*) conveyances taking effect by operation of law. [2]

54. Creation of interests in land by parol. —(1) All interests in land created by parol and not put in writing and signed by the persons so creating the same, or by their agents thereunto lawfully authorised in writing, have, notwithstanding any consideration having been given for the same, the force and effect of interests at will only.

2.   FORM OF DEED

(a) Individuals

LAW OF PROPERTY (MISCELLANEOUS PROVISIONS) ACT 1989

1. Deeds and their execution [3]

(1) Any rule of law which —

(*a*) restricts the substances on which a deed may be written;

(*b*) requires a seal for the valid execution of an instrument as a deed by an individual; or

(*c*) requires authority by one person to another to deliver an instrument as a deed on his behalf to be given by deed,

is abolished.

---

[19] But assents to the vesting of a legal estate in land must be in writing, signed by the personal representative: AEA 1925, s. 36(1)(4); *Re King's Will Trusts* [1964] Ch 542, [1964] 1 All ER 833; *Re Edwards' Will Trusts* [1982] Ch 30, [1981] 2 All ER 941; (1964) 28 Conv (NS) 298 (J. F. Garner); (1976) CLP 60 (E. C. Ryder); Farrand, *Contract and Conveyance* (4th edn), p. 106; Barnsley, *Conveyancing Law and Practice* (4th edn), p. 321. See Law Commission Working Paper on Title on Death 1987 (No. 105), paras 4.19–4.28. Law Commission Report on Title on Death 1989 (Law Com No. 184), paras 1.5–1.6. *Re King's Will Trusts* was not followed in *Mohay v Roche* [1991] 1 IR 560; [1992] Conv 383 (J. A. Dowling).

[20] As amended by Insolvency Act 1986, s. 439, Sch. 14.

[1] Reconveyances of mortgages by endorsed receipts, p. 902, post. As amended by LP (Miscellaneous Provisions) Act 1989, s. 1, Sch 1, para. 2.

[2] E.g. probates and letters of administration.

[3] This section is based on Law Commission Report on Deeds and Escrows 1987 (Law Com No 163. HC 1). It came into force on 31 July 1990 and is not retrospective: Commencement Order 1990 (SI 1990 No. 1175); [1990] Conv 1, 90. See Land Registration (Execution of Deeds) Rules 1990 (SI 1990 No. 1010); [1990] Conv 85 (D. N. Clarke) 321. See [1991] Lloyd's Maritime and Commercial Law Quarterly 209 (G. Virgo and C. Harpum) for a trenchant criticism of 'the recent reforms which have left the law of deeds both more complex and less rational than it was hitherto'. A seal is still required for deeds executed by corporations sole, and by corporations aggregate which are not companies within the Companies Act 1985; Foreign Companies (Execution of Documents) Regulations 1994 (SI 1994 No. 950). For precedents, see LR (Execution of Deeds) Rules 1990 (SI 1990 No. 1010); 1994 (SI 1994 No. 1130), paras. 4.19–4.28. See Law Commission Working Paper on Title on Death 1987 (Law Com No 105), paras. 4.19–4.28.

(2) An instrument shall not be a deed unless —

    (*a*) it makes it clear on its face that it is intended to be a deed by the person making it or, as the case may be, by the parties to it (whether by describing itself as a deed or expressing itself to be executed or signed as a deed or otherwise); and

    (*b*) it is validly executed as a deed by that person or, as the case may be, one or more of those parties.

(3) An instrument is validly executed as a deed by an individual if, and only if —

    (*a*) it is signed —

    (i) by him in the presence of a witness who attests the signature; or

    (ii) at his direction and in his presence and the presence of two witnesses who each attest the signature; and

    (*b*) it is delivered as a deed by him or a person authorised to do so on his behalf.

(4) In subsections (2) and (3) above 'sign', in relation to an instrument, includes making one's mark on the instrument and 'signature' is to be construed accordingly.

(5) Where a solicitor or licensed conveyancer, or an agent or employee of a solicitor or licensed conveyancer, in the course of or in connection with a transaction involving the disposition or creation of an interest in land, purports to deliver an instrument as a deed on behalf of a party to the instrument, it shall be conclusively presumed in favour of a purchaser that he is authorised so to deliver the instrument.

(b) Companies

COMPANIES ACT 1985

36A. Execution of documents: England and Wales. [4]—(1) Under the law of England and Wales the following provisions have effect with respect to the execution of documents by a company.

(2) A document is executed by a company by the affixing of its common seal.

(3) A company need not have a common seal, however, and the following subsections apply whether it does or not.

(4) A document signed by a director and the secretary of a company, or by two directors of a company, and expressed (in whatever form of words) to be executed by the company has the same effect as if executed under the common seal of the company.

(5) A document executed by a company which makes it clear on its face that it is intended by the person or persons making it to be a deed has effect, upon

---

[4]   Inserted by Companies Act 1989, s. 130(2). In 1996 the Law Commission published a Consultation Paper (No. 143) on The Execution of Deeds and Documents by or on behalf of Bodies Corporate, 'At present the existence of three different sets of rules based on common law and statute for the execution of documents by the three different types of corporation, some requiring the use of a seal, others not, appears to be needlessly complex. In addition, the rules governing the execution of documents by an attorney for a company and the delivery of a deed are uncertain': Law Commission Twenty-Ninth Annual Report 1994 (Law Com No 232), para. 2. 36. See Law Commission Report 1998 (Law Com No. 253) recommending detailed amendments: [1998] Conv 434. The Government has accepted all its recommendations: Law Commission Thirty-Sixth Annual Report 2001 (Law Com No. 275), para. 3.17. See also LPA 1925, s. 74 (execution of instruments by or on behalf of corporations); *Bolton Metropolitan Borough Council v Torkington* [2003] EWCA Civ 1634, [2004] 2 WLR 426.

delivery, as a deed; and it shall be presumed, unless a contrary intention is proved, to be delivered upon its being so executed.

(6) In favour of a purchaser a document shall be deemed to have been duly executed by a company if it purports to be signed by a director and the secretary of the company, or by two directors of the company, and, where it makes it clear on its face that it is intended by the person or persons making it to be a deed, to have been delivered upon its being executed.

A 'purchaser' means a purchaser in good faith for valuable consideration and includes a lessee, mortgagee or other person who for valuable consideration acquires an interest in property.

3. TITLE[5]

LAW OF PROPERTY ACT 1925

44. Statutory commencements of title.—(1) After the commencement of this Act thirty years shall be substituted for forty years as the period of commencement of title which a purchaser of land may require; nevertheless earlier title than thirty years may be required in cases similar to those in which earlier title than forty years might immediately before the commencement of this Act be required.

LAW OF PROPERTY ACT 1969

23. Reduction of statutory period of title.—Section 44(1) of the Law of Property Act 1925 ... shall have effect, in its application to contracts made after the commencement of this Act,[6] as if it specified fifteen years instead of thirty years as the period of commencement of title which may be so required.

4. CONVEYANCE TO SELF

LAW OF PROPERTY ACT 1925

72. Conveyances by a person to himself &c.—(3) After the commencement of this Act a person may convey land to or vest land in himself.

(4) Two or more persons (whether or not being trustees or personal representatives) may convey, and shall be deemed always to have been capable of conveying, any property vested in them to any one or more of themselves in like manner as they could have conveyed such property to a third party ...[7]

5. SAVINGS

LAW OF PROPERTY ACT 1925

55. Savings in regard to last two sections. —Nothing in the last two foregoing sections[8] shall —
  (*a*) invalidate dispositions by will; or
  (*b*) affect any interest validly created before the commencement of this Act; or
  (*c*) affect the right to acquire an interest in land by virtue of taking possession; or
  (*d*) affect the operation of the law relating to part performance.

---

5   C & B, pp. 819–820; M & W, paras. 5.021–5.022; MM, pp. 62–63. See also Law Commission Interim Report on Root of Title to Freehold Land 1967 (Law Com. No. 9).
6   1 January 1970; LPA 1969, s. 31(2).
7   *Rye v Rye* [1962] AC 496, [1962] 1 All ER 146; p. 521, post.
8   S. 53, p. 83, post; s. 54, pp. 78, 83, ante.

6. PRECEDENT

PRECEDENT OF A CONVEYANCE ON SALE OF A FREEHOLD [9]

THIS CONVEYANCE made the . . . . . day of . . . . . [*date*] BETWEEN *AB* of . . . . . [*Address and description*] (hereinafter called 'the Vendor') of the one part and *CD* of . . . . . [*address and description*] (hereinafter called 'the Purchaser') of the other part.

WHEREAS the Vendor is seised for his own sole benefit of the property hereby conveyed for a legal estate in fee simple in possession free from encumbrances and has agreed with the Purchaser for the sale thereof to him for the sum of £ . . . . . [*Price*].

NOW THIS DEED WITNESSETH as follows:

1. In pursuance of the said agreement and in consideration of the sum of £ . . . . . paid by the Purchaser to the Vendor (the receipt whereof the Vendor hereby acknowledges) the Vendor HEREBY CONVEYS with Full/Limited Title Guarantee [10] unto the Purchaser ALL . . . . . [*parcels*] TO HOLD unto the Purchaser in fee simple.

2. The Vendor HEREBY ACKNOWLEDGES the right of the Purchaser to the production of the documents mentioned in the Schedule hereto (the possession of which is retained by the Vendor) and to delivery of copies thereof AND HEREBY UNDERTAKES with the Purchaser for the safe custody of the same documents.

3. It is hereby certified that the transaction hereby effected does not form part of a larger transaction or of a series of transactions in respect of which the amount or value or the aggregate amount or value of the consideration exceeds [£30,000].

IN WITNESS whereof this document has been executed as a Deed [11] the day and year first above [*or* 'before'] written.

THE SCHEDULE

[*Here list the documents acknowledged*]
[*To be executed by the Vendor (and, if desired, the Purchaser) and attested*]

(b) Registered Land

The requirement of registration under the Land Registration Act 2002 are dealt with in Chapter 2.

The Land Registry Form (Form TR1) for the transfer of the whole of a registered title is set out below. Together with different forms for other transfers it is printed in Schedule 1 of the Land Registration Rules 2003.

---

[9]   Reproduced from Hallet's *Conveyancing Precedents* (1965), p. 192.
[10]   This incorporates the usual covenants for title. See LP (Miscellaneous Provisions) Act 1994, ss. 10–13. This was based on Law Commission Report on Implied Covenants for Title 1991 (Law Com No 199).
[11]   Law of Property (Miscellaneous Provisions) Act 1989, s. 1, p. 78, ante.

**Transfer of whole
of registered title(s)**

Land Registry

TR1

If you need more room than is provided for in a panel, use continuation sheet CS and attach to this form.

1.　Stamp Duty

Place "X" in the appropriate box or boxes and complete the appropriate certificate.

❑　It is certified that this instrument falls within category ☐ in the Schedule to the Stamp Duty (Exempt Instruments) Regulations 1987

❑　It is certified that the transaction effected does not form part of a larger transaction or of a series of transactions in respect of which the amount or value or the aggregate amount of value of the consideration exceeds the sum of £ ☐

❑　It is certified that this is an instrument on which stamp duty is not chargeable by virtue of the provisions of section 98 of the Finance Act 2001

2.　Title Number(s) of the Property *Leave blank if not yet registered.*

3.　Property

4.　Date

5.　Transferor *Give full names and company's registered number if any.*

6.　Transferee **for entry on the register** *Give full name(s) and company's registered number, if any. For Scottish companies use an SC prefix and for limited liability partnerships use an OC prefix before the registered number, if any. For foreign companies give territory in which incorporated.*

Unless otherwise arranged with Land Registry headquarters, a certified copy for the Transferee's constitution (in English or Welsh) will be required if it is a body corporate but is not a company registered in England and Wales or Scotland under the Companies Acts.

7.　Transferee's **intended address(es) for service (including postcode) for entry on the register** *You may give up to three addresses for service one of which must be a postal address but does not have to be within the UK. The other addresses can be any combination of a postal address, a box number at a UK document exchange or an electronic address.*

8.　**The Transferor transfers the Property to the Transferee**

9.　Consideration *Place "X" in the appropriate box. State clearly the currency unit if other than sterling. If non of the boxes applies, insert an appropriate memorandum in the additional provisions panel.*

❑　The Transferor has received from the Transferee for the Property the sum of *In words and figures.*

❑　*Insert other receipt as appropriate.*

❑　The transfer is not for money or anything which has a monetary value.

10.　The Transferor transfers with *Place "X" in the appropriate box and add any modifications.*

❑　full title guarantee　　　❑　limited title guarantee

11.　Declaration of trust *Where there is more than one Transferee, place "X" in the appropriate box.*

❑　The Transferees are to hold the Property on trust for themselves as joint tenants

❑　The Transferees are to hold the Property on trust for themselves as tenants in common in equal shares

❑　The Transferees are to hold the Property *Complete as necessary.*

12.　Additional provisions *Insert here any required or permitted statements, certificates or applications and any agreed covenants.*

13.　Execution *The Transferor must execute this transfer as a deed using the space below. If there is more than one Transferor, all must execute. Forms of execution are given in Schedule 9 to the Land Registration Rules 2003. If the transfer contains Transferee's covenants or declarations or contains an application by the Transferee (e.g. for a restriction), it must also be executed by the Transferee (all of them, if there is more than one).*

III. LEASES

(a) Formalities

LAW OF PROPERTY ACT 1925

52. Conveyances to be by deed.—(2)(*d*), p. 78, ante.

54. Creation of interests in land by parol. —(2) Nothing in the foregoing provisions of this Part of this Act shall affect the creation by parol of leases taking effcct in possession [12] for a term not exceeding three years (whether or not the lessee is given power to extend the term) at the best rent which can be reasonably obtained without taking a fine. [13]

205. General definitions.—(1)(ii), p. 9, ante.

(b) Title

This is dealt with later. [14]

(c) Savings

LAW OF PROPERTY ACT 1925

55. Savings in regard to last two sections. —p. 80, ante.

(d) Registered Land

The requirements of registration under the Land Registration Act 2002 are dealt with in Chapter 2.

B. Equitable Interests [15]

I. REQUIREMENT OF WRITING

LAW OF PROPERTY ACT 1925

53. Instruments required to be in writing. [16]—(1) Subject to the provisions hereinafter contained with respect to the creation of interests in land by parol —

    (*a*) no interest in land can be created or disposed of except by writing signed by the person creating or conveying the same, or by his agent thereunto lawfully authorised in writing, or by will, or by operation of law;

---

[12] A reversionary lease conferring no immediate right to take possession is excluded from the ambit of s. 54(2) and can take effect only if made by deed: *Long v Tower Hamlets Borough Council* [1996] 3 WLR 317 at 329–336, [1996] 2 All ER 683 at 694–701; [2001] Conv 213 (J.E.A.).

[13] I.e. a premium paid on the granting of the lease and operating in reduction of the rent; LP (Miscellaneous Provisions) Act 1989, s. 2, does not apply to a contract to grant such a lease: s. 2(5)(*a*), p. 68, ante.

[14] See p. 559, post.

[15] C & B, pp. 841–842; M & W, paras. 10.038–10.051.

[16] See generally H & M , pp. 79–94; M & B, *Trusts and Trustees* (6th edn, 2002), pp. 60–72.

(*b*)   a declaration of trust respecting any land or any interest therein must be manifested and proved by some writing signed by some person who is able to declare such trust or by his will;

(*c*)   a disposition of an equitable interest or trust subsisting at the time of the disposition, must be in writing [17] signed by the person disposing of the same, or by his agent thereunto lawfully authorised in writing or by will. [18]

(2) This section does not affect the creation or operation of resulting, implied or constructive trusts. [19]

II. SAVINGS

LAW OF PROPERTY ACT 1925

55.   Savings in regard to last two sections.—p. 80, ante.

C.   Creation and Transfer in Equity. Estate Contracts

I. AN ESTATE CONTRACT IS A GRANT IN EQUITY

An enforceable contract to convey or create a legal estate in land is one of the categories of contract which equity will specifically enforce. [20] If that remedy is available in respect of a particular contract, equity looks on that as done which ought to be done, and treats the situation as if the land were already conveyed. Such a contract is thus effective as a conveyance in equity. [1] This differs in various ways from a conveyance at law; just as interests in equity differ from estates and

---

[17]   This may be satisfied by joinder of documents: *Re Danish Bacon Co Ltd Staff Pension Fund Trusts* [1971] 1 WLR 248, [1971] 1 All ER 486; cf LPA 1925, s. 40(1), p. 66, ante; LP (Miscellaneous Provisions) Act 1989, s. 2(3), p. 67, ante; *Timmins v Moreland Street Property Co Ltd* [1958] Ch 110, [1957] 3 All ER 265; *Elias v George Sahely & Co (Barbados) Ltd* [1983] 1 AC 646, [1982] 3 All ER 801.

[18]   *Grey v IRC* [1960] AC 1, [1959] 3 All ER 603; (1960) 76 LQR 197 (R. E. Megarry); *Oughtred v IRC* [1960] AC 206, [1959] 3 All ER 623; *Bishop Square Ltd v IRC* (1997) 78 P & CR 169; *Neville v Wilson* [1997] Ch 144, [1996] 3 All ER 171; *Re Tyler* [1967] 1 WLR 1269, [1967] 3 All ER 389; *Vandervell v IRC* [1967] 2 AC 291 at 310–312, [1967] 1 All ER 1 at 6–8; [1966] CLJ 19 (G. H. Jones); *Re Vandervell's Trusts (No 2)* [1974] Ch 269, [1974] 3 All ER 205; (1975) 38 MLR 557 (J. W. Harris); see generally [1979] Conv 17; (1975) 7 Ottawa LR 483 (G. Battersby); (1984) 47 MLR 385 (B. Green).

[19]   *Bannister v Bannister* [1948] 2 All ER 133, p. 615, post; *Hodgson v Marks* [1971] Ch 892, [1971] 2 All ER 684; *Binions v Evans* [1972] Ch 359, [1972] 2 All ER 70, p. 617, post; *Ottaway v Norman* [1972] Ch 698, [1971] 3 All ER 1325.

[20]   On specific performance, see H & M, chap. 24; Snell, chap. 40; Spry, *Equitable Remedies* (4th edn, 1990); Jones and Goodhart, *Specific Performance* (2nd edn, 1996).

[1]   C & B, pp. 402–408; Gray, pp. 394, 580–586; M & W, paras. 14.039–14.053; Smith, pp. 384–386; *Lysaght v Edwards* (1876) 2 ChD 499, infra. See also *Earl of Egmont v Smith* (1877) 6 ChD 469; *Abdulla v Shah* [1959] AC 124 (vendor must not remove parts of the realty after the date of the contract); *Clarke v Ramuz* [1891] 2 QB 456 (removal of soil by trespasser); *Phillips v Lamdin* [1949] 2 KB 33, [1949] 1 All ER 770 (removal of door). The risk passes to the purchaser who should therefore insure: *Paine v Meller* (1801) 6 Ves 349; *Rayner v Preston* (1881) 18 ChD 1; LPA 1925, s. 47 (reversing the decision in *Rayner v Preston*); *Berkeley v Poulett* (1976) 241 EG 911, 242 EG 39 (discussing the rights of a sub-purchaser); *Ware v Verderber* (1978) 247 EG 1081 (duty of vendor to take reasonable care of property). Condition 5.1.4 Standard Conditions of Sale excludes LPA 1925, s. 47; [1989] Conv 1 (H. W. Wilkinson). See Law Commission Report on Risk of Damage After Contract of Sale 1990 (Law Com No 191). As to the effect of LP (Miscellaneous Provisions) Act 1989, s. 2 on this informal conveyance, see [1990] Conv 44 (J. Howell).

interests at law. The doctrine is applicable to contracts for the sale of land, contracts to grant a lease, a mortgage, an easement or profit, indeed a contract to convey or create a legal estate in any hereditament, corporeal or incorporeal. [2] Such a contract is termed an estate contract, and is defined in, and made registrable by, the Land Charges Act 1972, s. 2(4), Class C(iv). [3]

In **Lysaght v Edwards** (1876) 2 ChD 499 Sir George JESSEL MR, said at 506: 'The effect of a contract for sale has been settled for more than two centuries; certainly it was completely settled before the time of Lord Hardwicke, who speaks of the settled doctrine of the court as to it. What is that doctrine? It is that the moment you have a valid contract for sale the vendor becomes in equity a trustee for the purchaser of the estate sold, and the beneficial ownership passes to the purchaser, the vendor having a right to the purchase-money, a charge or lien on the estate for the security of that purchase-money, and a right to retain possession of the estate until the purchase-money is paid, in the absence of express contract as to the time of delivering possession.' [4]

WALSH v LONSDALE [5]
(1882) 21 ChD 9 (CA, Sir George JESSEL MR, COTTON and LINDLEY LJJ)

On 29 May 1879, the defendant agreed to grant to the plaintiff a lease of a mill for seven years at a rent which varied with the number of looms operated by the plaintiff, and at a rate per loom which depended on whether the lessor or lessee provided the steam power. The minimum rent payable was calculated on the smallest number of looms which the plaintiff was contractually bound to operate, and at the lowest rate was £810. The rent was payable in advance if demanded. The plaintiff entered and paid rent quarterly, not in advance. He was in arrears with rent due in January, 1882, and in March the defendant demanded a year's rent in advance. It was not paid, and the defendant distrained. The plaintiff brought this action for damages for illegal distress and also for specific performance of the agreement and for an interim injunction to restrain the distress.

Held. The landlord (defendant) had a right to distrain. An injunction to restrain the distress would be granted only on payment by the plaintiff of £810, the lowest sum that could be due for rent under the lease.

SIR GEORGE JESSEL MR: The question is one of some nicety. There is an agreement for a lease under which possession has been given. Now since the

---

[2] As to the distinction between grants of interests in real property and sales of chattels, see M & W, para. 12.026. The distinction also arises under LPA 1925, s. 40 with regard to the necessity for evidence in writing; and under LP (Miscellaneous Provisions) Act 1989, s. 2 for the requirement of writing. See also Chap. 9, post; *Wood v Manley* (1839) 11 Ad & El 34; *James Jones & Son Ltd v Earl of Tankerville* [1909] 2 Ch 440.

[3] See p. 32, ante.

[4] On the unpaid seller's lien, see *Barclays Bank plc v Estates & Commercial Ltd* [1997] 1 WLR 415 at 419–420 per MILLETT LJ; *Emmet on Title*, para 15.021; [1994] CLJ 263 (S. Worthington).

[5] *Tottenham Hotspur Football and Athletic Co Ltd v Princegrove Publishers Ltd* [1974] 1 WLR 113, [1974] 1 All ER 17; (1974) 90 LQR 149 (M. Albery); *Warmington v Miller* [1973] QB 877, [1973] 2 All ER 372; *Industrial Properties (Barton Hill) Ltd v Associated Electrical Industries Ltd* [1977] QB 580, [1977] 2 All ER 293, infra; (1988) 8 OJLS 350 (P. Sparkes); *Re A Company (No. 00792 of 1992), ex p Tredegar Enterprises Ltd* [1992] 2 EGLR 39.

Judicature Act[6] the possession is held under the agreement. There are not two estates as there were formerly, one estate at common law by reason of the payment of the rent from year to year, and an estate in equity under the agreement. There is only one court, and the equity rules prevail in it. The tenant holds under an agreement for a lease. He holds, therefore, under the same terms in equity as if a lease had been granted, it being a case in which both parties admit that relief is capable of being given by specific performance. That being so, he cannot complain of the exercise by the landlord of the same rights as the landlord would have had if a lease had been granted. On the other hand, he is protected in the same way as if a lease had been granted; he cannot be turned out by six months' notice as a tenant from year to year. He has a right to say, 'I have a lease in equity, and you can only re-enter if I have committed such a breach of covenant as would if a lease had been granted have entitled you to re-enter according to the terms of a proper proviso for re-entry.' That being so, it appears to me that being a lessee in equity he cannot complain of the exercise of the right of distress merely because the actual parchment has not been signed and sealed.

In **Industrial Properties (Barton Hill) Ltd v Associated Electrical Industries Ltd** [1977] QB 580, [1977] 2 All ER 293, the Parker trustees agreed in 1959 to sell part of an industrial estate to the plaintiff company. The purchase money was paid and the contract registered as a land charge, but, in order to save stamp duty, the legal estate was never conveyed to the company. In 1966 the company, which was a mere equitable owner, entered into negotiations with the defendants for the grant of a lease, and their solicitors inadvertently stated that the plaintiffs were the freeholders. The lease contained a covenant to keep the premises in good and tenantable repair and condition and so to yield them up at the determination of the term. When the lease expired, the defendants gave up possession, leaving the premises badly out of repair. The plaintiff company brought an action for damages for breach of the covenant. The defendants argued that the plaintiff company had no legal title to the premises.

The Court of Appeal (Lord DENNING MR, ROSKILL and LAWTON LJJ) held that the defendants were liable. There was a tenancy by estoppel under which the defendants were estopped from denying the plaintiff company's title.[7] The Court of Appeal also held that the defendants were liable under the doctrine of *Walsh v Lonsdale.* Lord DENNING said at 598, at 303;

'Thus far I have considered the position at common law. But in equity there is a much shorter way to a decision. It is quite plain that, if the lease to A.E.I. was defective in point of law, nevertheless it was good in equity, and for this simple reason. There were two agreements of which specific performance would be granted. One was the agreement by the Parker trustees to convey to the plaintiff company. The other was the agreement by the plaintiff company to grant a lease to A.E.I. In respect of each of these agreements, equity looks upon that as done

---

[6]   Supreme Court of Judicature Act 1873 provided for the creation of the Supreme Court of Judicature and for the application in all branches thereof of the rules both of law and of equity. In s. 25(1)–(10) rules applicable to particular points are laid down, and sub-s. (11) (now Supreme Court Act 1981, s. 49(1)) provides:

'Generally in all matters not herein-before particularly mentioned in which there is any conflict or variance between the Rules of Equity and the Rules of the Common Law with reference to the same matter, the Rules of Equity shall prevail.'

[7]   P. 515, post.

which ought to be done. It follows that, by combining the two agreements, the tenants, A.E.I., hold upon the same terms as if a lease had actually been granted by the Parker trustees to A.E.I. This is, of course, an extension of the doctrine of *Walsh v Lonsdale* where there was only one agreement. But I see no reason why the doctrine should not be extended to a case like the present, where there were two agreements, each of which was such that specific performance would be granted.' [8]

II. SPECIFIC PERFORMANCE IS DISCRETIONARY

In **Warmington v Miller** [1973] QB 877, [1973] 2 All ER 372, STAMP J said at 887, at 377,

'The equitable interests which the intended lessee has under an agreement for a lease do not exist in vacuo, but arise because the intended lessee has an equitable right to specific performance of the agreement. In such a situation that which is agreed to be and ought to be done is treated as having been done and carrying with it in equity the attendant rights'.

COATSWORTH v JOHNSON [9]
(1886) 54 LT 520 (CA, Lord ESHER MR, LINDLEY and LOPES LJJ)

The plaintiff entered into possession of the defendant's farm under an agreement to execute a lease in accordance with a draft lease which had already been signed but not sealed. This draft contained, among other covenants, a covenant by the tenant to use the land in a good and husbandlike manner, and there was a power of re-entry on breach of any of the covenants.

The plaintiff failed to cultivate the farm properly, and the defendant, before any rent was due or paid, gave notice to quit and, acting under the power of re-entry, turned the plaintiff out of possession. The plaintiff brought this action for damages for trespass, claiming protection under section 14 of the Conveyancing Act 1881. [10]

Held. The plaintiff was not entitled to the protection of the statute.

LOPES LJ: In this case the tenant, the plaintiff, who brings this action for trespass, is in possession of the land in question under an agreement for a lease. No rent has been paid, and that agreement contains a covenant to cultivate the land according to the approved course of husbandry—the usual covenant—and it has been found by the jury that that covenant has been broken. But, as I have said, no rent has been paid. If rent had been paid the position of things would have been

---

[8]   See also *McManus v Cooke* (1887) 35 Ch D 681 (easement of light); *Mason v Clarke* [1955] AC 778, [1955] 1 All ER 914 (profit à prendre); *Ex p Wright* (1812) 19 Ves 255 (mortgage by deposit of title deeds), where the contract was enforceable under the doctrine of part performance, p. 66, ante.

[9]   *Williams v Greatrex* [1957] 1 WLR 31, [1956] 3 All ER 705; *Cornish v Brook Green Laundry Ltd* [1959] 1 QB 394, [1959] 1 All ER 373; (1959) 75 LQR 168 (R.E.M.); *Kingswood Estate Co Ltd v Anderson* [1963] 2 QB 169, [1962] 3 All ER 593; (1963) 79 LQR 19 (R.E.M.); *Bell Street Investments v Wood* (1970) 216 EG 585; *Henry Smith's Charity Trustees v Hemmings* (1982) 45 P & CR 377; *Shelley v United Artists Corpn Ltd* [1990] 1 EGLR 103. For a criticism of the requirement of specific performance, see (1987) 7 OJLS 60 (S. Gardner).

On the jurisdiction of the county court to grant specific performance, see County Courts Act 1984, s. 23(*d*); County Courts Jurisdiction Order 1981 (SI 1981 No. 1123), as amended by High Court and County Courts Jurisdiction Order 1991 (SI 1991 No. 724).

[10]   See now LPA 1925, s. 146, p. 532, post.

very different. Then the plaintiff would have been a tenant from year to year on the terms of that agreement, so far as those terms are not inconsistent with a yearly tenancy. But no rent having been paid, I am clearly of opinion that the plaintiff is a tenant at will only.

But it is said in this case that he is more than a tenant at will, because the court of equity would have decreed specific performance of this agreement for a lease, and that he must be regarded as lessee for the term of years mentioned in that agreement on the ground that we must regard that as done which a court of equity would have done. No doubt that is perfectly correct. But then the point arises, would the court of equity have decreed specific performance under the particular circumstances of this case? The plaintiff, the tenant, when he went to the court of equity and asked for specific performance, would have had to admit that which has been proved here, namely, that he himself had failed to perform a material portion of the contract—in point of fact, that he had broken a portion of the agreement. I take it that, under those circumstances, it is perfectly clear that the court of equity would have refused specific performance. If that is so, he is only a tenant at will. The notice had been given; the tenancy was determined; and the landlord, the defendant, makes out the justification which he sets up in this action. It might have been that a very different and important question might have arisen under section 14 of the Conveyancing Act 1881. I do not think, however, that that arises under the circumstances of this case. It is not necessary for us to consider what the position of the tenant under the lease would have been, and I therefore do not give any opinion with regard to that section.

III. REGISTRATION

Estate contracts, being interests in equity only, are liable to destruction by a bona fide purchaser of the legal estate for value without notice.

Maitland, *Equity* (2nd edn) p. 158:

'An agreement for a lease is not equal to a lease. An equitable right is not equivalent to a legal right; between the contracting parties an agreement for a lease may be as good as a lease; just so between the contracting parties an agreement for the sale of land may serve as well as a completed sale and conveyance. But introduce the third party and then you will see the difference. I take a lease; my lessor then sells the land to X; notice or no notice my lease is good against X. I take a mere agreement for a lease, and the person who has agreed to grant the lease then sells and conveys to Y, who has no notice of my merely equitable right. Y is not bound to grant me a lease.'

In unregistered land X may protect his equitable interest against a third party by registering it as a land charge Class C (iv) under the Land Charges Act 1972. [11] In registered land X may protect it by the entry of a notice or caution under the Land Registration Act 1925,[12] or of a notice under the Land Registration Act 2002; failing that, by having an overriding interest as a person in actual occupation of the land. [13]

---

[11]   LCA 1972, s. 2(4), p. 32, ante.
[12]   LRA 1925, ss. 48–56; LRA 2002, s. 32; pp. 168 post.
[13]   Ibid., s. 70(1)(g); LRA 2002, Sch. 3. para. 2, pp. 131, 163 post.

IV. OPTION TO PURCHASE AND RIGHT OF PRE-EMPTION [14]

(a) Option to Purchase

An option to purchase has been analysed in two different ways. (1) As an offer to sell which 'the grantor is contractually precluded from withdrawing so long as the option remains exercisable'. [15] A contract to purchase is formed when the notice exercising the option is given to the grantor. (2) As 'a conditional contract which the grantee is entitled to convert into a concluded contract of purchase'. [16]

The option creates an immediate equitable interest in favour of the grantee as soon as it is granted. The grantee's right to call for a conveyance of the land is an equitable interest; as far as the grantor is concerned, 'his estate or interest is taken away from him without his consent, and the right to take it away being vested in another, the covenant giving the option must give that other an interest in the land'. [17]

SPIRO v GLENCROWN PROPERTIES LTD [18]
[1991] Ch 537, [1991] 1 All ER 600 (ChD, HOFFMANN J).

HOFFMANN J: This is an action for damages for breach of a contract to buy land. On 14 November 1989 the plaintiff granted an option to the first defendant ('the purchaser') to buy a property in Finchley for £745,000. The option was exercisable by notice in writing delivered to the vendor or his solicitors by 5 p.m. on the same day. The purchaser gave a notice exercising the option within the

---

[14] C & B, pp. 133–135; Gray, pp. 586–591; M & W, paras. 12.012–12.013; MM, p. 150; Smith, pp. 94–95. See generally Barnsley, *Land Options* (3rd edn), 1998); Kenny, *Tenant's Rights of Preemption* (1999); (1974) 38 Conv (NS) 8 (A. Pritchard); [1984] CLJ 55 (S. Tromans); (1991) Can BR (P. M. Perell); Blundell Memorial Lecture 1996 (T. Etherton and D. Beales).

[15] *Beesly v Hallwood Estates Ltd* [1960] 1 WLR 549 at 556, [1960] 2 All ER 314 at 321, per BUCKLEY J. See also *Brown v Gould* [1972] Ch 53 at 58, [1971] 2 All ER 1505 at 1509, p. 461, post. The option must be sufficiently certain in its terms: *Sudbrook Trading Estate Ltd v Eggleton* [1983] 1 AC 444, [1982] 3 All ER 1, p. 465, post.

[16] *Griffith v Pelton* [1958] Ch 205 at 225, [1957] 3 All ER 75 at 83, per JENKINS LJ.

[17] *London and South Western Rly Co v Gomm* (1882) 20 ChD 562 at 581, per JESSEL MR; *Griffith v Pelton* [1958] Ch 205 at 225; *Webb v Pollmount Ltd* [1966] Ch 584 at 597, [1966] 1 All ER 481 at 485; *Mountford v Scott* [1975] Ch 258, [1975] 1 All ER 198; *George Wimpey & Co Ltd v IRC* [1974] 1 WLR 975 at 980, [1974] 2 All ER 602 at 606; affd [1975] 1 WLR 995, [1975] 2 All ER 45; *Pritchard v Briggs* [1980] Ch 338 at 418, [1980] 1 All ER 294 at 328. See also *Di Luca v Juraise (Springs) Ltd* [1998] 2 EGLR 125 ('The rule that time is of the essence, a settled and invariable rule in relation to options to purchase', per NOURSE LJ.). For the application of the rule against perpetuities, see p. 409, post. If an option is registered, there is no need to register the ensuing contract when the option is exercised: *Armstrong & Holmes Ltd v Holmes* [1993] 1 WLR 1482, [1994] 1 All ER 826; [1994] Conv 483 (N. P. Gravells).

[18] [1990] Conv 9 (J. E. Adams); [1990] 47 EG 48 (C. Sydenham and M. Rodrigues); [1991] Conv 140 (P. F. Smith); [1991] CLJ 236 (A. J. Oakley); *Emmet on Title*, para. 2.118 A. See also *Bircham & Co Nominees (No 2) Ltd v Worrell Holdings Ltd* (2001) 82 P & CR 34 at 39–43 per CHADWICK LJ analysing and applying *Spiro v Glencrown Properties Ltd*; *Active Estates Ltd v Parness* [2002] 3 EGLR at 18–19 per NEUBERGER J (put option leads to same result).
     A put option is when it is the potential grantee or lessor who is to execute it: a call option (as in *Spiro v Glencrown*) is where it is the potential grantee or purchaser who can execute it. In registered land the option should be protected by entry on the register; if not, it may be an overriding interest if the grantee or his successors are in actual occupation: LRA 1925, s. 70(1)(g); LRA 2002, Schs. 1, 3. See *Freeguard v Royal Bank of Scotland plc* (1998) 79 P & CR 81 (an unregistered option to purchase lost priority against a later unregistered charge in 'a thoroughly artificial transaction' involving a ransom strip).

stipulated time. He failed to complete and the vendor, after serving a notice to complete and issuing a writ for specific performance, rescinded the contract. The second defendant, Mr. Berry, is guarantor of the purchaser's obligations. On 1 May 1990 the vendor obtained judgment in default of defence against the purchaser for damages to be assessed. There are now before me a summons by the vendor for judgment under R.S.C., Ord. 14 against Mr. Berry as guarantor and a summons by the purchaser to set aside the judgment against it. Since both summonses raise the same short point of law and there are no other issues in the case, the parties have agreed to treat this hearing as the trial of the action.

The only question for decision is whether the contract on which the vendor relies complied with the provisions of section 2 of the Law of Property (Miscellaneous Provisions) Act 1989, which came into force on 27 September 1989, some seven weeks before the grant and exercise of the option. It is a question which has produced a lively debate in conveyancing journals. The relevant provisions are as follows:

'(1) A contract for the sale or other disposition of an interest in land can only be made in writing and only by incorporating all the terms which the parties have expressly agreed in one document or, where contracts are exchanged, in each. (2) The terms may be incorporated in a document either by being set out in it or by reference to some other document. (3) The document incorporating the terms or, where contracts are exchanged, one of the documents incorporating them (but not necessarily the same one) must be signed by or on behalf of each party to the contract.'

If the 'contract for the sale ... of an interest in land' was for the purposes of section 2(1) the agreement by which the option was *granted*, there is no difficulty. The agreement was executed in two exchanged parts, each of which incorporated all the terms which had been agreed and had been signed by or on behalf of the vendor and purchaser respectively. But the letter which *exercised* the option was of course signed only on behalf of the purchaser. If the contract was made by this document, it did not comply with section 2.

Apart from authority, it seems to me plain enough that section 2 was intended to apply to the agreement which created the option and not to the notice by which it was exercised. Section 2, which replaced section 40 of the Law of Property Act 1925, was intended to prevent disputes over whether the parties had entered into a binding agreement or over what terms they had agreed. It prescribes the formalities for recording their mutual consent. But only the grant of the option depends upon consent. The exercise of the option is a unilateral act. It would destroy the very purpose of the option if the purchaser had to obtain the vendor's countersignature to the notice by which it was exercised. The only way in which the concept of an option to buy land could survive section 2 would be if the purchaser ensured that the vendor not only signed the agreement by which the option was granted but also at the same time provided him with a countersigned form to use if he decided to exercise it. There seems no conceivable reason why the legislature should have required this additional formality.

The language of section 2 places no obstacle in the way of construing the grant of the option as the relevant contract. An option to buy land can properly be described as a contract for the sale of that land conditional on the exercise of the option. A number of eminent judges have so described it. In *Helby v Matthews* [1895] AC 471 at 482, which concerned the sale of a piano on hire-purchase, Lord Macnaughten said:

'The contract, as it seems to me, on the part of the dealer was a contract of hiring coupled with a conditional contract or undertaking to sell. On the part of the customer it was a contract of hiring only until the time came for making the last payment.'

In *Griffith v Pelton* [1958] Ch 205, [1957] 3 All ER 75 which raised the question of whether the benefit of an option was assignable, Jenkins LJ said, at 225, at 83:

'An option in gross for the purchase of land is a conditional contract for such purchase by the grantee of the option from the grantor, which the grantee is entitled to convert into a concluded contract of purchase, and to have carried to completion by the grantor, upon giving the prescribed notice and otherwise complying with the conditions upon which the option is made exercisable in any particular case.'

In the context of section 2, it makes obvious sense to characterise it in this way. So far, therefore, the case seems to me to be clear.

The purchaser, however, submits that I am constrained by authority to characterise an option as an irrevocable offer which does not become a contract for the sale of land until it has been accepted by the notice which exercises the option. It follows that the 'contract for the sale ... of an interest in land' within the meaning of section 2 can only have been made by the letter.

[His Lordship referred to *Helby v Matthews* [1895] AC 471 and continued:]

But the concept of an offer is of course normally used as part of the technique for ascertaining whether the parties have reached that mutual consent which is a necessary element in the formation of a contract. In this primary sense, it is of the essence of an offer that by itself it gives rise to no legal obligations. It was for this reason that Diplock LJ said in *Varty v British South Africa Co* [1965] Ch 508, 523 [1964] 2 All ER 975, 982:

'To speak of an enforceable option as an "irrevocable offer" is juristically a contradiction in terms, for the adjective "irrevocable" connotes the existence of an obligation on the part of the offeror, while the noun "offer" connotes the absence of an obligation until the offer has been accepted.'

Here the underlying principles are clear enough. The granting of the option imposes no obligation on the purchaser and an obligation on the vendor which is contingent on the exercise of the option. When the option is exercised, vendor and purchaser come under obligations to perform as if they had concluded an ordinary contract of sale. And the analogy of an irrevocable offer is, as I have said, a useful way of describing the position of the purchaser between the grant and exercise of the option. Thus in *J Sainsbury plc v O'Connor* [1990] STC 516, Millet J used it to explain why the grantee of an option to buy shares did not become the beneficial owner until he had exercised the option.

But the irrevocable offer metaphor has much less explanatory power in relation to the position of the vendor. The effect of the 'offer' which the vendor has made is, from his point of view, so different from that of an offer in its primary sense that the metaphor is of little assistance. Thus in the famous passage in *London and South Western Rly Co v Gomm* (1882) 20 Ch D 562, 581, Sir George Jessel MR had no use for it in explaining why the grant of an option to buy land confers an interest in the land upon the grantee:

'The right to call for a conveyance of the land is an equitable interest or an equitable estate. In the ordinary case of a contract for purchase there is no doubt about this, and an option for repurchase is not different in its nature. A person exercising the option has to do two things, he has to give notice of his intention to purchase, and to pay the purchase money; but as far as the man who is liable to convey is concerned, his estate or interest is taken away from him without his consent, and the right to take it away being vested in another, the covenant giving the option must give that other an interest in the land.'

The fact that the option binds the vendor contingently to convey was the reason why an option agreement was held to fall within section 40 of the Law of Property Act 1925: see *Richards v Creighton Griffiths (Investments) Ltd* (1972) 225 EG 2104, where Plowman J rejected a submission that it was merely a contract not to withdraw an offer. Similarly in *Weeding v Weeding* (1861) 1 John & H 424, Page-Wood V-C held that the grant of an option to buy land was sufficient to deem that land converted into personalty for the purposes of the grantor's will, even though the option had not yet been exercised when he died. The Vice-Chancellor said, at 430–431:

'I cannot agree with the argument that there is no contract. It is as much a conditional contract as if it depended on any other contingency than the exercise of an option by a third person, such as, for example, the failure of issue of a particular person.'

Thus in explaining the vendor's position, the analogy to which the courts usually appeal is that of a conditional contract. This analogy might also be said to be imperfect, because one generally thinks of a conditional contract as one in which the contingency does not lie within the sole power of one of the parties to the contract. But this difference from the standard case of a conditional contract does not destroy the value of the analogy in explaining the *vendor's* position. So far as he is concerned, it makes no difference whether or not the contingency is within the sole power of the purchaser. The important point is that 'his estate or interest is taken away from him without his consent.'

[His Lordship referred to *Griffith v Pelton* [1958] Ch 205, [1957] 3 All ER 75; *Laybutt v Amoco Australia Pty Ltd* (1974) 48 ALJR 492, and continued:]

The purchaser's argument requires me to say that 'irrevocable offer' and 'conditional contract' are mutually inconsistent concepts and that I must range myself under one or other banner and declare the other to be heretical. I hope that I have demonstrated this to be a misconception about the nature of legal reasoning. An option is not strictly speaking either an offer or a conditional contract. It does not have *all* the incidents of the standard form of either of these concepts. To that extent it is a relationship sui generis. But there are ways in which it resembles each of them. Each analogy is in the proper context a valid way of characterising the situation created by an option. The question in this case is not whether one analogy is true and the other false, but which is appropriate to be used in the construction of section 2 of the Law of Property (Miscellaneous Provisions) Act 1989.

[His Lordship referred to *Beesly v Hallwood Estates Ltd* [1960] 1 WLR 549, 556, [1960] 2 All ER 314, 321; *London and South Western Rly Co v Gomm* (1882) 20 Ch D 562, 581, and *United Scientific Holdings Ltd v Burnley Borough Council* [1978] AC 904, [1977] 2 All ER 62, and continued:]

Perhaps the most helpful case for present purposes is *Re Mulholland's Will Trusts* [1949] 1 All ER 460. A testator had let premises to the Westminster Bank on a lease which included an option to purchase. He appointed the bank his executor and trustee and after his death the bank exercised the option. It was argued for his widow and children that the bank was precluded from exercising the option by the rule that a trustee cannot contract with himself. Wynn-Parry J was pressed with the irrevocable offer metaphor, which, it was said, led inexorably to the conclusion that when the bank exercised the option, it was indeed entering into a contract with itself. But Wynn-Parry J held that if one considered the purpose of the self-dealing rule, which was to prevent a trustee from being subjected to a conflict of interest and duty, the only relevant contract was the grant of the option. The rule could only sensibly be applied to a consensual transaction. While for some purposes it might be true to say that the exercise of the option brought the contract into existence, there could be no rational ground for applying the self-dealing rule to the unilateral exercise of a right granted before the trusteeship came into existence. Wynn-Parry J quoted, at p. 464, from Sir George Jessel MR in *Gomm's* case, 20 Ch D 562, 582, and said:

'As I understand that passage, it amounts to this, that, as regards this option, there was between the parties only one contract, namely, the contract constituted by the provisions in the lease which I have read creating the option. The notice exercising the option did not lead, in my opinion, to the creation of any fresh contractual relationship between the parties, making them for the first time vendors and purchasers, nor did it bring into existence any right in addition to the right conferred by the option. ...'

In my judgment there is nothing in the authorities which prevents me from giving section 2 of the Act of 1989 the meaning which I consider to have been the clear intention of the legislature. On the contrary, the purposive approach taken in cases like *Mulholland* [1949] 1 All ER 460 encourages me to adopt a similar approach to section 2. And the plain purpose of section 2 was, as I have said, to prescribe the formalities for recording the consent of the parties. It follows that in my view the grant of the option was the only 'contract for the sale or other disposition of an interest in land' within the meaning of the section and the contract duly complied with the statutory requirements. There must be judgment for the plaintiff against both defendants with costs.

(b) Right of Pre-emption

In **Kling v Keston Properties Ltd** (1983) 49 P & CR 212, the question was whether a right of pre-emption over a garage in Chelsea was enforceable by the grantee against a purchaser of the garage from the grantor. In holding that it was, Vinelott J followed the views of the majority of the Court of Appeal in *Pritchard v Briggs* [1980] Ch 338, [1980] 1 All ER 294 [19] that the right of pre-emption, although not initially an interest in land, became an equitable interest when the grantor agreed to sell the garage to the purchaser. He said at 215: [20]

'The question whether a right of pre-emption or first refusal over land creates an equitable interest in the land capable of binding a purchaser was for many years a controversial one. It was settled so far as this court is concerned by the decision of the Court of Appeal in *Pritchard v Briggs*. In that case, the owners of a piece of land granted the defendants' predecessor in title a right of first refusal. It was granted in the form of a negative stipulation "that so long as the [grantee] shall live and the [owners] or the survivors of them shall also be alive the [owners] will not nor will either of them sell or concur in selling all or any part of the [land] without giving to the [grantee] the option of purchasing [the land]"—at a stated price. Later the owners granted a lease to the plaintiff and the lease contained an option giving the plaintiff the right to purchase the land on three months' notice after the death of the survivor of the owners, again at a fixed price.

[19] (1980) 96 LQR 488 (H.W.R.W.); [1980] Conv 433 (J. Martin). See also *Manchester Ship Canal Co v Manchester Racecourse Co* [1901] 2 Ch 37; *Murray v Two Strokes Ltd* [1973] 1 WLR 823, [1973] 3 All ER 357; (1973) 89 LQR 462 (M. J. Albery); *First National Securities Ltd v Chiltern District Council* [1975] 1 WLR 1075, [1975] 2 All ER 766; cf. *Birmingham Canal Co v Cartwright* (1879) 11 ChD 421.

[20] The case concerned registered land. The right was not entered on the register, but was protected as an overriding interest under LRA 1925, s. 70(1)(g); p. 150, post. For an analysis of a right of pre-emption, see *Speciality Shops v Yorkshire and Metropolitan Estates Ltd* [2002] EWHC 2969 (Ch), [2003] 2 P &CR 410.

A further lease was subsequently granted and the option was repeated in it. Both the right of pre-emption and the option were registered as estate contracts under the Land Charges Act 1925. Under that Act, and under the Land Charges Act 1972 (which is a consolidating Act) the contracts registrable as estate contracts expressly include a contract conferring "a valid option or right of pre-emption or any other like right." The survivor of the owners, a Major Lockwood, in fact sold the land to the defendants, purportedly in pursuance of the right of pre-emption. After the death of Major Lockwood, the plaintiff gave notice exercising the option. Goff LJ was of the opinion that the right of pre-emption created a merely personal right and did not create an interest in land even after the conditions for its exercise had been satisfied. Accordingly the defendants could not claim priority over the plaintiff's option. In his opinion the Land Charges Act 1972, in so far as it provided for registration of a right of pre-emption as an estate contract, proceeded on a wrong view of the law.[1] However, Templeman and Stephenson LJJ took a different view of the nature and effect of a right of pre-emption. Templeman LJ explained the effect of a right of pre-emption in a passage which I should, I think, cite in full. He said at 418, at 328:

"Rights of option and rights of pre-emption share one feature in common; each prescribes circumstances in which the relationship between the owner of the property which is the subject of the right and the holder of the right will become the relationship of vendor and purchaser. In the case of an option, the evolution of the relationship of vendor and purchaser may depend on the fulfilment of certain specified conditions and will depend on the volition of the option holder. If the option applies to land, the grant of the option creates a contingent equitable interest which, if registered as an estate contract, is binding on successors in title of the grantor and takes priority from the date of its registration. In the case of a right of pre-emption, the evolution of the relationship of vendor and purchaser depends on the grantor, of his own volition, choosing to fulfil certain specified conditions and thus converting the pre-emption into an option. The grant of the right of pre-emption creates a mere spes which the grantor of the right may either frustrate by choosing not to fulfil the necessary conditions or may convert into an option and thus into equitable interest by fulfilling the conditions. An equitable interest thus created is protected by prior registration of the right of pre-emption as an estate contract but takes its priority from the date when the right of pre-emption becomes exercisable and the right is converted into an option and the equitable interest is then created. The holder of a right of pre-emption is in much the same position as a beneficiary under a will of a testator who is still alive, save that the holder of the right of pre-emption must hope for some future positive action by the grantor which will elevate his hope into an interest. It does not seem to me that the property legislation of 1925 was intended to create, or operated to create an equitable interest in land where none existed."

Accordingly the plaintiff's claim succeeded, for:

"After the grant of Mr Pritchard's option, Major Lockwood was not in a position to make an offer to Mr and Mrs Briggs or to grant an option to them pursuant to their right of pre-emption or at all save subject to Mr Pritchard's option. After the registration of Mr Pritchard's option, Mr and Mrs Briggs could not accept an offer or exercise an option granted by Major Lockwood pursuant to the right of pre-emption or at all save subject to Mr Pritchard's option. In short Major

---

[1]   For similar provisions, see LPA 1925, ss. 2(3)(iv), 186; SLA 1925, ss. 58(2), 61(2); PAA 1964, s. 9(2), p. 410, post. See also Housing Act 1925, s. 33.

Lockwood could only sell and the Briggs could only purchase subject to Mr Pritchard's option; ..."

Stephenson LJ said at 423, at 332:

'The 1944 conveyance—(which created the right of pre-emption)—refers to giving the option of purchasing but as a future act, not as a present right; and Mr Scott has satisfied me that what is granted as a right of pre-emption, on the true construction of the grant, is only properly called an option when the will of the grantor turns it into an option by deciding to sell and thereby binding the grantor to offer it for sale to the grantee. That it thereby becomes an interest in land is a change in the nature of the right to which, unlike Goff LJ, I see no insuperable objection in logic or in principle. And, as I understand his opinion on this point, its consequence would be that a right of pre-emption could never be enforceable against a successor in title whether it is registered or not.

I accordingly prefer the option of Templeman LJ on this point'. [2]

LAND REGISTRATION ACT 2002

115 Rights of pre-emption [3]

(1) A right of pre-emption in relation to registered land has effect from the time of creation as an interest capable of binding successors in title (subject to the rules about the effect of dispositions on priority).

(2) This section has effect in relation to rights of pre-emption created on or after the day on which this section comes into force. [4]

QUESTIONS

1. It has often been said that the Judicature Act effects a fusion of procedure but not of substantive law. 'But the two streams of jurisdiction, though they run in the same channel run side by side, and do not mingle their waters'. Ashburner, *Principles of Equity* (2nd edn, 1933), p. 18. What light is thrown on this question by the cases considered in this section? See also (1870) 14 SJ 548; (1954) 70 LQR 326 (Lord Evershed); (1961) 24 MLR 116 (V. T. H. Delany); (1977) 93 LQR 529 (P. V. Baker); (1977) 6 Anglo-Am 119 (T. G. Watkin); H & M, pp. 20–26; Meagher, Gummow and Lehane, *Equity: Doctrines and Remedies* (4th edn 2002), chap 2; Pettit, *Equity and the Law of Trusts* (8th edn, 1997), pp. 9–11; *United Scientific Holdings Ltd v Burnley Borough Council* [1978] AC 904, [1977] 2 All ER 62; *Tinsley v Milligan* [1994] 1 AC 340 at 370, 375, [1993] 3 All ER 65 at 86, 90.

2. Work out, step by step, the way in which the *Walsh v Lonsdale* litigation would have proceeded before 1875. H & M pp. 14–17.

3. Is a contract for a lease as good as a lease? p. 523, post. What is the effect on this of (a) the Land Charges Act 1972; (b) Law of Property (Miscellaneous Provisions) Act 1989, s. 2; [1990] Conv 44 (J. Howell); (c) Land Registration Act 2002?

---

[2]   For a detailed analysis of the right, see CHADWICK LJ in *Bircham & Co Nominees (No 2) Ltd v Worrell Holdings Ltd* [2001] 3 EGLR 83 at 86–89; *Tiffany Investments Ltd v Bircham & Co Nominees (No 2) Ltd* [2003] EWCA Civ 1759, [2004] EG 152; *Dear v Reeves* [2002] Ch 1 (right of preemption held to be an interest in land for the purposes of Insolvency Act 1986, s. 436 ('*Pritchard v Briggs* was a decision on the construction of LCA 1925', per MUMMERY LJ at para. 43); [2001] Conv 295 (P.H. Kenny).

[3]   H & B para. 3.40; R & R, paras. 15.026–15.027.

[4]   13 October 2003.

4.   How far do property rights and human rights overlap? Gray and Gray, *Land Law* (3rd edn), paras. 2.2–2.4, 2.11, 2.13; MM, pp. 92–93; Smith, pp. 16–19; Sparkes, *A New Land Law* (2nd edn), pp. 71–77; Rook, *Property Law and Human Rights*; [2002] Conv 316 (D. Rook) reviewing the first year of the Human Rights Act 1998.

5.   Does the Human Rights Act 1998 have a horizontal effect (it applies to disputes between private individuals), or a vertical effect (it only applies to relations between the state and individuals)? Rook, chap. 3; [1998] PL 423 (M. Hunt); [1999] Conv 287; Modern Studies in Property Law (ed. E. Cooke), chap. 9 (J. Howell); (2000) 116 LQR 48 (Sir Richard Buxton); (2000) 116 LQR 217 (H.W.R. Wade); (2001) 117 LQR (N. Bamforth); [2002] Conv 513 (P. Halstead); (2002) 118 LQR 623 (D. Beyleveld and S.D. Pattinson).

IV. Fixtures [5]

A. What is Land?

Since land and chattels are treated differently by the law and since a chattel may, by being affixed to land, become part of the land, it is necessary to have a test to determine whether or not such a change has taken place. For example, a brick in a builder's yard is a chattel; once used to build a wall, it becomes part of the land; and if the wall is knocked down the bricks become chattels again. When land is sold, the conveyance includes the land but not the chattels, [6] but includes those things which were once chattels but which have become land. [7]

The question whether a chattel remains a chattel or has become part of the land can arise in many contexts, namely whether it passes to a purchaser, [8]

---

[5]   C & B, pp. 151–157; Gray, pp. 44–55; M & W, paras. 14.311–14.328; MM, pp. 19–24; Smith, pp. 83–90; LPA 1925, s. 205(1)(ix) as amended by TLATA 1996, s. 25(2), Sch 4; SLA 1925, s. 117(1)(ix); as amended by TLATA 1996, s. 25(1), Sch 3, para. 2(13)(a); TA 1925, s 68(6) as amended by TLATA 1996, s. 25(2), Sch. 4; LRA 1925, s. 3(viii); LCA 1972 s. 17(1); as amended by TLATA 1996, s. 25(2), Sch. 4; Interpretation Act 1978, s. 5, Sch 1. as amended by TLATA 1996, s. 25(1), Sch. 3, para. 16.

[6]   By LPA 1925, s. 62, p. 722, post, a conveyance of land includes buildings, erections and fixtures, in the absence of a contrary intention: *HE Dibble Ltd v Moore* [1970] 2 QB 181, [1969] 3 All ER 1465 (greenhouses resting on own weight on concrete dollies held to be removable chattels).

[7]   See *Melluish v BMI (No 3) Ltd* [1996] AC 454, [1995] 4 All ER 453 (contractual term that object shall remain a chattel not decisive: 'The concept of a fixture which remains personal or removable property is a contradiction in terms and an impossibility in law; [1995] Ch 90 at 115 per DILLON LJ in CA).

[8]   *Colegrave v Dias Santos* (1823) 2 B & C 76 (fixtures, including those which a tenant could have removed, passed on sale of freehold); *Phillips v Lamdin* [1949] 2 KB 33, [1949] 1 All ER 770 (purchaser entitled to reinstatement of Adam door removed by vendor); *Hynes v Vaughan* (1985) 50 P & CR 444 (purchaser not entitled to chrysanthemum growing frame and sprinkler system); *Deen v Andrews* (1986) 52 P & CR 17 (purchaser not entitled to large prefabricated greenhouse bolted to concrete plinth resting by its own weight). For the effect of hire-purchase agreements, see (1963) 27 Conv (NS) 30 (A. G. Guest and J. Lever); [1990] Conv 275 (G. McCormack).

or sub-purchaser,[9] on a sale of the land; whether it is included as part security on a mortgage of the land, [10] whether it is owned by the estate tenant for life or passes to the remainderman, [11] whether it is owned by a tent for years or by the freeholder, [12] whether it passes on a death as realty or personalty, [13] and whether a drainpipe, placed underground in the exercise of an easement of drainage, remains the property of the party entitled to the easement. [14]

A related but separate question follows. [15] There are some occasions in which the owner of a one-time chattel may remove it even though it has now become part of the land. A tenant for years has long been able to remove trade, ornamental and domestic fixtures, and may now, by statute, remove agricultural fixtures also. [16] A tenant for life was in the same position at common law, but has not been given the statutory right to agricultural fixtures.

[9] *Berkley v Poulett* (1976) 241 EG 911, 242 EG 39. Cf. *Hamp v Bygrave* (1982) 266 EG 720 (stone and lead garden ornaments resting on own weight held to be fixtures because the vendors regarded them as 'features of, and part and parcel of, the garden'; alternatively, if the ornaments were chattels, the vendors were estopped from denying that they formed part of the sale); [1983] LSG 1773 (H. W. Wilkinson). *Berkley v Poulett* was not cited. See generally [1983] NZLJ 256 (H. W. Wilkinson); *Kennedy v Secretary of State for Wales* [1996] EGCS 17 (three massive ormulu bronze chandeliers and carillon turret clock at Neo-Gothic Grade II listed Leighton Hall, Welshpool, held to be fixtures).

[10] *Holland v Hodgson* (1872) LR 7 CP 328; *Hobson v Gorringe* [1897] 1 Ch 182 (machinery affixed. The judgment of Smith LJ contains a resumé of the cases up to that time); *Lyon & Co v London City and Midland Bank* [1903] 2 KB 135 (tip-up seats screwed to bolts fastened to floor and hired to mortgagors held to be chattels); *Vaudeville Electric Cinema Ltd v Muriset* [1923] 2 Ch 74 (similar seats owned by mortgagor held to be land); *Reynolds v Ashby & Sons* [1904] AC 466 (machines bolted to the floor held to be land); *Hulme v Brigham* [1943] KB 152, [1943] 1 All ER 204 (heavy printing machinery resting by its own weight held by Birkett J to be chattels); *Botham v TSB Bank plc* (1996) 73 P & CR D1 (CA held bathroom fittings, fitted kitchen units and sink to be fixtures, but not fitted carpets, curtains, blinds, gas fires, oven, hob, dishwasher, freezer and washing machine).

[11] *D'Eyncourt v Gregory* (1866) LR 3 Eq 382 (ornamental statues in park, resting by their weight on plinth, held to be part of realty); *Leigh v Taylor* [1902] AC 157 (tapestries stretched over canvas and tacked thereto held to remain chattels); *Re Lord Chesterfield's Settled Estates* [1911] 1 Ch 237 (proceeds of sale of ornamental wood carvings by Grinling Gibbons treated as capital money under SLA 1882).

[12] *Culling v Tufnal* (1694) Bull NP 34; *Elwes v Maw* (1802) 3 East 38 (Dutch barn resting by own weight in hollow of brick foundations remained a chattel); *Webb v Frank Bevis Ltd* [1940] 1 All ER 247 (similarly a corrugated iron building held to floor by iron strips); cf. *Elitestone v Morris*, infra (27 chalets resting on timber and block footing held to be part of land).

[13] *Bain v Brand* (1876) 1 App Cas 762 (machinery in colliery passed to heir and not to executor); *Re Whaley* [1908] 1 Ch 615 (pictures and tapestries in dining-room designed as a 'complete specimen of Elizabethan dwelling-house' passed under devise of house and not under bequest of chattels).

[14] *Simmons v Midford* [1969] 2 Ch 415, [1969] 2 All ER 1269 (plaintiff's drainpipe under road held to be chattel with which neighbour claiming an easement of drainage could not interfere); cf. *Montague v Long* (1972) 24 P & CR 240 (bridge over river).

[15] The two questions are not always kept separate: *Leigh v Taylor* [1902] AC 157; cf. Lords Halsbury and Macnaghten with Lord Shand. In the Court of Appeal, sub nom *Re De Falbe* [1901] 1 Ch 523, Stirling LJ said: 'It appears to me, therefore, both on principle and on authority that the exception from the rule extends to ornamental fixtures as well as to trade fixtures. Now, what are the objects as to which the dispute arises here? Tapestries. Photographs of some of them have been produced, and they shew that the tapestries are of an ornamental character, and, therefore, it appears to me that the exception from the rule applies'.

[16] Agricultural Holdings Act 1986, s. 10.

ELITESTONE LTD v MORRIS

([1997] 1 WLR 687, [1997] 2 All ER 513, HL, Lords BROWNE-WILKINSON, LLOYD OF BERWICK, NOLAN, NICHOLLS OF BIRKENHEAD and CLYDE)[17]

LORD LLOYD OF BERWICK: My Lords, the plaintiffs, Elitestone Ltd., are the freehold owners of land known as Holt's Field, Murton, Near Swansea. The land is divided into 27 lots. The defendant, Mr Morris, is the occupier of a chalet or bungalow on Lot No. 6. It is not known for certain when the chalet was built. But it seems likely that it was before 1945. Mr Morris has lived there since 1971.

The plaintiffs acquired the freehold in 1989 with a view to redevelopment. On 30 April 1991 they issued proceedings in the Swansea County Court claiming possession against all 27 occupiers. Five lead actions were selected, including that in which Mr Morris was defendant. They came on for trial before Mr Bidder, sitting as an assistant recorder, in November 1994. The assistant recorder had a number of issues to decide. He dealt with them in a most impressive manner. So far as Mr Morris is concerned, his defence was that he is a tenant from year-to-year, that he occupies the premises as his residence, and is therefore entitled to the protection of the Rent Act 1966. He claims a declaration to that effect.

The assistant recorder held, correctly, at the end of what was necessarily a very lengthy judgment that the question in Mr Morris's case turned on whether or not the bungalow formed part of the realty. If it did then Mr Morris was entitled to his declaration ...

[The assistant recorder held that the bungalow formed part of the realty, but the Court of Appeal disagreed.] The photographs show very clearly what the bungalow is, and especially what it is not. It is *not* like a Portakabin, or mobile home. The nature of the structure is such that it could not be taken down and re-erected elsewhere. It could only be removed by a process of demolition. This, as will appear later, is a factor of great importance in the present case. If a structure can only be enjoyed in situ, and is such that it cannot be removed in whole or in sections to another site, there is at least a strong inference that the purpose of placing the structure on the original site was that it should form part of the realty at that site, and therefore cease to be a chattel. ...

The sole remaining issue for your Lordships is whether Mr Morris's bungalow did indeed become part of the land, or whether it has remained a chattel ever since it was first constructed before 1945.

It will be noticed that in framing the issue for decision I have avoided the use of the word 'fixture.' There are two reasons for this. The first is that 'fixture,' though a hallowed term in this branch of the law, does not always bear the same meaning in law as it does in everyday life. In ordinary language one thinks of a fixture as being something fixed to a building. One would not ordinarily think of the building itself as a fixture. Thus in *Boswell v Crucible Steel Co* [1925] 1 KB 119 the question was whether plate glass windows which formed part of the wall of a warehouse were landlord's fixtures within the meaning of a repairing covenant. Atkin LJ said, at p. 123:

'... I am quite satisfied that they are not landlord's fixtures, and for the simple reason that they are not fixtures at all in the sense in which that term is generally understood. A fixture, as that term is used in connection with the house, means something which has been affixed to the freehold as accessory to the house. It does not include things which were made part of the house itself in the course of its construction.'

---

[17]   (1997) 147 NLJ 1031 (H. W. Wilkinson); [1997] CLJ 498 (S. Bridge).

Yet in *Billing v Pill* [1954] 1 QB 70, 75, [1953] 2 All ER 1061, 1063 Lord Goddard CJ said:

'What is a fixture? The commonest fixture is a house which is built into the land, so that in law it is regarded as part of the land. The house and the land are one thing.'

There is another reason. The term fixture is apt to be a source of misunderstanding owing to the existence of the category of so called 'tenants' fixtures' (a term used to cover both trade fixtures and ornamental fixtures), which are fixtures in the full sense of the word (and therefore part of the realty) but which may nevertheless be removed by the tenant in the course of or at the end of his tenancy. Such fixtures are sometimes confused with chattels which have never become fixtures at all. ...

For my part I find it better in the present case to avoid the traditional twofold distinction between chattels and fixtures, and to adopt the threefold classification set out in *Woodfall, Landlord and Tenant* (looseleaf ed.), vol. 1, para. 13.131:

'An object which is brought into land may be classified under one of three broad heads. It may be (a) a chattel; (b) a fixture; or (c) part and parcel of the land itself. Objects in categories (b) and (c) are treated as being part of the land.'

So the question in the present appeal is whether, when the bungalow was built, it became part and parcel of the land itself. The materials out of which the bungalow was constructed, that is to say, the timber frame walls, the feather boarding, the suspended timber floors, the chipboard ceilings, and so on, were all, of course, chattels when they were brought onto the site. Did they cease to be chattels when they were built into the composite structure? The answer to the question, as Blackburn J pointed out in *Holland v Hodgson* (1872) LR 7 CP 328, depends on the circumstances of each case, but mainly on two factors, the degree of annexation to the land, and the object of the annexation.

Degree of annexation

The importance of the degree of annexation will vary from object to object. In the case of a large object, such as a house, the question does not often arise. Annexation goes without saying. So there is little recent authority on the point, and I do not get much help from the early cases in which wooden structures have been held not to form part of the realty, such as the wooden mill in *R v Otley* (1830) 1 B & Ad 161, the wooden barn in *Wansbrough v Maton* (1836) 4 Ad & El 884 and the granary in *Wiltshear v Cottrell* (1853) 1 E & B 674. But there is a more recent decision of the High Court of Australia which is of greater assistance. In *Reid v Smith* (1905) 3 CLR 656, 659 Griffith CJ stated the question as follows:

'The short point raised in this case is whether an ordinary dwelling-house, erected upon an ordinary town allotment in a large town, but not fastened to the soil, remains a chattel or becomes part of the freehold.'

The Supreme Court of Queensland had held that the house remained a chattel. But the High Court reversed this decision, treating the answer as being almost a matter of common sense. The house in that case was made of wood, and rested by its own weight on brick piers. The house was not attached to the brick piers in any way. It was separated by iron plates placed on top of the piers, in order to prevent an invasion of white ants. There was an extensive citation of English and American authorities. It was held that the absence of any attachment did not prevent the house forming part of the realty. Two quotations, at p. 667, from the American authorities may suffice. In *Snedeker v Warring* 12 NY 170, 175 (1854) Parker J said: 'A thing may be as firmly affixed to the land by gravitation as by clamps or cement. Its character may depend upon the object of its erection.' In *Goff v O'Connor* 16 Ill 421, 423 (1855), the court said:

'Houses, in common intendment of the law, are not fixtures to, but part of, the land. ... This does not depend, in the case of houses, so much upon the particular mode of attaching, or fixing and connecting them with the land upon which they stand or rest, as it does upon the uses and purposes for which they were erected and designed.'

Purpose of annexation

Many different tests have been suggested, such as whether the object which has been fixed to the property has been so fixed for the better enjoyment of the object as a chattel, or whether it has been fixed with a view to effecting a permanent improvement of the freehold. This and similar tests are useful when one is considering an object such as a tapestry, which may or may not be fixed to a house so as to become part of the freehold: see *Leigh v Taylor* [1902] AC 157. These tests are less useful when one is considering the house itself. In the case of the house the answer is as much a matter of common sense as precise analysis. A house which is constructed in such a way so as to be removable, whether as a unit, or in sections, may well remain a chattel, even though it is connected temporarily to mains services such as water and electricity. But a house which is constructed in such a way that it cannot be removed at all, save by destruction, cannot have been intended to remain as a chattel. It must have been intended to form part of the realty. I know of no better analogy than the example given by Blackburn J in *Holland v Hodgson* (1872) LR 7 CP 328, 335:

'Thus blocks of stone placed one on the top of another without any mortar or cement for the purpose of forming a dry stone wall would become part of the land, though the same stones, if deposited in a builder's yard and for convenience sake stacked on the top of each other in the form of a wall, would remain chattels.'

Applying that analogy to the present case, I do not doubt that when Mr Morris's bungalow was built, and as each of the timber frame walls were placed in position, they all became part of the structure, which was itself part and parcel of the land. The object of bringing the individual bits of wood onto the site seems to be so clear that the absence of any attachment to the soil (save by gravity) becomes an irrelevance.

Finally I return to the judgment of the Court of Appeal. I need say no more about the absence of attachment, which was the first of the reasons given by the Court of Appeal for reversing the assistant recorder. The second reason was the intention which the court inferred from the previous course of dealing between the parties, and in particular the uncertainty of Mr Morris's tenure. The third reason was the analogy with the shed in *Webb v Frank Bevis Ltd* [1940] 1 All ER 247, and the greenhouse in *Deen v Andrews* [1986] 1 EGLR 262.

As to the second reason the Court of Appeal may have been misled by Blackburn J's use of the word 'intention' in *Holland v Hodgson*. But as the subsequent decision of the Court of Appeal in *Hobson v Gorringe* [1897] 1 Ch 182 made clear, and as the decision of the House in *Melluish v BMI (No 3) Ltd* [1996] AC 454 put beyond question, the intention of the parties is only relevant to the extent that it can be derived from the degree and object of the annexation. The subjective intention of the parties cannot affect the question whether the chattel has, in law, become part of the freehold, any more than the subjective intention of the parties can prevent what they have called a licence from taking effect as a tenancy, if that is what in law it is: see *Street v Mountford* [1985] AC 809, [1985] 2 All ER 289, p. 473, ante.

As for the third of the reasons, I have already pointed out that *Webb v Frank Bevis Ltd* does not support the Court of Appeal's conclusion, because the shed in that case was held to be a fixture, albeit a fixture which the tenant was entitled to remove.

In *Deen v Andrews* the question was whether a greenhouse was a building so as to pass to the purchaser under a contract for the sale of land 'together with the farmhouses and other buildings.' Hirst J held that it was not. He followed an earlier decision in *H E Dibble Ltd v Moore* [1970] 2 QB 181, [1969] 3 All ER 1465 in which the Court of Appeal, reversing the trial judge, held that a greenhouse was not an 'erection' within section 62(1) of the Law of Property Act 1925. I note that in the latter case Megaw LJ, at p. 187G, at p. 1469 drew attention to some evidence 'that it was customary to move such greenhouses every few years to a fresh site.' It is obvious that a greenhouse which can be moved from site to site is a long way removed from a two bedroom bungalow which cannot be moved at all without being demolished.

For the above reasons I would allow this appeal and restore the order of the assistant recorder. [18]

B. What Fixtures may be Removed?

Even if a chattel is affixed to the land so as to become part of the land, the person who affixed it or his successors in title may have a right to remove it. [19] At common law, a tenant for years and a tenant for life were entitled to remove trade, [20] ornamental or domestic fixtures. [1] By Agricultural Holdings Act 1986, section 10, replacing earlier legislation, a tenant for years may also remove agricultural fixtures. As between devisee and personal representative, vendor and purchaser and mortgagor and mortgagee there is no right of removal, and the question of entitlement is dependent upon the question of annexation to the land. [2]

---

[18]   *Chelsea Yacht and Boat Co Ltd v Pope* [2000] 1 WLR 1941, [2000] 2 All ER 409 (converted wooden D-Day landing craft fitted inside a steel Thames barge, moored to a pontoon and the bed and bank of a river in which it took the ground at about half tide, held not to be part of the land. 'It is common sense that a boat on a river is not part of the land. A boat, albeit one used as a home, is not of the same genus as real property' per TUCKEY LJ at 1946, at 414.

[19]   *Herbert v British Railways Board* (2000) 4 L&T Rev D13 (rails and sleepers held to be landlord's fixtures).

[20]   *Poole's Case* (1703) 1 Salk 368; *Climie v Wood* (1861) LR 4 Exch 328; *Penton v Robart* (1801) 2 East 88; *Wardell v Usher* (1841) 3 Scott NR 508; *Elliott v Bishop* (1854) 10 Exch 496; *Smith v City Petroleum Co Ltd* [1940] 1 All ER 260; *New Zealand Government Property Corpn v H M and S Ltd* [1982] QB 1145, [1982] 1 All ER 624; *Young v Dalgety plc* [1987] 1 EGLR 116; [1987] Conv 253 (G. Kodilinye). See *Mancetter Development Ltd v Garmaston Ltd* [1986] QB 1212, [1986] 1 All ER 449 p. 21, n. 9, ante.

[1]   *Grymes v Boweren* (1830) 6 Bing 437; *Buckland v Butterfield* (1820) 2 Brod & Bing 54; *Beck v Rebow* (1706) 1 P Wms 94; *Leach v Thomas* (1835) 7 C & P 327; *Spyer v Phillipson* [1931] 2 Ch 183; *Colegrave v Dias Santos* (1823) 2 B & C 76, 77; *Darby v Harris* (1841) 1 QB 895; *Lyde v Russell* (1830) 1 B & Ad 394.

[2]   See p. 96, ante.

2. Registered Land [1]

---

[1]   C & B, pp. 100–108, 855–878; Gray, chap. 9; M & W, paras. 4.066–4.072; MM, pp. 111–145;
Smith, chap. 11. The authoritative account of LRA 1925 is Ruoff and Roper (former Chief
Land Registrars), *Law and Practice of Registered Conveyancing*; (1991 edn. looseleaf, with the
last supplement in 2003); Wolstenholme and Cherry, *Conveyancing Statutes* (13th edn. 1972),
vol. 6; Barnsley, *Conveyancing Law and Practice* (4th edn. 1996), chaps. 2, 3, 4, 11, 15; Hayton,
Registered Land (3rd edn. 1981); Wontner's *Guide to Land Registry Practice* (9th edn.); Coveney
and Pain, *Practical Guide to Effective Protection and the Land Registry*. See also Potter, *Principles*

I. Introduction

We have seen that the basic doctrines of land law developed at common law under a system in which title to land was proved by the production of deeds recording the history of transactions affecting the land; this system is steadily being overtaken by a system which is based upon the registration of title to land. Under the latter system, all transfers of the legal title are required to be by registration in an individual register of the transferee's property, name and any charges on that property. The old cumbrous method of conveyancing by title deeds is dispensed with; and a registered title is thence-forth guaranteed by the State.

A system of registration of title was introduced into England as far back as 1862, but only on an optional basis. A revised system of registration of title was set out in the Land Registration Acts 1925[2] and the Land Registration Rules 1925[3]—which must be kept wholly distinct from systems of registration of deeds[4] and charges (such as that under the Land Charges Act 1972). Since 1990 it has been compulsory over the whole of England and Wales;[5] compulsory in the sense that dealings in land must now be carried out under the new and not the old system of conveyancing.[6]

There are now about 19 million registered titles and it is estimated that there are potentially a further 3 to 4 million titles which are not on the register. Computerisation is making further progress. Some key data, including the Index Map, are being computerised, and a new Computer Services Centre is being set up at Plymouth. A Land Registry Online is available whereby anyone can look at registers from their PC and pay for the service by credit card. In the run-up to full electronic conveyancing, a pilot scheme is operating for the automatic discharge of a registered charge.[7]

---

and Practice of Conveyancing under the Land Registration Act 1925 (1934; 2nd edn, 1948); Brickdale and Stewart-Wallace, *The Land Registration Act 1925* (4th edn, 1939). For specialist commentaires on LRA 2002, see p. 104, n. 8 post. The Chief Land Registrar publishes an Annual Report on H.M. Land Registry. The first report of the Law Commission was published in 1983 (Law Com No. 125, HC 86) on Identity and Boundaries, Conversion of Title, the Treatment of Leases and Minor Interests Index; its second report in 1985 on Inspection of the Register (Law Com No. 148, HC 551); its third report in 1987 on Overriding Interests, Rectification and Indemnity and Minor Interests (Law Com No. 158, HC 269) on which see [1987] Conv 334 (R.J. Smith). The recommendations on the last three topics of the 1983 Report were implemented in LRA 1986; and the 1985 Report was implemented in LRA 1988. Its fourth Report was in 1988 which presented a Land Registration Bill which incorporates the recommendations of the third report and 'is a modern, and we hope, simpler version of the 1925 Act'. In advance of this, the Law Commission published in 1995 a First Report on the Implementation of its Third and Fourth Reports (Law Com No. 235, Cm 2950); and this was implemented in LRA 1997.

2   As amended by LRA 1925, 1936, 1966, LR and LCA 1971, Parts I and III, LRA 1986, 1988, 1997, 1999, 1999 (No. 2), 1999 (No. 3), 2000, 2000 (No. 2); 2000 (No. 3), 2001 and 2002.

3   For further Rules see LRR 1956, 1964, 1967, 1976, 1978, 1989, 1990, 1993, 1995, 1995 (No. 2), 1995 (No. 3), 1996 and 1997; LR (Souvenir Land) R 1972; LR (Capital Transfer Tax) R 1975; LR (Companies and Insolvency) R 1986; LR (Powers of Attorney) R 1986; LR (Delivery of Applications) R 1986; LR (Charges) R 1990; LR (Open Register) R 1991, as amended by LRR 2001, Sch. 3; LR (Charities) R 1993; LR (Leasehold Reform) R 1993; LR (Official Searches) R 1993; LR (Execution of Deeds) R 1994; LR (Implied Covenants for Title) R 1995; LR (Matrimonial Home Rights) R 1997 as amended by LRR 2001, Sch. 3; LR Fees Order 2003; LR (Conduct of Business) Regs. 1997.

4   The Yorkshire Deeds Registries are closed: LPA 1969, Part II.

5   Land registration is being extended to Scotland by area: Land Registration (Scotland) Act 1979.

6   Registration of Title Order 1989.

7   Annual Report for 2002–2003, pp. 5, 9, 44.

The Land Registration Act 1925 and the Land Registration Rules 1925 were repealed and replaced by the Land Registration Act 2002 and the Land Registration Rules 2003. These came into force on 13 October 2003.[8] There are substantial transitional provisions which make the former Act and Rules relevant.[9]

The object of the new Act and Rules is to provide a legislative framework which will enable conveyancing to be carried out electronically. Conveyancing will thus take advantage of information technology and develop alongside similar transactions such as banking and business. To this end the register of a parcel of land must be as complete a mirror of title as possible.

The Law Commission said in its Report on *Land Registration for the Twenty-First Century*[10] that:

> 'The fundamental objective of the Act is that, under the system of electronic dealing with land that it seeks to create, the register should be a complete and accurate reflection of the state of the title of the land at any given time, so that it is possible to investigate title to land on line, with the absolute minimum of additional enquiries and inspections.'

A. Similarity of 1925 and 2002 Acts

There are similarities of policy and structure between the two Acts. The 2002 Act is presented in a more coherent and logical form.[11] The main similarities between the two Acts are:

---

8   On the Land Registration Act 2002, see Law Commission Consultative Document on Land Registration for the Twenty-First Century 1998 (Law Com No. 254, Cm 4027); Law Commission Report on Land Registration for the Twenty-First Century – A Conveyancing Revolution 2001 (Law Com No. 271 HC14); Ruoff and Roper, *Registered Conveyancing* (Looseleaf 2003); Harpum and Bignell, *Registered Land: The New Law* (2002) (Charles Harpum was the Law Commissioner responsible for the two Law Commission papers and for the Land Registration Act 2002); Harpum and Bignell, *Registered Land. Law and Practice under the Land Registration Act 2002* (2004); Abbey and Richards, *Blackstone's Guide to the Land Registration Act 2002*; Wolstenholme and Cherry: *Land Registration Act 2002* (ed. I. Clarke and J. Farrand), which contains LRA 1925 and 2002, and LRR 1925 and 2003; Current Law Statutes 2002 (ch. 9) annotated by P.H. Kenny; [2002] Conv 11 (E. Cooke); [2003] Conv 136 (M. Dixon). On the Land Registration Rules 2003, see Land Registry New Rules Consultation; Report on Responses to the Consultation. On E-Conveyancing, see A Land Registry Consultation; and A Land Registry Consultation Report. The Land Registry has issued 57 Practice Guides on the Act and Key Changes in Action Pact which contains Fact Sheets, which are also on CD Rom. Land Registry Forms are set out in LRR 2003 Sch. 1–9. On land registration systems in European countries, see Cooke, *The New Law of Land Registration* (2003), chap. 9.

9   For transitional provisions, see LRA 2002, s. 134, Sch. 12, paras. 1–3 (existing entries in the register); 4 (existing cautions against first registration); 5–6 (pending applications); 7–13 former overriding interests); p. 128 post; 14–16 (cautions against first registration); 17 (applications under ss. 34 or 43 by cautioners); 18 (adverse possession), p. 252 post; 19 (indemnities); 20 (implied indemnity covenants on transfer of pre-1996 leases); LRR 2003 (SI 2003 No. 1417) rr. 218–253 (cautions against dealings); 224 (registered rentcharges); LRA 2002 (Transitional Provisions) Order (SI 2003 No. 1953), arts 2–5 (general and administrative); 6–9 (disputes, objections, appeals and proceedings); 6–13 (souvenir land), p. 141, n. 18 post; 14–18 (cautions); 19 (outline applications); 20 (matrimonial home rights cautions); 21 (index of relating franchises and manors); 22–23 (compulsory first registration); 25 (obligation to make further advances); 26–27 (Forms); 28 (official searches and official copies); LRA 2002 (Transitional Provisions) Order 2003 (No. 2) (SI 2003 No. 2431) (right to repair a church chancel) p. 162 post.

10   2001 (Law Com No. 271), para. 1.5.

11   The LRA 1925 was the only part of the 1925 Legislation which was not drafted by Sir Benjamin Cherry.

1. A disposition of registered land will not take effect at law unless the registration requirements are met.
2. There is a tripartite register for each parcel of registered land.
3. There is voluntary and compulsory registration of title, with the latter being triggered by specified events.
4. The register of title is conclusive, but the effect of this is qualified by the court's powers of alteration and indemnity.
5. Indemnity is an integral part of the state guarantee of title.
6. The registrar is not to be affected with notice of a trust.
7. There is a distinction between registrable interests with an individual register and those interests which need protection on the register.
8. There are overriding interests which bind even though they do not appear on the register.

B. Main Changes in the Land Registration Act 2002

Important changes have been made by the Land Registration Act 2002 and the Land Registration Rules 2003. These are:
1. An increase in the number of triggers for first registration, with the promise of more to come until the register is complete.
2. The length of leases subject to compulsory registration is reduced from 21 to 7 years, so that most business leases now become registrable.
3. A decrease in the number and extent of overriding interests.
4. The Limitation Act 1980 is disapplied in relation to registered land, and is replaced by a new law of adverse possession. This is advantageous to a landowner, but disadvantageous to a squatter, so much so that a landowner may decide to take advantage of the reduced fees for voluntary registration and to register.[12]
5. Land held by Her Majesty the Queen as demesne land becomes registrable for the first time. This includes extensive parts of the foreshore in England and Wales.
6. The redrafting of classes of title, the methods of protection of minor interests, and the restructuring of rectification and indemnity.
7. A simplification of the principles of priority.
8. The creation of mortgages by demise and sub-demise, hitherto obsolescent, becomes obsolete.
9. The creation of a new system of independent adjudication arising out of disputed applications to the registrar.
10. No further land or charge certificates will be issued, and, if a certificate is lodged with the Land Registry, it will be destroyed.[12a] In its place a Title Information Document will be issued which comprises a copy of the register and a copy of the title plan.

These changes are designed to pave the way for the introduction of a system of paperless transfer of land by electronic conveyancing. This is a fundamental change and will not be fully implemented overnight.

[12a] LR Fee Order 2004 (SI 2004 No. 595), as amended by LR Fee (Amendment) Order 2004 (SI 2004 No. 1833).

[12] LRA 2002 (Transitional Provisions) Order 2003 (SI 2003 No 1953), art. 24 (abolition of land and charge certificates). For copies of the original land certificate and its successor, see the 7th edn of this book at pp. 105–108. The borders were decorated with the arms of six Lord Chancellors, Lords Birkenhead, Haldane, Halsbury, Cairns, Selborne and Westbury. See the tribute paid to these Lord Chancellors by Sir Leslie Scott when moving the second reading of the Law of Property Bill 1922; Scott, *The New Law of Property Acts Explained* (1925) 'It is not revolution, but evoluton.'

The new Act and Rules create a coherent framework in which the land law of England and Wales can develop.

C. Requirement of Registration for Effect at Law

LAND REGISTRATION ACT 2002

27   Disposition required to be registered

(1) If a disposition of a registered estate or registered charge is required to be completed by registration, it does not operate at law until the relevant registration requirements are met.

D. Conclusiveness of Register

Registration is conclusive of title to the legal estate and is said to confer a new root of title on the proprietor. There are limited powers of rectification of the register, subject to payment of an indemnity from public funds to any person suffering loss thereby.

LAND REGISTRATION ACT 2002

58   Conclusiveness[13]

(1) If on the entry of a person in the register as the proprietor of a legal estate, the legal estate would not otherwise be vested in him, it shall be deemed to be vested in him as a result of the registration.

(2) Subsection (1) does not apply where the entry is made in pursuance of a registrable disposition in relation to which some other registration requirement remains to be met.

Law Commission Report on Land Registration for the Twenty-First Century 2001 (Law Com No. 271), paras. 9.4–9.5.

'9.4   One of the most fundamental principles of registered conveyancing is that it is registration that vests the legal estate in the registered proprietor. Section 58 of the Act provides accordingly that if, on the entry of a person in the register as the proprietor of a legal estate, the legal estate would not otherwise be vested in him or her, it shall be deemed to be vested in him or her as a result of registration. Thus, for example, if a person is registered as proprietor on the strength of a forged transfer, the legal estate will vest in that transferee even though the transfer was a nullity.

9.6   The following events will exemplify how the provision in [section 58(2)] will operate, X applies to be registered as the grantee of a 99-year lease. The lease is registered with its own title. However, the registrar fails to enter a notice

---

[13]   R & R, paras. 3.009–3.009.1.; H & B, paras. 5.3–5.4. Cf. LRA 1925, s. 69. In *Argyle Building Society v Hammond* (1984) 49 P & CR 148 at 153, SLADE LJ referred to the 'statutory magic' of the section. If an interest, such as a restrictive covenant, is void for non-registration as a land charge under LCA 1972 prior to the first registration of title, it is not revived by an entry in the charges register of the registered title: *Kitney v MEPC Ltd* [1977] 1 WLR 981 (estate contract): R & R, para. 9.020.

of the lease on the superior freehold title. The legal estate is not vested in X by virtue of [section 58(1)]. The grant will, however, be effective in equity.'[14]

E. Trusts

LAND REGISTRATION ACT 2002

78 Notice of trust not to affect registrar
The registrar shall not be affected with notice of a trust.[15]

F. Critique of Land Registration Act 2002

Law Commission Consultative Document on Land Registration for the Twenty-First Century 1998 (Law Com No. 254), para. 11.9.

'As any system is likely to be introduced in stages, we regard it as essential that the eventual goal that we wish to achieve should be clear from the outset. Only in this way can developments be properly directed. That eventual goal is to eliminate so far as possible the present three-stage process by which a document is executed, lodged with the Registry and then registered. The only way to achieve this is to provide that the transaction should be executed electronically by registration. Thus any transfer would be completed by registering it, and any right that it was intended to create over registered land would not be created until it was registered. This is only possible with an electronic system.'

Law Commission Report on Land Registration for the Twenty-First Century 2001 (Law Com No. 271), para. 1.10.

'These changes will necessarily alter the perception of title to land. It will be the fact of registration and registration alone that confers title. This is entirely in accordance with the fundamental principle of a conclusive register which underpins the Bill.'

C. Harpum in Getzler, ed. *Rationalizing Property, Equity and Trusts*, p. 203

'LRA 2002 is a very different Act from its predecessor. First, it has the coherent objective of securing a conclusive register. Secondly, it creates a system under which, when electronic conveyancing is introduced, there will be title by registration rather than registration of title.[16] Thirdly, it sets out to create a system of substantive law that reflects the principles of registered conveyancing. The two Law Commission reports, that respectively preceded and accompanied the Land Registration Bill,[17] provide a substantial corpus of material to guide the courts in interpreting the new legislation and the mischief it is intended to

---

[14] *Malory Enterprises Ltd v Cheshire (UK) Ltd* [2002] Ch 216, and its criticism by C. Harpum in Getzler, ed. *Rationalizing Property, Equity and Trusts*, chap. 9; (2003) 119 LQR 31 (D. Sheehan).
[15] Cf. LRA 1925, s. 74.
[16] LRA 2002, s. 93, p. 199, post.
[17] *Land Registration for the Twenty-First Century: A Consultative Document* (Law Com No. 254) and *Land Registration for the Twenty-First Century: A Conveyancing Revolution* (Law Com No. 271).

remedy.[18] Furthermore, the draftsman of LRA 2002 went to considerable trouble to define the relationship between land registration and the general principles of real property law. It is much clearer under the new Act than it is under LRA 1925. However, no draftsman, however good, can foresee all possibilities, nor address all those situations that he can. The modern approach to statutory interpretation is purposive and, it is suggested, principles that might be applicable in unregistered conveyancing should not be applied to dealings with registered land if to do so would be inconsistent with the scheme found in the new Act. In the final report that accompanied the draft Land Registration Bill, the Law Commission commented that "unregistered land has had its day".[19] If LRA 2002 is to achieve its objective the registered system has to be recognised in its own right and can no longer be regarded as mere gloss on the unregistered system.'

II. Scope of Title Registration

LAND REGISTRATION ACT 2002

2   Scope of title registration
This Act makes provision about the registration of title to—
(a) unregistered legal estates which are interests of any of the following kinds—
  (i)   an estate in land,
  (ii) a rentcharge,[20]
  (iii) a franchise,[1]
  (iv) a profit a prendre in gross,[2] and
  (v)   any other interest or charge which subsists for the benefit of or is a charge on, an interest the title to which is registered, and
(b) interests capable of subsisting at law which are created by a disposition of an interest the title to which is registered.

III. The Register of Title

LAND REGISTRATION ACT 2002

1   Register of title
  (1) There is to continue to be a register of title kept by the registrar.[3]

---

[18] Although Lord Nicholls has warned that the use of external aids to the construction of legislation (including Law Commission Reports, which he expressly mentioned) need to be used with circumspection (*R v Secretary of State for the Environment, ex p Spath Holme Ltd* [2001] 2 AC 349 at 398), the courts can and do frequently refer to them. As Clarke LJ explained in *Yaxley v Gotts* [2000] Ch 162 at 182, [2000] 1 All ER 711 at 726, 'Where a statute has been enacted as a result of the recommendations of the Law Commission, it is, as I see it, both appropriate and permissible for the court to consider those recommendations in order to help to identify both the mischief which the Act is designed to cure and the public policy underlying it.'
[19] *Land Registration for the Twenty-First Century: A Conveyancing Revolution* (Law Com No. 271) s. 1.6.
[20] On rentcharges generally, see R & R, chap. 29.
[1]   A franchise is 'a royal privilege or branch of the royal prerogative subsisting in the hands of a subject by grant from the King': *Spook Erection Ltd v Secretary of State for the Environment* [1989] QB 300 at 305, per Nourse LJ. The most important franchise is that of the market.
[2]   Profits a prendre in gross (i.e. without a dominant tenement, p. 690, post) now become registrable with their own titles. Manors are no longer registrable.
[3]   R & R, chap. 4.

(2) Rules may make provision about how the register is to be kept and may, in particular, make provision about —
(a) the information to be included in the register,
(b) the form in which information included in the register is to be kept, and
(c) the arrangement of that information.

LAND REGISTRATION RULES 2003

Form and arrangement of the register of title

2.—(1) The register of title may be kept in electronic or paper form, or partly in one form and partly in the other.

(2) Subject to rule 3, the register of title must include an individual register for each registered estate which is—
(a) an estate in land, or
(b) a rentcharge, franchise, manor or profit a prendre in gross, vested in a proprietor.

Arrangement of individual registers

4.—(1) Each individual register must have a distinguishing number, or series of letters and numbers, known as the title number.

(2) Each individual register must consist of a property register, a proprietorship register and, where necessary, a charges register.

(3) An entry in an individual register may be made by reference to a plan or other document; in which case the registrar must keep the original or a copy of the document.

(4) Whenever the registrar considers it desirable, he may make a new edition of any individual register so that it contains only the subsisting entries, rearrange the entries in the register or alter its title number.

Contents of the property register

5.—(1) The property register of a registered estate must contain—
(a) a description of the registered estate which in the case of a registered estate in land, rentcharge or registered franchise which is an affecting franchise must refer to a plan based on the Ordnance Survey map and known as the title plan;[4]
(b) where appropriate, details of—
  (i)   the inclusion or exclusion of mines and minerals in or from the registration under rule 32,
  (ii) easements, rights, privileges, conditions and covenants benefiting the registered estate and other similar matters,
  (iii) all exceptions arising on enfranchisement of formerly copyhold land, and

---

[4]   LRA 2002, s. 60; the boundary as shown for the purposes of the register is a general boundary and does not determine the exact line of the boundary. That line, however, may be fixed in accordance with s. 60(3)(4); LRR 2003, rr. 117–123; R & R, chap. 5; Law Commission Report on Registered Land for the Twenty-First Century 2001 (Law Com No. 271), paras. 9.9–9.15; *Chadwick v Hauser Conveyancing* [2004] NPC 80 (reviewing the authorities). See also s. 61 (accretion and diluvion): their operation is not affected, *Southern Centre of Theosophy Inc v State of South Australia* [1982] AC 706, 716, [1982] 1 All ER 293, per Lord WILBERFORCE.
In *Alan Wibberley Building Ltd v Insley* [1999] 2 All ER 897, [1999] 1 WLR 894 at 895, Lord HOFFMANN said: 'Boundary disputes are a particularly painful form of litigation. Feelings run high as disproportionate amounts of money are spent. Claims to small and valueless pieces of land are pressed with the zeal of Fortinbras's army.'

(iv) any other matter required to be entered in any other part of the register which the registrar considers may more conveniently be entered in the property register, and

(c) such other matters as are required to be entered in the property register by these rules.

Property register of a registered leasehold estate

6.—(1) The property register of a registered leasehold estate must also contain sufficient particulars of the registered lease to enable the lease to be identified.

(2) If the lease contains a provision that prohibits or restricts dispositions of the leasehold estate, the registrar must make an entry in the property register stating that all estates, rights, interests, powers and remedies arising on or by reason of a disposition made in breach of that prohibition or restriction are excepted from the effect of registration.

Property register of a registered estate in a rentcharge, a franchise or a profit a prendre in gross

7. The property register of a registered estate in a rentcharge, franchise or a profit a prendre in gross must, if the estate was created by an instrument, also contain sufficient particulars of the instrument to enable it to be identified.

Contents of the proprietorship register

8.—(1) The proprietorship register of a registered estate must contain, where appropriate—

(a) the class of title,

(b) the name of the proprietor of the registered estate including, where the proprietor is a company registered under the Companies Acts, or a limited liability partnership incorporated under the Limited Liability Partnerships Act 2000, its registered number,

(c) an address for service of the proprietor of the registered estate in accordance with rule 198,

(d) restrictions under section 40 of the Act,[5] including one entered under section 86(4) of the Act, in relation to the registered estate,

(e) notices under section 86(2) of the Act in relation to the registered estate,[6]

(f) positive covenants by a transferor or transferee and indemnity covenants by a transferee entered under rules 64 or 65,

(g) details of any modification of the covenants implied by paragraphs 20(2) and (3) of Schedule 12 to the Act entered under rule 66,[7]

(h) details of any modification of the covenants implied under the Law of Property (Miscellaneous Provisions) Act 1994 entered under rule 67(6),

(i) where the class of title is possessory, the name of the first proprietor of the registered estate and, where that proprietor is a company registered under the Companies Acts, or a limited liability partnership incorporated under the Limited Liability Partnerships Act 2000, its registered number, and

(j) such other matters as are required to be entered in the proprietorship register by these rules.

(2) On first registration and on a subsequent change of proprietor, the registrar whenever practicable will enter in the proprietorship register the price paid or value declared and such entry will remain until there is a change of proprietor, or

---

[5]   P. 172, post.
[6]   Notice in respect of a pending action after registration of petition in bankruptcy.
[7]   Implied indemnity covenants on transfer of pre-1996 leases, p. 511, n. 20, post.

some other change in the register of title which the registrar considers would result in the entry being misleading.

Contents of the charges register

9. The charges register of a registered estate must contain, where appropriate—

(a) details of leases, charges, and any other interests which adversely affect the registered estate subsisting at the time of first registration of the estate or created thereafter,

(b) any dealings with the interests referred to in paragraph (a), or affecting their priority, which are capable of being noted on the register,

(c) sufficient details to enable any registered charged to be identified,

(d) the name of the proprietor of any registered charge including, where the proprietor is a company registered under the Companies Acts, or a limited liability partnership incorporated under the Limited Liability Partnerships Act 2000, its registered number,

(e) an address for service of the proprietor of any registered charge in accordance with rule 198,

(f) restrictions under section 40 of the Act,[8] including one entered under section 86(4) of the Act, in relation to a registered charge,

(g) notices under section 86(2) of the Act in relation to a registered charge,[9] and

(h) such other matters affecting the registered estate or any registered charge as are required to be entered in the charges register by these rules.

There is also:

(1) an Index which records all registered estates and land affected by any caution against first registration: LRA 2000, s. 68; LRR 2003, r. 10.

(2) an Index of proprietors' names: LRR 2003, r. 11

(3) The Day List showing the date and time at which every pending application was made and of every application for an official search with priority under LRR 2003 r. 147; LRR 2003, r. 12

(4) A Register of cautions against first registration. LRR 2002, s. 19, p. 119, post.

The Registers of title and cautions against first registration are open to the public; any person may inspect and make copies: LRA 2000, ss. 66, 67; but not if the document contains prejudicial information: LRR 2003, rr. 133, 136.

A purchaser may make an official search with priority of protection under LRA 2000 ss. 70, 72 and LRR 2003, rr. 147–160.

IV. First Registration of Title[10]

First registration of title may be either voluntary or compulsory. It has been compulsory throughout England and Wales since 1990 when there are dealings

---

8   P. 172, post.
9   P. 110, ante.
10   LRR 2003, rr. 21–38; R & R, chaps. 5–11; H & B, chap. 2: Law Commission Report on Land Registration for the Twenty-First Century 2001 (Law Com No. 271) Part III.

with unregistered land. The events which trigger compulsory registration of unregistered land were extended by the Land Registration Act 1997 and further extended by the Land Registration Act 2002. The Lord Chancellor has power under section 5 to add further triggers. The eventual aim is to have a complete register of title of all land by 2012.[11] We shall then have a second Domesday Book over nine hundred years after its more picturesque ancestor of 1086.

A. Voluntary First Registration

LAND REGISTRATION ACT 2002

3   When title may be registered

(1) This section applies to any unregistered legal estate which is an interest of any of the following kinds—

(a)   an estate in land,

(b)   a rentcharge,

(c)   a franchise, and

(d)   a profit a prendre in gross.

(2) Subject to the following provisions, a person may apply to the registrar to be registered as the proprietor of an unregistered legal estate to which this section applies if—

(a)   the estate is vested in him, or

(b)   he is entitled to require the estate to be vested in him.

(3) Subject to subsection (4), an application under subsection (2) in respect of a leasehold estate may only be made if the estate was granted for a term of which more than seven years are unexpired.

(4) In the case of an estate in land, subsection (3) does not apply if the right to possession under the lease is discontinuous.[11a]

(5) A person may not make an application under subsection (2)(a) in respect of a leasehold estate vested in him as a mortgagee where there is a subsisting right of redemption.

(6) A person may not make an application under subsection (2)(b) if his entitlement is as a person who has contracted to buy under a contract.

(7) If a person holds in the same right both—

(a)   a lease in possession, and

(b)   a lease to take effect in possession on, or within a month of, the end of
        the lease in possession,

then, to the extent that they relate to the same land, they are to be treated for the purposes of this section as creating one continuous term.

B. Compulsory First Registration[12]

LAND REGISTRATION ACT 2002

i. TRIGGERS FOR REGISTRATION

4   When title must be registered

(1)   The requirement of registration applies on the occurrence of any of the following events—

---

[11]   Land Registry Annual Report 2002–2003, p. 10.

[11a]   P. 506, post.

[12]   R & R, chaps. 8, 9; H & B, paras. 2.10–2.26; Law Commission Report on Land Registration for the Twenty-First Century 2001 (Law Com No. 271), paras. 3.22–3.65. Cf. LRA 1925, ss. 123, 123A.

   (a) the transfer of a qualifying estate—
      (i)   for valuable or other consideration,[13] by way of gift or in pursuance of an order of any court, or
      (ii) by means of an assent (including a vesting assent);
   (b) the transfer of an unregistered legal estate in land in circumstances where section 171A of the Housing Act 1985 applies (disposal by landlord which leads to a person no longer being a secure tenant);
   (c) the grant out of a qualifying estate of an estate in land—
      (i)   for a term of years absolute of more than seven years from the date of the grant, and
      (ii) for valuable or other consideration, by way of gift or in pursuance of an order of any court;[14]
   (d) the grant out of a qualifying estate of an estate in land for a term of years absolute to take effect in possession after the end of the period of three months beginning with the date of the grant;
   (e) the grant of a lease in pursuance of Part 5 of the Housing Act 1985 (the right to buy) out of an unregistered legal estate in land;
   (f) the grant of a lease out of an unregistered legal estate in land in such circumstances as are mentioned in paragraph (b);
   (g) the creation of a protected first legal mortgage of a qualifying estate.
   (2) For the purposes of subsection (1), a qualifying estate is an unregistered legal estate which is—
   (a) a freehold estate in land, or
   (b) a leasehold estate in land for a term which, at the time of the transfer, grant or creation, has more than seven years to run.
   (3) In subsection (1)(a), the reference to transfer does not include transfer by operation of law.
   (4) Subsection (1)(a) does not apply to—
   (a) the assignment of a mortgage term, or
   (b) the assignment or surrender of a lease to the owner of the immediate reversion where the term is to merge in that reversion.
   (5) Subsection (1)(c) does not apply to the grant of an estate to a person as a mortgagee.
   (6) For the purposes of subsection (1)(a) and (c), if the estate transferred or granted has a negative value, it is to be regarded as transferred or granted for valuable or other consideration.
   (7) In subsection (1)(a) and (c), references to transfer or grant by way of gift include transfer or grant for the purpose of—
   (a) constituting a trust under which the settlor does not retain the whole of the beneficial interest, or
   (b) uniting the bare legal title and the beneficial interest in property held under a trust under which the settlor did not, on constitution, retain the whole of the beneficial interest.[15]

---

[13] 'Valuable consideration' does not include marriage consideration or a nominal consideration in money: LRA 2002, s. 132(1): cf. LRA 1925, s. 3 (xxxi), which is inclusive of the first but not of the last.

[14] Leases granted for more than seven years (formerly 21 years) became subject to compulsory registration under LRA 2002. So did leases granted to take effect in possession more than three months in advance (reversionary leases) and discontinuous leases (p. 506, post).

[15] Thus a settlement by S to trustees on trust for S and B would amount to a gift triggering registration. Transfers to trustees on a bare trust would not.

(8) For the purposes of subsection (1)(g)—

(a) a legal mortgage is protected if it takes effect on its creation as a mortgage to be protected by the deposit of documents relating to the mortgaged estate,[16] and

(b) a first legal mortgage is one which, on its creation, ranks in priority ahead of any other mortgages then affecting the mortgaged estate.

(9) In this section—

'land' does not include mines and minerals held apart from the surface;
'vesting assent' has the same meaning as in the Settled Land Act 1925.

ii. SPECIAL CASE: THE CROWN[17]

Before the 2002 Act the Crown was unable to register its demesne land (land which it holds in its capacity as ultimate feudal overlord) because it had no *estate* in such land: 'a major, but unremarked, lacuna in the system of land registration in England and Wales', per Burnton QC in *Scmlla Properties Ltd v Gesso Properties (BVI) Ltd* [1995] BCC 793 at 798. Under LRA 2002, s. 79 the Crown can grant to itself a freehold estate which it can then register.[18]

LAND REGISTRATION ACT 2002

79 Voluntary registration of demesne land

(1) Her Majesty may grant an estate in fee simple absolute in possession out of demesne land to Herself.

80 Compulsory registration of grants out of demesne land

(1) Section 4(1) shall apply as if the following were included among the events listed—

(a) the grant by Her Majesty out of demesne land of an estate in fee simple absolute in possession, otherwise than under section 79;

(b) the grant by Her Majesty out of demesne land of an estate in land—

(i)   for a term of years absolute of more than seven years from the date of the grant, and

(ii) for valuable or other consideration, by way of gift or in pursuance of an order of any court.

(5) In its application by virtue of subsection (1), section 7 has effect with the substitution for subsection (2) of—

'(2) On the application of subsection (1), the grant has effect as a contract made for valuable consideration to grant the legal estate concerned".[19]

[16] P. 792, post.

[17] R & R, chap. 40; H & B, paras. 2.61–2.62; Law Commission Report on Registered Land for the Twenty-First Century 2001 (Law Com No. 271), paras. 11.1–11.38. See also s. 80 (compulsory registration of grants out of demesne land); 81 (demesne land: cautions against first registration); 82 (escheat etc.); 83 (Crown and Duchy land: representation); 84 (disapplication of requirements relating to Duchy land); 85 (bona vacantia).

[18] Souvenir land is no longer excluded from registration of title: LR and LCA 1971, s. 4 was repealed by LRA 2002, Sch. 13. For matters relating to registered land which immediately before 13 October 2003 was subject to a declaration that it was souvenir land under LR (Souvenir Land) Rules 1972 (SI 1972 No. 985, amended by SI 2002 No. 2539), see LR 2002 (Transitional Provisions) Order 2003 (SI 2003 No. 1953), arts. 10–13. R & R paras. 20.030–20.031.

[19] P. 115, post.

iii.   DUTY TO APPLY FOR REGISTRATION

6   Duty to apply for registration of title

(1) If the requirement of registration applies, the responsible estate owner, or his successor in title, must, before the end of the period for registration, apply to the registrar to be registered as the proprietor of the registrable estate.

(2) If the requirement of registration applies because of section 4(1)(g)—

(a)   the registrable estate is the estate charged by the mortgage, and

(b)   the responsible estate owner is the owner of that estate.

(3) If the requirement of registration applies otherwise than because of section 4(1)(g)—

(a)   the registrable estate is the estate which is transferred or granted, and

(b)   the responsible estate owner is the transferee or grantee of that estate.

(4) The period for registration is 2 months beginning with the date on which the relevant event occurs, or such longer period as the registrar may provide under subsection (5).

(5) If on the application of any interested person the registrar is satisfied that there is good reason for doing so, he may by order provide that the period for registration ends on such later date as he may specify in the order.

(6) Rules may make provision enabling the mortgagee under any mortgage falling within section 4(1)(g) to require the estate charged by the mortgage to be registered whether or not the mortgagor consents.

iv.   EFFECT OF FAILURE TO REGISTER[20]

7   Effect of non-compliance with section 6

(1) If the requirement of registration is not complied with, the transfer, grant or creation becomes void as regards the transfer, grant or creation of a legal estate.

(2) On the application of subsection (1)—

(a)   in a case falling within section 4(1)(a) or (b),[1] the title to the legal estate reverts to the transferor who holds it on a bare trust for the transferee, and

(b)   in a case falling within section 4(1)(c) to (g),[1] the grant or creation has effect as a contract made for valuable consideration to grant or create the legal estate concerned.

(3) If an order under section 6(5) is made in a case where subsection (1) has already applied, that application of the subsection is to be treated as not having occurred.

(4) The possibility of reverter under subsection (1) is to be disregarded for the purposes of determining whether a fee simple is a fee simple absolute.[2]

C.   Classes of Title[3]

LAND REGISTRATION ACT 2002

i.   FREEHOLD ESTATES

9   Titles to freehold estates

(1) In the case of an application for registration under this Chapter of a freehold estate, the classes of title with which the applicant may be registered as proprietor are—

---

[20]   R & R, paras. 8.013–8.016.
[1]   P. 112, ante.
[2]   On possibility of reverter, see LPA 1925, s. 7, p. 7, ante.
[3]   R & R, chap. 6; H & B, paras. 2.27–2.34. Law Commission Report on Land Registration for the Twenty-First Century 2001 (Law Com No. 271), paras. 3.42–3.52, cf. LRA 1925, ss. 5–12.

(a) absolute title,

(b) qualified title, and

(c) possessory title;

and the following provisions deal with when each of the classes of title is available.

(2) A person may be registered with absolute title if the registrar is of the opinion that the person's title to the estate is such as a willing buyer could properly be advised by a competent professional adviser to accept.

(3) In applying subsection (2), the registrar may disregard the fact that a person's title appears to him to be open to objection if he is of the opinion that the defect will not cause the holding under the title to be disturbed.

(4) A person may be registered with qualified title if the registrar is of the opinion that the person's title to the estate has been established only for a limited period or subject to certain reservations which cannot be disregarded under subsection (3).

(5) A person may be registered with possessory title if the registrar is of the opinion—

(a) that the person is in actual possession of the land, or in receipt of the rents and profits of the land, by virtue of the estate, and

(b) that there is no other class of title with which he may be registered.

ii. LEASEHOLD ESTATES

LAND REGISTRATION ACT 2002

10   Titles to leasehold estates[4]

(1) In the case of an application for registration under this Chapter of a leasehold estate, the classes of title with which the applicant may be registered as proprietor are—

(a) absolute title,

(b) good leasehold title,

(c) qualified title, and

(d) possessory title;

and the following provisions deal with when each of the classes of title is available.

(2) A person may be registered with absolute title if—

(a) the registrar is of the opinion that the person's title to the estate is such as a willing buyer could properly be advised by a competent professional adviser to accept, and

(b) the registrar approves the lessor's title to grant the lease.

(3) A person may be registered with good leasehold title if the registrar is of the opinion that the person's title to the estate is such as a willing buyer could properly be advised by a competent professional adviser to accept.

(4) In applying subsection (2) or (3), the registrar may disregard the fact that a person's title appears to him to be open to objection if he is of the opinion that the defect will not cause the holding under the title to be disturbed.

(5) A person may be registered with qualified title if the registrar is of the opinion that the person's title to the estate, or the lessor's title to the reversion, has been established only for a limited period or subject to certain reservations which cannot be disregarded under subsection (4).

(6) A person may be registered with possessory title if the registrar is of the opinion—

---

[4]   R & R, chap. 12. Cf. LRA 1925, s. 77 (as amended).

(a) that the person is in actual possession of the land, or in receipt of the rents and profits of the land, by virtue of the estate, and

(b) that there is no other class of title with which he may be registered.

iii. UPGRADING OF TITLES[4]

LAND REGISTRATION ACT 2002
62 Power to upgrade title

(1) Where the title to a freehold estate is entered in the register as possessory or qualified, the registrar may enter it as absolute if he is satisfied as to the title to the estate.

(2) Where the title to a leasehold estate is entered in the register as good leasehold, the registrar may enter it as absolute if he is satisfied as to the superior title.

(3) Where the title to a leasehold estate is entered in the register as possessory or qualified the registrar may—

(a) enter it as good leasehold if he is satisfied as to the title to the estate, and

(b) enter it as absolute if he is satisfied both as to the title to the estate and as to the superior title.

(4) Where the title to a freehold estate in land has been entered in the register as possessory for at least twelve years, the registrar may enter it as absolute if he is satisfied that the proprietor is in possession of the land.

(5) Where the title to a leasehold estate in land has been entered in the register as possessory for at lease twelve years, the registrar may enter it as good leasehold if he is satisfied that the proprietor is in possession of the land.

(6) None of the powers under subsections (1) to (5) is exercisable if there is outstanding any claim adverse to the title of the registered proprietor which is made by virtue of an estate, right or interest whose enforceability is preserved by virtue of the existing entry about the class of title.

(7) The only persons who may apply to the registrar for the exercise of any of the powers under subsections (1) to (5) are—

(a) the proprietor of the estate to which the application relates,

(b) a person entitled to be registered as the proprietor of that estate,

(c) the proprietor of a registered charge affecting that estate, and

(d) a person interested in a registered estate which derives from that estate.

(8) In determining for the purposes of this section whether he is satisfied as to any title, the registrar is to apply the same standards as those which apply under section 9 or 10 to first registration of title.

(9) The Lord Chancellor may by order amend subsection (4) or (5) by substituting for the number of years for the time being specified in that subsection such number of years as the order may provide.[5]

63 Effect of upgrading title

(1) On the title to a registered freehold or leasehold estate being entered under section 62 as absolute, the proprietor ceases to hold the estate subject to any estate, right or interest whose enforceability was preserved by virtue of the previous entry about the class of title.

(2) Subsection (1) also applies on the title to a registered leasehold estate being entered under section 62 as good leasehold, except that the entry does not affect or prejudice the enforcement of any estate, right or interest affecting, or in derogation of, the title of the lessor to grant the lease.

---

[5] See Law Commission Report on Limitation of Actions 2001 (Law Com No. 270), which recommends that the period of 12 years be reduced to 10 years; p. 242, post.

D. Effect of First Registration[6]

I.   FREEHOLD ESTATES

LAND REGISTRATION ACT 2002

11   Freehold estates[7]

(1)   This section is concerned with the registration of a person under this Chapter as the proprietor of a freehold estate.

(2)   Registration with absolute title has the effect described in subsections (3) to (5).

(3)   The estate is vested in the proprietor together with all interests subsisting for the benefit of the estate.

(4)   The estate is vested in the proprietor subject only to the following interests affecting the estate at the time of registration—

(a)   interests which are the subject of an entry in the register in relation to the estate,[8]

(b)   unregistered interests which fall within any of the paragraphs of Schedule 1,[9] and

(c)   interests acquired under the Limitation Act 1980 of which the proprietor has notice.[10]

(5)   If the proprietor is not entitled to the estate for his own benefit, or not entitled solely for his own benefit, then, as between himself and the persons beneficially entitled to the estate, the estate is vested in him subject to such of their interests as he has notice of.[11]

(6)   Registration with qualified title has the same effect as registration with absolute title, except that it does not affect the enforcement of any estate, right or interest which appears from the register to be excepted from the effect of registration.

(7)   Registration with possessory title has the same effect as registration with absolute title, except that it does not affect the enforcement of any estate, right or interest adverse to, or in derogation of, the proprietor's title subsisting at the time of registration or then capable of arising.

ii.   LEASEHOLD ESTATES

LAND REGISTRATION ACT 2002

12   Leasehold estates[12]

(1)   This section is concerned with the registration of a person under this Chapter as the proprietor of a leasehold estate.

(2)   Registration with absolute title has the effect described in subsections (3) to (5).

(3)   The estate is vested in the proprietor together with all interests subsisting for the benefit of the estate.

---

[6]   R & R, paras. 3.007–3.008; H & B, paras. 2.35–2.45.

[7]   Cf. LRA 1925, ss. 5, 6, 7(2).

[8]   For example, a notice entered by the registrar on the charges register of the servient land in respect of an easement.

[9]   Unregistered interests which override first registration; p. 159, post.

[10]   P. 206, post. See Explanatory Notes on the Land Registration Bill, cited Wolstenholme and Cherry, *Annotated Land Registration Act 2002*, para. 3.011.

[11]   This includes the rights of a person who has an equity arising by proprietary estoppel; p. 622, post.

[12]   Cf. LRA 1925, ss. 9, 10, 11, 12(2).

(4) The estate is vested subject only to the following interests affecting the estate at the time of registration—

    (a) implied and express covenants, obligations and liabilities incident to the estate,

    (b) interests which are the subject of an entry in the register in relation to the estate,

    (c) unregistered interests which fall within any of the paragraphs of Schedule 1, and

    (d) interests acquired under the Limitation Act 1980 of which the proprietor has notice.

(5) If the proprietor is not entitled to the estate for his own benefit, or not entitled solely for his own benefit, then, as between himself and the persons beneficially entitled to the estate, the estate is vested in him subject to such of their interests as he has notice of.

(6) Registration with good leasehold title has the same effect as registration with absolute title, except that it does not affect the enforcement of any estate, right or interest affecting, or in derogation of, the title of the lessor to grant the lease.

(7) Registration with qualified title has the same effect as registration with absolute title except that it does not affect the enforcement of any estate, right or interest which appears from the register to be excepted from the effect of registration.

(8) Registration with possessory title has the same effect as registration with absolute title, except that it does not affect the enforcement of any estate, right or interest adverse to, or in derogation of, the proprietor's title subsisting at the time of registration or then capable of arising.

E. Cautions Against First Registration

Any person who has an interest in unregistered land may apply for a caution against first registration of that land. The object is to ensure that on first registration his interest will be protected on the register. The caution gives the cautioner the right to be notified of the application to register and to object to it. It is a procedural device and gives no substantive right. The Land Registration Act 2002 replaces the caution against dealings under Section 53 of the Land Registration Act 1925 and creates a new special register of cautions.[13]

LAND REGISTRATION ACT 2002

15 Right to lodge

    (1) Subject to subsection (3), a person may lodge a caution against the registration of title to an unregistered legal estate if he claims to be—

    (a) the owner of a qualifying estate, or

    (b) entitled to an interest affecting a qualifying estate.

    (2) For the purposes of subsection (1), a qualifying estate is a legal estate which—

    (a) relates to land to which the caution relates, and

    (b) is an interest of any of the following kinds—

        (i) an estate in land,

---

[13]   LRR 2003, rr. 39–53; R & R, chap. 11; H & B, paras. 2.57–2.63; Law Commission Report on Land Registration for the Twenty-First Century 2001 (Law Com No. 271), paras. 3.54–3.65. See also LRA 2002, ss. 19 (cautions register); 20, 21 (alteration of register by court and by registrar). For transitional provisions, see Sch. 12, paras. 4, 14–17.

      (ii)   a rentcharge,
      (iii) a franchise, and
      (iv) a profit a prendre in gross.
  (3) No caution may be lodged under subsection (1)—
  (a) in the case of paragraph (a), by virtue of ownership of—
      (i)   a freehold estate in land, or
      (ii) a leasehold estate in land granted for a term of which more than
           seven years are unexpired;
  (b) in the case of paragraph (b), by virtue of entitlement to such a leasehold
      estate as is mentioned in paragraph (a)(ii) of this subsection.
  (4) The right under subsection (1) is exercisable by application to the registrar.

16 Effect

  (1) Where an application for registration under this Part relates to a legal estate which is the subject of a caution against first registration, the registrar must give the cautioner notice of the application and of his right to object to it.

  (2) The registrar may not determine an application to which subsection (1) applies before the end of such period as rules may provide, unless the cautioner has exercised his right to object to the application or given the registrar notice that he does not intend to do so.

  (3) Except as provided by this section, a caution against first registration has no effect and, in particular, has no effect on the validity or priority of any interest of the cautioner in the legal estate to which the caution relates.

  (4) For the purposes of subsection (1), notice given by a person acting on behalf of an applicant for registration under this Part is to be treated as given by the registrar if—
  (a) the person is of a description provided by rules, and
  (b) notice is given in such circumstances as rules may provide.

18 Cancellation

  (1) A person may apply to the registrar for cancellation of a caution against first registration if he is—
  (a) the owner of the legal estate to which the caution relates, or
  (b) a person of such other description as rules may provide.

V. Dispositions of Registered Land[14]

A. Powers of Disposition[15]

Part III of the Act is concerned with dispositions of registered land by an owner. Sections 23–26 set out the powers of disposition. Section 26 provides that an owner's right to exercise them is to be taken to be free from any limitation affecting the validity of the disposition, unless the limitation is reflected by an entry in the register (by a notice or a restriction). This follows from the fundamental basis of the registration system that those who rely on the register can assume that its contents are true.[16]

---

[14]   H & B, chap. 3. Law Commission Report on Registration for Land for the Twenty-First Century 2001 (Law Com No. 221), Part IV.
[15]   R & R, chap. 13; H & B, chap. 3. Law Commission Report, paras. 3.3–3.10.
[16]   See LRA 2002, s. 58, p. 106, ante.

LAND REGISTRATION ACT 2002

23 Owner's powers

(1) Owner's powers in relation to a registered estate consist of—

(a) power to make a disposition of any kind permitted by the general law in relation to an interest of that description, other than a mortgage by demise or sub-demise,[17] and

(b) power to charge the estate at law with the payment of money.[18]

24 Right to exercise owner's powers

A person is entitled to exercise owner's powers in relation to a registered estate or charge if he is—

(a) the registered proprietor, or

(b) entitled to be registered as the proprietor.[19]

26 Protection of disponees

(1) Subject to subsection (2), a person's right to exercise owner's powers in relation to a registered estate or charge is to be taken to be free from any limitation affecting the validity of a disposition.

(2) Subsection (1) does not apply to a limitation—

(a) reflected by an entry in the register, or

(b) imposed by, or under, this Act.

(3) This section has effect only for the purpose of preventing the title of a disponee being questioned (and so does not affect the lawfulness of a disposition).

———————

Harpum and Bignall, *Registered Land: The New Law,* paras. 3.9–3.10.

3.9 This example demonstrates that the protection given by the LRA 2002 does not apply to the transferor who has acted in breach of his obligations. It also shows that although the transferee's title is inviolable, he may be under other forms of liability if he was knowingly implicated in the breach of duty by the transferor.[20]

3.10 A and B hold registered land on trust for C for life, thereafter for D absolutely. Under the terms of the trust, A and B may not sell the land without the prior written consent of D. There is no restriction in the register to ensure that no sale can take place without D's consent. A and B sell the land to E without obtaining D's consent. E's title cannot be challenged by D. A and B are in breach of trust and D can take proceedings against them accordingly. If D could show that E knew that A and B were acting in breach of trust by transferring the land:

– she could not challenge E's title; but

– she could take proceedings against him on the basis that he was liable in equity for the knowing receipt of property transferred in breach of trust.[1]

Liability for knowing receipt is merely a personal liability to account for the loss suffered by D. It does not give rise to a proprietary claim by D against the land which E acquired.

———————

[17] Thereby abolishing the creation of a mortgage by demise or sub-demise; p. 795, post.

[18] Similarly for owner's powers in relation to a registered charge: LRA 2002, s. 23(2), (3), p. 795, post.

[19] On the mode of exercise of owner's powers, see LRA 2002, s. 25.

[20] Cf. Law Commission Report on Land Registration for the Twenty-First Century 2001 (Law Com No. 271), paras. 4.10, 4.11.

[1] See H & M, pp. 305–319; Maudsley & Burn, *Trusts and Trustees: Cass and Materials* (6th edn, 2002), pp. 303–313.

B. Registrable Dispositions[2]

Section 27 of the Land Registration Act 2002 provides that a disposition of a registered estate or charge is required to be completed by registration. Until it is registered, it does not take effect at law. However it may take effect in equity and be valid as an estate contract which needs to be protected by a notice, or as an overriding interest by actual occupation[3]

The section replaces similar but not identical provisions of the Land Registration Act 1925.[4]

LAND REGISTRATION ACT 2002

27 Dispositions required to be registered

(1) If a disposition of a registered estate or registered charge is required to be completed by registration, it does not operate at law until the relevant registration requirements are met.

(2) In the case of a registered estate, the following are the dispositions which are required to be completed by registration—

(a) a transfer,[5]

(b) where the registered estate is an estate in land, the grant of a term of years absolute—

(i)   for a term of more than seven years from the date of the grant,

(ii) to take effect in possession after the end of the period of three months beginning with the date of the grant,

(iii) under which the right to possession is discontinuous,[6]

(iv) in pursuance of Part 5 of the Housing Act 1985 (the right to buy), or

(v)   in circumstances where section 171A of that Act applies (disposal by landlord which leads to a person no longer being a secure tenant),

(c) where the registered estate is a franchise or manor, the grant of a lease,

(d) the express grant or reservation of an interest of a kind falling within section 1(2)(a) of the Law of Property Act 1925,[7] other than one which is capable of being registered under the Commons Registration Act 1965.

(e) the express grant or reservation of an interest of a kind falling within section 1(2)(b) or (e) of the Law of Property Act 1925,[8] and

(f) the grant of a legal charge.

(3) In the case of a registered charge, the following are the dispositions which are required to be completed by registration—

(a) a transfer, and

---

[2]   R & R, chap. 16; H & B, paras. 3.11–3.25. Law Commission Report on Land Registration for the Twenty-First Century 2001 (Law Com No. 271), paras. 4.12–4.31.

[3]   The importance of s. 27 will be diminished when electronic conveyancing is introduced. Dispositions will then occur and be registered simultaneously. Hence s. 27(1) is disapplied by s. 93(4), p. 200, post.

[4]   LRA 1925, ss. 18, 21, 123, 123A.

[5]   An effective gift can be made: *Mascall v Mascall* (1984) 50 P & CR 119 (where an intended donor of registered land executed transfer; and handed land certificate to donee, held to be a gift in equity even though not registered); following *Re Rose* [1952] Ch 499, [1952] 1 All ER 127. See also *Brown & Root Technology Ltd v Sun Alliance Insurance Co Ltd* [2001] Ch 733.

[6]   P. 506, post.

[7]   P. 6, ante.

[8]   P. 6, ante.

(b) the grant of a sub-charge.

(4)　Schedule 2 to this Act (which deals with the relevant registration requirements) has effect.[9]

(5) This section applies to dispositions by operation of law as it applies to other dispositions, but with the exception of the following—

(a)　a transfer on the death or bankruptcy of an individual proprietor,

(b)　a transfer on the dissolution of a corporate proprietor, and

(c)　the creation of a legal charge which is a local land charge.

(6)　Rules may make provision about applications to the registrar for the purpose of meeting registration requirements under this section.

(7)　In subsection (2)(d), the reference to express grant does not include grant as a result of the operation of section 62 of the Law of Property Act 1925.[9]

C. Registration Requirements

Section 27   SCHEDULE 2

REGISTRABLE DISPOSITIONS: REGISTRATION REQUIREMENTS

PART 1

REGISTERED ESTATES

Introductory

1 This Part deals with the registration requirements relating to those dispositions of registered estates which are required to be completed by registration.

Transfer

2(1)　In the case of a transfer of whole or part, the transferee, or his successor in title, must be entered in the register as the proprietor.

(2)　In the case of a transfer of part, such details of the transfer as rules may provide must be entered in the register in relation to the registered estate out of which the transfer is made.

Lease of estate in land

3(1)　This paragraph applies to a disposition consisting of the grant out of an estate in land of a term of years absolute.

(2)　In the case of a disposition to which this paragraph applies—

(a)　the grantee, or his successor in title, must be entered in the register as the proprietor of the lease, and

(b)　a notice in respect of the lease must be entered in the register.

Lease of franchise or manor

4 (1)　This paragraph applies to a disposition consisting of the grant out of a franchise or manor of a lease for a term of more than seven years from the date of the grant.

(2)　In the case of a disposition to which this paragraph applies—

(a)　the grantee, or his successor in title, must be entered in the register as the proprietor of the lease, and

(b)　a notice in respect of the lease must be entered in the register.

5 (1)　This paragraph applies to a disposition consisting of the grant out of a franchise or manor of a lease for a term not exceeding seven years from the date of the grant.

[9]　p. 722, post.

(2) In the case of a disposition to which this paragraph applies, a notice in respect of the lease must be entered in the register.

Creation of independently registrable legal interest

6(1) This paragraph applies to a disposition consisting of the creation of a legal rentcharge or profit a prendre in gross, other than one created for, or for an interest equivalent to, a term of years absolute not exceeding seven years from the date of creation.

(2) In the case of a disposition to which this paragraph applies—

(a) the grantee, or his successor in title, must be entered in the register as the proprietor of the interest created, and

(b) a notice in respect of the interest created must be entered in the register.

(3) In sub-paragraph (1), the reference to a legal rentcharge or profit a prendre in gross is to one falling within section 1(2) of the Law of Property Act 1925.[10]

Creation of other legal interest

7(1) This paragraph applies to a disposition which—

(a) consists of the creation of an interest of a kind falling within section 1(2)(a), (b) or (e) of the Law of Property Act 1925, and

(b) is not a disposition to which paragraph 4, 5 or 6 applies.

(2) In the case of a disposition to which this paragraph applies—

(a) a notice in respect of the interest created must be entered in the register, and

(b) if the interest is created for the benefit of a registered estate, the proprietor of the registered estate must be entered in the register as its proprietor.

(3) Rules may provide for sub-paragraph (2) to have effect with modifications in relation to a right of entry over or in respect of a term of years absolute.

Creation of legal charge

8 In the case of the creation of a charge, the chargee, or his successor in title, must be entered in the register as the proprietor of the charge.

PART 2

REGISTERED CHARGES

Introductory

9 This Part deals with the registration requirements relating to those dispositions of registered charges which are required to be completed by registration.[11]

Transfer

10 In the case of a transfer, the transferee, or his successors in title, must be entered in the register as the proprietor.

Creation of sub-charge

11 In the case of the creation of a sub-charge, the sub-chargee, or his successor in title, must be entered in the register as the proprietor of the sub-charge.

---

[10]   P. 6, ante.
[11]   P. 795, post.

D. Land Registry Form for Transfer of Whole of Registered Title

Transfer of whole
of registered title(s)

Land Registry

TR1

If you need more room than is provided for in a panel, use continuation sheet CS and attach to this form.

1. Stamp Duty

Place "X" in the appropriate box or boxes and complete the appropriate certificate.

❑ It is certified that this instrument falls within category ☐ in the Schedule to the Stamp Duty (Exempt Instruments) Regulations 1987

❑ It is certified that the transaction effected does not form part of a larger transaction or of a series of transactions in respect of which the amount or value or the aggregate amount of value of the consideration exceeds the sum of £ ☐

❑ It is certified that this is an instrument on which stamp duty is not chargeable by virtue of the provisions of section 98 of the Finance Act 2001

---

2. Title Number(s) of the Property *Leave blank if not yet registered.*

---

3. Property

---

4. Date

---

5. Transferor *Give full names and company's registered number if any.*

---

6. Transferee for entry on the register *Give full name(s) and company's registered number, if any. For Scottish companies use an SC prefix and for limited liability partnerships use an OC prefix before the registered number, if any. For foreign companies give territory in which incorporated.*

Unless otherwise arranged with Land Registry headquarters, a certified copy for the Transferee's constitution (in English or Welsh) will be required if it is a body corporate but is not a company registered in England and Wales or Scotland under the Companies Acts.

---

7. Transferee's intended address(es) for service (including postcode) for entry on the register *You may give up to three addresses for service one of which must be a postal address but does not have to be within the UK. The other addresses can be any combination of a postal address, a box number at a UK document exchange or an electronic address.*

---

8. The Transferor transfers the Property to the Transferee

9. Consideration *Place "X" in the appropriate box. State clearly the currency unit if other than sterling. If non of the boxes applies, insert an appropriate memorandum in the additional provisions panel.*

❑ The Transferor has received from the Transferee for the Property the sum of *In words and figures.*

❑ *Insert other receipt as appropriate.*

❑ The transfer is not for money or anything which has a monetary value.

---

10. The Transferor transfers with *Place "X" in the appropriate box and add any modifications.*

❑ full title guarantee   ❑ limited title guarantee

---

11. Declaration of trust *Where there is more than one Transferee, place "X" in the appropriate box.*

❑ The Transferees are to hold the Property on trust for themselves as joint tenants

❑ The Transferees are to hold the Property on trust for themselves as tenants in common in equal shares

❑ The Transferees are to hold the Property *Complete as necessary.*

---

12. Additional provisions *Insert here any required or permitted statements, certificates or applications and any agreed covenants.*

---

13. Execution *The Transferor must execute this transfer as a deed using the space below. If there is more than one Transferor, all must execute. Forms of execution are given in Schedule 9 to the Land Registration Rules 2003. If the transfer contains Transferee's covenants or declarations or contains an application by the Transferee (e.g. for a restriction), it must also be executed by the Transferee (all of them, if there is more than one).*

E. Effect of Registered Dispositions on Priorities[12]

'The present law governing the priority of competing interests in registered land is a patchwork of statute and common law. Where the Land Registration Act 1925 was silent—principally in relation to the priority of competing minor interests—the judges have filled the gaps as best they can by reference to the general principles of priority that apply to competing equitable interests, namely that where the equities are equal, the first in time prevails.'[13]

In sections 28–31 the Land Registration Act 2002 replaced these rules by a statutory scheme of priorities. In section 28 the basic rule is that the priority of any interest is determined by the date of its creation. To this there are two important exceptions. First, under section 29, where there is a registered disposition of a registered estate or charge which is made for valuable consideration, the Land Registration Act 2002 follows sections 20(1) and 23(1) of the Land Registration Act 1925. The basic rule of the order of creation does not apply. In effect, section 29 sets out what previously created interests are binding on a purchaser for value of the registered estate or charge.

The interests are:
(a) a registered charge;
(b) an interest which is the subject of a notice in the register;[14]
(c) an unregistered interest which overrides a registered disposition under Schedule 3;[15]
(d) an interest which appears from the register to be excepted from the effect of registration where title is other than absolute, for example, possessory title;
(e) an interest which is incident to a leasehold estate, for example, restrictive covenants in a lease which do not have to be protected by a notice on the register.

The definition of 'valuable consideration' has been narrowed by section 132(1) of the 2002 Act. Marriage and nominal consideration in money are no longer included. If the registrable disposition is made without valuable consideration, the basic rule of priority under section 28 applies, and a purchaser takes free of the interests.

The second exception to the basic rule in section 28 is the Inland Revenue charge for unpaid tax (section 31).

There are also three special cases where the Land Registration Act 2002 has classified the type of interest in such a way that its priority may be affected; a right of pre-emption, an equity arising by estoppel and a mere equity.[16]

---

[12] R & R, chap. 15; H & B, paras. 3.26–3.42; Law Commission Consultative Document on Land Registration for the Twenty-First Century 1998 (Law Com No. 254), paras. 7.15–7.19; Law Commission Report on Land Registration for the Twenty-First Century 2001 (Law Com No. 271), Part V. For a useful example on the operation of the principal rules, see R & R, paras. 15.032–15.039.

[13] H & B, para. 3.26.

[14] For the protection of interests under a trust by way of restriction, see p. 298, post.

[15] P. 163, post.

[16] Sections 115, p. 95, ante; 116, p. 686, post; p. 95, ante.

LAND REGISTRATION ACT 2002

28 Basic rule

(1) Except as provided by sections 29 and 30, the priority of an interest affecting a registered estate or charge is not affected by a disposition of the estate or charge.

(2) It makes no difference for the purposes of this section whether the interest or disposition is registered.

29 Effect of registered dispositions: estates

(1) If a registrable disposition of a registered estate is made for valuable consideration, completion of the disposition by registration has the effect of postponing to the interest under the disposition any interest affecting the estate immediately before the disposition whose priority is not protected at the time of registration.

(2) For the purposes of subsection (1), the priority of an interest is protected—

(a) in any case, if the interest—

    (i)   is a registered charge or the subject of a notice in the register,

    (ii) falls within any of the paragraphs of Schedule 3, or

    (iii) appears from the register to be excepted from the effect of registration, and

(b) in the case of a disposition of a leasehold estate, if the burden of the interest is incident to the estate.

(3) Subsection (2)(a)(ii) does not apply to an interest which has been the subject of a notice in the register at any time since the coming into force of this section.

(4) Where the grant of a leasehold estate in land out of a registered estate does not involve a registrable disposition, this section has effect as if—

(a) the grant involved such a disposition, and

(b) the disposition were registered at the time of the grant.

30 Effect of registered dispositions: charges

(1) If a registrable disposition of a registered charge is made for valuable consideration, completion of the disposition by registration has the effect of postponing to the interest under the disposition any interest affecting the charge immediately before the disposition whose priority is not protected at the time of registration.

(2) For the purposes of subsection (1), the priority of an interest is protected—

(a) in any case, if the interest—

    (i)   is a registered charge or the subject of a notice in the register,

    (ii) falls within any of the paragraphs of Schedule 3, or

    (iii) appears from the register to be excepted from the effect of registration, and

(b) in the case of a disposition of a charge which relates to a leasehold estate, if the burden of the interest is incident to the estate.

(3) Subsection (2)(a)(ii) does not apply to an interest which has been the subject of a notice in the register at any time since the coming into force of this section.

31 Inland Revenue charges

The effect of a disposition of a registered estate or charge on a charge under section 237 of the Inheritance Tax Act 1984 (charge for unpaid tax) is to be determined, not in accordance with sections 28 to 30 above, but in accordance with sections 237(6) and 238 of that Act (under which a purchaser in good faith for money or money's worth takes free from the charge in the absence of registration).

115   Rights of pre-emption
See p. 95 ante.

116   Proprietary estoppel and mere equities
See pp. 95, 686 ante.

VI. Overriding Interests[17]

A.   Introduction

Interests in land which cannot be registered as separate titles fall into the category of either overriding interests or interests which need protection on the register.

Overriding interests are enforceable without being protected on the register, and bind a registered proprietor and his transferee even though he does not know of their existence. They thus detract from the principle that the register should be a mirror of the title. They were listed in section 70(1) of the Land Registration Act 1925 and have been added to by later enactments.[18] They consist of third party rights which on policy grounds should bind a purchaser, but which for some reason or other do not fit into the pattern of the register. If, however, an overriding interest does appear on the register,[19] then its protection under this category is superfluous; it ceases to bind as an overriding interest and its protection is then the protection of a minor interest entered on the register.

There was criticism of the category of overriding interests under the Land Registration Act 1925,[20] especially of the wide-ranging safety-net of paragraph (g), which accorded protection to 'the rights of every person in actual occupation of the land or in receipt of the rents and profits thereof, save where enquiry is made of such person and the rights are not disclosed'. This

---

[17]   C & B, pp. 100–110, 855–870; Gray, pp. 971–1035; M & W, paras. 6.036–6.073; MM, pp. 121–129; Smith, pp. 241–259; R & R (1991 edn.), chap. 6; R & R, chaps. 10, 17; W & C, vol. 6, pp. 63–67; Barnsley (4th edn), pp. 50–69; Farrand (2nd edn), pp. 184–209; Hayton (3rd edn), chap. 6.

[18]   LRR 1925, r. 258, p. 132, post; Tithe Act 1936, s. 13(11), p. 130, n. 9, post; Coal Act 1938, s. 41; Coal Industry Nationalisation Act 1946, ss. 5, 8, Sch. 1; Leasehold Property (Temporary Provisions) Act 1951, s. 2(4); Coal Industry Act 1987, s. 1.

[19]   And it often does: R & R, para. 6–04; (1969) 32 MLR, at p. 129 (T.B.F. Ruoff). See *Re Dances Way, West Town, Hayling Island* [1962] Ch 490 at 507, [1962] 2 All ER 42 at 50, per UPJOHN LJ.

[20]   Part II of the Law Commission's Third Report on Land Registration (Law Com No. 158, HC 269), contains a valuable and critical account of the existing law. See *Overseas Investment Services Ltd v Simcobuild Construction Ltd* [1996] 1 EGLR 49 at 51, per PETER GIBSON LJ 'As overriding interests constitute an exception [to the mirror of title principle] the court should in my opinion, not be astute to give a wide meaning to any item constituting an overriding interest'.

paragraph protected an occupier who had failed either to register a title or to protect an interest by an entry on the register. This is diametrically opposed to the Draconian provisions of the Land Charges Act 1972 in the case of unregistered land under which a purchaser takes free of an unregistered land charge even if the person entitled thereto is in possession.[1]

Section 70(1) *(g)* is, in effect, an application of the rule in *Hunt v Luck*[2] to registered land; extended so as to include the rights of every person in receipt of the rents and profits of the land; and extended, it seems, in some of the decisions on the question of 'actual occupation'.[3] On principle, this type of rule is sounder than the Land Charges Act rule. In most cases, of course, vacant possession will be given to the purchaser on completion, and the problem does not arise. Where the purchaser completes when some other person is in occupation, he will almost always, if he is careful, discover the occupation.

B. Land Registration Act 1925

LAND REGISTRATION ACT 1925

3. Interpretation.—(xvi) 'Overriding interests' mean all the incumbrances, interests, rights, and powers not entered on the register but subject to which registered dispositions are by this Act to take effect, and in regard to land registered at the commencement of this Act include the matters which are by any enactment repealed by this Act declared not to be incumbrances; . . .

70. Liability of registered land to overriding interests.—(1) All registered land shall, unless under the provisions of this Act the contrary is expressed on the register,[4] be deemed to be subject to such of the following overriding interests as may be for the time being subsisting in reference thereto, and such interests shall not be treated as incumbrances within the meaning of this Act, (that is to say):—

    (a) Rights of common,[5] drainage rights, customary rights (until extinguished), public rights,[6] profits à prendre, rights of sheep-walk, rights of way, watercourses, rights of water, and other easements not being equitable easements required to be protected by notice on the register;[7]

---

[1]   LCA 1972, s. 4, p. 46, ante.
[2]   [1901] 1 Ch 45; affd. [1902] 1 Ch 428, p. 37, ante.
[3]   P. 150, et seq., post.
[4]   *Woolwich Building Society v Dickman* [1996] 3 All ER 204 (waiver of right by tenant held to have no effect on rights under s. 70(1) *(g)*, unless an entry to that effect has been made); (1996) 140 SJ 1108 (M. Draper).
[5]   Commons Registration Act 1965, s. 1(1), (2), p. 60, ante.
[6]   *Overseas Investment Services Ltd v Simcobuild Construction Ltd* (1995) 70 P & CR 322 (right to have road constructed under Highways Act 1980, s. 38).
[7]   *Celsteel Ltd v Alton House Holdings Ltd* [1985] 1 WLR 204, [1985] 2 All ER 562, p. 148, post; *Thatcher v Douglas* (1996) 146 NLJR 282; *Secretary of State for the Environment, Transport and the Regions v Baylis* (2000) 80 P & CR 324.

(b)   Liability to repair highways by reason of tenure, quit-rents, crown rents, heriots, and other rents and charges (until extinguished) having their origin in tenure;

(c)   Liability to repair the chancel of any church;[8]

(d)   Liability in respect of embankments, and sea and river walls;

(e)   . . .,[9] payments in lieu of tithe, and charges or annuities payable for the redemption of tithe rentcharges;

(f)   Subject to the provisions of this Act, rights acquired or in course of being acquired under the Limitation Acts;[10]

(g)   The rights of every person[11] in actual occupation of the land[12] or in

8   Law Commission Report on Liability for Chancel Repairs 1985 (Law Com No 152) recommended that liability should be abolished after 10 years; but, if not abolished promptly, it should be registered in Local Land Charges registers, and failure to register would exonerate a purchaser of the land; (1984) 100 LQR 185 (J.H. Baker). For the liability in unregistered land, see *Hauxton Parochial Church Council v Stevens* [1929] P 240; *Chivers & Sons Ltd v Air Ministry and Queen's College, Cambridge* [1955] Ch 585, [1955] 2 All ER 607. In *Aston Cantlow and Wilmcote Parish Church Council v Wallbank* [2004] 1 AC 546; HL held that the recovery of costs of chancel repair was not unlawful as being contrary to the Human Rights Act 1998.

9   As amended by Tithe Act 1936, s. 48, Sch. 8, and Finance Act 1963, ss. 68, 73(8)(b), Sch. 14, Pt. VI. Tithe redemption annuities were extinguished as from 2 October 1977; FA 1977, s. 56.

10   LRA 1925, s. 75, p. 245, post; *Re Chowood's Registered Land* [1933] Ch 574 at 581; *Bridges v Mees* [1957] Ch 475, [1957] 2 All ER 577.

11   *Hypo-Mortgage Services Ltd v Robinson* [1997] 2 FLR 71 (minors aged 1 and 3 with equitable beneficial interests under a trust for sale held not to be capable of being in actual occupation: "They were there because their parent is there. They have no right of occupation of their own . . . they are only there as shadows of occupation of their parents: per NOURSE LJ, citing *Bird v Syme-Thompson* [1979] 1 WLR 440, [1978] 3 All ER 1027, p. 139, post. But see *Williams & Glyn's Bank Ltd v Boland* [1981] AC 487, 505–506, [1980] 2 All ER 408, 413, per Lord WILBERFORCE, p. 139, post.

12   *National Provincial Bank Ltd v Ainsworth* [1965] AC 1175, [1965] 2 All ER 472, p. 688, post, (deserted wife's equity not overriding interest); *Strand Securities Ltd v Caswell* [1965] Ch 958, [1965] 1 All ER 820, p. 153, post (step-daughter's occupation on her own account of flat by gratuitous licence from step-father lessee not actual occupation); *Webb v Pollmount Ltd* [1966] Ch 584, [1966] 1 All ER 481, p. 142, post (option to purchase freehold reversion contained in lease held to be overriding interest); *London and Cheshire Insurance Co Ltd v Laplagrene Property Co Ltd* [1971] Ch 499, [1971] 1 All ER 766, p. 157, post (unpaid vendor's lien under lease-back from purchaser held to be overriding interest); *Hodgson v Marks* [1971] Ch 892, [1971] 2 All ER 684 (equitable fee simple under bare trust held to be overriding interest); *Lee-Parker v Izzet (No 2)* [1972] 1 WLR 775, [1972] 2 All ER 800 (overriding interest conceded where purchaser-occupier expended money at request of vendor in belief induced by vendor that purchaser was beneficial owner under contract of sale, later held void for uncertainty); *Epps v Esso Petroleum Co Ltd* [1973] 1 WLR 1071, [1973] 2 All ER 465, p. 189, post (intermittent parking of car on undefined space not actual occupation); *Williams & Glyn's Bank Ltd v Boland* [1981] AC 487, [1980] 2 All ER 408, p. 136, post (wife held to be in actual occupation of matrimonial home registered in sole name of husband); *Blacklocks v JB Developments (Godalming) Ltd* [1982] Ch 183 [1981] 3 All ER 392 (right to rectify contract and conveyance for mistake [1983] Conv 169, 257 (J.T.F.) or right to rectify the register [1983] Conv 361 (D.G. Barnsley) held to be overriding interest. No reference was made to *Smith v Jones* [1954] 1 WLR 1089, [1954] 2 All ER 823, p. 47, ante; which was distinguished in *Nurdin & Peacock plc v Ramsden & Co Ltd* [1999] 1 EGLR 119 as being a case on unregistered land; [1998] Conv 421 (S. Pascoe); *Bhullar v McArdle* (2001) 82 P&CR 481 (rectification of register); *Malory Enterprises Ltd v Cheshire Homes (UK) Ltd 2002* [2002] Ch 216 (rectification of document and of register held to be overriding interests); *Kling v Keston Properties Ltd* (1983) 49 P & CR 212 (right of pre-emption held to be overriding interest; see *Pritchard v Briggs* [1980] Ch 338, [1980] 1 All ER 294, p. 93, ante); *Chhokar v Chhokar* [1984] FLR 313, p. 157, post (wife evicted by fraudulent purchaser of matrimonial home from husband held to be in actual occupation); *Celsteel Ltd v Alton House Holdings Ltd* [1985] 1 WLR 204, [1985] 2 All ER 562 (lessee exercising right of way to garage held to be in actual occupation); *City of London*

receipt of the rents and profits thereof,[13] save where enquiry is made of such person and the rights are not disclosed;[14]

(h) In the case of a possessory, qualified, or good leasehold title[15] all estates, rights, interests and powers excepted from the effect of registration;

(i) Rights under local land charges unless and until registered or protected on the register in the prescribed manner,[16]

(j) Rights of fishing and sporting, seignorial and manorial rights of all descriptions (until extinguished), and franchises;

Building Society v Flegg [1988] AC 54, [1987] 3 All ER 435, p. 316, post (equitable interests of parents as tenants in common arising from contribution to purchase price of house, registered in names of their daughter and son-in-law, held to be overreachable by mortgagees under LPA 1925, s. 2(1)(ii); *Winkworth v Edward Baron Development Co Ltd* [1986] 1 WLR 1512, [1987] 1 All ER 114 (equitable interest of wife in occupation of matrimonial home, arising from contribution to purchase price paid by husband and wife to company controlled by them both, held to be overriding interest); *Paddington Building Society v Mendelsohn* (1985) 50 P & CR 244 (only *enforceable* rights of actual occupant at date of transfer are protected under para. *(g)*); *Abbey National Building Society v Cann* [1991] 1 AC 56, [1990] 1 All ER 1085, p. 143, post (relevant date for determining an overriding interest held by HL to be date of registration, except for para. *(g)* when it is date of completion); see (1987) 57 P & CR 381 where CA held that acts of a preparatory nature carried out by vendor prior to completion were not actual occupation); *Lloyds Bank plc v Rosset* [1989] Ch 350, [1988] 3 All ER 915, p. 150, post (semi-derelict house capable of actual occupation); *Nationwide Anglia Building Society v Ahmed and Balakrishnan* (1995) 70 P & CR 381 (vendor of premises who remained in possession of part under contractual licence after completion held not to have overriding interest); *Stockholm Finance Ltd v Garden Holdings Inc* [1995] NPC 162 (intermittent presence held to be 'pattern of alternating presence and absence rather than continuous occupation marked by absences', and therefore not an overriding interest).

Ferrishurst Ltd v Wallcite Ltd [1999] Ch 355 (actual occupation of part of land protects rights of occupier in whole); [1999] Conv 144 (S. Pascoe); [1999] CLJ 483 (L. Tee); (2000) 63 MLR 113 (J. Hill); [1999] All ER Rev 222 (P.J. Clarke); *Goodger v Willis* [1999] EGCS 302 (demolition of buildings and laying of concrete held to be actual occupation); *Collings v Lee* [2001] 2 All ER 332 (rights of beneficiary under bare trust arising as a result of transfer induced by fraudulent misrepresentation of transferee held to be within s. 70(1)(g)); [2001] CLJ 477 (R. Nolan); [2001] All ER Rev 253 (P.J. Clarke).

See also *Bridges v Mees*, supra (overlap between para. *(f)* and para. *(g)*). For statutory exclusions from para. *(g)* see Matrimonial Homes Act 1983, s. 2(8)(b), now Family Law Act 1996, s. 31(10)(b) as amended by LRA 2002, Sch. 11, para. 34(2) (spouse's right of occupation); Leasehold Reform Act 1967, s. 5(5) (tenant's right to acquire freehold or apply for extended lease, as amended by LRA 2002, Sch. 11, para. 30); Housing Act 1985 Sch. 9A, para. 6(1), inserted by Housing and Planning Act 1986, s. 8(2), Sch. 2 and amended by LRA 2002, Sch. 11, para. 18(10) (tenant's right to buy); Access to Neighbouring Land Act 1992, s. 5, as amended by LRA 2002, Sch. 11, para 26(4), p. 713, post; LRA 2002, s. 87(3) (pending land actions, units, orders and deeds of arrangement). And also excluded by implication is an interest under a strict settlement: LRA 1925, s. 86(2), p. 159, post.

[13] *Eden Park Estates Ltd v Longman* [1982] Conv 237 (P.H. Kenny) (payment in advance in respect of rent by tenant of original landlord held not to be overriding interest); *E S Schwab & Co Ltd v McCarthy* (1975) 31 P & CR 196 ('receipt' means actual receipt of rent from a tenant); *UCB Group Ltd v Hedworth* (2002) 23 EGCS 122 (rent must be from a legal estate: rent payable under a tenancy by estoppel granted by a beneficial owner of land under a bare trust held not to be rent issuing out of land within LRA 1925, s. 3(xxv), and therefore not an overriding interest under s. 70(1)(g).

[14] On the proviso, cf. in unregistered land *Midland Bank Ltd v Farmpride Hatcheries Ltd* (1980) 260 EG 493, p. 28, ante; *UCB Bank v Beasley and France* [1995] NPC 144 (unpaid vendor with lien held not to have overriding interest, because of failure to disclose interest in pre-contractual enquiries) *Habermann v Koehler (No. 2)* [2000] EGCS 125 (failure to disclose option to purchase).

[15] LRA 1925, ss. 6, 7, 10, 11, 12.

[16] Ibid., s. 49(1)(c), s. 59(2).

(k) Leases granted[17] for a term not exceeding twenty-one years[18] . . .

(kk) PPP leases[19]

(m) Any interest or right which is an overriding interest by virtue of paragraph 1(1) of Schedule 9 to the Coal Industry Act 1994;[20]

Provided that, where it is proved to the satisfaction of the registrar that any land registered or about to be registered is exempt from land tax, or tithe rentcharge or payments in lieu of tithe, or from charges or annuities payable for the redemption of tithe rentcharge, the registrar may notify the fact on the register in the prescribed manner.[1]

(2) Where at the time of first registration any easement, right, privilege, or benefit created by an instrument and appearing on the title adversely affects the land, the registrar shall enter a note thereof on the register.[2]

(3) Where the existence of any overriding interest mentioned in this section is proved to the satisfaction of the registrar or admitted, he may (subject to any prescribed exceptions) enter notice of the same or of a claim thereto on the register, but no claim to an easement, right, or privilege not created by an instrument shall be noted against the title to the servient land if the proprietor of such land (after the prescribed notice is given to him) shows sufficient cause to the contrary.

(3A) Neither subsection (2) nor subsection (3) of this section shall apply in the case of a PPP lease.[3]

(4) Neither subsection (2) nor subsection (3) of this section shall apply in the case of any such interest or right as is mentioned in subsection (1) *(m)* of this section.[4]

LAND REGISTRATION RULES 1925

258. Adverse easements treated as overriding interests.—Rights, privileges, and appurtenances appertaining or reputed to appertain to land or demised, occupied, or enjoyed therewith or reputed or known as part or parcel of or appurtenant thereto, which adversely affect registered land, are overriding interests within section 70 of the Act, and shall not be deemed incumbrances for the purposes of the Act.[5]

---

[17]   This does not include an agreement for a lease; *City Permanent Building Society v Miller* [1952] Ch 840, [1952] 2 All ER 621, p. 505, post; nor a statutory tenancy under the Rent Act 1977: *Barclays Bank plc v Zaroovabli* [1997] 2 WLR 729 at 736, [1997] 2 All ER 19 at 737: (1997) 113 LQR 390 (M. Robinson). But they may be overriding interests under para. *(g)*. No application can be made for the entry of a notice of a lease for 21 years or less: LRA 1925, s. 48(1).

[18]   As amended by LRA 1986, s. 4(1), following Law Commission Report on Land Registration Part IV Treatment of Leases 1983 (Law Com No. 121, HC 86), para. 4.37, which recommended that the exclusion of gratuitous leases and of leases granted at a premium should be removed.

[19]   Added by Greater London Authority Act 1999, s. 219(7). PPP are Public Private Partnerships relating to transport in London. See Law Commission Report on Land Registration for the Twenty-First Century 2001 (Law Com No. 27), paras 8.11–8.13.

[20]   As added by Coal Industry Act 1994, Sch. 9, para. 1(2).

[1]   Para. *(l)* specifies certain rights to mines and minerals existing before 1926.

[2]   See p. 717, post.

[3]   Added by Greater London Authority Act 1999, s. 219(7).

[4]   As added by Coal Industry Act 1994, Sch. 9, para. 1(2).

[5]   *Celsteel Ltd v Alton House Holdings Ltd* [1985] 1 WLR 204, [1985] 2 All ER 562, p. 148, post; *Thatcher v Douglas* [1996] NPC 206.

i. RATIONALE

Law Commission: Land Registration for the Twenty-First Century: A Consultative Document (1998) Law Com No. 254, paras. 4.4–4.10.

'4.4 The orthodox explanation for the existence of overriding interests is that they are—

> various minor liabilities which are not usually, or at any rate not invariably, shown in title-deeds or mentioned in abstracts of title, and as to which, therefore, it is impracticable to form a trustworthy record on the register . . . As to these, persons dealing with registered land must obtain information *aliunde* in the same manner and from the same sources as persons dealing with unregistered land obtain it.[6]

The way in which the law on overriding interests has developed over the last seventy-two years has demonstrated that overriding interests are by no means only "minor liabilities". Furthermore, as will become apparent from the analysis of individual overriding interests in Part V of this Report, this explanation of the rationale of such interests is no longer correct in all respects, whatever the position may have been perceived to be when the legislation was first enacted. Most overriding interests do appear to have one shared characteristic, however, that is related to the orthodox explanation of them, namely that *it is unreasonable to expect the person who has the benefit of the right to register it as a means of securing its protection.* As we shall explain, not every overriding interest can be justified on that basis, and this in itself is a reason for examining such interests in detail. An examination of the list of overriding interests — at least as they have come to be understood in practice — suggests that most of them fall into five tolerably clear categories.

Categories of overriding interests

Those which provide a means of accommodating rights which may be created informally or where the origins of the rights may be obscure

4.5 First, overriding interests provide a means of accommodating rights which can be created (or may arise) informally, and where registration at the time of creation may therefore be unrealistic. These include—

(1) easements that arise by prescription or by implied grant or reservation (LRA 1925, s.70(1)(a));
(2) the rights of adverse possessors (s. 70(1)(f)), and
(3) in the case of persons in actual occupation, rights arising by estoppel or constructive trust (s. 70(1)(g)).

4.6 The inclusion of customary and public rights as overriding interests (s. 70(1)(a)), is justifiable on a similar basis, namely the obscurity that may surround their origins. Customary rights can only be established by long user— in theory (but not in practice) this must be shown from the beginning of legal memory in 1189. Although public rights can of course arise in other ways, it is not uncommon for their origins to be uncertain and undocumented and, in effect, to depend upon proof of long exercise.

---

[6] Brickdale & Stewart Wallace's *Land Registration Act, 1925* (4th ed 1939), p. 190. The substance of the passage is retained in Ruoff & Roper, *Registered Conveyancing*, 6-04.

Rights that had overriding status prior to 1926

4.7 Secondly, rights which were the equivalent of overriding interests under the previous land registration legislation[7] became overriding interests under the Land Registration Act 1925.[8] Most of these rights were of a kind that could no longer be created. The overriding interests that fall within this category are—

(1) liability to repair highways by reason of tenure, quit-rents, crown rents, heriots, and other rents and charges having their origin in tenure (s. 70(1)(b));

(2) chancel repair liability (s. 70(1)(c));

(3) liability in respect of embankments, and sea and river walls (s. 70(1)(d));

(4) liability to make various payments in lieu of tithe or tithe rentcharge (s. 70(1)(e));

(5) seignorial and manorial rights and franchises (s. 70(1)(j));

(6) in relation to land registered—

    (a) prior to 1898, mineral rights created before that date; and

    (b) after 1897 and before 1926, mineral rights created prior to first registration (s. 70(1)(l)).

It would obviously have been unreasonable in those circumstances to impose an obligation to register such rights.[9]

Incorporeal rights in existence at the time of first registration but not registered

4.8 Thirdly, incorporeal rights such as easements and profits, which were in existence but were not noted on the register at the time of the first registration of the land burdened by them, take effect as overriding interests.[10] The status of overriding interest here acts as a "fail-safe" mechanism to protect such rights in case they do not come to light on first registration.[11]

Rights which it would be inconvenient or pointless to register

4.9 Fourthly, some rights are overriding interests because it would be either inconvenient or even pointless to register them. Leases granted for a term not exceeding 21 years (s. 70(1)(h)), and rights in coal (s. 70(1)(m)) both fall into this category.

---

[7] See Land Transfer Act 1875, s. 18, as amended by the Land Transfer Act 1897. The rights were rather clumsily described as interests which were not deemed to be encumbrances within the meaning of the Land Transfer Act 1875.

[8] The five categories of overriding interest that were introduced for the first time in the Land Registration Act 1925 were (I) customary and public rights (s. 70(1)(a)); (ii) the rights of adverse possessors (s. 70(1)(f)); (iii) the rights of persons in actual occupation (s. 70(1)(g)); (iv) the rights excepted from the effect of registration in cases where title was registered with some title other than absolute (s. 70(1)(h)); and (v) rights under local land charges (s. 70(1)(i)).

[9] There are other situations in the 1925 property legislation where a registration requirement was imposed prospectively, so as not to affect the existing method of protecting rights that had already been created. Thus restrictive covenants and equitable easements created before 1926 are not registrable as land charges in unregistered land, but continue to be protected by the doctrine of notice: see Land Charges Act 1972, s. 2(5)(ii), (iii).

[10] This can be inferred from Land Registration Act 1925, ss. 70(1)(a); 70(2); and 70(3).

[11] Cf. s. 70(2).

Rights which are otherwise protected

4.10 Finally, there are rights which are otherwise protected and where it may therefore be regarded as otiose to expect them to be registered. An obvious example of this is the category of local land charges which are protected by registration on a register kept by the relevant local authority (s. 70(1)(i). More controversially, the rights of those in actual occupation (s. 70(1)(g)) are also explicable on this basis. At common law, the rights over land of a person in occupation — and perhaps in possession as well — were protected by that occupation or possession.[12] The exact scope of this principle was never precisely defined.[13] Sometimes it was explained on the basis that occupation gave notice of the rights of the occupier.[14] On other occasions, it was formulated more widely. The mere *fact* of occupation, whether or not it was apparent, was notice of the rights of the occupier.[15] Whatever the extent of the principle, the idea that an occupier was not required to take any further steps to protect his or her rights in the property was an ancient and deeply engrained one.'

ii. THE LEGAL FRAMEWORK OF SECTION 70

In **National Provincial Bank Ltd v Ainsworth** [1965] AC 1175, [1965] 2 All ER 472 Lord WILBERFORCE said at 1261, at 503:

'[The Land Registration] Act is a registration Act concerned (in this instance) to provide that certain rights are to be binding without registration and without the necessity for actual notice. To ascertain what "rights" come within this provision, one must look outside the Land Registration Act and see what rights affect purchasers under the general law. To suppose that the subsection makes any right, of howsoever a personal character, which a person in occupation may have, an overriding interest by which a purchaser is bound, would involve two consequences: first that this Act is, in this respect, bringing about a substantive change in real property law by making personal rights bind purchasers; second, that there is a difference *as to the nature of the rights by which a purchaser may be bound* between registered and unregistered land; for purely personal rights including the wife's right to stay in the house (if my analysis of this is correct) cannot affect purchasers of unregistered land even with notice. One may have to accept that there is a difference between unregistered land and registered land as regards what kind of notice binds a purchaser, or what kind of inquiries a purchaser has to make. But there is no warrant in the terms of this paragraph or elsewhere in the Act for supposing that the nature of the rights which are to bind a purchaser is to be different, excluding personal rights in one case, including them in another. The whole frame of section 70, with the list that it gives of interests, or rights, which are overriding, shows that it is made against a background of interests or rights whose nature and whose transmissible character is known, or ascertainable, aliunde, i.e., under other statutes or under the common law. So, if the right of a deserted wife is a purely personal claim against her husband, not specifically related to the house in question, but merely, at its highest, to be

---

[12] For a discussion, see [1990] CLJ 277, 315–320 (C. Harpum).
[13] Nor, given the effect upon it of the provisions of the Law of Property Act 1925 and what is now the Land Charges Act 1972, is it ever likely to be.
[14] See, eg *Barnhart v Greenshields* (1853) 9 Moo PCC 18, 32.
[15] *Holmes v Powell* (1856) 8 De GM & G 572, 580–581.

provided with a home, there is no difficulty in seeing that this type of right cannot, any more than any purely contractual right, be an overriding interest.'

WILLIAMS & GLYN'S BANK LTD v BOLAND[16]
[1981] AC 487, [1980] 2 All ER 408 (HL, Lord WILBERFORCE, Viscount DILHORNE, Lords SALMON, SCARMAN and ROSKILL)

In each of two cases the husband was registered as sole proprietor of the matrimonial home where he and his wife lived. The wife had made a substantial contribution to the purchase, which entitled her to a share in the house. She had not protected her interest by entering a notice, caution or restriction on the register. The husband, without the wife's consent, charged the house to the plaintiff bank to secure his business indebtedness. The bank made no enquiry as to whether the wife had any interest in the house. It now claimed repayment of the loan and possession of the house. In both cases the wife claimed an overriding interest under Land Registration Act 1925, section 70(1) *(g)*.

Held. The wife had an overriding interest.

LORD WILBERFORCE. My Lords, these appeals, . . . raise for decision the same question: whether a husband or a wife, (in each actual case a wife) who has a beneficial interest in the matrimonial home, by virtue of having contributed to its purchase price, but whose spouse is the legal and registered owner, has an 'overriding interest' binding on a mortgagee who claims possession of the matrimonial home under a mortgage granted by that spouse alone. Although this statement of the issue uses the words 'spouse,' 'husband and wife,' 'matrimonial home,' the appeals do not, in my understanding, involve any question of matrimonial law, or of the rights of married women or of women as such. Exactly the same issue could arise if the roles of husband and wife were reversed, or if the persons interested in the house were not married to each other. The solution must be derived from a consideration in the light of current social conditions of the Land Registration Act 1925 and other property statutes.
. . .

The legal framework within which the appeals are to be decided can be summarised as follows:

Under the Land Registration Act 1925, legal estates in land are the only interests in respect of which a proprietor can be registered. Other interests take effect in equity as 'minor interests,' which are overriden by a registered transfer. But the Act recognises also an intermediate, or hybrid, class of what are called 'overriding interests': though these are not registered, legal dispositions take effect subject to them. The list of overriding interests is contained in section 70 and it includes such matters as easements, liabilities having their origin in tenure, land tax and tithe rentcharge, seignorial and manorial rights, leases for terms not exceeding 21 years, and finally, the relevant paragraph being section 70(1) *(g)*:

'The rights of every person in actual occupation of the land or in receipt of the rents and profits thereof, save where enquiry is made of such person and the rights are not disclosed; . . .'

The first question is whether the wife is a 'person in actual occupation' and if so, whether her right as a tenant in common in equity is a right protected by this provision.

---

[16]   [1980] Conv 361; [1981] Conv 84 (J. Martin); (1979) 95 LQR 501; (1981) 97 LQR 12 (R.J. Smith); (1980) 130 NLJ 896 (R.L. Deech); (1980) SJ 651, 670 (P.W. Smith).

The other main element arises out of the Law of Property Act 1925. Since that Act, undivided shares in land can only take effect in equity, behind a trust for sale upon which the legal owner is to hold the land. Dispositions of the land, including mortgages, may be made under this trust and, provided that there are at least two trustees, or a trust corporation, 'overreach' the trusts. This means that the 'purchaser' takes free from them, whether or not he has notice of them, and that the trusts are enforceable against the proceeds of sale: see Law of Property Act 1925, section 2(2) and (3) which lists certain exceptions.

The second question is whether the wife's equitable interest under the trust for sale, if she is in occupation of the land, is capable of being an overriding interest, or whether, as is generally the rule as regards equitable interests it can only take effect as a 'minor interest.' In the latter event a registered transferee, including a legal mortgagee, would take free from it.

The system of land registration, as it exists in England, which long antedates the Land Registration Act 1925, is designed to simplify and to cheapen conveyancing. It is intended to replace the often complicated and voluminous title deeds of property by a single land certificate, on the strength of which land can be dealt with. In place of the lengthy and often technical investigation of title to which a purchaser was committed, all he has to do is to consult the register; from any burden not entered on the register, with one exception, he takes free. Above all, the system is designed to free the purchaser from the hazards of notice—real or constructive—which, in the case of unregistered land, involved him in enquiries, often quite elaborate, failing which he might be bound by equities. The Law of Property Act 1925 contains provisions limiting the effect of the doctrine of notice, but it still remains a potential source of danger to purchasers. By contrast, the only provisions in the Land Registration Act 1925 with regard to notice are provisions which enable a purchaser to take the estate free from equitable interests or equities whether he has notice or not. (See, for example, section 3(xv) s.v. 'minor interests'). The only kind of notice recognised is by entry on the register.

The exception just mentioned consists of 'overriding interests' listed in section 70. As to these, all registered land is stated to be deemed to be subject to such of them as may be subsisting in reference to the land, unless the contrary is expressed on the register. The land is so subject regardless of notice actual or constructive. In my opinion therefore, the law as to notice as it may affect purchasers of unregistered land, whether contained in decided cases, or in a statute (the Conveyancing Act 1882, section 3, Law of Property Act, section 199) has no application even by analogy to registered land. Whether a particular right is an overriding interest, and whether it affects a purchaser, is to be decided upon the terms of section 70, and other relevant provisions of the Land Registration Act 1925, and upon nothing else.

In relation to rights connected with occupation, it has been said that the purpose and effect of section 70(1)(g) of the Land Registration Act 1925 was to make applicable to registered land the same rule as previously had been held to apply to unregistered land: see per Lord Denning MR in *National Provincial Bank Ltd v Hastings Car Mart Ltd* [1964] Ch 665 at 689, [1964] 1 All ER 688 at 697, and in this House [1965] AC 1175 at 1259, [1965] 2 All ER 472 at 501–502.

I adhere to this, but I do not accept the argument which learned counsel for the appellant sought to draw from it. His submission was that, in applying section

70(1) *(g)*, we should have regard to and limit the application of the paragraph in the light of the doctrine of notice. But this would run counter to the whole purpose of the Act. The purpose, in each system, is the same, namely, to safeguard the rights of persons in occupation, but the method used differs. In the case of unregistered land, the purchaser's obligation depends upon what he has notice of—notice actual or constructive. In the case of registered land, it is the fact of occupation that matters. If there is actual occupation, and the occupier has rights, the purchaser takes subject to them. If not, he does not. No further element is material.

I now deal with the first question. Were the wives here in 'actual occupation'? These words are ordinary words of plain English, and should, in my opinion, be interpreted as such. Historically they appear to have emerged in the judgment of Lord Loughborough LC in *Taylor v Stibbert* (1794) 2 Ves 437 at 439–440, in a passage which repays quotation:

'... whoever purchases an estate from the owner, knowing it to be in possession of tenants, is bound to inquire into the estates those tenants have. It has been determined, that a purchaser being told, particular parts of the estate were in possession of a tenant, without any information as to his interest, and taking it for granted it was only from year to year, was bound by a lease, that tenant had, which was a surprise upon him. That was rightly determined; for it was sufficient to put the purchaser upon inquiry, that he was informed, the estate was not in the *actual possession* of the person, with whom he contracted; that he could not transfer the ownership and possession at the same time; that there were interests, as to the extent and terms of which it was his duty to inquire.'

They were taken up in the judgment of the Privy Council in *Barnhart v Greenshields* (1853) 9 Moo PCC 18. The purpose for which they were used, in that case, was evidently to distinguish the case of a person who was in some kind of legal possession, as by receipt of the rents and profits, from that of a person actually in occupation as tenant. Given occupation, i.e. presence on the land, I do not think that the word 'actual' was intended to introduce any additional qualification, certainly not to suggest that possession must be 'adverse': it merely emphasises that what is required is physical presence, not some entitlement in law. So even if it were necessary to look behind these plain words into history, I would find no reason for denying them their plain meaning.

Then, were the wives in actual occupation? I ask: why not? There was physical presence, with all the rights that occupiers have, including the right to exclude all others except those having similar rights. The house was a matrimonial home, intended to be occupied, and in fact occupied by both spouses, both of whom have an interest in it: it would require some special doctrine of law to avoid the result that each is in occupation. Three arguments were used for a contrary conclusion. First, it was said that if the vendor (I use this word to include a mortgagor) is in occupation, that is enough to prevent the application of the paragraph. This seems to be a proposition of general application, not limited to the case of husbands, and no doubt, if correct, would be very convenient for purchasers and intending mortgagees. But the presence of the vendor, with occupation, does not exclude the possibility of occupation of others.[17] There are observations which suggest the contrary in the unregistered land case of *Caunce v Caunce* [1969] 1 WLR 286, [1969] 1 All ER 722, but I agree with the

---

17   'Occupation need not be in one single person. Two persons can be in actual occupation, by themselves jointly, or each of them severally': *Williams & Glyn's Bank Ltd v Boland* [1979] Ch 312 at 331, [1979] 2 All ER 697 at 705, per Lord DENNING MR.

disapproval of these, and with the assertion of the proposition I have just stated by Russell LJ in *Hodgson v Marks* [1971] Ch 892 at 934, [1971] 2 All ER 684 at 690. Then it was suggested that the wife's occupation was nothing but the shadow of the husband's—a version I suppose of the doctrine of unity of husband and wife. This expression and the argument flowing from it was used by Templeman J in *Bird v Syme-Thomson* [1979] 1 WLR 440 at 444, [1978] 3 All ER 1027 at 1030, a decision preceding and which he followed in the present case. The argument was also inherent in the judgment in *Caunce v Caunce* which influenced the decisions of Templeman J. It somewhat faded from the arguments in the present case and appears to me to be heavily obsolete. The appellant's main and final position became in the end this: that, to come within the paragraph, the occupation in question must be apparently inconsistent with the title of the vendor. This, it was suggested, would exclude the wife of a husband-vendor because her apparent occupation would be satisfactorily accounted for by his. But, apart from the rewriting of the paragraph which this would involve, the suggestion is unacceptable. Consistency, or inconsistency, involves the absence, or presence, of an independent right to occupy, though I must observe that 'inconsistency' in this context is an inappropriate word. But how can either quality be predicated of a wife, simply qua wife? A wife may, and everyone knows this, have rights of her own; particularly, many wives have a share in a matrimonial home. How can it be said that the presence of a wife in the house, as occupier, is consistent or inconsistent with the husband's rights until one knows what rights she has? And if she has rights, why, just because she is a wife (or in the converse case, just because an occupier is the husband), should these rights be denied protection under the paragraph? If one looks beyond the case of husband and wife, the difficulty of all these arguments stands out if one considers the case of a man living with a mistress, or of a man and a woman—or for that matter two persons of the same sex—living in a house in separate or partially shared rooms. Are these cases of apparently consistent occupation, so that the rights of the other person (other than the vendor) can be disregarded? The only solution which is consistent with the Act (section 70(1) *(g)*) and with common sense is to read the paragraph for what it says. Occupation, existing as a fact, may protect rights if the person in occupation has rights. On this part of the case I have no difficulty in concluding that a spouse, living in a house, has an actual occupation capable of conferring protection, as an overriding interest, upon rights of that spouse.

This brings me to the second question, which is whether such rights as a spouse has under a trust for sale are capable of recognition as overriding interests—a question to my mind of some difficulty.[18] The argument against this is based upon the structure of the Land Registration Act 1925 and upon specific provisions in it.

As to structure, it is said that the Act recognises three things: (a) legal estates, (b) minor interests, which take effect in equity, (c) overriding interests. These are mutually exclusive: an equitable interest, which is a minor interest, is incapable of being at the same time an overriding interest. The wife's interest, is incapable of being at the same time an overriding interest. The wife's interest, existing under or behind a trust for sale, is an equitable interest and nothing more. To give it the protection of an overriding interest would, moreover, contradict the principle according to which such an equitable interest can be overreached by an exercise of the trust for sale. As to the provisions of the Act,

---

[18]   The doctrine of conversion was abolished retrospectively by TLATA 1996, s. 3.

particular emphasis is placed on section 3(xv) which, in defining 'minor interests' specifically includes in the case of land held on trust for sale 'all interests and powers which are under the Law of Property Act 1925 capable of being overridden by the trustees for sale' and excludes, expressly, overriding interests. Reliance is also placed on section 86, which, dealing analogously, so it is said, with settled land, prescribes that successive or other interests created by or arising under a settlement take effect as minor interests and not otherwise, and on section 101 which, it is argued, recognises the exclusive character of minor interests, which in all cases can be overridden.

My Lords, I find this argument formidable. To reach a conclusion upon it involves some further consideration of the nature of trusts for sale, in relation to undivided shares. The trusts upon which, in this case, the land is to be held are defined—as 'statutory trusts'—in section 35 of the Law of Property Act 1925, i.e.:

'. . . upon trust to sell the same and to stand possessed of the net proceeds of sale, after payment of costs, and of the net rents and profits until sale after payment of rates, taxes, costs of insurance, repairs, and other outgoings, upon such trusts, and subject to such powers and provisions, as may be requisite for giving effect to the rights of the persons . . . interested in the land'.

In addition to this specific disposition, the general provisions as to trusts for sale in sections 23 to 31, where not inconsistent, appear to apply. The right of occupation of the land pending sale is not explicitly dealt with in these sections and the position as to it is obscure. Before the Act the position was that owners of undivided shares (which could exist at law) had concurrent rights of occupation. In *Bull v Bull* [1955] 1 QB 234, [1955] 1 All ER 253, it was held by the Court of Appeal, applying *Re Warren* [1932] 1 Ch 42, that the conversion of these legal estates into equitable interests by the Law of Property Act 1925 should not affect the mutual rights of the owners. Denning LJ, in a judgment which I find most illuminating, there held, at 238, at 255 in a factual situation similar to that of the instant cases, that 'when there are two equitable tenants in common, then, until the place is sold, each of them is entitled concurrently with the other to the possession of the land and to the use and enjoyment of it in a proper manner'. And he referred to section 14 of the Law of Property Act 1925 which provides that the Act 'shall not prejudicially affect the interest of any person in possession or in actual occupation of land to which he may be entitled in right of such possession or occupation'.

How then are these various rights to be fitted into the scheme of the Land Registration Act 1925? It is clear, at least, that the interests of the co-owners under the 'statutory trusts' are minor interests—this fits with the definition in section 3(xv). But I can see no reason why, if these interests, or that of any one of them, are or is protected by 'actual occupation' they should remain merely as 'minor interests'. On the contrary, I see every reason why, in that event, they should acquire the status of overriding interests. And, moreover, I find it easy to accept that they satisfy the opening, and governing, words of section 70, namely, interests subsisting in reference to the land. As Lord Denning MR points out, to describe the interests of spouses in a house jointly bought to be lived in as a matrimonial home as merely an interest in proceeds of sale, or rents and profits until sale, is just a little unreal: see also *Elias v Mitchell* [1972] Ch 652, [1972] 2 All ER 153, per Pennycuick V-C with whose analysis I agree, and contrast, *Cedar Holdings Ltd v Green* [1981] Ch 129, [1979] 3 All ER 117 (which I consider to have been wrongly decided).

There are decisions, in relation to other equitable interests than those of tenants in common, which confirm this line of argument. In *Bridges v Mees* [1957] Ch 475, [1957] 2 All ER 577, Harman J decided that a purchaser of land under a contract for sale, who had paid the price and so was entitled to the land in equity, could acquire an overriding interest by virtue of actual occupation, and a similar position was held by the Court of Appeal to arise in relation to a resulting trust: *Hodgson v Marks* [1971] Ch 892, [1971] 2 All ER 684. These decisions (following the law as it undoubtedly existed before 1925—see *Barnhart v Greenshields* (1853) 9 Moo PCC 18 at 32, *Daniels v Davison* (1809) 16 Ves 249, *Allen v Anthony* (1816) 1 Mer 282, 284 per Lord Eldon LC) provide an answer to the argument that there is a firm dividing line, or an unbridgeable gulf, between minor interests and overriding interests, and, on the contrary, confirm that the fact of occupation enables protection of the latter to extend to what without it would be the former. In my opinion, the wives' equitable interests, subsisting in reference to the land, were by the fact of occupation, made into overriding interests, and so protected by section 70(1) *(g)*. I should add that it makes no difference to this that these same interests might also have been capable of protection by the registration of a caution: see *Bridges v Mees* [1957] Ch 475 at 487, [1957] 2 All ER 577 at 582 and Land Registration Act 1925, section 59(6).

There was finally an argument based upon section 74 of the Land Registration Act 1925. The section provides:

'Subject to the provisions of this Act as to settled land, neither the registrar nor any person dealing with a registered estate or charge shall be affected with notice of a trust express implied or constructive, and references to trusts shall, so far as possible, be excluded from the register.'

The argument was that if the overriding interest sought to be protected is, under the general law, only binding on a purchaser by virtue of notice, the section has the effect of denying the protection. It is obvious—and indeed conceded—that if this is right, *Hodgson v Marks* and *Bridges v Mees* must have been wrongly decided.

I am of opinion that this section has no such effect. Its purpose is to make clear, as I have already explained, that the doctrine of notice has no application to registered conveyancing, and accordingly to establish, as an administration measure, that entries may not be made in the register which would only be appropriate if that doctrine were applicable. It cannot have the effect of cutting down the general application of section 70(1).

I would only add, in conclusion, on the appeal as it concerns the wives a brief observation on the conveyancing consequences of dismissing the appeal. These were alarming to Templeman J, and I can agree with him to the extent that whereas the object of a land registration system is to reduce the risks to purchasers from anything not on the register, to extend (if it be an extension) the area of risk so as to include possible interests of spouses, and indeed, in theory, of other members of the family or even outside it, may add to the burdens of purchasers, and involve them in enquiries which in some cases may be troublesome.

But conceded, as it must be, that the Act, following established practice, gives protection to occupation, the extension of the risk area follows necessarily from the extension, beyond the paterfamilias, of rights of ownership, itself following from the diffusion of property and earning capacity. What is involved is a departure from an easy-going practice of dispensing with enquiries as to occupation beyond that of the vendor and accepting the risks of doing so. To substitute for this a practice of more careful enquiry as to the fact of occupation, and if necessary, as to the rights of occupiers can not, in my view of the matter, be considered as unacceptable except at the price of overlooking the widespread development of shared interests of ownership. In the light of section 70 of the Act, I cannot believe that Parliament intended this, though it may be true that in 1925 it did not foresee the full extent of this development.[19]

iii. THE INTEREST

WEBB v POLLMOUNT LTD
[1966] Ch 584, [1966] 1 All ER 481 (ChD, UNGOED-THOMAS J)

The plaintiff held under a lease granted by the defendant's predecessor in title. The lease gave to the plaintiff the option to purchase the freehold but, as the register contained no mention of the option, the defendant claimed that it could not be exercised as against him. The issue was whether the option constituted an overriding interest within section 70(1) (g).

Held. The option was an overriding interest.

UNGOED-THOMAS J: The defendant submits that overriding interests or rights in section 70(1) (g) are limited to rights of a person in an estate in the land, and he makes this submission with a view to establishing that the plaintiff's overriding interest is here limited to his leasehold estate exclusive of the option to purchase. It was first sought to establish this by limiting 'land' in sub-paragraph (g) to an estate in the land. . . .

As a matter of first impression, 'land' in section 70(1) (g) does not appear to me to refer to an estate in land, but to the physical land. The references which are contained in the sub-paragraph to 'actual occupation' and 'receipt of the rents and profits thereof' indicate this conclusion: and (g) is not limited to the rights of every tenant or estate owner, but extends to the rights of every person in actual occupation. 'Registered land' and 'land' are by definition not limited to estates in land, but include physical land. . . .

As the definition of 'overriding interests' expressly excludes matters entered on the register, it indicates that matters registrable but not registered, are not excluded. Overriding interests may include registrable matters, provided they have not been entered on the register. . . .

The opening words of section 70(1) provide a further limit on overriding interests within the section, namely, that they be 'for the time being subsisting in reference' to the registered land. The result is that, so far as material to this case, rights within section 70(1) (g) must fall within such rights as (1) are 'not entered on the register', (2) are 'affecting the estate transferred' to the defendant, (3) 'may be for the time being subsisting in reference' to the registered land. The option was not entered on the register, and there is no difficulty about the first of these limitations. So, the question in this case is whether the option to purchase contained in the lease affects the reversion transferred to the defendant and subsists in reference to the registered land. The statute itself does not answer this question: it raises it. The answer is only to be found by reference to the general law in whose context the statute was enacted.

---

[19]   Cf. *City of London Building Society v Flegg* [1988] AC 54, [1987] 3 All ER 435, p. 316, post, where HL distinguished *Boland* (mortgage money paid to *two* trustees; equitable beneficial interests overreached under LPA 1925, s. 2(1)(ii) even though their holders were in actual occupation).

In *National Provincial Bank Ltd v Ainsworth* [1965] AC 1175, [1965] 2 All ER 472, the House of Lords, in considering the rights of a deserted wife in respect of the matrimonial home, dealt with section 70. Russell LJ's observations in the Court of Appeal in that case were quoted with approval in the House of Lords. He said:

'It seems to me that section 70 in all its parts is dealing with rights in reference to land which have the quality of being capable of enduring through different ownerships of the land, according to normal conceptions of title to real property.'

Lord Upjohn said:

'. . . notice itself does not create the right. To create a right over the land of another that right must (apart from statute) create a burden on the land, i.e., an equitable estate or interest in the land.'

Thus, for a right to be within section 70(1) *(g)*, it must be an 'interest in the land' capable of enduring through different ownerships of the land according to normal conceptions of title to real property.'

An option to purchase is an interest in the land in respect of which it is exercisable, whether contained in a lease or not . . . .

It was suggested for the defendant that 'the right of every person in actual occupation of the land' should be construed as the right by virtue of which a person is in actual occupation of the land. The short answer to this, it seems to me, is that it does not say so; and the wording is in marked contrast with the wording in section 14 of the Law of Property Act 1925, where reference is made to the interest of a person in possession or occupation of land 'to which he may be entitled in right of such possession or occupation'. It is neither, in my view, consistent with the wording of section 70(1) *(g)* of the Land Registration Act 1925, nor with the authorities from which I have quoted.

Although an option to purchase does not, like an option to renew, 'touch', 'concern' or 'affect' the land demised and regarded as the subject-matter of the lease' (so as, e.g., to bind the reversion under the Grantees of Reversions Act 1540), what we are concerned with here is not whether it so 'affects' 'the land demised' and is within the relationship of landlord and tenant as considered in the judgment of the Court of Appeal in *Woodall v Clifton* [1905] 2 Ch 257, p. 409, post, but whether within section 20(1) *(b)* it is an interest 'affecting the estate transferred' to the defendant. That it is capable of affecting the estate transferred to the defendant is not disputed; e.g., if the defendant had notice of it before transfer to him. So, it seems to me to fall within Russell LJ's test in *National Provincial Bank Ltd v Ainsworth* of 'being capable of enduring through different ownerships of the land according to normal conceptions of title to real property.' And if it, thus, in the circumstances of this case, is a right 'affecting the estate transferred', within the requirement of section 20(1) *(b)*, it seems to me that it is 'for the time being subsisting in reference to' registered land within the requirement of section 70(1). My conclusion, therefore, is that subject to deciding the question as to the effect of section 59, the option to purchase appears to be an overriding interest.[20]

iv. THE RELEVANT DATE FOR DETERMINING THE INTEREST

ABBEY NATIONAL BUILDING SOCIETY v CANN
[1991] 1 AC 56, [1990] 1 All ER 1085 (HL, Lords BRIDGE OF HARWICH, GRIFFITHS, ACKNER, OLIVER OF AYLMERTON and JAUNCEY OF TULLICHETTLE)[1]

---

[20] See also *Habermann v Koehler* (1996) 73 P & CR 515 (raising the question whether the equity created by proprietory estoppel is a right within LRA 1925, s. 70(1)*(g)*; p. 686, post.
[1] (1990) 106 LQR 32, 545 (R.J. Smith); [1990] CLJ 397 (A.J. Oakley); (1990) 87 LSG 19–24, 34–39 (M. Beaumont, junior counsel for Mrs Cann); [1991] Conv 116 (S. Baughen), 155 (P.T. Evans).

In May 1984 George Cann applied to the Building Society for a loan of £25,000 to be secured on a mortgage of a registered leasehold house, 7 Hillview, Mitcham, which he proposed to purchase. He stated that the house was being purchased for his sole occupation. He intended, however, that the house should be occupied by his elderly mother and her 81-year-old husband-to-be, Abraham. Of the £25,000 loan, only £4,000 was required for the purchase of the house, and George used the balance to pay his creditors. Completion was to be on 13 August.

On 6 August the Building Society gave a cheque for £25,000 to George's solicitors, and prior to 13 August, George executed a legal charge in their favour. On 13 August completion of the purchase and of the charge took place simultaneously at 12.30 p.m.

At that time Mrs Cann was on holiday in the Netherlands, but at 10.00 a.m. George and Abraham arrived at the house; and at 11.45 a.m., with the vendor's consent, carpet-layers, acting on behalf of Mrs Cann, laid the carpets, and her furniture was taken into the house. The house was thereafter occupied by Mrs Cann and Abraham. On 13 September George was registered as sole proprietor, and the Building Society as proprietors of the charge.

George defaulted in his payments and the Building Society brought an action for possession. Mrs Cann claimed that, by reason of a contribution which she had made to the purchase of a property previously purchased by George, and of an assurance given by him that she would always have a roof over her head, she had an equitable interest in the house; and that this interest took priority over the charge as an overriding interest under Land Registration Act 1925, section 70(1) (g) by virtue of her actual occupation at the date of registration.

Held (1) (upholding the Court of Appeal (1989) 57 P & CR 381) Mrs Cann had impliedly authorised George to obtain the charge so as to preclude her from relying on any interest as prevailing over that of the Building Society.[2]

(2) The relevant date for determining the existence of overriding interests was the date of registration,[3] but the date of actual occupation under paragraph (g) was that of completion.[4]

---

[2]   Mrs Cann was well aware that there was a shortfall which would have to be met from somewhere . . . Dillon LJ inferred that 'she left it to George Cann to raise the balance", from which he further inferred that George Cann had authority to raise that sum from the society': per Lord OLIVER OF AYLMERTON at 94, at 1101. See also *Bristol and West Building Society v Henning* [1985] 1 WLR 778, [1985] 2 All ER 606; *Paddington Building Society v Mendelsohn* (1985) 50 P & CR 244; *Equity and Law Home Loans Ltd v Prestidge* [1992] 1 WLR 137, [1992] 1 All ER 909; (1992) 108 LQR 371 (R.J. Smith) (X, sole legal owner of house in Penzance, mortgaged it to Britannia Building Society for £30,000, with the knowledge of Y, who had an equitable interest in the house arising from her contribution of £10,000 to its purchase price. X then remortgaged the house to the plaintiff for £43,000, without Y having any knowledge of the mortgagee's identity or of the mortgage details. CA held, extending *Henning*, that Y's interest was subject to that of the plaintiff to the extent of £30,000: 'the substituted encumbrance should rank ahead of the beneficial interest as far as, but no further than, the consent which was to be imputed to Y' per MUSTILL LJ); [1992] CLJ 223 (M. Dixon); [1992] Conv 206 (M.P. Thompson); (1992) 108 LQR 371 (R.J. Smith); *Locabail (UK) Ltd v Waldorf Investment Corpn* (1999) Times, 31 March; *Woolwich Building Society v Dickman* [1996] 3 All ER 204; [1996] All ER Rev 254 (P.J. Clarke); [1998] CLJ 1328 (L. Tee). And the mortgage itself may be invalid if the registered proprietor has no power to create it.

[3]   Or, more specifically, when the application for registration is delivered at the registry: LRR 1925, r. 83(2), as substituted by LRR 1978, r. 8.

[4]   As recommended by the Law Commission in its Third Report on Land Registration 1987 (Law Com No 115, Cmnd 8636), para. 2.77.

(3) There was no scintilla temporis between completion and charge, during which Mrs Cann's equitable interest could crystallise and then take priority over that of the Building Society (p. 519, post).

(4) In any event, Mrs Cann was not in actual occupation. (p. 150, post).

LORD OLIVER OF AYLMERTON: In the Court of Appeal Mrs Cann's claim failed because, in the view of all members of the court, she was aware that the balance of the purchase price of 7, Hillview, over and above the net amount to be produced by the sale of 30, Island Road, was going to be raised by George Cann by mortgage of the premises. Having thus impliedly authorised him to raise this amount on mortgage she must necessarily have authorised him to that extent to create a charge to the society having priority to her interest, and could not, as against the society, complain that George had exceeded a limitation on his authority of which the society was unaware. Dillon LJ, however, took the view that the events which took place between 11.45 a.m. and 12.20 p.m. on 13 August did constitute actual occupation of the property by Mrs Cann sufficient to enable her to claim an overriding interest, a proposition which was doubted by Ralph Gibson and Woolf LJJ.

If, of course, the ground upon which the Court of Appeal rejected Mr and Mrs Cann's claim to resist an order for possession in the society's favour is correct, it is strictly unnecessary to determine any of the other points which arise, but since they have been fully argued and having regard to the pending appeal in *Lloyds Bank plc v Rosset* [1991] 1 AC 107, [1990] 1 All ER 1111, p. 150, post which immediately follows this appeal, it is desirable that they should be decided.

First in logical order is the question of the appropriate date for ascertaining the existence of overriding interests under the Land Registration Acts. Curiously enough the point appears never to have arisen directly for decision in any reported case prior to *Rosset*, save in one case in 1985 in the Bristol County Court which was decided on appeal on a different point (*Paddington Building Society v Mendelsohn* (1985) 50 P & CR 244). In *Re Boyle's Claim* [1961] 1 WLR 339, 344, [1961] 1 All ER 620, 623 Wilberforce J expressed the view that the relevant date was the date of acquisition of the registered title, but the issue in that case was quite a different one and the point does not appear to have been argued. That case has, however, been used as the basis for statements in a number of leading conveyancing textbooks that that is the date at which occupation for the purposes of section 70(1)(g) has to be ascertained: see, e.g., *Wolstenholme and Cherry's Conveyancing Statutes*, 13th ed. (1972), vol. 6, p. 65; *Emmet on Title*, 19th ed. (1986), para. 5. 197. The question arose directly in *Rosset* in which the Court of Appeal [1989] Ch 350, [1988] 3 All ER 915 decided unanimously that the relevant date was the date of completion of the purchase and not that of registration. Your Lordships are now invited to overrule that decision.

My Lords, the conclusion at which the Court of Appeal arrived makes good conveyancing sense and, speaking for myself, I should be extremely reluctant to overrule it unless compulsively driven to do so, the more so because it produces a result which is just, convenient and certain, as opposed to one which is capable of leading to manifest injustice and absurdity. It has, I think, to be acknowledged that the interrelation between the provisions of sections 3(xvi), 20 and 23, 37, 69 and 70(1) is not altogether easy to understand, particularly in relation to the position of a chargee whose charge is created by a purchaser of land who is not yet himself the registered proprietor. The solution propounded by the trial judge and by counsel for the bank in *Rosset* depends upon the words 'affecting the estate transferred or created' in sections 20(1) *(b)* and 23(1) *(c)* and construes them as if there were added the words 'at the time at which it was transferred or created,' thus excluding from the category of interests affecting the estate the rights of a person entering into occupation after the transfer or creation of the estate effected by completion of the transaction. It will be convenient to refer to this as 'the judge's construction.'

This is an attractive solution because it is, as Nicholls LJ observed in the course of his judgment in *Rosset*, at 373, at 922 a conveyancing absurdity that, for instance, a mortgagee should, after completion and after having made all possible inquiries and parted with his money, be bound by the interest asserted by a newly-arrived occupant coming in between completion and the registration of his charge. So far as registered interests are concerned the chargee can protect himself by an official search which will preserve his priority over any further registered entries during a priority period well sufficient to enable him to have his charge stamped and lodged for registration: see rules 3 and 5 of the Land Registration (Official Searches) Rules 1981 (SI 1981 No. 1135). There is, however, no similar protection against overriding interests which are not recorded on the register and whose existence can be ascertained only by inquiry and there is, accordingly, good sense in so construing sections 20(1) and 23(1) as to preserve the priority of the purchaser or chargee as from the date of completion when both are irrevocably committed to the transaction, which only awaits the formal step of registration in order to vest the legal estate.

[His Lordship considered ss. 3(xvi), 20, 23, 37, 69 and 70(1), and continued:]

I conclude, therefore, like Nicholls LJ that the relevant date for determining the existence of overriding interests which will 'affect the estate transferred or created' is the date of registration. This does, of course, give rise to the theoretical difficulty that since a transferor remains the registered proprietor until registration of the transfer, it would be possible for him, in breach of trust, to create overriding interests, for instance, by grant of an easement or of a lease, which would be binding on the transferee and against which the transferee would not be protected by an official search. That would, of course, equally be the case in a purchase of unregistered land where the purchaser pays the price in advance of receiving a conveyance. I cannot, however, find in the theoretical possibility of so improbable an event a context for preferring the judge's construction.

The question remains, however, whether the date of registration is also the relevant date for determining whether a claimant to a right is in actual occupation. It is to be noted that it is not the actual occupation which gives rise to the right or determines its existence. Actual occupation merely operates as the trigger, as it were, for the treatment of the right, whatever it may be as an overriding interest. Nor does the additional quality of the right as an overriding interest alter the nature or quality of the right itself. If it is an equitable right it remains an equitable right. As was observed in *William's & Glyn's Bank Ltd v Boland* [1981] AC 487, 504, [1980] 2 All ER 408, 412, p. 136, ante the purpose of section 70(1) *(g)* was to make applicable to registered land the same rule for the protection of persons in actual occupation as had been applied in the case of unregistered land in, for instance, *Hunt v Luck* [1902] 1 Ch 428, p. 46, ante. In relation to legal rights it does nothing, for it is not easy to conceive of a legal right in the land which would not already be an overriding interest under some other head, as, for instance, paragraphs *(a)* or *(k)*. Again, as regards equitable rights in an occupier which arise before completion and are supported by occupation at that date there is no difficulty. A chargee who advances money and so acquires an equitable charge prior to the creation of the occupier's right does not lose his priority because the occupier's right becomes an overriding interest. That interest remains what it always was, an interest subject to the prior equity of the chargee which, on registration, is fortified by the legal estate. Equally, a chargee advancing his money after the creation of the occupier's equitable right is, as one would expect, subject to such right.

The case which does give rise to difficulty if the date of registration is the relevant date for determining whether there is a claimant in actual occupation is one in which the sequence of events is that the right, unaccompanied by occupation, is created before completion and before the chargee has advanced his money and then subsequently the claimant enters into actual occupation after completion and remains in occupation up to the date when the registration of the charge is effected. The chargee in that event would have no possibility of discovering the existence of the claimant's interest before advancing his money and taking his charge, but would nevertheless be subject, on registration, to the claimant's prior equitable interest which, ex hypothesi, would not have been subject to the charge at its creation.

This does indeed produce a conveyancing absurdity and there is, as Nicholls LJ observed, an internal context for supposing that the legislature, in enacting paragraph *(g)*, must have been contemplating an occupation which preceded and existed at completion of a transfer or disposition. Not only was the paragraph clearly intended to reflect the rule discussed in *Hunt v Luck* with regard to unregistered conveyancing, but the reference to inquiry and failure to disclose cannot make any sense unless it is related to a period in which such inquiry could be other than otiose. That absurdity can, I think, be avoided only by the route which the Court of Appeal adopted and by referring the 'actual occupation' in paragraph *(g)* to the date of completion of the transaction by transfer and payment of the purchase money. Section 70(1) refers to such interests 'as may be for the time being subsisting' and in order to affect 'the estate transferred or created' on registration such interests would no doubt require to be subsisting on that date. But I see no insuperable difficulty in holding that the actual occupation required to support such an interest as a subsisting interest must exist at the date of completion of the transaction giving rise to the right to be registered, for that is the only date at which the inquiry referred to in paragraph *(g)* could, in practice, be made and be relevant. I agree, therefore, with the conclusion of the Court of Appeal in *Rosset* [1989] Ch 350 [1988] 3 All ER 915, that it is at that moment that it falls to be determined whether there is an actual occupation for the purposes of paragraph *(g)*. I do not think that I can improve upon Nicholls LJ's analysis when he said, in the course of his judgment in *Rosset*, at 374, at 923:

'If this is right, the pieces of the jigsaw fit together reasonably well. A purchaser or mortgagee inspects and inquires before completion, in the established fashion. Or he fails to do so, at his own risk. He then completes the transaction, taking an executed transfer or mortgage. Whether or not an overriding interest under paragraph *(g)* subsists so far as his freehold or mortgage is concerned falls to be determined at that moment. If an overriding interest does subsist, then his estate when registered takes subject to that

---

5   See *Barclays Bank plc v Zaroovabli* [1997] 2 WLR 729 at 735, [1997] 2 All ER 19 at 25, per Sir RICHARD SCOTT V-C; [1997] CLJ 196 (D. G. Barnsley).

interest. If it does not, then subsequent entry of a person into occupation before the transfer or mortgage has been registered, and 'completed' for the purposes of section 19, does not have the consequence of creating an overriding interest under paragraph (*g*) in relation to that freehold or mortgage.'[5]

V. EQUITABLE EASEMENTS AND PROFITS A PRENDRE. SECTION 70(1)(*a*)

Legal easements are among the list of overriding interests but they may nevertheless appear in the property register of the dominant land. A note should also appear on the register of the servient land.[6]

Equitable easements, however, are not overriding interests under the ill-drafted section 70(1)(*a*) of the Land Registration Act 1925,[7] but may become so by virtue of rule 258 of the Land Registration Rules 1925, in spite of the conflict between the rule and the section.[8]

In **Celesteel Ltd v Alton House Holdings Ltd** [1985] 1 WLR 204, [1985] 2 All ER 562, Alton House Holdings Ltd (the first defendant) was the registered freeholder of Cavendish House, a large block of flats just North of Lord's cricket ground. The third plaintiff was the tenant of a flat and garage under a contract for a lease for 120 years from the predecessor in title of Alton House Holdings Ltd. The contract gave the third plaintiff rights of way from the garage (No. 52) to the street. The lease was never granted, nor was the right of way protected by any entry against the registered title of the freeholder. In 1982 Alton House Holdings Ltd granted to Mobil Oil Co Ltd (the second defendant) a lease of the ground floor of Cavendish House, including a part of the driveway over which the right of way had been given.

One question was whether the third plaintiff had an overriding interest in respect of his equitable easement of way. In holding that he had, SCOTT J said at 219, at 574:

'It is plain, also, that the third plaintiff, although in actual occupation of garage 52, was not in actual occupation of any part of the rear driveway. He cannot therefore protect his easement over the rear driveway under paragraph (*g*) of section 70(1) and the only paragraph of section 70(1) under which, arguably, he might protect that easement as an overriding interest is paragraph (*a*).

Paragraph (*a*) of section 70(1) protects as overriding interests the following rights:

[His Lordship read para. (*a*) and continued:]

The rights over the rear driveway which the third plaintiff acquired by virtue of the facts pleaded in the paragraphs of the statement of claim which I have mentioned were certainly rights of way. If they were legal rights of way then the second defendants are bound by them. If they were only equitable rights of way then it must decide whether or not they are excepted from paragraph (*a*) by the

---

6   C & B, pp. 633–634.
7   P. 130, ante.
8   Followed by CA in *Thatcher v Douglas* [1996] NLJR 282; [1986] Conv 31 (M.P. Thompson); [1999] Conv 31 (J. Greed); *Leeman v Mohammed* (2001) 82 P & CR 159, See [1986] Conv 296 (M. Davey); [1987] Conv 328 (A.M. Pritchard).

phrase "not being equitable easements required to be protected by notice on the register."

The third plaintiff's entitlement to the easements comprised in the intended lease of garage 52 for the intended 120 year term is an *equitable* entitlement. It could only become a *legal* entitlement by the grant to him of the lease contracted to be granted and the registration of that lease at Her Majesty's Land Registry. But the meaning and scope of the provision "equitable easements required to be protected by notice on the register" is somewhat obscure. In *Ives (E R) Investment Ltd v High* [1967] 2 QB 379, [1967] 1 All ER 504, p. 665, ante, it was held by the Court of Appeal that easements acquired in equity by proprietary estoppel were not equitable easements for the purposes of section 10(1) Class D (iii) of the Land Charges Act 1925. Lord Denning MR expressed the view that "equitable easements" referred simply to that limited class of rights which before the 1925 property legislation were capable of being conveyed or created at law but thereafter were capable of existing only in equity: see at 395, at 508. In *Poster v Slough Estates Ltd* [1969] 1 Ch 495, [1968] 3 All ER 257, Cross J declined, at 506–507, at 262, to disagree with Lord Denning MR's view of the meaning of the expression and held that a right to re-enter premises after termination of a lease and to remove fixtures therefrom was not an "equitable easement" for the purposes of the Land Charges Act 1925. These authorities might be thought to suggest by analogy that equitable easements in section 70(1) (*a*) should be given a similarly limited meaning. I am, however, reluctant to do that because in general the clear intention of the Land Registration Act 1925 is that equitable interests should be protected either by entry on the register or as overriding interests and, if equitable easements in general are not within the exception in paragraph (*a*), it would follow that they would rank as overriding interests and be binding upon registered proprietors of servient land even though such proprietors did not have and could not by any reasonable means have obtained any knowledge of them. That result could not possibly be supported. In my view, therefore, the dicta in the two cases are not applicable to the construction of "equitable easements" in paragraph (*a*) of section 70(1).

Mr. Purle submitted that the exception expressed in section 70(1) (*a*) applied only to those equitable easements in respect of which a positive requirement that they be protected by notice on the register could be found in the Act. He submitted further that the Act contained no such requirement and that accordingly the expression covered nothing. It seems, however, from paragraph (*c*) of the proviso to section 19(2) of the Act, that the draftsman assumed that easements would require to be protected either by registration as appurtenant to registered land or by entry of notice against the registered title of the servient land. I do not, therefore, feel able to accept these submissions.

In my opinion, the words "required to be protected" in paragraph (*a*) should be read in the sense "need to be protected". The exception in the paragraph was, in my view, intended to cover all equitable easements other than such as by reason of some other statutory provision or applicable principle of law, could obtain protection otherwise than by notice on the register. The most obvious example would be equitable easements which qualified for protection under paragraph (*g*) as part of the rights of a person in actual occupation. In my view I must examine the easement claimed by the third plaintiff and consider whether there is any statutory provision or principle of law which entitles it to protection otherwise than by entry of notice on the register.

The matter stands in my opinion thus. At the time when Mobil acquired its registered leasehold title the third plaintiff's right to an easement of way for the benefit of garage 52 over a part of the property enjoyed under that leasehold title was an equitable easement. It was not protected by any entry on the register. On the other hand, it was at the relevant time openly exercised and enjoyed by the third plaintiff as appurtenant to garage 52. Section 144 of the Land Registration Act 1925 contains power for rules to be made for a number of specified purposes. The Land Registration Rules 1925 were accordingly made and rule 258 provides:

[His Lordship read r. 258, p. 133 ante, and continued:]

The third plaintiff's equitable right of way over the rear driveway was, in my view, at the time when Mobil acquired its registered leasehold title, a right enjoyed with land for the purposes of this rule. It was plainly a right which adversely affected registered land including the part of the rear driveway comprised in Mobil's lease. Rue 258 categorises such a right as an overriding interest. Section 144(2) of the Act provides that "Any rules made in pursuance of this section shall be of the same force as if enacted in this Act." Accordingly, in my judgment, the third plaintiff's right ranks as an overriding interest, does not need to be protected by entry of notice on the register and is binding on Mobil.

Mr. Davidson submitted that there was no power under section 144(1) for rules to add to the overriding interests specified in the various paragraphs of section 70(1). He submitted that rule 258 was ultra vires and of no effect. I do not agree. Sub-paragraph (xxxi) of section 144(1) enables rules to be made,

"for regulating any matter to be prescribed or in respect of which rules are to or may be made under this Act and any other matter or thing, whether similar or not to those above mentioned, in respect of which it may be expedient to make rules for the purpose of carrying this Act into execution."

This is a power in very wide terms. In my view, it is in terms wide enough to justify rule 258 and I see no reason why it should be given a limited effect.

Accordingly, for these reasons, the third plaintiff's equitable right of way over the rear driveway enjoyed with garage 52 was and is, in my judgment, binding on Mobil.'

vi. ACTUAL OCCUPATION. SECTION 70(1)(*g*)

(a)   Nature and State of the Property

LLOYDS BANK PLC v ROSSET
[1989] Ch 350, [1988] 3 All ER 915 (CA, PURCHAS, MUSTILL and NICHOLLS LJJ)[9]

In 1982 Mr and Mrs Rosset decided to purchase a semi-derelict farmhouse in Thanet, Kent, which was registered land. The purchase was to be funded by Mr Rosset's family trust in Switzerland, and the legal estate was to be in his sole name. It was their common intention that the renovation should be a joint venture and that Mrs Rosset should have a beneficial interest in the farmhouse.

On 7 November the vendors allowed Mr and Mrs Rosset's builders to enter and start work. Mrs Rosset spent nearly every day on the site and generally urged on the builders. On 23 November contracts were exchanged. On 14 December, Mr Rosset, without his wife's knowledge, sought a short term loan from the Bank. On 17 December completion took place, and Mr Rosset executed a charge in favour of the Bank. On 3 February the transfer and the charge were registered.

[9]   [1988] Conv 453 (M.P. Thompson); [1989] CLJ 180 (P.G. McHugh); [1988] All ER Rev 163 (P.J. Clarke); (1988) 104 LQR 507 (R.J. Smith); [1989] Conv 342 (P. Sparkes).

Mr and Mrs Rosset and their two children moved into the farm house, where Mrs Rosset had been spending occasional evenings since completion.

Following matrimonial difficulties, Mr Rosset, who was a courier accompanying coach parties abroad, left the farm and his wife and children in May 1984. The loan to Mr Rosset was not repaid, and the Bank sought an order for possession. Mrs Rosset claimed an equitable beneficial interest under a trust, and an overriding interest under Land Registration Act 1925, section 70(1)(g).

Held (1) The relevant date for determining the overriding interest was the date of completion (17 December) and not registration (3 February).

(2) (MUSTILL LJ dissenting) Mrs Rosset was in actual occupation on 17 December.

The House of Lords affirmed (1) in [1991] 1 AC 107, [1990] 1 All ER 1111, following *Abbey National Building Society v Cann* [1991] 1 AC 56, [1990] 1 All ER 1085, p. 143, ante, but reversed the Court of Appeal on the ground that Mrs Rosset had no equitable beneficial interest under a trust. Accordingly, no views were expressed on the question of actual occupation.

NICHOLLS LJ: Lord Wilberforce observed in *Williams & Glyn's Bank Ltd v Boland* [1981] AC 487, 504, that the words 'actual occupation' are ordinary words of plain English and that they should be interpreted as such. The bank submitted that in ordinary, every day speech the wife would not have been regarded as being in occupation of Vincent Farmhouse on 17 December. Residential premises are occupied only by those who live in them.

I agree with this submission to the extent that I accept that in ordinary speech one normally does equate occupation in relation to a house with living there. If a person is intending to move into a house but has not yet done so, he would not normally be regarded as having gone into occupation. That is the normal position, with a house which is fit for living in. But that does not provide the answer in the present case, where the house was semi-derelict. In the first place, I do not think that in every day speech actual occupation of a house can never exist short of residence. Take Vincent Farmhouse. I do not think that it is as clear as the bank suggests that in every day speech the wife would not have been regarded as being in occupation on 17 December 1982 when the purchase was completed. Had the defendants been asked on the day 'are you in occupation?' I am not sure that their answer would have been a simple 'no'. Their answer might well have been to the effect 'We are not living there yet. The farmhouse was semi-derelict when we found it. No one could have lived there with the house as it was then. But we have the builders in. They have been there for over five weeks now. Diana spends almost every day there. Progress has been slower than we had hoped. We had intended to move in by Christmas but that will not be possible now.' Secondly, if the words 'actual occupation' are given the rigid, restricted meaning submitted by the bank in relation to residential premises, and that meaning is applied to a house in course of being built or renovated, the result in some cases will be to defeat the purpose intended to be achieved by paragraph (g) of section 70(1). If, day after day, workmen are actively building a house on a plot of land, or actively and substantially renovating a semi-derelict house, it would be contrary to the principle underlying paragraph (g) if a would be purchaser or mortgagee were entitled to treat that site as currently devoid of an occupant for the purpose of the paragraph. If, for example, the owner had granted a tenancy in return for a premium, so that the tenancy did not qualify as an overriding interest under section 70(1)(k), but the tenant himself and workmen employed by him were on site, building or renovating as I have described, why should he not be as much entitled to the protection afforded to occupants by section 70(1) (g) as he would be once the work had been finished and he was living in the house?

In my view, the test of residence propounded by the bank is too narrow. As the judge observed, what constitutes occupation will depend upon the nature and state of the property in question. I can see no reason, in principle or in practice, why a semi-derelict house such as Vincent Farmhouse should not be capable of actual occupation whilst the works proceed and before anyone has started to live in the building.

The bank further submitted that the presence of the builder and his men in the property could not constitute actual occupation by the defendants. I am unable to agree. I can detect nothing in the context in which the expression 'actual occupation' is used in paragraph (g) to suggest that the physical presence of an employee or agent cannot be regarded as the presence of the employer or principal when determining whether the employer or principal is in actual occupation. Whether the presence of an employee or agent is to be so regarded will depend on the function which the employee or agent is discharging in the premises in the particular case.

[His Lordship referred to *Williams & Glyn's Bank Ltd v Boland* [1979] Ch 312, 338, [1979] 2 All ER 697, 710, per Ormrod LJ: and *Strand Securities Ltd v Caswell* [1965] Ch 958, 981, 984, [1965] 1 All ER 820, 827, 829, p. 153, post, per Lord Denning MR and Russell LJ and continued:]

I turn to the facts of the present case, which I have already summarised. The vendors had ceased to be in actual occupation long before 17 December. The house was empty and semi-derelict. They permitted the husband to go on to the property before completion. From 7 November until after Christmas the builder and his men were there every working day. One of them slept in the property on most nights. The wife spent almost every weekday at the property, from 10 a.m. to 4 p.m. Thus, there was physical presence on the property throughout the period leading up to completion on 17 December and that physical presence was to the extent that one would expect of an occupier, having regard to the then state of the property.

Thus far I am in agreement with the judge. Where I feel obliged to part company from him is his conclusion that, although (as I read his judgment) the husband, through the presence of the building and his men, was in actual occupation of the property on 17 December, the wife was not. As appears from the second extract from his judgment that I have quoted above, in reaching that conclusion the judge attached importance to the answer which Mr Griffin, the builder, would have given to the question, 'who occupies the building?' With all respect to the judge, I do not think that was the right question to pose. What mattered was not the builder's views on who occupied the building, but on whose behalf the builder was in the building. The judge himself had observed earlier that that was the vital question. As to that, the facts seem reasonably clear. Mr Griffin regarded himself as being employed by both the husband and the wife. There was no clear evidence that in this he was mistaken. Mr Griffin addressed his invoices to both Mr and Mrs Rosset. He looked to both of them for payment. In those circumstances, even though the husband alone was the contracting purchaser of the property, it seems to me that the presence of the builder and his men on the property was as much on behalf of the wife as it was on behalf of the husband. Mr Griffin was working there under a contract made with both of them, renovating the property for both of them. He was there on behalf of both of them. There was no sound basis for distinguishing between the two of them. If the builder's presence was sufficient to constitute occupation by the husband, it was equally sufficient to constitute occupation by the wife. This was so even after the incident mentioned by the judge. A stage was reached when the workmen complained that both the husband and wife were giving them instructions. The husband then 'laid it down' that the workmen should take their instructions from him alone.

So the position was that the builder and his men were in the building, carrying out a contract made with the husband and the wife. Additionally, the wife herself was there almost every weekday. In my view, those facts amounted to actual occupation of the property by the wife on 17 December 1982. There was, I repeat, physical presence on the property by the wife and her agent of the nature, and to the extent, that one would expect of an occupier having regard to the then state of the property: namely, the presence involved in actively carrying out the renovation necessary to make the house fit for residential use.

In my view, therefore, the judge erred in the inference he drew from the primary facts which he found. The reality was that before completion the husband and the wife had already taken over this semi-derelict house, under a revocable licence granted to the husband by the vendors. By 17 December renovation was well under way. Completion took place on 17 December, but no physical change then took place in their use of the property, save that the wife slept there more frequently. Eventually in February 1983 the family began to live there.

This conclusion has the attraction that it gives effect to the purpose of paragraph *(g)*. Had a representative of the bank inspected the property before 17 December to check if anyone was in actual occupation, he would have seen that, indeed, someone was there. Builders were working there, day after day, plainly on behalf of someone. Had he gone up to the door, he would probably have found the wife in the house. In such circumstances the bank really has only itself to blame if it lends money without looking into the position further. In particular, I find it surprising that the bank, knowing that this was to be the matrimonial home, did not seek the wife's written consent to the grant of the charge. This was in December 1982. The *Boland* case [1981] AC 487 was decided by the House of Lords over two years earlier, in June 1980.[10]

(b)   Actual Occupation Through Others

STRAND SECURITIES LTD v CASWELL[11]
[1965] Ch 958, [1965] 1 All ER 820 (CA, Lord Denning MR and Harman and Russell LJJ)

The first defendant was the sub-lessee of a flat, the 42-year head lease of which had been registered with good leasehold title. The sub-lease of 39¼ years, less three days, was not, at the material date, entered in any way on the register. The question arose whether the first defendant had an overriding interest within

---

[10]   *Malory Enterprises Ltd v Cheshire Homes (UK) Ltd* [2002] Ch 216 (derelict block of flats only used for temporary storage; gates in fence kept locked and ground floor windows blocked up held to be actual occupation: 'The requisite physical presence must, as it seems to me, in fairness be such as to put a person inspecting the land on notice that there was some person in occupation', per Arden LJ at para. 81).

[11]   LRA 1925, s. 70(1)(*k*) did not apply; the first defendant's sub-lease exceeded 21 years; the second defendant was a gratuitous licensee.
    The decision was applied in *Lloyd v Dugdale* [2001] EWCA Civ 1754, [2002] 2 P C CR 13 (where D Ltd, rather than D, major shareholder and managing director of D Ltd, was in occupation as licensee of D, it was held that D was not in actual occupation. '*Strand Securities v Caswell* is clear authority for the proposition that where A permits B to occupy land on B's own behalf by way of gratuitous licence, A's capacity as licensor will not by itself entitle him to claim to be in actual occupation of the land': per Sir Christopher Slade at para 45. Nor did D's regular presence help, since he was there as managing director and not on his own account.

section 70(1) (g) which prevailed against a purchaser from the freeholders. He lived in the country but used the flat as a London base. He allowed his step-daughter, the second defendant (who had been deserted by her husband) to live in the flat rent free.

Held. The first defendant had no overriding interest.

RUSSELL LJ: It is to be remarked that if [the first defendant] . . . had moved up to London and occupied the bedroom or received from or demanded of his step-daughter . . . a penny a week for the privilege of remaining there, he would have had an unanswerable claim to his sublease being an overriding interest under section 70(1) (g) as he would be in the one case a person in actual occupation and in the other in receipt of the rents and profits. Of course he did neither of these things. Their possibility, however, serves to show how rare it must be that an actual sublessee entitled to possession is not a person either in actual occupation or in receipt of the rents and profits. . . .

On the facts, was the first defendant . . . a person in actual occupation, though he was not in any ordinary sense residing there or treating it as his home, and the second defendant and her family were allowed by him to reside there? As a matter of the ordinary use of language I would not consider the first defendant to be such. For him it was argued that the phrase 'in actual occupation' derives from cases in which 'actual occupation' and 'actual possession' are used indifferently to describe a condition of enjoyment of the land itself, and that the phrase 'actual occupation' here involves that form of the legal concept of possession as distinct from the other or notional forms of that concept consisting of the receipt of money payments derived from land, or of the right to possession though the land be vacant. And it was argued that 'actual possession' was avoided by the draftsman as a phrase because of the difficulty which would flow from the definition of 'possession', in section 3(xviii) of the Land Registration Act, 1925. Reference was made to the number of authorities, including cases in the fields of rating, poor law, and landlord and tenant, with a view to showing that possession, and therefore occupation, may be had through the medium of another. Suppose, it was said, that the first defendant employed a resident caretaker to look after the flat in question, would the first defendant not be a person in actual occupation? I think that is correct. Then, it was argued, that is because the caretaker would be his licensee, bound to go at his will, and that was the position of the second defendant. But I think that here is the distinction between occupation by the caretaker as a matter of duty on behalf of the first defendant and the occupation of the second defendant on her own behalf; both were licensees, but the former, by her occupation for which she was employed, was the representative of the first defendant and her occupation may therefore be regarded as his. The proposition that in each case the first defendant was in actual occupation because neither the caretaker nor the second defendant had a right to occupy independently of him seems to me too broadly stated and to ignore that distinction. I do not say that a contract of employment or agency with the person residing there is essential to actual occupation by the other person. I think that it might well be that if a house was used as a residence by a wife, separated from the tenant, her husband (whether or not in desertion), he could also be regarded as in actual occupation through her; the question whether the husband was also a

---

12   See *Chhokar v Chhokar* [1984] FLR 313, p. 156, post, where furniture was relevant.
13   The first defendant succeeded on another ground; when he had made application for first registration of his sub-lease, he was unable to produce the head-lessor's land certificate. CA held that there was no need to produce it, and that the register should be rectified. This gave the sub-lease priority over the transfer of the head-lease to the purchaser, which had not been registered until after the date of the first defendant's application.

person in actual occupation did not, of course, arise in *National Provincial Bank Ltd v Hastings Car Mart Ltd (No 3)* [1964] Ch 665, [1964] 3 All ER 93n. But this conception, even if valid, could not extend to the relationship in the present case.

Nor, it seems to me, can the presence on the premises of some of the first defendant's furniture,[12] nor the previously mentioned use by him and others of the family of the flat, nor the fact, which I am prepared to assume though it was not proved, that he had a key, nor a combination of those matters, constitute actual occupation by him.[13]

(c)   Acts of Preparatory Character

In **Abbey National Building Society v Cann** [1991] 1 AC 56, [1990] 1 All ER 1085, p. 143, *ante*, Lord OLIVER OF AYLMERTON said at 93, at 1101:

'I have, up to this point, been content to assume that the facts of the instant case justify the proposition which found favour with Dillon LJ, that [Mrs Cann] was in actual occupation of the property at the material time. This is, of course, essentially a question of fact, but there is the serious question of what, in law, can amount to "actual occupation" for the purposes of section 70(1) *(g)*. In *Williams & Glyn's Bank Ltd v Boland* [1981] AC 487, 504, [1980] 2 All ER 408, 412 Lord Wilberforce observed that these words should be interpreted for what they are, that is to say, ordinary words of plain English. But even plain English may contain a variety of shades of meaning. At the date of completion Mrs Cann was not personally even in England, leave alone in personal occupation of the property, and the trial judge held that the acts done by Mr Abraham Cann and Mr George Cann amounted to

"no more than the taking of preparatory steps leading to the assumption of actual residential occupation on or after completion, whatever the moment of the day when completion took place . . ."

For my part, I am content to accept this as a finding of fact which was amply justified by the evidence before him, and I share the reservations expressed by Ralph Gibson and Woolf LJJ in the Court of Appeal. It is, perhaps dangerous to suggest any test for what is essentially a question of fact, for "occupation" is a concept which may have different connotations according to the nature and purpose of the property which is claimed to be occupied. It does not necessarily, I think involve the personal presence of the person claiming to occupy. A caretaker or the representative of a company can occupy, I should have thought, on behalf of his employer. On the other hand, it does, in my judgment, involve some degree of permanence and continuity which would rule out mere fleeting presence. A prospective tenant or purchaser who is allowed, as a matter of indulgence, to go into property in order to plan decorations or measure for furnishings would not, in ordinary parlance, be said to be occupying it, even though he might be there for hours at a time. Of course, in the instant case, there was, no doubt, on the part of the persons involved in moving Mrs Cann's belongings, an intention that they would remain there and would render the premises suitable for her ultimate use as a residential occupier. Like the trial judge, however, I am unable to accept that acts of this preparatory character carried out by courtesy of the vendor prior to completion can constitute "actual occupation" for the purposes of section 70(1) *(g)*. Accordingly, all other considerations apart, Mrs Cann fails, in my judgment, to establish the necessary condition for the assertion of an overriding interest.'

(d)   Effect of Absence

1. ON ACQUISITION OF OVERRIDING INTEREST

In **Kingsnorth Finance Co Ltd v Tizard** [1986] 1 WLR 783, [1986] 2 All ER 54,[14] Mr and Mrs Tizard lived at Willowdown, Lechlade, Gloucestershire. The unregistered title was in the sole name of the husband, who held it on trust for sale for himself and his wife. In 1982 the marriage broke down, and the wife moved into the spare bedroom. She began to spend some nights at her sister's house, but returned to sleep at Willowdown, especially during the frequent absences of the husband on business. She still kept her clothes in cupboards in their bedroom, and frequently returned to the house in the mornings to look after their twin children and to prepare herself for work.

In March 1983, the husband negotiated a loan with the plaintiffs, describing himself on the application form as single. A surveyor, acting as agent for the plaintiffs, visited the house and saw only the husband, who told him that he was married, but that his wife had left him some months ago to live with someone nearby. No further enquiries were made, and on the basis of the surveyor's report, the plaintiffs granted a mortgage. The husband emigrated and they claimed possession of the house.

In rejecting the claim, Judge John Finlay QC held that the surveyor had constructive notice of the wife's equitable interest, and that this notice was imputed to the plaintiffs. He considered the position if it were a case of registered land, and said at 788, at 59:

'Mrs Tizard was, in my judgment, in occupation of Willowdown notwithstanding that Mr Tizard was living there also; and notwithstanding the fact that on numerous occasions she slept elsewhere. "The physical presence" to which Lord Wilberforce refers[15] does not connote continuous and uninterrupted presence; such a notion would be absurd. Nor, indeed, do I consider that the requisite "presence" is negatived by regular and repeated absence. I find that Mrs Tizard was in Willowdown virtually every day for some part of the day; that her life and activities were based on her presence, interrupted though it was, in Willowdown; there she prepared herself for work; there she cared for her children; she went in the morning and returned in the evening to discharge her duties as housewife and mother. It is clear that prior to the time, November 1982, when she ceased always to sleep in the house when her husband was there, she had been in occupation; and, in my judgment she did not cease to be in occupation simply because she made that change in her habits, significant though the change was.

Willowdown, however, is not registered land. If it were, my findings that Mrs Tizard had equitable rights in the house and was at the material time in occupation would protect those rights against the mortgagee by reason of section 70(1)(g) of the Land Registration Act 1925.'

---

[14]   [1987] CLJ 28 (P.G. McHugh); [1986] Conv 283 (M.P. Thompson); p. 29, n. 7, ante.
[15]   *Williams & Glyn's Bank Ltd v Boland* [1981] AC 487 at 505–506, [1980] 2 All ER 408 at 412–413.

In **Chhokar v Chhokar** [1984] FLR 313, [1984] Fam Law 269, a husband and wife purchased the registered freehold of 5 Lady Margaret Road, Southall, as a matrimonial home in 1977. Both contributed to the purchase price and upkeep of the house which was registered in the name of the husband only. In 1978 the husband and wife went to India, where the husband deserted his wife and returned home. She followed him a few weeks later, being seven months' pregnant. In December the husband, without the knowledge of his wife, arranged to sell the house to a Mr Parmar at a price well below market value. As CUMMING-BRUCE LJ said in the Court of Appeal 'there was an obvious similarity between this discussion and a discussion that might take place in similar circumstances in relation to property which was asserted to have fallen off the back of a lorry'. EWBANK J said at 317:

'On 19 February 1979, the date of completion, the husband made special arrangements to have the net proceeds of sale in cash in his hands. He paid his debts and then set off for India. That was the last the wife saw of him for some 2 years. The wife and the baby were discharged from hospital on 22 February. They went home. They found the locks had been changed and so they went to spend the night with an aunt with whom the elder child had been staying while the wife was in hospital. On the following day, 23 February, the wife went home. Mr Parmar, who had bought the house, ejected her. On 1 March 1979 Mr Parmar registered the conveyance to him at the Land Registry.[16] The wife on that date was not in the house because he had put her out, but some of her furniture was there. I have to consider whether she was in actual occupation on the day of the registration of the conveyance. I have no difficulty in deciding that she was in actual occupation. Her interest, accordingly, in the house is an overriding interest and Mr Parmar, in my judgment, took the conveyance of the house into his name subject to her overriding interest. He accordingly has held the house since then, subject to a half share belonging to the wife.'[17]

2. ON LOSS OF OVERRIDING INTEREST

In **London and Cheshire Insurance Co Ltd v Laplagrene Property Co Ltd** [1971] Ch 499, [1971] 1 All ER 766 the unpaid vendors of registered land,[18] who remained in occupation under a leaseback by the purchasers, were held to have an overriding interest under section 70(1)(g). This entitled the vendors to enforce their lien against chargees of the purchaser, even though they had gone out of occupation subsequent to the purchase. BRIGHTMAN J said at 505 at 771:

'I can see nothing in section 20, read with section 70, which causes a paragraph (g) overriding interest, subject to which a disposition was made, to be extinguished merely because the owner of the right ceases occupation after that disposition but before there has been any other material dealing with the land.

---

[16] The relevant date is now that of completion: *Abbey National Building Society v Cann* [1991] 1 AC 56, [1990] 1 All ER 1085, p. 143, ante.

[17] This part of the judgment was not challenged in the Court of Appeal, where Mr Parmar's application for sale under LPA 1925, s. 30 and for rent failed. 'Is there any room for crocodile tears because his unlawful enterprise did not succeed? I can see no room for giving him anything more than the court in an unreported case gave to the moneylender who had rights over a debtor. The proceedings are recorded in a play of Shakespeare.' The story had a happy ending: Mr and Mrs Chhokar were reconciled, and Mr Parmar was left owning a house which he could neither occupy nor sell and from which he could get no rent.

[18] (1971) 35 Conv (NS) 188 (F.R. Crane). On conveyancing liens generally, see [1997] Conv 336 (D. G. Barnsley), especially pp. 344–345.

The extinction of the overriding interest in such a case, for the fortuitous benefit of the proprietor of the land, seems to me both unsupported by the wording of the Act and an unreasonable result. A right exists as an overriding interest for the very good reason that the owner of the right is in occupation of the land, ought to have been asked to define his rights by the intending transferee or grantee, but is ignored and has no inquiry made of him. In such circumstances, it is reasonable to provide that the transferee or grantee takes subject to the right as an overriding interest. The transferee or grantee has no one but himself to blame for that result. If the overriding interest were extinguished when the owner of the right went out of occupation, that would be a windfall for the transferee or grantee. He would be freed from a burden for no good reason that I can discern.'[19]

B. Land Registration Act 2002[20]

The 2002 Act substantially changes the law on overriding interests in pursuance of its policy of creating as complete a register of land as possible. It reduces the number and extent of the interests. It does this by abolishing some of them, by phasing out others after ten years, and by reducing the extent of some of those that remain.

The Act provides for the continued existence of 14 categories of overriding interests; phases out five of these after ten years; and adds a new one — the Public-Private Partnership (PPP) lease for the London Underground Railway system. In three of the categories which remain (short leases, legal easements and profits à prendre, and the interests of persons in actual occupation), the requirements for the overriding interest are different and depend on whether it is a case of first registration (Schedule 1) or a case of subsequent registered disposition (Schedule 3). This division is new.

There are transitional provisions which preserve any overriding interests acquired under the 1925 Act;[1] and, in particular, the cases on 'rights in reference to land' and on 'actual occupation' in the 1925 Act are relevant to the interpretation of their equivalents in the 2002 Act.

i.   UNREGISTERED INTERESTS WHICH OVERRIDE FIRST REGISTRATION

When a person becomes the proprietor of registered land on first registration, he takes the estate subject to those overriding interests which are set out in Schedule 1 to the 2002 Act. Important changes from the 1925 Act arise in three cases:

(a) *Short leases for a term not exceeding seven years from the date of the grant (paragraph 1 of Schedules 1 and 3).* This is a reduction from 21 years under the 1925 Act (section 70(1)(k)). A notice of such a lease should be entered on the register of the title out of which it has been granted. There are exceptions which are not

---

[19]   For the protection of a lien by registration of a caution, see *Woolf Project Management Ltd v Woodtrek Ltd* (1987) 56 P & CR 134.
[20]   R & R, chaps. 10, 17 (prescription and abandonment); H & B, paras. 2.46–2.52, 3.92–3.109; Law Commission Report on Land Registration for the Twenty-First Century 2001 (Law Com No. 271), Part VIII.
[1]   For transitional provisions to preserve former overriding interests, see LRA 2002, Sch. 12, paras. 7–13. For reduction in unregistered interests with automatic protection, see s. 117.

overriding interests even if they are for seven years or less (LRA 2002, section 4(1)(d)-(f), p. 113 ante). These must be registered with their own individual titles.

(b)   Interests of persons in actual occupation (paragraph 2). There are three major changes from the equivalent interests in section 70(1)(g) of the 1925 Act. First, persons who are in receipt of the rent and profits of the land are no longer capable of having overriding interests. Secondly, the decision in *Ferrishurst Ltd v Wallcite Ltd* [1999] Ch 355, p 131, n. 12, ante, is reversed, so that if a person is in actual occupation of part of the land, he no longer has an overriding interest over the whole of that land. Thirdly, the exclusion of the rights of a beneficiary under the Settled Land Act 1925 is confirmed.[2] And, fourthly, the qualification in section 70(1)(g) 'save where enquiry is made of such person and the rights are not disclosed' is left out.

(c)   Legal easements and profits a prendre (paragraph 3). Section 70(1)(a) of the Land Registration Act 1925 is replaced. The effect of *Celsteel Ltd v Alton House Holdings Ltd* [1987] 1 WLR 291, [1987] 2 All ER 240, p. 148, ante, is reversed and so equitable easements and profits a prendre can no longer be overriding interests. There may be fewer legal easements and profits a prendre under paragraph 3, because of the duty of disclosure under section 71, p. 161, post.

There are no changes in paragraphs 4 to 9. The remaining miscellaneous interests in paragraphs 10 to 14 are to be phased out over ten years from the date when the Act came into force (13 October 2002). Section 117 permits those with the benefit of those rights to protect them on the register during the ten years without payment of fees; by a caution against first registration in the case of unregistered land, or by a notice in the case of registered land.

LAND REGISTRATION ACT 2002

SCHEDULE 1

UNREGISTERED INTERESTS WHICH OVERRIDE FIRST REGISTRATION

Leasehold estates in land
1   A leasehold estate in land granted for a term not exceeding seven years from the date of the grant, except for a lease the grant of which falls within section 4(1)(d), (e) or (f).

Interests of persons in actual occupation
2   An interest belonging to a person in actual occupation, so far as relating to land of which he is in actual occupation, except for an interest under a settlement under the Settled Land Act 1925.

Easements and profits a prendre
3   A legal easement or profit a prendre.

Customary and public rights
4   A customary right.
5   A public right.

Local land charges
6   A local land charge.

---

[2]   In spite of the recommendations of the Law Commission Consultative Document on Land Registration for the Twenty-First Century (Law Com No. 254), para. 5.63.

Mines and minerals
7   An interest in any coal or coal mine, the rights attached to any such interest
and the rights of any person under section 38, 49 or 51 of the Coal Industry
Act 1994.
8   In the case of land to which title was registered before 1898, rights to mines
and minerals (and incidental rights) created before 1898.
9   In the case of land to which title was registered between 1898 and 1925
inclusive, rights to mines and minerals (and incidental rights) created before
the date of registration of the title.

Miscellaneous
10   A franchise.
11   A manorial right.
12   A right to rent which was reserved to the Crown on the granting of any freehold
estate (whether or not the right is still vested in the Crown).
13   A non-statutory right in respect of an embankment or sea or river wall.
14   A right to payment in lieu of tithe.

II.   UNREGISTERED INTERESTS WHICH OVERRIDE REGISTERED DISPOSITIONS

There are 15 interests which override registered dispositions. They are set out
in Schedule 3; and a further interest is added by section 90 (PPP leases relating
to transport in London).

Of the 15 interests which are overriding interests on first registration under
Schedule 1, 12 are identical with those in Schedule 3. There are, however,
important changes in the other three:

(a)   Short leases (paragraph 1).

The three categories in Schedule 1 in which leases granted for a term not
exceeding seven years are not overriding interests on first registration also apply
in Schedule 3. To these are added five further exceptions in respect of
dispositions which are granted out of a registered estate; they cannot be overriding
interests because they are registrable in their own right; they are specified in
section 27 (p. 122, ante).

(b)   Interests of person in actual occupation (paragraph 2).

In this paragraph there is a new and very important replacement of section
70(1)(g) of the 1925 Act, which attempts to provide a fairer balance between the
interests of a person in actual occupation and that of a purchaser for valuable
consideration. The interest is not overriding if it (i) belongs to a person whose
occupation would not have been obvious on a reasonably careful inspection of
the land at the time of the disposition, and (ii) of which the person to whom the
disposition is made does not have actual knowledge at that time.   The Law
Commission in its Report,[3] makes three important points:
    '(1)   For the purposes of the Bill, it is not the *interest* that has to be apparent
            (as is the case in relation to contracts for the sale of land), but the
            occupation of the person having the interest.
    (2)   The test is not one of constructive notice of the occupation. It is the less
            demanding one (derived from the test applicable to intending buyers

---

[3]   Report on Land Registration for the Twenty-First Century 2001 (Law Com No. 271),
para. 8.62.

of land) that it should be obvious on a reasonably careful inspection of the land.[4]

(3) Even if a person's occupation is not apparent, the exception does not apply where a buyer has actual knowledge of that occupation.

The object of this exception is, therefore, to protect buyers and other registered disponees for valuable consideration in cases where the fact of occupation is neither subjectively known to them nor readily ascertainable. Once an intending buyer becomes aware of the occupation, he or she should make inquiry of the occupier because of the second exception mentioned above."

(c) Legal easements and profits a prendre (paragraph 3).

Far-reaching changes are made under Schedule 3 to the scope of overriding interests in relation to easements and profits a prendre. No such rights which are expressly created or reserved out of registered land[5] can take effect as overriding interests; and no equitable easements or profits, however created, are capable of overriding a registered disposition.[6] The only legal easements and profits which will be capable of being overriding interests are:

(i)   those already in existence at the time the 2002 Act came into force which have not been registered;

(ii) those arising by implied grant or reservation; and

(iii) those arising by prescription.

There is a further curtailment of the category. Legal easements and profits a prendre which are not easily discoverable cannot be overriding interests. The effect of paragraph 3 is that a purchaser of an interest for valuable consideration under a registered disposition is only bound by an easement or profit a prendre which is an overriding interest if:

(i)   he actually knows of it; or

(ii) if it would have been obvious on a reasonably careful inspection of the land over which the easement or profit a prendre is exercisable, so that the vendor of land would be obliged to disclose it; or

(iii) it has been exercised within one year before the disposition.

This is intended to cover the numerous invisible easements such as rights of drainage or the right to run a water supply over a neighbour's land.

There is a significant transitional provision. A period of grace is given for any legal easement or profit a prendre which has not been registered for three years after the Act came into force.

In effect, this protects those interests which arise during the period by prescription or by implied grant or reservation. Those created by express grant or by reservation do not qualify: they are only equitable rights unless and until they are registered.

---

[4]   See M & W, para. 12.068; Law Com No. 25, para. 5.72. Cf. the view of Wolstenholme and Cherry, *Annotated Land Registration Act 2002*, para 3.173: 'Not only does the asserted distinction from constructive notice seem elusive, but the assented derivation of the test is suspect': *Emmet on Title*, para. 5.130.

[5]   See p. 717, post, for the express or implied creation of easements and profits a prendre.

[6]   See R & R, para. 17.027.

LAND REGISTRATION ACT 2002

SCHEDULE 3

UNREGISTERED INTERESTS WHICH OVERRIDE REGISTERED DISPOSITIONS

Leasehold estates in land
1   A leasehold estate in land granted for a term not exceeding seven years from the date of the grant, except for —
   (a) a lease the grant of which falls within section 4(1)(d), (e) or (f);
   (b) a lease the grant of which constitutes a registrable disposition.

Interests of persons in actual occupation
2   An interest belonging at the time of the disposition to a person in actual occupation, so far as relating to land of which he is in actual occupation, except for —
   (a) an interest under a settlement under the Settled Land Act 1925;
   (b) an interest of a person of whom inquiry was made before the disposition and who failed to disclose the right when he could reasonably have been expected to do so;
   (c) an interest —
      (i) which belongs to a person whose occupation would not have been obvious on a reasonably careful inspection of the land at the time of the disposition, and
      (ii) of which the person to whom the disposition is made does not have actual knowledge at that time;
   (d) a leasehold estate in land granted to take effect in possession after the end of the period of three months beginning with the date of the grant and which has not taken effect in possession at the time of the disposition.

Easements and profits a prendre
3 (1)   A legal easement or profit a prendre, except for an easement, or a profit a prendre which is not registered under the Commons Registration Act 1965, which at the time of the disposition —
      (a) is not within the actual knowledge of the person to whom the disposition is made, and
      (b) would not have been obvious on a reasonably careful inspection of the land over which the easement or profit is exercisable.
   (2)   The exception in sub-paragraph (1) does not apply if the person entitled to the easement or profit proves that it has been exercised in the period of one year ending with the day of the disposition.

Customary and public rights
4   A customary right.
5   A public right.

Local land charges
6   A local land charge.

Mines and minerals
7   An interest in any coal or coal mine, the rights attached to any such interest and the rights of any person under section 38, 49 or 51 of the Coal Industry Act 1994.
8   In the case of land to which title was registered before 1898, rights to mines and minerals (and incidental rights) created before 1898.
9   In the case of land to which title was registered between 1898 and 1925 inclusive, rights to mines and minerals (and incidental rights) created before the date of registration of the title.

Miscellaneous

10 A franchise.

11 A manorial right.

12 A right to rent which was reserved to the Crown on the granting of any freehold estate (whether or not the right is still vested in the Crown).

13 A non-statutory right in respect of an embankment or sea or river wall.

14 A right to payment in lieu of tithe.

iii. ABOLITION OF CERTAIN OVERRIDING INTERESTS

Three categories of overriding interests are abolished: rights acquired or in course of being acquired under the Limitation Acts (LRA 1925, section 70(1) (*f*); a new scheme of adverse possession is introduced by the 2002 Act (p. 252, post). And, secondly, 'in the case of a possessory qualified or good leasehold title, all rights interests and powers excepted from the effect of registration' (section 70(1) (*f*)). The third category abolished, 'liability to repair the chancel of any church' (section 70(1) (*c*)), was reinstated in the light of the reversal of *Aston Cantlow Parochial Church Council v Wallbank* by the House of Lords.[7]

iv. DUTY TO DISCLOSE

There is a new duty of disclosure in an application for registration to provide information about overriding interests under both Schedules 1 and 3. Although there is no specific penalty for failure to do so, the object of section 71 of the Act is to ensure that as many rights as possible are brought onto the register.

––––––––––

LAND REGISTRATION ACT 2002

71 Duty to disclose unregistered interests

Where rules so provide[8]—

(a) A person applying for registration under Chapter 1 of Part 2 must provide to the registrar such information as the rules may provide about any interest affecting the estate to which the application relates which—

(i) falls within any of the paragraphs of Schedule 1, and

(ii) is of a description specified by the rules.

(b) a person applying to register a registrable disposition of a registered estate must provide to the registrar such information as the rules may provide about any unregistered interest affecting the estate which—

(i) falls within any of the paragraphs of Schedule 3, and

(ii) is of description specified by the rules.

v. SUMMARY

Abbey and Richards, *The Land Registration Act 2002*, para 12.6

'After ten years, the following overriding interests will remain:

7   [2003] 3 WLR 283, [2003] 3 All ER 1213; Land Registration Act 2002 (Transitional Provisions) (No. 2) Order 2003 (SI 2003 No. 2431).

8   LRR 2003, rr. 28, 57. Cf. the proviso to LRA 1925, s. 70(1) (*g*); R & R, para. 17.028.

- most leases granted for three years or less;[9]
- the interests of person in actual occupation where that actual occupation is apparent and the interest is either a beneficial interest under a trust or arose informally (for example an equity arising by estoppel);
- legal easements and profits a prendre that have arisen by implied grant or reservation or by prescription;
- customary and public rights;
- local land charges;
- certain mineral rights; and
- liability to repair the chancel of any church.'

QUESTIONS

1. (a) How far is notice of actual occupation relevant in interpreting section 70(1)(g) of the Land Registration Act 1925?
      Compare *Williams v Glyn's Bank Ltd v Boland* [1981] AC 487 at 503, [1980] 2 All ER 408 at 412 per Lord WILBERFORCE; *Hodgson v Marks* [1971] Ch 892 with *Lloyds Bank plc v Rosset* [1989] Ch 350 at 397, [1988] 3 All ER 915 at 949 per MUSTILL LJ; at 404, at 946, per PURCHAS LJ; *Abbey National Building Society v Cann* [1989] 2 FLR 265 at 278, per RALPH GIBSON LJ; at 278, per WOLFF LJ; *Malory Enterprises Ltd v Cheshire Homes (UK) Ltd* [2002] Ch 216 at para 81, per ARDEN LJ; *Emmet on Title*, para. 5.127.
   (b) How far is notice or actual knowledge relevant in the Land Registration Act 2002? See Law Commission Report on Land Registration for the Twenty-First Century (2000) (Law Com No. 274), paras. 5.16–5.27; H & B para. 3.38; *Emmet on Title*, para. 5.142. In particular, consider Sch. 3, para. 2(c) (interests of persons in actual occupation) p. 163, ante; and the effect of *Lyas v Prowsa Developments Ltd* [1982] 1 WLR 1044, [1982] 2 All ER 953 and *Peffer v Rigg* [1977] 1 WLR 285, [1977] 3 All ER 745, p. 176, post.
2. You are advising the mortgagee bank in a *Boland* situation.
   (a) How would you set about discovering whether there is a 'person in actual occupation'? And when would you inspect the property? Hayton, pp. 88–91. See the criticisms of VINELOTT J in *Kling v Keston Properties Ltd* (1983) 49 P & CR 212 at 221–222.
   (b) You discover an actual occupant who discloses to you a beneficial interest under a trust. The mortgagee nevertheless still wishes to lend money to the registered proprietor. How would you seek to neutralise the occupant's rights?

   Consider in particular
      (i) The appointment of an additional trustee.
          Should this entitle the bank to overreach the occupant's interest? *City of London Building Society v Flegg* [1988] AC 54, [1987] 3 All ER 435; Law Commission Report on Overreaching: Beneficiaries in Occupation 1989 (Law Com No 188, HC 61); p. 316, post.
      (ii) The express release of rights by the occupant:
          Gracegrove Estates v Boateng [1997] NPC 98
          Are there any difficulties —
          (a) If the occupant is a minor?

    (b) In the construction of the release given by the occupant: *Woolwich Building Society v Dickman* [1996] 3 All ER 204; (1996) 140 SJ 1108 (M. Draper); [1997] CLJ 37 (L. Tee).

  (iii) The implied release of rights by the occupant

    (a) By estoppel: *Spiro v Lintern* [1973] 1 WLR 1002, [1973] 3 All ER 319; *Emmet on Title*, para 11.031.

    (b) By an imputed intention that his interest is subject to the rights of the purchaser: *Abbey National Building Society v Cann* [1991] 1 AC 56, [1990] 1 All ER 1085 at 94, at 1101, p. 143, ante; *Bristol and West Building Society v Henning* [1985] 1 WLR 778, [1985] 2 All ER 606; *Paddington Building Society v Mendelsohn* (1985) 50 P & CR 244; *Equity and Law Homes Loans Ltd v Prestidge* [1992] 1 WLR 137, [1992] 1 All ER 909, p. 144, n. 2, ante.

3. In 1982 Lord HAILSHAM OF ST. MARYLEBONE LC, speaking in the House of Lords (Hansard volume 437 column 663, 15 December) made the point that, if the bank in *Boland* had made Mr Boland bankrupt, it could then have forced a sale of the property in spite of the wife's overriding interest.

  (a) Advise the bank on the possible success of this course of action: TLATA 1996, ss. 14, 15; *Re Lowrie* [1981] 3 All ER 353; *Re Citro* [1991] Ch 142, [1990] 3 All ER 952; Insolvency Act 1986, s. 335A, as added by TLATA 1996, s. 25(1), Sch. 3, para. 23; pp. 283–288, post.

  (b) What further advice would you give to the bank in the light of s. 267(1)(b) of the Insolvency Act 1986, which provides that the debt must be unsecured at the time of the presentation of the petition. If the bank wishes to make Mr Boland bankrupt, it must forego the priority afforded to him by the mortgage under s. 269.

4. You are advising the purchaser of a dwelling house. On inspection you discover on the premises the vendor and a baby in a pram. There are no other occupants. To what legal problems does the baby give rise? *Hypo-Mortgage Services Ltd v Robinson* [1997] 2 FLR 71, p. 130, n. 11, ante.

5. How would you decide the actual occupation point in the following cases, if the events took place after 12 October 2003:

  (a) *Chhokar v Chhokar* [1984] FLR 13, p. 157, ante;

  (b) *Kling v Keston Properties* (1983) 49 P & CR 212, p. 93, ante;

  (c) *Malory Enterprises Ltd v Cheshire Homes (UK) Ltd* [2002] Ch 216, p. 130, ante?

VII.   Interests which Require Protection on the Register. Minor Interests[1]

As we have seen, overriding interests do not stand in need of protection on the register, but all other interests do need entry on the register of the land affected if they are to bind purchasers for value; they were called minor interests and defined in section 3(xv) of the Land Registration Act 1925. As in unregistered

9   Assuming that the period for the registration of a lease will by then have been reduced from seven to three years.

1   C & B, pp. 107–108, 870–876; Gray, pp. 1035–1068; M & W, paras. 6.075–6.095; MM, pp. 129–134; Smith, pp. 235–241; Ruoff and Roper, chaps. 7–8, For detailed discussion of priorities of minor interests, see [1976] CLP 26 at pp. 37 et seq. (D.J. Hayton); (1977) 93 LQR 541 (R.J. Smith).

land, actual notice of the interest which should have been protected, but was not so protected, was irrelevant.[2]

A. Land Registration Act 1925

An entry on the register could be made by way of notice, restriction, caution or inhibition.[3] A notice was entered on the charges register of the land affected, and gave protection to and information about such interests as leases, agreements for leases, restrictive covenants and estate contracts.[4] Before a notice could be entered, the land certificate had to be lodged at the Registry,[5] and for this the registered proprietor's co-operation was required. But production was not necessary where the land was subject to a registered charge; in this case the land certificate would already be deposited at the Registry.[6] Nor was it necessary where a lease had been granted at a rent without taking a fine.[7] If a notice had been entered, any disposition of the land affected took effect subject to the estate or interest protected by the notice, but only if and so far as such estate or interest was valid.[8]

A restriction was an entry on the proprietorship register, which prevented dealings in registered land until certain conditions and requirements had been complied with.[9] A common example of a restriction was when it was used to ensure that a purchaser of the land complied with the rules relating to the overreaching provisions of the Settled Land Act 1925[10] and the Law of Property Act 1925,[11] thereby protecting the interests of the beneficiaries.[12]

A caution against dealings was entered on the proprietorship register, but, unlike a notice, the co-operation of the registered proprietor was unnecessary. Its effect was merely to achieve 'no dealing with the land', without notice being first served on the cautioner, so as to give him an opportunity to object.[13]

An inhibition rarely occurred, except where a bankruptcy inhibition was automatically entered by the Registrar.[14]

LAND REGISTRATION ACT 1925

3. Interpretation. —
    (xv) 'Minor interests' mean the interests not capable of being disposed of or created by registered dispositions and capable of being overridden[15]

2   P. 50, ante; LRA 1925, s. 59(6); *Hodges v Jones* [1935] Ch 657 at 671, per LUXMOORE J: *De Lusignan v Johnson* (1973) 117 SJ 854; see, however, *Peffer v Rigg* [1977] 1 WLR 285, [1978] 3 All ER 745, p. 176, ante.
3   For a chart showing the registration machinery which replaces that of LCA 1972, see Ruoff and Roper (1991 edn), para. 7.08, reproduced in the 7th edn. of this book at pp. 156–157.
4   LRA 1925, ss. 48–51, 59(2), 59(5).
5   Ibid., s. 64.
6   Ibid., s. 65.
7   Ibid., s. 64(1)(c).
8   Ibid., s 52(1), p. 167, post.
9   Ibid., s. 58(1), p. 167, post.
10   P. 310, post.
11   P. 293, post.
12   LRA 1925, s. 58; LRR 1925, r. 236.
13   Ibid., ss. 54, 55, 56, p. 168, post.
14   Ibid., s. 57; LRR 1925, r. 190.
15   See *City of London Building Society v Flegg* [1988] AC 54 at 85, [1987] All ER 435 at 464 where Lord OLIVER OF AYLMERTON says: 'Plainly here "overridden" is used as embracing interests which can be overreached under the provisions of section 2 of the Law of Property Act'.

(whether or not a purchaser has notice thereof) by the proprietors unless protected as provided by this Act, and all rights and interests which are not registered or protected on the register and are not overriding interests, and include —

   (a) in the case of land held subject to a trust of land, all interests and powers which are under the Law of Property Act, 1925, capable of being overridden by the trustees, whether or not such interests and powers are so protected;[16] and

   (b) in the case of settled land, all interests and powers which are under the Settled Land Act, 1925, and the Law of Property Act, 1925, or either of them, capable of being overridden by the tenant for life or statutory owner, whether or not such interests and powers are so protected as aforesaid.

i. NOTICES

LAND REGISTRATION ACT 1925

52. Effect of notices.—(1) A disposition by the proprietor shall take effect subject to all estates, rights, and claims which are protected by way of notice on the register at the date of the registration or entry of notice of the disposition, but only if and so far as such estates, rights, and claims may be valid[17] and are not (independently of this Act) overridden by the disposition.

(2) Where notice of a claim is entered on the register, such entry shall operate by way of notice only, and shall not operate to render the claim valid whether made adversely to or for the benefit of the registered land or charge.

LAND REGISTRATION RULES 1925

199. Entry as to trivial rights not required.—The Registrar shall not be required to enter notice of any liability, right, or interest which shall appear to him to be of a trivial or obvious character, or the entry of which on the register is likely to cause confusion or inconvenience.

ii. RESTRICTIONS

LAND REGISTRATION ACT 1925

58. Power to place restrictions on register.—(1) Where the proprietor of any registered land or charge desires to place restrictions on transferring or charging the land or on disposing of or dealing with the land or charge in any manner in which he is by this Act authorised to dispose of or deal with it, or on the deposit by way of security of any certificate, the proprietor may apply to the registrar to make an entry in the register that no transaction to which the application relates shall be effected, unless the following things, or such of them as the proprietor may determine, are done —

   (a) unless notice of any application for the transaction is transmitted by post to such address as he may specify to the registrar;

   (b) unless the consent of some person or persons, to be named by the proprietor, is given to the transaction;

---

[16] As amended by TLATA 1996, s. 25(1), Sch. 3, para. 5(2).

[17] *Cator v Newton and Bates* [1940] 1 KB 415, [1939] 4 All ER 457 (entry that freehold land is subject to positive covenant does not make covenant enforceable).

(c)   unless some such other matter or thing is done as may be required by the applicant and approved by the registrar: . . .

(2) The registrar shall thereupon, if satisfied of the right of the applicant to give the directions, enter the requisite restrictions on the register, and no transaction to which the restriction relates shall be effected except in conformity therewith; . . .

(5) Rules may be made to enable applications to be made for the entry of restrictions by persons other than the proprietor.[8]

iii. INHIBITIONS

LAND REGISTRATION ACT 1925

57. Power for court or registrar to inhibit registered dealings.—(1) . . .The registrar . . . may . . . issue an order or make an entry inhibiting for a time, or until the occurrence of an event to be named in such order or entry, or generally until further order or entry, the registration or entry of any dealing with any registered land or registered charge.

(2) The court or registrar may make or refuse to make any such order or entry, and annex thereto any terms or conditions the court or registrar may think fit, and discharge such order or cancel such entry when granted, with or without costs, and generally act in the premises in such manner as the justice of the case requires.

(4) The court or the registrar may, in lieu of an inhibition, order a notice or restriction to be placed on the register.

iv. CAUTIONS AGAINST DEALINGS

LAND REGISTRATION ACT 1925

54. Cautions against dealings.—(1) Any person interested under any unregistered instrument, or interested as a judgment creditor, or otherwise howsoever, in any land or charge registered in the name of any other person, may lodge a caution with the registrar to the effect that no dealing with such land or charge on the part of the proprietor is to be registered until notice has been served upon the cautioner.[9]

Provided that a person whose estate, right, interest, or claim has been registered or protected by a notice or restriction shall not be entitled (except with the consent of the registrar) to lodge a caution in respect of such estate, right, interest, or claim.[10]

55. Effect of cautions against dealings.—(1) After any such caution against dealings has been lodged[11] in respect of any registered land or charge, the registrar shall not, without the consent of the cautioner, register any dealing or make any entry on the register for protecting the rights acquired under a deposit of a land or charge

---

8   LRR 1925, r. 236.
9   *Re White Rose Cottage* [1965] Ch 940, [1965] 1 All ER 11 (equitable charge); *Parkash v Irani Finance Ltd* [1970] Ch 101, [1969] 1 All ER 930 (charging order); *Elias v Mitchell* [1972] Ch 652, [1972] 2 All ER 153 (equitable tenant in common under trust for sale); cf. *Myton Ltd v Schwab-Morris* [1974] 1 WLR 331, [1974] 1 All ER 326; *Lynton International Ltd v Noble* (1991) 63 P & CR 452 (contractual right to share proceeds of sale); *Clark v Chief Land Registrar* [1994] Ch 370, [1994] 4 All ER 96. On the effect of a caution, see s. 55(1); *Emmet on Title*, para. 36–04.
10   As amended by LRA 1986, s. 5(5)(a).
11   *Smith v Morrison* [1974] 1 WLR 659 at 682, [1974] 1 All ER 957 at 978.

certificate or other dealing by the proprietor with such land or charge until he has served notice on the cautioner, warning him that his caution will cease to have any effect after the expiration of the prescribed number of days next following the date at which such notice is served; and after the expiration of such time as aforesaid the caution shall cease unless an order to the contrary is made by the registrar, and upon the caution so ceasing the registered land or charge may be dealt with in the same manner as if no caution had been lodged.

B. Land Registration Act 2002[12]

This category of interests remains as a category but its name of minor interests does not appear in the Act. The scheme for their protection is reorganised. There are now only two types of entry on the register of the land affected: notices and restrictions. Cautions against dealings and inhibitions disappear, the former are subsumed under notices, and the latter under restrictions. Existing entries continue to have effect.

i.   NOTICES[13]

Under the Act notices are of two kinds: agreement notices and unilateral notices. These reflect the differences between notices and cautions against dealings under the 1925 Act. An agreement notice will be entered on the application of or with the agreement of the registered proprietor of the land affected. A unilateral notice, on the other hand, may be entered without his consent, but the registrar must inform him of the entry so that he may exercise his right to apply for its cancellation. This is more effective than the old caution; in the absence of an objection, a unilateral notice will protect the interest in the same way as an agreed notice does. The mere fact of registration of a notice does not mean that the interest is valid.[14]

   Section 33 sets out interests which cannot be protected by a notice. The most important are:
(a) beneficial interests under a trust of land or strict settlement.
(b) leases for a term of three years or less, the title to which is not required to be registered.
(c) restrictive covenants between lessor and lessee so far as relating to the demised premises.

LAND REGISTRATION ACT 2002

32   Nature and effect
   (1) A notice is an entry in the register in respect of the burden of an interest affecting a registered estate or charge.
   (2) The entry of a notice is to be made in relation to the registered estate or charge affected by the interest concerned.

----

[12]   R & R, chap. 42 (notices), 43 (cautions against dealings), 44 (restrictions),45 (the matrimonial home); H & B. paras. 3.43–3.89.
[13]   LRR 2003, Part 7.
[14]   LRA 2002, s. 32(3), infra.

(3) The fact that an interest is the subject of a notice does not necessarily mean that the interest is valid, but does mean that the priority of the interest, if valid, is protected for the purposes of sections 29 and 30.

33   Excluded interests

No notice may be entered in the register in respect of any of the following—
- (a) an interest under—
  - (i) a trust of land, or
  - (ii) a settlement under the Settled Land Act 1925[15]
- (b) a leasehold estate in land which—
  - (i) is granted for a term of years of three years or less from the date of the grant, and
  - (ii) is not required to be registered,[16]
- (c) a restrictive covenant made between a lessor and lessee, so far as relating to the demised premises,[17]
- (d) an interest which is capable of being registered under the Commons Registration Act 1965,[18] and
- (e) an interest in any coal or coal mine, the rights attached to any such interest and the rights of any person under section 38, 49 or 51 of the Coal Industry Act 1994.

34   Entry on application

(1) A person who claims to be entitled to the benefit of an interest affecting a registered estate or charge may, if the interest is not excluded by section 33, apply to the registrar for the entry in the register of a notice in respect of the interest.

(2) Subject to rules, an application under this section may be for—
- (a) an agreed notice,[1] or
- (b) a unilateral notice.

(3) The registrar may only approve an application for an agreed notice if—
- (a) the applicant is the relevant registered proprietor, or a person entitled to be registered as such proprietor.
- (b) the relevant registered proprietor, or a person entitled to be registered as such proprietor, consents to the entry of the notice, or
- (c) the registrar is satisfied as to the validity of the applicant's claim.

(4) In subsection (3), references to the relevant registered proprietor are to the proprietor of the registered estate or charge affected by the interest to which the application relates.

35   Unilateral notices

(1) If the registrar enters a notice in the register in pursuance of an application under section 34(2)(b) ("a unilateral notice"[2]), he must give notice of the entry to—
- (a) the proprietor of the registered estate or charge to which it relates, and
- (b) such other persons as rules may provide.

(2) A unilateral notice must—

---

[15]   P. 352, post.
[16]   P. 506, post.
[17]   P. 941, n. 13, post.
[18]   P. 60, ante.
[1]   LRR 2003, r. 81.
[2]   Ibid., r. 83.

(a) indicate that it is such a notice, and

(b) identify who is the beneficiary of the notice.

(3) The person shown in the register as the beneficiary of a unilateral notice, or such other person as rules may provide, may apply to the registrar for the removal of the notice from the register.

36   Cancellation of unilateral notices[3]

(1) A person may apply to the registrar for the cancellation of a unilateral notice if he is—

(a) the registered proprietor of the estate or charge to which the notice relates, or

(b) a person entitled to be registered as the proprietor of that estate or charge.

(2) Where an application is made under subsection (1), the registrar must give the beneficiary of the notice notice of the application and of the effect of subsection (3).

(3) If the beneficiary of the notice does not exercise his right to object to the application before the end of such period as rules may provide, the registrar must cancel the notice.

(4) In this section—

'beneficiary', in relation to a unilateral notice, means the person shown in the register as the beneficiary of the notice, or such other person as rules may provide;

'unilateral notice' means a notice entered in the register in pursuance of an application under section 34(2)(b).

37   Unregistered interests

(1) If it appears to the registrar that a registered estate is subject to an unregistered interest which—

(a) falls within any of the paragraphs of Schedule 1,[4] and

(b) is not excluded by section 33,

he may enter a notice in the register in respect of the interest.

(2) The registrar must give notice of an entry under this section to such persons as rules may provide.

38   Registrable dispositions

Where a person is entered in the register as the proprietor of an interest under a disposition falling within section 27(2)(b) to (e), the registrar must also enter a notice in the register in respect of that interest.[5]

39   Supplementary

Rules may make provision about the form and content of notices in the register.

LAND REGISTRATION RULES 2003

Certain interests to be protected by agreed notices

80. A person who applies for the entry of a notice in the register must apply for the entry of an agreed notice where the application is for—

(a) a matrimonial home rights notice,[6]

(b) an inheritance tax notice,

---

[3]   Ibid., r. 86.

[4]   An unregistered interest which overrides first registration; p. 158, ante.

[5]   The object is to provide for a cross-entry.

[6]   P. 312, post.

    (c) a notice in respect of an order under the Access to Neighbouring Land Act 1992,[7]

    (d) a notice of any variation of a lease effected by or under an order under section 38 of the Landlord and Tenant Act 1987 (including any variation as modified by an order under section 39(4) of that Act),

    (e) a notice in respect of a—

        (i) public right, or

        (ii) customary right.

Entry of a notice in the register

    84.—(1) A notice under section 32 of the Act must be entered in the charges register of the registered title affected.

ii. RESTRICTIONS

These are similar to restrictions under the 1925 Act.[8] They cannot be used to protect interests which are capable of being protected by a notice.

LAND REGISTRATION ACT 2002

40 Nature

    (1) A restriction is an entry in the register regulating the circumstances in which a disposition of a registered estate or charge may be the subject of an entry in the register.

    (2) A restriction may, in particular—

    (a) prohibit the making of an entry in respect of any disposition, or a disposition of a kind specified in the restriction;

    (b) prohibit the making of an entry—

        (i) indefinitely,

        (ii) for a period specified in the restriction, or

        (iii) until the occurrence of an event so specified.

    (3) Without prejudice to the generality of subsection (2)(b)(iii), the events which may be specified include—

    (a) the giving of notice,

    (b) the obtaining of consent, and

    (c) the making of an order by the court or registrar.

    (4) The entry of a restriction is to be made in relation to the registered estate or charge to which it relates.

41 Effect

    (1) Where a restriction is entered in the register, no entry in respect of a disposition to which the restriction applies may be made in the register otherwise than in accordance with the terms of the restriction, subject to any order under subsection (2).

    (2) The registrar may by order—

    (a) disapply a restriction in relation to a disposition specified in the order or dispositions of a kind so specified, or

    (b) provide that a restriction has effect, in relation to a disposition specified in the order or dispositions of a kind so specified, with modifications so specified.[9]

---

[7]   P. 713, post.

[8]   LRR 2003, Part 8, and Sch. 4 (Standard Forms of Restriction).

[9]   LRR 2003, r. 96.

(3) The power under subsection (2) is exercisable only on the application of a person who appears to the registrar to have a sufficient interest in the restriction.

42 Power of registrar to enter

(1) The registrar may enter a restriction in the register if it appears to him that it is necessary or desirable to do so for the purpose of—

    (a) preventing invalidity or unlawfulness in relation to dispositions of a registered estate or charge,

    (b) securing that interests which are capable of being overreached on a disposition of a registered estate or charge are overreached, or

    (c) protecting a right or claim in relation to a registered estate or charge.

(2) No restriction may be entered under subsection (1)(c) for the purpose of protecting the priority of an interest which is, or could be, the subject of a notice.

(3) The registrar must give notice of any entry made under this section to the proprietor of the registered estate or charge concerned, except where the entry is made in pursuance of an application under section 43.

(4) For the purposes of subsection (1)(c), a person entitled to the benefit of a charging order relating to an interest under a trust shall be treated as having a right or claim in relation to the trust property.

43 Applications

(1) A person may apply to the registrar for the entry of a restriction under section 42(1) if—

    (a) he is the relevant registered proprietor, or a person entitled to be registered as such proprietor,

    (b) the relevant registered proprietor, or a person entitled to be registered as such proprietor, consents to the application, or

    (c) he otherwise has a sufficient interest in the making of the entry.[10]

(2) Rules may—

    (a) require the making of an application under subsection (1) in such circumstances, and by such person, as the rules may provide;

    (b) make provision about the form of consent for the purposes of subsection (1)(b);

    (c) provide for classes of person to be regarded as included in subsection (1)(c);

    (d) specify standard forms of restriction.

(3) If an application under subsection (1) is made for the entry of a restriction which is not in a form specified under subsection (2)(d), the registrar may only approve the application if it appears to him—

    (a) that the terms of the proposed restriction are reasonable, and

    (b) that applying the proposed restriction would—

        (i) be straightforward, and

        (ii) not place an unreasonable burden on him.

(4) In subsection (1), references to the relevant registered proprietor are to the proprietor of the registered estate or charge to which the application relates.

44 Obligatory restrictions

(1) If the registrar enters two or more persons in the register as the proprietor of a registered estate in land, he must also enter in the register such restrictions

---

[10] LRR 2003, rr. 93, 94, p. 175, post.

as rules may provide for the purpose of securing that interests which are capable of being overreached on a disposition of the estate are overreached.

(2) Where under any enactment the registrar is required to enter a restriction without application, the form of the restriction shall be such as rules may provide.[11]

45 Notifiable applications

(1) Where an application under section 43(1) is notifiable, the registrar must give notice of the application, and of the right to object to it, to—

(a)   the proprietor of the registered estate or charge to which it relates, and

(b)   such other persons as rules may provide.

(2) The registrar may not determine an application to which subsection (1) applies before the end of such period as rules may provide,[12] unless the person, or each of the persons, notified under that subsection has exercised his right to object to the application or given the registrar notice that he does not intend to do so.

(3) For the purposes of this section, an application under section 43(1) is notifiable unless it is—

(a)   made by or with the consent of the proprietor of the registered estate or charge to which the application relates, or a person entitled to be registered as such proprietor,

(b)   made in pursuance of rules under section 43(2)(a), or

(c)   an application for the entry of a restriction reflecting a limitation under an order of the court or registrar, or an undertaking given in place of such an order.

46 Power of court to order entry

(1) If it appears to the court that it is necessary or desirable to do so for the purpose of protecting a right or claim in relation to a registered estate or charge, it may make an order requiring the registrar to enter a restriction in the register.

(2) No order under this section may be made for the purpose of protecting the priority of an interest which is, or could be, the subject of a notice.

(3) The court may include in an order under this section a direction that an entry made in pursuance of the order is to have overriding priority.

(4) If an order under this section includes a direction under subsection (3), the registrar must make such entry in the register as rules may provide.[13]

(5) The court may make the exercise of its power under subsection (3) subject to such terms and conditions as it thinks fit.

47 Withdrawal

A person may apply to the registrar for the withdrawal of a restriction if—

(a)   the restriction was entered in such circumstances as rules may provide, and

(b)   he is of such a description as rules may provide.[14]

LAND REGISTRATION RULES 2003

Persons regarded as having a sufficient interest to apply for a restriction

93. The following persons are to be regarded as included in section 43(1)(c) of the Act—

---

11   Ibid., r. 95.
12   Ibid., r. 92.
13   LRR 2003, r. 100.
14   Ibid., r. 98.

(a) any person who has an interest in a registered estate held under a trust of land where a sole proprietor or a survivor of joint proprietors (unless a trust corporation) will not be able to give a valid receipt for capital money, and who is applying for a restriction in Form A to be entered in the register of that registered estate,

(b) any person who has a sufficient interest in preventing a contravention of section 6(6) or section 6(8) of the Trusts of Land and Appointment of Trustees Act 1996[15] and who is applying for a restriction in order to prevent such a contravention,

(c) any person who has an interest in a registered estate held under a trust of land where the powers of the trustees are limited by section 8 of the Trusts of Land and Appointment of Trustees Act 1996, and who is applying for a restriction in Form B to be entered in the register of that registered estate,

(d) any person who has an interest in the due administration of the estate of a deceased person, where—
  (i) the personal representatives of the deceased hold a registered estate on a trust of land created by the deceased's will and the personal representatives' powers are limited by section 8 of the Trusts of Land and Appointment of Trustees Act 1996, and
  (ii) he is applying for a restriction in Form C to be entered in the register of that registered estate,

(e) the donee of a special power of appointment in relation to registered land affected by that power,

(f) the Charity Commissioners in relation to registered land held upon charitable trusts ...

iii. ANTI-ABUSE PROVISION

A person who fails to exercise reasonable care when applying for the entry of a notice or a restriction may be liable in damages to anyone who suffers damage thereby. Section 77(2) creates a statutory tort. The object is to dissuade anyone from using the procedure as tactics in neighbour or business disputes.

LAND REGISTRATION ACT 2002

77 Duty to act reasonably

(1) A person must not exercise any of the following rights without reasonable cause—

(a) the right to lodge a caution under section 15,[16]

(b) the right to apply for the entry of a notice or restriction,[17] and

(c) the right to object to an application to the registrar.

(2) The duty under this section is owed to any person who suffers damage in consequence of its breach.

---

15 P. 273, post.
16 P. 119, ante.
17 Pp. 169, 172, ante.

VIII. Registered Land and Constructive Trusts

The constructive trust has been used in two cases at first instance to avoid the consequences of the failure to register a right as a minor interest under the Land Registration Act 1925.[18]

A. Purchaser with Notice

In **Peffer v Rigg** [1977] 1 WLR 285, [1978] 3 All ER 745,[19] a purchaser with notice of an interest under a trust for sale was held to take subject to it, applying general equitable principles. By section 20(1) of the Land Registration Act 1925, a transferee for valuable consideration takes free from unprotected minor interests. GRAHAM J held that the requirement of good faith could be read into this provision, so that a transferee with notice of the minor interest could not rely on it; but that the same result could be achieved by the device of a constructive trust. He said at 294, at 752:

'On the evidence in this case I have found that the second defendant knew quite well that the first defendant held the property on trust for himself and the plaintiff in equal shares. The second defendant knew this was so and that the property was trust property when the transfer was made to her, and therefore she took the property on a constructive trust in accordance with general equitable principles: see *Snell's Principles of Equity* 27th edn. (1973), pp. 98–99. This is a new trust imposed by equity and is distinct from the trust which bound the first defendant. Even if, therefore, I am wrong as to the proper construction of sections 20 and 59, when read together, and even if section 20 strikes off the shackles of the express trust which bound the first defendant, this cannot invalidate the new trust imposed on the second defendant.'

In **Williams & Glyn's Bank Ltd v Boland** [1981] AC 487 at 504, [1980] 2 All ER 408 at 412, the House of Lords confirmed that the doctrine of notice has no relevance to registered land. As Lord WILBERFORCE said: 'The only kind of notice recognised is by entry on the register.'[20]

B. A Statute Cannot be Used as an Instrument of Fraud

In **Lyus v Prowsa Developments Ltd** [1982] 1 WLR 1044, [1982] 2 All ER 953, a development company was the registered proprietor of St Martin's Green Estate, Trimley, Suffolk. In 1978 it mortgaged the estate to the bank, and in 1979 contracted to build a house on Plot 29 and sell it to the plaintiffs. It then went insolvent, leaving the house unfinished. The bank, although not subject to the plaintiffs' contract, sold Plot 29 as mortgagees to Prowsa Developments Ltd (the first defendants) 'subject to and with the benefit of' the plaintiffs' contract. Prowsa

---

[18]   On resulting trusts and registered land, see [1995] Conv 383 (D. Wilde).
[19]   (1977) 41 Conv (NS) 207 (F.R. Crane); 93 LQR 341 (R.J. Smith); [1977] CLJ 227 (D. Hayton); (1977) 40 MLR 602 (S. Anderson); [1978] Conv 52 (J. Martin). See also *Orakpo v Manson Investments Ltd* [1977] 1 WLR 347 at 360; [1977] 1 All ER 666 at 678, 687; (1978) 94 LQR 239 (D.C. Jackson).
[20]   P. 136, ante. *Peffer v Rigg* was not cited.

Developments Ltd then contracted to re-sell Plot 29 to the second defendants, subject to the plaintiffs' contract of 1978 'so far, if at all, as it may be enforceable against' Prowsa Developments Ltd. The second defendants were registered as proprietors after a transfer which did not mention the contract of 1978.

The plaintiffs claimed for a declaration that the 1978 contract was binding on Prowsa Developments Ltd and on the second defendants, and for an order for specific performance.

DILLON J held that the defendants were bound by a constructive trust on the ground that the Land Registration Act was not to be used as an instrument of fraud. Having applied *Bannister v Bannister* [1948] 2 All ER 133 and a dictum of Lord DENNING MR in *Binions v Evans* [1972] Ch 359 at 368, [1972] 2 All ER 70 at 76, p. 617, post, his Lordship said at 1054, at 962:

'This does not, however, conclude the matter since I also have to consider the effect of the provisions of the Land Registration Act 1925, plot 29 having at all material times, as I have mentioned, been registered land. In the course of the argument, emphasis was laid on the effect of section 34(4) of the Land Registration Act 1925, which is concerned with the effect on subsequent interests of a transfer of registered land by a mortgagee. Section 34 has, however, to be read with section 20 (p. 113, ante), which is concerned with the effect of the registration of a transfer of registered land by the registered proprietor. The protection conferred by section 34 on a transfer by a mortgagee is thus additional to the protection which is conferred by section 20 on registration of a transfer by a registered proprietor.

It has been pointed out by Lord Wilberforce in *Midland Bank Trust Co Ltd v Green* [1981] AC 513 at 531, [1981] 1 All ER 153 at 159, p. 38, ante, that it is not fraud to rely on legal rights conferred by Act of Parliament. Under section 20, the effect of the registration of the transferee of a freehold title is to confer an absolute title subject to entries on the register and overriding interests, but, 'free from all other estates and interests whatsoever, including estates and interests of His Majesty . . .' In *Miles v Bull (No 2)* [1969] 3 All ER 1585, Bridge J expressed the view that the words which I have quoted embraced, prima facie, not only all kinds of legal interests, but all kinds of equitable interests: see 1589.[1] He therefore held, at 1590, as I read his judgment, that actual or constructive notice on the part of a purchaser of an unregistered interest would not have the effect of imposing a constructive trust on him. The interest in *Miles v Bull (No 2)* was the interest in the matrimonial home of a deserted wife who had failed to protect her interest by registration under the Matrimonial Homes Act 1967.[2] The contract for sale between the husband, who was the registered proprietor, and the purchaser provided that the house concerned was sold subject to such rights of occupation as might subsist in favour of the wife, with a proviso that this was not to imply that the wife had, or would after completion have any such rights as against the purchaser. Plainly, therefore, the cause was only included in the contract for the protection of the husband who was the vendor. The wife was to get no fresh rights, and it was not in *Miles v Bull (No 2)* a stipulation of the bargain between the vendor and the purchaser that the purchaser should give effect to the rights as

[1] See also *Ashburn Anstalt v Arnold (No. 2)* [1989] Ch 1, which upheld the decision in *Lyus v Prowsa*, at the same time holding that more than notice is required for the creation of the constructive trust: p. 612, post; cf. *Chalthey v Farndale Holdings Inc* (1996) 75 P & CR 298 (where a purchaser from the constructive trustee was not bound by mere knowledge of the trustee's obligation).

[2] Now Family Law Act 1996, p. 312, post.

against the vendor of the deserted wife. *Miles v Bull (No 2)* is thus distinguishable from the facts of the present case as I interpret those facts.

It seems to me that the fraud on the part of the defendants in the present case lies not just in relying on the legal rights conferred by an Act of Parliament, but in the first defendant reneging on a positive stipulation in favour of the plaintiffs in the bargain under which the first defendant acquired the land. That makes, as it seems to me, all the difference. It has long since been held, for instance, in *Rochefoucauld v Boustead* [1897] 1 Ch 196, that the provisions of the Statute of Frauds 1677 now incorporated in certain sections of the Law of Property Act 1925, cannot be used as an instrument of fraud, and that it is fraud for a person to whom land is agreed to be conveyed as trustee for another to deny the trust and relying on the terms of the statute to claim the land for himself. *Rochefoucauld v Boustead* was one of the authorities on which the judgment in *Bannister v Bannister* [1948] 2 All ER 133[3] was founded.

It seems to me that the same considerations are applicable in relation to the Land Registration Act 1925. If, for instance, the agreement of October 18, 1979, between the bank and the first defendant had expressly stated that the first defendant would hold Plot 29 upon trust to give effect for the benefit of the plaintiffs to the plaintiffs' agreement with the vendor company, it would be difficult to say that that express trust was over-reached and rendered nugatory by the Land Registration Act 1925. The Land Registration Act 1925 does not, therefore, affect the conclusion which I would otherwise have reached in reliance on *Bannister v Bannister* and the judgment of Lord Denning MR in *Binions v Evans* [1972] Ch 359, [1972] 2 All ER 70 had Plot 29 been unregistered land.

The plaintiffs are, therefore, entitled to succeed in this action. The appropriate relief in that event is that specific performance should be ordered as against the second defendants of the sale to the plaintiffs of Plot 29, with the completed house thereon, on the terms of the agreement of January 30, 1978, made between the plaintiffs and the vendor company.'

(1983) 46 MLR 96 (P.H. Kenny), at p. 98:

'The case is as important for what was omitted as for what was decided. Key sections of the Land Registration Act were not referred to: section 74 which states that no "person dealing with a registered estate or charge shall be affected with notice of a trust express implied or constructive" was ignored. Similarly, section 59(1) providing that matters registrable in the case of unregistered land under the Land Charges Act 1972 are to be "protected only by lodging a creditor's notice, a bankruptcy inhibition or a caution against dealings with the land or charge" was ignored.[4] Presumably, the same sweeping principles of equity would have sidestepped these provisions.

The court here showed the usual judicial reluctance to grapple firmly with the mechanics of land registration. This arm's-length approach to the registration system led it not to give effect to the prescriptive system of registration in the Land Registration Act 1925. In the same way that the effect of non-registration of an estate contract is prescribed by section 4 of the Land Charges Act 1972 and had to be given effect to in *Midland Bank Trust Co Ltd v Green*, so the

---

[3]   See generally [1984] CLJ 306 (T.G. Youdan).
[4]   *De Lusignan v Johnson* (1973) 230 EG 499 was also ignored although it could have been distinguished in the same way as *Miles v Bull (No 2)*.

need to register an equivalent interest in registered land is prescribed by section 59(1) of the Land Registration Act 1925 which, with section 20 and section 34(4), should have been given effect to by the court. The legislation for both registered and unregistered land makes mandatory provision for registration and is specific on the effect of non-registration. The estate contract could, under the Land Registration Act, have been protected against the charge only by registration giving priority over the charge with the bank's consent. If there is a principle of equity which allows such transparently clear provisions to be sidestepped it should at least be described with greater precision and result from a less cavalier treatment of the relevant legislation.'[5]

IX. Alteration of the Register and Indemnity[6]

A. Rectification of the Register and Indemnity under the Land Registration Act 1925

The Land Registration Act 1925 made detailed provisions for one particular type of alteration to the register, namely rectification. There were ten grounds on which rectification might be ordered under the Land Registration Act 1925 or the Land Registration Rules 1925. These were broadly as follows:[7]

(a) Where a court either made an order which gave effect to an established property right or interest, or ordered the removal from the register of an entry in respect of a right which had not been established (section 82(1)(a), (b)).

(b) Where the court or the registrar decided that the register was incorrect in some way (section 82(1)(d)–(h)).

(c) Where the registrar decided that a clerical error needed to be corrected (LRR 1925, rules 13, 14).

Under the Act rectification was always discretionary.

'Indemnity is the correlative of rectification. And is payable where a person suffers loss as a result of an error or omission in the register, whether or not the register is rectified, and in certain other circumstances (section 83, substituted by the Land Registration Act 1997, section 2).'The availability of indemnity is of great importance to the system of land registration. It is the basis of the so-called State Guarantee of title which registration confers.'[8]

In addition to rectification under section 82, there are provisions which enable the registrator to update the register, for example, the discharge of a restrictive covenant under section 50.[9]

---

[5] See Oakley, *Constructive Trusts* (3rd edn 1997), chap. 2; [1982] All ER Rev (P.J. Clarke); [1983] CLJ 54 (C.J. Harpum); [1983] Conv 64 (P. Jackson); (1983) 133 NLJ 798 (C.T. Emery and B. Smythe); cf. (1984) 47 MLR 476 (P. Bennett); [1985] CLJ 280 (M.P. Thompson). See also *Du Boulay v Raggett* (1988) 58 P & CR 138; *Emmet on Title*, para. 9.020. On constructive trusts generally, see H & M, chap. 12.

[6] C & B, pp. 107, 859–861; Gray, pp. 1068–1082; M & W, paras. 6.119–6.131; MM, pp. 138–143; Smith, pp. 259–260; Barnsley, chap. 4; Farrand (2nd edn), pp. 209–222; Hayton, chap. 9; R & R, chap. 40; H & B, paras. 5.46–5.79.

[7] Law Commission Report on Land Registration for the Twenty-First Century 2001 (Law Com No. 2741), para. 10.1.

[8] Ibid., para. 10.3.

[9] Ibid., para. 10.2.

LAND REGISTRATION ACT 1925

82. Rectification of the register.—(1) The register may be rectified pursuant to an order of the court or by the registrar, subject to an appeal to the court,[10] in any of the following cases, but subject to the provisions of this section: —

(a) Subject to any express provisions of this Act to the contrary, where a court of competent jurisdiction has decided that any person is entitled to any estate right or interest in or to any registered land or charge, and as a consequence of such decision such court is of opinion that a rectification of the register is required, and makes an order to that effect;[11]

(b) Subject to any express provision of this Act to the contrary, where the court, on the application in the prescribed manner of any person who is aggrieved by any entry made in, or by the omission of any entry from, the register, or by any default being made, or unnecessary delay taking place, in the making of any entry in the register, makes an order for the rectification of the register;[12]

(c) In any case and at any time with the consent of all persons interested;

(d) Where the court or the registrar is satisfied that any entry in the register has been obtained by fraud;[13]

(e) Where two or more persons are, by mistake, registered as proprietors of the same registered estate or of the same charge;

(f) Where a mortgagee has been registered as proprietor of the land instead of as proprietor of a charge and a right of redemption is subsisting;[14]

(g) Where a legal estate has been registered in the name of a person who if the land had not been registered would not have been the estate owner;[15] and

(h) In any other case where, by reason of any error or omission in the register, or by reason of any entry made under a mistake, it may be deemed just to rectify the register.[16]

(2) The register may be rectified under this section, notwithstanding that the rectification may affect any estates, rights, charges, or interests acquired or protected by registration, or by any entry on the register, or otherwise.[17]

---

[10] There is no jurisdiction to order rectification with retrospection effect: *Malory Enterprise Ltd v Cheshire Homes (UK) Ltd* [2002] Ch 216, per ARDEN LJ at para 79; (2004) 119 LQR 31 (D. Sheehan).

[11] *Chowood Ltd v Lyall (No 2)* [1930] 2 Ch 156 (rectification ordered to give effect to overriding interest acquired by adverse possession to part of land registered in name of proprietor); *Calgary and Edmonton Land Co Ltd v Discount Bank (Overseas) Ltd* [1971] 1 WLR 81, [1971] 1 All ER 551 (caution removed); *Proctor v Kidman* (1986) 51 P & CR 67. See also *Spectrum Investment Co v Holmes* [1981] 1 WLR 221, [1981] 1 All ER 6, p. 245, post.

[12] *Chowood Ltd v Lyall (No 2)*, supra at 168–169, per LAWRENCE LJ; *Calgary and Edmonton Land Co Ltd v Discount Bank (Overseas) Ltd*, supra; *Lester v Burgess* (1973) 26 P & CR 536 (caution removed).

[13] *Re Leighton's Conveyance* [1936] 1 All ER 667 (fraudulent misrepresentation and undue influence) p. 186, post; *Norwich and Peterborough Building Society v Steed* [1993] Ch 116; *Argyle Building Society v Hammond* (1984) 49 P & CR 148 (forgery), p. 183, post; LRA 1925, s. 114.

[14] Cf. for unregistered land LPA 1925, ss. 85(2), (3), 86(2), (3), p. 792, post.

[15] *Chowood Ltd v Lyall (No 2)*, supra.

[16] *Re Dances Way, West Town, Hayling Island* [1962] Ch 490, [1962] 2 All ER 42 (notice of adverse easement cancelled).

[17] *Freer v Unwins Ltd* [1976] Ch 288, [1976] 1 All ER 634 (where it was held that the rectification of the register of title to servient land by the entry of a notice of restrictive covenants does not operate retrospectively so as to bind a person taking under a prior registered disposition for valuable consideration). See (1976) 40 Conv (NS) 304 (F.R. Crane); 126 NLJ 523 (S.M. Cretney); R & R (1991 edn), para. 40–15; *Clark v Chief Land Registrar* [1993] Ch 294, [1993] 2 All ER 936; affd [1994] Ch 370, [1994] 4 All ER 96; [1993] Conv 225 (J. Martin); [1993] All ER Rev. 244 (P.J. Clarke).

(3)[18] The register shall not be rectified, except for the purpose of giving effect to an overriding interest[19] or an order of the court so as to affect the title of the proprietor who is in possession[20]

    (a) unless the proprietor has caused or substantially contributed to the error or omission by fraud or lack of proper care; or ....

    (c) unless for any other reason, in any particular case, it is considered that it would be unjust not to rectify the register against him.[1]

83.[2] **Indemnity for errors or omissions in the register.**—(1) Where the register is rectified under this Act, then, subject to the provisions of this Act—

    (a) any person suffering loss by reason of the rectification shall be entitled to be indemnified;[3] and

    (b) if, notwithstanding the rectification, the person in whose favour the register is rectified suffers loss by reason of an error or omission in the register in respect of which it is so rectified, he also shall be entitled to be indemnified.

(2) Where an error or omission has occurred in the register, but the register is not rectified, any person suffering loss by reason of the error or omission shall, subject to the provisions of this Act, be entitled to be indemnified.

(3) Where any person suffers loss by reason of the loss or destruction of any document lodged at the registry for inspection or safe custody or by reason of an error in any official search, he shall be entitled to be indemnified under this Act.

(4) Subject to the following provisions of this section, a proprietor of any registered land or charge claiming in good faith under a forged disposition shall, where the register is rectified, be deemed to have suffered loss by reason of such rectification and shall be entitled to be indemnified under this Act.

(5) No indemnity shall be payable under this Act—

    (a) on account of any loss suffered by a claimant wholly or partly as a result of his fraud or wholly as a result of his own lack of proper care;[4]

    (b) on account of any mines or minerals, or the existence of any right to work or get mines or minerals, unless it is noted on the register that the mines or minerals are included in the title; or

    (c) on account of any costs or expenses (of whatever nature) incurred without the consent of the registrar, unless—

---

[18] As amended by AJA 1977, s. 24; see Law Com Working Paper No. 45 (1972), pp. 36–74.

[19] *Re Chowood's Registered Land* [1933] Ch 574, p. 193, post; *Epps v Esso Petroleum Co Ltd* [1973] 1 WLR 1071, [1973] 2 All ER 465, p. 189, post.

[20] *Hayes v Nwajiaku* [1994] EGCS 106 (proprietor means proprietor of land, not of charges). The policy of the 1925 Act favours registered proprietors in possession being left with their title undisturbed . . . He is deemed to be in possession unless and until dispossessed: *Kingsalton Ltd v Thames Water Developments Ltd* [2001] 1 P & CR 184, at para. 51, per Sir Christopher SLADE.

[1] *Epps v Esso Petroleum Co Ltd*, supra; *Hounslow London Borough Council v Hare* (1990) 24 HLR 9; [1993] Conv 224 (J. Martin); *Horrill v Cooper* (1998) 78 P & CR 336.

[2] As substituted by LRA 1997, s. 2. It is based on the First Report of a Joint Working Group on the Implementation of the Law Commission's Third and Fourth Reports on Land Registration 1995 (Law Com No. 235); [1996] CLJ 241 (L. Tee); (1997) 127 NLJ 925 (H.W. Wilkinson); Land Registry Public Information Leaflet 015.

[3] The indemnity is payable by the Chief Land Registrar out of moneys provided by Parliament: LR & LCA 1971, s. 1. During 2002–2003, £2.507,854 million was paid for 712 claims; the largest single claim was for £184,000 loss arising from a forged transfer of a registered property. Annual Report for 2002–2003, p. 25. 'Still a modest sum in the context of the enormous value of the land on the register."'

[4] *Dean v Dean* (2000) 80 P & CR 457 (a 'but for' test is not the applicable test, since, even if satisfied, it does not exclude possible other causes; *Prestige Properties v Scottish Provident Institution* [2003] Ch 1, [2003] 2 All ER 1145 (indemnity reduced by 90% due to family emergency).

(i)   by reason of urgency it was not practicable to apply for the registrar's consent before they were incurred, and

(ii)   the registrar subsequently approves them for the purposes of this paragraph.

(6) Where any loss suffered by a claimant is suffered partly as a result of his own lack of proper care, any indemnity payable to him shall be reduced to such extent as is just and equitable having regard to his share in the responsibility for the loss.

(7) For the purposes of subsections (5) (*a*) and (6) above, any fraud or lack of proper care on the part of a person from whom the claimant derives title (otherwise than under a disposition for valuable consideration which is registered or protected on the register) shall be treated as if it were fraud or lack of proper care on the part of the claimant (and the reference in subsection (6) to the claimant's share in the responsibility for the loss shall be construed accordingly).

(8) Where an indemnity is paid in respect of the loss of an estate or interest in or charge on land, the amount so paid shall not exceed—

(*a*)   where the register is not rectified, the value of the estate, interest or charge at the time when the error or omission which caused the loss was made;

(*b*)   where the register is rectified, the value (if there had been no rectification) of the estate, interest or charge, immediately before the time of rectification.

(9) Subject to subsection (5) (c) above, as restricted by section 2(2) of the Land Registration and Land Charges Act 1971—

(*a*)   an indemnity under any provision of this Act shall include such amount, if any, as may be reasonable in respect of any costs or expenses properly incurred by the claimant in relation to the matter; and

(*b*)   a claimant for an indemnity under any such provision shall be entitled to an indemnity thereunder of such amount, if any, as may be reasonable in respect of any such costs or expenses, notwithstanding that no other indemnity money is payable thereunder.

(10) Where indemnity is paid to a claimant in respect of any loss, the registrar, on behalf of the Crown, shall be entitled—

(*a*)   to recover the amount paid from any person who caused or substantially contributed to the loss by his fraud; or

(*b*)   for the purpose of recovering the amount paid, to enforce—

(i)   any right of action (of whatever nature or however arising) which the claimant would have been entitled to enforce had the indemnity not been paid, and

(ii)   where the register has been rectified, any right of action (of whatever nature and however arising) which the person in whose favour the register has been rectified would have been entitled to enforce had it not been rectified.

(11) Subsection (10) above does not prejudice any other rights of recovery which by virtue of any enactment are exercisable by the registrar where he has made a payment of indemnity.

(12) A liability to pay indemnity under this Act shall be deemed to be a simple contract debt; and for the purposes of the Limitation Act 1980, the cause of action shall be deemed to arise at the time when the claimant knows, or but for his own default might have known, of the existence of his claim.

(13) This section applies to the Crown in like manner as it applies to a private person.

i. FRAUD. FORGERY

NORWICH AND PETERBOROUGH BUILDING SOCIETY v STEED (NO 2)
[1993] Ch 116, [1993] 1 All ER 330 (CA, Purchas, Butler-Sloss and Scott LJJ)[5]

In 1964 Mr Steed became the registered freehold proprietor of 2 Arlow Road, Winchmore Hill, London. In 1976 he went to the United States, leaving in the house his mother, and his sister and her husband, Mr and Mrs Hammond. He alleged that in 1979 his sister induced him to sign a power of attorney to enable his mother to sell the house on his behalf; and that a transfer of the house took place by way of a forged deed in favour of the sister and her husband who were then registered as joint proprietors. They borrowed £15,000 by way of registered legal charge from the Argyle Building Society. On default the Building Society obtained an order for possession. Mr Steed applied to have the registered charge rectified against the Building Society. The Court of Appeal in *Argyle Building Society v Hammond* (1984) 49 P & CR 148 held that it had jurisdiction under section 82 of the Land Registration Act 1925 to order rectification and stayed the order for possession.

In subsequent proceedings for possession by the Norwich Building Society (successor of the Argyle Building Society) Mr Steed no longer alleged forgery but relied on new pleas of non est factum and fraud. Knox J held that non est factum did not apply on the facts but that the transfer was voidable for fraud. He ordered rectification against the Hammonds but refused it against the Building Society. On appeal against this refusal.

Held. No rectification against the Building Society.

Scott LJ: The transfer of 4 September 1979 was induced by the fraud of Mr and Mrs Hammond. It was voidable but not void. The building society advanced £15,000 to the Hammonds on the security of the charge which they executed and which was subsequently registered. The question is whether the court has power under section 82 of the Land Registration Act 1925 to order the register to be rectified by deletion of the entry of the building society's registered charge in the charges register. The question is primarily one of construction of the statutory language used in section 82.

[His Lordship read ss. 82 and 83 and continued:]

If an order of rectification is to be made the case must be brought within at least one of paragraphs (*a*) to (*h*) of section 82(1). The dispute in the present case is as to the breadth of the power conferred by paragraphs (*a*) and (*b*) and, to a lesser extent, (*d*) and (*h*). There is no doubt but that, if Mrs Steed's signature had been forged or if the non est factum plea had been made good, the case would have fallen squarely within paragraph (*g*). In neither case, if the land had been unregistered, would the Hammonds or the building society have obtained a legal estate. I cannot see any reasonable basis on which an order of rectification could have been withheld. If, however, as is the case, the transfer is only voidable, paragraph (*g*) does not apply. It is plain that, if title to the property had been unregistered, Mr Steed would have had no remedy against the building society. He would have recovered the property from the Hammonds but the property would have remained subject to the charge. It is submitted, however, that paragraphs (*a*), (*b*), (*d*) or (*h*) can, since title is registered, be prayed in aid. This

5 On forgeries and registered land generally, see (1985) 101 LQR 79 (R.J. Smith); (1993) 109 LQR 187 (R.J. Smith); [1993] All ER Rev 245, (P.J. Clarke); [1992] Conv 293 (C. Davis).

submission is made on the footing that, under one or more of these paragraphs, the court is given a general discretion to order rectification in any case in which it may be thought just to do so. If the submission is right, then section 82, or its statutory predecessors, achieved a remarkable and unnoticed change in the substantive law. If the discretion can be exercised where there has been a fraudulent misrepresentation, as in the present case, it must be exercisable also where a merely innocent misrepresentation has been made. It would, as Mr Lloyd conceded, be exercisable also in a case where no misrepresentation inducing the transaction could be pointed to but where a registered proprietor had entered into a transaction under a misapprehension for which the other party to the transaction was not responsible, a misapprehension as to the value of the property, for example. Mr Lloyd said that in such a case the discretion to order rectification against a bona fide purchaser, such as the building society in the present case, would be very unlikely ever to be exercised. But the proposition that the discretionary power contended for can be spelled out of the statutory language is, to me, so startling as to require the premise of the proposition to be very carefully examined.

There is a sense in which the power to rectify under section 82 is undoubtedly discretionary. The words, in subsection (1) are 'may be rectified'. Section 83(2) shows that rectification is not automatic. The power to rectify may, in a particular case, be present but, nonetheless, there is a general discretion to refuse rectification. It does not follow, however, that there is, in every case, a general discretion to grant rectification. The power to grant rectification is limited in subsection (1) to 'any of the following cases.' The power to order rectification must, therefore, be found within one or other of the subsection (1) paragraphs and cannot be spelled out of the words 'may be rectified.'

Paragraphs *(a)* and *(b)* provide a power to rectify that can only be exercised by the court. The power conferred by the other paragraphs can be exercised either by the registrar or by the court. Paragraph *(a)* enables an order of rectification to be made where the court 'has decided that any person is entitled to any estate right or interest in or to any registered land or charge . . .' This, in my judgment, is a clear reference to an entitlement under the substantive law. An example would be a case, such as Mr Steed's case against the Hammonds, for the setting aside of a transaction on the ground of misrepresentation or some other sufficient cause. Another example would be the successful assertion of a possessory title. A third example might be the assertion of a right by a beneficiary under a trust who had become absolutely entitled to the land. In each of these cases, once the entitlement had been established the court would have power under paragraph *(a)* to order the register to be rectified so as to reflect the entitlement. But paragraph *(a)* does not, in my judgment, give any substantive cause of action where none before existed. It does not enable a voidable transaction to be set aside as against a bona fide purchaser who has acquired by registration a legal estate. And if no entitlement as against such a purchaser can be established, paragraph *(a)* does not, in my judgment, enable the register to be rectified as against such a purchaser. Paragraph *(a)* does not assist Mr Steed in his rectification claim against the building society.

Paragraph *(b)* is the paragraph on which Mr Lloyd pinned his main hopes. It applies, he submitted, whenever any person is 'aggrieved' by an entry on the register. Paragraph *(b)* is something of a puzzle, not least because the form of the 'application' is not 'prescribed' by any rules made under the Act. The same language was used in section 96 of the [Land Transfer] Act of 1875, but there, too, no form of application was 'prescribed'. The legislative intention underlying paragraph *(b)* and its statutory predecessor is difficult to identify with clarity. The reference to 'the application in the prescribed manner' makes me believe that it was contemplated that some form of summary process would be prescribed in order to enable speedy relief to be given in clear cases. Be that as it may, the real question at issue is whether the provision was intended simply to provide a remedy in respect of proprietary rights that either entitled the proprietor to have some entry made on the register or entitled the proprietor to have some entry removed from the register or whether the provision should be construed as creating a new cause of action entitling the court to make rectification orders as it might in its discretion think fit in favour of persons who would not under substantive law, apart from paragraph *(b)*, have any proprietary rights which they could assert against the registered proprietor or chargee. In my judgment, the question has only to be put for the answer to be apparent. Parliament could not have intended paragraph *(b)* to produce new substantive rights in respect of registered land, enabling registered dispositions to be set aside and removed from the register in circumstances where, if the land had not been registered, no cause of action would have existed. In my judgment, paragraph *(b)*, like paragraph *(a)*, provides a remedy but does not create any new substantive rights or causes of action.

The scope of paragraph *(c)* is self-evident but not relevant in the present case.

Paragraph *(d)* too was relied on by Mr Lloyd. He contended that since the transfer had been induced by the Hammonds' fraud, both the registration of the Hammonds as proprietors and the registration of the building society's legal charge could be described as having been 'obtained by fraud.' In my judgment, that is a misreading of the paragraph. The paragraph is directed, in my opinion, to fraud practised upon the Land Registry in order to obtain the entry in question. No fraud was used to obtain the entry on the charges register of the building society's legal charge.

This construction of paragraph *(d)* derives support from the language used in section 174(1) *(c)* of the Law of Property Act 1922, the statutory predecessor of paragraph *(d)*. Section 174(1) *(c)* enabled the register to be rectified:

'Where the court or the registrar is satisfied that the registration of . . . a charge, mortgage, or other entry in the register . . . has been obtained by fraud, by annulling the registration, notice or other entry . . .'

This provision was reduced to its present succinct form in the Law of Property (Amendment) Act 1924: see section 8 and Schedule 8, paragraph 16. It is the *registration* that must be obtained by fraud.

The registration of a forged transfer could, in my opinion, at least if the application for registration had been made by the forger, be annulled under paragraph *(d)*. The entry would have been obtained by fraud in the presenting of a forged transfer for registration. But if a voidable disposition were registered before being avoided, I would doubt whether the register could be rectified under paragraph *(d)*, even if the disposition were voidable on account of fraud. In such a case the entry on the register would not, it seems to me, have been obtained by fraud. Rectification could, of course, in such a case be obtained under paragraph *(a)* or paragraph *(b)*. Whether or not that is right, and it need not be decided in this case, a registered disposition made by the fraudster to a bona fide purchaser cannot in my judgment be removed from the register under paragraph *(d)*. The registration would not have been obtained by fraud. So paragraph *(d)* cannot in my judgment assist Mr Steed as against the building society.

Paragraphs *(e)* and *(f)* are self-explanatory and are of no relevance to this case.

Paragraph *(g)* does not, in the event that the transfer is voidable, assist Mr Steed as against the building society. It is, however, an important paragraph so far as an understanding of the scheme of section 82(1) is concerned.

In my opinion the scheme is reasonably clear. Paragraphs *(a)* and *(b)* give power to the court to make orders of rectification in order to give effect to property rights which have been established in an action or which are clear. Paragraph *(c)* enables orders to be made by consent. The remaining paragraphs, *(d)* to *(h)*, are intended to enable errors to be corrected. Paragraph *(d)*, paragraph *(e)*, paragraph *(f)* and paragraph *(g)* each deals with an error of a particular character. But, since these paragraphs might not cover comprehensively all errors, paragraph *(h)* was added as a catch-all provision to cover any other errors. The breadth of the catch-all provision was, I imagine, the reason why it was thought appropriate to make the power exercisable 'where . . . it may be deemed just to rectify the register.' There are no comparable words in any of the other paragraphs.

Paragraph *(h)* is relied on by Mr Lloyd. But in order for the paragraph to be applicable some 'error or omission in the register' or some 'entry made under a mistake' must be shown. The entry in the charges register of the building society's legal charge was not an error and was not made under a mistake. The legal charge was executed by the Hammonds, who were at the time transferees under a transfer executed by Mrs Steed as attorney for the registered proprietor. The voidable transfer had not been set aside. The registration of the Hammonds as proprietors took place at the same time as the registration of the legal charge. Neither registration was an error. Neither entry was made under a mistake. So the case for rectification cannot be brought under paragraph *(h)*.

As a matter of principle, if, as I think, the defendant's case for rectification as against the building society cannot be brought under any of the paragraphs of section 82(1), I would conclude that that must be an end to the rectification claim. Mr Lloyd, however, has relied strongly on passages in the judgment of Slade LJ in *Argyle Building Society v Hammond* (1984) 49 P & CR 148. Before I come to those passages, it is convenient to refer to such earlier authority as there is. [His Lordship referred to *Chowood v Lyall (No 2)* [1930] 2 Ch 156 and *Calgary & Edmonton Co Ltd v Discount Bank (Overseas) Ltd* [1971] 1 WLR 81, [1971] 1 All ER 551, and continued:]

In *Re Leighton's Conveyance* [1936] 1 All ER 667 a non est factum case was raised. The plaintiff sought rectification first, against her daughter, who had fraudulently induced the plaintiff to sign a transfer leading to the daughter's registration as proprietor and, secondly, against chargees who, without any notice of the daughter's fraud, had advanced money to the daughter on the security of registered charges. The case was, therefore, very similar to the present case. Luxmoore J ordered rectification as against the daughter but, having concluded that the non est factum plea failed, he dismissed the rectification claim against the chargees. He said, at p. 673:

'I am satisfied that there are no grounds on which I can say that these charges are bad, but with regard to the equity of redemption I am satisfied on the evidence that what Mrs Wardman did was at the request of and in reliance on her daughter, and under her influence . . . . It follows that the conveyance to Mrs Bergin can have no effect as against Mrs Wardman, and she is still entitled to the equity of redemption in the property. . . . With regard to the charges register, there is no ground for interfering with it and directing any rectification. They are good charges and remain enforceable against the property.'

It was not stated in the judgment which paragraph or paragraphs of section 82(1) Luxmoore J regarded as applicable, but the report of the argument of counsel and an editorial note at p. 667 suggest that the judge was invited to act under paragraph *(d)*. It appears also from the report of argument that rectification as against the daughter was conceded and that the only issue in the case against the chargees was the non est factum issue. In my opinion, paragraph *(a)*, rather than paragraph *(d)*, provided the power to rectify as against the daughter. If the non est factum case had succeeded, paragraph *(g)* also would have been in point, both against the daughter and against the chargees. It was not suggested by counsel for the mother that, if the non est factum plea failed, she might nonetheless be entitled to rectification against the chargees. And there is nothing in the judgment of Luxmoore J to indicate that, having rejected the non est factum plea, he thought that he had any discretionary power to order rectification of the charges register.

I now come to the judgment of Slade LJ in *Argyle Building Society v Hammond* (1984) 49 P & CR 148. For the purposes of his judgment Slade LJ assumed that the allegation of forgery would succeed. He assumed nothing else. References to the 'assumed facts' are references to the facts regarding the forgery. At p. 157, having set out the text of section 82(1), he said:

'First, registers of title made pursuant to the Act of 1925 consist of three parts, namely the property register, the proprietorship register and the charges register. The jurisdiction to rectify under the subsection plainly extends to all or any of these parts. Secondly, on the assumed facts in the present case, the court would, in our judgment, have clear jurisdiction to rectify the proprietorship register of the house by substituting the name of the appellant for that of Mr and Mrs Hammond, since the case would fall within all or any of sub-paragraphs *(a)*, *(b)*, *(d)*, *(g)* and *(h)* of section 82(1). The present argument relates to the possibility or otherwise of rectification of the charges register.'

At p. 158 he made clear the opinion of the court that, on the assumed facts, the court would have power to rectify the charges register against the mortgagees as well as the proprietorship register against the Hammonds. I would respectfully agree, save that, for the reasons I have given, I do not think the case would come within paragraph *(d)*. It would come, in my opinion, within paragraphs *(a)*, *(b)*, *(g)* and, perhaps, *(h)*.

Slade LJ then referred to *Re Leighton's Conveyance* [1936] 1 All ER 667, cited the passage from the judgment of Luxmoore J that I have cited and continued, at p. 160:

'Reverting to the decision at first instance in the *Leighton* case, the report of the argument shows that the provisions of section 82(1) and (2) of the Act of 1925 were drawn to the attention of Luxmoore J. We feel no doubt that he would have appreciated that, even in the absence of a successful plea of forgery or non est factum, the section would in terms have conferred a discretion on the court to rectify the charges register, even as against the innocent chargees. Nevertheless, it is readily intelligible that Luxmoore J should have considered that, when the discretion fell to be exercised, the equities were all on one side—that is to say in favour of the chargees, who had acted on the faith of a document of transfer which the mother had herself executed after having failed to make inquiries which would have revealed that the document related to the property. If the title to the land had not been registered, the title of the daughter would, at worst, have been voidable, not void; and under general principles of equity, mortgagees from the daughter in good faith and for value, without notice of the facts giving rise to the voidability, would have acquired a good title to their mortgages. We can see no reason why the court in the *Leighton* case should have regarded the equities as being any different, as between the mother and the chargees, merely because the land happened to be registered land.'

In my respectful opinion, this analysis of *Re Leighton's Conveyance* is not justified by Luxmoore J's judgment. There is nothing in the judgment or in the report of counsel's argument to suggest that the possibility of rectification against the chargees, in the absence of a successful plea of forgery or non est factum, was ever considered. At p. 162 of his judgment Slade LJ commented:

'in a case where one or more of the conditions of section 82(1) are fulfilled, the court always has at least theoretical discretion to rectify any part of the register, even as against innocent third parties. . .'

I would respectfully agree with this comment, based as it is on the premise that the case can be brought within one or other of the paragraphs of section 82(1). But Slade LJ then went on to distinguish the case of a party 'deprived of his title as a result of a forged document which he did not execute' from the case where the party 'has been deprived as a result of a document which he himself executed, albeit under a mistake induced by fraud' and commented that 'when the court comes to exercise its discretion, different considerations may well apply.' The paragraph of section 82(1) under which the latter case could be brought was not identified. On the true construction of section 82(1) there is not, in my opinion, any paragraph under which the latter case could be brought.

Mr Lloyd's argument that the court has a general discretionary power to order rectification of the register was based on the passages from Slade LJ's judgment to which I have referred. The passages were not part of the ratio of the decision by which we are bound and with which I respectfully agree. A voidable transfer was not part of the 'assumed facts' on which the ratio was based. In my judgment, the obiter passages, regarding voidable transfers and innocent third parties claiming thereunder, were based on an incorrect construction of section 82(1) and should not be followed.

In my opinion, if the defendant's non est factum case is rejected, the court has no power under section 82(1) to order rectification as against the building society.

It is strictly unnecessary for me to deal with the issue of discretion which only arises if the court has power to rectify. Knox J refused rectification as a matter of discretion. He held that as between the defendant and the building society 'all the equities are on the building society's side'. This would certainly be so if the land were unregistered. But under section 83(1) the building society, if rectification were ordered, would have what seems to me to be an unimpeachable statutory right to an indemnity against the loss it would thereby suffer. On the other hand, if rectification were refused, the defendant would not be able to claim an indemnity under section 83(2). Mr Lloyd accepted, rightly, that, since the registration of the building society's charge was not an 'error or omission,' the case would not come within section 83(2). The financial consequences to the parties of ordering or refusing rectification make it difficult to weigh the 'equities.' If rectification were ordered, the loss would fall not upon the building society but upon the public purse. If rectification were refused, the public purse would be saved the burden of paying an indemnity. I mention these matters not in order to indicate any disagreement with Knox J's conclusions on discretion but because the indemnity provisions in section 83 seem to me to underline that the legislature did not contemplate the power of rectification being exercisable under section 82 except in cases either where an error or omission had occurred in the register, i.e. paragraphs *(d)* to *(h)*, or where a substantive cause of action against the registered proprietor required the register to be rectified, i.e. paragraphs *(a)* and *(b)*.

In 'error or omission' cases, i.e. in cases coming within paragraphs *(d)* to *(h)*, an indemnity would, if rectification were refused, be available under section 83(2), subject always to section 83(5) *(a)*. In cases within paragraphs *(a)* and *(b)* but not within any of paragraphs *(d)* to *(h)*, e.g. cases in which voidable transactions are set aside and, as a consequence, rectification of the register is required, it is difficult to construct any scenario in which rectification could be withheld. The construction of section 82(1) that I have suggested seems to me to mesh with and to explain the scheme of indemnity contained in section 83. The 'general discretion' approach to section 82(1) does not.

For the reasons I have given I would dismiss this appeal.

ii. DOUBLE CONVEYANCE. OVERRIDING INTEREST

EPPS v ESSO PETROLEUM CO LTD
[1973] 1 WLR 1071, [1973] 2 All ER 465[6] (ChD, TEMPLEMAN J)

In 1935 Alfred Clifford owned 4 Darland Avenue, Gillingham, Kent, and, on the north side of it, the adjoining Darland Garage. In that year he leased both to Mr Jones. In 1955 his personal representatives conveyed the house to Mrs Jones in fee simple, together with an extra 11 foot strip of frontage on the north side of the wall dividing the home from the garage. The object was to provide space for a garage at the home. Mrs Jones covenanted to erect a new wall on the new boundary, but never did. In 1956 Clifford's personal representatives granted a new lease of Darland Garage to Mr Jones, and in error the plan included the 11 foot strip. In 1959 they conveyed the garage, subject to the lease, to Julian Ball, and included the strip. The Land Registration Act 1925 had become applicable, and Ball became first registered proprietor of the garage and strip, with the consequence that LRA 1925, section 5 deprived Mrs Jones of the strip and vested it in Ball, subject to any overriding interests affecting the strip. In 1964 Ball conveyed the garage and strip to the defendants who became the second registered proprietors with absolute title. In 1968 the personal representatives of Mrs Jones conveyed 4 Darland Avenue and the strip to Mr and Mrs Epps, who obtained first registration of the house without the strip.

On a summons by Mr and Mrs Epps for rectification of the register, so as to exclude the strip from the defendant's title on the register, the plaintiffs argued that Mrs Jones was in possession of the strip at the time of the conveyance to the defendant in 1964; and, therefore, Mrs Jones and her estate had an overriding interest under LRA 1925, section 70(1) *(g)* by virtue of that possession.

Held. Rectification refused.

TEMPLEMAN J: Section 82(1) of the Land Registration Act provides that the register may be rectified where, inter alia, as in the present case, a legal estate has been registered in the name of a person who, if the land had not been registered, would not have been the estate owner. That describes the defendants. Section 82(3) limits the exercise of the power of rectification conferred by section 82(1). The limitation is in these terms:

'The register shall not be rectified, except for the purpose of giving effect to an overriding interest, so as to affect the title of the proprietor who is in possession—unless . . .'

---

[6]   (1973) 37 Conv (NS) 284 (F.R. Crane).

and then it specifies three conditions,[7] one of which must be satisfied, if rectification is to be granted . . . .

Condition (c) provides for rectification and I quote:

'unless for any other reason, in any particular case, it is considered that it would be unjust not to rectify the register against . . .' [the registered proprietor]

Mr Cullen, for the plaintiffs, submitted that when Mrs Jones was deprived of her legal estate in fee simple by the mistaken registration of Mr Ball as proprietor, Mrs Jones retained or acquired, and her successors in title, down to and including the plaintiffs, acquired an equitable interest in fee simple. The registered proprietor, first Mr Ball and now the defendants, acquired the legal estate, subject to the equitable interest of Mrs Jones and her successors. Effect should be given to that equitable interest by rectification. The limitation on the exercise of the power of rectification, which is to be found in section 82(3), does not apply where rectification is required to give effect to an overriding interest. The equitable interest of Mrs Jones and her successors in title is an overriding interest.

By section 70(1) (g) overriding interests include the rights of every person in actual occupation of the land or in receipt of the rents and profits thereof, save where inquiry is made of such person and the rights are not disclosed. Mrs Jones and her successors in title were in actual occupation, because Mrs Jones, and later the plaintiffs, parked a car on the disputed strip. Mr Ball and the defendants acquired the disputed strip subject to the overriding interests of Mrs Jones and her successors constituted by an equitable interest protected by actual occupation. The defendants never were in possession or, at any rate, ceased to be in possession when the plaintiffs erected their fence in 1968. Thus far Mr Cullen . . . .

The claim put forward by Mr Cullen on behalf of the plaintiffs to an overriding interest depends on whether Mr Jones was in actual occupation of the disputed strip when the defendants became the registered proprietor of the disputed strip in 1964. The contention put forward by Mr Cullen that the defendants were not in possession depends on whether they went into possession of the disputed strip when they became the registered proprietor and remained in possession until after the plaintiffs completed their purchase in 1968. Mr Brodie for the defendants took up a position at the opposite pole. He submitted that even if Mr Jones was in actual occupation he occupied in his capacity as tenant of Mr Ball. Alternatively, the occupation of Mr Jones could not protect any equitable interest vested in the probate judge at the date when the defendants became the registered proprietors of the disputed strip in 1964.

I reject these submissions of Mr Brodie. If Mr Jones was in actual occupation when the defendants completed their purchase of the disputed strip then his occupation in the present circumstances sufficed to assert and protect any equitable interest of Mrs Jones and her estate so as to constitute an overriding interest, and sufficed also to defeat the claim by the defendants to be in possession. . . .

In my judgment, the fact that the defendants were not the original proprietors, but subsequent transferees, is only one element to be considered in the exercise of the discretion conferred by section 82(1) and section 82(3) (c) of the Land Registration Act 1925. In the confrontation envisaged by section 82(1) and in particular by section 82(1) (g), between, on the one hand, the registered proprietor, who is a victim of double conveyancing, and the first purchaser or his successors, deprived of the legal estate by registration, the court must first

---

[7]   Reduced to two two by AJA 1977, s. 24, p. 180, ante.

determine whether the registered proprietor is in possession. If the registered proprietor is not in possession then section 82(3) does not apply, and the court will normally grant rectification: see *Chowood Ltd v Lyall (No 2)* [1930] 2 Ch 156. A fortiori if the registered proprietor is not in possession but the applicant has an overriding interest constituted by an equitable interest protected by actual occupation, the court will grant rectification; see *Bridges v Mees* [1957] Ch 475 at 486, [1957] 2 All ER 577 at 581, 582. However, the power of rectification given by section 82(1) never ceases to be discretionary, so that where section 82(3) does not apply there may still be circumstances which defeat the claim for rectification.

If the registered proprietor is in possession, the applicant for rectification will not normally be in actual occupation, and one of the conditions specified in section 82(3) must be satisfied if rectification is to be granted. . . .

It follows that the crucial questions in the present case are, first, whether Mr Jones was in actual occupation of the disputed strip when the defendants completed purchase in 1964; secondly, whether the defendants were in possession at the date when the plaintiffs completed their purchase of 4 Darland Avenue in 1968; and if those questions are decided in favour of the defendants, thirdly, whether it would be unjust not to rectify against them.

In *Hodgson v Marks* [1971] Ch 892 at 931, [1971] 2 All ER 684 at 688, Russell LJ said, on actual occupation as an ingredient of an overriding interest, that he was prepared for the purpose of that case to assume, without necessarily accepting, that section 70(1)(g) of the Land Registration Act 1925 is designed only to apply to a case in which the occupation is such in point of fact as would in the case of unregistered land affect a purchaser with constructive notice of the rights of the occupier. Then Russell LJ said, at 932, at 688:

'I do not think it desirable to attempt to lay down a code or catalogue of situations in which a person other than the vendor should be held to be in occupation of unregistered land for the purpose of constructive notice of his rights, or in actual occupation of registered land for the purposes of section 70(1)(g). It must depend on the circumstances, and a wise purchaser or vendor will take no risks. Indeed, however wise he may be he may have no ready opportunity of finding out; but, nevertheless, the law will protect the occupier.'

In my judgment Mr Jones was not in actual occupation of the disputed strip when the defendants completed their purchase of Darland Garage and was not thereafter in actual occupation.

Mr Jones gave evidence that every night he parked his car on the disputed strip, and sometimes the car was there during the day. Mr Jones's recollection, not unnaturally, was not very reliable, and I find that he sometimes parked his car on the disputed strip, but how often and when no one can now determine with any certainty. But even if Mr Jones regularly parked his car on the disputed strip I do not consider that this constituted actual occupation of the disputed strip in the circumstances of the present case. I reach this conclusion for the following reasons: first, the parking of a car on a strip 11 feet wide by 80 feet long does not actually occupy the whole, or a substantial, or any defined part of that disputed strip for the whole or any defined time. Secondly, the parking of a car on an unidentified piece of land, apparently comprised in garage premises, is not an assertion of actual occupation of anything.

In addition to these two reasons there are circumstances which show that, not only was Mr Jones not in actual occupation, but on the contrary that the defendants were.

[His Lordship reviewed the evidence and continued:]

In my judgment, therefore, section 82(3) does apply because the Jones's and the plaintiffs had no overriding interest protected by actual occupation and because the defendants were in possession. There remains the question, under condition (c) of section 82(3) whether it would be unjust not to rectify against the defendants.

In my judgment, justice in the present case lies wholly with the defendants and not with the plaintiffs. . . .

In my judgment, whereas the defendants bought the disputed strip, the plaintiffs bought a law suit, thanks to the default of their vendor in not taking steps to assert ownership and possession of the disputed strip, and thanks to the failure of the plaintiffs to make before completion the inquiries which they made immediately after completion.

Mr Cullen put forward one additional circumstance which he argued, with some force, tilted the balance of justice in favour of rectification. That circumstance, he submitted, was that if the register is rectified the defendants can recover compensation based on the 1973 value of the disputed strip, but if the register is not rectified the plaintiffs cannot recover compensation. This argument is founded on section 83 of the Land Registration Act 1925 which deals with compensation. Section 83(1) provides that, subject to the provisions of the Act to the contrary, any person suffering loss by reason of any rectification of the register under the Act shall be entitled to be indemnified.

That will be the position of the defendants if I rectify. Section 83(2) provides that where an error or omission has occurred in the register but the register is not rectified, any person suffering loss by reason of such error or omission shall, subject to the provisions of the Act, be entitled to be indemnified. That is the position of the plaintiffs, if I do not rectify.

By section 83[8][8] where indemnity is paid in respect of the loss of an estate or interest in or charge on land the amount so paid shall not exceed (a), where the register is not rectified the value of the estate interest or charge at the time when the error or omission which caused the loss was made. In other words, if I do not rectify then the plaintiffs' indemnity is reduced to the value of the disputed strip as at 1959 when the error was made. Subsection [8] *(b)*, on the other hand, says that where the register is rectified the indemnity is not to exceed the value if there had been no rectification of the estate, interest or charge immediately before the time of rectification. This would apply to the defendants. So that the legislature provides 1959 values for the plaintiffs and 1973 values for the defendants. The matter does not end there, however, because by subsection [12] there is a further limitation on indemnity. Subsection [12] provides that a liability to pay indemnity under the Act shall be deemed a simple contract debt and for the purposes of the Limitation Act the cause of action shall be deemed to arise at the time when the claimant knows or, but for his own default, might have known of the existence of his claim. Whether or not that applies to the plaintiffs, it clearly does not affect the defendants; first, because they are not claimants; and, secondly, because they must have been in complete innocence of anything wrong until the plaintiffs came on the scene and raised the question of where the true boundary lay ...

This is a case, in my judgment, in which if an order for rectification is made the defendants will be entitled to indemnity on 1973 values, and if the claim for rectification is refused then they will keep the land, but the plaintiffs will not get compensation.

---

[8]   These sections are renumbered as a result of the substituted s. 83 by LRA 1997, s. 2.

The question I have to determine is whether that is sufficient to upset the justice of the defendants' claim that there should not be rectification in the present instance. Is it sufficient—and this is the test—to make it unjust not to rectify the register against the defendants? Mr Cullen pointed out that as far as the defendants are concerned the disputed strip formed, he calculated, 4 per cent of the garage premises. He said it could not make a lot of difference to the defendant's garage; on the other hand, it was of importance to 4 Darland Avenue because it provided a private garage, an asset which is important in commuter territory.

In my judgment, however, this cannot be solved merely on the question of money. The defendants bought the land; they bought it to exploit for their commercial purposes; they did not buy it in order to sell a strip for a 1973 value, which in real terms will not, in my judgment, adequately indemnify them. Although the strip is at the back of the garage, in the same way as it could be used as a private garage for 4 Darland Avenue, so it could be used by the defendants for commercial purposes, and in fact they say now they intend to use it in connection with a car wash; if they are deprived of it they will be in considerable difficulty, and will not have all the facilities which a modern garage requires. I think that may be putting it a bit high, but the fact of the matter is that this strip is worth more to the defendants than the pounds, shillings and pence which they will receive by indemnity, even on a 1973 basis.

Accordingly, in my judgment, that argument is not sufficient to overturn all the other arguments in favour of the defendants, and I decline to order rectification of the register.[9]

RE CHOWOOD'S REGISTERED LAND[10]
[1933] Ch 574 (ChD, CLAUSON J)

Lyall had, before the registration of Chowood Ltd (the purchaser of certain freeholds from Ralli) as proprietor of those freeholds with an absolute title, acquired a right under the Limitation Acts to a part thereof. The register was rectified and Chowood Ltd claimed an indemnity under section 83.

Held. Chowood Ltd was not entitled to be indemnified.

CLAUSON J: Chowood's title was all along subject to the rights which Lyall has succeeded in establishing; and the loss, if it may properly be so called, which Chowood has suffered is that they have not got, and since the Act of 1925 came into force (whatever may have been the position before) have never had title to the strip, except subject to an overriding right in Lyall. That loss was occasioned by Chowood failing to ascertain that, when they bought, Lyall was in possession, and in possession under such circumstances that Ralli could not make a title to the strip. The loss was occasioned by paying Ralli for a strip to which Ralli could not make title. The rectification of the register merely recognised the existing position, and put Chowood in no worse a position than they were in before.

In these circumstances I must hold that Chowood have suffered no loss by reason of the rectification of the register.

---

9   See *Malory Enterprises Ltd v Cheshire Homes (UK) Ltd* [2002] Ch 216; H & B, para. 5.3, n 2; p. 107, n. 14, ante.
10 Followed in *Re Boyle's Claim* [1961] 1 WLR 339, [1961] 1 All ER 620.

B. Alteration of the Register and Indemnity under the Land Registration Act 2002[11]

i.   ALTERATION OF THE REGISTER

The provisions for alteration of the register have been recast so as to reflect the present practice in relation to rectification and amendment of the register. The basic concept is *alteration* of the register, with rectification as one form of alteration. Rectification is defined in paragraph 1 of Schedule 4 to the 2002 Act as an alteration which:

(a) involves the correction of a mistake; and

(b) prejudicially affects the title of a registered proprietor.

In respect of this kind of alteration, the proprietor of land may have a claim to an indemnity under Schedule 8.

Cases under the 1925 Act will be relevant in interpreting the new provisions under Schedule 4.

Schedule 8 sets out the eight grounds which govern the payment of indemnity. They reflect the similar grounds under section 83 of the 1925 Act, which were amended by section 2 of the Land Registration Act 1997. Although redrafted in the 2002 Act, their substance is unimpaired.

LAND REGISTRATION ACT 2002

65 Alteration of register

Schedule 4 (which makes provision about alteration of the register) has effect.

SCHEDULE 4

ALTERATION OF THE REGISTER

Introductory

1   In this Schedule, references to rectification, in relation to alteration of the register, are to alteration which—

(a) involves the correction of a mistake, and

(b) prejudicially affects the title of a registered proprietor.

Alteration pursuant to a court order

2(1) The court may make an order for alteration of the register for the purpose of—

(a) correcting a mistake,

(b) bringing the register up to date, or

(c) giving effect to any estate, right or interest excepted from the effect of registration.

(2) An order under this paragraph has effect when served on the registrar to impose a duty on him to give effect to it.

3   (1) This paragraph applies to the power under paragraph 2, so far as relating to rectification.

(2) If alteration affects the title of the proprietor of a registered estate in land, no order may be made under paragraph 2 without the proprietor's consent in relation to land in his possession unless—

(a) he has by fraud or lack of proper care caused or substantially contributed to the mistake, or

---

[11]   R & R, chaps. 46, 47; H & B, paras. 5.46–5.65: Law Commission Report on Land Registration for the Twenty-First Century (2001), Part X.

(b) it would for any other reason be unjust for the alteration not to be made.

(3) If in any proceedings the court has power to make an order under paragraph 2, it must do so, unless there are exceptional circumstances which justify its not doing so.

(4) In sub-paragraph (2), the reference to the title of the proprietor of a registered estate in land includes his title to any registered estate which subsists for the benefit of the estate in land.

4   Rules may—

(a) make provision about the circumstances in which there is a duty to exercise the power under paragraph 2, so far as not relating to rectification;

(b) make provision about the form of an order under paragraph 2;

(c) make provision about service of such an order.[12]

Alteration otherwise than pursuant to a court order

5   The registrar may alter the register for the purpose of—

(a) correcting a mistake,

(b) bringing the register up to date,

(c) giving effect to any estate, right or interest excepted from the effect of registration, or

(d) removing a superfluous entry.

6   (1) This paragraph applies to the power under paragraph 5, so far as relating to rectification.

(2) No alteration affecting the title of the proprietor of a registered estate in land may be made under paragraph 5 without the proprietor's consent in relation to land in his possession[13] unless—

(a) he has by fraud or lack of proper care caused or substantially contributed to the mistake, or

(b) it would for any other reason be unjust for the alteration not to be made.[14]

(3) If on an application for alteration under paragraph 5 the registrar has power to make the alteration, the application must be approved, unless there are exceptional circumstances which justify not making the alteration.

(4) In sub-paragraph (2), the reference to the title of the proprietor of a registered estate in land includes his title to any registered estate which subsists for the benefit of the estate in land.

7   Rules may[15]—

(a) make provision about the circumstances in which there is a duty to exercise the power under paragraph 5, so far as not relating to rectification;

(b) make provision about how the register is to be altered in exercise of that power;

(c) make provision about applications for alteration under that paragraph, including provision requiring the making of such applications;

(d) make provision about procedure in relation to the exercise of that power, whether on application or otherwise.

---

12   LRR 2003, Part 12.
13   See LRA 1925, s. 82(3), p. 181, ante.
14   Ibid., s. 82(3), p. 181, ante.
15   LRR 2003, rr. 126–130.

Rectification and derivative interests
8   The powers under this Schedule to alter the register, so far as relating to rectification, extend to changing for the future the priority of any interest affecting the registered estate or charge concerned.

ii.   INDEMNITY

LAND REGISTRATION ACT 2002

103 Indemnities

Schedule 8 (which makes provision for the payment of indemnities by the registrar) has effect.

SCHEDULE 8

INDEMNITIES

Entitlement
1   (1)   A person is entitled to be indemnified by the registrar if he suffers loss by reason of—
   (a) rectification of the register,
   (b) a mistake whose correction would involve rectification of the register,
   (c) a mistake in an official search,
   (d) a mistake in an official copy,
   (e) a mistake in a document kept by the registrar which is not an original and is referred to in the register,
   (f) the loss or destruction of a document lodged at the registry for inspection or safe custody,
   (g) a mistake in the cautions register, or
   (h) failure by the registrar to perform his duty under section 50.
   (2)   For the purposes of sub-paragraph (1)(a)—
   (a) any person who suffers loss by reason of the change of title under section 62 is to be regarded as having suffered loss by reason of rectification of the register, and
   (b) the proprietor of a registered estate or charge claiming in good faith under a forged disposition is, where the register is rectified, to be regarded as having suffered loss by reason of such rectification as if the disposition had not been forged.
   (3)   No indemnity under sub-paragraph (1)(b) is payable until a decision has been made about whether to alter the register for the purpose of correcting the mistake; and the loss suffered by reason of the mistake is to be determined in the light of that decision.

Mines and minerals
2   No indemnity is payable under this Schedule on account of—
   (a) any mines or minerals, or
   (b) the existence of any right to work or get mines or minerals,
   unless it is noted in the register that the title to the registered estate concerned includes the mines or minerals.

Claimant's fraud or lack of care
5   (1)   No indemnity is payable under this Schedule on account of any loss suffered by a claimant—
   (a) wholly or partly as a result of his own fraud, or
   (b) wholly as a result of his own lack of proper care.

(2) Where any loss is suffered by a claimant partly as a result of his own lack of proper care, any indemnity payable to him is to be reduced to such extent as is fair having regard to his share in the responsibility for the loss.

(3) For the purposes of this paragraph any fraud or lack of care on the part of a person from whom the claimant derives title (otherwise than under a disposition for valuable consideration which is registered or protected by an entry in the register) is to be treated as if it were fraud or lack of care on the part of the claimant.

Valuation of estates etc.

6   Where an indemnity is payable in respect of the loss of an estate, interest or charge, the value of the estate, interest or charge for the purposes of the indemnity is to be regarded as not exceeding—

(a) in the case of an indemnity under paragraph 1(1)(a), its value immediately before rectification of the register (but as if there were to be no rectification), and

(b) in the case of an indemnity under paragraph 1(1)(b), its value at the time when the mistake which caused the loss was made.

Determination of indemnity by court

7   (1) A person may apply to the court for the determination of any question as to—

(a) whether he is entitled to an indemnity under this Schedule, or

(b) the amount of such an indemnity.

(2) Paragraph 3(1) does not apply to the costs of an application to the court under this paragraph or of any legal proceedings arising out of such an application.

Time limits

8   For the purposes of the Limitation Act 1980—

(a) a liability to pay an indemnity under this Schedule is a simple contract debt, and

(b) the cause of action arises at the time when the claimant knows, or but for his own default might have known, of the existence of his claim.

Interest

9   Rules may make provision about the payment of interest on an indemnity under this Schedule, including[16]—

(a) the circumstances in which interest is payable, and

(b) the periods for and rates at which it is payable.

Recovery of indemnity by registrar

10   (1) Where an indemnity under this Schedule is paid to a claimant in respect of any loss, the registrar is entitled (without prejudice to any other rights he may have)—

(a) to recover the amount paid from any person who caused or substantially contributed to the loss by his fraud, or

(b) for the purpose of recovering the amount paid, to enforce the rights of action referred to in sub-paragraph (2).

(2) Those rights of action are—

(a) any right of action (of whatever nature and however arising) which the claimant would have been entitled to enforce had the indemnity not been paid, and

---

[16]   LRR 2003, r. 195.

(b) where the register has been rectified, any right of action (of whatever nature and however arising) which the person in whose favour the register has been rectified would have been entitled to enforce had it not been rectified.

(3) References in this paragraph to an indemnity include interest paid on an indemnity under rules under paragraph 9.

Interpretation

11 (1)   For the purposes of this Schedule, references to a mistake in something include anything mistakenly omitted from it as well as anything mistakenly included in it.

(2) In this Schedule, references to rectification of the register are to alteration of the register which—
  (a) involves the correction of a mistake, and
  (b) prejudicially affects the title of a registered proprietor.

X. Electronic Conveyancing

The changes made by the Land Registration Act 2002 prepare the way for the move from a paper-based system of conveyancing to one which is entirely electronic. The enabling provisions for its introduction are set out in Part 8 of the Act (sections 91 to 95). Schedule 5 sets out the details for the Land Registry network agreement under which electronic conveyancing takes place.[17]

The full system will take time to introduce. It is already possible to notify the Registry of the discharge of a registered charge by electronic means, and applications to register dealings with registered land can be lodged electronically.

A Land Registry Consultation Paper on E-conveyancing was published in 2002.

LAND REGISTRATION ACT 2002

91   Electronic dispositions: formalities

(1)   This section applies to a document in electronic form where—
  (a) the document purports to effect a disposition which falls within subsection (2), and
  (b) the conditions in subsection (3) are met.

(2)   A disposition falls within this subsection if it is—
  (a) a disposition of a registered estate or charge,
  (b) a disposition of an interest which is the subject of a notice in the register, or
  (c) a disposition which triggers the requirement of registration, which is of a kind specified by rules.

(3)   The conditions referred to above are that—
  (a) the document makes provision for the time and date when it takes effect,

---

[17]   LRR 2003, rr. 54–79; R & R, chap. 19; H & B, chap. 7; Law Commission Report on Land Registration for the Twenty-First Century 2001 (Law Com No. 271), Part XIII.

      (b) the document has the electronic signature of each person by whom it purports to be authenticated,

      (c) each electronic signature is certified, and

      (d) such other conditions as rules may provide are met.

(4)   A document to which this section applies is to be regarded as—

      (a) in writing, and

      (b) signed by each individual, and sealed by each corporation, whose electronic signature it has.

(5)   A document to which this section applies is to be regarded for the purposes of any enactment as a deed.

(6)   If a document to which this section applies is authenticated by a person as agent, it is to be regarded for the purposes of any enactment as authenticated by him under the written authority of his principal.

(7)   If notice of an assignment made by means of a document to which this section applies is given in electronic form in accordance with rules, it is to be regarded for the purposes of any enactment as given in writing.

(8)   The right conferred by section 75 of the Law of Property Act 1925 (purchaser's right to have the execution of a conveyance attested) does not apply to a document to which this section applies.

(9)   If subsection (4) of section 36A of the Companies Act 1985 (execution of documents) applies to a document because of subsection (4) above, subsection (6) of that section (presumption of due execution) shall have effect in relation to the document with the substitution of 'authenticated' for 'signed'.

(10) In this section, references to an electronic signature and to the certification of such a signature are to be read in accordance with section 7(2) and (3) of the Electronic Communications Act 2000.

92 Land registry network

(1) The registrar may provide, or arrange for the provision of, an electronic communications network for use for such purposes as he thinks fit relating to registration or the carrying on of transactions which—

      (a) involve registration, and

      (b) are capable of being effected electronically.

(2) Schedule 5 (which makes provision in connection with a network provided under subsection (1) and transactions carried on by means of such a network) has effect.

93 Power to require simultaneous registration

(1)   This section applies to a disposition of—

      (a) a registered estate or charge, or

      (b) an interest which is the subject of a notice in the register,

    where the disposition is of a description specified by rules.

(2)   A disposition to which this section applies, or a contract to make such a disposition, only has effect if it is made by means of a document in electronic form and if, when the document purports to take effect—

      (a) it is electronically communicated to the registrar, and

      (b) the relevant registration requirements are met.

(3)   For the purposes of subsection (2)(b), the relevant registration requirements are—

      (a) in the case of a registrable disposition, the requirements under Schedule 2,[18] and

---

[18]   P. 123, ante.

> (b) in the case of any other disposition, or a contract, such requirements as rules may provide.
>
> (4)   Section 27(1) does not apply to a disposition to which this section applies.[19]
>
> (5)   Before making rules under this section the Lord Chancellor must consult such persons as he considers appropriate.
>
> (6)   In this section, "disposition", in relation to a registered charge, includes postponement.

94   Electronic settlement

> The registrar may take such steps as he thinks fit for the purpose of securing the provision of a system of electronic settlement in relation to transactions involving registration.

95   Supplementary

> Rules may—
>
> (a) make provision about the communication of documents in electronic form to the registrar;
>
> (b) make provision about the electronic storage of documents communicated to the registrar in electronic form.

Law Commission Report on Land Registration for the Twenty-First Century 2001 (Law Com No. 271), paras. 2.48 to 2.59.

'Electronic conveyancing: the anticipated model[20]

Introduction

2.48   Before examining how a typical dematerialised conveyancing transaction involving registered land[1] might work, two points should be emphasised.

2.49   The first is that the Land Registry's involvement in the conveyancing process will begin earlier than at present. This will be either—

(1) before the parties to a disposition of either—

(a)   registered land; or

(b)   unregistered land that will trigger compulsory registration;

conclude a contract that is to precede that disposition;[2] or if there is no such contract,[3]

(2)   before the relevant disposition is made.

2.50   In many cases the disposition and, where title is already registered, its simultaneous registration will be the *last* stage of the conveyancing process. That means that all the conveyancing work must be completed by that date.[4] One of the intended objectives of the new system is to identify errors and

---

19   P. 122, ante.
20   See also LR Consultation: e-conveyancing.
1   For electronic conveyancing and applications for first registration, see below, para. 2.65.
2   In other words, an estate contract such as contract to sell land.
3   As where a registered proprietor intends to charge his land, or where (as is commonly the case) there is to be a lease without any prior agreement for a lease.
4   Ironically, this will bring the registered system into line with what formerly happened with unregistered conveyancing, where the deed of conveyance was the final stage of the conveyancing process. Many dispositions of unregistered land now trigger compulsory registration, so that the deed of conveyance is no longer the final stage. There has to be an application for first registration and the registrar will need to be satisfied as to the title before he can register the disposition. See Ruoff & Roper, *Registered Conveyancing*, 12–45.

discrepancies at the earliest possible stage, and to resolve any difficulties so far as possible before registration.[5]

2.51 The second point is that changes to the register will be made as a result of the actions of the solicitors or licensed conveyancers acting for the parties to the transactions. This is explained more fully below.[6] We also explain that do-it-yourself conveyancers will not be excluded from electronic conveyancing.[7]

How a typical conveyancing transaction might operate

2.52 The manner in which electronic conveyancing might operate may be illustrated by the example of a typical contract to sell a parcel of registered land and its subsequent completion. It should be stressed that this is necessarily tentative and that what eventually appears is likely to differ in some details at least from what is set out here. The system is likely to be based on a secure electronic communications network that will only be accessible by contractually authorised professionals, whether those are solicitors, licensed conveyances, estate agents or mortgage lenders.[8] The network will not just be used for the specifically legal stages of the transaction, but also for the provision of information about the property. It is also likely to be employed to co-ordinate and manage chains of transactions,[9] provided that those transactions are dispositions of registered land or are of a kind that will trigger the requirement of compulsory registration. It is anticipated that some body — which might or might not be the Land Registry — will be made responsible for managing chain sales in order to facilitate them. When a party instructs a solicitor or licensed conveyancer to act on his or her behalf in a purchase or sale of a property in circumstances in which there is likely to be a chain, that agent will be required[10] to notify the "chain manager" of the fact of that instruction. There will be further requirements for that agent to provide information to the chain manager as to the completion of the various precontractual stages of the transaction, such as investigating title, carrying out local searches, obtaining mortgage offers, etc. The chain manager will then be able to build up a picture of the chain and so that he can identify any persons in the chain who are delaying the process. This information will be made available via the secure Intranet to all parties in the chain. Although it is not anticipated that the chain manager will have any compulsive powers,[11] he will be able to encourage the offending parties to complete the steps that are still to be performed. There will inevitably be pressure from others in the chain who are ready to contract. The power to manage chains in this way

---

[5] We have been told by many practitioners that it is not always possible for them to finalise the details of ancillary rights (typically cross-easements) in a complex conveyancing transaction. However, in future, such matters could be resolved by contract between the parties. That contract will be protected in the register, so that its priority is preserved. When the details are finalised between the parties, the easements or other rights can then be entered in the register.

[6] See below, para. 2.57.

[7] See below, para. 2.68.

[8] The extent to which professionals may be permitted to access the secure Intranet will obviously depend on their role.

[9] In particular a chain of house sales. There may be no need for 'chain management' in relation to a chain of commercial transactions.

[10] The basis of this requirement will be contractual.

[11] Indeed, it is not easy to see what effective forms of compulsion there could be.

is an important feature of our proposals on electronic conveyancing. Chains are a major cause of disquiet in the conveyancing process, particularly in relation to domestic conveyancing. By providing a means of controlling and expediting chains, the Bill should do much to alleviate the frustrations that are suffered by so many buyers and sellers of land. It is anticipated that it should prevent chains from collapsing.

2.53   When the parties have agreed the terms of the contract,[12] they will send a copy in electronic form to HM Land Registry, where it will be checked electronically. This will enable any discrepancies in the contract on matters such as property address, title number and seller's name to be identified at that stage and rectified before the contract is concluded.

2.54   The contract will be made in electronic form and signed electronically by the parties or their agents. It is anticipated that, under the Bill, estate contracts will be required to be protected in the register by the entry of a notice as pre-requisite to their validity. This noting in the register will occur simultaneously with the making of the contract and one effect of it will be to confer priority protection on the buyer.[13] The form of notice will have been agreed with the Registry in advance. The Registry will store the contract in electronic form and this is likely to be for a period that will be set in accordance with rules and is likely to reflect the nature of the contract.[14]

2.55   In relation to the disposition itself, a similar process will be undertaken. The draft transfer and any charge will be prepared in electronic form and agreed between the parties. Once again, the draft will be submitted to the Registry. The details in the transfer will be checked electronically against the contract to ensure that there are no discrepancies. A "notional" register will then be prepared by the Registry in consultation with the parties to indicate the form that the register will take when the transaction is completed. Completion, when it occurs, will entail the simultaneous occurrence of the following events—

(1)   the execution of the transfer and any charges in electronic form and their transmission to the Registry, where they will be stored;

(2)   the registration of the dispositions so that the register conforms with the notional register previously agreed with the Registry; and

(3)   the appropriate (and automatic) movement of funds[15] and the payment of stamp duty[16] and Land Registry fees.

2.56   The proposed system will eliminate the "registration gap". There will no longer be any period of time between the disposition and its registration. In time it will also mean that the register becomes conclusive as to the priority of all expressly created interests. This is because, if it is only possible to create interests validly if they are registered simultaneously, the date on which they are created will be the date of their registration. The register will therefore become a record of the priority of such rights.

2.57   As we have indicated above—

---

[12]   The draft contract will be an electronic document.
[13]   See clause 72(6)(a)(ii) of the Bill, below, para. 9.68.
[14]   In the case of a normal estate contract, the period of storage is likely to be comparatively short. This is because most contractual obligations are merged on completion. Where the contract is likely to have a longer life, such as an option or a right of pre-emption, the period of storage will be longer. It will be possible to obtain official copies of such contracts.
[15]   See below, para. 2.62.
[16]   See below, para. 2.64. See FA 2003, s. 48(1), (2).

(1)   Changes to the register will be made automatically as a consequence of electronic documents and applications created by solicitors or licensed conveyancers, who are acting for the parties to the transactions.[17]

(2)   Only those solicitors or licensed conveyancers who have been authorised do so will be permitted to conduct electronic conveyancing.[18] The relationship with the Registry will be contractual, under a "network access agreement",[19] and the Registry will be obliged to contract with any solicitor or licensed conveyancer who meets the specified criteria.[20] Those specified criteria will be the subject of wide consultation and discussion with the relevant professional and other interested bodies. One of the important aims of those criteria is, as we explain in Part XIII of this Report, to raise the standards of conveyancing.[1]

2.58   However, it will also be noted from the examples given above,[2] that the Registry will still exercise a substantial measure of control over the registration process. This is because it will not be possible to change the register except in the form agreed in advance with the Registry.

Compulsory use of electronic conveyancing

2.59   There is power in the Bill to make the use of electronic conveyancing compulsory. The way that the power will operate, if exercised, is that a disposition (or a contract to make such a disposition) will only have effect if it is—

(1)   made by means of an electronic document;

(2)   communicated in electronic form to the Registry; and

(3)   simultaneously registered.[3]

2.60   This is a power that will not be exercised lightly. When solicitors and licensed conveyancers enter into network access agreements with the Registry, they will be required to conduct electronic conveyancing in accordance with network transaction rules.[4] Those transaction rules are likely to provide that the dispositions and contracts to make dispositions are made in the manner explained in the previous paragraph. In other words, those rules will ensure that electronic dispositions are simultaneously registered, which is the single most important technical objective of the Bill. However, as we explain in Part XIII of this Report,[5] it may be necessary to exercise the statutory power to secure that technical objective notwithstanding what can be done under the network transaction rules.[6]

2.61   There are, in any event, other reasons why the Bill has to contain a power to make electronic conveyancing compulsory. It is inevitable that the move from a paper-based to an all-electronic system of conveyancing will take some years and that the two systems will necessarily co-exist during this period of

---

[17]   See below, para. 2.51.
[18]   See below, para. 2.52.
[19]   For such agreements, see Sch. 5, para. 1; below, para. 13.36.
[20]   The criteria are necessary to ensure the integrity of the register. For the criteria, see Sch. 5, para. 10; below, paras. 13.40 and following.
[1]   See below, para. 13.42.
[2]   See below, paras. 2.54, 2.55.
[3]   S. 93; below, para. 13.75.
[4]   See Sch. 5, paras. 2, 5; below, paras. 13.47, 13.52.
[5]   See below, paras. 13.74 and following.
[6]   This could be quite important in relation to priorities: see above, para. (2).

transition. However, that period of transition needs to be kept to a minimum for two principal reasons. The first is that it will be very difficult both for practitioners and for the Land Registry to have to operate two distinct systems side by side. Secondly, if electronic conveyancing is to achieve its true potential and deliver the savings and benefits that it promises, it must be the only system. This can be illustrated by the example of a typical chain of domestic sales. As we have indicated above, it will be possible to manage chains in an all-electronic system.[7] However, if just one link in that chain is conducted in the conventional paper-based manner, the advantages of electronic chain management are likely to be lost. A chain moves at the speed of the slowest link. A paper-based link is in its nature likely to be slower than an electronic one[8] and will not be subject to the scrutiny and controls of those links in the chain that are electronic and therefore managed. There must, therefore, be a residual power to require transactions to be conducted in electronic form. It is hoped that the eventual exercise of the power will be merely a formality because solicitors and licensed conveyancers will have chosen to conduct conveyancing electronically in view of the advantages that it offers to them and to their clients. Not only will it make the conduct of conveyancing easier and faster for them, but they will also have to compete with other practitioners who have elected to adopt the electronic system."

XI. Land Registry: Administration and Adjudication[9]

The office of Her Majesty's Land Registry continues in its present form under section 99 of the Land Registration Act 2002. Its headquarters is in Lincoln's Inn Fields, London, and it controls 24 District Land Registries throughout England and Wales.[10]

The Registrar has both administrative and judicial powers.[11] Section 107 of the Act creates a new office of Adjudicator to Her Majesty's Land Registry. His function is to determine any contested application to the Registrar which cannot be disposed of by agreement between the parties. This replaces the present system of determination by the Solicitor to the Land Registry. Anyone aggrieved by a decision of the Adjudicator may appeal to the High Court.[12]

LAND REGISTRATION ACT 2002

99   The land registry
(1) There is to continue to be an office called Her Majesty's Land Registry which is to deal with the business of registration under this Act.

[7]   See para. 2.52.
[8]   Because it will not be able to take advantage of the time-saving features that electronic conveyancing will be able to offer.
[9]   R & R, chap. 48; H & B, chap. 9; Law Commission Report on Land Registration for the Twenty-First Century 2001 (Law Com No. 274), Part 16. See also LRA 2002, ss. 99–106 (administration of the Land Registry), 107–114 (adjudication).
[10]   Land Registration (Proper Offices) Order 2003 (SI 2003 No. 2040). The Headquarters in Lincoln's Inn Fields is illustrated on the front cover of this edition.
[11]   For the power of the registration to compel the production of documents see LRA 2002, s. 75.
[12]   LRA 2002, ss. 107–114; The Adjudicator to Her Majesty's Land Registry (Practice and Procedure) Rules 2003 (SI 2003 No. 2171); LR (Referral to Adjudicator to HM Land Registry) Rules 2003 (SI 2003 No. 2114); Land Registration (Acting Adjudicator) Regs. 2003 (SI 2003 No. 2342).

(2) The land registry is to consist of—
(a) the Chief Land Registrar, who is its head, and
(b) the staff appointed by him;
and references in this Act to a member of the land registry are to be read accordingly.
(3) The Lord Chancellor shall appoint a person to be the Chief Land Registrar.
(4) Schedule 7 (which makes further provision about the land registry) has effect.

107 The adjudicator
(1) The Lord Chancellor shall appoint a person to be the Adjudicator to Her Majesty's Land Registry.
. . .
(3) Schedule 9 (which makes further provision about the adjudicator) has effect.

108 Jurisdiction
(1) The adjudicator has the following functions—
(a) determining matters referred to him under section 73(7), and
(b) determining appeals under paragraph 4 of Schedule 5.
(2) Also, the adjudicator may, on application, make any order which the High Court could make for the rectification or setting aside of a document which—
(a) effects a qualifying disposition of a registered estate or charge,
(b) is a contract to make such a disposition, or
(c) effects a transfer of an interest which is the subject of a notice in the register.
(3) For the purposes of subsection (2)(a), a qualifying disposition is—
(a) a registrable disposition, or
(b) a disposition which creates an interest which may be the subject of a notice in the register.
(4) The general law about the effect of an order of the High Court for the rectification or setting aside of a document shall apply to an order under this section.

QUESTIONS

1. Legal and equitable estates in land have existed for centuries. Since 1925, we speak of legal estates and equitable interests. To what extent is this nomenclature meaningful in the context of:
    (a) Unregistered Land;
    (b) Registered Land?
    See Maitland, *Equity*, pp. 210–215.
2. Is the Land Registration Act 2002 evolutionary or revolutionary?
3. How far is a purchaser bound, and how far should he be bound, by an unregistered registrable interest of which he actually knows?
    (a) Unregistered land. LPA 1925, s. 199; LCA 1972, s. 4; *Hollington Bros Ltd v Rhodes* [1951] 2 TLR 691, p. 46, ante; *Industrial Properties (Barton Hill Ltd) v Associated Electrical Industries Ltd* [1977] QB 580 at 608–609, [1977] 2 All ER 293 at 312–313, per ROSKILL LJ; *Midland Bank Trust Co Ltd v Green* [1981] AC 513, [1981] 1 All ER 153, p. 38, ante.
    (b) Registered land. *Hodges v Jones* [1935] Ch 657 at 671, per LUXMOORE J; *De Lusignan v Johnson* (1973) 117 SJ 854, p. 165, n.2, ante; *Peffer v Rigg* [1977] 1 WLR 285, [1978] 3 All ER 745, pp. 176, ante; *Lyus v Prowsa Developments Ltd* [1982] 1 WLR 1044, [1982] 2 All ER 953, p. 176, ante.
    See Question 1 on p. 164, ante.

3. Limitation of Actions [1]

Since the Land Registration Act came into force on 13 October 2003, there have in effect been three statutes which govern the rights of a squatter who is in adverse possession of someone else's land. They are the Limitation Act 1980 for unregistered land, and the Land Registration Acts 1925 and 2002 for registered land. The Land Registration Act 2002 displaces the law in the Land Registration Act 1925 and substitutes a new scheme which reflects the principles underlying registered conveyancing. The details of the new scheme are set out in Schedule 6 to the 2002 Act and rules 187–194 of the Land Registration Rules 2003. [2]

I. Limitation Act 1980

The Limitation Act 1980 [3] consolidates the law of limitation of civil actions. [4] The general principle is that no action may be brought for the recovery of land after the expiration of a prescribed period from the time when the right of action first

---

[1]   C & B, chap. 27; Gray, chap. 3; M & W, chap. 21; MM, chap. 14; Smith, pp. 64–83. See the annotation of the Limitation Act 1980 in Current Law Statutes (D. Morgan), and generally McGee, *Limitation Periods* (4th edn, 2002); Preston and Newsom, *Limitation of Actions* (3rd edn 1953); (4th edn 1989); Franks, *Limitation of Actions* (1959); Josling, *Periods of Limitation* (6th edn 1986); Prime and Scanlon, *Modern Law of Limitation* (1993); Redmond-Cooper, *Limitation of Actions* (1997); Oughton, *Limitation of Actions* (1998). For the history of the old law: Holdsworth, vol. iv, pp. 484–486, vol. vii, p. 29, et seq.; Simpson, *History of The Land Law* (2nd edn 1986), pp. 141–145; Hayes, *Introduction to Conveyancing* (5th edn.), pp. 222 et seq. In 1998 the Law Commission published a detailed Consultation Paper on Limitation of Actions (Law Com No 151); see especially paras. 6.1–6.50 and 13.113–13.136. See now Law Commission Report on Limitation of Actions 2001 (Law Com No 270), p. 242, post.

[2]   R & R, chap. 35; H & B, chap. 87. Law Commission Report on Land Registration for the Twenty-First Century, Part XIV. On transitional provisions; see LRA 2002, Sch. 12, para. 18; R & R, paras. 33.009–33.015; (2004) 148 SJ 141 (W. Hanbury).

[3]   As amended by the Latent Damage Act 1986; p. 219, n. 5, post.

[4]   Previous statutes on actions to recover were: Limitation Act 1623; Real Property Limitation Acts 1833, 1874; Limitation Act 1939 (based upon Law Revision Committee Fifth Interim Report (Statutes of Limitation) 1936 (Cmd. 5334)); Limitation Amendment Act 1980 (based upon Law Reform Committee 21st Report (Final Report on Limitations of Actions) 1977 (Cmnd 6923), which contains a valuable discussion of all aspects of limitation).

accrues. This period is now in general twelve years,[5] and the Act deals specifically with the accrual of the right of action in the case of present interests, future interests, settled land and land held under a trust of land, forfeiture or breach of condition, and tenancies. For an action to accrue, and consequently for time to start running, there must be an 'adverse possessor' against whom an action can be brought.[6]

The policy of limitation was stated by Streatfield J in *R B Policies at Lloyd's v Butler*.[7] 'It is a policy of the Limitation Acts that those who go to sleep upon their claims should not be assisted by the courts in recovering their property, but another, and, I think, equal policy behind these Acts, is that there shall be an end of litigation . . .'[8] What is the effect of such a policy? What is the effect of the expiration of the limitation period on D (the person who has been dispossessed or has discontinued his possession) and on A (the person in adverse possession)?[9]

(a) On D

The effect of the Limitation Act is purely negative. Not only is D's right of action to recover the land from A extinguished, but also his title to the land.[10] D cannot revive his title by a later acknowledgement or payment made to him,[11] nor by a judgment obtained by default.[12] He cannot restore his position by re-entry on the land (in this case, he can only regain it by lapse of time as an adverse possessor), and if he brings an action for recovery of the land, A need not plead the Limitation Act.[13]

(b) On A

Here the Act is silent. It is now clear that D's title is not transferred to A: there is no 'Parliamentary Conveyance'.[14] But by a combination of the negative effect of the Act on D's title, and the positive effect of his adverse possession, A has a new estate of his own, a fee simple subject to the unextinguished rights of other persons.[15] If D is a fee simple owner, then, as Megarry and Wade say,[16] 'A's

---

[5] Limitation Act 1980, s. 15(1); the general period of 20 years, fixed by the Real Property Limitation Act 1833, was reduced to 12 years by the Real Property Limitation Act 1874.

[6] Ibid., s. 15(6), Sch. 1, para. 8; *Buckinghamshire County Council v Moran* [1990] Ch 623, [1989] 2 All ER 225.

[7] [1950] 1 KB 76 at 81, [1949] 2 All ER 226 at 229; *A'Court v Cross* (1825) 3 Bing 329 at 332, per BEST CJ 'It is ... an Act of peace. Long dormant claims have often more of cruelty than of justice in them.'

[8] See [1985] Conv 272 (M. Dockray).

[9] C & B, pp. 950–984; Gray, pp. 238–250; M & W, paras. 3.115–3.126, 21.055–21.070; MM, pp. 559–564; Smith, pp. 79–83; Pollock and Wright, *Possession* (1888), pp. 93–100; Franks, pp. 131–133, 141–143; (1925) 41 LQR 139 (S.A. Wiren); (1940) 56 LQR 376 (A.D. Hargreaves), 479 (W.S. Holdsworth); (1962) 78 LQR 541 (H.W.R. Wade); (1964) 80 LQR 63 (B. Rudden); (1973) 32 Conv (NS) 85 (J.A. Omotola); Section VII, post.

[10] Limitation Act 1980, s. 17, p. 233, post; s. 25(3) (advowsons).

[11] *Sanders v Sanders* (1881) 19 ChD 373, p. 232, post; *Nicholson v England* [1926] 2 KB 93.

[12] *Irish Land Commission v Ryan* [1900] 2 IR 565.

[13] *Dawkins v Lord Penrhyn* (1878) 4 App Cas 51; *Dismore v Milton* [1938] 3 All ER 762; Franks, pp. 131, 265.

[14] *Tichborne v Weir* (1892) 67 LT 735, p. 241, post.

[15] Co Litt 271a (also 2a, 297a) 'For a disseisor, abator, intruder, usurper, etc., have a fee simple, but it is not a lawful fee'; *Leach v Jay* (1878) 9 ChD 44 at 45; *Rankin v M'Murtry* (1889) 24 LR Ir 290; (1962) 78 LQR at 543–545.

[16] At paras. 3.122–3.123. The symbols have been changed.

possession at once gives him all the rights and powers of ownership.[17] A has, in fact, a legal estate, a fee simple absolute in possession. But so also has D, until such time as his title is extinguished by limitation . . . . There is thus no absurdity in speaking of two or more [18] adverse estates in the land, for their validity is relative. If D allows his title to become barred by lapse of time, A's title becomes the better, and A then becomes "absolute owner". But if D brings his action within the time allowed, he can successfully assert his better title based on his prior possession; as against D, A's legal estate is nothing.'

If D is a lessee of L, and A has been in adverse possession for twelve years, A's possession extinguishes D's title. This has no effect on L's title, because L's right of action does not accrue until the end of the lease.[19] 'A has a legal estate (probably a fee simple) subject to L's right of entry at the end of the original term.'[20] But A may be evicted before then (a) by L, if he has taken a surrender of the lease from D,[1] or if he has forfeited the lease,[2] (b) by D, if he has taken a conveyance of the fee simple from L.[3] If, however, A acknowledges L as the freeholder, he may become a tenant for a term of years, or a yearly tenant or a tenant at will.

Whatever interest A gets, it is subject to the legal and equitable rights of third parties which run with the land and have not themselves been independently extinguished e.g. easements and restrictive covenants.[4] If the land is leasehold and A has extinguished the title of the lessee but not that of the lessor, he is not an assignee of the lease, and so is not bound by any covenants in the lease, unless they are enforceable as restrictive covenants. If A pays rent to the lessor and becomes a yearly tenant, he is not, by the mere payment of rent, estopped from denying that he is bound by the terms of the original lease.[5]

The Limitation Act 1980, then, operates negatively; not positively as does the Prescription Act 1832.[6] It does not create a title in A, it merely prevents D from enforcing his. The effect of this as between vendor and purchaser is that a title based on adverse possession alone for the limitation period or longer is not necessarily a good title. The claims of the reversioner or a remainderman may have yet to be extinguished:[7] the reversion may be on a 99 year lease, the remainderman's interest may not vest in possession for over 100 years.[8] But if a

---

[17] If A dies, the land passes under his will or intestacy; *Asher v Whitlock* (1865) LR 1 QB 1, p. 233, post; *Allen v Roughley* (1955) 94 CLR 98; [1956] CLJ 177 (H.W.R. Wade).

[18] In the case of successive adverse possessors, the last in possession may be evicted by an earlier adverse possessor, until that possessor's title has itself been extinguished by lapse of time. See *Mount Carmel Investments Ltd v Peter Thurlow Ltd* [1988] 1 WLR 1078, [1988] 3 All ER 129, where D was dispossessed by A, who in turn transferred his possession to X, another squatter; CA held that X could add both periods and acquire title by limitation.

[19] Limitation Act 1980, s. 15(2), p. 220, post.

[20] M & W, para. 21.067.

[1] *Fairweather v St Marylebone Property Co Ltd* [1963] AC 510, [1962] 2 All ER 288; p. 237, post. For a different solution in registered land, see *Spectrum Investment Co v Holmes* [1981] 1 WLR 221, [1981] 1 All ER 6, p. 245, post.

[2] *Tickner v Buzzacott* [1965] Ch 426, [1964] 1 All ER 131 (adverse possessor not entitled to apply to court for relief against forfeiture of lease for non-payment of rent).

[3] *Taylor v Twinberrow* [1930] 2 KB 16; *Chung Ping Kwan v Lam Island Development Co Ltd* [1997] AC 38, p. 234, post.

[4] *Re Nisbet and Potts' Contract* [1906] 1 Ch 386, p. 241, post; *Scott v Scott* (1854) 4 HL Cas 1065.

[5] *Tichborne v Weir* (1892) 67 LT 735, p. 241, post.

[6] See *Buckinghamshire County Council v Moran* [1990] Ch 623 at 644, [1989] 2 All ER 225 at 238, per NOURSE LJ.

[7] Limitation Act 1980, s. 15(2). Time runs against the landlord even if the lease is immediately renewed; p. 226, post.

[8] *Cadell v Palmer* (1833) 1 Cl & Fin 372: vesting postponed for over 100 years (note to *Re Villar* [1928] Ch 471 at 478).

vendor can establish that the flaw in an otherwise good title is one that can be cured by the running of time in his favour under the Act, he can force a purchaser to take the title.[9] Proof that rival claims have been extinguished by the lapse of time may be very difficult, and in practice a purchaser often agrees to accept an imperfect title.

LIMITATION ACT 1980

15. Time limit for actions to recover land. — (6) Part I of Schedule 1[10] to this Act contains provisions for determining the date of accrual of rights of action to recover land in the cases there mentioned.

(7) Part II of that Schedule[11] contains provisions modifying the provisions of this section in their application to actions brought by, or by a person claiming through, the Crown or any spiritual or eleemosynary corporation sole.

SCHEDULE 1

Right of action not to accrue or continue unless there is adverse possession

8. — (1) No right of action to recover land shall be treated as accruing unless the land is in the possession of some person in whose favour the period of limitation can run (referred to below in this paragraph as 'adverse possession'); and where under the preceding provisions of this Schedule any such right of action is treated as accruing on a certain date and no person is in adverse possession on that date, the right of action shall not be treated as accruing unless and until adverse possession is taken of the land.[12]

(2) Where a right of action to recover land has accrued and after its accrual, before the right is barred, the land ceases to be in adverse possession, the right of action shall no longer be treated as having accrued and no fresh right of action shall be treated as accruing unless and until the land is again taken into adverse possession.[13]

(3) For the purposes of this paragraph —

(a) possession of any land subject to a rentcharge by a person (other than the person entitled to the rentcharge) who does not pay the rent shall be treated as adverse possession of the rentcharge; and

(b) receipt of rent under a lease by a person wrongfully claiming to be entitled to the land in reversion immediately expectant on the determination of the lease[14] shall be treated as adverse possession of the land.[15]

(4) For the purpose of determining whether a person occupying land is in

---

9   *Re Atkinson's and Horsell's Contract* [1912] 2 Ch 1; *Re Spencer and Hauser's Contract* [1928] Ch 598, distinguished in *George Wimpey & Co Ltd v Sohn* [1967] Ch 487, [1966] 1 All ER 232; Farrand, *Contract and Conveyance* (4th edn, 1983), pp. 108–109.

10   Paras. 1–9.

11   Paras. 10–13.

12   *Smith v Lawson* [1997] NPC 87 (occupant of land protected by estoppel held not to be in adverse possession).

13   Enacting the rule in *Trustees, Executors and Agency Co Ltd v Short* (1888) 13 App Cas 793. The mere sending and receipt of a letter demanding possession of land does not amount to termination of adverse possession: *Mount Carmel Investments Ltd v Peter Thurlow Ltd* [1988] 1 WLR 1078, [1988] 3 All ER 129. Cf *BP Properties Ltd v Buckler* (1987) 55 P & CR 337 where possession ceased to be adverse when claimant occupied by unilateral licence from true owner; [1994] Conv 196 (H. Wallace); *Sze To Chun Keung v Kung Kwok Wai David* [1997] 1 WLR 1232 (the last appeal to PC from Hong Kong); *Smith v Lawson* (1997) 75 P & CR 466 (time held not to run against freeholder in favour of occupier of land protected by promissory estoppel).

14   See p. 220, post.

15   *Bligh v Martin* [1968] 1 WLR 804, [1968] 1 All ER 1157.

adverse possession of the land it shall not be assumed by implication of law that his occupation is by permission of the person entitled to the land merely by virtue of the fact that his occupation is not inconsistent with the latter's present or future enjoyment of the land.

This provision shall not be taken as prejudicing a finding to the effect that a person's occupation of any land is by implied permission of the person entitled to the land in any case where such a finding is justified on the actual facts of the case.[16]

38. Interpretation.— (1) In this Act, unless the context otherwise requires — 'land' includes corporeal hereditaments, tithes and rentcharges and any legal or equitable estate or interest therein, but except as provided above in this definition does not include any incorporeal hereditament.[17]

(5) Subject to subsection (6) below, a person shall be treated as claiming through another person if he became entitled by, through, under, or by the act of that other person to the right claimed, and any person whose estate or interest might have been barred by a person entitled to an entailed interest in possession shall be treated as claiming through the person so entitled.

(6) A person becoming entitled to any estate or interest by virtue of a special power of appointment shall not be treated as claiming through the appointor.

II. Adverse Possession

In order to establish a title by adverse possession, a squatter must be shown to have both factual possession and the requisite intention to possess (animus possidendi). In *JA Pye (Oxford) Ltd v Graham* [2003] 1 AC 419, at para. 43, [2003] 3 All ER 865 at 877, Lord BROWNE-WILKINSON approved the test, set out by SLADE LJ in *Buckinghamshire County Council v Moran* [1990] Ch. 623 at 640, [1989] 2 All ER 225 at 235, that the requisite intention was 'an intention to exclude the world at large, including the owner with the paper title, so far as reasonably practicable and so far as the processes of the law will allow.'[18]

J A PYE (OXFORD) LTD v GRAHAM
[2003] 1 AC 419, [2002] 3 All ER 865 (HL, LORDS BINGHAM OF CORNHILL, MACKAY OF CLASHFERN, BROWNE-WILKINSON, HOPE OF CRAIGHEAD and HUTTON)[19]
In February 1983 the claimants entered into a written grazing agreement with Graham in respect of 25 hectares of agricultural land at Henwick, Thatcham in Berkshire, which adjoined Graham's farmland. The land was enclosed by hedges and was only accessible, save on foot, through a gate kept padlocked by Graham. The agreement expired in December 1993 and the claimants required Graham

---

[16]　As added by Limitation Amendment Act 1980, s. 4. This reverses the doctrine of implied or hypothetical licence suggested by LORD DENNING MR in *Wallis's Cayton Bay Holiday Camp Ltd v Shell-Mex and BP Ltd* [1975] QB 94, [1974] 3 All ER 575; *Gray v Wykeham-Martin and Goode* [1977] Bar Library Transcript No 10A (CA, affirming the decision of GOULDING J, who had followed *Wallis* by implying a licence without any factual basis). In *Powell v McFarlane* (1979) 38 P & CR 452, at 484 SLADE J explained 'the substantial conceptual difficulties of the doctrine.'

[17]　As amended by TLATA 1996, s. 25(2), Sch. 4.

[18]　See also *Powell v McFarlane* (1977) 38 P & CR 452 at 470, per SLADE J.
　　The statutory provisions relating to adverse possession are not incompatible with Art. 1 Protocol 1 or Art. 6 of the European Convention on Human Rights: *Family Housing Association v Donnellan* [2002] 1 P & CR 34; *Stubbings v United Kingdom* [1996] 25 EHRR 213.

[19]　[2003] CLJ 36 (L. Tee).

to vacate the land. They refused requests to renew the agreement, indicating that they did not want the land to be grazed while they applied for planning permission to develop it. Graham continued to use the land and in August 1984, with the claimants' permission, took a cut of hay for payment. In 1984 and 1985 Graham's further requests to renew the agreement and to take cuts of hay were not answered, but he continued to occupy and maintain all the year round the land which he farmed as a unit with his adjoining land. ✍

In June 1997 Graham registered cautions against the claimants' title to the land. In August 1997 the claimants applied to warn off the cautions and in April 1998 issued an originating summons to cancel them. In January 1999 the claimants brought possession proceedings against Graham.

Held (reversing the Court of Appeal [2001] Ch. 804 and restoring NEUBERGER J [2002] Ch 676). G had established a possessory title under the Limitation Act 1980, section 15(1), Schedule 1, paragraphs 1, 8(1).

LORD BROWNE-WILKINSON:

The issues

27 The action was brought by Pye at the earliest on 30 April 1998. The question therefore is whether, prior to that date, there was a period of 12 years during which the Grahams were in possession of the disputed land to the exclusion of Pye. More accurately, there are two questions viz: (1) did Pye discontinue possession or was it 'dispossessed' of the disputed land (within the meaning of paragraph 1 of Schedule 1 to the 1980 Act) before 30 April 1986; and if so (2) did the Grahams thereafter remain in possession of the land for a period of 12 years?

28 It is common ground that Pye did not 'discontinue' possession within the meaning of the Act. Further I did not understand there to be any claim by Pye that, if the Grahams had at any time prior to 30 April 1986 dispossessed Pye, the Grahams thereafter ceased to be in possession for the purposes of the Act.

29 It was further common ground that so long as the Grahams were occupying the disputed land with Pye's consent, they could not be treated as having dispossessed Pye. Accordingly no relevant right of action can have accrued to Pye under Schedule 1, paragraph 1 until after the expiry on or about 31 August 1984 of the grass-cutting permission.

30 The relevant question therefore is whether at some time between 1 September 1984 and 30 April 1986 Pye were 'dispossessed' of the disputed land so that, at that date, Pye's right of action accrued for the purposes of Schedule 1, paragraph 1 to the 1980 Act.

The law

31 The apparently straight forward statutory provisions have given rise to considerable difficulties, most of which flow from the remarks of the Court of Appeal in *Leigh v Jack* (1879) 5 Ex D 264 and *Littledale v Liverpool College* [1900] 1 Ch 19. In a remarkable judgment at first instance, *Powell v McFarlane* (1977) 38 P & CR 452,[1] Slade J traced his way successfully through a number of Court of Appeal judgments which were binding on him so as to restore a degree of order to the subject and to state clearly the relevant principles. Although there are

[1]   Infant who at age of 14 began to graze the cow Kashla, otherwise known as Ted's cow, held not to have requisite intent.

one or two minor points on which (unlike Slade J) your Lordships are not bound by authority and can therefore make necessary adjustments, for the most part the principles set out by Slade J as subsequently approved by the Court of Appeal in *Buckinghamshire County Council v Moran* [1990] Ch 623, [1989] 2 All ER 225 cannot be improved upon. Hereafter I adopt them without specific recognition beyond marking with inverted commas those passages which I have quoted verbatim.

Possession, dispossession, ouster and adverse possession

32 In *Powell's* case Slade J was considering the Limitation Act 1939. However, apart from paragraph 8(4) of Schedule 1 to the 1980 Act the statutory provisions applicable in the present case are identical in the 1939 Act and the 1980 Act. Slade J first addressed himself to the question what was the meaning of possession and dispossession in the statutory provisions. After noticing that possession and dispossession were not defined in the 1939 Act he continued, at p. 469:

'Possession of land, however, is a concept which has long been familiar and of importance to English lawyers, because (inter alia) it entitles the person in possession, whether rightfully or wrongfully, to maintain an action of trespass against any other person who enters the land without his consent, unless such other person has himself a better right to possession. In the absence of authority, therefore, I would for my own part have regarded the word "possession" in the 1939 Act as bearing the traditional sense of that degree of occupation or physical control, coupled with the requisite intention commonly referred to as animus possidendi, that would entitle a person to maintain an action of trespass in relation to the relevant land; likewise I would have regarded the word "dispossession" in the Act as denoting simply the taking of possession in such sense from another without the other's licence or consent; likewise I would have regarded a person who has "dispossessed" another in the sense just stated as being in "adverse possession" for the purposes of the Act.'

Save as to the last sentence I have quoted (as to which I will make certain further comments below), I entirely agree with that statement of the law. Slade J felt doubts whether, in the light of certain Court of Appeal judgments then binding on him, he could properly adhere to the view that he expressed. Decisions (for example *Wallis's Cayton Bay Holiday Camp Ltd v Shell-Mex and BP Ltd* [1975] QB 94, [1974] 3 All ER 575) appeared to hold that use of the land by a squatter which would have been sufficient to constitute possession in the ordinary sense of the word was not enough: it was said that such use by the squatter did not constitute 'adverse possession' which was required for the purposes of limitation unless the squatter's use conflicted with the intentions of the paper title owner as to his present or future use of the disputed land. In those cases it was held that the use by the squatter was, as a matter of law, to be treated as enjoyed with the implied consent of the paper owner. Not surprisingly, Slade J found this line of reasoning difficult to follow. It is hard to see how the intentions of the paper title owner (unless known to the squatter) can affect the intention of the squatter to possess the land. In my judgment, Slade J was right and the decision of the Court of Appeal in those cases wrong. In any event Parliament (on the advice of the Law Reform Committee) has intervened to reverse the principle of implied licence: see the 1980 Act, Schedule 1, paragraph 8(4). However there remains a long standing confusion as to what constitutes 'dispossession' and the place, if any, of 'adverse possession' in the modern law.

33 The root of the problem is caused by the concept of 'non-adverse possession'. This was a concept engrafted by the common law and equity onto the limitation statute of James I (21 Jac 1, c 16). Before the passing of the Real Property Limitation Acts 1833 (3 & 4 Will 4, c 27) and 1874 (37 & 38 Vict c 57), the rights of the paper owner were not taken away save by a 'disseisin' or an ouster and use of the land by the squatter of a kind which was clearly inconsistent with the paper title. Such inconsistent use was called adverse possession: see Professor Dockray, 'Adverse Possession and Intention' [1982] Conveyancer 256, 260. Under the 1833 Act (sections 2 and 3 of which were substantially to the same effect as the 1980 Act, section 15(1) and Schedule 1, paragraph 1) the right of action was barred 20 years after 'the right ... to bring such action shall have first accrued' and 'such right shall be deemed to have first accrued at the time of such dispossession or discontinuance of possession'. Soon after the passing of the 1833 Act it was held that 'the second and third sections of that Act ... have done away with the doctrine of non-adverse possession, and ... the question is whether 20 years have elapsed *since the right accrued,* whatever the nature of the possession': Denman CJ in *Nepean v Doe d Knight* (1837) 2 M & W 894, 911. The same statement of the new law was made in *Culley v Doe d Taylerson* (1840) 11 Ad & E 1008, 1015 where Denman CJ said:

'The effect of [section 2] is to put an end to all questions and discussions, whether the possession of lands, etc, be adverse or not; and, if one party has been in the actual possession for 20 years, whether adversely or not, the claimant, whose original right of entry accrued above 20 years before bringing the ejectment, is barred by this section.'

34 The same was held to be the law by the Privy Council in a carefully reasoned advice delivered by Lord Upjohn in *Paradise Beach and Transportation Co Ltd v Price-Robinson* [1968] AC 1072; [1968] 1 All ER 530 see also Professor Dockray [1982] Conveyancer 256.

35 From 1833 onwards, therefore, old notions of adverse possession, disseisin or ouster from possession should not have formed part of judicial decisions. From 1833 onwards the only question was whether the squatter had been in possession in the ordinary sense of the word. That is still the law, as Slade J rightly said. After 1833 the phrase 'adverse possession' did not appear in the statutes until, to my mind unfortunately, it was reintroduced by the Limitation Act 1939, section 10 of which is in virtually the same words as para. 8(1) of Schedule 1 to the 1980 Act. In my judgment the references to 'adverse possession' in the 1939 and 1980 Acts did not reintroduce by a side wind after over 100 years the old notions of adverse possession in force before 1833. Paragraph 8(1) of Schedule 1 to the 1980 Act defines what is meant by adverse possession in that paragraph as being the case where land is in the possession of a person in whose favour time 'can run'. It is directed not to the nature of the possession but to the capacity of the squatter. Thus a trustee who is unable to acquire a title by lapse of time against the trust estate (see section 21) is not in adverse possession for the purposes of paragraph 8. Although it is convenient to refer to possession by a squatter without the consent of the true owner as being 'adverse possession' the convenience of this must not be allowed to reintroduce by the back door that which for so long has not formed part of the law.

36 Many of the difficulties with these sections which I will have to consider are due to a conscious or subconscious feeling that in order for a squatter to gain title by lapse of time he has to act adversely to the paper title owner. It is said that he has to 'oust' the true owner in order to dispossess him; that he has to intend to exclude the whole world including the true owner; that the squatter's use of

the land has to be inconsistent with any present or future use by the true owner. In my judgment much confusion and complication would be avoided if reference to adverse possession were to be avoided so far as possible and effect given to the clear words of the Acts. The question is simply whether the defendant squatter has dispossessed the paper owner by going into ordinary possession of the land for the requisite period without the consent of the owner.

37 It is clearly established that the taking or continuation of possession by a squatter with the actual consent of the paper title owner does not constitute dispossession or possession by the squatter for the purposes of the Act. Beyond that, as Slade J said, the words possess and dispossess are to be given their ordinary meaning.

38 It is sometimes said that ouster by the squatter is necessary to constitute dispossession: see for example *Rains v Buxton* (1880) 14 Ch. D 537, 539 per Fry J. The word 'ouster' is derived from the old law of adverse possession and has overtones of confrontational, knowing removal of the true owner from possession. Such an approach is quite incorrect. There will be a 'dispossession' of the paper owner in any case where (there being no discontinuance of possession by the paper owner) a squatter assumes possession in the ordinary sense of the word.[1a] Except in the case of joint possessors, possession is single and exclusive. Therefore if the squatter is in possession of the land but the squatter's subsequent occupation of it in law constitutes possession the squatter must have 'dispossessed' the true owner for the purposes of Schedule 1, paragraph 1: see *Taylor v Nute* [1976] 1 WLR 1295, 1300 [1977] 1 All ER 230, 234; Professor Dockray [1982] Conveyancer 256. Therefore in the present case the relevant question can be narrowed down to asking whether the Grahams were in possession of the disputed land, without the consent of Pye, before 30 April 1986. If they were, they will have 'dispossessed' Pye within the meaning of paragraph 1 of Schedule 1 to the 1980 Act.

39 What then constitutes 'possession' in the ordinary sense of the word?

Possession

40 In *Powell's* case 38 P & CR 470 Slade J said, at p. 470:
'(1) In the absence of evidence to the contrary, the owner of land with the paper title is deemed to be in possession of the land, as being the person with the prime facie right to possession. The law will thus, without reluctance, ascribe possession either to the paper owner or to persons who can establish a title as claiming through the paper owner. (2) If the law is to attribute possession of land to a person who can establish no paper title to possession, he must be shown to have both factual possession and the requisite intention to possess ("animus possidendi").'

Counsel for both parties criticised this definition as being unhelpful since it used the word being defined – possession – in the definition itself. This is true: but Slade J was only adopting a definition used by Roman law and by all judges and writers in the past. To be pedantic the problem could be avoided by saying there are two elements necessary for legal possession: (1) a sufficient degree of physical custody and control ('factual possession'); (2) an intention to exercise such custody and control on one's own behalf and for one's own benefit ('intention to possess'). What is crucial is to understand that, without the requisite intention, in law there can be no possession. Remarks made by Clarke LJ in

---

[1a]   *Purbrick v Hackney London Borough* [2004] 1 P & CR 34 (placing makeshift door with two locks on entrance to dilapidated 'burnt-out shell' held to be adverse possession, even though squatter was aware that he was liable to be dispossessed).

Lambeth London Borough Council v Blackburn (2001) 82 P & CR 494, 499 ('It is not perhaps immediately obvious why the authorities have required a trespasser to establish an intention to possess as well as actual possession in order to prove the relevant adverse possession') provided the starting point for a submission by Mr Lewison for the Grahams that there was no need, in order to show possession in law, to show separately an intention to possess. I do not think that Clarke LJ was under any misapprehension, but in any event there has always, both in Roman law and in common law, been a requirement to show an intention to possess in addition to objective acts of physical possession. Such intention may be, and frequently is, deduced from the physical acts themselves, but there is no doubt in my judgment that there are two separate elements in legal possession. So far as English law is concerned intention as a separate element is obviously necessary. Suppose a case where A is found to be in occupation of a locked house. He may be there as a squatter, as an overnight trespasser, or as a friend looking after the house of the paper owner during his absence on holiday. The acts done by A in any given period do not tell you whether there is legal possession. If A is there as a squatter he intends to stay as long as he can for his own benefit: his intention is an intention to possess. But if he only intends to trespass for the night or has expressly agreed to look after the house for his friend he does not have possession. It is not the nature of the acts which A does but the intention with which he does them which determines whether or not he is in possession.

Factual possession

41 In *Powell's* case Slade J said at pp. 470–471:

'(3) Factual possession signifies an appropriate degree of physical control. It must be a single and [exclusive] possession, though there can be a single possession exercised by or on behalf of several persons jointly. Thus an owner of land and a person intruding on that land without his consent cannot both be in possession of the land at the same time. The question what acts constitute a sufficient degree of exclusive physical control must depend on the circumstances, in particular the nature of the land and the manner in which land of that nature is commonly used or enjoyed ... Everything must depend on the particular circumstances, but broadly, I think what must be shown as constituting factual possession is that the alleged possessor has been dealing with the land in question as an occupying owner might have been expected to deal with it and that no-one else has done so.'

I agree with this statement of the law which is all that is necessary in the present case. The Grahams were in occupation of the land which was within their exclusive physical control. The paper owner, Pye, was physically excluded from the land by the hedges and the lack of any key to the roadgate. The Grahams farmed it in conjunction with Manor Farm and in exactly the same way. They were plainly in factual possession before 30 April 1986.

Intention to possess

(a) To own or to possess?

42 There are cases in which judges have apparently treated it as being necessary that the squatter should have an intention to own the land in order to be in possession. In *Littledale v Liverpool College* [1900] 1 Ch 19, 24 Sir Nathaniel Lindley MR referred to the plaintiff relying on 'acts of ownership': see also *George Wimpey & Co Ltd v Sohn* [1967] Ch 487, 510, [1966] 1 All ER 232, 240. Even Slade J in *Powell*, at pp. 476 and 478, referred to the necessary intention as being an 'intention to own'. In the *Moran* case (1988) 86 LGR 472, 479 the trial judge

(Hoffmann J) had pointed out that what is required is 'not an intention to own or even an intention to acquire ownership but an intention to possess'. The Court of Appeal in that case [1990] Ch. 623, 643, [1989] 2 All ER 225, 238 adopted this proposition which in my judgment is manifestly correct. Once it is accepted that in the Limitation Acts, the word 'possession' has its ordinary meaning (being the same as in the law of trespass or conversion) it is clear that, at any given moment, the only relevant question is whether the person in factual possession also has an intention to possess: if a stranger enters on to land occupied by a squatter, the entry is a trespass against the possession of the squatter whether or not the squatter has any long term intention to acquire a title.

43 A similar manifestation of the same heresy is the statement by Sir Nathaniel Lindley MR in *Littledale v Liverpool College* [1900] 1 Ch 19, 23 that the paper owners 'could not be dispossessed unless the plaintiffs obtained possession themselves; and possession by the plaintiffs involves an animus possidendi – ie, occupation with the intention of excluding the owner as well as other people'. This requirement of an intention to exclude the owner as well as everybody else has been repeated in subsequent cases. In *Powell's* case 38 P & CR 452, 471–472 Slade J found difficulty in understanding what was meant by this dictum since a squatter will normally know that until the full time has run the paper owner can recover the land from him. Slade J reformulated the requirement (to my mind correctly) as requiring an 'intention, in one's own name and on one's own behalf, to exclude the world at large, including the owner with the paper title if he be not himself the possessor, so far as is reasonably practicable and so far as the processes of the law will allow'.

(b) Must the acts of the squatter be inconsistent with the intentions of the paper owner?

44 The decision of the Court of Appeal in *Leigh v Jack* 5 Ex D 264 has given rise to repeated trouble in later cases. In that case the plaintiff's predecessor in title (Mr Leigh) had laid out part of his estate as proposed streets to be known as Grundy Street and Napier Place. He conveyed to the defendant certain land described as being 'bounded by' Grundy Street and Napier Place: therefore the intention to use the adjoining land for streets was known to all parties. Within the 20-year limitation period, both Mr Leigh and the defendant had carried out work on a fence separating Grundy Street from other land of Mr Leigh, Regent Road. From 1854 onwards the defendant had placed on Grundy Street and Napier Place old graving dock materials, screw propellers, boilers and refuse from his foundry. In 1872 (four years before action brought) the defendant completely enclosed Grundy Street and Napier Place. The Court of Appeal held that the defendant had not acquired title to the enclosed land under the Limitation Act 1833.

45 The decision on the facts is not a surprising one. Quite apart from anything else, during the 20-year limitation period relied on, the paper owner (Mr Leigh) carried out works on the fence separating Grundy Street from Regent Road. This was inconsistent with a claim that he had either discontinued possession or been dispossessed. Unfortunately, other reasons were given. Cockburn CJ said that the defendant's storage of goods on the disputed land was not 'done with the view of defeating the purpose of the parties to the conveyances'. It will be noted that the defendant was well aware of Mr Leigh's intention to use the land as a public road since he was party to the conveyance so stating. Cotton LJ relied solely on the repair of the fence by Mr Leigh which I have mentioned as showing that there had been possession by him during the limitation period. The real difficulty has arisen from the judgment of Bramwell LJ. He said, at p. 273:

'I do not think that there was any dispossession of the plaintiff by the acts of the defendant: acts of user are not enough to take the soil out of the plaintiff and her predecessors in title and to vest it in the defendant; in order to defeat a title by dispossessing the former owner, acts must be done which are inconsistent with his enjoyment of the soil for the purposes for which he intended to use it ...'

The suggestion that the sufficiency of the possession can depend on the intention not of the squatter but of the true owner is heretical and wrong. It reflects an attempt to revive the pre-1833 concept of adverse possession requiring inconsistent user. Bramwell LJ's heresy led directly to the heresy in the *Wallis's Cayton Bay* line of cases to which I have referred, which heresy was abolished by statute. It has been suggested that the heresy of Bramwell LJ survived this statutory reversal but in the *Moran* case the Court of Appeal rightly held that however one formulated the proposition of Bramwell LJ as a proposition of law it was wrong[2] The highest it can be put is that, if the squatter is aware of a special purpose for which the paper owner uses or intends to use the land and the use made by the squatter does not conflict with that use, that may provide some support for a finding as a question of fact that the squatter had no intention to possess the land in the ordinary sense but only an intention to occupy it until needed by the paper owner. For myself I think there will be few occasions in which such inference could be properly drawn in cases where the true owner has been physically excluded from the land. But it remains a possible, if improbable, inference in some cases.

(c) Squatters' willingness to pay if asked

46 In a number of cases (such as the present case) squatters have given evidence that if they had been asked by the paper owner to pay for their occupation of the disputed land or to take a lease they would have been prepared to do so. In *Ocean Estates Ltd v Pinder* [1969] 2 AC 19, 24 Lord Diplock giving the advice of the Privy Council said that an admission by the squatter to that effect 'which any candid squatter hoping in due course to acquire a possessory title would be almost bound to make' did not indicate an absence of an intention to possess. In my judgment in the present case the Court of Appeal did not give full weight to that decision. In my judgment the decision of the Court of Appeal in *R v Secretary of State for the Environment, Ex p Davies* (1990) 61 P & CR 487 (the decision in *Pinder* not having been cited) was wrong. The decision in *Pinder* is to be preferred because it is consistent with principle. Once it is accepted that the necessary intent is an intent to possess not to own and an intention to exclude the paper owner only so far as is reasonably possible, there is no inconsistency between a squatter being willing to pay the paper owner if asked and his being in the meantime in possession. An admission of title by the squatter is not inconsistent with the squatter being in possession in the meantime. ...

[His Lordship reviewed the judgments of NEUBERGER J and the Court of Appeal and continued:]

64 Despite Pye's notification to quit the land in December 1983, its peremptory refusal of a further grazing licence in 1984 and the totally ignored later requests for a grazing licence, after 31 December 1983 the Grahams stayed in occupation of the disputed land using it for what purposes they thought fit. Some of those purposes (ie the grazing) would have fallen within a hypothetical grazing agreement. But the rest are only consistent with an intention, verified by

---

[2] Similarly disapproved in *London Borough of Hounslow v Minchinton* (1997) 74 P & CR 221.

Mr Michael Graham, to use the land as they thought best. That approach was adopted from the outset. In my judgment, when the Grahams remained in factual possession of the fully enclosed land after the expiry of the mowing licence they manifestly intended to assert their possession against Pye.

65 Finally I should mention one further point. In the Court of Appeal Pye unsuccessfully contended that the Human Rights Act 1998 affected the appeal which came on for hearing on 4 December 2000, ie after the Act had come into effect on 2 October 2000. Before your Lordships' House, it was conceded that the Human Rights Act 1998 did not have a retrospective effect.[3] But Pye submitted that, even under the common law principles of construction applicable before the Human Rights Act 1998 came into effect, the court should seek to apply the law so as to make it consistent with the European Convention for the Protection of Human Rights and Fundamental Freedoms. Any such old principle of construction only applied where there was an ambiguity in the language of a statute. No such ambiguity in the 1980 Act was demonstrated to your Lordships.

66 For these reasons I would allow the appeal and restore the judgment of Neuberger J.[4]

[3]   See *Rook, Property Law and Human Rights*, pp. 205–208.
[4]   On factual possession, see *Seddon v Smith* (1877) 36 LT 168; *Littledale v Liverpool College* [1900] 1 Ch 19; *George Wimpey & Co Ltd v Sohn* [1967] Ch 487, [1966] 1 All ER 22 (where the plaintiff had an easement over the land in question); *Bligh v Martin* [1968] 1 WLR 804, [1968] 1 All ER 1157; *Tecbild Ltd v Chamberlain* (1969) 20 P & CR 633 (playing by children and tethering of ponies held to be acts too trivial for adverse possession): *Basildon District Council v Manning* (1975) 237 EG 879 (erecting fence and dumping poultry manure held not to be adverse possession); *Red House Farms (Thorndon) Ltd v Catchpole* (1976) 244 EG 295 (shooting over marshy ground held to be adverse possession); *Treloar v Nute* [1976] 1 WLR 1295, [1976] 1 All ER 230 (grazing of two cows and a yearling, storing timber and stone and filling in a gully held to be adverse possession); *Hyde v Pearce* [1982] 1 WLR 560, [1982] 1 All ER 1029 (continued occupation by purchaser, after termination of licence to occupy pending completion, held not to be adverse possession since 'he had at no time made it clear that he was no longer bound by the contract of sale') cf. *Bridges v Mees* [1957] Ch 475, [1957] 2 All ER 577 (contracting purchaser having equitable ownership held adverse possessor); [1982] Conv 383 (J.E.M.); 46 MLR 89 (M. Dockray); *Bills v Fernandez-Gonzalez* (1981) 132 NLJ 60 (compost pens, bonfires, free-ranging chickens and planting trees and shrubs, together with adjoining owner's walking along line of fence for purposes of *his* garden, held not to be adverse possession); *Williams v Usherwood* (1983) 45 P & CR 235 (enclosure of land by fence, parking of three cars in enclosed curtilage of private dwelling-house and paving of driveway with decorative crazy-paving stones held to be adverse possession); [1983] Conv 398 (M. Dockray); (1984) 134 NLJ 144 (H. Wilkinson); *Buckinghamshire County Council v Moran* [1990] Ch 623, [1989] 2 All ER 225 (placing of new lock and chain on access gate held to be adverse possession); [1990] CLJ 23 (C. Harpum); [1989] Conv 211 (G. McCormack); [1989] All ER 176 (P. J. Clarke); *Bladder v Phillips* [1991] EGCS 109 (cleaning of ditch at defendant's request ('thinking it was my ditch') held not to be adverse possession; *Dear v Woods* [1984] CA Transcript 318 (playing of children, single perambulation by male plaintiff and laying of tar macadam on strip half the width of a brick held not to be adverse possession: this note was cited by Sir David CAIRNS as containing examples of trivial acts that will not suffice); *Boosey v Davis* (1987) 55 P & CR 83 (grazing of goats, cutting down of scrub and erection of secondary wire mesh fence held not to be adverse possession); *Maddern v Atkins* [1992] EGCS 82 (use of river and its northern bank held to be adverse possession by owner of southern bank); *Marsden v Miller* (1992) 64 P & CR 239 (erection of fence for 24 hours held not to be adverse possession by person having no documentary title against another such person); *Wilson v Martin's Executors* [1993] 1 EGLR 178 (walking boundary, cutting chestnuts for repair of fence, clearing fallen timber for firewood, repairing wire fence and cutting trees for sale held not to be adverse possession); *Stacey v Gardner* [1994] CLY 568 (incinerator on concrete base on small part of land held not to be adverse possession, even though it was a substantial piece of machinery and a prominent feature); *Hughes v Cork* [1994] EGCS 25 (enclosure of triangular shaped plot 'most cogent evidence' of adverse possession; *Basildon District Council v Charge* [1996] CLY 4929 (keeping of geese

III. Accrual of Right of Action [5]

A. Present Interests

LIMITATION ACT 1980

SCHEDULE I

Part I

Accrual of right of action in case of present interests in land

1. Where the person bringing an action to recover land, or some person through whom he claims, has been in possession of the land, and has while entitled to the land been dispossessed or discontinued his possession, the right of action shall be treated as having accrued on the date of the dispossession or discontinuance.

2. Where any person brings an action to recover any land of a deceased person (whether under a will or on intestacy) and the deceased person —

   (a)   was on the date of his death in possession of the land or, in the case of a rentcharge created by will or taking effect upon his death, in possession of the land charged; and

   (b)   was the last person entitled to the land to be in possession of it;

the right of action shall be treated as having accrued on the date of his death.

3. Where any person brings an action to recover land, being an estate or interest in possession assured otherwise than by will to him, or to some person through whom he claims, and —

   (a)   the person making the assurance was on the date when the assurance took effect in possession of the land or, in the case of a rentcharge created by the assurance, in possession of the land charged; and

within chestnut paling fence, digging of vegetable patch and storage of sawed wood held not to be adverse possession); *London Borough of Hounslow v Minchinton* (1997) 74 P & CR 221 (keeping of compost heap, trimming of hawthorn and elderberry hedges and erection of fencing to prevent dogs from escaping held to be adverse possession); (1997) 147 NLJ 1662 (H. W. Wilkinson); *Prudential Assurance Co Ltd v Waterloo Real Estate Inc* [1999] 2 EGLR 85 (adverse possession of one face of a divided wall); *Burns v Anthony* (1997) 74 P & CR D41 (concreting over an enclosed area and parking cars regularly and apparently as of right, close to someone else's conservatory, held to be adverse possession); *Central Midlands Estates Ltd v Leicester Dyers Ltd* [2003] 2 P & CR D2 (no possession where car parking was on an unenclosed strip of land with no erection of car parking signs); *Inglewood Investment Co Ltd v Baker* [2003] 2 P&CR 319 (erection of portakabins for use as lavatories for those attending car boot sales; shooting of rabbits and foxes; children playing and deposit of rubbish held not to be adverse possession; nor was the erection of a fence, the object of which was to keep sheep in and not to keep the paper owner out.

On animus possidendi, see *Pavledes v Ryesbridge Properties Ltd* (1989) 58 P & CR 459 (intention to possess absent where claimant of land for car-parking asked the true owner 'to do its duty as the person entitled to possession to keep out trespassers'); *Battersea Freehold and Leasehold Property Co Ltd v Battersea London Borough Council* (2001) 82 P & CR 137 (distribution of access keys to other persons entitled to use land indicates lack of animus); *Ellis v Lambeth London Borough Council* (1999) 32 HLR 596 (squatter not estopped by failure to return community charge forms sent to the property). *Wills v Wills* [2003] UKPC 84, 2004] 1 P & CR 612 (dispossession or discontinuance, where co-owner husband acquired title by possession from co-owner wife: only possession of wife on premises was her discarded wedding ring). See also [2001] Conv 155 (O. Radley-Gardner and C. Harpum).

[5]   C & B, pp. 967–978; Gray, pp. 252–258; M & W, paras. 21.013–21.043; MM, pp. 550–557. For accrual in negligence cases in respect of latent damage to property, see the Latent Damage Act 1986, which is based on the recommendations of the Law Reform Committee 24th Report on Latent Damage (1984 Cmnd 9390). See McGee, *Limitation Periods* (3rd edn), chap. 6; (1991) 54 MLR 349 (N.J. Mullany); *Emmet on Title*, para. 1063A.

(b)   no person has been in possession of the land by virtue of the assurance;
           the right of action shall be treated as having accrued on the date when
           the assurance took effect.

B. Future Interests

LIMITATION ACT 1980

SCHEDULE I
PART I
Accrual of right of action in case of future interests

4. The right of action to recover any land shall, in a case where —
   (a) the estate or interest claimed was an estate or interest in reversion or
       remainder or any other future estate or interest; and
   (b) no person has taken possession of the land by virtue of the estate or interest
       claimed;
be treated as having accrued on the date on which the estate or interest fell into
possession by the determination of the preceding estate or interest.

15.   Time limit for actions to recover land. — (2) Subject to the following
provisions of this section, where —
   (a)   the estate or interest claimed was an estate or interest in reversion or
           remainder or any other future estate or interest and the right of action
           to recover the land accrued on the date on which the estate or interest
           fell into possession by the determination of the preceding estate or
           interest; and
   (b)   the person entitled to the preceding estate or interest (not being a term
           of years absolute) was not in possession of the land on that date;
no action shall be brought by the person entitled to the succeeding estate or
interest after the expiration of twelve years from the date on which the right of
action accrued to the person entitled to the preceding estate or interest or six
years from the date on which the right of action accrued to the person entitled
to the succeeding estate or interest, whichever period last expires.
      (3) Subsection (2) above shall not apply to any estate or interest which falls
into possession on the determination of an entailed interest and which might
have been barred by the person entitled to the entailed interest. [6]

PART II

MODIFICATIONS OF SECTION 15 WHERE CROWN OF CERTAIN CORPORATIONS SOLE
ARE INVOLVED

13. Section 15(2) of this Act shall apply in any case where the Crown or a spiritual
or eleemosynary corporation sole is entitled to the succeeding estate or interest
with the substitution —
      (a) for the reference to twelve years of a reference to thirty years; and

---

[6]   See also ss. 15(1) and 38(5); M & W, para. 21.025. The combined effect of these three
       sections is that a 'reversioner or remainderman expectant upon an entail in possession
       is not entitled to the alternative six-year period, if his interest could have been barred by
       the tenant in tail.'

(b)   for the reference to six years of a reference to twelve years.

C. Settlements and Trusts of Land

LIMITATION ACT 1980

18. Settled land and land held on trust. — (1) Subject to section 21(1) and (2) of this Act, the provisions of this Act shall apply to equitable interests in land, as they apply to legal estates. [7]

Accordingly a right of action to recover the land shall, for the purposes of this Act but not otherwise, be treated as accruing to a person entitled in possession to such an equitable interest in the like manner and circumstances, and on the same date, as it would accrue if his interest were a legal estate in the land (and any relevant provision of Part I of Schedule 1 to this Act shall apply in any such case accordingly).

(2) Where the period prescribed by this Act has expired for the bringing of an action to recover land by a tenant for life or a statutory owner of settled land —

(a)   his legal estate shall not be extinguished if and so long as the right of action to recover the land of any person entitled to a beneficial interest in the land either has not accrued or has not been barred by this Act: and

(b)   the legal estate shall accordingly remain vested in the tenant for life or statutory owner and shall devolve in accordance with the Settled Land Act 1925;

but if and when every such right of action has been barred by this Act, his legal estate shall be extinguished.

(3) Where any land is held upon trust and the period prescribed by this Act has expired for the bringing of an action to recover the land by the trustees, the estate of the trustees shall not be extinguished if and so long as the right of action to recover the land of any person entitled to a beneficial interest in the land either has not accrued or has not been barred by this Act; but if and when every such right of action has been so barred the estate of the trustees shall be extinguished. [7]

(4) Where —

(a)   any settled land is vested in a statutory owner; or

(b)   any land is held upon trust;

an action to recover the land may be brought by the statutory owner or trustees on behalf of any person entitled to a beneficial interest in possession in the land whose right of action has not been barred by this Act, notwithstanding that the right of action of the statutory owner or trustees would apart from this provision have been barred by this Act. [7]

SCHEDULE I

PART I

Possession of beneficiary not adverse to others interested in settled land or land held on trust

9. Where any settled land or any land subject to a trust of land [8] is in the possession of a person entitled to a beneficial interest in the land (not being a person solely or absolutely entitled to the land), no right of action to recover the land shall be

---

[7]   As amended by TLATA 1996, s. 25(2), Sch. 4.
[8]   As amended by TLATA 1996, s. 25(1), Sch. 3, para. 18.

treated for the purposes of this Act as accruing during that possession to any person in whom the land is vested as tenant for life, statutory owner or trustee, or to any other person entitled to a beneficial interest in the land. [9]

21. Time limit for actions in respect of trust property. — (1) No period of limitation prescribed by this Act shall apply to an action by a beneficiary under a trust, being an action —
(a)   in respect of any fraud or fraudulent breach of trust to which the trustee was a party or privy [10]; or
(b)   to recover from the trustee trust property or the proceeds of trust property in the possession of the trustee or previously received by the trustee and converted to his use. [11]

(2) Where a trustee who is also a beneficiary under the trust receives or retains trust property or its proceeds as his share on a distribution of trust property under the trust, his liability in any action brought by virtue of sub-section (1)(*b*) above to recover that property or its proceeds after the expiration of the period of limitation prescribed by this Act for bringing an action to recover trust property shall be limited to the excess over his proper share.

This subsection only applies if the trustee acted honestly and reasonably in making the distribution.

(3) Subject to the preceding provisions of this section, an action by a beneficiary to recover trust property or in respect of any breach of trust, not being an action for which a period of limitation is prescribed by any other provision of this Act, shall not be brought after the expiration of six years from the date on which the right of action accrued.

For the purposes of this subsection, the right of action shall not be treated as having accrued to any beneficiary entitled to a future interest in the trust property until the interest fell into possession. [12]

D. Forfeiture

LIMITATION ACT 1980

SCHEDULE I

Part I

Accrual of right of action in case of forfeiture or breach of condition

7. — (1) Subject to sub-paragraph (2) below, a right of action to recover land by virtue of a forfeiture or breach of condition shall be treated as having accrued on

---

[9]   As amended by TLATA 1996, s. 25(2), Sch. 4. *Bridges v Mees* [1957] Ch 475, [1957] 2 All ER 577; *Re Cussons Ltd* (1904) 73 LJ Ch 296; M & W, para. 21.040; *Earnshaw v Hartley* [2000] Ch 155 (beneficial interest in unadministered estate held to be sufficient for purposes of para. 9); (2000) 150 NLJ 940 (G. Miller).

[10]   *Armitage v Nurse* [1998] Ch 241, [1997] 2 All ER 705 (deliberate but honest breach by trustee not fraud); *Paragon Finance plc v Thakerer & Co* [1999] 1 All ER 400. On constructive trustees and breach of fiduciary duty, see *Paragon Finance v Thakerer & Co*; *Coulthard v Disco Mix Club Ltd* [2000] 1 WLR 707, [1999] 2 All ER 457; *Cia de Seguros Imperio v Health (REBX) Ltd* [2001] 1 WLR 112, [2000] 2 All ER (Comm) 787; Maudsley and Burn, *Trusts and Trustees: Cases and Materials* (6th edn, 2000), pp. 934–936.

[11]   Ibid. (beneficiaries under discretionary trust did not have an interest in possession).

[12]   The section does not apply to an action by the Attorney-General to enforce a charitable trust, because there is no relevant beneficiary: *A-G v Cocke* [1988] Ch 414, [1988] 2 All ER 391.

the date on which the forfeiture was incurred or the condition broken.

(2) If any such right has accrued to a person entitled to an estate or interest in reversion or remainder and the land was not recovered by virtue of that right, the right of action to recover the land shall not be treated as having accrued to that person until his estate or interest fell into possession, as if no such forfeiture or breach of condition had occurred.

E. Tenancies

i. PERIODIC TENANCIES

LIMITATION ACT 1980

15. Time limit for actions to recover land. — (2) p. 220, ante.

SCHEDULE 1

PART I

Accrual of right of action in case of future interests

4. P. 220, ante.

5. — (1) Subject to sub-paragraph (2) below, a tenancy from year to year or other period, without a lease in writing, [13] shall for the purposes of this Act be treated as being determined at the expiration of the first year or other period; and accordingly the right of action of the person entitled to the land subject to the tenancy shall be treated as having accrued at the date on which in accordance with this sub-paragraph the tenancy is determined. [14]

(2) Where any rent has subsequently been received in respect of the tenancy, the right of action shall be treated as having accrued on the date of the last receipt of rent.

6. — (1) Where —

(a)   any person is in possession of land by virtue of a lease in writing by which a rent of not less than ten pounds a year is reserved; and

(b)   the rent is received by some person wrongfully claiming to be entitled to the land in reversion immediately expectant on the determination of the lease; and

(c)   no rent is subsequently received by the person rightfully so entitled;

the right of action to recover the land of the person rightfully so entitled shall be treated as having accrued on the date when the rent was first received by the person wrongfully claiming to be so entitled and not on the date of the determination of the lease.

(2) Sub-paragraph (1) above shall not apply to any lease granted by the Crown.

---

[13]   A document is not a lease in writing unless it is dispositive, that is a document which at law creates, of and by itself, a leasehold estate in land. A document which is merely an agreement for a lease, or merely evidential of the terms of a lease is not a lease in writing. *Long v Tower Hamlets London Borough Council* [1996] 3 WLR 317 at 327, [1996] 2 All ER 683 at 692.

[14]   *Moses v Lovegrove* [1952] 2 QB 533, [1952] All ER 1279 (rent-book is not a lease in writing: and the Rent Acts do not prevent time from running); *Jessamine Investment Co v Schwartz* [1978] QB 264, [1976] 3 All ER 521; *Smith v Lawson* [1997] NPC 87.

In **Hayward v Chaloner** [1968] 1 QB 107, [1967] 3 All ER 122, the Saville Estate leased in 1938 to the rector of the parish of Bilsthorpe part of Redcote Farm for use as a garden on an oral tenancy at the rent of 10s. a year. The rent was paid by successive rectors until 1942, but not subsequently. In 1955 the plaintiffs purchased Redcote Farm including the part let to the rector.

In 1966 the incumbent rector, the defendant, claimed title under the Limitation Act 1939. The plaintiffs' application for possession failed before the Court of Appeal (Lord DENNING MR dissenting). RUSSELL LJ said at 122, at 127:

'In the present case there was a periodic tenancy, not in writing: the last payment of rent was in May, 1942, by the then rector, Mr McCormick, so that the right of action must by section 9(2) [15] for the purposes of the Limitation Act be deemed to have then accrued, and the plaintiffs' action in 1966 to recover possession was clearly forbidden by section 4(3). [16]

It was argued for the plaintiffs, and the argument found favour with the county court judge, that section 10(1) [17] operated to prevent the right of action being deemed to accrue at any time because no person was in adverse possession at any time, adverse possession being the label applied by section 10 to "the possession of some person in whose favour the period of limitation can run." I do not think it necessary to discuss here the history of the conception of "adverse possession" beyond a reference to Preston and Newsom's Limitation of Actions, 3rd edn. (1953), p. 86. I have no doubt that for this purpose the possession of a tenant is to be considered adverse once the period covered by the last payment of rent has expired so that section 10(1) does not bear further upon section 9(2). Nor do I doubt the applicability of section 9(2) to the present case just because the freeholders were content that the rector should not pay his rent and did not bother to ask for it for all those years. In *Moses v Lovegrove* [1952] 2 QB 533, [1952] 1 All ER 1279, in this court it was assumed on all hands that when section 9 apparently operates, adverse possession starts: see especially Lord Evershed, and Romer LJ, at 538–540, 543, at 1282–1283, 1285. The principle clearly accepted was that once the period covered by the last payment of rent expired, the tenant ceased to be regarded by the Limitation Acts as the tenant. This case was not cited to the county court judge. A similar assumption was made in *Nicholson v England* [1926] 2 KB 93 under the then existing principles which section 10(1) was designed to embody. Textbooks to the same effect include Cheshire's Modern Law of Real Property, 9th edn. (1962), pp. 797, 798; Megarry and Wade's Textbook of the Law of Real Property, 3rd edn. (1966), p. 1010; and Preston and Newsom on Limitation of Actions, 3rd edn. (1953), p. 89. I am not aware that the contrary view has been anywhere expressed, and in my judgment the cases relied upon by the county court judge of *Leigh v Jack* (1879) 5 Ex D 264, and *Williams Bros Direct Supply Ltd v Raftery* [1958] 1 QB 159, [1957] 3 All ER 593, have no bearing on a question arising under section 9(2) of the Act. In my judgment, therefore, a possessory title has been acquired to this property . . . .

The generous indulgence of the plaintiffs and their predecessors in title, loyal churchmen all, having resulted in a free accretion at their expense to the lands of their church, their reward may be in the next world. But in this

---

[15]   Now Limitation Act 1980, s. 15(6), Sch. 1, para. 5, supra.
[16]   Ibid. s. 15(1), p. 228, post.
[17]   Ibid., s. 15(6), Sch. 1, para. 8(1), p. 209, ante.

jurisdiction we can only qualify them for that reward by allowing the appeal and dismissing their action.'[18]

ii. OCCUPATION FOR BENEFIT OF LANDLORD

SMIRK v LYNDALE DEVELOPMENTS LTD
[1975] Ch 317, [1975] 1 All ER 690
(ChD, PENNYCUICK V-C, and CA, CAIRNS and LAWTON LJJ and WALTON J)

A tenant of a house, first of British Railways, and, from 1967, of the defendants, occupied other land belonging to British Railways which adjoined the house (the blue land) and enclosed it. The defendants in 1973 began to develop the blue land, and the plaintiff brought this action claiming (i) that he had a good possessory title to the land, or alternatively (ii) that he held it as an extension of the tenanted land.

Held. (i) (expressly agreeing with PENNYCUICK V-C) the plaintiff held the land as an addition to the demised land; and (ii) (reversing PENNYCUICK V-C) the purchase of the blue land by the defendants in 1967 did not, on the facts, operate as a surrender and regrant of the lease.

PENNYCUICK V-C:[19] I turn now to the law applicable where a tenant takes possession of adjoining land — a tenant, during the currency of his tenancy, who takes possession of adjoining land belonging to his landlord. The law on this point, if I may respectfully say so, has got into something of a tangle. [His Lordship referred to *Kingsmill v Millard* (1855) 11 Exch 313 and quoted from the judgments of Alderson and Parke BB and continued:]

It will be observed that in his judgment Parke B in terms states that the presumption that the tenant has inclosed for the benefit of the landlord applies, irrespective of whether the inclosed land is part of the waste or belongs to the landlord; and indeed he uses the word 'encroachment' as appropriate in either case. He then goes on to state in terms, following and agreeing what Alderson B said in the course of the argument, that in order to displace the presumption there must be communication to the landlord. That decision of high authority seems to me to be in accordance with justice and common sense, and unless I were compelled to do otherwise by subsequent authority, I would certainly adopt it. I should add, as is perhaps obvious, as appears in some of the later cases, that the presumption may be rebutted by any form of express or implied agreement or, in some cases, as Parke B says, by estoppel.

The next case is *Whitmore v Humphries* (1871) LR 7 CP 1, where Willes J says, at 4–5:

'This case raises a question upon a branch of the law which involves considerations of some nicety. By the rule of law applicable to this subject the landlord is entitled at the determination of the tenancy to recover from the tenant, not only the land originally demised, but also any land which the tenant may have added to it by encroachment from the waste, such encroachment being deemed to be made by him as tenant as an addition to his holding, and consequently for the benefit of his landlord, unless it is made under

---

[18] *Lodge v Wakefield Metropolitan City Council* [1995] 2 EGLR 124 (occupier who wrongly believed that he was a rent paying tenant held to have necessary animus possidendi); *Price v Hartley* [1995] EGCS 74; *Williams v Jones* [2002] 3 EGLR 69 (former tenant holding over without payment of rent in continuous possession did not have to satisfy requirements of animus possidendi).

[19] The present extract covers the judgment of PENNYCUICK V-C on the first point.

circumstances which show an intention to hold it for his own benefit alone, and not as part of his holding under the landlord. This rule undoubtedly applies when the encroachment is made over land belonging to the landlord, and no inquiry appears ever to have been made in such cases, whether it was made with the consent of the landlord or not. In such cases the reasonableness of the rule is very obvious; it only gives back to the landlord that which is rightly his, and prevents the tenant, who has taken advantage of his tenancy to encroach, from keeping that which it would be a breach of the duty arising from the relation of the landlord and tenant not to give up. The rule, however, goes further than this. It is not confined to cases where the encroachment is upon land to which the landlord is entitled, it applies to cases where the land encroached upon does not belong to the landlord' and he then goes on to deal with the position where the encroachment is upon land to which the landlord is not entitled. Willes J continues, at 5:

'The rule is based upon the obligation of the tenant to protect his landlord's rights, and to deliver up the subject of his tenancy in the same condition, fair wear and tear excepted, as that in which he enjoyed it. There is often great temptation and opportunity afforded to the tenant to take in adjoining land which may or may not be his landlord's and it is considered more convenient and more in accordance with the rights of property that the tenant who has availed himself of the opportunity afforded him by his tenancy to make encroachments, should be presumed to have intended to make them for the benefit of the reversioner, except under circumstances pointing to an intention to take the land for his own benefit exclusively. The result is to avoid questions which would otherwise frequently arise as to the property in land, and to exclude persons who have come in as tenants, and who are likely to encroach, from raising such questions. The reason of the rule appears on the one hand to be entirely independent of any notion of encroachment being a wrong done, and so also on the other hand it appears to be quite independent of the question, whether the encroachment was made with the assent of the landlord.'

[His Lordship said that this principle was applied also in *Tabor v Godfrey* (1895) 64 LJQB 245. But statements in other cases (*Lord Hastings v Saddler* (1898) 79 LT 355 and *JF Perrott & Co Ltd v Cohen* [1951] 1 KB 705, [1950] 2 All ER 939) apply the presumption only to cases where the land occupied by the tenant is waste and adjacent to the demised land.]

Having been through the authorities I propose, as I have said earlier, to adopt and apply the principle laid down in *Kingsmill v Millard* (1855) 11 Exch 313.

To return to the present case, there is nothing on the facts which could in any way rebut the presumption, which it seems to me is applicable here, namely, that the tenant, the plaintiff, was occupying the plots by way of an addition to land comprised with his tenancy, and not otherwise adversely to the landlord. I need only add on this point that if, contrary to my view, the unilateral intention of the plaintiff was relevant, the plaintiff's very candid evidence of intention would be fatal to his own case.

iii. TIME RUNS EVEN IF THE LEASE IS IMMEDIATELY RENEWED

In **Gray v Wykeham-Martin and Goode** [1977] Bar Library Transcript No. 10A GEOFFREY LANE LJ said:

'A person coming to this type of situation freshly may well wonder by what possible rule of law a life tenant [20] could be affected [where there have been

---

[20]   The landlord.

continual renewals]. It would seem to the uninitiated that the land has been in the possession of tenants throughout and that even if the freeholder had wanted to remove the chicken houses or the rabbit hutches from the land and to ensure thereby that the plaintiff had no claim to the land, he could not have done so. Such it seems is not the case; because it is not disputed by the defendants that the decision of the House of Lords in *Ecclesiastical Comrs of England and Wales v Rowe* (1880) 5 App Cas 736 governs the situation and that, where a tenancy comes to an end, even if it is followed immediately by a fresh tenancy, there is a moment of time, however short, in which the freeholder notionally regains possession of the land and a moment when time can start to run against the freeholder or life tenant; . . . Consequently if during that moment of time, or one of those moments of time, the squatter is in the necessary adverse possession of the disputed land, time under the Limitation Act starts to run against the life tenant.'

IV. Limitation Period [1]

LIMITATION ACT 1980

2. Time limit for actions founded on tort. — (1) An action founded on tort shall not be brought after the expiration of six years from the date on which the cause of action accrued.

5. Time limit for actions founded on simple contract. — An action founded on simple contract shall not be brought after the expiration of six years from the date on which the cause of action accrued.

8. Time limit for actions on a specialty. — (1) An action upon a specialty [2] shall not be brought after the expiration of twelve years from the date on which the cause of action accrued.

(2) Subsection (1) above shall not affect any action for which a shorter period of limitation is prescribed by any other provision of this Act.

36. Equitable jurisdiction and remedies. — (1) The following time limits under this Act, that is to say —
  (a) the time limit under section 2 for actions founded on tort;
  (b) the time limit under section 5 for actions founded on simple contract; . . .
  (d) the time limit under section 8 for actions on a specialty. . .
shall not apply to any claim for specific performance of a contract or for an injunction or for other equitable relief, except in so far as any such time limit may be applied by the court by analogy in like manner as the corresponding time limit under any enactment repealed by the Limitation Act 1939 was applied before 1st July 1940.

---

[1] C & B, pp. 963–984; M & W, paras. 21.004–21.012; MM, pp. 549–550.
[2] This includes a covenant under seal: *Re Compania de Electricidad de la Provincia de Buenos Aires Ltd* [1980] Ch 146, [1978] 3 All ER 668 (the obligation must be created or secured by the specialty); *Collin v Duke of Westminster* [1985] QB 581, [1985] 1 All ER 463 (tenant's claim to enfranchisement under Leasehold Reform Act 1967 held to be a claim upon a specialty. See *Global Financial Recoveries Ltd v Jones* (2000) Times, 23 February (claim to recover shortfall on personal covenant after realisation of mortgage held to be on a specialty, where loan founded on express agreement under seal, and therefore subject to a limitation period of 12 years under Limitation Act 1980, s. 8(1)).

(2) Nothing in this Act shall affect any equitable jurisdiction to refuse relief on the ground of acquiescence or otherwise. [3]

15. Time limit for actions to recover land. — (1) No action shall be brought by any person to recover any land after the expiration of twelve years from the date on which the right of action accrued to him or, if it first accrued to some person through whom he claims, to that person. [4]

SCHEDULE I
PART II
MODIFICATIONS OF SECTION 15 WHERE CROWN OR CERTAIN
CORPORATIONS SOLE ARE INVOLVED

10. Subject to paragraph 11 below, section 15(1) of this Act shall apply to the bringing of an action to recover any land by the Crown or by any spiritual or eleemosynary corporation sole with the substitution for the reference to twelve years of a reference to thirty years. [5]

11. — (1) An action to recover foreshore may be brought by the Crown at any time before the expiration of sixty years from the date mentioned in section 15(1) of this Act. . . .

12. Notwithstanding section 15(1) of this Act, where in the case of any action brought by a person other than the Crown or a spiritual or eleemosynary corporation sole the right of action first accrued to the Crown or any such corporation sole through whom the person in question claims, the action may be brought at any time before the expiration of—

(a)   the period during which the action could have been brought by the Crown or the corporation sole; or

(b)   twelve years from the date on which the right of action accrued to some person other than the Crown or the corporation sole;

whichever period first expires.

16. Time limit for redemption actions. — When a mortgagee of land has been in possession of any of the mortgaged land for a period of twelve years, no action to redeem the land of which the mortgagee has been so in possession shall be brought after the end of that period by the mortgagor or any person claiming through him. [6]

---

[3]   This preserves the equitable doctrine of laches; Snell, para. 3.19; Brunyate, *Limitation of Actions in Equity*; Maudsley & Burn, *Trusts and Trustees, Cases and Materials* (6th edn, 2002), p. 944; *Re Dixon* [1900] 2 Ch 561; *Re Eyre-Williams* [1923] 2 Ch 533; *GL Baker Ltd v Medway Building and Supplies Ltd* [1958] 1 WLR 1216, [1958] 3 All ER 540; *Nelson v Rye* [1996] 1 WLR 1378, [1996] 2 All ER 186 (where defence succeeded); *Kershaw v Whelan (No 2)* (1997) Times, 10 February (where defence failed). For the modern approach to the doctrine, see *Nelson v Rye* [1996] 1 WLR 1378 at 1382, [1996] 2 All ER 186 at 200, per LADDIE J; *Frawley v Neill* (1999) Times, 5 April, per ALDOUS J.

[4]   The same period applies in the case of a spiritual or eleemosynary corporation sole. On advowsons, see Limitation Act 1980, s. 25. After a judgment for possession has been obtained in an action begun in due time, the successful plaintiff has twelve years from the date of judgment: *BP Properties Ltd v Buckler* (1987) 55 P & CR 337.

[5]   *Secretary of State for Foreign and Commonwealth Affairs v Tomlin* (1990) Times, 4 December (former embassy of Government of Cambodia in St John's Wood, London). *Filrose Securities Ltd v Midgeley* [1998] 3 EGLR 43 (equitable set-off held to be within s. 36(2) and not statute barred).

[6]   *Young v Clarey* [1948] Ch 191, [1948] 1 All ER 197.

19. Time limit for actions to recover rent. — No action shall be brought, or distress made, to recover arrears of rent, or damages in respect of arrears of rent, after the expiration of six years from the date on which the arrears became due. [7]

20. Time limit for actions to recover money secured by a mortgage or charge or to recover proceeds of the sale of land. — (1) No action shall be brought to recover —

(a)   any principal sum of money secured by a mortgage or other charge on property (whether real or personal); or

(b)   proceeds of the sale of land;

after the expiration of twelve years from the date on which the right to receive the money accrued. [8]

(3) The right to receive any principal sum of money secured by a mortgage or other charge and the right to foreclose on the property subject to the mortgage or charge shall not be treated as accruing so long as that property comprises any future interest or any life insurance policy which has not matured or been determined.

(4) Nothing in this section shall apply to a foreclosure action in respect of mortgaged land, but the provisions of this Act relating to actions to recover land shall apply to such an action.

(5) Subject to subsections (6) and (7) below, no action to recover arrears of interest payable in respect of any sum of money secured by a mortgage or other charge or payable in respect of proceeds of the sale of land, or to recover damages in respect of such arrears shall be brought after the expiration of six years from the date on which the interest became due. [9]

(6) Where —

(a)   a prior mortgagee or other incumbrancer has been in possession of the property charged; and

(b)   an action is brought within one year of the discontinuance of that possession by the subsequent incumbrancer;

the subsequent incumbrancer may recover by that action all the arrears of interest which fell due during the period of possession by the prior incumbrancer or damages in respect of those arrears, notwithstanding that the period exceeded six years.

(7) Where —

(a)   the property subject to the mortgage or charge comprises any future interest or life insurance policy; and

(b)   it is a term of the mortgage or charge that arrears of interest shall be treated as part of the principal sum of money secured by the mortgage or charge;

interest shall not be treated as becoming due before the right to recover the principal sum of money has accrued or is treated as having accrued.

---

[7]   *Romain v Scuba TV Ltd* [1997] QB 887, [1996] 2 All ER 117 (time limit applies to guarantor in respect of his undertaking to pay rent reserved by lease); *Tabarrok v EDC Lord & Co* (1997) Times, 14 February (where negligent advice causes plaintiff to guarantee another's debts, time runs as soon as plaintiff suffers loss).

[8]   *British & West plc v Bartlett* [2003] 1 WLR 284, [2002] 4 All ER 1067, (even if mortgagee has exercised power of sale before issuing proceedings for recovery of principal and interest); *Scottish Equitable plc v Thompson* [2003] 07 EG 137 (CS).

[9]   *Barclays Bank plc v Walters* (1988) Times, 20 October; McGee (4th edn), paras. 12.016–21.010.

V. Effect of Disability [10]

LIMITATION ACT 1980

28. Extension of limitation period in case of disability. — (1) Subject to the following provisions of this section, if on the date when any right of action accrued for which a period of limitation is prescribed by this Act, the person to whom it accrued was under a disability, the action may be brought at any time before the expiration of six years from the date when he ceased to be under a disability or died (whichever first occurred) notwithstanding that the period of limitation has expired.

(2) This section shall not affect any case where the right of action first accrued on some person (not under a disability) through whom the person under a disability claims.

(3) When a right of action which has accrued to a person under a disability accrues, on the death of that person while still under a disability, to another person under a disability, no further extension of time shall be allowed by reason of the disability of the second person.

(4) No action to recover land or money charged on land shall be brought by virtue of this section by any person after the expiration of thirty years from the date on which the right of action accrued to that person or some person through whom he claims.

38. Interpretation. — (2) For the purposes of this Act a person shall be deemed to be under a disability while he is an infant, or of unsound mind. . . .

VI. Effect of Fraud, Concealment and Mistake [11]

LIMITATION ACT 1980

32. Postponement of limitation period in case of fraud, concealment or mistake. — (1) Subject to subsection (3) below, where in the case of any action for which a period of limitation is prescribed by this Act, either —
  (a)   the action is based upon the fraud of the defendant,[12] or
  (b)   any fact relevant to the plaintiff's right of action has been deliberately concealed from him by the defendant,[13] or

---

[10]   C & B, pp. 984–985, M & W, para. 21.044; MM, pp. 557–558.
[11]   C & B, pp. 985–987; M & W, paras. 21.048–21.050; MM, p. 558.
[12]   *Beaman v ARTS Ltd* [1949] 1 KB 550 at 558, [1949] 1 All ER 465 at 467, per Lord GREENE MR.
[13]   *Rains v Buxton* (1880) 14 Ch D 537; *Vane v Vane* (1873) 8 Ch App 383; *Clark v Woor* [1965] 1 WLR 650, [1965] 2 All ER 353; *Applegate v Moss* [1971] 1 QB 406, [1971] 1 All ER 747; *King v Victor Parsons & Co* [1973] 1 WLR 29, [1973] 1 All ER 206; *Tito v Waddell (No 2)* [1977] Ch 106 at 224–225, [1977] 3 All ER 129 at 244–245; *Lewisham London Borough v Leslie & Co Ltd* (1978) 250 EG 1289; *Bartlett v Barclays Bank Trust Co Ltd* [1980] Ch 515 at 537, [1980] 1 All ER 139 at 154–155; *Westlake v Bracknell District Council* [1987] 1 EGLR 161; *Johnson v Chief Constable of Surrey* (1992) Times 23 November; *Sheldon v RHM Outhwaite (Underwriting Agencies) Ltd* [1995] 2 WLR 570 (even though time started to run after cause of action arose, subsequent concealment starts time running again)); *Brocklesby v Armitage* [2001] 1 WLR 598, [2001] 1 All ER 172.

(c) the action is for relief from the consequences of a mistake, [14]
the period of limitation shall not begin to run until the plaintiff has discovered the fraud, concealment or mistake (as the case may be) or could with reasonable diligence have discovered it. [15]

References in this subsection to the defendant include references to the defendant's agent and to any person through whom the defendant claims [16] and his agent.

(2) For the purposes of subsection (1) above, deliberate commission of a breach of duty in circumstances in which it is unlikely to be discovered for some time amounts to deliberate concealment of the facts involved in that breach of duty.[17]

(3) Nothing in this section shall enable any action —
(a) to recover, or recover the value of, any property; or
(b) to enforce any charge against, or set aside any transaction affecting, any property;
to be brought against the purchaser of the property or any person claiming through him in any case where the property has been purchased for valuable consideration by an innocent third party since the fraud or concealment or (as the case may be) the transaction in which the mistake was made took place.

(4) A purchaser is an innocent third party for the purposes of this section —
(a) in the case of fraud or concealment of any fact relevant to the plaintiff's right of action, if he was not a party to the fraud or (as the case may be) to the concealment of that fact and did not at the time of the purchase know or have reason to believe that the fraud or concealment had taken place; and
(b) in the case of mistake, if he did not at the time of the purchase know or have reason to believe that the mistake had been made.

VII. Effect of Acknowledgment and Part Payment [18]

LIMITATION ACT 1980

29. Fresh accrual of action on acknowledgment or part payment. — (1) Subsections (2) and (3) below apply where any right of action (including a

---

[14] See *Phillips-Higgins v Harper* [1954] 1 QB 411, [1954] 1 All ER 116, per PEARSON J. Mistake must be an essential ingredient of the cause of action, for example, an action to recover money paid under a mistake: see *Kleinwort Benson Ltd v Lincoln City Council* [1999] 2 AC 349, [1998] 4 All ER 513; [1999] CLJ 478 (G. Virgo) (s. 32(1)(c) held to apply to claim for recovery of money paid under a mistake of *law*, including cases where mistake based on a settled understanding of the law which is shown by a later judicial decision to have been mistaken). See also *Nurdin & Peacock plc v DB Ramsden & Co Ltd* [1999] 1 WLR 1249, [1999] 1 All ER 941.

[15] See *Peco Arts Inc v Hazlitt Gallery Ltd* [1983] 1 WLR 1315 at 1322–1323, [1983] 3 All ER 193 at 199 (drawing Études Pour le Bain Turc by Ingres), per WARNER J.

[16] *Eddis v Chichester Constable* [1969] 2 Ch 345, [1969] 2 All ER 912 (painting attributed to Caravaggio).

[17] *Cave v Robinson Jarvis & Rolf* [2003] 1 AC 384 (deliberate concealment does not include failure to disclose a negligent breach of duty which the actor was unaware of committing). See *Emmet on Title*, para. 1.010B.

[18] C & B, pp. 987–988; M & W, paras. 21.051–21.054; MM, p. 559 *Colchester Borough Council v Smith* [1992] Ch 421, [1992] 2 All ER 561 (claimant estopped from asserting that he had title under Limitation Act 1980).

foreclosure action) to recover land or an advowson [19] . . . has accrued.

(2) If the person in possession of the land . . . acknowledges the title of the person to whom the right of action has accrued —

(*a*)the right shall be treated as having accrued on and not before the date of the acknowledgment . . .

(3) In the case of a foreclosure or other action by a mortgagee, if the person in possession of the land, . . . or the person liable for the mortgage debt makes any payment in respect of the debt (whether of principal or interest) the right shall be treated as having accrued on and not before the date of the payment.

(4) Where a mortgagee is by virtue of the mortgage in possession of any mortgaged land and either —

(*a*)   receives any sum in respect of the principal or interest of the mortgage debt; or

(*b*)   acknowledges the title of the mortgagor, or his equity of redemption; an action to redeem the land in his possession may be brought at any time before the expiration of twelve years from the date of the payment or acknowledgment.

(5) Subject to subsection (6) below, where any right of action has accrued to recover —

(*a*)   any debt or other liquidated pecuniary claim, [20] or

(*b*)   any claim to the personal estate of a deceased person or to any share or interest in any such estate;

and the person liable or accountable for the claim acknowledges the claim [1] or makes any payment in respect of it the right shall be treated as having accrued on and not before the date of the acknowledgment or payment.

(6) A payment of a part of the rent or interest due at any time shall not extend the period for claiming the remainder then due, but any payment of interest shall be treated as a payment in respect of the principal debt.

(7) Subject to subsection (6) above, a current period of limitation may be repeatedly extended under this section by further acknowledgments or payments, but a right of action, once barred by this Act, shall not be revived by any subsequent acknowledgment or payment. [2]

30. Formal provisions as to acknowledgments and part payments. — (1) To be effective for the purposes of section 29 of this Act, an acknowledgment must be in writing and signed by the person making it. [3]

(2) For the purposes of section 29, any acknowledgment or payment —

(*a*)   may be made by the agent of the person by whom it is required to be made under that section; and

---

[19]   Limitation Act 1980, s. 25.

[20]   As, for example, rent due under a lease.

[1]   *Good v Parry* [1963] 2 QB 418, [1963] 2 All ER 59; *Dungate v Dungate* [1965] 1 WLR 1477, [1965] 3 All ER 818; *Surrendra Overseas Ltd v Government of Sri Lanka* [1977] 1 WLR 565, [1977] 2 All ER 481; *Kamouh v Associated Electrical Industrial International Ltd* [1980] QB 199; *Re Overmark Smith Warden Ltd* [1982] 1 WLR 1195, [1982] 3 All ER 513.

[2]   *Sanders v Sanders* (1881) 19 ChD 373; *Nicholson v England* [1926] 2 KB 93.

[3]   See *Browne v Perry* [1991] 1 WLR 1297 at 1301, per Lord TEMPLEMAN; *Bigden v Lambeth London Borough Council* [2000] EGCS 147; *Archangel v Lambeth London Borough Council* [2000] EGCS 149.

(b)   shall be made to the person, or to an agent of the person, whose title or claim is being acknowledged or, as the case may be, in respect of whose claim the payment is being made. [4]

31. Effect of acknowledgment or part payment on persons other than the maker or recipient. — (1) An acknowledgment of the title to any land . . . by any person in possession of it shall bind all other persons in possession during the ensuing period of limitation.

(2) A payment in respect of a mortgage debt by the mortgagor or any other person liable for the debt, or by any person in possession of the mortgaged property, shall, so far as any right of the mortgagee to foreclose or otherwise to recover the property is concerned, bind all other persons in possession of the mortgaged property during the ensuing period of limitation.

VIII. Effect of Expiration of Limitation Period [5]

LIMITATION ACT 1980

17. Extinction of title to land after expiration of time limit. — Subject to —
(a)   section 18 of this Act, [6] and
(b)   section 75 of the Land Registration Act 1925; [7]
at the expiration of the period prescribed by this Act for any person to bring an action to recover land (including a redemption action) [8] the title of that person to the land shall be extinguished. [9]

A. Disposition by Squatter

ASHER v WHITLOCK
(1865) LR 1 QB 1 (Ct Exch Ch, COCKBURN CJ and MELLOR and LUSH JJ)
In 1842 Williamson enclosed some manorial land, which he occupied until his death in 1860. At that time (the period of limitation being 20 years) the title of the Lord of the Manor was not yet extinguished. He devised the land by will to his widow so long as she remained unmarried, with remainder to his daughter in fee simple. After his death the widow remained in possession, and in 1861 married the defendant, who came to live with the widow and daughter. The daughter died in February and the widow in May 1863. The defendant remained in possession of the property, and in 1865 the daughter's heir-at-law brought ejectment against him.

---

[4]   *Edginton v Clark* [1964] 1 QB 367, [1963] 3 All ER 468 (letter to owner's agent offering to purchase land held to be effective acknowledgment); *Re Compania de Electricidad de la Provincia de Buenos Aires Ltd* [1980] Ch 146, [1978] 3 All ER 668 (balance sheet effective acknowledgment if received by creditor).
[5]   See p. 107, n. 9, ante.
[6]   See p. 221, ante.
[7]   See p. 228, post.
[8]   Limitation Act 1980, s. 16, p. 204, ante.
[9]   The extinguishment of title also extinguishes the rights to claim rent and mesne profits during the period of adverse possession: *Mount Carmel Investments Ltd v Peter Thurlow Ltd* [1988] 1 WLR 1078, [1988] 3 All ER 129.

Held. The heir-at-law was entitled to recover the property.

COCKBURN CJ: Assuming the defendant's possession to have been adverse, we have then to consider how far it operated to destroy the right of the devisee and her heir-at-law. . . . I take it as clearly established, that possession is good against all the world except the person who can shew a good title: and it would be mischievous to change this established doctrine. In *Doe d Hughes v Dyeball* (1829) Mood & M 346 one year's possession by the plaintiff was held good against a person who came and turned him out; and there are other authorities to the same effect. Suppose the person who originally inclosed the land had been expelled by the defendant, or the defendant had obtained possession without force, by simply walking in at the open door in the absence of the then possessor, and were to say to him, 'You have no more title than I have, my possession is as good as yours', surely ejectment could have been maintained by the original possessor against the defendant. All the old law on the doctrine of disseisin was founded on the principle that the disseisor's title was good against all but the disseisee. It is too clear to admit of doubt, that if the devisor had been turned out of possession he could have maintained ejectment. What is the position of the devisee? There can be no doubt that a man has a right to devise that estate, which the law gives him against all the world but the true owner. Here the widow was a prior devisee, but *durante viduitate* only, and as soon as the testator died, the estate became vested in the widow; and immediately on the widow's marriage the daughter had a right to possession; the defendant however anticipates her, and with the widow takes possession. But just as he had no right to interfere with the testator, so he had no right against the daughter, and had she lived she could have brought ejectment; although she died without asserting her right, the same right belongs to her heir. Therefore I think the action can be maintained, inasmuch as the defendant had not acquired any title by length of possession. The devisor might have brought ejectment, his right of possession being passed by will to his daughter, she could have maintained ejectment, and so therefore can her heir, the female plaintiff. We know to what extent encroachments on waste lands have taken place; and if the lord has acquiesced and does not interfere, can it be at the mere will of any stranger to disturb the person in possession? I do not know what equity may say to the rights of different claimants who have come in at different times without title; but at law, I think the right of the original possessor is clear. On the simple ground that possession is good title against all but the true owner, I think the plaintiffs entitled to succeed. . . . [10]

B. Landlord, Tenant and Squatter

CHUNG PING KWAN v LAM ISLAND DEVELOPMENT CO LTD
[1997] AC 38 (PC, LORDS KEITH OF KINKEL, JAUNCEY OF TULLICHETTLE, NICHOLLS OF BIRKENHEAD AND STEYN and SIR Christopher SLADE)

The Crown granted a lease of land on an island in the New Territories of Hong Kong for a term of 75 years from 1 July 1898 to Lam Island Development Co Ltd. The lease expired in 1973 but was renewable for a further term of 24 years less

---

[10]   *Perry v Clissold* [1907] AC 73. For this shift to possession as the basis of title, see M & W para 3.1200; *Ezekiel v Fraser* (2002) 4 October, where Judge Rich followed *Oxford Meat Pty Co Ltd v McDonald* (1963) 63 SR (NSW) 423.

three days. Chung Ping Kwan had been in continuous possession adverse to Liam Island Development Co Ltd since 1959.

The question was whether the tenant, having exercised its option to renew the lease could recover possession from the squatter, who had, by virtue of his adverse possession, barred its rights against him under the original lease.

Held. For Chung Ping Kwan, the squatter.

LORD NICHOLLS OF BIRKENHEAD: Their Lordships will consider first the basic principles applicable in this area of the law, before turning to the provisions of the Renewable Leases Ordinance. The Limitation Ordinance is closely modelled on the Limitation Act 1980.[11] [His Lordship read the relevant provisions and continued:]

From these provisions several conclusions emerge. Time begins to run against a lessee when he is dispossessed by a trespasser. In the present case time ran against the plaintiff's predecessor Mak Yung from the date when the defendants took possession and thereby dispossessed him: section 8(1) [Limitation Act 1980, Sch. 1, para. 1]. If continued for the prescribed period of 20 years, this adverse possession would have barred the right of Mak Yung to recover possession. It would similarly have barred those claiming under him.

However, dispossession of a lessee by a squatter does not set time running against the lessee's landlord. The landlord's right to recover possession from the squatter on the determination of the lease is not barred by a squatter's adverse possession against the lessee, however long this continues. In the ordinary course the landlord's right of action accrues when, but only when, the lease ends and the landlord's reversionary interest falls into possession: [Limitation Act 1980, Sch. 1, para. 4, p. 220, ante]. Only then does time start running against the landlord.

The rationale of this provision is that so long as the legal estate created by the lease remains in existence, the landlord has no right to obtain possession of the land from a squatter. The squatter dispossessed the lessee, not his landlord. If the lessee seeks to recover possession it will be sufficient for him to prove he was in possession and that the squatter dispossessed him. But if the landlord, not having been dispossessed by the squatter, comes along and seeks to eject the squatter he must set up and rely upon his title. He has to show a better title to possession than the squatter. Herein will be his difficulty. So long as the lease is extant, his title to present possession of the land is deficient. This is so even if the title of the lessee, as between himself and the squatter, has been extinguished by [Limitation Act 1980, s. 17(1), p. 233, ante]. These established principles are conveniently displayed in *Megarry & Wade, The Law of Real Property*, 5th ed. (1984), pp. 103–109, 1037.

On the determination of the lease, therefore, the landlord is entitled to oust the squatter however long he may have been on the land. Those claiming through the landlord are similarly entitled: their right to possession is no better, and no worse, than the right of the landlord from whom they derive their title. So if the landlord grants a new lease, the lessee of the new lease may eject the squatter.

In principle the position cannot be different if the lessee under the new lease is the same person as the lessee under the original lease. There seems to be no sensible reason why the landlord's ability to confer on a new lessee a title as good as his own should be subject to an exception when the new lessee is the original lessee. Lord Bledisloe argued otherwise. He submitted that the combined

---

[11] The sections of the Limitation Act 1980 have been substituted for those of the Ordinance.

effect of [Limitation Act 1980, s. 15(1), p. 228, ante and Sch. 1, para. 1, p. 219, ante] is that once the prescribed period of 20 years has run against a lessee,, the lessee is barred from bringing an action to recover the land from the squatter and that he remains barred even if he acquires another source of title he did not have when the 20-year period expired. It would be extraordinary, so the argument runs, if a lessee whose right to bring possession proceedings against a squatter has become time-barred could set time running anew against the same squatter by obtaining another lease.

Their Lordships are unable to accept this submission. A lessee's ability to regain possession in reliance on a new lease is no more than a striking illustration of the principle that dispossession of a lessee sets time running against the lessee and those claiming through him as lessee, but not against the landlord and those claiming through him as reversioner. A trespasser on leased property is more vulnerable than a trespasser on property occupied by the freeholder. In the latter case the title which the squatter bars is the freehold title. In the former case the title which is barred is leasehold only, because that is the extent of the title of the person who has been dispossessed. Adverse possession defeats the rights, whatever they may be, of the person against whom the possession is adverse. It does not defeat the rights of others.

Their Lordships consider that *Taylor v Twinberrow* [1930] 2 KB 16 was correctly decided. It is unnecessary for their Lordships to express a view on the controversial decision in *Fairweather v St Marylebone Property Co Ltd* [1963] AC 510, [1962] 2 All ER 288, p. 237, post: see the powerful critique by Professor H.W.R. Wade in 'Landlord, Tenant and Squatter', (1962) 78 LQR 541. The actual decision in that case turned on the effect of the surrender of a lease by a lessee whose title has been barred by a trespasser's adverse possession. The answer to that conundrum throws no light on the problem arising in the present appeal.

A right to renew

Thus far consideration has been given to the straightforward position of a simple lease for a term of years. The next step is to consider the case of a lease containing an option for the lessee to renew the lease. Mr Nugee submitted this makes no difference. In such a case, just as much as in the case where there is no option to renew, the estate to which the squatter's possession was adverse was the term of years created by the lease. Only that estate was extinguished. As between the landlord and the lessee the lease still subsists, and the lessee can still enforce the option. If he does so, he acquires from the landlord a new legal estate, and in respect of that estate time runs from the determination of the original lease, in accordance with [Sch. 1, para. 4]. The lessee's claim for possession is then based on the new lease, not the original lease. The pre-existing contractual right of renewal is not itself an estate.

Clearly, until the new lease is granted the lessee does not have a legal estate in the property for the term of years which is the subject of the option. Equally clearly, in the ordinary course the option will be specifically enforceable. The lessee has a right in respect of the property which he can enforce against the landlord. Thus the question to be addressed is whether adverse possession bars the lessee from asserting against the squatter this specifically enforceable right, *and the legal estate which flows from this right,* as much as it bars the lessee from asserting against the squatter the other rights granted to him by the lease.

Their Lordships consider that an affirmative answer to this question will accord better with the legislative intention inherent in the scheme of the Limitation Act 1980 and the Limitation Ordinance. The principle underlying [Sch. 1, para.4] is that time should not run against a reversioner so long as there is a prior estate or interest standing between him and the right to retake the property. Until the preceding estate or interest determines, and the reversionary estate or interest falls into possession, the reversioner is not sleeping on his rights.

This principle applies to a prior legal estate such as a lease. This principle seems apt to be applied also to a specifically enforceable prior right to call for a legal estate, such as a lessee's renewal option, when the person having the right is already lawfully in possession. In the latter case, as much as the former, the reversioner has no right to enter and eject the trespasser. If the lessee validly exercises the option the landlord is bound to renew the lease. He can be compelled to do so. He is not entitled to eject the lessee at the expiration of the lease. This is the crucial feature. The landlord is not entitled to possession. This pre-existing interest of the lessee, precluding the landlord from ejecting the lessee, would be a fatal flaw in a claim by the landlord to oust a trespasser. The trespasser is as much entitled to set up and rely upon this interest as a deficiency in the landlord's right to possession as he is entitled to set up and rely upon a lease for this purpose.

Conversely, and unlike the reversioner, the lessee has slept on his rights. There seems to be no compelling reason why, as between him and the trespasser, his rights under the renewal option in the lease should not be defeated just as much as his other rights under the lease. It is true that when he exercises the option the lessee obtains a new legal estate, but this is no more than implementation of a pre-existing contract. He acquires a new legal estate by virtue only of a right included in the lease whose title has been extinguished as against the trespasser. To ignore the legal source of the lessee's entitlement to his new legal estate would be to exalt form (a new legal estate) over substance (a pre-existing right to the estate).

There seems to be no authority on this point. The point was not raised clearly in the recent Hong Kong cases until the present one. Some assistance can be derived from considering the closely analogous situation which arose in the Australian case of *Bree v Scott* (1904) 29 VLR 692. . . .

In their Lordships' view, where a new lease is granted pursuant to a lessee's option in the original lease the right to bring an action to recover the land from a trespasser within the meaning of section [15] accrues to the lessee on the date of the dispossession. [Sch. 1, para. 1] is applicable in such a case, and as against the trespasser section 17 operates to extinguish his title to the new lease as much as the original lease. Conversely, in such a case [Sch. 1, para. 4] is inapplicable and does not operate to set a new limitation period running in favour of the lessee. The lessee's claim in right of the new lease is not a claim to an estate or interest in reversion within the meaning of [Sch. 1, para. 4], because the lessee's right to the new lease, subject to satisfying any prescribed conditions, was a right he already had as lessee.

C. Surrender of Lease by Squatter

FAIRWEATHER v ST MARYLEBONE PROPERTY CO LTD
[1963] AC 510, [1962] 2 All ER 288 (HL, Lords RADCLIFFE, DENNING, MORRIS OF BORTH-Y-GEST [12] and GUEST)

LORD DENNING: My Lords, at the back of a leasehold house in Hampstead there is a shed. In the year 1920 the next-door neighbour, Mr Millwood, saw it was unused and out of repair. He went in and repaired it and has treated it as his own ever

---

[12] Lord MORRIS dissented. For criticism of the majority view, see (1962) 78 LQR 541 (H.W.R. Wade).

since. Mr Millwood has actually sub-let it as part of his own house. Now a property company has bought the freehold of the property on which the shed stands and wants to recover possession of the shed. Can it do so? or is it barred by the Statutes of Limitation? There are three important persons to consider:

(1) The *freeholder* who, in 1893, let the premises on which the shed stands on a lease for 99 years at a ground rent with a repairing covenant and a proviso for re-entry. The 99 years will not expire till 1992.

(2) The *leaseholder* who has taken no steps for more than 12 years to recover possession of the shed which stands on part of his leasehold premises. His right of action first accrued in 1920. So the 12 years for him to sue expired in 1932.

(3) The *squatter*, who has been in possession of the shed since 1920, by himself or his sub-tenants.

And there is one important event to consider. The *surrender* in 1959 by the *leaseholder* to the *freeholder* of the rest of the term of 99 years. Whereupon the freeholder claims that he is entitled to possession of the shed. But the *squatter* says he is entitled to stay in it until 1992.

It is quite clear from the Statutes of Limitation that in the year 1932 the 'title' of the leaseholder to the land was 'extinguished'. What does this mean? There are four suggestions to consider.

The first suggestion is that the title of the leaseholder to the shed is extinguished completely, not only against the squatter, but also against the freeholder. So that the leasehold interest disappears altogether, and the freeholder becomes entitled to the land. I reject this suggestion completely. It would mean in this case that the freeholder would have become entitled to possession of the shed in the year 1932 and time would have begun to run against him from 1932. So that 12 years later the title of the freeholder to the shed would have been extinguished, that is, in 1944. That cannot be right, and it was not seriously suggested. In 99 cases out of 100, the freeholder has no knowledge that the squatter is on the premises at all. It would be utterly wrong if the title of the freeholder could be eroded away during the lease without his knowledge. The correct view is that the freehold is an estate in reversion within section 6(1) of the Act of 1939, [13] and time does not run against the freeholder until the determination of the lease: see *Doe d Davy v Oxenham* (1840) 7 M & W 131.

The second suggestion is that the title of the leaseholder to the shed is extinguished so far as the leaseholder is concerned — so that he is no longer entitled to the shed — but that the leasehold interest itself persists and is vested in the squatter. In other words, the squatter acquired a title which is 'commensurate' with the leasehold interest which has been extinguished. This suggestion was made in 1867 in the first edition of Darby and Bosanquet's book [Statutes of Limitation] at p. 390, and it was accepted in 1889 as correct by the court in Ireland in *Rankin v M'Murtry* (1889) 24 LR Ir 290. But it has since been disapproved. If it were correct, it would mean that the squatter would be in the position of a statutory assignee of the shed, and he would by reason of privity of estate, be liable on the covenants and subject to the conditions of the lease. I reject this suggestion also: for the simple reason that the operation of the Statutes of Limitation is merely negative. It destroys the leaseholder's title to the land but does not vest it in the squatter. The squatter is not liable on the repairing covenants: see *Tichborne v Weir* (1892) 67 LT 735, p. 241, post. Nor, when the leasehold is a tenancy from year to year, does he step into the shoes of the tenant so as to be himself entitled to six month's notice to quit: see *Taylor v Twinberrow* [1930] 2 KB 16.

---

[13]   Now Limitation Act 1980, s. 15(6), Sch. 1, para. 4, p. 220, ante.

The third suggestion is that the *title* of the leaseholder is extinguished but that his *estate* in the land is not. This is too fine a distinction for me. And so it was for Parliament. For Parliament itself uses the two words as if they meant the same: see section 16 of the Limitation Act 1939, and section 75 of the Land Registration Act 1925.

The fourth suggestion is that the title of the leaseholder to the shed is extinguished as *against the squatter*, but remains good as *against the freeholder*. This seems to me the only acceptable suggestion. If it is adopted, it means that time does not run against the freeholder until the lease is determined — which is only just. It also means that until that time the freeholder has his remedy against the leaseholder on the covenants, as he should have; and can also re-enter for forfeiture, as he should be able to do: see *Humphry v Damion* (1612) Cro Jac 300, and can give notice to determine on a 'break' clause or notice to quit, as the case may be. Further, it means that if the leaseholder should be able to induce the squatter to leave the shed — or if the squatter quits and the leaseholder resumes possession — the leaseholder is at once in the same position as he was originally, being entitled to the benefits and subject to the burdens of the lease in regard to the shed. All this seems to me eminently reasonable but it can only be achieved if, despite the presence of the squatter, the title of the leaseholder remains good as against the freeholder.

On this footing it is quite apparent that at the date of the surrender, the leaseholder had something to surrender. He still had his title to the shed as against the freeholder and was in a position to surrender it to him. The maxim nemo dat quod non habet has no application to the case at all.

But there still remains the question: What was the effect of the surrender? [14] There are here two alternatives open:

(1) On the one hand, it may be said that the surrender operated to *determine* the term, just as a forfeiture does. If this is correct, it would mean that the freeholder would be entitled to possession at once as soon as the leaseholder surrendered the house. He could evict the squatter by virtue of his freehold estate against which the squatter could say nothing. And time would begin to run against the freeholder as soon as the surrender took place. This view is based on *Ecclesiastical Comrs of England and Wales v Rowe* (1880) 5 App Cas 736, and section 6(1) of the Limitation Act 1939.

(2) On the other hand, it may be said that the surrender operated as an *assignment* by the leaseholder to the freeholder of the rest of the 99 years. If this is correct, it would mean that the freeholder could not evict the squatter because the freeholder would be 'claiming through' the leaseholder and would be barred for the rest of the 99 years, just as the leaseholder would be: see section 4(3) of the Limitation Act. Time would not begin to run against the freeholder until the 99 years expired. This view is based on *Walter v Yalden* [1902] 2 KB 304.

My Lords, I have come to the clear conclusion that a surrender operates as a determination of the term. It is not an assignment of it. I am aware that no less an authority than Lindley LJ once said that 'the surrender of the term only operated as an assignment of the surrenderor's interest in it': see *David v Sabin* [1893] 1 Ch 523, 533. But if that be true, it is not by any rule of the common law, only by force of statute: and then only in the case of underleases, not in the case of trespasser or squatter.

At common law, if a leaseholder made an underlease and afterwards surrendered his term to the freeholder, then the freeholder could not evict the

---

[14] On surrender generally, see C & B, pp. 497–499, 840–841; Gray, 423–429; M & W, paras. 14.172–14.175; MM, pp. 364–365.

underlessee during the term of the underlease: see *Pleasant (Lessee of Hayton) v Benson* (1811) 14 East 234. But this was not because there was any assignment from surrenderor to surrenderee. It is clear that, upon the surrender, the head term was determined altogether. It was extinguished completely, so much so that the freeholder could not sue the underlessee on the covenants or enforce the proviso for re-entry: see *Webb v Russell* (1789) 3 Term Rep 393. The underlessee could enjoy the property without payment of rent and without performance of the covenants and conditions until the end of the term of the underlease: see *Ecclesiastical Comrs for England v Treemer* [1893] 1 Ch 166. This was remedied by the statutes of 1740 and 1845, which have been re-enacted in sections 139 and 150 of the Law of Property Act 1925. Under those statutes, on a surrender of the head lease, an underlessee becomes a direct tenant of the freeholder on the terms of his underlease. So that the surrender does operate as if it were an assignment of the surrenderor's interest. But those statutes have no application to trespassers or squatters.

The question may be asked: why did the common law on a surrender protect the underlessee from eviction? The answer is to be found in Coke upon Littleton II, p. 338b, where it is said that 'having regard to the parties to the surrender, the estate is absolutely drowned ... But having regard to strangers, who were not parties or privies thereunto, lest by a voluntary surrender they may receive prejudice touching any right or interest they had before the surrender, the estate surrendered hath in consideration of law a continuance.' This passage applies in favour of an underlessee so as to protect him from eviction during the term of his underlease: but it does not apply in favour of a trespasser. The reason for the difference is because the underlessee comes in under a grant from the lessee; and the lessee cannot, by a surrender, derogate from his own grant: see *Davenport's case* (1610) 8 Co Rep 144b and *Mellor v Watkins* (1874) LR 9 QB 400 at 405, by Blackburn J. But a trespasser comes in by wrong and not by grant of the lessee. If the lessee surrenders his term, the freeholder is at once entitled to evict the trespasser for the simple reason that, on the surrender, the lease is determined, and there is no bar whatever to the freeholder recovering possession: see *Ecclesiastical Comrs of England and Wales v Rowe* (1880) 5 App Cas 736. And I see no reason why the same reasoning should not apply even though, at the date of the surrender, the trespasser is a squatter who has been there more than 12 years. For, as against the freeholder, he is still a trespasser. The freeholder's right to possession does not arise until the lease is determined by the surrender. It then comes into being and time begins to run against him under section 6(1) of the Limitation Act, 1939.

The only reason, it seems to me, which can be urged against this conclusion is that it means that a squatter's title can be destroyed by the leaseholder and freeholder putting their heads together. It is said that they can by a surrender — or by a surrender and regrant — destroy the squatter's title completely and get rid of him. So be it. There is no way of preventing it. But I would point out that, if we were to deny the two of them this right, they could achieve the same result in another way. They could easily do it by the leaseholder submitting to a forfeiture. If the leaseholder chooses not to pay the rent, the freeholder can determine the lease under the proviso for re-entry. The squatter cannot stop him. He cannot pay the rent without the authority of the leaseholder. He cannot apply for relief against forfeiture. The squatter's title can thus be defeated by a forfeiture — or by a forfeiture and regrant — just as it can by a surrender — or by a surrender and regrant. So there is nothing in the point.

My Lords, so far as these questions under the Limitation Acts are concerned, I must say that I see no difference between a surrender or merger or a forfeiture.

On each of those events the lease is determined and the freeholder is entitled to evict the squatter, even though the squatter has been on the land during the lease for more than 12 years: and on the determination of the lease, time then begins to run against the freeholder. It follows that, in my opinion, *Walter v Yalden* [1902] 2 KB 304 was wrongly decided and *Taylor v Twinberrow* [1930] 2 KB 16 was rightly decided . . . . I would dismiss this appeal.[15]

D. Covenants

In **Tichborne v Weir** (1892) 67 LT 735[16] KAY LJ, said, at 737:

'On the occasion of the conveyance [between Giraud and Weir] Giraud made a statement that he had no assignment of the lease, but only a title by a possession of forty years. The question is, what is the effect of that title. There is no doubt that covenants running with the land would bind anyone coming into possession of the estate which Baxter had, and if the lease is anyhow vested in the defendant, he would be bound by such covenants. Therefore the question is, whether Baxter's estate is vested in the defendant. It was argued that the effect of the statute was to transfer the term from Baxter to Giraud, and so it would be vested in the defendant. Under section 34 of 3 & 4 Will 4, c27,[17] "the right and title" of Baxter to "the land" (which by the interpretation clause includes chattel interest) was "extinguished". That is the operation of the section, and we are now asked to construe the Act of Parliament so as to make it say that Baxter's right and title was transferred to Giraud . . . . The defendant got an estate in the land which he has admitted, by paying rent, is not the fee simple, and by operation of the statute Baxter's right to claim the term was extinguished. It follows that Giraud during the test of the term was free from liability to Baxter or anyone claiming under him, but it does not follow that he acquired Baxter's estate. There is another point as to whether the defendant is estopped from denying that he was in possession of Baxter's lease. He admits he is in possession of the land, he and Giraud have paid rent agreed on in the lease of 1802, and they have claimed possession for the rest of the term. The landlord's title to the land has been completely admitted, but there is no other evidence of the defendant's being bound by all the terms of the lease, or of his holding all Baxter's estate. There being no such admission, either express or implied, we must hold that there is no evidence of such an extensive estoppel as that which has been contended for.[18] I think that the defendant, for the reasons I have stated, is not liable on the covenants of the lease, and that this appeal should be dismissed.'

In **Re Nisbet and Potts' Contract** [1906] 1 Ch 386,[19] COZENS-HARDY LJ said at 409:

'The suggestion which is at the root of the appellant's argument is this, that a squatter can wholly disregard restrictive covenants affecting a building estate. That

---

[15]   *Jessamine Investment Co v Schwartz* [1978] QB 264, [1976] 3 All ER 521 (sub-tenant, protected as statutory tenant under Rent Acts, acquired possessory title against his immediate landlord, whose title continued to exist as against the freeholder until head lease expired. Sub-tenant held still protected under Rent Acts thereafter against freeholder); (1977) 41 Conv (NS) 213 (F.R. Crane).

[16]   See p. 946, post, where the facts are given.

[17]   Reproduced with amendments as Limitation Act 1980, s. 17, p. 223, ante.

[18]   *Tickner v Buzzacott* [1965] Ch 426, [1964] 1 All ER 131 (payment of rent due under lease not estoppel); *Ashe v Hogan* [1920] 1 IR 159; *O'Connor v Foley* [1906] 1 IR 20.

[19]   P. 947, post, where the facts are given.

is so startling a proposition, and so wide-reaching, that it must be wrong. The value of estates in the neighbourhood of London and all large towns, and the amenity of those estates, depend almost entirely upon the continuance of the mutual restrictive covenants affecting the user and the enjoyment of the property; and when we are told that the squatter, notwithstanding that he is a mere trespasser, is to be in a better position than that occupied by a person deriving a title strictly through the original covenantor, one feels that there must be an answer to the argument; and I think the authorities, when carefully examined, make the answer quite plain. The benefit of a restrictive covenant of this kind is a paramount right in the nature of a negative easement not in any way capable of being affected by the provisions of the Statute of Limitations on which the squatter relies. The only rights extinguished for the benefit of the squatter under section 34[20] are those of persons who might, during the statutory period, have brought, but did not in fact bring, an action to recover possession of the land. But the person entitled to the benefit of a restrictive covenant like this never had any cause of action which he could have brought, because unless and until there is a breach, or a threatened breach, of such a covenant, it is impossible for the person entitled to the benefit of it to bring any action. It appears, therefore, so far as the squatter is himself concerned, that both during the currency of the twelve years and after the expiration of the twelve years, there could be no possible answer to the claim of anyone seeking to enforce the covenant. In fact, there would, so far as he is concerned, be no difference between this covenant, which is in the nature of an equitable easement, and a legal easement strictly and properly so called. But although the squatter took the property subject to this equitable burden, it may be that the present vendor, who purchased from or through the squatter, is able to say that the burden does not affect the property in his hands. But what must he prove in order to claim this exemption? He must prove that he is a purchaser for value of the legal estate without notice. . . . Now can the present vendor allege and prove that he was a purchaser for value without notice? I think not.'

IX. Law Reform

In 2001 the Law Commission recommended that the provisions on actions to recover land should be redrafted. The main recommendation was that such actions should be subject to a long-stop period of ten years; a reduction from the 12 years of the Limitation Act 1980. The ten years would be from the date on which the action accrued to the claimant.

Law Commission Report on Limitation of Actions Part VI 2001 (Law Com No. 270)

Summary of Recommendations

(1)   The primary limitation period should start to run from the 'date of knowledge' rather than, for example, the date the cause of action accrues (Para. 3.7).

---

[20]   Reproduced with amendments as Limitation Act 1980, s. 17.

(15)   The primary limitation period applying under the core regime should be three years (Para. 3.98).

(16)   A claim, other than in respect of a personal injury, should be subject to a long-stop period of ten years (Para. 16).

(59)   A long-stop limitation period of ten years commencing on the date that the claimant's right to recover the land accrued (or, if later, the date on which the claimant's interest becomes an interest in possession) should apply to, and (subject to the recommendation in paragraph 65 below) be the sole limitation period for claims to recover land[1] (Para. 4.135).

(60)   A claimant entitled to a future interest to land which was in adverse possession before that interest fell into possession should be subject to a limitation period of ten years from the date on which his or her interest fell into possession rather than a reduced period (Para. 4.135).

(61)   The expiry of the limitation period will extinguish the claimant's rights to the land in question, and after that period, no claim may be made (Para. 4.135).

(62)   The limitation period in relation to all claims to recover equitable interests in land should be the same as that which applies in relation to claims to recover legal interests in land. The further provisions presently contained in section 18(2) to 18(4) of the Limitation Act 1980 should be retained (Para. 4.137).

(63)   Claims brought by, or by a person claiming through, the Crown (subject to paragraph 65 below) or any spiritual or eleemosynary corporation sole to recover land should be subject to the same limitation period applying to a claim by any other party to recover land (Para. 4.144).

(64)   In any case where the land is vested in the incumbent from time to time of a benefice as a spiritual corporation sole but the benefice is vacant a claim to recover the land or any part of it may be made by
   (a)   the priest-in-charge of the benefice, or
   (b)   by the sequestrators of the benefice (Para. 4.144).

(65)   The limitation period applicable to claims by the Crown to recover foreshore should be
   (a)   sixty years from the date of accrual of the right of action or
   (b)   ten years from the date when the land ceased to be foreshore
   whichever period first expires (Para. 4.147).

(66)   Where the identify of the person in adverse possession of the land changes, a new cause of action shall accrue to the claimant, unless anyone in adverse possession of the land before the change continues to be in adverse possession after that date.
   However, no new cause of action will accrue to the claimant
   (a)   where the second person in adverse possession claims possession through his or her predecessor and
   (b)   where the squatter coming into possession is recovering possession of the land from a squatter who had previously dispossessed him or her (Para. 4.150).

(67)   Claims to recover the proceeds of the sale of land should not be subject to the primary limitation period of three years from the date of knowledge but only to the long-stop limitation period of ten years running from the date when the vendor became entitled to recover the proceeds (by, for example, enforcing a lien over the land) (Para. 4.151).

[1]   Subject to the exceptions presently set out in Limitation Act 1980, s. 15(3) and (5).

(68) The core regime should apply to claims to recover rent, claims to recover damages in respect of arrears of rent, and the levying of distress for unpaid rent (Para. 4.157).

(69) The primary limitation period should not apply to claims to enforce a mortgage or charge over land; and
the long-stop limitation period should apply to claims to enforce a mortgage or charge over land, running from the date on which the mortgagee's or chargee's right to enforce the mortgage or charge accrues (Para. 4.166).

(70) Claims to enforce a mortgage or charge over personal property should be subject to the core regime (Para. 4.169).

(71) The primary limitation period should not apply to claims to enforce a mortgage or charge over both land and personal property; and
the long-stop limitation period should apply to claims to enforce a mortgage or charge over land and personal property, running from the date on which the mortgagee's or chargee's right to enforce the mortgage or charge, *vis-à-vis* the land, accrues (Para. 4.173).

(72) Only the long-stop limitation period should apply to claims to enforce an obligation secured by a mortgage or charge by suing on the covenant to repay (Para. 4.177).

(73) Where a mortgage or charge comprises a future interest or a life insurance policy, the limitation period applying to claims to enforce the mortgage or charge should not begin to run until the future interest determines or the life insurance policy matures (Para. 4.181).

(74) Where a prior mortgagee is in possession of the property which is subject to the mortgage, the limitation period applicable to a claim by the subsequent mortgagee to recover arrears of interest (or damages in lieu) should (if necessary) be extended so that it does not end before the date one year after the prior mortgagee ceases to be in possession (Para. 4.184).

(75) The limitation period applying to foreclosure proceedings should be suspended during the period that the mortgagee is in possession of the mortgaged property (Para. 4.185).

(76) No limitation period should apply to claims by the mortgagor to redeem a mortgage over land (Para. 4.189).

(77) Claims to redeem mortgaged personal property should not be subject to a limitation period (Para. 4.194).

(78) The expiry of the limitation period applying to claims to enforce a mortgage should extinguish the claimant's interest in the mortgaged property (Para. 4.196).[2]

X. Land Registration Act 1925[3]

The limitation provisions in the Land Registration Act 1925 were based on the principles applicable to unregistered land under the Limitation Act 1980.

---

[2]   In July 2002 the Government accepted in principle the recommendations in the Report; Law Commission Annual Report 2002–2003 (Law Com No. 280), para. 3.14.

LAND REGISTRATION ACT 1925

70. Liability of registered land to overriding interests. — (1) (*f*), p. 130, ante.[4]

75. Acquisition of title by possession.—(1) The Limitation Acts shall apply to registered land in the same manner and to the same extent as those Acts apply to land not registered, except that where, if the land were not registered, the estate of the person registered as proprietor would be extinguished, such estate shall not be extinguished but shall be deemed to be held by the proprietor for the time being in trust for the person who, by virtue of the said Acts, has acquired title against any proprietor, but without prejudice to the estates and interests of any other person interested in the land whose estate or interest is not extinguished by those Acts.

(2) Any person claiming to have acquired a title under the Limitation Acts to a registered estate in the land may apply to be registered as proprietor thereof.

(3) The registrar shall, on being satisfied as to the applicant's title, enter the applicant as proprietor either with absolute, good leasehold, qualified, or possessory title, as the case may require, but without prejudice to any estate or interest protected by any entry on the register which may not have been extinguished under the Limitation Acts, and such registration shall, subject as aforesaid, have the same effect as the registration of a first proprietor; but the proprietor or the applicant or any other person interested may apply to the court for the determination of any question arising under this section.

SPECTRUM INVESTMENT CO v HOLMES
[1981] 1 WLR 221, [1981] 1 All ER 6 (ChD, Browne-Wilkinson J)[5]

In 1902 the registered freeholder of 43 Mount Pleasant Lane, London granted a 99 year lease to K; the leasehold interest was registered. In 1939 K granted a monthly tenancy to Mrs Holmes who lived there with her daughter. In 1944 K assigned her lease to Mrs David who was registered as proprietor of it. Subsequent tenders of rent by Mrs Holmes were refused, and after her death in 1951, Miss Holmes remained in the house without paying rent. In 1968 Miss Holmes, who had acquired a possessory title against Mrs David under the Limitation Act 1939, was registered as proprietor of the leasehold interest with possessory title, and Mrs David's registered title was closed.

In 1975 Mrs David 'woke up' and purported to surrender her lease to the plaintiff (a company controlled by her family), who was the freeholder's successor in title. The plaintiff claimed possession of the house from Miss Holmes; and Mrs David, who was joined as plaintiff, claimed rectification of the register by the cancellation of Miss Holmes's possessory title and the restoration of her own.

Held. Both claims fail. Since Mrs David's title had been closed, she was no longer the registered proprietor of the lease and was therefore unable to surrender it. Rectification failed because the registrar had registered Miss Holmes's possessory title under the mandatory duty imposed on him by the Land Registration Act 1925, s. 75.

---

[3]   C & B, pp. 989–992; M & W, paras. 6.116–6.117; MM, pp. 549–550, 559–563; R & R (1991), chap. 29; R & R (2003), chap. 33.
[4]   For overlap with para (*g*), see *Bridges v Mees* [1957] Ch 475, [1957] 2 All ER 577.
[5]   [1981] Conv 155 (R.E. Annand); (1981) 131 NLJ 718 (P.F. Smith), 774 (E.G. Nugee); [1982] Conv 201 (P.H. Kenny).

BROWNE-WILKINSON J: I can now shortly state the contentions of the plaintiff. The plaintiff submits that the Land Registration Act 1925 introduces mere machinery for proving title to and transferring land and does not affect the substantive rights which parties enjoy under the general law. Accordingly, it is said that the rights of the plaintiff (as established by *Fairweather v St Marylebone Property Co Ltd* [1963] AC 510, [1962] 2 All ER 288, p. 237, ante) must be reflected in the provisions of the Act of 1925 and are preserved by the words in section 11 which expressly provide that registration with possessory title 'shall not affect or prejudice the enforcement of any estate, right, or interest (whether in respect of the lessor's title or otherwise) adverse to or in derogation of' the property with possessory title. So, it is said, having obtained a surrender of the lease from Mrs David, the plaintiff's right to possession as against the defendant is preserved.

There is in my judgment a short answer to the claim by the plaintiff. Accepting for the moment the broad proposition that the Act of 1925 was not intended to alter substantive rights, it undoubtedly was intended to alter the manner in which such rights were to be established and transferred. The surrender by Mrs David to the plaintiff is the linchpin of the plaintiff's claim. But in my judgment that surrender has not been effected by the only means authorised by the Land Registration Act 1925 for the disposal of a registered leasehold interest by act of the parties. At the date of the alleged surrender the lease was registered under title no. NGL 65073 in the name of the defendant. Mrs David was not registered as proprietor, her title no. LN 66166 having been taken off the register. By virtue of section 69(1) the effect of the registration of the defendant as proprietor of the lease was, as against Mrs David, to vest the term or deem it to be vested in the defendant.

Section 69(4) provides: 'The estate for the time being vested in the proprietor shall only be capable of being disposed of or dealt with by him in manner authorised by this Act.'

In my judgment the effect of these provisions is that, so long as the defendant is registered as proprietor of the lease, only she can dispose of it. Moreover by virtue of sections 21 and 22, even the defendant can only do so by a registered disposition. Accordingly, in my judgment there has, as yet, been no valid surrender of the lease and the plaintiff's claim fails in limine.

Mr Tager for the plaintiff sought to avoid this result by saying that a surrender was not a registrable disposition and referred me to section 46 of the Act. This argument does not meet the point that Mrs David was not registered as proprietor when she purported to surrender the lease. But even if she had been, in my judgment the surrender would have had to be effected by a registered disposition. Section 69(4) makes it clear that even a registered proprietor only has power to deal with any estate vested in him in the manner authorised by the Act. The only powers of disposition are those conferred by section 21 of the Act which authorises the transfer of the registered estate. In my judgment the word 'transfer' in this section must include surrendering the term, otherwise the Act does not authorise a surrender. Any disposition under section 21 has to be completed by registration: section 22. Section 46 on which Mr Tager relied merely directs the registrar to note on the register the determination of the lease, however that occurs, which will include determination by effluxion of time or operation of law. Section 46 does not purport to lay down the ways in which the determination can be effected by disposition of one of the parties.

Mr Tager submitted further that there ought to have been two registered titles to the lease, of which Mrs David was the proprietor of one and the defendant was the proprietor of the other. This suggestion seems to have no warrant in any provision of the Act and in my judgment runs contrary to the whole scheme of the Act, which is intended to ensure that there shall be one title for any interest in registered land and anyone dealing with that land can treat the registered proprietor of that interest as the owner of that interest.

For these reasons, in my judgment there has, as yet, been no surrender of the term by Mrs David to the plaintiff. Therefore, the plaintiff's claim fails since, so long as the term exists, it has no immediate right to possession. However, in order to determine the real issue between the parties I gave leave for Mrs David to be joined as co-plaintiff. If she is entitled to rectification of the register, she may thereafter be able to execute the necessary registered surrender and, if she can, the plaintiff's claim to possession would be unanswerable.

Mr Charles's submission for the defendant were very far-reaching. He submitted that the whole scheme of the Land Registration Act 1925 shows that the position of the squatter on registered land is totally different from that of a squatter on unregistered land as laid down by the House of Lords in *Fairweather v St Marylebone Property Co Ltd*. He submits that section 75(2) makes it clear that the squatter who has obtained title against the documentary lessee is entitled to apply to be registered as proprietor of the documentary lessee's registered estate in the land, i.e. as proprietor of the lease itself. Section 75(3) then requires the registrar, if satisfied of the facts, to effect such registration. Accordingly it is said that what was done in the present case was quite correct: the defendant is rightly registered as proprietor of the lease itself. As a result, it is said, the legal term of years is vested in the defendant by parliamentary conveyance contained in section 69 of the Act. By virtue of sections 9 and 11 of the Act the defendant as registered proprietor is deemed to have vested in her the possession of the leasehold interest, subject to the express and implied obligations in the lease and subject to any rights of the freeholder adverse to her interest. Therefore, Mr Charles submits, the scheme of the Land Registration Act 1925 is to produce exactly the result which the House of Lords held was not the result in relation to unregistered land, namely, to make the squatter the successor in title to the documentary lessee by parliamentary conveyance, the squatter taking subject to and with the benefit of the covenants in the lease.

This is a formidable and far-reaching submission. But, on the other side I was strongly pressed with authority suggesting that squatter's rights were the same over both registered and unregistered land.

[His Lordship referred to *Fairweather v St Marylebone Property Co Ltd* at 542–543, at 296, per Lord RADCLIFFE, at 548, at 299, per Lord DENNING, and to *Jessamine Investment Co v Schwartz* [1978] QB 264 at 275, [1976] 3 All ER 521 at 530, per Sir John PENNYCUICK, and continued:]

Finally, the words of section 75(1) itself state that the Limitation Acts shall apply to registered land 'in the same manner and to the same extent' as it applies to unregistered land, and then goes on to state exceptions.

On the other hand, I take into account the recent decision of the House of Lords in *Williams & Glyn's Bank Ltd v Boland* (decided since the conclusion of the argument in this case) [1981] AC 487, [1980] 2 All ER 408, p. 136, ante which shows that, if the words of the Land Registration Act 1925 are clear, they are to be given their natural meaning and not distorted so as to seek to produce uniformity in the substantive law as between registered and unregistered land. I therefore approach this question on the basis that one would expect that substantive legal rights would be the same whether the land is registered or unregistered but that clear words in the Act of 1925 must be given their natural meaning even if this leads to a divergence.

I do not find it necessary to reach any conclusion on the far-reaching propositions which Mr Charles put forward, since I think that I can decide this case on quite a narrow ground, leaving it to others to resolve the more fundamental questions. In my judgment, if Mrs David is to succeed in any claim to have the defendant deleted from the register as proprietor of the lease, she (Mrs David) must show at least that the registration of the defendant was not a mandatory requirement of the provisions of the Land Registration Act 1925. It is clear from the references in section 75(3) that section 75 applies to a leasehold interest. Under section 75(3) the registrar is under a mandatory duty to register the squatter on the application made by the squatter under section 75(2) if the registrar is satisfied as to the squatter's title. For what does the squatter make application? I will read section 75(2) again: 'Any person claiming to have acquired a title under the Limitation Acts to a registered estate in the land may apply to be registered as proprietor thereof.'

To my mind the words are clear and unequivocal: the squatter claims to have acquired a title to 'a registered estate in the land' (i.e. the leasehold interest) and applies to be registered as a proprietor '*thereof*' (my emphasis). Therefore under section 75(2), references to the squatter having acquired title to a registered estate must include the rights which under the Limitation Act 1939 the squatter acquires in relation to leasehold interests. Section 75(2) then refers to the squatter applying to be registered as proprietor 'thereof'. This word can, in my judgment, only refer back to the registered estate in the land against which the squatter has acquired title under the Act of 1939, i.e. the leasehold interest. The clear words of the Act therefore seem to require that, once the 12 years have run, the squatter is entitled to be registered as proprietor of the lease itself, and is bound to be so registered if he applies for registration. It follows that in my judgment the defendant (as the squatter) is correctly registered as proprietor of the lease itself in accordance with the clear requirements of section 75. If that is right, Mrs David cannot be entitled to rectification of the register as against the defendant, and she can therefore never get into a position in which she is competent to surrender the lease to the plaintiff.

I am conscious that in so deciding I am reaching a conclusion which produces at least a limited divergence between squatter's rights over registered and unregistered land. Once the squatter is rightly registered as proprietor under section 75(3) the documentary lessee and the freeholder can no longer defeat the squatter's rights by a surrender. But I am not deciding anything as to the position during the period between the date when the squatter obtains his title by adverse possession and the date on which he obtains registration of it. This is the period covered by section 75(1) which is the subsection on which Lord Radcliffe in *Fairweather v St Marylebone Property Co Ltd* [1963] AC 510 at 542, [1962] 2 All ER 588 at 296 and Sir John Pennycuick in *Jessamine Investment Co v Schwartz* [1978] QB 264 at 275, [1976] 3 All ER 521 at 530, were commenting. It may well be, as their dicta suggest, that during the period preceding any registration of the squatter's rights, the documentary lessee (as registered proprietor of the lease) and the freeholder can deal with the legal estate without reference to a person whose rights are not recorded on the register. But once the Act provides for registration of the squatter's title, it must in my judgment follow that the squatter's rights (once registered) cannot be overridden. The difference between registered and unregistered land in this respect is an inevitable consequence of the fact that the Land Registration Act 1925 provides for registration of the squatter as proprietor and that registered proprietors have rights.

I can summarise my conclusion as follows:

(*a*) The plaintiff cannot, under section 11 of the Act, have any estate right or interest adverse to or in derogation of the title of the defendant (as registered proprietor of the lease with possessory title) unless and until the lease has come to an end.

(*b*) The lease has not come to an end by virtue of the purported surrender of May 7, 1975, since at that date the leasehold interest was registered land and the surrender was not made in accordance with the provisions of the Act.

(*c*) Mrs David is not entitled to rectification of the register reinstating her as registered proprietor of the lease, since the defendant is registered in accordance with the mandatory requirements of section 75 of the Act.

Therefore (*d*) Mrs David can never surrender the term so as to merge it in the freehold, and accordingly the plaintiff cannot become entitled to possession by reason of such a surrender.

In these circumstances it is not necessary for me to consider the argument that in exercising my discretion whether or not to rectify the register, I should not in any event order rectification against the defendant, the registered proprietor in possession, at the suit of those whose disregard of their own property interest has led to the defendant's registration.

I therefore dismiss the claim by the plaintiff. [6]

In **Central London Commercial Estates Ltd v Kato Kagaku Ltd** [1998] 4 All ER 948, [7] a freeholder, predecessor in title of Central London Commercial Estates Ltd, granted a long lease in 1953 of land forming part of Bush House in the Strand. Both titles were registered. The squatter, Kato Kagaku Ltd, had been in continuous adverse possession of a courtyard for more than 12 years before 1996, using it as a paying car park. Unlike its counterpart in *Spectrum*, the squatter had not applied to register its possessory title.

Axia, a successor in title of the lessee, purported to surrender the lease, to the freeholder, with the intention of preventing Kato from excluding Central from the courtyard until the expiry of the head lease in 2028.

In an action for possession of the courtyard SEDLEY J held for Kato. Axia held the estate on trust for Kato under section 75 of the Land Registration Act 1925, and its rights under the trust were overriding interests under section 70(1) (*f*) or (*g*) or both. Any disposition by Axia (and a surrender is a disposition) was ineffective to override the rights of Kato.

SEDLEY J said at 958:

'I approach the construction of s. 75(1) in the same way as Browne-Wilkinson J in the *Spectrum* case, by regarding it as creating a specified exception to a general rule that limitation should affect registered and unregistered land similarly. The ordinary principle that legislation alters the general law is inverted by the opening words of s. 75(1). If therefore the effect of limitation on unregistered land has turned out, on authority, to be other than it was believed to be at the time of enactment, then (as Mr Tager says) it is the construction of the statute and not

---

[6]   See also *Mount Carmel Investments Ltd v Peter Thurlow Ltd* [1988] 1 WLR 1078 at 1089, [1988] 3 All ER 129 at 137 (original squatter forged a long lease from the registered freeholder and assigned it to another squatter).

[7]   (1999) 115 LQR 187 (C. Harpum); (1999) 149 NLJ 118 (H. W. Wilkinson); [1999] Conv 136 (E. J. Cooke), 329 (S. Pascoe); [1998] All ER Rev 272 (P. J. Clarke).

the general law which must give way. I do not consider, however, that any other assumptions should be brought to bear on the exercise. In particular, in spite of the regard paid in places by Lord Radcliffe and Lord Denning to the potential factual merits of the rival submissions in *Fairweather*'s case, the law seems to me to adopt and in turn to demand a stance of neutrality as between disseisor and disseised. Parliament has prescribed the effects of a sufficient period of adverse possession without reference to circumstances, and enough examples have been canvassed in the course of the submissions to demonstrate that the deserving and the undeserving alike may be caught or spared by the operation of the Limitation Acts. The law, correspondingly, leans neither towards nor against the extinction of titles by prescription: for policy reasons it simply provides for it to happen in certain situations (see Ruoff and Roper *Registered Conveyancing*, para. 29–03 and *Megarry and Wade's The Law of Real Property* (5th edn, 1984) p. 1030). This is why, for example, I have received no evidence about how Kato came to occupy the car park.

The situation before the court for the purposes of the exception in s. 75(1) is that, were the leasehold estate in the courtyard unregistered, s. 17 of the Limitation Act 1980 would by now have extinguished as much of the leasehold estate as entitles Axia to exclude Kato, but not as much of it as was held of the freeholder and has now been surrendered: see *Fairweather*'s case. Is the element of the estate which would otherwise be extinguished all that the statute saves, or is the estate indivisible for the purposes of the exception and so wholly subject to the trust?

I do not consider that Mr Tager's distinction between estate and title is material here, though it may be elsewhere. If estate were not synonymous with title in s. 75 (as both Lord Radcliffe and Lord Denning in *Fairweather*'s case clearly thought it was), the linkage of the Limitation Acts to the extinction of estates would be meaningless, since the Limitation Acts speak not of estates but of titles. In the bipartite situation of freeholder and disseisor, it is common ground that to bar the title is to bar the estate. The two must mean the same in the present context.

What then is the estate or title which, but for the disapplication of the effects of the Limitation Acts on registered land, 'would be extinguished' on the expiry of 12 years' adverse possession? The relevant unit of registration is 'the land', which by s. 3(viii) includes land of any tenure – in a case like the present, the leasehold estate. Such an estate is divisible for many purposes, but nothing in s. 75 suggests to me that it is divisible for the statutory purpose: on the contrary, what is evidently contemplated is the substitution of one registered proprietor for another without more, placing the second in the same relationship to the freeholder as had been enjoyed by the first. In the state of the decided cases in 1922 and 1925, this is unsurprising. The difficulty is to fit the statute to the post-*Fairweather* situation.

To split the leasehold interest after 12 years' adverse possession into an element related entirely to the freehold and another related solely to the squatter, as is now known to happen with unregistered land, does not seem to me to marry up with either the purpose or the operation of s. 75(1). The squatter, unlike an underlessee, has no legal relationship at all with the leaseholder during the 12 initial years of trespass (except in the negative sense that the leaseholder may at any time evict him and claim damages); and at the end of the 12 years by operation of law the leaseholder's right and title to do even this are extinguished wherever the Limitation Acts apply. At law the squatter is then in a position to make a good title, independent of the lease although always subject to the freeholder's eventual reversion. In relation to a registered leasehold, however, s. 75 lifts the extinguishing effect of the Limitation Act and substitutes a trust of the leasehold interest, benefits and burdens alike, from the moment of extinction of the leasehold title. The squatter becomes entitled, without regard to merits, to be placed in the same relationship with the freeholder as had previously been enjoyed by the leaseholder. The trust preserves not the squatter's common law title but a new statutory right to be substituted by registration for the leaseholder – carrying with it, as Mr Nugee accepts, an obligation to indemnify the leaseholder against outgoings. This is to all appearances a statutory conveyance of the entire leasehold interest.

There is apparent force in Mr Nugee's submission that Mr Etherton's ostensibly equally straightforward construction has hidden traps in it. Because Mr Etherton seeks to construe 'where' as focusing on the facts of a particular transaction, it is only when subsequent events are known that it becomes possible to say whether a statutory trust exists: if the leaseholder sues the squatter for possession, the trust intervenes; if the leaseholder surrenders to the freeholder, no trust arises (as distinct from there being no breach of trust). But it may be that in the end this does no more than carry into effect the dichotomy of the leasehold interest which Axia and Central assert characterises registered as it does unregistered land. The real question is whether, as Mr Tager and Mr Etherton argue, the material estate for the present statutory purpose is as much of the whole estate as would not be extinguished if the land were not registered – that is to say the leasehold interest shorn of the right to possession. If it is, then there is no doubt that it falls outside the exception, so that surrendering it extinguishes the squatter's title.

I appreciate that the search for the true meaning of a statute, especially the Land Registration Act 1925, is not the same thing as a search for simplicity. But it is realistic, I think, to see in s. 75 the relatively straightforward purpose which I have described. Such a purpose becomes unattainable if the leasehold estate is split up into two tranches, one the right to possession which after 12 years passes to the squatter; the other the interest held of the freeholder, which can be disposed of so as to frustrate the right to possession – unless the disseisor, following the giving of the necessary notices by the Registrar, first succeeds in obtaining registration in lieu of the leaseholder. The conceded fact that what the disseisor in the latter case obtains by virtue of s. 75(2) is the entirety of the leasehold interest seems to me a strong indicator that this is the estate intended to be preserved from extinction by the exception contained in s. 75(1). So is the fact that the s. 75(1) exception begins by nullifying the squatter's common law freehold if the land is registered: why should registration be given this effect unless the loss is to be made good by another means? By contrast, a trust of a bare right not to be evicted seems almost pointless. I accept the submission of Mr Tager and Mr Etherton that the race to register which their case entails is not unthinkable or unique; but when the result is less like a race than like a game of double or quits, one has to ask if it can be what Parliament meant to happen. I am persuaded that it is not.

If, as I hold, the leasehold interest was impressed by 1996 with the statutory trust, it must follow that the trusteeship passed to the freeholder upon the merger of the leasehold with the freehold interest by surrender. The full incidents of this trust, which are far from clear, do not fall for decision by me. It is sufficient to hold, as I do, that the beneficial interest of Kato under s. 75 was an overriding interest under s. 70(1)(f) or (g) or both, and that by virtue of ss. 23(1)(c) and 69 it now binds Central. Section 74 cannot intervene: see *Williams & Glyn's Bank Ltd v Boland* [1981] AC 487 at 508, [1980] 2 All ER 408 at 415.

QUESTIONS

1.   What weight do you think should be given, in determining whether adverse possession has been taken, to the fact that
    (a)   the owner did not currently need the land but had plans for future development
    (b)   the trespasser did or did not intend to acquire the land as his own
    (c)   the owner knew or did not know or should have known of the trespass?
2.   Consider the very difficult questions which arise in determining whether the owner (plaintiff) impliedly permitted the defendant to occupy; and whether an earlier express permission is still operative. A similar question arises in connection with the acquisition of easements by prescription. *Healey v Hawkins* [1968] 1 WLR 1967, [1968] 3 All ER 836, p. 745, post; Limitation Act 1980, s. 15(6), Sch. 1, para 8(4), p. 210, ante; Law Reform Committee 21st Report (1977), paras. 3.47–3.52.

XI. Land Registration Act 2002

The Land Registration Act 2002 disapplies the law of adverse possession in relation to registered land under the Land Registration Act 1925. It substitutes a new scheme which reflects the principles underlying registered conveyancing. The details of the scheme are set out in Schedule 6 to the Act, as supplemented by the Land Registration Rules 2003. [8]

Law Commission Report on Land Registration for the Twenty-First Century 2001 (Law Com No. 271), paras. 1.13, 14.5–14.7.

'Adverse possession
1.13   The Bill abandons the notion that a squatter acquires title once he or she has been in adverse possession for 12 years. It creates new rules in relation to registered land that will confer greater protection against the acquisition of title by persons in adverse possession. This is consistent with one of the objectives of the Bill – that it is registration alone that should confer title. The essence of the new scheme is that a squatter will be able to apply to be registered as proprietor after 10 years' adverse possession. However, the registered proprietor will be notified of that application and will, in most cases, be able to object to it. [9] If he or she does, the application will be rejected. However, the proprietor will then have to take steps to evict the squatter or otherwise regularise his or her position within two years. If the squatter is still in adverse possession after two years, he or she will be entitled to be registered as proprietor. We consider that this new scheme strikes a fairer balance between landowner and squatter than does the present law. It also reflects the fact that the basis of title to registered land is the fact of registration, not (as is the case with unregistered land) possession.

---

[8]   LRR 2003, rr. 187–194. R & R (2003) chap. 33; H & B, chap. 8; Law Commission Report on Land Registration for the Twenty First Century 2001 (Law Com No. 271), Part XIV. For transitional provisions, see LRA 2002, s. 134, Sch. 12, para. 18.

14.5 The essence of the scheme is that—

(1) adverse possession of itself, for however long, will not bar the owner's title to a registered estate;

(2) a squatter will be entitled to apply to be registered as proprietor after 20 years' adverse possession, and the registered proprietor, any registered chargee, and certain other persons interested in the land will be notified of the application;

(3) if the application is not opposed by any of those notified the squatter will be registered as proprietor of the land;

(4) if any of those notified oppose the application it will be refused, unless the adverse possessor can bring him or herself within one of three limited exceptions;[10]

(5) if the application for registration is refused but the squatter remains in adverse possession for a further two years,[11] he or she will be entitled to apply once again to be registered and will this time be registered as proprietor whether or not the registered proprietor objects;

(6) where the registered proprietor brings proceedings to recover possession from a squatter, the action will succeed unless the squatter can establish certain limited exceptions which are consistent with those in (4) above.

There are certain particular rules for special cases and there are transitional provisions to protect the rights of squatters who had barred the rights of the registered proprietor prior to the coming into force of the legislation.[12]

14.6 The aims of the scheme are as follows.

(1) Registration should of itself provide a means of protection against adverse possession, though it should not be unlimited protection. Title to registered land is not possession-based as is title to unregistered land. It is registration that vests the legal estate in the owner and the person's ownership is apparent from the register. The registered proprietor and other interested persons, such as the proprietor of a registered charge, are therefore given the opportunity to oppose an application by a squatter to be registered as proprietor.

(2) If the application is not opposed, however, whether because the registered proprietor has disappeared or is unwilling to take steps to evict the squatter, the squatter will be registered as proprietor instead. This ensures that land which has (say) been abandoned by the proprietor, or which he or she does not consider to be worth the price of possession proceedings, will remain in commerce.

(3) If the registered proprietor (or other interested person) opposes the registration, then it is incumbent on him or her to ensure that the squatter is either evicted or his or her position regularised[13] within two years. If the squatter remains in adverse possession for two years after such objection has been made, he or she will be entitled to apply

---

9   If there is no objection to the application, the squatter will be registered.
10 Para. 14.7 infra.
11 Which might happen if no steps were taken to evict the squatter, or to regularise his or her possession so that it would no longer be adverse, as where the squatter agreed to be the tenant or licensee of the registered proprietor.
12 LRR 2003, s. 134, Sch. 12, para. 18; the squatter can protect this right by being in actual occupation: para. 18(2).
13 In other words, where the squatter agrees to become the tenant or licensee of the registered proprietor.

once again to be registered, and this time the registered proprietor will not be able to object. In other words, the scheme provides a registered proprietor with one chance, but only one chance, to prevent a squatter from acquiring title to his or her land. The proprietor who fails to take appropriate action following his or her objection will lose the land to the squatter.

(4)   Consistently with the approach set out above, a registered proprietor who takes possession proceedings against a squatter will succeed, unless the squatter can bring him or herself within some very limited exceptions.

It will be apparent from this summary that one of the essential features of the scheme is that it must produce a decisive result. Either the squatter is evicted or otherwise ceases to be in *adverse* possession, or he or she is registered as proprietor of the land.

14.7   As we have mentioned above, there are certain very limited cases in which either—

(1)   a squatter's application to be registered will be successful notwithstanding the registered proprietor's objections; or

(2)   he or she may successfully resist possession proceedings brought by the proprietor.

This will be so where the squatter—

(a) was otherwise entitled to the land, as for example—

(i) where he or she was a purchaser in possession who had paid the whole of the contract price; or

(ii) by application of the principles of proprietary estoppel; or

(b) had been in adverse possession of land adjacent to his or her own under the mistaken but reasonable belief that he or she was the owner of it.

The situation in (a) is self-evident, but that in (b) needs explanation. As mentioned above, the register is not normally conclusive as to boundaries. Furthermore, cases often occur where the physical boundaries of the land and the legal boundaries as they appear from the register do not coincide. A common case is where a developer lays out an estate and constructs the fences between properties otherwise than in accordance with the boundaries as they are set out on the plan on the register. In these cases, we think that the squatter, whose conduct has been perfectly reasonable, should prevail over the registered proprietor.

LAND REGISTRATION ACT 2002

96 Disapplication of periods of limitation

(1) No period of limitation under section 15 of the Limitation Act 1980 [14] (time limits in relation to recovery of land) shall run against any person, other than a chargee, in relation to an estate in land or rentcharge the title to which is registered.

(2) No period of limitation under section 16 of that Act [15] (time limits in relation to redemption of land) shall run against any person in relation to such an estate in land or rentcharge.

---

[14]   P. 228, ante.
[15]   P. 228, ante.

(3) Accordingly, section 17[16] of that Act (extinction of title on expiry of time limit) does not operate to extinguish the title of any person where, by virtue of this section, a period of limitation does not run against him.

97 Registration of periods of limitation

Schedule 6 (which makes provision about the registration of an adverse possessor of an estate in land or rentcharge) has effect.[17]

98 Defences

(1) A person has a defence to an action for possession of land if—

(a)   on the day immediately preceding that on which the action was brought he was entitled to make an application under paragraph 1 of Schedule 6 to be registered as the proprietor of an estate in the land, and

(b)   had he made such an application on that day, the condition in paragraph 5(4) of that Schedule would have been satisfied.

(2) A judgment for possession of land ceases to be enforceable at the end of the period of two years beginning with the date of the judgment if the proceedings in which the judgment is given were commenced against a person who was at that time entitled to make an application under paragraph 1 of Schedule 6.

(3) A person has a defence to an action for possession of land if on the day immediately preceding that on which the action was brought he was entitled to make an application under paragraph 6 of Schedule 6 to be registered as the proprietor of an estate in the land.

(4) A judgment for possession of land ceases to be enforceable at the end of the period of two years beginning with the date of the judgment if, at the end of that period, the person against whom the judgment was given is entitled to make an application under paragraph 6 of Schedule 6 to be registered as the proprietor of an estate in the land.

(5) Where in any proceedings a court determines that—

(a)   a person is entitled to a defence under this section, or

(b)   a judgment for possession has ceased to be enforceable against a person by virtue of subsection (4).

the court must order the registrar to register him as the proprietor of the estate in relation to which he is entitled to make an application under Schedule 6.

(6) The defences under this section are additional to any other defences a person may have.

(7) Rules may make provision to prohibit the recovery of rent due under a rentcharge from a person who has been in adverse possession of the rentcharge.[18]

SCHEDULE 6

REGISTRATION OF ADVERSE POSSESSOR

Right to apply for registration

1 (1)   A person may apply to the registrar to be registered as the proprietor of a registered estate in land if he has been in adverse possession of the estate for the period of ten years ending on the date of the application.

---

[16]   P. 233, ante.
[17]   Infra. See LRR 2003, rr. 187–194.
[18]   LRR 2003, rr. 191–193.

(2)   A person may also apply to the registrar to be registered as the proprietor of a registered estate in land if—
   (a) he has in the period of six months ending on the date of the application ceased to be in adverse possession of the estate because of eviction by the registered proprietor, or a person claiming under the registered proprietor,
   (b) on the day before his eviction he was entitled to make an application under sub-paragraph (1), and
   (c) the eviction was not pursuant to a judgment for possession.
(3)   However, a person may not make an application under this paragraph if—
   (a) he is a defendant in proceedings which involve asserting a right to possession of the land, or
   (b) judgment for possession of the land has been given against him in the last two years.
(4)   For the purposes of sub-paragraph (1), the estate need not have been registered throughout the period of adverse possession.

Notification of application

2 (1)   The registrar must give notice of an application under paragraph 1 to—
   (a) the proprietor of the estate to which the application relates,
   (b) the proprietor of any registered charge on the estate,
   (c) where the estate is leasehold, the proprietor of any superior registered estate,
   (d) any person who is registered in accordance with rules as a person to be notified under this paragraph, and
   (e) such other persons as rules may provide.
(2)   Notice under this paragraph shall include notice of the effect of paragraph 4.

Treatment of application

3 (1)   A person given notice under paragraph 2 may require that the application to which the notice relates be dealt with under paragraph 5.
(2)   The right under this paragraph is exercisable by notice to the registrar given before the end of such period as rules may provide.
4   If an application under paragraph 1 is not required to be dealt with under paragraph 5, the applicant is entitled to be entered in the register as the new proprietor of the estate.
5 (1)   If an application under paragraph 1 is required to be dealt with under this paragraph, the applicant is only entitled to be registered as the new proprietor of the estate if any of the following conditions is met.
(2)   The first condition is that—
   (a) it would be unconscionable because of an equity by estoppel for the registered proprietor to seek to dispossess the applicant, and
   (b) the circumstances are such that the applicant ought to be registered as the proprietor.
(3)   The second condition is that the applicant is for some other reason entitled to be registered as the proprietor of the estate.
(4)   The third condition is that—
   (a) the land to which the application relates is adjacent to land belonging to the applicant,

¹⁹   P. 109, n. 4, ante; LRR 2003 rr. 117–123.

    (b) the exact line of the boundary between the two has not been determined under rules under section 60, [19]

    (c) for at least ten years of the period of adverse possession ending on the date of the application, the applicant (or any predecessor in title) reasonably believed that the land to which the application relates belonged to him, and

    (d) the estate to which the application relates was registered more than one year prior to the date of the application.

(5) In relation to an application under paragraph 1(2), this paragraph has effect as if the reference in sub-paragraph (4)(c) to the date of the application were to the day before the date of the applicant's eviction.

Right to make further application for registration

6 (1) Where a person's application under paragraph 1 is rejected, he may make a further application to be registered as the proprietor of the estate if he is in adverse possession of the estate from the date of the application until the last day of the period of two years beginning with the date of its rejection.

  (2) However, a person may not make an application under this paragraph if—

    (a) he is a defendant in proceedings which involve asserting a right to possession of the land,

    (b) judgment for possession of the land has been given against him in the last two years, or

    (c) he has been evicted from the land pursuant to a judgment for possession.

7   If a person makes an application under paragraph 6, he is entitled to be entered in the register as the new proprietor of the estate.

Restriction on applications

8 (1) No one may apply under this Schedule to be registered as the proprietor of an estate in land during, or before the end of twelve months after the end of, any period in which the existing registered proprietor is for the purposes of the Limitation (Enemies and War Prisoners) Act 1945—

    (a) an enemy, or

    (b) detained in enemy territory.

  (2) No-one may apply under this Schedule to be registered as the proprietor of an estate in land during any period in which the existing registered proprietor is—

    (a) unable because of mental disability to make decisions about issues of the kind to which such an application would give rise, or

    (b) unable to communicate such decisions because of mental disability or physical impairment.

  (3) For the purposes of sub-paragraph (2), 'mental disability' means a disability of disorder of the mind or brain, whether permanent or temporary, which results in an impairment or disturbance of mental functioning.

  (4) Where it appears to the registrar that sub-paragraph (1) or (2) applies in relation to an estate in land, he may include a note to that effect in the register.

Effect of registration

9 (1) Where a person is registered as the proprietor of an estate in land in pursuance of an application under this Schedule, the title by virtue of adverse possession which he had at the time of the application is extinguished.

(2) Subject to sub-paragraph (3), the registration of a person under this Schedule as the proprietor of an estate in land does not affect the priority of any interest affecting the estate.

(3) Subject to sub-paragraph (4), where a person is registered under this Schedule as the proprietor of an estate, the estate is vested in him free of any registered charge affecting the estate immediately before his registration.

(4) Sub-paragraph (3) does not apply where registration as proprietor is in pursuance of an application determined by reference to whether any of the conditions in paragraph 5 applies.

Appointment and discharge of charges

10 (1) Where—

(a) a registered estate continues to be subject to a charge notwithstanding the registration of a person under this Schedule as the proprietor, and

(b) the charge affects property other than the estate,

the proprietor of the estate may require the chargee to apportion the amount secured by the charge at that time between the estate and the other property on the basis of their respective values.

(2) The person requiring the apportionment is entitled to a discharge of his estate from the charge on payment of—

(a) the amount apportioned to the estate, and

(b) the costs incurred by the chargee as a result of the apportionment.

(3) On a discharge under this paragraph, the liability of the chargor to the chargee is reduced by the amount apportioned to the estate.

(4) Rules may make provision about apportionment under this paragraph, in particular, provision about—

(a) procedure,

(b) valuation,

(c) calculation of costs payable under sub-paragraph (2)(b), and

(d) payment of the costs of the chargor.

Meaning of 'adverse possession'

11 (1) A person is in adverse possession of an estate in land for the purposes of this Schedule if, but for section 96, a period of limitation under section 15 of the Limitation Act 1980 would run in his favour in relation to the estate.

(2) A person is also to be regarded for those purposes as having been in adverse possession of an estate in land—

(a) where he is the successor in title to an estate in the land, during any period of adverse possession by a predecessor in title to that estate, or

(b) during any period of adverse possession by another person which comes between, and is continuous with, periods of adverse possession of his own.

(3) In determining whether for the purposes of this paragraph a period of limitation would run under section 15 of the Limitation Act 1980, there are to be disregarded—

(a) the commencement of any legal proceedings, and

(b) paragraph 6 of Schedule 1 to that Act.

Trusts

12   A person is not to be regarded as being in adverse possession of an estate for the purposes of this Schedule at any time when the estate is subject to

a trust, unless the interest of each of the beneficiaries in the estate is an interest in possession.

Crown foreshore

13 (1) Where—
      (a) a person is in adverse possession of an estate in land,
      (b) the estate belongs to Her Majesty in right of the Crown or the Duchy of Lancaster or to the Duchy of Cornwall, [20] and
      (c) the land consists of foreshore,
    paragraph 1(1) is to have effect as if the reference to ten years were to sixty years.
  (2) For the purposes of sub-paragraph (1), land is to be treated as foreshore if it has been foreshore at any time in the previous ten years.
  (3) In this paragraph, 'foreshore' means the shore and bed of the sea and of any tidal water, below the line of the medium high tide between the spring and neap tides.

Rentcharges

14   Rules must make provision to apply the preceding provisions of this Schedule to registered rentcharges, subject to such modifications and exceptions as the rules may provide.

Procedure

15   Rules may make provision about the procedure to be followed pursuant to an application under this Schedule

QUESTION

What is meant by saying that the new scheme of adverse possession under the Land Registration Act 2002 reflects the fact that the basis of title to registered land is the fact of registration, not (as is the case with unregistered land) possession? (Law Commission Report on Land Registration for the Twenty-First Century 2001 (Law Com No. 271), para. 1.13).

---

[20]   P. 114, ante.

Part Two. Family Interests

4.   Trusts of Land [1]

I. Successive and Concurrent Interests

A system of private ownership of property must provide for something more sophisticated than absolute ownership of the property by one person. A property owner needs to be able to do more than own it during his lifetime and pass it on to someone else on his death. He may wish to give it to his children, subject to an annuity for his widow, or to give a life interest to the widow and a remainder to the children; or to provide, on his son's marriage, a life interest for his son, and after his death for the daughter-in-law and after her death for their children. He may wish to set up a form of family dynasty, such as was popular among the aristocracy in the 17th, 18th and 19th centuries. The law should make possible the satisfaction of an owner's reasonable wishes on these lines. Limits are imposed on the extent to which property can be tied up in this way. We will see that dispositions are void unless they vest within the period of a life in being plus twenty-one years, or, if a fixed period of years is chosen, a period not exceeding eighty years.

But a system which allows successive interests in property necessarily raises a number of problems. Who is to manage the property during the period of the working out of the various interests? Above all, who is the person to take the decision to sell the property and to transfer title? And what is to happen, when the land is sold, to the interests of the beneficiaries?

The problem is simplest with a fund of money. The common law never developed a system of limited estates in personalty. But in equity a fund could be vested in trustees, who would receive the income and pay it to the income

---

[1] For pre-1997 trusts for sale, see C & B, pp. 69–70, 95–97, 187–188, 215–225; Gray, pp. 653–665; M & W, paras. 8.001–8.002, 8.005–8.010; M M, pp. 7–8, 250; Smith, chap 14; H & M, chap. 11; Harvey, *Settlements of Land* (1973). See Bonfield, *Marriage Settlements 1601–1740* (1983); English and Saville, *Strict Settlement* (1983) which contains details of several dynastic settlements of land; and essays in Rubin and Sugarman, *Law, Economy and Society* (1984) pp. 1–123 (D. Sugarman and G.R. Rubin), 124–167 (M.R. Chesterman), 168–191 (E. Spring) and 209–210 (B. English). The Law Commission reviewed the whole subject of trusts of land. Its Working Paper in 1985 (No. 94) contains a useful outline of the problems arising from the former system of successive and concurrent interests. See the Law Commission Report on Trusts of Land 1989 (Law Com. No. 181).

beneficiary and hand over the capital to the person who was absolutely entitled at the conclusion of the limited interests. Similarly there was no problem in equity with investments. The trustees could buy and sell them, the purchaser taking a good title from the trustees, and the purchase money being added as capital to the trust fund. Chattels can be held in trust; but there has always been doubt as to the forms of limited ownership which could exist in personalty; and heirlooms used to be settled on trusts conforming as far as possible to the devolution of the land with which they were connected. [2] In a trust, it is important to state what powers are to be given to the trustees; powers of management and investment, and the power to sell and to give a good receipt to the purchaser free from the trusts of the settlement. Much of this is now covered by statute.

Successive interests in land provided a special case. The common law system of estates provided for life estates, fees tail, remainders and reversions. When uses and trusts of land developed, equity, generally speaking, followed the law, and allowed similar interests in equity behind a use or a trust. But, when the legal fee simple of land was split up between successive limited owners, there was no provision for the proper management of the land and, above all, no provision for selling. If land were limited to A for life, with remainder to B for life, with remainder to C in fee simple, who would sell the land? The same problem arose if similar limitations were created behind a trust; for, unless special powers were given to the trustees, they could not give a clear title to anyone other than a purchaser of the legal estate for value without notice, because any other purchaser would take the legal estate with notice of the trusts and would be bound by them. [3] Of course, all the legal estate owners in the case of a limitation of legal estates, or all the beneficiaries in the case of a trust, could combine to sell. That might not be difficult where there was a simple limitation, such as one to A for life with remainder to B. But it becomes highly impracticable if there is a long series of limitations, and impossible if the limitations include an entail in a minor or if they create interests which are designed to vest on the happening of some contingencies which have not yet been worked out. [4]

What is needed therefore is a system which meets both these difficulties; which allows a property owner to create future successive and contingent interests in the property (always within the perpetuity rule [5]) and, at the same time, provides for proper management of the fund and the power to sell and to pass a good title to the purchaser free from the trusts affecting the property. The problem is most acute where the capital consists of one single unique piece of property, like a piece of land. How can the interests of the beneficiaries and those of a purchaser be reconciled?

The solution is found by the application of the principle of 'overreaching', and this is applied in each of two forms of procedure used before 1997 for the purpose, the strict settlement and the trust for sale. 'Overreaching' is a principle by which, on a sale of property which is subject to successive interests, the interests of the beneficiaries leave the property and attach to the purchase money. The interests of the beneficiaries are said to be overreached. The beneficiaries do not lose economically out of the sale. A ton of feathers weighs the same as a ton

---

[2]   *Shelley v Shelley* (1868) LR 6 Eq 540; *Re Morrison's Settlement* [1974] Ch 326, [1973] 3 All ER 1094.

[3]   P. 14, ante.

[4]   [1972] Duke Law Journal 517 (W.M. Fratcher); (1977) 42 Missouri LR 355 (R.H. Maudsley).

[5]   Chap. 7, p. 368, post.

of lead. A life interest in remainder in £50,000 worth of land is worth exactly the same as the same interest in £50,000; indeed, more valuable if the money is invested more profitably; less valuable, though, if the land proved to be the better investment. The question is one of choice of investment of the family capital.

The two procedures or methods by which this result could be achieved before 1997 were the strict settlement and the trust for sale.[6] In the context of family holdings of land, the strict settlement is historically the more significant; because it was in this way that the great families held their ancestral lands. Legislation providing for the application of the overreaching principle to successive interests in land first came in 1882.[7] Under the Settled Land Act 1925, where there are successive interests in land, the legal estate was vested in the tenant for life (the income beneficiary) and he had the powers of management and of sale of the fee simple; and on such a sale the beneficial interests in the land were overreached and thus transferred from the land to the proceeds of sale.

On the other hand, land held on trust for sale was vested in trustees upon trust to sell and to hold the income until sale and the proceeds of the sale on trust for the beneficiaries according to their interests under the terms of the limitation. Under the doctrine of conversion, by which land subject to a trust for sale was treated in equity as being personalty, the interests of the beneficiaries were already interests in personalty. Overreaching was therefore automatic, but the Law of Property Act 1925 section 2 made express provision for it.[8] The existence of the trust for sale did not mean that the trustees must sell forthwith, for, although they were under a duty to sell, they were given by statute a discretionary power to postpone sale; and they could retain the land under this power as long as they wished. They were also given the same powers of management and sale as the tenant for life in the case of a strict settlement.

The trust for sale before 1997 was thus an alternative method of dealing with successive interests in land. It was more convenient than a strict settlement for various reasons, the most important of which were: land and personalty could be held together, and most family trusts contained both; decisions were taken by a group of persons in a fiduciary position and not by one interested beneficiary; it was equally convenient where there were concurrent as opposed to successive interests; and it proved more flexible and able to accommodate special forms of trusts developed to reduce taxation. Income tax, estate duty (replaced by capital transfer tax in 1974 and by inheritance tax in 1986) and capital gains tax have all played their part in developing the modern law of settlements.[9]

Concurrent interests used to create a similar problem for a purchaser. To get a good title, he had to buy from all the co-owners. This problem was overcome in 1925 by providing that all concurrent interests, other than landholding by trustees, existed only behind a trust for sale which, if not created expressly, was implied as a trust for sale by statute.[10] There could not be more than four trustees

---

[6]   For the problems arising from the pre 1997 dual system of strict settlement and trust for sale, see Law Commission Report on Trusts of Land Part I: Law Com No 181 (1989): and for some suggested solutions, see (1928) 166 LT 45; (1938) 85 LJ News 353 (J.M.L.); (1938) 54 LQR 576 (M.M. Lewis); (1944) 8 Conv (NS) 147 (H. Potter); (1957) CLP 152 (E.H. Scamell); (1961) 24 MLR 123 (G.A. Grove); (1962) CLP 104 (E.C. Ryder).

[7]   SLA 1882.

[8]   It makes provision also for overreaching interests prior to the trust for sale where the trustees are either two or more individuals approved or appointed by the court or a trust corporation: LPA 1925, s. 2(2), p. 294, post.

[9]   See generally H & M, chap. 9; M & B, *Trusts and Trustees* (6th edn, 2002), Part III; Thomas, *Taxation and Trusts* (1981).

[10]   Chap. 5, p.300, post.

of land. [11] So, even if land was beneficially owned by 130 tenants in common, the purchaser bought from not more than four trustees for sale, who passed the title, as with successive interests, free from the beneficial interests of the co-owners. Their interests attached to the purchase money.

Before 1997 all cases of successive or concurrent ownership were thus subject to either a trust for sale or a strict settlement. Conveyancers used the trust for sale almost exclusively, but many titles, especially those deriving from large family landholdings, were still dependent upon the Settled Land Act conveyancing.

In 1996 the first change in the structure of English land law since 1925 was made by the Trusts of Land and Appointment of Trustees Act 1996. [12] The Act applies to trusts of land created before or after the date of its commencement on 1 January 1997. Under it the dual system of strict settlement and trust for sale is replaced by a trust of land which applies to both successive and concurrent interests. Existing strict settlements continue, but no new strict settlements can be created. Existing express trusts for sale, whether of successive or of concurrent interests, also continue, and may still be expressly created so as to come within the wide definition of the trust of land. [13] If, however, trusts of concurrent interests were implied by statute, they are converted into trusts of land. Under the trust of land the legal estate to the land is vested in trustees who are given all the powers of an absolute owner for the purpose of exercising their functions as trustees. The trustees have a power, but not a duty, to sell, and the interests of the beneficiaries are still overreachable on sale, as they were under the previous dual system. The doctrine of conversion is abolished in respect of all trusts for sale, whenever created, [14] and consequently the interests of the beneficiaries cease to be interests in personalty and become interests in land. The Act is another and welcome measure in the long line of measures which over the centuries have sought to develop and simplify the land law; it is an important gloss on the 1925 legislation, and gives to the trustees broad and flexible powers to enable them to manage the land more effectively, and to the beneficiaries more scope in the control of those powers.

II. Meaning of Trust of Land

A. Trust of Land

'Trust of land' is widely drawn so as to include any trust of property which consists of or includes land; whether created or arising before 1997 or after 1996. It includes a trust for sale: new strict settlements are excluded. [15]

---

[11]   TA 1925, s.34.
[12]   C & B, pp. 227–240; Gray, pp. 889–941; M & W, paras. 8.123–8.168; MM, pp. 283–289; Smith, pp. 304–341. For commentaries on the Act, see Whitehouse and Hassall, *The Trusts of Land and Appointment of Trustees Act 1996: A Practical Guide* (2nd edn) (a very useful commentary which is referred to throughout this chapter); Barraclough and Matthews, *Trusts of Land and Appointment of Trustees Act 1996;* Kenny and Kenny, *The Trusts of Land and Appointment of Trustees Act 1996* (2nd edn) (with the principal sections of the 1925 legislation as amended, and the Law Commission Report on Trusts of Land 1988 (Law Com No. 181)); Sydenham and Sydenham, *Trusts of Land—The New Law.* See also *Emmet on Title,* chap. 22; R & R (1991 edn), chap. 37; (2003 edn), chap. 32; [1986] Conv 401 (A.J. Oakley); (1998) 61 MLR 56 (L. M. Clements).
[13]   P. 267, post. See (1997) 113 LQR 207 (P. H. Pettit).
[14]   Except for a trust for sale created in the will of a testator dying before 1997.
[15]   W & H, paras. 2.1–2.17. For strict settlements, see chap. 5.

TRUSTS OF LAND AND APPOINTMENT OF TRUSTEES ACT 1996

1. Meaning of 'Trust of Land'—(1) In this Act—

(a) 'trust of land' means (subject to subsection (3)) any trust of property which consists of or includes land, and

(b) 'trustees of land' means trustees of a trust of land. [16]

(2) The reference in subsection (1)(a) to a trust—

(a) is to any description of trust (whether express, implied, resulting or constructive), including a trust for sale and a bare trust, and

(b) includes a trust created, or arising, before the commencement of this Act.

(3) The reference to land in subsection (1)(a) does not include land which (despite section 2) is settled land or which is land to which the Universities and College Estates Act 1925 applies.

B. Exclusion of Strict Settlements

TRUSTS OF LAND AND APPOINTMENT OF TRUSTEES ACT 1996

2. Trusts in place of settlements—(1) No settlement created after the commencement of this Act is a settlement for the purpose of the Settled Land Act 1925; and no settlement shall be deemed to be made under that Act after that commencement.

(2) Subsection (1) does not apply to a settlement created on the occasion of an alteration in any interest in, or of a person becoming entitled under, a settlement which—

(a) is in existence at the commencement of this Act, or

(b) derives from a settlement within paragraph (a) or this paragraph.

(3) But a settlement created as mentioned in subsection (2) is not a settlement for the purposes of the Settled Land Act 1925 if provision to the effect that it is not is made in the instrument, or any of the instruments, by which it is created.

(4) Where at any time after the commencement of this Act there is in the case of any settlement which is a settlement for the purposes of the Settled Land Act 1925 no relevant property which is, or is deemed to be, subject to the settlement, the settlement permanently ceases at that time to be a settlement for the purposes of that Act.

In this subsection 'relevant property' means land and personal chattels to which section 67(1) of the Settled Land Act 1925 (heirlooms) applies.

(5) No land held on charitable, ecclesiastical or public trusts shall be or be deemed to be settled land after the commencement of this Act, even if it was or

---

[16] Trustees are usually appointed by the settlor when creating the trust; in default the court may appoint them. See Trustee Act 1925, ss. 34–43, as amended by TLATA 1996, s. 25(1) Sch. 3, paras. 3(9)–(14); TLATA 1996 Part II: ss. 19 (appointment and retirement of trustee at instance of beneficiaries); 20 (appointment of substitute for incapable trustee); 21 (supplementary); Trustee Delegation Act 1999, s.8 (incorporated into TA, s.36, as (6A)–(6D); appointment of additional trustee by attorney). See generally M & B, *Trusts and Trustees*, chap. 16; M & W, paras. 10.052–10.065; W & H, paras. 3.1–3.33; Law Commission Report on Trustees' Powers and Duties 1999 (Law Com No. 260).

In respect of deaths after 1996, the provisions of Part I of the Act relating to trustees apply to personal representatives, other than ss. 10, p. 277, post; 11, p. 277, post; and 14, p. 282, post: s.18.

was deemed to be settled land before that commencement.

(6) Schedule 1 has effect to make provision consequential on this section (including provision to impose a trust in circumstances in which, apart from this section, there would be a settlement for the purposes of the Settled Land Act 1925 (and there would not otherwise be a trust)). [17]

C. Trust for Sale

I. DEFINITION

LAW OF PROPERTY ACT 1925

205. General definitions.—(1)

(xxix) 'Trust for sale', in relation to land, means an immediate trust for sale, whether or not exercisable at the request or with the consent of any person; 'trustees for sale' mean the persons (including a personal representative) holding land on trust for sale.

Before 1997 it was necessary to distinguish between a trust for sale and a strict settlement. An interest in succession created a strict settlement unless it satisfied the then definition of a trust for sale which included the word 'binding' between 'immediate' and 'trust'. There must be a trust which imposes on the trustees a duty to sell and not merely a power of sale; the trust for sale must be immediate in that a trust to sell at some future date does not prevent land from being settled land for the time being. [18] It must also be binding. The apparent tautology of this word caused difficulty; trusts are by their very nature binding. [19]

After 1996 it is necessary to discover whether an interest in succession is a trust for sale within the overall definition of a trust of land. To do this it must satisfy the amended definition which excises the word binding (s. 25(2), Sch 4). If it does not satisfy the definition, it still comes within the provisions of the new Act, but if it does, it imposes on the trustees a duty to sell with a mandatory power to postpone sale (under section 4, infra).

II. EXPRESS TRUSTS FOR SALE AS TRUSTS OF LAND

Before 1997 section 25 of the Law of Property Act 1925 gave to trustees for sale the power to postpone sale indefinitely, unless a contrary intention was

---

[17]   Paras 1 and 2 (minors); 3 (family charges); 4 (charitable, ecclesiastical and public trusts); 5 (entailed interests), p. 13, ante; 6 (property held on settlement ceasing to exist).

[18]   See *Re Hanson* [1928] Ch 96; *Bacon v Bacon* [1947] P 151, [1947] 2 All ER 327; *Re Herklots' Will Trusts* [1964] 1 WLR 583, [1964] 2 All ER 66 (trust for sale subject to X's right to occupy house for life held to be immediate trust for sale subject to X's consent); *Re Nierop's Will Trusts* (23 April 1986, unreported), discussed in *Williams on Wills* (7th edn) pp. 1008, 1174–1178 (trust to sell with consent of beneficiary combined with trust to permit beneficiary to reside while property remains unsold qualifies as trust for sale).

[19]   See the 6th edn of this book, pp. 225–229; C & B, pp. 228–230; M & W, (5th edn), pp. 386–389; MM, p. 280; *Emmet on Title*, para. 23.012; *Re Parker's Settled Estates* [1928] Ch 247; cf. *Re Leigh's Settled Estates* [1926] Ch 852. It may be necessary to interpret the word when deciding whether there is a pre-existing strict settlement on 1 January 1997, but this will be very rare.

expressed in the trust instrument. After 1996 this power still exists but cannot be excluded by the settlor. The sale can only be postponed if the trustees for sale unanimously decide to exercise the power; [20] if they are not unanimous, then the land must be sold. [1]

Trusts for sale can still be expressly created. It has been suggested that it may be desirable to create an express trust for sale where there is a trust in the residue clause of a will, or where there is a conveyance to co-owners. [2] In any event section 4 of the Trusts of Land and Appointment of Trustees Act 1996 ensures that if a trust for sale is created in ignorance of the new legislation it will be valid under it.

Express trusts for sale created before 1997 continue, but are subject to the mandatory power of postponement in section 4 (1).

TRUSTS OF LAND AND APPOINTMENT OF TRUSTEES ACT 1996

4. Express trusts for sale as trusts of land.—(1) In the case of every trust for sale of land created by a disposition there is to be implied, despite any provision to the contrary made by the disposition, a power for the trustees to postpone sale of the land; and the trustees are not liable in any way for postponing sale of the land, in the exercise of their discretion, for an indefinite period.

(2) Subsection (1) applies to a trust whether it is created, or arises, before or after the commencement of this Act.

(3) Subsection (1) does not affect any liability incurred by trustees before that commencement.

III. IMPLIED TRUSTS FOR SALE AS TRUSTS OF LAND

All trusts for sale which are implied by statute, including those arising before 1997, are converted into trusts of land by section 5 (1) of the Trusts of Land and Appointment of Trustees Act 1996. Schedule 2 of the Act identifies these statutory trusts for sale. Statutory provisions have been amended to replace the duty to sell by a power to sell and a power to retain. [3]

TRUSTS OF LAND AND APPOINTMENT OF TRUSTEES ACT 1996

5. Implied trusts for sale as trusts of land.—(1) Schedule 2 has effect in relation to statutory provisions which impose a trust for sale of land in certain circumstances so that in those circumstances there is instead a trust of the land (without a duty to sell).

(2) Section 1 of the Settled Land Act 1925 does not apply to land held on any trust arising by virtue of that Schedule (so that any such land is subject to a trust of land).

---

[20] *Re Mayo* [1943] Ch 302 (where the power to retain required unanimity).
[1] Subject to an order of the court under TLATA 1996, ss. 14 and 15, p. 281, post. Charitable Trustees may act by a majority: *Re Whiteley* [1910] 1 Ch 600 at 607.
[2] W & H, paras. 6.40–6.41; Sydenham, *Trusts of Land*, para. 3.8.3; *Emmet on Title*, para. 22.035; [1987] Conv 84 (R. Mitchell) doubting whether a trust for sale should continue to be used in a will.
[3] LPA 1925, s.35 which sets out the meaning of the statutory trusts for sale is repealed: TLATA 1996, s. 25(2), Sch. 4.

Schedule 2 refers to
  (a) Mortgaged property held by trustees after redemption barred (LPA 1925, s.31).
  (b) Land purchased by trustees of personal property (LPA 1925, s.32).
  (c) Dispositions to tenants in common (LPA 1925, s. 34, pp. 300, post).
  (d) Joint tenancies (LPA 1925, s. 36, pp. 301, post).
  (e) Intestacy (AEA 1925, s. 33).
  (f) Reverter of sites (Reverter of Sites Act 1987, s. 1, p. 7, n.4, ante).

D. Bare Trusts

Snell: Principles of Equity (30th edn) para. 6.30

'A simple (or bare [4]) trust is one in which property is vested in one person on trust for another, the nature of the trust not being prescribed by the settlor but being left to the construction of the law, as where property is transferred to T "on trust for B absolutely". In such a case, T must permit B to enjoy the property, and must obey his instructions as to disposing of it.' [5]

Before 1997 bare trusts fell outside the dual system of trust for sale and strict settlement. This caused difficulty, especially in that interests under bare trusts could not be overreached (p. 293, post). After 1996 bare trusts came within the definition of a trust of land (TLATA 1996, s. 1(2)(a), p. 267, ante) and interests under them are therefore now overreachable.

III. Doctrine of Conversion

Before 1997 the doctrine of conversion applied as soon as a trust for sale came into operation; the interests of the beneficiaries were thus automatically interests in the proceeds of sale of land and not in the land itself. Cross LJ said in **Irani Finance Ltd v Singh** [1971] Ch 59 at 80, [1970] 3 All ER 199 at 204:
  'The whole purpose of the trust for sale is to make sure, by shifting the equitable interests away from the land and into the proceeds of sale, that a purchaser of the land takes free from the equitable interests. To hold these to be equitable interests in the land itself would be to frustrate this purpose. Even to hold that they have equitable interests in the land for a limited period, namely, until the land is sold, would, we think, be inconsistent with the trust for sale being an "immediate" trust for sale working an immediate conversion, which is what the Law of Property Act, 1925 envisages (see section 205(1)(xxix)).' [6]
  But this view gives rise to difficulties and in certain situations it was found undesirable to apply the full logic of the doctrine of conversion. [7]

---

[4]   See *Re Cunningham and Frayling* [1891] 2 Ch 567 at 572; *Tomlinson v Glyns Executor and Trustee Co* [1970] Ch 112 at 125–126.
[5]   For another example of a bare trust, see *Hodgson v Marks* [1971] Ch 892, [1971] 2 All ER 684.
[6]   P. 268, ante. This statement was expressly approved and relied upon by Lord OLIVER OF AYLMERTON in *City of London Building Society v Flegg* [1988] AC 54 at 82, [1987] 3 All ER 435 at 447; p. 316, post.
[7]   For analysis of the doctrine and its difficulties, see pp. 292–301 of the 6th edn of this book; C & B, p. 230; M & W 8.007, 8.118–8.121.

Lord WILBERFORCE said in *Williams & Glyn's Bank Ltd v Boland* [1981] AC 487 at 507, [1980] 2 All ER 408 at 414, p. 136, ante:

'To describe the interests of spouses in a house jointly bought to be lived in as a matrimonial home as merely an interest in proceeds of sale, or rents and profits until sale, is just a little unreal'.

Section 3 of the Trusts of Land and Appointment of Trustees Act 1996 abolished the doctrine retrospectively in this area, and the interests of beneficiaries under a trust of land are now interests in the land itself.

TRUSTS OF LAND AND APPOINTMENT OF TRUSTEES ACT 1996

3. Abolition of doctrine of conversion. [8] —(1) Where land is held by trustees subject to a trust for sale, the land is not to be regarded as personal property; and where personal property is subject to a trust for sale in order that the trustees may aquire land, the personal property is not to be regarded as land.

(2) Subsection (1) does not apply to a trust created by a will if the testator died before the commencement of this Act.

(3) Subject to that, subsection (1) applies to a trust whether it is created, or arises, before or after that commencement.

IV. Functions of Trustees of Land

A. General Powers of Trustees of Land

Before 1997 section 28 of the Law of Property Act 1925 gave to trustees for sale 'all the powers of a tenant for life and the trustees of a settlement under the Settled Land Act 1925.' This section is repealed and replaced by section 6 of the Trusts of Land and Appointment of Trustees Act 1996, which applies to all trusts of land whether arising before or after the commencement of the Act. The scope of the new section is much wider than its predecessor and is designed 'to make the scheme of powers as broadly based and as flexible as possible.' [9]

TRUSTS OF LAND AND APPOINTMENT OF TRUSTEES ACT 1996

6. General powers of trustees.—(1) For the purpose of exercising their functions [10] as trustees, the trustees of land have in relation to the land subject to the trust all the powers of an absolute owner.

(2) Where in the case of any land subject to a trust of land each of the beneficiaries interested in the land is a person of full age and capacity who is absolutely entitled to the land, the powers conferred on the trustees by subsection (1) include the power to convey the land to the beneficiaries even though they have not required the trustees to do so; and where land is conveyed by virtue of this subsection—

(a) the beneficiaries shall do whatever is necessary to secure that it vests in them, and

---

[8]   W & H, paras. 2.18–2-24. See also TLATA 1996 s. 25(5). The side heading of s. 3 is misleading. The doctrine still subsists for example, in specifically enforceable contracts for the sale of land: (1997) 113 LQR 207 at p. 209 (P. H. Pettit).

[9]   Law Commission Report No 181, paras 10.4, 10.5.

[10] This includes both powers and duties of trustees.

(b) if they fail to do so, the court may make an order requiring them to do so. [11]

(3) The trustees of land have power to acquire land under the power conferred by section 8 of the Trustee Act 2000. [12]

(4) The power conferred by subsection (3) may be exercised by trustees to purchase land—

(a) by way of investment,

(b) for occupation by any beneficiary, or

(c) for any other reason.

(5) In exercising the powers conferred by this section trustees shall have regard to the rights of the beneficiaries.

(6) The powers conferred by this section shall not be exercised in contravention of, or of any order made in pursuance of, any other enactment or any rule of law or equity.

(7) The reference in subsection (6) to an order includes an order of any court or of the Charity Commissioners.

(8) Where any enactment other than this section confers on trustees authority to act subject to any restriction, limitation or condition, trustees of land may not exercise the powers conferred by this section to do any act which they are prevented from doing under the other enactment by reason of the restriction, limitation or condition.

(9) The duty of care under section 1 of the Trustee Act 2000 applies to trustees of land when exercising the power conferred by this section. [13]

B. Partition by Trustees of Land

TRUSTS OF LAND AND APPOINTMENT OF TRUSTEES ACT 1996

7. Partition by trustees. [14] —(1) The trustees of land may, where beneficiaries of full age are absolutely entitled in undivided shares to land subject to the trust, partition the land, or any part of it, and provide (by way of mortgage or otherwise) for the payment of any equality money.

(2) The trustees shall give effect to any such partition by conveying the partitioned land in severalty (whether or not subject to any legal mortgage created for raising equality money), either absolutely or in trust, in accordance with the rights of those beneficiaries.

(3) Before exercising their powers under subsection (2) the trustees shall obtain the consent of each of those beneficiaries. [15]

(4) Where a share in the land is affected by an incumbrance, the trustees may either give effect to it or provide for its discharge from the property allotted to that share as they think fit.

(5) If a share in the land is absolutely vested in a minor, subsections (1) to (4) apply as if he were of full age, except that the trustees may act on his behalf and retain land or other property representing his share in trust for him.

---

11   On the difficulties of this ss., see W & H, paras 2.45–2.51.

12   As amended bty TA 2000, s. 40 Sch 2 Pt II para. 45.See s. 17(2) for its use by trustees of a trust of proceeds of sale of land.

13   For the duty of care, see p. 275, post.

14   Replacing LPA 1925, s.28 (3), (4), which with amendments is extended to all trusts of land.

15   A purchaser of land is not concerned to see that the requirements of consent have been obtained: *Booth v Ellard* [1980] 1 WLR 1443, [1980] 3 All ER 569; but cf. TLATA 1996, s. 10(3).

C. Exclusion and Restriction of Powers

The powers given under sections 6 and 7 may be excluded or restricted by the disposition creating the trust. They apply to all existing trusts and cannot be excluded. Similarly, they will apply to all implied trusts wherever arising. It is therefore only in express trusts of land created after 1996 that advantage can be taken of section 8. [16]

TRUSTS OF LAND AND APPOINTMENT OF TRUSTEES ACT 1996

8. Exclusion and restriction of powers.—(1) Sections 6 and 7 do not apply in the case of a trust of land created by a disposition in so far as provision to the effect that they do not apply is made by the disposition.

(2) If the disposition creating such a trust makes provision requiring any consent to be obtained to the exercise of any power conferred by section 6 or 7, the power may not be exercised without that consent. [17]

(3) Subsection (1) does not apply in the case of charitable, ecclesiastical or public trusts. [18]

(4) Subsections (1) and (2) have effect subject to any enactment which prohibits or restricts the effect of provision of the description mentioned in them. [19]

D. Delegation to Beneficiaries by Trustees of Land Collectively

Under section 29 of the Law of Property Act 1925 trustees for sale were empowered to delegate revocably their powers of leasing, accepting surrenders of leases and management to any person of full age for the time being beneficially entitled in possession to the net rents and profits of the land during his life or for any less period. The duty to sell could not be delegated. The trustees were not liable for the acts or defaults of the delegate, but he was, in relation to the exercise of the power by him, deemed to be in the position and to have the duties and liabilities of a trustee.

This section has been repealed by the Trusts of Land and Appointment of Trustees Act 1996, [20] and replaced by a wider provision for delegation by the trustees acting together. [1]

---

[16]   W & H, paras. 2.68–2.99; [1997] Conv 263 (G. Watt).

[17]   For the position of purchasers, see ss. 10, 16(3), pp. 276, 296, post.

[18]   This was introduced as an amendment at the Report stage of the Bill to enable these trusts to take advantage of the general powers of trustees of land.

[19]   In particular this refers to Pensions Act 1995, s.35 (4) which prevents the powers of occupational pensions scheme trustees being fettered by reference to requirements to obtain the consent of the employer.

[20]   S. 25(2), Sch. 4. See W & H, paras. 2.72–2.99.

[1]   It seems that the power to delegate under s. 9 cannot be excluded: Kenny and Kenny, para. 47–11. For delegation by an individual trustee for a limited period only, see Trustee Act 1925, ss. 25, 29, as substituted by Trustee Delegation Act 1999, s. 5(1), and Enduring Powers of Attorney Act 1985 (as amended) by Trustee Delegation Act, s. 6. For delegation of general powers by trustees, see TA 2000, Part IV, which creates a new statutory regime. For delegation by trustees of land who are also beneficiaries, see Trustee Delegation Act 1999, ss. 1 and 2. See generally M & B, *Trusts and Trustees* (6th edn), pp. 799–804; H & M, 576–585; Law Commission Report on Delegation by Individual Trustees 1994 (Law Com No. 220); Law Commission Report on Trustees' Powers and Duties 1997 (Law Com. No. 260).

TRUSTS OF LAND AND APPOINTMENT OF TRUSTEES ACT 1996

9. Delegation by trustees.—(1) The trustees of land may, by power of attorney delegate to any beneficiary or beneficiaries of full age and beneficially entitled to an interest in possession in land [2] subject to the trust any of their functions as trustees which relate to the land. [3]

(2) Where trustees purport to delegate to a person by a power of attorney under subsection (1) functions relating to any land and another person in good faith deals with him in relation to the land, he shall be presumed in favour of that other person to have been a person to whom the functions could be delegated unless that other person has knowledge at the time of the transaction that he was not such a person.

And it shall be conclusively presumed in favour of any purchaser whose interest depends on the validity of that transaction that that other person dealt in good faith and did not have such knowledge if that other person makes a statutory declaration to that effect before or within three months after the completion of the purchase.

(3) A power of attorney under subsection (1) shall be given by all the trustees jointly and (unless expressed to be irrevocable and to be given by way of security) may be revoked by any one or more of them; and such a power is revoked by the appointment as a trustee of a person other than those by whom it is given (though not by any of those persons dying or otherwise ceasing to be a trustee).

(4) Where a beneficiary to whom functions are delegated by a power of attorney under subsection (1) ceases to be a person beneficially entitled to an interest in possession in land subject to the trust—

(a) if the functions are delegated to him alone, the power is revoked,

(b) if the functions are delegated to him and to other beneficiaries to be exercised by them jointly (but not separately), the power is revoked if each of the other beneficiaries ceases to be so entitled (but otherwise functions exercisable in accordance with the power are so exercisable by the remaining beneficiary or beneficiaries), and

(c) if the functions are delegated to him and to other beneficiaries to be exercised by them separately (or either separately or jointly), the power is revoked in so far as it relates to him.

(5) A delegation under subsection (1) may be for any period or indefinite.

(6) A power of attorney under subsection (1) cannot be an enduring power within the meaning of the Enduring Powers of Attorney Act 1985. [4]

(7) Beneficiaries to whom functions have been delegated under subsection (1) are, in relation to the exercise of the functions, in the same position as trustees (with the same duties and liabilities); but such beneficiaries shall not be regarded as trustees for any other purposes (including, in particular, the purposes of any enactment permitting the delegation of functions by trustees or imposing requirements relating to the payment of capital money).

(8) ... [5]

(9) Neither this section nor the repeal by this Act of section 29 of the Law of Property Act 1925 (which is superseded by this section) affects the operation after the commencement of this Act of any delegation effected before that commencement.

---

[2]   On the meaning of beneficiary, see s. 22, p. 276, post.
[3]   See ss. 6 and 7, pp. 271–272, ante.
[4]   On powers of attorney generally, see Cretney and Lush, *Enduring Powers of Attorney* (4th edn.).
[5]   Repealed by TA 2000, s. 40(1), (3), Sch. 2, Pt II, para. 46, Sch. 4, Pt II.

9A. Duties of trustees in connection with delegation etc. [6]—(1) The duty of care under section 1 of the Trustee Act 2000 applies to trustees of land in deciding whether to delegate any of their functions under section 9.

(2) Subsection (3) applies if the trustees of land—

(a) delegate any of their functions under section 9, and

(b) the delegation is not irrevocable.

(3) While the delegation continues, the trustees—

(a) must keep the delegation under review,

(b) if circumstances make it appropriate to do so, must consider whether there is a need to exercise any power of intervention that they have, and

(c) if they consider that there is a need to exercise such a power, must do so.

(4) 'Power of intervention' includes—

(a) a power to give directions to the beneficiary;

(b) a power to revoke the delegation.

(5) The duty of care under section 1 of the 2000 Act applies to trustees in carrying out any duty under subsection (3).

(6) A trustee of land is not liable for any act or default of the beneficiary, or beneficiaries, unless the trustee fails to comply with the duty of care in deciding to delegate any of the trustees' functions under section 9 or in carrying out any duty under subsection (3).

(7) Neither this section nor the repeal of section 9(8) by the Trustee Act 2000 affects the operation after the commencement of this section of any delegation effected before that commencement.

TRUSTEE ACT 2000

1. The duty of care

(1) Whenever the duty under this subsection applies to a trustee, he must exercise such care and skill as is reasonable in the circumstances, having regard in particular—

(a) to any special knowledge or experience that he has or holds himself out as having, and

(b) if he acts as trustee in the course of a business or profession, to any special knowledge or experience that it is reasonable to expect of a person acting in the course of that kind of business or profession.

(2) In this Act the duty under subsection (1) is called 'the duty of care'. [7]

V. Beneficiaries under a Trust of Land

Sections 10 to 13 of the Trusts of Land and Appointment of Trustees Act 1996 are mainly concerned with the rights of beneficiaries under a trust of land and with the duties owed to them by their trustees.

---

[6]   As inserted by TA 2000, s. 40(1), Sch. 2, Pt II, para. 47.

[7]   For the application of the duty of care, see TA 2000, 52, Sch. 1; W & H, paras. 10.1–10.21; M & B, *Trusts and Trustees* (6th edn), pp. 679–684.

A. Meaning of Beneficiary

TRUSTS OF LAND AND APPOINTMENT OF TRUSTEES ACT 1996

22. Meaning of 'beneficiary'.—(1) In this Act 'beneficiary', in relation to a trust, means any person who under the trust has an interest in property subject to the trust (including a person who has such an interest as a trustee or a personal representative).

(2) In this Act references to a beneficiary who is beneficially entitled do not include a beneficiary who has an interest in property subject to the trust only by reason of being a trustee or personal representative.

(3) For the purposes of this Act a person who is a beneficiary only by reason of being an annuitant is not to be regarded as entitled to an interest in possession in land subject to the trust. [8]

B. Consents

Section 10 of the Trusts of Land and Appointment of Trustees Act 1996 is based on section 26 of the Law of Property Act 1925 which has been repealed. [9] Settlors may wish to make the sale of trust land dependent on the consent of the interest in possession beneficiary who will then be able to enjoy the use of the land and so prevent the trustees from selling it over his head and thereby overreaching his interest.

TRUSTS OF LAND AND APPOINTMENT OF TRUSTEES ACT 1996

10. Consents.—(1) If a disposition creating a trust of land requires the consent of more than two persons to the exercise by the trustees of any function relating to the land, the consent of any two of them to the exercise of the function is sufficient in favour of a purchaser.

(2) Subsection (1) does not apply to the exercise of a function by trustees of land held on charitable, ecclesiastical or public trusts.

(3) Where at any time a person whose consent is expressed by a disposition creating a trust of land to be required to the exercise by the trustees of any functions relating to the land is not of full age—

(a) his consent is not, in favour of a purchaser, required to the exercise of the function, but

(b) the trustees shall obtain the consent of a parent who has parental responsibility for him (within the meaning of the Children Act 1989) or of a guardian of his.

In **Re Inns** [1947] Ch 576, [1947] 2 All ER 308 there was an application by a widow under the Inheritance (Family Provision) Act 1938, section 1 for an increased provision from her deceased husband's very substantial estate. The widow argued that it was the testator's intention that she should reside during widowhood in a luxurious mansion 'Springfield' which was expensive to run and would consume more than the financial provision made for her. The house was held on trust for sale, but could only be sold with the consent both of the

---

[8]   For a detailed analysis, see W & H, paras. 2.60, 4.1–4.9.
[9]   S. 25 (2), Sch. 4.

widow and of the Stevenage Urban District Council, to whom the house was to be offered, on the widow's remarriage or death, for use as a hospital, with £10,000 in addition for maintenance and equipment if they accepted the gift.

WYNN-PARRY J refused to hold, on the facts, that the financial provision for the widow was unreasonable, but at no stage was doubt cast upon the validity of the requirement of the consent of the widow and of the Council. WYNN-PARRY J said at 582, at 312:

'After an exhaustive consideration of all the circumstances I come to the conclusion that while, if I had been sitting in the testator's armchair, I might well have avoided tying up "Springfield" so that only the plaintiff's consent to its sale in her lifetime would have been required, and I might well have provided a somewhat larger fund than the 85,000*l* in view of the size of the estate; yet, bearing in mind the principles upon which I am directed to proceed by the authorities which I regard as binding on me, and with which I am respectfully in agreement, I cannot bring myself to the conclusion that what has been provided is so little as to be unreasonable. From the plaintiff's point of view the provisions regarding "Springfield" are unfortunate in that neither she nor the trustees can bring about a sale during her lifetime.'

C. Consultation with Beneficiaries

Section 11 of the Trusts of Land and Appointment of Trustees Act 1996 [10] is based on section 26(3) of the Law of Property Act 1925, which has been repealed and extends to express trusts a rule which applied before 1997 to implied trusts for sale only. [11] It applies to trusts expressly created after 1996 unless excluded by the disposition; it also applies to implied trusts, whenever arising. As far as pre-1997 express trusts are concerned, the section does not apply unless it is included by a deed made by the settlor after 1996. It does not apply to trusts created by will before 1997.

TRUSTS OF LAND AND APPOINTMENT OF TRUSTEES ACT 1996

11. Consultation with beneficiaries.—(1) The trustees of land shall in the exercise of any function relating to land subject to the trust—

(a) so far as practicable, consult the beneficiaries of full age and beneficially entitled to an interest in possession in the land, and

(b) so far as consistent with the general interest of the trust, give effect to the wishes of those beneficiaries, or (in case of dispute) of the majority (according to the value of their combined interests). [12]

(2) Subsection (1) does not apply—

(a) in relation to a trust created by a disposition in so far as provision that it does not apply is made by the disposition,

(b) in relation to a trust created or arising under a will made before the commencement of this Act, or

(c) in relation to the exercise of the power mentioned in section 6(2).

[10] See W & H, paras. 2.107–2.119.

[11] S. 25(2), Sch. 4.

[12] If the trustees fail to consult the beneficiaries it may be a breach of trust; *Re Jones* [1931] 1 Ch 375 at 377 per BENNETT J; *Crawley Borough Council v Ure* [1996] QB 13, [1996] 1 All ER 724 (notice to quit given to landlord by one joint tenant without consultation with other joint tenant not a 'positive' act for which consultation was necessary, and therefore, not a breach of trust).

(3) Subsection (1) does not apply to a trust created before the commencement of this Act by a disposition, or a trust created after that commencement by reference to such a trust, unless provision to the effect that it is to apply is made by a deed executed—

(a) in a case in which the trust was created by one person and he is of full capacity, by that person, or

(b) in a case in which the trust was created by more than one person, by such of the persons who created the trust as are alive and of full capacity.

(4) A deed executed for the purposes of subsection (3) is irrevocable.

D. Right to Occupy

Section 12 of the Trusts of Land and Appointment of Trustees Act 1996[13] gives to a beneficiary, who is beneficially entitled to an interest in possession of land, the right to occupy trust land. Section 13 provides that the trustees may exclude, restrict or impose conditions on such occupation.[14]

Before 1997 there were difficulties concerning the occupation of beneficiaries under a trust for sale, especially where the beneficiaries were co-owners under an implied trust. This was due to the doctrine of conversion under which the interests of beneficiaries under a trust for sale were in the proceeds of sale and not in the land itself. As we have seen the courts regarded the doctrine as artificial.[15]

In **Bull v Bull**,[16] for example, a mother and son were equitable tenants in common of residential accommodation and the son was trustee of the legal estate which he held upon an implied trust for sale in favour of his mother and himself. The question was whether the son could obtain vacant possession against his mother. In holding that the son failed, Lord DENNING treated the mother as having an interest in land, and a right to occupy it. The doctrine of conversion has been abolished[17] retrospectively, and the matter is now regulated by sections 12 and 13.

TRUSTS OF LAND AND APPOINTMENT OF TRUSTEES ACT 1996

12. The right to occupy.—(1) A beneficiary who is beneficially entitled to an interest in possession in land subject to a trust of land is entitled by reason of his interest to occupy the land at any time if at that time—

(a) the purposes of the trust include making the land available for his occupation (or for the occupation of beneficiaries of a class of which he is a member or of beneficiaries in general), or

(b) the land is held by the trustees so as to be so available.

(2) Subsection (1) does not confer on a beneficiary a right to occupy land if it is either unavailable or unsuitable for occupation by him.

(3) This section is subject to section 13.

---

13   [1998] CLJ 123 (D. G. Barnsley).
14   W & H, paras. 2.120–2.138; [1997] Conv 254 (J.G. Ross Martyn).
15   P. 210, ante.
16   [1955] 1 QB 234, [1955] 1 All ER 253; cf. *Barclay v Barclay* [1970] 2 QB 677 (express testamentary trust for sale of bungalow intended to be sold and the proceeds divided). Before 1926 the answer depended very much on the discretion of the trustees: (1955) 19 Conv (NS) 146 at p. 147 (F.R. Crane).
17   TLATA 1996, s. 5.

13. Exclusion and restriction of right to occupy.—(1) Where two or more beneficiaries are (or apart from the subsection would be) entitled under section 12 to occupy land, the trustees of land may exclude or restrict the entitlement of any one or more (but not all) [18] of them.

(2) Trustees may not under subsection (1)—

(a) unreasonably exclude any beneficiary's entitlement to occupy land, or

(b) restrict any such entitlement to an unreasonable extent.

(3) The trustees of land may from time to time impose reasonable conditions on any beneficiary in relation to his occupation of land by reason of his entitlement under section 12.

(4) The matters to which trustees are to have regard in exercising the powers conferred by this section include—

(a) the intentions of the person or persons (if any) who created the trust,

(b) the purposes for which the land is held, and

(c) the circumstances and wishes of each of the beneficiaries who is (or apart from any previous exercise by the trustees of those powers would be) entitled to occupy the land under section 12.

(5) The conditions which may be imposed on a beneficiary under subsection (3) include, in particular, conditions requiring him—

(a) to pay any outgoings or expenses in respect of the land, or

(b) to assume any other obligation in relation to the land or to any activity which is or is proposed to be conducted there.

(6) Where the entitlement of any beneficiary to occupy land under section 12 has been excluded or restricted, the conditions which may be imposed on any other beneficiary under subsection (3) include, in particular, conditions requiring him to—

(a) make payments by way of compensation to the beneficiary whose entitlement has been excluded or restricted, or

(b) forgo any payment or other benefit to which he would otherwise be entitled under the trust so as to benefit that beneficiary.

(7) The powers conferred on trustees by this section may not be exercised—

(a) so as prevent any person who is in occupation of land (whether or not by reason of an entitlement under section 12) from continuing to occupy the land, or

(b) in a manner likely to result in any such person ceasing to occupy the land,

unless he consents or the court has given approval.

(8) The matters to which the court is to have regard in determining whether to give approval under subsection (7) include the matters mentioned in subsection (4)(a) to (c).

———————

In **Rodway v Landy** [2001] Ch 703, Rodway and Landy were medical practitioners who were the joint owners of a property which they developed as a surgery. They were trustees of land holding the property on a trust of land for themselves as beneficial tenants in common in equal shares. When the practice came to an end, Rodway sought either an order under section 14 of the 1996 Act for the partitioning of the property between them, or an order under section 13 that the parties exercise their powers to exclude or restrict each other's

[18] *Rodway v Landy* [2001] Ch 703, infra.

entitlement. The Court of Appeal held that partition was prohibited by the National Health Service Act 1977, but that an order should be made under section 13.

PETER GIBSON LJ said at 712:

'31 The main argument of Mr Berry related to section 13 of the 1996 Act. He submitted that the judge erred in concluding that he could make an order excluding or restricting each of the two doctors from a part of the property. This point turns on the construction of the words in parenthesis in section 13(1), "(but not all)". The judge said of those words:

"The words should not be read in isolation. Section 13 is a limiting provision. It further limits the right of occupation expressly conferred by section 12(1). An exercise of the power so as to exclude or restrict the entitlement of all of the beneficiaries in respect of some part of the land subject to the trust would render section 12(1) nugatory to that extent. The ... words therefore prohibit so extensive an exercise of the power. Accordingly, an exercise of the power to exclude or restrict the entitlement to occupation of one of two beneficiaries in relation to part is not offensive to section 12(1) so long as the other beneficiary is entitled to enjoy his right of occupation of that part. There is no ambiguity. The construction merely reflects that every part of a piece of land is unique."

32 Mr Pearce supported the reasoning and conclusion of the judge. He said that to construe the subsection literally, as Mr Berry urged, would produce an irrational limitation on section 13(1) as it would mean that the trustees can exclude one of two beneficiaries entirely from the occupation of trust property but not limit each of them to occupation of only part of it. Mr Pearce urged that the words "but not all" mean that the trustees may not exclude or restrict the entitlement of the beneficiaries collectively; after the trustees have exercised their powers the beneficiaries collectively must have rights which are as extensive as those which the beneficiaries collectively had previously. Mr Berry on the other hand submitted that the limitation on the power to exclude or restrict is in terms on the number of beneficiaries who may be excluded or restricted, and it is not related to the land which happens to be the subject of the restriction.

33 I accept that the limitation on the power to exclude or restrict is expressed as a limitation on the number of beneficiaries who may be excluded or restricted. Plainly it would make no sense if there was no beneficiary left entitled to occupy land subject to a trust of land as a result of the exercise of the power under section 13. That is the force of the words "(but not all)". But if an estate consisting of adjoining properties, Blackacre and Whiteacre, was held subject to a trust of land and A and B were entitled to occupy the estate, it would be very surprising if the trustees were not able under section 13 to exclude or restrict B's entitlement to occupy Blackacre and at the same time to exclude or restrict A's entitlement to occupy Whiteacre. So also I do not see why, in relation to a single building which lends itself to physical partition, the trustees could not exclude or restrict one beneficiary's entitlement to occupy one part and at the same time exclude or restrict the other beneficiary's entitlement to occupy the other part. Each part is land subject to a trust of land and the beneficiaries are entitled to occupy that part until the entitlement of a beneficiary is excluded or restricted by the exercise of the power under section 13. So construed section 3(1) seems to me to make good sense and to provide a useful power which trustees might well wish to exercise in appropriate circumstances so as to be even-handed between beneficiaries. In contrast, I can see no good reason why Parliament should want to confine the trustees to the all or nothing approach urged by Mr Berry. I therefore agree with the conclusion of the judge on this point.'

VI. Powers of the Court

A. General

Section 14 of the Trusts of Land and Appointment of Trustees Act 1996 gives to the court wide powers to interfere with the trustees' exercise of any of the trust powers, to dispense with any consents, or to regulate occupation of land by the beneficiaries. Section 15 sets out the matters to which the court must have regard in determining an application under section 14.

The sections apply to all applications whether made before or after the commencement of the Act. In particular, an application may be made by a trustee; an interest in possession beneficiary; a remainderman (whether vested or contingent); a discretionary beneficiary; the secured creditor of a beneficiary; and trustees (and beneficiaries) of a sub-trust (because the 'interest' does not have to be owned beneficially). [19]

There is a considerable body of case law on section 30 of the Law of Property Act 1925, which has been repealed. [20] Those decisions were influenced by the primacy of the trustees' *duty* to sell. The courts invented the doctrine of a secondary or collateral purpose to help them to decide whether that primary purpose could be displaced. They could then exercise their discretion as to whether to make an order for sale or not. As the Law Commission Report said: 'there is something odd about a doctrine whose essential purpose is so obviously the circumvention of an inconvenient position'. [1]

Section 15 puts on a statutory footing the criteria which the courts developed for settling disputes over trusts for sale. The leading cases on section 30 are set out in the sixth edition of this book [2] and are not repeated here except for an extract from *Re Evers' Trust*. The width of section 15 makes it unlikely that much resort will need to be made to them. [3]

In **Re Evers' Trust** [1980] 1 WLR 1327, [1980] 3 All ER 399, ORMROD LJ said at 1330, at 401:

'When asked to exercise its discretionary powers under section 30 to execute the trust, the court must have regard to its underlying purpose: see *Re Buchanan-Wollaston's Conveyance* [1939] Ch 217, and in this court at 738, [1939] 2 All ER 302. In that case four adjoining landowners purchased a plot of land to prevent it being built on and held it on trust for sale. They also covenanted with one another that the land would not be dealt with except with the unanimous agreement of the trustees. Subsequently one of them wished to sell, but some of the other trustees objected so the plaintiff applied to the court under section 30 for an order for sale. At first instance, Farwell J refused the order.

---

[19] W & H, paras. 2.139–2.164. S.4 also applies in relation to a trust of proceeds of sale of land: s. 17(1).
[20] S. 25(2), Sch. 4; *Fisher v Fisher* [1997] 9 CL 303.
[1] Law Com. No. 181, para, 12.3.
[2] 6th edn., pp. 238–250.
[3] H & M, p. 294. *Mortgage Corporation v Shaire* [2001] Ch 743, [2001] 4 All ER 364, p. 289, post.

His decision was upheld in this court, but on a broader basis, Sir Wilfred Greene MR said, at 308:

"....it seems to me that the court of equity, when asked to enforce the trust for sale, whether one created by a settlement or a will or one created by the statute, must look into all the circumstances of the case and consider whether or not, at the particular moment and in the particular circumstances when the application is made to it, it is right and proper that such an order shall be made. In considering a question of that kind, in circumstances such as these, the court is bound to look at the contract into which the parties have entered and to ask itself the question whether or not the person applying for execution of the trust for sale is a person whose voice should be allowed to prevail."

Some 20 years later, in *Jones v Challenger* [1961] 1 QB 176, [1960] 1 All ER 785, Devlin LJ reviewed the authorities and affirmed this principle. He said, at 181, at 787:

" 'But this simple principle' i.e., that in a trust for sale there is a duty to sell 'cannot prevail where the trust itself or the circumstances in which it was made show that there was a secondary or collateral object besides that of sale. Simonds J, in his judgment in *Re Mayo* [1943] Ch 302, [1943] 2 All ER 440, said that if there were mala fides, the position would be different. If it be not mala fides, it is at any rate wrong and inequitable for one of the parties to the trust to invoke the letter of the trust in order to defeat one of its purposes, whether that purpose be written or unwritten, and the court will not permit it.' "

In that case a house had been purchased by a husband and wife jointly as a home. Subsequently, the marriage broke down, the wife left and committed adultery and applied to the court for an order for sale of the property, a leasehold with only a few years to run. The husband continued to live in the house on his own; there were no children. In these circumstances the court decided that the house should be sold. Devlin LJ said, at 183, at 789:

"In the case we have to consider, the house was acquired as the matrimonial home. That was the purpose of the joint tenancy and, for so long as that purpose was still alive, I think that the right test to be applied would be that in *Re Buchanan-Wollaston's Conveyance* [1939] Ch 738, [1939] 2 All ER 302. But with the end of the marriage, that purpose was dissolved and the primacy of the duty to sell was restored.'" [4]

TRUSTS OF LAND AND APPOINTMENT OF TRUSTEES ACT 1996

14. Applications for order.—(1) Any person who is a trustee of land or has an interest in property subject to a trust of land may make an application to the court for an order under this section.

(2) On an application for an order under this section the court may make any such order—

(a) relating to the exercise by the trustees of any of their functions (including an order relieving them of any obligation to obtain the consent of, or to consult, any person in connection with the exercise of any of their functions),[5] or

---

[4]   See *Bank of Baroda v Dhillon* (1997) Times, 4 March (on application by the bank, court had jurisdiction under LPA 1925, s. 30 to order sale of matrimonial home, even though wife had overriding interest under LRA 1925, s. 70(1)(g), which ranked before that of the bank. The bank's interest would, however, have defeated a claim for possession).

[5]   *Abbey National Mortgages plc v Powell* (1999) 78 P & CR D16.

(b) declaring the nature or extent of a person's interest in property subject to the trust,

as the court thinks fit.

(3) The court may not under this section make any order as to the appointment or removal of trustees.

(4) The powers conferred on the court by this section are exercisable on an application whether it is made before or after the commencement of this Act. [6]

15. Matters relevant in determining applications.—(1) The matters to which the court is to have regard in determining an application for an order under section 14 include—

(a) the intentions of the person or persons (if any) who created the trust,

(b) the purposes for which the property subject to the trust is held,

(c) the welfare of any minor who occupies or might reasonably be expected to occupy any land subject to the trust as his home, and

(d) the interests of any secured creditor of any beneficiary.

(2) In the case of an application relating to the exercise in relation to any land of the powers conferred on the trustees by section 13, [7] the matters to which the court is to have regard also include the circumstances and wishes of each of the beneficiaries who is (or apart from any previous exercise by the trustees of those powers would be) entitled to occupy the land under section 12.

(3) In the case of any other application, other than one relating to the exercise of the power mentioned in section 6(2) [8], the matters to which the court is to have regard also include the circumstances and wishes of any beneficiaries of full age and entitled to an interest in possession in property subject to the trust or (in case of dispute) of the majority (according to the value of their combined interests).

(4) This section does not apply to an application if section 335A of the Insolvency Act 1986 (which is inserted by Schedule 3 and relates to applications by a trustee of a bankrupt) applies to it. [9]

B. Bankruptcy

Where an application is made by a trustee in bankruptcy under section 14 of the Trusts of Land and Appointment of Trustees Act 1996, the court must take into account the considerations set out in section 335A of the Insolvency Act 1986, which was added to that Act by the 1996 Act. [10] These new powers are exercisable whether the application is made before or after the commencement of the section. Pre-1997 cases are relevant when discussing the attitude of the courts to bankruptcy situations.

INSOLVENCY ACT 1986

335A. Rights under trusts of land.—(1) Any application by a trustee of a bankrupt's estate under section 14 of the Trusts of Land and Appointment of Trustees Act 1996 (powers of court in relation to trusts of land) for an order

---

[6]   S. 14 also applies in relation to a trust of proceeds of sale: TLATA 1996 s. 17(1).
[7]   P. 279, ante.
[8]   P. 271, ante.
[9]   Infra.
[10] TLATA 1996, s. 25(1), Sch. 3, para. 23.

under that section for the sale of land shall be made to the court having jurisdiction in relation to the bankruptcy.

(2) On such an application the court shall make such order as it thinks just and reasonable having regard to—
   (a) the interests of the bankrupt's creditors;
   (b) where the application is made in respect of land which includes a dwelling house which is or has been the home of the bankrupt or the bankrupt's spouse or former spouse—
       (i) the conduct of the spouse or former spouse, so far as contributing to the bankruptcy,
       (ii) the needs and financial resources of the spouse or former spouse, and
       (iii) the needs of any children; and
   (c) all the circumstances of the case other than the needs of the bankrupt.

(3) Where such an application is made after the end of the period of one year beginning with the first vesting under Chapter IV of this Part of the bankrupt's estate in a trustee, the court shall assume, unless the circumstances of the case are exceptional, that the interests of the bankrupt's creditors outweigh all other considerations.

(4) The powers conferred on the court by this section are exercisable on an application whether it is made before or after the commencement of this section.

RE CITRO
[1991] Ch 142, [1990] 3 All ER 952 (CA, Nourse and Bingham LJJ and Sir George Waller) [11]

In 1985 the two Citro brothers, Domenico and Carmine, who ran a garage business as panel beaters and car sprayers, were declared bankrupt. The trustee in bankruptcy of their joint and several estates applied for an order under section 30 of the Law of Property Act 1925 for possession and sale. In each case the house was jointly owned by the bankrupt and his wife in equal shares. Domenico was judicially separated from his wife Mary in December 1984 and she lived in their house with their three children, but Carmine lived in his house together with his wife Josephine and their three children. The youngest child of Domenico was aged 12, and that of Carmine 10. The debts owed by each of the brothers exceeded the value of their interests in their houses.

Hoffmann J made an order for possession and sale, postponed until the youngest child in each case became 16 (i.e. until 1994 and 1995).

Held. (Sir George Waller dissenting) Order confirmed, but period of postponement not to exceed 6 months.

Nourse LJ: In the leading case of *Jones v Challenger* [1961] 1 QB 176, [1960] 1 All ER 785, it was held by this court that on an application under section 30 of the Law of Property Act 1925 in relation to property acquired jointly as a matrimonial home neither spouse has a right to demand a sale while that purpose still exists. That is now a settled rule of law, applicable to property owned jointly by joint occupants, whether married or unmarried. But its application depends on the whole of the beneficial interest being vested in the occupants. If one of them has become bankrupt, so that part of the beneficial interest is vested in his or her trustee, there arises a conflict between the interests of the occupants and

---

[11]   (1991) 107 LQR 177 (S.M. Cretney); [1991] CLJ 45 (J.C. Hall); [1991] Conv 302 (A. M. M. Lawson); (1992) 15 MLR 284 (D. Brown).

the statutory obligation of the trustee to realise the bankrupt's assets for the benefit of the creditors.

In a series of bankruptcy decisions relating to matrimonial homes subsequent to *Jones v Challenger* it has been held that the interests of the husband's creditors ought usually to prevail over the interests of the wife and any children and, with one exception, *Re Holliday* [1981] Ch 405, [1980] 3 All ER 385, a sale within a short period has invariably been ordered ...

Hoffmann J carefully considered the personal circumstances of each wife and her children. He observed that they had very little money coming in and that Mary Citro was not well. In evidence they had both said that their children's education would be upset if they had to move. The judge was clearly concerned, more so perhaps in the case of Mary Citro, that, if the houses had to be sold, the half shares of the proceeds received by the wives would not enable them to find proper accommodation for themselves and their families. He expressed his decision thus:

'The balancing which one is required to do between the interests of the creditors and the interests of the wives and families – who are of course entirely innocent parties – is by no means an easy thing to do. The two interests are not in any sense commensurable. On the one hand, one has the financial interests of the Crown, some banking institutions and a few traders. On the other, one has personal and human interests of these two families. It is very hard to see how they can be weighed against each other, except in a way which involves some value judgment on the part of the tribunal.

If one was considering the rights of these two wives to their matrimonial homes in the event of a breakdown of their marriages, I think that it would be accepted that, in so far as the Family Division did not order the interest of the husband to be transferred to the wife, it would be unlikely to make an order for the sale of the house to allow the husband to realise his share until at any rate such time as the youngest child of the marriage had attained the age of 16. It is of course true that the vesting of the husband's share in the trustee brings a new factor into the equation. It requires the interests of the creditors too to be taken into account. Nevertheless the normal practice in the Family Division seems to me a fair indication of the way in which the court might deal with the husband's property rights as property rights, and it is after all to his property rights that the trustee has succeeded. It therefore appears to me that it would be wrong to refuse altogether to make an order for sale. That would be treating the wives as having a permanent right to reside in the houses and to prevent the husband or his trustee from realising their interests. That, in my view, would be inequitable. On the other hand, I think it would be equally wrong to make an immediate order for sale, having regard to the hardship which this would cause to the two families.'

In order to see whether the judge's decision can be supported, it is necessary to give close consideration to the earlier authorities.

[His Lordship referred to *Jones v Challenger* [1961] 1 QB 176, [1960] 1 All ER 785; *Re Mayo* [1943] Ch 302, [1943] 2 All ER 440; *Re Buchanan-Wollaston's Conveyance* [1939] Ch 738, [1939] 2 All ER 302; *Re Solomon* [1967] Ch 573, [1966] 3 All ER 255; *Boydell v Gillespie* (1970) 216 EG 1505; *Re Hardy's Trust* (1970) Times, 23 October; *Re Turner* [1974] 1 WLR 1556, [1975] 1 All ER 5; *Re Densham* [1975] 1 WLR 1519, [1975] 3 All ER 726; *Re Bailey* [1977] 1 WLR 278, [1977] 2 All ER 26; *Re Holliday* [1981] Ch 405, [1980] 3 All ER 385; *Re Lowrie* [1981] 3 All ER 353; p. 288, post; and continued:]

The broad effect of these authorities can be summarised as follows. Where a spouse who has a beneficial interest in the matrimonial home has become bankrupt under debts which cannot be paid without the realisation of that interest, the voice of the creditors will usually prevail over the voice of the other spouse and a sale of the property ordered within a short period. The voice of the other spouse will only prevail in exceptional circumstances. No distinction is to be made between a case where the property is still being enjoyed as the matrimonial home and one where it is not.

What then are exceptional circumstances? As the cases show, it is not uncommon for a wife with young children to be faced with eviction in circumstances where the realisation of her beneficial interest will not produce enough to buy a comparable home in the same neighbourhood, or indeed elsewhere. And, if she has to move elsewhere, there may be problems over schooling and so forth. Such circumstances, while engendering a natural sympathy in all who hear of them, cannot be described as exceptional. They are the melancholy consequences of debt and improvidence with which every civilised society has been familiar. It was only in *Re Holliday* that they helped the wife's voice to prevail, and then only, as I believe, because of one special feature of that case. One of the reasons for the decision given by Sir David Cairns was that, it was highly unlikely that postponement of payment of the debts would cause any great hardship to any of the creditors, a matter of which Buckley LJ no doubt took account as well. Although the arithmetic was not fully spelled out in the judgments, the net value of the husband's half share of the beneficial interest in the matrimonial home was about £13,250, against which had to be set debts of about £6,500 or £7,500 as the sum required to obtain a full discharge. Statutory interest at 4 per cent. on £6,500 for five years would have amounted to no more than £1,300 which, when added to the £7,500, would make a total of less than £9,000, well covered by the £13,250. Admittedly, it was detrimental to the creditors to be kept out of a commercial rate of interest and the use of the money during a further period of five years. But if the principal was safe, one can understand that that detriment was not treated as being decisive, even in inflationary times. It must indeed be exceptional for creditors in a bankruptcy to receive 100p in the £ plus statutory interest in full and the passage of years before they do so does not make it less exceptional. On the other hand, without that special feature, I cannot myself see how the circumstances in *Re Holliday* could fairly have been treated as exceptional. I am confirmed in that view by the belief that it would be shared by Balcombe LJ, who in *Harman v Glencross* [1986] Fam 81, 95, [1986] 1 All ER 545, 556, said that the decision in *Re Holliday* was very much against the run of the recent authorities. I would not myself have regarded it as an exceptional circumstance that the husband had presented his own petition, even 'as a tactical move'. That was not something of the creditors' choosing and could not fairly have been held against them. [12] I do not say that in other cases there might not be other exceptional circumstances. They must be identified if and when they arise.

If *Re Holliday* is put on one side, are the bankruptcy cases, all of which were

---

[12]   See *Re Lowrie* [1981] 3 All ER 353, p. 288, post, where LAWTON J said at 355: ' The petition in bankruptcy had been presented by the husband himself as a tactical move, and quite clearly as a tactical move, to avoid a transfer of property order in favour of his wife, or ex-wife, at a time when no creditors whatsoever were pressing and he was in a position in the course of a year or so out of a very good income to discharge whatever debts he had. He had gone off leaving the wife in the matrimonial home, which was the subject matter of the application, with responsibility for all the children on her own. One can scarcely, I think, imagine a more exceptional set of facts, and the court gave effect to those exceptional facts.'

decided at first instance or in the Divisional Court in Bankruptcy, consistent with the principles stated in *Jones v Challenger* [1961] 1 QB 176, [1960] 1 All ER 785?
...

I am therefore of the opinion that the earlier authorities, as I have summarised them, correctly state the law applicable to the present case. Did Hoffmann J correctly apply it to the facts which were before him? I respectfully think that he did not. First, for the reasons already stated, the personal circumstances of the two wives and their children, although distressing, are not by themselves exceptional. Secondly, I think that the judge erred in fashioning his orders by reference to those which might have been made in the Family Division in a case where bankruptcy had not supervened. That approach, which tends towards treating the home as a source of provision for the children, was effectively disapproved by the earlier and uncontroversial part of the decision of this court in *Re Holliday*. Thirdly, and perhaps most significantly, he did not ask himself the critical question whether a further postponement of payment of their debts would cause hardship to the creditors. It is only necessary to look at the substantial deficiencies referred to earlier in this judgment in order to see that it would. Since then a further 18 months' interest has accrued and the trustee has incurred the costs of these proceedings as well.

In all the circumstances, I think that these cases are clearly distinguishable from *Re Holliday* and ought to have been decided accordingly. Part at least of the reason why they were not was that the points with which we have been concerned were not as fully argued below as they have been here. In particular, a close examination of the figures in order to see whether a postponement would cause increasing hardship to the creditors was not undertaken. This is not to imply any criticism of counsel. It is a characteristic of our system that the higher court often seems partial towards thinking that the important point is the one which was not taken in the lower court. [13]

Finally, I refer to section [335A] of the Insolvency Act 1986 which, although it does not apply to either of these cases, will apply to such cases in the future. In subsection (3) of that section the court is required, in the circumstances there mentioned, to 'assume, unless the circumstances of the case are exceptional, that the interests of the bankrupt's creditors outweigh all other considerations.' I have no doubt that that section was intended to apply the same test as that which has been evolved in the previous bankruptcy decisions, and it is satisfactory to find that it has. ...

I would allow both appeals by deleting the provisos for postponement from Hoffmann J's orders and substituting short periods of suspension, the length of which can be discussed with counsel.

(1991) 107 LQR 177 at p. 179 (S.M. Cretney)

'The decision of the Court of Appeal is clearly defensible in analytical terms. But it seems inevitable that its effect will be to discourage the exercise of the judicial flexibility which has been found so valuable by the courts in cases involving the family home. *Re Gorman* [1990] 1 WLR 616, [1990] 1 All ER 717, provides an instructive recent example of the judicial readiness to be inventive

---

[13]   Nourse LJ referred to Insolvency Act 1986, s. 336, which is in part repealed by TLATA 1996, Sch. 4. S. 336 now applies only to occupation orders under FLA 1996, s. 33 in cases of bankruptcy; p. 315, post.

and constructive in cases involving a competition between creditor and family interests which now seems unlikely to be favoured: the Divisional Court indicated that it would be prepared to postpone sale of the former family home (on terms) pending the outcome of legal action by the wife which might furnish her with the funds to buy out the husband's interest. But the court did not decide that it would *impose* such a solution against the wishes of the trustee, and in the light of *Re Citro* it seems difficult to believe that it could now properly do so.'

In **Re Mott** [1987] CLY 212, Q had lived in a house for over 40 years with each of her late husbands. She was 70. The house was full of memories and she had done a lot of work on it. She was in poor health which the doctor said would deteriorate if she was forced to move. She and her son, M, had purchased the freehold in 1980 from the local authority. M's creditors were largely the State in the form of the Inland Revenue and the DHSS. M had left home in 1986 and disappeared. In a claim by M's trustee in bankruptcy under section 30 for an order for sale of the house, Q sought postponement of sale until after her death.

HOFFMANN J dismissed the trustee's claim. He held that it was necessary to balance the legal and moral claims of the creditors and the mother and to take into account the hardship which the latter would suffer. It would be difficult to imagine a more extreme case of hardship than this one. The creditors should wait until after Q's death. [14]

In **Re Lowrie** [1981] 3 All ER 353, the Divisional Court granted an order to the trustee in bankruptcy. WALTON J said at 356: [15]

'I think it is desirable to step back for a moment and look at the situation which must in these cases inevitably occur, or at any rate must occur so frequently as to be almost inevitable. The first one is of course that the whole family are going to be rendered homeless. That is not an exceptional circumstance. It is a normal circumstance and is the result, the all too obvious result, of a husband having conducted the financial affairs of the family in a way which has led to bankruptcy. The second result almost invariably is that it is going to be incredibly hard and incredibly bad luck on the co-owner, the wife, who is in most cases a totally innocent person who has done nothing to bring about the bankruptcy. Of course, as against that, one has to realise that she has been enjoying over whatever period it may be the fruits of the debts which the bankrupt has contracted and which debts are not at the moment being paid. So that although it may be very bad luck on her, she at any rate has had some enjoyment of the fruits which led to the bankruptcy.'

---

[14]   *Judd v Brown* [1998] 2 FLR 360 (cancer); *Re Raval* [1998] 2 FLR 718 (mental illness of wife). See *Re Bennett* [2000] EGCS 41, applying the same test for exceptional circumstances as was applied in pre-1996 Act decisions; *Claughton v Charalambers* [1998] BPIR 558 (60-year-old with chronic disease, who had great difficulty in walking in house adapted to her needs): *Re Bremner* [1999] 1 FLR 912; *Re Raval* [1998] 2 FLR 718 (sale postponed for a year to allow accommodation to be found for paranoid schizophrenic with three children).
[15]   [1982] Conv 374 (A. Sydenham): [1983] Conv 219 (C. Hand).

C. Relationship with Pre-1997 Case Law

In **Mortgage Corporation v Shaire** [2001] Ch 743, [2001] 4 All ER 364,[16] the claimant bank, as equitable chargee of the defendant's house, sought possession and sale of it by reason of arrears of payment on the mortgage. In deciding not to make an order until the parties had had an opportunity to consider the consequences of the court's conclusions on the law, NEUBERGER J said at 756, at 381:

'The question here is: ought I to make an order for sale of the house and, if not, what order ought I to make? Until the 1996 Act came into force on 1 January 1997, property owned by more than one person, not held on a strict settlement, was held on trust for sale, and section 30 of the Law of Property Act 1925 applied. In that connection the law had developed in the following way. In *Re Citro* [1991] Ch 142, 157, [1990] 3 All ER 952, 961 Nourse LJ said:

[His Lordship read the paragraph "The broad effect of these authorities" ... p. 285, ante, and continued:]

In *Lloyds Bank plc v Byrne* [1993] 1 FLR 369, the Court of Appeal had to consider a number of grounds advanced for distinguishing between a case (such as *Re Citro*) where the trustee in bankruptcy of one of the owners of a beneficial interest in the property wanted to sell and a case (such as *Lloyds Bank plc v Byrne*) where a mortgagee or chargee of one of the parties' beneficial interests wished to sell. Those differences were recorded, at p. 372, including lastly: "a trustee in bankruptcy is under a statutory duty to realise the assets of the bankrupt whereas there is no such duty upon a chargee under a charging order." Parker LJ went on to say:

[His Lordship cited Parker LJ at, 377, at 757, and continued:]

Accordingly, there was, in relation to trusts for sale and before the 1996 Act came into force, no difference between the two types of case considered in *Re Citro* and *Lloyds Bank plc v Byrne*. The normal rule in such cases was that, save in exceptional circumstances, the wish of the person wanting the sale, be it a trustee in bankruptcy or a chargee, would prevail, and that the interests of children and families in occupation would be unlikely to prevail. These conclusions were applied in a number of cases at first instance, including *Barclays Bank plc v Hendricks* [1996] 1 FLR 258 (Laddie J) and *Zandfarid v Bank of Credit and Commerce International SA* [1996] 1 WLR 1420 (Jonathan Parker J).

However, trusts for sale and section 30 have now been effectively replaced by the 1996 Act.

[His Lordship read sections 14(1) and (2) and 15 and continued:]

Two questions of principle have been canvassed. First, as a result of the 1996 Act, has the law, relating to the way in which the court will exercise its power to order a sale at the suit of a chargee of the interest of one of the owners of the beneficial interest in property, changed? In other words, does section 15 change the law from how it had been laid down in *Re Citro* and *Lloyds Bank plc v Byrne*? Secondly, does section 15(3) apply in the present case?

The effect of the 1996 Act

To my mind, for a number of reasons, Mr Asif is correct in his submission on behalf of Mrs Shaire that section 15 has changed the law. First, there is the rather trite point that, if there was no intention to change the law, it is hard to see why

---

[16]   [2002] Conv 329 (M. Thompson); [2000] Conv 315 (S. Pascoe); [2001] CLJ 43 (M. Oldham); [2001] All ER Rev 258 (P. J. Clarke).

Parliament has set out in section 15(2) and, indeed, on one view, section 15(3), the factors which have to be taken into account specifically, albeit not exclusively, when the court is asked to exercise its jurisdiction to order a sale.

Secondly, it is hard to reconcile the contention that Parliament intended to confirm the law as laid down in *Lloyds Bank plc v Byrne* with the fact that, while the interest of a chargee is one of the four specified factors to be taken into account in section 15(1)(d), there is no suggestion that it is to be given any more importance than the interests of the children residing in the house: see section 15(1)(c). As is clear from the passage I have quoted from the judgment of Nourse LJ in *Re Citro* as applied to a case such as this in light of *Lloyds Bank plc v Byrne*, that would appear to represent a change in the law.

Thirdly, the very name "trust for sale" and the law as it has been developed by the courts suggest that under the old law, in the absence of a strong reason to the contrary, the court should order sale. Nothing in the language of the new code as found in the 1996 Act supports that approach.

Fourthly, it is clear from the reasons in *Lloyds Bank plc v Byrne*, and indeed the later two first instance cases to which I have referred, that the law, as developed under section 30 of the Law of Property Act 1925, was that the court should adopt precisely the same approach in a case where one of the co-owners was bankrupt (*Re Citro*) and a case where one of the co-owners had charged his interest (*Lloyds Bank plc v Byrne*). It is quite clear that Parliament now considers that a different approach is appropriate in the two cases – compare section 15(2) and section 15(3) of the 1996 Act with section 15(4) and the new section 335A of the Insolvency Act 1986.

Fifthly, an indication from the Court of Appeal that the 1996 Act was intended to change the law is to be found in (an albeit plainly obiter) sentence in the judgment of Peter Gibson LJ in *Bankers Trust Co v Namdar* (unreported) 14 February 1997; Court of Appeal (Civil Division) Transcript No 349 of 1997. Having come to the conclusion that the wife's appeal against an order for sale had to be refused in light of the reasoning in *Re Citro* and *Lloyds Bank plc v Byrne*, Peter Gibson LJ said: "It is unfortunate for Mrs Namdar that the very recent Trusts of Land and Appointment of Trustees Act 1996 was not in force at the relevant time" – ie at the time of the hearing at first instance. Of course it would be dangerous to build too much on that observation, but it is an indication from the Court of Appeal, and indeed from a former chairman of the Law Commission, as to the perceived effect of the 1996 Act.

Sixthly, the leading textbooks support the view that I have reached. In *Megarry & Wade, The Law of Real Property*, para 9-064, one finds:

"Although the authorities on the law prior to 1997 will therefore continue to provide guidance, the outcome will not in all cases be the same as it would have been under the previous law. This is because the legislation is much more specific as to the matters which a court is required to take into account ..."

And in *Emmet on Title*, 19th ed. looseleaf, vol 2, para. 22-035:

"Cases decided on pre-1997 law may be disregarded as of little, if any, assistance ... because the starting point ... was necessarily a trust for sale implied or expressed as a conveyancing device enabling the convenient co-ownership of the property ..."

Seventhly, the Law Commission Report which gave rise to the 1996 Act, Transfer of Land, Trusts of Land (1989) (Law Com No. 181), tends to support this view as well. It is fair to say that the Law Commission did not propose a new section in a new Act such as section 15 of the 1996 Act, but a new section 30 of the 1925 Act. It is also fair to say that the terms of the proposed new section 30 were slightly different from those of section 15. However, in my judgment, the way in which the terms of the 1996 Act, and in particular section 15, have been drafted suggests that the Law Commission's proposals were very much in the mind of, and were substantially adopted by, the legislature. In paragraph 12.9 of the report the Law Commission describe the aim as being to "consolidate *and rationalise*" (emphasis added) the current approach. When commenting on the proposed equivalents of what are now section 15(2) and section 15(3) the Law Commission said, in footnote 143:

"Clearly, the terms of these guidelines may influence the exercise of discretion in some way. For example, it may be that the courts' approach to creditors' interests will be altered by the framing of the guideline as to the welfare of children. If the welfare of children is seen as a factor to be considered independently of the beneficiaries' holdings, the courts may be less ready to order the sale of the home than they are at present."

Finally the Law Commission said, at paragraph 13.6:

"Within the new system, beneficiaries will be in a comparatively better position than beneficiaries of current trusts of land. For example, given that the terms governing applications under section 30 will be less restrictive than they are at present, beneficiaries will have greater scope to challenge the decisions of the trustees and generally influence the management of the trust land."

Eighthly, to put it at its lowest, it does not seem to me unlikely that the legislature intended to relax the fetters on the way in which the court exercised its discretion in cases such as *Re Citro* and *Lloyds Bank plc v Byrne*, and so as to tip the balance somewhat more in favour of families and against banks and other chargees. Although the law under section 30 was clear following *Re Citro* and *Lloyds Bank plc v Byrne*, there were indications of judicial dissatisfaction with the state of the law at that time. Although Bingham LJ agreed with Nourse LJ in *Re Citro*, he expressed, at p. 161F, unhappiness with the result and Sir George Waller's dissatisfaction went so far as led him to dissent: see his judgment, at pp. 161–163. Furthermore, there is a decision of the Court of Appeal in *Abbey National plc v Moss* [1994] 1 FLR 307 which suggests a desire for a new approach.

All these factors, to my mind, when taken together point very strongly to the conclusion that section 15 has changed the law. As a result of section 15, the court has greater flexibility than heretofore, as to how it exercises its jurisdiction on an application for an order for sale on facts such as those in *Re Citro* and *Lloyds Bank plc v Byrne*. There are certain factors which must be taken into account: see section 15(1) and, subject to the next point, section 15(3). There may be other factors in a particular case which the court can, indeed should, take into account. Once the relevant factors to be taken into account have been identified, it is a matter for the court as to what weight to give to each factor in a particular case.

[His Lordship referred to *TSB Bank v Marshall* [1998] 2 FLR 769, 771–772, and continued:]

A difficult question, having arrived at this conclusion, is the extent to which the old authorities are of assistance, and it is no surprise to find differing views expressed in the two textbooks from which I have quoted. On the one hand, to throw over all the wealth of learning and thought given by so many eminent judges to the problem which is raised on an application for sale of a house where competing interests exist seems somewhat arrogant and possibly rash. On the other hand, where one has concluded that the law has changed in a significant respect so that the court's discretion is significantly less fettered than it was, there are obvious dangers in relying on authorities which proceeded on the basis that the court's discretion was more fettered than it now is. I think it would be wrong to throw over all the earlier cases without paying them any regard. However, they have to be treated with caution, in light of the change in the law, and in many cases they are unlikely to be of great, let alone decisive, assistance.

Section 15(3)

The second question of principle can be dealt with more shortly. The question is whether section 15(3) applies in a case such as this. That turns on the meaning of the words "In the case of any other application". Mr Harry for TMC said that those words mean any application which does not fall within subsection (1) or subsection (2) and, as the present application falls within subsection (1), subsection (3) does not apply. Mr Asif for Mrs Shaire contended that the reference to "any other application" is to any application not falling within subsection (2), and given that the present application falls within subsection (1), subsection (3) applies.

Looking at the matter as one of pure language, either construction appears to me to be acceptable and, if anything, I would tend to favour that preferred by Mr Harry. However, once one looks at the matter more widely in the context of the 1996 Act as a whole, it seems to me clear that Mr Asif is right and subsection (3) does apply to a case such as this. In my judgment, the essential clue is that section 14 is the only section specifically dealing with applications to the court for an order. Many of the other sections are, as I have mentioned, concerned with exercise of powers of duties by trustees, and certain other sections are concerned with the rights of beneficiaries. However, section 14 is the section which deals with the rights of the parties to make applications to the court. If one reads subsection (3) in the way for which Mr Harry contends, it seems to me very difficult to give it any meaning at all in those circumstances, because any application would seem to be governed by section 14 and therefore to fall within subsection (1).

In my judgment, therefore, the position is as follows. When considering any application under the Act, subsection (1) always applies. When considering any application made under the Act relating to section 13, subsection (2) applies. When considering any application other than one made under section 13 or one made under section 6(2), subsection (3) applies. It also seems to me that, bearing in mind the factors which the legislature has said should be taken into account, on any view, when considering an application for sale such as the present, namely the four matters specified in subsection (1), it would be surprising if the legislature intended the factor identified in subsection (3) to be ignored.

An order for sale?

Bearing in mind these conclusions as to the effect of the 1996 Act, ought I to make an order for sale?

[His Lordship considered the facts and continued:]

An idea which attracts me is that put forward by Mr Lawrence on behalf of the solicitors, and accepted by Mr Harry, if there is no order for sale. This idea is that the house is valued at a specific figure (rather than the range I have mentioned) and that The Mortgage Corporation is effectively taken out by having its equity converted into loan, and Mrs Shaire then has to pay interest on that loan. In my judgment, unless Mrs Shaire is in a position to agree that course and to meet the payments which that course would involve, I would not be prepared to refuse the order for sale. If she is prepared to agree that course and she is in a position to meet the repayments as and when they fall due, then I would be prepared to refuse an order for sale. ...

I appreciate that this leaves matters slightly up in the air, but I do not believe that I should make an order without a little more information. At the risk of adding further to the time and costs of this case, I would rather make the order on the basis of the parties having an opportunity to consider my conclusions, work out their consequences and, if necessary, argue about their consequences.' [17]

VII. Protection of Purchasers

Purchasers are protected by the doctrine of overreaching and also by limitations on powers and consent requirements.

TRUSTS OF LAND AND APPOINTMENTS OF TRUSTEES ACT 1996

23. Other interpretation provisions.—(1) In this Act 'purchaser' has the same meaning as in Part I of the Law of Property Act 1925. [18]

A. Overreaching [19]

The main object of the doctrine is a compromise between, on the one hand, the interest of the public in securing that land held in trust is freely marketable and, on the other hand, the interests of the beneficiaries in preserving their rights under the trust. The overreaching provisions under the Law of Property Act 1925, section 2 (1) are routinely amended by the Trust of Land and Appointment of Trustees Act 1996, and continue to operate. [20] They are improved in that bare trusts are included in the definition of a trust of land by section 1(2)(a).

LAW OF PROPERTY ACT 1925

2. Conveyances overreaching certain equitable interests and powers. —(1) A conveyance to a purchaser of a legal estate in land shall overreach any equitable interest or power affecting that estate, whether or not he has notice thereof, if —

> (ii) the conveyance is made by trustees of land and the equitable interest or power is at the date of the conveyance capable of being overreached by such trustees under the provisions of subsection (2) of this section or independently of that subsection [1] and the requirements of section 27

---

[17] *Bank of Ireland Home Mortgages Ltd v Bell* [2001] 2 All ER (Comm) 920 (sale ordered: purpose for which matrimonial home was purchased ceased when husband left); [2001] All ER Rev 262 (P. J. Clarke).

[18] 'A person who acquires an interest in or charge on property for money or money's worth; and in reference to a legal estate includes a chargee by way of legal mortgage': LPA 1925 s. 205 (1) (xxi).

[19] C & B, pp. 96, 889–892; Gray, pp. 215–218; M & W, paras. 4.073–4.082, 8.165–168; MM, pp. 210, 530–535; W & H, paras. 1.18–1.29, 6.64. See *City of London Building Society v Flegg* [1988] AC 54, [1987] 3 All ER 435, p. 316, post; *Birmingham Midshire's Mortgage Services Ltd v Sabherwal* (1999) 80 P & CR 256, p. 310, post, and for a critical analysis of the statutory provisions on overreaching, see [1990] CLJ 277, at pp. 287–310 (C.J. Harpum), [1998] Conv 168; [2000] Conv 221; (G. Ferris and G. Battersby); W & H, para. 2.175. See also (2003) 119 LQR 94 at p. 125: 'When viewed as a whole the statutory reforms contained in TLATA 1996, TA 2000, and LRA 2002 create a legal environment in which the law of overreaching will continue to operate as a central support to the marketability of land.'

[20] [1997] Conv 81 (N. Hopkins).

[1] *Re Ryder and Steadman's Contract* [1927] 2 Ch 62.

of this Act respecting the payment[2] of capital money arising on such a conveyance are complied with. [3]

(iii) the conveyance is made by a mortgagee or personal representative in the exercise of his paramount powers, and the equitable interest or power is capable of being overreached by such conveyance, and any capital money arising from the transaction is paid to the mortgagee or personal representative;

(iv) the conveyance is made under an order of the court and the equitable interest or power is bound by such order, and any capital money arising from the transaction is paid into, or in accordance with the order of the court.

(1A) An equitable interest in land subject to a trust of land which remains in, or is to revert to, the settlor shall (subject to any contrary intention) be overreached by the conveyance if it would be so overreached were it an interest under the trust. [4]

(2) [5] Where the legal estate affected is subject to a trust of land, then if at the date of a conveyance made after the commencement of this Act by the trustees, the trustees (whether original or substituted) are either —

(*a*) two or more individuals approved or appointed by the court or the successors in office of the individuals so approved or appointed; or

(*b*) a trust corporation[6]

any equitable interest or power having priority to the trust of land, shall, notwithstanding any stipulation to the contrary, be overreached by the

---

2   *State Bank of India v Sood* [1997] Ch 276, [1997] 1 All ER 169, p. 322, post, (overreaching even when no capital money advanced at time when mortgage was created).
3   As amended by TLATA 1996, s. 25 (1), Sch. 3, para. 4 (2).
4   As inserted by TLATA 1996, s. 25 (1), Sch. 3, para.. 4 (2).
5   This subsection was amended by LP(A)A 1926, Sch and TLATA 1996, s. 25(1), Sch. 3, para. 4(2). The trust of land then becomes 'ad hoc' with additional overreaching powers. See SLA 1925, s. 21, p. 337, post for 'ad hoc' settlements.
6   Defined in LPA 1925, s. 205(1)(xxviii) as follows: 'Trust corporation' means the Public Trustee or a corporation either appointed by the court in any particular case to be a trustee or entitled by rules made under subsection (3) of section four of the Public Trustee Act, 1906, to act as custodian trustee.
     Corporations which are entitled under the Public Trustee Rules 1912, r. 30, as substituted by the Public Trustee (Custodian Trustee) Rules 1975 (SI 1975 No. 1189, as amended by SI 1976 No. 836; SI 1981 No. 358; SI 1984 No. 109; SI 1985 No. 132; SI 1987 No. 1891), include 'any corporation constituted under the law of the United Kingdom and empowered by its constitution to undertake trust business and having one or more places of business there', and being a registered company 'having a capital (in stock or shares) for the time being issued of not less than £250,000, of which not less than £100,000 has been paid up in cash'.
     The definition was extended by LP (A) A 1926, s. 3 to include the 'Treasury Solicitor, the Official Solicitor, and any person holding any other official position prescribed by the Lord Chancellor, and, in relation to the property of a bankrupt and property subject to a deed of arrangement, includes the trustee in bankruptcy and the trustee under the deed respectively, and, in relation to charitable, ecclesiastical and public trusts, also includes any local or public authority so prescribed, and any other corporation constituted under the laws of the United Kingdom or any part thereof which satisfies the Lord Chancellor that it undertakes the administration of any such trusts without remuneration, or that by its constitution it is required to apply the whole of its net income after payment of outgoings for charitable, ecclesiastical or public purposes, and is prohibited from distributing, directly or indirectly, any part thereof by way of profits amongst any of its members, and is authorised by him to act in relation to such trusts as a trust corporation.' See also SLA 1925, s. 117(1)(xxx), as amended by TLATA 1996, s. 25(1), Sch. 3; TA 1925, s. 68(18); AEA 1925, s. 55(1)(xxvi); Supreme Court Act 1981, s. 128, as amended by TLATA 1996, Sch. 4.

conveyance, and shall, according to its priority, take effect as if created or arising by means of a primary trust affecting the proceeds of sale and the income of the land until sale.

(3) The following equitable interests and powers are excepted from the operation of subsection (2) of this section, namely —

    (i) Any equitable interest protected by a deposit of documents relating to the legal estate affected;

    (ii) The benefit of any covenant or agreement restrictive of the user of land;

    (iii) Any easement, liberty, or privilege over or affecting land and being merely an equitable interest (in this Act referred to as an 'equitable easement');

    (iv) The benefit of any contract (in this Act referred to as an 'estate contract') to convey or create a legal estate, including a contract conferring either expressly or by statutory implication a valid option to purchase, a right of pre-emption, or any other like right;

    (v) Any equitable interest protected by registration under the Land Charges Act, 1925,[7] other than —

        (*a*) an annuity within the meaning of Part II of that Act;

        (*b*) a limited owner's charge or a general equitable charge within the meaning of that Act.

(4) Subject to the protection afforded by this section to the purchaser of a legal estate, nothing contained in this section shall deprive a person entitled to an equitable charge of any of his rights or remedies for enforcing the same.

(5) So far as regards the following interests, created before the commencement of this Act (which accordingly are not within the provisions of the Land Charges Act 1925[7]), namely —

    (*a*) the benefit of any covenant or agreement restrictive of the user of the land;

    (*b*) any equitable easement;

    (*c*) the interest under a puisne mortgage within the meaning of the Land Charges Act, 1925,[7] unless and until acquired under a transfer made after the commencement of this Act;

    (*d*) the benefit of an estate contract, unless and until the same is acquired under a conveyance made after the commencement of this Act;

a purchaser of a legal estate shall only take subject thereto if he has notice thereof, and the same are not overreached under the provisions contained or in the manner referred to in this section.

27. Purchaser not to be concerned with the trust of the proceeds of sale.—(1) A purchaser of a legal estate from trustees of land shall not be concerned with the trusts affecting the land, the net income of the land or the proceeds of sale of the land whether or not those trusts are declared by the same instrument as that by which the trust of land is created.[8]

(2) Notwithstanding anything to the contrary in the instrument (if any) creating a trust of land or in any trust affecting the net proceeds of sale of the land if it is sold, the proceeds of sale or other capital money shall not be paid to or applied by the direction of fewer than two persons as trustees, except where the trustee is a trust corporation, but this subsection does not affect the right of

---

7   Now LCA 1972. The annuity referred to in (*a*) is one created before 1926 and registered in the Register of Annuities which then existed: LCA 1972, Sch. 1.

8   As substituted by TLATA 1996, s. 25(1), Sch. 3, para. 8(a).

a sole personal representative as such to give valid receipts for, or direct the application of, proceeds of sale or other capital money, nor, except where capital money arises on the transaction, render it necessary to have more than one trustee. [9]

B. Limitation on Powers and Consent Requirements

Further protection is given to a purchaser by section 16 of the Trusts of Land and Appointment of Trustees Act 1996. This section only applies to unregistered land. [10]

TRUSTS OF LAND AND APPOINTMENT OF TRUSTEES ACT 1996

16. Protection of purchasers.—(1) A purchaser of land which is or has been subject to a trust need not be concerned to see that any requirement imposed on the trustees by section 6(5), 7(3) or 11(1) [11] has been complied with.

(2) Where—
   (a) trustees of land who convey land which (immediately before it is conveyed) is subject to the trust contravene section 6(6) or (8), [12] but
   (b) the purchaser of the land from the trustees has no actual notice of the contravention,

the contravention does not invalidate the conveyance.

(3) Where the powers of trustees of land are limited by virtue of section 8—
   (a) the trustees shall take all reasonable steps to bring the limitation to the notice of any purchaser of the land from them, but
   (b) the limitation does not invalidate any conveyance by the trustees to a purchaser who has no actual notice of the limitation.

(4) Where trustees of land convey land which (immediately before it is conveyed) is subject to the trust to persons believed by them to be beneficiaries absolutely entitled to the land under the trust and of full age and capacity—
   (a) the trustees shall execute a deed declaring that they are discharged from the trust in relation to that land, and
   (b) if they fail to do so, the court may make an order requiring them to do so.

(5) A purchaser of land to which a deed under subsection (4) relates is entitled to assume that, as from the date of the deed, the land is not subject to the trust unless he has actual notice that the trustees were mistaken in their belief that the land was conveyed to beneficiaries absolutely entitled to the land under the trust and of full age and capacity.

(6) Subsections (2) and (3) do not apply to land held on charitable, ecclesiastical or public trusts.

(7) This section does not apply to registered land.

---

[9]   As amended by TLATA 1996, s. 25(1), Sch. 3, para. 8(b). Sub-s. 2 was substituted by LP (A) A 1926, s. 7 and Sch. See also TA 1925, s. 14; as amended by TA 2000, 5.40, Sch. 2, Pt. II, para. 19.
[10]   W & H, paras. 2.165–2.175.
[11]   Pp. 272, 277, ante.
[12]   Pp. 272, 273, ante.

VIII. Registered Land[13]

Title to land subject to a trust of land must be registered in the name of the trustees (not exceeding four in number), and the purchaser is informed of the necessity to pay capital moneys to at least two trustees or to a trust corporation by entry of a restriction on the register. [14]

If the interests of beneficiaries under a trust of land have not been protected by entry on the register, they may nevertheless be overriding interests under section 70(1)(*g*) of the Land Registration Act 1925 or under Schedules 1 and 3 of the Land Registration Act 2002. [15] These interests may, however, be overreached. [16]

LAND REGISTRATION ACT 2002

4 When title must be registered

(7) In subsection (1)(a) and (c), references to transfer or grant by way of gift include transfer or grant for the purpose of—

    (a) constituting a trust under which the settlor does not retain the whole of the beneficial interest, [17] or

    (b) uniting the bare legal title and the beneficial interest in property held under a trust under which the settlor did not, on constitution, retain the whole of the beneficial interest.

11 Freehold estates

(5) If the proprietor is not entitled to the estate for his own benefit, or not entitled solely for his own benefit, then, as between himself and the persons beneficially entitled to the estate, the estate is vested in him subject to such of their interests as he has notice of. [18]

33 Excluded interests

No notice may be entered in the register in respect of any of the following—

    (a) an interest under—

        (i)   a trust of land, or

        (ii)   a settlement under the Settled Land Act 1925

---

[13]   C & B, p. 266; M & W, para. 6.093; R & R, chap. 32; [1996] Conv 411, at pp. 427–428 (N. Hopkins).

[14]   For the provisions of LRA 1925, see ss. 58, 94, 95, LRR 1925 Statutory Form 62.

[15]   Pp. 158–162, ante.

[16]   *City of London Building Society v Flegg* [1988] AC 54, [1987] 3 All ER 435, p. 316, post.

[17]   R&R, 37.001–37.011 Law Commission Report on Land Registration for the Twenty-First Century 2001 (Law Com No. 271), p. 466; '... If S transfers an unregistered estate in land to T1 and T2, to hold on trust of land for S and U in equal shares, that transfer will trigger compulsory registration. However, a transfer by S to T1 and T2 to hold on trust for her as nominee will not trigger compulsory registration. Secondly, a transfer by way of a gift includes a transfer for the purpose of uniting the legal title and a beneficial interest in property held under a trust under which the settlor did not, on constitution, retain the whole of the beneficial interest (see s. 4(7)(b)). Thus, if T1 and T2 hold an unregistered estate in land on trust for A for life, thereafter to B absolutely, and A dies, so that the trustees hold the land on trust for B absolutely, a transfer of that land by T1 and T2 to B will trigger compulsory registration. However, where T1 and T2 hold on trust for the settlor absolutely, and the land is transferred eitehr to him or to the person entitled to the interest (as for example, under the settlor's will or intestacy), this will not trigger compulsory registration.'

[18]   Similarly for leasehold estates: s. 12(5).

42 Power of registrar to enter

(1) The registrar may enter a restriction in the register if it appears to him that it is necessary or desirable to do so for the purpose of—

(a) preventing invalidity or unlawfulness in relation to dispositions of a registered estate or charge.

(b) securing that interests which are capable of being overreached on a disposition of a registered estate or charge are overreached, or

(c) protecting a right or claim in relation to a registered estate or charge.

43 Applications

(1) A person may apply to the registrar for the entry of a restriction under section 42(1) if—

(a) he is the relevant registered proprietor, or a person entitled to be registered as such proprietor,

(b) the relevant registered proprietor, or a person entitled to be registered as such proprietor, consents to the application, or

(c) he otherwise has a sufficient interest in the making of the entry.

78 Notice of trust not to affect registrar

The registrar shall not be affected with notice of a trust. [19]

LAND REGISTRATION RULES 2003

Persons regarded as having a sufficient interest to apply for a restriction

93. The following persons are to be regarded as included in section 43(1)(c) of the Act—

(a) any person who has an interest in a registered estate held under a trust of land where a sole proprietor or a survivor of joint proprietors (unless a trust corporation) will not be able to give a valid receipt for capital money, and who is applying for a restriction in Form A to be entered in the register of that registered estate,

(b) any person who has a sufficient interest in preventing a contravention of section 6(6) or section 6(8) of the Trusts of Land and Appointments of Trustees Act 1996 [20] and who is applying for a restriction in order to prevent such a contravention,

(c) any person who has an interest in a registered estate held under a trust of land where the powers of the trustees are limited by section 8 of the Trusts of Land and Appointment of Trustees Act 1996, [1] and who is applying for a restriction in Form B to be entered in the register of that registered estate.

SCHEDULE 4

STANDARD FORMS OF RESTRICTION

Form A (Restriction on dispositions by sole proprietor)

No disposition by a sole proprietor of the registered estate (except a trust corporation) under which capital money arises is to be registered unless authorised by an order of the court.

Form B (Dispositions by trustees—certificate required)

[19]   See LRA 1925, s. 74.
[20]   P. 272, post.
[1]   P. 273, post.

No disposition [*or specify details*] by the proprietors of the registered estate is to be registered unless they make a statutory declaration, or their conveyancer gives a certificate, that the disposition [*or specify details*] is in accordance with [*specify the disposition creating the trust*] or some variation thereof referred to in the declaration or certificate.

IX. Discharge of Trusts of Land

Section 16 (4) and (5) make provision for a new deed of discharge, thereby remedying the defective procedure before 1997. Section 23 of the Law of Property Act has been repealed. [2]

TRUSTS OF LAND AND APPOINTMENT OF TRUSTEES ACT 1996

16. Protection of purchasers. – (4) (5), p. 296, ante.

LAND REGISTRATION RULES 2003

Cancellation of a restriction relating to a trust

99. When registering a disposition of a registered estate, the registrar must cancel a restriction entered for the purpose of protecting an interest, right or claim arising under a trust of land if he is satisfied that the registered estate is no longer subject to that trust of land.

------

[2] Cf. deed of charge in the case of a strict settlement: SLA 1925, s. 17.

5. Concurrent Interests After 1925[1]

I. The Scheme of the 1925 Legislation

The sections of the 1925 legislation applicable to concurrent interests are a further manifestation of the basic principles of that legislation. They attempt to simplify conveyancing by presenting to the purchaser a single title, however numerous and complicated the beneficial interests are, and by applying the overreaching principle to beneficial interests. In short, this is achieved by providing that the only form of co-ownership that can exist *at law* is a form of unseverable joint tenancy such as trustees hold. This is held on trust, and every form of *beneficial* co-ownership can only exist behind the trust.

Before 1997 co-ownership was governed either by an express trust for sale or by a statutory trust for sale. After 1996 the statutory trust for sale imposed by the 1925 legislation has been modified to become a trust of land, and the statutory trusts (for sale) under section 35 of the Law of Property Act 1925 have been abolished.

The Land Registry recommended the following wording for the creation of the trust under the Land Registration Act 1925:[2]

(a) For a beneficial joint tenancy:
The land is to be held by A and B in trust for C and D[3] as joint tenants.

(b) For a beneficial tenancy in common:
The land is to be held by A and B in trust for C and D[4] in equal shares (or in other specified shares).

These formulae now appear in the Land Registration Rules 2003 in Panel 11 of Form TR 1 for the Transfer of whole of registered title(s), p. 81, ante.

TRUSTS OF LAND AND APPOINTMENT OF TRUSTEES ACT 1996

5. Implied trusts for sale as trusts of land. p. 269, ante.

LAW OF PROPERTY ACT 1925

1. Legal estates and equitable interests.—(6) p. 7, ante.

34. Effect of future dispositions to tenants in common. —(1) An undivided share

---

[1]   C & B, pp. 241–268; Gray, pp. 821–889; M & W, paras. 9.001–9.109; MM, pp. 303–332; Smith, chap. 13; Thompson, *Co-ownership* (1988). For the nature and characteristics of different types of co-ownership, and for the pre-1926 law, see C & B, pp. 241–253; Gray, pp. 821–889; M & W, paras. 9.001–9.035, 9.051–9.054, and, on co-parcenary, pp. 456–459 (5th edn). MM, pp. 303–332. The present chapter assumes an understanding of this material.
[2]   Practice Advice Leaflet No. 13 Part B3.
[3]   The land may also be held in either case 'for themselves'.
[4]   The land may also be held in either case 'for themselves'.

in land shall not be capable of being created except as provided by the Settled Land Act, 1925[5] or as hereinafter mentioned.

(2) Where, after the commencement of this Act, land is expressed to be conveyed to any persons in undivided shares and those persons are of full age, the conveyance shall (notwithstanding anything to the contrary in this Act) operate as if the land had been expressed to be conveyed to the grantees, or, if there are more than four grantees, to the four first named in the conveyance, as joint tenants in trust for the persons interested in the land.[6]

Provided that, where the conveyance is made by way of mortgage the land shall vest in the grantees or such four of them as aforesaid for a term of years absolute (as provided by this Act) as joint tenants subject to cesser on redemption in like manner as if the mortgage money had belonged to them on a joint account, but without prejudice to the beneficial interests in the mortgage money and interest.

(3) A devise bequest or testamentary appointment, coming into operation after the commencement of this Act, of land to two or more persons in undivided shares shall operate as a devise bequest or appointment of the land to the personal representatives of the testator, and (but without prejudice to the rights and powers of the personal representatives for purposes of administration) in trust for the persons interested in the land.[7]

(3A) In subsections (2) and (3) of this section references to the persons interested in the land include persons interested as trustees or personal representatives (as well as persons beneficially interested).[8]

36. Joint tenancies.[9]—(1) Where a legal estate (not being settled land)[10] is beneficially limited to or held in trust for any persons as joint tenants, the same shall be held in trust,[11] in like manner as if the persons beneficially entitled were tenants in common, but not so as to sever their joint tenancy in equity.

(2) No severance of a joint tenancy of a legal estate, so as to create a tenancy in common in land, shall be permissible, whether by operation of law or otherwise, but this subsection does not affect the right of a joint tenant to release his interest to the other joint tenants, or the right to sever a joint tenancy in an equitable interest whether or not the legal estate is vested in the joint tenants:

Provided that, where a legal estate (not being settled land) is vested in joint tenants beneficially, and any tenant desires to sever the joint tenancy in equity,[12] he shall give to the other joint tenants a notice in writing[13] of such desire or do such other acts or things as would, in the case of personal estate, have been effectual to sever the tenancy in equity, and thereupon the land shall be held in

5   SLA 1925, s. 36(1), (2), p. 302, post
6   As amended by TLATA 1996, s. 5, Sch. 2, para. 3(2).
7   As amended by TLATA 1996, s. 5, Sch. 2, para. 3(3).
8   As added by TLATA 1996, s. 5, Sch. 2, para. 3(4).
9   As to whether beneficial joint tenancies should be abolished, see [1987] Conv 29, 225 (M. P. Thompson) in favour; 273 (A. M. Prichard) against.
10   The definition of settled land is the same as that in SLA 1925, s. 1, p. 326, post; *Re Gaul and Houlston's Contract* [1928] Ch 689.
11   As amended by TLATA 1996, s. 5, Sch. 2, para. 4(2).
12   See pp. 303–309, post.
13   *Re 88 Berkeley Road, NW9* [1971] Ch 648, [1971] 1 All ER 254 (notice properly served by recorded delivery, even if not received by addressee); LPA 1925, s. 196(4); (1971) 87 LQR 155; *Kinch v Bullard* [1999] 1 WLR 423, [1998] 4 All ER 650 (severance although wife posted notice to husband but destroyed it before he received it); [1999] Conv 60 (M. Percival); [1998] All ER Rev 261 (P. J. Clarke). See also p. 532, n. 7 ante.

trust on terms which would have been requisite for giving effect to the beneficial interests if there had been an actual severance.[14]

Nothing in this Act affects the right of a survivor of joint tenants, who is solely and beneficially interested, to deal with his legal estate as if it were not held in trust.[15]

37. Rights of husband and wife.—A husband and wife shall, for all purposes of acquisition of any interest in property, under a disposition made or coming into operation after the commencement of this Act, be treated as two persons.

SETTLED LAND ACT 1925

36. Undivided shares to take effect behind a trust of land.—(1) If and when, after the commencement of this Act, settled land is held in trust for persons entitled in possession under a trust instrument[16] in undivided shares, the trustees of the settlement (if the settled land is not already vested in them) may require the estate owner in whom the settled land is vested (but in the case of a personal representative subject to his rights and powers for purposes of administration), at the cost of the trust estate, to convey the land to them, or assent to the land vesting in them as joint tenants, and in the meantime the land shall be held on the same trusts as would have been applicable thereto if it had been so conveyed to or vested in the trustees.

(2) If and when the settled land so held in trust in undivided shares is or becomes vested in the trustees of the settlement, the land shall be held by them (subject to any incumbrances affecting the settled land which are secured by a legal mortgage, but freed from any incumbrances affecting the undivided shares or not secured as aforesaid, and from any interests, powers and charges subsisting under the trust instrument which have priority to the trust for the persons entitled to the undivided shares) in trust for the persons interested in the land.[17]

(4) An undivided share in land shall not be capable of being created except under a trust instrument or under the Law of Property Act 1925, and shall then only take effect behind a trust of land.[18]

(6) In subsections (2) and (3) of this section references to the persons interested in the land include persons interested as trustees or personal representatives (as well as persons beneficially interested).[19]

Before 1997 the scheme of the Act was to subject to a trust for sale all forms of concurrent ownership except for joint owners taking as tenants for life, in which case the land remained settled land.[20] The question arose, however, of the position of a form of concurrent ownership which did not come within the terms

---

[14]   As amended by TLATA 1996, s. 5, Sch. 2, para. 4(3)(a).
[15]   As added by LP(A)A 1926, s. 7 and Sch., and amended by TLATA 1996, s. 5, Sch. 2, para. 4(3)(b). For the protection given to the purchaser of a legal estate from a surviving joint tenant of unregistered land, see LP (Joint Tenants) Act 1964, as amended by LP (Miscellaneous Provisions) Act 1994, s. 21(1), para. 3; and LRA 2002, s. 133, Sch. 11, para. 5; [2004] Conv 41 (E.J. Cooke).
[16]   P. 339, post.
[17]   As amended by TLATA 1996, s. 25(1), Sch. 3, para. 2(11)(a).
[18]   As substituted by TLATA 1996, s. 25(1), Sch. 3, para. 2(11)(b).
[19]   As substituted by TLATA 1996, s. 25(1), Sch. 3, para. 2(11)(c).
[20]   SLA 1925, s. 19(2), p. 289, post.

of the Law of Property Act 1925, sections 34 and 36.[1] For example, land conveyed in undivided shares to an adult and an infant; or where a tenancy in common exists although the land is not 'expressed to be conveyed in undivided shares'.

Since 1996 the gap in the legislation has been plugged. 'Because implied trusts are included within the all embracing definition of a trust of land, these situations are within the Trusts of Land and Appointment of Trustees Act 1996.'[2]

II.   Severance[3]

LAW OF PROPERTY ACT 1925

36. Joint Tenancies. —(1), (2) p. 301, ante.

The provision in Law of Property Act 1925, section 36(2) for the severance of equitable joint tenancies by the giving of notice to the other joint tenants was new in 1925; and is additional to other methods of severance.[4] It is still not possible to effect severance by will.

RE DRAPER'S CONVEYANCE[5]
[1969] 1 Ch 486, [1967] 3 All ER 853 (ChD, PLOWMAN J)

A house was conveyed to a husband and wife as joint tenants. The wife obtained a divorce, and issued a summons under section 17 of the Married Women's Property Act 1882, asking for an order that the house be sold and the proceeds distributed according to the interests of the spouses. The order was made but the husband remained in occupation. The husband died and the question was whether the wife was entitled to the house absolutely by survivorship or whether she and her husband's estate were entitled in equal shares.

Held. The wife held the legal estate on trust for herself and her husband's estate in equal shares.

PLOWMAN J: It is common ground that the answer to the question asked by originating summons in this case depends upon whether a beneficial joint tenancy which subsisted between two persons who were formerly husband and wife in a certain house was severed in the lifetime of the husband. ... Mr Cooke, on behalf of the defendants, submits that the joint tenancy was severed, and he puts the matter in two ways, either that it was severed by notice in writing, or it was severed by conduct, and in order to explain those submissions I should, I think, refer to section 36(2) of the Law of Property Act 1925. ...

---

1   (1945) 9 Conv (NS) 37; (1963) 27 Conv (NS) 51 (B. A. Rudden); *Bull v Bull* [1955] 1 QB 234, [1995] 1 All ER 253; *Re Buchanan-Wollaston's Conveyance* [1939] Ch 217; affd [1939] Ch 238, [1939] 2 All ER 302; *Re Kempthorne* [1930] 1 Ch 268.
2   W & H, para. 2.3.
3   See Law Commission Working Paper: Trusts of Land No. 94 (1988) paras. 16.11–16.14; Gray, pp. 851–877; Smith, pp. 291–300; [1995] Conv 105 (L. Tee).
4   *Carr-Glynn v Frearsons* [1999] 2 WLR 1046, [1998] 4 All ER 225; (solicitor, who failed to advise 81 year old testatrix promptly to sever joint tenancy in conjunction with execution of her will, held liable to compensate specific legatee for loss suffered thereby); (1999) 115 LQR 201; [1999] Conv 399 (R. Kerridge and A. H. R. Brierley).
5   (1968) 84 LQR 462 (PVB).

Mr Cooke, as I say, puts it in two ways: first, he submits that the wife's conduct was such as to effect a severance of the joint tenancy, and in relation to that matter he relies on the summons of 11 February 1966, in the Probate, Divorce and Admiralty Division, coupled with the orders which were made by that court, coupled with the plaintiff's solicitor's letter of 7 June 1966. And he says, either as a result of those three matters or as a result of any of them, the joint tenancy became severed by conduct, and he referred me to the decision of Havers J in *Hawkesley v May* [1956] 1 QB 304, [1955] 3 All ER 353. The part of that case which is relevant for present purposes depends upon these facts, which I read from the headnote: 'A settled fund was held by trustees upon trusts under which on attaining the age of 21 the plaintiff and his younger sister became absolutely entitled as joint tenants.' The question was whether that joint tenancy had become severed, and Havers J said:

'The joint tenancy was capable of being severed by the plaintiff on attaining the age of 21. There are a number of ways by which a joint tenancy may be severed. In *Williams v Hensman* (1861) 1 John & H 546 Page Wood V-C, in the course of his judgment, said: "A joint-tenancy may be severed in three ways: in the first place, an act of any one of the persons interested operating upon his own share may create a severance as to that share.[6] The right of each joint-tenant is a right by survivorship only in the event of non severance having taken place of the share which is claimed under the jus accrescendi. Each one is at liberty to dispose of his own interest in such manner as to sever it from the joint fund – losing, of course, at the same time, his own right of survivorship. Secondly, a joint-tenancy may be severed by mutual agreement. And, in the third place, there may be a severance by any course of dealing sufficient to intimate that the interests of all were mutually treated as constituting a tenancy in common. When the severance depends on an inference of this kind without any express act of severance, it will not suffice to rely on an intention, with respect to the particular share, declared only behind the backs of the other persons interested".'

Havers J continued:

'The first method indicated, namely, an act of any one of the persons interested operating upon his own share, obviously includes a declaration of intention to sever by one party.'

Then, after referring to *Walmsley v Foxhall* (1870) 40 LJ Ch 28 he said:

'This being the state of the authorities, I hold that on the plaintiff attaining the age of 21 he was entitled to the income of his share of the fund. As regards the severance, I hold that when the sister wrote the letter dated 18 March 1942, in which she said: "Thank you for your letter of 17th instant with the particulars of the investments. I should like the dividends to be paid into my account at

---

[6]   E.g. by sale or mortgage or settlement of the share; *First National Securities Ltd v Hegerty* [1985] QB 850, [1984] 1 All ER 139, 641 (joint tenancy held to be severed where husband purported to mortgage jointly-owned property by forging wife's signature); *Ahmed v Kendrick and Ahmed* (1987) 56 P & CR 120 (severance where husband sold jointly owned house by forging wife's signature on both contract and registered transfer); cf. *Penn v Bristol and West Building Society* [1995] 2 FLR 938 (no severance where purchaser colluded in forgery by husband joint tenant of his wife's signature on the conveyance); *Monarch Aluminium v Rickman* [1989] CLY 1526 (charging order nisi held to be severance). See also [2000] Conv 208 (L. Fox); [2001] Conv 477 (S. Nield).

For severance by involuntary alienation, as where a joint tenant is adjudicated bankrupt and his interest vests in his trustee in bankruptcy, see *Re Dennis* [1996] Ch 80, [1995] 3 All ER 171; [1995] All ER Rev 292 (S.M. Cretney); *Re Gorman* [1990] 1 WLR 616, [1990] 1 All ER 717; *Re Pavlou* [1993] 1 WLR 1046, [1993] 3 All ER 955; cf. *Re Palmer* [1994] Ch 316, [1994] 3 All ER 835 (insolvency administration order); [1995] Conv 68 (M. Haley); [1995] CLJ 52 (L. Tee); *Emmet on Title*, para. 11.145A.

Martins Bank, 208 Kensington High Street" (which was a letter in reply to the first defendant), that was a sufficient act on her part to constitute a severance of the joint tenancy. If I am wrong about that, there clearly was a severance when her share of the trust funds were transferred to her in September 1942.'

So from that case I derive this; a declaration by one of a number of joint tenants of his intention to sever operates as a severance. Mr Cooke also, as I have said, relied upon the notice in writing which under section 36(2) of the Law of Property Act, 1925, is allowed in the case of a joint tenancy in land, although not in personalty, and he submits that the summons to which I have already referred, although not signed, amounted to a notice in writing on the part of the wife that she desired to sever the joint tenancy in equity. I say 'although not signed by the wife or by anybody on her behalf' because there is no requirement in the subsection of a signature.

Dealing with the matter there, and ignoring for a moment certain matters which were submitted by Mr McCulloch, it seems to me that Mr Cooke's submissions are right whether they are based on the new provision in section 36(2) of the Law of Property Act, 1925, or whether they are based on the old law which applied to severing a joint tenancy in the case of a personal estate. It seems to me that that summons, coupled with the affidavit in support of it, clearly evinced an intention on the part of the wife that she wished the property to be sold and the proceeds distributed, a half to her and a half to the husband. And if that is right then it seems to me that that is wholly inconsistent with the notion that a beneficial joint tenancy in that property is to continue, and therefore, apart from these objections to which I will refer in a moment, I feel little doubt that in one way or the other this joint tenancy was severed in equity before the end of February 1966, as a result of the summons which was served on the husband and as a result of what the wife stated in her affidavit in support of the summons.

But then certain matters were submitted to me by Mr McCulloch on behalf of the wife, which I think fall under two heads. In the first place I was referred to certain observations which were made by Lord Denning MR in *Bedson v Bedson* [1965] 2 QB 666, [1965] 3 All ER 307. That was a case in which a wife, in September 1964, applied to the county court under section 17 of the Married Women's Property Act 1882, for an order that the property together with the fixtures, fittings, car, stock and goodwill be sold, and the proceeds divided between herself and her husband in equal shares. And then the headnote goes on to state that no matrimonial proceedings had at any relevant date been begun.

But Lord Denning in the course of his judgment had certain things to say about the severance of the joint tenancy in the matrimonial home. He said:

'(3) So long as the house is in the possession of the husband and wife as joint tenants or one of them, there can be no severance of their equitable interests: see section 36(1)(3).' That is a reference to the Law of Property Act 1925. 'Neither of them can sell his or her equitable interest separately. If he or she could do so, it would mean that the purchaser could insist on going into possession himself – with the other spouse there – which is absurd. It would mean also that one of them could, of his own head, destroy the right of survivorship which was the essence of the joint tenancy. That cannot be correct.'

If I may say so, it is not easy to understand what it is in section 36(1) and (3) of the Law of Property Act 1925, on which Lord Denning was relying as authority for the proposition that so long as the house is in the possession of the husband and wife as joint tenants or one of them there can be no severance of their equitable interests.

Then Lord Denning MR added:

'One further point: I am of opinion that, while the husband is in possession of the house, there can be no severance of the joint tenancy. The wife cannot sell her interest separately. In case I am wrong about this, I think we should make an order restraining the wife from doing so. It would be quite intolerable that she should, for instance, be able to sell her interest to her mother and get her to turn him out. The jurisdiction in this behalf is amply covered by *Lee v Lee* [1952] 2 QB 489n, [1952] 1 All ER 1299, which has been approved by the House of Lords.'

Mr McCulloch points out that in the present case the husband continued in possession until January of 1967 which was some time after the orders of the Divorce court had been made. However, Russell LJ in the same case took a different view about the severance of beneficial joint tenancies. He said:

'I am unable to accept the legal position of Lord Denning MR, that when husband and wife are joint tenants of the legal estate in the matrimonial home and also beneficial joint tenants in respect of it, neither can, so long as one is in possession, sell his or her beneficial interest therein or otherwise sever the beneficial joint tenancy. The proposition is, I think, without the slightest foundation in law or in equity. If anything, it appears to be an attempt to revive to some extent the long defunct tenancy by entireties which, as I have already remarked, was doomed by the Married Women's Property Act, 1882, itself. It may indeed be that either the wife's claim in this case, or the notation in the business accounts of the husband of her interest has long since operated as a severance.'

If I have to choose between those two statements I respectfully express my preference for that of Russell LJ.[7] It is interesting to note that he referred to the possibility that the wife's claim in that case might have operated by itself as a severance, and, as I have already stated, I take the view that in this case the summons issued by the wife in the Divorce Division coupled with the affidavit which she swore in support of that summons did operate to sever her beneficial joint tenancy.[8]

BURGESS v RAWNSLEY
[1975] Ch 429, [1975] 3 All ER 142 (CA, Lord DENNING MR, BROWNE LJ and Sir John PENNYCUICK)[9]

Lord DENNING MR: In 1966 there was a scripture rally in Trafalgar Square. A widower, Mr Honick, went to it. He was about 63. A widow, Mrs Rawnsley, the defendant, also went. She was about 60. He went up to her and introduced himself. He was not much to look at. 'He looked like a tramp,' she said. 'He had

7   So did CA in *Harris v Goddard* [1983] 1 WLR 1203 at 1208, [1983] 2 All ER 242 at 245, per LAWTON LJ. See also (1966) 82 LQR 29 (R.E.M.); (1976) 40 Conv (NS) 77 (J. F. Garner).

8   Cf. *Harris v Goddard* [1983] 1 WLR 1203, [1982] 3 All ER 242 (a wife's prayer in a divorce petition for a property adjustment order to be made in respect of the former matrimonial home did not operate); [1984] Conv 148 (S. Coneys); *Grindal v Hooper* [1999] EGCS 150 (notice of severance effective, even though not endorsed on conveyance). Whether a unilateral act not amounting to notice under s. 36(2) can effect severance is a matter of dispute; *Burgess v Rawnsley* [1975] Ch 429, [1975] 3 All ER 142; [1976] CLJ 20 (D. J. Hayton); (1977) Conv (NS) 243 (S. M. Bandali).

9   (1975) 39 Conv (NS) 443 (F. R. Crane); [1976] CLJ 20 (D. J. Hayton); (1977) 41 Conv (NS) 243 (S. M. Bandali).

been picking up fag-ends.' They got on well enough, however, to exchange addresses. His was 36 Queen's Road, Waltham Cross, Hertfordshire. Hers was 74 Downton Avenue, Streatham Hill, London, SW2. Next day he went to her house with a gift for her. It was a rose wrapped in a newspaper. Afterwards their friendship grew apace. She was sorry for him, she said. She smartened him up with better clothes. She had him to meals. She went to his house: he went to hers. They wrote to one another in terms of endearment. We were not shown the letters, but counsel described them as love letters.

A few months later Mr Honick had the opportunity of buying the house where he lived at 36 Queen's Road, Waltham Cross. He had been the tenant of it for some years, but his wife had died and his married daughter had left; so that he was alone there. He talked it over with Mrs Rawnsley. He told her that the owner was willing to sell the house to him for £800. Mrs Rawnsley said that she would go half shares: she would have the upper flat and he the lower flat.

[In 1967 they bought the house in their joint names 'as joint tenants', each providing half the purchase price. Mr Honick was minded to marry Mrs Rawnsley, but it was clear that she was not minded to marry him. In fact they did not marry and Mrs Rawnsley did not move into the house. There was evidence of an oral agreement between them in 1968 whereby she agreed to sell her share to him for £750 but that she later refused to sell. Mr Honick died and the question was whether his estate was entitled to a half share in the house. In holding that it was, because there had been a severance of the joint tenancy, Lord DENNING MR continued:]

Was there a severance of the beneficial joint tenancy? The judge said:

'I hold that there has been a severance of the joint tenancy brought about by the conduct of the defendant in asking £750 for her share which was agreed to.'

In making that statement the judge made a little slip. She did not ask £750. But it was a slip of no importance. The important finding is that there was an agreement that she would sell her share to him for £750. Almost immediately afterwards she went back upon it. Is that conduct sufficient to effect a severance?

Mr Levy submitted that it was not. He relied on the recent decision of Walton J in *Nielson-Jones v Fedden* [1975] Ch 222, [1974] 3 All ER 38, given subsequently to the judgment of the judge here. Walton J held that no conduct is sufficient to sever a joint tenancy unless it is irrevocable. Mr Levy said that in the present case the agreement was not in writing. It could not be enforced by specific performance. It was revocable and was in fact revoked by Mrs Rawnsley when she went back on it. So there was, he submitted, no severance.

Walton J founded himself on the decision of Stirling J in *Re Wilks* [1891] 3 Ch 59. He criticised *Hawkesley v May* [1956] 1 QB 304, [1955] 3 All ER 353 and *Re Draper's Conveyance* [1969] 1 Ch 486, [1967] 3 All ER 853, and said that they were clearly contrary to the existing well-established law. He went back to *Coke upon Littleton*, 189a, 299b and to *Blackstone's Commentaries*. Those old writers were dealing with legal joint tenancies. *Blackstone* said, 8th edn. (1778), vol. II, pp. 180, 185:

'The properties of a joint estate are derived from its unity, which is fourfold; the unity of interest, the unity of title, the unity of time, and the unity of possession: . . . an estate in joint tenancy may be severed and destroyed . . . by destroying any of its constituent unities.'

And he gives instances of how this may be done. Now that is all very well when you are considering how a legal joint tenancy can be severed. But it is of no application today when there can be no severance of a legal joint tenancy; and you are only considering how a beneficial joint tenancy can be severed. The thing to remember today is that equity leans against joint tenants and favours tenancies in common.

Nowadays everyone starts with the judgment of Sir William Page Wood V-C in *Williams v Hensman* (1861) 1 John & H 546, 557, where he said:

'A joint tenancy may be severed in three ways: in the first place, an act of any one of the persons interested operating upon his own share may create a severance as to that share. . . . Secondly, a joint tenancy may be severed by mutual agreement. And, in the third place, there may be a severance by any course of dealing sufficient to intimate that the interests of all were mutually treated as constituting a tenancy in common. When the severance depends on an inference of this kind without any express act of severance, it will not suffice to rely on an intention, with respect to the particular share, declared only behind the backs of the other persons interested. You must find in this class of cases a course of dealing by which the shares of all the parties to the contest have been affected, as happened in the cases of *Wilson v Bell* (1843) Ir 5 Eq R 501 and *Jackson v Jackson* (1804) 9 Ves 591.'

In that passage Page Wood V-C distinguished between severance 'by mutual agreement' and severance by a 'course of dealing.' That shows that a 'course of dealing' need not amount to an agreement, expressed or implied, for severance. It is sufficient if there is a course of dealing in which one party makes clear to the other that he desires that their shares should no longer be held jointly but be held in common. I emphasise that it must be made clear to the other party. That is implicit in the sentence in which Page Wood V-C says:

'it will not suffice to rely on an intention, with respect to the particular share, declared only behind the backs of the other persons interested.'

Similarly it is sufficient if both parties enter on a course of dealing which evinces an intention by both of them that their shares shall henceforth be held in common and not jointly. As appears from the two cases to which Page Wood V-C referred to of *Wilson v Bell* and *Jackson v Jackson*.

I come now to the question of notice. Suppose that one party gives a notice in writing to the other saying that he desires to sever the joint tenancy. Is that sufficient to effect a severance? I think it is.

[His Lordship read LPA 1925, section 36(2), p. 301, ante, and continued:]

The word 'other' is most illuminating. It shows quite plainly that, in the case of personal estate one of the things which is effective in equity to sever a joint tenancy is 'a notice in writing' of a desire to sever. So also in regard to real estate.

Taking this view, I find myself in agreement with Havers J in *Hawkesley v May* [1956] 1 QB 304, 313–314, [1955] 3 All ER 353, 356, and of Plowman J in *Re Draper's Conveyance* [1969] 1 Ch 486, [1967] 3 All ER 853. I cannot agree with Walton J in *Nielson-Jones v Fedden* [1975] Ch 222 at 234–235, [1974] 3 All ER 38 at 48–49, that those cases were wrongly decided. It would be absurd that there should be a difference between real estate and personal estate in this respect. Suppose real estate is held on a joint tenancy on a trust for sale and is sold and converted into personal property. Before sale, it is severable by notice in writing. It would be ridiculous if it could not be severed afterwards in like manner. I look upon section 36(2) as declaratory of the law as to severance by notice and not as a new provision confined to real estate. A joint tenancy in personal estate can be severed by notice just as a joint tenancy in real estate.

[His Lordship referred to *Nielson-Jones v Fedden* and *Re Wilks* [1891] 3 Ch 59, and continued:]

It remains to apply these principles to the present case. I think there was evidence that Mr Honick and Mrs Rawnsley did come to an agreement that he would buy her share for £750. That agreement was not in writing and it was not specifically enforceable. Yet it was sufficient to effect a severance.[10] Even if there was not any firm agreement but only a course of dealing, it clearly evinced an intention by both parties that the property should henceforth be held in common and not jointly.

On these grounds I would dismiss the appeal.[11]

III. Legal Estate in One Person with Beneficial Interest in Two or More

Complicated situations arise where the legal estate in land is held by one person, but the beneficial interest is held by two or more. Such a case occurs usually, but not exclusively, in the context of the matrimonial home. A number of problems can arise, and it will sometimes be relevant to determine the true nature of the beneficiary's interest. Thus, a husband takes a conveyance, in his own name, of a house which is paid for partly by him and partly by his wife, or where there has been an agreement to hold in joint names.[12] Or, as in *Bull v Bull* [1955] 1 QB 234, [1955] 1 All ER 253, where a house was conveyed to the plaintiff who provided the bulk of the purchase money, but his mother, the defendant, also contributed. The plaintiff married, and he attempted to evict his mother. Or, as in *Barclay v Barclay* [1970] 2 QB 677, [1970] 2 All ER 676, where a trust for sale in a will provided for the sale of a bungalow and division of the proceeds. The sole trustee was a daughter-in-law of the testator. She wished to sell with vacant possession, but one of the beneficiaries, the testator's son, remained in possession throughout.

A. Co-ownership in Equity

In these situations, the first question is whether there is co-ownership in equity of the house. In *Bull v Bull*, there was, because the mother had provided part of the purchase money, and was entitled in equity to a share of the beneficial ownership, which related to her share of the purchase money. Similarly, in the matrimonial situation.[13] A spouse may obtain a beneficial interest by making a

---

[10] Followed in *Hunter v Babbage* (1994) 69 P & CR 548 (draft agreement); cf. *Edwards v Hastings* [1996] NPC 87 (agreement to sever conditional on sale of family home).

[11] Cf. *Greenfield v Greenfield* (1979) 38 P & CR 570 (conversion of house jointly owned by brothers into two self-contained maisonettes occupied separately held not to be severance by a course of dealing); *Barton v Morris* [1985] 1 WLR 1257, [1985] 2 All ER 1032 (inclusion of property as a partnership asset in the partnership accounts for tax purposes held not severance by a course of dealing); *Gore and Snell v Carpenter* (1990) 60 P & CR 456 (negotiations between husband and wife with a view to settling claims for ancillary relief in divorce proceedings held not to be severance in absence of a final agreement between them); *Re Denny* (1947) 177 LT 291; *McDowell v Hirschfield* [1992] 2 FLR 126 (onus of proof on party who desires to establish course of dealing).

For severance by homicide, see *Re K* [1985] Ch 85, [1985] 1 All ER 403; affd [1986] Ch 180, [1985] 2 All ER 833; Maudsley and Burn, *Trusts and Trustees* (6th edn.), pp. 288–292.

[12] *Caunce v Caunce* [1969] 1 WLR 286, [1969] 1 All ER 722; *Williams & Glyn's Bank Ltd v Boland* [1981] AC 487, [1980] 2 All ER 408.

[13] H & M, pp. 271–284; *Emmet on Title*, paras. 12.009–12.012; Oakley, *Constructive Trusts* (3rd edn), pp. 64–83; Bromley, *Family Law* (9th edn, 1998), chap. 4; Cretney and Masson,

contribution [14] in money or money's worth to the purchase price, whether towards the initial deposit or to the mortgage instalments; or by substantially contributing in money or money's worth to the improvement of the property. [15] If some person, as well as the legal estate owner, is entitled to a beneficial proprietary interest in the house, there is co-ownership in equity. [16] Beneficial joint tenancy or tenancy in common can only exist in equity; and we have seen that a tenancy in common can only take effect behind a trust of land. [17]

B. Right to Possession against Trustee

Assuming that there is a trust of land, whether express or implied, a further question is whether the equitable co-owners can remain in possession as against the trustee. Before 1997 there were conceptual difficulties due to the doctrine of conversion. In *Bull v Bull* [1955] 1 QB 234, [1955] 1 All ER 253, and in *Barclay v Barclay* [1970] 2 QB 677, [1970] 2 All ER 676, the sole trustee sued for possession. The action failed in the former case because Mrs Bull, it was said, had an interest in the land; but succeeded in the latter because, it was said, the brother-in-law had an interest only in the proceeds of sale. [18] After 1996 the doctrine of conversion no longer applies, [19] and the occupation rights of beneficiaries are now governed by the Trusts of Land and Appointment of Trustees Act 1996, sections 12, 13, p. 278, ante. Thus, a conceptual analysis could reach either result.

C. Overreaching on Sale

Where a trustee is suing a beneficiary for possession, he usually does so in order to be able to sell with vacant possession. He does not need possession in order

---

Principles of Family Law (6th edn, 1999) chap. 5; Mee, *The Property Rights of Cohabitees* (1999).

In 2002 the Law Commission published a Discussion Paper on Sharing Homes (Law Com No. 278). Its conclusion was summarised in Law Commission Annual Report 2002–03 (Law Com No. 280) at para. 7.2:

'In this project, the Law Commission had attempted to devise a scheme for the ascertainment and quantification of rights in the shared home which would apply whenever the parties had failed to make express legally enforceable arrangements. The aim was to recommend a scheme that would operate fairly and evenly across the diversity of domestic circumstances – not only to married and unmarried couples, but also to friends, to relatives, and to all others sharing a home outside commercial relationships such as landlord and tenant or lodger. It was however concluded that this was not possible, and that the common law, by adopting a broader approach to the valuation of shares in the home, had greater potential to apply to the wide range of relationships than any statutory scheme.'

See also Smith, p. 164.

14   *Lloyds Bank plc v Rossett* [1991] 1 AC 107 at 133, [1990] 1 All ER 1111 at 1119, per Lord BRIDGE OF HARWICH, who thought it 'extremely doubtful' whether indirect contributions could suffice, for example, those made by a wife in helping with the housekeeping expenses, 'or keeping house, giving birth to and looking after and helping to bring up the children'.

15   Matrimonial Proceedings and Property Act 1970, s. 37.

16   P. 302, ante.

17   SLA 1925, s. 36(4), p. 302, ante.

18   At 684, at 678, per Lord DENNING MR. See *Irani Finance Ltd v Singh* [1971] Ch 59 at 79–80, [1970] 3 All ER 199 at 203–204; (1970) 34 Conv (NS) 344 (F. R. Crane).

19   P. 210, ante.

to be able to sell. For a sale by trustees overreaches the interests of the beneficiaries, including the interest of a beneficiary in possession; even if that interest is valid against the trustee's claim for possession, it would have no effect against the purchaser. But, to effect a sale as trustees, there must be at least two trustees. [20] A second trustee therefore needs to be appointed. A sale could then be made; though it would leave the purchaser with the unattractive problem of evicting the remaining beneficiary, and that would reduce the price which could be obtained.

D. Order of Court Under Trusts of Land and Appointment of Trustees Act 1996, section 14

The 1925 legislation on co-ownership assumes that the beneficial co-owners (or the first four mentioned) are the trustees. [1] They would have to agree upon a sale. If they disagree, there can be an application to the court under the Trusts of Land and Appointment of Trustees Act 1996, section 14; the guidelines are set out in section 15. [2]

If, however, there is one trustee only and more than one beneficial owner, as where the legal title is in a husband and he and his wife are beneficial owners, a second trustee for sale should be appointed in order to effect a sale. The wife would be appropriate. But if there is disagreement, she cannot insist on being appointed. She may, however, as one who has an interest in property subject to a trust of land, apply to the court under section 14 for an order of sale.

E. Sale by Single Owner

i. UNREGISTERED LAND

A further problem arises if the sale is made by one trustee only. The overreaching provisions do not apply. [3] This was illustrated in *Caunce v Caunce* [1969] 1 WLR 286, [1969] 1 All ER 722, where a husband and wife agreed that the wife would make a capital payment towards the purchase of a house, that the husband would pay the instalments to the building society, and that the conveyance would be in their joint names. The house was, however, conveyed to the husband alone, and, without the wife's knowledge, he further charged it in favour of Lloyds Bank. On the husband's bankruptcy, one question was whether the bank took subject to, or free from, the wife's equitable interest. STAMP J held that the bank took free, as a bona fide purchaser of a legal estate for value without notice. [4] Thus, in that

---

[20]   LPA 1925, s. 27, as amended by TLATA 1996, s. 25(1), Sch. 3, para. 8, p. 295, ante. On overreaching, see p. 293, post.

[1]   LPA 1925, s. 34(2), p. 301, ante.

[2]   P. 281, ante.

[3]   See *Williams & Glyn's Bank Ltd v Boland* [1979] Ch 312 at 330, [1979] 2 All ER 697 at 703–704, per Lord DENNING MR; *City of London Building Society v Flegg* [1988] AC 54, [1987] 3 All ER 271, p. 316, post.

[4]   *Caunce v Caunce* was disapproved in *Williams & Glyn's Bank Ltd v Boland* [1981] AC 487, [1980] 2 All ER 408: Lord SCARMAN at 511, at 418 'was by no means certain that *Caunce v Caunce* was rightly decided.' So too RUSSELL LJ in *Hodgson v Marks* [1971] Ch 892 at 924–925, [1971] 2 All ER 684 at 690. It was not followed in *Kingsnorth Finance Co Ltd v Tizard* [1986] 1 WLR 783, [1986] 2 All ER 54, p. 29, n. 7; ante. See the instructive decision of the Eire Supreme Court in *Northern Bank Ltd v Henry* [1981] IR 1 (noted *Emmet on Title*, para. 5.145) where a bank mortgagee from a husband was held to have constructive notice of resident wife's equitable interest: apart from a deeds registry search, it had made no enquiries or investigation of title. See also (1980) 15 Ir Jur 211 (R. A. Pearce).

situation, whether or not a purchaser is bound by the interest of the beneficial co-owner depends upon the application of the old doctrine of the bona fide purchaser without notice. If the bank had had notice, actual or constructive, of the wife's interest, the mortgage would have been subject to it.[5]

II. REGISTERED LAND

This type of situation arises in a different form in the case of registered land. Notice there is irrelevant; or should be. The question is whether the wife has an overriding interest under Land Registration Act 1925, section 70(1)(g) or under Land Registration Act 2002, Sch. 3, para. 2. Such an interest must be in the nature of a proprietary interest at the date of completion; and the spouse claiming it must be in actual occupation.[6]

F. Right of Occupation. Family Law Act 1996

A wife however has a further means of protection. She may rely, not upon her ownership, but upon the statutory right of occupation given to a spouse under the Family Law Act 1996, Part IV. This supersedes the Matrimonial Homes Act 1983, which had itself superseded Matrimonial Homes Act 1967.[7] She may protect the right against purchasers by registration of a land charge, Class F in the case of unregistered land. With registered land, the right must be protected by entry of a notice.[8] In these situations, that is to say, in respect of the statutory protection given to the wife under the Family Law Act 1996, all depends on following the correct procedure for protection. Failure to register or to protect by notice involves the loss of the right against a purchaser. But the loss of that right still leaves open any claim which the wife may have in respect of her beneficial ownership.

FAMILY LAW ACT 1996

30. Rights concerning matrimonial home where one spouse has no estate, etc.—
(1) This section applies if—
  (a) one spouse is entitled to occupy a dwelling-house by virtue of
    (i) a beneficial estate or interest or contract; or
    (ii) any enactment giving that spouse the right to remain in occupation; and
  (b) the other spouse is not so entitled.
  (2) Subject to the provisions of this Part, the spouse not so entitled has the following rights ('matrimonial home rights')—

---

[5]   *Kingsnorth Finance Co Ltd v Tizard*, supra.
[6]   *Williams & Glyn's Bank Ltd v Boland* [1980] AC 487 at 507, [1980] 2 All ER at 414, per Lord WILBERFORCE, p. 136, ante; LRA 2002, Schs. 1 and 3, p. 158, ante. Interests under a strict settlement can never be overriding interests: LRA 1925, s. 86(2); (1958) 22 Conv (NS) 14, at pp. 23–24 (F. R. Crane); p. 159, post.
[7]   The Act is based on the Law Commission Report on Domestic Violence and Occupation of the Family Home 1992 (Law Com No 207, HC 1). On the matrimonial home in registered land, see R & R, chap. 45.
[8]   It cannot be an overriding interest, even if the spouse is in actual occupation. The difference between a wife who has an equitable interest (protected as an overriding interest: *Williams & Glyn's Bank Ltd v Boland* [1981] AC 487, [1980] 2 All ER 408) and a wife who has only her rights of occupation under the Act is therefore considerable.

(a) if in occupation, a right not to be evicted or excluded from the dwelling-house or any part of it by the other spouse except with the leave of the court given by an order under section 33;

(b) if not in occupation, a right with the leave of the court so given to enter into and occupy the dwelling-house. [9]

(3) If a spouse is entitled under this section to occupy a dwelling-house or any part of a dwelling-house, any payment or tender made or other thing done by that spouse in or towards satisfaction of any liability of the other spouse in respect of rent, mortgage payments or other outgoings affecting the dwelling-house is, whether or not it is made or done in pursuance of an order under section 40, as good as if made or done by the other spouse.

(5) If a spouse ('the first spouse')—

(a) is entitled under this section to occupy a dwelling-house or any part of a dwelling-house, and

(b) makes any payment in or towards satisfaction of any liability of the other spouse ('the second spouse') in respect of mortgage payments affecting the dwelling-house,

the person to whom the payment is made may treat it as having been made by the second spouse, but the fact that that person has treated any such payment as having been so made does not affect any claim of the first spouse against the second spouse to an interest in the dwelling-house by virtue of the payment.

(6) If a spouse is entitled under this section to occupy a dwelling-house or part of a dwelling-house by reason of an interest of the other spouse under a trust, all the provisions of subsections (3) to (5) apply in relation to the trustees as they apply in relation to the other spouse.

(7) This section does not apply to a dwelling-house which has at no time been, and which was at no time intended by the spouses to be, a matrimonial home of theirs.

(8) A spouse's matrimonial home rights continue—

(a) only so long as the marriage subsists, except to the extent that an order under section 33(5) otherwise provides; and

(b) only so long as the other spouse is entitled as mentioned in subsection (1) to occupy the dwelling-house, except where provision is made by section 31 for those rights to be a charge on an estate or interest in the dwelling-house.

(9) It is hereby declared that a spouse—

(a) who has an equitable interest in a dwelling-house or in its proceeds of sale, but

(b) is not a spouse in whom there is vested (whether solely or as joint tenant) a legal estate in fee simple or a legal term of years absolute in the dwelling-house,

is to be treated only for the purpose of determining whether he has matrimonial home rights, as not being entitled to occupy the dwelling-house by virtue of that interest. [10]

---

[9]   *Watts v Waller* [1973] QB 153, [1972] 3 All ER 257 (spouse out of occupation can register before getting leave of court to re-enter); *Barnett v Hassett* [1981] 1 WLR 1385, [1982] 1 All ER 80 (spouse having no intention to occupy not permitted to register in attempt to freeze proceeds of intended sale).

[10]   For powers of the courts to make occupation orders, see ss. 33–41.

31. Effect of matrimonial home rights as charge on dwelling-house.—(1) Subsections (2) and (3) apply if, at any time during a marriage, one spouse is entitled to occupy a dwelling-house by virtue of a beneficial estate or interest.

(2) The other spouse's matrimonial home rights are a charge on the estate or interest.

(3) The charge created by subsection (2) has the same priority as if it were an equitable interest created at whichever is the latest of the following dates—

(a) the date on which the spouse so entitled acquires the estate or interest;

(b) the date of the marriage; and

(c) 1st January 1968 (the commencement date of the Matrimonial Homes Act 1967).

(4) Subsections (5) and (6) apply if, at any time when a spouse's matrimonial home rights are a charge on an interest of the other spouse under a trust, there are, apart from either of the spouses, no persons, living or unborn, who are or could become beneficiaries under the trust.

(5) The rights are a charge also on the estate or interest of the trustees for the other spouse.

(6) The charge created by subsection (5) has the same priority as if it were an equitable interest created (under powers overriding the trusts) on the date when it arises.

(7) In determining for the purposes of subsection (4) whether there are any persons who are not, but could become, beneficiaries under the trust, there is to be disregarded any potential exercise of a general power of appointment exercisable by either or both of the spouses alone (whether or not the exercise of it requires the consent of another person).

(8) Even though a spouse's matrimonial home rights are a charge on an estate or interest in the dwelling-house, those rights are brought to an end by—

(a) the death of the other spouse, or

(b) the termination (otherwise than by death) of the marriage,

unless the court directs otherwise by an order made under section 33(5).

(9) If—

(a) a spouse's matrimonial home rights are a charge on an estate or interest in the dwelling-house, and

(b) that estate or interest is surrendered to merge in some other estate or interest expectant on it in such circumstances that, but for the merger, the person taking the estate or interest would be bound by the charge,

the surrender has effect subject to the charge and the persons thereafter entitled to the other estate or interest are, for so long as the estate or interest surrendered would have endured if not so surrendered, to be treated for all purposes of this Part as deriving title to the other estate or interest under the other spouse or, as the case may be, under the trustees for the other spouse, by virtue of the surrender.

(10) If the title to the legal estate by virtue of which a spouse is entitled to occupy a dwelling-house (including any legal estate held by trustees for that spouse) is registered under the Land Registration Act 2002 or any enactment replaced by that Act—

(a) registration of a land charge affecting the dwelling-house by virtue of this Part is to be effected by registering a notice under that Act and

(b) a spouse's matrimonial home rights are not to be capable of falling within paragraph 2 of Schedule 1 or 3 to that Act. [11]

---

[11]   As amended by LRA 2002, s. 133, Sch. 11, para. 34(1), (2)(a), (b), ie the rights cannot be overriding interests.

(12) If—

(a) a spouse's matrimonial home rights are a charge on the estate of the other spouse or of trustees of the other spouse, and

(b) that estate is the subject of a mortgage,

then if, after the date of the creation of the mortgage ('the first mortgage'), the charge is registered under section 2 of the Land Charges Act 1972, the charge is, for the purposes of section 94 of the Law of Property Act 1925 [12] (which regulates the rights of mortgagees to make further advances ranking in priority to subsequent mortgages), to be deemed to be a mortgage subsequent in date to the first mortgage.

(13) It is hereby declared that a charge under subsection (2) or (5) is not registrable under subsection (10) or under section 2 of the Land Charges Act 1972 unless it is a charge on a legal estate.

54. Dwelling-house subject to mortgage.—(1) In determining for the purposes of this Part whether a person is entitled to occupy a dwelling-house by virtue of an estate or interest, any right to possession of the dwelling-house conferred on a mortgagee of the dwelling-house under or by virtue of his mortgage is to be disregarded.

(2) Subsection (1) applies whether or not the mortgagee is in possession.

SCHEDULE 4

Release of matrimonial home rights

5.—(1) A spouse entitled to matrimonial home rights may by a release in writing release those rights or release them as respect part only of the dwelling-house affected by them. [13]

Postponement of priority of charge

6. —A spouse entitled by virtue of section 31 to a charge on an estate or interest may agree in writing that any other charge on, or interest in, that estate or interest shall rank in priority to the charge to which that spouse is so entitled.

INSOLVENCY ACT 1986

336. Rights of occupation etc. of bankrupt's spouse. —(2) Where a spouse's matrimonial home rights under the Act of 1996 are a charge on the estate or interest of the other spouse, or of trustees for the other spouse, and the other spouse is adjudged bankrupt —

(*a*) the charge continues to subsist notwithstanding the bankruptcy and, subject to the provisions of that Act, binds the trustee of the bankrupt's estate and persons deriving title under that trustee, and

(*b*) any application for an order under section 33 of that Act [14] shall be made to the court having jurisdiction in relation to the bankruptcy.

---

[12]   P. 918, post.
[13]   *Holmes v H Kennard & Son* (1984) 49 P & CR 202; [1985] Conv 293 (N. S. Price), where purchaser's solicitors were held liable in negligence for failure to obtain release of vendor's wife's right of occupation by correct conveyancing procedure.
[14]   As amended by TLATA 1996, s. 25(2), Sch. 4; Sch.8, para. 57(3), (4).

(4) On such an application as is mentioned in subsection (2) the court shall make such order under section 33 of the Act of 1996 as it thinks just and reasonable having regard to —

(*a*) the interests of the bankrupt's creditors,

(*b*) the conduct of the spouse or former spouse, so far as contributing to the bankruptcy,

(*c*) the needs and financial resources of the spouse or former spouse,

(*d*) the needs of any children, and

(*e*) all the circumstances of the case other than the needs of the bankrupt.

(5) Where such an application is made after the end of the period of one year beginning with the first vesting under Chapter IV of this Part of the bankrupt's estate in a trustee, the court shall assume, unless the circumstances of the case are exceptional, that the interests of the bankrupt's creditors outweigh all other considerations.

IV. Legal Estate in Two Persons with Beneficial Interest in One or More

Where the legal estate in land is held by two trustees for sale, but the beneficial interest is held by at least one person who is not a trustee, a difficult problem arises when the land is sold or mortgaged by the two trustees, and the purchase or mortgage money is paid to them. If a beneficiary is in possession or in actual occupation at the time of the sale or mortgage, can he prevent the sale or mortgage without giving his consent; or can the purchaser or mortgagee claim that the overreaching provisions apply and that, by paying the moneys to the two trustees of the legal estate, he can overreach and take free from the beneficial interest?

In *City of London Building Society v Flegg* [1988] AC 54, [1987] 3 All ER 435, the House of Lords reversed the Court of Appeal [1986] Ch 605, [1986] 1 All ER 989 and decided the issue in favour of a mortgagee of registered land. In 1989 the Law Commission in its Report on Overreaching: Beneficiaries (Law Com No. 188) had recommended that the interest of an adult beneficiary of full capacity who has a right to occupy trust land and is in actual occupation of it should only be overreached if he consents; in effect reversing the decision of the House of Lords. [15] The recommendation was not followed in the Trusts of Land and Appointment of Trustees Act 1996.

A. Overreaching and Overriding

CITY OF LONDON BUILDING SOCIETY v FLEGG

[1988] AC 54, [1987] 3 All ER 435 (HL, Lords BRIDGE OF HARWICH, TEMPLEMAN, MACKAY OF CLASHFERN, OLIVER OF AYLMERTON and GOFF OF CHIEVELEY) [16]

LORD TEMPLEMAN: My Lords, the appellants, City of London Building Society, are the mortgagees under a charge by way of legal mortgage of registered land held at the date of the charge by two trustees upon trust for sale and to stand possessed

---

[15]   [1990] CLJ 277 at pp. 311–333 (C. Harpum); (1988) 104 LQR 367 (S. Gardner).
[16]   [1987] All ER Rev 149 (P. J. Clarke); (1988) 51 MLR 365 (S. Gardner); [1988] Conv 108 (M. P. Thompson), 141 (P. Sparkes).

of the net proceeds of sale and rents and profits until sale upon trust for four tenants in common including the respondents, Mr and Mrs Flegg. The legal charge was entered into by the trustees in breach of trust, although the appellants were unaware of this. The respondents who were in actual occupation of the mortgaged land claim that the appellants' legal charge is subject to the respondents' overriding interest. The Court of Appeal declined to order the respondents to deliver up possession of the land to the appellants; hence this appeal.

By a conveyance dated 18 October 1977 the land appropriately named Bleak House was conveyed to Mr and Mrs Maxwell-Brown in fee simple upon trust for sale and to stand possessed of the net proceeds of sale and rents and profits until sale upon trust for the Maxwell-Browns as joint tenants. In fact, the purchase price paid by the Maxwell-Browns for Bleak House, amounting to £34,000, had been provided as to £18,000 or more by the respondents who were the parents of Mrs Maxwell-Brown. In consequence and notwithstanding the express trusts set out in the conveyance, Bleak House was held by the Maxwell-Browns on trust for sale and to stand possessed of the net proceeds of sale and rents and profits until sale upon trust for the Maxwell-Browns and the respondents as tenants in common in the proportions in which they had respectively contributed to the purchase price. The respondents were entitled to occupy Bleak House together with the Maxwell-Browns as tenants in common under the trust for sale and all four beneficiaries duly went into occupation.

By a legal charge by way of mortgage dated 8 January 1982 the Maxwell-Browns charged Bleak House to secure £37,500 advanced by the appellants to the Maxwell-Browns. The respondents knew nothing of the legal charge which was granted by the Maxwell-Browns for their own purposes and in breach of trust. The appellants knew nothing of the respondents.

By section 27 of the Law of Property Act 1925 (as amended by the Law of Property (Amendment) Act 1926, Schedule): [17]

'(1) A purchaser of a legal estate from trustees for sale shall not be concerned with the trusts affecting the proceeds of sale of land subject to a trust for sale .... or affecting the rents and profits of the land until sale ... (2) Notwithstanding anything to the contrary in the instrument (if any) creating a trust for sale of land or in the settlement of the net proceeds, the proceeds of sale or other capital money shall not be paid to or applied by the direction of fewer than two persons as trustees for sale, except where the trustee is a trust corporation ...'....

[His Lordship read section 28(1) of the Law of Property Act 1925 and section 17 of the Trustee Act 1925, and continued:]

Thus the appellants advancing money in good faith to two trustees for sale on the security of a charge by way of legal mortgage of Bleak House were not concerned with the trusts affecting the proceeds of sale of Bleak House or with the propriety of the trustees entering into the legal charge. As a result of the legal charge the interests of the beneficiaries in Bleak House pending sale were transferred to the equity of redemption vested in the Maxwell-Browns and to the sum of £37,500 received by the Maxwell-Browns from the appellants in consideration for the grant of the legal charge. The Maxwell-Browns did not account to the respondents for any part of the sum of £37,500 and defaulted in the performance of their obligations to the appellants under the legal charge. The appellants seek possession of Bleak House with a view to enforcing its security.

[17] And now amended by TLATA 1996, s. 25(1), Sch. 3, para. 8.

The respondents resist the claim of the appellants to possession of Bleak House and rely on section 14 of the Law of Property Act 1925. Sections 27 and 28 of that Act which overreach the interests of the respondents under the trust for sale of Bleak House are to be found in Part I of the Act. Section 14 provides:

'This Part of this Act shall not prejudicially affect the interest of any person in possession or in actual occupation of land to which he may be entitled in right of such possession or occupation.'

The respondents were in actual occupation of Bleak House at the date of the legal charge. It is argued that their beneficial interests under the trust for sale were not overreached by the legal charge or that the respondents were entitled to remain in occupation after the legal charge and against the appellants despite the overreaching of their interests.

My Lords, the respondents were entitled to occupy Bleak House by virtue of their beneficial interests in Bleak House and its rents and profits pending the execution of the trust for sale. Their beneficial interests were overreached by the legal charge and were transferred to the equity of redemption held by the Maxwell-Browns and to the sum advanced by the appellants in consideration of the grant of the legal charge and received by the Maxwell-Browns. After the legal charge the respondents were only entitled to continue in occupation of Bleak House by virtue of their beneficial interests in the equity of redemption of Bleak House and that equity of redemption is subject to the right of the appellants as mortgagees to take possession. . . .

It follows that when the legal charge in the present case is registered, the appellants will take free from all the interests of the beneficiaries interested under the trust for sale in the proceeds of sale and rents and profits until sale of Bleak House but subject to any overriding interest.

Section 70(1) of the Land Registration Act 1925 defines overriding interests which include:

'(g) The rights of every person in actual occupation of the land or in receipt of the rents and profits thereof, save where inquiry is made of such person and the rights are not disclosed; . . .'

In my view the object of section 70 was to reproduce for registered land the same limitations as section 14 of the Law of Property Act 1925 produced for land whether registered or unregistered. The respondents claim to be entitled to overriding interests because they were in actual occupation of Bleak House on the date of the legal charge. But the interests of the respondents cannot at one and the same time be overreached and overridden and at the same time be overriding interests. The appellants cannot at one and the same time take free from all the interests of the respondents yet at the same time be subject to some of those interests. The right of the respondents to be and remain in actual occupation of Bleak House ceased when the respondents' interests were overreached by the legal charge save in so far as their rights were transferred to the equity of redemption. As persons interested under the trust for sale the respondents had no right to possession as against the appellants and the fact that the respondents were in actual occupation at the date of the legal charge did not create a new right or transfer an old right so as to make the right enforceable against the appellants.

One of the main objects of the legislation of 1925 was to effect a compromise between on the one hand the interests of the public in securing that land held in trust is freely marketable and, on the other hand, the interests of the beneficiaries in preserving their rights under the trusts. By the Settled Land Act 1925 a tenant for life may convey the settled land discharged from all the trusts powers and provisions of the settlement. By the Law of Property Act 1925 trustees for sale may convey land held on trust for sale discharged from the trusts affecting the proceeds of sale and rents and profits until sale. Under both forms of trust the protection and the only protection of the beneficiaries is that capital money must be paid to at least two trustees or a trust corporation. Section 14 of the Law of Property Act 1925 and section 70 of the Land Registration Act 1925 cannot have been intended to frustrate this compromise and to subject the purchaser to some beneficial interests but not others depending on the waywardness of actual occupation. The Court of Appeal took a different view, largely in reliance on the decision of this House in *Williams & Glyn's Bank Ltd v Boland* [1981] AC 487, [1980] 2 All ER 408, p. 136, ante. In that case the sole proprietor of registered land held the land as sole trustee upon trust for sale and to stand possessed of the net proceeds of sale and rents and profits until sale upon trust for himself and his wife as tenants in common. This House held that the wife's beneficial interest coupled with actual possession by her constituted an overriding interest and that a mortgagee from the husband, despite the concluding words of section 20(1), took subject to the wife's overriding interest. But in that case the interest of the wife was not overreached or overridden because the mortgagee advanced capital moneys to a sole trustee. If the wife's interest had been overreached by the mortgagee advancing capital moneys to two trustees there would have been nothing to justify the wife in remaining in occupation as against the mortgagee. There must be a combination of an interest which justifies continuing occupation plus actual occupation to constitute an overriding interest. Actual occupation is not an interest in itself.

For these reasons and for the reasons to be given by my noble and learned friend, Lord Oliver of Aylmerton, I would allow this appeal and restore the order of Judge Thomas who ordered the respondents to deliver up Bleak House to the appellants.

LORD OLIVER OF AYLMERTON: Considered in the context of a transaction complying with the statutory requirements of the Law of Property Act 1925 the question of the effect of section 70(1)(g) of the Land Registration Act 1925 must, in my judgment, be approached by asking first what are the 'rights' of the person in occupation and whether they are, at the material time, subsisting in reference to the land. In the instant case the exercise by the registered proprietors of the powers conferred on trustees for sale by section 28(1) of the Law of Property Act 1925 had the effect of overreaching the interests of the respondents under the statutory trusts upon which depended their right to continue in occupation of the land. The appellants took free from those trusts (section 27) and were not, in any event, concerned to see that the respondents' consent to the transaction was obtained (section 26). If, then, one asks what were the subsisting rights of the respondents referable to their occupation, the answer must, in my judgment, be that they were rights which, vis-à-vis the appellants, were, eo instante with the creation of the charge, overreached and therefore subsisted only in relation to the equity of redemption. I do not, for my part, find in *Boland's* case anything which compels a contrary conclusion. Granted that the interest of a co-owner pending the execution of the statutory trust for sale is, despite the equitable doctrine of conversion, an interest subsisting in reference to the land the subject matter of the trust and granted also that *Boland's* case establishes that such an interest, although falling within the definition of minor interest and so liable to be overridden by a registered disposition, will, so long as it subsists, be elevated to the status of an overriding interest if there exists also the additional element of occupation by the co-owner, I cannot for my part accept that, once what I may call the parent interest, by which alone the occupation can be justified, has been overreached and thus subordinated to a legal estate properly created by the trustees under their statutory powers, it can, in relation to the proprietor of the legal estate so created, be any longer said to be a right 'for the time being subsisting.' Section 70(1)(g) protects only the rights in reference to the land of the occupier whatever they are at the material time – in the instant case the right to enjoy in specie the rents and profits of the land held in trust for him. Once the beneficiary's rights have been shifted from the land to capital moneys in the hands of the trustees, there is no longer an interest in the land to which the occupation can be referred or which it can protect. If the trustees sell in accordance with the statutory provisions and so overreach the beneficial interests in reference to the land, nothing remains to which a right of occupation can attach and the same result must, in my judgment, follow vis-à-vis a chargee by way of legal mortgage so long as the transaction is carried out in the manner prescribed by the Law of Property Act 1925, overreaching the beneficial interests by subordinating them to the estate of the chargee which is no longer 'affected' by them so as to become subject to them on registration pursuant to section 20(1) of the Land Registration Act 1925. In the instant case, therefore, I would for my part, hold that the charge created in favour of the appellants overreached the beneficial interests of the respondents and that there is nothing in section 70(1)(g) of the Land Registration Act 1925 or in *Boland's* case which has the effect of preserving against the appellants any rights of the respondents to occupy the land by virtue of their beneficial interests in the equity of redemption which remains vested in the trustees.

In **Birmingham Midshire's Mortgage Services Ltd v Sabherwal** (2000) 80 P & CR 256,[18] the two sons of Mrs Sabherwal were the registered owners of a house in Gerard's Cross. They had borrowed £225,000 from Midshire's Mortgage Services Ltd secured on the house. Mrs Sabherwal had a significant equitable interest under a common intention constructive trust, or by way of proprietary estoppel (the sons had told their mother that she would always have a roof over her head). She was in actual occupation of the house under section 70(1)(g) of the Land Registration Act 1925. The sons defaulted on the loan.

The question was whether the lender had overreached the equitable interests of Mrs Sabherwal. In holding that it had, the Court of Appeal held that *City London Building Society v Flegg* had not been affected by the Trusts of Land and Appointment of Trustees Act 1996. WALKER LJ said at 260:

'22. The judge gave ten reasons for concluding that the decision in *Flegg* has not been affected by the 1996 Act. Since that conclusion is not directly challenged in this court, at any rate on the grounds that the judge considered, it is sufficient to mention three of the most cogent of his reasons. First, the overreaching effect of the legal charges took place when they were executed in July 1990, and cannot be ousted by the coming into force of the 1996 Act over six years later. Second, the 1996 Act contains nothing to exclude the essential overreaching provision contained in section 2(1)(ii) of the Law of Property Act 1925.[19] On the contrary,

---

[18]   (2000) 116 LQR 341 (C. Harpum); [2000] Conv 267 (M. Dixon); [2001] Conv 221 (G. Ferris and G. Battersby).
[19]   P. 293, ante.

that provision is amended so as to meet the new terminology of the 1996 Act (see section 25(1) and Schedule 3 paragraph 4(1)) and so is in effect confirmed, with that new terminology, by the 1996 Act. Third, the abolition of the doctrine of conversion (by section 3 of the 1996 Act[20]) is irrelevant for reasons stated by Lord Oliver in *Flegg* (see p. 90G–H)[1]. However, the abolition of that doctrine does explain the amendment of s. 27(1) of the Law of Property Act 1925, on which some reliance has been placed.

23. Instead in this court Mr Marc Beaumont (for Mrs Sabherwal) has in his skeleton argument (in amplification of a very terse notice of appeal) sought to distinguish *Flegg* on two grounds. The first is based on proprietary estoppel. The second is based on Article 8 of the European Convention of Human Rights. The first of these grounds was not argued before the judge but this court has (perhaps over-indulgently) permitted the point to be argued, on the footing that no further findings of fact are required.

24. On the facts of this case, Mrs Sabherwal plainly made a substantial financial contribution to all the properties successively owned by the family. She could rely on a resulting trust and had no need to rely on proprietary estoppel (if and so far as the two are, in the context of the family home, distinct doctrines: see the observations of Sir Nicolas Browne-Wilkinson V.-C. in *Grant v Edwards* [1986] Ch. 638, 656, [1985] 2 All ER 426, 438). If she had made no financial contribution, but had nevertheless acted to her detriment in reliance on her sons' promises, she might have obtained (through the medium of estoppel rather than through the medium of a trust) equitable rights of a proprietary nature. Her actual occupation of the house would then have promoted those rights into an overriding interest. That, I think, is not conceded by counsel for the respondents but I assume that to be the case. On that basis, it would have been a remarkable result if those more precarious rights were incapable of being overreached, on a sale by trustees, under section 2(1)(ii) of the Law of Property Act 1925.

25. Mr Beaumont has however contended for that result, citing what Lord Wilberforce said in *Shiloh Spinners v Harding* [1973] AC 691, at 721 [1973] 1 All ER 90, at 99:

"All this seems to show that there may well be rights, of an equitable character, outside the provisions as to registration and which are incapable of being overreached."

26. Lord Wilberforce had just before referred to *ER Ives Investment Ltd v High* [1967] 2 QB 379, [1967] 1 All ER 504. In that case a boundary dispute between neighbours had been settled by an informal agreement including the grant of a right of way. The agreement about the right of way was never completed by a deed of grant, and was never registered. The Court of Appeal held that it was binding despite the lack of registration. Similarly, *Shiloh Spinners v Harding* was concerned with an equitable right of entry for enforcement of a covenant arising in what Lord Wilberforce called a "dispute ... of a commonplace character between neighbours".

27. Equitable interests of that character ought not to be overreached, since they are rights which an adjoining owner enjoys over the land itself, regardless of its ownership from time to time. The principle is in my view correctly stated in Megarry and Wade, *The Law of Real Property* 5th ed. p. 409:

"In fact the only examples of such equities likely to occur are commercial (as opposed to family) interests, which it is absurd to speak of overreaching.

---

[20]   P. 220, ante.
[1]   P. 295, post.

Two instances are an equitable right of way which is yet not an equitable easement, and an equitable right of entry to secure performance of a covenant, and there are probably others. To overreach such interests is to destroy them ..."

28. The footnotes to this passage refer to *ER Ives Investment Ltd v High* and *Shiloh Spinners v Harding* (cases which were cited to the House of Lords in *Flegg* – see especially counsel's argument at p. 63 – but are not referred to in any of the speeches of their Lordships). The essential distinction is, as the authors of Megarry and Wade note, between commercial and family interests. An equitable easement or an equitable right of entry cannot sensibly shift from the land affected by it to the proceeds of sale. An equitable interest as a tenant in common can do so, even if accompanied by the promise of a home for life, since the proceeds of sale can be used to acquire another home.

29. Mr Beaumont has also argued that, although in *Grant v Edwards* the Vice-Chancellor regarded interests in the family home created by equitable estoppel or by a constructive trust as closely similar, if not interchangeable, his remarks do not apply to a resulting trust arising from a monetary contribution. This is an area of the law in which the terminology is unfortunately far from uniform, but I do not accept that the Vice-Chancellor's remarks were limited in that way. On the contrary, immediately after his reference to proprietary estoppel he said (see [1986] Ch. at 657H–658A):

30. "Identifiable contributions to the purchase [price] of the house will of course be an important factor in many cases."

31. Similarly, in *Lloyds Bank v Rosset* [1991] 1 AC 107, [1990] 1 All ER 1111 Lord Bridge (in a very well-known passage at pp. 132–133, at pp. 1118–1119) referred to "direct contributions to the purchase price by [a party] who is not the legal owner", as readily justifying the creation of a constructive trust. Such a trust, however labelled, does not then leave room for a separate interest by way of equitable estoppel: compare the remarks of Morritt LJ in *Lloyds Bank v Carrick* [1996] 4 All ER 630 at p. 639C–E. To do so would cause vast confusion in an area which is already quite difficult enough. The confusion is avoided if what Lord Wilberforce said in *Shiloh Spinners v Harding* is limited, as in my judgment it must be, to some unusual types of equitable interest arising in commercial situations. In this type of family situation, the concepts of trust and equitable estoppel are almost interchangeable, and both are affected in the same way by the statutory mechanism of overreaching, the substance of which is not affected by the 1996 Act.

32. In these circumstances I do not find it necessary to consider how far the judge's findings in this area (which were largely limited to a general acceptance of Mrs Sabherwal's evidence) would establish the necessary conditions for proprietary estoppel. I assume in favour of Mrs Sabherwal that they would do so.'

[His Lordship held that Article 8 of the Human Rights Act 1988 was of no assistance.]

B. No Advance of Capital Money

In **State Bank of India v Sood** [1997] 2 WLR 421, [1997] 1 All ER 169,[2] PETER GIBSON LJ, in holding that the interests of beneficiaries were overreached even when no capital money had been advanced at the time when the mortgage was created, said at 424, at 172:

---

[2]   [1997] CLJ 494 (M. Oldham); [1997] Conv 134 (M. P. Thompson).

'Before I turn to the statutory provisions, I would make a few general observations on overreaching. As is explained by Charles Harpum in his illuminating article, "Overreaching, Trustees' Powers and the Reform of the 1925 Legislation" [1990] CLJ 277, overreaching is the process whereby existing interests are subordinated to a later interest or estate created pursuant to a trust or power. Mr Harpum arrived at that statement of the true nature of overreaching by a consideration of the effect of the exercise of powers of disposition in a settlement, referring to *Sugden on Powers*, 8th edn. (1861), pp. 482, 483. He argued cogently that a transaction made by a person within the dispositive powers conferred upon him will overreach equitable interests in the property the subject of the disposition, but ultra vires dispositions will not, and the transferee with notice will take the property subject to those interests. Mr Harpum expressed the view that the exercise intra vires of a power of disposition which does not give rise to any capital money, such as an exchange of land, overreaches just as much as a transaction which does. There is every reason to think that the draftsman of the 1925 property legislation fully appreciated the true nature of overreaching. A principal objective of the 1925 property legislation was to simplify conveyancing and the proof of title to land. To this end equitable interests were to be kept off the title to the legal estate and could be overreached on a conveyance to a purchaser who took free of them.

The statutory provision governing overreaching is section 2 of the Law of Property Act 1925 (p. 293, ante): ...

Much though I value the principle of overreaching as having aided the simplification of conveyancing, I cannot pretend that I regard the resulting position in the present case as entirely satisfactory. The safeguard for beneficiaries under the existing legislation is largely limited to having two trustees or a trust corporation where capital money falls to be received. But that is no safeguard at all, as this case has shown, when no capital money is received on and contemporaneously with the conveyance.

Further, even when it is received by two trustees as in *City of London Building Society v Flegg* [1986] Ch 605; revsd [1988] AC 54, it might be thought that beneficiaries in occupation are insufficiently protected. Hence the recommendation for reform in the Law Commission's report, "Transfer of Land, Overreaching: Beneficiaries in Occupation" (1989) Law Com No 188, that a conveyance should not overreach the interest of a sui juris beneficiary in occupation unless he gives his consent. Mr Harpum in the article to which reference has been made proposed an alternative reform, limiting the power of trustees to mortgage. Whether the legislature will reform the law remains to be seen. I should add for completeness that we were assured by counsel that the recent Trusts of Land and Appointment of Trustees Act 1996 was of no assistance and we have not considered its effect.'

QUESTIONS

1. Can land be made inalienable under the Trusts of Land and Appointment of Trustees Act 1996? Can a settlor of an express trust of land exclude the power of sale? TLATA 1996, s. 8(1); p.273, ante; [1997] Conv 263 (G. Watt). Can an argument be made on the basis of decisions on conditions which restrain alienation: *Re Brown* [1954] Ch 39, [1953] 2 All ER 1342, p. 9, ante?

2. What considerations should a settlor have in mind when creating a trust of land under the Act?
   Barraclough and Matthews: *A Practitioner's Guide to the Trusts of Land and Appointment of Trustees Act 1996*, chap 12, especially pp. 139–140, and

Precedents in Appendix 8; Kenny and Kenny, *The Trusts of Land and Appointment of Trustees Act 1996*, Part II, especially paras. 9.1 to 9.5; Sydenham, *Trusts of Land —The New Law*, pp. 136–138 and Precedents pp. 139–155; Whitehouse and Hassall: *The Trusts of Land and Appointment of Trustees Act 1996: A Practical Guide*, Part IV (Precedents).

3.   Is the exercise of powers conferred on trustees of land under section 6 subject to the rule against perpetuities? P & AA 1964, s. 8 (1); *Emmet on Title*, para. 22.032.

4.   In view of *City of London Building Society v Flegg* [1988] AC 54, [1987] 3 All ER 435 and *State Bank of India v Sood* [1997] 2 WLR 421, [1997] 1 All ER 169, do you think that overreaching gives sufficient protection to beneficiaries?

5.   How far can a strict settlement be reproduced today: Law Commission Report on Trusts of Land, 1989 (Law Com No. 181), para. 4.5; W & H, paras. 2.11–2.17.

6.   Consider the difficulties arising from the registrability of Class F land charges in *Wroth v Tyler* [1974] Ch 30, [1973] 1 All ER 897, p. 66, ante; *Watts v Waller* [1973] QB 153, [1972] 3 All ER 257; and in *Barnett v Hassett* [1981] 1 WLR 1385, [1982] 1 All ER 80. Do you think that registration is a suitable mechanism for the protection of interests of a family character? Cretney and Masson, *Principles of Family Law* (6th edn.), pp. 187–189; Barnsley, *Conveyancing Law and Practice* (7th edn.), para. 6.008; [1974] 38 Conv (NS) 110; (1975) 39 Conv (NS) 78 (D. J. Hayton); [1974] CLP 76 (D. G. Barnsley); [1976] CLP 26 at pp. 31–33, 43–50 (D. J. Hayton).

6. Strict Settlements [1]

Under the Trusts of Land and Appointment of Trustees Act 1996, no new strict settlements can be created or be deemed to be made after 1996. [2] However, existing strict settlements remain, and where a settlement exists on 1 January 1997, any later resettlement creates a new settlement. The settlement comes to an end when there is no longer any land or heirlooms subject to it. The strict settlement is being phased out, but it will be a long time before it finally disappears. It is therefore essential to know whether a pre-1997 instrument has created a strict settlement.

A settlement exists whenever successive interests exist in land (not being land held upon trust for sale). Successive interests are interests less than a fee simple, and cannot exist as legal estates. They are therefore equitable interests, existing behind a trust. These elementary propositions are the key to understanding the definition of a settlement for the purposes of the Settled Land Act 1925. With a single exception, it will be seen that the definition in section 1 includes an element of successive ownership. The exception is the case where land is held by a minor; the Settled Land Act machinery is then imposed in order to make possible dealings with the legal estate.

It should also be noted that by virtue of subsection 7 of section 1, settlements and trusts for sale are alternatives.

Under a strict settlement the life tenant is master in his own house. The legal title is vested in him by statute; and he alone has the power to sell and to manage the land. His powers are indefeasible, inalienable and fiduciary.

---

[1]   C & B, pp. 69–80, 95–96, 188–215, 882–884, 893; Gray, pp. 646–653; M & W, paras. 8.001–8.004, 8.011, 8.108–8.168; MM, pp. 6–7, 247–302; Harvey, *Settlements of Land* (1973); Arnold, *The Settled Land Acts* (1937); Bonfield, *Marriage Settlements 1601–1740* (1983); English and Saville, *Strict Settlement* (1983); and essays in Rubin and Sugarman, *Law, Economy and Society* (1984) at pp. 1–123 (D. Sugarman and G.R. Rubin), 124–167 (M.R. Chesterman), 168–191 (E. Spring) and 209–210 (B. English); Spring, *Strict Settlement, Role in History* (1989) EHR 454; Spring, *Law, Land and Family* (1997); (1998) 61 MLR 162 (A. Pottage).

[2]   TLATA 1996, s. 2 and Sch. 1, p. 268, ante.

I. Definition of a Settlement under the Settled Land Act 1925[3]

SETTLED LAND ACT 1925

1. What constitutes a settlement.—(1) Any deed, will, agreement for a settlement or other agreement,[4] Act of Parliament, or other instrument,[5] or any number of instruments, whether made or passed before or after, or partly before and partly after, the commencement of this Act, under or by virtue of which instrument or instruments any land, after the commencement of this Act, stands for the time being—

  (i)   limited in trust[6] for any persons by way of succession; or

  (ii) limited in trust for any person in possession—

    (a) for an entailed interest whether or not capable of being barred or defeated;[7]

    (b) for an estate in fee simple or for a term of years absolute subject to an executory limitation, gift, or disposition over on failure of his issue or in any other event;

    (c) for a base or determinable fee (other than a fee simple absolute by virtue of section 7 of the Law of Property Act 1925)[8] or any corresponding interest in leasehold land;

    (d) being an infant, for an estate in fee simple or for a term of years absolute,[9] or

  (iii) limited in trust for any person for an estate in fee simple or for a term of years absolute contingently on the happening of any event; or ....

  (v)   charged, whether voluntarily or in consideration of marriage or by way of family arrangement, and whether immediately or after an interval, with the payment of any rentcharge for the life of any person, or any less period,[10] or

---

3   C & B, pp. 188–191; Gray, pp. 646–648; M & W, paras. 8.047–8.057; MM, pp. 252–255.

4   *Bacon v Bacon* [1947] P 151, [1947] 2 All ER 327 (a separation agreement giving the wife the right to remain in the house for her life).

5   *Martin v Martin* [1978] Fam 12, [1977] 3 All ER 762; [1978] Conv 229 (P. Smith); *Griffiths v Williams* (1977) 248 EG 947, p. 673, post.

6   It need not be expressly limited. The trust may arise by operation of law, as, for instance, where there is a constructive trust under which the court gives protection to a licensee for the period of his life: pp. 615–622, post: *Bannister v Bannister* [1948] 2 All ER 133, p. 615; post; *Binions v Evans* [1972] Ch 359, [1972] 2 All ER 70, p, 617, post (Lord DENNING MR dissented on this point at 366, at 74); *Ungurian v Lesnoff* [1990] Ch 206; especially at p. 224, per VINELOTT J [1990] CLJ 25 (M. Oldham); [1990] Conv 223 (P. Sparkes); [1991] Conv 596 (J. Hill); *Costello v Costello* (1994) 70 P & CR 297; [1994] Conv 391 (M.P. Thompson). See now TLATA 1996, s. 2, p. 267, post; cf. *Ivory v Palmer* [1975] ICR 340; *Dent v Dent* [1996] 1 WLR 683 [1996] 1 All ER 659; [1996] All ER Rev. 258 (P.J. Clarke). See Harvey, pp. 54, 82 et seq.; *Emmet on Title*, para. 22.004; (1977) 93 LQR 561 (J.A. Hornby). On avoidance of an unintentional creation of a strict settlement in this situation, see *Griffiths v Williams* (1977) 248 EG 947, p. 673, post; [1978] Conv 250. For similar problems arising in connection with settlements on divorce, see p. 340, n. 11, post. See also Law Commission Report on Trusts of Land 1989 (Law Com No. 118), para 4.2.

7   For the effect of a purported entailed interest after 1996, see TLATA 1996, s. 2, Sch. 1, para. 5, p. 13, ante.

8   As added by TLATA 1996, s. 25(1), Sch. 3, para. 2(2).

9   For the effect of a conveyance of a legal estate to a minor after 1996, see TLATA 1996, s. 2, Sch. 1, para. 1.

10   See *Re Austen* [1929] 2 Ch 155. See also AJA 1982, s. 22, which provides that in the case of a will of a testator who dies after 1982, there is a rebuttable presumption that 'if a testator devises or bequeaths property to his spouse in terms which in themselves would give an absolute interest to the spouse, but by the same instrument purports to give his issue an interest in the same property, the gift to the spouse is absolute notwithstanding the purported gift to the issue.' This was recommended by the Law Reform Committee on the Interpretation of Wills 1973 (Cmnd 5301).

of any capital, annual, or periodical sums for the portions, advancement, maintenance, or otherwise for the benefit of any persons, with or without any term of years for securing or raising the same, [11]

creates or is for the purposes of this Act a settlement and is in this Act referred to as a settlement, or as the settlement, as the case requires;

Provided that, where land is the subject of a compound settlement, references in this Act to the settlement shall be construed as meaning such compound settlement, unless the context otherwise requires.

(2) Where an infant is beneficially entitled to land for an estate in fee simple or for a term of years absolute and by reason of an intestacy or otherwise there is no instrument under which the interest of an infant arises or is acquired, a settlement shall be deemed to have been made by the intestate, or by the person whose interest the infant has acquired.

(4) An estate or interest not disposed of by a settlement and remaining in or reverting to the settlor, or any person deriving title under him, is for the purposes of this Act an estate or interest comprised in the subject of the settlement and coming to the settlor or such person under or by virtue of the settlement.

(5) Where —

(a) a settlement creates an entailed interest which is incapable of being barred or defeated, or a base or determinable fee, whether or not the reversion or right of reverter is in the Crown, or any corresponding interest in leasehold land; or

(b) the subject of a settlement is an entailed interest, or a base or determinable fee, whether or not the reversion or right of reverter is in the Crown, or any corresponding interest in leasehold land;

the reversion or right of reverter upon the cesser of the interest so created or settled shall be deemed to be an interest comprised in the subject of the settlement, and limited by the settlement.

(6) Subsections (4) and (5) of this section bind the Crown.

(7) This section does not apply to land held upon trust for sale. [12]

2. What is settled land.—Land which is or is deemed to be the subject of a settlement is for the purposes of this Act settled land, and is in relation to the settlement referred to in this Act as the settled land.

The Law of Property (Amendment) Act 1926, Schedule, amending Law of Property Act 1925, section 7(1), provides that 'a fee simple subject to a legal or equitable right of entry or re-entry is for the purposes of this Act a fee simple absolute.' [13]

Other types of settlement also arise:

i. Compound settlements: [14] Where new trusts are declared of land which is already subject to a settlement, as, for example, where a settlement is followed by

[11]   For the effect of a family charge after 1996, see TLATA 1996, s. 2, Sch. 1, para. 3.
[12]   Sub-s. 7 was added by LP(A)A 1926, Sch.
[13]   See p. 7, n. 4, ante, where this amendment is commented upon.
[14]   C & B, pp. 209–211; M & W, paras. 8.069–8.070.

a resettlement, the land is subject to a compound settlement. Normally the same person would be tenant for life under both settlements; but, even if he was tenant for life under the resettlement only, he could act as tenant for life under the compound settlement. The Settled Land Act 1925, section 31(1) [15] provides that the trustees of the original settlement or, if there are none, [16] the trustees of the resettlement shall be trustees of the compound settlement.

ii. Referential settlements: i.e. a settlement which incorporates by reference an earlier settlement. [17]

iii. Derivative settlements: i.e. a settlement which is created out of the beneficial interest of one of the beneficiaries of another settlement.

In **Re Ogle's Settled Estates** [1927] 1 Ch 229, ROMER J held that where the owner of an estate subject to family charges sold plots subject to the charges, the land retained and the plots sold were subject to separate settlements. ROMER J said at 232:

'In some parts of the Act no doubt "settlement" means merely the document or documents creating the settlement: see, for example, sections 1 subsection 4, 47 and 64. But in general a settlement, for the purposes of the Act, is a state of affairs in relation to certain land, brought about, or deemed to have been brought about by one or more documents, the particular state of affairs being one or more of those specified in subsections (i) to (v) of section 1 subsection 1. A document may, therefore, create more than one settlement. If by means of one and the same document, Blackacre and Whiteacre stand limited in trust for A and his children, in strict succession, and for B and his children in strict succession respectively, there are two settlements.'

II. Machinery. The Curtain Principle [18]

The Settled Land Act 1925 introduced the 'curtain principle', shutting off the purchaser's view of matters which do not concern him, such as the beneficial interests, and providing him with all the information he needs for the purpose of being certain to obtain the legal estate.

Dealings with the legal estate and equitable interests are contained in separate documents.

SETTLED LAND ACT 1925

4. Authorised method of settling land inter vivos.—(1) Every settlement of a legal estate in land inter vivos, shall, save as in this Act otherwise provided, be effected by two deeds, namely, a vesting deed and a trust instrument and if effected in any other way shall not operate to transfer or create a legal estate.

(2) By the vesting deed the land shall be conveyed to the tenant for life or

---

[15]   See p. 355, post. This section is retrospective: *Re Symons* [1927] 1 Ch 344.
[16]   This provision was added by LP(A)A 1926, Sch.
[17]   SLA 1925, s. 32, also retrospective.
[18]   C & B, pp. 191–195, 883–888; M & W, paras. 8.017–8.022; MM, pp. 258–265

statutory owner (and if more than one as joint tenants) for the legal estate the subject of the intended settlement:

Provided that, where such legal estate is already vested in the tenant for life or statutory owner, it shall be sufficient, without any other conveyance, if the vesting deed declares that the land is vested in him for that estate.

(3) The trust instrument shall —

(a) declare the trusts affecting the settled land;

(b) appoint or constitute trustees of the settlement;

(c) contain the power, if any, to appoint new trustees of the settlement;

(d) set out, either expressly or by reference, any powers intended to be conferred by the settlement in extension of those conferred by this Act;

(e) bear any ad valorem stamp duty which may be payable (whether by virtue of the vesting deed or otherwise) in respect of the settlement. [19]

TRUST INSTRUMENT ON THE SETTLEMENT OF LAND [20]

This Trust Instrument is made [&c.] between *John H.* of [&c.] (hereinafter called the Settlor) of the first part, *Jane W.* of [&c.] of the second part, and X of [&c.], Y of [&c.] and Z of [&c.] (hereinafter called the trustees) of the third part.

Whereas by a deed (hereinafter called the Vesting Deed) bearing even date with but executed contemporaneously with these presents, and made between the same parties and in the same order as these presents, certain heriditaments situated at . . . . in the county of . . . . were vested in the Settlor Upon the trusts declared concerning the same by a trust instrument of even date therein referred to (meaning these presents).

Now in consideration of the intended marriage between the Settlor and *Jane W.*, this Deed witnesseth as follows: —

1. The Settlor hereby agrees that he will hold the heriditaments and property comprised in the Vesting Deed In trust for himself until the solemnisation of the said marriage and thereafter Upon the trusts following, that is to say: —

2. Upon trust for the Settlor during his life without impeachment of waste with remainder Upon trust if *Jane W.* Survives him that she shall receive out of the premises during the residue of her life a yearly jointure rentcharge of [&c.] and subject thereto Upon trust for the trustees for a term of 800 years from the date of the death of the Settlor without impeachment of waste Upon the trusts hereinafter declared concerning the same. And subject to the said term and the trusts thereof Upon trust for the first and other sons of the said intended marriage successively according to seniority in tail male with remainder [&c.] *with an ultimate remainder in trust for the Settlor in fee simple.*

[Here add the requisite trusts of the portions term, and any other proper provisions including the appointment of the trustees to be trustees of the settlement for the purposes of the

---

[19] See LRR 1925, rr. 99, as substituted by LRR 1999, r. 2(1), Sch. 1, para. 5.

[20] SLA 1925, 1st Sch. Form No. 3. For the proposed repeal of Sch. 1 and Forms 2 and 3, see Law Commission Statute Law Revision: Seventeenth Report 2003 (Law Com No. 285) on the ground that their guidance, necessary in 1925 when the SLA was new, is no longer necessary, as there are now modern precedents in relation to the dwindling number of strict settlements in existence.

Settled Land Act, 1925, extension of Settled Land Act powers, and a power for the tenant for life for the time being of full age to appoint new trustees of the settlement.]
    In witness [&c.].
    [Note.—The Vesting Deed and the Trust Instrument can be executed as escrows till the marriage.]

---

5. Contents of Vesting deeds.—(1) Every vesting deed for giving effect to a settlement or for conveying settled land to a tenant for life or statutory owner during the subsistence of the settlement (in this Act referred to as a 'principal vesting deed') shall contain the following statements and particulars, namely: —
    (a) A description, either specific or general, of the settled land;
    (b) A statement that the settled land is vested in the person or persons to whom it is conveyed or in whom it is declared to be vested upon the trusts from time to time affecting the settled land;
    (c) The names of the persons who are the trustees of the settlement;
    (d) Any additional or larger powers conferred by the trust instrument relating to the settled land which by virtue of this Act operate and are exercisable as if conferred by this Act on a tenant for life;
    (e) The name of any person for the time being entitled under the trust instrument to appoint new trustees of the settlement.
    (2) The statements or particulars required by this section may be incorporated by reference to an existing vesting instrument, and, where there is a settlement subsisting at the commencement of this Act, by reference to that settlement and to any instrument whereby land has been conveyed to the uses or upon the trusts of that settlement, but not (save as last aforesaid) by reference to a trust instrument nor by reference to a disentailing deed.
    (3) A principal vesting deed shall not be invalidated by reason only of any error in any of the statements or particulars by this Act required to be contained therein. [1]

VESTING DEED ON THE SETTLEMENT OF LAND [2]

This Vesting Deed made [&c.] between *John H.* of [&c.] of the first part, *Jane W.* of [&c.] of the second part, and *X* of [&c.], *Y* of [&c.], and *Z* of [&c.] (hereinafter called the trustees) of the third part.
    Witnesseth and it is hereby declared as follows: —
    1. In consideration of the intended marriage between *John H.* and *Jane W.* the said *John H.* as Settlor hereby declares that
    All that (*setting out the parcels by reference to a schedule or otherwise*) are vested in *John H.* In fee simple (*or in the case of leaseholds refer to the terms*).
    Upon the trusts declared concerning the same by a Trust Instrument bearing even date with but intended to be executed contemporaneously with these presents and made between the same parties and in the same order as these

---

[1]   SLA 1925, s. 110(2); see p. 361, post.
[2]   Ibid., 1st Sch. Form No. 2. See p. 329, n. 20, ante.

presents or upon such other trusts as the same ought to be held from time to time.

2. The trustees are the trustees of the settlement for the purposes of the Settled Land Act, 1925.

3. The following additional or larger powers are conferred by the said trust instrument in relation to the settled land and by virtue of the Settled Land Act, 1925, operate and are exercisable as if conferred by that Act on a tenant for life. [*Here insert the additional powers.*]

4. The power of appointing a new trustee or new trustees of the settlement is vested in the said [*John H.*] during his life.

In witness [&c.].

---

6. Procedure in the case of settlements by will.—Where a settlement is created by the will of an estate owner who dies after the commencement of this Act —

(*a*) the will is for the purposes of this Act a trust instrument; and

(*b*) the personal representatives of the testator shall hold the settled land on trust, if and when required so to do, to convey it to the person who, under the will, or by virtue of this Act, is the tenant for life [3] or statutory owner, [4] and, if more than one, as joint tenants. [5]

8. Mode and costs of conveyance, and saving of rights of personal representatives and equitable chargees.—(1) A conveyance by personal representatives under either of the last two preceding sections [6] may be made by an assent in writing signed by them which shall operate as a conveyance. [7]

9. Procedure in the case of settlements and of instruments deemed to be trust instruments.—(1) Each of the following settlements or instruments shall for the purposes of this Act be deemed to be a trust instrument, and any reference to a trust instrument contained in this Act shall apply thereto, namely: —

(i) An instrument executed, or, in case of a will, coming into operation, after the commencement of this Act which by virtue of this Act is deemed to be a settlement;

(ii) A settlement which by virtue of this Act is deemed to have been made by any person after the commencement of this Act, [8]

(iii) An instrument inter vivos intended to create a settlement of a legal estate in land which is executed after the commencement of this Act, and does not comply with the requirements of this Act with respect to the method of effecting such a settlement; and

(iv) A settlement made after the commencement of this Act (including a settlement by the will of a person who dies after such commencement) of any of the following interests —

(*a*) an equitable interest in land which is capable, when in possession, of subsisting at law; or

---

3   SLA 1925, ss. 19, 20; see pp. 339–340, post.
4   Ibid., s. 20.
5   Ibid., s. 19(2).
6   For s. 7, see p. 359, post.
7   The vesting assent performs the same function as a vesting deed; but it need not be sealed: AEA 1925, s. 36.
8   For instruments deemed to be settlements or settlements deemed to have been made after the commencement of the Act, see SLA 1925, ss. 1(2), (3), 20(3), 29(1).

(*b*)   an entailed interest; or

(*c*)   a base or determinable fee or any corresponding interest in leasehold land,

but only if and when the interest settled takes effect free from all equitable interests and powers under every prior settlement (if any).

(2) As soon as practicable after a settlement, or an instrument which for the purposes of this Act is deemed to be a trust instrument, takes effect as such, the trustees of the settlement may, and on the request of the tenant for life or statutory owner shall, execute a principal vesting deed, containing the proper statements and particulars, declaring that the legal estate in the settled land shall vest or is vested in the person therein named, being the tenant for life or statutory owner, and including themselves if they are the statutory owners, and such deed shall, unless the legal estate is already so vested, operate to convey or vest the legal estate in the settled land to or in the person or persons aforesaid and, if more than one, as joint tenants.

(3) If there are no trustees of the settlement, then (in default of a person able and willing to appoint such trustees) an application under this Act shall be made to the court for the appointment of such trustees.

III. Registered Land

The detailed provisions on the treatment of settled land where the title is registered were set out in sections 86–92 of the Land Registration Act 1925. [9] They are now contained in section 89 of the Land Registration Act 2002 and in Schedule 7 of the Land Registration Rules 2003. There is no change in their substance. The legal estate in the settled land is registered in the name of the tenant for life or statutory owner; the beneficial interests under the settlement are protected by restrictions entered in the proprietorship register; [10] but they cannot be overriding interests. Under section 86(2) of the Land Registration Act 1925 the successive or other interests created by or arising under a settlement 'shall ... take effect as minor interests and not otherwise'. Similarly in paragraphs 2 of each of Schedules 1 and 3, the Land Registration Act 2002 provides that the interests are not overriding.

LAND REGISTRATION ACT 2002

89 Settlements

(1) Rules may make provision for the purposes of this Act in relation to the application to registered land of the enactments relating to settlements under the Settled Land Act 1925.

(2) Rules under this section may include provision modifying any of those enactments in its application to registered land.

---

[9]   Law Com Report on Land Registration for the Twenty-First Century (Law Com No. 271), paras. 8.17, 11.45; H & B, para. 3.117; R&R, paras. 31.05, 37.012–37.018.

[10]   A notice cannot be entered: LRA 2002, s. 33(a)(i).

LAND REGISTRATION RULES 2003

SCHEDULE 7

SETTLEMENTS

General

   1. Registered land which is settled land must be registered in the name of the tenant for life or the statutory owner.

SCHEDULE 4

STANDARD FORMS OF RESTRICTION

Form G (Tenant for life as registered proprietor of settled land, where there are trustees of the settlement)
No disposition is to be registered unless authorised by the Settled Land Act 1925, or by any extension of those statutory powers in the settlement, and no disposition under which capital money arises is to be registered unless the money is paid to (*name*) and (*address*) and (*name*) and (*address*), (the trustees of the settlement, who may be a sole trust corporation or, if individuals, must number at least two but not more than four) or into court.

Form H (Statutory owners as trustees of the settlement and registered proprietors of settled land)
No disposition is to be registered unless authorised by the Settled Land Act 1925, or by any extension of those statutory powers in the settlement, and, except where the sole proprietor is a trust corporation, no disposition under which capital money arises is to be registered unless the money is paid to at least two proprietors.

Form I (Tenant for life as registered proprietor of settled land—no trustees of the settlement)
No disposition under which capital money arises, or which is not authorised by the Settled Land Act 19235 or by any extension of those statutory powers in the settlement, is to be registered.

IV. Dispositions of Settled Land [11]

A. No Vesting Instrument. Paralysis

SETTLED LAND ACT 1925

13. Dispositions not to take effect until vesting instrument is made.—Where a tenant for life or statutory owner has become entitled to have a principal vesting deed or a vesting assent executed in his favour, then until a vesting instrument is executed or made pursuant to this Act in respect of the settled land, any purported disposition thereof inter vivos by any person, other than a personal representative (not being a disposition which he has power to make in right of

---

[11]   C & B, pp. 194–195, 885–888; M & W, paras. 8.023–8.026, 8.042–8.046; MM, pp. 260–263.

his equitable interests or powers under a trust instrument), shall not take effect except in favour of a purchaser of a legal estate [without notice of such tenant for life or statutory owner having become so entitled as aforesaid], [12] but, save as aforesaid, shall operate only as a contract for valuable consideration to carry out the transaction after the requisite vesting instrument has been executed or made, and a purchaser of a legal estate shall not be concerned with such disposition unless the contract is registered as a land charge. [13]

By virtue of Law of Property (Amendment) Act 1926, section 1, a person beneficially entitled in possession to land for an estate in fee simple or term of years absolute subject to charges [14] which would normally make the land settled land [15] may sell the land subject to such charges without complying with the Settled Land Act procedure and section 13. Alternatively he can overreach the charges by complying with the statutory procedure.

B. Subject to Vesting Instrument

SETTLED LAND ACT 1925

18. Restrictions on dispositions of settled land where trustees have not been discharged.—(1) Where land is the subject of a vesting instrument and the trustees of the settlement have not been discharged under this Act, then —

(a) any disposition by the tenant for life or statutory owner of the land, other than a disposition authorised by this Act or any other statute, or made in pursuance of any additional or larger powers mentioned in the vesting instrument, shall be void, [16] except for the purpose of conveying or creating such equitable interests as he has power, in right of his equitable interests and powers under the trust instrument, to convey or create; and

(b) if any capital money is payable in respect of a transaction, a conveyance to a purchaser of the land shall only take effect under this Act if the capital money is paid to or by the direction of the trustees of the settlement or into court; and

(c) notwithstanding anything to the contrary in the vesting instrument, or the trust instrument, capital money shall not, except where the trustee is a trust corporation, be paid to or by the direction of fewer persons than two as trustees of the settlement. [17]

(2) The restrictions imposed by this section do not affect —

(a) the right of a personal representative in whom the settled land may be vested to convey or deal with the land for the purposes of administration;

(b) the right of a person of full age who has become absolutely entitled (whether beneficially or as trustee of land [18] or personal representative

---

[12]   As amended by LP(A)A 1926, Sch.
[13]   See W & C, vol. 3, pp. 54–57.
[14]   SLA 1925, s. 20(1)(ix).
[15]   Ibid., s. 1(1)(v).
[16]   *Bevan v Johnston* [1990] 2 EGLR 33; [1991] Conv 601 (J. Hill).
[17]   See also SLA 1925, s. 94; and as to receipts, s. 95, p. 338, post. For the definition of a trust corporation, see p. 294, n. 6, ante.
[18]   As amended by TLATA 1996, s. 25(1), Sch. 3, para. 2(7).

or otherwise) to the settled land, free from all limitations, powers, and charges taking effect under the trust instrument, to require the land to be conveyed to him.

The question arises of the position of the purchaser if he fails to comply with these requirements in circumstances in which he did not know and could not have known that the land was subject to a settlement. Is the conveyance 'void' under section 18? Or, should a purchaser be protected under section 110(1) (p. 361, post)?

In **Weston v Henshaw** [1950] Ch 510, three generations of Westons, W 1, W 2, and W 3, were successively interested in Blackacre. In 1921 W 1 sold Blackacre to W 2, who in 1927 sold it back to W 1. By his will W 1 settled it on Mrs W 1 for life and then on W 2 for life and to a grandson (W 3) contingently on attaining the age of 25. W 1 died in 1931, and Mrs W 1 in 1940, and on her death the fee simple was vested by vesting assent in W 2.

W 2 charged Blackacre to the defendants by way of legal mortgage to secure a number of personal advances, making title on each occasion by showing the deeds up to the sale to him in 1921, and suppressing all subsequent documents. Thus, W 2 appeared to be the absolute owner of the fee simple. In reality, he was only a tenant for life. There was no way in which the defendant, by enquiries, could have found out.

W 3 brought this action, after the death of W 2, as his administrator, for a declaration that the charges were void against him.

DANCKWERTS J held that they were, because the land was settled land, and the mortgagee had not complied with the provisions of section 18. The mortgagee was by any standards a bona fide purchaser of a legal estate for value without notice; and, if the decision is correct, his position, under an Act which was intended to help him, is worse than it was before 1926.

The decision was doubted in **Re Morgan's Lease** [1972] Ch 1, [1971] 2 All ER 235 [19] where UNGOED-THOMAS J said at 7, at 241:

'I come now to the third issue on the first question, whether section 110 of the Settled Land Act 1925 only applies if the purchaser knows that the other party to the transaction is a tenant for life. The landlords' submission was founded on *Weston v Henshaw* [1950] Ch 510.

[His Lordship referred to *Mogridge v Clapp* [1892] 3 Ch 382, which 'unfortunately was not brought to DANCKWERTS J's notice' and continued:]

Here Kay LJ, sitting in the Court of Appeal with Lindley LJ and Bowen LJ, seems to me to treat it as self-evident that a person dealing with a life tenant without knowing that he was a life tenant would be entitled to rely on section 110 of the Settled Land Act 1925; and, with the greatest respect for the decision in *Weston v Henshaw* [1950] Ch 510, that is the conclusion to which I would come independently of authority. There is, in the section, no express provision limiting

---

[19]   (1971) 87 LQR 338 (D. W. Elliott); (1973) 36 MLR 25 at p. 28 (R. H. Maudsley).

its benefit to a purchaser who knows that the person with whom he is dealing is a tenant for life. On its face it reads as free of limitation and as applicable to a person without such knowledge as to a person who has it. There is a limitation, namely, that the purchaser must act in good faith; but that limitation reads as applicable to a purchaser with such knowledge as without. So, despite the insertion of the limitation of good faith on the part of the purchaser, there is no insertion of the limitation for which the landlords contend. Thus, my conclusion is that section 110 applies whether or not the purchaser knows that the other party to the transaction is tenant for life.'

V. Overreaching[20]

A. Under an Ordinary Conveyance

If the correct machinery is used, a sale by a tenant for life 'overreaches' the beneficial interests under the settlement and passes the title to a purchaser free from them. The beneficial interests are transferred from the land to the purchase money.[1]

LAW OF PROPERTY ACT 1925

2. Conveyances overreaching certain equitable interests and powers.—(1) A conveyance to a purchaser of a legal estate in land shall overreach any equitable interest or power affecting that estate, whether or not he has notice thereof, if —
  (i) the conveyance is made under the powers conferred by the Settled Land Act, 1925,[2] or any additional powers conferred by a settlement, and the equitable interest or power is capable of being overreached thereby, and the statutory requirements respecting the payment of capital money arising under the settlement are complied with;[3]

SETTLED LAND ACT 1925

72. Completion of transactions by conveyance.—(1) On a sale, exchange, lease, mortgage, charge, or other disposition, the tenant for life may, as regards land sold, given in exchange, leased, mortgaged, charged, or otherwise disposed of, or intended so to be, or as regards easements or other rights or privileges sold, given in exchange, leased, mortgaged or otherwise disposed of, or intended so to be, effect the transaction by deed to the extent of the estate or interest vested or declared to be vested in him by the last or only vesting instrument affecting the settled land or any less estate or interest, in the manner requisite for giving effect to the sale, exchange, lease, mortgage, charge, or other disposition, but so that a mortgage shall be effected by the creation of a term of years absolute in the settled land or by charge by way of legal mortgage, and not otherwise.

---

[20] C & B, pp. 96, 885–887, 892–893; Gray, pp. 215–218; M & W, paras. 8.157–8.164; MM, pp. 258–265.
[1] SLA 1925, s. 75(5), p. 357, post.
[2] Ibid., s. 72, infra.
[3] Ibid., s. 18(1)(b), p. 334, ante.

(2) Such a deed, to the extent and in the manner to and in which it is expressed or intended to operate and can operate under this Act, is effectual to pass the land conveyed, or the easements, rights, privileges or other interests created, discharged from all the limitations, powers, and provisions of the settlement, and from all estates, interests, and charges subsisting or to arise thereunder, but subject to and with the exception of —

(i) all legal estates and charges by way of legal mortgage having priority to the settlement; and

(ii) all legal estates and charges by way of legal mortgage which have been conveyed or created for securing money actually raised at the date of the deed; and

(iii) all leases and grants at fee-farm rents or otherwise, and all grants of easements, rights of common, or other rights or privileges which —

(a) were before the date of the deed granted or made for value in money or money's worth, or agreed so to be, by the tenant for life or statutory owner, or by any of his predecessors in title, or any trustees for them, under the settlement, or under any statutory power, or are at that date otherwise binding on the successors in title of the tenant for life or statutory owner; and

(b) are at the date of the deed protected by registration under the Land Charges Act, 1925, [4] if capable of registration thereunder.

(3) Notwithstanding registration under the Land Charges Act, 1925[4] of —

(a) an annuity within the meaning of Part II of that Act;

(b) a limited owner's charge or a general equitable charge within the meaning of that Act;

a disposition under this Act operates to overreach such annuity or charge which shall, according to its priority, take effect as if limited by the settlement.

(4) Where a lease is by this Act authorised to be made by writing under hand only, such writing shall have the same operation under this section as if it had been a deed.

B. Ad Hoc Settlements

SETTLED LAND ACT 1925

21. Absolute owners subject to certain interests to have the powers of tenant for life.—(1) Where a person of full age is beneficially entitled in possession to a legal estate subject to any equitable interests or powers, then, for the purpose of overreaching such interests or powers, he may, notwithstanding any stipulation to the contrary, by deed (which shall have effect as a principal vesting deed within the meaning of this Act) declare that the legal estate is vested in him on trust to give effect to all equitable interests and powers affecting the legal estate, and that deed shall be executed by two or more individuals approved or appointed by the court or a trust corporation, [5] who shall be stated to be the trustees of the settlement for the purposes of this Act.

Thereupon so long as any of the equitable interests and powers are subsisting the following provisions shall have effect: —

---

[4] Now LCA 1972.
[5] See p. 294, n. 6, ante.

(a) The person so entitled as aforesaid and each of his successors in title being an estate owner shall have the powers of a tenant for life and the land shall be deemed to be settled land;

(b) The instrument (if any) under which his estate arises or is acquired, and the instrument (if any) under which the equitable interests or powers are subsisting or capable of taking effect shall be deemed to be the trust instrument:

Provided that where there is no such instrument as last aforesaid then a deed (which shall take effect as a trust instrument) shall be executed contemporaneously with the vesting deed, and shall declare the trusts affecting the land;

(c) The persons stated in the principal vesting deed to be the trustees of the settlement for the purposes of this Act shall also be the trustees of the trust instrument for those purposes; and

(d) Capital money arising on any disposition of the land shall be paid to or by the direction of the trustees of the settlement or into court, and shall be applicable towards discharging or providing for payment in due order of any principal money payable in respect of such interests or charges as are overreached by such disposition, and until so applied shall be invested or applied as capital money under the trust instrument, and the resultant profits[6] shall be applied as the income of such capital money, and be liable for keeping down in due order any annual or periodical sum which may be overreached by the disposition.

(2) The following equitable interests and powers are excepted from the operation of subsection (1) of this section, namely —

(i) an equitable interest protected by a deposit of documents relating to the legal estate affected;

(ii) the benefit of a covenant or agreement restrictive of the user of land;

(iii) an easement, liberty or privilege over or affecting land and being merely an equitable interest;

(iv) the benefit of a contract to convey or create a legal estate, including a contract conferring either expressly or by statutory implication a valid option of purchase, a right of pre-emption, or any other like right;

(v) any equitable interest protected by registration under the Land Charges Act 1925,[7] other than —

(a) an annuity within the meaning of Part II of that Act;

(b) a limited owner's charge or a general equitable charge within the meaning of that Act.

(3) Subject to the powers conferred by this Act on a tenant for life, nothing contained in this section shall deprive an equitable chargee of any of his rights or of his remedies for enforcing those rights.

---

6   As amended by TA 2000, s. 40, Sch. 2, Part II, para. 7.
7   Now LCA 1972.

VI. The Tenant for Life[8]

A. Who is Tenant for Life and Who has Powers of Tenant for Life

I. TENANT FOR LIFE AND OTHER LIMITED OWNERS

SETTLED LAND ACT 1925

19. Who is tenant for life.—(1) The person of full age who is for the time being beneficially entitled under a settlement to possession of settled land for his life is for the purposes of this Act the tenant for life of that land and the tenant for life under that settlement.

(2) If in any case there are two or more persons of full age so entitled as joint tenants, they together constitute the tenant for life for the purposes of this Act.

(3) If in any case there are two or more persons so entitled as joint tenants and they are not all of full age, such one or more of them as is or are for the time being of full age is or (if more than one) together constitute the tenant for life for the purposes of this Act, but this subsection does not affect the beneficial interests of such of them as are not for the time being of full age.

(4) A person being tenant for life within the foregoing definitions shall be deemed to be such notwithstanding that, under the settlement or otherwise, the settled land, or his estate or interest therein, is incumbered or charged in any manner or to any extent, and notwithstanding any assignment by operation of law or otherwise of his estate or interest under the settlement, whether before or after it came into possession, other than an assurance which extinguishes that estate or interest.

20. Other limited owners having powers of tenant for life.—(1) Each of the following persons being of full age shall, when his estate or interest is in possession, have the powers of a tenant for life under this Act, (namely): —

   (i)   A tenant in tail, including a tenant in tail after possibility of issue extinct, and a tenant in tail who is by Act of Parliament restrained from barring or defeating his estate tail, and although the reversion is in the Crown, but not including such a tenant in tail where the land in respect whereof he is so restrained was purchased with money provided by Parliament in consideration of public services;

   (ii)   A person entitled to land for an estate in fee simple or for a term of years absolute with or subject to, in any of such cases, an executory limitation, gift, or disposition over on failure of his issue or in any other event;

   (iii)   A person entitled to a base or determinable fee, although the reversion or right of reverter is in the Crown, or to any corresponding interest in leasehold land;

   (iv)   A tenant for years determinable on life, not holding merely under a lease at a rent;

   (v)   A tenant for the life of another, not holding merely under a lease at a rent;

---

[8]   C & B, pp. 195–208; Gray, pp. 648–653; M & W, paras. 8.058–8.106; MM, pp. 255–256, 268–278.

(vi) A tenant for his own or any other life, or for years determinable on life, whose estate is liable to cease in any event during that life, whether by expiration of the estate, or by conditional limitation, or otherwise, or to be defeated by an executory limitation, gift, or disposition over, or is subject to a trust for accumulation of income for any purpose;

(vii) A tenant by the curtesy;

(viii) A person entitled to the income of land under a trust or direction for payment thereof to him during his own or any other life, whether or not subject to expenses of management or to a trust for accumulation of income for any purpose, or until sale of the land, or until forfeiture, cesser or determination by any means of his interest therein, unless the land is subject to a trust of land; [9]

(ix) A person beneficially entitled to land for an estate in fee simple or for a term of years absolute subject to any estates, interests, charges, or powers of charging, subsisting or capable of being exercised under a settlement. [10]

117. Definitions.— (1) ...

(xxviii) 'Tenant for life' includes a person (not being a statutory owner) who has the powers of a tenant for life under this Act, and also (where the context requires) one of two or more persons who together constitute the tenant for life, or have the powers of a tenant for life, [11] ...

ii. STATUTORY OWNERS

SETTLED LAND ACT 1925

23. Powers of trustees, &c., when there is no tenant for life.—(1) Where under a settlement there is no tenant for life, nor, independently of this section, a person having by virtue of this Act the powers of a tenant for life then —

(*a*) any person of full age on whom such powers are by the settlement expressed to be conferred; [12] and

---

[9]   As amended by TLATA 1996, s. 25(1), Sch. 3, para. 2(8).

[10]   Such persons may, however, convey the land subject to a prior interest as if the land had not been settled land: LP(A)A 1926, s. 1.

[11]   *Re Jeffreys* [1939] Ch 205, [1938] 4 All ER 120 (an annuitant is not a tenant for life); *Re Carne's Settled Estates* [1899] 1 Ch 324 ('to occupy the land rent free so long as she might wish to do so,' held to be a tenant for life); *Ayer v Benton* (1967) 204 EG 359; *Re Catling* [1931] 2 Ch 359 (wife as tenant at a nominal annual sum, the tenancy not to be determined so long as she made the property her principal place of residence held not to be a tenant for life; and indeed there was no settlement); *Re Waleran Settled Estates* [1927] 1 Ch 522 (a term to a woman 'for 99 years if she should so long life' held to be a tenant for life); *Re Ogle's Settled Estates* [1927] 1 Ch 229, p. 328, *ante*; *Re Cayley and Evans' Contract* [1930] 2 Ch 143; *Re Gallenga Will Trusts* [1938] 1 All ER 106. Questions also arise in connection with settlements on divorce: *Morss v Morss* [1972] Fam 264, [1972] 1 All ER 1121 (agreement incorporated in court order allowing a wife the use of house 'rent free for her life or until . . . debarred by court from access to the children' held a licence); *Martin v Martin* [1978] Fam 12, [1977] 3 All ER 762 (court order giving house on trust to wife for life or until remarriage or such earlier date as she should cease to live there, and thereafter on trust for the parties in equal shares. This would presumably make the wife a tenant for life; the inconveniences of such a decision are pointed out in [1978] Conv 229 (P. Smith)). See also *Allen v Allen* [1974] 1 WLR 1171, [1974] 3 All ER 385, where a similar result was achieved through the machinery of a trust for sale. A similar problem arises where the court gives protection to a licensee for the period of his life; p. 326, n. 6, *ante*, pp. 673–678, *post*.

[12]   *Re Craven Settled Estates* [1926] Ch 985; *Re Norton* [1929] 1 Ch 84; *Re Beaumont Settled Estates* [1937] 2 All ER 353.

(b)   in any other case the trustees of the settlement;
shall have the powers of a tenant for life under this Act. [13]

26. Infants, how to be affected. [14]—(1) Where an infant is beneficially entitled in possession to land for an estate in fee simple or for a term of years absolute or would if of full age be a tenant for life of or have the powers of a tenant for life over settled land, then, during the minority of the infant—

(a)   if the settled land is vested in a personal representative, the personal representative, until a principal vesting instrument has been executed pursuant to the provisions of this Act; and

(b)   in every other case, the trustees of the settlement;

shall have, in reference to the settled land and capital money, all the powers conferred by this Act and the settlement on a tenant for life, and on the trustees of the settlement.

117. Definitions.—(1) ...

(xxvi) 'Statutory owner' means the trustees of the settlement or other persons who, during a minority, or at any other time when there is no tenant for life, have the powers of a tenant for life under this Act, but does not include the trustees of the settlement, where by virtue of an order of the court or otherwise the trustees have power to convey the settled land in the name of the tenant for life.

B. Powers of the Tenant for Life

i. POWERS

The tenant for life's powers are given in detail in Settled Land Act 1925, Part II. The most important sections are set out below.

---

[13]   SLA 1925, s. 104(1) as amended by TA 2000, s. 40(1), (3), Sch. 2, Pt II, para. 16 provides that the powers of a tenant for life are not capable of assignment or release. A person who becomes a 'statutory owner' under s. 23(1) may release his powers and the trustees then become statutory owners: *Re Craven Settled Estates* [1926] Ch 985, p. 359, post.

[14]   Ibid., ss. 1(1)(ii)(d), 1(2), 102 as amended by TA 2000, s. 40(1), Sch. 2, Pt II, para 15. The Family Law Reform Act 1969, s. 1 provides that as from January 1, 1970, 'a person shall attain full age on attaining the age of eighteen instead of on attaining the age of twenty-one; and a person shall attain full age on the date if he has then already attained the age of eighteen but not the age of twenty-one'. On minors generally, see C & B, pp. 999–1006; M & W, paras. 20.002–20.019; MM, pp. 301–304. A minor cannot hold a legal estate in land, although he may hold an equitable interest: LPA 1925, s. 1(6); LRA 1925, s. 3(iv); *Kingston-upon-Thames London Borough Council v Prince* [1998] EGCS 179 (infant succeeds to secure tenancy held by her grandmother, with equitable interest during her minority). For the effect of a conveyance of a legal estate to a minor before 1997: LPA 1925, s. 19; SLA 1925, s. 27, both sections repealed by TLATA 1996, s. 25(2), Sch. 4; LRA 1925, s. 111, as amended by TLATA 1996, s. 25(1), Sch. 3, para. 11. For the trust of land after 1996, see TLATA 1996, s. 2, Sch. 1, para. 1. See Law Commission Report on Minors' Contracts 1984 (Law Com No. 134, HC 494), paras. 5.13–5.16 on leases granted to minors, explaining supposed difficulties. He cannot be appointed a trustee: LPA 1925, s. 20, nor an executor: Supreme Court Act 1981, s. 118; nor an administrator: *Re Manuel* (1849) 13 Jur 664. He cannot make a will: Wills Act 1837, s. 7, except as provided by Wills (Soldiers and Sailors) Act 1918. Any disposition by a minor of any interest in land is voidable at his option, on his attaining his majority, or within a reasonable time thereafter.

38. Powers of sale and exchange.—A tenant for life —

(i) May sell the settled land, or any part thereof, or any easement, right or privilege of any kind over or in relation to the land; and

(iii) May make an exchange of the settled land, or any part thereof, or of any easement, right, or privilege of any kind, whether or not newly created, over or in relation to the settled land, or any part thereof, for other land, or for any easement, right or privilege of any kind, whether or not newly created, over or in relation to other land, including an exchange in consideration of money paid for equality of exchange. [15]

41. Power to lease for ordinary or building or mining or forestry purposes.—A tenant for life may lease the settled land, or any part thereof, or any easement, right or privilege of any kind over or in relation to the land, for any purpose whatever, whether involving waste or not, for any term not exceeding —

(i) In case of a building lease, nine hundred and ninety-nine years;

(ii) In case of a mining lease, one hundred years;

(iii) In case of a forestry lease, nine hundred and ninety-nine years;

(iv) In case of any other lease, fifty years. [16]

51. Power to grant options.—(1) A tenant for life may at any time, either with or without consideration, grant by writing an option to purchase or take a lease of the settled land, or any part thereof, or any easement, right, or privilege over or in relation to the same at a price or rent fixed at the time of the granting of the option. [17]

(2) Every such option shall be made exercisable within an agreed number of years not exceeding ten.

71. Power to raise money by mortgage.—(1) Where money is required for any of the following purposes namely: —

(i) Discharging an incumbrance on the settled land or part thereof;

(ii) Paying for any improvement authorised by this Act or by the settlement;

(iii) Equality of exchange;

(vi) Redeeming a compensation rentcharge in respect of the extinguishment of manorial incidents and affecting the settled land;

(vii) Commuting any additional rent made payable on the conversion of a perpetually renewable leasehold interest into a long term;

(viii) Satisfying any claims for compensation on the conversion of a perpetually renewable leasehold interest into a long term by any officer, solicitor, or other agent of the lessor in respect of fees or remuneration which would have been payable by the lessee or underlessee on any renewal;

(ix) Payment of the costs of any transaction authorised by this section or either of the two last preceding sections;

the tenant for life may raise the money so required, on the security of the settled land, or of any part thereof, by a legal mortgage, and the money so raised shall be capital money for that purpose, and may be paid or applied accordingly.

---

[15] For further details concerning the powers of sale and exchange, see ss. 39, 40.

[16] For further details concerning the power of leasing, see ss. 42—48. As to whether a tenant for life has power to insert a rent renewal clause in the lease, see [1979] Conv 258 (M. Dockray).

[17] *Re Morgan's Lease* [1972] Ch 1, [1971] 2 All ER 235.

Law Reform Committee 23rd Report (The Powers and Duties of Trustees) 1982 Cmnd. 8733, para. 9.1. VIII. 52—56.

'52. A tenant for life of settled land should be empowered to grant a lease of that land or any part of it at a rent initially ascertained by arbitration or valuation, or any other generally recognised method of arriving at the best rent. (para. 8.4)

53. A tenant for life should be given statutory authority to grant concurrent leases.[18] (para. 8.5)

54. Section 41 of the Settled Land Act 1925 should be amended to give the tenant for life the power to grant ordinary leases of 99 years. (para. 8.6)

55. Trustees of a settlement should be empowered to require a tenant for life to obtain valuations in respect of transactions under section 101 of the Settled Land Act 1925 [19] so enabling them to control transactions with the settled land more effectively. (para 8.9)

56. Section 51 of the Settled Land Act 1925 [20] should be amended so as to enable the tenant for life of a settlement to grant options at a price to be fixed by valuation, arbitration or any other generally recognised method. (para. 8.10)

ii. NOTICE TO TRUSTEES

When a tenant for life exercises his powers of sale, exchange, leasing, mortgaging, charging or granting an option, he is usually required to give notice to the trustees.[1] In the case of the sale of a mansion house, their consent is required.

iii. SPECIAL CONSENTS [2]

SETTLED LAND ACT 1925

65. Power to dispose of mansion.—(1) The powers of disposing of settled land conferred by this Act on a tenant for life may be exercised as respects the principal mansion house, if any, on any settled land, and the pleasure grounds and park and lands, if any, usually occupied therewith:

Provided that those powers shall not be exercised without the consent of the trustees of the settlement or an order of the court —

    (a) if the settlement is a settlement made or coming into operation before the commencement of this Act and the settlement does not expressly provide to the contrary; or

    (b) if the settlement is a settlement made or coming into operation after the commencement of this Act and the settlement expressly provides that these powers or any of them shall not be exercised without such consent or order.

(2) Where a house is usually occupied as a farmhouse, or where the site of any house and the pleasure grounds and park and lands, if any, usually occupied therewith do not together exceed twenty-five acres in extent, the house is not to be deemed a principal mansion house within the meaning of this section, and may accordingly be disposed of in like manner as any other part of the settled land.

---

[18] P. 520, post.
[10] Infra.
[20] Supra.
[1] SLA 1925, s. 101.
[2] See also s. 66(1) (cutting and sale of timber by tenant for life impeachable for waste); s. 58 (compromising claims); s. 67(3) (order of the court needed for the sale of settled chattels); s. 64 (general power to effect any transaction under a court order, infra).

iv. GENERAL POWER FOR THE BENEFIT OF THE SETTLED LAND

SETTLED LAND ACT 1925

64. General power for the tenant for life to effect any transaction under an order of the court.—(1) Any transaction affecting or concerning the settled land, or any part thereof, or any other land (not being a transaction otherwise authorised by this Act, or by the settlement) which in the opinion of the court could be for the benefit of the settled land, or any part thereof, or the persons interested under the settlement, may, under an order of the court, be effected by a tenant for life, if it is one which could have been validly effected by an absolute owner.

(2) In this section 'transaction' includes any sale, . . . grant, lease . . . or other disposition, and any purchase or other acquisition, and any covenant, contract, or option, and any application of capital money . . ., and any compromise or other dealing, or arrangement [3] . . . ;

This section is applicable both to settlements and trusts for sale. [4]

The wide definition of 'transaction' has enabled the power given by the section to be exercised in the following situations:

In **Re White-Popham Settled Estates** [1936] Ch 725, [1936] 2 All ER 1486, approval was given to a scheme for paying off debts incurred in keeping up the estate. The Court of Appeal (reversing EVE J) held that the section was wide enough to cover schemes which were for the benefit of persons interested under the settlement as well as those for the benefit of the settled land.

In **Re Scarisbrick Re-settlement Estates** [1944] Ch 229, [1944] 1 All ER 404, approval was given to a scheme to raise £10,000 out of capital to enable the tenant for life to continue to live in the mansion house.

In **Re Earl of Mount Edgcumbe** [1950] Ch 615, [1950] 2 All ER 242, approval was given in the expenditure of £10,000, being compensation for chattels and heirlooms destroyed by war, upon such furniture and chattels for a rebuilt mansion house as the trustees (other than the tenant for life) thought suitable.

In **Re Rycroft's Settlement** [1962] Ch 263, [1961] 3 All ER 581, intended leases were held to be outside the statutory powers of the tenant for life, and WILBERFORCE J said at 273, at 587:

'Therefore it must either be discarded altogether or it must be brought forward by means of some individual scheme justified on its merits and sanctioned by the court, either under the general provisions of section 64 of this Act, or . . . the rather more special provisions which apply to building leases contained in section 46.'

In **Raikes v Lygon** [1988] 1 WLR 281, [1988] 1 All ER 884, approval was given to a scheme to establish a maintenance fund for the benefit of Madresfield Court near Malvern in Worcestershire, a mansion house of outstanding architectural and historical interest, so that the fund would qualify for exemption from inheritance tax, even though there would be additional potential beneficiaries under the settlement.

---

[3]   Sub-s. 2 has been amended by Settled Land and Trustee Acts (Court's General Powers) Act 1943, s. 2. See also s. 1.

[4]   *Re Simmons' Trusts* [1956] Ch 125, [1955] 3 All ER 818.

In **Hambro v Duke of Marlborough** [1994] Ch 158, [1994] 3 All ER 332, it was held that the court had jurisdiction to authorise the tenant for life to vary the beneficial interest of an ascertained beneficiary of full age and capacity, even if that beneficiary did not consent. The present tenant for life of the Blenheim Parliamentary Estates could execute a conveyance which would deprive his heir of the right to live in and manage the palace and estates. [5]

This section also enables the court to approve on behalf of those who, being minor, incompetent or unborn, cannot consent to schemes which adjust beneficial interests under a settlement, [6] where the object of the adjustment is to reduce liability to taxation. Its jurisdiction is wider than that of the Trustee Act 1925, section 57. [7] However, the Variation of Trusts Act 1958, section 1 gives the court power to approve an 'arrangement' varying the trusts or the powers of the trustees on behalf of persons covered by the section: this section is now most commonly used for the ordinary case of adjustment or re-distribution of capital for the purpose of reducing liability to taxation. [8] If the 1958 Act does not apply to a particular case, and if the settlement includes land, Settled Land Act 1925, section 64 may be used.

C. Reductions from and Additions to the Powers of the Tenant for Life

SETTLED LAND ACT 1925

106. [9] **Prohibition or limitation against exercise of powers void, and provision against forfeiture.**—(1) If in a settlement, will, assurance, or other instrument executed or made before or after, or partly before and partly after, the commencement of this Act a provision is inserted —

    (a) purporting or attempting, by way of direction, declaration, or otherwise, to forbid a tenant for life or statutory owner to exercise any power under this Act, or his right to require the settled land to be vested in him; or

    (b) attempting, or tending or intended, by a limitation, gift, or disposition over of settled land, or by a limitation, gift, or disposition of other real or any personal property, or by the imposition of any condition, or by forfeiture, or in any other manner whatever, to prohibit or prevent him from exercising, or to induce him to abstain from exercising, or to put him into a position inconsistent with his exercising any power under this Act, or his right to require the settled land to be vested in him;

that provision, as far as it purports, or attempts, or tends, or is intended to have, or would or might have, the operation aforesaid, shall be deemed to be void.

(2) For the purposes of this section an estate or interest limited to continue so long as a person abstains from exercising any such power or right as aforesaid shall be and take effect as an estate or interest to continue for the period for which it would continue if that person were to abstain from exercising the power or right, discharged from liability to determination or cesser by or on his exercising the same.

---

[5]   [1994] Conv 492 (E. Cooke). The substantive application was approved on 22 July 1994.
[6]   *Re Downshire Settled Estates* [1953] Ch 218, [1953] 1 All ER 103.
[7]   *Chapman v Chapman* [1954] AC 429, [1954] 1 All ER 798.
[8]   H & M, chap. 22; Snell, paras. 11.66–11.77; M & B, *Trusts and Trustees* (6th edn, 2002), chap. 19; Harris, *Variation of Trusts* (1975).
[9]   [1978] Conv 229 (P. Smith).

(3) Notwithstanding anything in a settlement, the exercise by the tenant for life or statutory owner of any power under this Act shall not occasion a forfeiture.

108. Saving for and exercise of other powers.—(1) Nothing in this Act shall take away, abridge, or prejudicially affect any power for the time being subsisting under a settlement, or by statute or otherwise, exercisable by a tenant for life, or (save as hereinafter provided) by trustees with his consent, or on his request, or by his direction, or otherwise, and the powers given by this Act are cumulative.

(2) In case of conflict between the provisions of a settlement and the provisions of this Act, relative to any matter in respect whereof the tenant for life or statutory owner exercises or contracts or intends to exercise any power under this Act, the provisions of this Act shall prevail; and, notwithstanding anything in the settlement, any power (not being merely a power of revocation or appointment) relating to the settled land thereby conferred on the trustees of the settlement or other persons exercisable for any purpose, whether or not provided for in this Act, shall, after the commencement of this Act, be exercisable by the tenant for life or statutory owner as if it were an additional power conferred on the tenant for life within the next following section of this Act and not otherwise.

109. Saving for additional or larger powers under settlement.—(1) Nothing in this Act precludes a settlor from conferring on the tenant for life, or (save as provided by the last preceding section) on the trustees of the settlement, any powers additional to or larger than those conferred by this Act.

(2) Any additional or larger powers so conferred shall, as far as may be, notwithstanding anything in this Act, operate and be exercisable in the like manner, and with all the like incidents, effects, and consequences, as if they were conferred by this Act, and, if relating to the settled land, as if they were conferred by this Act on a tenant for life.

In **Re Jeffreys** [1939] Ch 205, [1938] 4 All ER 120, FARWELL J held that a power given to an annuitant to restrain a sale by trustees of the settlement as statutory owners was not a 'power exercisable by trustees with' the consent of the tenant for life [10] and was not therefore saved by section 108(1); the annuitant's power to restrain a sale was thus in conflict with the powers given to the statutory owners by the Act. [11] The statutory power of sale thus prevailed under section 108(2); and, even if the annuitant consented, sales by the statutory owners were sales under their statutory power, and the provisions of the Settled Land Act 1925 as to capital money must be complied with. [12]

In **Re Ames** [1893] 2 Ch 479, personalty was bequeathed for the upkeep of settled land; the surplus income being applicable to the tenant for life, but, if the tenant for life should become disentitled to the possession or income of the settled land, the settled personalty should fall into residue.

NORTH J held the proviso void under the Settled Land Act 1882, section 51 (the predecessor of section 106) and the tenant for life continued to be entitled to the income of the personalty after the sale of the settled land.

[10]   See p. 340, n. 11, ante.
[11]   See p. 340, ante.
[12]   SLA 1925, s. 18(1), p. 334, ante; s. 73, p. 358, ante; s. 75, p. 356, post; (1939) 55 LQR 22 (H.P.).

In **Re Acklom** [1929] 1 Ch 195, the testator gave his leasehold house and its contents on trust for Mrs Hawkins for life; with a direction to the trustees that if 'and when she shall not wish to reside or continue to reside there', the house should be sold, and the proceeds divided between certain charities.

The testator died in 1918 and Mrs Hawkins went into possession. In 1925, she went abroad for health reasons, and her return was delayed by a serious illness in the spring of 1926. In 1927 she sold the premises in exercise of her Settled Land Act powers and the trustees sold the contents.

In holding that she had not forfeited her interest in the property, and could receive the income from the proceeds of sale, MAUGHAM J said at 198:

'There is no doubt at all that under section 106 of the Settled Land Act, 1925, which applies to the provisions of wills made before or after the Act, a provision which limits or prevents the tenant for life from exercising his power of sale is void. Accordingly it is reasonably clear to my mind in this case that if Mrs Hawkins was in a position to exercise the powers of a tenant for life on 29 June 1927, a provision whereby the proceeds of sale should under the terms of the will pass to be charities is void. If authority were needed for that it would be found in *Re Paget's Settled Estates* (1885) 30 ChD 161, *Re Trenchard* [1902] 1 Ch 378 and *Re Gibbons* [1920] 1 Ch 372. By parity of reasoning it cannot be denied that so long as Mrs Hawkins was a person having the powers of a tenant for life she was entitled to let Wiseton Court without incurring any forfeiture even if she ceased thereupon to reside or to continue to reside within the meaning of the words contained in the clause I have read. The argument for the charities does not dispute this proposition. They maintain that on the evidence and in the events which happened Mrs Hawkins must be taken to have ceased to reside or to continue to reside at a date considerably anterior to the sale, and accordingly that she had forfeited her interest in the property prior to the sale, and therefore that they are entitled to the proceeds of sale. Now the evidence as to this is unsatisfactory; . . . I have no evidence that at any particular date it can be established that prior to the sale she had finally and irrevocably decided not only not to continue to reside, but not to let the house under her powers as tenant for life. The question of intention is affected by section 106; and if a tenant for life or person entitled to possession, so long as he enjoys it, is careful to exercise the powers as under the Act so that section 106 applies, the intention is wholly immaterial. I hold that Mrs Hawkins was entitled temporarily to give up possession if it was for the purpose of exercising her powers under the Settled Land Act or of procuring a tenant or effecting a sale, and that on the evidence before me Mrs Hawkins has so acted that the trustees had not the power of sale of the property. Of course it is material in that connection to bear in mind that they never purported to exercise any such power. They are to be presumed to have allowed her to sell without interference by any one. Accordingly I answer the first question by saying that she has not forfeited her interest in the proceeds of sale of the leasehold property.' [13]

---

[13]   See also *Re Orlebar* [1936] Ch 147; and *Re Aberconway's Settlement Trusts* [1953] Ch 647, [1953] 2 All ER 350.

D. Non-Assignability

SETTLED LAND ACT 1925

104. Powers not assignable, and contract not to exercise powers void.—(1) The powers under this Act of a tenant for life are not capable of assignment or release, and do not pass to a person as being, by operation of law or otherwise, an assignee of a tenant for life, and remain exercisable by the tenant for life after and notwithstanding any assignment, by operation of law or otherwise, of his estate or interest under the settlement.

This subsection applies notwithstanding that the estate or interest of the tenant for life under the settlement was not in possession when the assignment was made or took effect by operation of law.

(2) A contract by a tenant for life not to exercise his powers under this Act or any of them shall be void.

(4) Where such an assignment for value [14] is made or comes into operation after the commencement of this Act, the consent of the assignee shall not be requisite for the exercise by the tenant for life of any of the powers conferred by this Act:

Provided that—

(a) the assignee shall be entitled to the same or the like estate or interest in or charge on the land, money, or securities for the time being representing the land, money, or securities comprised in the assignment, as he had by virtue of the assignment in the last-mentioned land, money, or securities; and

(b) if the assignment so provides, or if it takes effect by operation of the law of bankruptcy, and after notice thereof to the trustees of the settlement, the consent of the assignee shall be required to an investment of capital money for the time being affected by the assignment in investments other than securities, and to any application of such capital money, [15] and

(c) notice of the intended transaction shall, unless the assignment otherwise provides, be given to the assignee, but a purchaser shall not be concerned to see or inquire whether such notice has been given.

(10) An assignment by operation of the law of bankruptcy, where the assignment comes into operation after the commencement of this Act, shall be deemed to be an assignment for value for the purposes of this section.

105. Effect of surrender of life estate to the next remainderman.—(1) Where the estate or interest of a tenant for life under the settlement has been or is absolutely assured with intent to extinguish the same, either before or after the commencement of this Act, to the person next entitled in remainder or reversion under the settlement, [16] then, the statutory powers of the tenant for life under this Act shall, in reference to the property affected by the assurance, and notwithstanding the provisions of the last preceding section, cease to be exercisable by him, and the statutory powers shall thenceforth become exercisable as if he were dead, but without prejudice to any incumbrance affecting the estate or interest assured, and to the rights to which any incumbrancer would have been entitled if those powers had remained exercisable by the tenant for life . . . .

---

[14]   I.e., an assignment for value of the beneficial interest of the tenant for life (sub-s. 3).

[15]   As amended by TA 2000, s. 40, Sch. 2, Pt II, para. 9; SLA 1925, ss. 73, 74; TA 2000, Sch. 2, Part II, p. 350, post.

[16]   A remainderman or reversioner does not qualify if there is an intervening limitation which may take effect: *Re Maryon-Wilson's Instruments* [1971] Ch 789, [1969] 3 All ER 558.

In **Re Shawdon Estates Settlement** [1930] 2 Ch 1, it was held by the Court of Appeal (Lord HANWORTH MR, LAWRENCE AND ROMER LJJ, affirming EVE J) that section 105(1) applied also to the case where the 'assurance' was made by the trustee in bankruptcy of the tenant for life. The tenant for life refused to execute a vesting deed in favour of the tenant in tail in remainder, the 'person next entitled', who was held to be entitled to call for a vesting order in his favour under the Settled Land Act 1925, section 12(1)(*a*).

SETTLED LAND ACT 1925

24. As to a tenant for life who has parted with his interest.—(1) If it is shown to the satisfaction of the court that a tenant for life, who has by reason of bankruptcy, assignment, incumbrance, or otherwise ceased in the opinion of the court to have a substantial interest in his estate or interest in the settled land or any part thereof, has unreasonably refused to exercise any of the powers conferred on him by this Act, or consents to an order under this section, the court may, on the application of any person interested in the settled land or the part thereof affected, make an order authorising the trustees of the settlement, to exercise, in the name and on behalf of the tenant for life, any of the powers of a tenant for life under this Act, in relation to the settled land or the part thereof affected, either generally and in such manner and for such period as the court may think fit, or in a particular instance, and the court may by the order direct that any documents of title in the possession of the tenant for life relating to the settled land be delivered to the trustees of the settlement.

(2) While any such order is in force, the tenant for life shall not, in relation to the settled land or the part thereof affected, exercise any of the powers thereby authorised to be exercised in his name and on his behalf, but no person dealing with the tenant for life shall be affected by any such order, unless the order is for the time being registered as an order affecting land. [17]

(3) An order may be made under this section at any time after the estate or interest of the tenant for life under the settlement has taken effect in possession, and notwithstanding that he disposed thereof when it was an estate or interest in remainder or reversion.

RE THORNHILL'S SETTLEMENT
[1941] Ch 24, [1940] 4 All ER 83, 249 (ChD, BENNETT, J, affirmed in five lines by CA Sir Wilfrid GREENE MR, CLAUSON and GODDARD LJJ).

Michael Christopher Wright McCreagh, the tenant for life, was bankrupt. He neglected the management of the property, and the mansion house and three farms were derelict.

The summons asked that the Public Trustee, as trustee of the settlement, should be authorised by order under the Settled Land Act 1925, section 24(1) to exercise the tenant for life's powers of leasing and sale.

Held. The tenant for life had unreasonably refused to exercise his powers, and the order should be made.

BENNETT J: The real question which I have to determine is whether the applicant has satisfied me that the tenant for life, the bankrupt, has

---

[17] LCA 1972, s. 6, p. 43, ante.

unreasonably refused to exercise the powers which the Settled Land Act 1925 gives to him as a tenant for life. . . .

There is evidence which satisfies me that for some years past the land comprised in the settlement has been neglected. . . .

The fact that the land has been allowed to fall into this deplorable condition is not a ground for exercising the jurisdiction which section 24 of the Settled Land Act 1925 confers on this court. I have been satisfied by evidence that the tenant for life has unreasonably refused to exercise the powers which that Act gives him—namely, the powers of sale and the powers of leasing and other powers concerned with the disposal of the land comprised in the settlement.

There are three respects in which, in my judgment, the applicant has proved that the bankrupt has unreasonably refused to exercise his powers. . .

[His Lordship referred to occasions on which the bankrupt unreasonably refused to let farms, to sell to the War Office land which it had requisitioned, and to let some allotments. The tenant for life was acting in this way because he felt aggrieved that the settlor, his mother, had given him only a life interest under the settlement.]

On the evidence I think that it is plain that in the interests of everybody interested in the settled land an order should be made authorizing the trustees of the settlement to exercise on behalf of the tenant for life some of the tenant for life's powers. I do not propose, as at present advised and on the evidence before me, to make an order which will authorize the trustees of the settlement to exercise powers of sale over the whole of the settled land, because, as I understand it, the settled land has been in the possession of the ancestors of the present tenant for life since the days of King John. It may well be that the bankrupt might have objections founded on reason against the whole of the estate being disposed of. The order which I propose to make under the section is one which will enable the Public Trustee, as trustee of the settlement, to exercise in the name and on behalf of the tenant for life the powers of sale in relation to any of the land comprised in the settlement and requisitioned by or on behalf of the War Office, and the powers of the tenant for life to lease any part of the settled land and to exercise all powers conferred on a tenant for life by the Act ancillary to the powers of leasing. I will also make an order on the tenant for life to deliver to the trustee documents of title in his possession relating to the settled land. I will authorize the trustee to exercise the powers of the tenant for life to make a contract to sell the land requisitioned by the War Office and to sell it, and I will vest in the trustee the power to direct investment.

E. Fiduciary Nature of the Powers of the Tenant for Life

SETTLED LAND ACT 1925

107. Tenant for life trustee for all parties interested.—(1) A tenant for life or statutory owner shall, in exercising any power under this Act, have regard to the interests of all parties entitled under the settlement, and shall, in relation to the exercise thereof by him, be deemed to be in the position and to have the duties and liabilities of a trustee for those parties.

(1A) The following provisions apply to the tenant for life as they apply to the trustees of the settlement—

    (a) sections 11, 13 to 15 and 21 to 23 of the Trustee Act 2000 (power to employ agents subject to certain restrictions),

(b) section 32 of that Act (remuneration and expenses of agents etc.),

(c) section 19 of the Trustee Act 1925 (power to insure), and

(d) in so far as they relate to the provisions mentioned in paragraphs (a) and (c), Part I of and Schedule 1 to, the Trustee Act 2000 (the duty of care). [18]

In **Wheelwright v Walker** (1883) 23 ChD 752, the defendant was tenant for life of land which was settled within the Settled Land Act 1882, and his daughter was entitled in remainder. [19] The daughter sold her interest in remainder to the plaintiff. The defendant intended to sell under his Settled Land Act powers, the result of such sale being to deprive the plaintiff of his right to occupy the land when the defendant died. [20] No Settled Land Act trustees had been appointed.

PEARSON J granted an injunction on the ground that, since no Settled Land Act trustees had been appointed, the provisions of the Act would not be complied with. On the question of the tenant for life's power to sell, he said at 758:

'So far as I can see, there is no restriction whatever in the Act on the power of a tenant for life to sell. There is nothing that I can see in the Act to enable the Court to restrain him from selling, whether he desires to sell because he is in debt, and wishes to increase his income; or whether he desires to sell from mere unwillingness to take the trouble involved in the management of landed property; or whether he acts from worse motives, as from mere caprice or whim, or because he is desirous of doing that which he knows would be very disagreeable to those who expect to succeed him at his death. There is not, so far as I can see, any power either in the Court or in trustees to interfere with his power of sale. [1]
. . . Now if *Elizabeth France*, instead of selling the property to the Plaintiff *J. W. Wheelwright*, had simply settled it, on her marriage, on herself as tenant for life, with remainder to her children, I am of opinion that this Act would have applied, and her father, as tenant for life under the will, could have exercised the power of sale as tenant for life under the Act. I think it makes no difference that *Elizabeth France* simply sold to the Plaintiff *J. W. Wheelwright* instead of settling her interest. I find nothing whatever in the Act which gives any person entitled in remainder any power of any sort or description to interfere with the right of the tenant for life to sell. So far as I can see, the object of the Act is to enable the tenant for life of real estate comprised in a settlement to take it out of the settlement, and to substitute for it, *ex mero motu*, the value of it in pounds, shillings, and pence. I come now to the next question which has been raised. It was said that the tenant for life may have a power to sell, but that there are no trustees here; that trustees are required to be in existence under the Act, and that the tenant for life cannot sell unless there be trustees under the Act, because he is required to give them notice... Although I do not see exactly what power or control they have over the tenant for life in regard to selling the property, it is quite plain from the whole scope of the Act that the trustees are considered as having an important duty to perform; at all events, I think it clear that even as regards a sale they have this

---

[18] As inserted by TA 2000, s. 40, Sch. 2, Part II, para. 17. On the duty of care, see p. 275, ante.

[19] Subject to partial divestment if, as was most unlikely, her father had further children.

[20] The plaintiff's interest would be overreached on sale and transferred to the purchase money: SLA 1882, s. 22(5); SLA 1925, s. 75(5), p. 357, post.

[1] See also *Cardigan v Curzon-Howe* (1885) 30 ChD 531 at 540, per CHITTY J.

important duty to perform, that if a tenant for life attempted to commit what may be called a fraud, and proposed to sell the property for something infinitely below its real value, it would be the duty of the trustees to come to the Court and ask for an injunction to restrain a sale. I do not think it would be right for them to leave the remainderman to take the objection at some remote period when the evidence might be very conflicting as to the circumstances under which the sale was made, and as to the value of the property; but I think it would be the trustees' duty to bring the matter before the Court, and the Court would have power in that case of controlling the sale, and the more so because the 53rd section of the Act[2] states that "a tenant for life shall in exercising any power under this Act . . . be deemed to be in the position and to have the duties and liabilities of a trustee for" all parties. I assent to Mr *William Pearson's* argument that a tenant for life in selling under the Act must sell as fairly as trustees must sell for the tenant for life and for those in remainder. . . . Now, there are certainly no trustees here who come within the meaning of the Act. But by the 38th section [3] power is given to "the tenant for life", or any other person having an interest in the settled land, to come to the Court, and then the Court "may, if it thinks fit, . . . appoint fit persons to be trustees under the settlement for the purposes of this Act". I think, therefore, that *John Walker*, the tenant for life, has himself power to sell the fee simple and inheritance of this property if he should comply with the provisions of the Act, but I also think that he has been proceeding, up to the present moment, precipitately, because there are no trustees to whom he can give notice, and therefore I shall grant an injunction to restrain him from selling or offering for sale the property until such time as there shall have been appointed proper trustees of the will for the purposes of the Act, to whom notice can be given and until due notice shall have been given to them of the intention to sell.'

In **Middlemas v Stevens** [1901] 1 Ch 574, the defendant was entitled under her deceased husband's will to the enjoyment of a house during widowhood and so long as she resided therein. Intending to marry again, she proposed to grant, under her Settled Land Act powers, a 21 year lease to her intended husband. The remainderman objected, and JOYCE J held that her proposed action was not a bona fide exercise of her powers. He said at 577:

'I have no doubt in this case. A tenant for life in exercising any of the powers conferred by the Settled Land Acts must have regard to the interests of all parties entitled under the settlement. Here is a lady who is tenant for life during widowhood. Apart from any question as to her relationship to the gentleman who is the intended lessee, if I found a person, whose interest in the settled property would come to an end tomorrow, persisting in granting a lease which was objected to by all those entitled in remainder, I should regard the case with considerable suspicion. But this case goes beyond suspicion. It is clear from the correspondence that the real object of the lady in granting the lease is that she may herself continue in occupation of the premises. That, in my opinion, is not a bona fide exercise of her powers as tenant for life. But it does not rest there, because it is admitted by the correspondence that she has no intention of granting the lease in the event of her not marrying the gentleman in question. I think the

---

2   Replaced by SLA 1925, s. 107(1) p. 351, ante.
3   Replaced by SLA 1925, s. 34, p. 355, post.

plaintiffs are entitled to an injunction restraining the defendant from granting the lease without their consent or the sanction of the Court.'[4]

Subject to restrictions, the tenant for life may however deal with the settled land for his own purposes.

SETTLED LAND ACT 1925

68. Provision enabling dealings with tenant for life.—(1) In the manner mentioned and subject to the provisions contained in this section —
- (a) a sale, grant, lease, mortgage, charge or other disposition of settled land, or of any easement, right, or privilege over the same may be made to the tenant for life; or
- (b) capital money may be advanced on mortgage to him; or
- (c) a purchase may be made from him of land to be made subject to the limitations of the settlement; or
- (d) an exchange may be made with him of settled land for other land; and
- (e) any such disposition, advance, purchase, or exchange as aforesaid may be made to, from, or with any persons of whom the tenant for life is one.

(2) In every such case the trustees of the settlement shall, in addition to their powers as trustees, have all the powers of a tenant for life in reference to negotiating and completing the transaction, and shall have power to enforce any covenants by the tenant for life, or, where the tenant for life is himself one of the trustees, then the other or others of them shall have such power, and the said powers of a tenant for life may be exercised by the trustees of the settlement in the name and on behalf of the tenant for life.[5]

(3) This section applies, notwithstanding that the tenant for life is one of the trustees of the settlement, or that an order has been made authorising the trustees to act on his behalf, or that he is suffering from mental disorder,[6] but does not apply to dealings with any body of persons which includes a trustee of the settlement, not being the tenant for life, unless the transaction is either previously or subsequently approved by the court.

VII.   Trustees of the Settlement[7]

SETTLED LAND ACT 1925

30. Who are trustees for purposes of Act.—(1) Subject to the provisions of this Act, the following persons are trustees of a settlement for the purposes of this

---

[4]   See also later proceedings in *Wheelwright v Walker* (1883) 31 WR 912, where a malicious attempt to sell at a deflated price was restrained; *Re Handman and Wilcox's Contract* [1902] 1 Ch 599 (best rent not obtained as required by SLA 1882, s. 7, now SLA 1925, s. 42); *Re Earl Somers* (1895) 11 TLR 567 (lease of public house by teetotal tenant for life containing a term that intoxicating liquors should not be sold).

[5]   See *Re Pennant's Will Trusts* [1970] Ch 75, [1969] 2 All ER 862.

[6]   Amended by Mental Health Act 1959, s. 149(1) and Sch. 7, Part I.

[7]   C & B, pp. 208–211; Gray, p. 619; M & W, paras. 8.065–8.010, 8.106–8.108; MM, 256–257.

Act, and are in this Act referred to as the 'trustees of the settlement' or 'trustees of a settlement', namely —
  (i)   the persons, if any, who are for the time being under the settlement, trustees with power of sale of the settled land (subject or not to the consent of any person), or with power of consent to or approval of the exercise of such a power of sale, or if there are no such persons; then
  (ii) the persons, if any, for the time being, who are by the settlement declared to be trustees thereof for the purposes of the Settled Land Acts 1882 to 1890, or any of them, or this Act, or if there are no such persons; then
  (iii) the persons, if any, who are for the time being under the settlement trustees with a power or duty to sell [8] any other land comprised in the settlement and subject to the same limitations as the land to be sold or otherwise dealt with, or with power of consent to or approval of the exercise of such a power of sale, or, if there are no such persons; then
  (iv) the persons, if any, who are for the time being under the settlement trustees with a future power or duty to sell the settled land, or with power of consent to or approval of the exercise of such a future power of sale, and whether the power or duty takes effect in all events or not, or, if there are no such persons; then
  (v)   the persons, if any, appointed by deed to be trustees of the settlement by all the persons who at the date of the deed were together able, by virtue of their beneficial interests or by the exercise of an equitable power, to dispose of the settled land in equity for the whole estate the subject of the settlement.

(2) Paragraphs (i), (iii) and (iv) of the last preceding subsection take effect in like manner as if the powers therein referred to had not by this Act been made exercisable by the tenant for life or statutory owner.

(3) Where a settlement is created by will, or a settlement has arisen by the effect of an intestacy, and apart from this subsection there would be no trustees for the purposes of this Act of such settlement, then the personal representatives of the deceased shall, until other trustees are appointed, be by virtue of this Act the trustees of the settlement, but where there is a sole personal representative, not being a trust corporation, it shall be obligatory on him to appoint an additional trustee to act with him for the purposes of this Act, and the provisions of the Trustee Act, 1925, [9] relating to the appointment of new trustees and the vesting of trust property shall apply accordingly.

31. As to trustees of compound settlements.—(1) Persons who are for the time being trustees for the purposes of this Act of an instrument which is a settlement, or is deemed to be a subsisting settlement for the purposes of this Act, shall be the trustees for the purposes of this Act of any settlement constituted by that instrument and any instruments subsequent in date or operation.

Where there are trustees for the purposes of this Act of the instrument under which there is a tenant for life or statutory owner but there are no trustees for these purposes of a prior instrument, being one of the instruments by which a compound settlement is constituted, those trustees shall, unless and until trustees are appointed of the prior instrument or of the compound settlement, be the trustees for the purposes of this Act of the compound settlement. [10]

---

[8]   As amended by TLATA 1996, s. 25(1), para. 2(9).
[9]   TA 1925, ss. 36–44, as amended by TLATA 1996, s. 25(1), para. 3(11)–(14).
[10] As added by LP(A)A 1926, Sch.

34. Appointment of trustees by court.—(1) If at any time there are no trustees of a settlement, or where in any other case it is expedient, for the purposes of this Act, that new trustees of a settlement be appointed, the court may, if it thinks fit, on the application of the tenant for life, statutory owner, or of any other person having, under the settlement, an estate or interest in the settled land, in possession, remainder or otherwise, or, in the case of an infant, of his testamentary or other guardian or next friend, appoint fit persons to be trustees of the settlement.

(2) The persons so appointed, and the survivors and survivor of them, while continuing to be trustees or trustee, and, until the appointment of new trustees, the personal representatives or representative for the time being of the last surviving or continuing trustee, shall become and be the trustees or trustee of the settlement.

35. Procedure on appointment of new trustees.—(1) Whenever a new trustee for the purposes of this Act is appointed of a trust instrument or a trustee thereof for the purposes aforesaid is discharged from the trust without a new trustee being appointed, a deed shall be executed supplemental to the last or only principal vesting instrument containing a declaration that the persons therein named, being the persons who after such appointment or discharge, as the case may be, are the trustees of the trust instrument for the purposes aforesaid, are the trustees of the settlement for those purposes; and a memorandum shall be endorsed on or annexed to the last or only principal vesting instrument in accordance with the Trustee Act, 1925.

(2) Every such deed as aforesaid shall, if the trustee was appointed or discharged by the court, be executed by such person as the court may direct, and, in any other case, shall be executed by —

(i) the person, if any, named in the principal vesting instrument as the person for the time being entitled to appoint new trustees of the settlement, or if no person is so named, or the person is dead or unable or unwilling to act, the persons who if the principal vesting instrument had been the only instrument constituting the settlement would have had power to appoint new trustees thereof;

(ii) the persons named in the deed of declaration as the trustees of the settlement; and

(iii) any trustee who is discharged as aforesaid or retires.

(3) A statement contained in any such deed of declaration as is mentioned in this section to the effect that the person named in the principal vesting instrument as the person for the time being entitled to appoint new trustees of the settlement is unable or unwilling to act, or that a trustee has remained outside the United Kingdom for more than twelve months, or refuses or is unfit to act, or is incapable of acting, shall in favour of a purchaser of a legal estate be conclusive evidence of the matter stated.

95. Trustees' receipts. The receipt or direction in writing of or by the trustees of the settlement, or where a sole trustee is a trust corporation, of or by that trustee, or of or by the personal representatives of the last surviving or continuing trustee, for or relating to any money or securities, paid or transferred to or by the direction of the trustees, trustee, or representatives, as the case may be, effectually discharges the payer or transferor therefrom, and from being bound to see to the application or being answerable for any loss or misapplication thereof, and, in case of a mortgagee or other person advancing money, from being concerned to see that any money advanced by him is wanted for any purpose of this Act, or that no more than is wanted is raised.

Provisions relating to the protection of trustees are contained in Settled Land Act 1925, sections 95–98. [11]

VIII. Capital Money [12]

A. Application

SETTLED LAND ACT 1925

75. Regulations respecting investment, devolution, and income of securities, &c. [13]—(1) Capital money arising under this Act [14] shall, in order to its being invested or applied as aforesaid, be paid either to the trustees of the settlement or into court at the option of the tenant for life, and shall be invested or applied by the trustees, or under the direction of the court, as the case may be, accordingly.

(2) Subject to Part IV of the Trustee Act 2000, to section 75A of this Act and to the following provisions of this section—

(a) the investment or other application by the trustees shall be made according to the discretion of the trustees, but subject to any consent required or direction given by the settlement with respect to the investment or other application by the trustees of trust money of the settlement, and

(b) any investment shall be in the names or under the control of the trustees. [15]

(3) The investment or other application under the direction of the court shall be made on the application of the tenant for life, or of the trustees.

(4) The trustees, in exercising their power to invest or apply capital money, shall—

(a) so far as practicable, consult the tenant for life; and

(b) so far as consistent with the general interest of the settlement, give effect to his wishes.

(4A) Any investment or other application of capital money under the direction of the court shall not during the subsistence of the beneficial interest of the tenant for life be altered without his consent.

(4B) The trustees may not under section 11 of the Trustee Act 2000 authorise a person to exercise their functions with respect to the investment or application of capital money on terms that prevent them from complying with subsection (4) of this section.

(4C) A person who is authorised under section 11 of the Trustee Act 2000 to exercise any of their functions with respect to the investment or application of capital money is not subject to subsection (4) of this section.

(5) Capital money arising under this Act while remaining uninvested or unapplied, and securities on which an investment of any such capital money is made shall for all purposes of disposition, transmission and devolution be treated as land, and shall be held for and go to the same persons successively, in the same manner and for and on the same estates, interests, and trusts, as the land

---

[11]   As amended by TA 2000, s. 40, Sch. 2, Part II, paras. 11, 12.
[12]   C & B, pp. 211–214; M & W, para. 8.094; MM, pp. 89–90.
[13]   As to investment of capital money, see SLA 1925, ss. 73, as amended by TA 2000, s. 40, Sch. 2, Part II, para. 9 and TA 2000 Part III, p. 358, post.
[14]   For the meaning of capital money, see W & C, vol. 2, pp. 156–157.
[15]   As substituted by TA 2000, s. 40, Sch. 2, Part II, para. 10.

wherefrom the money arises would, if not disposed of, have been held and have gone under the settlement.

(6) The income of those securities shall be paid or applied as the income of that land, if not disposed of, would have been payable or applicable under the settlement.

(7) Those securities may be converted into money, which shall be capital money arising under this Act.

(8) All or any part of any capital money paid into court may, if the court thinks fit, be at any time paid out to the trustees of the settlement.

75A. Power to accept charge as security for part payment for land sold.—(1) Where—

    (a) land subject to the settlement is sold by the tenant for life or statutory owner, for an estate in fee simple or a term having at least five hundred years to run, and

    (b) the proceeds of sale are liable to be invested,

the tenant for life or statutory owner may, with the consent of the trustees of the settlement, contract that the payment of any part, not exceeding two-thirds, of the purchase money shall be secured by a charge by way of legal mortgage of the land sold, with or without the security of any other property.

(2) If any buildings are comprised in the property secured by the charge, the charge must contain a covenant by the mortgagor to keep them insured for their full value against loss or damage due to any event.

(3) A person exercising the power under subsection (1) of this section, or giving consent for the purposes of that subsection—

    (a) is not required to comply with section 5 of the Trustee Act 2000 before giving his consent, and

    (b) is not liable for any loss incurred merely because the security is insufficient at the date of the charge.

(4) The power under subsection (1) of this section is exercisable subject to the consent of any person whose consent to a change of investment is required by the instrument, if any, creating the trust.

(5) Where the sale referred to in subsection (1) of this section is made under the order of the court, the power under that subsection applies only if and as far as the court may by order direct. [16]

B. Improvements

SETTLED LAND ACT 1925

83. Description of improvements authorised by Act.—Improvements authorised by this Act are the making or execution on, or in connexion with, and for the benefit of settled land, of any of the works mentioned in the Third Schedule to this Act, or of any works for any of the purposes mentioned in that Schedule, and any operation incident to or necessary or proper in the execution of any of those works, or necessary or proper for carrying into effect any of those purposes, or for securing the full benefit of any of those works or purposes.

84. Mode of application of capital money.—(1) Capital money arising under this Act may be applied in or towards payment for any improvement authorised by this Act or by the settlement, without any scheme for the execution of the

---

[16]   As added by TA 2000, s. 40, Sch. 2, Part II, para. 11.

improvement being first submitted for approval to, or approved by, the trustees of the settlement or the court.

The Third Schedule is divided into three Parts:

I   Improvements, the costs of which are not liable to be replaced by instalments.

II   Improvements, the costs of which the trustees of the settlement or the court may require to be replaced by instalments.

III   Improvements, the costs of which the trustees of the settlement or the court must require to be replaced by instalments. [17]

C. Receipts

SETTLED LAND ACT 1925

94. Number of trustees to act.—(1) Notwithstanding anything in this Act, capital money arising under this Act shall not be paid to fewer than two persons as trustees of the settlement, unless the trustee is a trust corporation.[18]

D. Investment [19]

The Settled Land Act 1925, section 73 [20] gives a list of investments or other authorised applications of capital money under the Act.[1] There are 21 such headings, of which the most important are:

(i)   In investment in Government securities, or in other securities in which the trustees of the settlement are by the settlement or by law authorised to invest trust money of the settlement;

(ii)   In discharge, purchase, or redemption of incumbrances affecting the whole estate the subject of the settlement . . .

(iii)   In payment for any improvement authorised by this Act;

(xi–xii)   In purchase of land in fee simple, or of leasehold land held for sixty years or more unexpired at the time of purchase, with or without mines and minerals; or of mines and minerals separately, convenient to be held or worked with the settled land;

(xxi)   In any other mode authorised by the settlement with respect to money produced by the sale of the settled land.

---

[17]   Law Reform Committee 23rd Report (The Powers and Duties of Trustees) 1982 (Cmnd 8733), paras. 8–11, suggested that the provisions of the Third Schedule 'undoubtedly require modernisation.'

[18]   See SLA 1925, s. 95, p. 355, ante.

[19]   H & M, pp. 532–549; *Lewin on Trusts* (17th edn), pp. 405–420; *Snell's Equity* (30th edn), paras. 11.06–11.34; M&B, *Trusts and Trustees* (6th edn), pp. 735–757.

[20]   As amended by TA 2000, Sch. 2, Part II, para. 9.

[1]   See also Coal Mining (Subsidence) Act 1957, s. 11(7); Leasehold Reform Act 1967, s. 6(5), Sch. 2, para. 9.

Maudsley and Burn, *Trusts and Trustees: Cases and Materials* (6th edn), p. 735

'Trustees are under a duty to invest the trust fund and so make it productive.[2] For many years it has been usual to give trustees a wide power of investment in the trust instrument setting up the trust.[3] Otherwise their powers were limited to those which were provided by statute. Until recently the relevant statute was the Trustee Investment Act 1961, which was described by the Law Reform Committee in 1982 as "tiresome, cumbrous and expensive in operation with the result that its provisions are now seen to be inadequate".[4] Similarly, the Law Commission described the operation of the Act as "positively detrimental to most trusts to which it applies."[5] Much of this Act has now been repealed by the Trustee Act 2000,[6] Part II of which creates a regime which is more in keeping with modern investment practice.[7] This Act has substantially widened the investment powers of trustees. It is, however, still possible either to limit these statutory powers of investment in the trust instrument[8] or expand them.'[9]

IX. Change of Ownership

SETTLED LAND ACT 1925

7. Procedure on change of ownership.—(1) If, on the death of a tenant for life or statutory owner, or of the survivor of two or more tenants for life or statutory owners, in whom the settled land was vested, the land remains settled land, his personal representatives shall hold the settled land on trust, if and when required so to do, to convey it to the person who under the trust instrument or by virtue of this Act becomes the tenant for life or statutory owner and, if more than one, as joint tenants.

(2) If a person by reason of attaining full age becomes a tenant for life for the purposes of this Act of settled land, he shall be entitled to require the trustees of the settlement, personal representatives, or other persons in whom the settled land is vested, convey the land to him.

(3) If a person who, when of full age, will together with another person or other persons constitute the tenant for life for the purposes of this Act of settled land attains that age, he shall be entitled to require the tenant for life, trustees of the settlement, personal representatives or other persons in whom the settled land is vested to convey the land to him and the other person or persons who together with him constitute the tenant for life as joint tenants.

(4) If by reason of forfeiture, surrender, or otherwise the estate owner of any settled land ceases to have the statutory powers of a tenant for life and the land remains settled land, he shall be bound forthwith to convey the settled land to

---

[2] *Re Wragg* [1919] 2 Ch. 58 at 64, per P. O. Lawrence J.
[3] Such clauses are construed strictly: *Re Harari's ST* [1949] 1 All ER 430.
[4] The Powers and Duties of Trustees (1982) Cmnd 8733, para. 3.20.
[5] *Trustees' Powers and Duties*, 1999 (Law Com No. 260), p. 16.
[6] Following the recommendations of the Law Commission: *Trustees' Powers and Duties*, ibid.
[7] Most notably 'portfolio theory' by virtue of which investment decisions are to be made by reference to the whole portfolio of investments. See (1995) TLI 71 (Lord Nicholls of Birkenhead); (1996) 10 TLI 102 (E. Ford); (2000) 14 TLI 75 (I. Legair). See also Law Com. No. 260 (1999), p. 23; H & M, p. 537.
[8] TA 2000, s. 6(1)(b).
[9] To include, for example, investment in land situated abroad. See TA 2000, s. 8.

the person who under the trust instrument, or by virtue of this Act, becomes the tenant for life or statutory owner and, if more than one, as joint tenants.

(5) If any person of full age becomes absolutely entitled to the settled land (whether beneficially, or as personal representative, or as trustee of land, [10] or otherwise) free from all limitations, powers, and charges taking effect under the settlement, he shall be entitled to require the trustees of the settlement, personal representatives, or other persons in whom the settled land is vested, to convey the land to him, and if more persons than one being of full age become so entitled to the settled land they shall be entitled to require such persons as aforesaid to convey the land to them as joint tenants.

8. Mode and costs of conveyance, and saving of rights of personal representatives and equitable chargees.—(1) A conveyance by personal representatives under either of the last two preceding sections may be made by an assent in writing signed by them which shall operate as a conveyance.

(4) Where the land is or remains settled land a conveyance under either of the last two preceding sections [11] shall —
   (a) if by deed, be a principal vesting deed; and
   (b) if by an assent, be a vesting assent, which shall contain the like statements and particulars as are required by this Act in the case of a principal vesting deed.

ADMINISTRATION OF ESTATES ACT 1925

22. Special executors as respects settled land.—(1) A testator may appoint, and in default of such express appointment shall be deemed to have appointed, as his special executors in regard to settled land, the persons, if any, who are at his death the trustees of the settlement thereof, and probate may be granted to such trustees specially limited to the settled land.

In this subsection 'settled land' means land vested in the testator which was settled previously to his death and not by his will. [12]

(2) A testator may appoint other persons either with or without such trustees as aforesaid or any of them to be his general executors in regard to his other property and assets.

24. Power for special personal representatives to dispose of settled land.—(1) The special personal representatives may dispose of the settled land without the concurrence of the general personal representatives, who may likewise dispose of the other property and assets of the deceased without the concurrence of the special personal representatives.

(2) In this section the expression 'special personal representatives' means the representatives appointed to act for the purposes of settled land and includes any original personal representative who is to act with an additional personal representative for those purposes.

---

[10]   As amended by TLATA 1996, s. 25(1), Sch. 3, para. 2(4).
[11]   For s. 6, see p. 331, ante.
[12]   *Re Bridgett and Hayes' Contract* [1928] Ch 163, p. 363, post. For similar result in the case of intestacy, see Supreme Court Act 1981, s. 116. See too W & C, vol. 5, pp. 36–38.

X. Protection of Purchasers [13]

SETTLED LAND ACT 1925

110. Protection of purchasers, &c.—(1) On a sale, exchange, lease, mortgage, charge, or other disposition, a purchaser dealing in good faith with a tenant for life or statutory owner shall, as against all parties entitled under the settlement, be conclusively taken to have given the best price, consideration, or rent, as the case may require, that could reasonably be obtained by the tenant for life or statutory owner, and to have complied with all the requisitions of this Act. [14]

(2) A purchaser of a legal estate in settled land shall not, except as hereby expressly provided, be bound or entitled to call for the production of the trust instrument or any information concerning that instrument or any ad valorem stamp duty thereon, and whether or not he has notice of its contents he shall, save as hereinafter provided, be bound and entitled if the last or only principal vesting instrument contains the statements and particulars required by this Act to assume that —

(a) the person in whom the land is by the said document vested or declared to be vested is the tenant for life or statutory owner and has all the powers of a tenant for life under this Act, including such additional or larger powers, if any, as are therein mentioned;

(b) the persons by the said instrument stated to be the trustees of the settlement, or their successors appearing to be duly appointed, are the properly constituted trustees of the settlement;

(c) the statements and particulars required by this Act and contained (expressly or by reference) in the said instrument were correct at the date thereof;

(d) the statements contained in any deed executed in accordance with this Act declaring who are the trustees of the settlement for the purposes of this Act are correct;

(e) the statements contained in any deed of discharge, executed in accordance with this Act, are correct;

Provided that, as regards the first vesting instrument executed for the purpose of giving effect to —

(a) a settlement subsisting at the commencement of this Act; or

(b) an instrument which by virtue of this Act is deemed to be a settlement, [15] or

(c) a settlement which by virtue of this Act is deemed to have been made by any person after the commencement of this Act, or

(d) an instrument inter vivos intended to create a settlement of a legal estate in land which is executed after the commencement of this Act and does not comply with the requirements of this Act with respect to the method of effecting such a settlement;

---

[13]　C & B, pp. 885–888; Gray, pp. 650–653; M & W, paras. 8.028–8.035; MM, pp. 260-265.

[14]　See *Weston v Henshaw* [1950] Ch 510, p. 335, ante; *Re Morgan's Lease* [1972] Ch 1, [1971] 2 All ER 235, p. 335, ante; see also *Gilmore v O'Conor* [1947] IR 462; *Davies v Hall* [1954] 1 WLR 855, [1954] 2 All ER 330, raising the question whether the purchaser can claim to be acting in good faith when the tenant for life's failure to observe the statutory requirements was discoverable; *Re Handman and Wilcox's Contract* [1902] 1 Ch 599 (transferee from lessee).

[15]　See p. 326, n. 6, ante.

a purchaser shall be concerned to see —
(i)   that the land disposed of to him is comprised in such settlement or instrument;
(ii)   that the person in whom the settled land is by such vesting instrument vested, or declared to be vested, is the person in whom it ought to be vested as tenant for life or statutory owner;
(iii) that the persons thereby stated to be the trustees of the settlement are the properly constituted trustees of the settlement.
(3) A purchaser of a legal estate in settled land from a personal representative shall be entitled to act on the following assumptions: —
(i)   If the capital money, if any, payable in respect of the transaction is paid to the personal representative, that such representative is acting under his statutory or other powers and requires the money for purposes of administration;
(ii)   If such capital money is, by the direction of the personal representative, paid to persons who are stated to be the trustees of a settlement, that such persons are the duly constituted trustees of the settlement for the purposes of this Act, and that the personal representative is acting under his statutory powers during a minority;
(iii) In any other case, that the personal representative is acting under his statutory or other powers.
(4) Where no capital money arises under a transaction, a disposition by a tenant for life or statutory owner shall, in favour of a purchaser of a legal estate, have effect under this Act notwithstanding that at the date of the transaction there are no trustees of the settlement.
(5) If a conveyance of or an assent relating to land formerly subject to a vesting instrument does not state who are the trustees of the settlement for the purposes of this Act, a purchaser of a legal estate shall be bound and entitled to act on the assumption that the person in whom the land was thereby vested was entitled to the land free from all limitations, powers, and charges taking effect under that settlement, absolutely and beneficially, or, if so expressed in the conveyance or assent, as personal representative, or trustee of land [16] or otherwise, and that every statement of fact in such conveyance or assent is correct.

The scheme of the Settled Land Act 1925 with the exceptions as shown in the proviso to section 110(2), is based on the assumption that the purchaser of settled land is unaffected by the beneficial interests of the settlement. The scheme assumes that the appropriate machinery is correctly used; and the Act does not provide answers to the problems that will arise if mistakes are made. [17] Problems are most likely to arise in connection with a vesting instrument. Fraudulent suppression of deeds is another hazard, not however confined to settled land. [18]

---

[16]   As amended by TLATA 1996, s. 25(1), Sch. 3, para. 2(12).
[17]   Similar problems have arisen in connection with AEA 1925, s. 36(1); *Re Duce and Boots Cash Chemists (Southern) Ltd's Contract* [1937] Ch 642, [1937] 3 All ER 788; *Re Alefounder's Will Trusts* [1927] 1 Ch 360.
[18]   *Pilcher v Rawlins* (1872) 7 Ch App 259, p. 26, ante; *Weston v Henshaw* [1950] Ch 510, p. 335, ante.

(1946) 62 LQR 167, at pp. 168–169 (A.H. Withers)

'Conveyancers also assume that, in connexion with settled land, abstracted documents purporting to be vesting deeds, vesting assents by personal representatives of deceased tenants for life, deeds of declaration and deeds of discharge operate according to their tenor, except (1) in the case of the first vesting instrument made to give effect to a pre-1926 settlement, and (2) where facts or events are disclosed which suggest that some mistake has been made.

In practice conveyancers must make these assumptions, though . . . unless section 110 of the Settled Land Act 1925 is benevolently construed by the court, such assumptions are not justified.'

RE BRIDGETT AND HAYES' CONTRACT
[1928] Ch 163 (ChD, ROMER J)

At the date of her death on 17 January 1926, Mrs Thornley was tenant for life of settled land, and Jackson was sole surviving trustee of the settlement, which came to an end on Mrs Thornley's death.

Mrs Thornley appointed Bridgett as her sole executor, and he entered into an agreement to sell the land to Hayes. Hayes objected on the ground that title should have been made by Mrs Thornley's special representative under the Administration of Estates Act, 1925, section 22(1).

Held. Bridgett was able to give a good title to the land.

ROMER J: It is common ground that up to the date of her death Mrs Emily Margaret Thornley, who was the tenant for life of the property now in question, had vested in her the legal estate in the property. It is common ground that, that being so, on her death this legal estate passed to her personal representative by virtue of subsections 1 and 3 of section 1 of the Administration of Estates Act, 1925. But then it is said that by virtue of section 22, subsection 1, of that Act, in such a case as this the lady must be deemed to have appointed as her special executor in regard to this land the person who up to the date of her death was sole surviving trustee for the purposes of the Settled Land Act. Let me assume that this was so. On 17 January 1926, she died, and on 7 April 1926, a general grant of probate of her will was made to Thomas William Bridgett, a person whom she had thereby appointed as executor. As from that date, at any rate, wherever the legal estate in this property may have been as between the date of her death and this act of probate, the legal estate in this land vested in Thomas William Bridgett, and, while that act of probate remains unrevoked, he can in my opinion properly convey the legal estate to the purchaser. Section 204 of the Law of Property Act, 1925, subsection 1, says this: 'An order of the Court under any statutory or other jurisdiction shall not, as against a purchaser, be invalidated on the ground of want of jurisdiction, or of want of any concurrence, consent, notice, or service, whether the purchaser has notice of any such want or not.' Section 22, subsection 1 (if the purchaser is right as to its application at all to this case), provided that probate might have been granted to this sole surviving trustee. In point of fact the Court of Probate did not grant probate to him, but granted probate to Thomas William Bridgett. That being so, it appears to me that section 204 of the Law of Property Act applies to the case with regard to the taking of a conveyance from the legal personal representative. Further, the purchaser would be protected in the event of any subsequent revocation of that grant of probate by section 37, subsection 1, of the Administration of Estates Act, 1925. It can hardly be doubted that in this case, if the purchaser does take a conveyance from the person to whom the grant of probate was granted, he would be acting in good faith, within the meaning of section 55, subsection 1(xviii), of the Act. . . .

The point still remains as to whether section 22, subsection 1, applies to the present case, it being conceded on both sides that on the death of this lady the settlement came to an end.

[His Lordship read section 22(1) and continued:]

Section 22 is the first of three sections which are introduced under the general heading 'Special Provisions as to Settled Land'. In sections 23 and 24 it is I think reasonably clear that 'settled land' means land which after the death of the testator continues to be settled land, and the words in section 22, subsection 1, ' "settled land" means land vested in the testator which was settled previously to his death and not by his will' refer in terms only to that particular subsection. I cannot help thinking that these words were merely designed for the purpose of making it clear that section 22, subsection 1, did not apply to a case where the land was settled by the will of a testator. However, I have to deal with the words as I find them, and that being so I must read the earlier part of the sub-section as follows: 'A testator may appoint and in default of such express appointment shall be deemed to have appointed as his special executors in regard to land vested in the testator which was settled previously to his death the persons if any who are at his death the trustees of the settlement thereof.' So far down to the words 'previously to his death' the section applies to the present case, because here land was vested in the testatrix and it had been settled previously to her death. Then the sub-section says she shall be deemed to have appointed as her special executors the persons, if any, who are at her death the trustees of the settlement. Now before any one can go to the Court of Probate and get probate specially limited to the settled land granted to him, he must be in a position to say to the Court that he is to be deemed to have been appointed special executor of this land, because at the death of the testator he was trustee of the settlement thereof. But in my opinion he is not in a position to make that statement if the settlement comes to an end the moment the testator dies. It is to be observed that the subsection does not refer to the persons who immediately before the death of the testator were the trustees of the settlement, but to the persons who at his death are the trustees of the settlement.

The words 'persons who are at his death the trustees of the settlement' connote to my mind persons who are trustees notwithstanding his death, especially when it is realised that the section is dealing with the testator's will, which comes into operation only when he is dead.

For these reasons I think this sub-section does not apply in a case like the present, where, upon the death of the testatrix in question, the settlement existing up to that date comes to an end.

It has been seen that difficulties can arise where a vesting instrument is executed by those who appear to the purchaser to be the wrong persons. Similarly there may be doubt as to whether or not the land is settled land and whether, if it is settled, it has been vested in the right person as tenant for life. There seems little doubt that a purchaser who follows the correct Settled Land Act machinery is intended to be protected; but, as he is a purchaser with notice of the existence of trusts affecting the land, statutory authority is needed to protect him. And if he discovers the flaw on the title by extraneous enquiries or by chance and objects to the title, it will be odd if he is compelled to take a bad title. [19]

Megarry and Wade, *Law of Real Property* (6th edn), para. 8.029

'A vesting deed or transfer is not invalidated by any mistake in the particulars required to be contained in it, [20] and it is provided by section 110(2) of the Act [1] that a purchaser of a legal estate in settled land is bound and entitled to assume that those particulars are correct as to the persons who are the tenant for life and the trustees. [2] There is no statutory provision to indicate what is to happen if any of the matters is wrongly stated in the vesting instrument. An example is where, prior to 1997, land was settled on W for life or until remarriage, with remainder to X in fee simple. If W is widowed and secretly remarries, she will cease to be a tenant for life, the land would no longer be settled, and she would hold the property on a bare trust for X; yet this would not be apparent to any person dealing with the land. If W purported as tenant for life to exercise some power of disposition, would P, a purchaser of a legal estate, obtain a good title if he both dealt with W on the assumption that she was a tenant for life and paid any capital monies to the trustees? One view is that because P is not a purchaser of a legal estate in settled land, he is not entitled to treat the vesting deed as conclusive that W is the tenant for life. P purchases the land with notice that the land is held on trust and therefore, it is said, takes the land subject to X's interest. A number of solutions to this problem have been offered. [3] First, both from the wording of section 110(2) itself [4] and from other provisions of the Act, [5] there is reason to think that P would in fact be regarded as a purchaser of a legal estate in settled land and could therefore claim the protection of the section. Secondly, although P would have notice that the property was held on trust, there would be nothing to put him on inquiry that the settlement had terminated so that the conveyance to him was in breach of trust. [6]

The spread of registration of title is likely to eliminate such slight risk as there may be that this problem may arise. If the title to the land is registered and the settlement is protected by the usual restriction, [7] W will have all the powers of

---

[19] See (1939) 83 SJ 45 (A.H. Withers); (1946) 10 Conv (NS) 135 (H. Potter); (1947) 11 Conv (NS) 91 (H. Potter), 159 (B.B. Benas); (1958) 22 Conv (NS) 78 (F.R. Crane).

[20] SLA 1925, s. 5(3). But a vesting deed executed by the wrong person is inoperative: para. 8–020 ante.

[1] Subject to certain exceptions.

[2] Where the title is registered, a purchaser will not see the vesting transfer. There is no statutory provision to indicate whether he is bound and entitled to make the same assumptions about the restrictions on the register.

[3] See [1984] Conv 354 (P. A. Stone); and the previous edition of this work at p. 335; cf. [1985] Conv 377 (R. Warrington).

[4] See s. 110(2)(e), which provides that a purchaser of a legal estate in settled land is bound and entitled to assume that any statements contained in any deed of discharge are correct. If there is a deed of discharge, and land cannot be settled land: para. 8–036, post.

[5] See s. 36(1), where 'settled land' includes land which is notionally treated as if it were settled: see the previous edition of this work at p. 452, cf. para. 9–090, post.

[6] [1984] Conv 354 at 360 (P. A. Stone).

[7] Para. 8–022, ante.

disposition conferred by the Settled Land Act 1925. Any transaction made by W in exercise of those powers will necessarily confer a good title on P.'[8]

XI. Termination of Settlements[9]

A. Duration

SETTLED LAND ACT 1925

3. Duration of settlements.—Land which has been subject to a settlement which is a settlement for the purposes of this Act[10] shall be deemed for the purposes of this Act to remain and be settled land, and the settlement shall be deemed to be a subsisting settlement for the purposes of this Act so long as —

(a) any limitation, charge, or power of charging under the settlement subsists, or is capable of being exercised; or

(b) the person who, if of full age, would be entitled as beneficial owner to have that land vested in him for a legal estate is an infant.

7. Procedure on change of ownership.—(5), p. 359, ante.

B. Deed of Discharge

SETTLED LAND ACT 1925

17. Deed of discharge on termination of settlement.—(1) Where the estate owner of any settled land holds the land free from all equitable interests and powers under a trust instrument, the persons who in the last or only principal vesting instrument or the last or only endorsement on or annex thereto are declared to be the trustees of the settlement or the survivors of them shall, save as hereinafter mentioned, be bound to execute, at the cost of the trust estate, a deed declaring that they are discharged from the trust so far as regards that land: . . .

Where the land is affected by a derivative settlement or trust of land, the deed of discharge shall contain a statement that the land is settled land by virtue of such vesting instrument as aforesaid and the trust instrument therein referred to, or is subject to a trust of land.[11]

110. Protection of purchasers, &c.—(5), p. 361, ante.

C. Property held on Settlement Ceasing to Exist

TRUSTS OF LAND AND APPOINTMENT OF TRUSTEES ACT 1996

Schedule 1

Property held on settlement ceasing to exist

6. Where a settlement ceases to be a settlement for the purposes of the Settled Land Act 1925 because no relevant property (within the meaning of section 2(4)) is, or is deemed to be, subject to the settlement, any property which is or later becomes subject to the settlement is held in trust for the persons interested under the settlement.

---

[8]   LRA 1925, s. 20(1), para. 6.105, ante.

[9]   C & B, p. 884; M & W, paras. 8.036–8.040; MM, pp. 267–268.

[10]   TLATA 1996, s. 25(1), Sch. 3, para. 2(3).

[11]   As amended by TLATA 1996, s. 25(1), Sch. 3, para. 2 (6). For the termination of a trust of land, see p. 299, ante.

D. Registered Land

LAND REGISTRATION RULES 2003

SCHEDULE 7

Discharge of registered land from beneficial interests and powers under a settlement

14. Where the trustees of a settlement desire to discharge registered land from the beneficial interests and powers under the settlement they may do so by any document sufficient to discharge it.

Discharge from liability in respect of beneficial interests and powers under a settlement

15. Where a proprietor or the personal representatives of a deceased proprietor has or have, in good faith, complied with the requirements of this Schedule in executing a transfer of settled land or discharge of trustees and in applying for the appropriate restrictions that may be required for the protection of the beneficial interests and powers under a settlement—
    (a) he is or they are absolutely discharged from all liability in respect of the equitable interests and powers taking effect under the settlement, and
    (b) he is or they are entitled to be kept indemnified at the cost of the trust estate from all liabilities affecting the settled land.

QUESTIONS

(a) T died in 1916, having appointed the Public Trustee sole trustee of her will, and devising land to her husband for life, and after his death to her sister A, and on A's death to the Public Trustee on trust to sell and divide the proceeds between six nieces of her husband. Her husband died in 1929. A vesting assent duly vested the legal estate in A as tenant for life. A, after giving notice to the Public Trustee, sold the land to various purchasers at a time of rapidly rising prices and in circumstances which showed that the sales were commercially most imprudent. The nieces did not know of the sales until A's death. Advise the nieces whether they have a basis of complaint against A's estate, the Public Trustee, or the purchasers.

If the nieces had known of the intention to sell, could they have prevented the sale?

See *England v Public Trustee* (1967) 205 EG 651, where SELLERS LJ suggested that it would be desirable to provide that notice of an intended sale should be given to the beneficiaries under a settlement. See also SLA 1925, ss. 30(3), 97, 101.

(b) What arguments would you put forward on behalf of the purchaser in the hypothetical case on p. 365, ante?

(c) Would a purchaser from personal representatives obtain a good title on facts which were identical with those of *Re Bridgett and Hayes' Contract* [1928] Ch 163, p. 363, ante except for the fact that, as the purchaser later discovered, the settlement had not come to an end?

(d) A purported to convey land to B for life and after B's death to C in fee. Later A executed a vesting deed vesting the land in B as tenant for life under the settlement and executed also a trust instrument. B, relying on the vesting deed, sold the land to X. Is X entitled to the protection of SLA 1925, s. 110(2)? See SLA 1925, ss. 4, 5, 9, 18, 110(2); (1946) 10 Conv (NS) 139–140.

7. Perpetuities and Accumulations [1]

I. General

The policy of the law has always been to prevent property from being tied up in perpetuity. The problem has been met in various forms. Conditions preventing

---

[1] C & B, pp. 309–358; M & W, paras. 7.015–7.136; Gray, chap. 16; MM, pp. 210–246; John Chipman Gray, *Rule Against Perpetuities* (4th edn. 1942); Maudsley, *Modern Law of Perpetuities* (1979); Morris and Leach, *Rule Against Perpetuities* (2nd edn., 1962 and supplement, 1964); Lynn, *The Modern Rule Against Perpetuities* (1965); *Theobald on Wills* (16th edn, 2001), chap. 44; Holdsworth, HEL, vol. vii, pp. 81–144, 193–238; Simpson, *History of the Land Law* (2nd edn. 1986) pp. 208–241.

In 1998 the Law Commission published a Report on the Rules Against Perpetuities and Excessive Accumulations (Law Com No 251), recommending major changes in both Rules, p. 426, post.

alienation are void, [2] as are non-charitable trusts of perpetual duration; [3] estates tail have been barrable since *Taltarum's Case* in 1472, [4] in which a condition against barring was held void; [5] and the subsequent device of the creation of successive life estates was prevented by a rule which is one aspect of the rule against double possibilities, but which is better known under its 19th century title of the rule in *Whitby v Mitchell*. [6] The emergence of the modern rule against perpetuities was inevitable once it was established that executory limitations were valid at law, and were indestructible by a tortious feoffment by the tenant in possession; [7] the power to project estates into the future was unlimited.

The rule was therefore concerned with the extent to which estates could be made to vest in the future, and the period finally established was that of a life or lives in being plus 21 years plus a period of gestation in respect of a life in being or of a beneficiary if a posthumous child were born. [8]

A. Relationship between Vesting and Living Persons

John Chipman Gray's famous and authoritative statement of the Rule is: 'No interest is good unless it must vest, if at all, not later than twenty-one years after some life in being at the creation of the interest.' This is one author's formulation and not a statute. There are special situations, dealt with below, [9] where exceptions have to be made. It does not mean that an interest will be invalid, unless it is certain to vest within the period of a life in being plus 21 years. The rule is concerned with contingent interests, and, by definition, such an interest may never vest at all. The point is that, to comply with the Rule, the interest must be such that, if it does vest in the future, it must necessarily do so within the period. Put another way, and in a way which is sometimes thought to be easier to comprehend, an interest is void if it might by any possibility vest outside the period.

It is amazing that the Rule, so simple on its face, has caused such difficulty in its operation. What has to be appreciated is that the Rule requires the *recognition of a relationship* between the vesting and the lives of living people. The question is: is it certain that the interest must vest, if it vest at all, within 21 years of the death of some person now living? That is a simple legal formulation. The difficulty is in the recognition of the *relationship* between the vesting and the lives, that is, in being able to say for certain whether a particular contingent interest is certain to vest within 21 years of someone's death; or, to put it in the other way, whether the contingent interest might vest outside the period.

---

[2]   Litt s. 306; Co Litt 206b, 223a; and cases quoted in C & B, pp. 367–368; M & W, para. 3.071; MM, p. 43.

[3]   *Carne v Long* (1860) 2 De GF & J 75; *Gilmour v Coats* [1949] AC 426, [1949] 1 All ER 848; *Leahy v A-G for New South Wales* [1959] AC 457, [1959] 2 All ER 300; *Macaulay v O'Donnell* [1943] Ch 435n; M & B, *Trusts and Trustees* (6th edn, 2002), chap 8; H & M, chap. 14; Maudsley, pp. 166–178; Morris and Leach, pp. 307–327.

[4]   (1472) YB 12 Edw 4 Ed 19.

[5]   *Corbet's Case* (1600) 1 Co Rep 83b; *Mildmay's Case* (1605) 6 Co Rep 40a; *Portington's Case* (1613) 10 Co Rep 35b.

[6]   (1889) 42 ChD 494; affd (1890) 44 ChD 85. The rule was abolished in 1925: LPA 1925, s. 161.

[7]   *Pells v Brown* (1620) Cro Jac 590; Gray, s. 159; Morris and Leach, chap. 1.

[8]   *Duke of Norfolk's Case* (1683) 3 Cas in Ch 1; *Lloyd v Carew* (1697) Show Parl Cas 137, 1 Moo PCC 133n; *Stephens v Stephens* (1736) Cas temp Talb 228; *Thellusson v Woodford* (1805) 11 Ves 112; *Cadell v Palmer* (1833) 1 Cl & Fin 372; *Re Wilmer's Trusts* [1903] 2 Ch 411; *Re Stern* [1962] Ch 732, [1961] 3 All ER 1129.

[9]   P. 412, post.

As will be seen in the discussion which follows, there is no need to attempt to define who the 'lives in being' may be. Anyone will do; so long as the interest must vest, if at all, within 21 years of the dropping of that life. The life (or lives) in being is (are), therefore, that person (those persons) within 21 years of whose death (deaths) the interest must vest, if it vest at all. They are the lives who validate the gift. There are no 'lives in being' in the case of void gifts. The only problems in relation to 'lives in being' are those in which the settlor has himself expressly selected the persons whose lives are to be used for the purpose.

Thus a gift

(i)   to the first child of A (who is alive) to marry was void at common law, because the first child of A to marry might be a future born child, and that future born child was not certain to marry, if at all, within 21 years of the death of a person living at the date of the gift.

(ii) to the first child of A to attain the age of 21. This is valid whether A is alive or dead. If A is alive, it is valid because A's first child must attain the age of 21 within 21 years of A's death (a period of gestation is added in the case of posthumous children). A is the 'life in being'. If A is dead, the first child to attain the age of 21 must be a child of A living at the date of the gift. The child is the 'life in being'.

(iii) to the first great-grandchild of A to go for a walk with X. This is valid, because it must happen, if at all (and however unlikely in fact), during X's lifetime. X is the 'life in being'.

(iv) to the first child of A (who is alive) to marry a person now living. This is valid, because the marriage must take place, if at all, within the lifetime of a living person (though not yet identified).

(v)   to the first grandchild of A (who is alive) to attain the age of 21. This is void, because the first grandchild of A to attain the age of 21 might be a child of a future born child of A, and may attain the age of 21 more than 21 years after the death of any person alive at the date of the gift.

(vi) to the first grandchild of A (who is deceased) to attain the age of 21. This is valid, because any grandchild of A, whether born at the date of the gift or not, must attain the age of 21 within 21 years of the death of a child of A. A's children are the 'lives in being'. If a child (or all the children) of A be dead, his (their) children must be alive and they would be the 'lives in being'.

B. Vesting in Interest. Vesting in Possession

The requirement of vesting is that the gift must vest in interest but not necessarily in possession. This means that the beneficiary or beneficiaries must be ascertained and that all prior conditions have been satisfied.[10] In the case of class gifts, the size and the share of each beneficiary must be known before the class gift is considered to vest for the purposes of the perpetuity rule;[11] a class gift does not therefore vest for this purpose until there can be no possibility of the membership of the class increasing or decreasing. Thus, a gift 'to the children of A' does not 'vest', as a class gift in this context, until A dies; for A may have further children after the date of the gift. And a gift 'to the children of A who

[10]   Maudsley, p. 10; Morris and Leach, p. 1.
[11]   See p. 394, post; *Pearks v Moseley* (1880) 5 App Cas 714; *Re Dawson* (1888) 39 ChD 155; *Ward v Van der Loeff* [1924] AC 653.

survive both their parents' does not vest, as a class gift in this context, until the death of both parents; for, although there can be no more children of those parents after the death of either of them, the number of members of the class may be reduced at any time before the death of the survivor, and this possibility prevents vesting until that time.

C. Remorseless Application

The rule has been applied remorselessly,[12] defeating the intention of the testator, and has invalidated many gifts because of the recognition of the most extreme and unlikely possibilities, which would allow an interest to vest outside the period. This converted the rule into an object of ridicule; and one of the worst aspects of arbitrary application is, as Professor Leach has pointed out, that the vice of a void limitation is one that could have been prevented by competent drafting. The fault is the lawyer's, but the intended beneficiary is the sufferer.[13] However, apart from these anomalous cases which have become well-known draftsman's 'traps', the rule has by and large performed a useful function in holding a balance between the claims of the property owner to control the disposition of his property, and the policy in favour of free alienation.[14]

D. Subject Matter

A remarkable feature of its history is that it was established in the context of the control and disposition of family land, and has survived the change from land to stocks and shares as the basic form of capitalistic wealth. In this new context, the question of the tying up of property appears in a new light; in the old context of the tying up of land, the particular piece of land was inalienable during the period of the family settlement. In a settlement of stocks and shares, no property is tied up or made inalienable; for, even if successive interests under the settlement continued in perpetuity, the stocks and shares which formed the trust would remain alienable by the trustees, and would be bought and sold as the trustees decided to vary the investments.

E. Reform

In spite of much criticism, the rule proved itself obstructive to reform, and various attempts over the years to amend it in the United States have met with difficulties, and many states abandoned the attempt and re-established the common law rule.[15] In recent years, largely through Leach's influence, various jurisdictions in the Commonwealth and the United States have, in various ways, passed legislation reforming the Rule.[16] The methods selected are basically of three types, though some jurisdictions combine the methods —

[12] See pp. 381, et seq., post; Maudsley, p. 36.
[13] (1952) 68 LQR 35 (W.B. Leach).
[14] Simes, *Public Policy and the Dead Hand* (1953) 52 Mich LR 179; (1955) 103 U of Penn LR 707.
[15] Morris and Leach, pp. 13,33.
[16] Maudsley, Appendix D.

(i) Patching Up: that is to say, to provide specific solutions to the specific situations which have caused problems in the working of the Rule. The most common situation is that in which the vesting is postponed to an age greater than 21 and the interest thereby invalidated. England dealt with this case in 1925. [17]

(ii) Cy-Près: that is, to give to a court the power, on the analogy of the cy-près power in connection with charitable trusts, to alter the terms of a void gift so as to make it conform to the Rule. After all, the testator did not intend to make a void gift. Altering the terms would meet his intention. This solution was considered by the Law Reform Committee in 1956, and rejected.

(iii) Wait and See. This, on its face, is the most attractive solution. Much of the criticism directed at the common law rule related to cases where the interest was held void on the ground that it might conceivably vest outside the period, but did in fact vest next year. Thus, to return to example (i) above, assume that A is a lady of 56 and has three children, all engaged to be married. They all marry within the year. But the gift would be void at common law because of the possibility that A's present children may die. A may have another child, and the first child of A to marry may do so outside the period. The policy behind the Rule is to prevent remote vesting; not to hold void gifts which vest within the period merely because they might have vested outside. Why not, therefore, wait and see whether or not the gift vests within the period; and hold it valid if it does, but void if it does not? This is the principle recommended by the Law Reform Committee and adopted by the Perpetuities and Accumulations Act 1964; along with some 'patching up' provisions also.

Canada has provided the first example of legislation to abolish, and not merely to reform, the rule against perpetuities. In 1983 Manitoba abolished the rule, and in its place widened the jurisdiction of the court to vary trusts. [18]

In 1998 the Law Commission recommended that the rule against perpetuities should only apply to interests and rights arising under wills and trusts. [19] There should be one fixed and overriding period of 125 years. It also recommended that the rule against accumulations should be abolished except in relation to charitable trusts. Thus there will co-exist three different rules against perpetuities; for instruments made (a) prior to the coming into force of the 1964 Act; [20] (b) after the coming into force of that Act but before the recommended

---

[17]   LPA 1925, s. 163; p. 393, post.

[18]   Perpetuities and Accumulations Act 1983 (SM 1982–1983, c43); Manitoba Law Reform Commission Report on the Rules against Accumulations and Perpetuities (1982 No. 49), which was largely the work of D. W. M. Waters; see (1984) OJLS 454 (R. Deech) for a detailed review and criticism of this legislation, p. 422, post; (1983) Manitoba LJ 245 (A. I. McClean) 'Abolition is a great step into the unknown . . . the Manitoba Law Reform Commission and the Manitoba Legislature are not to be numbered amongst the law's timorous souls'; (1984) 62 Can Bar Rev 618 (J. M. Glenn), criticizing the legislation.
       Abolition has also been recommended by the Law Reform Committee of South Australia (73rd Report, *Relating to the Reform of the Law of Perpetuities* (1984)) and the Law Reform Commission of Saskatchewan (*Proposals Relating to the Rules Against Perpetuities and Accumulations* (1987). For reforms in other jurisdictions, see Law Commission Report on the Rules against Perpetuities and Excessive Accumulations 1998 (Law Com No. 251), Appendix B.

[19]   Report on the Rules against Perpetuities and Excessive Accumulations, supra; see Lord Chancellor's Department: Consultation Paper on the Rule against Excessive Accumulations 2002 (CP10/02); p. 428, post.

[20]   The 1964 Act is not retrospective: PAA 1964, s. 15(5).

reforms are implemented; and (c) after the coming into force of those reforms. Except in one instance, the reforms are not retrospective.

F. Perpetuities and Accumulations Act 1964

The Perpetuities and Accumulations Act 1964 came into force on 16 July 1964, and applies only to instruments coming into effect on or after that date.[1] The common law rule still applies to other limitations. Litigation on pre-1964 dispositions will become less likely as the years go by; but will remain possible for many years because questions for decision do not arise until the time for payment arrives, and this may await the termination of a life interest or the attainment of a specified age by beneficiaries.

Further, Wait and See applies, according to the terms of the Act, to void gifts; that is, to dispositions which are void under the common law rule on the ground that they might vest outside the period. To follow this method, it is necessary to apply the common law rule first, in order to discover whether the disposition is valid or void under the common law rule. Thus, there are two rules to apply; and the common law rule still survives in spite of the introduction of Wait and See.

The question is whether the retention of the common law rule was necessary or sensible; whether, in other words, there is any advantage in knowing that a disposition complies with the common law rule. It is submitted here that compliance with the common law rule is irrelevant once Wait and See is enacted; and it should be noted that all jurisdictions which have enacted Wait and See, except those which have effectively copied the English Act, have abolished the common law rule and relied solely on Wait and See. In these circumstances, the common law rule would phase peacefully out, and validity would depend on Wait and See alone.

The issue turns on the question whether or not, in a Wait and See jurisdiction, there is any advantage in knowing whether a disposition complies with the common law rule. The legislators assumed that there was. The contrary view, argued in detail elsewhere,[2] can only be presented shortly here. The point is that a contingent interest which is valid under the common law rule remains contingent; the beneficiary does not take until the contingency occurs. Thus, before paying out, even with 'valid' gifts, you have to wait and see whether they do in fact vest. If the gift is to the first child of A to attain the age of 21, and A has a child of 16, then, you wait and see if the child attains 21. If he does, you pay out; if he does not, the gift fails. The current value of the gift depends on the statistical likelihood of vesting. Similarly with all gifts under a Wait and See system. Treat the gift as valid until it is known that it will not vest within the period. The value of the interest depends on the statistical likelihood of vesting within the period. Presumably, 'valid' gifts are more likely to vest within the period than 'void' gifts; but the added value which they acquire is due to their increased likelihood of vesting, and not to their happening to comply with the Rule. Compare two gifts: —

(i) To such of the children and grandchildren of A as shall return from the Moon within 21 years of the death of X. A has 2 children and 4 grandchildren (none of them astronauts).

---

[1] Section 15(5). An arrangement under the Variation of Trusts Act 1958 will, with the court order approving it, constitute an 'instrument' for the purposes of the subsection: *Re Holt's Settlement* [1969] 1 Ch 100, [1968] 1 All ER 470.

[2] Maudsley, chap. 4.

(ii) To the first grandchildren of A (who is alive) to attain the age of 21. A has 2 children and also 4 grandchildren, all healthy and aged 20.

The first gift is valid under the common law rule, because it must vest, if at all, during X's lifetime; but it would be valueless to the children and grandchildren, because the trustees would be unlikely to make an advancement, and the grandchildren would be unable to offer it as security for a loan. The second gift is void (see above), but would have value, especially in the case of the eldest grandchild. In the era of Wait and See, compliance with the common law rule is irrelevant. Likelihood of vesting is crucial.

The common law rule is logically irrelevant, because Wait and See necessarily takes it over. The common law rule asks and answers the question: Is the limitation one which must vest, if at all, within the period? Wait and See asks whether it does in fact vest within the period. If an interest *must* vest, if at all, within the period, then it *will* vest, if at all, within the period. Wait and See takes over the common law rule. Unless, that is, you can detect situations in which the periods are different: as where a life in being might validate the gift at common law, but is not a person whom the statute allows to be used as a measuring life under Wait and See. There are, tragically, a few such situations under the English Act. That should be dealt with either by adding such lives to the statutory list of measuring lives applicable to Wait and See; or by letting the disposition stand or fall by the use of the statutory lives alone. It makes no sense to perpetuate for ever the learning of the common law rules just to deal with such situations. We should look, one way or another, to a system in which we have to deal with Wait and See alone.

G. Impact of Taxation

However you look at it, the great days of the perpetuity rule are over. There is a further reason for simplification. It is indeed paradoxical that, after waiting so long for reform of the law of perpetuities, the Act eventually comes when wealthy families no longer attempt to provide a series of successive limited interests projecting into the future. It was noted above that the problem of perpetuity became less acute when family settlements became settlements of variable securities rather than a specific piece of land; and, in the last few decades, the severity of the rates of estate duty, coupled with the rule that duty was payable at a life tenant's death upon the full value of the capital sum, greatly decreased the attractiveness of settlements containing successive limited interests. Discretionary settlements in various forms, which had substantial fiscal attractions prior to the Finance Act 1969, involve the use of the perpetuity rule only in respect of the measurement of the duration of the discretionary trust; and the provision of an alternative period of 80 years in section 1 of the Perpetuities and Accumulations Act 1964 is most welcome in this respect as an escape from a period based upon royal lives. The capital transfer tax system, introduced in the Finance Act 1975 (and consolidated in the Capital Transfer Tax Act 1984), made the tying-up of property in family settlements even less attractive. The position was somewhat alleviated by the abolition of capital transfer tax and its replacement by inheritance tax in 1986. [3]

---

[3]   See M & B, *Trusts and Trustees* (6th edn 2002), pp. 640–641.

II. The Perpetuity Period

A. At Common Law [4]

In **Cadell v Palmer** (1833) 1 Cl & Fin 372, BAYLEY B, in tendering advice to the House of Lords, discussed a number of cases [5] and continued at 416:

'We would not wish the House to suppose, that there were not expressions in other cases about the same period, from which it might clearly be collected, that minority was originally the foundation of the limit, [6] and to raise some presumption that the limit of 21 years after a life in being was confined to cases in which there was such a minority; but the manner in which the rule was expressed in the instances to which I have referred, as well as in text writers, appears to us to justify the conclusion, that it was at length extended to the enlarged limit of a life or lives in being, and 21 years afterwards. It is difficult to suppose, that men of such discriminating minds, and so much in the habit of discrimination, should have laid down the rule, as they did, without expressing minority as a qualification of the limit, particularly when, in many of the instances, they had minority before their eyes, had it not been their clear understanding, that the rule of 21 years was general, without the qualification of minority.

[His Lordship then referred to *Beard v Westcott* (1813) 5 Taunt 393, in which the Court of Common Pleas upheld an executory limitation which was not to take effect until 21 years after a life in being; but Lord ELDON sent the case to the King's Bench (1822) 5 B & Ald 801 where it was held void, on the ground however that it followed a prior void limitation. He continued:]

Upon the direct authority, therefore, of the decision of the Court of Common Pleas, in *Beard v Westcott*, and the *dicta* by LC Justice Willes, Lord Mansfield and Lord Kenyon, and the rules laid down in Blackstone and Fearne, we consider ourselves warranted in saying that the limit is a life or lives in being, and 21 years afterwards, without reference to the infancy of any person whatever. This will certainly render the estate unalienable for 21 years after lives in being, but it will preserve in safety any limitations which may have been made upon authority of the *dicta* or text writers I have mentioned; and it will not tie up the alienation an unreasonable length of time.

Upon the second and third questions proposed by your Lordships, whether a limitation by way of executory devise is void, as too remote, or otherwise, if it is not to take effect until after the determination of a life or lives in being, and upon the expiration of a term of 21 years afterwards, together with the number of months equal to the ordinary or longest period of gestation, but the whole of such years and months to be taken as a term in gross, and without reference to the infancy of any person whatever, born or *en ventre sà mere*, the unanimous opinion of the Judges is, that such a limitation would be void, as too remote. They

---

[4]   C & B, pp. 316–319; M & W, paras. 7.018–7.019; MM, pp. 219–221; Maudsley, pp. 42–45; Morris and Leach, pp. 56–70; *Duke of Norfolk's Case* (1681) 3 Cas in Ch 1; *Lloyd v Carew* (1697) Show Parl Cas 137; *Stephens v Stephens* (1736) Cas temp Talb 228; *Thellusson v Woodford* (1805) 11 Ves 112.

[5]   *Lloyd v Carew,* supra; *Marks v Marks* (1718) 10 Mod Rep 419; *Taylor v Biddall* (1677) 2 Mod Rep 289; *Stephens v Stephens,* supra; *Goodtitle d Gurnall v Wood* (1740) Willes 211; *Thellusson v Woodford,* supra; *Goodman v Goodright* (1759) 2 Burr 873; *Buckworth v Thirkell* (1785) 3 Bos & P 652n; *Jee v Audley* (1787) 1 Cox Eq Cas 324; *Long v Blackall* (1797) 7 Term Rep 100; *Wilkinson v South* (1798) 7 Term Rep 555.

[6]   To 21 years.

consider 21 years as the limit, and the period of gestation to be allowed in those cases only in which the gestation exists.'

Their Lordships affirmed the decision of the court below. [7]

B. Perpetuities and Accumulations Act 1964

PERPETUITIES AND ACCUMULATIONS ACT 1964

1. Power to specify perpetuity period. [8]—(1) Subject to section 9(2) of this Act and subsection (2) below, where the instrument by which any disposition is made so provides, the perpetuity period applicable to the disposition under the rule against perpetuities, instead of being of any other duration, shall be of a duration equal to such number of years not exceeding eighty as is specified in that behalf in the instrument.

(2) Subsection (1) above shall not have effect where the disposition is made in exercise of a special power of appointment, but where a period is specified under that subsection in the instrument creating such a power the period shall apply in relation to any disposition under the power as it applies in relation to the power itself.

15. Short title, interpretation and extent.—(2) In this Act—
'disposition' includes the conferring of a power of appointment and any other disposition of an interest in or right over property, and references to the interest disposed of shall be construed accordingly. [9]

(6) This Act shall apply in relation to a disposition made otherwise than by an instrument as if the disposition had been contained in an instrument taking effect when the disposition was made.

In **Re Green's Will Trusts** [1985] 3 All ER 455, Mrs Green made a codicil to her will stating that 'the period from the date of my death to the 1st day of January 2020 is hereby specified as the Perpetuity Period for the purpose of the trusts of the residue of my estate contained in my said Will'. She died on 1 February 1976. In holding that this was a valid specification, NOURSE J said at 460:

'That was an attempt to attract the operation of s. 1(1) of the Perpetuities and Accumulations Act 1964, . . .

Counsel submits that the attempt was unsuccessful, on the ground that what was here specified was not a number of years but a period expiring on a particular date. He did not go so far as to submit that a number of years plus a fraction of another, for example 79½, could not be a number of years for this purpose. What he said was that a period which can only be reduced to a number of years by making a calculation is not a specified number of years. For that he relied on *White v Whitcher* [1928] 1 KB 453, a once well-known authority on the meaning of

---

[7]   *Bengough v Edridge* (1827) 1 Sim 173. See note to ASTBURY J's judgment in *Re Villar* [1928] Ch 471, p. 380, n. 14, post.

[8]   This section does not apply to options: s. 9(2); C & B, pp. 338–339; M & W, paras. 7.042–7.043; MM, p. 224; Maudsley, pp. 111–115; Morris and Leach, Supplement, pp. 2–3.

[9]   *Re Thomas Meadows & Co. Ltd and Subsidiary Companies* (1960) *Staff Pension Scheme Rules* [1971] Ch 278, [1971] 1 All ER 239 (entry of employees' names in register for pension purposes held to be a disposition).

"some specified age" in what later became s. 228 of the Income Tax Act 1952. I find that authority to be of no assistance in the present case. There is plenty of other authority, including that of common sense, to the effect that "specified" merely means "unambiguously identified" or "made clear". Speaking from Mrs Green's death on 1 February 1976 and looking forward to 1 January 2020, I think that the codicil unambiguously identified, or made clear, a period of $43^{11}/_{12}$ years as the perpetuity period for the purposes of the trusts of residue. In my judgment that was a specified number of years within s. 1(1) of the 1964 Act.'

III. Lives in Being at Common Law [10]

A. Validating Lives

(1955) University of Florida LR at p. 470 (B.M. Sparks) [11]

'There are possibly those who will say . . . that they can never figure out this business about lives in being. They will ask how they are to determine who are the measuring lives. The best answer to that is that you may determine the measuring lives any way you desire. Do the lives have to be named in the instrument? No. Do the lives have to be lives of persons taking an interest under the will or deed? No. Is there a limit to the number of lives? No, not so long as they are reasonably ascertainable. Instead of searching for measuring lives it will probably be more profitable to concentrate on an examination of the property interest you are creating. The proper question to ask is: Can I point to some person or persons now living and say that this interest will by the very term of its creation be vested in an identified individual within twenty-one years after that person dies?'

American Bar Association Legislation Handbook (3rd edn, 1967), p. 4

'. . . at common law, if vesting were certain to occur within 21 years after *any* life in being, it was valid. But if *no* person could be identified, within 21 years of whose death an interest was certain to vest, the interest was void.'

RE GAITE'S WILL TRUSTS
[1949] 1 All ER 459 (ChD, Roxburgh J)

A testatrix left gifts by will in favour of such of the grandchildren of Mrs Gaite 'as shall be living at my death or born within five years therefrom who shall attain the age 21 years or being female marry under that age in equal shares'. At the date of the death, there were two children and one grandchild of Mrs Gaite alive.
Held. The gifts were valid as no grandchildren could take outside the perpetuity period unless that grandchild was born, within 5 years of the testatrix's

---

[10]   C & B, pp. 316–319; M & W, paras. 7.037–7.041; MM, pp. 219–221; Maudsley, pp. 88–92; Morris and Leach, pp. 60–63, 67–68.
[11]   Used by permission; Copyright 1955, by the University of Florida Law Review.

death, of a child of Mrs Gaite born after the testatrix's death; this was legally impossible as it is not lawful to marry under the age of 16 years.

ROXBURGH J: I must assume that Mrs Hagar Gaite, who was alive at the date of the death of the testatrix, might have had a child within five years after the death of the testatrix. What is impossible is that the child of Mrs Hagar Gaite, *ex hypothesi* born after the death of the testatrix, could itself have had a child within that period of five years, and that is essential to qualify for membership of the class. I do not base my judgment on physical impossibility. I leave all questions of that sort open for consideration when they arise because the matter is, in my judgment, concluded—and counsel for the second defendant admitted it was concluded— by the Age of Marriage Act 1929, section 1(1), [12] which provides:

'A marriage between persons either of whom is under the age of sixteen shall be void.'

Ex hypothesi, the child of Mrs Hagar Gaite born after the death of the testatrix must be under the age of 16 years at the expiration of five years from the death of the testatrix, and, therefore, that child could not lawfully be married and have lawful children. In construing the rule, I must have regard to the statute law of England, and, therefore, I hold that the rule is not infringed. [13]

Who were the lives in being? Who were the persons within 21 years of whose death (children of future-born children being eliminated) the interest must vest if at all?

Mrs Gaite's living children were the lives in being, though nowhere mentioned in the instrument (nor in the judgment). Further grandchildren of Mrs Gaite might attain the age of 21 more than 21 years after the death of the testatrix and Mrs Gaite; but it was certain that they would do so, if at all, within 21 years of the death of the living children of Mrs Gaite.

B. Expressly Selected Lives

The same principle applies where the settlor or testator selects the persons within 21 years of whose death the interest must vest, if at all. It will be seen that this was done in the following cases in this section. A gift would be void if it were made, for example, to 'such of the great-grandchildren of A (who is alive) as shall attain the age of 25. The measuring lives for the purposes of this limitation

---

[12]   Now Marriage Act 1949, s. 2.

[13]   For criticisms of the reasoning of ROXBURGH J, see (1949) 13 Conv (NS) 289 (J. H. C. Morris); Morris and Leach, pp. 85–86; *Theobald on Wills* (16th edn. 2001), para. 44–11; (1952) 68 LQR 35, 46 (W. B. Leach).

In respect of dispositions made on or after 1 January 1970, Family Law Reform Act 1969, s. 15, provides that, in the absence of a contrary intention, references to children and other relatives include references to any illegitimate child and to any persons descended through an illegitimate person.

In respect of dispositions made after 3 April 1988, Family Law Reform Act 1987, s. 1(1) provides that references to any relationship between two persons shall, unless a contrary intention appears, be construed in accordance with the general principle of the Act that it is immaterial whether or not a person's parents have or had been married to each other at any time: see Law Commission Reports: Illegitimacy 1982 (Law Com No 118, HC 98); Illegitimacy (Second Report) 1986 (Law Com No. 157, Cmnd 9913); Cretney Masson and Bailey-Harris, *Principles of Family Law* (7th edn 2002), paras. 18.027–10.036.

shall be X, Y and Z.' The vesting is not, in that situation, *related* to the lives. Where it is so related, there is the further question of the number and complexity of the lives who may be selected.

RE VILLAR
[1928] Ch 471 (Ch D, ASTBURY J); affirmed [1929] 1 Ch 243
(CA, Lord HANWORTH, LAWRENCE and RUSSELL LJJ)

By a will dated 1921 and confirmed by a codicil of 1926 the testator, who died in 1926, left his property upon certain trusts and provided that interests in the capital should not vest until the termination of the period of restriction which was defined as 'the period ending at the expiration of 20 years from the day of the death of the last survivor of all the lineal descendants of Her late Majesty Queen Victoria who shall be living at the time of my death'.

It was established that, in view of the fact that there were about 120 known descendants of Queen Victoria, some of whom had been dispersed and might be living in obscurity, and some whose fate was unknown, the ascertainment of the date of the dropping of these lives would be extremely difficult and expensive. The question was whether the testator could properly select such lives in 1926.

Held. The ascertainment of the lives was not impracticable and the trust was valid.

ASTBURY J: The real question is whether the period of restriction is one that can be given effect to in the circumstances. I feel the gravest doubt as to the validity of this will, having regard to the period of restriction and the circumstances now surrounding the lineal descendants of the late Queen Victoria. This form of restriction has appeared in many books of forms for many years, and the testator in 1921 adopted this form, which having regard to the war and the events during the war and subsequent thereto, is extremely difficult to carry out ...

The whole matter turns upon the true meaning of the law as explained in *Thellusson v Woodford* (1799) 4 Ves 227; affd. (1805) 11 Ves 112. In that case the judges were called in to advise the House of Lords, and their unanimous opinion was pronounced by Macdonald CB. It is upon the true meaning of that opinion and that of Lord Eldon LC that the question must be decided ...

The joint effect [of the tests applied by Lord Eldon LC and Macdonald CB in *Thellusson v Woodford*] is that, if, in the circumstances of the particular gift and the lives selected, it is substantially impracticable to ascertain the date of the extinction of the lives described, the gift is bad; but if, although the lives are numerous and the ascertainment of the date of the survivor's death is or may be difficult and expensive, the gift will not be rendered invalid if ordinary legal testimony can be applied, and will be available to determine that date.

Now, in this case the testator has in 1921 used an old form or precedent, restraining the distribution of his estate to a period expiring twenty years from the death of the last survivor of all the lineal descendants of the late Queen Victoria living on 6 September 1926. That must postpone the vesting for a very long period, but having regard to the character of this class, I have come to the conclusion that I cannot say it will be impracticable, having regard to the legal testimony probably available, to ascertain the period when the capital becomes distributable twenty years after the survivor's death. The expense involved will probably be very great. The trust operates very hardly upon the testator's five children. If I could have seen my way to hold this tying up invalid I would gladly have done so, but in my opinion I am not at liberty to do so.

It must be borne in mind that there are probably many other gifts and trusts now in existence with similar limitations. Years ago this was a very common form of limitation. Its application has presented increasing difficulties as time has gone on, and now, having regard to the war, the difficulties are still more serious. But I feel myself unable to hold that the determination of the period of vesting is beyond the scope of legal testimony in the ordinary sense, and for these reasons this capital gift is good. There will be liberty to apply for an inquiry to ascertain the existing descendants, but that inquiry will be unnecessary, if, as I hope, my judgment is reversed on appeal. [14]

In **Re Moore** [1901] 1 Ch 936, an attempt was made to stretch the period of perpetuity to the utmost: 'for the longest period allowed by law, that is to say, until the period of twenty-one years from the death of the last survivor of all persons who shall be living at my death'. JOYCE J held the gift void for uncertainty. [15] The gift was for the maintenance of a tomb.

In **Re Kelly** [1932] IR 255, the question concerned the validity of a bequest to expend '£4 sterling on the support of each of my dogs per year . . . and on the death of the last of my dogs' any balance to charitable purposes. MEREDITH J held that the gift was void for remoteness, and said at 260:

'It will be more convenient to deal first with the gift of any possible surplus remaining over on the death of the last of the dogs. Here the question, so far as there can be any question, is strictly one of remoteness. If the lives of the dogs or other animals could be taken into account in reckoning the maximum period of "lives in being and twenty-one years afterwards" any contingent or executory interest might be properly limited, so as only to vest within the lives of specified carp, or tortoises, or other animals that might live for over a hundred years, and for twenty-one years afterwards, which, of course, is absurd. "Lives" means human lives. It was suggested that the last of the dogs could in fact not outlive the testator by more than twenty-one years. I know nothing of that. The court does not enter in the question of a dog's expectation of life. In point of fact neighbours' dogs and cats are unpleasantly long-lived; but I have no knowledge of their precise expectation of life. Anyway the maximum period is exceeded by the lives of specified butterflies and twenty-one years afterwards. And even, according to my decision—and, I confess, it displays this weakness on being pressed to a logical conclusion—the expiration of the life of a single butterfly, even without the twenty-one years, would be too remote, despite all the world of poetry that may be thereby destroyed. In *Robinson v Hardcastle* (1786) 2 Bro CC 22 at 30 Lord Thurlow defined a perpetuity in these words: "What is a perpetuity, but the extending the estate beyond a life in being, and twenty-one years after?" Of course

---

[14]   It was not. A footnote to the case at [1928] Ch 478 adds: 'For a somewhat similar impracticability argument see *Cadell v Palmer* (1833) 1 Cl & Fin 372, 397; *Tudor's Real Property Cases* 3rd edn., pp. 424, 443. In that case the testator died in April 1818, and on 16 May 1918, his estate was finally wound up by ASTBURY J, in *Bengough v Edridge*, a few months after the period of 28 lives and 20 years had expired.' For other cases on royal lives, see *Re Leverhulme (No 2)* [1943] 2 All ER 274 (testator died in 1925 and life tenant in 1943. MORTON J held the gift valid, but warned testators not to use the descendants of Queen Victoria in the future); *Re Warren's Will Trusts* (1961) 105 SJ 511 (gift upheld in spite of MORTON J's warning. Testator died in 1944). Modern precedents use the descendants of King George V (or, preferably a period not exceeding 80 years, p. 376, ante).

[15]   And not even valid for 21 years, e.g. *Muir v IRC* [1966] 1 WLR 1269 at 1282, [1966] 3 All ER 38 at 44.

by a "life" he means lives; and there can be no doubt that "lives" means lives of human beings, not of animals or trees in California.

[His Lordship then considered the gift for the support of the dogs and said:] I adhere to the view that in the present case there is a valid severable trust for twenty-one years succeeding the death of the testator, provided any of the dogs live so long.'

If there are no lives in being, the period of 21 years may be allowed. In **Re Hooper** [1932] 1 Ch 38, a gift for the upkeep of certain monuments 'so far as [the trustees] legally can do so . . .' was upheld by MAUGHAM J for a period (in respect of non-charitable objects) of 21 years.

A child en ventre sa mère [16] may be a life in being, and a period of gestation, if it exists, [17] may also be added to the perpetuity period of a life in being plus 21 years.

In **Re Wilmer's Trusts** [1903] 1 Ch 874; affd [1903] 2 Ch 411, BUCKLEY J said at 886:
'*Thellusson v Woodford* is to be found again reported in 11 Ves 112, and at 143 Macdonald CB says: "The case of *Long v Blackall* (1797) 7 Term Rep 100 seems to have decided that an infant in ventre matris is a life in being. The established length of time, during which the vesting may be suspended, is during a life or lives in being, the period of gestation, and the infancy of such posthumous child".'

IV. Possible Not Actual Events. The Requirement of Certainty [18]

The rule requires that the interest must be certain to vest, if it vest at all, within the period. This requirement has been applied remorselessly; and limitations have been struck down where the only chance of vesting outside the period is

---

[16] 'In simple English, it is an unborn child inside the mother's womb': *Royal College of Nursing of the United Kingdom v Department Health and Social Security* [1981] AC 800 at 802, [1981] 1 All ER 545 at 554, per Lord DENNING MR. For the effect on the rule against perpetuities of delayed posthumous births by means of sperm banks or other devices, see (1979) 53 ALJ 311 (C. Sappideen). See also Human Fertilisation and Embryology Act 1992; as amended by Human Fertilisation and Embryology (Deceased Fathers) Act 2003; Human Fertilisation and Embryology (Disclosure of Information) Act 1992; Law Commission Report on The Rules against Perpetuities and Excessive Accumulations 1993 (Law Com No. 133), paras. 2.20, n. 30; 2.21, n. 45; 5.79.

[17] *Cadell v Palmer* (1833) 1 Cl & Fin 372, p. 375, ante; *Re Stern* [1962] Ch 732, [1961] 3 All ER 1129 (conception equivalent to birth).

[18] C & B, pp. 320–322; M & W, paras.7.024–7.029; Maudsley, pp. 35, 45–56; Morris and Leach, pp. 70–95.

fantastic, and even physically impossible. A number of such limitations are now well known.

A. The Fertile Octogenarian; [19] or the Conclusive Presumption of Fertility [20]

I. THE COMMON LAW RULE

In **Jee v Audley** (1787) 1 Cox Eq Cas 324, the testator gave £1,000 'unto my niece Mary Hall and the issue of her body lawfully begotten, and to be begotten, and in default of such issue, I give the same £1,000 to be equally divided between the daughters then living of my kinsman John Jee and his wife Elizabeth Jee.'

Mary Hall was about 40 and the Jees were 70, and had four living daughters. But, because the provision related to a general failure of issue (i.e. failure at any time in the future) it was theoretically possible that Mary Hall's issue might die at a time in the future, and because the daughters of the Jees *then* living might include a future born daughter of that old couple, the give was held void. [1]

WARD v VAN DER LOEFF

[1924] AC 653 (HL, Viscounts Haldane LC and Cave,
Lords Dunedin, Phillimore and Blanesburgh)

By his will the testator devised and bequeathed his residuary real and personal estate on trust for his widow for life and then for their children, and, if none (as happened), on trust for the children of his brothers and sisters.

By a codicil he declared that his widow's life interest should be terminable on her remarriage unless such remarriage should be with a natural born British subject; and that on her death the trustees should hold the residuary estate on trust for the children of his brothers and sisters who should be living at the death of his wife or born at any time afterwards before any one of them . . . attained a vested interest and who being a son attained 21 or being a daughter attained that age or married. The widow married a Dutchman.

At the date of the testator's death (without issue) his parents were both aged 66. All his brothers and sisters were over 30 years old and all had infant children, one of whom was born after the remarriage of the widow.

Held. (i) The gift in the codicil was void for perpetuity. (ii) The codicil did not revoke the gift in the will which was valid.

Viscount Haldane LC: On the construction of the will and codicil, two questions arise. The first is, whether the limitation in favour of children, contained in the concluding words of the codicil, is valid, having regard to the rule against perpetuities. The second is whether, if invalid, this new limitation and the wording of the codicil have been at all events efficacious as expressing a revocation of his bequest to children contained in the will. If the limitation to

---

[19]   Prof. Barton Leach labelled these categories: (1938) 51 HLR 1329; (1952) 65 HLR 721; (1952) 68 LQR 44; *Re Dawson* (1888) 39 ChD 155, p. 396, post.

[20]   On the law's different approach to this matter in a non-perpetuity context, see *Re Widdow's Trusts* (1871) LR 11 Eq 408; *Re White* [1901] 1 Ch 570; *Re Eve* [1909] 1 Ch 796; *Re Fletcher* [1949] Ch 473, [1949] 1 All ER 732; *Re Wohlgemuth* [1949] Ch 12, [1948] 2 All ER 882; *Re Herwin* [1953] Ch 701, [1953] 2 All ER 782; *Re Gilpin* [1954] Ch 1, [1953] 2 All ER 1218; *Re Westminster Bank's Declaration of Trust* [1963] 1 WLR 820, [1963] 2 All ER 400n; *Re Pettifor's Will Trusts* [1966] Ch 257, [1966] 1 All ER 913.

[1]   *Re Sayer's Trusts* (1868) LR 6 Eq 319; *Re Deloitte* [1926] Ch 56; *Figg v Clarke* [1997] 1 WLR 603 (1963 settlement; capital gains; CGTA 1979, s. 54(1)); [1997] Conv 237 (I. Ferrier).

children in the codicil be invalid, and that in the will has not been revoked, then a further question arises, whether the gift in the will operated in favour of any children of the brothers and sisters who were not born until after the testator's death. Philip Ponsonby Burnyeat, who is one of the parties to these appeals, was a son of the testator's brother, Myles Fleming Burnyeat, but was not born until after the testator's death and the remarriage of his widow. It is argued against his claim that the life interest of the widow was effectively determined by the provision in the codicil and that the class of children to take was finally ascertained at that date as the time of distribution. If this be so, Philip Ponsonby Burnyeat is excluded.

P.O. Lawrence J was the judge before whom this summons came in the first instance. He decided that the gift in the codicil in favour of the children of the testator's brothers and sisters was so framed as to be void for perpetuity. He held further, that the codicil operated to revoke the residuary gift in the will only so far as the substituted provision in the codicil was valid, and that the gift in the will in favour of these children, therefore, took effect, but merely in favour of such of the children as were born before the remarriage of the testator's widow. Philip Ponsonby Burnyeat was thus excluded. A majority of the Court of Appeal, Lord Sterndale MR and Warrington LJ, agreed with him in holding that the gift in the codicil in favour of the children of brothers and sisters was void for perpetuity, but held that the codicil revoked the gift in their favour contained in the will, and that there was an intestacy as regarded the residuary estate of the testator as from the remarriage of his widow. Atkin LJ dissented, holding that the testator must be taken, as matter of construction, to have been referring in his codicil only to the brothers and sisters of the whole blood in existence when he died, just as if he had designated them individually. The provision in the codicil was therefore valid, that in the will having been revoked.

My Lords, the principle to be applied in construing instruments for the purpose of ascertaining whether the direction they contain infringes the rule against perpetuity is a well settled one. It was repeated with emphasis in this House in *Pearks v Moseley* (1880) 5 App Cas 714, where it was laid down that in construing the words the effect of the rule must in the first instance be left out of sight, and then, having in this way defined the intention expressed, the court had to test its validity by applying the rule to the meaning thus ascertained. It is only therefore if, as a matter of construction, the words in the codicil, taken in the natural sense in which the testator used them, do not violate the rule that they can be regarded as giving a valid direction. Looking at the language of the testator here, I am wholly unable to read it as not postponing the ascertainment of possible members of the class beyond the period of a life in being and twenty-one years afterwards. No doubt if we were warranted in interpreting the testator as having referred only to the children of those of his brothers and sisters who were alive at his death we might read his language in a way which would satisfy the law. But for so restricting the natural meaning of his words there is no justification in the language used in the context. He speaks of his brothers and sisters generally, and there is no expression which excludes the children of other possible brothers and sisters of the whole or half blood who might in contemplation of law be born. He has nowhere indicated an intention that his words are not to be construed in this, their natural meaning. I think, therefore, that the class to be benefited was not one all the members of which were, as a necessary result of the words used, to be ascertained within the period which the law prescribes, and that the gift in the codicil in favour of children of brothers and sisters is wholly void.

The next question is whether the codicil, although inoperative to this extent, was yet operative to revoke the gift to children of brothers and sisters contained in the will. After consideration, I have come to the conclusion that it was not so operative. There is indeed a revocation expressed in the codicil, but it is confined to the power of appointment given to the wife. It does not extend to what follows. That is, in terms, an attempt at a substantive and independent gift, and, as it is wholly void, I think, differing on this point from the Court of Appeal, that the provision in the will stands undisturbed. There is nothing else in the codicil which purports to affect it. It can make no difference that the class of children is a new and different class if the constitution of the new class is wholly inoperative in law. If it fails, then unless an independent and valid intention to revoke has been independently of it expressed, no revocation can take place. There is no such independent expression of intention here.

The only other point is at what period the class of children of brothers and sisters who took under the will is to be ascertained. I think that according to a well-known rule, the period is that of distribution; in other words, taking the valid alteration in the codicil into account, the remarriage of the widow with a foreign subject. Philip Ponsonby Burnyeat is thus excluded.

The result is that the judgment of P.O. Lawrence J should be restored. As the difficulty has been entirely caused by the testator himself, I think that the costs here and below should be taxed as between solicitor and client and paid out of the residuary estate.

LORD BLANESBURGH: My Lords, I too have arrived at the same conclusions as the rest of your Lordships. I am of opinion that the ultimate gift of residue contained in this testator's codicil is void as transgressing the rule against perpetuities, and I think it is also inoperative to revoke those residuary dispositions of his will which rank subsequent to the interest thereby given to his widow.

We have in this case, my Lords, an extreme but by no means uncommon illustration of the stringency—I might even describe it as the penal character—of this rule. At no time was there here any practical possibility that a perpetuity could eventuate as a result of the complete fulfilment of the terms of the gift in question; while, by the time any contest as to the validity of the gift arose, it had become, by reason of the death of the testator's father, inconceivable that any infraction of the rule could be involved in it. If we consider matters as they stood at the testator's death, which is, of course, the really relevant date, it was necessary before anything obnoxious to the rule could take place in connection with this residuary gift, that the following remarkable conjunction of events should supervene. The testator's father and mother were then each upwards of sixty-six years of age; to them, after a family of five, no child had been born for more than thirty years. It was, nevertheless, necessary that they should have another child. Alternatively it was necessary that their marriage should be dissolved otherwise than by the death of the father, and that he should marry again, and have a child by the second marriage. That child, in turn, had to have a child born after the death of the testator's widow—one born in her lifetime would not have been excluded by the rule. And even a child so born would have brought about an infraction of the rule, only if it had also eventuated that no one of the already substantial and apparently increasing families of the testator's four living brothers and sisters had survived his widow having married or attained twenty-one.

So much, as matters stood at the testator's death, had to happen before any nephew or niece excluded by the rule could appear. By the date of the summons on which the orders under appeal were made, this new event had to take place before the rule could be infringed. The testator's mother had survived her husband; she, then a widow lady of upwards of seventy-two years of age, had to marry again and have issue.

It is, I think, only fair to the draftsman of this codicil, manifestly prepared under severe pressure of time, to give this indication of the apparent remoteness of any provision contained in it from the danger of a perpetuity. It is quite certain, I make bold to say, that no idea of such a possibility entered anybody's mind. In its application to the present case, the rule has been really a snare, useless so far as its legitimate purpose is concerned, but operative in the view of the Court of Appeal and operative also in the view of this House (but for a fortunate accident for which the rule is entitled to no credit), to produce an intestacy under which certainly one person would greatly benefit, whose interests it was the permissible and express purpose of the testator by his codicil to circumscribe and reduce.

In my own experience nearly all modern manifestations of the rule are of this character, and have this result. The rule has so schooled testators into compliance with, perhaps even into approval of, its requirements, that deliberate attempts to push their privileges beyond its strict limits are now rarely made. So far as the Courts are concerned, the existence of the rule in these days is usually made manifest only in cases where nothing of the kind having been desired or suspected, and where by nothing short of a miracle could a perpetuity at any time have supervened, even that possibility has, by the time of the contest, ceased to be existent. All the same in these cases the rule is fatal even to gifts so innocuous, and I cannot doubt that such a result is both mischievous and unfortunate, in many directions—in this notably, that it brings a sound principle into entirely gratuitous discredit. Nevertheless I most fully agree that the rule is not to be whittled away by the Courts even for such a reason as that. It is too well authenticated in all its recognised incidents to be any longer under the control of any Court. It is the Legislature alone, which, maintaining the salutary purpose of the rule in its proper application, can, if it pleases, remove from it those incidents or excrescences which, without assisting to achieve its legitimate object, have done much mischief in other directions.

In the present case, and notwithstanding the actual conditions to which I have referred, I am, like the rest of your Lordships, satisfied that on the construction of the words here used by the testator, it is impossible to say that this gift is not within the prohibition of the rule as we have inherited it. It is agreed that the only conceivable means of escape is, either by construction or otherwise, to confine the apparently general expression 'my brothers and sisters' to the brothers and sisters of the testator in being at the date of his codicil. On construction it is not, I think, open to your Lordships so to limit these words. Nor is it, in my judgment, permissible, by reference to surrounding circumstances, to confine them, as Atkin LJ thought he could, to those same brothers and sisters as being the only brothers and sisters the testator knew, and as being in consequence and in the circumstances those with reference to whom alone he must be taken to have spoken. [2]

The problem of the 'precocious toddler', dealing with the minimum age of reproduction, is dealt with in *Re Gaite's Will Trusts* [1949] 1 All ER 459, p. 377, ante.

[2] *Cooper v Laroche* (1881) 17 ChD 368; *Re Dawson* (1888) 39 ChD 155, p. 396, post.

II. PERPETUITIES AND ACCUMULATIONS ACT 1964 [3]

PERPETUITIES AND ACCUMULATIONS ACT 1964

2. Presumptions and evidence as to future parenthood.—(1) Where in any proceedings there arises on the rule against perpetuities a question which turns on the ability of a person to have a child at some future time, then —

    (a) subject to paragraph (b) below, it shall be presumed that a male can have a child at the age of fourteen years or over, but not under that age, and that a female can have a child at the age of twelve years or over, but not under that age or over the age of fifty-five years; but

    (b) in the case of a living person evidence may be given to show that he or she will or will not be able to have a child at the time in question. [4]

(2) Where any such question is decided by treating a person as unable to have a child at a particular time, and he or she does so, the High Court may make such order as it thinks fit for placing the persons interested in the property comprised in the disposition, so far as may be just, in the position they would have held if the question had not been so decided.

(3) Subject to subsection (2) above, where any such question is decided in relation to a disposition by treating a person as able or unable to have a child at a particular time, then he or she shall be so treated for the purpose of any question which may arise on the rule against perpetuities in relation to the same disposition in any subsequent proceedings.

(4) In the foregoing provisions of this section references to having a child are references to begetting or giving birth to a child, but those provisions (except subsection (1)(b)) shall apply in relation to the possibility that a person will at any time have a child by adoption, [5] legitimation [6] or other means [7] as they apply to his or her ability at that time to beget or give birth to a child.

QUESTIONS

1.   As a lawyer who is trained to construe a will in accordance with the intention of the testator, how would you have construed the will in *Ward v Van der Loeff?* See Morris and Leach, p. 79; Restatement of Property, vol. 4, section 377, comment (c); *Re Powell* [1898] 1 Ch 227; *Re Cockle's Will Trusts* [1967] Ch 690, [1967] 1 All ER 391.

2.   Redraft the codicil in *Ward v Van der Loeff* so as to comply with the testator's true intention.

3.   (For thought now; answer later). If the codicil was void in *Ward v Van der Loeff,* why was the will not void too?

4.   What would be the decision on the facts of *Re Gaite's Will Trusts* if the testatrix had died in 1970—i.e. after the coming into force of Family Law Reform Act 1969, section 15?

---

[3]   C & B, p. 339–340; M & W, paras. 7.035–7.036; MM, pp. 217–218; Maudsley, pp. 116–118; (1964) 80 LQR 489–491; Morris and Leach Supp., pp. 3–4.

[4]   For a precedent authorising trustees to assume that no child will be born to a woman over the usual age of child-bearing, see Conv. Prec. 11–20.

[5]   Children Act 1975, s. 8, Sch. 1, paras. 3–5. See Adoption Act 1976, s. 39.

[6]   Legitimacy Act 1976, s. 5, Schs., 1,2.

[7]   See, for illegitimate children, Family Law Reform Act 1969, ss. 14, 15; Family Law Reform Act 1987, s. 1(1); p. 378, n. 13, ante.

B. The Unborn Widow under the Common Law Rule

RE FROST

(1889) 43 ChD 246 (ChD, Kay J)

The testator devised a freehold estate to his spinster daughter Emma for life, and after her decease, to the use of any husband she may hereafter marry for his life and, subject to a power of appointment, to the use of such of Emma's children as should be living at the death of the survivor of Emma and such husband . . . with further gifts over. The question was whether, on the death of Emma and her husband, without issue, the subsequent limitations were valid.

Held. All the limitations subsequent to the life interests to the spouses were void.

Kay J: [Emma] might have married after the death of the testator a person who was not born in his lifetime, and it might therefore have been a limitation to *Emma Frost* for life, remainder to an unborn person for life, with a contingent remainder over to the children of *Emma Frost* living at the death of that unborn person, of such of them as should be then dead leaving issue then living, and an alternative limitation to other persons, still to be living at the death of that unborn person, or leaving issue then living. That clearly would be a limitation which would offend against the rule of perpetuity, because it would tie up the estate, not merely during the life of *Emma Frost*, who was in existence at the death of the testator, but during the life of *Emma Frost's* husband, who might possibly not be living at the death of the testator. So that it would not merely be tied up for a life in being and twenty-one years after, but for a life in being, with remainder for a life not in being, with a contingent gift over. [8]

In **Re Garnham** [1916] 2 Ch 413, the limitation was to A (a bachelor) for life, then to any woman he might marry for life, and then to the children of A at 21 or on marriage, and in default of children (as happened) then to certain other persons. The gift was upheld. It differed from *Re Frost*, in that, as Neville J, at 416, said:

'It seems to me that upon the determination of the tenancy for life given to an existing person the class is ascertained, although the enjoyment may be postponed during a life tenancy of a person who may have been unborn at the date of the gift.'

In other words, in this case, the limitation vested in interest on the death of A, and not, as in *Re Frost*, on the death of the survivor. The vesting in possession would be the same in either case, but this is not relevant in the application of the perpetuity rule.

This distinction was further illustrated in *Re Garnham*. The land was to be held on trust for sale on the death of the survivor of A and such wife. Neville J decided that the trust for sale was void and that the property was received by those entitled to it in its unconverted form.

---

[8] The limitation was void also under the rule in *Whitby v Mitchell* (1890) 44 ChD 85. If Emma was married at the date of the gift, it would be a question of construction whether the gift to the husband was limited to her present husband, who would be a life in being, or would include other future husbands who might not be.

The Perpetuities and Accumulations Act 1964 makes provision for dealing with the unborn widow problem in section 5. [9] The section however applies only where the gift has not been saved under the 'wait and see' principle introduced in section 3. The sections will be considered in the order in which they are to be applied.

C. Administrative Contingencies under the Common Law Rule

In **Re Wood** [1894] 2 Ch 310; affd [1894] 3 Ch 381, [10] the testator, a gravel contractor, directed his trustees to 'carry on my said business of a gravel contractor until my gravel-pits are worked out,' and then to sell them and to hold the proceeds of sale amongst his children 'then living' and the living issue of (deceased) children who being sons attain 21, or, being daughters, attain 21 or marry.

At the date of the will it was clear that the testator knew that the gravel pits would soon be worked out and they were in fact worked out within six years. KEKEWICH J and the Court of Appeal held the gift void for perpetuity because the gravel pits might not have been worked out within the perpetuity period.

In **Re Atkins' Will Trusts** [1974] 1 WLR 761, [1974] 2 All ER 1, a testator, who died in 1957, devised his farm on trust to allow his stepson, Ernest Alexander Double, to have the full use and enjoyment thereof and on his death or his ceasing to work the farm the trustees were directed to sell it 'and to divide the net proceeds of sale equally and per capita amongst such of the following as shall be living at the date of the completion of the said sale', namely, the grandchildren of a deceased brother of the testator, a niece of the testator and the four children of another niece. After the death of the stepson on 30 March 1972, the bulk of the farm was sold on 7 September 1972. In holding that the remainder was valid, PENNYCUICK V-C said at 767, at 6:

'Having reached the conclusion which I have expressed on the first two points—namely, that the proceeds of sale of the farm became divisible amongst the beneficiaries living at the date of completion of the sale and that the duty of the bank was to sell within one year, at latest, from the death of Ernest Alexander Double—then one comes to the question: was such a disposition void on the ground of perpetuity, namely, that the interest of the beneficiaries might not vest within 21 years from the death of Ernest Alexander Double, who was a life in being at the death of the testator?

Counsel for the last two defendants stressed, as is undoubtedly true, that in applying the rule against perpetuities as it stood before the Perpetuities and Accumulations Act 1964, one must look at possible and not actual events (see, for instance, *Theobald, Wills,* 13th edn. (1971), para. 1483), and there is no doubt that the court over the years has sometimes taken into account some very remote possibilities. Counsel relied in particular on *Re Wood* [1894] 3 Ch 381, in the Court of Appeal, a decision which has come in for a good deal of textbook

---

[9]   P. 399, post.
[10]   *Thomas v Thomas* (1902) 87 LT 58. This is so, even if the gift is charitable; *Re Lord Stratheden and Campbell* [1894] 3 Ch 265 (annuity of £100 to be provided to the Central London Rangers on the appointment of the next lieutenant-colonel).

criticism since, but which I suppose in comparable circumstances I should be bound to follow. It seems to me, however, that there is a critical distinction to be made between the possibility of delay owing to physical causes such as were considered in *Re Wood* and the possibility of delay owing to a breach of trust on the part of the trustee concerned. In the former case one must, I suppose, take into account anything physically capable of happening. I should myself wish to reserve consideration on that matter in relation to certain highly improbable events. On the other hand, where there is a possibility that delay can arise only should there be a breach of trust, that is a possibility which it seems to me the court must clearly disregard. The court will act on the basis that equity regards that as done which ought to be done, and it will treat the trustees as having done whatever they were bound to do. It will not allow the rights of beneficiaries to be defeated because the trustees failed to carry out their fiduciary duties.

So, in the present case, the duty of the trustee was to sell this farm immediately, and that means at the latest, as I have held, within one year of the death of Ernest Alexander Double, and the court should not and cannot properly take into account the possibility that the bank, in breach of trust, might fail to realise within the time in which it was bound to realise. The result is that one must treat the sale as something which must be completed within, at the most, 12 months from the death of Ernest Alexander Double, and accordingly the vesting of the interests of the beneficiaries would take effect within one year of the death of Ernest Alexander Double, and there can be no question of a perpetuity.'

V. Wait and See

A. General

It will be observed that all of the limitations in the examples given which failed did so because they *might* have vested outside the perpetuity period; not because they did so. This was necessitated by the common law's requirement of certainty; an interest is valid under the common law rule only if it is possible to postulate, at the date when the gift takes effect, that *if* the gift ever vests, it *must* do so within the perpetuity period. Of course, it may never vest at all. This is the risk of all contingent interests. The common law rule is concerned with the time within which it *must* vest if it ever does.

We have seen that, by making a judicious selection of measuring lives, a competent draftsman can extend the rule to its fullest extent. It will be observed that all the illustrations so far given could have been validated if the draftsman had made use of the opportunities available to him. He could have made use of selected lives; or, he could have included a simple catch-all provision, such as 'provided that no beneficiary shall be entitled to take unless his interest shall vest within 21 years of the death of . . . .' [11] Such a provision would not restrict the donor's freedom of disposition, because in nearly all the cases the interests given will in fact vest within the period. It should be appreciated that, however many lives are selected, the period is the same: a life in being plus 21 years. For, as Twisden used to say, 'the candles are all lighted at once.' [12]

---

[11]   (1961) 74 HLR 1141 (W. B. Leach and J. K. Logan).
[12]   *Scatterwood v Edge* (1699) 1 Salk 229.

What, then, is the sense in holding void a gift which vests within the period, merely because it might have vested outside, but did not? We saw that a gift to the first child of A to marry is void, if A is alive and has no married child; because A's first child to marry *might* do so more than 21 years after the death of any persons now living. But if the gift is made on the eve of A's eldest daughter's wedding day, and she does marry on that day, why should the gift be held void for perpetuity?

In other words, why insist on certainty of vesting, if at all, within the period? Why not wait and see whether the disposition does in fact vest within the period? The adoption of a wait and see rule was enacted by the Perpetuities and Accumulations Act 1964, section 3.

PERPETUITIES AND ACCUMULATIONS ACT 1964

3. [13] **Uncertainty as to remoteness.**—(1) Where, apart from the provisions of this section and sections 4 and 5 of this Act, a disposition would be void on the ground that the interest disposed of might not become vested until too remote a time, the disposition shall be treated, until such time (if any) as it becomes established that the vesting must occur, if at all, after the end of the perpetuity period, as if the disposition were not subject to the rule against perpetuities; and its becoming so established shall not affect the validity of anything previously done in relation to the interest disposed of by way of advancement, application of intermediate income or otherwise.

(2) Where, apart from the said provisions, a disposition consisting of the conferring of a general power of appointment would be void on the ground that the power might not become exercisable until too remote a time, the disposition shall be treated, until such time (if any) as it becomes established that the power will not be exercisable within the perpetuity period, as if the disposition were not subject to the rule against perpetuities.

(3) Where, apart from the said provisions, a disposition consisting of the conferring of any power, option or other right would be void on the ground that the right might be exercised at too remote a time, the disposition shall be treated as regards any exercise of the right within the perpetuity period as if it were not subject to the rule against perpetuities and, subject to the said provisions, shall be treated as void for remoteness only if, and so far as, the right is not fully exercised within that period.

B. Measuring Lives [14]

The introduction of the Wait and See principle requires a total reconsideration of the question of measuring lives. The common law lives obviously will not do; because the only persons recognised as common law lives are those who have already validated the gifts. If we only used them, we 'would never wait and see at all.' [15] If the statute does not make some selection, it could be argued that any

---

[13]   C & B, pp. 340–344; M & W, paras. 7.030–7.034; MM, pp. 222–223; Maudsley, pp. 120–122; (1964) 80 LQR 492–495; Morris and Leach Supp., pp. 5–8. For the first judicial application, see *Re Thomas Meadows & Co Ltd and Subsidiary Companies* (1960) *Staff Pension Scheme Rules* [1971] Ch 278, [1971] 1 All ER 239.

[14]   Maudlsey, pp. 87–109, 123–139.

[15]   (1965) 81 LQR 106, 108 (D. E. Allan).

living person would do, [16] but this 'would send potential beneficiaries ransacking the registers of births and deaths throughout the world' in order to find a centenarian capable of validating a gift which vested after 121 years.

It is obvious that the lives to be used should be known, and known precisely. If gifts are to be held valid or void, dependent on whether or not they do in fact vest within a period of lives in being plus 21 years, the system can only operate if you know how long the period is, and you only know that, if you know whose lives are to be used. The statute enacting Wait and See must lay down who the measuring lives are. They need have no relation to common law lives; it is best to discard all thoughts based on the common law situation; and to consider what, in the new situation, is required of the measuring lives. The new situation is trying to allow a limitation to be effective if it vests within a life in being plus 21 years (or 80 years). Any life? No, because of the inconvenience of following up every life; but the policy is to include every life that is reasonably connected with the limitation and identifiable at the date of the gift. In a gift 'to the grandchildren of A' (a living person) why not include a present living grandchild if such inclusion enables the limitation to be valid, or allows the testator's intention to be more accurately followed; or, indeed, the donee of a power? On the other hand, an 'unborn widow' is not included even if she turns out to have been alive at the date of the gift, because of the clearly sound principle that lives in being must be ascertainable at the beginning of the period. The Act of 1964 was the first in the world to recognise the problem and to produce a workable list. [17]

PERPETUITIES AND ACCUMULATIONS ACT 1964

3. Uncertainty as to remoteness.—(4) Where this section applies to a disposition and the duration of the perpetuity period is not determined by virtue of section 1 or 9(2) of this Act, it shall be determined as follows:—

(a) where any persons falling within subsection (5) below are individuals in being and ascertainable at the commencement of the perpetuity period the duration of the period shall be determined by reference to their lives and no others, but so that the lives of any description of persons falling within paragraph (b) or (c) of that subsection shall be disregarded if the number of persons of that description is such as to render it impracticable to ascertain the date of death of the survivor;

(b) where there are no lives under paragraph (a) above the period shall be twenty-one years.

(5) The said persons are as follows:—

(a) the person by whom the disposition was made;

(b) a person to whom or in whose favour the disposition was made, that is to say —

---

[16] (1953) 52 Mich LR 179 (L. M. Simes); (1963) 6 U of WALR 21 (L. M. Simes); 27 (D. E. Allan); (1965) 81 LQR 106 (D. E. Allan); (1970) 86 LQR 357 (R. H. Maudsley); (1981) 97 LQR 593 (R. L. Deech) which contains a useful summary and discussion of the conflicting views; (1986) 102 LQR 250 (J. Dukeminier).

[17] And followed with or without minor changes, in Northern Ireland, Alberta, British Columbia and New Zealand; Maudsley, Appendix D. In 1987 the American Uniform Act of Perpetuities adopted a period of 90 years as the wait and see period, in preference to a life in being and 21 years: (1987) Real Property, Probate & Trust Journal 569; [1987] CLJ 234 (L. W. Waggoner).

   (i) in the case of a disposition to a class of persons, any member or potential member of the class;

  (ii) in the case of an individual disposition to a person taking only on certain conditions being satisfied, any person as to whom some of the conditions are satisfied and the remainder may in time be satisfied;

 (iii) in the case of a special power of appointment exercisable in favour of members of a class, any member or potential member of the class;

 (iv) in the case of a special power of appointment exercisable in favour of one person only, that person or, where the object of the power is ascertainable only on certain conditions being satisfied, any person as to whom some of the conditions are satisfied and the remainder may in time be satisfied;

  (v) in the case of any power, option or other right, the person on whom the right is conferred;

  (c) a person having a child or grandchild within sub-paragraphs (i) to (iv) of paragraph (b) above, or any of whose children or grandchildren, if subsequently born, would by virtue of his or her descent, fall within those sub-paragraphs;

  (d) any person on the failure or determination of whose prior interest the disposition is limited to take effect.

15. Short title, interpretation and extent.—(3) For the purposes of this Act a person shall be treated as a member of a class if in his case all the conditions identifying a member of the class are satisfied, and shall be treated as a potential member if in his case some only of those conditions are satisfied but there is a possibility that the remainder will in time be satisfied.

With this compare:

VICTORIA PERPETUITIES AND ACCUMULATIONS ACT 1968

6—(4) Nothing in this section[18] makes any person a life in being for the purposes of ascertaining the perpetuity period unless the life of that person is one expressed or implied as relevant for this purpose by the terms of the disposition and would have been reckoned a life in being for such purpose if this section had not been enacted:

Provided however that in the case of a disposition to a class of persons or to one or more members of a class, any person living at the date of the disposition whose life is so expressed or implied as relevant for any member of the class may be reckoned a life in being in ascertaining the perpetuity period.

KENTUCKY REVISED STATUTES[19]

381.216 Wait-and-see doctrine; reformation. In determining whether an interest would violate the rule against perpetuities the period of perpetuities shall be measured by actual rather than possible events; provided, however, the period shall not be measured by any lives whose continuance does not have a causal relationship to the vesting or failure of the interest. Any interest which would

---

[18]   Introducing a 'wait and see' rule.
[19]   (1960) 49 Kentucky LR 62 (J. Dukeminier); Dukeminier, *Perpetuities in Action*; Maudsley, p. 107, nn. 13, 14.

violate said rule as thus modified shall be reformed, within the limits of that rule, to approximate most closely the intention of the creator of the interest.

VI. Reduction of Age Contingencies

A. Before 1964[20]

A common cause of violation of the rule was the postponement of vesting until an age greater than 21.

LAW OF PROPERTY ACT 1925

163. Validation of certain gifts void for remoteness.—(1) Where in a will, settlement or other instrument the absolute vesting either of capital or income of property, or the ascertainment of a beneficiary or class of beneficiaries, is made to depend on the attainment by the beneficiary or members of the class of an age exceeding twenty-one years, and thereby the gift to that beneficiary or class or any member thereof, or any gift over, remainder, executory limitation, or trust arising on the total or partial failure of the original gift, is, or but for this section would be, rendered void for remoteness, the will, settlement, or other instrument shall take effect for the purposes of such gift over, remainder, executory limitation, or trust as if the absolute vesting or ascertainment aforesaid had been made to depend on the beneficiary or member of the class attaining the age of twenty-one years, and that age shall be substituted for the age stated in the will, settlement, or other instrument.

(2) This section applies to any instrument executed after the commencement of this Act and to any testamentary appointment (whether made in exercise of a general or special power), devise, or bequest contained in the will of a person dying after such commencement, whether the will is made before or after such commencement.

(3) This section applies without prejudice to any provision whereby the absolute vesting or ascertainment is also made to depend on the marriage of any person, or any other event which may occur before the age stated in the will, settlement, or other instrument is attained.

B. Perpetuities and Accumulations Act 1964[1]

A different solution was needed after the introduction of a principle of 'wait and see' into the perpetuity rule by the 1964 Act.

PERPETUITIES AND ACCUMULATIONS ACT 1964

4. Reduction of age and exclusion of class members to avoid remoteness.—
(1) Where a disposition is limited by reference to the attainment by any person or persons of a specified age exceeding twenty-one years, and it is apparent at the time the disposition is made or becomes apparent at a subsequent time —

---

[20] C & B, p. 320; M & W, paras. 7.070–7.072; MM, p. 221; Morris and Leach, pp. 52–56.
[1] C & B, pp. 348–349; M & W, paras. 7.073–7.078; MM, p. 223; Maudsley, pp. 139–143; (1964) 80 LQR 508–510; Morris and Leach, Supp. pp. 10–12.

(a) that the disposition would, apart from this section, be void for remoteness, but

(b) that it would not be so void if the specified age had been twenty-one years, the disposition shall be treated for all purposes as if, instead of being limited by reference to the age in fact specified, it had been limited by reference to the age nearest to that age which would, if specified instead, have prevented the disposition from being so void.

(2) Where in the case of any disposition different ages exceeding twenty-one years are specified in relation to different persons —

(a) the reference in paragraph *(b)* of subsection (1) above to the specified age shall be construed as a reference to all the specified ages, and

(b) that subsection shall operate to reduce each such age so far as is necessary to save the disposition from being void for remoteness.

(6) Section 163 of the Law of Property Act 1925 (which saves a disposition from remoteness arising out of a condition requiring the attainment of an age exceeding twenty-one years) is hereby repealed.

(7) [2] For the avoidance of doubt it is hereby declared that a question arising under section 3 of this Act or subsection (1) *(a)* above of whether a disposition would be void apart from this section is to be determined as if subsection (6) above had been a separate section of this Act.

VII. Class Gifts [3]

A. The Common Law Rule

Many of the gifts which have been held void, in the illustrations so far discussed, have been class gifts; and they have been held void because there was a theoretical possibility that the interest of a member of the class might vest outside the period. The fact that the interests of most (and probably all) the members of the class vested well within the period did not help the gift, nor did it help the prospects of those whose interests did in fact vest. When the rule says that 'an interest . . . must vest', it refers in the case of a class gift to the vesting of the class and not to the interests of individual members. [4] It means that the composition of the class and the share of each member must be known within the period. The gift is void if, outside the period, the number of members of the class might increase and the size of each share thus be reduced; or if the number of members of the class might be reduced, and the size of each share be increased. [5]

It is important to appreciate that the question of 'vesting', when asked in a perpetuity context, is different from that asked in the more usual context

---

[2]   As added by Children Act 1975, s. 108, Sch. 3, para. 43; (1965) 81 LQR 346 (J. D. Davies); (1976) 120 SJ 498 (F. A. R. Bennion).

[3]   C & B, pp. 322–325; M & W, paras. 7.059–7.062; MM, p. 227; Maudsley, pp. 15–25, 36–39; Morris and Leach, pp. 101–133; (1938) 51 HLR 1329 (W. B. Leach).

[4]   Lord SELBORNE LC in *Pearks v Moseley* (1880) 5 App Cas 714 said at 723: 'A gift is said to be to a "class" of persons, when it is to all those who shall come within a certain category or description defined by a general or collective formula, and who, if they take at all, are to take one divisible subject in proportionate shares; and the rule is, that the vice of remoteness affects the class as a whole, if it may affect an unascertained number of its members.' See also American Law Institute: *Restatement of Property*, chap. 22.

[5]   *Jee v Audley* (1787) 1 Cox Eq Cas 324; *Leake v Robinson* (1817) 2 Mer 363; *Pearks v Moseley*, supra; *Ward v Van der Loeff* [1924] AC 653 and cases cited in this section.

unaffected by the perpetuity rule; when, for example, the question is whether or not one member is yet qualified to claim an admittedly valid gift, and whether it is therefore safe for an executor or trustee to pay a share to him. For example: 'To the children of A at 21.' When A's eldest son is 21, he will have a 'vested' interest and can be paid his share. If the question were whether or not the gift had 'vested' in a perpetuity context, however, the answer would have to be 'no'; the gift will not vest until 21 years from the death of A'. For until A's death, there may be more children so as to increase the class; and, after A's death, there may be fewer, if some die under 21, and this would reduce the membership.

To return to the trustee paying out under the gift to the children of A at 21. What share can he properly pay to the eldest son? There may be more children. Either the eldest must wait until A's death, at which time the maximum number of claimants would be known; and for this purpose it does not matter that the number may be later reduced; [6] or the eldest must be allowed to claim his share now, based upon the existing number of children, and to the exclusion of later born children. The problem would be presented more dramatically if the limitation were 'to all the grandchildren of X at 21.' X has died, leaving a grandchild Y who is 21, and a son Z who is 10. Must Y wait until the death of all his uncles and aunts, including Z, and perhaps a further 21 years before claiming? For only then will it be known how many grandchildren of X will attain 21.

The law solves the problem by closing the class of potential takers to those possible claimants who are alive at the period of distribution—i.e. when the trustees wish to start paying out. This provides a maximum number of takers and the smallest possible share; and this is what the trustees need to know. Those who are alive at that time will be paid when they vest; future born are excluded. The rule is only a rule of construction, and gives way to an expression of contrary intention and it seems that the courts are becoming more ready to find such contrary intention. [7] It is known as the rule of convenience; it is highly convenient for the trustees and for those who are alive at the period of distribution; highly inconvenient for future born. The class-closing rules have been much criticized. [8] It is important to appreciate that they are arbitrary; and inevitable.

Finally, let it be noted that the rule against perpetuities and the class-closing rules sometimes interact. Sometimes, as it were by a fluke, a class artificially closed must vest, if at all, within the period, although if left to close naturally, members might join outside. Some of these cases will be examined at p. 399 et seq., post.

---

[6] For the share of each would then be increased.

[7] *Re Bleckly* [1951] Ch 740, [1951] 1 All ER 1064; *Re Cockle's Will Trusts* [1967] Ch 690, [1967] 1 All ER 391; *Re Kebty-Fletcher's Will Trusts* [1969] 1 Ch 339, [1967] 3 All ER 1076; *Re Harker's Will Trusts* [1969] 1 WLR 1124, [1969] 3 All ER 1; *Re Henderson's Trusts* [1969] 1 WLR 651, [1969] 3 All ER 769; *Re Edmondson's Will Trusts* [1972] 1 WLR 183, [1972] 1 All ER 444; *Re Deeley's Settlement* [1974] Ch 454, [1973] 3 All ER 1127; (1970) 34 Conv (NS) 393 (J. G. Riddall); *Re Chapman's Settlement Trusts* [1977] 1 WLR 1163, [1978] 1 All ER 1122; [1978] Conv 73 (F. R. Crane); *Re Clifford's Settlement Trusts* [1981] Ch 63, [1980] 1 All ER 1013; *Re Tom's Settlement* [1987] 1 WLR 1021, [1987] 1 All ER 1081; *Re Drummond* [1988] 1 WLR 234, [1988] 1 All ER 449; [1988] Conv 427 (P. Luxton).

[8] For a statement of the class-closing rules, see C & B, pp. 324–325; M & W, paras. 7.063–7.067; MM, p. 228; Maudsley, pp. 17–25; Morris and Leach, pp. 109–125; (1954) 70 LQR 61 (J. H. C. Morris); [1958] CLJ 39 (S. J. Bailey); *Theobald on Wills* (16th edn, 2001), chap. 32, and note that, where the members of a class are to take vested interests at birth and no member of the class exists at the time when the property is available for distribution, the class remains open indefinitely: *Shepherd v Ingram* (1764) Amb 448; (1954) 70 LQR 66, 67. Otherwise the first born would automatically take the whole at birth. On balance that would be less satisfactory than the inconvenience of allowing the class to remain open: *Re Bleckly, supra.*

RE DAWSON
(1888) 39 Ch D 155 (Ch D, CHITTY J)

A testator, by his will, provided an annuity for the plaintiff, his daughter, and after her death the residue was to be held on trust for her children at 21, or (being daughters) at that age or on marriage, and also for such child or children of any son of the plaintiff who should die under 21, as shall live to attain the age of 21, or being daughters live to attain that age or marry, such children to take their parent's share.

The plaintiff was 60 years of age on the testator's death, and her children were all over 21.

She brought this action claiming that the trusts of the will subsequent to her death were void for remoteness.

Held. Since the plaintiff could in law give birth to further children, membership of the class would not be determined until a time beyond the period and the whole class gift was void.

CHITTY J: The question in this case is whether the trust in favour of the children and grandchildren of the testator's daughter, the Plaintiff *Mary Elizabeth Johnston,* is or is not void for remoteness.

Putting aside for a moment the question that has been argued as to the admissibility of evidence to shew that the daughter was at the time of the testator's death past child-bearing, it appears to me to be clear this trust is void. The gift is in favour of one class, but made up of two generations. The first generation is the daughter's own children. As to that no objection can be raised. The children are to take at twenty-one or marriage. But the limitation in favour of the next generation, that is the daughter's grandchildren, is plainly void. The gift, to read it shortly, is for such children of any son of the daughter who should die under the age of twenty-one as shall live to attain the age of twenty-one years, or being a daughter or daughters live to attain that age or marry. Admitting the possibility of the testator's daughter having a son born after the testator's death, then I should get to a life not in being at his death; and as that child might die under twenty-one more than twenty-one years after the death of the testator that limitation to his children at twenty-one is obviously too remote . . . . [9]

Then it is argued that the Court in applying the rule against perpetuities looks at the state of things as they existed at the testator's death, and it appears that the testator's daughter at his death was sixty years and three months old, or thereabouts; and thereupon it is said that she was past child-bearing, and consequently that there could be no son of hers born after the testator's death.
. . .

[His Lordship, relying especially on *Jee v Audley* (1787) 1 Cox Eq Cas 324, p. 382, ante, and *Re Sayer's Trusts* (1868) LR 6 Eq 319, held that evidence as to capacity for child-bearing was inadmissible, and then continued:]

Another argument was adduced with reference to what appears to be the practice of the Court of Chancery in former times and of the Chancery Division of the High Court in the present day with reference to payment out where there is a married woman whose children are to take and the lady has attained a certain age. Those are cases I think, when examined from the beginning down to the present time, in which the Court does not assume the impossibility of issue, but

---

[9]   The question so far was the same as that decided by the House of Lords in *Pearks v Moseley* (1880) 5 App Cas 714, where however there was not the complication of the physical impossibility of the appearance of new members.

as a mere matter of convenience of administration regards the high degree of improbability, and it has come now to be fixed somewhere about the age of fifty-four, although the circumstances may still be inquired into. [10] But with regard to the rule against perpetuities a high degree of probability or improbability will not do. The rule with regard to perpetuities is that the limitation must be such that every member of the class, where it is a question of a class gift, must of necessity take within the time allowed.

In **Re Hooper's Settlement Trusts** [1948] Ch 586, [1948] 2 All ER 261, [11] the same fate befell a gift where the limitation was for the sons and daughters of the settlor . . . 'provided always that if any son of the settlor shall die . . .leaving him a child or children who shall attain the age of twenty-one years. . .' JENKINS J held that the fact that the grandchildren were introduced by way of proviso was not sufficient to distinguish the case from *Pearks v Mosley* (1880) 5 App Cas 714.

However, a different construction may save parts of the gift.

In **Cattlin v Brown** (1853) 11 Hare 372, WOOD V-C said at 373:
    'The question arises on a short devise to *Thomas Bannister Cattlin* for life, and after his decease to all and every his children or child, for their lives, in equal shares, and after the decease of any or either of them, the part or share of the child so dying unto his, her, or their children or child, and his, her or their heirs for ever . . .
    The fifth and last rule to which I need to advert is this,—that where there is a gift or devise of a given sum of money or property to each member of a class, and the gift to each is wholly independent of the same or similar gift to every other member of the class, and cannot be augmented or diminished whatever be the number of the other members, then the gift may be good as to those within the limits allowed by law. This was settled in the case of *Storrs v Benbow* . . . . [12]
    The testator devises the estate to *Thomas Bannister Cattlin* for life, with remainder to all his children as tenants in common for life, with remainder as to every share of every child to the children of that child in fee. Now, to follow the respective shares of the property, suppose *Thomas Bannister Cattlin* to have four sons, A. B. C. and D. and A. and B. to be living at the testator's death and the others to be born afterwards. A. and B. on the testator's death take an immediate vested interest in the remainder for life, expectant on their father's death, with remainder to their respective children in fee, subject to their respective moieties being diminished on the birth of C. and D., but their exact shares are ascertained within the legal limits at the death of their father, and neither their life interests nor the remainder in fee are capable of being wholly divested in favour of any party beyond the legal limits, neither could any one intended by the testator to take an interest, but at a period beyond the legal limits, possibly take in lieu of A. or B.; their shares are not therefore within the third rule, or governed by the judgment in the case of *Lord Dungannon v Smith* (1846) 12 Cl & Fin 546 as might have been the case if the devise had been to the sons of *Thomas Bannister Cattlin*

---

10   See p. 382, n. 20, ante.
11   *Re Lord's Settlement* [1947] 2 All ER 685; *Haworth v IRC* [1974] STC 378.
12   (1853) 3 De GM & G 390; *Wilkinson v Duncan* (1861) 30 Beav 111.

living at his decease, with remainder to their sons in fee, for then there might possibly, at the death at *Thomas Bannister Cattlin*, have been no son who was in existence at the testator's death. Neither, again, can any possible event happening after the death of *Thomas Bannister Cattlin*, augment or diminish the share of A. or B. Here then A. and B. are respectively persons in esse at the death of the testator, who are to take a share that must be ascertained in a manner incapable of augmentation or diminution at the expiration of another life in esse. What is there to prevent the limitation of that share to him for life, with remainder to his children in fee? For this share must of necessity vest, if at all, within the legal limits, and complies, therefore, with the rule. It is in reality the case of *Storrs v Benbow*, substituting a given share for a given sum of money. . . .

The limitation as to the shares of C. and D. in the case I have supposed would be clearly void, as their children might be born at a period exceeding the limits which the law allows, they themselves not being in esse at the death of the testator.
. . .

The declaration will be that the estate was by the will of the testator well limited in fee to the children of those children of *Thomas Bannister Cattlin* who were living at the death of the testator.'

In **Re Russell** [1895] 2 Ch 698, [13] there was a gift to all the daughters of Mary Dorrell who shall attain 21 . . . provided that . . . the share of any daughter shall be held on trust for her for life and after her death on trust for her children.

Mary Dorrell's only daughter, the plaintiff, who was born in the testator's lifetime and had attained 21, claimed that the proviso was void and that she was entitled absolutely.

The Court of Appeal (Lord HALSBURY LC, LINDLEY and RIGBY LJJ) construed the proviso as being a condition of defeasance of the original gift to the daughters; and held it to apply independently to the separate share of each daughter; so that, while it would have been void in the case of a daughter born after the testator's death, it was valid in the plaintiff's case.

B. Perpetuities and Accumulations Act 1964 [14]

PERPETUITIES AND ACCUMULATIONS ACT 1964

4. Reduction of age and exclusion of class members to avoid remoteness.—(2) p. 394, ante.

(3) Where the inclusion of any persons, being potential members of a class or unborn persons who at birth would become members or potential members of the class, prevents the foregoing provisions of this section [15] from operating to save a disposition from being void for remoteness, those persons shall thenceforth be deemed for all the purposes of the disposition to be excluded from the class, and the said provisions shall thereupon have effect accordingly.

(4) Where, in the case of a disposition to which subsection (3) above does not apply, it is apparent at the time the disposition is made or becomes apparent

13   *Re Morrison's Will Trusts* [1940] Ch 102, [1939] 4 All ER 332.
14   C & B, pp. 349–350; M & W, paras. 7.073–7.079; MM, p. 225; Maudsley, pp. 140–143; (1964) 80 LQR 510–512; Morris and Leach Supp., pp. 10–12.
15   Section 4(1), (2), p. 393, ante, relating to reduction of age contingencies.

at a subsequent time that, apart from this subsection, the inclusion of any persons, being potential members of a class or unborn persons who at birth would become members or potential members of the class, would cause the disposition to be treated as void for remoteness, those persons shall, unless their exclusion would exhaust the class, thenceforth be deemed for all the purposes of the disposition to be excluded from the class.

(5) Where this section has effect in relation to a disposition to which section 3 above applies, [16] the operation of this section shall not affect the validity of anything previously done in relation to the interest disposed of by way of advancement, application of intermediate income or otherwise.

5. Condition relating to death of surviving spouse.—Where a disposition is limited by reference to the time of death of the survivor of a person in being at the commencement of the perpetuity period and any spouse of that person, and that time has not arrived at the end of the perpetuity period, the disposition shall be treated for all purposes, where to do so would save it from being void for remoteness, as if it had instead been limited by reference to the time immediately before the end of that period.

QUESTIONS

1.   Do you prefer the English, or the Victorian or the Kentucky treatment of the problem of the selection of measuring lives for the purposes of the perpetuity rule in a 'wait and see' context?
2.   Which limitations, if any, are valid at common law, but may be void under 'wait and see'? Should the statutory list be made to include everyone who would be implied as a life in being at common law? If this were done, would there be any need to apply to instruments coming into operation after 15 July 1964, any parts of the common law rule, other than those relating to the selection of 'express' lives in being? See Maudsley, pp. 156–160; (1975) 60 Cornell LR 355; C & B, pp. 344–347; M & W, paras. 7.043–7.056.
3.   Which measuring lives do you think should be used for Wait and See?

VIII. Class Closing Rules [17]

It may sometimes happen that a class gift is saved at common law by the fortuitous operation of the class closing rules discussed above. [18] It cannot be emphasised too strongly that the purpose of the class closing rules is to do something quite different. But it sometimes has this effect.

PICKEN v MATTHEWS
(1878) 10 ChD 264 (ChD, Malins V-C)

The testator gave real and personal property on trust for the children of his daughters Helen and Charlotte who should attain 25. At the date of the testator's death Helen had three children, one of whom had attained 25 and Charlotte

---

[16]   P. 390, ante.
[17]   See p. 395, n. 8, ante.
[18]   See pp. 394–395, ante; [1988] Conv 339 (P. Sparkes and R. Snape).

had two infant children.

Held. A valid gift to such of the daughters' children living at the testator's death who should attain 25.

MALINS V-C: If the two daughters of the testator had had no children living at his death, the gift would have been void for remoteness; because it would not be certain that the property would vest within a life or lives in being and twenty-one years after. But this is a gift to living grandchildren . . . . Now, the rules . . . . applicable to this case are, first, that a gift to a class not preceded by any life estate is a gift to such of the class as are living at the death of the testator. . . .

The second rule is, that where you have a gift for such of the children of A. as shall attain a specified age, only those who are in esse when the first of the class attains the specified age can take. All afterborn children are excluded. This also is a rule of convenience . . .

Here there is a gift to such of a class as shall attain twenty-five. The class was ascertained at the death of the testator because one of them had then attained twenty-five. The two infant children of *Charlotte* . . . who were alive at the death of the testator are entitled to take provided they attain the age of twenty-five years . . .

Here I hold that there is a valid gift because one of the children of *Helen* . . . had attained twenty-five at the death of the testator; the maximum number to take was, therefore, then ascertained, and the gift in question is not void for remoteness.

A class may be closed by the existence of the estate of a deceased member of the class who held a vested interest before his death.

In **Re Chartres** [1927] 1 Ch 466, the testator gave two-fifths of the residue, after the expiration of 21 years, in trust for the children or remote issue of his son Richard as Richard should by will appoint, and in default of appointment in trust for all Richard's children who being sons attain 21 or being daughters attain 21 or marry.

On 11 March 1905 the testator died, so that the 21 year period expired on 11 March 1926.

On 18 March 1916, Richard's only child, Archibald, attained 21.

On 12 March 1924, Richard released his testamentary power.

On 26 February 1925, Archibald died having bequeathed his property to Richard.

Richard was still alive and the question was whether, having released his testamentary power, he could claim the two-fifths of the estate given to his children. ASTBURY J held that the class closed at the period of distribution, which would be at the expiry of the 21 year period, or the attainment of 21 by one of Richard's children, whichever was the later. Archibald's interest had 'vested'; the period of distribution was therefore the expiry of the 21 year period on 11 March 1926, and the trustees were to pay the money over to Archibald's estate, to the exclusion of possible future born children of Richard. [19] The two-fifths share thus passed under Archibald's will to Richard.

----

[19]   See the criticism of the application of the class-closing rules to a case where a life interest is released: *Re Kebty-Fletcher's Will Trusts* [1969] 1 Ch 339, [1967] 3 All ER 1076; *Re Harker's Will Trusts* [1969] 1 WLR 1124, [1969] 3 All ER 1; (1970) 34 Conv (NS) 393, 398, 407 (J. G. Riddall).

The Perpetuities and Accumulations Act 1964 makes no reference to the class closing rules. They will apply in exactly the same way as they did before the Act. Where they would previously have saved a gift from invalidity, their effect now is to avoid the necessity of applying the Act.

Where a limitation is void at common law and consequently the wait and see rule applies under section 3(1), there is new scope for the operation of the class closing rules. A class gift which comes within section 3(1) may remain open for lives in being plus 21 years, and after that time potential members who have not yet joined the class will be excluded: section 4(4). Many class gifts will not however wait so long; for, at the period of distribution, the class will close to include only those potential members who are in being at the time.

Thus, suppose a gift: 'To such of the grandchildren of A. (a living person), as shall attain the age of 21.' A. has two sons, B. and C. and a grandson X., all of whom will be measuring lives under section 3(5). Without rules for artificial closing of the class, any grandchildren could join it who attained 21 within 21 years of the dropping of the last of those lives. However, on X.'s 21st birthday, he will be able to demand payment of his share; and the class will close to include only those grandchildren who are alive at the time.[20]

QUESTIONS

1. On what principle was the gift in the will in *Ward v Van der Loeff* [1924] AC 653, p. 382, ante, held valid?
2. What alteration in the facts would have enabled the gift in the codicil to be upheld on the same ground as that on which the gift in the will was upheld? (1954) 70 LQR 61, 84 (J. H. C. Morris); *Re Cockle's Will Trusts* [1967] Ch 690, [1967] 1 All ER 391; Maudsley, pp. 53–56.
3. A testator bequeathed his residuary estate upon trust to be divided equally between such of his nephews and nieces as were living at the date of his death for their lives and after the death of any such nephew or niece upon trust for the child or children of such nephews or nieces who shall attain the age of 21 years.

   One nephew, Geoffrey, having no need of the income, released to the trustees all his interest to the intent that the trustees should hold the income on the same trusts as would be applicable if he were dead. The elder of Geoffrey's two daughters attained the age of 21. Is she entitled to claim half of the fund? See *Re Kebty-Fletcher's Will Trusts* [1969] 1 Ch 339, [1967] 3 All ER 1076; *Re Harker's Will Trusts* [1969] 1 WLR 1124, [1969] 3 All ER 1.
4. What would be the solution to *Ward v Van der Loeff* if the testator had died after 1964?

[20] If there is no grandchild alive at the testator's death, there is some doubt whether or not the class closes when the first grandchild attains 21. The better view is that it does: *Pearse v Catton* (1839) 1 Beav 352; Morris and Leach, p. 114; (1954) 70 LQR 61, 68–69 (J. H. C. Morris); *Re Bleckly* [1951] Ch 740 at 749, [1951] 1 All ER 1064 at 1069.

IX. Powers of Appointment

A. Before 1964[1]

I. GENERAL POWERS

(a) Validity of Power

A general power is one by which the donee of the power may appoint to any person, including himself. Thus, the giving of a general power to a donee is, in a sense, equivalent to giving the property to him. Hence, a general power is valid if it must become exercisable by the donee, if at all, within the perpetuity period. It is not relevant that he may exercise it outside the period.

(b) Validity of Exercise of Power

In the case of the general power, the perpetuity period runs from the time of the exercise of the power.

II. SPECIAL POWERS

(a) Validity of Power

A special power is one in which the class of appointees is restricted. The donor of the power is exercising an element of control over the appointment. A stricter rule applies.

In **Re De Sommery** [1912] 2 Ch 622, PARKER J said at 630: 'A special power which, according to the true construction of the instrument creating it, is capable of being exercised beyond lives in being and twenty-one years afterwards is, by reason of the rule against perpetuities, absolutely void; but if it can only be exercised within the period allowed by the rule, it is a good power, even although some particular exercise of it might be void because of the rule.

If a power be given to a person alive at the date of the instrument creating it, it must, of course, if exercised at all, be executed during his life, and is therefore valid. Again, if a power can be exercised only in favour of a person living at the date of the instrument creating it, it must, if exercised at all, be exercised during the life of such person, and is therefore unobjectionable. Further, the instrument itself may expressly limit a period, not exceeding the legal limits, for the exercise of the power. Lastly, where the settlor has used language from which the Court may fairly infer that he contemplated the creation, not of a single power, but of two distinct powers, one of which only is open to objection because of the rule against perpetuities, the Court will avoid the latter only and will give effect to the power which is not open to this objection. Thus, although a power vested in the trustees for the time being of a settlement has, so far as I can discover, been uniformly looked on as a single and indivisible power, it may be otherwise if the power be limited to A. and B. or other trustees of the settlement for the time being. In this case the Court may treat the settlor as having created one power vested in A. and B. while trustees, and a distinct power vested in their successors,

---

[1]   C & B, pp. 325–329; M & W, paras. 7.102–7.112; MM, pp. 232–235; Maudsley, pp. 59–64; Morris and Leach, pp. 134–163.

in which case the power vested in A. and B. would be open to no objection on the ground of remoteness: *Attenborough v Attenborough* (1855) 1 K & J 296.

In the present case the testatrix devised all her real and residuary personal estate to two named persons, thereinafter called her "trustees", upon trust for sale, and, after payment of her debts and funeral and testamentary expenses and a certain charitable legacy, to divide the proceeds into thirteen parts, and, as to two such parts, to hold the same, upon trust to pay the capital and income thereof, or neither, to her nephew Eugene de Sommery, or to apply the capital or income thereof for his benefit, or for the benefit of his wife or any child or children of his, as her trustees should consider advisable, and, subject thereto, to pay any capital or income which might remain in their hands under that trust to such of her nephews and nieces, and in such shares, as her trustees should think proper. In my opinion, the power or powers thus created in favour of Eugene de Sommery, his wife and children, are conferred on the trustees of the will for the time being, and not on the original trustees only (see *Re Smith* [1904] 1 Ch 139); and this being so, there is, I think, no possibility of applying the principle of *Attenborough v Attenborough*. Further, if there be one power only vested in these trustees, it is fairly obvious that it may, according to the true construction of the will, be exercised during the life of any child of Eugene de Sommery, whether alive at the testatrix's death or born afterwards, and would therefore be avoided by the rule against perpetuities. I have come to the conclusion, however, that there are in fact two powers vested in the trustees for the time being of the will—first, a power of paying either capital or income to Eugene de Sommery, which is only capable of being exercised during his life, and secondly, a power of applying either capital or income for the benefit of Eugene de Sommery, his wife or children, which is capable of being exercised beyond the period allowed by law. I see no reason on principle which precludes me from upholding the former and rejecting the latter power.'

(b) Validity of Exercise of Power

The appointment must be read back into the instrument containing the power; that is the perpetuity period must run from the date of the creation of the power.

RE BROWN AND SIBLY'S CONTRACT
(1876) 3 ChD 156 (ChD, MALINS V-C)

By a marriage settlement in 1821, land was conveyed to trustees to the use of W.M. for life and after his death as he shall appoint among his issue with a gift over in default.

W.M. appointed by will in 1867 to his son W.E.M. in fee; but in case W.E.M. should have no child who should attain 21, then in fee to W.M.B. (a grandson through a daughter, and unborn at the date of the settlement).

W.E.M. sold part of the land to Brown, who then entered into a contract with Sibly to sell part of the land to him. The question was whether W.E.M. could give a good title to the fee simple without the concurrence of W.M.B.

Held. He could; because the executory gift over to W.M.B. was void for remoteness.

MALINS V-C: The point I have to decide under this settlement is free from doubt. The law is settled, that where a person takes property by virtue of the execution of a special or limited power of appointment, he takes directly under the instrument creating the power. Consequently, when *W. Metford* made his will, it was the same as if the words he there used had formed part of the settlement, and as if the property had been conveyed by that settlement to trustees to the use of himself for life, with remainder to the use of his (unborn) son in fee, with a direction that in case his son should have no child who should attain twenty-one, then that the estate should, after the son's death, go over to the settlor's grandson in fee. That is an attempt to make the property inalienable for a period which might extend to twenty-one years after the determination of the life of a person not in being at the date of the settlement. The law does not allow a man to tie up property for longer than a life or lives in being and twenty-one years; and this is clearly an attempt to do what is contrary to the law.

I need not do more than refer to my decision in *Stuart v Cockerell* (1869) LR 7 Eq 363, afterwards affirmed on appeal (1870) 5 Ch App 713, which shews that the law is as I have stated it. My opinion, therefore, is that the appointment by the testator to his son in fee is good, and the attempt to give the estate over is void. It is precisely the same as if a man were to give property to his son for life, and after his decease to his son's children, as tenants in common in fee, with a proviso that if any of the children should die under twenty-five the property should go over. In that case the proviso carrying over the shares would be void. The gift to the son in fee is therefore good, and the executory devise over is void. [2]

But the court will take into consideration certain facts existing at the date on which the appointment is made.

In **Re Paul** [1921] 2 Ch 1, a testator who died in 1895 left a share of his residuary estate to his daughter Mrs A. for life and after her death as she should appoint by will among her children.

Mrs A., by will, appointed the share to her son A.J.A. on attaining 25 years. She died in 1919 when A.J.A. was 18 or 19.

SARGANT J upheld the appointment and said at 5:

'There is ample and quite conclusive authority in favour of the appointment being good. *Wilkinson v Duncan* (1861) 30 Beav 111 and *Von Brockdorff v Malcolm* (1885) 30 ChD 172 are direct decisions in favour . . . Having regard to the fact that the son in this case was 18 or 19 years old at the time of his mother's death, so that his interest must vest in him in six or seven years after her death, I decide that the gift to him is good, contingently, of course, on his attaining the age of 25 years . . .'

In **Wilkinson v Duncan** (1861) 30 Beav 111, [3] there was a bequest to such of the children of George Wilkinson as he should appoint. He appointed the fund upon trust to pay £2,000 to each of his daughters as and when they attained 24, and to divide the residue among his sons equally as and when they attained 24. George Wilkinson left ten children, two of whom were under the age of three years at his death. Sir John ROMILLY MR held that the gift to the sons was void; but

---

[2]   The same principle was applied to a statutory power of advancement (TA 1925, s. 32) in *Pilkington v IRC* [1964] AC 612 at 642, [1962] 3 All ER 622 at 632: 'I think that the important point for the purpose of the rule against perpetuities is that the new settlement is only effected by the operation of a fiduciary power which itself "belongs" to the old settlement;' *Re Hastings-Bass* [1975] Ch 25, [1974] 2 All ER 193.

[3]   *Permanent Trustee Co of New South Wales Ltd v Richardson* (1948) 48 SRNSW 313.

the gift to the daughters was valid in respect of such of the daughters as were three years old at his death.

B. Perpetuities and Accumulations Act 1964[4]

PERPETUITIES AND ACCUMULATIONS ACT 1964

1. Power to specify perpetuity period.—(2) p. 376, ante.

3. Uncertainty as to remoteness.—(2) p. 390, ante.
   (3) p. 390, ante.

7. Powers of appointment.—For the purposes of the rule against perpetuities, a power of appointment shall be treated as a special power unless —

    (a) in the instrument creating the power it is expressed to be exercisable by one person only, and

    (b) it could, at all times during its currency when that person is of full age and capacity, be exercised by him so as immediately to transfer to himself the whole of the interest governed by the power without the consent of any other person or compliance with any other condition, not being a formal condition relating only to the mode of exercise of the power;

Provided that for the purpose of determining whether a disposition made under a power of appointment exercisable by will only is void for remoteness, the power shall be treated as a general power where it would have fallen to be so treated if exercisable by deed.[5]

15. Short title, interpretation and extent.—(2) In this Act . . . 'power of appointment' includes any discretionary power to transfer a beneficial interest in property without the furnishing of valuable consideration; . . .

(5) The foregoing sections of this Act . . . in the case of an instrument made in the exercise of a special power of appointment shall apply only where the instrument creating the power takes effect after [the commencement of the Act].

Provided that section 7 above shall apply in all cases for construing the foregoing reference to a special power of appointment.

X. Administrative Powers of Trustees[6]

PERPETUITIES AND ACCUMULATIONS ACT 1964

8. Administrative powers of trustees.—(1) The rule against perpetuities shall not operate to invalidate a power conferred on trustees or other persons to sell, lease, exchange or otherwise dispose of any property for full consideration, or to do any other act in the administration (as opposed to the distribution) of any

---

[4]   C & B, pp. 342–343; M & W, paras. 7.102–7.112; MM, pp. 234–235; Maudsley, pp. 162–166; (1964) 80 LQR 518–521; Morris and Leach Supp., pp. 7, 14–15.

[5]   Thus avoiding the difficulties in cases such as *Re Churston Settled Estates* [1954] Ch 334, [1954] 1 All ER 725; *Re Earl of Coventry's Indentures* [1974] Ch 77, [1973] 3 All ER 1 (joint power and consent power held special power for purposes of the rule).

[6]   C & B, pp. 336–337, 352; M & W, para. 7.101; MM, p. 231; Maudsley, pp. 58–59, 183–185; Morris and Leach, pp. 232–242.

property, and shall not prevent the payment to trustees or other persons of reasonable remuneration for their services.

(2) Subsection (1) above shall apply for the purpose of enabling a power to be exercised at any time after the commencement of this Act notwithstanding that the power is conferred by an instrument which took effect before that commencement.

XI. Expectant and Dependent Limitations

A. Before 1964[7]

In **Re Hubbard's Will Trusts** [1963] Ch 275, [1962] 2 All ER 917, the testator gave a share of the 'sisters' fund' to each of his sisters and their issue (clause 9(iv)) by trusts which included discretionary trusts in favour of the sisters' grandchildren, which were void for remoteness (clause 9(v)). The will, by clause 9(vi), directed that, on the failure or determination of any of the sisters' shares, there should be an accruer to the other shares, and, subject thereto, the property was given to charity.

The question was whether the gifts over on the failure of the discretionary trusts were valid. BUCKLEY J held that the accruer provision, being dependent upon the same provision as that which terminated the trusts, was void. But the gift to charity was a vested gift, not dependent, and was valid. He said at 283, at 920:

'It is said that it is settled law that any limitation dependent or expectant on a prior limitation which is void for remoteness is itself invalid *Re Abbott* [1893] 1 Ch 54, and *Re Canning's Will Trusts* [1936] Ch 309, but it is not very easy to discover from the authorities what is meant by the expression "dependent or expectant on" in this context. In *Re Thatcher's Trusts* Sir John Romilly MR used the following language (1859) 26 Beav 365 at 370: "On the other hand if the limitations are ulterior to or expectant upon limitations which are too remote, they are void also, although made to a person in existence at the date of the will."

It is clear from the comparatively modern decision of *Re Coleman* [1936] Ch 528, [1936] 2 All ER 225 that the mere fact that a trust is ulterior to another which is invalid for remoteness, in the sense that the benefit under the former trust can only fall into possession when any possible benefit under the latter, had it been valid, would have ceased, is not sufficient to render the ulterior trust invalid. Accordingly, I think that it is necessary to look at the cases to see to what kind of case the rule applies . . .

I think that the cases in which the problem with which I am concerned has been considered, where the trusts were such that successive interests existed or could have come into existence, can be divided into three categories.

If a testator or other settlor settles property in such a way as to create a series of successive interests, each intended to take effect upon and only upon the exhaustion or termination of all antecedent interests in the chain, and one of those interests is void for remoteness, all the ulterior interests will fail, and this will be so even in the case of such an interest as a life interest given to a living

---

[7]   C & B, pp. 329–333; M & W, paras. 7.080–7.085; MM, pp. 225–226; Maudsley, pp. 64–67; Morris and Leach, pp. 173–181; (1950) 10 CLJ 392 (J.H.C. Morris); (1950) 14 Conv (NS) 148 (A.K. Kiralfy).

person which, if it were ever to take effect at all, would necessarily do so within the limits of perpetuity. In such a case the invalidity of one of the successive interests for perpetuity breaks the chain and all interests below the point of fracture fall away. This rule seems to be based on the intention of the settlor demonstrated by the nature of the trusts. It was explained by Stirling J in *Re Abbott* [1893] 1 Ch 54 at 57, as follows: "The reason appears to be that the persons entitled under the subsequent limitation are not intended to take unless and until the prior limitation is exhausted; and as the prior limitation which is void for remoteness can never come into operation, much less be exhausted, it is impossible to give effect to the intentions of the settlor in favour of the beneficiaries under the subsequent limitation."

In such a case, if an ulterior interest were accelerated to fill the void created by the failure of the preceding interest on the ground of perpetuity, the result would be that someone would be in possession whom the settlor did not mean to be in possession in the existing circumstances. Alternatively, the gap might be left void. Each alternative would be contrary to the intention of the settlor.

The leading case on this subject is *Beard v Westcott* (1822) 5 B & Ald 801, explained in *Monypenny v Dering* (1852) 2 De GM & G 145. Sir John Romilly MR in *Re Thatcher's Trusts* (1859) 26 Beav 365 treated himself as following *Beard v Westcott*, and Astbury J in *Re Hewett's Settlement* [1915] 1 Ch 810 purported to follow both *Beard v Westcott* and *Re Thatcher's Trusts*. *Re Backhouse* [1921] 2 Ch 51 was presumably decided on similar grounds; and see *Re Mortimer* [1905] 2 Ch 502 where a vested legal remainder subsequent to a remote estate tail was held to fail. So far as these authorities result in an interest which, if it ever falls into possession, must do so within the perpetuity period being rendered invalid by the remoteness of some earlier interest in the chain, they have been subjected to criticism in Gray on Perpetuities, 4th edn., pp. 276–281, paras. 252–257, which seems to me to be cogent, but there is no doubt that they are binding on me. In such cases the ulterior interest may truly be said to fail by reason of contagion with or of dependency on the remote interest if, as in *Beard v Westcott*, the ulterior interest is one which is expressed to take effect on some contingency which is not itself remote. This is, I believe, the only kind of case to be found in the books in which this rule has been applied. They are to be distinguished from the kinds of cases which I now proceed to notice.

Where the testator or settlor so frames his trusts as to create an interest which will not take effect in possession until a future date but must vest in interest within the perpetuity limit, either on a stated date or on some event which must occur within that limit, and the enjoyment of that interest in possession is not dependent on the prior exhaustion of the antecedent interests, such future interest will be unaffected by remoteness in any of the antecedent interests. Thus in *Re Coleman* [1936] Ch 528, [1936] 2 All ER 225, where a testator settled a share of his residue on discretionary trusts for his son W. during his life, and after his death on similar discretionary trust for any widow W. might leave and for all or any of the children of W. and after the death of such widow on trust for the children of W. at 21 or marriage, in equal shares, it was held that though the discretionary trust in favour of W.'s widow was void for remoteness, as W. might marry a woman who was not born at the death of the testator, the ultimate trust in favour of W.'s children being vested, and not contingent or dependent on the void trust, was valid. . . .

Another case falling within this class is *Re Allan* [1958] 1 WLR 220, [1958] 1 All ER 401, where although the interest there in question was expressed to take effect "on the determination of the trusts hereinbefore declared," Danckwerts J contrued those words as equivalent to "on the death of such widow."

A third class of cases is exemplified by *Re Abbott* [1893] 1 Ch 54, and *Re Canning's Will Trusts* [1936] Ch 309. Where a testator or settlor gives property to A. either immediately or at some future date which is not too remote, but so frames his trusts that the interest of A. may be displaced by the exercise of some power or discretion, the interest of A. will be unaffected by any invalidity of that power or discretion on the ground of remoteness.

[His Lordship referred to *Re Abbott* and to *Re Canning's Will Trusts* and continued:]

I now return to considering the testator's will. As I have pointed out, the accruer provision in clause 9(vi) must take effect, if at all, while the trusts declared by clause 9(iv) and (v) remain in operation in respect of the appropriate share of one of the testator's sisters. That is to say, it must take effect, if at all, while a sister of the testator or a child of a sister of the testator is alive. It must and could only take effect in respect of a particular share upon there ceasing to be a sister of the testator or any child of hers entitled in respect of that share under clause 9(iv) and, ignoring perpetuity for the present purpose, any grandchild of that sister entitled in respect of that share under clause 9(v). In other words, it could only take effect upon the exhaustion of the objects of the preceding trusts. The accruer provision is, in my judgment, dependent on the preceding trusts and expectant on their failure, as indeed the opening words of clause 9(vi) suggest.

The disposition of capital in the second half of clause 9(vi),[8] however, appears to me to stand on a different footing. The earlier trusts are trusts for a limited period which must end on or before an ascertainable date, namely, the death of the last survivor of the testator's sisters and their children. This event is not dependent on the exhaustion of objects of the antecedent trusts. The fact that theoretically this date might be more than 21 years after the end of a life in being at the testator's death is, I think, irrelevant: *Re Coleman*. The gift of the capital of the sisters' fund contained at the end of clause 9(vi) is the only disposition of the capital of this fund, it vested in interest immediately on the death of the testator, and the enjoyment by the charities of that interest in possession is merely postponed because and to the extent that the testator has for a limited time given the income elsewhere. I see no ground upon which this gift could be said itself to fail for perpetuity, nor do I think that the facts of the case bring it within the principle of what I may call dependent invalidity.

The only case which may perhaps be said to be awkward to reconcile with this view is *Re Backhouse* [1921] 2 Ch 51. . . .

If *Re Backhouse* and *Re Coleman* conflict, I prefer the decision of Clauson J in *Re Coleman*. At any rate, *Re Backhouse* is clearly distinguishable on its facts from the present case, and as Eve J gave no reasons for the relevant part of his decision in that case I am not embarrassed by it.'[9]

B. Perpetuities and Accumulations Act 1964

PERPETUITIES AND ACCUMULATIONS ACT 1964[10]

6. Saving and acceleration of expectant interests.—A disposition shall not be treated as void for remoteness by reason only that the interest disposed of is

---

8   I.e., the gift over to charity.

9   On the question whether 'failure' of the trusts includes failure because of the application of the perpetuity rule, see *Re Robinson's Will Trusts* [1963] 1 WLR 628, [1963] 1 All ER 777 (held to include); *Re Buckton's Settlement Trusts* [1964] Ch 497, [1964] 2 All ER 487 (held not to include); (1964) 80 LQR 323 (R.E. Megarry).

10   C & B, p. 352; M & W, para. 7.085; MM, p. 226; Maudsley, p. 185; (1964) 80 LQR 517–518. Morris and Leach Supp. pp. 13–14.

ulterior to and dependent upon an interest under a disposition which is so void, and the vesting of an interest shall not be prevented from being accelerated on the failure of a prior interest by reason only that the failure arises because of remoteness.

XII. Contracts and Options

A. Before 1964 [11]

In **Woodall v Clifton** [1905] 2 Ch 257, the question was whether the rule applied to a covenant in a 99 year lease to purchase the fee simple, in such a way as to prevent the assignee of the lease from being able to enforce the covenant against an assignee of the freehold.

WARRINGTON J held that it did. In the Court of Appeal the result was affirmed on the ground that the covenant did not run with the reversion under 32 Hen 8, c34; [12] the perpetuity question was not referred to in the judgments on appeal.

LONDON AND SOUTH WESTERN RAILWAY CO v GOMM
(1882) 20 ChD 562 (CA, JESSEL MR, Sir James HANNEN, LINDLEY LJ)

In 1865 the London and South Western Railway Co conveyed to Powell for £100 the fee simple of certain land which was no longer required for the purposes of the railway. Powell covenanted with the company that he, his heirs and assigns would at any time thereafter whenever the land might be required for the railway and upon receiving £100, reconvey the land to the company. In 1879 Gomm purchased the land from Powell's heir with notice of the covenant, and in 1880 the company brought an action for specific performance of the covenant.

Held (inter alia). The covenant was void, as it created an interest in land and might be exercised outside the perpetuity period.

JESSEL MR: If then the rule as to remoteness applies to a covenant of this nature, this covenant clearly is bad as extending beyond the period allowed by the rule. Whether the rule applies or not depends upon this as it appears to me, does or does not the covenant give an interest in the land? If it is a bare or mere personal contract it is of course not obnoxious to the rule, but in that case it is impossible to see how the present Appellant can be bound. He did not enter into the contract, but is only a purchaser from *Powell* who did. If it is a mere personal contract it cannot be enforced against the assignee. Therefore the company must admit that it somehow binds the land. The right to call for a conveyance of the land is an equitable interest or equitable estate. In the ordinary case of a contract for purchase there is no doubt about this, and an option for repurchase is not different in its nature. [13] A person exercising the option has to do two things, he

---

[11]   C & B, pp. 333–334; M & W, paras. 7.113–7.122; MM, pp. 235–236; Maudsley, pp. 72–75; Morris and Leach, pp. 219–228; (1954) 18 Conv (NS) 576 (J.H.C. Morris and W.B. Leach).
[12]   See p. 564, post.
[13]   *Mountford v Scott* [1975] Ch 258, [1974] 1 All ER 148; affd [1975] 1 All ER 198 (option to purchase); *George Wimpey & Co Ltd v IRC* [1974] 1 WLR 975, [1974] 2 All ER 602; cf. *Murray v Two Strokes Ltd* [1973] 1 WLR 823, [1973] 3 All ER 357 (right of pre-emption); *Pritchard v Briggs* [1980] Ch 338, [1980] 1 All ER 294; Barnsley, *Land Options*, (2nd edn.) chap. 7; p. 93, ante.

has to give notice of his intention to purchase, and to pay the purchase-money; but as far as the man who is liable to convey is concerned, his estate or interest is taken away from him without his consent, and the right to take it away being vested in another, the covenant giving the option must give that other an interest in the land.

It appears to me therefore that this covenant plainly gives the company an interest in the land, and as regards remoteness there is no distinction that I know of (unless the case falls within one of the recognised exceptions, such as charities) between one kind of equitable interest and another kind of equitable interest. In all cases they must take effect as against the owners of the land within a prescribed period.

Specific performance was held to be obtainable between the original contracting parties: *Hutton v Watling*[14] [1948] Ch 26, [1947] 2 All ER 641; affd on other grounds [1948] Ch 398, [1948] 1 All ER 803; and even if the defendant is no longer in possession of the land, damages for breach of contract could be obtained: *Worthing Corpn v Heather* [1906] 2 Ch 532.[15]

B. Perpetuities and Accumulations Act 1964[16]

PERPETUITIES AND ACCUMULATIONS ACT 1964

9. Options relating to land.—(1) The rule against perpetuities shall not apply to a disposition consisting of the conferring of an option to acquire for valuable consideration an interest reversionary (whether directly or indirectly) on the term of a lease if—

    (a) the option is exercisable only by the lessee or his successors in title, and

    (b) it ceases to be exercisable at or before the expiration of one year following the determination of the lease.

This subsection shall apply in relation to an agreement for a lease as it applies in relation to a lease, and 'lessee' shall be construed accordingly.

(2) In the case of a disposition consisting of the conferring of an option to acquire for valuable consideration any interest in land, the perpetuity period under the rule against perpetuities shall be twenty-one years, and section 1 of this Act shall not apply:[17]

Provided that this subsection shall not apply to a right of pre-emption conferred on a public or local authority in respect of land used or to be used for religious purposes where the right becomes exercisable only if the land ceases to be used for such purposes.

10. Avoidance of contractual and other rights in cases of remoteness.—Where a disposition inter vivos would fall to be treated as void for remoteness if the rights

---

[14] (1948) 12 Conv (NS) 258 (E.O. Walford).

[15] See also *South Eastern Rly Co v Associated Portland Cement Manufacturers (1900) Ltd* [1910] 1 Ch 12; *Dunn v Blackdown Properties Ltd* [1961] Ch 433, [1961] 2 All ER 62. *Dunn v Blackdown Properties Ltd* [1961] Ch 433, [1961] 2 All ER 62; (1961) 25 Conv (NS) 415 (G. Battersby); *Newham v Lawson* (1971) 22 P & CR 852. The right may however be construed as an immediate right which has not yet been exercised, and not as a future right: *South Eastern Rly Co v Associated Portland Cement Manufacturers (1900) Ltd* [1910] 1 Ch 12; cf. *Sharpe v Durant* [1911] WN 158. See Morris and Leach, pp. 228–231.

[16] C & B, pp. 351–352; M & W, paras. 7.113–7.122; MM, p. 235–236; Maudsley, pp. 186–189; (1964) 80 LQR 522–525; Morris and Leach, Supp., pp. 16–17.

[17] *Wilson v Truelove* [2003] 23 EG 136 unlimited 'right to repurchase' held void).

and duties thereunder were capable of transmission to persons other than the original parties and had been so transmitted, it shall be treated as void as between the person by whom it was made and the person to whom or in whose favour it was made or any successor of his, and no remedy shall lie in contract or otherwise for giving effect to it or making restitution for its lack of effect.

XIII. Possibilities of Reverter and Conditions Subsequent [18]

A. Before 1964 [19]

LAW OF PROPERTY ACT 1925

4. Creation and disposition of equitable interests.—(3) All rights of entry affecting a legal estate which are exercisable on condition broken or for any other reason may after the commencement of this Act, be made exercisable by any person and the persons deriving title under him, but, in regard to an estate in fee simple (not being a rentcharge held for a legal estate) only within the period authorised by the rule relating to perpetuities. [20]

The rule was usually held not to apply to a possibility of reverter. [1] An executory gift over, outside the period, will of course be void; the interest reverts to the grantor who can dispose of it by a grant inter vivos or by his will: *Brown v Independent Baptist Church of Woburn*. [2] The view was strongly held before 1964 that the rule ought to be applied to possibilities of reverter; and in *Hopper v Liverpool Corpn* (1943) 88 SJ 213, the Vice-Chancellor of the Lancaster County Palatine Court held that it did.

B. Perpetuities and Accumulations Act 1964 [3]

PERPETUITIES AND ACCUMULATIONS ACT 1964

12. Possibilities of reverter, conditions subsequent, exceptions and reservations.—(1) In the case of —
  (*a*) a possibility of reverter on the determination of a determinable fee simple, or
  (*b*) a possibility of a resulting trust on the determination of any other determinable interest in property,

[18] For the distinction between a determinable and a conditional fee, see C & B, pp. 364–367; M & W, paras. 3.060–3.076; MM, pp. 42–44; see also p. 23, ante.
[19] C & B, pp. 335–343; M & W, paras. 7.089–7.097; MM, pp. 229–231; Maudsley, pp. 69–71; Morris and Leach, pp. 209–219.
[20] *Re Trustees of Hollis' Hospital and Hague's Contract* [1899] 2 Ch 540; *Re Da Costa* [1912] 1 Ch 337; *Re Bowen* [1893] 2 Ch 491; *Re Peel's Release* [1921] 2 Ch 218.
[1] *Re Randell* (1888) 38 ChD 213; *Re Blunt's Trusts* [1904] 2 Ch 767; *Re Chardon* [1928] Ch 464; *Re Wightwick's Will Trusts* [1950] Ch 260, [1950] 1 All ER 689; *Re Chambers' Will Trusts* [1950] Ch 267; *Re Cooper's Conveyance Trusts* [1956] 1 WLR 1096, [1956] 3 All ER 28.
[2] 325 Mass 645, 91 NE (2d) 922 (1950); (1952) 65 HLR 721, 741 (W.B. Leach) (a residuary gift held in Massachusetts to include such an interest).
[3] C & B, pp. 361, 365–366; M & W, paras. 7.092–7.097; MM, p. 231; Maudsley, pp. 190–191; (1964) 80 LQR 525–527; Morris and Leach Supp., p. 18.

the rule against perpetuities shall apply in relation to the provision causing the interest to be determinable as it would apply if that provision were expressed in the form of a condition subsequent giving rise, on breach thereof, to a right of re-entry or an equivalent right in the case of property other than land, and where the provision falls to be treated as void for remoteness the determinable interest shall become an absolute interest.

(2) Where a disposition is subject to any such provision, or to any such condition subsequent, or to any exception or reservation, the disposition shall be treated for the purposes of this Act as including a separate disposition of any rights arising by virtue of the provision, condition subsequent, exception and reservation.

XIV. Exceptions to the Rule [4]

Morris and Leach, *The Rule Against Perpetuities* (2nd edn.), pp. 242–243

'It may be useful to enumerate here some of the more important exceptions to the Rule. Most of these have already been considered. [5]
  (1) Gifts over from one charity to another. [6]
  (2) Limitations which must vest at or before the termination of an entailed interest. [7]
  (3) Contracts, unless they create contingent interests in land or other property. [8]
  (4) Covenants for renewal in leases. [9]
  (5) Mortgages. [10]
  (6) Certain easements. [11]
  (7) Certain rights of entry for non-payment of rentcharges. [12]
  (8) Trusts for the payment of debts. [13]
  (9) Accumulations for reducing the National Debt. [14]
  (10) Trusts of 'registered funds' the main purpose of which is to provide superannuation allowances or widows' pensions or children's allowances for employees or the assurance of capital sums on the death of employees. [15]
  (11) Trusts of a personal or occupational pension scheme.' [16]

[4]   C & B, pp. 333–337, 352–353; M & W, paras. 7.123–7.135; MM, pp. 237–238.
[5]   The footnotes refer to pages in Morris and Leach.
[6]   Ante, pp. 189–194.
[7]   Ante, pp. 195–196.
[8]   Ante, pp. 219, 227, 228.
[9]   Ante, pp. 223.
[10]   Ante, pp. 227.
[11]   Ante, pp. 229–230.
[12]   LPA 1925, ss. 121 (6), 162; ante, p. 218.
[13]   Ante, pp. 240–241.
[14]   Superannuation and Other Trust Funds (Validation) Act 1927, s. 9.
[15]   Social Security Act 1973, s. 69; Personal and Occupational Pension Schemes (Perpetuities) Regs 1990 (SI 1990 No. 1143). Similar legislation is in force in many other parts of the British Commonwealth; Maudsley, p. 191.
[16]   Pension Schemes Act 1993, s. 163; Personal and Occupational Pension Schemes (Perpetuities) Regs 1990 (SI 1990 No. 1143), reg. 3. For a perceptive criticism, see (1995) Private Client Business, pp. 133–145, 223–232 (G. Thomas); *Thomas on Powers*, paras. 4.44–4.65. S. 163; Personal and Occupational Pension Schemes (Perpetuities) Regs 1990 (S.I. 1990 No. 1143) reg. 3. For a perceptive criticism, see (1995) Private Client Business, pp. 133–145, 223–232 (G. Thomas). See also *Air Jamaica Ltd v Charlton* [1999] 1 WLR 1399; [2000] Conv 170 (C. Harpum).

XV. Rule Against Accumulations [17]

A. Introduction

The rule against accumulations was introduced by the Accumulations Act 1800, as a result of *Thellusson v Woodford* (1799) 4 Ves 227; affd (1805) 11 Ves 112; see p. 414, post, and these statutory provisions were re-enacted and amended by sections 164–166 Law of Property Act 1925. The general effect is to limit those accumulations, to which the Act applies, [18] to any one of four periods: first, the life of the grantor or settlor; second, twenty-one years from the death of the grantor, settlor or testator, and third and fourth, two alternative periods of certain specified minorities. The main differences between the third and fourth periods [19] are that the third is limited to persons alive at the death of the testator or settlor, while the fourth period includes accumulations *(a)* during the minorities of persons born after the death of the grantor, settlor or testator, provided that accumulation is not directed to begin until such person is born and *(b)* during successive minorities; but it is confined to the minorities of those who would, if of full age, have been entitled to the income which is being accumulated. [20]

Two further periods of accumulation were added by the Perpetuities and Accumulations Act 1964, section 13(1) [1] for the benefit of a living settlor, namely twenty-one years from the date of the disposition, and the minority or respective minorities of any person or persons in being at that date. This provision offered considerable advantages to a settlor who wished to establish an inter vivos discretionary trust for his family. Previously the only periods applicable to inter vivos trusts were accumulations during minorities (third and fourth periods); or during the life of the settlor (first period) which attracted estate duty on the settlor's death. [2] Under the present tax system, inheritance tax is payable when an interest in possession under a trust ends on or within seven years before the beneficiary's death. In the case of discretionary trusts, the tax is payable upon capital distributed from the trust. It is also payable upon the whole of the capital of the trust on each tenth anniversary of the transfer of the property to the trust; but tax is chargeable at only 30% of the rate which would be chargeable upon actual distribution. [3]

The effect of a direction which breaks the rule against accumulations depends on whether it also breaks the rule against perpetuities. If it breaks both rules, then the direction is totally void i.e. there is no accumulation at all. If, however, it satisfies the rule against perpetuities but only breaks the rule against accumulations, then it is good pro tanto and only void as to the excess beyond the appropriate statutory period. There is, then, a gap from the end of the

---

[17]   C & B, pp. 353–358; M & W, paras. 7.152–7.178; MM, pp. 240–246; Gray, *Rule Against Perpetuities* (4th edn, 1942), ss. 671–679. 1, Appendix B, ss. 686–714; Maudsley, chap. 7; Morris and Leach, pp. 266–306; Simes, *Public Policy and the Dead Hand,* chap. 4; *Theobald on Wills* (16th edn, 2001), paras. 44.59–44.70; (1953) 17 Conv (NS) 199 (G.B. Graham); [1958] CLJ 39 (S.J. Bailey); Law Reform Committee Fourth Report 1958 (Cmnd. 18), Section C.

[18]   For exemptions, see LPA 1925, s. 164 (2), p. 419, post.

[19]   *Re Cattell* [1914] 1 Ch 177, p. 416, post. For the relationship between LPA 1925, s. 165, as interpreted in *Re Maber* [1928] Ch 88 and the fourth period under s. 164, see Morris and Leach, pp. 276–278.

[20]   *Re Cattell* [1914] 1 Ch 177 at 189.

[1]   Following the recommendations of the Law Reform Committee Fourth Report, paras. 56, 57; (1964) 80 LQR 529–530; Morris and Leach Supp., 19.

[2]   FA 1894, s. 2(1)(*b*); FA 1969, s. 36 (the 'substituted section 2(1)(*b*)(iv).').

[3]   IHTA 1984, ss. 64, 66. See also s. 71, excluding accumulation and maintenance trusts from this provision.

statutory period until the end of the period chosen during which the income is in effect undisposed of; during this gap the income so released either reverts to the settlor or his representatives or falls into residue or goes to the next of kin. There is no acceleration of the interests of those entitled after the accumulation is over. [4]

B. Before 1964

THELLUSSON v WOODFORD [5]
(1805) 11 Ves 112 (HL, Lord ELDON LC)

Peter Thellusson, who died in 1797, devised real estates of the annual value of about £1,000, and other estates, directed to be purchased with the residue of the personal estate, amounting to above £600,000 to trustees upon trust to accumulate the rents and profits at compound interest during the lives of his sons, grandsons and great-grandsons living at his death or born in due time [6] afterwards, and on the death of the survivor to divide the said estates into three lots, each of which was to be strictly settled on the eldest male lineal descendant then living of each of his three sons. He directed that the trustees should stand seised, upon the failure of male lineal descendants, upon trust to sell and pay the produce to His Majesty, his heirs, and successors, to the use of the Sinking Fund: and that all the persons becoming entitled should use the surname of Thellusson only. At the time of the testator's death, there were alive his widow, three sons and four grandsons: two more grandsons, who were en ventre at the time of his death, were born later.

   Held (affirming the decision of Lord LOUGHBOROUGH (1799) 4 Ves 227). The limitations and the direction to accumulate were valid, being confined to lives in being.

   Counsel for the appellants: 'Mr *Thellusson's* will is morally vicious; as it was a contrivance of a parent to exclude every one of his issue from the enjoyment even of the produce of his property during almost a century; and it is politically injurious; as during the whole of that period it makes an immense property unproductive both to individuals and the community at large; and by the time, when the accumulation shall end, it will have created a fund, the revenue of which will be greater than the civil list; and will therefore give its processor the means of disturbing the whole economy of the country. The probable amount of the accumulated fund, in the events, which have happened, is stated in the Appellant's bill, and admitted in the answer, to be 19,000,000*l*; and in case any of the persons, answering the description of heir male, when the period of suspense ends, should be a minor, and his minority should continue 10 years, it would increase the amount of that third of the sum of 10,802,373*l*; so that, if the whole property should centre in one person, and that person should have a minority of 10 years, after the end of the period of suspense (a circumstance by no means improbable, particularly as Mr *George Woodford Thellusson* had been long

---

4   *Green v Gascoyne* (1865) 4 De GJ & Sm 565, p. 420, post.
5   For a general history of the Thellusson family litigation, see (1970) 21 NILQ 131 (G.W. Keeton); (1997) 147 NLJ 1046 (S. Hooper).
6   I.e. the period of gestation.

married and has no son), the whole accumulated fund will amount to 32,407,120*l.*'[7]

LORD ELDON LC: Another question arises out of this will; which is a pure question of equity: Whether a testator can direct the rents and profits to be accumulated for that period, during which he may direct, that the title shall not vest, and the property shall remain unalienable; and, that he can do so, is most clear law. A familiar case may be put. If this testator had given the residue of his personal estate to such person as should be the eldest male descendant of *Peter Isaac Thellusson* at the death of the survivor of all the lives, mentioned in this will, without more, that simple bequest would in effect have directed accumulation, until it should be seen, what individual would answer the description of that male descendant; and the effect of the ordinary rule of law, as applied in equity, would have supplied everything, that is contained in this will, as to accumulation; for the first question would be, Is the executory devise of the personal estate to the future individual, so described, good? If it is, wherever a residue of personal estate is given, the interest goes with the bulk; and there is no more objection to giving that person, that, which is only forming another capital, than to giving the capital itself. But the constant course of a Court of Equity is to accumulate interest from time to time without a direction, and to hand over the accumulation to that person, who is to take the capital. Take another instance of accumulation: Suppose, the nine persons, named in this will, had been lunatics: without any direction there would been an accumulation of the interests and profits of all these estates. In truth there is no objection to accumulation upon the policy of the law, applying to perpetuities: for the rents and profits are not to be locked up, and made no use of, for the individuals, or the public. The effect is only to invest them from time to time in land: so that the fund is, not only in a constant course of accumulation, but also in a constant course of circulation. To that application what possible objection can there be at law? . . . Therefore, as to giving the property at the expiration of nine lives and the accumulation, I never could doubt upon these points.

LAW OF PROPERTY ACT 1925

164. General restrictions on accumulation of income.—(1) No person[8] may by any instrument or otherwise settle or dispose of any property in such manner that the income thereof shall, save as hereinafter mentioned, be wholly or partially accumulated for any longer period than one of the following, namely—

  (a) the life of the grantor or settlor; or

  (b) a term of twenty-one years from the death of the grantor, settlor or testator; or

  (c) the duration of the minority[9] or respective minorities of any person or persons living or en ventre sa mere at the death of the grantor, settlor or testator; or

---

[7] 'On the death of the last surviving grandson in 1856, the estate was divided (not without more litigation) between the two male representatives of the two of Peter Thellusson's sons who had left issue. But owing to mismanagement and costs of litigation, the estate realised a comparatively small amount': Holdsworth, vii, p. 230; (1970) 21 NILQ at pp. 169–174.

[8] A corporate settlor is not a 'person' within the section: *Re Dodwell & Co Ltd's Trust Deed* [1979] Ch 301, [1978] 3 All ER 738.

[9] In the case of dispositions taking effect after 1969, minority ends at the age of 18; Family Law Reform Act 1969, s. 1. There are transitional provisions so that the change from 21 to 18 shall not invalidate any direction for accumulation in a settlement or other disposition made by a deed, will or other instrument, which was made before 1970: ss. 1, 4, Sch. 3, para. 7.

(d) the duration of the minority or respective minorities only of any person or persons who under the limitations of the instrument directing the accumulations would, for the time being, if of full age, be entitled to the income directed to be accumulated. [10]

In every case where any accumulation is directed [11] otherwise than as aforesaid, the direction shall (save as hereinafter mentioned) be void; and the income of the property directed to be accumulated shall, so long as the same is directed to be accumulated contrary to this section, go to and be received by the person or persons who would have been entitled thereto if such accumulation had not been directed.

(3) The restrictions imposed by this section apply to instruments made on or after the twenty-eighth day of July, eighteen hundred, but in the case of wills only where the testator was living and of testamentary capacity after the end of one year from that date.

165. Qualification of restrictions on accumulation.—Where accumulations of surplus income are made during a minority under any statutory power or under the general law, the period for which such accumulations are made is not (whether the trust was created or the accumulations were made before or after the commencement of this Act) to be taken into account in determining the periods for which accumulations are permitted to be made by the last preceding section, and accordingly an express trust for accumulation for any other permitted period shall not be deemed to have been invalidated or become invalid, by reason of accumulations also having been made as aforesaid during such minority. [12]

166. Restriction on accumulation for the purchase of land.—(1) No person may settle or dispose of any property in such manner that the income thereof shall be wholly or partially accumulated for the purchase of land only, for any longer period than the duration of the minority or respective minorities of any person or persons who, under the limitations of the instrument directing the accumulation, would for the time being, if of full age, be entitled to the income so directed to be accumulated.

(2) This section does not, nor do the enactments which it replaces, apply to accumulations to be held as capital money for the purposes of the Settled Land Act, 1925, or the enactments replaced by that Act, whether or not the accumulations are primarily liable to be laid out in the purchase of land.

(3) This section applies to settlements and dispositions made after the twenty-seventh day of June eighteen hundred and ninety-two.

In **Re Cattell** [1914] 1 Ch 177, the question was whether an accumulation was limited to the minority of persons born in the lifetime of the testator. The Court of Appeal (LORD PARKER OF WADDINGTON, LORD SUMNER and WARRINGTON J) held that the fourth period extended to the minorities of persons born after the testator's death and to successive minorities. Lord PARKER OF WADDINGTON said at 186:

'In construing the Thellusson Act, it must be remembered that it is not an enabling but a disabling Act. Prior to the passing of the Act a testator had the

[10]   See *Re Cattell* [1914] 1 Ch 177, p. 416, post.
[11]   This includes a power to accumulate: PAA 1964, s. 13(2), p. 418, post; affirming *Re Robb* [1953] Ch 459, [1953] 1 All ER 920. The same point was so decided in Scotland under Trusts (Scotland) Act 1961, s. 5(2); *Baird v Lord Advocate* [1979] AC 666, [1979] 2 All ER 28.
[12]   See n. 9, supra.

right to direct an accumulation for any period he chose, provided he did not exceed the time which was allowed by the perpetuity rule—that is to say, lives in being, and twenty-one years afterwards. The Act was passed in order to disable testators from taking full advantage of the liberty which they had hitherto enjoyed in that respect. The terms of the Act are "That no person or persons shall after the passing of this Act, by any deed or deeds, surrender or surrenders, will, codicil or otherwise howsoever, settle or dispose of any real or personal property so and in such manner that the rents, issues, profits or produce thereof shall be wholly or partially accumulated for any longer term than"—then there are four alternative periods given, and it has been held, and I think rightly held, that of those four periods one only can be selected by the testator. The difficulty arises in this case in regard to the fourth period. The first contemplates the case of a man who settles property otherwise than by will, in which case he may direct that the rents and profits be accumulated during his life. The settlor cannot direct an accumulation during his life and some further period. The second period contemplates an accumulation which is to commence from the death of the settlor, and includes the case of a settlor by will. No such accumulation is to go on for more than twenty-one years. Then the third alternative is a period—almost the same period of twenty-one years from the death of the settlor—during the minority or respective minorities of any person or persons "who shall be living or en ventre sa mère" at the time of the death of the settlor. That of course must be limited to twenty-one years, and some further period representing gestation in the case of a child yet unborn. Then there is the fourth alternative, which gives rise to the difficulty in the present case . . . [His Lordship read the fourth period [13] and continued:] It is to be observed that this last alternative clause closely follows and seems to be contrasted with the alternative with regard to the minority or respective minorities of any person or persons who should be living or en ventre sa mère at the time of the death of the settlor. One would not therefore expect it to be limited (as contended by the appellant) to children living or en ventre sa mère at the settlor's death. Indeed if so limited it would in effect add nothing to the preceding alternative. The reason urged in support of the appellant's contention rests mainly on certain decisions which it is said we ought to follow and to which I will now refer.

[His Lordship referred to *Haley v Bannister* (1820) 4 Madd 275, *Ellis v Maxwell* (1841) 3 Beav 587 and *Bryan v Collins* (1852) 16 Beav 14 and continued:] In my opinion the fourth alternative period covers not only children who are born or en ventre sa mère at the death of the settlor, but children who are subsequently born, and I think the fact that the fourth alternative comes immediately after, and in contrast with, the third alternative, which refers only to born children, and children en ventre sa mère, at the time of the death of the settlor, points strongly to this conclusion. . . .

It is said—and I think said with some truth—that in this case if we adopt the construction which allows a child who is not born at the death of the settlor to be one of the children during whose minority or respective minorities the accumulations are directed to be made, then we allow successive accumulations to be made of what practically, if not theoretically, is the same fund, which accumulations taken together may last for a considerable time. I think that may be true, but at the same time it is worth bearing in mind that though these periods may when added together amount to a considerable time, yet the periods in

---

[13] Which was in substance the same as LPA 1925, s. 164(1)(*d*), p. 416, *ante*.

question are not really within the vice against which the Act is directed . . . and there being nothing in the express words of the Act to prevent us giving effect to the old powers which were possessed by testators before the Act, there is no reason to construe the fourth alternative in any other way than I have suggested. It is well known that settlements are and have been drawn up on this footing. A testator may often direct a settlement of property upon A. for life, and after his death upon his children on attaining twenty-one, and if he goes on to provide that during the minority or respective minorities of his children the income of the property shall be accumulated, it is only a clause in common form. I have never known any doubt to be thrown on the validity of such a clause, but if the appellant's contention prevailed its validity would be open to question. It seems to me, therefore, that Neville J was right in his decision, and that this appeal ought to be dismissed.'

See also Trustee Act 1925, section 31, [14] which gives power to trustees to apply income for the maintenance of beneficiaries, vested or contingent, during their minority, and requires the unapplied part of the income to be accumulated.

C. Perpetuities and Accumulations Act 1964

PERPETUITIES AND ACCUMULATIONS ACT 1964

13. Amendment of s. 164 of Law of Property Act 1925.—(1) The periods for which accumulations of income under a settlement or other disposition are permitted by section 164 of the Law of Property Act 1925 shall include —

(a) a term of twenty-one years from the date of the making of the disposition, and

(b) the duration of the minority or respective minorities [15] of any person or persons in being at that date.

(2) It is hereby declared that the restrictions imposed by the said section 164 apply in relation to a power to accumulate income whether or not there is a duty to exercise that power, and that they apply whether or not the power to accumulate extends to income produced by the investment of income previously accumulated.

14. Right to stop accumulations.—Section 2 above shall apply to any question as to the right of beneficiaries to put an end to accumulations of income under any disposition as it applies to questions arising on the rule against perpetuities. [16]

---

[14]   As amended by TA 2000, s. 40, Sch. 2, Part II, para. 25.
[15]   See p. 415, n. 9, ante.
[16]   Beneficiaries of full age holding an absolute beneficial interest in a trust fund may terminate the accumulation and the trust and require the trustees to pay the capital of the fund to them: *Saunders v Vautier* (1841) Cr & Ph 240. *Re Deloitte* [1926] Ch 56 had held that evidence of infertility was inadmissible to help beneficiaries to terminate a trust under this rule.

Compare, with these provisions:

VICTORIA PERPETUITIES AND ACCUMULATIONS ACT 1968

19. Accumulation of income.—(1) Where property is settled or disposed of in such manner that the income thereof may be or is directed to be accumulated wholly or in part the power or direction to accumulate that income shall be valid if the disposition of the accumulated income is or may be valid but not otherwise.

D. Exemptions from Restrictions on Accumulation

I. BY STATUTE

LAW OF PROPERTY ACT 1925
164. General restrictions on accumulation of income.—(2) This section does not extend to any provision —
  (i) for payment of the debts of any grantor, settlor, testator or other person;
  (ii) for raising portions for —
  (*a*) any child, children or remoter issue of any grantor, settlor or testator; or
  (*b*) any child, children or remoter issue of a person taking any interest under any settlement or other disposition directing the accumulations or to whom any interest is thereby limited;
  (iii) respecting the accumulation of the produce of timber or wood; and accordingly such provisions may be made as if no statutory restrictions on accumulation of income had been imposed.

II. OTHER EXEMPTIONS

Maudsley, *Modern Law of Perpetuities*, pp. 210–211.

'COMMERCIAL ARRANGEMENTS; CONTRACTS OF INSURANCE; UNIT TRUSTS

Various commercial arrangements have been held to be outside the Act, even though they involve in some sense an accumulation. Thus, in the leading case of *Bassil v Lister*[17] a testator directed his trustees to pay the premiums on a policy of insurance on his son's life out of the income of the residuary estate. Turner V-C held that this was not an accumulation of the type to which the Thellusson Act was directed; and that it was valid for the son's life, and not merely for a period of 21 years. In *Re AEG Unit Trust (Managers) Ltd's Deed*,[18] the question concerned a provision in a trust deed to the effect that surplus income in any accounting period, over and above that available for distribution to unit holders, should be added to capital and should thereupon cease to be available for distribution. Again, this, in a sense, involved an accumulation of such income. Wynn-Parry J held that the Law of Property Act 1925, section 164, did not apply. An investor, purchasing units in a unit trust, did not "settle or dispose" of property, nor was such a transaction within the scope of the section. Nor would the section be applicable where the unit holders were able at any time to amend or terminate the trust.[19] Nor does the section apply where a corporation is the settlor.[20]

---

[17] (1851) 9 Hare 177; similarly with a partnership agreement: (1851) 9 Hare at 184; *Re AEG Unit Trust (Managers) Ltd's Deed* [1957] Ch 415 at 421, [1957] 2 All ER 506 at 508.
[18] Supra.
[19] At 421, at 508: *Wharton v Masterman* [1895] AC 186.
[20] *Re Dodwell & Co Ltd's Trust Deed* [1979] Ch 301, [1978] 3 All ER 738.

MAINTENANCE OF PROPERTY [1]

A provision for the application of income for the upkeep of property is also outside the scope of the Act. This is not really an exception; for it covers only the maintenance of the value of depreciating property, whether by way of provision for repairs, [2] or by way of provision for the replacement of leaseholds as they expire. [3] It does not include a fund for the accumulation of income for the improvement of land, or by the construction of buildings on it. [4] Where the exception applies, the provision must of course comply with the perpetuity period.' [5]

E. Excessive Accumulations

GREEN v GASCOYNE
(1864) 4 De GJ & Sm 565 (Lord WESTBURY LC)

LORD WESTBURY LC: The case is that of a testator directing an accumulation during the lives of his wife and sister and the life of the survivor of them of the rents and profits of certain freehold estates.

The first question is, what is the operation of the statute upon that trust for accumulation? The second, what will be its effect upon the construction and interpretation of the will?

The first effect of the statute I apprehend to be that the trust for accumulation is reduced to a term of twenty-one years, and that I must take the trust as if it had been expressed 'for a period of twenty-one years, provided my wife and my sister *Sarah* or the survivor of them shall so long live.' Secondly, I take it that the words of the statute which direct that the rents released by its effect from the operation of the trust for accumulation shall 'go to and be received by such person or persons as would have been entitled thereto if such accumulation had not been directed'. The meaning of the words therefore is brought to be the same as it would have been had the accumulations been directed for twenty-one years only.

I am not at liberty to apply or use the statute so as in any manner to accelerate the enjoyment of any gift or disposition contained in the will, nor can I use the statute for the purpose of giving to any term or description contained in the will a meaning which it would not have had the trust for accumulation been good instead of bad. Although the trust for accumulation is cut down and reduced to a limited period, the whole of the rest of the will remains in point of disposition, in point of meaning, effect and true interpretation of its language, precisely as if there had been no such operation performed by the statute. . . .

The result is that there is a hiatus between the period when the accumulation ceases by law and the period when the accumulation is directed to cease by the will; there is nothing in the will to catch the rents which arise during that hiatus; and those rents accordingly belong to the heir at law.

---

1   See generally M & W, para. 07.176; Morris and Leach, p. 280.
2   *Vine v Raleigh* [1891] 2 Ch 13; *Re Mason* [1891] 3 Ch 467.
3   *Re Gardiner* [1901] 1 Ch 697; *Re Hurlbatt* [1910] 2 Ch 553.
4   *Vine v Raleigh* [1891] 2 Ch 13 at 26; *Re Gardiner* [1901] 1 Ch 697 at 700.
5   *Curtis v Lukin* (1842) 5 Beav 147.

Sometimes the problem is to know which of the permitted periods should be applied.

In **Re Ransome** [1957] Ch 348, [1957] 1 All ER 690, there was a testamentary direction in a will coming into operation in 1935 that 'the income . . . shall be accumulated until the youngest child of my [living grandson R] shall attain the age of 21 years.' R had by his first marriage a son D, who attained 21 in 1951. By R's second marriage in 1953, there were no children at the date of the proceedings. UPJOHN J held that the gift did not vest absolutely in D on his attaining 21. This meant that the direction to accumulate was excessive, and one question was the proper period of accumulation.

UPJOHN J said at 361, at 696:

'The next question is as to the impact of the rule against accumulations on the direction to accumulate until the youngest child attains 21. Plainly, that direction infringes the rule and it is necessary to determine for what period the term is valid. The test is stated to be that you have first to determine which of the four periods set out in section 164 the testatrix has seemingly selected, determining that question according to the language employed and the facts of the case; see *Re Watt's Will Trusts* [1936] 2 All ER 1555 at 1562. That seems to me an artificial and difficult test. The trouble in this case and in most cases dealing with the rule against accumulations is that the testatrix has given directions clearly not having the rule in mind at all. The competing periods in this case are section 164(1) (*b*), a term of 21 years from the death of the testatrix, which brings the period of valid accumulation to an end on 6 July 1956, on the one hand, and, on the other, sub-paragraph (*c*) of the section, the duration of the minority or respective minorities of anyone living at the death of the testatrix. If that period is selected, it is submitted that it came to an end when the eldest child, David, attained 21 on 24 June 1951.

Neither sub-paragraph fits in, in the least degree, with the direction of the testatrix. However, in directing accumulations until Robert's youngest child should attain 21, the testatrix can hardly have contemplated that the period of accumulations would in fact come to an end by the attainment by Robert's eldest child of the age of 21 years, and I propose to hold that sub-paragraph (*b*) is the relevant paragraph; the difference is not of great importance.'

QUESTIONS

1. What periods would you expect to be applied in the following testamentary dispositions:
   (*a*) '. . . during the minority of the children of Gerald,': *Re Watt's Will Trusts* [1936] 2 All ER 1555.
   (*b*) '. . . so much of the dividends as shall accrue due to Elizabeth Mary Griffiths (a beneficiary) during the life of John Griffiths, her husband, . . . shall be accumulated': *Griffiths v Vere* (1803) 9 Ves 127.
   (*c*) 'to be accumulated . . . until the decease of the last survivor of the said several annuitants, or during such portion of such surviving annuitant's life as the rules of law will permit . . .': *Talbot v Jevers* (1875) LR 20 Eq 255.
   (*d*) Upon trust 'to invest the same in the Funds, and to receive the Dividends thereof and to invest the same in the Funds, so as the same might accumulate, by way of Compound Interest until (the testator's) Great Nephew, Philip Crawley, [aged 3] should attain 25': *Longdon v Simson* (1806) 12 Ves 295; *Crawley v Crawley* (1835) 7 Sim 427.
   (*e*) 'To my wife during widowhood, but if she should marry again, then from and after such marriage, I direct that all bequests in her favour shall cease,

and that in lieu thereof the trustees shall pay to my wife an annuity of £500 and shall accumulate the surplus income during the remainder of the life of my wife': *Weatherall v Thornburgh* (1878) 8 ChD 261.

(f)   '. . . as and when each of them the said Ann Webb and William Adams shall respectively die, the annuity and annuities so given by me to or for her or him respectively as aforesaid, shall be laid out from time to time, until the death of the last survivor of them the said two last-named annuitants, as an addition to the said capital of the said rest, residue, and remainder of my said stock of three per cent consolidated Bank annuities . . . shall be and shall be taken as an increase and accumulation to the said capital stock, until the death of the last survivor of them, the said two last-mentioned annuitants': *Webb v Webb* (1840) 2 Beav 493.

(g)   And a gift inter vivos:
'. . . to receive and accumulate the dividends . . . during the joint lives of James Campbell and Jane, his wife, and, after the death of James Campbell, if his wife should survive him . . . for her life, and, after her decease, whether the same should happen in the lifetime or after the decease of her husband, to stand possessed of the capital and accumulations in trust for their daughter, Charlotte Campbell . . .': *Re Lady Rosslyn's Trust* (1848) 16 Sim 391.

(h)   By a settlement dated 6 December 1951 'to accumulate the income during the life of the settlor or until the beneficiary [born 1950] attains the age of 22': *Re Erskine's Settlement Trusts* [1971] 1 WLR 162, [1971] 1 All ER 572. Would the answer be different if all the facts had taken place after 1964?

2.   Do you think that restrictive rules, such as those currently applicable, are required? The present trend in countries abroad is to return to the common law rule: or even to abolish the rule altogether: PAA 1983 of Manitoba (SM 1982–83, c. 43); p. 372, n.18, ante, p. 424, post. Maudsley p. 202, Appendix D; (1984) 4 OJLS 454 (R. Deech), infra.

3.   Does Wait and See apply to the question of the validity, under the perpetuity rule, of a provision for the accumulation of income? Can you see any reason why, if Wait and See is introduced in respect of disposition generally, it should not also apply to accumulation? C & B, p. 356, n. 4; M & W, paras. 7.162–7.166; Maudsley, pp. 206–208. See Victoria Perpetuities and Accumulations Act 1968, s. 19(1), p. 419, ante; and others included in Maudsley, Appendix D.

XVI. Abolition or Retention and Reform of the Two Rules

(1984) 4 OJLS 454 (R. Deech) at pp. 454, 458–463:

'The Perpetuities and Accumulations Act 1983 of Manitoba (SM 1982–83, c. 43) [6] has abolished the rule against perpetuities, the rule in *Whitby v Mitchell* and the Thellusson Act as they applied in that province (sections 2, 3) and it has transformed successive legal interests into equitable interests, belatedly following

---

[6]   See also Manitoba Law Reform Commission Report on the Rules against Accumulations and Perpetuities (1982 No. 49); (1983) Manitoba LJ 245 (A.I. McClean) 'Abolition is a great step into the unknown. The Manitoba Law Reform Commission and the Manitoba Legislator are not to be numbered amongst this law's timorous souls'; (1984) 62 Can Bar Rev 618 (J.M. Glenn), criticizing the legislation.

section 1 of the Law of Property Act 1925. Coming into force on the same day, 1 October 1983, was an Act to Amend the Trustee Act 1983 (SM 1982–83, c. 38), which abolishes the rule in *Saunders v Vautier* (1841) 4 Beav 115, and subjects any proposal to vary a trust to the approval of the court . . .

Is there still a case for retention and reform of the rule rather than abolition? The case for reform, but never for abolition, has been exhaustively argued by writers and law reform reports. The 1956 Law Reform Committee Report simply stated that it was "beyond argument" that there should be a time limit on the vesting of future interests (para. 4); the case for abolition was not argued by Morris and Leach, *The Rule Against Perpetuities* (2nd edn.), both of whom had assisted in the preparation of the Fourth Report . . . . Maudsley (*The Modern Law of Perpetuities* 221) considered abolition briefly but was daunted by the risk of dynastic trusts created by testators unafraid of tax liability. This risk was considered remote by the Manitobans: whatever social conditions might prevail in England to make this a genuine problem, they were absent in Canada, and even if a few offenders emerged after abolition of the rule, they could not be numerous enough to outweigh the disadvantages of its complications and unforeseeable effect. The harm, if any, in long delayed vesting would be to the taxpayer himself, and not widespread. In Manitoba the days are long gone when an owner wished to keep a fortune in his family over as many generations as possible. In a country of immigration, of nuclear families and of marriage breakdowns calling for property reallocation, it was estimated that there was no significant risk of any ill effect if the rule were to be abolished and, moreover, with retroactive effect. Legislation would deal with specific problems when and if they arose and the balancing of the interests of the living and the dead would henceforth be achieved more satisfactorily by the power of the courts to consent to variation and revocation of trust.

Among the weightiest arguments in favour of abolition were the internal inconsistencies of wait and see itself. To repair is to assert that the rule is the right response to a genuine problem; yet the need to remove well known traps and to provide a safety net, as in the English statute, is an indictment of the rule. Wait and see creates uncertainty for lawyer and client; it also tends to prolong the actual period allowed for vesting and may well validate all gifts. If wait and see is so praiseworthy in its removal of restraint and in achieving closer fulfilment of the testator's wishes, then abolition must be even more acceptable. As Mechem said, if there is a widespread desire to liberalize the rule and a feeling of triumph when a limitation escapes its clutches, then abandonment must be the welcome culmination of the trend. If the law permits, at least to a limited extent, that a testator may make bequests that appear unreasonable to his family then, the rule having been abolished, it can be no worse to allow present disinheritance in favour of beneficiaries living a century hence.

The arguments for keeping the rule, reformed or otherwise, are undeniably less forceful. Partly it is fear; the attitude of Simes: "I do not think there is any way in which the property institutions of a civilised country can be completely wiped out and a new set of institutions established at one stroke of the legislative pen" (103 *U Pa L Rev* 707, 732), to which the 1925 Acts must stand as a refutation. More specifically, Gray in *The Rule Against Perpetuities* (4th edn., s. 871): "It is a dangerous thing to make such a radical change in a part of the law which is concatenated with almost mathematical precision." American jurisdictions that had substantially amended the rule admittedly had to revert to the original, but these experiments were confined to length of perpetuity period, not the concept itself. There is also disquiet about the legislative or other response to new problems emerging if the rule is abolished, whether it be retrospective legislation or the courts' reformulation of a rule against perpetuities, thus starting the historical cycle afresh. The most solid reason for keeping the rule is its alleged power of restraint. The dissenting view in the *Report* was that the rule regulated remoteness of vesting in a fair and intelligible form, and any occasional inappropriate result could be avoided by amending legislation. The frustration of the intention of settlors is no good argument for abolition for the rule exists precisely in order to thwart certain intentions. After all, many wills are defeated because the testator failed to comply with essential formalities, such as the signature of acceptable witnesses, yet there is no demand for wholesale relaxation of the law of wills because it embodies sound policy. It is unlikely that evidence of success would be found because the rule would, if properly applied, prevent the emergence of perpetuities problems and, so far as can be estimated, it has performed its role successfully for three centuries.

Manitoba's abolition of the rule is linked to a widened jurisdiction to vary trusts, which is to take its place and fulfil such balancing effect as the rule might be claimed to have had. If the arguments for abolition cannot be resisted, then the crucial test for the new law is whether variation of trusts can do all that is expected of it. The *Report* assumed that a combination of the rule in *Saunders v Vautier* and the Variation of Trusts Act 1958 already ensured that trusts could only remain in effect in England with the consent of the beneficiaries and the court's consent on behalf of the incapacitated:[7] the parallel legislation in Manitoba was section 61 of the Trustee Act (CCSM, T160), derived from the Sixth Report of the English Law Reform Committee, (Cmnd 310 (1957), *Court's Power to Sanction Variation of Trusts*). The Manitoba *Report* recommended amendment of section 61 to define the "benefit" that the court must find in the proposed arrangement on behalf of the beneficiary and to make it clear that the court must also consider the intentions of the settlor or testator in creating the trust and the circumstances that prevail at the time of application under section 61.

What would motivate courts to give or to withhold approval of variation remains to be seen. There could be problems in this. The existing English law, although of a different scope, works in tandem with perpetuities: once gone, would considerations such as postponed vesting or length of trust and restrictions on spending affect Manitoban or English courts? The nature of the term "benefit" is chameleon-like—if perpetuities cease to be an issue, it is hard to predict whether the court would regard it as of benefit to future possible beneficiaries to end a trust now and divide the capital amongst those presently alive, the difficulty being that one cannot assume that future "beneficiaries" do *not* have a right to enjoy capital once the rule against perpetuities has been abolished. There would arise the question of compensation of remote future beneficiaries. The issue is overshadowed by clouds of possibly unborn entitled persons, and their entitlement would complicate valuation of future shares of capital. Since the settlor's intentions are relevant under the new Manitoba law, his possible desire to establish a dynastic trust will be influential and perhaps weigh so heavily that there will appear no way to terminate it. The moral and social issues involved in trusts (Harris, *Variation of Trusts* 47; *Re Remnant's Settlement Trusts* [1970] Ch 560, [1970] 2 All ER 554) will lose what certainty they have if the perpetuity period is removed as a guideline.

---

[7]   See generally H & M, chap. 22; M & B, *Trusts and Trustees* (6th edn, 2002), chap. 19, p. 418, n. 16, ante.

The tax assumptions also bear questioning. The accepted wisdom is that tax laws serve to curb a man's otherwise greedily dynastic instincts and that tax avoidance dominates *inter vivos* trust establishment. It must nevertheless be conceded that settlements will continue to be deployed when the settlor's prime purpose is not so much tax avoidance but rather control over his capital and beneficiaries. So far at least it is evident that existing tax laws have not prevented large fortunes from descending through the generations, . . . There is, moreover, no foundation for the assumption that tax laws do, and always will, bite on long delayed future interests so as to act as an alternative to or a reinforcement of the perpetuities rule. . . .

Tax efficiency is at the moment regarded as an important reason for variation, even if the House of Lords is less generous than hitherto in approving tax avoidance schemes: *WT Ramsay Ltd v IRC* [1982] AC 300, [1981] 1 All ER 865; *IRC v Burmah Oil Co Ltd* (1981) 54 TC 200; *Furniss v Dawson* [1984] AC 474, [1984] 1 All ER 530.[8] The combination of tax legislation and the abolition of the rule against perpetuities could lead to the establishment of lengthy trusts with resort to the court every generation for variation to suit the demands of the moment. The uncertainties of this process might produce a result even less acceptable than the rule against perpetuities, whose common law rigidities, once mastered, had much to commend them from the point of view of certainty. The unanswerable question is whether the courts would assume that delayed vesting was a good or bad thing in deciding variation questions without the rule, which has provided a framework for trusts questions in the past. The American verdict on such a scheme is adverse; (Sparks, 45 *Va L Rev* 493, considering the parallel *Claflin* doctrine, 20 NE 454 (1889)); but only practice can tell. It could be that a few early cases concerning variation of long-running trusts established by wealthy Manitobans will set the pattern for future attitudes. If abolition of the rule against perpetuities were to be considered in this country then, likewise, the Variation of Trusts Act would have to be altered in scope.

Accumulations law has also been reformed in Manitoba and in the rest of Canada. The arguments against lengthy accumulations were treated by Manitoba in the same way as those relating to perpetuities with the result that restrictive legislation is to be dispensed with the tax laws relied on to deter over-ambitious plans. Accumulation was regarded as a sensible plan in certain cases and the old Thellusson Act applying in Manitoba unsatisfactorily frustrating. Elsewhere in Canada there has been a reversion to the common law rule that accumulation is acceptable as long as the accumulated fund vests within the perpetuity period, following the suggestions of Simes (Alberta, Perpetuities Act, RSA 1980, cP–4, section 240; British Columbia: Perpetuity Act 1975, c. 53, section 24(1); see also W. Australia: Law Reform (Property, Perpetuities and Succession) Act 1962, section 17) but in Ontario six accumulation periods have been provided (Accumulations Act, RSO 1980, c. 5) in emulation of English law. In Manitoba the Accumulations Act has simply been repealed and not replaced (section 2).'

---

[8]   See, however, *Craven v White* [1989] AC 398, [1988] 3 All ER 495; *MacNiven v Westmoreland Investments Ltd* [2001] 2 WLR 377, [2001] 1 All ER 865. On the taxation of trusts, see H & M, chap. 9; M & B, *Trusts and Trustees* (6th edn. 2002), Part III.

Law Commission Report on the Rules Against Perpetuities and Excessive Accumulations 1998 (Law Com No 251), Part XI: Summary of Recommendations [9]

'11.1   The rule against perpetuities should not apply except as provided by statute. (Para. 7.30; Draft Bill, Cl 1(1).)

11.2   The rule against perpetuities should only apply—
(1)   to successive estates and interests in property held in trust, including an estate or interest which—
(a)   is subject to a condition precedent; or
(b)   arises under either a right of reverter on the determination of a determinable fee simple, or under a resulting trust on the determination of a determinable interest;
(2)   where property is held on trust for an estate or interest subject to a condition subsequent, a right of re-entry (or the equivalent right in property other than land) that is exercisable on breach of that condition;
(3)   to powers of appointment; and
(4)   where a will limits chattels in such a way as to create successive legal interests in them under the doctrine of executory bequests, to those interests. (Para. 7.31; Draft Bill, Cl 1(2)–(6).)

11.3   Interests created by instruments which either nominate benefits under a pension scheme or by the exercise of a power of advancement under such a scheme should be subject to the rule against perpetuities. (Para. 7.33; Draft Bill, Cl 2(5).)

11.4   We recommend that the rule against perpetuities should not apply to an interest or right arising under—
(1)   an occupational pension scheme;
(2)   a personal pension scheme;
(3)   a public service pension scheme; or
(4)   a self-employed pension arrangement. (Para. 7.36; Draft Bill, Cls 2(4); 20(5).)

11.5   The Lord Chancellor should have power to specify further exceptions to the rule against perpetuities by statutory instrument. (Para. 7.52; Draft Bill, Cl 3).)

11.6   The restrictions on the scope of the rule against perpetuities that we recommend in paragraphs 11.2–11.4 above, should only apply to instruments taking effect on or after the date on which any legislation is brought into force. (Para. 7.53; Draft Bill, Cl 15(1), (3), 22.)

11.7   There should be one fixed perpetuity period of 125 years. (Para. 8.13; Draft Bill, Cl 5(1).)

11.8   The 125-year period should be overriding and should apply whatever the instrument creating the estate or interest may provide. (Para. 8.14; Draft Bill, Cl 5(2).)

11.9   The perpetuity period should comence when the instrument creating the estate, interest, right or power to which the rule applies takes effect. (Para. 8.15; Draft Bill, Cl 6(1).)

---

[9]   (1998) Trust Law International 148 (P. Sparkes).

11.10 In relation to any estate, right or interest created by the exercise of a special power of appointment, the perpetuity period should commence when the instrument creating the power takes effect. (Para. 8.16; Draft Bill, Cl 6(2).)

11.11 In respect of interests created where a nomination or advancement is made under a pension scheme, the perpetuity period shall be taken to start on the date on which the person making the nomination became a member of the scheme. (Para 8.17; Draft Bill, Cl 6(3).)

11.12 Subject to two exceptions set out in the following paragraphs, the 125-year perpetuity period—
   (1) should only apply prospectively to instruments taking effect on or after the date on which any legislation is brought into force; (Para. 8.18; Draft Bill, Cl 15(1)) but
   (2) should not apply to wills that were executed before that date, but where the testator died afterwards. (Para. 8.18; Draft Bill Cls 15(1), 16.)

11.13 The first exception is that trustees of a trust that was in existence at the time when the legislation was brought into force should have a power to elect by means of an irrevocable deed that the trust should be subject to—
   (1) the statutory 125-year perpetuity period; and
   (2) those other provisions of the legislation in Clauses 6–11 of the Draft Bill that relate to the operation of the rule against perpetuities.

11.14 This power should be exercisable only if—
   (1) the trust contained an express perpetuity period of lives in being plus 21 years; and
   (2) the trustees believe that it is difficult or impracticable to ascertain the existence or whereabouts of the measuring lives in being so that they could not determine the date at which the perpetuity period would come to an end. (Para. 8.20; Draft Bill, Cl 12.)

11.15 The second exception is that where a disposition is made under a special power of appointment, then whether or not that special power was created before or after the commencement of the legislation, the perpetuity period applicable to the disposition should be 125 years commencing on the effective date of the instrument which created the special power of appointment. (Para. 8.23; Draft Bill, Cl 6(2).)

11.16 For the purposes of the recommendation in paragraph 11.15, a nomination of benefits made under a pension scheme should be treated in a similar way to a special power. (Para. 8.24; Draft Bill, Cl 6(3).)

11.17 In relation to the 125-year perpetuity period, the principle of "wait and see" should apply to those estates, interests, rights and powers which are subject to the rule aginst perpetuities, in the same way as it does under the 1964 Act. (Para 8.25; Draft Bill, Cl 7.)

11.18 The legislation should not affect the rule of law which limits the duration of non-charitable purpose trusts. (Para. 8.36; Draft Bill, Cl 18.)

11.19 Subject to the exception explained below, in paragraph 11.21, the statutory restrictions on accumulations should be repealed. (Para. 10.15; Draft Bill, Cls 13 and 21.)

11.20 The rule would cease to apply only in relation to instruments taking effect after the date on which any legislation was brought into force, including any special power of appointment created before but exercised after that date. (Paras. 10.15, 10.16; Draft Bill, Cl 15(1).)

11.21 Where an instrument confers a power or duty to accumulate on trustees of property that is held in trust for charitable purposes, the direction to accumulate should cease to have effect 21 years after the day on which the income must or may be accumulated. (Draft Bill, Cl 14(1)–(3).)

11.22 This limitation should apply whether the settlor was an individual or a corporation, but it would be applicable only to instruments taking effect after the legislation was brought into force. (Draft Bill, Cl 14(1), 15(1).)

11.23 Where the power or duty came to an end, the income should be applied for the persons or purposes for whom or which it would have been applicable had there been no power or duty to accumulate. (Draft Bill, Cl 14(4).)'

———————

On 6 March 2001 the Government accepted the recommendations in the Law Commission Report. In September 2002 the Lord Chancellor's Department published a Consultation Paper on The Rule against Excessive Accumulations, in which it suggested one change to the Report. It is proposed that, in the case of charitable trusts, the accumulation of income be restricted to a period of 21 years, subject to derogations at the discretion of the Charity Commissioners.

Part Three. Commercial Interests

8.   Terms of Years [1]

[1]   C & B, pp. 34–36, chap. 16; Gray, pp. 319–448, chap. 11; M & W, pp. 3.009–3.016, chaps. 14, 15; MM, chap. 9; Smith, chaps. 16, 17 and 18; Aldridge, *Leasehold Law;* Foa, *Law of Landlord and Tenant* (8th edn. 1957); Hill and Redman, *Law of Landlord and Tenant;* Woodfall, *Landlord and Tenant;* Evans and Smith, *Law of Landlord and Tenant* (6th edn. 2002); Hill and Redman: *Guide to Landlord and Tenant Law* (1999); Partington, *Landlord and Tenant* (2nd edn. 1980).

The Law Commission has published reports on the law of landlord and tenant (*a*) The Obligations of Landlords and Tenants 1975 (Law Com No. 67, HC 377); (*b*) Covenants Restricting Dispositions, Alterations and Change of User 1985 (Law Com No. 141, HC 278); (1985) 135 NLJ 991, 1015 (P. F. Smith); (*c*) Forfeiture of Tenancies (1985) (Law Com No. 142, HC 279); (*d*) Landlord and Tenant: Reform of the Law 1987 (Law Com No. 162, Cm 145) which reviews the law and identifies areas which require reform; (*e*) Leasehold Conveyancing 1987 (Law Com No. 161, HC 360); (*f*) Privity of Contract and Estate 1988 (Law Com No 174, HC 8); (*g*) Compensation for Tenants' Improvements 1989 (Law Com No. 178, HC 291); (*h*) Distress for Rent 1991 (Law Com No. 194, HC 138); (*i*) Business Tenancies: A Periodic Review of the LTA 1925 Part II 1992 (Law Com No. 208, HC 224); (*j*) Termination of Tenancies Bill 1994 (Law Com No. 221, HC 135); (*k*) Implied Covenants for Title 1991 (Law Com No. 199, HC 437); (*l*) Responsibility for State and Condition of Property 1996 (Law Com No. 238, HC 236).

Consultation Papers have been published by

(a) the Law Commission on Land, Valuation and Housing Tribunals 2003 (Law Com No. 170); see Appendices C (The Agricultural Land Tribunal), F (The Leasehold Valuation Tribunal), G (The Rent Assessment Committee), H (The Rent Tribunal), and I (The Valuation Tribunal); and on Renting Homes 1. Status and Security and 2. Co-occupation, Transfer and Succession 2002 (Law Com Nos. 162 and 168), recommending two types of residential tenancy: long-term with a considerable degree of statutorily supported security of tenure, and short term where the contract will be the key document, supplemented by minimal statutory protection. This Consultation Paper has been followed by a narrative Report' on Renting Homes 2003 (Law Com No. 284), p. 502, post; Termination of Tenancies for Tenant Default 2004 (Law Com No. 174); p. 588, post.

(b) The Lord Chancellor's Department on Distress for Rent 2001 (Cm 5096).

(c) The DTLR on Landlord and Tenant: Responsibility for State and Condition of Property (2001); and on Business Tenancies Legislation in England and Wales: The Government's proposals for reform (2001); [2002] Conv 261 (R. Hewitson). On the voluntary Code of Practice for Commercial Leases, see (2002) 152 NLJ 1033 (J. Keating).

(d) The Department of the Environment in 1992 on the Reform of the Caravan Sites Act 1968; [1993] Conv 39,111 (G. Holgate) and in 1996 on the Landlord and Tenant Act 1954 Part II; [1993] Conv 334 (M. Haley).

Several cases on leases are reported only in the Property and Compensation Reports and the Estates Gazette (issued weekly) and thence in Estates Gazette Digest (published annually until 1984) and thereafter in the Estates Gazette Law Reports. Specialist periodicals are Landlord & Tenant Law Review (which began in 1997), and Rent Review and Lease Journal (1981).

I. General Background

Other than the estate in fee simple absolute in possession, the only *legal* estate which can subsist after 1925 is the term of years absolute. [2] These two legal estates are different in nature, in that the former is a freehold, the latter a leasehold estate; the former, in other words, is held, theoretically, of a feudal superior by

---

[2]   LPA 1925, s. 1(1), p. 6, ante.

freehold tenure, the latter is held of the freeholder by leasehold tenure. The two estates can therefore exist contemporaneously in one piece of land,[3] the fee simple being held by the freeholder.

It was essential for the feudal system of landholding that one person or a group of feoffees to uses should be responsible for each piece of land; as freeholders they were protected, in the days before the action of trespass, by the Real Actions, the Writs of Right, Writs of Entry and the Possessory Assizes, all of which were available to, and only to, persons seised.[4] The leaseholder's position was not important to the feudal system, and he never received the protection of the Real Actions; his interest never became 'Real' property, and is, to the present day, personalty; he was never seised; he was originally left to his action on the covenant against his landlord, the freeholder, if he were evicted.[5]

Better remedies became available to the leaseholder as soon as remedies dependent on *possession*, as opposed to *seisin*, were developed in the King's Court. Trespass was such an action, and a leaseholder, being *possessed* of the land, could bring the writ of trespass, without being *seised*.[6] By the thirteenth century,[7] the action of trespass *quare clausum fregit* was available to persons in possession of land and lay for damages against anyone who was guilty of unlawful physical interference with land. This was an improvement, but the leaseholder needed something more than damages; he needed an action by which he could recover his lease. This came with Ejectment at the end of the fifteenth century.[8] From that time a leaseholder has had a 'real' remedy; but leasehold property was already established as 'personalty' and it was too late then for it to become 'realty' for the purposes of the general law.

The tables were now turned on the freeholder. He had a 'real' remedy, but it was cumbrous and old-fashioned. The leaseholder now had a modern action for specific recovery, the action of Ejectment. Freeholders began to use this action by alleging a fictitious lease. This practice began in the sixteenth century, and continued until the abolition of the old Real Actions in the first half of the nineteenth century. A possession claim now lies in respect of any wrongful deprivation of possession of land.[9]

This chapter deals with some of the principles of the law relating to leases. Superimposed upon the general law is a large body of statutory material dealing with specialised topics. The general policy of these statutes is to limit the rent which a landlord can obtain, and restrict his right to recover possession of the premises at the end of the lease. The Leasehold Reform Act 1967 goes further, and grants to certain long leaseholders of residential premises at low rents the right to acquire their freehold or an extended lease.[10] These statutes and books

---

[3]   LPA 1925, s. 1(5).
[4]   Maitland, *Forms of Action at Common Law*, pp. 20 et seq; Simpson, *A History of the Land Law* (2nd edn. 1986), pp. 25–46; M & W, pp. 1440–1447.
[5]   Pollock and Maitland, *History of English Law* (2nd edn., reissued 1968), vol. ii, pp. 106–117; Plucknett, *Concise History of the Common Law* (5th edn. 1956), pp. 570–574; Jouon des Longrais, *La Conception Anglaise de la Saisine*, pp. 141–148; Simpson, pp. 71–78.
[6]   In the ordinary case of land being owned by A, the freeholder, and leased to B, the leaseholder, A is seised and B possessed of the land.
[7]   Maitland, *Forms of Action*, p. 48; C & B, pp. 26–29; M & W, pp 1442–1444.
[8]   *Trespass de ejectione firmae*, Pollock and Maitland, p. 109; Simpson, pp. 144–147.
[9]   Maitland, *Forms of Action*, pp. 57–60; C & B, p. 86; M & W, pp. 1445–1447; Simpson, pp. 147–151. On the modern law, see Walter and Harris; *Claims to the Possession of Land* (3rd edn. 1996); Civil Procedure Rules Part 55; (2001) 5 L & T Rev 103, 122 (G. Webb).
[10] See p. 937, post.

dealing with them must be consulted before a working knowledge of the law of leaseholds can be obtained; but lack of space forbids their treatment here. [11]

Central Statistical Office Social Trends 27 (2004 edn.), pp. 152–154

'The increase in owner-occupation has been a notable feature of the past century. At the start of the 20th century, almost all dwellings in England, 89 per cent, were privately rented and only a small proportion, 10 per cent, were owner-occupied. The 1950s saw a period of growth in prosperity alongside initiatives to improve housebuilding; this was accompanied by deregulation in both planning and the building industry. Thus, owner-occupation increased from 29 per cent in 1951 to 45 per cent in 1964. Between 1981 and 2002 the number of owner-occupied dwellings in Great Britain increased by almost 43 per cent to reach 17.4 million, more than double the number of rented dwellings. During the same period the number of private rented dwellings increased by 5 per cent to 2.5 million and the number of dwellings rented in the social sector decreased by 23 per cent to 5.1 million.

The growth in owner occupation since the early 1980s has in part been due to a number of schemes that aim to increase low-cost home ownership, such as

[11]   C & B, pp. 509–561; Gray, pp. 1342–1360; M & W, paras 22.062–22.303; MM, pp. 580–619; Aldridge, *Leasehold Law; Practical Lease Precedents*; Hill and Redman, *Law of Landlord and Tenant*; Woodfall, *Landlord and Tenant*. The main statutes are:
(a) *Agricultural Lettings*
    (i)   Agricultural Holdings before September 1985: Agricultural Holdings Act 1986.
    (ii)   Farm Business Tenancies after August 1995: Agricultural Tenancies Act 1995.
    (iii) Agricultural Tied Accommodation. Rent (Agriculture) Act 1976.
    Lennon, *Agricultural Law, Tax and Tenancies*; Watt, *Agricultural Holdings* (14th edn. 1998); Rodgers, *Agricultural Law* (2nd edn. 1998); Scammell and Densham's *Law of Agricultural Holdings* (8th edn. 1997).
(b) *Business Tenancies.* Landlord and Tenant Act 1954, Part II as amended by Regulatory Reform (Business Tenancies) (England and Wales) Order 2003 (SI 2003 No 3096); (2004) 148 SJ 520, 565, 593, 617, 651, 679 (G. Webber). LPA 1969, Part I. Aldridge, *Letting Business Premises* (7th edn. 1996); Levison, *Drafting Business Leases* (6th edn. 2001); Ross, *Drafting and Negotiating Commercial Leases* (4th edn. 1994); Tromans, *Commercial Leases* (2nd edn. 1996); Reynolds and Clark, *Renewal of Business Tenancies* (2002 2nd edn.); Williams, Brand and Hubbard, *Handbook of Business Tenancies*.
(c) *Private Residential Lettings before 15 January 1989.* Rent Act 1977; Housing Act 1980; Rent (Amendment) Act 1985. Megarry, *Rent Acts* vols 1 and 2.
(d) *Private Residential Lettings on and after 15 January 1989.* Housing Act 1988; on and after *28 Feb. 1987* Housing Act 1996 Part III (assured tenancies and assured shorthold tenancies); Megarry, *Rent Acts*, vol. 3; Martin, *Residential Security* (2nd edn. 1996); Rodgers, *Private Sector Housing Law*; Bridge, Assured Tenancies (1999).
(e) *Public Sector Housing (Secure Tenancies).* Housing Act 1985, Parts IV and V, Leasehold Reform, Housing and Urban Development Act 1993, Part II; Housing Act 1996, Part V.
(f) Long Tenancies. Landlord and Tenant Act 1954, Part I; Leasehold Reform Act 1967, Part I; Leasehold Reform Act 1979: Leasehold Reform, Housing and Urban Development Act 1993; Housing Act 1996, Part III; Commonhold and Leasehold Reform Act 2002, p. 938, post. Barnes, *Leasehold Reform Act 1967*; Hague, *Leasehold Enfranchisement* (4th edn. 2003); Megarry, *Rent Acts*, chap. 13. Aldridge, (*Commonhold Law* (2002).
    See *James v United Kingdom* (Application 8793/79) (1986) 8 EHRR 123, where the European Court of Human Rights held that the Leasehold Reform Act 1967 was not in breach of the European Convention on Human Rights. The trustees of the Grosvenor Estate in Mayfair had been compelled under the Act to sell 80 houses to long-lease tenants at a loss of £2,529,903; *Di Palma v United Kingdom* (1988) 10 EHRR 149. For the possible effect of the Human Rights Act 1998 on leasehold law. See Rook, *Property Law and Human Rights* paras. 8.1–8.3; (2002) 4 L&T Rev 4, 29 (C. Harpum).
(g) *Mobile Homes.* Caravan Sites and Control of Development Act 1960; Caravan Sites Act 1968; Mobile Homes Act 1983. Brand, *Mobile Homes and the Law* (1986); Gordon, *Mobile Homes and Caravans* (1985).

the right to buy scheme. Owner occupation is lower in Scotland (64 per cent) than in either England or Wales (70 and 73 per cent, respectively). The only sector where there has been a decline in stock since 1981 is in dwellings rented from local authorities. This reflects large scale stock transfers to registered social landlords whose stock rose by 256 per cent during this period.

The Census provided a comprehensive picture of the type of tenure and accommodation. In April 2001, 81 per cent of households in England and Wales lived in a house or bungalow, with semi-detached and terraced being the most common type of dwelling. The type of accommodation varies by tenure. Owner occupiers are far more likely to live in houses than renters in either the social or private sectors. The proportion of those in shared ownership properties (part-rent part-buy) who lived in a house of bungalow was lower than for those who owned outright or with a mortgage. In contrast social sector renters were far more likely than owners to live in purpose-built flats. Those living in shared ownership properties were also more likely than other owner occupiers to live in a flat, although less likely to do so than social renters.

Tenure varies markedly according to the type of household. In 2001 lone parents with dependent children were far more likely than any other type of household to rent their property. While only 34 per cent of lone parents with dependent children households lived in owner-occupier property, 46 per cent lived in accommodation rented from the social sector and 19 per cent rented privately. In contrast, 80 per cent of households comprising a couple with dependent children owned their own property and only 13 per cent rented from the social sector. Similarly, 81 per cent of pensioner households were owner occupiers, compared with only 58 per cent of lone pensioner households.

Owner occupation in the United Kingdom, at 71 per cent, is just above the average for all EU countries. In 2000 the highest rates of owner occupation in the EU were in Spain, Greece and Ireland, at over 80 per cent. Germany had the lowest level of owner occupation at just over 40 per cent. In all EU countries owner occupiers were more likely to live in a house than a flat. On average, 80 per cent of those living in a house in the EU were owner occupiers compared with only 38 per cent of those living in a flat. Tenure is also linked to economic activity status. At the time of the 2001 Census, over thee quarters of employed, self-employed and retired heads of household were owner occupiers. In contrast, less than a third of unemployed heads of household and just over a fifth of full-time students who were also in paid employment owned their own home, either outright or with a mortgage. Renting from a council was the most common form of tenure among those who were looking after a home or family, or those who were permanently sick or disabled. In contrast, less than a tenth of employed or self-employed heads of household rented from a council.'

II. General Characteristics

A. A Lease may be a Legal Estate

LAW OF PROPERTY ACT 1925

1. Legal estates and equitable interests.—(1) The only estates in land which are capable of subsisting or of being conveyed or created at law are—

    (*a*) An estate in fee simple absolute in possession; [12]

---

[12]   See p. 6, ante.

(b) A term of years absolute.

205. General definitions.—(1) ... (xxvii) 'Term of years absolute' means a term of years (taking effect in possession or in reversion whether or not at a rent) with or without impeachment for waste, [13] subject or not to another legal estate, and either certain or liable to determination by notice, re-entry, [14] operation of law, or by a provision for cesser on redemption, [15] or in any other event (other than the dropping of a life, or the determination of a determinable life interest); but does not include any term of years determinable with life or lives or with the cesser of a determinable life interest, [16] nor, if created after the commencement of this Act, a term of years which is not expressed to take effect in possession within twenty-one years after the creation thereof where required by this Act to take effect within that period, [17] and in this definition the expression 'term of years' includes a term for less than a year, [18] or for a year or years and a fraction of a year or from year to year.

B. Contractual Nature of a Lease

A lease is not only an estate; it is also a contract between landlord and tenant. In recent years the courts have emphasised the contractual nature of a lease and in some cases have applied contractual rules, for example, the doctrines of frustration and repudiation.

'A lease is a hybrid, part contract, part property'. [19] In the controversial case of *Bruton v London & Quadrant Housing Trust* [2000] 1 AC 406, [1999] 3 All ER 481, p. 441 post, the House of Lords has created a hybrid within a hybrid. An agreement with an occupant by an owner which had the capacity but not the power to grant a lease was held to create a lease as between the parties without creating any property relationship so as to bind third parties. [20]

---

[13]   See p. 18, ante.
[14]   See p. 526, post.
[15]   See pp. 792–793, post.
[16]   LPA 1925, s. 149(6), p. 455, post.
[17]   Ibid., s. 149(3), p. 454, post.
[18]   See *Re Land and Premises at Liss, Hants* [1971] Ch 986 at 991, [1971] 3 All ER 380 at 382, per GOULDING J; *Trustees of Henry Smith's Charity Trustees v Willson* [1983] QB 316 at 326–328, [1983] 1 All ER 73 at 81–82, per SLADE J.
[19]   *Linden Gardens Trust Ltd v Lenester Sludge Disposals Ltd* [1994] 1 AC 85 at 108, [1993] 3 All ER 417 at 431, per Lord BROWNE-WILKINSON. See S. Bridge in *Land Law, Issues, Debates, Policy*, ed. L. Tee, chap. 4.
        The Unfair Contract Terms Act 1977 does not apply to a covenant in a lease 'in so far as it relates to the creation or transfer of an interest in land': Sch 1, para 1(b); *Electricity Supply Nominees Ltd v IAF Group Ltd* [1993] 1 WLR 1059, [1993] 3 All ER 372 (anti-set off clause excluded); Conv Bulletin 1993/6, p. 9 (P. H. Kenny); *Star Rider Ltd v Inntrepreneur Pub Co* [1998] 1 EGLR 53 (agreement for lease). But the Unfair Terms in Consumer Contracts Regulations 1999 *do* apply to contracts relating to land, and therefore to a lease: *London Borough of Newham v Kaun* [2004] EWCA Civ 55, Times, 27 February.
[20]   See Smith, pp. 390–393. In *Prudential Assurance Co Ltd v London Residuary Body* [1992] 2 AC 386, [1993] 3 All ER 504, p. 447, post, HL rejected a contractual approach; *PW & Co v Milton Gate Investments Ltd* [2004] 2 WLR 443, where NEUBERGER J held that as a matter of law it was not possible to contract out of the general rule in *Pennell v Payne* [1995] QB 192, [1995] 2 All ER 592 and *Barrett v Morgan* [1999] 1 WLR 1109, [2000] 1 All ER 481 that a subtenancy comes to an end on determination of the head tenancy, p. 532, n. 3.

In **Hussein v Mehlman** [1992] 2 EGLR 87, [1] Mehlman granted to the plaintiff tenants a three-year assured shorthold tenancy of 27 Kenneth Crescent, Brent, London. The tenancy was subject to a covenant to repair on the part of the landlord implied by section 11 of the Landlord and Tenant Act 1985. By March 1991 one of the bedrooms had been made uninhabitable by the collapse of its ceiling; the sitting-room was letting in rainwater and part of its ceiling was bulging dangerously; the outside toilet was unusable and the hall wall was affected by damp. This situation was not improved by ill-fitting doors and windows and the effects of burst pipes. The landlord refused to carry out repairs in spite of several complaints by the tenants, who in the end returned the keys to the landlord's agents and vacated the property.

SMEDLEY QC, in holding that there had been a repudiatory breach by the landlord of the implied covenant to repair, and that the tenants had accepted that repudiation as putting an end to the tenancy, said at 88:

'The single most important point in the case is this: is it possible in law for a contract of letting to be terminated by one party's acccptance of the other's repudiatory conduct? ...

Although a contract of letting, whether for a term of years certain or for a periodic "springing" term, differs from other contracts in creating an estate in land, it is nevertheless a contract: see *United Scientific Holdings Ltd v Burnley Borough Council* [1978] AC 904, at pp. 929E, 935B, 944B, 947B–C, 956F–H, 962A and 963H–964B, [1977] 2 All ER 62 at 71j, 76c, 83e, 86a–b, 93d–f, 97f, and 99e–d, approving *C H Bailey Ltd v Memorial Enterprises Ltd* [1974] 1 WLR 728, [1974] 1 All ER 1003; and, most recently, *Hammersmith and Fulham London Borough Council v Monk* [1992] 1 AC 478 at 483B and 492G, 493D–E, and [1992] 1 All ER 1 at 3d, h, and 492d, 493h–j. [2] Since, in the ordinary way, any contract may be brought to an end by one party's repudiatory conduct, the question to be answered is whether a contract of letting is an exception to the rule.

In *C H Bailey Ltd v Memorial Enterprises Ltd* [1974] 1 WLR 728 at 732C, at 1007a, Lord Denning MR said:

"It is time to get away from the medieval concept of rent. That appears from a passage in *Holdsworth, A History of English Law*, vol. VII (1900), p 262....... in modern law, rent is not conceived of as a thing, but rather as a payment which a tenant is bound by his contract to make to his landlord for the use of the land.

The time and manner of the payment is to be ascertained according to the true construction of the contract, and not by reference to out-dated relics of medieval law."

Sir Eric Sachs at p 735E, at p. 1010a, said:

"Whatever the position last century, the word 'rent' today can often simply refer to any contractual sum to which a landlord becomes entitled for the use of his land."

He endorsed the following passage in *Foa, General Law of Landlord and Tenant* (8th ed, 1957) at p 101:

"There has been a considerable development from the medieval conception of rent as a 'thing' or proprietary interest to the modern conception of rent as a contractual obligation to pay for the use of property let, and the notion that 'rent' must have the quality that it can be distrained for is more appropriate to the medieval than the modern conception. Accordingly, the question in each case is to determine

---

[1]   [1995] Conv 379 (M. Pawlowski); [1993] Conv 71 (S. Bright); [1993] CLJ 212 (C. J. Harpum). See also *WG Clark (Properties) Ltd v Dupre Properties Ltd* [1992] Ch 297, [1992] 1 All ER 596 (tenant's disclaimer of lease a repudiation); *GS Fashions Ltd v B & Q plc* [1995] 1 WLR 1088, [1995] 4 All ER 899; *Progressive Mailing House Pty Ltd v Tabili Pty Ltd* (1985) 157 CLR 17; [1986] Conv 262 (J.W. Carter and J. Hill); (1988) 14 Monash LR 83 (J. Effron).

[2]   P. 512, post.

what in substance is the subject-matter of the tenancy granted to the tenant by the contract: *prima facie* rent is the monetary compensation payable by the tenant in consideration for the grant, however it be described or allocated ..."

It seems clear, then, that, although the modern law of landlord and tenant has not made obsolete the availability of distress for rent or the concept of an estate in land arising out of the relationship, these are no longer the foundation of the relationship but are its incidents: its foundation is the contract to pay money or give other consideration in return for the exclusive right to occupy land. (It may or may not be that the rent free tenancy is an anomaly in this context, but that rare species cannot swim very far against the tide of the general law.)

The anchor by which Mr Russen, in his able argument, seeks to secure his client's boat against this tide is the decision of the Court of Appeal in *Total Oil Great Britain Ltd v Thompson Garages (Biggin Hill) Ltd* [1972] 1 QB 318, [1971] 3 All ER 1226 ...

Lord Denning MR said at 324A, at 1229e:

"A lease is a demise. It conveys an interest in land. It does not come to an end like an ordinary contract on repudiation and acceptance. There is no authority on the point, but there is one case which points that way. It is *Cricklewood Property & Investment Trust Ltd v Leighton's Investment Trust Ltd* [1945] AC 221, [1945] 1 All ER 252. Lord Russell of Killowen and Lord Goddard at pp 234 and 244, at pp. 258 and 264 were both of opinion that frustration does not bring a lease to an end. [3] Nor I think does repudiation and acceptance. ..."

The *Total Oil* decision, at its fullest, is therefore to be found in the judgment of Lord Denning. If it stood by itself it would, at this level, be binding authority for the proposition that because of the special character of a demise of land a lease is not terminable by frustration nor, therefore, by repudiation and acceptance.

However, since the *Total Oil* case was decided in 1971, both the major and the minor premises upon which Lord Denning's second holding was based appear to have been destroyed by decisions of the House of Lords. As I have already indicated, the major premise that a lease of land is in its essence different from other contracts has been overset, in particular by the decision of the House of Lords in *United Scientific Holdings Ltd v Burnley Borough Council*. The minor premise that a lease cannot be determined by frustration has been overset by the decision of the House of Lords in *National Carriers Ltd v Panalpina (Northern) Ltd* [1981] AC 675, [1981] 1 All ER 161, in which a demised warehouse became unusable because of a street closure, and the tenants withheld rent, claiming that the lease had been frustrated. The House of Lords (Lord Russell of Killowen dissenting) held that the doctrine of frustration was in principle applicable to leases but that it did not operate on the facts of the instant case. Their lordships declined to follow the *dicta* in the

---

[3]   The third Lord RUSSELL OF KILLOWEN, with filial piety, dissented, and followed the views of the second Lord RUSSELL and Lord GODDARD in the *Cricklewood* case. For him also "the second answer of the *Pinafore*'s captain on the subject of mal de mer is to be preferred to his first." See C & B, pp 503–505.

Lord RUSSELL OF KILLOWEN at 223, at 258 recognised obiter that there may be excuses for the non-performance of a building covenant short of full frustration:

'It may well be that circumstances may arise during the currency of the term which render it difficult, or even impossible, for one party or the other to carry out some of its obligations as landlord or tenant, circumstances which might afford a defence to a claim for damages for their breach, but the lease would remain.'

This dictum was applied in *John Lewis Properties plc v Viscount Chelsea* [1993] 2 EGLR 77 where a tenant was unable to perform a covenant to demolish and rebuild property owing to his inability to obtain planning permission, which had become necessary on its subsequent listing as a Grade II building (25 Cadogan Gardens, once described as the most beautiful building in the world).

Cricklewood case. The *Total Oil* case was cited but was not referred to in the speeches. Lord Hailsham, at p 690D, at p. 168b, said:

"I conclude that the matter is not decided by authority and that the question is open to your Lordships to decide on principle. In my view your Lordships ought now so to decide it. Is there anything in principle which ought to prevent a lease from ever being frustrated? I think there is not. In favour of the opposite opinion, the difference in principle between real and chattel property was strongly urged. But I find it difficult to accept this, once it has been decided, as has long been the case, that time and demise charters even of the largest ships and of considerable duration can in principle be frustrated."

Lord Wilberforce at p 694E, at p. 171b, said:

"It was pointed out, however, by Atkin LJ in *Matthey v Curling* [1922] 2 AC 180, 200, in a passage later approved by Viscount Simon [1945] AC 221, 230, [1945] 1 All ER 252, 256 that as a lease can be determined, according to its terms, upon the happening of certain specified events, there is nothing illogical in implying a term that it should be determined on the happening of other events—namely, those which in an ordinary contract work a frustration …

A man may desire possession and use of land or buildings for, and only for, some purpose in view and mutually contemplated. Why is it an answer, when he claims that this purpose is 'frustrated', to say that he has an estate if that estate is unusable and unsaleable? In such a case the lease, or the conferring of an estate, is a subsidiary means to an end, not an aim or end of itself."

He concluded at p 696G, at p. 172h:

"It was not until the *Cricklewood* case that the argument was put on principle and fully explored. The governing decision (of the Court of Appeal) was summary, unargued, and based upon previous cases which will not bear the weight of a generalisation. I think that the movement of the law of contract is away from a rigid theory of autonomy towards the discovery—or I do not hesitate to say imposition—by the Courts of just solutions, which can be ascribed to reasonable men in the position of the parties."

This reasoning, it seems to me, not only takes away the minor premise of the *Total Oil* judgment but has fundamental implications for its major premise: it continues the process, to which I have referred, of assimilating leases to other contracts. It follows, in my judgment, that unless some special exception can be established for acts of repudiation, not only has *Total Oil* ceased to be authority for the proposition that a lease cannot be repudiated: the decisions which have rendered it obsolete point powerfully in the direction of repudiation being a legitimate ground for termination of a lease. I bear in mind, however, that the House of Lords was extremely cautious about the range of situations in which it would allow the doctrine of frustration to operate on a lease and that Lord Hailsham posed the choice, in the language of *HMS Pinafore*, as lying only between 'never' and 'hardly ever', coming down in favour of the latter.

Very recently the Court of Appeal has held, apparently without argument to the contrary and without any citation of authority, that a tenancy agreement which one party is induced to enter into by the fraud of the other can be rescinded at the innocent party's election: *Killick v Roberts* [1991] 1 WLR 1146 at 1150a, [1991] 4 All ER 289, at p 292d. [4]

It is perhaps a relief that the *Total Oil* case is no longer good law, because it appears to have silently overruled an important line of cases (not cited in argument) in which, throughout the 19th century, the courts took it as axiomatic

---

[4]   [1992] Conv 269 (J. Martin); [1992] CLJ 21 (L. Tee).

that a contract of letting could be terminated by the innocent party without notice if the other party failed to fulfil a fundamental term of the contract. I will refer to them because they are of assistance in deciding the next question, namely what breaches of a lessor's covenant are of a sufficiently fundamental character to amount to repudiation.

[His Lordship referred to *Edwards v Etherington* (1825) Ry & M 268; *Collins v Barrow* (1831) 1 Mood &R 112; *Izon v Gorton* (1839) 5 Bing NC 501; and *Arden v Pullen* (1842) 10 M & W 321; and continued:]

It was this well-established line of authority that the Court of Exchequer followed in the celebrated case of *Smith v Marrable* (1843) 11 M & W 5. The defendant had taken a furnished house for his family, who found it infested with bugs and left. On an action for the rent for the remainder of the term of five weeks, Lord Abinger CB directed the jury that:

"in point of law every house must be taken to be let upon the implied condition that there was nothing about it so noxious as to render it uninhabitable."

Parke B, giving the leading judgment on a motion for a new trial, cited a number of the authorities to which I have referred and concluded:

"These authorities appear to me fully to warrant the position, that if the demised premises are incumbered with a nuisance of so serious a nature that no person can reasonably be expected to live in them, the tenant is at liberty to throw them up."

Lord Abinger CB, sitting as was the custom on the appeal against his own direction to the jury, expressed relief that authorities supported what he had taken to be a proposition of common sense and concluded:

"I entertain no doubt whatever on the subject, and think the defendant was fully justified in leaving these premises as he did: indeed, I only wonder that he remained so long, and gave the landlord so much opportunity of remedying the evil."

It will be seen that this case is authority not only for the proposition for which it is known, that there is an implied covenant of fitness for habitation in a letting of a furnished house, but also for the proposition that a contract of tenancy may be repudiated by a breach of such a condition, and—incidentally—that it is not to be held against the tenant that he has endured the breach for longer than he needed to.

Although the vocabulary of repudiation is not consistently used in these cases—the earliest, for example, speaks of "exempting" the defendant from the demand for rent and others speak of the tenant being allowed to "throw up" the letting or "to withdraw", by 1842 Lord Abinger is using the phrase "the contract of letting" and Alderson B is speaking about the tenant "avoiding" the lease for the landlord's default. When in 1877 the Exchequer division decided *Wilson v Finch Hatton* (1877) 2 Ex D 336 and followed *Smith v Marrable*, all three barons used the language of repudiation and Pollock B sought to cut away furnished lettings from the doctrine that rent issues out of the realty and to hold instead that this was simply "a sum paid for the accommodation afforded by the use of the house". (The divergent patch which Parke B charted in relation to demises of real property in *Hart v Windsor* (1843) 12 M & W 68, shortly after he decided *Smith v Marrable*, has now, it appears, all but converged again with the path of contract, at least since the decision in *C H Bailey Ltd v Memorial Enterprises Ltd*.) ...

I recognise that the proposition that a contract of tenancy can be repudiated like any other contract has a number of important implications, which it is not appropriate to explore on the facts of this case. For example, if the obligation to pay rent is as fundamental as the obligation to keep the house habitable, it will follow that a default in rent payments is a repudiatory act on the tenant's part. That this may follow is not, however, a reason for going back on what appears to me to be the inexorable effect of binding authority. It will, however, have effect subject not only to all the statutory provisions which now hedge the right to recover possession but also, I would think, to the provisions contained in the contract of letting itself in relation to forfeiture (where there is a term certain): in other words, the right to terminate by acceptance of repudiatory conduct may itself be modified by further contractual provisions which lay down conditions, supported by statute, for the exercise of the right.'

BRUTON v LONDON & QUADRANT HOUSING TRUST

[2000] 1 AC 406, [1999] 3 All ER 481 [5] (HL, Lords SLYNN OF HADLEY, JAUNCEY OF TULLYCHETTLE, HOFFMANN, HOPE OF CRAIGHEAD and HOBHOUSE OF WOODBOROUGH).

The London Borough of Lambeth owned a block of flats in Brixton of which it had no statutory authority to grant a tenancy. It therefore entered into a licence agreement with the Housing Trust, which prohibited it from granting a tenancy. The Trust then entered into a 'weekly licence agreement' with Mr Bruton, who had exclusive possession of the flat. He brought an action against the Trust for breach of repairing obligations implied by section 11 of the Landlord and Tenant Act 1985. The section only applied to 'a lease of dwelling-house for a term of less than seven years'.

Held (reversing the Court of Appeal [1988] QB 834; [1997] 4 All ER 970) for Mr Bruton. The fact that the Trust had no estate in the land to support a lease binding on third parties was irrelevant.

LORD HOFFMANN: 'Did this agreement create a 'lease' or 'tenancy' within the meaning of the Landlord and Tenant Act 1985 or any other legislation which refers to a lease or tenancy? The decision of this House in *Street v Mountford* [1985] AC 809 [1985] 2 All ER 289, p. 473, post is authority for the proposition that a 'lease' or 'tenancy' is a contractually binding agreement, not referable to any other relationship between the parties, by which one person gives another the right to exclusive occupation of land for a fixed or renewable period or periods of time, usually in return for a periodic payment in money. An agreement having these characteristics creates a relationship of landlord and tenant to which the common law or statute may then attach various incidents. The fact that the parties use language more appropriate to a different kind of agreement, such as a licence, is irrelevant if upon its true construction it has the identifying characteristics of a lease. The meaning of the agreement, for example, as to the extent of the possession which it grants, depends upon the intention of the parties, objectively ascertained by reference to the language and relevant background. The decision of your Lordships' House in *Westminster City Council v Clarke* [1992] 2 AC 288, [1992] 1 All ER 695, p. 471, n.16, post, is a good example of the importance of background in deciding whether the agreement grants exclusive possession or not. But the classification of the agreement as a lease

---

[5]   [1998] Conv 524 (D. Rook); [1999] All ER Rev 225 (P. J. Clarke); (1999) 3 L&TR 124 (M. Pawlowski); (2000) 116 LQR 7 (S. Bright), p. 445, post; [2002] CLJ 25 (M. Dixon); (2000) 4 L&TR 118 (M. Pawlowski and J. Brown).

does not depend upon any intention additional to that expressed in the choice of terms. It is simply a question of characterising the terms which the parties have agreed. This is a question of law.

In this case, it seems to me that the agreement, construed against the relevant background, plainly gave Mr Bruton a right to exclusive possession. There is nothing to suggest that he was to share possession with the trust, the council or anyone else. The trust did not retain such control over the premises as was inconsistent with Mr Bruton having exclusive possession, as was the case in *Westminster City Council v Clarke.* The only rights which it reserved were for itself and the council to enter at certain times and for limited purposes. As Lord Templeman said in *Street v Mountford* at 818, at 293 such an express reservation 'only serves to emphasise the fact that the grantee is entitled to exclusive possession and is a tenant.' Nor was there any other relationship between the parties to which Mr Bruton's exclusive possession could be referable.

Mr Henderson, who appeared for the trust, submitted that there were 'special circumstances' in this case which enabled one to construe the agreement as a licence despite the presence of all the characteristics identified in *Street v Mountford.* These circumstances were that the trust was a responsible landlord performing socially valuable functions, it had agreed with the council not to grant tenancies. Mr Bruton had agreed that he was not to have a tenancy and the trust had no estate out of which it could grant one.

In my opinion none of these circumstances can make an agreement to grant exclusive possession something other than a tenancy. The character of the landlord is irrelevant because although the Rent Acts and other Landlord and Tenant Acts do make distinctions between different kinds of landlords, it is not by saying that what would be a tenancy if granted by one landlord will be something else if granted by another. The alleged breach of the Trust's licence is irrelevant because there is no suggestion that the grant of a tenancy would have been ultra vires either the trust or the council: see section 32(3) of the Housing Act 1985. If it was a breach of a term of the licence from the council, that would have been because it was a tenancy. The licence could not have turned it into something else. Mr Bruton's agreement is irrelevant because one cannot contract out of the statute. The trust's lack of title is also irrelevant, but I shall consider this point at a later stage. In *Family Housing Association v Jones* [1990] 1 WLR 779, [1990] 1 All ER 385 where the facts were very similar to those in the present case, the Court of Appeal construed the 'licence' as a tenancy. Slade LJ gave careful consideration to whether any exceptional ground existed for making an exception to the principle in *Street v Mountford* and came to the conclusion that there was not. I respectfully agree. For these reasons I consider that the agreement between the trust and Mr Bruton was a lease within the meaning of section 11 of the Landlord and Tenant Act 1985.

My Lords, in my opinion, that is the end of the matter. But the Court of Appeal did not stop at that point. In the leading majority judgment, Millet LJ said [1998] QB 834, 845, [1997] 4 All ER 970, 979 that an agreement could not be a lease unless it had a further characteristic, namely that it created a legal estate in the land which 'binds the whole world.' If, as in this case, the grantor had no legal estate, the agreement could not create one and therefore did not qualify as a lease. The only exception was the case in which the grantor was estopped from denying that he could not create a legal estate. In that case, a 'tenancy by estoppel' came into existence. But an estoppel depended upon the grantor having purported to grant a lease and in this case the trust had not done so. It had made it clear that it was only purporting to grant a licence.

My Lords, I hope that this summary does justice to the closely reasoned judgment of Millett LJ. But I fear that I must respectfully differ at three critical steps in the argument.

First, the term 'lease' or 'tenancy' describes a relationship between two parties who are designated landlord and tenant. It is not concerned with the question of whether the agreement creates an estate or other proprietary interest which may be binding upon third parties. A lease may, and usually does, create a proprietary interest called a leasehold estate or, technically, a 'term of years absolute.' This will depend upon whether the landlord had an interest out of which he could grant it. Nemo dat quod non habet. But it is the fact that the agreement is a lease which creates the proprietary interest. It is putting the cart before the horse to say that whether the agreement is a lease depends upon whether it creates a proprietary interest.

[His Lordship referred to *Lewisham Borough Council v Roberts* [1949] 2 QB 608, and continued:]

Millett LJ, at p. 846, at p. 980 distinguished *Family Housing Association v Jones*, where, as I have said, the facts were very similar to those in the present case, on the ground that 'the fact that the grantor had no title was not referred to in argument or the judgments.' In my opinion this is easily explained by the fact that the grantor's title or lack of title was irrelevant to the issue in the case.

Secondly, I think that Millett LJ may have been misled by the ancient phrase 'tenancy by estoppel' into thinking that it described an agreement which would not otherwise be a lease or tenancy but which was treated as being one by virtue of an estoppel. In fact, as the authorities show, it is not the estoppel which creates the tenancy, but the tenancy which creates the estoppel. The estoppel arises when one or other of the parties wants to deny one of the ordinary incidents or obligations of the tenancy on the ground that the landlord had no legal estate. The basis of the estoppel is that having entered into an agreement which constitutes a lease or tenancy, he cannot repudiate that incident or obligation. So in *Morton v Woods* (1869) LR 4 QB 293, a factory owner granted a second mortgage to a bank to secure advances. But the mortgagor had no legal estate, having conveyed it to the first mortgagee, and therefore could not confer one upon the second mortgagee. As additional security, the borrower 'attorned tenant' to the second mortgagee, that is to say, acknowledged a relationship of landlord and tenant between them. This was a device commonly used in old mortgages to give the mortgagee the rights of a landlord—a speedier procedure for recovery of possession which was then available and the right to levy distress upon goods and chattels on the mortgaged premises: see *Megarry & Wade, The Law of Real Property*, 5th ed. (1984), p. 946. When the borrower failed to pay, the bank levied a distress. The owner of the goods sued for damages, claiming that the bank had no right to levy distress because that ancient common law remedy was available only to the holder of a legal estate. A recital to the mortgage made it plain that the bank was a second mortgagee and therefore had no legal estate. The Court of Queen's Bench held that the mortgagor was estopped from denying the bank's legal title. Kelly CB said, at p. 304:

'it is the creation of the tenancy, or the estoppel, which arises from the creation of the relation of landlord and tenant by agreement between the parties, that makes the actual legal estate unnecessary to support the distress ...'

Thus it is the fact that the agreement between the parties constitutes a tenancy that gives rise to an estoppel and not the other way round. It therefore seems to me that the question of tenancy by estoppel does not arise in this case. The issue is simply whether the agreement is a tenancy. It is not whether either party is entitled to deny some obligation or incident of the tenancy on the ground that the trust had no title.

Thirdly, I cannot agree that there is no inconsistency between what the trust purported to do and its denial of the existence of a tenancy. This seems to me to fly in the face of *Street v Mountford*. In my opinion, the trust plainly did purport to grant a tenancy. It entered into an agreement on terms which constituted a tenancy. It may have agreed with Mr Bruton to say that it was not a tenancy. But the parties cannot contract out of the Rent Acts or other landlord and tenant statutes by such devices. Nor in my view can they be used by a landlord to avoid being estopped from denying that he entered into the agreement he actually made.

For these reasons I would allow the appeal and declare that Mr Bruton was a tenant. I should add that I express no view on whether he was a secure tenant or on the rights of the council to recover possession of the flat.

LORD HOBHOUSE OF WOODBOROUGH. My Lords, I agree that this appeal should be allowed as proposed by my noble and learned friend, Lord Hoffmann, and for the reasons which he has given. I would add only this.

The claim made in the action seeks to enforce a contractual cause of action. ...

Counsel for the housing trust accepted before your Lordships that a contractual relationship of landlord and tenant suffices to make the provisions of the Act applicable. The question therefore is whether the agreement creates such a relationship. The answer to this question is, in my judgment, determined by the decision in *Street v Mountford*. The agreement was an agreement to give Mr Bruton the exclusive possession of the flat for a period or periods of time in return for the periodic payment of money; the grant of exclusive possession was not referable to any other relationship between the parties. It follows that the relationship created was that of landlord and tenant and the provisions of the Act apply to the agreement. Mr Bruton is entitled to succeed.

The relevant question is simply one of ascertaining the effect in law of the agreement which the parties made. It is true that before the court construes an agreement it must inform itself of the surrounding circumstances existing at the time that the contract was made: *Reardon Smith Line Ltd v Yngvar Hansen-Tangen* [1976] 1 WLR 989, [1976] 3 All ER 570. This rule applies as much to contracts relating to property as to any other contract. In the present case, it is correct that both parties knew that the housing trust was a mere licensee of the council and, in so far as they may have thought about it, should have realised that for the housing trust to grant Mr Bruton the exclusive possession of the flat probably amounted to a breach of the housing trust's obligations to the council. But this cannot contradict what was actually agreed between the housing trust and Mr Bruton or its legal effect as between them (*Family Housing Association v Jones*). It would be different if it could be shown that the housing trust had no capacity to make the agreement (*Minister of Agriculture and Fisheries v Matthews* [1950] 1 KB 148). Lack of capacity renders an apparent agreement without legal effect; this is an application of the ordinary principles of the law of contract. But the present case is not such a case. The housing trust had the requisite capacity to make the agreement with Mr Bruton (as for that matter had the council: section 44(1) of the Housing Act 1985).

S. Bridge in *Land Law Issues, Debates, Policy*, (ed. L. Tee), pp. 116–120

'The process of contractualisation of leases was now growing apace. Frustration, rescission for fraud, termination for breach, implication of terms for business efficacy (contractual doctrines all) have been applied in recent years to leases, unobjectionably in my view, on the ground that a lease is as much a contract as an estate. [6] But the *coup de grace*, or some might say the *reductio ad absurdum*, of the contractualists, was to come in the decision of the House of Lords in *Bruton v London & Quadrant Housing Trust*. A lease is a contract, and it may be nothing more than a contract. It need not be an estate at all. ...

Lord Hoffmann, giving the leading speech, held that the agreement conferred exclusive possession on the occupier. Under normal *Street v Mountford* principles, therefore, this would be a tenancy unless "special circumstances" could be shown. Lord Hoffmann rightly rejected the defendant's argument that the identity of the landlord, or its agreement with the council not to grant tenancies, or the plaintiff's agreement that he was not to be a tenant, comprised "special circumstances". But he went on to hold, much more controversially, that the defendant's lack of any property interest in the land was immaterial. Although the defendant trust could not grant a legal estate in the land, the plaintiff had nevertheless obtained a lease in the flat.

Lord Hoffmann advanced two arguments in support of this result. First, the term "lease" (or "tenancy") refers to a bilateral relationship between the landlord and the tenant, and nothing more:

"It is not concerned with the question of whether the agreement creates an estate or other proprietary interest which may be binding upon third parties. A lease may, and usually does, create a proprietary interest called a leasehold estate or, technically, a 'term of years absolute'. This will depend upon whether the landlord had an interest out of which he could grant it. Nemo dat quod non habet. But it is the fact that the agreement is a lease which creates the proprietary interest. It is putting the cart before the horse to say that whether the agreement is a lease depends upon whether it creates a proprietary interest." [7]

This has been aptly described as advancing a "relative" or "relational" concept of exclusive possession, pursuant to which the court asks simply whether the occupier has exclusive possession as against their immediate landlord. [8] By adopting this focused approach, it is possible to concentrate on the two parties to the contract and to disregard wider issues such as capacity to grant a proprietary interest. But its undoubted effect is to recognise that an agreement which does not confer an estate in the property can nevertheless be a lease. This kind of lease, being non-proprietary, is unique.

Lord Hoffmann held that a tenancy also arose by virtue of estoppel. Here, the articulation of principle ("it is not the estoppel which creates the tenancy, but the tenancy which creates the estoppel") is unexceptionable. [9] But its application to the facts of the case is. While it may be necessary for there to be a tenancy to create the estoppel, there was no tenancy in *Bruton*, for the reasons

---

[6] See also the central role assumed by contract in the future version of he landlord occupier relationship in Law Commission Consultation Paper No. 162, *Renting Homes*, 132 et seq, Part VI.

[7] [2001] 1 AC 406 at 415.

[8] See Bright (2000) 116 LQR 7.

[9] For subsequent citation by way of approval, see *Wroe (t/a Telepower) v Exmos Cover Ltd* [2000] EGLR 66.

given above. There are two accepted circumstances in which a tenancy by estoppel may arise. The estoppel may be by deed (the grantor being precluded from disputing the validity of his or her grant [10]), or by representation (the grantor being estopped by an unambiguous and material representation as to his or her title on the strength of which the tenant takes a lease [11]). The facts of *Bruton* cannot be forced into either analysis. The trust took great care to communicate the limited nature of their interest in the flat to the plaintiff, and throughout the agreement referred to him only as a licensee. The trust had never purported to grant the plaintiff a tenancy – on the contrary . . . [12]

The one speech that takes a slightly different tack is that of Lord Hobhouse. As befits a commercial judge, he adopts what might be described as a "contractual" approach. The claim was to enforce a contractual course of action. The existence of a contractual relationship of landlord and tenant sufficed to trigger the statutory implication of the repairing covenant. The housing trust had capacity to enter into the contractual agreement. No problem arose from the fact that the trust had no legal estate, as no interest was being asserted by the plaintiff against any third party to the agreement. Lord Hobhouse's speech does not satisfactorily answer the objections already outlined, but it may indicate a possible way for future courts to deal with the precedent set by *Bruton*. Indeed, on policy grounds – that a landlord should not be able to escape statutorily repairing obligations by denying that they had capacity to grant a tenancy – the decision is perfectly acceptable. As a precedent it is much more difficult, as it creates a hybrid interest of a seemingly non-proprietary nature, the full implications of which we will only come to understand and appreciate with its further judicial exposition . . . [13]

Prior to *Bruton*, one would have thought that the conferment of a proprietary interest was absolutely essential to the characterisation of an agreement as a lease. The bare minima of a lease would have seemed to be the grant of exclusive possession for a term, and the capacity to make a grant of exclusive possession in the absolute sense (so that the tenant can defend his or her possession against all-comers) of the very essence. In an earlier House of Lords decision, *Prudential Assurance Co Ltd v London Residuary Body*, [14] an attack was made on the necessity for the "term" of a lease to fulfil the requirement of certainty. Previous cases had held that it must be possible to say, at the beginning of a lease, when it would terminate by effluxion of time. [15] However, despite argument that the contractual autonomy of the parties should be respected and their freely negotiated agreement duly enforced, the House of Lords held that the principle must prevail. This assertion of the power of property law to limit the extent to which parties can modify property interests was welcomed in some quarters. [16] Most

---

[10]   *First National Bank plc v Thompson* [1996] Ch 231 at 237.

[11]   See Harpum, *Megarry & Wade: The Law of Real Property*, 6th edn (2000) para. 14.095.

[12]   Millett LJ set out the position lucidly in the Court of Appeal: 'In the present case both parties knew that the trust had no title and could not grant a tenancy. That is not sufficient to prevent the creation of a tenancy by estoppel. But the trust did not purport to grant a tenancy. The document was carefully drawn by the trust and accepted by Mr Bruton as a licence. There is no inconsistency between the terms of the document and the trust's assertion that it has not granted a tenancy. There is no ground for holding that the parties must be taken to have adopted an assumed basis for the transaction. They did not agree that the trust should grant a tenancy even though it had no title; they agreed that it should grant a licence because it could not grant a tenancy.'

[13]   See Bright (2000) 116 LQR 7 at 9.

[14]   [1992] 2 AC 386, [1992] 3 All ER 504.

[15]   *Lace v Chantler* [1944] KB 368, [1944] 1 All ER 305.

[16]   Sparkes (1993) 109 LQR 93.

conveyancers would agree that freedom of contract must occasionally be sacrificed on the altar of property, and Lord Templeman did not seem unduly concerned by the consequences of applying strict property principles to the facts before him. However, Lord Browne-Wilkinson, while accepting that under the current law it was necessary for an effective lease to satisfy tests of certainty, considered that the result in *Prudential Assurance* was unsatisfactory, and proposed that the issue should be referred to the Law Commission so that it could contemplate future reform. [17] The decision in *Bruton* presents a further challenge for those who believe that the division between contract and property should be clear and easily drawn.'

C. Time Certain [18]

A lease must commence at, [19] and exist for, [20] a 'time certain', or at or for a time which can be rendered certain. It may even be for a single discontinuous term, for example, a single letting for three successive bank holidays, [1] or where possession is limited to certain hours of the day. [2]

The rule of certainty applies both to fixed and to periodic tenancies.

PRUDENTIAL ASSURANCE CO LTD v LONDON RESIDUARY BODY [3]
[1992] 2 AC 386, [1992] 3 All ER 504 (HL, Lords TEMPLEMAN, GRIFFITHS, GOFF OF CHIEVELEY, BROWNE-WILKINSON and MUSTILL).

In 1930 the London County Council, predecessor in title of the London Residuary Body, entered into a sale and lease back agreement with Mr. Nathan concerning a strip of land with a frontage of 36 feet to Walworth Road, Southwark, at a rent of £30 a year. Mr. Nathan retained the freehold of his adjacent shop premises (Nos. 263–265). The tenancy was to continue 'until the said land is required by the council for the purposes of the widening of Walworth Road,' in which case the landlord could recover possession on giving two months' notice.

---

[17] [1992] 2 AC 386 at 396, [1992] 3 All ER 504 at 512, infra.

[18] C & B, pp. 396–399; Gray, pp. 657–660; M & W, paras. 14.055–14.065; MM, pp. 342, 346, 350–352, 411–413; Smith, pp. 352–356.

[19] *Harvey v Pratt* [1965] 1 WLR 1025, [1965] 2 All ER 786 (a contract for a lease failed to specify the date of its commencement); *James v Lock* (1977) 246 EG 395; cf. *Secretary of State for Social Services v Beavington* (1981) 262 EG 551. See generally *Liverpool City Council v Walton Group plc* [2001] 1 EGLR 149.

[20] *Birrell v Carey* (1989) 58 P & CR 184 (grant for a term 'so long as the company is trading' held uncertain); [1990] Conv 288 (J. E. Martin).

[1] *Smallwood v Sheppards* [1895] 2 QB 627; *Cottage Holiday Associates Ltd v Customs and Excise Comrs* [1983] QB 735 (lease of holiday cottage on time sharing basis of one week in each year for 80 consecutive years held to be lease for a discontinuous term of 80 weeks); [1983] All ER Rev. 229 (P. J. Clark).

  See Timeshare Act 1992; Timeshare Regulations 1997 (SI 1997 No. 1081); The Act and the Regs were both amended by Timeshare Act 1992 (Amendment) Regulations 2003 (SI 2003 No. 1922); Timeshare (Cancellation Information) 2003 (SI 2003 No. 2579); [1992] Conv 30; [1993] Conv 248 (H. W. Wilkinson).

[2] *Graysim Holdings Ltd v P&O Property Holdings Ltd* [1994] 1 WLR 992, [1994] 3 All ER 897.

[3] (1993) 109 LQR 93 (P. Sparkes); [1993] Conv 461 (P. F. Smith); (1994) 57 MLR 117 (D. Wilde); [1993] CLJ 26 (S. Bridge); [1992] 13 LS 38 (S. Bright); [1992] All ER 229 (P. J. Clarke); [1993] CLP Part I 69 (P. Kohler). For the subsequent holding that the purported lease was valid as a periodic tenancy on the terms of the agreement in so far as they were consistent with a yearly tenancy, see p. 512, post.

In 1988 the landlord issued a notice, and the tenant sought a declaration that the tenancy could only be determined on the land being required for road widening.

Held (reversing the Court of Appeal). Declaration refused.
  (i) The term was of uncertain duration
  (ii) A periodic tenancy arising from payment and acceptance of rent failed since its terms were inconsistent with those of a yearly tenancy.

LORD TEMPLEMAN: The agreement was clearly intended to be of short duration and could have been secured by a lease for a fixed term, say five or ten years with power for the landlord to determine before the expiry of that period for the purposes of the road widening. Unfortunately the agreement was not so drafted. Over 60 years later Walworth Road has not been widened, and it does not appear that the road will ever be widened. The agreement purported to grant a term of uncertain duration which, if valid, now entitles the tenant to stay there for ever and a day at the 1930 rent of £30; valuers acting for both parties have agreed that the annual current commercial rent exceeds £10,000.

A demise for years is a contract for the exclusive possession and profit of land for some determinate period. Such an estate is called a 'term.' Thus *Co.Litt.*, 19th ed. (1832), vol. 1, para. 45b said that:

'["Terminus"] in the understanding of the law does not only signify the limits and limitation of time, but also the estate and interest that passes for that time.'

Blackstone's Commentaries on the Laws of England, 2nd ed. (1766), vol. II, said, at p. 143:

'Every estate which must expire at a period certain and prefixed, by whatever words created, is an estate for years. And therefore this estate is frequently called a term, *terminus*, because its duration or continuance is bounded, limited and determined: for every such estate must have a certain beginning, and certain end.'

In *Say v Smith* (1563) 1 Plowd 269 a lease for a certain term purported to add a term which was uncertain; the lease was held valid only as to the certain term. Anthony Brown J is reported to have said, at p. 272:

'every contract sufficient to make a lease for years ought to have certainty in three limitations, viz. in the commencement of the term, in the continuance of it, and in the end of it; so that all these ought to be known at the commencement of the lease, and words in a lease, which don't make this appear, are but babble ... And these three are in effect but one matter, showing the certainty of the time for which the lessee shall have the land, and if any of these fail, it is not a good lease, for then there wants certainty.'

The Law of Property Act 1925, taking up the same theme provided, by section 1(1), that:

'The only estates in land which are capable of subsisting or of being conveyed or created at law are—(*a*) An estate in fee simple absolute in possession; (*b*) A term of years absolute.'

Section 205(1)(xxvii) was in these terms:

'"Term of years absolute" means a term of years ... either certain or liable to determination by notice, re-entry, operation of law, or by a provision for cesser on redemption, or in any other event (other than the dropping of a life, or the determination of a determinable life interest); ... and in this definition the expression "term of years" includes a term for less than a year, or for a year or years and a fraction of a year or from year to year; ...'

The term expressed to be granted by the agreement in the present case does not fall within this definition.

Ancient authority, recognised by the Act of 1925, was applied in *Lace v Chantler* [1944] KB 368. A dwelling house was let at the rent of 16s. 5d. per week. Lord Greene MR (no less) said, at pp. 370–371:

'Normally there could be no question that this was an ordinary weekly tenancy, duly determinable by a week's notice, but the parties in the rent-book agreed to a term which appears there expressed by the words "furnished for duration," which must mean the duration of the war. The question immediately arises whether a tenancy for the duration of the war creates a good leasehold interest. In my opinion, it does not. A term created by a leasehold tenancy agreement must be expressed either with certainty and specifically or by reference to something which can, at the time when the lease takes effect, be looked to as a certain ascertainment of what the term is meant to be. In the present case, when this tenancy agreement took effect, the term was completely uncertain. It was impossible to say how long the tenancy would last. Mr Sturge in his argument has maintained that such a lease would be valid, and that, even if the term is uncertain at its beginning when the lease takes effect, the fact that at some future time it will be rendered certain is sufficient to make it a good lease. In my opinion, that argument is not to be sustained. I do not propose to go into the authorities on the matter, but in *Foa's Landlord and Tenant*, 6th ed. (1924), p. 115, the law is stated in this way, and, in my view, correctly: "The habendum in a lease must point out the period during which the enjoyment of the premises is to be had; so that the duration, as well as the commencement of the term, must be stated. The certainty of a lease as to its continuance must be ascertainable either by the express limitation of the parties at the time the lease is made, or by reference to some collateral act which may, with equal certainty, measure the continuance of it, otherwise it is void."'

The legislature concluded that it was inconvenient for leases for the duration of the war to be void and therefore by the Validation of Wartime Leases Act 1944 Parliament provided, by section 1(1), that any agreement entered into before or after the passing of the Act which purported to grant a tenancy for the duration of the war:

'shall have effect as if it granted or provided for the grant of a tenancy for a term of 10 years, subject to a right exercisable either by the landlord or the tenant to determine the tenancy, if the war ends before the expiration of that term, by at least one month's notice in writing given after the end of the war; ...'

Parliament granted the fixed and certain term which the agreements between the parties lacked in the case of tenancies for the duration of the war and which the present agreement lacks.

When the agreement in the present case was made, it failed to grant an estate in the land. The tenant however entered into possession and paid the yearly rent of £30 reserved by the agreement. The tenant entering under a void lease became by virtue of possession and the payment of a yearly rent, a yearly tenant holding on the terms of the agreement so far as those terms were consistent with the yearly tenancy. A yearly tenancy is determinable by the landlord or the tenant at the end of the first or any subsequent year of the tenancy by six months' notice unless the agreement between the parties provides otherwise. Thus in *Doe d Rigge v Bell* (1793) 5 Term Rep 471 a parol agreement for a seven year lease did not comply with the Statute of Frauds 1677 (29 Car. 2, c.3) but the tenant entered and paid a yearly rent and it was held that he was tenant from year to year on the terms of the agreement. Lord Kenyon CJ said, at p. 472:

'Though the agreement be void by the Statute of Frauds as to the duration of the lease, it must regulate the terms on which the tenancy subsists in other respects, as to the rent, the time of year when the tenant is to quit, etc. ... Now, in this case, it was agreed, that the defendant should quit at Candlemas; and though the agreement is void as to the number of years for which the defendant was to hold, if the lessor chooses to determine the tenancy before the expiration of the seven years, he can only put an end to it at Candlemas.'

Now it is said that when in the present case the tenant entered pursuant to the agreement and paid a yearly rent he became a tenant from year to year on the terms of the agreement including clause 6 which prevents the landlord from giving notice to quit until the land is required for road widening. This submission would make a nonsense of the rule that a grant for an uncertain term does not create a lease and would make nonsense of the concept of a tenancy from year to year because it is of the essence of a tenancy from year to year that both the landlord and the tenant shall be entitled to give notice determining the tenancy.

In *Doe d Warner v Browne* (1807) 8 East 165 there was an agreement to lease at a rent of £40 per annum and it was agreed that the landlord, W. Warner, should not raise the rent nor turn out the tenant 'so long as the rent is duly paid quarterly, and he does not expose to sale or sell any article that may be injurious to W. Warner in his business.' The tenant duly paid his rent and did not commit any breach of covenant. The landlord gave six months' notice and it was held that the notice was good. These were the days when it was possible to have a lease for life. Lord Ellenborough CJ asked, at p. 166:

'What estate the defendant was contended to have? And whether he was not in this dilemma; that either his estate might enure for life, at his option; and then according to Lord Coke such an estate would, in legal contemplation, be an estate for life; which could not be created by parol: or if not for life, being for no assignable period, it must operate as a tenancy from year to year; in which case it would be inconsistent with, and repugnant to the nature of such an estate, that it should not be determinable at the pleasure of either party giving the regular notice.'

Lawrence J said, at p. 167:

'If this interest be not determinable so long as the tenant complies with the terms of the agreement, it would operate as an estate for life; which can only be created by deed ... The notion of a tenancy from year to year, the lessor binding himself not to give notice to quit, which was once thrown out by Lord Mansfield, has been long exploded.'

In *Cheshire Lines Committee v Lewis & Co* (1880) 50 LJQB 121 an agreement for a weekly tenancy contained an undertaking by the landlord not to give notice to quit until the landlord required to pull down the demised buildings. Lush J, after citing *Doe d Warner v Browne* [1807] 8 East 165 said of that case, 50 LJQB 121, 124:

'This reasoning applies with at least equal force to the present case. This is not a mere constructive tenancy as that was. It is as explicit as words can make it that the defendants are to hold 'upon a weekly tenancy at a weekly rental, and that the tenancy is to be determined by either of the parties on giving a week's notice to the other.' There is this difference between the two cases, that in *Doe d Warner v Browne* the lessor engaged not to turn out the tenant so long as he observed the conditions, and in this case [the company's agent] engages that the tenant shall hold until the company require to pull down the buildings. But, as that is an event which may never happen, the distinction is merely between the contingency of the tenant breaking the conditions and the contingency of the company wanting the premises in order to pull them down. The restriction is as repugnant to the nature of the tenancy in the one case as in the other. It is therefore no legal answer to the ejectment to say that the contingency provided for has not happened.'

These authorities indicate plainly enough that the agreement in the present case did not create a lease and that the tenancy from year to year enjoyed by the tenant as a result of entering into possession and paying a yearly rent can be determined by six months' notice by either landlord or tenant. The landlord has admittedly served such a notice. The Court of Appeal have however concluded that the notice was ineffective and that the landlord cannot give a valid notice until the land is required 'for the purposes of the widening of Walworth Road' in conformity with clause 6 of the agreement.

The notion of a tenancy from year to year, the landlord binding himself not to give notice to quit, which was exploded long before 1807 according to Lawrence J in *Doe d Warner v Browne* [1807] 8 East 165, 167, was however revived and applied by the Court of Appeal in *Re Midland Rly Co's Agreement* [1971] Ch 725, [1971] 1 All ER 1007. In that case a lease for a period of six months from 10 June 1920 was expressed to continue from half year to half year until determined. The agreement provided for the determination of the agreement by three months' written notice given by either party to the other subject to a proviso that the landlords should not exercise that right unless they required the premises for their undertaking. The successors to the landlords served a six months' written notice to quit under section 25 of the Landlord and Tenant Act 1954 although they did not require the premises for their undertaking. The Court of Appeal, upholding Foster J, declared that the notice to quit was invalid and of no effect because the landlords did not require the premises for their undertaking. The Court of Appeal held that the decision in *Lace v Chantler* [1944] KB 368 did not apply to a periodic tenancy and declined to follow *Doe d Warner v Browne* [1807] 8 East 165 or *Cheshire Lines Committee v Lewis & Co* (1880) 50 LJQB 121. Russell LJ delivering the judgment of the court held that the decision in *Lace v Chantler* [1944] KB 368 did not apply to a tenancy from year to year and said [1971] Ch 725, 733:

'we are persuaded that, there being no authority to prevent us, it is preferable as a matter of justice to hold parties to their clearly expressed bargain rather than to introduce for the first time in 1971 an extension of a doctrine of land law so as to deny the efficacy of that bargain.'

My Lords, I consider that the principle in *Lace v Chantler* [1944] KB 368 reaffirming 500 years of judicial acceptance of the requirement that a term must be certain applies to all leases and tenancy agreements. A tenancy from year to year is saved from being uncertain because each party has power by notice to determine at the end of any year. The term continues until determined as if both parties made a new agreement at the end of each year for a new term for the ensuing year. A power for nobody to determine or for one party only to be able to determine is inconsistent with the concept of a term from year to year: see *Doe d Warner v Browne* [1807] 8 East 165 and *Cheshire Lines Committee v Lewis & Co* (1880) 50 LJQB 121. In *Re Midland Rly Co's Agreement* there was no 'clearly expressed bargain' that the term should continue until the crack of doom if the demised land was not required for the landlord's undertaking or if the undertaking ceased to exist. In the present case there was no 'clearly expressed bargain' that the tenant shall be entitled to enjoy his 'temporary structures' in perpetuity if Walworth Road is never widened. In any event principle and precedent dictate that it is beyond the power of the landlord and the tenant to create a term which is uncertain.

A lease can be made for five years subject to the tenant's right to determine if the war ends before the expiry of five years. A lease can be made from year to year subject to a fetter on the right of the landlord to determine the lease before the expiry of five years unless the war ends. Both leases are valid because they create a determinable certain term of five years. A lease might purport to be made for the duration of the war subject to the tenant's right to determine before the end of the war. A lease might be made from year to year subject to a fetter on the right of the landlord to determine the lease before the war ends. Both leases would be invalid because each purported to create an uncertain term. A term must either be certain or uncertain. It cannot be partly certain because the tenant can determine it at any time and partly uncertain because the landlord cannot determine it for an uncertain period. If the landlord does not grant and the tenant does not take a certain term the grant does not create a lease.

The decision of the Court of Appeal in *Re Midland Rly Co's Agreement* [1971] Ch 725 was taken a little further in *Ashburn Anstalt v Arnold* [1989] Ch 1, [1988] 2 All ER 147. That case, if it was correct, would make it unnecessary for a lease to be of a certain duration. In an agreement for the sale of land the vendor reserved the right to remain at the property after completion as licensee and to trade therefrom without payment of rent

'save that it can be required by Matlodge [the purchaser] to give possession on not less than one quarter's notice in writing upon Matlodge certifying that it is ready at the expiration of such notice forthwith to proceed with the development of the property and the neighbouring property involving, inter alia, the demolition of the property.'

The Court of Appeal held that this reservation created a tenancy. The tenancy was not from year to year but for a term which would continue until Matlodge certified that it was ready to proceed with the development of the property. The Court of Appeal held that the term was not uncertain because the vendor could either give a quarter's notice or vacate the property without giving notice. But of course the same could be said of the situation in *Lace v Chantler* [1944] KB 368. The cumulative result of the two Court of Appeal authorities *Re Midland Rly Co's Agreement* and *Ashburn's* case would therefore destroy the need for any term to be certain.

In the present case the Court of Appeal were bound by the decisions in *Re Midland Rly Co's Agreement* and *Ashburn's* case. In my opinion both these cases were wrongly decided. A grant for an uncertain term does not create a lease. A grant for an uncertain term which takes the form of a yearly tenancy which cannot be determined by the landlord does not create a lease. I would allow the appeal. The trial judge, Millett J, reached the conclusion that the six months' notice served by the London Residuary Body was a good notice. He was of course bound by the Court of Appeal decisions but managed to construe the memorandum of agreement so as to render clause 6 ineffective in fettering the right of the landlord to serve a notice to quit after the landlord had ceased to be a road widening authority. In the circumstances this question of construction need not be considered. For the reasons which I have given the order made by Millett J must be restored. The plaintiffs must pay the costs of the second to fourth defendants before the House and in the courts below.

LORD BROWNE-WILKINSON. My Lords, I agree with the speech of my noble and learned friend, Lord Templeman, that this appeal must be allowed for the reasons he gives. However, I reach that conclusion with no satisfaction.

Before 1930, Mr. Nathan owned shop premises, 263–265 Walworth Road, with a frontage to the street. The agreement made in 1930 between the London County Council and Mr Nathan was part of a sale and leaseback arrangement whereby a part of Mr Nathan's land ('the strip') was sold to the L.C.C. for road widening. Mr Nathan retained the freehold of the remainder of No. 263–265. By the agreement, the strip was leased back to Mr Nathan for continued use, with the rest of 263–265, Walworth Road until required for road widening as commercial premises. Up until today, the remainder of No. 263–265 together with the strip has been let and occupied as one single set of retail shop premises with a frontage to the Walworth Road. As a result of our decision Mr Nathan's successor in title will be left with the freehold of the remainder of No. 263–265 which, though retail premises, will have no frontage to a shopping street: the L.C.C.'s successors in title will have the freehold to a strip of land with a road frontage but probably incapable of being used save in conjunction with the land from which it was severed in 1930, i.e. the remainder of No. 263–265.

It is difficult to think of a more unsatisfactory outcome or one further away from what the parties to the 1930 agreement can ever have contemplated. Certainly it was not a result their contract, if given effect to, could ever have produced. If the 1930 agreement had taken effect fully, there could never have come a time when the freehold to the remainder of No. 263–265 would be left without a road frontage.

This bizarre outcome results from the application of an ancient and technical rule of law which requires the maximum duration of a term of years to be ascertainable from the outset. No one has produced any satisfactory rationale for the genesis of this rule. No one has been able to point to any useful purpose that it serves at the present day. If, by overruling the existing authorities, this House were able to change the law for the future only I would have urged your Lordships to do so. But for this House to depart from a rule relating to land law which has been established for many centuries might upset long established titles. I must therefore confine myself to expressing the hope that the Law Commission might look at the subject to see whether there is in fact any good reason now for maintaining a rule which operates to defeat contractually agreed arrangements between the parties (of which all successors in title are aware) and which is capable of producing such an extraordinary result as that in the present case. [4]

i. INTERESSE TERMINI

LAW OF PROPERTY ACT 1925

149. Abolition of interesse termini, and as to reversionary leases and leases for lives.—(1) The doctrine of interesse termini is hereby abolished.

(2) As from the commencement of this Act all terms of years absolute shall, whether the interest is created before or after such commencement, be capable of taking effect at law or in equity, according to the estate interest or powers of the grantor, from the date fixed for commencement of the term, without actual entry.

---

[4]   Lords GRIFFITHS and MUSTILL concurred with this view.

ii. REVERSIONARY LEASES [5]

LAW OF PROPERTY ACT 1925

149. Abolition of interesse termini, and as to reversionary leases and leases for lives.—(3) A term, at a rent or granted in consideration of a fine, [6] limited after the commencement of this Act to take effect more than twenty-one years from the date of the instrument purporting to create it, shall be void, and any contract made after such commencement to create such a term shall likewise be void; but this subsection does not apply to any term taking effect in equity under a settlement, or created out of an equitable interest under a settlement, or under an equitable power for mortgage, indemnity or other like purposes.

RE STRAND AND SAVOY PROPERTIES LTD [7]
[1960] Ch 582, [1960] 2 All ER 327 (ChD, BUCKLEY J)

A 35 year lease contained a provision that the lessors would 'at the written request of the lessee made 12 months before the expiration of the term hereby created' grant a further term of 35 years at the same rent.

The tenants took out a summons to determine whether the Law of Property Act 1925, section 149(3) invalidated their option to renew the lease on the ground that it was a contract to take effect more than 21 years from the date of the lease granting the option.

Held. The option for renewal was valid.

BUCKLEY J: Sir Milner Holland, who appears for the tenants, ... says that subsection (3) makes it impossible for any man to create a reversionary term—that is to say, a term to take effect more than 21 years from the date of the instrument creating the term—and that it also invalidates any contract by which a man undertakes to create a reversionary term, that is to say, a term which will not commence until 21 years after the date of the instrument creating such a term. He says that the subsection does not invalidate a contract to create a lease, at however remote a date in the future, which, when it is granted, will create a term which will take effect within 21 years of the date of that lease. ...

Mr Albery, on the other hand, points out that the contention advanced by Sir Milner really gives no operative effect to that part of subsection (3) which deals with contracts at all, because if a lease granting a term to commence at a date later than 21 years from the date of the lease is void, a contract to grant such a lease must also necessarily be void without any express provision to that effect in the statute. ...

On [its true] terms the subsection is confined, so far as contracts are concerned, to contracts to create terms which, when created, will only take effect more than 21 years from the dates of the instruments creating them; that is to say, it invalidates contracts for the granting of leases which will, when granted, be reversionary leases, the postponement of the commencement of the term being for more than 21 years from the date of the lease.

---

[5]   I.e., a lease which is to take effect at a future time. A reversionary lease can take effect only if created by deed: *Long v Tower Hamlets London Borough Council* [1996] 3 WLR 317, [1996] 2 All ER 683, p. 83, n. 12, ante.

[6]   P 455, n. 9, ante.

[7]   (1960) 76 LQR 352 (R.E.M.).

WEG MOTORS LTD v HALES

[1962] Ch 49, [1961] 3 All ER 181 (CA, Lord EVERSHED MR, HARMAN and DONOVAN LJJ)

In July 1938 the plaintiffs were granted a lease of premises for a term of 21 years from December 1938, with an option of 'taking a further lease' of the premises for a period of 21 years from the date of the exercise of the option; and the option was expressed to be exercisable at any time before 25 December 1959. The defendants claimed that the option agreement was void under section 149(3).

Held. The option agreement was valid.

LORD EVERSHED MR: The question is, in our judgment, an extremely short one—namely, does the option agreement of July, 1938, fall within the scope of the language in subsection (3) of section 149 of the Act of 1925 as being a contract 'to create such a term' as therein mentioned? The view of the learned author of the note to the section in volume 1 of Wolstenholme and Cherry's *Conveyancing Statutes*, 12th edn. (1932), p. 497, appears clearly to have been that a contract to create a term of years, which might begin to take effect more than 21 years from the date of the contract, fell within the vice of the subsection. It was this view that Buckley J rejected in the case already cited;[8] and he did so upon the basis that the phrase 'such a term' could in its context refer, and refer only, to a term commencing more than 21 years from the instrument purporting to create the term, that is to say, the lease executed in pursuance of the contract and not the contract itself. We must not be taken to be expressing any doubt of the correctness of Buckley J's decision. But in the present case we are concerned not with a contract, that is a binding agreement, to grant and take a lease but with an option which might never be exercised and cannot, until exercised, be in any event said, in our judgment, to create a term of years at all. It follows, therefore, in our view, that the option agreement with which we are concerned cannot be said to be such a contract as is comprehended in section 149(3) of the Act of 1925. The challenge to the plaintiffs based upon that section must, therefore, fail.

iii. LEASES FOR LIVES

LAW OF PROPERTY ACT 1925

149. Abolition of interesse termini, and as to reversionary leases and leases for lives.—(6) Any lease or underlease, at a rent, or in consideration of a fine,[9] for life or lives or for any term of years determinable with life or lives, or on the marriage of the lessee, or any contract therefor, made before or after the commencement of this Act, or created by virtue of Part V of the Law of Property Act, 1922, shall take effect as a lease, underlease or contract therefor, for a term of ninety years determinable after the death or marriage (as the case may be) of the original lessee, or of the survivor of the original lessees, by at least one month's notice in writing given to determine the same on one of the quarter days applicable to the tenancy, either by the lessor or the persons deriving title under

---

8   *Re Strand and Savoy Properties Ltd* [1960] Ch 582, [1960] 2 All ER 327, p. 454, ante.

9   A fine is usually the single payment of a lump sum made by the tenant, and is additional to the rent. By statute the word includes 'a premium or foregift and any payment, consideration or benefit in the nature of a fine, premium or foregift': LPA 1925, s. 205(1)(xxiii); *Skipton Building Society v Clayton* (1993) 66 P & CR 223. The rent or fine excludes beneficial tenancies for life under a settlement; these are equitable interests and subject to SLA 1925: *Binions v Evans* [1972] Ch 359 at 366, [1972] 2 All ER 70 at 74, p. 617, post; *Ivory v Palmer* [1975] ICR 340.

him, to the person entitled to the leasehold interest, or if no such person is in existence by affixing the same to the premises, or by the lessee or other persons in whom the leasehold interest is vested to the lessor or the persons deriving title under him:

Provided that—

(a) this subsection shall not apply to any term taking effect in equity under a settlement or created out of an equitable interest under a settlement for mortgage, indemnity, or other like purposes; ...

(d) if there are no quarter days specially applicable to the tenancy, notice may be given to determine the tenancy on one of the usual quarter days. [10]

In **Bass Holdings Ltd v Lewis** [1986] 2 EGLR 40, Bass Holdings Ltd, the respondent, entered into a tenancy agreement with Lewis, by which it sub-let to him the Railway Tavern, Deptford for three years, terminable by Bass on giving six months' notice, or, if Lewis died, not less than fourteen days' notice to his personal representatives. In November 1984, Bass served a notice to quit on Lewis who denied Bass's right to possession, on the ground that under section 149(6) the term granted to him had been converted into one for 90 years, determinable only by notice after his death. In rejecting this claim, Nourse LJ said at 40:

'The essence of Hoffmann J's decision is to be found at p 3 B–C of the transcript where, having described the appellant's claim and its consequences in tones of some irony, he said this: "In my judgment the short answer to this remarkable claim is that Mr Lewis's tenancy was not granted for life or lives or any term of years determinable with life or lives within the meaning of section 149(6) of the Law of Property Act 1925. The statute is dealing with leases which are granted either for a term limited by reference to a life or lives, or for a term of years limited conditionally upon the survival of a life or lives."

I entirely agree. I add by way of illustration that the simplest example of a term of years limited conditionally upon the survival of a life or lives is a lease "to A for a term of 20 years if he shall so long live."

The learned judge [11] then went on to consider the aim of the 1925 property legislation, implemented in part by section 149(6), to reduce the legal estates which are capable of existing in land to estates in fee simple absolute in possession and to terms of years absolute. He pointed out, correctly, that a lease for a fixed period with a proviso which allows for its determination by notice, even if the dropping of a life is a condition precedent to the service of a valid notice, is none the less a term of years absolute.

The appellant's construction of section 149(6) as advanced by Mr Wood on his behalf, necessitates reading the words "for any term of years determinable with life or lives" as including a term of years determinable by notice after the dropping of a life or lives. It seems to me that there are a number of conclusive objections to that construction.

---

[10]   Lady Day (March 25), Midsummer Day (June 24); Michaelmas Day (September 29) or Christmas Day (December 25).

[11]   See Hoffmann J (unreported) who said: 'Why should a term of 3 years "if X shall so long live" automatically become a term of 90 years determinable by notice after X's death? It is possible (although one hardly dare whisper such a suggestion about the great conveyancers who drafted the statute) that it was simply a mistake.'

First, the word "determinable" is capable of meaning "liable to determine" and no more. It does not necessarily also mean "determinable by notice" or by some other positive act.

Second, it seems to me to be very important to pay attention to the prepositions which are used in the two parts of the subsection. In describing the leases to which it is to apply, the subsection refers to leases determinable *with* life or lives, or *on* the marriage of the lessee. That suggests that it is referring to leases which will determine automatically, in the one case on death and in the other on marriage. By contrast, when you get to the provision dealing with the new lease, you find that it is to be determinable by notice *after* the death or marriage as the case may be of the lessee. That is a distinction which I do not think can be ignored and it is further emphasised by the terms of proviso (*c*).

Third, the contrast between the use of the word "determinable" *simpliciter* in the first part of the subsection and the reference to determinability after the death or marriage *by notice* in the second conclusively confirms that in the first part "determinable" does not mean determinable by notice.

For these reasons, as well as for those given by the learned judge, it seems to me that this is a very clear case. In my view the learned judge arrived at an entirely correct decision. I would therefore dismiss this appeal.'

iv. PERPETUALLY RENEWABLE LEASES

Perpetually renewable leases are converted into terms of 2,000 years; those existing on 1 January 1926 date from the commencement of the existing tenancy, and those created after 1925 from the date fixed for the commencement of the tenancy. Perpetually renewable subleases are converted into terms of 2,000 years less one day. [12]

In **Caerphilly Concrete Products Ltd v Owen** [1972] 1 WLR 372, [1972] 1 All ER 248, [13] a grant in 1963 of a five year term of 4,800 square feet in an industrial area of Caerphilly at £10 a year contained a provision that 'the landlord will on the written request of the tenant ... grant to him a lease of the said demised land for the further term of five years from the expiration of the said term hereby granted at the same rent and containing the like covenants and provisos as are herein contained (including an option to renew such lease for the further term of five years at the expiration thereof)'. The Court of Appeal (RUSSELL, SACHS and STAMP LJJ) held that the grant took effect as a lease for 2,000 years.

RUSSELL LJ said at 374, at 251:

'The approach to the question whether a lease is perpetually renewable is not in doubt. The language used must plainly lead to that result: though the fact that an argument is capable of being sustained at some length against that result does not of course suffice. As a matter of history, when a covenant by a lessor conferred a right to renewal of the lease, the new grant to contain the same or the like covenants and provisos as were contained in the lease, the courts refused to give literal effect to that language, which if taken literally would mean that the second lease would contain the same covenant (or option) to renew, totidem verbis, and so on perpetually. The reference to the same covenants was construed

[12] LPA 1922, s. 145 and Sch. 15.
[13] (1972) 88 LQR 173.

as not including the option covenant itself. This limited the tenant's right to one renewal. In order therefore to make it plain that the covenants to be contained in the second lease (to be granted under the exercise of the option to renew) were to include also the covenant to renew, draftsmen were accustomed to insert phrases such as (including this covenant), so as to achieve a perpetually renewable lease. As I have indicated, if they did not do this, the second lease would not contain any option clause.

The operation of the words of inclusion was not limited to requiring the second lease to contain a covenant to renew once more only, which would have been the outcome if the words of inclusion had been omitted in the second lease. This was because the words of inclusion could not properly be construed as requiring the second lease to contain the same covenants other than the covenant to renew but additionally to include an option to renew once more only—a total of three terms. The words of inclusion defined or explained what was meant by "the same covenants," that is to say, as including the covenant to renew. Consequently in the second lease, in order to comply with the words of definition or explanation, the covenants referred to therein to be contained in the second lease must contain the same wording including the inclusion.

In the present case the brackets make it abundantly plain that the parties are explaining that "containing the like covenants and provisos" is a phrase intended to embrace an option. That is to say that the covenants and provisos contained in the first lease, which the first lease requires the second lease to contain, are not to be construed as a reference to those covenants and provisos other than an option to renew, but as a reference to all those covenants including an option to renew. If the words ... are repeated in the second lease without the words in parenthesis the second lease will not be carrying out the requirement of the first lease: it will not be granting an option for a further lease containing "the like covenants" as defined.'

Sachs LJ said at 375, at 252: 'I, too, have underlined the words in brackets. It is trite to say that when construing a document such as a lease it is the prime purpose of the courts to seek to adopt a meaning that conforms to the intentions of the parties. Not even the most impeccable conveyancing logic, however neatly expressed, can convince me that in the instant case it was the mutual intention of the parties that the lease should be perpetually renewable. So far as the landlord is concerned it seems to me highly unlikely that he really intended that this particular lease could or should be "for ever". My doubts on that question of intention extend also to the tenant—for I would acquit him of any intent to lay a trap through the operation of the words enclosed in the brackets, which we know to have been added to the draft at the very last moment by his solicitors. It is difficult indeed, at any rate so far as I am concerned, to think that two business men would be talking in terms of five years if both—or indeed either—of them truly meant that a lease should be granted which went on ad infinitum.

Were I in a position to give effect to the views just expressed that would result in the landlord succeeding in this appeal: but it is necessary to consider whether the authorities which were so fully and so helpfully cited to us permit such a result. An examination of the relevant decisions discloses an area of law in which the courts have manoeuvred themselves into an unhappy position ... [They] appear to have bound themselves to hold that the use of a certain set of words (to which I will refer as "the formula") causes the lease to be perpetually renewable, even when no layman—at least if he has some elementary knowledge of business—would dream of granting such a lease and, if aware of the technical meaning of the particular phraseology would almost certainly be aghast at its devastating effect and refuse to sign. One reason for the courts so binding themselves is said to be that the formula is one the effect of which is well known to trained coveyancers, and that this is advantageous, however much of a trap it may constitute for others.

As already mentioned, the prime purpose of the courts when construing a lease is to interpret it according to the true intentions of the parties. Already 20 years ago judicial unease at having to determine those intentions in cases of the instant type by a blinkered approach is reflected in the judgments in *Parkus v Greenwood*, both at first instance [1950] Ch 33, [1949] 2 All ER 743 and on appeal [1950] Ch 644, [1950] 1 All ER 436.

[His Lordship referred to *Green v Palmer* [1944] Ch 328, [1944] 1 All ER 670 and continued:]

The judicial unease of 1950 is, so far as I am concerned, by now increased by two factors. First, more and more leases over the two succeeding decades have tended to come from pens not fully trained in the art of conveyancing. Secondly, over the same period the value of the pound sterling has been decreasing rapidly, thus making it even more unlikely that a man of business in the course of a normal transaction would knowingly part "for ever" with his rights over land in return for a static rent. Moreover, when residential property is concerned a landlord could indeed now find himself in the position of having to relinquish a freehold when the document which he signed appeared on the face of it to be a lease for relatively short periods of years.

In those circumstances I, too, have great sympathy with the line of approach adopted by Uthwatt J in *Green v Palmer* and Harman J in *Parkus v Greenwood*. I could wish that the courts had followed the apparent preference of Lord FitzGerald in *Swinburne v Milburn* (1884) 9 App Cas 844 at 855 for confining interpretations of perpetual renewability to leases where words such as "for ever" or "from time to time for ever hereafter" or some equivalent were used in the relevant document. This approach would have avoided that sort of path by which good logic can on occasion make bad law, and would have been in accord with the aphorism that at times "logic is only the art of going wrong with confidence".

Having, however, examined the authorities, I feel bound in this court to say that the matter is concluded by them in that the words in brackets, as inserted at the last moment, have in law the same effect as those considered in *Parkus v Greenwood*.'

In **Marjorie Burnett Ltd v Barclay** (1980) 258 EG 642,[14] there was a grant in 1971 of a seven year lease of a shop with residential accommodation above in Boscombe at a yearly rent of £650. Clause 6 contained a covenant to renew. The plaintiff sought a declaration that this was not perpetually renewable. In holding that it was not, Nourse J said:

'[Clause 6] reads as follows:

"If the tenant shall be desirous of taking a new lease of the demised premises after the expiration of the term hereby granted ..."

There are then provisions which are in a not very elegant form, but the effect of them is clear enough. It is that the tenant can give the landlord notice of the desire to take a new lease. Then clause 6 goes on as follows:

[14]   (1981) 131 NLJ 683 (H. W. Wilkinson).

"Then the landlord will at or before the expiration of the term hereby granted, if there shall then be no subsisting breach of any of the tenant's obligations under this present lease"—and now I come to some important words—"grant to the tenant a new lease of the premises hereby demised for a further term of seven years, to commence from and after the expiration of the term hereby granted at a rent to be agreed between the parties."

There are then provisions for the rent to be fixed in default of agreement. Then come the final words of the clause, which are also important. They read as follows:

"And such lease shall also contain a like covenant for renewal for a further term of seven years on the expiration of the term thereby granted. ..."

[His Lordship referred to *Parkus v Greenwood* [1950] Ch 33, [1949] 2 All ER 743 and *Caerphilly Concrete Products Ltd v Owen* [1972] 1 WLR 372, [1972] 1 All ER 248 and continued:]

In construing clause 6 of the lease in the present case I must therefore approach the matter in this way. I must bear in mind that the leaning of the courts has been against perpetual renewals. I have to find expressly in the lease a covenant or obligation for perpetual renewal. And I have to look ahead to see what the second lease will contain when the requirements of the covenant for renewal in the first have been duly observed.

I now return to clause 6 of the lease. What the landlord has to do, if the tenant gives it notice of his desire to take a new lease, is to grant to the tenant a new lease of the demised premises for a further term of seven years at a rent to be agreed, and if not agreed to be fixed in the manner specified. Then it is provided that such lease shall also contain a like covenant for renewal for a further term of seven years on the expiration of the term thereby granted.

Mr Henty really puts his case on this primary question in two ways. First, he takes the simple course of asking me to see what provisions the second lease would contain if it were to be granted pursuant to clause 6. He says that it would inevitably be at a different rent from the £650 reserved by the first lease. Then he says that the second lease would contain a like covenant for renewal for a further term of seven years as that contained in clause 6 of the first lease. But that covenant ends with the part of clause 6 which deals with the provisions for fixing the rent in default of agreement. It does not seem to me that the second lease could possibly contain the words "and such lease shall also contain a like covenant for renewal for a further term of seven years on the expiration of the term thereby granted," because those words are not part of the covenant for renewal and to include them would be to go further than clause 6 requires. And so I agree with Mr Henty that the second lease would be at a new rent and that it would contain the whole of clause 6, except for the last three lines or so which I have just quoted. On that footing it is clear that there is no express covenant or obligation for perpetual renewal. Indeed the contrary is the case. There is an express provision in the lease to the effect that it can be renewed twice only.

That would in itself be enough to dispose of the primary question in these proceedings. But Mr Henty goes on to take a second point, which appears to me to be one of equal force, and that is this. He says that even supposing his first argument were wrong I must bear in mind that what will happen if this is a perpetually renewable lease is that it will be converted by the 1922 Act into a lease for a term of 2,000 years. He says, and I can see no answer to this, that the notion of a 2,000-year term is completely inimical to a lease which contains provisions for rent review every seven years. And so again he says that as a matter of construction clause 6 could not possibly have the effect for which the defendant has contended. I agree with that contention also.'

D. Certainty of Rent

The rent must be certain. [15] That does not mean that it must be certain at the date of the lease. Rent is sufficiently certain if it can be calculated with certainty at the time when payment comes to be made. [16] This problem has been considered in connexion with options to renew a lease and rent revision at the time of renewal. [17]

i. OPTION TO RENEW LEASE

BROWN v GOULD[18]
[1972] Ch 53, [1971] 2 All ER 1505 (ChD, MEGARRY J)

In 1949 Margaret Gould leased part of Albion Granaries, 250 High Road, Loughton, Essex to Frank Brown [19] for 21 years from 29 September 1949, at a rent of £500 a year. Clause 3(c) of the lease granted to the tenant an option to renew the tenancy for a further term of 21 years at a rent 'to be fixed having regard to the market value of the premises at the time of exercising the option taking into account to the advantage of the tenant any increased value of such premises attributable to structural improvements made by the tenant during the currency of this present lease'. Frank Brown spent nearly £30,000 rebuilding the premises, and in 1969 served notice in accordance with the terms of the lease purporting to exercise the option. The trustees of Margaret Gould, in whom the reversion had vested on her death, contended that the option was void for uncertainty.

Held. The option was valid.

MEGARRY J: The landlords ... contend that the option for renewal contained in the lease is void for uncertainty. That is the sole question that I have to

---

[15] On the meaning of rent, see [1991] Conv 270 (R. G. Lee).

[16] *Greater London Council v Connolly* [1970] 2 QB 100, [1970] 1 All ER 870 ('rent liable to be increased or decreased on notice being given' held to be valid); *CH Bailey Ltd v Memorial Enterprises Ltd* [1974] 1 WLR 728, [1974] 1 All ER 1003 (increased rent ascertained retrospectively); *Bradshaw v Pawley* [1980] 1 WLR 10, [1979] 3 All ER 273 (rent payable from a date prior to execution of lease). For the validity of an index linked rent, see *Blumenthal v Gallery Five Ltd* (1971) 220 EG 31 (index of retail prices); *Cumshaw Ltd v Bowen* [1987] 1 EGLR 30; (1987) 132 NLJ 288 (H. W. Wilkinson); (1994) 138 SJ 552 (R. Castle and A. MacFarquhar); *Lambert v HTV Cymru (Wales) Ltd* [1998] EMLR 629 (clause obliging purchaser 'to use all reasonable endeavours to obtain rights of first negotiation from any assignee' for benefit of seller held not enforceable for lack of certainty).

[17] See *United Scientific Holdings Ltd v Burnley Borough Council* [1978] AC 904, [1977] 2 All ER 62, where HL held that there was a presumption that time was not of the essence in construing clauses which specify time limits for the operation of the rent review procedure. See generally C & B, pp. 428–430; Aldridge, *Leasehold Law*, paras. 4.038–48; Reynolds and Fetherstonhaugh, *Handbook of Rent Review,* Bernstein and Reynolds, *Essentials of Rent Review* (1995); Clarke and Adams, *Rent Reviews and Variable Rents* (3rd edn. 1990); Reynolds and Clark, *Renewal of Business Tenancies* (2002); *Emmet on Title*, paras. 26.031–26.051; Barnsley, *Land Options* (3rd edn., 1998), chap. 10; Rent Review Journal (which began in 1981 and was superseded in 1992 by Rent Review and Lease Renewal Journal). For precedents see Aldridge, P. 011–020; Conv Precedents vol. 1,2108–9; 5–57.

[18] (1972) 36 Conv (NS) 317 (P. Robertshaw).

[19] 'He had the good fortune to live at Arabin House, High Beech, Essex', at 55, at 1506. See Megarry, *Arabinesque-at-law* (1969), p. xi.

determine. Stated briefly, the proper approach, I think, is that the court is reluctant to hold void for uncertainty any provision that was intended to have legal effect. In this case it is very properly accepted that the option was intended to have business efficacy.

In an unreported case, *Re Lloyd's Trust Instruments* (1970) 24th June, to which I referred counsel, I endeavoured to state the basic principles applicable in cases of uncertainty. What I said there was:

'I think the starting point on any question of uncertainty must be that of the court's reluctance to hold an instrument void for uncertainty. Lord Hardwicke LC once said "A court never construes a devise void, unless it is so absolutely dark, that they cannot find out the testator's meaning": *Minshull v Minshull* (1737) 1 Atk 411 at 412. Lord Brougham said: "The difficulty must be so great that it amounts to an impossibility, the doubt so grave that there is not even an inclination of the scales one way": *Doe d Winter v Perratt* (1843) 9 Cl & F 606 at 689. In a well-known statement, Sir George Jessel MR said that the court would not hold a will void for uncertainty "unless it is utterly impossible to put a meaning upon it. The duty of the court is to put a fair meaning on the terms used, and not, as was said in one case, to repose on the easy pillow of saying that the whole is void for uncertainty": *Re Roberts* (1881) 19 ChD 520 at 529. That this is not a doctrine confined to wills but is one which applies to other instruments, such as planning permissions, is shown by cases such as *Fawcett Properties Ltd v Buckingham County Council* [1961] AC 636, [1960] 3 All ER 503, where, by a majority, the delphic language of a condition in a planning permission escaped from being held void for uncertainty largely because of its resemblance to a section to be found in a modern Act of Parliament. The second question is that of the types of uncertainty. The basic type (and on one view the only true type) is uncertainty of concept, as contrasted with mere difficulty of application: see, for example, *Re Gape* [1952] Ch 418, affirmed at 743, where the question was one of a condition subsequent, in which special considerations apply. In *Fawcett's* case [1961] AC 636 at 670, [1960] 3 All ER 503 at 513, Lord Keith of Avonholm said: "The point is one of uncertainty of concept. If it is impossible, on construction of the condition, to reach a conclusion as to what was in the draftsman's mind, the condition is meaningless and must be read as pro non scripto." Putting it another way, the question is one of linguistic or semantic uncertainty, and not of difficulty of ascertainment: see *Re Baden's Deed Trusts* [1971] AC 424 at 457, [1970] 2 All ER 288 at 427, per Lord Wilberforce. If there is a trust for "my old friends," all concerned are faced with uncertainty as to the concept or idea enshrined in these words. It may not be difficult to resolve that "old" means not "aged" but "of long standing"; but then there is the question how long is "long". Friendship, too, is a concept with almost infinite shades of meaning. Where the concept is uncertain, the gift is void. Where the concept is certain, then mere difficulty in tracing and discovering those who are entitled normally does not invalidate the gift.'

To the authorities mentioned in that passage must now be added *Greater London Council v Connolly* [1970] 2 QB 100, [1970] 1 All ER 870, a landlord and tenant case concerning a condition on the rent card of a council tenant. This condition provided that the rent and other sums shown on the rent card 'are liable to be increased or decreased on notice being given'; and the Court of Appeal unanimously held that the condition was not void for uncertainty. Lord Denning MR said, at 108, at 874: 'The courts are always loath to hold a condition bad for uncertainty. They will give it a reasonable interpretation whenever possible. It is possible here.' ... No doubt there may be cases in which the draftsman's ineptitude will succeed in defeating the court's efforts to find a meaning for the provision in question; but only if the court is driven to it will it be held that a provision is void for uncertainty.

With that in mind, I approach the attack made on the present clause. Mr Scamell [counsel for the defendants] concentrated on three phrases in the clause, the words 'a rent to be fixed', the words 'having regard to' the market value of the premises at the time of exercising the option, and the words 'taking into account' to the advantage of the tenant any increased value of the premises attributable to his structural improvements. In addition, he pointed to the absence of any machinery for working out this formula, by contrast with the other provisions in the lease that I have mentioned. Taken together, he said, these considerations showed that the clause provided neither a clear basis for determining the rent nor any means of quantifying that basis, and accordingly the option was void for uncertainty.

At least three types of option may be distinguished. First, the option may be for renewal simply 'at a rent to be agreed'. In that case, no formula for quantifying the rent is laid down, and prima facie the option will, as in *King's Motors (Oxford) Ltd v Lax* [1970] 1 WLR 426, [1969] 3 All ER 665, be void as being a mere contract to make a contract, or, perhaps more properly, as being an agreement to make a contract, or a contract dependent upon the making of an agreement. [20] In *Smith v Morgan* [1971] 1 WLR 803, [1971] 2 All ER 1500, my brother Brightman held that a right of pre-emption in a conveyance 'at a figure to be agreed upon' was not void for uncertainty, but imposed upon the person granting it an obligation to offer the land to the grantee at the price at which she was willing to sell it. On this, I would make two comments. First, it illustrates the attitude of the court in striving to avoid holding a provision void for uncertainty. Second, it illustrates one of the differences between an option and a right of pre-emption. Under an option, only one step is normally needed to constitute a contract, namely, the exercise of the option. Under a right of pre-emption, two steps will usually be necessary, the making of the offer in accordance with the right of pre-emption, and the acceptance of that offer. The failure to provide either a price or a formula for ascertaining the price is accordingly far more serious in the case of an option than under a pre-emption: he who exercises such an option may well be virtually signing a blank cheque, whereas he who is entitled to a right of pre-emption can at least refrain from accepting the grantor's offer if the price be too high. [1]

The second type of option is one that is expressed to be exercisable at a price to be determined according to some stated formula, without any effective machinery being in terms provided for the working out of that formula. That is

---

[20]   See also *Courtney and Fairbairn Ltd v Tolaini Bros (Hotels) Ltd* [1975] 1 WLR 297, [1975] 1 All ER 716 (building agreement 'to negotiate fair and reasonable contract sums' held to be void for uncertainty); *Bushwall Properties Ltd v Vortex Properties Ltd* [1976] 1 WLR 591, [1976] 2 All ER 283 (contract for sale of 51½ acres of land for £50,000 payable in three unequal instalments held unenforceable because of provision that on each payment 'a proportionate part of the land shall be released'); *Walford v Miles* [1992] 2 AC 128, [1992] 1 All ER 453, p. 77, ante (agreement 'to continue to negotiate in good faith' held to be void for uncertainty). Cf. *Hackney London Borough Council v Thompson* [2001] L & TR 7 (covenant requiring transferee to 'pay a due proportion of management costs' held valid: construable as meaning an appropriate or reasonable proportion). See Farrand, *Contract and Conveyance* (4th edn.), pp. 40–41.

[1]   See pp. 89–95, ante. *Smith v Morgan* was doubted in *Miller v Lakefield Estates Ltd* (1988) 57 P & CR 104, where MAY LJ thought it arguable that 'the judge there might have implied too much into the option clause.'

the present case. Thirdly, the option may be one which provides both a formula and the machinery, as, for example, arbitration. In this last case, it may be that the machinery can do something to cure defects in the formula: I do not have to decide that. What is before me is a formula that is assailed for its uncertainty, and the absence of any specified machinery that can do anything to cure that uncertainty. I shall consider the question of machinery first.

[His Lordship rejected the landlords' argument that there was no adequate machinery for determining the rent, and continued:]

I readily accept that the words of clause 3(c) might have been more precise. But that is not the point: the point is whether it is void for uncertainty. If one approaches the formula stated in the clause with reasonable goodwill, as I think I am entitled and, indeed, required to do, does it appear to embody such uncertainty of concept as to make it void? Without saying that there is no room for argument on the details, I would answer No to that question, or, indeed, to any other reasonable way of formulating the question that I can conceive. The question is not, I think, whether the clause is proof against wilful misinterpretation, but whether someone genuinely seeking to discover its meaning is able to do so. To that question I would answer Yes.

In **Corson v Rhuddlan Borough Council** (1989) 59 P & CR 185, [2] the lease of Prestatyn Golf course included an option to renew for a further lease 'and at a rent to be agreed', such rent not to exceed the previous rent of £1,150. The Court of Appeal rejected the landlord's claim that the option was void for uncertainty, and implied a term for a fair rent with an upper limit of £1,150. RALPH GIBSON LJ said at 194:

'It seems plain to me, therefore, that, in the absence of authority requiring us to take a different course, it is proper to apply to this clause the principle applied by Lord Tomlin to the document in *Hillas & Co v Arcos* (1932) 147 LT 503 namely that the court should, if it can: "so balance matters that without violation of essential principle the dealings of men may as far as possible be treated as effective."

In *Brown v Gould*, Megarry J referred to the reluctance of the court to hold an instrument void for uncertainty as a basic principle. If we are free to do so, I would hold that in this case the contractual intention of the parties is clear that, upon proper notice being given, the council should be under an obligation to grant a new lease at a fair rent to be agreed between the parties, that fair rent not to be in excess of £1,150. It is just and necessary to imply the provision for the rent to be a fair rent.

There is said to be authority in the way of taking that course. In *King's Motors (Oxford) Ltd v Lax* the option clause was contained in a seven-year lease of a petrol station and provided for a further term of seven years. As in this case, there was a requirement as to the giving of notice six months before the end of the term and of due performance of the covenants in the lease, but the rent

---

[2]   [1990] Conv 290 (J. E. Martin). See also *Miller v Lakefield Estates Ltd*, supra (option to purchase 'at a price to be agreed', but if no sale took place within six months of notice given to exercise option, then property should be sold at public auction, held valid). Cf. *ARC Ltd v Schofield* [1990] 2 EGLR 52 (option to renew lease at a rent 'to be agreed between the landlord and tenant, being a fair and reasonable market rent at that time' held valid).

was to be "as may be agreed between the parties." There was no statement as to the maximum rent. Mr Orr submitted that that case had been approved in *Beer v Bowden* [1981] 1 WLR 522n, [1981] 1 All ER 1070 p. 467, post, by this court and that the reference in the option clause in this case to a maximum rent did not serve to distinguish this case from the grounds of decision in *Lax's* case. As was pointed out in the course of argument by Balcombe LJ, the correctness of the decision in *Lax's* case was not treated as a matter of decision for this court in *Beer v Bowden*. The *Lax* case was concerned with an option clause, as contrasted with the rent revision clause before the court in *Beer v Bowden*, and was thus regarded as distinguishable. It is, again, I think, not necessary for this court to decide whether the decision in the *Lax* case was correct because the provision for a maximum rent is, in my judgment, a material distinction. For my part, however, I incline to the view that it was, as Mr George submitted, wrongly decided, and I would respectfully differ from the view of Goff LJ that the option clause was in that case precluded from being a valid contract because the rent was not ascertainable. I see no reason why different principles should be applicable to the construction, so far as concerns voidness for uncertainty, of a rent revision clause in an existing lease as contrasted with an option for a "new" lease or further lease in an existing lease. *Foley v Classique Coaches Ltd* [1934] 2 KB 1, established that the presence of the words "to be agreed by the parties" is not fatal to the existence of an enforceable contract if it is otherwise plain, upon the construction of the whole of the document in its context, including of course those words, that there was a clear contractual intention of the parties to be bound by the clause. A provision that the rent should be a fair rent could, I think, have been implied in the *Lax* case. I can see no risk of difficulty arising from such a conclusion. If parties intend an option clause to be no more than an indication that the landlord will be willing to consider a request for a new lease without obligation and on terms to be agreed, there is no difficulty in making that intention clear if there is thought to be any utility in including such a statement in the document.'

SUDBROOK TRADING ESTATE LTD v EGGLETON

[1983] 1 AC 444, [1982] 3 All ER 1 [3] (HL, Lords Diplock, Fraser of Tullybelton, Russell of Killowen, Scarman and Bridge of Harrow)

In a series of leases of industrial properties in Gloucester, the lessees were granted an option 'to purchase the reversion in fee simple in the premises hereby demised ... at such price not being less than £12,000 as may be agreed upon by two valuers one to be nominated by the lessor and the other by the lessee and in default of such agreement by an umpire appointed by the valuers.' The lessees purported to exercise the option, but the lessors refused to appoint a valuer, claiming that machinery for the ascertainment of the option price was defectively uncertain. The lessees sought specific performance of the options.

Held. (Lord Russell of Killowen dissenting). Specific performance granted.

Lord Fraser of Tullybelton: I recognise the logic of the reasoning which has led to the courts' refusing to substitute their own machinery for the machinery which has been agreed upon by the parties. But the result to which it leads is so remote from that which parties normally intend and expect, and is so inconvenient in practice, that there must in my opinion be some defect in

---

[3]   [1983] Conv 76 (K. Hodkinson); (1982) 98 LQR 539 (J. Murdoch).

the reasoning. I think the defect lies in construing the provisions for the mode of ascertaining the value as an essential part of the agreement. That may have been perfectly true early in the 19th century, when the valuer's profession and the rules of valuation were less well established than they are now. But at the present day these provisions are only subsidiary to the main purpose of the agreement which is for sale and purchase of the property at a fair or reasonable value. In the ordinary case parties do not make any substantial distinction between an agreement to sell at a fair value, without specifying the mode of ascertaining the value, and an agreement to sell at a value to be ascertained by valuers appointed in the way provided in these leases. The true distinction is between those cases where the mode of ascertaining the price is an essential term of the contract, and those cases where the mode of ascertainment, though indicated in the contract, is subsidiary and non-essential: see *Fry on Specific Performance*, 6th edn. (1921), pp. 167, 169, paragraphs 360, 364. The present case falls, in my opinion, into the latter category. Accordingly when the option was exercised there was constituted a complete contract for sale, and the clause should be construed as meaning that the price was to be a fair price. On the other hand where an agreement is made to sell at a price to be fixed by a valuer who is named, or who, by reason of holding some office such as auditor of a company whose shares are to be valued, will have special knowledge relevant to the question of value, the prescribed mode may well be regarded as essential. Where, as here, the machinery consists of valuers and an umpire, none of whom is named or identified, it is in my opinion unrealistic to regard it as an essential term. If it breaks down there is no reason why the court should not substitute other machinery to carry out the main purpose of ascertaining the price in order that the agreement may be carried out.

In the present case the machinery provided for in the clause has broken down because the respondents have declined to appoint their valuer. In that sense the breakdown has been caused by their fault, in failing to implement an implied obligation to co-operate in making the machinery work. The case might be distinguishable in that respect from cases where the breakdown has occurred for some cause outside the control of either party, such as the death of an umpire, or his failure to complete the valuation by a stipulated date. But I do not rely on any such distinction. I prefer to rest my decision on the general principle that, where the machinery is not essential, if it breaks down for any reason the court will substitute its own machinery.

The appropriate means for the court to enforce the present agreements is in my opinion by ordering an inquiry into the fair value of the reversions. That was the method used in *Talbot v Talbot* [1968] Ch 1, [1967] 2 All ER 920 [option to purchase 'at a reasonable valuation' held valid by CA]. The alternative of ordering the respondents to appoint a valuer would not be suitable because in the event of the order not being obeyed, the only sanction would be imprisonment for contempt of court which would clearly be inappropriate.

For these reasons the decisions in *Agar v Macklew* (1825) 2 Sim & St 418 and *Vickers v Vickers* (1867) LR 4 Eq 529 should in my opinion be overruled.

I agree with the order proposed by my noble and learned friend, Lord Diplock, allowing this appeal.

LORD RUSSELL OF KILLOWEN (dissenting): I felt considerable sympathy for counsel for the respondents when he was told that he had all the law on his side, but was (in effect) facing the prophets. (This is a paraphrase of my own remark in argument, when he was told that he had all equity behind him and I intervened to suggest that he had less in front of him.)

In the result I would dismiss this appeal. I can only exclaim with Macduff—'What! All my pretty chickens and their dam, at one fell swoop?' (Macbeth, Act IV, Sc. 3) [4]

ii. RENT REVIEW

In **Beer v Bowden** [1981] 1 WLR 522n, [1981] 1 All ER 1070, a lease was granted in 1956 for 14 years. The rent was £1,250 for the first five years and was to be reviewed every five years thereafter, being 'such rent as shall thereupon be agreed between the landlord and the tenant'. The lease contained no machinery for fixing the rent in default of agreement. On failure to agree at the end of the first five years, the question arose as to what rent was payable. The Court of Appeal held that the rent should be a fair rent.

GOFF LJ said at 525, at 1074: '*King's Motors (Oxford) Ltd v Lax* [1970] 1 WLR 426, [1969] 3 All ER 665 ... , in my judgment, is wholly distinguishable and does not really assist at all. That was a case of an option to renew, and the exercise of the option could operate, if at all, only to create a contract. Valid contract it could not be, because an essential term—namely, the rent—was neither agreed nor ascertainable. That, in my judgment, poses an entirely different problem from that which arises where one starts with the premise that there is a subsisting lease which creates an estate in the land and with the premise that the court must imply some term, because it is conceded that rent is payable.'

BUCKLEY LJ said at 528, at 1076: 'It appears to me that the introduction by implication of a single word in the clause in the lease relating to the rent to be payable solves the problem of this case; that is, the insertion of the word " fair" between the words "such" and "rent." If some such implication is not made, it seems to me that this would be a completely inoperative rent review provision, because it is not to be expected that the tenant would agree to an increase in the rent if the rent to be agreed was absolutely at large. Clearly the parties contemplated that at the end of five years some adjustment might be necessary to make the position with regard to the rent a fair one, and the rent review provision with which we are concerned was inserted in the lease to enable such an adjustment to be made. The suggestion that upon the true construction of the clause it provides that the rent shall continue to be at the rate of £1,250 a year

---

[4] *Re Malpass* [1985] Ch 42, [1984] 2 All ER 313 (testamentary option to purchase farm 'at the agricultural value thereof determined for agricultural purposes ... as agreed with the District Valuer'; the valuer declined to act). See also *Trustees of National Deposit Friendly Society v Beatties of London Ltd* [1985] 2 EGLR 59, where GOULDING J held valid an option agreement for a new lease in favour of tenants who had carried on a business of selling model railways for 75 years 'the rent payable ... to be the greater of £33,000 per annum exclusive or such rent as may be agreed as from the architect's certificate of completion'. In rejecting claims that it was void for uncertainty in regard to the date of the commencement of the term, the amount of rent and the covenants and conditions, he said at 61: 'There has been such performance on the tenant's side as to justify the court in a much more liberal approach to the validity of the document than in the case of a purely executory option where nothing but perhaps a nominal consideration has been given on either side'; *Campbell v Edwards* [1976] 1 WLR 403, [1976] 1 All ER 785 (valuation fixed by an agreed valuer); *R & A Millett (Shops) Ltd v Leon Allan International Fashions Ltd* [1989] 1 EGLR 138 (sublease rent to be 78/85ths of head lease rent where head lease had been surrendered); *Harben Style Ltd v Rhodes Trust* [1995] 1 EGLR 118 (only landlord had power to apply to President of RCIS for appointment of third party to determine rent; on his refusal to apply, tenant not entitled to have rent determined by court); cf *Royal Bank of Scotland v Jennings* [1997] 1 EGLR 101 (where both landlord and tenant had such power); *Addin v Secretary of State for the Environment* [1997] 1 EGLR 99; *Black Country Housing Association v Shand and Shand* [1998] NPC 92 (land to be transferred at a price which reflected its use being restricted as a garden held valid).

unless the parties otherwise agree would, in my opinion, render the provision entirely inoperative, because, as I say, one could not expect the tenant voluntarily to agree to pay a higher rent.'[5]

In **Thomas Bates & Son Ltd v Wyndham's (Lingerie) Ltd** [1981] 1 WLR 505, [1981] 1 All ER 1077, a seven year lease was granted in 1970 with an option for a further lease 'of the demised premises ... at a rent to be agreed between the lessor and the lessees but in default of such agreement at a rent to be fixed by a single arbitrator appointed by the President for the time being of the Royal Institution of Chartered Surveyors.' In 1963 the option was exercised and a further lease was granted with an option in terms identical to the original lease. In 1970, when the lessees exercised the option, the lessor sought to introduce a review clause. A new lease was executed for 14 years with a review at the fifth and tenth years. By a mistake, the lease contained no provision for arbitration in default of agreement on the rent review, and merely provided that the rent during the second five years and the final four years should be 'such rents as shall have been agreed between the Lessor and the Lessees.' The lessees, though aware of the omission, did not bring it to the lessor's notice.

In proceedings for rectification, the Court of Appeal held:
  (i) the rent review clause should be rectified by inserting a reference to arbitration;
  (ii) the arbitrator should assess not the market rent but the rent which it would have been reasonable for the parties themselves to have agreed under the lease.

BUCKLEY LJ said at 519, at 1088: 'In my judgment, in default of agreement between the parties, the arbitrator would have to assess what rent it would have been reasonable for these landlords and these tenants to have agreed under this lease having regard to all the circumstances relevant to any negotiations between them of a new rent from the review date.

If I were wrong on a point of rectification, then, on construction and by a process of implication, the rent to be ascertained in default of agreement must, I think, be a fair rent as between the landlords and the tenants. It would be most unjust that the landlords should receive no rent because of failure of the parties to agree. The landlords have granted a 14-year term and the court must endeavour to fill any gap in the terms of the lease by means of a fair and reasonable implication as to what the parties must have intended their bargain to be. See in this connection the decision of this court in F & G Sykes (Wessex) Ltd v Fine Fare Ltd [1967] 1 Lloyd's Rep 53, which was a case very different on its facts from the present, but in which the court explained the function of any court of construction where parties have embarked upon any commercial relationship but under terms that are not altogether adequate to cover the eventualities. The court would ascertain by inquiry what rent the landlords and the tenants, as willing negotiators anxious to reach agreement, would arrive at for each of the two rent review periods. In short, the standard would be the same, as I see it, as would have to be adopted by an arbitrator under the clause if it is rectified in the way in which I consider that it should be rectified.'[6]

---

[5]   See *Corson v Rhuddlan Borough Council* (1989) 59 P & CR 185, p. 464, ante; *Coventry Motor Mart Ltd v Corner Coventry Ltd* [1997] NPC 48.

[6]   *Lear v Blizzard* [1983] 3 All ER 662 where there was an option to renew a lease for a further term of 21 years 'at a rent to be agreed between the parties or in default of agreement at a rent to be determined by a single arbitrator.' TUDOR EVANS J held that the rent to be determined by the arbitrator was to be a fair rent for the particular tenant and

E. Lease and Licence[7]

i. THE DISTINCTION

In the 19th century the critical issue was whether the party in question had exclusive possession of the land.[8] If a person were in exclusive possession (other than a freeholder or copyholder) he was a tenant, if not he was a licensee.[9] In the mid 20th century the emphasis shifted from the simple test of exclusive possession to that of the intention of the parties to be inferred from all the circumstances. Contrary to views expressed in many of the older cases, exclusive possession did not necessarily mean that the person in enjoyment must be a tenant and not a licensee. As SACHS LJ said in *Barnes v Barratt* [1970] 2 QB 657 at 669, [1970] 2 All ER 483 at 487: 'In this case, as always, it is necessary to give weight to the fact that exclusive possession has been given to the occupiers ... That, however, is a factor which is no longer conclusive and, indeed, appears nowadays to have diminishing weight ... The law has adapted itself so as to deal with the complexities of the Rent Acts without causing patently unintended injustice to landlords, whilst guarding against improper avoidance by the latter of the provisions of those Acts.[10]

---

the particular landlord, account being taken of all considerations which would affect the mind of either party to negotiations between them. Cf. *Ponsford v HMS Aerosols Ltd* [1979] AC 63, [1978] 2 All ER 837, where HL, by a majority of 3 to 2, applied an objective test; 'a reasonable rent for the demised premises' was construed as that which was reasonable for the premises and not what would be reasonable for the tenant to pay. See [1983] All ER Rev 239 (P. H. Pettit).

[7] C & B, pp. 386–396; Gray, pp. 353–383; M & W, paras. 14.010–14.027; MM, pp. 339–342; Smith, pp. 356–378; Megarry, *Rent Acts* (10th edn.), pp. 53–64; Martin, *Residential Security* (2nd edn, 1995), pp. 7–31; Evans and Smith, *Law of Landlord and Tenant* (6th edn, 2002), chap. 3. On the distinction between a lease and a sale, see *Paper Properties Ltd v Power Corporation plc* (1994) 69 P & CR D16 ('It is clear that at one end of the range of possibilities a letting at a rack rent for no premium cannot be a sale. At the other end the grant of a leasehold interest at a peppercorn rent for a premium of £6.5 million would be a sale.').

[8] The giving of a right of exclusive possession should be distinguished from the giving of an exclusive or sole right to use the premises for a particular purpose which has never been held to create a tenancy: *Hill v Tupper* (1863) 2 H & C 121, p. 693, post; *Wilson v Tavener* [1901] 1 Ch 578; *Clore v Theatrical Properties Ltd and Westby & Co Ltd* [1936] 3 All ER 483.

[9] In *Lynes v Snaith* [1899] 1 QB 486, LAWRENCE J said: 'As to the first question, I think it is clear [the defendant] was a tenant at will and not a licensee; for the admissions state that she was in exclusive possession, a fact which is wholly inconsistent with her having been a mere licensee'; *Allan v Liverpool Overseers* (1874) LR 9 QB 180, p. 476, post; *Glenwood Lumber Co Ltd v Phillips* [1904] AC 405, p. 475, post. Cf. *Taylor v Caldwell* (1863) 3 B & S 826, p. 476, post.

[10] The distinction is also relevant in the application of the Landlord and Tenant Act 1954 (business tenancies), p. 485, post; the duty of care owed to an occupier in respect of his chattels by a licensor but not by a landlord: *Appah v Parncliffe Investments Ltd* [1964] 1 WLR 1064, [1964] 1 All ER 838; and the warranty of suitability of premises for their intended purpose implied into a licence: *Wettern Electric Ltd v Welsh Development Agency* [1983] QB 796, [1983] 2 All ER 629; (1983) 80 LSG 2195 (H. W. Wilkinson); there is no such warranty in respect of a lease, apart from express guarantee by the landlord; the length of notice required for the termination of a licence: *Smith v Northside Developments Ltd* [1987] 2 EGLR 151; and, under FA 2003, s. 48(1) and (2) a lease is a stamp duty chargeable interest, but not a licence to use or occupy land, nor, in England and Wales or Northern Ireland, a tenancy at will. And, more importantly, a lease is enforceable against third parties as a legal estate or an equitable interest, whereas a contractual licence is not, unless the circumstances give rise to a constructive trust or proprietary estoppel: *Ashburn Anstalt v Arnold* [1989] Ch 1, [1988] 2 All ER 147, p. 618, post; for the meaning of a licence to occupy land for the purposes of value added tax, see VAT Act 1994, Sch 9 Group 1, and Bulletins of HM Customs and Excise theron. A difference was removed by *National Carriers Ltd v Panalpina Ltd* [1981] AC 675, [1981] 1 All ER 161, where HL held that the doctrine of frustration is applicable to a lease; for licences, see *Krell v Henry* [1903] 2 KB 740; C & B, pp. 503–505.

The high water-mark of this approach was seen in the line of Court of Appeal decisions which began with *Somma v Hazelhurst* [1978] 1 WLR 1014, [1978] 2 All ER 1011, in which agreements were drafted as licences and exclusive possession was denied to the occupier by the device of reserving to the licensor the right to enter upon the premises himself or to introduce other licensees. The general principle was stated by CUMMING-BRUCE LJ at 1024, at 1020: 'We can see no reason why an ordinary landlord should not be able to grant a licence to occupy an ordinary house. If that is what both he and the licensee intend and if they can frame any written agreement in such a way as to demonstrate that it is not really an agreement for a lease masquerading as a licence, we can see no reason in law or justice why they should be prevented from achieving that object.' The House of Lords Appellate Committee refused leave to appeal from the decision in *Somma v Hazelhurst*, [11] and subsequent decisions in the Court of Appeal continued to re-state the principle, even when the agreement was held to be a sham. [12]

In *Street v Mountford* [1985] AC 809, [1985] 2 All ER 289, infra, the House of Lords (in the first case to be heard there on the distinction) decisively rejected this approach. In this case there was a licence agreement, under which the occupant was given exclusive possession but had signed a statement at the end of the agreement that she accepted that it 'does not and is not intended to give me a tenancy protected under the Rent Acts'. As SLADE LJ said in the Court of Appeal (1984) 271 EG 1261 at 1262: 'It was a plain expression of the intentions of both parties that what she was being given was a licence rather than a tenancy. There is no plea by her of misrepresentation, undue influence or *non est factum* and no claim for rectification.' The House of Lords reversed the Court of Appeal and held that the agreement was a tenancy. It also disapproved of the 'sham device and artificial transaction' of *Somma v Hazlehurst* at 825, at 299.

Street v Mountford thus decides that 'where the only circumstances are that residential accommodation is offered and accepted with exclusive possession for a term at a rent, [13] the result is a tenancy [14] ... The courts will, save in exceptional

---

[11]   [1978] 2 All ER 1011 at 1025 (Lords WILBERFORCE, SALMON and FRASER OF TULLYBELTON).

[12]   Followed in *Aldrington Garages Ltd v Fielder* (1978) 247 EG 557; *Sturolson & Co v Weniz* (1984) 272 EG 326. Cf. *O'Malley v Seymour* (1978) 250 EG 1083; *Walsh v Griffiths-Jones* [1978] 2 All ER 1002, where the agreements were held to be sham. For a detailed review, see (1980) 130 NLJ 939, 959 (A. Waite).

[13]   Rent is not essential for a lease; LPA 1925, s. 205(1)(xxvii); *Ashburn Anstalt v Arnold*, [1989] Ch 1, [1988] 2 All ER 147, p. 618, post (occupier let into possession for business purposes under rent-free arrangement pending re-development; only outgoings payable during occupation; held to be a tenant); *Skipton Building Society v Clayton* (1993) 66 P & CR 223; [1983] Conv 478 (L. Crabb).

For a residential tenancy to be protected under the Rent Act 1977, the rent must be not less than two-thirds of the rateable value or, if not in money, quantifiable: *Barnes v Barratt* [1970] 2 QB 657, [1970] 2 All ER 483; *Bostock v Bryant* (1990) 61 P & CR 23 (Uncle Joe who owned a house and lived in one room paid general and water rates in respect of the whole house, and the respondents, who lived in the rest of the house, the gas and electricity likewise for the whole; CA held that, assuming the respondents were tenants, the rent was not quantifiable).

Where no rent is payable, a licence may be the more likely construction: *Barnes v Barratt*, supra; *Onyx (UK) Ltd v Beard* [1996] EGCS 55.

[14]   A simple example of the rule is *Caplan v Mardon* [1986] CLY 1873 (held in the county court that three students were joint tenants in spite of a signed agreement that nothing in it should create a tenancy). Cf. *Mehta v Royal Bank of Scotland* [1999] 3 EGLR 153 (licence even though the three hallmarks of *Street v Mountford* were present; ten other equally significant factors based on the parties' intentions and surrounding circumstances to be taken into account; no deliberate intention to exclude the Rent Acts); (1999) 3 L & TR 64.

circumstances, only be concerned to inquire whether as a result of an agreement relating to residential accommodation the occupier is a lodger or a tenant': at 827, at 300.[15] Lord TEMPLEMAN (who delivered the only speech) identified as exceptional cases those where:

> (*a*) the occupancy is within one of a number of special categories, for example,[16] 'under a contract for the sale of land,[17] or pursuant to a contract of employment or referable to the holding of an office'[18] at 827, at 300.

---

[15]   'He will be a lodger if the landlord provides attendance or services which require the landlord or his servants to have unrestricted access to the premises': *Royal Philanthropic Society v County* (1985) 276 EG 1068 at 1071, per Fox LJ; *Brillouet v Landless* [1996] 5 CL 327. But the fact that the occupier chooses not to avail himself of the attendance or services cannot convert a licence into a tenancy *Uratemp Ventures Ltd v Collins* [2002] 1 EGLR 156 at 157H per PETER GIBSON LJ. The presence or absence of cooking facilities is not relevant: *Uratemp Ventures Ltd v Collins* [2002] 1 AC 301.

[16]   The categories are 'illustrative and not exhaustive': *Dellneed Ltd v Chin* (1986) 53 P & CR 172 at 187, per MILLETT J. See *Royal Philanthropic Society v County* [1985] 2 EGLR 109, where CA rejected a number of submitted exceptional circumstances; [1986] Conv 215 (P. F. Smith); *Whitbread West Pennines Ltd v Reedy* [1988] ICR 807.

   Another possible exception is homeless persons: *Westminster City Council v Clarke* [1992] 2 AC 288, [1992] 1 All ER 695; [1992] Conv 112 (J. E. Martin), 285 (D. S. Cowan); [1992] All ER Rev 225 (P. J. Clarke) (grant of 'licence to occupy' to occupant of single room in men's hostel run by appellant council, in pursuance of its duty to house the homeless under Housing Act 1985, s. 65(2), held to be a licensee and not a secure tenant; 'a very special case which depends on the peculiar nature of the hostel maintained by the council, the use of the hostel by the council, the totality, immediacy, and objectives of the powers exercisable by the council and the immediate restrictions imposed on Mr. Clarke. The decision in this case will not allow a landlord, private or public, to free himself from the Rent Acts or from the restrictions of a secure tenancy merely by adopting or adapting the language of the licence to occupy': per Lord TEMPLEMAN at 238); *Parkins v Westminster City Council* [1998] 13 EG 145; *Bruton v London and Quadrant Housing Trust* [2000] 1 AC 456, [1999] 3 All ER 481, p. 441, ante (not a special circumstance that the Trust was a responsible landlord performing socially valuable functions). See also Housing Act 1985, s. 79(3), Sch 1, para 4 and Housing Act 1988, s. 1(6), which exclude most tenancies granted in such circumstances from statutory protection.

[17]   See *Bretherton v Paton* [1986] 1 EGLR 172, where CA interpreted this exception narrowly, in holding that a *potential* purchaser of a dwelling house who had entered into exclusive possession for a term at a rent under an arrangement with the ultimate intention of negotiating for its sale was held to be a tenant. See also *Essex Plan Ltd v Broadminster Ltd* (1988) 56 P & CR 353 (licence where occupier continued in possession after expiry of option; no exclusive possession); [1989] Conv 55 (J. E. Martin); cf. *Heslop v Burns* [1974] 1 WLR 1241, [1974] 3 All ER 406, p. 507, post, where SCARMAN LJ held that occupation prior to a contract of sale was a paradigm case of a tenancy at will; *Vandersteen v Agius* (1992) 65 P & CR 266 (occupation pursuant to sale of goodwill of osteopathy practice not an exception).

[18]   *Mayhew v Suttle* (1854) 4 E & B 347; *Smith v Seghill Overseers* (1875) LR 10 QB 422, p. 477, post. Distinguish a service occupant who is a licensee from a service tenant who is not. The latter is a person to whom a dwelling-house is let in consequence of his employment, but who is not required to live there for the better performance of his duties: *Torbett v Faulkner* [1952] 2 TLR 659. See *Royal Philanthropic Society v County*, supra; *Norris v Checksfield* [1991] 1 WLR 1241, [1991] 4 All ER 327 (semi-skilled mechanic held to be service licensee, even though he was never in a position to perform the duties required of him); *Burgoyne v Griffiths* [1991] 13 EG 164 (farm cottage); [1991] All ER Rev 214 (P. J. Clarke); *South Glamorgan County Council v Griffiths* [1992] 2 EGLR 232; *Hughes v Greenwich London Borough Council* [1994] 1 AC 170, [1993] 4 All ER 517; *Surrey County Council v Lamond* [1999] 1 EGLR 32 (employer providing facility but not imposing obligation). The occupant may also be an object of charity; *Gray v Taylor* [1998] 1 WLR 1093, [1998] 4 All ER 17 (occupant of Peterborough Almshouse held to be a licensee); [1998] 2 L & TR 40.

(b) the owner has no power to grant a tenancy. [19]

(c) the circumstances show that there is no intention to create legal relationships as, for example, 'where there has been something in the circumstances such as a family arrangement, an act of friendship or such like, to negative any intention to create a tenancy'. [20]

It would appear that the test of intention is relevant in deciding whether there is an intention to create a legal relationship, but irrelevant in deciding which legal relationship is created.

Five years later the House of Lords considered the matter further in joint appeals: *A G Securities v Vaughan* and *Antoniades v Villiers* [1990] 1 AC 417, [1988] 3 All ER 1058, pp. 486–493, post. The House followed and elaborated *Street v Mountford* in the complex area of multiple occupation.

The effect of *Street v Mountford* and the subsequent cases is to prevent a landlord from driving a coach and horses through the Rent Acts. [1] Its rejection of the relevance of the *intention* of the parties is of paramount importance; and the consequent rigidity of the test for distinguishing between a lease and a licence may have led to the overprotection of the tenant at the expense of the landlord.

The crux of the matter is that an owner of residential property is reluctant to grant a lease to a tenant which will have the consequences of rent control and of security of tenure after the end of the contractual term. A status of irremovability is particularly unattractive to an owner. The Housing Act of 1988 phased out the Rent Act 1977 by introducing the assured and the assured shorthold tenancy. Tenancies created before 15 January 1989 were not affected. The object was to

---

[19]   *Street v Mountford* [1985] AC 809 at 821, [1985] 2 All ER 289 at 300; *Camden London Borough Council v Shortlife Community Housing Ltd* (1992) 90 LGR 358 (which contains a critique on the exceptions by MILLETT J); [1993] Conv 157 (D. S. Cowan); *Bruton v London and Quadrant Housing Trust*, p. 441 ante (whittling down this exception).

[20]   *Facchini v Bryson* [1952] 1 TLR 1386 at 1389–1390, per DENNING LJ, cited in *Street v Mountford* at 821, at 296, p. 479, post; *Ramnarace v Lutchman* [2001] 1 WLR 1651, p. 508, post. See *Booker v Palmer* [1942] 2 All ER 674, p. 477, post; *Marcroft Wagons Ltd v Smith* [1951] 2 KB 496, [1951] 2 All ER 271; p. 478, post; *Heslop v Burns* [1974] 1 WLR 1241, [1974] 3 All ER 406, p. 507, post; *Sharp v McArthur* (1986) 19 HLR 364 (where owner of flat, with 'For Sale' notice board prominently displayed, let defendant into possession as a favour pending sale. Held by CA to be a licence, even though defendant had exclusive possession and was given a rent book for the purpose of enabling him to obtain payment from the D.H.S.S. for outgoings for accommodation); *Carr Gomm Society v Hawkins* [1990] CLY 2811 (self-employed gardener held to be licensee of registered charity which had 60 homes in London and a continuing need to move people if necessary); *Westminster City Council v Basson* [1991] 1 EGLR 277 (girl friend who remained in exclusive possession of flat after her boy friend's tenancy had been terminated held to be licensee, even though she had received rent rebates from the council, which had made it clear that no tenancy was intended); [1992] Conv 113 (J. E. Martin); *Colchester Borough Council v Smith* [1992] Ch 421, [1991] 2 All ER 29 (no intention to create legal relations where occupant's implied offer to pay reasonable rent was rejected, and where there was insistence on his occupation at his own risk and on his giving up possession at short notice if land required for other purposes). Cf *Nunn v Dalrymple* (1989) 59 P & CR 231; *Ward v Warnke* (1990) 22 HLR 496 (in both cases a *family* arrangement in which exclusive possession of a cottage in return for regular payments was held to be a tenancy). See also *Abbeyfield (Harpenden) Society v Woods* [1968] 1 WLR 374, [1968] 1 All ER 352n, p. 481, post; *Barnes v Barratt* [1970] 2 QB 657, [1970] 2 All ER 483 (house-sharing arrangement without rent or fixed term held to be licence).

[1]   At 819, at 294. In *Brooker Settled Estates Ltd v Ayers* [1987] 1 EGLR 50, O'CONNOR LJ said at 51: 'Lord Templeman reviewed the authorities dealing with this tortured question, and sought to introduce some order into the law for the better administration of the law and guidance of the learned judges, particularly in the county courts, who have to deal with this problem.'

provide an incentive to landlords to let premises and to ease the housing shortage in the private rented sector. The new regime preserved the basic principle of security of tenure, but the grounds of possession were strengthened and only minimal rights of succession and rent control were provided. The Housing Act 1996 reduced the rights of tenants still further, by providing that, subject to limited exceptions, future tenancies (save those outside the Act) were to take effect as assured shortholds, which offer less security than assured tenancies.

There is now less incentive for the landlord of residential property to create a licence instead of a lease. There will, however, be many cases of licences created before *Street v Mountford* which will have to be interpreted in the light of that decision.

ii. RESIDENTIAL TENANT OR LODGER

STREET v MOUNTFORD [2]
[1985] AC 809, [1985] 2 All ER 289 (HL, Lords SCARMAN, KEITH OF KINKEL, BRIDGE OF HARWICH, BRIGHTMAN and TEMPLEMAN)

LORD TEMPLEMAN: My Lords, by an agreement dated 7 March 1983, the respondent Mr Street granted the appellant Mrs Mountford the right to occupy the furnished rooms numbers 5 and 6 at 5, St. Clements Gardens, Boscombe, from 7 March 1983 for £37 per week, subject to termination by 14 days' written notice and subject to the conditions set forth in the agreement. The question raised by this appeal is whether the agreement created a tenancy or a licence.

A tenancy is a term of years absolute. This expression, by section 205(1) (xxvii) of the Law of Property Act 1925, reproducing the common law, includes a term from week to week in possession at a rent and liable to determination by notice or re-entry. Originally a term of years was not an estate in land, the lessee having merely a personal action against his lessor. But a legal estate in leaseholds was created by the Statute of Gloucester 1278 and the Act of 1529 21 Hen VIII, c 15. Now by section 1 of the Law of Property Act 1925 a term of years absolute is an estate in land capable of subsisting as a legal estate. In the present case if the agreement dated 7 March 1983 created a tenancy, Mrs Mountford having entered into possession and made weekly payments acquired a legal estate in land. If the agreement is a tenancy, the occupation of Mrs Mountford is protected by the Rent Acts.

A licence in connection with land while entitling the licensee to use the land for the purposes authorised by the licence does not create an estate in the land. If the agreement dated 7 March 1983 created a licence for Mrs Mountford to occupy the premises, she did not acquire any estate in the land. If the agreement is a licence then Mrs Mountford's right of occupation is not protected by the Rent Acts. Hence the practical importance of distinguishing between a tenancy and a licence.

In the course of argument, nearly every clause of the agreement dated 7 March 1983 was relied upon by the appellant as indicating a lease and by the respondent as indicating a licence. The agreement, in full, was in these terms:

---

[2] C & B, p. 387; [1985] All ER Rev 190 (P. J. Clarke); [1985] Conv 328 (R. Street); [1985] CLJ 351 (S. Tromans); 48 MLR 712 (S. Anderson); (1986) 130 SJ 3, 27 (P. M. Rank); [1986] Conv 39 (D. N. Clarke); [1986] Conv 344 (S. Bridge); Lewison, *Lease or Licence, The Law after Street v Mountford* (1985).

'I Mrs Wendy Mountford agree to take from the owner Roger Street the single furnished room number 5 and 6 at 5 St. Clements Gardens, Boscombe, Bournemouth, commencing 7 March 1983 at a licence fee of £37 per week.

'I understand that the right to occupy the above room is conditional on the strict observance of the following rules:

'1. No paraffin stoves, or other than the supplied form of heating, is allowed in the room.

'2. No one but the above-named person may occupy or sleep in the room without prior permission, and this personal licence is not assignable.

'3. The owner (or his agent) has the right at all times to enter the room to inspect its condition, read and collect money from meters, carry out maintenance works, install or replace furniture or for any other reasonable purpose.

'4. All rooms must be kept in a clean and tidy condition.

'5. All damage and breakages must be paid for or replaced at once. An initial deposit equivalent to 2 weeks' licence fee will be refunded on termination of the licence subject to deduction for all damage or other breakages or arrears of licence fee, or retention towards the cost of any necessary possession proceedings.

'6. No nuisance or annoyance to be caused to the other occupiers. In particular, all music played after midnight to be kept low so as not to disturb occupiers of other rooms.

'7. No children or pets allowed under any circumstances whatsoever.

'8. Prompt payment of the licence fee must be made every Monday in advance without fail.

'9. If the licence fee or any part of it shall be seven days in arrear or if the occupier shall be in breach of any of the other terms of this agreement or if (except by arrangement) the room is left vacant or unoccupied, the owner may re-enter the room and this licence shall then immediately be terminated (without prejudice to all other rights and remedies of the owner).

'10. This licence may be terminated by 14 days' written notice given to the occupier at any time by the owner or his agent, or by the same notice by the occupier to the owner or his agent.

'Occupier's signature

'Owner/agent's signature

'Date 7 March 1983

'I understand and accept that a licence in the above form does not and is not intended to give me a tenancy protected under the Rent Acts.

'Occupier's signature.'

On 12 August 1983 on Mrs Mountford's application a fair rent was registered. Mr Street then made application under section 51 (*a*) of the County Courts Act for a declaration that Mrs Mountford's occupancy was a licence and not a tenancy. The recorder in the county court held that Mrs Mountford was a tenant entitled to the protection of the Rent Acts and made a declaration accordingly. The Court of Appeal held that Mrs Mountford was a licensee not entitled to the protection of the Rent Acts. Mrs Mountford appeals.

On behalf of Mrs Mountford her counsel, Mr Hicks QC seeks to reaffirm and re-establish the traditional view that an occupier of land for a term at a rent is a tenant providing the occupier is granted exclusive possession. It is conceded on behalf of Mr Street that the agreement dated 7 March 1983 granted exclusive possession to Mrs Mountford. The traditional view that the grant of exclusive possession for a term at a rent creates a tenancy is consistent with the elevation of a tenancy into an estate in land. The tenant possessing exclusive possession is able to exercise the rights of an owner of land, which is in the real sense his land albeit temporarily and subject to certain restrictions. A tenant armed with exclusive possession can keep out strangers and keep out the landlord unless the landlord is exercising limited rights reserved to him by the tenancy agreement to enter and view and repair. A licensee lacking exclusive possession can in no sense call the land his own and cannot be said to own any estate in the land. The licence does not create an estate in the land to which it relates but only makes an act lawful which would otherwise be unlawful.

On behalf of Mr Street his counsel, Mr Goodhart QC, relies on recent authorities which, he submits, demonstrate that an occupier granted exclusive possession for a term at a rent may nevertheless be a licensee if, in the words of Slade LJ in the present case (1984) 271 EG 1261 at 1264: 'there is manifested the clear intention of both parties that the rights granted are to be merely those of a personal right of occupation and not those of a tenant.'

In the present case, it is submitted, the provisions of the agreement dated 7 March 1983 and in particular clauses 2, 4, 7 and 9 and the express declaration at the foot of the agreement manifest the clear intention of both parties that the rights granted are to be those of a personal nature and not those of a tenant.

My Lords, there is no doubt that the traditional distinction between a tenancy and a licence of land lay in the grant of land for a term at a rent with exclusive possession. In some cases it was not clear at first sight whether exclusive possession was in fact granted. For example, an owner of land could grant a licence to cut and remove standing timber. Alternatively the owner could grant a tenancy of the land with the right to cut and remove standing timber during the term of the tenancy. The grant of rights relating to standing timber therefore required careful consideration in order to decide whether the grant conferred exclusive possession of the land for a term at a rent and was therefore a tenancy or whether it merely conferred a bare licence to remove the timber.

In *Glenwood Lumber Co Ltd v Phillips* [1904] AC 405, the Crown in exercise of statutory powers 'licensed' the respondents to hold an area of land for the purpose of cutting and removing timber for the term of 21 years at an annual rent. Delivering the advice of the Judicial Committee of the Privy Council, Lord Davey said, at 408–409:

'The appellants contended that this instrument conferred only a licence to cut timber and carry it away, and did not give the respondent any right of occupation or interest in the land itself. Having regard to the provisions of the Act under the powers of which it was executed and to the language of the document itself, their Lordships cannot adopt this view of the construction or effect of it. In the so-called licence itself it is called indifferently a licence and a demise, but in the Act it is spoken of as a lease, and the holder of it is described as the lessee. It is not, however, a question of words but of substance. If the effect of the instrument is to give the holder an exclusive right of occupation of the land, though subject to certain reservations or to a restriction of the purposes for which it may be used, it is in law a demise of the land itself. By [the Act] it is enacted that the lease shall vest in the lessee the right to take and keep exclusive possession of the lands described therein subject to the conditions in the Act provided or referred to, and the lessee is empowered (amongst other things) to bring any actions or suits against any party unlawfully in possession of any land so leased, and to prosecute all trespassers thereon. The operative part and habendum in the licence is framed in apt language to carry out the intention so expressed in the Act. And their Lordships have no doubt that the effect of the so-called licence was to confer a title to the land itself on the respondent.'

This was a case in which the court after careful consideration of the purposes of the grant, the terms of the grant and the surrounding circumstances, came to the conclusion that the grant conferred exclusive possession and was therefore a tenancy.

A contrary conclusion was reached in *Taylor v Caldwell* (1863) 3 B & S 826 in which the defendant agreed to let the plaintiff have the use of the Surrey Gardens and Music Hall on four specified days giving a series of four concerts and day and night fetes at the gardens and hall on those days, and the plaintiff agreed to take the gardens, and the hall and to pay £100 for each day. Blackburn J said, at 832:

'The parties inaccurately call this a "letting," and the money to be paid a "rent," but the whole agreement is such as to show that the defendants were to retain the possession of the hall and gardens so that there was to be no demise of them, and that the contract was merely to give the plaintiffs the use of them on those days.'

That was a case where the court after considering the purpose of the grant, the terms of the grant and the surrounding circumstances came to the conclusion that the grantee was not entitled to exclusive possession but only to use the land for limited purposes and was therefore a licensee.

In the case of residential accommodation there is no difficulty in deciding whether the grant confers exclusive possession. An occupier of residential accommodation at a rent for a term is either a lodger or a tenant. [3] The occupier is a lodger if the landlord provides attendance or services which require the landlord or his servants to exercise unrestricted access to and use of the premises. [4] A lodger is entitled to live in the premises but cannot call the place his own. In *Allan v Liverpool Overseers* (1874) LR 9 QB 180 at 191–192 Blackburn J said:

'A lodger in a house, although he has the exclusive use of rooms in the house, in the sense that nobody else is to be there, and though his goods are stowed there, yet he is not in exclusive occupation in that sense, because the landlord is there for the purpose of being able, as landlords commonly do in the case of lodgings, to have his own servants to look after the house and the furniture, and has retained to himself the occupation, though he has agreed to give the exclusive enjoyment of the occupation to the lodger.'

If on the other hand residential accommodation is granted for a term at a rent with exclusive possession, the landlord providing neither attendance nor services, the grant is a tenancy; any express reservation to the landlord of limited rights to enter and view the state of the premises and to repair and maintain the premises only serves to emphasise the fact that the grantee is entitled to exclusive possession and is a tenant. In the present case it is conceded that Mrs Mountford is entitled to exclusive possession and is not a lodger. Mr Street provided neither attendance nor services and only reserved the limited rights of inspection and maintenance and the like set forth in clause 3 of the agreement. On the traditional view of the matter, Mrs Mountford not being a lodger must be a tenant.

---

[3]   'I think it wiser and safer to say that the question whether a man is a lodger, or whether he is occupying as a tenant, must depend on the circumstances of each case': *Bradley v Baylis* (1881) 8 QBD 195 at 218, per JESSEL MR.

[4]   'This does not mean that an occupier is a lodger, if and only if such attendance or services are provided: *Crancour Ltd v De Silvaesa* [1986] 1 EGLR 80 at 85, per RALPH GIBSON LJ; *Brooker Settled Estates Ltd v Ayers* (1987) 54 P & CR 165; *Huwyler v Ruddy* (1996) 72 P & CR D3 (provision of cleaning and linen once a week which entailed only twenty minutes labour held to be unrestricted access).

There can be no tenancy unless the occupier enjoys exclusive possession; but an occupier who enjoys exclusive possession is not necessarily a tenant. He may be owner in fee simple, a trespasser, a mortgagee in possession, an object of charity or a service occupier. To constitute a tenancy the occupier must be granted exclusive possession for a fixed or periodic term certain in consideration of a premium or periodical payments. The grant may be express, or may be inferred where the owner accepts weekly or other periodical payments from the occupier.

Occupation by service occupier may be eliminated. A service occupier is a servant who occupies his master's premises in order to perform his duties as a servant. In those circumstances the possession and occupation of the servant is treated as the possession and occupation of the master and the relationship of landlord and tenant is not created; see *Mayhew v Suttle* (1854) 4 E & B 347. The test is whether the servant requires the premises he occupies in order the better to perform his duties as a servant:

'Where the occupation is necessary for the performance of services, and the occupier is required to reside in the house in order to perform those services, the occupation being strictly ancillary to the performance of the duties which the occupier has to perform, the occupation is that of a servant'; per Mellor J in *Smith v Seghill Overseers* (1875) LR 10 QB 422 at 428.

The cases on which Mr Goodhart relies begin with *Booker v Palmer* [1942] 2 All ER 674. The owner of a cottage agreed to allow a friend to install an evacuee in the cottage rent free for the duration of the war. The Court of Appeal held that there was no intention on the part of the owner to enter into legal relationships with the evacuee. Lord Greene MR said at 677:

'To suggest there is an intention there to create a relationship of landlord and tenant appears to me to be quite impossible. There is one golden rule which is of very general application, namely, that the law does not impute intention to enter into legal relationships where the circumstances and the conduct of the parties negatives any intention of the kind. It seems to me that this is a clear example of the application of that rule.'

The observations of Lord Greene MR were not directed to the distinction between a contractual tenancy and a contractual licence. The conduct of the parties (not their professed intentions) indicated that they did not intend to contract at all.

In the present case, the agreement dated 7 March 1983 professed an intention by both parties to create a licence and their belief that they had in fact created a licence. It was submitted on behalf of Mr Street that the court cannot in these circumstances decide that the agreement created a tenancy without interfering with the freedom of contract enjoyed by both parties. My Lords, Mr Street enjoyed freedom to offer Mrs Mountford the right to occupy the rooms comprised in the agreement on such lawful terms as Mr Street pleased. Mrs Mountford enjoyed freedom to negotiate with Mr Street to obtain different terms. Both parties enjoyed freedom to contract or not to contract and both parties exercised that freedom by contracting on the terms set forth in the written agreement and on no other terms. But the consequences in law of the agreement, once concluded, can only be determined by consideration of the effect of the agreement. If the agreement satisfied all the requirements of a tenancy, then the agreement produced a tenancy and the parties cannot alter the effect of the agreement by insisting that they only created a licence. The manufacture of a five-pronged implement for manual digging results in a fork even if the manufacturer, unfamiliar with the English language, insists that he intended to make and has made a spade. [5]

It was also submitted that in deciding whether the agreement created a tenancy or a licence, the court should ignore the Rent Acts. If Mr Street has succeeded, where owners have failed these past 70 years, in driving a coach and horses through the Rent Acts, he must be left to enjoy the benefit of his ingenuity unless and until Parliament intervenes. I accept that the Rent Acts are irrelevant to the problem of determining the legal effect of the rights granted by the agreement. Like the professed intention of the parties, the Rent Acts cannot alter the effect of the agreement.

In *Marcroft Wagons Ltd v Smith* [1951] 2 KB 496, [1951] 2 All ER 271 the daughter of a deceased tenant who lived with her mother claimed to be a statutory tenant by succession and the landlords asserted that the daughter had no rights under the Rent Acts and was a trespasser. The landlords expressly refused to accept the daughter's claims but accepted rent from her while they were considering the position. If the landlords had decided not to apply to the court for possession but to accept the daughter as a tenant, the moneys paid by the daughter would have been treated as rent. If the landlords decided, as they did decide, to apply for possession and to prove, as they did prove, that the daughter was not a statutory tenant, the moneys paid by the daughter were treated as mesne profits. The Court of Appeal held with some hesitation that the landlords never accepted the daughter as tenant and never intended to contract with her although the landlords delayed for some six months before applying to the court for possession. Roxburgh J said, at 507, at 277:

'Generally speaking, when a person, having a sufficient estate in land, lets another into exclusive possession, a tenancy results, and there is no question of a licence. But the inference of a tenancy is not necessarily to be drawn where a person succeeds on a death to occupation of rent-controlled premises and a landlord accepts some rent while he or the occupant, or both of them, is or are considering his or their position. If this is all that happened in this case, then no tenancy would result.'

In that case, as in *Booker v Palmer* the court deduced from the conduct of the parties that they did not intend to contract at all.

Errington v Errington and Woods [1952] 1 KB 290, [1952] 1 All ER 149 concerned a contract by a father to allow his son to buy the father's house on payment of the instalments of the father's building society loan. Denning LJ referred, at 297, at 154, to the judgment of Lord Greene MR in *Booker v Palmer* [1942] 2 All ER 674 at 677 where, however, the circumstances and the conduct of the parties negatived any intention to enter into legal relationships. Denning LJ continued, at 297–298, at 154–155:

'We have had many instances lately of occupiers in exclusive possession who have been held to be not tenants, but only licensees. When a requisitioning authority allowed people into possession at a weekly rent: ... when a landlord told a tenant on his retirement that he could live in a cottage rent free for the rest of his days: ... when a landlord, on the death of the widow of a statutory tenant,

---

[5]   See *Antoniades v Villiers* [1990] 1 AC 417 at 444, [1988] 2 All ER 309 at 315, where BINGHAM LJ said: 'The House of Lords [in *Street v Mountford*] has not, I think, held that assertions in a document that it is a licence should be ignored. It has held that the true legal nature of a transaction is not to be altered by the description the parties choose to give it. A cat does not become a dog because the parties have agreed to call it a dog. But in deciding whether an animal is a cat or a dog the parties' agreement that it is a dog may not be entirely irrelevant.'

allowed her daughter to remain in possession, paying rent for six months: *Marcroft Wagons Ltd v Smith* [1951] 2 KB 496; when the owner of a shop allowed the manager to live in a flat above the shop, but did not require him to do so, and the value of the flat was taken into account at £1 a week in fixing his wages: ... in each of those cases the occupier was held to be a licensee and not a tenant. ... The result of all these cases is that, although a person who is let into exclusive possession is prima facie to be considered a tenant, nevertheless he will not be held to be so if the circumstances negative any intention to create a tenancy. Words alone may not suffice. Parties cannot turn a tenancy into a licence merely by calling it one. But if the circumstances and the conduct of the parties show that all that was intended was that the occupier should be granted a personal privilege, with no interest in the land, he will be held to be a licensee only.'

In *Errington v Errington and Woods* and in the cases cited by Denning LJ at 297, at 154 there were exceptional circumstances which negatived the prima facie intention to create a tenancy, notwithstanding that the occupier enjoyed exclusive occupation. The intention to create a tenancy was negatived if the parties did not intend to enter into legal relationships at all, or where the relationship between the parties was that of vendor and purchaser, master and service occupier, or where the owner, a requisitioning authority, had no power to grant a tenancy. These exceptional circumstances are not to be found in the present case where there has been the lawful, independent and voluntary grant of exclusive possession for a term at a rent.

If the observations of Denning LJ are applied to the facts of the present case it may fairly be said that the circumstances negative any intention to create a mere licence. Words alone do not suffice. Parties cannot turn a tenancy into a licence merely by calling it one. The circumstances and the conduct of the parties show that what was intended was that the occupier should be granted exclusive possession at a rent for a term with a corresponding interest in the land which created a tenancy.

In *Cobb v Lane* [1952] 1 TLR 1037, [1952] 1 All ER 1199, an owner allowed her brother to occupy a house rent free. The county court judge, who was upheld by the Court of Appeal, held that there was no intention to create any legal relationship and that a tenancy at will was not to be implied. This is another example of conduct which negatives any intention of entering into a contract, and does not assist in distinguishing a contractual tenancy from a contractual licence.

In *Facchini v Bryson* [1952] 1 TLR 1386, an employer and his assistant entered into an agreement which, inter alia, allowed the assistant to occupy a house for a weekly payment on terms which conferred exclusive possession. The assistant did not occupy the house for the better performance of his duty and was not therefore a service occupier. The agreement stipulated that 'nothing in this agreement shall be construed to create a tenancy between the employer and the assistant.' Somervell LJ said, at 1389:

'If, looking at the operative clauses in the agreement, one comes to the conclusion that the rights of the occupier, to use a neutral word, are those of a lessee, the parties cannot turn it into a licence by saying at the end "this is deemed to be a licence;" nor can they, if the operative paragraphs show that it is merely a licence, say that it should be deemed to be a lease.'

Denning LJ referred to several cases including *Errington v Errington and Woods* and *Cobb v Lane* and said, at 1389–1390:

'In all the cases where an occupier has been held to be a licensee there has been something in the circumstances, such as a family arrangement, an act of friendship or generosity, or such like, to negative any intention to create a tenancy. … In the present case, however, there are no special circumstances. It is a simple case where the employer let a man into occupation of a house in consequence of his employment at a weekly sum payable by him. The occupation has all the features of a service tenancy, and the parties cannot by the mere words of their contract turn it into something else. Their relationship is determined by the law and not by the label which they choose to put on it: …'

The decision, which was thereafter binding on the Court of Appeal and on all lower courts, referred to the special circumstances which are capable of negativing an intention to create a tenancy and reaffirmed the principle that the professed intentions of the parties are irrelevant. The decision also indicated that in a simple case a grant of exclusive possession of residential accommodation for a weekly sum creates a tenancy.

In *Murray, Bull & Co Ltd v Murray* [1953] 1 QB 211, [1952] 2 All ER 1079 a contractual tenant held over, paying rent quarterly. McNair J found at 217, at 1082:

'both parties intended that the relationship should be that of licence and no more … The primary consideration on both sides was that the defendant, as occupant of the flat, should not be a controlled tenant.'

In my opinion this case was wrongly decided. McNair J citing the observations of Denning LJ in *Errington v Errington and Woods* [1952] 1 KB 290 at 297, [1952] 1 All ER 149 at 154–155 and *Marcroft Wagons Ltd v Smith* [1951] 2 KB 496, [1951] 2 All ER 271 failed to distinguish between first, conduct which negatives an intention to create legal relationships, secondly, special circumstances which prevent exclusive occupation from creating a tenancy and thirdly, the professed intention of the parties. In *Murray, Bull & Co Ltd v Murray* the conduct of the parties showed an intention to contract and there were no relevant special circumstances. The tenant holding over continued by agreement to enjoy exclusive possession and to pay a rent for a term certain. In those circumstances he continued to be a tenant notwithstanding the professed intention of the parties to create a licence and their desire to avoid a controlled tenancy.

In *Addiscombe Garden Estates Ltd v Crabbe* [1958] 1 QB 513, [1957] 3 All ER 563, the Court of Appeal considered an agreement relating to a tennis club carried on in the grounds of a hotel. The agreement was:

'described by the parties as a licence … the draftsman has studiously and successfully avoided the use either of the word "landlord" or the word "tenant" throughout the document' per Jenkins LJ at 522, at 567.

On analysis of the whole of the agreement the Court of Appeal came to the conclusion that the agreement conferred exclusive possession and thus created a tenancy. Jenkins LJ said, at 522, at 565:

'The whole of the document must be looked at; and if, after it has been examined, the right conclusion appears to be that, whatever label may have been attached to it, it in fact conferred and imposed on the grantee in substance the rights and obligations of a tenant, and on the grantor in substance the rights and obligations of a landlord, then it must be given the appropriate effect, that is to say, it must be treated as a tenancy agreement as distinct from a mere licence.'

In the agreement in the *Addiscombe* case it was by no means clear until the whole of the document had been narrowly examined that exclusive possession was granted by the agreement. In the present case it is clear that exclusive possession was granted and so much is conceded. In these circumstances it is unnecessary to analyse minutely the detailed rights and obligations contained in the agreement.

In the *Addiscombe* case Jenkins LJ referred, at 528, at 571, to the observations of Denning LJ in *Errington and Errington and Woods* to the effect that 'The test of exclusive possession is by no means decisive.' Jenkins LJ continued:

'I think that wide statement must be treated as qualified by his observations in *Facchini v Bryson* [1952] 1 TLR 1386 at 1389; and it seems to me that, save in exceptional cases of the kind mentioned by Denning LJ in that case, the law remains that the fact of exclusive possession, if not decisive against the view that there is a mere licence, as distinct from a tenancy, is at all events a consideration of the first importance.'

Exclusive possession is of first importance in considering whether an occupier is a tenant; exclusive possession is not decisive because an occupier who enjoys exclusive possession is not necessarily a tenant. The occupier may be a lodger or service occupier or fall within the other exceptional categories mentioned by Denning LJ in *Errington v Errington and Woods*.

In *Isaac v Hotel de Paris Ltd* [1960] 1 WLR 239, [1960] 1 All ER 348 an employee who managed a night bar in a hotel for his employer company which held a lease of the hotel negotiated 'subject to contract' to complete the purchase of shares in the company and to be allowed to run the nightclub for his own benefit if he paid the head rent payable by the company for the hotel. In the expectation that the negotiations 'subject to contract' would ripen into a binding agreement, the employee was allowed to run the nightclub and he paid the company's rent. When negotiations broke down the employee claimed unsuccessfully to be a tenant of the hotel company. The circumstances in which the employee was allowed to occupy the premises showed that the hotel company never intended to accept him as a tenant and that he was fully aware of that fact. This was a case, consistent with the authorities cited by Lord Denning in giving the advice of the Judicial Committee of the Privy Council, in which the parties did not intend to enter into contractual relationships unless and until the negotiations 'subject to contract' were replaced by a binding contract.

In *Abbeyfield (Harpenden) Society Ltd v Woods* [1968] 1 WLR 374, [1968] 1 All ER 352n the occupier of a room in an old people's home was held to be a licensee and not a tenant. Lord Denning MR said, at 376, at 353:

'The modern cases show that a man may be a licensee even though he has exclusive possession, even though the word "rent" is used, and even though the word "tenancy" is used. The court must look at the agreement as a whole and see whether a tenancy really was intended. In this case there is, besides the one room, the provision of services, meals, a resident housekeeper, and such like. The whole arrangement was so personal in nature that the proper inference is that he was a licensee.'

As I understand the decision in the *Abbeyfield* case the court came to the conclusion that the occupier was a lodger and was therefore a licensee not a tenant.

In *Shell-Mex and BP Ltd v Manchester Garages Ltd* [1971] 1 WLR 612, [1971] 1 All ER 841 the Court of Appeal after carefully examining an agreement whereby the defendant was allowed to use a petrol company's filling station for the purposes of selling petrol, came to the conclusion that the agreement did not grant exclusive possession to the defendant who was therefore a licensee. [6] At

---

[6]   *Esso Petroleum Co Ltd v Fumegrange Ltd* [1994] 2 EGLR 90 (three year "partnership licence" agreement, which reserved control to licensor over physical layout of premises and way in which the business was run held to be licence).

615, at 843 Lord Denning MR in considering whether the transaction was a licence or a tenancy said:

'Broadly speaking, we have to see whether it is a personal privilege given to a person (in which case it is a licence), or whether it grants an interest in land (in which case it is a tenancy). At one time it used to be thought that exclusive possession was a decisive factor. But that is not so. It depends on broader considerations altogether. Primarily on whether it is personal in its nature or not: see *Errington v Errington and Woods.*'

In my opinion the agreement was only 'personal in its nature' and created 'a personal privilege' if the agreement did not confer the right to exclusive possession of the filling station. No other test for distinguishing between a contractual tenancy and a contractual licence appears to be understandable or workable.

Heslop v Burns [1974] 1 WLR 1241, [1974] 3 All ER 406 was another case in which the owner of a cottage allowed a family to live in the cottage rent free and it was held that no tenancy at will had been created on the ground that the parties did not intend any legal relationship. Scarman LJ cited with approval, at 1252, at 415, the statement by Denning LJ in *Facchini v Bryson* [1952] 1 TLR 1386, at 1389:

'In all the cases where an occupier has been held to be a licensee there has been something in the circumstances, such as a family arrangement, an act of friendship or generosity, or such like, to negative any intention to create a tenancy.'

In *Marchant v Charters* [1977] 1 WLR 1181, [1977] 3 All ER 918, a bedsitting room was occupied on terms that the landlord cleaned the rooms daily and provided clean linen each week. It was held by the Court of Appeal that the occupier was a licensee and not a tenant. The decision in the case is sustainable on the grounds that the occupier was a lodger and did not enjoy exclusive possession. But Lord Denning MR said, at 1185, at 922:

'What is the test to see whether the occupier of one room in a house is a tenant or a licensee? It does not depend on whether he or she has exclusive possession or not. It does not depend on whether the room is furnished or not. It does not depend on whether the occupation is permanent or temporary. It does not depend on the label which the parties put upon it. All these are factors which may influence the decision but none of them is conclusive. All the circumstances have to be worked out. Eventually the answer depends on the nature and quality of the occupancy. Was it intended that the occupier should have a stake in the room or did he have only permission for himself personally to occupy the room, whether under a contract or not? In which case he is a licensee.'

But in my opinion in order to ascertain the nature and quality of the occupancy and to see whether the occupier has or has not a stake in the room or only permission for himself personally to occupy, the court must decide whether upon its true construction the agreement confers on the occupier exclusive possession. If exclusive possession at a rent for a term does not constitute a tenancy then the distinction between a contractual tenancy and a contractual licence of land becomes wholly unidentifiable.

In *Somma v Hazlehurst* [1978] 1 WLR 1014, [1978] 2 All ER 1011, a young unmarried couple H. and S. occupied a double bedsitting room for which they paid a weekly rent. The landlord did not provide services or attendance and the couple were not lodgers but tenants enjoying exclusive possession. But the Court of Appeal did not ask themselves whether H. and S. were lodgers or tenants and did not draw the correct conclusion from the fact that H. and S. enjoyed exclusive possession. The Court of Appeal were diverted from the correct inquiries by the fact that the landlord obliged H. and S. to enter into separate agreements and reserved power to determine each agreement separately. The landlord also insisted that the room should not in form be let to either H. or S. or to both H. and S. but that each should sign an agreement to share the room in common with such other persons as the landlord might from time to time nominate. The sham nature of this obligation would have been only slightly more obvious if H. and S. had been married or if the room had been furnished with a double bed instead of two single beds. If the landlord had served notice on H. to leave and had required S. to share the room with a strange man, the notice would only have been a disguised notice to quit on both H. and S. The room was let and taken as residential accommodation with exclusive possession in order that H. and S. might live together in undisturbed quasi-connubial bliss making weekly payments. The agreements signed by H. and S. constituted the grant to H. and S. jointly of exclusive possession at a rent for a term for the purposes for which the room was taken and the agreement therefore created a tenancy. Although the Rent Acts must not be allowed to alter or influence the construction of an agreement, the court should, in my opinion, be astute to detect and frustrate sham devices and artificial transactions [7] whose only object is to disguise the grant of a tenancy and to evade the Rent Acts. I would disapprove of the decision in this case that H. and S. were only licensees and for the same reason would disapprove of the decision in *Aldrington Garages Ltd v Fielder* (1978) 37 P & CR 461 and *Sturolson & Co v Weniz* (1984) 272 EG 326.

In the present case the Court of Appeal, 271 EG 1261 held that the agreement dated 7 March 1983 only created a licence. Slade LJ at 1262 accepted that the agreement and in particular clause 3 of the agreement 'shows that the right to occupy the premises conferred on the defendant was intended as an exclusive right of occupation, in that it was thought necessary to give a special and express power to the plaintiff to enter. ...' Before your Lordships it was conceded that the agreement conferred the right of exclusive possession on Mrs Mountford. Even without clause 3 the result would have been the same. By the agreement Mrs Mountford was granted the right to occupy residential accommodation. The landlord did not provide any services or attendance. It was plain that Mrs Mountford was not a lodger. Slade LJ proceeded to analyse all the provisions of the agreement, not for the purpose of deciding whether his finding of exclusive possession was correct, but for the purpose of assigning some of the provisions of the agreement to the category of terms which he thought are usually to be found in a tenancy agreement and of assigning other provisions to the category of terms which he thought are usually to be found in a licence. Slade LJ may or may not have been right that in a letting of a furnished room it was 'most unusual to find a provision in a tenancy agreement obliging the tenant to keep his rooms in a "tidy condition" ': at 1262. If Slade LJ was right about this and other provisions there is still no logical method of evaluating the results of his survey. Slade LJ reached the conclusion that 'the agreement bears all the hallmarks of a licence, rather than a tenancy, save for the one important feature of exclusive occupation': at 1262. But in addition to the hallmark of exclusive occupation of residential accommodation there were the hallmarks of weekly payments for a periodical

---

[7]   'It would have been more accurate and less liable to give rise to misunderstandings if I had substituted the word "pretence" for the references to "sham devices" and "artificial transactions"; *AG Securities v Vaughan* [1990] 1 AC 417 at 462, [1988] 3 All ER 1058 at 1067, per Lord TEMPLEMAN, p. 488, post. See also *Stribling v Wickham* [1989] 2 EGLR 35 at 38, per Sir Denys BUCKLEY, p. 493, post.

term. Unless these three hallmarks are decisive, it really becomes impossible to distinguish a contractual tenancy from a contractual licence save by reference to the professed intention of the parties or by the judge awarding marks for drafting. Slade LJ was finally impressed by the statement at the foot of the agreement by Mrs Mountford 'I understand and accept that a licence in the above form does not and is not intended to give me a tenancy protected under the Rent Acts.' Slade LJ said, at 1262:

'it seems to me that if the defendant is to displace the express statement of intention embodied in the declaration, she must show that the declaration was either a deliberate sham or at least an inaccurate statement of what was the true substance of the real transaction agreed between the parties; …'

My Lords, the only intention which is relevant is the intention demonstrated by the agreement to grant exclusive possession for a term at a rent. Sometimes it may be difficult to discover whether, on the true construction of an agreement, exclusive possession is conferred. [8] Sometimes it may appear from the surrounding circumstances that there was no intention to create legal relationships. Sometimes it may appear from the surrounding circumstances that the right to exclusive possession is referable to a legal relationship other than a tenancy. Legal relationships to which the grant of exclusive possession might be referable and which would or might negative the grant of an estate or interest in the land include occupancy under a contract for the sale of the land, occupancy pursuant to a contract of employment or occupancy referable to the holding of an office. But where as in the present case the only circumstances are that residential accommodation is offered and accepted with exclusive possession for a term at a rent, the result is a tenancy.

The position was well summarised by Windeyer J sitting in the High Court of Australia in *Radaich v Smith* (1959) 101 CLR 209 at 222, where he said:

'What then is the fundamental right which a tenant has that distinguishes his position from that of a licensee? It is an interest in land as distinct from a personal permission to enter the land and use it for some stipulated purpose or purposes. And how is it to be ascertained whether such an interest in land has been given? By seeing whether the grantee was given a legal right of exclusive possession of the land for a term or from year to year or for a life or lives. If he was, he is a tenant. And he cannot be other than a tenant, because a legal right of exclusive possession is a tenancy and the creation of such a right is a demise. To say that a man who has, by agreement with a landlord, a right of exclusive possession of land for a term is not a tenant is simply to contradict the first proposition by the second. A right of exclusive possession is secured by the right of a lessee to maintain ejectment and, after his entry, trespass. A reservation to the landlord, either by contract or statute, of a limited right of entry, as for example to view or repair, is, of course, not inconsistent with the grant of exclusive possession. Subject to such reservations, a tenant for a term or from year to year or for a life or lives can exclude his landlord as well as strangers from the demised premises. All this is long established law: see *Cole on Ejectment* (1857) pp. 72, 73, 287, 458.'

---

[8]   See *Appah v Parncliffe Investments Ltd* [1964] 1 WLR 1064, [1964] 1 All ER 838; *University of Reading v Johnson-Houghton* (1985) 276 EG 1353; *Wigan Borough Council v Green & Son (Wigan) Ltd* [1985] 2 EGLR 242.

My Lords, I gratefully adopt the logic and the language of Windeyer J. Henceforth the courts which deal with these problems will, save in exceptional circumstances, only be concerned to inquire whether as a result of an agreement relating to residential accommodation the occupier is a lodger or a tenant. In the present case I am satisfied that Mrs Mountford is a tenant, that the appeal should be allowed, that the order of the Court of Appeal should be set aside and that the respondent should be ordered to pay the costs of the appellant here and below.[9]

iii. BUSINESS TENANT OR LICENSEE

The decision in *Street v Mountford,* which related to residential accommodation, has been applied to business tenancies not only where the three indicia of exclusive possession and payment of rent for a term are present, but even where the indicium of rent is lacking.[10]

In **Dresden Estates Ltd v Collinson** [1987] 1 EGLR 45,[11] where 'an unusual provision' in a licence agreement reserved to the licensor of an industrial unit the right to relocate the licensee to an adjoining unit, the Court of Appeal held that this effectively deprived the licensee of the right to exclusive possession. GLIDEWELL LJ said at 47:

'*Street v Mountford* was concerned with residential premises. Mr. Coveney conceded that there was no material difference, at least for present purposes, between the law applicable to residential premises and the law applicable to business premises. As a broad, general proposition that may be right, but I am not sure that his concession may not have gone too far in this respect, that the attributes of residential premises and business premises are often quite different.'

And LLOYD LJ said at 55:

'I would only add, like my Lord, that our decision today should not be regarded as providing a way round the decision of the House of Lords in *Street v Mountford.* It will only be in a limited class of case that a provision, such as is found in clause 4(b), would be appropriate. If it is included in an agreement where it is not appropriate, then it will not carry the day.'

---

[9]   'The original rent of £37 per week was a compromise between Mr Street's suggestion for £39 and Mrs Mountford's suggestion for £35. The rent officer then fixed a "fair" rent of £14. Costs as claimed (but not yet taxed) at the county court, Court of Appeal and House of Lords amount to some £40,000. Meanwhile, Mrs Mountford has vacated in return for a cash sum of £1,800. This can, in effect, be deducted from the £2,410 rent she paid whilst occupying the flat for 2½ years.' (1985) 129 SJ 852 in a letter from G. Cutting, Chairman, Small Landlords Association.

For a check-list of the points raised by Lord TEMPLEMAN, see *Crancour Ltd v De Silvaesa* [1986] 1 EGLR 80 at 88; (1987) 50 MLR 226 (A. J. Waite).

[10]   *Ashburn Anstalt v Arnold* [1989] Ch 1, [1985] 2 All ER 147, p. 618, post. 'We are unable to read Lord Templeman's speech in *Street v Mountford* as laying down a principle of "no rent, no lease",' per Fox LJ at 9, at 154.

[11]   [1987] Conv 220 (P. F. Smith); (1987) 50 MLR 655 (S. Bridge).

In **London and Associated Investment Trust plc v Calow** (1986) 53 P & CR
340, Judge Paul Baker QC said at 352:
'Certainly it seems to me that self-contained business offices stand in the same
case as do residential properties. Lord Templeman mentioned residence
because that was the actual case that he was dealing with there. It was not meant
to lay down a separate doctrine for residential properties as opposed to business
properties. There might be special cases of some sort of trading properties, areas
in shops and so forth, or stalls in markets, and there might be difficulties with
agricultural properties, where licences are frequent, but I cannot see
differentiation for this purpose between a residence on the one hand and a
solicitor's office on the other.'[12]

iv. MULTIPLE OCCUPATION. SHAM DEVICES OR PRETENCE[13]

Before 1985 some landlords drafted occupation agreements in terms designed
to ensure that the premises were occupied under a licence and not under a
tenancy. Their object was to avoid the application of the Rent Acts. A simple device
was to deny the occupant the right to exclusive possession of the premises by
incorporating a term that their use was 'to be in common with the licensor and
such other licensees as the licensor may permit from time to time to use the said

---

[12]   [1987] Conv 137 (S. Bridge); *Dellneed Ltd v Chin* (1986) 53 P & CR 172 (Mai Toi
        agreement); [1987] Conv 298 (S. Bridge); cf *Smith v Northside Developments Ltd* [1987] 2
        EGLR 151 (*oral* agreement where occupier said that he 'would take unit 17 on my own'
        held not to be grant of exclusive possession). See also *Bracey v Read* [1962] 3 All ER 472
        at 475, per CROSS J; *University of Reading v Johnson-Houghton* (1985) 276 EG 1353 (grant of
        right to 'gallop' for racehorses at Blewbury in Berkshire' held to be a lease on the balance
        of probabilities ... despite its title ('licence') and much of its language, per LEONARD J at
        1356; [1986] Conv 275 (C. P. Rodgers); *Wigan Borough Council v Green & Son (Wigan) Ltd*
        [1985] 2 EGLR 242 ('permission to use exclusively' stalls in covered market for 'a very
        substantial butcher's shop' held to be tenancy); *Essex Plan Ltd v Broadminster Ltd* (1988)
        56 P & CR 353; *McCarthy v Bence* [1990] 1 EGLR 1 (joint venture in form of sharing milk
        arrangement held to be licence for purposes of s. 2(2)(*b*) of the Agricultural Holdings
        Act 1986; agreement would not involve "exclusive occupation", and area of land and fields
        available for licensee's cows might be altered from time to time by the licensor, who also
        enjoyed access for several purposes such as the exercise of sporting rights, felling dead
        elm trees, hedging and ditching and "walking with his dog, taking his thistle spud in the
        thistle season to pull out thistles or doing any other minor tidying up that caught his
        eye" [1991] Conv 58 (C. Rodgers), 207 (M. Slater)); *Graysim Holdings Ltd v P & O Property
        Holdings Ltd* [1994] 1 WLR 992, [1994] 3 All ER 897 (stallholder in covered market at
        Wallasey held to be tenant); *Hunts Refuse Disposals v Norfolk Environmental Waste Services
        Ltd* [1997] 03 EG 139 (agreement giving waste disposal firm access to part of active quarry
        for 21 years for disposal of waste on payment held to be licence); *Venus Investment Ltd v
        Stocktop Ltd* [1996] EGCS 173 (vendor of garage permitted to remain after completion
        under written agreement intended to create licence and not lease held to be licensee);
        National Car Parks Ltd v Trinity Development Co (Banbury) Ltd [2001] 2 EGLR 43 (agreement
        to operate shoppers' car park held to be licence because grantee had no right to exclude
        grantor), following *Esso Petroleum Co Ltd v Fumegrange Ltd* [1994] 2 EGLR 90 p. 481, n. 6,
        ante [2001] Conv 348 (M. Haley)..
[13]   P 483, n. 7, ante. See *Snook v London and West Riding Investments Ltd* [1967] 1 All ER 518
        at 528, where DIPLOCK LJ defines 'this popular and pejorative word': 'If it has any meaning
        in law, it means acts done or documents executed by the parties to the "sham" which are
        intended by them to give to third parties or to the court the appearance of creating
        between the parties legal rights and obligations different from the actual legal rights
        and obligations (if any) which the parties intend to create.'
            Cf the similar approach in the House of Lords to tax avoidance schemes which involve
        'a pre-ordained series of transactions (whether or not they include the achievement of
        a legitimate commercial end) into which there are inserted steps which have no

rooms'. This term was upheld by the Court of Appeal in *Somma v Hazlehurst* [1978] 1 WLR 1014, [1978] 2 All ER 1011, p. 470, ante. A further green light was given when the Appellate Committee of the House of Lords refused leave to appeal: [1978] 2 All ER 1011 at 1025.

As we have seen, the House of Lords in *Street v Mountford* [1985] AC 809 [1985] 2 All ER 289, p.473, ante, strongly disapproved of *Somma v Hazelhurst*, and in two cases in 1990 reversed it as being a mere pretence and inconsistent with the Rent Acts,[14] *AG Securities v Vaughan* and *Antoniades v Villiers* [1990] 1 AC 417, [1988] 3 All ER 1058, infra, which were heard simultaneously.[15] Both concerned separate flat-sharing agreements, both were described as 'licences', and both denied exclusive possession (in terms drafted before *Street v Mountford*). In both cases the House of Lords reversed the Court of Appeal, holding that in the first there was a licence, and in the second a joint tenancy.

In **AG Securities v Vaughan** four young men signed separate agreements on different dates with different amounts of payment. The documents were described as licences, denied exclusive possession of any part and required the occupier to share with not more than three other persons. When there was a change, there was a pecking order for the best rooms. The House of Lords held that the four occupiers were individual licensees, and not joint tenants. The differences of date and payment made it impossible for the four unities (of possession, interest, time and title) of a joint tenancy to exist.[16] As Lord BRIDGE OF HARWICH said at 454, at 1061:

---

commercial purpose apart from the avoidance of a liability to tax which in the absence of those particular steps would have been payable': *IRC v Burmah Oil Co Ltd* [1982] STC 30 at 32, per Lord DIPLOCK. See also *WT Ramsay Ltd v IRC* [1982] AC 300, [1981] 1 All ER 865; *Furniss v Dawson* [1984] AC 474, [1984] 1 All ER 530; *Craven v White* [1989] AC 398, [1988] 3 All ER 495; *Hatton v IRC* [1992] STC 140; *IRC v Fitzwilliam* [1993] 1 WLR 1189; *IRC v McGuckian* [1997] 1 WLR 991, [1997] 3 All ER 817; *MacNiven v Westmoreland Investments Ltd* [2001] 2 WLR 377, [2001] 1 All ER 865. See M & B, *Trusts and Trustees* (6th edn, 2002), pp. 613–621. See also *Gisborne v Burton* [1989] QB 390, [1988] 3 All ER 760, where CA invoked the tax doctrine to strike down a scheme to deny a sub-tenant the protection of the Agricultural Holdings Act 1948, s. 24(1); cf. *Barrett v Morgan* [2000] 2 AC 264, [2000] 1 All ER 481; [2000] CLJ 251 (L. Tee); *Hilton v Plustitle Ltd* [1989] 1 WLR 149, [1988] 3 All ER 1051 (company let scheme held not to be a sham because the company tenant, rather than the occupier, performed all the obligations under the tenancy); distinguished in *Bankway Properties Ltd v Pensfold-Dunsford* [2001] EWCA Civ 528, [2001] 1 WLR 1369; [2001] CLJ 146 (S. Bright); *Kaye v Massbetter Ltd* (1990) 62 P & CR 558 (letting to limited company tenant with a view to excluding the Rent Acts held to be genuine); [1992] Conv 58 (P. Luther); *Estavest Investments Ltd v Commercial Express Travel Ltd* [1988] 2 EGLR 91: [1991] 11 OJLS 136 (S. Bright); *Belvedere Court Management v Frogmore Developments Ltd* [1997] QB 858, [1996] 1 All ER 312. See also the 1986 Blundell Memorial Lecture, summarised at (1986) 83 LSG 3736 (K. Lewison); (1987) 84 LSG 403 (P. Freedman) (2001) 117 LQR 575 (Lord TEMPLEMAN); Getzler, ed., *Rationalizing Property, Equity and Trusts*; chap. 7 (Lord TEMPLEMAN); chap. 8 (B. McFarlane and E. Simpson).

[14] *Aldrington Garages Ltd v Fielder* (1978) 37 P & CR 461, *Sturolson v Weniz* (1984) 272 EG 326, and *Hadjiloucus v Crean* [1988] 1 WLR 1006, [1987] 3 All ER 1008 were also reversed.
[15] [1989] CLJ 19 (C. Harpum); (1989) 105 LQR 165 (P. V. Baker); (1989) Conv 128 (P. F. Smith); (1989) 52 MLR 408 (J. Hill); [1988] All ER Rev 171 (P. J. Clarke).
[16] On the four unities, see C & B, pp. 242–243; Gray, pp. 830–833; M & W, paras. 9.004–9.008; MM, pp. 304–306.

'The arrangement seems to have been a sensible and realistic one to provide accommodation for a shifting population of individuals who were genuinely prepared to share the flat with others introduced from time to time who would, at least initially, be strangers to them. There was no artificiality in the contracts concluded to give effect to this arrangement.'

In **Antoniades v Villiers** there were two separate agreements based on the *Somma v Hazelhurst* precedent. They were entered into by a man and a woman who wished to live together in a small flat in undisturbed quasi-connubial bliss. [17] They chose a double rather than a single bed. They were to use the flat in common with the owner or other licensees permitted by him. Unlike *AG Securities v Vaughan*, 'the two agreements were interdependent, not independent of one another. Both would have been signed or neither. The two agreements must therefore be read together' (per Lord TEMPLEMAN at 460, at 1066). The sharing term was 'contrary to the provisions of the Rent Acts and, in addition was, in the circumstances, a pretence intended only to get round the Rent Acts.'

AG SECURITIES v VAUGHAN
ANTONIADES v VILLIERS

[1990] 1 AC 417, [1988] 3 All ER 1058 (Lords BRIDGE OF HARWICH, TEMPLEMAN, ACKNER, OLIVER OF AYLMERTON and JAUNCEY OF TULLICHETTLE)

LORD TEMPLEMAN: My Lords, ever since 1915 the Rent Acts have protected some tenants of residential accommodation with security of tenure and maximum rents. The scope and effect of the Rent Acts have been altered from time to time and the current legislative protection is contained in the Rent Act 1977. Section 1 of the Act of 1977, reproducing earlier enactments, provides:

'Subject to this Part of this Act, a tenancy under which a dwelling-house (which may be a house or part of a house) is let as a separate dwelling is a protected tenancy for the purposes of this Act.'

Parties to an agreement cannot contract out of the Rent Acts; if they were able to do so the Acts would be a dead letter because in a state of housing shortage a person seeking residential accommodation may agree to anything to obtain shelter. The Rent Acts protect a tenant but they do not protect a licensee. Since parties to an agreement cannot contract out of the Rent Acts, a document which expresses the intention genuine or bogus of both parties or of one party to create a licence will nevertheless create a tenancy if the rights and obligations enjoyed and imposed satisfy the legal requirements of a tenancy. A person seeking residential accommodation may concur in any expression of intention in order to obtain shelter. Since parties to an agreement cannot contract out of the Rent Acts, a document expressed in the language of a licence must nevertheless be examined and construed by the court in order to decide whether the rights and obligations enjoyed and imposed create a licence or a tenancy. A person seeking residential accommodation may sign a document couched in any language in order to obtain shelter. Since parties to an agreement cannot contract out of the

---

[17]   *Street v Mountford* [1985] AC 809 at 825, [1985] 2 All ER 289 at 299, per Lord TEMPLEMAN.

Rent Acts, the grant of a tenancy to two persons jointly cannot be concealed, accidentally or by design, by the creation of two documents in the form of licences. Two persons seeking residential accommodation may sign any number of documents in order to obtain joint shelter. In considering one or more documents for the purpose of deciding whether a tenancy has been created, the court must consider the surrounding circumstances including any relationship between the prospective occupiers, the course of negotiations and the nature and extent of the accommodation and the intended and actual mode of occupation of the accommodation. If the owner of a one-bedroomed flat granted a licence to a husband to occupy the flat provided he shared the flat with his wife and nobody else and granted a similar licence to the wife provided she shared the flat with the husband and nobody else, the court would be bound to consider the effect of both documents together. If the licence to the husband required him to pay a licence fee of £50 per month and the licence to the wife required her to pay a further licence fee of £50 per month, the two documents read together in the light of the property to be occupied and the obvious intended mode of occupation would confer exclusive occupation on the husband and wife jointly and a tenancy at the rent of £100.

Landlords dislike the Rent Acts and wish to enjoy the benefits of letting property without the burden of the restrictions imposed by the Acts. Landlords believe that the Rent Acts unfairly interfere with freedom of contract and exacerbate the housing shortage. Tenants on the other hand believe that the Acts are a necessary protection against the exploitation of people who do not own the freehold or long leases of their homes. The court lacks the knowledge and the power to form any judgment on these arguments which fall to be considered and determined by Parliament. The duty of the court is to enforce the Acts and in so doing to observe one principle which is inherent in the Acts and has been long recognised, the principle that parties cannot contract out of the Acts.

LORD OLIVER OF AYLMERTON:

ANTONIADES v VILLIERS

The appellants in this appeal are a young couple who at all material times were living together as man and wife. In about November 1984 they learned from a letting agency that a flat was available in a house at 6 Whiteley Road, London S. E. 19, owned by the respondent, Mr. Antoniades. They inspected the flat together and were told that the rent would be £174 per month. They were given the choice of having the bedroom furnished with a double bed or two single beds and they chose a double bed. So, right from the inception, there was never any question but that the appellants were seeking to establish a joint home and they have, at all material times, been the sole occupants of the flat.

There is equally no question but that the premises are not suitable for occupation by more than one couple, save on a very temporary basis. The small living-room contains a sofa capable of being converted into a double bed and also a bed-table capable of being opened out to form a narrow single bed. The appellants did in fact have a friend to stay with them for a time in what the trial judge found to be cramped conditions, but the size of the accommodation and the facilities available clearly do not make the flat suitable for multiple occupation. When it came to drawing up the contractual arrangements under which the appellants were to be let into possession, each was asked to and did sign a separate licence agreement in the terms set out in the speech of my noble and learned friend, Lord Templeman, under which each assumed an individual, but not a joint, responsibility for payment of one half of the sum of £174 previously quoted as the rent.

There is an air of total unreality about these documents read as separate and individual licences in the light of the circumstance that the appellants were together seeking a flat as a quasi-matrimonial home. A separate licensee does not realistically assume responsibility for all repairs and all outgoings. Nor in the circumstances can any realistic significance be given to clauses 16 and 17[18] of the document. It cannot realistically have been contemplated that the respondent would either himself use or occupy any part of the flat or put some other person in to share accommodation specifically adapted for the occupation by a couple living together. These clauses cannot be considered as seriously intended to have any practical operation or to serve any purpose apart from the purely technical one of seeking to avoid the ordinary legal consequences attendant upon letting the appellants into possession at a monthly rent. The unreality is enhanced by the reservation of the right of eviction without court order, which cannot seriously have been thought to be effective, and by the accompanying agreement not to get married, which can only have been designed to prevent a situation arising in which it would be quite impossible to argue that the 'licensees' were enjoying separate rights of occupation.

The conclusion seems to me irresistible that these two so-called licences, executed contemporaneously and entered into in the circumstances already outlined, have to be read together as constituting in reality one single transaction under which the appellants became joint occupiers. That of course does not conclude the case because the question still remains, what is the effect?

The document is clearly based upon the form of document which was upheld by the Court of Appeal as an effective licence in *Somma v Hazlehurst* [1978] 1 WLR 1014, [1978] 2 All ER 1011, p. 470, ante. That case, which rested on what was said to be the impossibility of the two licensees having between them exclusive possession, was overruled in *Street v Mountford* [1985] AC 809, [1985] 2 All ER 289. It was, however, a case which related to a single room and it is suggested that a similar agreement relating to premises containing space which could, albeit uncomfortably, accommodate another person is not necessarily governed by the same principle. On the other hand, the trial judge found that apart from the few visits by the respondent (who, on all but one occasion, sought admission by knocking on the door) no one shared with the appellants and that they had exclusive possession. He held that the licences were 'artificial transactions designed to evade the Rent Acts,' that a tenancy was created and that the appellants occupied as joint tenants.

His decision was reversed by the Court of Appeal, [1990] 1 AC 417–438E [1988] 2 All ER 173, on, broadly, the grounds that he had erred in treating the subsequent conduct of the parties as admissible as an aid to construction of the agreements and that in so far as the holding above referred to constituted a finding that the licences were a sham, that was unsupported by the evidence inasmuch as the appellants' intention that they should enjoy exclusive possession was not shared by the respondent. The licences could not, therefore,

---

[18]   '(16) The licensor shall be entitled at any time to use the rooms together with the licensee and permit other persons to use all of the rooms together with the licensee ... (17) This licence is personal to the licensee and shall not permit the use of the rooms by any person whatsoever and only the licensor will have the right to use or permit the use of the room as described in clause 16. The licensee under no circumstances will have the right to allow any other people of his choice to use the rooms in any way ...'

be said to mask the real intention of the parties and fell to be construed by reference to what they said in terms.

If the documents fall to be taken seriously at their face value and to be construed according to their terms, I see, for my part, no escape from the conclusion at which the Court of Appeal arrived. If it is once accepted that the respondent enjoyed the right—whether he exercised it or not—to share the accommodation with the appellants, either himself or by introducing one or more other persons to use the flat with them, it is, as it seems to me, incontestable that the appellants cannot claim to have had exclusive possession. The appellants' case therefore rests, as Mr. Colyer frankly admits, upon upholding the judge's approach that the true transaction contemplated was that the appellants should jointly enjoy exclusive possession and that the licences were mere sham or window-dressing to indicate legal incidents which were never seriously intended in fact, but which would be inconsistent with the application to that transaction of the Rent Acts. Now to begin with, I do not, for my part, read the notes of the judge's judgment as showing that he construed the agreement in the light of what the parties subsequently did. I agree entirely with the Court of Appeal that if he did that he was in error. But though subsequent conduct is irrelevant as an aid to construction, it is certainly admissible as evidence on the question of whether the documents were or were not genuine documents giving effect to the parties' true intentions. Broadly what is said by Mr Colyer is that nobody acquainted with the circumstances in which the parties had come together and with the physical lay-out and size of the premises could seriously have imagined that the clauses in the licence which, on the face of them, contemplate the respondent and an apparently limitless number of other persons moving in to share the whole of the available accommodation, including the bedroom with what, to all intents and purposes, was a married couple committed to paying £174 a month in advance, were anything other than a smoke-screen; and the fact that the respondent, who might be assumed to want to make the maximum profit out of the premises, never sought to introduce anyone else is at least some indication that that is exactly what it was. Adopting the definition of a sham formulated by Purchas LJ in *Hadjiloucas v Crean* [1988] 1 WLR 1006, 1013 [1987] 3 All ER 1008, 1014, Mr Colyer submits that the licences clearly incorporate clauses by which neither party intended to be bound and which were obviously a smoke-screen to cover the real intentions of both contracting parties. In the Court of Appeal, [1990] 1 AC 417, at 446–447A, [1988] 2 All ER 309, at 317, Bingham LJ tested the matter by asking two questions, viz (1) on what grounds, if one party had left the premises, could the remaining party have been made liable for anything more than the £87 which he or she had agreed to pay, and (2) on what ground could they have resisted a demand by the respondent to introduce a further person into the premises? For my part, however, I do not see how this helps. The assumed negative answers prove nothing, for they rest upon the assumption that the licences are not sham documents, which is the very question in issue.

If the real transaction was, as the judge found one under which the appellants became joint tenants with exclusive possession, on the footing that the two agreements are to be construed together, then it would follow that they were together jointly and severally responsible for the whole rent. It would equally follow that they could effectively exclude the respondent and his nominees.

Although the facts are not precisely on all fours with *Somma v Hazlehurst* [1978] 1 WLR 1014, [1978] 2 All ER 1011, they are strikingly similar and the judge was, in my judgment, entitled to conclude that the appellants had exclusive possession of the premises. I read his finding that, 'the licences are artificial transactions designed to evade the Rent Acts' as a finding that they were sham documents designed to conceal the true nature of the transaction. There was, in my judgment, material on which he could properly reach this conclusion and I, too, would allow the appeal.

AG SECURITIES v VAUGHAN

The facts in this appeal are startlingly different from those in the case of *Antoniades*. To begin with the appeal concerns a substantial flat in a mansion block consisting of four bedrooms, a lounge, a sitting-room and usual offices. The trial judge found, as a fact, that the premises could without difficulty provide residential accommodation for four persons. There is no question but that the agreements with which the appeal is concerned reflect the true bargain between the parties. It is the purpose and intention of both parties to each agreement that it should confer an individual right on the licensee named, that he should be liable only for the payment which he had undertaken, and that his agreement should be capable of termination without reference to the agreements with other persons occupying the flat. The judge found that the agreements were not shams and that each of the four occupants had arrived independently of one another and not as a group. His finding was that there was never a group of persons coming to the flat all together. That has been challenged because, it is said, the evidence established that initially in 1977 and 1978 there was one occupant who was joined by three others who, although they came independently and not as a trio, moved in at about the same time. Central heating was then installed, so that the weekly payments fell to be increased and new agreements were signed by the four occupants contemporaneously. Speaking for myself, I cannot see how this can make any difference to the terms upon which the individuals were in occupation. If they were in as licensees in the first instance, the mere replacement of their agreements by new agreements in similar form cannot convert them into tenants, and the case has, in my judgment, to be approached on the footing that agreements with the occupiers were entered into separately and individually. The only questions are those of the effect of each agreement vis-à-vis the individual licensee and whether the agreements collectively had the effect of creating a joint tenancy among the occupants of the premises for the time being by virtue of their having between them exclusive possession of the premises.

Taking first, by way of example, the position of the first occupier to be let into the premises on the terms of one of these agreements, it is, in my judgment, quite unarguable, once any question of sham is out of the way, that he has an estate in the premises which entitles him to exclusive possession. His right, which is, by definition, a right to share use and occupation with such other persons not exceeding three in number as the licensor shall introduce from time to time, is clearly inconsistent with any exclusive possession in him alone even though he may be the only person in physical occupation at a particular time. He has no legal title which will permit him to exclude other persons to whom the licensor may choose to grant the privilege of entry. That must equally apply to the additional licensees who join him. None of them has individually nor have they collectively the right or power lawfully to exclude a further nominee of the licensor within the prescribed maximum.

I pause to note that it has never been contended that any individual occupier has a tenancy of a particular room in the flat with a right to use the remainder of the flat in common with the tenants of other rooms. I can envisage that as a possibility in cases of arrangements of this kind if the facts support the marking out with the landlord's concurrence of a particular room as the exclusive domain of a particular individual. But to support that there would, I think, have to be proved the grant of an identifiable part of the flat and that simply does not fit with the system described in the evidence of the instant case.

The real question—and it is this upon which the respondents rely—is what is the position when the flat is occupied concurrently by all four licensees? What is said then is that since the licensor has now exhausted, for the time being, his right of nomination, the four occupants collectively have exclusive possession of the premises because they can collectively exclude the licensor himself. Because, it is argued, (1) they have thus exclusive possession and, (2) there is an ascertainable term during which all have the right to use and occupy, and (3) they are occupying in consideration of the payment of periodic sums of money, *Street v Mountford* [1985] AC 809, [1985] 2 All ER 289 shows that they are collectively tenants of the premises. They are not lodgers. Therefore they must be tenants. And because each is not individually a tenant, they must together be joint tenants.

My Lords, there appear to me to be a number of fallacies here. In the first place, the assertion of an exclusive possession rests, as it seems to me, upon assuming what it is sought to prove. If, of course, each licence agreement creates a tenancy, each tenant will be sharing with other persons whose rights to be there rest upon their own estates which, once they have been granted, they enjoy in their own right independently of the landlord. Collectively they have the right to exclude everyone other than those who have concurrent estates. But if the licence agreement is what it purports to be, that is to say, merely an agreement for permissive enjoyment as the invitee of the landlord, then each shares the use of the premises with other invitees of the same landlord. The landlord is not excluded for he continues to enjoy the premises through his invitees, even though he may for the time being have precluded himself by contract with each from withdrawing the invitation. Secondly, the fact that under each agreement an individual has the privilege of user and occupation for a term which overlaps the term of user and occupation of other persons in the premises, does not create a single indivisible term of occupation for all four consisting of an amalgam of the individual overlapping periods. Thirdly, there is no single sum of money payable in respect of use and occupation. Each person is individually liable for the amount which he has agreed, which may differ in practice from the amounts paid by all or some of the others.

The respondents are compelled to support their claims by a strange and unnatural theory that, as each occupant terminates his agreement, there is an implied surrender by the other three and an implied grant of a new joint tenancy to them together with the new incumbent when he enters under his individual agreement. With great respect to the majority in the Court of Appeal, this appears to me to be entirely unreal. For my part, I agree with the dissenting judgment of Sir George Waller in finding no unity of interest, no unity of title, certainly no unity of time and, as I think, no unity of possession. I find it impossible to say that the agreements entered into with the respondents created either individually or collectively a single tenancy either of the entire flat or of any part of it. I agree that the appeal should be allowed.

V. SHIFTING POPULATION OF INDIVIDUALS

AG Securities v Vaughan was applied in **Stribling v Wickham** [1989] 2 EGLR 35, [19] where PARKER LJ, in holding that the agreement was a licence, said at 35:

[19]   [1989] Conv 192 (J. E. Martin).

'The appellant, Mr Nigel Stribling, is the freehold owner of a large flat known as Garden Flat, 10a St Quintin Avenue, London W10. On May 23 1987, by three separate agreements each of which was in identical terms, he granted (or purported to grant) to each of the two respondents and a Mr Wickham a licence to use the premises on a shared basis from May 24 1987 to April 23 1988 in consideration of the payment by each of £1,254 by 11 instalments of £114, payable on May 24 1987 and thereafter on the 24th of each month until March 24 1988.

The respondents and Mr Wickham occupied the premises on a shared basis and duly paid the amounts provided for by the agreements. On the expiry of the agreements, despite the appellant's demand, the respondents and Mr Wickham refused to leave the premises and on May 16 1988 the appellant commenced proceedings for possession against them in the Bloomsbury County Court.

The action was tried in September 1988 by Mr Assistant Recorder Harris. By that time Mr Wickham had left the premises and did not defend. The respondents resisted the claim, contending that the three agreements, notwithstanding their terms, had created a joint tenancy of the flat in the respondents and Mr Wickham, and that they were accordingly entitled to protection under the Rent Act 1977.

It was, and is, common ground that if the respondents' contention is correct, the claim for possession fails but that if the contention fails the claim for possession succeeds.

The assistant recorder upheld the contention and accordingly dismissed the claim. The appellant now appeals to this court. ...

[His Lordship referred to *AG Securities v Vaughan* and *Antoniades v Villiers* and continued:]

In the two above-mentioned appeals, their lordships were dealing with two very different factual situations described by Lord Oliver as being at different ends of the scale. The present situation falls midway between the two. ...

It is not, and could not be, suggested that each agreement constituted a tenancy of a particular room together with a right to share living-room, kitchen and bathroom. The contest is between three individual licences and a joint tenancy.

As a matter of pure construction, it could not, in my view, possibly be suggested that, taken together, the agreements created a joint tenancy. One has therefore to see if any, and if so which, parts of the agreement should be regarded as a pretence or a sham or window dressing, the purpose of which was to disguise the grant of a tenancy.

The flat was suitable for use by a multiple but shifting population and was so used. Each occupant was given a specific right to terminate on 28 days' notice, and James Mavor specifically did so. His letter makes it plain that he considered that he was intending to terminate his own rights and obligations only, and that the positions of the other two would be unaffected. The owner was given a specific right against each to terminate on notice, and each agreement was expressed to terminate automatically if the "licensee" were in breach. Each licensee had a specific obligation to pay the amount reserved by his agreement only.

In my judgment, there is no process of "legal alchemy" by which the agreements can be placed into the mould of a tenancy. They represent the realities of the transaction and a genuine and sensible arrangement for the benefit of both sides.

The three licences were in substance and reality just what they purported to be. The right, specifically given under each of termination on 28 days' notice by either side, and the provision whereby each was responsible only for a specific sum which was in fact one-third of the total required by the landlord, are wholly inconsistent with a joint tenancy. That they were intended to operate is clear from events. They cannot be ignored nor can they, in my judgment, be converted by any legitimate process into a joint obligation to pay the whole rent or a form of authority to each occupant by the others to terminate a joint tenancy on notice by him, but by some magical process to re-create on the instant a joint tenancy in the remaining two until expiry of the current agreements.

I would allow this appeal, set aside the judgment and order that judgment for possession should be entered against the respondents.'

SIR DENYS BUCKLEY said at 38: 'I only want to add very few words in relation to the passage in the speech of Lord Templeman in *Street v Mountford* [1985] AC 809 at 825, [1985] 2 All ER 289, at 299 where he refers to the court being astute to detect and frustrate sham devices. Of course a court should always be astute to give effect to the intention of Parliament, although the word "astute" may be a rather emotive one to use in such a context. This does not mean that the court should lean in favour of any particular approach to construction, or any particular inference from the facts of the case.

The question whether there is a sham device, an artificial transaction or a pretence involved in the transaction under consideration must be approached evenhandedly. Only if an even-handed approach to all the relevant considerations leads to the conclusion that some feature of the transaction in question is in fact a pretence can the court proceed to consider whether that constitutes a ground for holding that that feature amounts to an attempt to evade the Rent Acts. I am satisfied that Lord Templeman did not intend to imply anything other than this in the passage to which I have referred'.

vi. SHARING PART OF DEMISED PREMISES

Street v Mountford principles also apply as between a tenant and the occupant of part of his demised premises.

In **Monmouth Borough Council v Marlog** [1994] 2 EGLR 68, Mr Roberts became the tenant of 5 Charles Close, Abergavenny. He moved in, accompanied by Mrs Marlog and her two children. Mr Roberts occupied one bedroom; Mrs Marlog and her children occupied the other two bedrooms. The kitchen, bathroom and living accommodation were shared. Mrs Marlog paid Mr Roberts £20 a week.

The Court of Appeal held that, although Mrs Marlog and her children had exclusive occupation of their two bedrooms, she was not the sub-tenant of Mr Roberts, but his licensee. She was therefore not entitled to remain as a secure tenant when Mr Roberts's tenancy from the local authority ended.

NOURSE LJ said at 241: 'Where two persons move into residential premises together under a tenancy granted to one but not the other of them, each occupying a bedroom or bedrooms and the remainder of the premises being shared between them, the court will be slow to infer a common intention that the one who is not the tenant shall be the subtenant of the one who is. The natural inference is that what is intended is a contractual house-sharing arrangement under the tenancy of one of them. The inference is greatly strengthened where, as here, there is a written agreement between the landlord and the tenant and none between the tenant and the other occupant.'

vii. JOINT AND SEVERAL LIABILITY FOR PAYMENT

In **Mikeover Ltd v Brady** [1989] 3 All ER 618, Mr Brady and Miss Guile
occupied the plaintiff's second floor flat (which had been advertised in the
Evening Standard as a flat for two people to share on the basis of two separate
but identical agreements). Each agreement provided that the 'Owner grants
to the Licensee the right to use in common with others who had been granted
the like right the rooms on the second floor, and also that the Licensee shall
pay the sum of £86.66 per month for the right to share in the use of the said
rooms.' Two years later Miss Guile moved out, but Mr Brady remained and with
the consent of the plaintiffs, paid £86.66 a month. When he fell into arrears,
the plaintiffs sought possession of the flat. The defendant argued that the
agreements together created a joint tenancy and that he was entitled to Rent
Act protection.

In rejecting the claim, SLADE LJ said at 623:

'The agreements have to be construed against the plaintiffs who proffered
them. If they wished to reserve the right to impose on the defendant or Miss
Guile a substitute co-occupant during the currency of the agreements, it was, in
our judgment, incumbent on the plaintiffs to do so in much clearer terms.

It follows that, in our judgment, the defendant's agreement on its true
construction conferred on him the *right* (by cl 1) to exclusive occupation of the
flat in common only with Miss Guile during its currency. Clause 2(4) is to be
read simply as imposing on him a corresponding *obligation* not to impede the
use of the rooms etc by Miss Guile during the currency of the term. Thus it is not
necessary or relevant to consider the alternative argument of the defendant's
counsel to the effect that, in so far as the agreement purported to reserve to the
plaintiffs the right to impose on the defendant a substitute co-occupier in place
of Miss Guile, it was a "sham".

We have already given reasons for concluding that the agreements in the
present case did not on their proper reading purport to reserve to the plaintiffs
the right to impose a co-occupant on the defendant or Miss Guile during the
term of either agreement. Nevertheless, their effect was to confer on the
defendant and Miss Guile together, so long as Miss Guile remained, a right of
joint exclusive occupation of the property. The decision in *Street v Mountford*
[1985] AC 809, [1985] 2 All ER 289, establishes that the enjoyment by one person
of exclusive occupation of premises for a term in consideration of periodical
payments creates a tenancy save in exceptional circumstances not relevant to
this appeal: see *Antoniades v Villiers* [1990] AC 417 at 459, [1988] 3 All ER 1058
at 1065, per Lord Templeman. Similarly, as the last-mentioned decision
illustrates, the enjoyment by more than one person of joint exclusive occupation
of premises for the same term in consideration of periodical payments is capable
of creating a joint tenancy.

It is, however, well settled that four unities must be present for the creation
of a joint tenancy, namely the unities of possession, interest, title and time: see
Megarry and Wade *The Law of Real Property* (5th edn, 1984) pp. 419–422. In the
present case there is no dispute that the two agreements of 6 June 1984 operated
to confer on the defendant and Miss Guile unity of possession and title. Likewise,
there was unity of time in that each of their interests arose simultaneously and
was expressed to endure for six months. The dispute concerns unity of interest.
The general principle, as stated in *Megarry and Wade* p. 240, is:

"The interest of each joint tenant is the same in extent, nature and duration,
for in theory of law they hold but one estate". "Interest" in this context must, in

our judgment, include the bundle of rights and obligations representing that interest. The difficulty, from the defendant's point of view, is that the two agreements, instead of imposing a joint liability on him and Miss Guile to pay a deposit of £80 and monthly payments of £173.32, on their face imposed on each of them individual and separate obligations to pay only a deposit of £40 and monthly payments of only £86.66. On the face of it, the absence of joint obligations of payment is inconsistent with the existence of a joint tenancy.

Counsel for the defendant sought to meet this difficulty in three ways. First, he contended that the two agreements were, as he put it, "interdependent" and must be read together. When so read, he submitted, they should be construed as placing on the two parties joint obligations. However, it seems to us quite impossible to rewrite the two agreements in this manner as a matter of construction: cf *Aldrington Garages Ltd v Fielder* (1978) 37 P & CR 461 at 471 per Geoffrey Lane LJ. One cannot add up two several obligations to pay £X so as to construct a joint obligation to pay £2X.

In agreement with the judge we thus conclude that as a matter of substance and reality each of the two parties to the agreements placed himself or herself under merely individual obligations to pay monthly sums of £86.66 and a deposit of £40, but no joint monetary obligations. What then is the effect?

Counsel for the defendant, as his last line of defence, submitted that even on this footing the defendant and Miss Guile were in law capable of being (and were in fact) joint tenants. In this context he invoked the authority of a dictum of Lord Templeman in *Antoniades v Villiers* [1990] 1 AC 417 at 461, [1988] 3 All ER 1058 at 1066, where he said:

"Mr Antoniades required each of them, Mr Villiers and Miss Bridger, to agree to pay one-half of each aggregate periodical payment, but this circumstance cannot convert a tenancy into a licence. A tenancy remains a tenancy even though the landlord may choose to require each of two joint tenants to agree expressly to pay one-half of the rent."

Lord Templeman was saying this in the context of two agreements which he regarded as shams. With great respect, however, if he was intending to say that a joint tenancy can exist even though the supposed joint tenants are not jointly liable for the whole rent, the weight of authority appears to go the other way. In *Antoniades v Villiers* at 469, at 1073, Lord Oliver said:

"If the real transaction was, as the judge found, one under which the appellants became joint tenants with exclusive possession, on the footing that the two agreements are to be construed together, then it would follow that they were together jointly and severally responsible for the whole rent. It would equally follow that they could effectively exclude the respondent and his nominees."

In the same case Lord Jauncey said at 473, at 1075:

"Normal attributes of a lease to joint tenants include a demise for a specific period with exclusive possession at a single rent for payment of which each joint tenant is liable to the lessor in full subject to relief from his co-tenants.

Finally, very recently in *Stribling v Wickham* [1989] 2 EGLR 35, p. 493, ante, Parker LJ, with whose judgment Fox LJ and Sir Denys Buckley agreed, said:

"The three licences were in substance and reality just what they purported to be. The right, specifically given under each of termination on 28 days' notice by either side, and the provision whereby each was responsible only for a specific sum which was in fact one-third of the total required by the landlord, are wholly inconsistent with a joint tenancy."

The entire inconsistency with a joint tenancy of a provision rendering each licensee responsible only for one-third of the total required by the landlord was, as we read *Stribling v Wickham*, part of the essential reasoning which led this court to its final decision.

On these authorities, it appears to us that unity of interest imports the existence of joint rights and joint obligations. We therefore conclude that the provisions for payment contained in these two agreements (which were genuinely intended to impose and did impose on each party an obligation to pay no more than the sums reserved to the plaintiffs by his or her separate agreement) were incapable in law of creating a joint tenancy, because the monetary obligations of the two parties were not joint obligations and there was accordingly no complete unity of interest. It follows that there was no joint tenancy. Since inter se Miss Guile and the defendant had no power to exclude each other from occupation of any part of the premises, it also follows that their respective several rights can never have been greater than those of licensees during the period of their joint occupation. It has not been submitted (and we think in all the circumstances it could not be submitted) that the defendant's status became that of tenant after Miss Guile's departure, if it was not that before.
...

Every case where the question of lease or licence arises must depend on its own facts. All we need say is that in our view and on the judge's findings, on the particular facts of the present case, no sham device or artificial transaction is involved. At first sight it appeared to us that the employment of two forms of agreement, rather than one, had an air of artificiality about it. However, once it is accepted that the monetary obligations of each licensee were genuinely intended to be entirely independent from those of the other, it seems to us that this course was understandable, even though not essential, and is not fairly open to criticism. We have already accepted that each agreement has to be construed in the light of the other. However, we do not accept the submission of counsel for the defendant that they were "interdependent". While each had to be read with the other, each was perfectly capable of being operated on its own.

For the reasons stated, and despite counsel's admirable argument for the defendant, we dismiss this appeal.'

viii. CONSTRUCTION OF TERMS OF OCCUPATION. INTRODUCTION OF OTHERS. RETENTION OF KEYS

Antoniades v Villiers was applied in *Aslan v Murphy* and *Duke v Wynne* [1990] 1 WLR 766, [1989] 3 All ER 130 (a joint appeal to the Court of Appeal).

In **Aslan v Murphy** [20] the plaintiff was the owner of a small basement room in Redcliffe Gardens, London. It was occupied by the defendant under a written agreement which provided that 'the Licensor is not willing to grant the Licensee exclusive possession of any part of the room'; that the licensor might permit others to use the room; and that he had no occupation rights at all between 10.30 a.m and 12 noon each day; and that the licensor would retain the keys to the room and have absolute right of entry at all times. Virtually no services were provided by the plaintiff during the defendant's occupation. The plaintiff obtained an order for possession of the room.

[20]   [1989] All ER Rev 172 (P. J. Clarke). It was also applied in *Nicolaou v Pitt* [1989] 1 EGLR 84 ('after a certain amount of humming and hawing the owner said he did contemplate introducing a stranger into the flat. I do not believe him'. CA held that there was a tenancy, even though the flat had a spare bedroom and had been previously occupied by three persons).

In **Duke v Wynne**, the plaintiff was the owner of a three bedroom house in Dunkeld Road, South Norwood, London. It was occupied by the defendants and their two sons. The written agreement recited that the owner wished to be able to obtain vacant possession at very short notice, that the occupiers accepted as a fundamental term of the agreement that they had no right of exclusive occupation in any part of the house, but would have to share it with other persons as directed by the plaintiff who retained a key and reserved the right to enter the house at any time. The plaintiff wished to emigrate to Canada and to sell the house with vacant possession. Negotiations took place with a view to the defendants buying the house, but agreement could not be reached on the price. Eventually the plaintiff obtained an order for possession.

In holding that in both cases the occupiers were tenants and therefore protected under the Rent Acts, LORD DONALDSON OF LYMINGTON said at 770, at 133:

'General principles

The status of a tenant is essentially different from that of a lodger and owners of property are free to make accommodation available on either basis. Which basis applies in any particular case depends upon what was the true bargain between the parties. It is the ascertainment of that true bargain which lies at the heart of the problem.

Labelling

The labels which parties agree to attach to themselves or to their agreements are never conclusive and in this particular field, in which there is enormous pressure on the homeless to agree to any label which will facilitate the obtaining of accommodation, they give no guidance at all. As Lord Templeman said in *Street v Mountford* [1985] AC 809, 819, [1985] 2 All ER 289, 294.

"The manufacture of a five-pronged implement for manual digging results in a fork even if the manufacturer, unfamiliar with the English language, insists that he intended to make and has made a spade."

Exclusive or non-exclusive occupation

This is the touchstone by which the "spade" of tenancy falls to be distinguished from the "fork" of lodging. In this context it is necessary to consider the rights and duties of the person making the accommodation available ("the owner") and the rights of other occupiers. The occupier has in the end to be a tenant or a lodger. He cannot be both. But there is a spectrum of exclusivity ranging from the occupier of a detached property under a full repairing lease, who is without doubt a tenant, to the overnight occupier of a hotel bedroom who, however up-market the hotel, is without doubt a lodger. The dividing line—the sorting of the forks from the spades—will not necessarily or even usually depend upon a single factor, but upon a combination of factors.

Pretences

Quite apart from labelling, parties may succumb to the temptation to agree to pretend to have particular rights and duties which are not in fact any part of the true bargain. Prima facie, the parties must be taken to mean what they say, but given the pressures on both parties to pretend, albeit for different reasons, the courts would be acting unrealistically if they did not keep a weather eye open for pretences, taking due account of how the parties have acted in performance of their apparent bargain. This identification and exposure of such pretences does not necessarily lead to the conclusion that their agreement is a sham, but only to the conclusion that the terms of the true bargain are not wholly the same as those of the bargain appearing on the face of the agreement. It is the true rather than the apparent bargain which determines the question "tenant or lodger?"

The effect of the Rent Acts

If an occupier would otherwise be protected by the Rent Acts, he does not lose that protection by agreeing that he will surrender it either immediately or in the future and whether directly and in terms or indirectly, e.g. by agreeing to substitute a shared for an exclusive right of occupation should the owner so require: *Antoniades v Villiers* [1990] AC 417, 461, [1988] 3 All ER 1058, 1066.

Aslan v Murphy (No. 1)

In fairness to the judge, it should be said that he gave judgment before the House of Lords reversed the decision of this court in *Antoniades v Villiers*, and therefore without the benefit of the guidance contained in the speeches. In the light of that guidance, the judge's decision is unsupportable on this ground and no attempt was made to support it.

The judge was, of course, quite right to approach the matter on this basis that it is not a crime, nor is it contrary to public policy, for a property owner to license occupiers to occupy a property on terms which do not give rise to a tenancy. Where he went wrong was in considering whether the whole agreement was a sham and, having concluded that it was not, giving effect to its terms i.e. taking it throughout at face value. What he should have done, and I am sure would have done if he had known of the House of Lords approach to the problem, was to consider whether the whole agreement was a sham and, if it was not, whether in the light of the factual situation the provisions for sharing the room and those depriving the defendant of the right to occupy it for 90 minutes out of each 24 hours [1] were part of the true bargain between the parties or were pretences. Both provisions were wholly unrealistic and were clearly pretences.

In this court an attempt to uphold the judge's decision was made upon a different basis, namely, the landlord's right to retain the keys. ... Provisions as to keys are often relied upon in support of the contention that an occupier is a lodger rather than a tenant. Thus in *Duke v Wynne*, to which we turn next, the agreement required the occupier "not to interfere with or change the locks on any part of the premises, [or] give the key to any other than an authorised occupier of the premises." Provisions as to keys, if not a pretence which they often are, do not have any magic in themselves. It is not a requirement of a tenancy that the occupier shall have exclusive possession of the keys to the property. What matters is what underlies the provisions as to keys. Why does the owner want a key, want to prevent keys being issued to the friends of the occupier or want to prevent the lock being changed?

A landlord may well need a key in order that he may be able to enter quickly in the event of emergency: fire, burst pipes or whatever. He may need a key to enable him or those authorised by him to read meters or to do repairs which are

---

[1]   'A similar provision in *Crancour Ltd v Da Silvaesa* [1986] 1 EGLR 80 was described by NICHOLLS LJ at 86 as being "so extraordinary in a grant of a right to use residential accommodation for a period of six months that it calls for an explanation".'

his responsibility. None of these underlying reasons would of themselves indicate that the true bargain between the parties was such that the occupier was in law a lodger. On the other hand, if the true bargain is that the owner will provide genuine services which can only be provided by having keys, such as frequent cleaning, daily bed-making, the provision of clean linen at regular intervals and the like, there are materials from which it is possible to infer that the occupier is a lodger rather than a tenant. But the inference arises not from the provisions as to keys, but from the reason why those provisions formed part of the bargain. On the facts of this case, the argument based upon the provisions as to keys must and does fail for the judge found that "during the currency of the present agreement virtually 'no services' had been provided." These provisions may or may not have been pretences, but they are without significance in the context of the question which we had to decide. [2]

Duke v Wynne

Here the facts were very different from those in *Aslan v Murphy* ...

Tenants or lodgers?

Were the defendants tenants or lodgers? Unlike the facts in *Aslan v Murphy* it would have been possible for them to have shared the house with another occupant. There were three bedrooms. One could have been used by the defendants, one by the children and the third, which was a very small room, by a lodger. However, the evidence did not disclose any immediate intention on the part of the plaintiff to make such an arrangement and she never in fact did so. Meanwhile, the defendants in fact occupied the whole house. In cases such as this the court has to determine whether the true bargain is that the occupiers are entitled to exclusive possession of the premises, unless and until the owner requires them to share, or whether the true bargain is that their entitlement is only to their share in the right to occupy, although, as there is currently no other occupant, it will be impracticable and unreasonable to seek to prevent their de facto occupation of the whole premises. If the former is the case and, for the time being, they have an entitlement to exclusive occupation, they are tenants and their status cannot at some future date be unilaterally converted into that of lodgers by the owner requiring them to share their occupation: *Antoniades v Villiers*. If the latter is the case, they never achieve the status of tenants.

In the instant appeal it is quite clear that the true bargain was that the defendants should be entitled to exclusive occupation unless and until the plaintiff wanted to exercise her right to authorise someone else to move in as a lodger and she never suggested that this was a serious possibility. The provision about the key was no pretence in the sense that the plaintiff retained a key and no doubt did not wish the defendants to change the locks without at least giving her new keys. But her wish to have a key was not dictated by any obligation to provide services or anything else from which it could be inferred that she was herself occupying the house as well as the defendants.

But the situation could have been different. If the plaintiff had determined to have two couples as lodgers, she might not have been able to find them simultaneously. The first couple might have de facto occupation of the whole house meanwhile, but could not have claimed to be tenants since the plaintiff

---

[2] *Family Housing Association v Jones* [1990] 1 WLR 779 at 789, [1990] 1 All ER 385 at 392.

would de jure herself have been a co-occupier until the second pair of lodgers arrived. Applying the test of what was the true bargain between the parties, the court would have wanted to know what steps (if any) were being taken by the owner to fill the vacancy. If the owner was not actively seeking another occupant, it would be inherently more likely that the first couple were *entitled* to exclude possession of the whole in the meanwhile and so were tenants.

On the facts of this case and the law as now declared by the House of Lords, the defendants are clearly to be regarded as tenants, their appeal must be allowed and the order for possession set aside.'

F. Law Reform

In 2003 the Law Commission published its Narrative Report on Renting Homes (Law Com No. 284).[3] Its recommendations for the reform of housing law represent radical legislative change to the regulation of the rented sector of the housing market. 'The proposed Bill will not only include detailed changes to the existing rules, but also fundamental change to the legislative approach to the regulation of this sector of the housing market. In particular, the historic linkage between principles of property law and housing legislation will, so far as practicable, be abandoned; instead a new approach based on contract which incorporated consumer law principles of fairness and transparency is proposed.' (para. 2.5.)

It is recommended that there should be two basic agreement types:

(1) Type 1 agreements with a high degree of security of tenure protected by the Act; these would be periodic agreements only.

(2) Type II agreements with a low degree of tenure provided by statute. Landlords would be able to enter either fixed-term or periodic agreements.

Type 1 is similar to the existing (local authority) secure tenancy; Type II is based on the existing assured shorthold tenancy agreement. (para 3.7.)

The broad objective is that, unless there are compelling reasons for excluding them, all occupation agreements should come within the scheme. A number of types of agreement currently outside the principal statutory scheme would be brought within it; for example, service occupancies and student accommodation provided by universities and local authorities. There would, however, be two classes of exemption from the scheme:

(1) Agreements covered by other statutory schemes; these include business tenancies, agricultural holdings, all leases for 21 years or more and mobile homes.

(2) Certain types of agreement excluded on social policy grounds, such as holiday lettings; agreements granted as a temporary expedient to persons who entered the premises as trespassers; agreements where the occupier is sharing accommodation with the landlord, agreements relating to certain categories of sheltered accommodation; and agreements relating to accommodation provided on a temporary basis to meet duties to house the homeless under Part VII of the Housing Act 1996. (paras. 3.14–3.16); 6.26–6.29.)

Under the scheme there must be a contractual agreement between the landlord and the occupier; if it is made orally, a written statement of it must be provided by the landlord to the occupier. There would be model agreements which would, by definition, comply with the Unfair Terms in Consumer Contracts

---

[3]   The Report followed two Consultation Papers: (a) Renting Homes (1) Status and Security 2002 (Law Com No. 162; and (b) Renting Homes (2) Co-occupation, Transfer and Succession 2002 (Law Com No. 168). See (2003) 7 L & T Rev 60; (2004) 8 L & T Rev 26 (M. Partington).

Regulations 1999. (para. 3.29.) The agreements would contain a clear statement of the rights and obligations of both landlords and occupiers and the grounds for possession. This would replace the present situations where the grounds for possession are prescribed in detail in statutory instruments which operate outside the agreement. (Part IX). There would also be special provision to facilitate the ability of landlords to enter into agreements with 16 and 17 year-olds. (para. 3.18.)

It is also recommended that existing agreements should, as far as possible, be brought within the scope of the new scheme. To this there would be two exceptions, tenancies still covered by the Rent Act 1977, and by the Rent (Agriculture) Act 1976.

On the distinction between a lease and a licence, which has attracted so much judicial interpretation, the Report says:

"While the practical importance of the distinction has receded in recent years, [4] it nonetheless retains its potential for complexity. We think this distinction is out of place in a modern system of housing law. We recommend that our scheme should apply to all contractual occupation agreements, not just those classifiable as tenancies.

While we seek to render the lease-licence distinction irrelevant so far as the question of which arrangements fall within our proposed scheme are concerned, it will remain of significance in the determination of certain third-party rights, where it will still be important to rely on established principles of property law."'

QUESTIONS

1. Is there any good reason why freedom of contract should not prevail in:
   (*a*) a *Street v Mountford* situation;
   (*b*) a *Somma v Hazlehurst* situation? Is the unlikely but possible intrusion into quasi-connubial bliss (*Street v Mountford* [1985] AC 809 at 825, [1985] 2 All ER 289 at 299) a sufficient reason for preventing the parties from being held to a genuine bargain?
2. Draft an occupation agreement so as to avoid granting exclusive possession to the occupant.
3. How far is professional drafting relevant when construing an agreement for the occupation of business premises? *IDC Group Ltd v Clark* [1992] 1 EGLR 187; affd [1992] 2 EGLR 184, p. 620, post.
4. Do you think that the agreements in *AG Securities v Vaughan* [1990] 1 AC 417, [1988] 3 All ER 1058 and *Stribling v Wickham* [1989] 2 EGLR 35 are joint tenancies or tenancies in common? If they are tenancies in common, what would the effect be? (1992) 142 NLJ 575 (S. Bright).

III. Creation [5]

A. Statutory Requirements

i. LAW OF PROPERTY ACT 1925

LAW OF PROPERTY ACT 1925

54. Creation of interest in land by parol.—(1) p. 18, ante.
   (2) p 83, ante.

---

[4]   Pp. 472, ante.
[5]   C & B, pp. 399–415; Gray, pp. 391–413; M & W, paras. 14.029–14.107; MM, pp. 342–353; Smith, pp. 102–104.

52. Conveyances to be by deed.—(1) p. 77, ante.

(2) (*d*) p. 77, ante.[6]

In **Crago v Julian** [1992] 1 WLR 372, [1992] 1 All ER 744,[7] Sir Donald
NICHOLLS V-C, in holding that a legal assignment of an oral lease created within
the ambit of section 54(2) of the Law of Property Act 1925 must be by deed, said
at 375, at 746:

'I turn first to the question of law: could this tenancy be assigned effectively
only by deed? I can start with the summary of the law set out in *Megarry & Wade on
the Law of Real Property*, 5th ed. (1984), p. 665:

"A legal lease, once created, can be transferred inter vivos only by deed, in
accordance with the general rule. This applies to all legal leases, even those
created orally, e.g. a yearly tenancy. However, on principles similar to those
applicable to the creation of leases, an oral or written assignment will be effective
in equity as between the assignor and the assignee as a contract to assign, if
sufficiently evidenced by writing or part performance."

In the present case nothing less than an assignment at law will assist Mrs
Julian. The view stated in *Megarry & Wade* is also expressed in all the other
leading textbooks on this subject. Undaunted, Mr Phillips contended that these
views are erroneous. The general rule mentioned by *Megarry & Wade* is a
reference to certain provisions in the Law of Property Act 1925. Mr Phillips
submitted that, properly interpreted, these provisions do not preclude a valid
assignment otherwise than by deed of a lease which has been created orally.

The statutory provisions are to be found in Part II of the Law of Property Act
1925. The material part of the relevant sections, sections 52 to 54, provide:

[His Lordship cited ss. 52 (p. 77, ante); 53 (p. 83, ante); 54(1) (p. 78, ante)
and 54(2) (p. 83, ante) and continued:]

This is a hotchpotch of sections reproducing, with some amendments,
provisions which before 1925 were to be found in the Statute of Frauds 1677 and
the Real Property Act 1845. I consider section 53 first. The grant of a tenancy is
the creation of an interest in land. An assignment of a tenancy of land is the
disposal of an interest in land. Thus, both the grant of a tenancy, and the
assignment of a tenancy, fall four-square within section 53(1) (*a*). A tenancy of
land cannot be created or assigned save by writing, or by will, or by operation of
law. Paragraph (*a*), however, is expressed to be "subject to the provisions
hereinafter contained with respect to the *creation* of interests in land by parol."
(Emphasis added.) Section 54(2) is such a provision. Section 54(2) provides
that the statutory requirements of Part II of the Act do not affect "the creation" by
parol of leases taking effect in possession for a term not exceeding three years at
a full market rent.

I pause to observe that, thus far, there can be no doubt as to the meaning of
the statutory provisions: interests in land cannot be created or disposed of except
in writing, but a lease in possession at a market rent for up to three years can be
validly created orally. Hence, and this is to be noted, the effect of these statutory

---

[6]   This includes a lease for a period exceeding three years even though it may be
determinable within the period: *Kushner v Law Society* [1952] 1 KB 264, [1952] 1 All ER
404.

[7]   [1992] Conv 375 (P. Sparkes); *London Borough of Camden v Alexandrou* (1997) 74 P & CR
D33.

provisions is indubitably to draw a distinction between the manner in which a short lease may be created and the manner in which it may be assigned.

The point is not wholly free from authority. Section 53(1)(*a*) derives from section 3 of the Statute of Frauds, and section 54 derives from sections 1 and 2. In *Botting v Martin* (1808) 1 Camp 317 Serjeant Best argued that by the leases mentioned in section 3, as requiring to be assigned in writing, must be intended such leases as are required by sections 1 and 2 to be created in writing, viz., leases conveying a larger interest to the party than a term for three years. He submitted:

"As a lease from year to year could be originally made by parol, there was no reason why it might not be assigned by parol, and the words of the statute would bear this interpretation, which was clearly consistent with its general import."

McDonald CB rejected the submission.

In my view section 53 provides an insuperable obstacle for Mrs Julian in the present case. Like McDonald CB, I consider the statutory language really leaves no room for reaching a different conclusion, even though the result is the curious distinction I have mentioned. Even if there were room for doubt I would be slow to upset an interpretation of statutory provisions which has been accepted by conveyancers for a very long time.

This conclusion is sufficient to dispose of this appeal, because here there was no assignment in writing.'

ii. LAND REGISTRATION ACTS [8]

(a) Land Registration Act 1925

A term of years absolute is registrable as a separate title, provided that it was a term of more than 21 years, or, in the case of an assignment of an existing lease, had more than 21 years to run. A notice of the lease itself had to be entered on the register of the lessor's title. Where the lease was registered as a separate title, the notice was entered automatically by the Registrat at the time of registration. But where the lease was incapable of registration, because it was a lease of 21 years or less, it was an overriding interest under section 70(1)(*k*) of the Land Registration Act 1925,[9] and no other protection was necessary.

Where the lease had not been noted on the register, a lessee who was in actual occupation would be protected by virtue of an overriding interest under section 70(1)(*g*) of the Land Registration Act 1925.[10]

In **City Permanent Building Society v Miller** [1952] Ch 840, [1952] 2 All ER 621, the Court of Appeal held that an agreement for a lease was not within LRA 1925, s. 70(1)(*k*). JENKINS LJ said at 852, at 628:[11]

'Mr Marsh relied on the definition of "lease" contained in section 3(x) of the Land Registration Act, 1925, which is in these terms: "Lease" includes an underlease and any tenancy "or agreement for a lease underlease or tenancy." He argued that the word "leases" in section 70(1)(*k*) of the same Act must

---

[8]   See LRA 1925, ss. 3(x), 8, 9, 10, 19, 22, 23, 48, 70(1)(*k*), 123. C & B, pp. 561–563; Gray, pp. 395–400; M & W, paras. 6.017–6.019; MM, pp. 115–134; Smith, pp. 224–225, 228, 242; R & R, chap. 25; H & B, paras. 2.15–2.20.
[9]   P. 130, ante.
[10]   P. 131, ante.
[11]   See now LRA 2002, Sch s. 1, para. 1 and 3, para. 1.

accordingly be construed as including agreements for leases; but, as my Lord has pointed out, the definitions in section 3 are prefaced by the familiar form of words. "In this Act, unless the context otherwise requires, the following expressions have the meanings hereby assigned to them respectively, that is to say." In my view, the context afforded in section 70(1)(*k*) does "otherwise require." It refers to "leases for any term or interest not exceeding 21 years, granted at a rent without taking a fine." In my judgment, the use there of the word granted clearly imports the actual creation of a term of years, whether it is done by deed or by an agreement under hand only, in that class of cases in which a legal term can be created by a document not under seal, or indeed by parol in any case in which an actual tenancy taking effect at law may be created without writing. But in my judgment the word "granted" necessarily imports the actual creation of a term, and that excludes, by force of the context, the case of a mere agreement for a lease, having no more than a contractual effect. To include such a case, in my judgment, section 70(1)(*k*) should have read "granted or agreed to be granted."'

(b) Land Registration Act 2002

The Land Registration Act 2002 makes significant changes. First, the period of 21 years is shortened to seven years; and, secondly, two types of lease become registrable for the first time.

1. A reversionary lease of any duration which is to take effect in possession more than three months after the date of the grant; and

2. A discontinuous lease of any length granted out of a registered title, such as a lease of land for two weeks in every year from 2003–2024 (a timeshare lease). [12]

The Lord Chancellor has power to shorten the seven-year period still further (section 4). The effect of the shorter period is that most business leases, which are usually granted for 10 or 15 years, will now become registrable.

Leases of land granted for a term not exceeding 7 years from the date of the grant (formerly 21 years) continue to be interests which may override; on first registration (Schedule 1, paragraph 1) and on a registered disposition (Schedule 2, paragraph 1). [13] Such a lease cannot be protected by a notice (section 33(b)).

An agreement for a lease under the doctrine of *Walsh v Lonsdale* (p 85, ante) cannot be registered with an individual title; it is not a legal estate; nor can it be an overriding interest under para 1 of either Schedule 1 or Schedule 3. The position of the tenant is similar to that under the Land Registration Act 1925. He may be protected by a notice against a purchaser for valuable consideration from the landlord, or, failing that by being in discoverable actual occupation under paragraph 2 of Schedule 3 to the Land Registration Act 2002. [14]

LAND REGISTRATION ACT 2002

3. When title may be registered, p. 111 ante.

4. When title must be registered, p. 112 ante.

10. Titles to leasehold estates, p. 116 ante.

---

[12]   A discontinuous lease created out of unregistered land may be voluntarily registered, except where the total of the lease periods exceeds 7 years.

[13]   P. 163, ante.

[14]   R & R, para. 25.014.

12. Leasehold estates, p. 118 ante.

27. Dispositions required to be registered, p. 122 ante.

Schedule 1, paragraph 1, p. 159 ante.

Schedule 3, paragraphs 1 and 2, p. 163 ante.

B. Tenancies at Common Law

i. TENANCIES AT WILL AND AT SUFFERANCE

Entry into possession as a tenant, or holding over with the landlord's consent after the expiration of the tenancy, creates a tenancy at will. [15]

A tenant who holds over without the landlord's consent becomes a tenant at sufferance.

There is a presumption that such tenancies expand to become weekly, monthly or yearly tenancies where rent is paid and accepted, the length of the tenancy being related to the period in respect of which the rent is paid. [16]

In **Wheeler v Mercer** [1957] AC 416, [1956] 3 All ER 631 Viscount SIMONDS said at 426, at 634:

'It may, I think, be truly said that, since a tenant at will is regarded at law as being in possession by his own will and at the will, express or implied, of his landlord, he is a tenant by their mutual agreement. ... He is distinguished from a tenant at sufferance in that such a tenant is said to be in possession without either the agreement or disagreement of the landlord. ... A tenancy at will ... has been properly described as a personal relation between the landlord and his tenant: it is determined by the death of either of them or by any one of a variety of acts, even by an involuntary alienation, which would not affect the subsistence of any other tenancy.' [17]

---

[15]   It is occasionally created by express agreement: *Morgan v William Harrison Ltd* [1907] 2 Ch 137; *Manfield & Sons Ltd v Botchin* [1970] 2 QB 612, [1970] 3 All ER 143; *Hagee (London) Ltd v A B Erikson and Larson* [1976] QB 209, [1975] 3 All ER 234; *Cardiothoracic Institute v Shrewdcrest Ltd* [1986] 1 WLR 368, [1986] 3 All ER 633; *Javad v Mohammed Aqil* [1991] 1 WLR 1007, [1991] 1 All ER 243, p. 510, post; *Dean and Chapter of the Cathedral and Metropolitan Church of Canterbury v Whitbread plc* (1995) 72 P & CR 9.

[16]   *Clayton v Blakey* (1798) 8 Term Rep 3; *Dougal v McCarthy* [1893] 1 QB 736; *Marcroft Wagons Ltd v Smith* [1951] 2 KB 496, [1951] 2 All ER 271; *Longrigg, Burrough and Trounson v Smith* (1979) 251 EG 847; *Javad v Mohammed Aquil, infra; Dreamgate Properties Ltd v Arnot* [1997] EGCS 121 (new tenancy not implied after expiry of lease; demand for rent computer generated and not result of conscious decision); *London Baggage Co (Charing Cross Ltd) v Railtrack plc* [2000] EGCS 57 (test of intention objective); cf. *Walji v Mount Cook Land Ltd* (2001) 81 P & CR D47.

[17]   Cf. the tolerated trespasser, who is a public sector tenant who remains in possession after the tenancy has been ended by a possession order, and pays for occupation, without the local authority taking any active steps to evict: *Burrows v Brent London Borough Council* [1996] 1 WLR 1448, [1996] 4 All ER 577; (2003) 119 LQR 495 (S. Bright). He was described by CLARKE LJ in *Pemberton v Southwark London Borough Council* [2000] 1 WLR 1672 at 1683, [2000] 3 All ER 924 at 934 as 'a recent, somewhat bizarre, addition to the dramatis personae of the law.'

In **Heslop v Burns** [1974] 1 WLR 1241, [1974] 3 All ER 406, SCARMAN LJ said at 1253, at 416:

'It may be that the tenancy at will can now serve only one legal purpose, and that is to protect the interests of an occupier during a period of transition. If one looks to the classic cases in which tenancies at will continue to be inferred, namely, the case of someone who goes into possession prior to a contract of purchase, or of someone who, with the consent of the landlord, holds over after the expiry of his lease, [18] one sees that in each there is a transitional period during which negotiations are being conducted touching the estate or interest in the land that has to be protected, and the tenancy at will is an apt legal mechanism to protect the occupier during such a period of transition: he is there and can keep out trespassers: he is there with the consent of the landlord and can keep out the landlord as long as that consent is maintained.'

In **Ramnarace v Lutchman** [2001] 1 WLR 1651, Lord MILLETT, in delivering the judgment of the Privy Council on appeal from the Court of Appeal of Trinidad and Tobago, said at 1656:

'16 A tenancy at will is of indefinite duration, but in all other respects it shares the characteristics of a tenancy. As Lord Templeman observed in *Street v Mountford* [1985] AC 809, 818 [1985] 2 All ER 289. p. 473 ante there can be no tenancy unless the occupier enjoys exclusive possession; but the converse is not necessarily true. An occupier who enjoys exclusive possession is not necessarily a tenant. He may be the freehold owner, a trespasser, a mortgagee in possession, an object of charity or a service occupier. Exclusive possession of land may be referable to a legal relationship other than a tenancy or to the absence of any legal relationship at all. A purchaser who is allowed into possession before completion and an occupier who remains in possession pending the exercise of an option each has in equity an immediate interest in the land to which his possession is ancillary. They are not tenants at will: see *Essex Plan Ltd v Broadminster* (1988) 56 P & CR 353, 356 per Hoffmann J.

17 A person cannot be a tenant at will where it appears from the surrounding circumstances that there was no intention to create legal relations. A tenancy is a legal relationship; it cannot be created by a transaction which is not intended to create legal relations. This provides a principled rationalisation of the statement of Denning LJ in *Facchini v Bryson* [1952] 1 TLR 1386, 1389 p. 479, ante, on which the Court of Appeal relied in the present case. Before an occupier who is in exclusive occupation of land can be treated as holding under a licence and not a tenancy there must be something in the circumstances such as a family arrangement, an act of friendship or generosity or suchlike, to negative any intention to create legal relations.

18 In the present case the plaintiff was allowed into occupation of the land as part of a family arrangement and at least in part as an act of generosity. But not wholly so, for the plaintiff testified that the intention of the parties was that she would buy the land when she could afford to do so, and the judge accepted her

---

[18]   Under Landlord and Tenant Act 1730, s. 1, a tenant who wilfully holds over after demand made and written notice given for delivery up of possession, is liable to pay double the yearly value of the lands for the time the premises are detained: *French v Elliott* [1960] 1 WLR 40, [1959] 3 All ER 866; *Dun & Bradstreet v Provident Mutual* [1996] NPC 57. See also Distress for Rent Act 1737, s. 18; *Ballard (Kent) Ltd v Oliver Ashworth (Holdings) Ltd* [1999] 2 EGLR 23.

evidence. Her uncle was generous in that he allowed her to remain indefinitely and rent-free pending her purchase, and in that he did not press her to negotiate. But a tenancy at will commonly arises where a person is allowed into possession while the parties negotiate the terms of a lease or purchase. He has no interest in the land to which his possession can be referred, and if in exclusive and rent-free possession is a tenant at will. In *Hagee (London) Ltd v AB Erikson and Larson* [1976] QB 209, 217, [1975] 3 All ER 234, Scarman LJ described this as one of the "classic circumstances" in which a tenancy at will arose.

19 Whether the parties intended to create legal relations, and whether there was any genuine intention on their part to negotiate a sale of the land when the plaintiff could afford to buy it, were questions of fact for the judge. Although he made no express findings in this regard, there was evidence which he accepted from which he could properly conclude that the plaintiff entered into possession as tenant at will.'

ii. YEARLY BASIS

ADLER v BLACKMAN
[1952] 2 All ER 41 (QBD, ORMEROD J) [19]

Blackman had held shop premises under a weekly tenancy until December 1947, from which date the tenancy was changed to a yearly tenancy on the following terms: 'To hold for the term of one year ... at the exclusive weekly rent of £3 payable weekly ...'. After the expiration of the year, Blackman held over and Adler served on him a notice to quit, which was valid if he held a weekly, void if he held a yearly, tenancy. The notice to quit was first accepted by Blackman, whose first reaction was to claim compensation or a new lease under the Landlord and Tenant Act 1927. He subsequently claimed that the notice was invalid.

Held. Notice valid, as Blackman was a weekly tenant.

ORMEROD J: The questions to be decided are: Was the tenant holding these premises as a tenant from year to year, in which case, of course, this notice was invalid, or was he holding them on a weekly tenancy, in which case admittedly the notice is good? Secondly, even if the notice was invalid, as the tenant elected to treat it as valid by taking proceedings under the Landlord and Tenant Act, 1927, can he now say that the notice was invalid and that he is entitled to remain in possession of the premises? So far as the first point is concerned, it is clearly established that, if a tenant holds over with the consent of the landlord at the expiration of a period reserved by a lease or tenancy agreement, an implied tenancy is set up, and the presumption is that that tenancy is a yearly tenancy on the terms of the instrument creating the original tenancy so far as they are consistent with a yearly tenancy, but that presumption may be rebutted by various circumstances including, of course, the terms of the agreement itself. I am asked by the landlord to say that the fact that the original tenancy was admittedly a weekly tenancy is a circumstance which should be taken into account in rebutting this presumption. The agreement for a tenancy for twelve months, in which the rent was expressed to be payable by the week and was calculated by the week and not by the year, says the landlord, is also a very strong circumstance to take into account. Further, he says that the conduct of the parties after the expiration of the period of tenancy, and, particularly, when the notice to quit was served by

---

[19] Affirmed by CA (SOMERVELL, JENKINS and HODSON LJJ) [1953] 1 QB 146, [1952] 2 All ER 945, where the decision of MACNAGHTEN J in *Covered Markets Ltd v Green* [1947] 2 All ER 140 was overruled.

the landlord on the tenant, establishes beyond doubt the inference that the tenancy was not a tenancy from year to year. ...

In *Covered Markets Ltd v Green* [1947] 2 All ER 140 a tenant held over at the expiration of a tenancy for seven years at a rent of £3, payable weekly. Macnaghten J decided that the presumption was that the tenancy was a yearly one, and he saw no reason to rebut that presumption. He distinguished that case from Maugham J's decision on the ground that the premises were a fishmonger's shop, whereas the premises in the *Ladies' Hosiery* case [1930] 1 Ch 304 were merely a piece of ground. I find it difficult to appreciate the distinction, but Macnaghten J very clearly held that the proper inference from the circumstances was that there was a yearly tenancy on the termination of the seven years.

I have to consider whether in the present case there is a yearly tenancy or whether the circumstances are such that the presumption of a yearly tenancy has been rebutted and the tenant holds the premises on a weekly tenancy only. I have come to the conclusion that I ought to hold that the presumption has been rebutted and that the tenancy is a weekly one. I am not influenced by the situation before the agreement for a yearly tenancy was entered into. I do not think I ought to regard that as relevant to the consideration of the circumstances because it may well be that the parties decided that they would have the tenancy on an entirely new basis. There is no evidence about that one way or the other. The terms of the tenancy under the agreement were very different from the terms of the tenancy before it, including the rent, the terms relating to repairs, and so on, but I do take into consideration strongly the fact that the rent was expressed to be the rent of £3 per week and was never calculated by reference to a yearly sum. It was always paid weekly, and, after the term of the agreement had expired, it continued to be paid weekly right up to the time when the notice to quit was given. ... The notice to quit was served on the basis that the tenancy was a weekly one, and was accepted without question by the tenant. Clearly the tenant's view was that he was holding on a weekly tenancy and not on a yearly tenancy, and I see no reason why that should not be taken into account in deciding whether the presumption of a yearly tenancy has been rebutted. Even if that were not the case, however, I think that, where as here, the original tenancy is not for a period of years, but is for only one year, and where the rent payable is expressed as a weekly sum and not by reference to a yearly rent, the presumption is rebutted that there is a yearly tenancy and the tenant must be taken to be holding over on the basis of a weekly tenancy on the terms of the agreement so far as they are consistent therewith. It follows that the notice was valid and the landlord is entitled to succeed in this action.

[ORMEROD J found it unnecessary to decide the second question. If it had been necessary to decide it, he would have held that the tenant, by claiming a new lease under the Landlord and Tenant Act 1927, had elected to accept the notice and could not now say that it was invalid.]

In **Javad v Mohammed Aqil** [1991] 1 WLR 1007, [1991] 1 All ER 243, [20] the defendant was let into occupation of business premises owned by the plaintiff while negotiations proceeded for the grant to him of a 10 year lease. On three occasions he paid rent on a quarterly basis before negotiations broke down, and the plaintiff told him to leave. The question was whether the defendant was a tenant at will, in which case the notice to quit was valid, or whether he was a

[20]   (1990) 140 NLJ 1538 (H. W. Wilkinson); [1991] CLJ 232 (S. Bridge); *Brent London Borough Council v O'Bryan* [1993] 1 EGLR 59; *Walji v Mount Cook Land Ltd* [2002] 1 P & CR 163.

quarterly tenant, in which case he was protected under the Landlord and Tenant Act 1954 Part II. In holding that the defendant was a tenant at will, NICHOLLS LJ said at 1012:

'A tenancy, or lease, is an interest in land. With exceptions immaterial for present purposes, a tenancy springs from a consensual arrangement between two parties: one person grants to another the right to possession of land for a lesser term than he, the grantor, has in the land. The extent of the right thus granted and accepted depends primarily upon the intention of the parties.

As with other consensually-based arrangements, parties frequently proceed with an arrangement whereby one person takes possession of another's land for payment without having agreed or directed their minds to one or more fundamental aspects of their transaction. In such cases the law, where appropriate, has to step in and fill the gaps in a way which is sensible and reasonable. The law will imply, from what was agreed and all the surrounding circumstances, the terms the parties are to be taken to have intended to apply. Thus if one party permits another to go into possession of his land on payment of a rent of so much per week or month, failing more the inference sensibly and reasonably to be drawn is that the parties intended that there should be a weekly or monthly tenancy. Likewise, if one party permits another to remain in possession after the expiration of his tenancy. But I emphasise the qualification: "failing more." Frequently there will be more. Indeed, nowadays there normally will be other material surrounding circumstances. The simple situation is unlikely to arise often, not least because of the extent to which statute has intervened in landlord-tenant relationships. Where there is more than the simple situation, the inference sensibly and reasonably to be drawn will depend upon a fair consideration of all the circumstances, of which the payment of rent on a periodical basis is only one, albeit a very important one. This is so however large or small may be the amount of the payment.

To this I add one observation, having in mind the facts of the present case. Where parties are negotiating the terms of a proposed lease, and the prospective tenant is let into possession or permitted to remain in possession in advance of, and in anticipation of, terms being agreed, the fact that the parties have not yet agreed terms will be a factor to be taken into account in ascertaining their intention. It will often be a weighty factor. Frequently in such cases a sum called "rent" is paid at once in accordance with the terms of the proposed lease: for example, quarterly in advance. But, depending on all the circumstances, parties are not to be supposed thereby to have agreed that the prospective tenant shall be a quarterly tenant. They cannot sensibly be taken to have agreed that he shall have a periodic tenancy, with all the consequences flowing from that, at a time when they are still not agreed about the terms on which the prospective tenant shall have possession under the proposed lease, and when he has been permitted to go into possession or remain in possession merely as an interim measure in the expectation that all will be regulated and regularised in due course when terms are agreed and a formal lease granted.

Of course, when one party permits another to enter or remain upon his land on payment of a sum of money, and that other has no statutory entitlement to be there, almost inevitably there will be some consensual relationship between them. It may be no more than a licence determinable at any time, or a tenancy at will. But when and so long as such parties are in the throes of negotiating larger terms, caution must be exercised before inferring or imputing to the parties an intention to give to the occupant more than a very limited interest, be it licence or tenancy. Otherwise the court would be in danger of inferring or imputing from conduct, such as payment of rent and the carrying out of repairs, whose explanation lies in the parties' expectation that they will be able to reach agreement on the large terms, an intention to grant a lesser interest, such as a periodic tenancy, which the parties never had in contemplation at all.'

iii. THE TERMS OF A YEARLY TENANCY

Where a tenant obtains a yearly (or other periodic) tenancy by entry followed by payment of rent in pursuance of an agreement to grant a lease or of a purported grant which is void for lack of a seal, the terms of the tenancy include such of those of the void grant as are consistent with a tenancy for the period in question. [1]

iv. TERMINATION OF PERIODIC JOINT TENANCY

HAMMERSMITH AND FULHAM LONDON BOROUGH COUNCIL v MONK
[1992] 1 AC 478, [1992] 1 All ER 1 (HL, Lords BRIDGE OF HARWICH, BRANDON OF OAKBROOK, ACKNER, JAUNCEY OF TULLICHETTLE and BROWNE-WILKINSON) [2]

LORD BRIDGE OF HARWICH. My Lords, the issue in this appeal is whether a periodic tenancy held by two or more tenants jointly can be brought to an end by a notice to quit by one of the joint tenants without the consent of the others. ...

Before examining the relevant authorities I think it helpful to consider whether the application of first principles suggests the answer to the question at issue. For a large part of this century there have been many categories of tenancy of property occupied for agricultural, residential and commercial purposes where the legislature has intervened to confer upon tenants extra-contractual rights entitling them to continue in occupation without the consent of the landlord, either after the expiry of a contractual lease for a fixed term or after notice to quit given by the landlord to determine a contractual periodic tenancy. It is primarily in relation to joint tenancies in these categories that the question whether or not notice to quit given by one of the joint tenants can determine the tenancy is of practical importance, particularly where, as in the instant case, the effect of the determination will be to deprive the other joint tenant of statutory protection. This may appear an untoward result and may consequently provoke a certain reluctance to hold that the law can permit one of two joint tenants unilaterally to deprive his co-tenant of 'rights' which both are equally entitled to enjoy. But the statutory consequences are in truth of no relevance to the question which your Lordships have to decide. That question is whether, at common law, a contractual periodic tenancy granted to two or more joint tenants is incapable of termination by a tenant's notice to quit unless it is served with the concurrence of all the joint tenants. That is the proposition which the appellant must establish in order to succeed.

As a matter of principle I see no reason why this question should receive any different answer in the context of the contractual relationship of landlord and tenant than that which it would receive in any other contractual context. If A and B contract with C on terms which are to continue in operation for one year in the first place and thereafter from year to year unless determined by notice at the

---

[1]   *Doe d Rigge v Bell* (1793) 5 Term Rep 471; *Doe d Thomson v Amey* (1840) 12 Ad & El 476; C & B, pp. 413–414; M & W, para. 14.066; MM, pp. 347–348.
[2]   [1992] 1 AC 478, [1992] 1 All ER 1; [1992] Conv 279 (S. Goulding); CLJ 218 (L. Tee); 108 LQR 375 (J. Dewar).

end of the first or any subsequent year, neither A nor B has bound himself contractually for longer than one year. To hold that A could not determine the contract at the end of any year without the concurrence of B and vice versa would presuppose that each had assumed a potentially irrevocable contractual obligation for the duration of their joint lives, which, whatever the nature of the contractual obligations undertaken, would be such an improbable intention to impute to the parties that nothing less than the clearest express contractual language would suffice to manifest it. Hence, in any ordinary agreement for an initial term which is to continue for successive terms unless determined by notice, the obvious inference is that the agreement is intended to continue beyond the initial term only if and so long as all parties to the agreement are willing that it should do so. In a common law situation, where parties are free to contract as they wish and are bound only so far as they have agreed to be bound, this leads to the only sensible result.

Thus the application of ordinary contractual principles leads me to expect that a periodic tenancy granted to two or more joint tenants must be terminable at common law by an appropriate notice to quit given by any one of them whether or not the others are prepared to concur. But I turn now to the authorities to see whether there is any principle of the English law of real property and peculiar to the contractual relationship of landlord and tenant which refutes that expectation or whether the authorities confirm it. A useful starting point is the following passage from *Blackstone's Commentaries*, Book II (1766), ch. 9, pp. 145–147:

[His Lordship read the passage and continued:]

Hence, from the earliest times a yearly tenancy has been an estate which continued only so long as it was the will of both parties that it should continue, albeit that either party could only signify his unwillingness that the tenancy should continue beyond the end of any year by giving the appropriate advance notice to that effect. Applying this principle to the case of a yearly tenancy where either the lessor's or the lessee's interest is held jointly by two or more parties, logic seems to me to dictate the conclusion that the will of the joint parties is necessary to the continuance of the interest.

In *Doe d Aslin v Summersett* (1830) 1 B & Ad 135, the freehold interest in land let on a yearly tenancy was vested jointly in four executors of a will to whom the land had been jointly devised. Three only of the executors gave notice to the tenant to quit. It was held by the Court of King's Bench that the notice was effective to determine the tenancy. Delivering the judgment, Lord Tenterden CJ said, at pp. 140–141:

'Upon a joint demise by joint tenants upon a tenancy from year to year, the true character of the tenancy is this, not that the tenant holds of each the share of each so long as he and each shall please, but that he holds the *whole* of *all* so long as he *and all* shall please; and as soon as any one of the joint tenants gives a notice to quit, he effectually puts an end to *that* tenancy; the tenant has a right upon such a notice to give up *the whole*, and unless he comes to a new arrangement with the other joint tenants as to their shares, he is compellable so to do. The hardship upon the tenant, if he were not entitled to treat a notice from one as putting an end to the tenancy as to the whole, is obvious; for however willing a man might be to be sole tenant of an estate, it is not very likely he should be willing to hold undivided shares of it; and if upon such a notice the tenant is entitled to treat it as putting an end to the tenancy as to the whole, the other joint tenants must have the same right. It cannot be optional on one side, and on one side only.' ...

There are three principal strands in the argument advanced for the appellant. First, reliance is placed on the judgment in *Gandy v Jubber* (1865) 9 B & S 15, for the proposition that a tenancy from year to year, however long it continues, is a single term, not a series of separate lettings. ...

The passage relied on reads, at p. 18:

'There frequently is an actual demise from year to year so long as both parties please. The nature of this tenancy is discussed in 4 Bac. Abr. tit. *Leases and Terms for Years*, pp. 838, 839, 7th ed.; and this article has always been deemed of the highest authority being said to be the work of Gilbert C.B. It seems clear that the learned author considered that the true nature of such a tenancy is that it is a lease for two years certain, and that every year after it is a springing interest arising upon the first contract and parcel of it, so that if the lessee occupies for a number of years, these years by computation from time past, make an entire lease for so many years, and that after the commencement of each new year it becomes an entire lease certain for the years past and also for the year so entered on, and that it is not a reletting at the commencement of the third and subsequent years. We think this is the true nature of a tenancy from year to year created by express words, and that there is not in contemplation of law a recommencing or reletting at the beginning of each year.'

It must follow from this principle, Mr Reid submits, that the determination of a periodic tenancy by notice is in all respects analogous to the determination of a lease for a fixed term in the exercise of a break clause, which in the case of joint lessees clearly requires the concurrence of all. But reference to the passage from *Bacon's Abridgment*, 7th ed., vol. IV, p. 839, on which the reasoning is founded shows that this analogy is not valid. ...

Thus the fact that the law regards a tenancy from year to year which has continued for a number of years, considered retrospectively, as a single term in no way affects the principle that continuation beyond the end of each year depends on the will of the parties that it should continue or that, considered prospectively, the tenancy continues no further than the parties have already impliedly agreed upon by their omission to serve notice to quit.

The second submission for the appellant is that, whatever the law may have been before the enactment of the Law of Property Act 1925, the effect of that statute, whereby a legal estate in land vested in joint tenants is held on trust for sale for the parties beneficially entitled, coupled with the principle that trustees must act unanimously in dealing with trust property, is to reverse the decision in *Summersett's* case, and to prevent one of two joint tenants determining a periodic tenancy without the concurrence of the other. It is unnecessary to consider the position where the parties beneficially entitled are different from those who hold the legal interest. But where, as here, two joint tenants of a periodic tenancy hold both the legal and the beneficial interest, the existence of a trust for sale can make no difference to the principles applicable to the termination of the tenancy. At any given moment the extent of the interest to which the trust relates extends no further than the end of the period of the tenancy which will next expire on a date for which it is still possible to give notice to quit. If before 1925 the implied consent of both joint tenants, signified by the omission to give notice to quit, was necessary to extend the tenancy from one period to the next, precisely the same applies since 1925 to the extension by the joint trustee beneficiaries of the periodic tenancy which is the subject of the trust.[3]

---

[3]   The position is not changed by TLATA 1996, s. 11. The giving of a notice is not an exercise of any *function* relating to land subject to the trust: *Notting Hill Housing Trust v Brackley* [2001] 3 EGLR 11. Nor is the failure to consult a breach of trust: *Crawley Borough Council v Ure* [1996] QB 13, [1996] 1 All ER 724.

Finally, it is said that all positive dealings with a joint tenancy require the concurrence of all joint tenants if they are to be effective. Thus, a single joint tenant cannot exercise a break clause in a lease, [4] surrender the term, make a disclaimer, exercise an option to renew the term or apply for relief from forfeiture. [5] All these positive acts which joint tenants must concur in performing are said to afford analogies with the service of notice to determine a periodic tenancy which is likewise a positive act. But this is to confuse the form with the substance. The action of giving notice to determine a periodic tenancy is in form positive; but both on authority and on the principle so aptly summed up in the pithy Scottish phrase 'tacit relocation' the substance of the matter is that it is by his omission to give notice of termination that each party signifies the necessary positive assent to the extension of the term for a further period.

For all these reasons I agree with the Court of Appeal that, unless the terms of the tenancy agreement otherwise provide, notice to quit given by one joint tenant without the concurrence of any other joint tenant is effective to determine a periodic tenancy.

v. TENANCY BY ESTOPPEL [6]

In **Webb v Austin** (1844) 7 Man & G 701, TINDAL CJ said at 724:

'The doctrine on this subject, as it has been generally understood by the profession, may be collected from Mr *Preston's Treatise on Abstracts* vol. ii, p. 210, and the authorities there cited. That general understanding appears to be, that "An indenture of lease, or a fine *sur concessit*, for years, will be an estoppel only during the term. It first operates by way of estoppel, and finally, when the grantor obtains an ownership, it attaches on the seisin and creates an interest, or produces the relation of landlord and tenant; and there is a term *commencing* by estoppel, but *for all purposes* it becomes an estate or interest. It binds the estate of the lessor, &c. and therefore continues in force against the lessor, his heirs, &c. It also binds the assigns of the lessor and of the lessee".'

(a) Determination of the Tenant's Estate

INDUSTRIAL PROPERTIES (BARTON HILL) LTD v ASSOCIATED ELECTRICAL INDUSTRIES LTD
[1977] QB 580, [1977] 2 All ER 293 (CA, LORD DENNING MR, ROSKILL and LAWTON LJJ) [7]

LORD DENNING MR: In the course of the discussion we were referred to many authorities, old and new. I have considered them all [8]—and others, too—but the result can be stated thus: If a landlord lets a tenant into possession under a lease,

---

[4] *Hounslow London Borough Council v Pilling* [1993] 1 WLR 1242, [1994] 1 All ER 432.

[5] On the unilateral grant of a tenancy, see [2000] Conv 208 (L. Fox).

[6] Spencer Bower and Turner, *The Law Relating to Estoppel by Representation* (4th edn, 2004), vi. 3.12–3.15, ix. 3.29–3.32; C & B, pp. 414–415; M & W, paras. 14.095–14.102; MM, pp. 352–353; (1964) 80 LQR 370 (A. M. Prichard); *Industrial Properties (Barton Hill) Ltd v Associated Electrical Industries Ltd* [1977] QB 580, [1977] 2 All ER 293, p. 86, ante; infra; (1977) 40 MLR 718 (P. Jackson); [1978] Conv 137 (J. Martin). A tenant by estoppel of business premises is entitled to the protection of L & TA 1954; *Bell v General Accident Fire & Life Assurance Corpn Ltd* [1997] EGCS 174.

[7] The facts are stated at p. 86, ante. (1977) 40 MLR 718 (P. Jackson); [1978] Conv 137 (J. Martin).

[8] His Lordship approved *Cuthbertson v Irving* (1859) 4 H & N 742; affd (1860) 6 H & N 135, and overruled *Harrison v Wells* [1967] 1 QB 263, [1966] 3 All ER 524, on the ground that it was decided per incuriam.

then, so long as the tenant remains in possession *undisturbed by any adverse claim*—then the tenant cannot dispute the landlord's title. Suppose the tenant (not having been disturbed) goes out of possession and the landlord sues the tenant on the covenant for rent or for breach of covenant to repair or to yield up in repair. The tenant cannot say to the landlord: 'You are not the true owner of the property.' Likewise, if the landlord, on the tenant's holding over, sues him for possession or for use and occupation or mesne profits, the tenant cannot defend himself by saying: 'The property does not belong to you, but to another.'

But if the tenant is disturbed *by being evicted by title paramount or the equivalent* of it, then he can dispute the landlord's title. Suppose the tenant is actually turned out by the third person—or if the tenant, without going out, acknowledges the title of the third person by attorning to him—or the tenant contests the landlord's claim on an indemnity from the third person—or there is anything else done which is equivalent to an eviction by title paramount then the tenant is no longer estopped from denying the landlord's title: see *Wilson v Anderton* (1830) 1 B & Ad 450 at 457, per Littledale J. The tenant, being thus disturbed in his possession, can say to the landlord: 'You were not truly the owner at the time when you demanded and received the rent from me. I am liable to pay mesne profits to this other man. So you must repay me the rent which I overpaid you. Nor am I liable to you on the covenants during the time you were not the owner.' See *Newsome v Graham* (1829) 10 B & C 234, *Mountnoy v Collier* (1853) 1 E & B 630 and *Watson v Lane* (1856) 11 Exch 769. The tenant can also claim damages for the eviction if there is, as here, an express covenant for quiet enjoyment covering interruption by title paramount.

Short of eviction by title paramount, or its equivalent, however, the tenant is estopped from denying the title of the landlord. It is no good his saying: 'The property does not belong to you but to a third person' unless that third person actually comes forward and successfully makes an adverse claim—by process in the courts or by the tenant's attornment; or acknowledgment of it as by the tenant defending on an indemnity. If the third person, for some reason or other, makes no adverse claim or is debarred from making it, the tenant remains estopped from denying the landlord's title. This is manifestly correct: for, without an adverse claim, it would mean that the tenant would be enabled to keep the property without paying any rent to anybody or performing any covenants. That cannot be right. That was the reasoning adopted by the Court of Queen's Bench in *Biddle v Bond* (1865) 6 B & S 225, a case of a bailor and bailee, but the court treated it as the same as landlord *v* tenant. ...

In the present case the tenants, A.E.I., are not subject to any adverse claim whatever. The lessor to A.E.I. was the plaintiff company which was the equitable owner. The legal owners were the Parker trustees. They were also the directors and shareholders of the plaintiff company. They acquiesced in the lease being made by the plaintiff company to A.E.I. They could not by any possibility make any adverse claim against A.E.I. on their own account. Not only that. They have actually come in as plaintiffs in these proceedings jointly with the plaintiff company—so as to make sure that the benefit of these proceedings goes to the plaintiff company only.

Seeing that A.E.I. are absolved from any adverse claim by the legal owners, it is a very proper case for the doctrine of tenancy by estoppel. A.E.I. have had the full benefit of the lease for the stipulated term of years. They should perform the covenants—or pay damages in lieu—to the only persons entitled to sue them, namely, the plaintiff company. Even though A.E.I. have gone out of possession, they cannot avoid their responsibilities by reliance on a technical rule of law—which on investigation is found to be groundless.

(b)   Determination of the Landlord's Estate

NATIONAL WESTMINSTER BANK LTD v HART
[1983] QB 773, [1983] 2 All ER 177 (CA, Waller LJ and Sir David Cairns) [9]

42 Haggard Road, Twickenham, was let under a 99 year lease expiring in 1967. In 1921 Cowles acquired the residue of the lease, and in 1947 sub-let the house to Hart. The sub-lease expired in 1965. Thereafter Hart continued to pay rent to Cowles until 1978, when, on the death of Cowles, he claimed that Cowles's title had expired in 1967. He refused to pay rent to Cowles's executor, the plaintiff bank, until it proved title. In the county court the plaintiff recovered arrears of rent on the ground that Hart was estopped from denying its title, since there was no third party claim to a better title.

Held (reversing the county court judge). Hart was not estopped from denying the bank's title.

Waller LJ: The defendants submit that they became tenants of this house before 1965, at which time they became tenants of the Cowles, and that the Cowles made no communication to them in 1967 when the headlease expired. The defendants cannot be estopped by the fact that they paid rent from March 1967 until August 1978, because they did not know the facts, and the Cowles did not tell them. They submit that neither the Cowles nor their personal representatives have title to 42, Haggard Road. They rely on *Fenner v Duplock* (1824) 2 Bing 10 and *Serjeant v Nash, Field & Co* [1903] 2 KB 304, and submit that the judge was in error in his conclusions.

The bank submit that the defendants are not entitled to succeed because they are unable to prove an adverse claim by a third party. They rely on *Carlton v Bowcock* (1884) 51 LT 659 and *Hindle v Hick Bros Manufacturing Co Ltd* [1947] 2 All ER 825.

The judge, being of opinion that the reasoning in *Carlton's* case and *Hindle's* case was inconsistent with *Fenner's* case and *Serjeant's* case, preferred *Carlton* and *Hindle*, and since there was no adverse claim by a third party on the facts of this case, gave judgment for the bank. ...

Can the reasoning of these two lines of cases be reconciled? The bank submit that they are not inconsistent because in *Fenner v Duplock*, and in *Serjeant v Nash, Field & Co* although in neither case did the judges mention it, there was in each case a third party claimant. There was in each case a possible third party claimant, but in my judgment the existence of such a person was not regarded by the judge as important. In *Fenner's* case, Best CJ, having said that a tenant may show that his title has expired, said, at 11, that the rule was founded on good sense, 'because if it were otherwise, the tenant might be called on to pay his rent twice over.' And in *Serjeant v Nash, Field & Co* the observations of each member of the court were quite specific, and I cannot believe that the necessity would have gone unmentioned by each member of the court if it was regarded as a requirement.

Mr Parker, on behalf of the defendants, submits that the decisions are quite consistent because when considering estoppel there is a great difference between the case of the landlord's title determining without informing a tenant so that the tenant in ignorance continues to pay rent, and the case of the landlord assigning his interest and the tenant, aware that there has been an assignment, paying rent to the assignee. In the latter case he is on notice that there has been

[9]   [1984] Conv 64 (J. W. Price).

a change of landlord and it is for him to decide whether to pay his rent to the assignee or not. If he does, he cannot be heard to complain about the assignee's title unless there is somebody else claiming title. It is clear from the care with which Cave J set out the receipts in his judgment that he regarded them as important because they gave notice of the change. In the former case of the landlord's title determining, the tenant does not know because nothing has happened to give him notice of the change. There can be no estoppel unless the tenant knows the facts or he has had notice which should have warned him.

As Mr Parker pointed out, there is a logical difference between the assignee and the landlord whose title has determined. When the tenant has freely entered into a tenancy agreement with the landlord and has as a consequence entered into possession, so long as he is in possession he is estopped from denying his landlord's title. However, the tenant whose landlord has assigned the tenancy and he, with notice, has accepted the assignee, cannot challenge the assignee's title unless there is a third party claiming to be the landlord.

Finally, in the case of the landlord whose title has determined and who has not informed the tenant:

'It is clear law that though a tenant cannot deny the title of his landlord to deal with the premises, he may prove that the title has determined.' (See per Sir Richard Henn Collins MR in *Serjeant's* case [1903] 2 KB 304 at 312.)

In the present case in my opinion if the Cowles had told the defendants in 1967 that title had determined, the tenants would have been under no obligation to pay rent to them. The Cowles not having disclosed the fact that their title had determined, the defendants cannot now be estopped from relying on the determination. I have come to the conclusion that the defendants are not liable to pay rent to the bank, and I would allow this appeal.

SIR DAVID CAIRNS: I would add that it seems to me that the bank in this case might have contended that they and their predecessors had been in possession of the rents and profits for more than 12 years, paying no rent and in no way recognising the rights of whoever may have been the freeholder, and that in that way they might have acquired a possessory title. But no such case was open to them on the pleadings, nor discussed in the court below.

(c) Feeding the Estoppel

If, after creating a tenancy by estoppel, the owner/lessor later acquires the legal estate, for example, where he purchases the fee simple, the effect is to feed the estoppel; the lessee then at once acquires a legal lease and ceases to rely on the estoppel.

Suppose that P agrees to purchase a house from V and is let into possession by V before completion of the purchase. He grants a lease of the house to T, and, later on completion, mortgages the house to M in order to raise the purchase price. The question arises whether the lease (which, until it is fed by completion of the purchase, is only a lease by estoppel) is binding on M. It is common practice for the conveyance of the house by V to P and the mortgage by P to M to be executed simultaneously. It is now settled that there is no *scintilla temporis* between the conveyance and the mortgage, which would enable a legal lease to be acquired by T and so take priority over M's mortgage.

This was decided by the House of Lords in **Abbey National Building Society v Cann** [1991] 1 AC 56, [1990], 1 All ER 1085, p. 143, ante, [10] where it was held that there was no possibility of a prior equitable interest gaining priority over such a mortgage through the doctrine of feeding the estoppel. Lord OLIVER OF AYLMERTON said at 89, at 1098:

'It is argued, however, that because the creation of a charge on property in favour of the society necessarily posits that the chargor has acquired an interest out of which the charge can be created, there must notionally be a point of time at which the estate vested in him free from the charge and in which the estoppel affecting him could be "fed" by the acquisition of the legal estate so as to become binding on and take priority over the interest of the chargee. This is a puzzling problem upon which it is not easy to reconcile the authorities.

The appellants rely upon the decision of the Court of Appeal in *Church of England Building Society v Piskor* [1954] Ch 553, [1954] 2 All ER 85, a case concerned with unregistered conveyancing. On the other side of the line are *Re Connolly Bros Ltd (No 2)* [1912] 2 Ch 25 and *Security Trust Co v Royal Bank of Canada* [1976] AC 503, [1976] 1 All ER 381. …

One is therefore presented with a stark choice between them. Of course, as a matter of legal theory, a person cannot charge a legal estate that he does not have, so that there is an attractive legal logic in the ratio in *Piskor's* case. Nevertheless, I cannot help feeling that it flies in the face of reality. The reality is that, in the vast majority of cases, the acquisition of the legal estate and the charge are not only precisely simultaneous but indissolubly bound together. The acquisition of the legal estate is entirely dependent upon the provision of funds which will have been provided before the conveyance can take effect and which are provided only against an agreement that the estate will be charged to secure them. Indeed, in many, if not most, cases of building society mortgages, there will have been, as there was in this case, a formal offer of acceptance of an advance which will ripen into a specifically enforceable agreement immediately the funds are advanced which will normally be a day or more before completion. In many, if not most, cases, the charge itself will have been executed before the execution, let alone the exchange, of the conveyance or transfer of the property. This is given particular point in the case of registered land where the vesting of the estate is made to depend upon registration, for it may well be that the transfer and the charge will be lodged for registration on different days so that the charge, when registered, may actually take effect from a date prior in time to the date from which the registration of the transfer takes effect: see section 27(3) of the Act of 1925 and the Land Registration Rules 1925, rule 83(2). Indeed, under rule 81 of the Rules of 1925, the registrar is entitled to register the charge even before registration of the transfer to the chargor if he is satisfied that both are entitled to be registered. The reality is that the purchaser of land who relies upon a building society or bank loan for the completion of his purchase never in fact acquires anything but an equity of redemption, for the land is, from the very inception, charged with the amount of the loan without which it could never have been transferred at all and it was never intended that it should be otherwise. The "scintilla temporis" is no more than a legal artifice and, for my part, I would adopt the reasoning of the Court of Appeal in *Re Connolly Bros Ltd* and of Harman J in *Coventry Permanent Economic Building Society v Jones* [1951] 1 All ER 901 and hold

---

[10]   (1992) 108 LQR 380 (G. Goldberg).

that *Piskor's* case was wrongly decided. It follows, in my judgment, that Mrs. Cann can derive no assistance from this line of argument.'[11]

vi. CONCURRENT LEASES [12]

LAW OF PROPERTY ACT 1925

149. Abolition of interesse termini, and as to reversionary leases and leases for lives.—
(2) See p. 453, ante.
(5) Nothing in this Act affects the rule of law that a legal term, whether or not being a mortgage term, may be created to take effect in reversion expectant on a longer term, which rule is hereby confirmed.

When a landlord grants a lease, and then later grants another lease of the same land (for more or less than the period of the first lease), there are concurrent leases, and he is said to have granted a lease of the reversion.[13] This creates the relationship of landlord and tenant between the first and second lessees; the second lessee does not need to go into possession,[14] but, by virtue of his legal estate, he can as reversioner claim rent, distrain, and enforce covenants. This is so, even if the second lease is for a term shorter than the first one.[15] If his lease continues after the end of the first lease, he is entitled to possession when the first lease terminates.

In **Re Moore and Hulm's Contract** [1912] 2 Ch 105, leaseholds were mortgaged by sub-demise for the residue of the original term less one day. Afterwards by another mortgage they were sub-demised to a second mortgagee (Worrell) for the same period, subject to the first mortgage. The second mortgage was paid off during the continuance of the first mortgage and the deed effecting the second mortgage was handed back to the mortgagor. A purchaser of the freeholds from the mortgagor declined to complete without a formal surrender being obtained of the term created by the second mortgage. JOYCE J held that a surrender was necessary and said at 109:
'[Counsel for the vendor] says, first, that there was no necessity or reason for Worrell, the second mortgagee, to surrender the term granted to him by the second mortgage because no legal term or interest passed to him. Bearing in

---

11   *Walthamstow Building Society v Davies* (1989) 60 P & CR 99 (where mortgagee took a second charge to replace a first charge, held no scintilla temporis between discharge of first and creation of second charge during which unauthorised tenancy granted by mortgagor became binding on mortgagee).
    The doctrine also applies in registered land: *First National Bank plc v Thompson* [1996] 1 All ER 140 (creation of charge of registered land); (1995) 139 SJ 1040 (P. Cowell); [1996] All ER 253 (P. J. Clarke).
    See also *Bruton v London and Quadrant Housing Trust* [1997] 4 All ER 970 per MILLETT LJ; reversed in HL [2000] 1 AC 406, [1999] 3 All ER 481, p. 441, ante.
12   M & W, paras. 14.103–14.107.
13   Distinguish a reversionary lease, p. 454, n. 5, ante.
14   LPA 1925, s. 149(2), p. 453, ante.
15   *Neale v Mackenzie* (1836) 1 M & W 747; *Re Moore and Hulm's Contract* [1912] 2 Ch 195, infra.

mind, however, the case cited to me by [counsel for the purchaser], I think that a legal estate or interest did pass to the second mortgagee. I think that Worrell acquired a legal reversion upon the term created by the first mortgage. I think that he got a legal term under his mortgage. If the money secured by the earlier mortgage had been paid to the first mortgagee on the date fixed for payment I think that the second mortgagee, would have had a right to the actual possession of the leasehold premises, [16] and if the lease granted by the first mortgage had been terminated in any manner during the continuance of the second mortgage, the second mortgagee would have been entitled to possession for the rest of the term created by his mortgage. Therefore I think that the argument for the vendor on the first point fails. ...

There must be a declaration that the vendor is bound to obtain a surrender of the term created by the second mortgage.'

C. Lease to Self

LAW OF PROPERTY ACT 1925

72. Conveyances by a person to himself, &c.—
(3) See p. 80, ante.
(4) See p. 80, ante.

RYE v RYE [17]
[1962] AC 496, [1962] 1 All ER 146 (HL, Viscount SIMONDS, Lords MACDERMOTT, REID, RADCLIFFE and DENNING)

In 1942 Arthur Rye, the appellant, and his brother Frank, who were in partnership as solicitors, became owners of freehold premises in London as tenants in common in equal shares. They decided to transfer the practice there and orally agreed that the firm should be granted a yearly tenancy of the premises at a rent of £500 a year to be paid out of the partnership assets. In 1948 Frank died, and the freehold was vested in Arthur and the two trustees of Frank's will, one of whom was Frank's son, Ralph, the respondent. In 1950 Arthur took Ralph into a partnership, which was dissolved in 1957. Ralph refused to leave the premises, where he continued to occupy a room. Arthur claimed possession of the room, on the ground that the firm was the tenant under the oral yearly tenancy of 1942, and that he was the surviving partner.

Held (affirming CA). No tenancy was created in 1942, and, therefore, the claim for possession failed.

VISCOUNT SIMONDS: The first [question] is whether it is competent for two persons orally to grant to themselves an annual tenancy of premises of which they are the owners. ...

It is common ground, my Lords, that before the Law of Property Act 1925 came into force it could not [be granted]. But the appellant claims that the law has been altered by the combined effect of sections 72 and 205 of that Act. In the courts below the meaning and effect of section 205(1)(ii), p. 9, ante, has been the main topic of discussion, and it appears to have been readily assumed that, if 'conveyance' includes the oral grant (or agreement to make a grant) of an

---

[16] For a mortgagee's right to possession, see p. 835, post.
[17] (1962) 78 LQR 175 (P.V.B.); 177 (R.E.M.).

annual tenancy, then either subsection (3) or subsection (4) of section 72 validates the transaction. I do not differ from those of your Lordships who think that section 205(1)(ii) has not this effect, nor do I think that any assistance is given by section 52 or section 54. But I would briefly examine the position if the contrary view prevails and an oral grant of a tenancy is a 'conveyance' within the meaning of the Act and 'convey' has a corresponding meaning.

I turn, then, to section 72 ... Let me take subsection (4) first. In this subsection I do not find it provided that two persons may convey property to themselves or three persons to themselves. On the contrary, I read the subsection literally as meaning that where property is vested in two persons they may convey it to one of themselves and where it is vested in three persons they may convey it to one or two of themselves. I see no reason for giving a more extended meaning to this subsection, and I would point out that, if it did have the meaning claimed for it, it would add nothing to subsection (3) except to provide a plain inconsistency in respect of the date of commencement. I come back to subsection (3). I accept that in this subsection the singular 'person' must include the plural so that two persons may now convey land to, or vest land in, themselves. What, then, is the scope of this subsection? It is said on behalf of the appellant that it enables A., the owner of property, to grant a lease of it to himself and similarly enables A. and B., the joint owners of property, to grant a lease of it to themselves. It was not, I think, suggested that A. and B. could do what A. could not do. The question, then, can conveniently be examined by asking whether the subsection enables A. to grant a lease to himself of land of which he is the owner, or, in other words, to carve out of his larger estate a lesser estate which creates (I know not how to put it otherwise) the relationship of landlord and tenant between himself and himself. I find this a strange conception. In *Grey v Ellison* (1856) 1 Giff 438, 444, Stuart V-C describes as fanciful and a whimsical transaction the proposal that a man should grant a lease to himself. He had, no doubt, in mind that a lease is in one aspect contractual. Of things necessary to a lease, says Sheppard's Touchstone of Assurances (see 7th edn., vol. II. p. 268), one is that: 'There must be an acceptance, [actual or presumed], of the thing demised.' Yet it is meaningless to say that a man accepts from himself something which is already his own. I recognise that a lease not only has a contractual basis between lessor and lessee, but operates also to vest an estate in the lessee. But what sort of estate is in these circumstances vested in the lessee? I will assume that it will not at once merge in the higher estate from which it springs, though I see no reason why it should not. Yet it must be an estate hitherto unknown to the law. Even a bare demise implies certain covenants at law: but to such an estate as this no covenants can be effectively attached. Nor can the common law remedy of distress operate to enable the lessor to distrain on his own goods. Again, at law in the absence of some special provision the lessee is entitled to exclusive possession of the demised premises. What meaning is to be attributed to this where the lessee is also the lessor? My Lords, my mind recoils against an interpretation of the Act which leads to so fanciful and whimsical a result, and it appears to me to be quite unnecessary.[18]

[18]   A person who holds land as a nominee for his principal may grant a valid lease to that principal: *Ingram v IRC* [2000] 1 AC 293, [1999] 1 All ER 297 (as part of an inheritance tax avoidance scheme HL held that Lady Ingram's solicitor, as nominee for her, granted a valid lease to her. The tax advantage has been negatived by FA 1999, s. 104); (1999) 115 LQR 351 (R. Kerridge). The convincing dissenting judgment of MILLETT LJ in CA was approved: [1997] STC 1234 at 1255, [1997] 4 All ER 395 at 419. See also Lord RADCLIFFE in *Rye v* Rye at 511, at 153: 'In effect, putting aside conveyancing forms, a man was able

If, then, it is asked what meaning can be given to the subsection, I think that the answer is that it is intended partly to supersede the old conveyancing device of a conveyance to uses or of a grant and regrant and partly to provide an essential step in the new machinery set up by the series of Acts passed in 1925. To the latter the word 'vest' itself supplies a clue. It appears to refer to the statutory provisions for vesting the legal estate in a tenant for life or statutory owner, which are to be found, for example, in Schedule II, paragraph 1, to the Settled Land Act 1925.

Thirty-five years have now passed since the Law of Property Act came into operation. I have not found in any of the textbooks that I have been able to consult dealing with real property or the relation of landlord and tenant any suggestion that section 72 of the Act has given birth to such a monstrous child … I am not prepared in this case to give it currency, and for this reason I would dismiss this appeal.

D. The Position in Equity

Where there is an enforceable agreement to grant a lease, of which equity is prepared, in the circumstances, to grant specific performance, equity (following the maxim that equity looks on that as done which ought to be done) will treat the intended tenant as having already, in equity, a lease. This is so where there is:

   (i) an agreement in writing which satisfies the requirement of formalities for its creation;[19] or

  (ii) a 'void' lease, i.e. a lease in writing for more than three years which is void at law owing to the lack of a seal, but is construed in equity as an agreement for a lease;[20]

 (iii) a lease in registered land which has not satisfied the requirements for registration.

E. The Doctrine of *Walsh v Lonsdale*[1]

This doctrine is one aspect of the general doctrine of estate contracts which is discussed in detail above.[2] A question which is commonly discussed is the extent to which an agreement for a lease is as good as a lease.

F. The Differences between a Lease and an Agreement for a Lease[3]

i. THE BONA FIDE PURCHASER

An agreement for a lease is an equitable interest, and, as such, liable to destruction by a bona fide purchaser of a legal estate for value without notice.[4]

---

to convey to himself before the 1925 Act. He could, of course, put land in trust for himself by conveying it to a nominee, and, I suppose, if there was any conceivable point in the operation, he could similarly demise land to a nominee. Cf *Kildrummy (Jersey) Ltd v IRC* [1990] STC 657, where it was held by the Court of Session that land could not be demised to a nominee. *Rye v Rye* was not cited; See also *Clydesdale Bank plc v Davidson* [1998] SLT 522 (under Scots law pro diviso heritable proprietors cannot create a lease over a property in favour of one of their number).

[19] Pp. 65 et seq, ante.

[20] *Parker v Taswell* (1858) 2 De G & J 559; *Bond v Rosling* (1861) 1 B & S 371; *Tidey v Mollett* (1864) 16 CBNS 298.

[1] (1882) 21 ChD 9, p. 85 ante.

[2] See p. 84 et seq., ante.

[3] C & B, pp. 403–408; Gray, pp. 580–586; M & W, paras. 14.041–14.053; MM, pp. 343–346; Smith, pp. 384–386.

[4] *Pilcher v Rawlins* (1872) 7 Ch App 259, p. 26, ante; Maitland, p. 158; p. 88, ante.

The doctrine of the bona fide purchaser is modified, in the case of unregistered land, by the introduction of a system of registration of land charges by the Land Charges Act 1925,[5] and has no part to play in the context of registered land.[6]

ii. LAW OF PROPERTY ACT 1925, SECTION 62

An agreement for a lease is not a 'conveyance' within the meaning of the Law of Property Act 1925, section 62.[7]

BORMAN v GRIFFITH
[1930] 1 Ch 493 (ChD, MAUGHAM J)

In 1923 James agreed to grant a lease to Borman of a house which was situated in a large park containing a mansion. The house was approached only by the drive leading to the mansion and not by a public road. The agreement contained no express grant of a right of way over the drive. In 1926 James leased the mansion to Griffith for 14 years.

Subsequent to the agreement of 1923, James constructed an unmetalled road to the rear of Borman's house. The road was not adequate for heavy traffic, and was unsuitable for Borman's trade as a poultry dealer, and Borman continued to use the drive. In 1928 Griffith obstructed Borman's use of the drive, and Borman sued to establish his right of way.

Held. (i) Section 62 of the Law of Property Act 1925 did not apply to an agreement for a lease, and the plaintiff could not claim an easement on that ground.

(ii) The plaintiff was entitled to claim the right of way under the rule in *Wheeldon v Burrows* (1879) 12 ChD 31, p. 718, post.

MAUGHAM J: ... The date of the contract is a date before the coming into force of the Law of Property Act 1925, and is a date at which the Conveyancing Act, 1881, was still in force. The plaintiff relies on section 62, subsections 1 and 2 of the Law of Property Act 1925, under which certain general words are deemed to be included in a conveyance, and, in particular, the words 'ways ... reputed to appertain to the land, houses, etc.' and 'reputed or known as part or parcel of or appurtenant to the land, houses, etc,': he asserts that the way along the drive in the front of his house, and the branch drive leading directly to the back of his house, were ways enjoyed with the premises demised by the contract; and he points out that under subsection 6, the section applies to conveyances executed after 31 December 1881, and that 'conveyance' is defined in section 205, subsection 1 (ii), to include 'a lease ... and every other assurance of property or of an interest therein by any instrument, except a will'. ...

On the whole, I think that it is not a 'conveyance', because it is not an 'assurance of property or of an interest therein'. It is true that, under the decision in *Walsh v Lonsdale* (1882) 21 ChD 9 at 14, p. 85, ante it has been held that, where there is an agreement for a lease under which possession has been given, the tenant holds, for many purposes, as if a lease had actually been granted. [His Lordship then quoted from the judgment of Jessel MR and continued:] That is the well known judgment of Sir George Jessel MR, with which Cotton and Lindley LJJ agreed. But no court has yet declared that an agreement for a lease for a term

---

[5]   P. 29, ante. Now LCA 1972.
[6]   P. 25, ante.
[7]   'Conveyance' is defined in LPA 1925, s. 205(1)(ii), p. 9, ante. For s. 62, see p. 722, post.

of more than three years is an 'assurance'. It has to be borne in mind that a lease for any term of more than three years must be by deed, and it is well known that, under section 3 of the Real Property Act, 1845, '... a lease required by law to be in writing, of any tenements or hereditaments ... shall ... be void at law unless made by deed.' (See now section 52 of the Law of Property Act, 1925, and the repeal section.)

In my opinion, a contract for a lease exceeding a term of three years does not come within the meaning of the phrase 'assurance of property or of an interest therein' as that phrase is used in section 205, subsection 1(ii), of the Law of Property Act, 1925: and accordingly I am unable to construe the agreement of 10 October 1923, as if the general words of section 62 of that Act were included in it ...

In my view, the principles laid down in such cases as *Wheeldon v Burrows* (1879) 12 ChD 31; *Brown v Alabaster* (1887) 37 ChD 490; and *Nicholls v Nicholls* (1899) 81 LT 811 are applicable. Without going through all those cases in detail, I may state the principle as follows—namely, that where, as in the present case, two properties belonging to a single owner and about to be granted are separated by a common road, or where a plainly visible road exists over the one for the apparent use of the other, and that road is necessary for the reasonable enjoyment of the property, a right to use the road will pass with the quasi-dominant tenement, unless by the terms of the contract that right is excluded: and in my opinion, if the present position were that the plaintiff was claiming against the lessor specific performance of the agreement of 10 October 1923, he would be entitled to be given a right of way for all reasonable purposes along the drive, including the part that passes the farm on the way to the orchard.

iii. AVAILABILITY OF SPECIFIC PERFORMANCE [8]

The doctrine of *Walsh v Lonsdale* is dependent upon the availability of specific performance, which is discretionary.

iv. THE EFFECT OF AN ASSIGNMENT

See p. 560, post. [9]

v. REGISTERED LAND

See p. 506, ante.

---

[8] *Coatsworth v Johnson* (1885) 55 LJQB 220, p. 87, ante; *Foster v Reeves* [1892] 2 QB 255; *Cornish v Brook Green Laundry Ltd* [1959] 1 QB 394, [1959] 1 All ER 373; (1959) 75 LQR 168 (R.E.M.); *Kingswood Estate Co Ltd v Anderson* [1963] 2 QB 169, [1962] 3 All ER 593; (1963) 79 LQR 19 (R.E.M.); *Rushton v Smith* [1976] QB 480, [1975] 2 All ER 905; *Industrial Properties (Barton Hill) Ltd v Associated Electrical Industries Ltd* [1977] QB 580, [1977] 2 All ER 293, p. 86, ante; *Warmington v Miller* [1973] QB 877 at 877, [1973] 2 All ER 372 at 377, p. 87, ante; *Bell Street Investments v Wood* (1970) 216 EG 585; *Henry Smith's Charity Trustees v Hemmings* (1982) 265 EG 383.

[9] A further difference was removed by *National Carriers Ltd v Panalpina (Northern) Ltd* [1981] AC 675, [1981] 1 All ER 161, where HL held that the doctrine of frustration is applicable to a lease; for an agreement for a lease, see *Rom Securities Ltd v Rogers (Holdings) Ltd* (1967) 205 EG 427.

IV. Remedies of the Landlord

It is not possible, in the available space, to deal with all the landlord's remedies. This section will be confined to a consideration of some of the restrictions upon the landlord's right to recover possession of the demised premises.

A. Statutory Restrictions on Recovery of Possession [10]

When a lease comes to an end, whether by the expiry of the term or by notice to quit, the landlord's common law right to recover possession is subject to certain statutory restrictions. [11]

(*a*) The landlord may be liable criminally, under Criminal Law Act 1977, section 6; [12] under Protection from Eviction Act 1977, section 1, [13] for unlawful eviction and harassment, and under Protection from Harassment Act 1997.

(*b*) The landlord may be liable under Housing Act 1988, sections 27 and 28 to pay damages when he has committed acts which amount to unlawful eviction and harassment. [14]

(*c*) The tenant may be protected under the statutory codes set out on p. 434, n. 11, ante.

(*d*) Or, more generally, under the following provisions:

PROTECTION FROM EVICTION ACT 1977 [15]

2. Restriction on re-entry without due process of law.—Where any premises are let as a dwelling on a lease which is subject to a right of re-entry or forfeiture it shall not be lawful to enforce that right otherwise than by proceedings in the court while any person is lawfully residing in the premises or part of them. [16]

3. Prohibition of eviction without due process of law.—(1) Where any premises have been let as a dwelling [17] under a tenancy which is neither a statutorily

---

[10]   C & B, pp. 500, 530–531; Gray, pp. 1257–1260; M & W, para.14.203; MM, pp. 616–617; Report of the Committee on the Rent Acts (1971) (Cmnd 4609), pp. 105–106.

[11]   On the landlord's right to terminate by physical re-entry, see Law Commission Consultation Paper on Termination of Tenancies for Tenant Default 2004 (Law Com No. 174, p. 558, post). On human rights, see *Harrow London Borough Council v Qazi* [2003] 3 WLR 792 (where the landlord has an unqualified right to possession under domestic law on proof that tenancy has been terminated, held no breach of Art. 8 of European Convention on Human Rights; (2004) 120 LQR 398 (S. Bright); nor of Art. 14 *Newham London Borough Council v Kibata* [2003] EWCA Civ 1785, [2004] 1 EGLR 56).

[12]   The Forcible Entry Acts 1381–1623 were abolished by s. 13. See Law Commission Report, Conspiracy and Criminal Law Reform, Part II (Law Com. No. 76, 1976).

[13]   As amended by Housing Act 1988, s. 29. See *R v Burke* [1991] 1 AC 135, [1990] 2 All ER 385.

[14]   For the measure of damages, see *Tagro v Cafane* [1991] 1 WLR 378, [1991] 2 All ER 235 (£31,000); [1991] Conv 297 (C. Rogers); *Jones v Miah* [1992] 2 EGLR 50 (£8,000); [1993] Conv 84 (S. Bridge); *Haniff v Robinson* [1993] QB 419 (£26,000 for Rent Act tenant); *Keen v McSpadden* (1996) 1 L & TR D41 (£94,000); *Regalgrand Ltd v Dickerson* (1996) 74 P & CR 312 (reduction by mitigating conduct); *King v Jackson* [1998] 03 EG 138. Such decisions are reported regularly in the monthly issues of Legal Action. For a recent review, see (1995) 145 NLJ 937, 1061 (N. Madge). See also *Sampson v Wilson* [1996] Ch 39 (landlord's agent not liable).

[15]   See generally Martin, *Residential Security* (2nd edn, 1995), chap. 3; [2001] Conv 249 (D. Cowan).

[16]   *Iperion Investments Corpn v Broadwalk House Residents Ltd* [1992] 2 EGLR 235 (tenants' housekeeper resident in premises).

[17]   See also *National Trust v Knipe* [1997] 4 All ER 627.

protected tenancy nor an excluded tenancy [18] and—
    (*a*) the tenancy (in this section referred to as the former tenancy) has come to an end, but
    (*b*) the occupier continues to reside in the premises or part of them,
it shall not be lawful for the owner to enforce against the occupier, otherwise than by proceedings in the court, his right to recover possession of the premises. [19]

(2) In this section 'the occupier', in relation to any premises, means any person lawfully residing in the premises or part of them at the termination of the former tenancy.

(2B) Subsections (1) and (2) above apply in relation to any premises occupied as a dwelling under a licence, other than an excluded licence, as they apply in relation to premises let as a dwelling under a tenancy, and in those subsections the expressions 'let' and 'tenancy' shall be construed accordingly. [20]

5. Validity of notices to quit.—Subject to subsection (1B) below no notice by a landlord or a tenant to quit any premises let (whether before or after the commencement of this Act) as a dwelling shall be valid unless—
    (*a*) it is writing and contains such information as may be prescribed, and
    (*b*) it is given not less than 4 weeks before the date on which it is to take effect. [1]

(1A) [2] Subject to subsection (1B) below, no notice by a licensor or a licensee to determine a periodic licence to occupy premises as a dwelling (whether the licence was granted before or after the passing of this Act) shall be valid unless—
    (*a*) it is in writing and contains such information as may be prescribed, and
    (*b*) it is given not less than 4 weeks before the date on which it is to take effect. [3]

(1B) Nothing in subsection (1) or subsection (1A) above applies to—
    (*a*) premises let on an excluded tenancy which is entered into on or after the date on which the Housing Act 1988 came into force unless it is entered into pursuant to a contract made before that date; or
    (*b*) premises occupied under an excluded licence.

8. Interpretation.—(1) In this Act 'statutorily protected tenancy' means—
    (*a*) a protected tenancy within the meaning of the Rent Act 1977 or a tenancy to which Part I of the Landlord and Tenant Act 1954 applies;
    (*b*) a protected occupancy or statutory tenancy as defined in the Rent (Agriculture) Act 1976;
    (*c*) a tenancy to which Part II of the Landlord and Tenant Act 1954 applies;
    (*d*) a tenancy of an agricultural holding within the meaning of the Agricultural Holdings Act 1986, which is a tenancy in relation to which that Act applies; [4]
    (*e*) an assured tenancy or assured agricultural occupancy under Part I of the Housing Act 1988; [5]

---

[18] As amended by Housing Act 1988, s. 30(1). For a definition of excluded tenancies and licences, see s. 3A, added by Housing Act 1988, s. 31. The most important exclusion is where accommodation is shared with either the landlord or with a member of the landlord's family (in the latter case the landlord must also reside in the same building, which must not be a purpose built block of flats).

[19] *Warder v Cooper* [1970] Ch 495, [1970] 1 All ER 1112.

[20] As added by Housing Act 1988, s. 30(2).

[1] As amended by Housing Act 1988, s. 32(1).

[2] As amended by Housing Act 1988, s. 32(2).

[3] *Norris v Checksfield* [1991] 1 WLR 1241, [1991] 4 All ER 327.

[4] As amended by the Agricultural Holdings Act 1986, Sch. 14, para. 61; Agricultural Tenancies Act 1995, s. 40, Sch. 8, para. 29(a).

[5] As amended by Housing Act 1988, s. 33(2).

(*f*) a tenancy to which Schedule 10 to the Local Government and Housing Act 1989 applies;[6]

(*g*) a farm business tenancy within the meaning of the Agricultural Tenancies Act 1995.[7]

(2) For the purposes of Part I of this Act a person who, under the terms of his employment, had exclusive possession of any premises other than as a tenant shall be deemed to have been a tenant and the expressions 'let' and 'tenancy' shall be construed accordingly.

(3) In Part I of this Act 'the owner', in relation to any premises, means the person who, as against the occupier, is entitled to possession thereof.

9. The court for purposes of Part I.—(3) Nothing in this Act shall affect the jurisdiction of the High Court in proceedings to enforce a lessor's right of re-entry or forfeiture[8] or to enforce a mortgagee's right of possession in a case where the former tenancy was not binding on the mortgagee.[9]

B. Forfeiture and Relief against Forfeiture[10]

A lease usually includes a forfeiture clause which provides for the landlord's right to forfeit the remainder of the lease if there is a breach by the tenant of any covenants in the lease.[11] The burden of proof lies on the landlord to establish an act of forfeiture on the part of the tenant.[12]

Unlimited application of such a clause could inflict hardship on the tenant out of all proportion to the damage suffered by the landlord. For example, a tenant, who is in arrears with his rent, may subsequently pay everything that is due with interest; a breach of a covenant to insure may cause no loss to the landlord, but it used to be treated as sufficient to produce forfeiture under a forfeiture clause.

It has long been settled that equity will relieve a tenant against forfeiture in respect of non-payment of rent, but as a general rule not in other cases. The position is now regulated by statute.

Under the Civil Procedure Rules 1998 all claims for the recovery of possession of land, including those by a landlord, must be started in the County Court; they

---

[6]   As amended by Local Government and Housing Act 1989, Sch. 11, para. 54.

[7]   As inserted by Agricultural Tenancies Act 1995, s. 40, Sch. 8, para. 29(b).

[8]   *Borzak v Ahmed* [1965] 2 QB 320, [1965] 1 All ER 808.

[9]   See p. 853, post.

[10]   C & B, pp. 456–475; Gray, pp. 1253–1294; M & W, paras. 14.118–14.171; MM, pp. 354–384; Smith, pp. 407–423; Pawlowski, *The Forfeiture of Leases* (1993). See Anti-Social Behaviour Act 2003, under which a public sector landlord may apply to the county court for a demotion order, which temporarily removes security of tenure from an anti-social tenant: (2004) 148 SJ 771 (D. Underwood); Collins and Cattermole, *Anti-Social Behaviour: Powers and Remedies* (2004).

[11]   See *Richard Clarke & Co Ltd v Widnall* [1976] 1 WLR 845, [1976] 3 All ER 301, where a clause in a lease under which the landlord was entitled to serve a notice to terminate in the event of a breach of a covenant to pay rent was construed as a forfeiture clause. Cf. *Clays Lane Housing Co-operative Ltd v Patrick* (1984) 49 P & CR 72 (for a clause to be a forfeiture clause it must bring the lease to an end earlier than the actual termination date). A forfeiture may also be incurred where the tenant denies his landlord's title: *WG Clark Properties Ltd v Dupre Properties Ltd* [1992] Ch 297, [1992] 1 All ER 596 (disclaimer of title as to part of demised premises held not sufficient); [1993] Conv 299 (J.E. Martin); *British Telecommunications plc v Department of the Environment* [1996] NPC 148 (denial must be unequivocal); *Abidogun v Frolan Health Cares Ltd* [2001] 45 EG 138 (CS); [2001] Conv 399 (M. Pawlowski).

[12]   *Doe d Bridger v Whitehead* (1838) 8 Ad & El 571; *Hagee (London) Ltd v Co-operative Insurance Society Ltd* [1992] 1 EGLR 57; [1992] Conv 345 (J. E. Martin).

may only be started in the High Court where there are complicated disputes of fact or points of law of general importance. [13] It is the issue of the claim form by the Court which is equivalent to re-entry by the landlord.

i. NON-PAYMENT OF RENT [14]

COMMON LAW PROCEDURE ACT 1852

210. Proceedings in ejectment by landlord for non-payment of rent.—In all cases between landlord and tenant, as often as it shall happen that one half year's rent shall be in arrear, and the landlord or lessor, to whom the same is due, hath right by law to re-enter for the non-payment thereof, such landlord or lessor shall and may without any formal demand or re-entry, serve a writ in ejectment for the recovery of the demised premises which service shall stand in the place and stead of a demand and re-entry; [15] and in case of judgment against the defendant for non-appearance, if it shall be made appear to the court where the said action is depending, by affidavit, or be proved upon the trial in case the defendant appears, that half a year's rent was due before the said writ was served, and that no sufficient distress was to be found on the demised premises, countervailing the arrears then due, and that the lessor had power to re-enter, then and in every such case the lessor shall recover judgment and execution, in the same manner as if the rent in arrear had been legally demanded, and a re-entry made; and in case the lessee or his assignee, or other person claiming or deriving under the said lease, shall permit and suffer judgment to be had and recovered on such trial in ejectment, and execution to be executed thereon, without paying the rent and arrears, together with full costs, and without proceeding for relief in equity within six months after such execution executed, then and in such case the said lessee, his assignee, and all other persons claiming and deriving under the said lease, shall be barred and foreclosed from all relief or remedy in law or equity, other than by bringing error for reversal of such judgment, in case the same shall be erroneous, and the said landlord or lessor shall from thenceforth hold the said demised premises discharged from such lease ...

211. Lessee proceeding in equity not to have injunction or relief without payment of rent and costs.—In case the said lessee, his assignee, or other person claiming any right, title, or interest, in law or equity, of, in, or to the said lease, shall, within

---

13   CPR 55; PD 1.3.
14   For a useful summary of the law, see *Billson v Residential Apartments Ltd* [1991] 3 WLR 264 at 277, per Sir Nicolas BROWNE-WILKINSON V-C.
15   *Canas Property Co Ltd v KL Television Services Ltd* [1970] 2 QB 433, [1970] 2 All ER 795; *Richards v De Freitas* (1975) 29 P & CR 1; *Ashton v Sobelman* [1987] 1 WLR 177, [1987] 1 All ER 755; *Hammersmith and Fulham London Borough Council v Top Shop Centres Ltd* [1990] Ch 237, [1989] 2 All ER 655; *Capital and City Holdings Ltd v Dean Warburg Ltd* (1988) 58 P & CR 346; *GS Fashions Ltd v B&Q Ltd* [1995] 1 WLR 1088, [1995] 4 All ER 899.
      The forfeiture does not become final until the landlord has obtained unconditional judgment for possession. Until then the covenants in the lease remain potentially good in favour of the tenant: *Driscoll v Church Comrs for England* [1957] 1 QB 330, [1956] 3 All ER 802; *Peninsular Maritime Ltd v Padseal Ltd* (1981) 259 EG 860 (landlord's covenant to repair lift held enforceable by tenant while seeking relief against forfeiture). See also *Meadows v Clerical Medical and General Life Assurance Society* [1981] Ch 70, [1980] 1 All ER 454; ('The tenancy has a trance-like existence pendente lite; none can assert with assurance whether it is alive or dead', per Sir Robert MEGARRY at 75, at 457); *Associated Deliveries Ltd v Harrison* (1984) 50 P & CR 91; [1985] Conv 285 (J. E. Martin); *Official Custodian for Charities v Mackey (No 2)* [1985] 1 WLR 1308, [1985] 2 All ER 1016; *Hillgate House Ltd v Expert Clothing Service and Sales Ltd* [1987] 1 EGLR 65; *Ivory Gate Ltd v Spetale* (1998) 77 P & CR 141.

the time aforesaid, proceed for relief in any court of equity, such person shall not have or continue any injunction against the proceedings at law on such ejectment, unless he does or shall, within forty days next after a full and perfect answer shall be made by the claimant in such ejectment, bring into court, and lodge with the proper officer such sum and sums of money as the lessor or landlord shall in his answer swear to be due and in arrear over and above all just allowances, and also the costs taxed in the said suit, there to remain till the hearing of the cause, or to be paid out to the lessor or landlord on good security, subject to the decree of the court; and in case such proceedings for relief in equity shall be taken within the time aforesaid, and after execution is executed, the lessor or landlord shall be accountable only for so much and no more as he shall really and bona fide, without fraud, deceit, or wilful neglect, make of the demised premises from the times of his entering into the actual possession thereof; and if what shall be so made by the lessor or landlord happen to be less than the rent reserved on the said lease, then the said lessee or his assignee, before he shall be restored to his possession, shall pay such lessor or landlord what the money so by him made fell short of the reserved rent for the time such lessor or landlord held the said lands.

212. Tenant paying all rent, with costs, proceedings to cease.—If the tenant or his assignee do or shall, at any time before the trial in such ejectment, pay or tender to the lessor or landlord, his executors or administrators, or his or their attorney in that cause, or pay into the court where the same cause is depending, all the rent and arrears, [16] together with the costs, then and in such case all further proceedings on the said ejectment shall cease and be discontinued; and if such lessee, his executors, administrators, or assigns, shall, upon such proceedings as aforesaid, be relieved in equity, he and they shall have, hold, and enjoy the demised lands, according to the lease thereof made, without any new lease.

LAW OF PROPERTY ACT 1925

146. Restrictions on and relief against forfeiture of leases and underleases.—
(4) p. 533, post.

SUPREME COURT ACT 1981

38. Relief against forfeiture for non-payment of rent. [17]—(1) In any action in the High Court for the forfeiture of a lease for non-payment of rent, the court

---

[16]   *Standard Pattern Co Ltd v Ivey* [1962] Ch 432, [1962] 1 All ER 452 (limiting the tenant's right to cases where at least half a year's rent is in arrear); (1962) 78 LQR 168 (R. E. Megarry).

[17]   See *Belgravia Insurance Co Ltd v Meah* [1964] 1 QB 436, [1963] 3 All ER 828; *Stanhope v Haworth* (1886) 3 TLR 34; *Re Brompton Securities Ltd (No 2)* [1988] 3 All ER 677, where VINELOTT J said at 680: 'Save in very exceptional circumstances, the court will grant relief against forfeiture to a tenant, and will do so notwithstanding that actions have been brought on previous occasions to recover the rent'. The court will refuse relief if 'the landlord has, not unreasonably or precipitously, granted rights in the premises to third parties; *Silverman v AFCO (UK) Ltd* [1988] 1 EGLR 51 at 53, per SLADE LJ.
        Under the ancient jurisdiction of the Court of Chancery, the court has power, independent of statute, to grant relief from forfeiture where there has been a peaceable entry; *Howard v Fanshawe* [1895] 2 Ch 581; *Lovelock v Margo* [1963] 2 QB 786, [1963] 2 All ER 13; *Thatcher v CH Pearce & Sons (Contractors) Ltd* [1968] 1 WLR 748 (tenant granted relief, in spite of bringing action six months and four days after landlord regained possession); *Ladup Ltd v Williams & Clyn's Bank plc* [1985] 1 WLR 851, [1985] 2 All ER 577. See [1969] JPL pp. 251–252. See also *Billson v Residential Apartments Ltd* [1992] 1

shall have power to grant relief against forfeiture in a summary manner, and may do so subject to the same terms and conditions as to the payment of rent, costs or otherwise as could have been imposed by it in such an action immediately before the commencement of this Act. [18]

(2) Where the lessee or a person deriving title under him is granted relief under this section, he shall hold the demised premises in accordance with the terms of the lease without the necessity for a new lease.

ii. BREACH OF COVENANTS OTHER THAN NON-PAYMENT OF RENT

(a) Law of Property Act 1925, section 146

Before a landlord can enforce a right of forfeiture for breach of covenant other than one for the payment of rent, he must serve a notice on the tenant under section 146(1) of the Law of Property Act 1925. Whether a breach is capable of remedy under para. (*b*) has given rise to difficulty. If the covenant is positive, e.g. to repair, the breach is clearly capable of remedy. [19] In the case of a negative covenant, 'the attractive and easy ratio' of MACKINNON J in *Rugby School (Governors) v Tannahill* [1934] 1 KB 695 at 700–701 was to hold that all negative covenants are incapable of remedy, and that recovery of possession by the landlord depends solely on whether the tenant can persuade the court to grant relief from forfeiture under section 146(2). In *Scala House and District Property Co Ltd v Forbes* [1974] QB 575, [1973] 3 All ER 308, p. 537, post, the Court of Appeal held that the breach of a covenant not to assign, underlet or part with possession without the consent of the landlord is incapable of remedy. 'It is a complete breach once for all. [20] The Court also considered that the breach of a user covenant, e.g. not to use the premises for illegal or immoral purposes, where the user has ceased before the service of a section 146 notice, is also incapable of remedy; the stigma attaching to the premises cannot be removed by mere cesser of the immoral or illegal user.' [1]

AC 494 at 516, [1991] 3 All ER 265 at 276, where CA held that there was no similar inherent jurisdiction in the case of relief for breach of covenant other than the covenant to pay rent; p. 551, post.

For the statutory jurisdiction of the County Court to grant relief, see the County Courts Act 1984, s. 138, as amended by AJA 1985, s. 55; High Court and County Courts Jurisdiction Order 1991, art. 2 (SI 1991 No. 724); *United Dominions Trust Ltd v Shellpoint Trustees Ltd* [1993] 4 All ER 310 (containing a detailed examination of the sections); (1994) 110 LQR 15 (N. P. Gravells); *Maryland Estates Ltd v Bar-Joseph* [1999] 1 WLR 83,[1998] 3 All ER 193; *Croydon (Unique) Ltd v Wright* [2001] Ch 318 (charging order).

[18] *Khar v Delbounty Ltd* [1997] EGCS 183 (no difference in substance between covenant to pay service charges and covenant to pay rent).

[19] *Expert Clothing Service and Sales Ltd v Hillgate House Ltd* [1986] Ch 340, [1985] 2 All ER 998, p. 542, post.

[20] At 588, at 315, per RUSSELL LJ, p. 540, post; *Billson v Residential Apartments Ltd* [1992] 1 AC 494, [1991] 3 All ER 265, (where Sir NICOLAS BROWNE-WILKINSON V-C doubted whether breach of covenant not to make alterations without prior consent of landlord was irremediable).

[1] *Rugby School (Governors) v Tannahill* [1935] 1 KB 87, p. 536, post; *Egerton v Esplanade Hotels, London Ltd* [1947] 2 All ER 88; *Hoffmann v Fineberg* [1949] Ch 245, [1948] 1 All ER 592, p. 538, post; *Borthwick-Norton v Romney Warwick Estates Ltd* [1950] 1 All ER 798; *Glass v Kencakes Ltd* [1966] 1 QB 611, [1964] 3 All ER 807, p. 538, post; *Dunraven Securities Ltd v Holloway* (1982) 264 EG 709 (keeping in tenant's Soho sex shop obscene articles for publication for gain contrary to Obscene Publications Act 1959); (1983) 133 NLJ 485 (H. W. Wilkinson); *British Petroleum Pension Trust Ltd v Behrendt* (1985) 52 P & CR 117, p. 539, n. 7, post; *Van Haarlam v Kasner* [1992] 2 EGLR 59 (paraphernalia for spying found in flat).

In *Savva v Houssein*, [1996] 2 EGLR 65, p. 541, post, however, the Court of Appeal, in holding that the breach of a covenant not to make alterations without the consent of the landlord was capable of remedy, changed tack and considered whether the harm caused by the breach was remediable, rather than whether the breach itself could be remedied.

The effect of the grant of relief to a tenant by the court is to reinstate the old lease, which is deemed to have been continuously in force. The court may impose conditions on granting relief.[2] Where a lease is forfeited, any under-leases created out of it automatically come to an end.[3] But an underlessee or mortgagee has the same right of applying to the court for relief against forfeiture of the head lease as the tenant has under the head lease. In this case, however, the effect of granting relief to an under-lessee is to grant and vest a new term in him; the lease forfeited by the landlord is not revived and continued.[4]

LAW OF PROPERTY ACT 1925

146. Restrictions on and relief against forfeiture of leases and underleases.—
(1) A right of re-entry or forfeiture under any proviso or stipulation in a lease for a breach of any covenant or condition in the lease[5] shall not be enforceable, by action or otherwise, unless and until the lessor serves on the lessee[6] a notice[7] —

---

[2]   *Hoffman v Fineberg* [1949] Ch 245 at 254, [1948] 1 All ER 592 at 596, per HARMAN J. See *Bank of Ireland Home Mortgages v South Lodge Developments* [1996] 1 EGLR 91.

[3]   *Pennell v Payne* [1995] QB 192 at 197, [1995] 2 All ER 592; *Barrett v Morgan* [1998] 4 All ER 179; *PW & CO v Milton Gate Investments Ltd* [2004] 2 WLR 443, p. 436, n. 20.

[4]   The new term cannot be any longer than the one forfeited, and the words 'any longer term ... sub-lease' in LPA 1925 s. 146(4) refer to the position immediately before forfeiture: *Cadogan v Dimovic* [1984] 1 WLR 609, [1984] 2 All ER 168 (sub-lease terminated by forfeiture of head lease, which was a business tenancy subject to extension under L & T Act 1954 (see C & B, pp. 546–554); sub-lessee granted a new term of appropriate duration but within the limits of the extension imposed by the 1954 Act); *Official Custodian for Charities v Mackey* [1985] Ch 168, [1984] 3 All ER 689 (rent for under-leases payable to lessor during period between forfeiture of the old lease and the creation of the new one); [1985] Conv 50 (J. Martin).

[5]   A s. 146 notice cannot be validly served under a long lease of a dwelling, unless the fact that there has been a breach has been determined by a court or admitted by the tenant: Commonhold and Leasehold Reform Act 2002, ss. 168, 169; for further restrictions, see s. 167 (failture to pay small amount for short period); s. 170 (forfeiture for failure to pay service charge etc.), amending Housing Act 1996, ss. 81, 82.

[6]   Where a lessee assigns his lease in breach of covenant, the assignment is effective, and the notice must be served on the assignee and not on the original lessee: *Old Grovebury Manor Farm Ltd v W Seymour Plant Sales and Hire Ltd (No 2)* [1979] 1 WLR 1397, [1979] 3 All ER 504; *Governors of the Peabody Donation Fund v Higgins* [1983] 1 WLR 1091, [1983] 3 All ER 122; *Fuller v Judy Properties Ltd* [1992] 1 EGLR 75; [1992] Conv 343 (J. E. Martin) (second notice served on assignee after taking possession held invalid); *Greenwich London Borough Council v Discreet Selling Estates Ltd* [1990] 2 EGLR 65; [1991] Conv 222 (J. E. Martin) (a landlord, who had served notice for breach of covenant to repair and then waived breach by acceptance of rent, need not serve a fresh notice). It is not necessary to serve a notice on a mortgagee of the term: *Church Commissioners for England v Ve-Ri-Best Manufacturing Co Ltd* [1957] 1 QB 238; *Smith v Spaul* [2003] 17 EG 148.

[7]   The notice may be served under LPA 1925 s. 196: it may be left at the tenant's address even though he is in prison and unlikely to receive it, *Van Haarlam v Kasner* [1992] 2 EGLR 59; and even though he is suffering from mental disorder (*Tadema Holdings Ltd v Ferguson* [1999] NPC 144. It may be sent there by registered letter or recorded delivery (Recorded Delivery Service Act 1962, s. 1); *WX Investments Ltd v Begg* [2002] 3 EGLR 47 (deemed delivery in the ordinary course of post); [2007] Conv 90 (M. Haley). *Blunden v Frogmore Investments Ltd* [2002] 2 EGLR 29 (notice affixed to premises); [2002] Conv 312 (J. E. Adams). See also p. 301, n. 13.

(*a*) specifying the particular breach complained of;[8] and

(*b*) if the breach is capable of remedy, requiring the lessee to remedy the breach; and

(*c*) in any case requiring the lessee to make compensation in money for the breach,[9]

and the lessee fails, within a reasonable time thereafter,[10] to remedy the breach, if it is capable of remedy, and to make reasonable compensation in money, to the satisfaction of the lessor, for the breach.

(2) Where a lessor is proceeding,[11] by action[12] or otherwise,[13] to enforce such a right of re-entry or forfeiture, the lessee[14] may, in the lessor's action, if any, or in any action brought by himself, apply to the court for relief; and the court may grant or refuse relief, as the court, having regard to the proceedings and conduct of the parties under the foregoing provisions of this section, and to all the other circumstances, thinks fit; and in case of relief may grant it on such terms, if any, as to costs, expenses, damages, compensation, penalty, or otherwise, including the granting of an injunction to restrain any like breach in the future, as the court, in the circumstances of each case, thinks fit.[15]

(4) Where a lessor is proceeding by action or otherwise to enforce a right of re-entry or forfeiture under any covenant, proviso, or stipulation in a lease, or for non-payment of rent, the court may, on application by any person

---

[8]   The landlord is not required to give particulars of each defect: *Fox v Jolly* [1916] 1 AC 1; *Adagio Properties Ltd v Ansari* [1998] 2 EGLR 69.

[9]   This does not make it necessary for the lessor to claim compensation if he does not want it: *Lock v Pearce* [1893] 2 Ch 271; *Rugby School (Governors) v Tannahill*, p. 536, post.

[10]   *Civil Service Co-operative Society Ltd v McGrigor's Trustee* [1923] 2 Ch 347; *Scala House and District Property Co Ltd v Forbes* [1974] QB 575, [1973] 3 All ER 308 (fourteen days held to be sufficient where breach of covenant against assigning or sub-letting held to be incapable of remedy); *Cardigan Properties Ltd v Consolidated Property Investments Ltd* [1991] 1 EGLR 64 (ten days to comply with insurance covenant held to be insufficient); [1991] Conv 223 (J. E. Martin); *Bhojwani v Kingsley Investment Trust Ltd* [1992] 2 EGLR 70; [1993] Conv 296 (J. E. Martin); *Fuller v Judy Properties Ltd* [1992] 1 EGLR 75 (seven days reasonable for breach of covenant against assignment); *Van Haarlam v Kasner* [1992] 2 EGLR 59 (twenty days reasonable for breach of covenant not to use premises for illegal or immoral purposes); *Courtney Lodge Management Ltd v Blake* [2004] EWCA Civ 975, (2004) Times, 15 July (one month inadequate for tenant to remedy nuisance caused by sub-tenants to neighbours).

[11]   The right to relief does not terminate upon peaceable re-entry by the lessor: *Rogers v Rice* [1892] 2 Ch 170. *Billson v Residential Apartments Ltd* [1992] 1 AC 494, [1992] 2 All ER 141, p. 551, post.

[12]   Such an action is a pending land action under LCA 1972, s. 17(1) and is registrable under s. 5; and, in the case of registered land, is required to be protected by a caution under LRA 1925, s. 59(1), (5); *Selim Ltd v Bickenhall Engineering Ltd* [1981] 1 WLR 1318, [1981] 3 All ER 210; or by a notice under LRA 2002, s. 87.

[13]   I.e., by the service of a notice under s. 146: *Pakwood Transport Ltd v 15 Beauchamp Place Ltd* (1977) 36 P & CR 112.

[14]   Where there are joint lessees, relief cannot be granted on the application of only one of them: *TM Fairclough & Sons Ltd v Berliner* [1931] 1 Ch 60.

[15]   In some circumstances the court may be able to grant relief as to part of the demised premises by restricting the order for possession to a party only: *GMS Syndicate Ltd v Gary Elliot Ltd* [1982] Ch 1, [1981] 1 All ER 619. Nourse J said at 12, at 626: 'I emphasise that I do not intend to go beyond the circumstances of the present case, where the two parts of the demised property are physically separated one from the other and are capable of being distinctly enjoyed, and where the breaches complained of were committed on one part of the property and on that part alone'.

claiming as under-lessee [16] any estate or interest in the property comprised in the lease or any part thereof, either in the lessor's action (if any) or in any action brought by such person for that purpose, make an order vesting, for the whole term of the lease or any less term, the property comprised in the lease or any part thereof in any person entitled as under-lessee to any estate or interest in such property upon such conditions as to execution of any deed or other document, payment of rent, costs, expenses, damages, compensation, giving security, or otherwise, as the court in the circumstances of each case may think fit, but in no case shall any such under-lessee be entitled to require a lease to he granted to him for any longer term than he had under his original sub-lease. [17]

(5) For the purposes of this section—

    (*a*) 'Lease' includes an original or derivative under-lease; also an agreement for a lease where the lessee has become entitled to have his lease granted; also a grant at a fee farm rent, or securing a rent by condition;

    (*b*) 'Lessee' includes an original or derivative under-lessee, and the persons deriving title under a lessee, [18] also a grantee under any such grant as aforesaid and the persons deriving title under him;

    (*c*) 'Lessor' includes an original or derivative under-lessor, and the persons deriving title under a lessor; also a person making such grant as aforesaid and the persons deriving title under him;

    (*d*) 'Under-lease' includes an agreement for an under-lease where the under-lessee has become entitled to have his under-lease granted;

---

[16]   See *Grand Junction Co Ltd v Bates* [1954] 2 QB 160, [1954] 2 All ER 385, p. 795, n. 3, post, where it was held that a mortgagee by way of legal charge can claim as underlessee. So can an equitable chargee: *Re Good's Lease* [1954] 1 WLR 309, [1954] 1 All ER 275.

    On relief for underlessees generally, see [1986] Conv 187 (S. Tromans). If relief is granted to a head-tenant's mortgagee, any sub-lease is forfeited, but the subtenant in turn has a right to relief: *Hammersmith and Fulham London Borough Council v Top Shop Centres Ltd* [1990] Ch 237, [1989] 2 All ER 655; [1989] All ER Rev 194 (P. J. Clarke); *Escalus Properties Ltd v Robinson* [1996] QB 231, [1995] 4 All ER 852 (relief granted retrospectively under s. 146(2) to mortgagee by sub-demise); [1995] All ER Rev 334 (P. J. Clarke); cf. *Pellicano v MEPC plc* [1994] 1 EGLR 104 (vesting order under s. 146(4) not retrospective; sub-lessee had no right to possession between date of forfeiture and grant of relief); *Barclays Bank plc v Prudential Assurance Ltd* [1998] 10 EG 159 (disclaimer of lease held not to prevent granting of relief to mortgagee as under-lessee).

    On relief for the holder of an equitable charge over a lease, see *Bland v Ingrams Estates Ltd* [2001] Ch 767, [2002] 1 All ER 224; [2002] All ER Rev 737 (P. H. Pettit) *Emmet on Title*, para. 26.224; leave to appeal to HL refused; [2003] 1 WLR 1810.

[17]   For the inherent jurisdiction of the court to grant relief outside sub-s. (4) where the lessor has re-entered peaceably for breach of covenant to pay a sum of money other than for payment of rent, see *Billson v Residential Apartments Ltd* [1991] 3 WLR 264, [1991] 3 All ER 265, (reversed on other grounds by HL, [1992] 1 AC 494, [1992] 1 All ER 141, p. 551, post, inherent jurisdiction not being raised), where CA preferred *Smith v Metropolitan City Properties Ltd* (1985) 277 EG 753, where WALTON J held that the inherent jurisdiction has been replaced by s. 146(2) (otherwise 'it would make complete nonsense of subsection (2)') and *Official Custodian for Charities v Parway Estates Developments Ltd* [1985] Ch 151, [1984] 3 All ER 679, where CA held that it had no inherent jurisdiction where the lessee was outside the time limits for relief under sub-s. 10, infra; [1984] All ER Rev 195 (P. H. Pettit) and rejected *Abbey National Building Society v Maybeech Ltd* [1985] Ch 190, [1984] 3 All ER 262. But the mortgagee can apply outside the time limits under sub-s. (4): *Official Custodian for Charities v Mackey (No 2)* [1985] 2 All ER 1016, 274 EG 398.

    RSC (Amendment No 2) 1986 (SI 1986 No. 1187) rr 2 and 3 require a landlord to notify any person entitled to relief against forfeiture of whom he is aware.

[18]   *High Street Investments Ltd v Bellshore Property Investments Ltd* [1996] 2 EGLR 40 (equitable assignee); *Escalus Properties Ltd v Robinson*, supra (mortgagee by subdemise).

(*e*) 'Under-lessee' includes any person deriving title under an under-lessee.

(8) This section does not extend—

(i) To a covenant or condition against assigning, underletting, parting with the possession, or disposing of the land leased where the breach occurred before the commencement of this Act; or

(ii) In the case of a mining lease, to a covenant or condition for allowing the lessor to have access to or inspect books, accounts, records, weighing machines or other things, or to enter or inspect the mine or the workings thereof.

(9) This section does not apply to a condition for forfeiture on the bankruptcy of the lessee [19] or on taking in execution of the lessee's interest if contained in a lease of—

(*a*) Agricultural or pastoral land;

(*b*) Mines or minerals;

(*c*) A house used or intended to be used as a public-house or beershop;

(*d*) A house let as a dwelling-house, with the use of any furniture, books, works of art, or other chattels not being in the nature of fixtures;

(*e*) Any property with respect to which the personal qualifications of the tenant are of importance for the preservation of the value or character of the property, [20] or on the ground of neighbourhood to the lessor, [1] or to any person holding under him.

(10) Where a condition of forfeiture on the bankruptcy of the lessee or on taking in execution of the lessee's interest is contained in any lease, other than a lease of any of the classes mentioned in the last subsection, then—

(*a*) if the lessee's interest is sold within one year from the bankruptcy or taking in execution, this section applies to the forfeiture condition aforesaid;

(*b*) if the lessee's interest is not sold before the expiration of that year, this section only applies to the forfeiture condition aforesaid during the first year from the date of the bankruptcy or taking in execution. [2]

(11) This section does not, save as otherwise mentioned, affect the law relating to re-entry or forfeiture or relief in case of non-payment of rent.

(12) This section has effect notwithstanding any stipulation to the contrary.

LAW OF PROPERTY (AMENDMENT) ACT 1929

1. Relief of under-lessees against breach of covenant.—Nothing in subsection (8), subsection (9) or subsection (10) of section one hundred and forty-six of the Law of Property Act, 1925 ... shall affect the provisions of subsection (4) of the said section.

---

[19]   But it does apply on the bankruptcy of a lessee's surety: *Halliard Property Co Ltd v Jack Segal Ltd* [1978] 1 WLR 377, [1978] 1 All ER 1219.

[20]   *Earl of Bathurst v Fine* [1974] 1 WLR 905, [1974] 2 All ER 1160; (1974) 90 LQR 441.

[1]   *Hockley Engineering Co Ltd v V & P Midlands Ltd* [1993] 1 EGLR 76.

[2]   See *Official Custodian for Charities v Parway Estates Developments Ltd* [1985] Ch 151, [1984] 3 All ER 679, p. 534, n. 17, ante.

1. BREACH OF NEGATIVE COVENANT

(a)   Not to Use Premises for Immoral or Illegal User. Stigma

RUGBY SCHOOL (GOVERNORS) v TANNAHILL
[1935] 1 KB 87 (CA, GREER, MAUGHAM and ROCHE LJJ) [3]

The Governors of Rugby School let premises in London to tenants who assigned them with their consent to the defendant, a woman who was convicted of using the premises for the purpose of habitual prostitution. The lease contained a covenant that the premises should not be used for illegal or immoral purposes, and contained a proviso for re-entry for breach of covenant. The Governors served a notice under Law of Property Act 1925, s. 146, requiring the defendant to surrender possession. The defence was that the notice to quit was bad in that it did not require the defendant to remedy the breach under s. 146(1)(b), nor to make compensation in money under s. 146(1)(c).

Held. (i) The breach was not capable of remedy and omission to require it to be remedied did not invalidate the notice;

(ii) As the landlords did not require compensation, omission to demand it did not invalidate the notice.

GREER LJ: The first point is, whether this particular breach is capable of remedy. In my judgment MacKinnon J was right in coming to the conclusion that it was not. I think perhaps he went further than was really necessary for the decision of this case in holding that a breach of any negative covenant the doing of that which is forbidden—can never be capable of remedy. [4] It is unnecessary to decide the point on this appeal; but in some cases where the immediate ceasing of that which is complained of, together with an undertaking against any further breach, it might be said that the breach was capable of remedy. This particular breach, however—conducting the premises, or permitting them to be conducted, as a house of ill-fame—is one which in my judgment was not remedied by merely stopping this user. I cannot conceive how a breach of this kind can be remedied. The result of committing the breach would be known all over the neighbourhood and seriously affect the value of the premises. Even a money payment together with the cessation of the improper use of the house could not be a remedy. Taking the view as I do that this breach was incapable of remedy, it was unnecessary to require in the notice that the defendant should remedy the breach.

The further question is whether the absence of any statement in the notice requiring compensation in money in respect of the breach is fatal to the validity of the notice. As to that, the decision of the Court of Appeal in *Lock v Pearce* [1893] 2 Ch 271 binds us to hold that the plaintiffs were under no obligation to require compensation in money. I can well understand that a body like the plaintiffs would be averse to touch money coming from a tenant in such circumstances. In any event, whatever might have been our view in the absence of authority, it is plain from the judgments in *Lock v Pearce* that the point is not open in this court.

---

3   *British Petroleum Pension Trust Ltd v Behrendt* (1985) 52 P & CR 117, where PURCHAS LJ said at 124: 'I have found nothing in the recent authorities which enables me to accede to Mr Brook's submissions that the concept that breaches of the negative covenant in 'stigma' cases are irremediable has in any way been relaxed.'

4   [1934] 1 KB 695 at 701: 'A promise to do a thing, if broken, can be remedied by the thing being done. But breach of a promise not to do a thing cannot in any sense be remedied; that which was done cannot be undone. There cannot truly be a remedy; there can only be abstention, perhaps accompanied with apology.'

Lindley LJ there used these words at 279: 'Then, as regards the notices required by s. 14, sub-s. 1 [of the Conveyancing Act 1881], the statute requires notice to be given specifying the breach complained of, as the first thing, and, if the breach is capable of remedy, requiring the lessee to remedy it, and 'in any case requiring the lessee to make compensation in money for the breach.' Supposing the lessor does not want compensation, is the notice to be held bad because he does not ask for it? There is no sense in that. The meaning is to be found by looking a little further on. The sub-section begins by saying that the right of re-entry or forfeiture shall not be enforceable unless proper notice is given and the lessee fails within a reasonable time afterwards to remedy the breach and to make reasonable compensation in money to the satisfaction of the lessor. The sense of that is that the lessor must tell the lessee what he wants done. The lessee is entitled to know what his landlord complains of, and, if his landlord is entitled to compensation, whether he wants compensation.' The Lord Justice there concluded his judgment in a paragraph of two sentences which are specially applicable to the present case; he said: 'On these grounds I am of opinion that this appeal fails. Upon the merits as well as upon the technicalities, all the points are against the appellants.' In the later case of *Civil Service Co-operative Society Ltd v McGrigor's Trustee* [1923] 2 Ch 347, Russell J followed *Lock v Pearce* as applicable to a case where the breach was incapable of remedy. The appeal must be dismissed.

(b)   Not to Assign or Sublet Without Consent of Landlord. Once for All Breach

SCALA HOUSE AND DISTRICT PROPERTY CO LTD v FORBES [5]
[1974] QB 575, [1973] 3 All ER 308 (CA, RUSSELL and JAMES LJJ and PLOWMAN J)

By a lease dated 8 February 1968, the lessees covenanted not to assign underlet or part with the possession of a shop in Dean Street, London, without the permission of the landlords. The lease contained a proviso for re-entry on breach of covenant. In March the lease was assigned to the first defendant with the landlords' consent. He used the premises as a restaurant, and then in November entered into an agreement with Pierto and Elisa Delpoio, the second and third defendants, to manage the restaurant for him. This agreement, which was intended to be a management agreement, in fact created a sub-lease in breach of the covenant. The plaintiff, who had acquired the reversion of the lease, served on the defendants a notice under Law of Property Act 1925, section 146(1), requiring them to remedy the breach, and 14 days later then issued a writ for possession. NIELD J held that the breach was capable of remedy, and since 14 days was insufficient time for the defendants to remedy the breach, dismissed the action. On appeal by the plaintiff.

Held. (i) The breach was not capable of remedy, and therefore 14 days was a sufficient time.

(ii) Relief from forfeiture was granted to the first defendant.

RUSSELL LJ: It is a remarkable fact that this case raises questions under section 146 of the Law of Property Act 1925, which, except in a case at first instance reported only in the Estates Gazette Digest, [6] have never been considered for decision. ...

---

[5]   (1973) 89 LQR 460 (P.V.B.); (1973) 57 Conv (NS) 445 (D. Macintyre).
[6]   *Capital and Counties Property Co Ltd v Mills* [1966] EGD 96, p. 539, post.

So the first question is whether a breach of covenant such as is involved in the present case is capable of remedy. If it is capable of remedy, and is remedied in reasonable time, the lessor is unable to prove that a condition precedent to his ability to seek to forfeit by action or otherwise has been fulfilled. Here at once is a problem. An unlawful subletting is a breach once and for all. The subterm has been created.

I turn to the authorities. In *Jackson v Simons* [1923] 1 Ch 373 there was a breach of a covenant against sharing the premises let: such a breach was not excluded from section 14 of the Act of 1881: no notice at all was served before the writ for possession issued and this was fatal to the action. The sharing apparently ended shortly after the writ: but there was no discussion whether a subsequent notice based on a 'past' breach, followed by a writ, would have resulted in either forfeiture or relief. *Rugby School (Governors) v Tannahill* [1935] 1 KB 87 was a case of user by the lessee for immoral purposes contrary to covenant in the lease sought to be forfeited. Apparently before the section 146 notice the prostitutes had left and the premises had ceased to be used for immoral purposes. The notice did not call upon the lessee to remedy the breach. At first instance the judge decided in favour of the lessor on the short ground that breach of a negative covenant could never be remedied. This court did not call upon counsel for the lessor, who thus had no opportunity to support the judge's short ground: this court expressed the view that breach of negative covenants might be capable of remedy, but not this one, on the ground that the stigma attaching to the premises would not be removed by mere cesser of the immoral user. I observe that it does not appear to have been considered whether the breach in that case was incapable of remedy on another ground, viz.: that the wrongful user had ceased before the section 146 notice. It might perhaps be argued that reliance by this court on the 'stigma' point suggests that it was considered that a wrongful user in breach wholly in the past, without continuing adverse effect, would not entitle the lessor to seek to forfeit at all. But the question does not seem to have been canvassed.

[His Lordship referred to *Borthwick-Norton v Romney Warwick Estates Ltd* [1950] 1 All ER 798, and continued:]

In *Hoffman v Fineberg* [1949] Ch 245, [1948] 1 All ER 592 (Harman J), the lessee, in breach of user covenants, allowed the premises to be used for illegal gambling, for which there were convictions. The section 146 notice did not call for the breach to be remedied. It is not clear whether the illegal user continued at the date of the notice. Again the decision was based on the 'stigma' aspect as making the breach incapable of remedy within a reasonable time. Harman J said, at 257 at 597: '... on the facts of this case this is a breach where mere cesser is no remedy.' The judgment referred to another immoral user case of *Egerton v Esplanade Hotels London Ltd* [1947] 2 All ER 88 (Morris J), in which the notice did not call for the breach to be remedied: it was decided on the stigma point, on the facts of that case, that the breach was not capable of remedy within a reasonable time. Morris J said, at 91: 'Merely desisting from the wrongful user or not continuing to commit further breaches is not, ... on the facts of this case, a way of remedying the breach.' Neither case was considered on the possible shorter ground that a user covenant breach when the user had ceased before the section 146 notice was incapable of remedy for that very reason.

Glass v Kencakes Ltd [1966] 1 QB 611, [1964] 3 All ER 807, a decision of Paull J was of this nature. The lease forbade the use of the upper part of the premises otherwise than for residential purposes. The lessee sublet that part to D, who caused and permitted their use for the business of prostitution unknown to the lessee. The sublease contained a similar covenant. The section 146 notice was simply based upon the fact of business use. It asserted that the breach was incapable of remedy. The judge held that the breach of the sublease by D was incapable of remedy by him: apparently he considered that the person who caused or permitted such a use could not, by the cesser of such use, remedy the breach, because the stigma on the premises could not be blotted out within a reasonable time so long as the man responsible remained subtenant. He therefore could not remedy his breach. Paull J pointed out that in the *Rugby School* case [1934] 1 KB 695, in *Egerton v Esplanade Hotels London Ltd* [1947] 2 All ER 88 (both cases of immoral user) and in *Hoffman v Fineberg* [1949] Ch 245, [1948] 1 All ER 592 (the illegal gambling case) it was in each case the tenant under the lease sought to be forfeited who was directly responsible for the breach: and that in the *Borthwick-Norton* case [1950] 1 All ER 798 the lessee had in breach suffered and permitted the immoral user by a subtenant. Paull J decided, however, that where the breach alleged was merely of a user by a subtenant for which the lessee whose lease was sought to be forfeited could not be said to have permitted or suffered or to be in any way responsible for, the breach was not incapable of remedy by that lessee, the remedy required being not only the cesser of the user in breach but also the ending of the subterm with all expedition by forfeiture. Paull J was much impressed by the argument that where there was a lease for a large block of flats, one of which, without any fault of the lessee, was used for a short time in breach of the user covenant in the lease by a subtenant, he should not be put in the situation that he was not capable of remedying the breach and must therefore be put to the expense of seeking relief from forfeiture. He held in that case that the notice was bad since it asserted that the breach was not capable of remedy. [7]

Two points are to be noticed in that case. First: Paull J did not address his mind, particularly in the case of the large block of flats mentioned, to the possible situation of the lessee if the subletting in question, and therefore the unlawful user, had come to an end before discovery by the head lessor, when no remedial step would have been available to the lessee, and whether in such case the lessee could only have sought relief. Second: the decision in terms says nothing of a case (other than 'stigma' cases) where the lessee is directly responsible for the breach by a business user contrary to covenant. ...

In summary upon the cases we have therefore a number of cases of user of premises in breach of covenant in which the decision that the breach is not capable of remedy has gone upon the 'stigma' point, without considering whether a short answer might be—if the user had ceased before the section 146 notice— that it was ex hypothesi incapable of remedy, leaving the lessee only with the ability to seek relief from forfeiture and the writ unchallengeable as such. If a user in breach has ceased before the section 146 notice (quite apart from the stigma cases) then either it is incapable of remedy and after notice there is nothing in the way of a writ: or the cesser of use has somehow deprived the lessor of his ability to seek to forfeit though he has done nothing to waive the breach, a situation in law which I find extremely difficult to spell out of section 146. But whatever may be the position in user breach cases, which are of a continuing nature, there is no authority, other than that of *Capital and Counties Property Co Ltd v Mills* [1966] EGD 96 to suggest that the creation of a subterm in breach of

---

[7]   Cf. *British Petroleum Pension Trust Ltd v Behrendt* (1985) 52 P & CR 117, where 'the tenant either knew of or deliberately shut his eyes to the use of the premises for prostitution' by his licensee.

covenant is capable of remedy. I would make two particular comments on that decision, as reported. First: I find it difficult to see how a breach is said to be capable of remedy because the lessor can waive the breach, which would be involved in the suggestion that he could post hoc consent to the subletting. Second: I do not see how a breach by unlawful subletting can be said to be remedied by the lessee when he does nothing except wait for the subterm to come to an end by effluxion of time.

After this review of the cases I come to the conclusion that breach by an unlawful subletting is not capable of remedy at all. In my judgment the introduction of such breaches into the relevant section for the first time by section 146 of the Act of 1925 operates only to confer a statutory ability to relieve the lessee from forfeiture on that ground. The subterm has been effectively created subject only to risks of forfeiture: it is a complete breach once for all: it is not in any sense a continuing breach. If the law were otherwise a lessee, when a subtenancy is current at the time of the section 146 notice, would have a chance of remedying the situation without having to apply for relief. But if the unlawful subletting had determined before the notice, the lessee could only seek relief from forfeiture. The only escape from that wholly unsatisfactory difference would be to hold that in the second example by some analogy the lessor was disabled from issuing a writ for possession. But I can find nothing in the section to justify that limitation on the common law right of re-entry, bearing especially in mind that a lessor might discover a whole series of past expired unlawful sublettings which might well justify a refusal to grant relief in forfeiture proceedings.

I stress again that where there has been an unlawful subletting which has determined (and which has not been waived) there has been a breach which at common law entitles the lessor to re-enter: nothing can be done to remedy that breach: the expiry of the subterm has not annulled or remedied the breach: in such case the lessor plainly need not, in his section 146 notice, call upon the lessee to remedy the breach which is not capable of remedy, and is free to issue his writ for possession, the possibility of relief remaining. Can it possibly be that, while that is the situation in such case, it is otherwise if the lessee has failed to get rid of the subterm until after a notice served? Is the lessee then in a stronger position and the lessor in a weaker position? In my judgment not so. These problems and questions arise only if such a breach is capable of remedy, which in my judgment it is not. [8] I consider that *Capital and Counties Property Co Ltd v Mills* [1966] EGD 96, if correctly reported, was wrongly decided. I should add that I find some support for my opinion in the comments of Fraser J in *Abrahams v MacFisheries Ltd* [1925] 2 KB 18, 35, who expressed the view that the exceptions in section 14(6) of the Act of 1881 (as to, inter alia, subletting) were made to cover cases where the breach cannot be remedied specifically.

In those circumstances in judging whether the 14 days that here elapsed between the section 146 notice and the writ, the time which it might reasonably take the lessee to come to terms with the subtenants, the second and third defendants, so as to end the subterm, which in fact was done in June 1972, is irrelevant. In those circumstances it is in my view plain that the writ was not

---

[8]   See the general criticism of this reasoning in *Expert Clothing Service and Sales Ltd v Hillgate House Ltd* [1986] Ch 340 at 364, [1985] 2 All ER 998 at 1015, per O'CONNOR LJ: 'It seems to me that it cannot be right to describe a breach which has been remedied as a breach which *is* incapable of remedy, and thereafter to say that it was incapable of remedy before it was remedied. To my mind a breach which has been remedied has been demonstrated to have been a breach which was ab initio capable of remedy.'

prematurely issued, even assuming, as with all familial piety I must having regard to *Civil Service Co-operative Society Ltd v McGrigor's Trustee* [1923] 2 Ch 347, citing *Horsey Estate v Steiger* [1899] 2 QB 79, that reasonable time in the case of an irremediable breach is related to something other than making compensation in money, notwithstanding the language of the section.

(c) Other Breaches of Negative Covenants

SAVVA v HOUSSEIN
[1996] 2 EGLR 65 (CA, STAUGHTON and ALDOUS LJJ and Sir John MAY) [9]

In 1991 Mr and Mrs Savva granted a lease of premises to Mr Houssein for their use as a cafe, a snack bar and a place for operating mini-cabs. Mr Hussein covenanted not to display on the outside of the premises any sign or advertisement and not to make any alterations or additions to them without the prior consent of the landlords. The tenant broke both covenants. The landlords served a section 146 notice asserting the breach of the covenants and claiming that they were incapable of remedy.

Held. The breaches were capable of remedy; the notice was invalid because it did not require the tenant to remedy the breach.

STAUGHTON LJ: In this case the question is whether the breaches, if there were breaches, were capable of remedy. They amount to doing things without the consent of the landlord. That is what the covenant did not allow. In the case of *Billson v Residential Apartments Ltd* (1990) 60 P & CR 392, Mummery J touched on the question whether such a breach could ever be capable of remedy. He said at p. 406:

'I reject the defendants' arguments on the ground that the breach of covenant committed by making the alterations in the property without the plaintiffs' consent "first had and obtained" was not capable of remedy by the defendants. It was a breach of the covenant for the defendants to embark on alterations to the property without first applying for and seeking to obtain the plaintiffs' consent. Now that the alterations have been made without consent it is impossible for the defendants to comply with the covenant which required them first to apply for consent so that they could either obtain it or, if they did not obtain it, be in a position to contend that they were entitled to make improvements because the plaintiffs had unreasonably withheld consent. In those circumstances I hold that the breach was not capable of remedy …'

When that case reached the Court of Appeal, the Vice Chancellor said:

'The judge held, first, that since the alterations had been started without *prior* consent of the plaintiffs the breach was irremediable. Second, he held that even if he were wrong on the first point, remedying the breach would consist, not in doing the works of reinstatement but in stopping the works, submitting the necessary plans and specifications and then awaiting the giving or unreasonable withholding of consent.

I prefer to express no view on the judge's first ground of decision, beyond expressing some doubt as to whether he was right in holding that the breach was irremediable.'

It is established law in this court that the breach of a covenant not to assign without consent cannot be remedied. That was decided in *Scala House & District Property Co Ltd v Forbes* [1974] QB 575, [1973] 3 All ER 308, p. 137, ante. Even then relief from forfeiture was granted, so that may not be of any great consequence.

---

[9]   [1997] 1 L & TLR 70 (J. Brown and R. Duddridge).

In my judgment, except in a case of breach of a covenant not to assign without consent, the question is: whether the remedy referred to is the process of restoring the situation to what it would have been if the covenant had never been broken, or whether it is sufficient that the mischief resulting from a breach of the covenant can be removed. When something has been done without consent, it is not possible to restore the matter wholly to the situation which it was in before the breach. The moving finger writes and cannot be recalled. That is not to my mind what is meant by a remedy, it is a remedy if the mischief caused by the breach can be removed. In the case of a covenant not to make alterations without consent or not to display signs without consent, if there is a breach of that, the mischief can be removed by removing the signs or restoring the property to the state it was in before the alterations.

I would hold that all the breaches complained of in this case were capable of remedy. It follows that the notice under section 146 should have required them to be remedied.

AULD LJ: In one sense a breach can never be remedied because there must have been non-compliance with the covenant for there to be a breach. That cannot be the solution. Thus, the fact there has been a breach does not determine whether it can be remedied in the way contemplated by the Law of Property Act 1925 section 146. That was decided in *Expert Clothing Service & Sales Ltd v Hillgate House Ltd* [1986] Ch 340, [1985] 2 All ER 998, infra, Slade LJ p. 357F, p. 1010b:

'… breach of a positive covenant to do something … can ordinarily, for practical purposes, be remedied by the thing being actually done …'

I can see no reason why similar reasoning should not apply to some negative covenants. An important purpose of section 146 is to give tenants, who have not complied with their obligations, one last chance to do so before the landlord re-enters. Slade LJ in *Expert Clothing* proposed this test at p. 358D, at p. 1010g:

'… if the section 146 notice had required the lessee to remedy the breach and the lessors had then allowed a reasonable time to elapse to enable the lessee fully to comply with the relevant covenant, would such compliance, coupled with the payment of any appropriate monetary compensation, have effectively remedied the harm which the lessors had suffered or were likely to suffer from the breach?'

It is only if the answer to that question is 'no' can it be said that the breach is not capable of being remedied.

What was proposed as the question to ask by Slade LJ, albeit in relation to a case of dispute about a positive covenant, is relevant to consideration as to whether a negative covenant can be remedied. There is, in my view, nothing in the statute, nor in logic, which require different considerations between a positive and negative covenant, although it may be right to differentiate between particular covenants. The test is one of effect. If a breach has been remedied then it must have been capable of being remedied.

For the reasons given by Staughton LJ I agree with the order proposed.

2. BREACH OF POSITIVE COVENANT

EXPERT CLOTHING SERVICE AND SALES LTD v HILLGATE HOUSE LTD
[1986] Ch 340, [1985] 2 All ER 998 (CA, O'CONNOR and SLADE LJJ and BRISTOW J)

In 1972 the plaintiff landlords granted a 25 year lease of Hillgate House, London W8 to the defendants, who covenanted to reconstruct the premises into a gymnasium and health club and to make them ready for occupation by or before

28 September 1982. The defendants failed to carry out the work. The plaintiffs served a s. 146 notice, alleging the breach of covenant and stating that the breach was incapable of remedy. They then brought proceedings claiming possession of the premises.

Held (reversing Judge Paul Baker QC). Claim for possession refused. The breach was capable of remedy, and, therefore the notice was invalid. [10]

SLADE LJ: In a case where the breach is 'capable of remedy' within the meaning of the section, the principal object of the notice procedure provided for by section 146(1), as I read it, is to afford the lessee two opportunities before the lessor actually proceeds to enforce his right of re-entry, namely (1) the opportunity to remedy the breach within a reasonable time after service of the notice, and (2) the opportunity to apply to the court for relief from forfeiture. In a case where the breach is not 'capable of remedy,' there is clearly no point in affording the first of these two opportunities; the object of the notice procedure is thus simply to give the lessee the opportunity to apply for relief.

Unfortunately the authorities give only limited guidance as to what breaches are capable of remedy within the meaning of the section. As Harman J pointed out in *Hoffman v Fineberg* [1949] Ch 245 at 253:

'In one sense, no breach can ever be remedied, because there must always, ex concessis, be a time in which there has not been compliance with the covenant, but the section clearly involves the view that some breaches are remediable, and therefore it cannot mean that.'

[His Lordship referred to MacKinnon J in *Rugby School (Governors) v Tannahill* [1934] 1 KB 695 at 701, p. 536, n. 4, ante, and to Greer LJ in [1935] 1 KB 87 at 90–91, p. 536, ante, and Maugham LJ at 93, and continued:]

In supporting the judge's conclusion that the breach relating to reconstruction of the premises was irremediable, Mr Collins, on behalf of the plaintiffs, has submitted to us three principal arguments. First, he pointed out that (as is common ground) the first defendant's failure to build by 28 Sept-ember 1982 was a 'once and for all' breach of the relevant covenant, and not a continuing breach: see, for example, *Stephens v Junior Army and Navy Stores Ltd* [1914] 2 Ch 516 at 523, per Lord Cozens-Hardy MR. He submitted that the breach of a covenant such as this, which can only be broken once, is ex hypothesi in no case capable of remedy.

Some superficial support for this conclusion is perhaps to be found in the judgments in *Scala House and District Property Co Ltd v Forbes* [1974] QB 575, [1973] 3 All ER 308, p.557, ante, in which the Court of Appeal held that the breach of a covenant not to assign, underlet or part with possession was not a breach capable of remedy within the meaning of section 146(1). ...

[His Lordship referred to RUSSELL LJ at 588, at 315, p.539, ante, and continued:]

It might well be regarded as anomalous if the once and for all breach of a negative covenant not to sublet were to be regarded as 'capable of remedy' within section 146, provided that the unlawful subtenancy was still current at the date of the section 146 notice, but (as Russell LJ considered) were not to be regarded as 'capable of remedy' if the unlawful subtenancy had been determined at that date. Russell LJ and James LJ who agreed with his reasoning (see particularly at 591C–D, at 317), were clearly much influenced by this anomaly in reaching the

---

[10]   The court further held that the plaintiffs had not waived their right to forfeit the lease.

conclusion that the breach of a covenant against underletting is never capable of remedy.

However, in the *Scala House* case this court was addressing its mind solely to the once and for all breach of a negative covenant. No corresponding anomaly arises if the once and for all breach of a positive covenant is treated as capable of remedy. While the *Scala House* decision is, of course, authority binding on this court for the proposition that the breach of a negative covenant not to assign, underlet or part with possession is never 'capable of remedy,' it is not, in my judgment, authority for the proposition that the once and for all breach of a positive covenant is never capable of remedy.

Mr Neuberger, on behalf of the defendants, did not feel able to go so far as to support the view of MacKinnon J that the breach of a positive covenant is *always* capable of remedy. He accepted, for example, that the breach of a covenant to insure might be incapable of remedy at a time when the premises had already been burnt down. Another example might be the breach of a positive covenant which in the event would be only capable of being fully performed, if at all, after the expiration of the relevant term.

Nevertheless, I would, for my part, accept Mr Neuberger's submission that the breach of a positive covenant (whether it be a continuing breach or a once and for all breach) will ordinarily be capable of remedy. As Bristow J pointed out in the course of argument, the concept of capability of remedy for the purpose of section 146 must surely be directed to the question whether the harm that has been done to the landlord by the relevant breach is for practicable purposes capable of being retrieved. In the ordinary case, the breach of a promise to do something by a certain time can for practical purposes be remedied by the thing being done, even out of time. For these reasons I reject the plaintiffs' argument that the breach of the covenant to reconstruct by 28 September 1982 was not capable of remedy *merely* because it was not a continuing breach. ...

[His Lordship rejected the second main argument that the breach of covenant was incapable of remedy because of the operation of a rent review clause and continued:]

I therefore turn to the third, and far the most important point, relied on by Mr Collins in support of the decision of the court below. His submissions in this context were to the following effect. The judgment of Maugham LJ in the *Rugby School* case [1935] 1 KB 87 at 93 and other judicial dicta indicate that if a breach is to be 'capable of remedy' at all within the meaning of section 146, it must be capable of remedy *within a 'reasonable time.'* As was observed by Lord Herschell LC in *Hick v Raymond and Reid* [1893] AC 22 at 29: 'there is of course no such thing as a reasonable time in the abstract. It must always depend upon circumstances.' In the present case, it was submitted, what was a reasonable time was a question of fact. In deciding that the breach of the covenant to reconstruct was not capable of remedy within a reasonable time, the judge expressed himself as 'having regard to the facts as I have found them.' ...

In my opinion, in considering whether or not remedy within a reasonable time is possible, a crucial distinction (which I infer from the judgment did not feature prominently in argument before the judge) falls to be drawn between breaches of negative user covenants, such as those under consideration in the *Rugby School* and the *Esplanade Hotels* [1947] 2 All ER 88 cases, and breaches of positive covenants. In the two last-mentioned cases, where the relevant breaches consisted of allowing premises to be used as a brothel, even full compliance with the covenant within a reasonable time and for a reasonable time would not have remedied the breach. As Maugham LJ pointed out in the *Rugby School* case, at 94:

'merely ceasing for a reasonable time, perhaps a few weeks or a month, to use the premises for an immoral purpose would be no remedy for the breach of covenant which had been committed over a long period.'

On the facts of cases such as those, mere cesser by the tenant of the offending use within a reasonable period and for a reasonable period of time could not have remedied the breaches because it could not have removed the stigma which they had caused to attach to the premises. The harm had been irretrievably done. In such cases, as Harman J pointed out in *Hoffman v Fineberg* [1949] Ch 245 at 257, [1948] 1 All ER 592 at 597, mere cesser will not enable the tenant to 'make his record clean, as he could by complying, though out of time, with a failure to lay on the prescribed number of coats of paint.'

In contrast with breaches of negative user covenants, the breach of a positive covenant to do something (such as to decorate or build) can ordinarily, for practical purposes, be remedied by the thing being actually done if a reasonable time for its performance (running from the service of the section 146 notice) is duly allowed by the landlord following such service and the tenant duly does it within such time.

In the present case there is no question of the breach of the covenant to reconstruct having given rise to any 'stigma' against the lessors or the premises. Significantly, the lease in 1982 still had 20 years to run. Mr Collins has, I think, been able to suggest no convincing reasons why the plaintiffs would still have suffered irremediable damage if (i) the section 146 notice had required the lessee to remedy the breach and (ii) the lessors had then allowed a reasonable time to elapse sufficient to enable the lessee to comply with the relevant covenant, and (iii) the lessee had complied with the covenant in such reasonable time and had paid any appropriate monetary compensation. Though he has submitted that a requirement directed to the defendants to remedy the breach would have been purposeless, on the grounds that they had neither the financial means nor the will to do the necessary work, these are matters which, in my opinion, a landlord is not entitled to prejudge in drafting his notice. An important purpose of the section 146 procedure is to give even tenants who have hitherto lacked the will or the means to comply with their obligations one last chance to summon up that will or find the necessary means before the landlord re-enters. In considering what 'reasonable time' to allow the defendants, the plaintiffs, in serving their section 146 notice, would, in my opinion, have been entitled to take into account the fact that the defendants already had enjoyed 15 months in which to fulfil their contractual obligations to reconstruct and to subject the defendants to a correspondingly tight time-table running from the date of service of the notice, though, at the same time, always bearing in mind that the contractual obligation to reconstruct did not even arise until 29 June 1981, and that as at 8 October 1982 the defendants had been in actual breach of it for only some 10 days. However, I think they were not entitled to say, in effect: 'We are not going to allow you any time at all to remedy the breach, because you have had so long to do the work already.'

In my judgment, on the remediability issue, the ultimate question for the court was this: if the section 146 notice had required the lessee to remedy the breach and the lessors had then allowed a reasonable time to elapse to enable the lessee fully to comply with the relevant covenant, would such compliance, coupled with the payment of any appropriate monetary compensation, have effectively remedied the harm which the lessors had suffered or were likely to suffer from the breach? If, but only if, the answer to this question was 'No,' would the failure of the section 146 notice to require remedy of the breach have been justifiable. In *Rugby School (Governors) v Tannahill* [1935] 1 KB 87; *Egerton v Esplanade Hotels, London Ltd* [1947] 2 All ER 88 and *Hoffman v Fineberg* [1949] Ch 245, [1948] 1 All ER 592 the answer to this question plainly would have been 'No.' In the present case, however, for the reasons already stated, I think the answer to it must have been 'Yes.'

My conclusion, therefore, is that the breach of the covenant to reconstruct ...was 'capable of remedy.' In reaching this conclusion, I find it reassuring that no reported case has been brought to our attention in which the breach of a positive covenant has been held incapable of remedy, though I do not suggest that cases of this nature, albeit perhaps rarely, could not arise.

In **Plymouth Corpn v Harvey** [1971] 1 WLR 549, [1971] 1 All ER 623, the tenant executed an undated deed of surrender in escrow. When he was in breach, the landlord dated the deed and demanded possession. The deed was held void as being a device to circumvent section 146. The statutory notices were required. 'A forfeiture in the guise of a surrender ... remains a forfeiture for the purposes of section 146,' said PLOWMAN J.

3. COVENANTS TO REPAIR

LANDLORD AND TENANT ACT 1927

18. Provisions as to covenants to repair.—(2) A right of re-entry or forfeiture for a breach of any such covenant or agreement as aforesaid shall not be enforceable, by action or otherwise, unless the lessor proves that the fact that such a notice as is required by section one hundred and forty-six of the Law of Property Act, 1925, had been served on the lessee was known either—

(*a*) to the lessee; or

(*b*) to an under-lessee holding under an under-lease which reserved a nominal reversion only to the lessee; or

(*c*) to the person who last paid the rent due under the lease either on his own behalf or as agent for the lessee or under-lessee;

and that a time reasonably sufficient to enable the repairs to be executed had elapsed since the time when the fact of the service of the notice came to the knowledge of any such person.

Where a notice has been sent by registered post[11] addressed to a person at his last known place of abode in the United Kingdom, then, for the purposes of this subsection, that person shall be deemed, unless the contrary is proved, to have had knowledge of the fact that the notice had been served as from the time at which the letter would have been delivered in the ordinary course of post.

This subsection shall be construed as one with section one hundred and forty-six of the Law of Property Act, 1925.

---

[11] The recorded delivery service may be used as an alternative to registered post; Recorded Delivery Service Act 1962, s. 1(1). [1990] Conv 47 (J. E. Adams); *Beanby Estates Ltd v Egg Stores (Stamford Hill) Ltd* [2003] 1 WLR 2064 (where notice sent by recorded delivery to addressee at place of abode, it was irrebuttably deemed to have been served); see *C. A. Webber (Transport) Ltd v Railtrack plc* [2004] 1 WLR 320 (*Beanby Estates Ltd* nor inconsistent with Human Rights Act 1998).

Where the landlord sues for damages or to enforce a forfeiture in respect of a covenant to keep or put the premises in repair, he is subject to a further statutory restriction under the Leasehold Property (Repairs) Act 1938.[12]

LEASEHOLD PROPERTY (REPAIRS) ACT 1938

1.[213] **Restriction on enforcement of repairing covenants in long leases of small houses.**—(1) Where a lessor serves on a lessee under subsection (1) of section one hundred and forty-six of the Law of Property Act, 1925, a notice that relates to a breach of a covenant or agreement to keep or put in repair[14] during the currency of the lease all or any of the property comprised in the lease, and at the date of the service of the notice three years or more of the term of the lease remain unexpired, the lessee may within twenty-eight days from that date serve on the lessor a counter-notice to the effect that he claims the benefit of this Act.

(2) A right to damages[215] for a breach of such a covenant as aforesaid shall not be enforceable by action commenced at any time at which three years or more of the term of the lease remain unexpired unless the lessor has served on the lessee not less than one month before the commencement of the action such a notice as is specified in subsection (1) of section one hundred and forty-six of the Law of Property Act, 1925,[16] and where a notice is served under this subsection, the lessee may, within twenty-eight days from the date of the service thereof, serve on the lessor a counter-notice to the effect that he claims the benefit of this Act.

(3) Where a counter-notice is served by a lessee under this section, then, notwithstanding anything in any enactment or rule of law, no proceedings, by action or otherwise, shall be taken by the lessor for the enforcement of any right of re-entry or forfeiture under any proviso or stipulation in the lease for breach of the covenant or agreement in question, or for damages for breach thereof, otherwise than with the leave of the court.

(4) A notice served under subsection (1) of section one hundred and forty-six of the Law of Property Act, 1925, in the circumstances specified in subsection (1) of this section, and a notice served under subsection (2) of this section shall not be valid unless it contains a statement, in characters not less conspicuous than those used in any other part of the notice,[17] to the effect that the lessee is entitled under this Act to serve on the lessor a counter-notice claiming the benefit of this Act, and a statement in the like characters specifying the time

---

12   For the special provisions relating to internal decorative repair, see LPA 1925, s. 147.

13   As amended by Landlord and Tenant Act 1954, s. 5(2), (5). On the Act generally, see [1986] Conv 85 (P. F. Smith).

14   *Starrokate Ltd v Burry* (1982) 265 EG 871 ('an obligation to cleanse is not an obligation to repair').

15   A landlord's action to recover a sum expended on carrying out repairs for which the tenant was liable was held to be for debt and not for damages and therefore no leave of the court is required under the Act: *Hamilton v Martell Securities Ltd* [1984] Ch 266, [1984] 1 All ER 665; *Jervis v Harris* [1996] 1 All ER 303; [1997] Conv 299 (R. Hewitson). See also *SEDAC Investments Ltd v Tanner* [1982] 1 WLR 1342, [1982] 3 All ER 646; (1984) 134 NLJ 791 (H. W. Wilkinson).

16   A notice cannot be served after the breach has been remedied, even if it is remedied by the landlord, since the s. 146 notice cannot then require the tenant to remedy the breach; *SEDAC Investments Ltd v Tanner* [1982] 1 WLR 1342, [1982] 3 All ER 646 ('a conclusion reached' by Michael Wheeler QC 'with surprise and regret'). In *Hamilton v Martell Securities Ltd*, supra, VINELOTT J was 'not persuaded that the decision was wrong.' [1983] Conv 72 (P. F. Smith).

17   To be read as 'equally readable': *Middlegate Properties Ltd v Messimeris* [1973] 1 WLR 168, [1973] 1 All ER 645.

within which, and the manner in which, under this Act a counter-notice may be served and specifying the name and address for service of the lessor. [18]

(5) Leave for the purposes of this section shall not be given unless the lessor proves [19] —

(a)   that the immediate remedying of the breach in question is requisite for preventing substantial diminution in the value of his reversion, or that the value thereof has been substantially diminished by the breach;

(b)   that the immediate remedying of the breach is required for giving effect in relation to the premises to the purposes of any enactment, or of any byelaw or other provision having effect under an enactment, or for giving effect to any order of a court or requirement of any authority under any enactment or any such byelaw, or other provision as aforesaid;

(c)   in a case in which the lessee is not in occupation of the whole of the premises as respects which the covenant or agreement is proposed to be enforced, that the immediate remedying of the breach is required in the interests of the occupier of those premises or of part thereof;

(d)   that the breach can be immediately remedied at an expense that is relatively small in comparison with the much greater expense that would probably be occasioned by postponement of the necessary work; or

(e)   special circumstances which in the opinion of the court, render it just and equitable that leave should be given. [20]

(6) The court may, in granting or in refusing leave for the purposes of this section, impose such terms and conditions on the lessor or on the lessee as it may think fit.

iii. WAIVER

(a)   *The Doctrine*

In **Matthews v Smallwood** [1910] 1 Ch 777, PARKER J said at 786:

'I think that the law on the subject of waiver is reasonably clear. The right to re-enter is a legal right which, apart from release or abandonment or waiver, will exist and can be exercised, at any time within the period fixed by the Statutes of Limitation; and if a defendant in an action of ejectment based upon that right of re-entry alleges a release or abandonment or waiver, logically speaking the onus ought to lie on him to shew the release or the abandonment or the waiver. Waiver of a right of re-entry can only occur where the lessor, with knowledge of the facts upon which his right to re-enter arises, does some unequivocal act recognizing the continued existence of the lease. It is not enough that he should do the act which recognizes, or appears to recognize, the continued existence of the lease, unless, at the time when the act is done, he has knowledge of the facts under which, or from which, his right of entry arose. Therefore we get the principle that, though an act of waiver operates with regard to all known breaches, it does not operate with regard to breaches which were unknown to the lessor at the

---

[18]   *Middlegate Properties Ltd v Messimeris,* supra; *BL Holdings Ltd v Marcolt Investments Ltd* (1978) 249 EG 849.

[19]   The landlord has to prove one of the statutory grounds on the balance of probabilities; *Associated British Ports v C H Bailey plc* [1990] 2 AC 703, [1990] 1 All ER 929; [1990] CLJ 401 (S. Bridge); [1990] Conv 305 (P. F. Smith). The relevant date for proving one or more of the s. 1(5) grounds is the date of the application for leave to bring forfeiture proceedings: *Landmaster Properties Ltd v Thackeray Property Service* [2003] 35 EG 83.

[20]   *Landmaster Properties Ltd v Thackeray Property Services,* supra.

time when the act took place. It is also, I think, reasonably clear upon the cases that whether the act, coupled with the knowledge, constitutes a waiver is a question which the law decides, and therefore it is not open to a lessor who has knowledge of the breach to say "I will treat the tenancy as existing, and I will receive the rent, or I will take advantage of my power as landlord to distrain; but I tell you that all I shall do will be without prejudice to my right to re-enter, which I intend to reserve". That is a position which he is not entitled to take up. If, knowing of the breach, he does distrain, or does receive the rent, then by law he waives the breach, and nothing which he can say by way of protest against the law will avail him anything. Logically, therefore, a person who relies upon waiver ought to shew, first, an act unequivocally recognizing the subsistence of the lease, and secondly, knowledge of the circumstances from which the right of re-entry arises at the time when the act is performed. [1]

LAW OF PROPERTY ACT 1925

148. Waiver of a covenant in a lease.—(1) Where any actual waiver by a lessor or the persons deriving title under him of the benefit of any covenant or condition in any lease is proved to have taken place in any particular instance, such waiver shall not be deemed to extend to any instance, or to any breach of covenant or condition save that to which such waiver specially relates, nor operate as a general waiver of the benefit of any such covenant or condition.

(2) This section applies unless a contrary intention appears and extends to waivers effected after the twenty-third day of July, eighteen hundred and sixty.

---

[1] *Goodright d Charter v Cordwent* (1795) 6 Term Rep 219; *Dendy v Nicholl* (1858) 4 CBNS 376; *Ward v Day* (1864) 5 B & S 359; *Grimwood v Moss* (1872) LR 7 CP 360; *Segal Securities Ltd v Thoseby* [1963] 1 QB 887, [1963] 1 All ER 500 (demand for rent made without prejudice held to be waiver); cf. *Expert Clothing Service and Sales Ltd v Hillgate House Ltd* [1986] Ch 340, [1985] 2 All ER 998, p. 542, ante (proferring of negotiating document held not to be waiver where no acceptance of rent or demand for rent involved); *Re National Jazz Centre Ltd* [1988] 2 EGLR 57 (mere entry into negotiations held not to be waiver); *Church Comrs for England v Nodjoumi* (1985) 51 P & CR 155 (service of s. 146 notice held not to be waiver of right to forfeit lease on grounds other than those set out in notice); *Central Estates (Belgravia) Ltd v Woolgar (No 2)* [1972] 1 WLR 1048, [1972] 3 All ER 610 (clerk of landlord's agents accepted rent by mistake); *David Blackstone Ltd v Burnetts (West End) Ltd* [1973] 1 WLR 1487, [1973] 3 All ER 782, p. 550, post (demand for future rent); *Welch v Birrane* (1974) 29 P & CR 102; (1976) 40 Conv (NS) 327; (1977) 41 Conv (NS) 220 (E. L. G. Tyler); (1988) 138 NLJ (H. W. Wilkinson); *Metropolitan Properties Co Ltd v Cordery* (1979) 39 P & CR 10 (landlords' acceptance of rent for flat with knowledge, through their porters, of facts which pointed to breach of covenant held to be waiver); *Cornillie v Saha* [1996] EGCS 21. Cf. *Trustees of Henry Smith's Charity v Willson* [1983] QB 316, [1983] 1 All ER 73 (uncommunicated rent demand); *Re A Debtor (No 13A)* [1995] 1 WLR 1127 (demand for rent due before right to forfeit not waiver); *Official Custodian for Charities v Parway Estates Development Ltd* [1985] Ch 151, [1984] 3 All ER 679 (publication in London Gazette of compulsory liquidation held not to be imputed knowledge so as to constitute waiver); *Chrisdell Ltd v Johnson* [1987] 2 EGLR 123 (landlord's failure to take action because he thinks that he will not be able to prove suspected breach of contract held not to be waiver); *Van Haarlam v Kasner* [1992] 2 EGLR 59; *Iperion Investments Corpn v Broadwalk House Residents Ltd* [1992] 2 EGLR 235.

In **David Blackstone Ltd v Burnetts (West End) Ltd** [1973] 1 WLR 1487, [1973] 3 All ER 782, SWANWICK J, in holding that there had been waiver by a landlord who was demanding future rent, said at 1498, at 792:

'My view, both on principle and on such persuasive authority as has been cited to me, is that an unambiguous demand for future rent in advance such as was made here does in law amount to an election and does constitute a waiver if, at the time when it is made, the landlord has sufficient knowledge of the facts to put him to his election. To my perhaps simple mind there is a fundamental inconsistency between contending that a lease has been determined and demanding rent on the basis of its future continuance.

This leads me to the second main issue in this case: what knowledge must the landlord or his agent be proved to have had in order that a demand for rent should amount to a waiver; what is the point in time at which such knowledge is to be assessed; and, therefore, are the second plaintiffs proved to have had the necessary knowledge at the relevant time so as to make their demand a waiver?

I will deal first with the appropriate point in time. ...

I consider that ... for there to be a valid election to waive a breach, the landlord or his agent must have sufficient knowledge of the breach before despatching the document making the election, but that such election does not become effective until it is communicated to the tenant. ...

This leaves the final branch of the final question. At the relevant time, did the second plaintiffs possess sufficient knowledge of the breach to render the demand a waiver in law? ...

In my judgment, again without the guidance of any direct authority, the knowledge required to put a landlord to his election is knowledge of the basic facts which in law constitute a breach of covenant entitling him to forfeit the lease. Once he or his agent knows those facts an appropriate act by himself or any agent will in law effect a waiver or a forfeiture. His knowledge or ignorance of the law is, in my judgment, irrelevant. If it were not so, a vast gap would be opened in the administration of the law of landlord and tenant and a facile escape route for landlords would be provided. Indeed, if this were the position unscrupulous landlords could hardly have failed in the past to take advantage of it long before now.'

(b) Waiver of Continuing Breach

In **City and Westminster Properties (1934) Ltd v Mudd** [1959] Ch 129, [1958] 2 All ER 733[2] a lease contained a covenant by the tenant 'to use the demised premises as showrooms, workrooms and offices only'. The tenant admitted that he was sleeping there. In an action for forfeiture for breach of covenant, the tenant alleged, inter alia, a release or waiver by the landlord by reason of his knowledge of the breach prior to and during the currency of the lease. In refusing the claim of waiver, HARMAN J said at 143, at 741:

'The next issue is that of waiver. Now residence, contrary to the covenants of the lease, is a continuing breach and therefore prima facie it is only waived by the acceptance of rent down to the date of that acceptance and there is a new breach immediately thereafter which is not waived. My attention was called to a number of cases which show that acts of waiver may be so continuous that the court is driven to the conclusion that there has been a new agreement for letting or a licence or a release of the covenant. The cases cited on this subject show

---

[2]   *Cooper v Henderson* (1982) 263 EG 592.

acquiescence continuing for a very long period of years. For instance, in *Gibson v Doeg* (1857) 2 H & N 615 the period was 20 years, in *Gibbon v Payne* (1905) 22 TLR 54 it was 40 years, and in *Hepworth v Pickles* [1900] 1 Ch 108, 24 years. In the more recent case of *Lloyds Bank Ltd v Jones* [1955] 2 QB 298, [1955] 2 All ER 409, Singleton LJ points out that no particular period such as 20 years is required. ...

Again, in *Wolfe v Hogan* [1949] 2 KB 194, [1949] 1 All ER 570 I find this in the headnote: "The mere acceptance of rent by the landlord from the tenant, after he had knowledge of the change of user by the tenant, though it continues for some time, does not, by itself, constitute such acceptance by the landlord of the changed position as to show that the house has been let as a separate dwelling"; and Denning LJ, after dealing with the facts, says this at 205, at 575: "A house or a part of a house originally let for business purposes does not become let for dwelling purposes unless it can be inferred from the acceptance of rent that the landlord has affirmatively consented to the change of user. Let me illustrate that from the common law doctrine as to waiver of forfeiture. A breach of covenant not to use premises in a particular way is a continuing breach. Any acceptance of rent by the landlord, after knowledge, only waives the breaches up to the time of the acceptance of rent. It does not waive the continuance of the breach thereafter and, notwithstanding his previous acceptance of rent, the landlord can still proceed for forfeiture on that account. Indeed, in the case of a continuing breach, the acceptance of rent, after knowledge, is only a bar to a claim for forfeiture if it goes on for so long, or is accepted in such circumstances, that it can be inferred that the landlord has not merely waived the breach but has affirmatively consented to the tenant continuing to use the premises as he has done. I cannot think that anything proved here amounts to a release by the landlord of his rights. He knew, indeed, that the tenant was using the property to sleep in, but I do not think he knew more than that. At that he was willing to wink, but I am unable to find a release of the covenant or an agreement for a new letting. In my judgment, therefore, the plea of waiver fails.'

iv. RELIEF AGAINST FORFEITURE

BILLSON v RESIDENTIAL APARTMENTS LTD [3]
[1992] 1 AC 494, [1992] 2 All ER 141 (HL, Lords KEITH OF KINKEL, TEMPLEMAN, OLIVER OF AYLMERTON, GOFF OF CHIEVELEY and JAUNCEY OF TULLICHETTLE)

The plaintiff landlords owned the freehold reversion of 17 Gledlow Gardens in London, of a lease which was assigned to the defendant tenants in May 1989 for £280,000. The lease contained a covenant by the tenant against alterations or additions without the written consent of the landlords. The defendants started on a major conversion scheme at a cost of between £260,000 and £375,000 without written consent. After correspondence between the parties, the landlords eventually served a notice under section 146 of the Law of Property Act 1925 on 4 July, requiring the breaches of covenant to be remedied 'within a reasonable time ... in so far as they are capable of remedy'. The tenants however continued their building works. At 6 a.m. on 18 July the landlords peaceably re-entered the vacant premises and changed the locks. By 10 a.m. on the same day the tenants regained possession. The landlords successfully claimed possession on the

---

[3]   [1992] CLJ 216 (S. Bridge); [1992] Conv 273 (P. F. Smith); (1992) 02 EG 154 (P. Dollar and C. Peet).

ground that the court had no jurisdiction to grant relief against forfeiture under section 146(2) of the Law of Property Act 1925.

Held (reversing the Court of Appeal [1991] 3 WLR 264, [1991] 3 All ER 264). The court had jurisdiction. Application for relief was remitted to the High Court.[4]

LORD TEMPLEMAN: By the writ in this action dated 19 July 1989 the landlords claim possession, damages for breach of covenant and damages for trespass. By their defence and counterclaim the tenants counterclaim for relief against forfeiture. By their reply the landlords claim that the court has no jurisdiction to grant the tenants relief from forfeiture. The trial judge, Mummery J (1990) 60 P & CR 392, and the Court of Appeal (Sir Nicolas Browne-Wilkinson V-C, and Parker and Nicholls LJJ), considered that they were constrained by authority to hold that the court had no jurisdiction to grant the tenants relief against forfeiture pursuant to section 146(2) because the tenants had not applied to the court for relief prior to the re-entry into possession by the landlords on 18 July 1989.[5] The tenants now appeal.

By the common law, when a tenant commits a breach of covenant and the lease contains a proviso for forfeiture, the landlord at his option may either waive the breach or determine the lease. In order to exercise his option to determine the lease the landlord must either re-enter the premises in conformity with the proviso or must issue and serve a writ claiming possession. The bringing of an action to recover possession is equivalent to an entry for the forfeiture. Thus in *Jones v Carter* (1846) 15 M & W 718, 726, Parke B said:

'the bringing of an ejectment for a forfeiture, and serving it on the lessee in possession, must be considered as the exercise of the lessor's option to determine the lease; and the option must be exercised once for all ... for after such an act, by which the lessor treats the lessee as a trespasser, the lessee would know that he was no longer to consider himself as holding under the lease, and bound to perform the covenants contained in it; ...' This observation was cited and applied by Lord Denning MR in *Canas Property Co Ltd v KL Television Services Ltd* [1970] 2 QB 433, 440, [1970] 2 All ER 795.[6]

Before the intervention of Parliament, if a landlord forfeited by entering into possession or by issuing and serving a writ for possession, equity could relieve the tenant against forfeiture but only in cases under the general principles of equity whereby a party may be relieved from the consequences of fraud, accident or mistake or in cases where the breach of covenant entitling the landlord to forfeit was a breach of the covenant for payment of rent.

Mr Reid, who appeared for the landlords, conceded that where equity claimed power to relieve against forfeiture, the tenant could apply for relief irrespective of the method by which the landlord had exercised his option to determine the lease. Relief could be granted whether the landlord had forfeited by entering into possession or had forfeited by issuing and serving a writ claiming possession.

---

4   This was refused: [1993] EGCS 150.
5   CA also held that (NICHOLLS LJ dissenting) that the court had no inherent jurisdiction to grant relief. This was not raised in HL. See p. 530, n. 17, ante.
6   And also in *GS Fashions Ltd v B & Q plc* [1995] 1 WLR 1088, [1995] 4 All ER 899; *Kingston upon Thames London Borough Council v Marlow* [1996] 1 EGLR 101 (tenant by relinquishing tenancy in response to forfeiture proceedings no longer entitled to possession, nor liable to pay rates).

In 1881 Parliament interfered to supplement equity and to enable any tenant to be relieved from forfeiture. The need for such intervention was and is manifest because otherwise a tenant who had paid a large premium for a 999-year lease at a low rent could lose his asset by a breach of covenant which was remediable or which caused the landlord no damage. The forfeiture of any lease, however short, may unjustly enrich the landlord at the expense of the tenant. In creating a power to relieve against forfeiture for breach of covenant Parliament protected the landlord by conferring on the court a wide discretion to grant relief on terms or to refuse relief altogether. In practice this discretion is exercised with the object of ensuring that the landlord is not substantially prejudiced or damaged by the revival of the lease.

Section 14(1) and (2) of the Conveyancing and Law of Property Act 1881 were provisions which conferred on the court power to relieve against forfeiture and those provisions were reproduced in section 146(1) and (2) of the Law of Property Act 1925 in identical terms. In referring to a section 146 notice I shall therefore mean and include a notice served under section 14(1) of the Act of 1881 and in referring to section 146(1) and (2) I shall mean and include section 14(1) and (2) of the Act of 1881 where appropriate.

Section 146(1) prevents the landlord from enforcing a right of re-entry or forfeiture by action or otherwise so that the landlord cannot determine the lease by issuing and serving a writ or by re-entering the premises until the tenant has failed within a reasonable time to remedy the breach and make reasonable compensation. Section 146(2) enables the tenant to apply to the court for relief where the landlord 'is proceeding, by action or otherwise' to enforce his right of re-entry or forfeiture. If the landlord 'is proceeding' to determine the lease by issuing and serving a writ, the tenant may apply for relief after the writ has been served. If the landlord 'is proceeding' to determine the lease by re-entering into possession, the tenant may apply for relief after the landlord has re-entered.

Mr Reid submitted and referred to authority for the proposition that on the true construction of section 146(2) a tenant cannot apply for relief against forfeiture after the landlord has re-entered without obtaining a court order. Thereafter the landlord is no longer 'proceeding' to enforce his rights; he has succeeded in enforcing them. The proposition is in my opinion historically unsound because the effect of issuing and serving a writ is precisely the same as the effect of re-entry; in each case the lease is determined. The landlord is entitled to remain in possession if he has re-entered and he is entitled to possession if he has issued and served a writ because the lease no longer exists. In each case the tenant seeks relief because the lease has been forfeited. The proposition is also inconsistent with the language of section 146(2). The tenant may apply for relief where the landlord is 'proceeding, by action or otherwise' to enforce his rights. The tenant may apply for relief where the landlord is 'proceeding' by action and also where the landlord is proceeding 'otherwise' than by action. This can only mean that the tenant may apply for relief where the landlord is proceeding to forfeit by re-entry after the expiry of a section 146 notice. If re-entry bars relief, the right of the tenant to apply for relief where the landlord is proceeding otherwise than by action is substantially inoperative and the words 'or otherwise' in section 146(2) have no application. In my opinion those words must have been included because Parliament intended that a tenant should be able to obtain relief against a landlord whether the landlord has asserted his rights by a writ or by re-entering. It is said that a tenant served with a section 146 notice could during and after the expiration of the notice apply for relief under section 146(2) but if he fails to do so he is at the mercy of the landlord who decides to re-enter and whose rights are therefore, it is said, quite unaffected by the provisions of section 146(2) designed to relieve tenants from the consequences of breach of covenant. In my opinion the ambiguous words 'is proceeding' can mean 'proceeds' and should not be construed so as to produce the result that a tenant served with a section 146 notice can only ensure that he will be able to apply for relief if he does so before he knows whether or not the landlord intends to proceed at all or whether, if the landlord decides to proceed, he will issue and serve a writ or will attempt to re-enter.

When a tenant receives a section 146 notice he will not know whether the landlord can be persuaded that there is no breach or persuaded to accept in due course that any breach has been remedied and that he has been offered adequate and satisfactory compensation or whether the landlord will seek to determine the lease by issuing and serving a writ or will seek to determine the lease by re-entering the premises. The tenant will not wish to institute proceedings seeking relief from forfeiture if those proceedings will be aggressive and hostile and may be premature and unnecessary. Parliament cannot have intended that if the landlord employs the civilised method of determining the lease by issuing and serving a writ, then the tenant will be entitled to apply for relief, but if the landlord employs the dubious and dangerous method of determining the lease by re-entering the premises, then the tenant will be debarred from applying for relief.

Mr Reid concedes that re-entry can only avail the landlord if the entry is lawful. Re-entry is unlawful where the premises are occupied by the tenant but not unlawful where the premises are occupied by the tenant's goods. If the argument of the landlords is correct, section 146 provides a method by which a landlord can sneak up on a shop at night, break into the shop, and install new locks so that the tenant loses his lease and can only press his nose against the shop window being unable to obtain the assistance of the court because he has become a trespasser entitled to no rights and to no relief. The farce in the present case when the landlords occupied the premises for four hours should not be allowed to defeat the statutory rights of the tenants.

The right conferred by section 146(2) on a tenant to apply for relief against forfeiture may without violence to the language, be construed as a right to apply 'where a lessor *proceeds*, by action or otherwise' to enforce a right of re-entry. So construed, section 146(2) enables the tenant to apply for relief whenever and however the landlord claims that the lease has been determined for breach of covenant. I have no doubt that this was the object and intention and is the effect of section 146.

In *Quilter v Mapleson* (1882) 9 QBD 672 a landlord forfeited a lease before the Act of 1881 came into force by issuing and serving a writ for possession. He recovered judgment, the tenant appealed and the Act of 1881 came into force before the appeal was heard. The Court of Appeal held that the Act was retrospective and granted relief to the tenant. Lindley LJ, at p. 676, decided that section 146(2) was applicable:

'The action was brought by the landlord on the ground of breaches committed before the Act, and he obtained judgment before the Act came into operation, but execution was stayed, so that he has never obtained possession. The original action then is not yet at an end. ... So long as the tenant has not been turned out of possession he is within the terms of the enactment, for the lessor is proceeding to enforce his right of re-entry. The enactment then being in terms retrospective must be construed according to its terms as being retrospective.'

The judgments of Sir George Jessel MR and Bowen LJ were to the like effect and it is now settled law that where a landlord forfeits a lease by issuing and serving a writ for possession the tenant may apply for relief before but not after the landlord has recovered judgment and re-entered. But although the court limited the time during which a tenant could apply for relief against forfeiture constituted by the issue and service of the writ, the court had no power and in my opinion did not intend to deprive a tenant of any right to apply for relief after a forfeiture constituted by re-entry without judgment. *Quilter v Mapleson* is authority for a case where the landlord forfeits by issue and service of a writ but is not authority for a case where the landlord forfeits by re-entry.

In *Rogers v Rice* [1892] 2 Ch 170 a landlord forfeited by the issue and service of a writ, recovered judgment and re-entered pursuant to the writ of possession then issued and was held to be no longer 'proceeding by action' within section 146(2). The tenant sought and was refused leave to set aside the verdict and the judgment. The tenant later issued an originating summons seeking relief from forfeiture under section 146(2). Lord Coleridge CJ said that a section 146 notice had been given and ignored, and continued, at pp. 171–172:

'The action proceeded to judgment, the judgment was executed, so far as possession was concerned, and at the time when the present proceeding was commenced the lessor was in possession. The action then, so far as related to enforcing the right of re-entry, was at an end, and it cannot be said that the landlord was 'proceeding' to enforce his right of re-entry. The case is clear on the terms of the Act, but I cannot omit to notice that the same view was taken by the judges of the Court of Appeal in *Quilter v Mapleson*, 9 QBD 672, 677, where all three judges gave their opinion to this effect, though that was not the point on which their decision turned.'

The decision can be supported on the grounds that no court could properly exercise its discretion to relieve against forfeiture after the landlord had issued and served a writ, recovered judgment in the action and entered into possession pursuant to that judgment. The decision can also be supported on the grounds set out in the speech of my noble and learned friend, Lord Oliver of Aylmerton. But the court had no power and in my opinion did not intend to deprive a tenant of any right to apply for relief after a forfeiture constituted by re-entry without judgment.

In *Pakwood Transport Ltd v 15, Beauchamp Place Ltd* (1977) 36 P & CR 112 the Court of Appeal rejected an argument by a landlord who had served a section 146 notice that the tenant could not apply for relief from forfeiture until proceedings for forfeiture has been instituted by the landlord. All three Lords Justices derived from *Quilter v Mapleson* and *Rogers v Rice* the proposition that, in the words of Orr LJ, at 117:

'a lessee could not apply for relief against re-entry or forfeiture after the landlord had obtained a judgment of the court entitling him to re-enter on a forfeiture; and it is claimed, and in my judgment rightly claimed, that the same principle must apply where the landlord has peaceably recovered possession. In other words, once he has either recovered possession or obtained an order for possession he can no longer be said to be "proceeding by action or otherwise to enforce a right of re-entry or forfeiture." '

My Lords, I accept that it is now settled law that a tenant cannot apply for relief after the landlord has recovered judgment for possession and has re-entered in reliance on that judgment. But I do not accept that any court has deprived or is entitled to deprive a tenant of any right to apply for relief if the landlord proceeds to forfeit otherwise than by an action instituted for that purpose. Orr LJ continued, at p. 117:

'On this basis the argument for the lessor appears to me to involve an absurdity, in that if the landlord has done no more than serve a section 146 notice, it is too early for the tenant to apply for relief; but if the landlord's next step is peaceably to recover possession, it is then too late for the tenant to apply. For my part, I am not prepared to accept an argument which leads to this absurdity, and I have no hesitation in holding that a landlord who serves a section 146 notice is at that stage 'proceeding to enforce a right of re-entry or forfeiture' in that the service of such a notice is a step which the law requires him to take in order to re-enter or forfeit.'

My Lords, I accept the conclusion that a landlord who serves a notice under section 146(1) can be said, for the purposes of section 146(2) to be proceeding to enforce his rights under the lease. A tenant authorised by section 146(2) to apply to the court for relief against forfeiture if he fails to comply with a section 146 notice may make that application after service of the notice for the purpose of elucidating the issues raised by the notice, ascertaining the intentions of the landlord, and setting in train the machinery by which the dispute between the landlord and the tenant can be determined by negotiation or by the court. But the fact that the tenant may apply to the court for relief after service of the section 146 notice does not mean that if he does not do so he loses the right conferred on him by section 146(2) to apply for relief if and when the landlord proceeds, not by action but 'otherwise' by exercising a right of re-entry. No absurdity follows from a construction which allows the tenant to apply for relief before and after a landlord re-enters without first obtaining a court order.

In the words of Laskin JA in *Re Rexdale Investments Ltd and Gibson* [1967] 1 OR 251, 259 dealing with provisions in the Ontario legislation indistinguishable from section 146(2), the argument that a tenant cannot apply for relief after a landlord has determined the lease by re-entry:

'depends on a detached grammatical reading of the phrase "is proceeding" … which makes nonsense of the phrase "or otherwise" (as covering physical re-entry) by making ineffective, in any practical sense, the provision for relief from forfeiture applicable to such re-entry. We do not construe statutes, especially when they are remedial … to the point of self-contradiction. In my opinion, the phrase "is proceeding" is more properly read in the sense of "has proceeded," and I am fortified in this view by the fact that the exercise of the power of termination is manifested effectively by the mere taking of proceedings as well as by physical re-entry. What [section 146(2)] means, therefore, is that when the landlord has terminated the lease by action or by actual re-entry without action, the tenant may seek relief from forfeiture in the pending action, if any, or, if none, by proceedings initiated by him. In the latter case, one would expect prompt reaction by the tenant. … The English cases relied on … [*Rogers v Rice* [1892] 2 Ch 170; *Lock v Pearce* [1893] 2 Ch 271 and *Quilter v Mapleson*, 9 QBD 672] are distinguishable, if need be … by the fact … that they relate to re-entry in pursuance of a judgment for possession.'

These observations by a distinguished Canadian judge who subsequently became Chief Justice of the Supreme Court of Canada, support the views which I have formed concerning the construction of section 146 and the ambit and effect of the earlier decisions.

Mr Reid argued that your Lordships should not interfere with 19th century decisions and for my part I do not intend to do so on this occasion or to question the result of the decision of the Court of Appeal in *Pakwood Transport Ltd v 15, Beauchamp Place Ltd* (1977) 36 P & CR 112. But the authorities were never directed to the point now in issue and certainly never decided that issue.

It was suggested that Parliament in 1925 accepted the views expressed in the 19th century cases. I agree that Parliament accepted that a tenant cannot apply for relief under section 146(2) after the landlord has forfeited the lease by issuing and serving a writ for possession and in his action has recovered and enforced judgment. The 19th century cases were not directed to the problem which has now emerged.

We were informed that the researches of counsel had not disclosed any reported case in which a landlord has forfeited by re-entry and then successfully denied the right of the tenant to apply for relief.

The landlords or their advisers, perhaps incensed by the activities of the tenants in the present case, conceived and carried out a dawn raid which fortunately did not result in bloodshed. Since the decision of the Court of Appeal in the instant case there has been a proliferation of section 146 notices followed by pressure on tenants to surrender on terms favourable to the landlord. If this appeal were not allowed, the only safe advice for a tenant would be to issue proceedings for relief against forfeiture as soon as a section 146 notice is received at a time when the tenant cannot know whether relief will be necessary. A tenant ignorant of the development in the law pioneered by the landlords in the present case will be at the mercy of an aggressive landlord. The conclusions which I have reached will not entail these consequences and will not again involve Parliament in correcting judicial constructions of statute by further legislation.

The results of section 146 and the authorities are as follows. A tenant may apply for appropriate declarations and for relief from forfeiture under section 146(2) after the issue of a section 146 notice but he is not prejudiced if he does not do so. A tenant cannot apply for relief after a landlord has forfeited a lease by issuing and serving a writ, has recovered judgment and has entered into possession pursuant to that judgment. If the judgment is set aside or successfully appealed the tenant will be able to apply for relief in the landlord's action but the court in deciding whether to grant relief will take into account any consequences of the original order and repossession and the delay of the tenant. A tenant may apply for relief after a landlord has forfeited by re-entry without first obtaining a court order for that purpose but the court in deciding whether to grant relief will take into account all the circumstances, including delay, on the part of the tenant. Any past judicial observations which might suggest that a tenant is debarred from applying for relief after the landlord has re-entered without first obtaining a court order for that purpose are not to be so construed.

I would therefore allow the appeal and set aside the orders of the trial judge and the Court of Appeal. [7]

---

[7] See also *Shiloh Spinners Ltd v Harding* [1973] AC 691, [1973] 1 All ER 90, p. 34, ante (refusal of relief in 'a case of clear and wilful breaches of more than one covenant'); *Scala House and District Property Co Ltd v Forbes* [1974] QB 575 at 584, [1973] 3 All ER 308 at 315, p. 537, ante; *Southern Depot Co Ltd v British Railways Board* [1990] 2 EGLR 39 (relief granted despite wilful breaches involving 'a thoroughly deceptive course of conduct towards the landlord'). For the grant of relief in wholly exceptional circumstances in favour of a tenant who was in breach of a covenant against immoral user, see *Central Estates (Belgravia) Ltd v Woolgar (No 2)* [1972] 1 WLR 1048, [1972] 3 All ER 610; *Ropemaker Properties Ltd v Noonhaven Ltd* [1989] 2 EGLR 50; (1989) 139 NLJ 1747 (H. W. Wilkinson) cf. *British Petroleum Pension Trust Ltd v Behrendt* (1985) 52 P & CR 117.

V. LAW REFORM

Law Commission Consultation Paper on Termination of Tenancies for Tenant Default 2004 (Law Com No. 174)

(2004) 154 NLJ 113 (S. Bridge)

'The proposed scheme would apply to all tenancies, except residential tenancies granted for a term of less than 21 years (such tenancies having already been the subject of reform recommendations in the Law Commission Report on Renting Homes, Law Com No. 284, p. 502, ante). It would therefore impact on tenancies of commercial premises and on long leases (that is, terms certain exceeding 21 years) of residential property.

The central provisional proposals of the consultation paper are as follows: [8]

1.   Any breach of covenant will comprise tenant default, entitling the landlord to commence action to terminate the tenancy. There will be no need to rely upon, and construe, forfeiture clauses.

2.   In every case, whatever the kind of breach, the landlord will be required to serve a "pre-action notice", in prescribed form, on the tenant and on any sub-tenants or mortgagees. This will inform those most likely to be affected by the landlord's action. The notice will give the tenant particulars of the alleged default, and require the tenant to put right the breaches complained of.

3.   At any time, the tenant, or others served with the notice, will be able to refer the notice to the court.

4.   If the landlord wishes to terminate the tenancy he may apply for an order, known as a "termination order", from the court. This order will only be available on proof of a specific ground for termination, the most important of which will be that the tenant default is so serious, and/or so frequent, as to make the tenant so unsatisfactory that he ought not to remain tenant of the property.

5.   In exceptional circumstances, a landlord of commercial premises (or residential premises which are no longer occupied) may be permitted to exercise self-help and to recover possession without prior sanction of the court. Prior service of a pre-action notice stating intention to use this procedure is essential. Once possession has been recovered, the tenancy will then terminate within one month, unless the tenant refers the landlord's action to the court.

6.   Otherwise, a tenancy will only terminate if and when an order of the court terminating the tenancy takes effect.

These are important proposals that should make a very substantial difference to the existing law. The universal requirement of written notice, and the insistence on full details of the tenant's default being provided, will promote the exchange of information between the parties, thereby facilitating compromise.

The pivotal role of the court and its judicious exercise of case management powers should lead to faster disposal of cases and, where appropriate, to greater protection for tenants and those others affected by attempts to forfeit leases.

Where premises are let and occupied as a dwelling, the only means of termination will be by order of the court. Landlord self-help will be restricted to premises that are not, or are no longer, residentially occupied, and even in those circumstances the tenant has the absolute right to due process by referring the pre-action notice to the court. Most importantly, the procedure will be simple and easy to follow.'

[8]   For previous proposals, see Law Commission Reports on Forfeiture of Tenancies 1985 (Law Com No. 142); and on Termination of Tenancies Bill 1994 (Law Com No. 221).

V. The Title to the Freehold [9]

A. Unregistered Land

LAW OF PROPERTY ACT 1925

44. Statutory commencements of title.—(2) Under a contract to grant or assign a term of years, whether derived or to be derived out of freehold or leasehold land, the intended lessee or assign shall not be entitled to call for the title to the freehold.

(3) Under a contract to sell and assign a term of years derived out of a leasehold interest in land, the intended assign shall not have the right to call for the title to the leasehold reversion.

(4) On a contract to grant a lease for a term of years to be derived out of a leasehold interest, with a leasehold reversion, the intended lessee shall not have the right to call for the title to that reversion.

(4A) Subsections (2) and (4) of this section do not apply to a contract to grant a term of years if the grant will be an event within section 4(1) of the Land Registration Act 2002 (events which trigger compulsory first registration of title). [10]

(5) Where by reason of any of subsections (2) to (4) of this section [11] an intending lessee or assign is not entitled to call for the title to the freehold or to a leasehold reversion, as the case may be, he shall not, where the contract is made after the commencement of this Act, be deemed to be affected with notice of any matter or thing of which, if he had contracted that such title should be furnished, he might have had notice.

(12) Nothing in this section applies in relation to registered land or to a term of years to be derived out of registered land. [12]

SHEARS v WELLS
[1936] 1 All ER 832 (ChD, Luxmoore J)

The first defendant was the owner, and the second defendant, Cooper, the tenant of premises under a tenancy commencing in 1929. [13] The plaintiff brought this action for an injunction to restrain the breach of a restrictive covenant contained in the conveyance to the first defendant. The second defendant pleaded that he had no notice of the restrictive covenant. On the question of his liability.

Held. By virtue of the Law of Property Act 1925, section 44(5), the second defendant was only bound by matters of which the plaintiff could prove he had notice at the commencement of his tenancy.

Luxmoore J: I think that Cooper is not liable under the covenant at all. He took the tenancy of the garage in 1929 after the passing of the Law of Property Act 1925. Section 44 enacts as follows:—

[His Lordship read section 44(2), (4), (5):] It follows that the onus of proving that the defendant Cooper had notice when he took the tenancy is on the

---

[9] C & B, pp. 822–823; M & W, paras. 14.295–14.300.
[10] Added by LRA 2002, s. 133, Sch. 11, para. 2(1)(2).
[11] Substituted by LRA 2002, s. 133, Sch. 11, para. 2(1)(3).
[12] Added by LRA 2002, s. 133, Sch. 11, para. 2(1)(4).
[13] In the statement of facts this date is given as 1931 but this is at variance with the date given in the judgment which is used here.

plaintiff. There is no evidence here that he had notice and the onus is not discharged. The defendant Cooper is therefore not subject to the covenants in the deed.

This case illustrates the reversal of the rule in *Patman v Harland* (1881) 17 ChD 353, where Sir George JESSEL MR held that a tenant had constructive notice of a restrictive covenant affecting the freehold, which covenant was disclosed in the deeds. The tenant was not protected even if the lessor told her that there was no such covenant, nor by the Vendor and Purchaser Act 1874, section 2 which provides 'subject to any stipulation to the contrary' that 'under a contract to grant or assign a term of years, whether derived or to be derived out of a freehold or leasehold estate, the intended lessee or assign shall not be entitled to call for the title to the freehold.'

Shears v Wells does not, however, solve all the problems. The person entitled to the benefit of the covenant needs to ensure that the lessee has notice of the covenant. Presumably he could do this by registration and rely on the provisions of the Law of Property Act 1925, section 198(1) that registration is deemed to constitute 'actual notice ... to all persons ... connected with the land affected.' [14] The result is not satisfactory; for the procedure for registration under the Land Charges Act 1925 provides for registration under personal names and not under the land concerned. Unless therefore the incumbrance is registered against the present lessor, the tenant (a fortiori, a sub-tenant), not seeing the earlier deeds, will not know under whose name to search. And neither pre-1926 covenants nor covenants originally entered into between landlord and tenant are registrable. [15]

B. Land Registration Act 2002

Section 44(12) of the Land Registration Act 2002 disapplies section 44 of the Law of Property Act 1925 (p. 559, ante) as regards registered land for a term of years to be derived out of registered land. This follows from the register being proof of the title of a registered estate, and therefore any prospective lessee can inspect the title of his landlord. [16]

VI. The Effect of Assignment on Covenants [17]

The Landlord and Tenant (Covenants) Act 1995 radically changed the law relating to the enforcement of covenants in leases. [18] It is not retrospective. It

---

[14]   In *White v Bijou Mansions* [1937] Ch 610 at 619, [1937] 3 All ER 269 at 273, SIMONDS J suggested 'that s. 198 ... appears, notwithstanding the unqualified language of s. 44, sub-s. 5, to affect a lessee with notice of all those charges which are registered under the Land Charges Act 1925'.

[15]   (1940) 56 LQR 361 (D. W. Logan); [1956] CLJ 230–234 (H. W. R. Wade).

[16]   Law Com Report No. 217, paras. 12.9–12.13; H & B, para. 6.7.

[17]   C & B, pp. 475–497; Gray, pp. 1302–1341; M & W, paras. 14,050–14.052, 14.108–14.114, chap. 15; MM, pp. 381–406; Smith, chap. 18.

[18]   (1996) 59 MLR (M. Davey); [1996] CLJ 313 (S. Bridge); [1996] Conv 432 (P. Walter); (1996) 49 CLP Part I 95 (A. Clarke). See generally Fancourt: *Enforceability of Landlord and Tenant Covenants* (1997).

provides a new code for covenants in leases granted after 1995. The existing law continues where the lease was created before 1996.[19]

A. Covenants in Pre-1996 Leases

i. COVENANTS WHICH TOUCH AND CONCERN THE LAND

The only covenants which can be enforced by or against assignees of the leasehold estate or the reversion, are those which touch and concern the land,[20] or (which means the same thing) have 'reference to the subject-matter of the lease.'[1] In Lord Ellenborough's words, the test is satisfied if the covenant 'affected the nature, quality or value of the thing demised, independently of collateral circumstances; or if it affected the mode of enjoying it.'[2] The simplest test is that put forward by Cheshire,[3] that is to consider whether the covenant affects 'the landlord *qua* landlord or the tenant *qua* tenant'.[4]

In **P & A Swift Investments v Combined English Stores Group plc** [1989] AC 632, [1988] 2 All ER 885, the House of Lords held that a covenant in a lease by a surety who guaranteed payment of the rent by the tenant was a covenant which touched and concerned the land. Lord TEMPLEMAN said at 637, at 887:

'The landlord replies that a covenant by a surety, in whatever form or expression the surety covenant may take, is a covenant that the tenant's covenants shall be performed and observed. A covenant by a surety that a tenant's covenant which touches and concerns the land shall be performed and observed must itself be a covenant which touches and concerns the land; the benefit of that surety's covenant will run with the reversion, and the covenant is therefore enforceable without express assignment. I agree. A surety for a tenant is a quasi tenant who volunteers to be a substitute or twelfth man for the tenant's team and is subject to the same rules and regulations as the player he replaces. A covenant which runs with the reversion against the tenant runs with the reversion against the surety.[5]

Lord OLIVER OF AYLMERTON said at 642, at 890.

'Formulations of definite tests are always dangerous, but it seems to me that, without claiming to expound an exhaustive guide, the following provides a satisfactory working test for whether, in any given case, a covenant touches and concerns the land: (1) the covenant benefits only the reversioner for time being, and if separated from the reversion ceases to be of benefit to the covenantee;

---

[19] Sections 17–20 apply to all leases whenever granted; p. 573, post. In *First Penthouse Ltd v Channel Hotels & Properties (UK) Ltd* [2003] EWHC 2713 (Ch), [2004] 05 EG 148, LIGHTMAN J said at para. 42: 'The 1995 Act is the product of rushed drafting, and its provisions create exceptional difficulties.'

[20] *Spencer's Case* (1583) 5 Co Rep 16a, p. 563, post; *Smith's Leading Cases* (13th edn. 1929), vol. 1, p. 51.

[1] LPA 1925, ss. 141, 142; *Davis v Town Properties Investment Corpn Ltd* [1903] 1 Ch 797.

[2] *Congleton Corpn v Pattison* (1808) 10 East 130 at 135.

[3] Infra. This was approved in *Breams Property Investment Co Ltd v Stroulger* [1948] 2 KB 1 at 7, [1948] 1 All ER 758 at 759; *Hua Chiao Commercial Bank Ltd v Chiaphua Industries Ltd* [1987] AC 99 at 107, [1985] 1 All ER 1110 at 1112, infra.

[4] C & B, pp. 476–480; M & W, paras. 15.025–15.028; MM, pp. 387–388.

[5] See *Milverton Group Ltd v Warner World Ltd* [1995] 2 EGLR 28 at 31.

(2) the covenant affects the nature, quality, mode of user or value of the land of the reversioner; (3) the covenant is not expressed to be personal (that is to say neither being given only to a specific reversioner nor in respect of the obligations only of a specific tenant[6]); (4) the fact that a covenant is to pay a sum of money will not prevent it from touching and concerning the land so long as the three foregoing conditions are satisfied and the covenant is connected with something to be done on, to or in relation to the land.'[7]

In **Hua Chiao Commercial Bank Ltd v Chiaphua Industries Ltd** [1987] AC 99, [1987] 1 All ER 1110, the Privy Council held that a covenant by a tenant to pay the landlord a substantial security deposit on the terms that it would be repayable at the end of the lease if there was no breach of the tenant's covenants, did not touch and concern the land. Lord OLIVER OF AYLMERTON said at 107, at 1112:

'Their Lordships have been referred to and are content to adopt the following passage from *Cheshire and Burn's Modern Law of Real Property*, 13th ed. (1982), pp. 430–431:

"If the covenant has direct reference to the land, if it lays down something which is to be done or is not to be done upon the land, or, and perhaps this is the clearest way of describing the test, if it affects the landlord in his normal capacity as landlord or the tenant in his normal capacity as tenant, it may be said to touch and concern the land.

Lord Russell CJ [in *Horsey Estate Ltd v Steiger* [1899] 2 QB 79, 89] said: 'The true principle is that no covenant or condition which affects merely the person, and which does not affect the nature, quality, or value of the thing demised or the mode of using or enjoying the thing demised, runs with the land;' and Bailey J at an earlier date asserted the same principle [in *Congleton Corpn v Pattison* (1808) 10 East 130, 138]: 'In order to bind the assignee, the covenant must either affect the land itself during the term, such as those which regard the mode of occupation, or it must be such as per se, and not merely from collateral circumstances, affects the value of the land at the end of the term.'

If a simple test is desired for ascertaining into which category a covenant falls, it is suggested that the proper inquiry should be whether the covenant affects either the landlord qua landlord or the tenant qua tenant. A covenant may very well have reference to the land, but, unless it is reasonably incidental to the relation of landlord and tenant, it cannot be said to touch and concern the land so as to be capable of running therewith or with the reversion." '

ii. COVENANTS RUNNING WITH THE LEASEHOLD ESTATE

The common law rule was that covenants which touched and concerned the land were enforceable by and against the assignee of the tenant. There was however an exception to the effect that a covenant relating to something not in esse at

---

[6]   *System Floors Ltd v Ruralpride Ltd* [1995] 1 EGLR 48 (benefit of covenant runs against assignee of reversion even though personal to original tenant).

[7]   See also *Kumar v Dunning* [1989] QB 193, [1987] 2 All ER 801, approved by Lord OLIVER; *Coronation Street Industrial Properties Ltd v Ingall Industries plc* [1989] 1 WLR 304, [1989] 1 All ER 979 (covenant to accept a new lease on the disclaimer of the lease by the tenant's liquidator held to touch and concern); *Clegg v Hands* (1890) 44 Ch D 503; *Caerns Motor Services Ltd v Texaco Ltd* [1994] 1 WLR 1249, [1995] 1 All ER 247 (solus agreement to purchase products held to touch and concern).

the date of the covenant only ran with the leasehold estate if assigns were expressly mentioned; this exception was abolished in 1925. [8]

SPENCER'S CASE
(1583) 5 Co Rep 16a (KB)

Spencer and his wife leased land to S for 21 years. S covenanted for him, his executors and administrators that he, his executors, administrators, or assigns would build a brick wall thereon. He assigned his lease to J, who assigned it to the defendant Clark. The question is as to the liability of Clark on the covenant to build.

Held. Since the covenant was in respect of something to be done on the land demised, and was not made expressly on behalf of the assigns the defendant was not liable.

The report records that after many arguments at the Bar, the case was excellently argued and debated by the justices at the Bench. Three of the resolutions were:

'1. When the covenant extends to a thing *in esse*, parcel of the demise, the thing to be done by force of the covenant is *quodammodo* annexed and appurtenant to the thing demised, and shall go with the land, and shall bind the assignee although he be not bound by express words: but when the covenant extends to a thing which is not in being at the time of the demise made, it cannot be appurtenant or annexed to the thing which hath no being: as if the lessee covenants to repair the houses demised to him during the term, that is parcel of the contract, and extends to the support of the thing demised, and therefore is *quodammodo* annexed appurtenant to houses, and shall bind the assignee although he be not bound expressly by the covenant: but in the case at bar, the covenant concerns a thing which was not *in esse* at the time of the demise made, but to be newly built after, and therefore shall bind the covenantor, his executors, or administrators, and not the assignee, for the law will not annex the covenant to a thing which hath no being.

2. It was resolved that in this case, if the lessee had covenanted for him and his assigns, that they would make a new wall upon some part of the thing demised, that for as much as it is to be done upon the land demised, that it should bind the assignee; for although the covenant doth extend to a thing to be newly made, yet it is to be made upon the thing demised, and the assignee is to take the benefit of it, and therefore shall bind the assignee by express words. So on the other side, if a warranty be made to one, his heirs and assigns, by express words, the assignee shall take benefit of it, and shall have *a Warrantia chartae*. ... But although the covenant be for him and his assigns, yet if the thing to be done be merely collateral to the land, and doth not touch or concern the thing demised in any sort, there the assignee shall not be charged. As if the lessee covenants for him and his assigns to build a house upon the land of the lessor which is no parcel of the demise, or to pay any collateral sum to the lessor, or to a stranger, it shall not bind the assignee, because it is merely collateral, and in no manner touches or concerns the thing that was demised, or that is assigned over; and therefore in such case the assignee of the thing demised cannot be charged with it, no more than any other stranger.

---

[8]　LPA 1925, s. 79, p. 564, post; and, in respect of covenants entered into before 1996, L & T(C)A 1995, s. 3(7), p. 584, post.

4. It was resolved, that if a man makes a feoffment by this word *dedi*, which implies a warranty, the assignee of the feoffee shall not vouch; but if a man makes a lease for years by this word *concessi* or *demisi*, which implies a covenant, if the assignee of the lessee be evicted, he shall have a writ of covenant; for the lessee and his assignee hath the yearly profits of the land which shall grow by his labour and industry for an annual rent, and therefore it is reasonable when he hath applied his labour, and employed his cost upon the land, and be evicted (whereby he loses all), that he shall take such benefit of the demise and grant, as the first lessee might, and the lessor hath no other prejudice than what his special contract with the first lessee hath bound him to.'

LAW OF PROPERTY ACT 1925 [9]

78. Benefit of covenants relating to land.—(1) A covenant relating to any land of the covenantee shall be deemed to be made with the covenantee and his successors in title and the persons deriving title under him or them, and shall have effect as if such successors and other persons were expressed.

For the purposes of this subsection in connexion with covenants restrictive of the user of land 'successors in title' shall be deemed to include the owners and occupiers for the time being of the land of the covenantee intended to be benefited.

(2) This section applies to covenants made after the commencement of this Act, but the repeal of section fifty-eight of the Conveyancing Act, 1881, does not affect the operation of covenants to which that section applied.

79. Burden of covenants relating to land.—(1) A covenant relating to any land of a covenantor or capable of being bound by him, shall, unless a contrary intention is expressed, be deemed to be made by the covenantor on behalf of himself his successors in title and the persons deriving title under him or them, and, subject as aforesaid, shall have effect as if such successors and other persons were expressed.

This subsection extends to a covenant to do some act relating to the land, notwithstanding that the subject-matter may not be in existence when the covenant is made.

(2) For the purposes of this section in connexion with covenants restrictive of the user of land 'successors in title' shall be deemed to include the owners and occupiers for the time being of such land.

(3) This section applies only to covenants made after the commencement of this Act.

iii. COVENANTS RUNNING WITH THE REVERSION

At common law the benefit and burden of covenants other than 'usual' or 'implied' covenants did not run with the landlord's reversion. Statutory provision was made in 32 Hen 8 c 34 and in the Conveyancing Act 1881. These provisions were superseded by the Law of Property Act 1925.[8a]

[8a]   See also LPA 1925, s 63 (which provides that, subject to a contrary intention in the conveyance, 'Every conveyance is effectual to pass all the estate, right, title, interest, claim, and demand which the conveying parties respectively have, in, to, or on the property conveyed, or expressed or intended so to be, or which they respectively have power to convey in, to, or on the same; *Harbour Estates Ltd v HSBC Bank plc* [2004] EWHC 1714 (Ch0, [2004] 3 ALl ER 1057, [2004] 32 EG 62 (CS) (benefit of break clause in lease held to touch and concern land, and therefore, to pass to assignee).

(a) Benefit

LAW OF PROPERTY ACT 1925

141. Rent and benefit of lessee's covenants to run with the reversion.—(1) Rent reserved by a lease, and the benefit of every covenant or provision therein contained, having reference to the subject-matter thereof, and on the lessee's part to be observed or performed, and every condition of re-entry and other condition therein contained, shall be annexed and incident to and shall go with the reversionary estate in the land, or in any part thereof, immediately expectant on the term granted by the lease, notwithstanding severance of that reversionary estate,[10] and without prejudice to any liability affecting a covenantor or his estate.

(2) Any such rent, covenant or provision shall be capable of being recovered, received, enforced, and taken advantage of, by the person from time to time entitled, subject to the term, to the income of the whole or any part, as the case may require, of the land leased.

(3) Where that person becomes entitled by conveyance or otherwise, such rent, covenant or provision may be recovered, received, enforced or taken advantage of by him notwithstanding that he becomes so entitled after the condition of re-entry or forfeiture has become enforceable, but this subsection does not render enforceable any condition of re-entry or other condition waived or released before such person becomes entitled as aforesaid.[11]

(4) This section applies to leases made before or after the commencement of this Act, but does not affect the operation of—

(*a*) any severance of the reversionary estate; or

(*b*) any acquisition by conveyance or otherwise of the right to receive or enforce any rent covenant or provision;

effected before the commencement of this Act.

RE KING [12]

[1963] Ch 459, [1963] 1 All ER 781 (CA, Lord DENNING MR, UPJOHN and DIPLOCK LJJ)

In 1895 Edward Graves-Tagg granted a lease of land and a factory in Bethnal Green to Mrs Elven, who covenanted for herself, her executors, administrators and assigns (*a*) to keep the premises in repair, (*b*) to insure the premises and keep them insured against loss or damage by fire and (*c*) to lay out all moneys received under any such policy in rebuilding or repairing the premises destroyed or damaged by fire and, if necessary, to reinstate the premises. In 1907 the lease was assigned to King. In 1944 the factory was severely damaged by fire, but could not be repaired or rebuilt owing to wartime restrictions. The insurance moneys were duly paid. In 1946 Edward Graves-Tagg assigned his reversion to Edward

---

9   See also pp. 948–949, 951–954, 959–966, post.

10   When the reversion is severed i.e. different parts come into different ownerships, the benefit of any covenant, condition or right of entry is apportioned and annexed to the severed parts: LPA 1925, s. 140. The severance must be genuine: *Persey v Bazley* (1983) 267 EG 519 (landlord conveyed part of reversion to bare trustees for himself); [1985] Conv 292 (J. Martin). The tenancy itself remains a single tenancy: *Jelley v Buckman* [1974] QB 488, [1973] 3 All ER 853; *Nevill Lang & Co (Boards) Ltd v Firmenich & Co* (1983) 268 EG 572. See also *Lester v Ridd* [1990] 2 QB 430, [1989] 1 All ER 1111 (severance of tenancy).

11   *Kataria v Safeland plc* [1998] 1 EGLR 39.

12   (1966) 30 Conv (NS) 429 (D. Macintyre). On the construction of a covenant to insure, see *Farimani v Gates* (1984) 271 EG 887; *Beacon Carpets Ltd v Kirby* [1985] QB 755, [1984] 2 All ER 726.

Ernest Graves-Tagg ('Tagg') and in 1949 King died. The factory had never been repaired or rebuilt. In 1960 Tagg assigned his reversion to the London County Council as a result of a compulsory purchase order. In 1961, during negotiations between the London County Council and King's executors for the transfer of the lease to the London County Council, King's executors issued a summons to determine, inter alia, whether Tagg could still sue them for the breach of the covenant to repair and to reinstate, which had occurred before the assignment of 1960. If he could, then King's executors argued that an indemnity by the London County Council should be included in the transfer of the lease.

Held. King's executors were not liable to Tagg.

UPJOHN LJ: The first question may be briefly stated in this way: Can a landlord, who has assigned his reversion to a lease, after the date of such assignment, sue the lessee in respect of breaches of covenant which occurred before the assignment? ...

This case is concerned with express covenants in a lease, and in such case it cannot possibly be doubted that section 141 of the Law of Property Act 1925 governs the situation. [His Lordship read sections (1) and (2) and continued:]

I turn, then, to a consideration of the meaning of section 141 and construe the language used in its ordinary and natural meaning, which seems to me quite plain and clear. To illustrate this, consider the case of a lease containing a covenant to build a house according to certain detailed specifications before a certain day. Let me suppose that after that certain day the then lessor assigns the benefit of the reversion to an assignee, and at the time of the assignment the lessee has failed to perform the covenant to build. Who can sue the lessee for breach of covenant? It seems to me clear that the assignee alone can sue. Upon the assignment the benefit of every covenant on the lessee's part to be observed and performed is annexed and incident to and goes with the reversionary estate. The benefit of that covenant to build, therefore, passed; as it had been broken, the right to sue also passed as part of the benefit of the covenant and, incidentally, also the right to re-enter, if that has not been waived. I protest against the argument that because a right to sue is itself a chose in action it, therefore, has become severed from, and independent of, the parent covenant; on the contrary it remains part of it. The right to sue on breach is merely one of the bundle of rights that are contained in the concept 'benefit of every covenant'. ... To return to my example. Suppose the right to sue for breach of that covenant did not pass, and that right remained in the assignor, then the assignee would take the lease without the benefit of that covenant and he could never enforce it. So he has not got the benefit of every covenant contained in the lease and the words of the section are not satisfied. That cannot be right. ...

Then suppose the lease contains a covenant to keep in repair which is broken at the date of the assignment, and that at all material times the premises were out of repair; that is, a continuing breach. It is an a fortiori case to the example I have just dealt with. Indeed, with all respect to the argument to the contrary, you cannot give any sensible meaning to the words of the section unless the entire benefit of a repairing covenant had passed, leaving the assignor without remedy against the lessee. Look at the absurd results if that were not so. The assignor of the reversion remains at liberty to sue the lessee for breaches down to the moment of the assignment. After assignment he sues and obtains judgment for certain damages. But then the premises are still out of repair and the breach continues. The assignee claims to re-enter or to sue because the premises are out of repair. What is the situation of the lessee? Either he has to pay damages twice or pay damages to the assignor and then reinstate the premises because otherwise the assignee will re-enter. This is impossible. Alternatively, the assignee's right to re-enter or to sue in respect of post assignment breaches is in some way adversely affected by reason of the fact that the assignor has recovered a judgment for damages for pre-assignment breaches; therefore, the benefit of the covenant to keep in repair did not pass wholly to him even in respect of post-assignment breaches. That directly contradicts the words of the section. ...

In my judgment Tagg's claims fail and I would allow this part of the appeal.

In **London and County (A and D) Ltd v Wilfred Sportsman Ltd** [1971] Ch 764, [1970] 2 All ER 600 the Court of Appeal held that section 141 should be similarly interpreted in the case of a covenant to pay rent. RUSSELL LJ said at 784, at 606:

'The language of section 141 (substantially re-enacting the earlier legislation from 1881 onwards) is such as, in my judgment, to indicate plainly that an assignee of the reversion may sue and re-enter for rent in arrear at the date of the assignment when the right of re-entry has arisen before the assignment.[13] The decision in *Rickett v Green* [1910] 1 KB 253, p. 578, post was, therefore, correct.'

(b)   Burden

LAW OF PROPERTY ACT 1925

142. Obligation of lessor's covenants to run with reversion.—(1) The obligation under a condition or of a covenant entered into by a lessor with reference to the subject-matter of the lease[14] shall, if and as far as the lessor has power to bind the reversionary estate immediately expectant on the term granted by the lease, be annexed and incident to and shall go with that reversionary estate, or the several parts thereof, notwithstanding severance of that reversionary estate, and may be taken advantage of and enforced by the person in whom the term is from time to time vested by conveyance, devolution in law, or otherwise; and, if and as far as the lessor has power to bind the person from time to time entitled to that reversionary estate, the obligation aforesaid may be taken advantage of and enforced against any person so entitled.

(2) This section applies to leases made before or after the commencement of this Act, whether the severance of the reversionary estate was effected before or after such commencement:

Provided that, where the lease was made before the first day of January eighteen hundred and eighty-two, nothing in this section shall affect the operation of any severance of the reversionary estate effected before such commencement.

This section takes effect without prejudice to any liability affecting a covenantor or his estate.

---

[13]   *Arlesford Trading Co Ltd v Servansingh* [1971] 1 WLR 1080, [1971] 3 All ER 113 (assignee of reversion recovered rent against lessee who had assigned his lease before the reversion was assigned, so that there was neither privity of contract nor of estate between the parties).

[14]   The obligation may be expressed in a side-letter; *System Floors Ltd v Ruralpride Ltd* [1995] 1 EGLR 48; *Lotteryking Ltd v AMEC Properties Ltd* [1995] NPC 55; cf. s. 141, where the covenant must be contained in the lease: *Weg Motors Ltd v Hales* [1962] Ch 49 at 73, [1961] 3 All ER 181 at 189.

Section 142 has been interpreted differently from section 141. It is the tenant and not the assignee who is entitled to sue for breach of a covenant by the landlord before the tenant assigns the lease.

In **City and Metropolitan Properties Ltd v Greycroft Ltd** [15] [1987] 1 WLR 1085, [1987] 3 All ER 839 the landlord bought a flat in Belsise Court, London NW3 subject to a 99 year lease. In 1982 the tenant acquired the lease by assignment when the landlord was in serious breach of the covenant to repair. In 1984 the tenant sold the lease again and claimed damages for losses suffered while it was tenant. In holding that the landlord was liable, John MOWBRAY QC said at 1086, at 840:

'The landlord's first defence is that, when the tenant assigned the lease, all its rights passed to the assignee, including any right to damages such as are claimed under the pre-existing specially indorsed writ, so the tenant has no cause of action left to support its claim. In my view that defence is not well founded. No authority was cited on the precise question whether a tenant who has assigned his lease can afterwards recover damages from the landlord for breaches of the landlord's covenants committed while the tenant held the lease. It is common ground, though, that a tenant (not the original lessee) who has assigned his lease again remains liable to the landlord for breaches of covenant which he committed while tenant: see *Megarry and Wade, The Law of Real Property*, 5th ed. (1984), p. 750, para. 5, *Woodfall, Landlord and Tenant*, 28th ed. (1978), vol. 1, para. 1–1095 and *Halsbury's Laws of England*, 4th ed., vol. 27 (1981), para. 395. Both this liability and the benefit of the landlord's covenants run with the lease at common law by privity of estate under *Spencer's Case* (1583) 5 Co.Rep. 16a: see *Smith's Leading Cases*, 13th ed. (1929), vol. 1, p. 51. There is a close analogy between the two. I take the view that, by this analogy, the landlord's liability to the tenant for existing breaches survives the assignment of the lease, in the same way as the tenant's liability to the landlord.

Mr Moss argued for the landlord here that the tenant's rights against the landlord did not survive the assignment of the lease, because on the assignment section 142(1) of the Law of Property Act 1925 made a statutory transfer of the tenant's rights to the assignee of the lease. Section 142(1) reads: ...

Mr Moss argued that the middle part of section 142(1) carried out the transfer, that is the words "and may be taken advantage of and enforced by the person in whom the tenant is from time to time vested by conveyance, devolution in law, or otherwise." He pointed out that the Court of Appeal has held section 141(1) to make a statutory transfer of the whole benefit of a tenant's covenant to an assignee of the reversion: *Re King* [1963] Ch 459, [1963] 1 All ER 781 and *London and County (A & D) Ltd v Wilfred Sportsman Ltd.* [1971] Ch 764, [1970] 2 All ER 600, p. 565, ante. He asked me to apply that principle by analogy to an assignment of the lease.

It is not possible to apply those decisions. They turned on words corresponding to the first part of section 142(1), "shall ... be annexed and incident to and shall go with that reversionary estate ..." The middle passage of section 142(1) is quite different. It does not say that the right to take advantage of the landlord's covenants is annexed or incident to the term, or "shall go with" it, the graphic phrase specially relied on by Diplock LJ in *Re King* [1963] Ch.

15   [1987] Conv 374 (P. F. Smith).

459, 497, [1963] 1 All ER 781, 798. It is not possible to apply the Court of Appeal decisions to the middle passage. If the intention had been to effect a statutory transfer of the right to an assignee of the term, I should have expected words to have been used similar to those in section 141(1) and the beginning of section 142(1) itself. What is more, the middle passage of section 142(1) does not on its separate interpretation show any intention to restrict a tenant's proceedings to any particular period. The words "from time to time" mean as occasion may require. If the intention had been to limit the tenant's right to recover damages to the time when he was tenant, I should have expected the subsections to say "for the time being."

Mr Moss said that these conclusions could lead to anomaly and injustice, particularly that both assignor and assignee tenants might attack the landlord for the disrepair and both recover damages for it, which could overlap. He very reasonably referred to *Re King*, on this point, in the judgment of Upjohn LJ, at p. 489, at p. 793, and Diplock LJ, at p. 498, at p. 799. I do not see how there can be any overlap in the present case, because the repairs were done before the assignment. The mere consequential damages of the assignor are personal and could not overlap any consequential damages of an assignee, who, in the present case, could not suffer any damage anyhow. It is true that a possible overlap of rights could occur in a case where disrepair continued over the assignment, but section 142 would not prevent the assignee's damages from being reduced to allow for his having bought cheaply because of the disrepair: contrast section 141(1) and *Re King* at p. 489, at p. 793.

Mr Moss also said that there could be several successive assignors who sold at depressed prices during the disrepair and each sued the landlord for the shortfall. I think this is a rather fanciful apprehension. It could only arise if the landlord delayed so long that a number of successive tenants sold in despair or disgust. Even where the disrepair lasted over the assignment, I do not see how any consequential damage to assignor or assignee could overlap, because each would be personal damages arising from the plaintiff's personal circumstances. I conclude that the first defence which I have been considering, based on section 142(1) of the Law of Property Act 1925, fails.'

iv. PRIVITY OF ESTATE AND PRIVITY OF CONTRACT

Subject to the situation discussed in (*e*) below, liability under, and the right to sue upon, covenants running with the land or the reversion exists only between persons between whom there is privity of estate. The original contracting parties are liable to each other contractually and remain so liable: assignees are liable and able to sue only if, and so long as, they hold the estate with which the covenant runs; and such persons must be assignees and not sub-lessees[16] or squatters.[17]

(*a*) *General Principles*

In **City of London Corpn v Fell** [1994] 1 AC 458, [1993] 4 All ER 968, Lord TEMPLEMAN said at 464, at 972:

'The principle that the benefit and burden of covenants in a lease which touch and concern the land run with the term and with the reversion is necessary

---

[16]   *South of England Dairies Ltd v Baker* [1906] 2 Ch 631, p. 574 post; *Hemingway Securities Ltd v Dunraven Ltd* [1995] 1 EGLR 61 (breach of covenant against sub-letting).
[17]   *Tichborne v Weir* (1892) 67 LT 735, p. 946, post.

for the effective operation of the law of landlord and tenant. Common law, and statute following the common law, recognise two forms of legal estate in land, a fee simple absolute in possession and a term of years absolute: see section 1 of the Act of 1925. Common law, and statute following the common law, were faced with the problem of rendering effective the obligations under a lease which might endure for a period of 999 years or more beyond the control of any covenantor. The solution was to annex to the term and the reversion the benefit and burden of covenants which touch and concern the land. The covenants having been annexed, every legal owner of the term granted by the lease and every legal owner of the reversion from time to time holds his estate with the benefit of and subject to the covenants which touch and concern the land. The system of leasehold tenure requires that the obligations in the lease shall be enforceable throughout the term, whether those obligations are affirmative or negative. The owner of a reversion must be able to enforce the positive covenants to pay rent and keep in repair against an assignee who in turn must be able to enforce any positive covenants entered into by the original landlord. Common law retained the ancient rule that the burden of a covenant does not run with the land of the covenantor except in the case of a lease, but even that rule was radically modified by equity so far as negative covenants were concerned: see *Tulk v Moxhay* (1848) 2 Ph 774, p. 942, post.

The effect of common law and statute on a lease is to create rights and obligations which are independent of the parallel rights and obligations of the original human covenantor who and whose heirs may fail or the parallel rights and obligations of a corporate covenantor which may be dissolved. Common law and statute achieve that effect by annexing those rights and obligations so far as they touch and concern the land to the term and to the reversion. Nourse LJ neatly summarised the position when he said in an impeccable judgment [1993] QB 589, 604, [1993] 2 All ER 449, 454:

"The contractual obligations which touch and concern the land having become imprinted on the estate, the tenancy is capable of existence as a species of property independently of the contract."

The common law did not release the original tenant from liability for breaches of covenant committed after an assignment because of the sacred character of covenant in English law. I understand that Scots law releases the original tenant once he has been replaced by a permitted or accepted assignee. This only means that the fortunate English landlord has two remedies after an assignment, namely his remedy against the assignee and his remedy against the original tenant. It does not follow that if the liability of the original tenant is released or otherwise disappears then the term granted by the lease will disappear or that the assignee will cease to be liable on the covenants.

As between landlord and assignee the landlord cannot enforce a covenant against the assignee because the assignee does not covenant. The landlord enforces against the assignee the provisions of a covenant entered into by the original tenant, being provisions which touch and concern the land, because those provisions are annexed by the lease to the term demised by the lease. The assignee is not liable for a breach of covenant committed after the assignee has himself in turn assigned the lease because once he has assigned over he has ceased to be the owner of the term to which the covenants are annexed.

Covenants are introduced on the creation of a lease but are not necessary to sustain a lease. Upon an assignment of a lease, the provisions of the covenants by the original tenant continue to attach to the term because those provisions touch and concern the land and not because there continues to exist an original tenant who has ceased to own any interest in the demised land but remains liable in contract to fulfil the promises he made under covenant.'

(b) Plight of Original Parties

1. ORIGINAL TENANT

The continuing liability of an original tenant in contract is a serious hazard. He may have long since disposed of his property and then find himself being made liable for breaches of covenant which occurred after the assignment, in particular, where an assignee over whom he has no control *breaks* the covenant to pay rent or to repair.[18]

(1996) 59 MLR 79 at pp. 81–83 (M. Davey)

'The original tenant had very few means of protecting himself save by verifying the creditworthiness of his immediate assignee as well as insisting on the presence of a clause in the original lease which compelled the landlord to take a direct covenant from that assignee.[19] The most obvious form of protection was for the first assignor to take an express indemnity[20] from his assignee who on a further assignment would have taken an indemnity from his assignee and so on, enabling liability to be ultimately revisited on the assignee in default. In addition the original tenant had a quasi-contractual claim against the defaulting assignee.[1] The weakness of these remedies was obvious. As far as the express (or statutory) indemnity was concerned it was always possible that there would turn out to have been an assignment at some stage where an indemnity had not been taken, thereby breaking the chain. But even more serious, in the case of both the express (or statutory) indemnity and the quasi-contractual claim, was the fact that the assignee in default would prove to be not worth suing. Indeed this would usually be the case if the landlord had felt it necessary to resort to the original tenant. Furthermore, if the defaulting tenant became insolvent and the lease was disclaimed by the trustee in bankruptcy, the assignee and his guarantor would

---

[18] See *City of London Corpn v Fell* [1994] 1 AC 458, [1993] 4 All ER 968 (where lease assigned by original tenant had run its term and been extended under Landlord and Tenant Act 1954, Part II, original tenant's obligations held to cease on completion of term); [1994] CLJ 28 (S. Bridge); cf. *Herbert Duncan Ltd v Cluttons* [1993] QB 589, [1993] 2 All ER 449; [1993] Conv 164 (P. F. Smith). See also *Norwich Union Life Insurance Society v Low Profile Fashions Ltd* [1992] 1 EGLR 86; [1992] CLJ 425 (S. Bridge) (no duty of care on landlord to ensure solvency of assignee when consenting to assignment, and no equitable principle which obliges landlord to sue assignees and his surety before original tenant).

[19] By this means the assignee could be made liable for breaches which occurred even after any further disposal of the lease by assignment when privity of estate between himself and the landlord would have ceased: *Estates Gazette Ltd v Benjamin Restaurants Ltd* [1994] 1 WLR 1528, [1995] 1 All ER 129. Qualified covenants against disposition have usually made this a condition of granting a licence to assign. By contrast it was not usual practice for an assignee of the reversion to covenant directly with the original tenant.

[20] An express indemnity would extend the liability of the assignee to breaches of any of the lease covenants committed at any time during the remainder of the term. A statutory indemnity to the same effect applied in the case of assignments for valuable consideration of leases to which title was unregistered: LPA 1925, s 77(1)(c), Sch 2, Pt IX whilst in the case of registered titles the indemnity applied to all transfers by way of assignment: LRA 1925, s 24(1). The implied statutory covenant is one of indemnity and not guarantee; *Scottish & Newcastle plc v Raguz* [2003] 33 EG 62 (CS).

[1] *Moule v Garrett* (1872) LR 7 Exch 101, 104.

be freed from liability. [2] But this afforded no relief to the former tenant, because his liability (and that of his surety [3] remained unaffected. [4] Even if the former tenant was in a position to have recourse by way of indemnity to an insolvent tenant he would only have been an ordinary creditor of the insolvent estate. However, a small measure of relief was provided by the rule that if there were a solvent guarantor of a later assignee, an original tenant who was sued was entitled to be indemnified by that guarantor. [5]

The unfortunate plight of former tenants was highlighted by a series of reported cases in the early 1980s when a number of tenants were held liable for very large sums attributable to breaches of covenant by assignees.' [6]

2. ORIGINAL LANDLORD

In **Stuart v Joy** [1904] 1 KB 362, Cozens-Hardy LJ said at 368:

'In my opinion, the position of the lessor with respect to covenants running with the reversion is now precisely similar to the position of the lessee with respect to covenants running with the lease. In neither case is liability extinguished by assignment.' [7]

---

[2]   Insolvency Act 1986, s. 315. A similar rule applies in relation to a disclaimer by the liquidator of an insolvent company; s. 178.
[3]   *Warnford Investments v Duckworth* [1979] Ch 127, [1978] 2 All ER 517.
[4]   See *Hindcastle Ltd v Barbara Attenborough Associates Ltd* [1995] QB 95, [1994] 4 All ER 129; affd [1997] AC 70, [1996] 1 All ER 737.
[5]   *Becton Dickinson UK Ltd v Zwebner* [1989] QB 208, 217. *Re A Debtor (No 21 of 1995)* [1995] NPC 170.
       Other defences available are fraught with difficulty:
       (a) surrender and regrant: *Jenkin R. Lewis Ltd v Kerman* [1971] Ch 477, [1970] 3 All ER 414; [1995] Conv 124 (A. Dowling); *Friends' Provident Life Office v British Railways Board* [1996] 1 All ER 336;
       (b) release by accord and satisfaction: *Deanplan Ltd v Mahmoud* [1993] Ch 151, [1992] 3 All ER 945, [1993] 143 NLJ 23 (H. W. Wilkinson); *Sun Life Assurance Society plc v Tantofex (Engineers) Ltd* [1999] 2 EGLR 135; *Allied London Investments Ltd v Hambro Life Assurance Ltd* [1984] 1 EGLR 16; *Mytre Investments Ltd v Reynolds* [1995] 3 All ER 588; *March Estates plc v Gunmark Ltd* [1996] 2 EGLR 38.
       (c) disclaimer by liquidator or trustee in bankruptcy: *Hindcastle Ltd v Barbara Attenborough Associates Ltd*, supra. [1997] Conv 24 (T. Taylor). *Scottish Widows plc v Tripipatkul* [2003] EWHC 1874 (Ch), [2004] 1 P & CR 461. See generally [1996] CLJ 313 at 319 (S. Bridge).
[6]   See the examples cited by the Law Commission which included claims against a retired couple whose income was barely above social security level and a former shopkeeper who faced a claim for £10,000 under a lease which he had assigned when the rent was £450 a year. Law Com No 174, (1988) para 3.8.
       The catalyst for the Landlord and Tenant (Covenants) Act 1995 was *Centrovincial Estates plc v Bulk Storage Ltd* (1983) 46 P & CR 393, where an original tenant was held to be contractually liable for a substantial increase in rent due to the operation by the landlord and his assignee of a rent review clause in the lease. This decision was undermined by CA in *Friends Provident Life Office v British Railways Board* [1996] 1 All ER 336.; *Beegas Nominees Ltd v BHP Petroleum Ltd* [1998] 2 EGLR 57. See now Landlord and Tenant (Covenants) Act 1995, s. 18, p. 574, post.
       On release of a surety by variation, see *Metropolitan Properties Co Ltd v Bartholomew* [1996] 1 EGLR 82; *Howard de Walden Estates Ltd v Pasta Place Ltd* [1995] 1 EGLR 79.
[7]   See *City and Metropolitan Properties Ltd v Greycroft Ltd* [1987] 1 WLR 1085, [1987] 3 All ER 839, p. 568, ante; *Celsteel Ltd v Alton House Holdings Ltd (No 2)* [1987] 1 WLR 291 at 296, [1987] 2 All ER 240 at 244.

(1996) 59 MLR 79 at p. 83 (M. Davey)

'The precarious position of former tenants was in marked contrast to that of the landlord who would invariably have reserved to himself the power to approve the identity of a proposed assignee. In addition the landlord had the powerful remedy of forfeiture in the event of non compliance with a covenant by the present tenant. Even worse from the tenant's point of view, were cases where the landlord preferred to have recourse to the original tenant for unpaid rent because market rental levels had fallen since the lease was granted and therefore he would not benefit by repossessing and reletting the property which might be occupied by the tenant in default or have been abandoned. In those circumstances the original tenant might have preferred to be able to have recourse to the leasehold property, but was unable to do so in the absence of a provision for re-entry in the assignment itself.

Finally, it should be noted that it had long been standard practice for landlords to require a tenant or, in cases where a direct covenant was required, an assignee, to provide a surety for performance of the tenant's covenants in the lease. The contractual liability of such a surety was normally, unless restricted, co-extensive with that of the principal debtor.[8] The benefit of such a covenant would pass to any subsequent assignee of the landlord's estate by virtue of the common law rules governing covenants affecting freehold land.'[9]

(c)   Statutory Protection for Original Tenant

The Landlord and Tenant (Covenants) Act 1995 imposes restrictions on the contractual liability of a former tenant or his guarantor after assignment of the tenancy. Sections 17–20, which apply to all tenancies whether created before or after the Act, are mentioned in brief outline.

1. RESTRICTION ON LIABILITY FOR FIXED CHARGE

Under section 17 there can only be liability for a 'fixed charge' (i.e. arrears of rent or service charge, or liquidated damages for breach of a tenant covenant) if the landlord serves a prescribed notice[10] on the former tenant or his guarantor within six months of the date when the fixed charge becomes due.

2. RIGHT TO OVERRIDING LEASE

Under sections 19 and 20 a former tenant or his guarantor who has paid a fixed charge under section 17 may have an overriding lease granted to him. He can

---

[8]   *Thames Manufacturing Co Ltd v Perrotts (Nichol & Peyton) Ltd* (1984) 271 EG 284, 287, cf *Johnsey Estates Ltd v Webb* [1990] 1 EGLR 80. But note that under the general law, if the obligation of the principal debtor were changed or if the creditor allowed him any time or indulgence, his guarantor was released unless, as was frequently the case in practice, the guarantee provided otherwise.

[9]   *P & A Swift Investments v Combined English Stores Group plc* [1989] AC 632, [1988] 2 All ER 885, p. 561, ante.

[10] Landlord and Tenant (Covenants) Act 1995 (Notices) Regulations 1995, Sch., Form 1 (SI 1995 No. 2964) Notices: *Cheverell Estates Ltd v Harris* [1998] 02 EG 127 (where guarantor is to be sued, notice need not also be served on former tenant as well); *Commercial Union Life Assurance Co Ltd v Moustafa* [1999] 2 EGLR 44 (notice is properly served if sent to intended recipient at his last residential address, whether it was received by that recipient or not). The amount recoverable may be less than the amount specified in the notice under s. 17(4); *Kellogg v Tobin* (8 April 1997, unreported); see [1999] EG 25 May p. 152 (D. Stevens) (former tenants must receive notices from landlord in order to obtain indemnity).

then pursue remedies directly against the defaulting tenant, if he is still in occupation, or take possession and make use of the property so that he can set off the return against his liability. In estate terms the former tenant is slotted into the hierarchy of interests.

3. RESTRICTION ON LIABILITY FOR POST-ASSIGNMENT VARIATION

Under section 18 a former tenant or his guarantor are not liable to pay any amount which is attributable to the variation of a covenant effected after assignment.

(d) Assignees and Sub-tenants

Assignees are liable and able to sue only if, and so long as, they hold the estate with which the covenant runs; and such persons must be assignees and not sub-lessees [11] or squatters. [12]

In **South of England Dairies v Baker** [1906] 2 Ch 631, the freeholder of certain property demised it for 21 years and covenanted to pay all rates and taxes (except one third of the water rate). In the following year, the lessee sub-demised the premises to the plaintiff (a company formed by the lessee) for the remainder of his term less three days. Seven years later the freeholder sold the fee simple subject to the lease to the defendant, who in the following year accepted the surrender of the lease from the original lessee. The plaintiff, the sub-tenant, was compelled by the Local Authority to pay the rates, and sought to recover damages from the defendant under the landlord's covenant to pay all rates and taxes. JOYCE J held that the defendant was not liable since the plaintiff was not an assignee of the original lessee and was unable therefore to enforce the covenant originally given to the lessee.

In **Milmo v Carreras** [1946] KB 306, [1946] 1 All ER 288, the plaintiff was tenant of a flat under a 7 year lease, expiring on 28 November 1944. In October 1943, he agreed to sublet the flat to the defendant for one year from 1 November 1943, 'and thereafter quarterly until such time as' one of the parties should give three months' notice to terminate. The plaintiff gave such notice on returning from active service in 1945.

The Court of Appeal (Lord GREENE MR, MORTON and BUCKNILL LJJ) held that the notice was bad because the plaintiff retained no reversion. Lord GREENE MR said at 310, at 290:

'For the purposes of this case, I think it is sufficient to say that, in accordance with a very ancient and established rule, where a lessee, by a document in the form of a sub-lease, divests himself of everything that he has got (which he must necessarily do if he is transferring to his so-called sub-lessee an estate as great as, or purporting to be greater than, his own) he from that moment is a stranger to the land, in the sense that the relationship of landlord and tenant, in respect of

---

[11]   *South of England Dairies Ltd v Baker* [1906] 2 Ch 631. A restrictive covenant can be enforced against a sub-tenant: *Hemingway Securities Ltd v Dunraven Ltd* [1995] 1 EGLR 61 (breach of covenant against sub-letting).
[12]   *Tichborne v Weir* (1892) 67 LT 735, p. 946, post.

tenure, cannot any longer exist between him and the so-called sub-lessee. That relationship must depend on privity of estate. I myself find it impossible to conceive of a relationship of landlord and tenant which has not got that essential element of tenure in it, and that implies that the tenant holds of his landlord, and he can only do that if the landlord has a reversion. You cannot have a purely contractual tenure. Tenure exists by reason of privity of estate. That seems to me to be the effect of all the decisions, and that position is recognised by all the decisions.'[13]

(e) Agreements for Leases

The question of the enforcement of covenants after assignment raises different issues where there has been no grant of a lease, but merely an agreement for a lease.[14] First, it used to be said that covenants could run with land at common law only if created under seal,[15] but this rule has since been changed.[16] Secondly, there is no privity of estate between persons who have entered into a contract for a lease or between their assigns;[17] nor between the lessor and one who has contracted to take an assignment from a lessee.[18]

Since the benefit of a covenant can be assigned at law, there is no difficulty in holding that the benefit of a covenant runs with the freehold reversion;[9] and it appears that the benefit will run also by virtue of Law of Property Act 1925, section 141,[20] and, if this is so, the burden will run also with the reversion under section 142. It is usually held that the benefit but not the burden of covenants will run on the assignment of an agreement for a lease;[1] an assignee may be liable under an implied agreement if he enters into possession and pays rent,[2] or on grounds of estoppel.[3] His freedom from liability under the covenant may cause great hardship to the lessor, and the question is whether this is a necessary limitation.

The rule seems to have developed from the independence of law and equity before the Judicature Acts. There could be no liability at law after the assignment because there was no privity of estate; in equity, the question was whether or not specific performance of the agreement would be given, and the question of monetary liability under the covenants pending the grant of specific performance did not arise. There appears to be no reason why, since the Judicature Acts, the doctrine of *Walsh v Lonsdale* should not be applied and the monetary liability of the defendant determined *as if* the decree of specific performance had been granted. The dicta in *Boyer v Warbey* [1953] 1 QB 234, [1952] 2 All ER 976, p. 580, post indicate that 'nowadays' the rules relating to the running of covenants

[13] *Parc Battersea Ltd v Hutchinson* [1999] 2 EGLR 35 (oral sub-tenancy effective on assignment by operation of law).
[14] See pp. 84, 523, ante.
[15] *Manchester Brewery Co v Coombs* [1901] 2 Ch 608, p. 516, post.
[16] LPA 1925, s. 154; *Boyer v Warbey* [1953] 1 QB 234, [1952] 2 All ER 976, p. 580, post.
[17] *Purchase v Lichfield Brewery Co* [1915] 1 KB 184, p. 579, post.
[18] *Cox v Bishop* (1857) 8 De GM & G 815, p. 578, post; *Friary, Holroyd, and Healey's Breweries Ltd v Singleton* [1899] 1 Ch 86.
[19] *Manchester Brewery Co v Coombs*, supra.
[20] *Rickett v Green* [1910] 1 KB 253; *Rye v Purcell* [1926] 1 KB 446; *London and County (A and D) Ltd v Wilfred Sportsman Ltd* [1971] Ch 764, [1970] 2 All ER 600.
[1] *Marquis of Camden v Batterbury* (1860) 7 CBNS 864; *Purchase v Lichfield Brewery Co*, supra.
[2] *Buckworth v Simpson* (1835) 1 Cr M & R 834; *Cornish v Stubbs* (1870) LR 5 CP 334 at 338–339.
[3] *Ashe v Hogan* [1920] 1 IR 159; *Rodenhurst Estates Ltd v WH Barnes Ltd* [1936] 2 All ER 3.

should be the same, whether the lease which has been assigned is legal or equitable. Further, as has been seen, the Court of Appeal in *Industrial Properties (Barton Hill) Ltd v Associated Electrical Industries Ltd* [1977] QB 580, [1977] 2 All ER 293, p. 86, ante held, as an alternative ground for supporting the judgment, that the doctrine of *Walsh v Lonsdale* applied where an equitable owner had purported to grant a lease; the effect was to treat the equitable lease as a legal lease, and thus enable the owner to sue for damages for breach of covenant in the lease.

The older cases are to the contrary. The only case in which the issue appears to have arisen since the Judicature Act is *Purchase v Lichfield Brewery* [1915] 1 KB 184, which was, however, one of assignment by way of mortgage. It is submitted that the trend of the modern cases should be supported, and that the court should hold that the liability, both of the assignee of an equitable lease and that of the equitable assignee of a legal lease, is the same as it would be if specific performance had been granted. [4]

These problems disappear where a lease or an agreement for a lease are created after 1995. Under section 28(1) of the Landlord and Tenant (Covenants) Act 1995, p. 582, post, equitable leases and equitable assignments are treated in the same way as their legal counterparts.

1. BENEFIT

MANCHESTER BREWERY CO v COOMBS
[1901] 2 Ch 608 (ChD, FARWELL J)

By an agreement under seal dated 10 December 1892 between the defendant and Broadbents Ltd, who were brewers, the defendant, who alone executed the deed, undertook to take a yearly tenancy of a hotel, and covenanted with 'Broadbents Ltd and their successors in business' to buy all his liquor from them. The covenant did not mention 'assigns'.

In June 1899, Broadbents sold their business to the plaintiffs, who gave notice of the purchase to the defendant. The defendant continued to take his supplies from the plaintiffs until December, when he ceased to buy from them. They brought this action for an injunction to restrain a breach of the covenant contained in the deed of 1892.

Held. The plaintiffs were entitled to the benefit of the covenant.

FARWELL J (after holding that the covenant was not, on its construction, a mere personal covenant confined to beer brewed at the original brewery which no longer operated): The last point taken by Mr Younger rests on the fact that the agreement of 10 December 1892 was not executed by the landlords. Having regard to the construction that I have put on the covenant, it could not be contended that it is not of such a nature as to run with the land. But it is said that, in order to arrive at the conclusion that it does run with the land, the Court must first find that an estate has been duly created at law in the land with which the covenant can run, or, in other words, that there must be privity of estate between lessor and lessee, and that such estate can only be created by deed duly executed by the lessor, and that this is borne out by 32 Hen 8, c 34, which applies only to leases by deed. This is undoubtedly sound—e.g., it has been held that a lease by mortgagor and mortgagee, in which the covenants to repair were with the mortgagor and his assigns, did not enable an assign of the mortgagee to maintain

---

an action on the covenant. [His Lordship referred to *Webb v Russel* (1789) 3 Term Rep 393 per Lord Kenyon at 402, and to *Standen v Christmas* (1847) 10 QB 135, and continued:] ... But it by no means follows that the plaintiffs would have failed in every form of action, even before the Judicature Acts; still less that they must fail now. Before the Judicature Acts the plaintiffs might have succeeded if they had sued on the new contract implied from the conduct of the tenant and the assignee of the landlord, instead of suing on the original contract between the tenant and the landlord.

[His Lordship then found that the defendant agreed that the plaintiffs should occupy the position of landlords to him in the same way as Broadbents Ltd had done, and continued:]

There is, moreover, another point which is fatal to the defendant. The defendant holds under an agreement for a lease from Broadbents Limited, under which he has been in possession and paid rent for several years. The whole contract has been performed up to the present time, except that the legal estate has not been actually demised. The defendant would have no defence to an action for specific performance, the sole object of which would be to compel him to accept the legal estate. If Broadbents Limited had not parted with the legal estate, I see no reason why they should not now execute the deed in order to complete the transaction. The present plaintiffs are the assigns of the benefit of the agreement both by implication from the conveyance of the land subject to the lease, and by the express words of clause 26 of the agreement of 29 March 1899. The plaintiffs could, therefore, obtain specific performance in this court of the contract so far as it is incomplete ... Holding, therefore, as I do, that the plaintiffs could obtain specific performance against the defendant, I find it laid down by the Court of Appeal that since the Judicature Acts there are not in such a case as this two estates as there were formerly, one at common law by reason of the payment of the rent, and another in equity under the agreement, but the tenant holds under the same terms, and has the same rights and liabilities as if a lease had been granted: *Walsh v Lonsdale* (1882) 21 ChD 9, approved by Cotton LJ in *Lowther v Heaver* (1889) 41 ChD 248 at 264, and explained by Lord Esher in *Swain v Ayres* (1888) 21 QBD 289 at 292 and *Foster v Reeves* [1892] 2 QB 255. Although it has been suggested that the decision in *Walsh v Lonsdale* takes away all differences between the legal and equitable estate, it, of course, does nothing of the sort, and the limits of its applicability are really somewhat narrow. It applies only to cases where there is a contract to transfer a legal title, and an act has to be justified or an action maintained by force of the legal title to which such contract relates. It involves two questions: (1) Is there a contract of which specific performance can be obtained? (2) If Yes, will the title acquired by such specific performance justify at law the act complained of, or support at law the action in question? It is to be treated as though before the Judicature Acts there had been, first, a suit in equity for specific performance, and then an action at law between the same parties; and the doctrine is applicable only in those cases where specific performance can be obtained between the same parties in the same court, and at the same time as the subsequent legal question falls to be determined. Thus, in *Walsh v Lonsdale*, the landlord under an agreement for a lease for a term of seven years distrained. Distress is a legal remedy and depends on the existence at law of the relation of landlord and tenant; but the agreement between the same parties, if specifically enforced, created that relation. It was clear that such an agreement would be enforced in the same court and between the same parties: the act of distress was therefore held to be lawful. So in the present case I have already stated that specific performance can be granted between the parties to this action. I must treat it therefore as granted, and I then find that the result justifies this action. It is not necessary to call in aid this doctrine in matters that are purely equitable; its existence is due entirely to the divergence of legal and equitable rights between the same parties, nor does it affect the rights of third parties. Thus, a contract by a landowner to sell the fee simple of land in possession to A. would not enable A. to maintain an action of ejectment or trespass against a third person because such actions are purely legal actions requiring the legal estate and possession respectively to support them, and the contract relied on is not made with the defendant. ...

I hold, therefore, on this point, that the plaintiffs, being clearly entitled in this court against the defendant to specific performance of the agreement under which the defendant has been for years and still is in possession of the land, can sue him on the covenants in the same manner as they could have done if Broadbents had actually executed the original agreement. ...

The result is that I grant the injunction as asked, and order the defendant to pay the costs of the action.

In **Rickett v Green** [1910] 1 KB 253, one of the questions was whether or not the plaintiff, as assignee of the freehold, was entitled to demand rent from the defendant who held the premises under an agreement for a lease. DARLING and PHILLIMORE JJ held that he was entitled to sue by virtue of the Conveyancing Act 1881, section 10 (now Law of Property Act 1925, section 141). DARLING J said at 259:

'The question occurred to [the county court judge] whether this tenancy agreement was a "lease" within the meaning of section 10 of the Act of 1881, inasmuch as the agreement was dated 19 December 1907, and the three years were to run from 25 December 1907, so that the lease was one exceeding three years from the making thereof and, not being under seal, was void at law under section 3 of the Real Property Act 1845. Though at law it may be void as a lease, still in equity it is looked upon as a lease, and in my judgment it must be treated, as between the parties, as if it were a lease under seal. A Court of Equity would look upon the matter as if a lease under seal had been granted. Upon the case to which we have been referred the county court judge came to a right conclusion upon this point, and the agreement must be treated as a "lease" for the purposes of section 10 of the Act of 1881, and for other purposes also.'

2. BURDEN

In **Cox v Bishop** (1857) 8 De GM & G 815, the freeholder brought an action for rent due and for breaches of covenant in a lease. The lessees had contracted to assign the lease to persons who assigned to the defendants. KNIGHT BRUCE and TURNER LJJ held that the defendants were not liable on the covenants, TURNER LJ, saying at 823:

'If, on the other hand, these Defendants are not at law liable to the Plaintiffs, what are the grounds alleged by this bill upon which they are in equity to be made liable? Simply that they have contracted to purchase interests in the lease and have been in possession. The contracts to purchase, however, are not contracts with the Plaintiffs, and there is nothing in the bill to shew that the Plaintiffs are in any manner entitled to the benefit of those contracts, and if the Defendants are liable by virtue of their possession, the liability, as I apprehend, is to be enforced at law and not in equity. Courts of equity do not, as I think, in ordinary cases, decree the payment of rent or the performance of covenants upon a mere agreement for a lease. In such cases the Court does not treat the relation of landlord and tenant as completed by the agreement, and decree the rent to be paid and the covenants to be performed accordingly, but it decrees the execution of the lease, and leaves the parties to their remedies at law consequent upon the relation created by the execution of it. To take, however, a case more near to the present, suppose, in the case of an agreement for a lease the intended lessee has assigned the benefit of the contract, can this Court, at the instance of the intended lessor, enforce the payment of the rent or the performance of the covenants by the assignee of the contract. I take it most clearly not; for there is no privity of contract between the lessor and the assignee; but if this cannot be done where there is a mere contract for a lease, upon what principle it is to be done where there is an actual lease and the lessee has agreed to assign.'

PURCHASE v LICHFIELD BREWERY CO
[1915] 1 KB 184 (KBD, HORRIDGE and LUSH JJ)

The plaintiff, in writing but not under seal, purported to grant to Lunnis a 15-year lease of a house, the agreement containing a proviso that Lunnis would not assign the term without the plaintiff's consent, such consent not to be unreasonably refused.

On the following day Lunnis assigned by way of mortgage his interest to the defendant, who never went into possession. The rent being unpaid, the plaintiff claimed from the defendant (mortgagee) the rent due under the agreement.

Held. In the absence of privity of contract or estate the defendant was not liable.

LUSH J (agreeing with HORRIDGE J): I am of the same opinion. The only point which the county court judge decided was that the present case was governed by *Williams v Bosanquet* (1819) 1 Brod & Bing 238. In my view that case does not apply. The lease in question there was under seal. It was assigned by deed to mortgagees. That was a valid assignment. The only question was whether the mortgagees, not having taken possession, were bound by the covenants in the lease. It was held that they were bound. In this case there was no lease under seal. No term was created as between lessor and lessee. Therefore the question decided in *Williams v Bosanquet* does not arise in this case. Consequently the judgment of the county court judge cannot stand on the grounds on which he has based it.

Then can the judgment be supported on other grounds? I do not think it is necessary to say how the case might have stood if the defendants had ever taken possession. They are liable, if at all, on the principle of *Walsh v Lonsdale* (1882) 21 ChD 9. In that case the tenant was in possession under the agreement. In the present case the defendants never did take possession. The agreement contained a provision against assigning. The defendants were only mortgagees. It does not follow from *Walsh v Lonsdale* that a court of equity would decree specific performance against mere mortgagees who only took an assignment by way of security. In my opinion it would leave the parties to their position at law. Accordingly the matter stands thus: A tenant under an agreement, whose only title to call himself a lessee depends on his right to specific performance of the agreement, assigns his right to assignees. The assignees never had a term vested in them because no term was ever created; therefore there was never privity of estate. They never went into possession or were recognised by the landlord, therefore there was never privity of contract. It is impossible that specific performance of a contract can be decreed against a person with whom there is neither privity of contract nor privity of estate. Therefore these assignees are not liable to perform the terms of the agreement and this appeal must be allowed.

In **Boyer v Warbey** [1953] 1 QB 234, [1952] 2 All ER 976 (CA, EVERSHED MR, DENNING and ROMER LJJ), one question was whether a covenant by a tenant in a written lease of a flat within the Rent Restriction Acts to pay £40 towards the cost of redecoration 'immediately after the expiration or determination of the tenancy' was binding on an assignee of the tenant.

The lease was for 3 years; within nine days of the expiration of term, the lessee assigned the lease to the defendant who, on the expiry of the nine days, became a statutory tenant, subject to all the terms of the original tenancy 'so far as the same are consistent with the provisions of this Act.'[5] It was held, inter alia, that the covenant to pay the £40 became a term of the statutory tenancy.

DENNING LJ said at 245:

'Seeing that the agreement touched and concerned the thing demised, it ran with the land so as to bind the assignee, the tenant, as soon as he entered into possession. I know that before the Judicature Act 1873, it was said that the doctrine of covenants running with the land only applied to covenants under seal and not to agreements under hand. See *Elliot v Johnson* (1868) LR 2 QB 120. But since the fusion of law and equity, the position is different. The distinction between agreements under hand and covenants under seal has been largely obliterated. There is no valid reason nowadays why the doctrine of covenants running with the land—or with the reversion—should not apply equally to agreements under hand as to covenants under seal; and I think we should so hold, not only in the case of agreements for more than three years which need the intervention of equity to perfect them, but also in the case of agreements for three years or less which do not.'

QUESTION

A. agreed to grant a lease for 99 years to B. of valuable land at a rent of £25,000 a year. B. assigned his interest to C., and disappeared. C has not yet taken possession. Is he liable for the rent? See C & B, p. 407; Gray, pp. 1337–1340; M & W, paras. 14.051-14.052; Smith, pp. 386, 451–453; *Purchase v Lichfield Brewery Co* [1915] 1 KB 184; (1978) 37 CLJ 9 (R.J. Smith).

B.   Covenants in Post 1995 Leases

i.   GENERAL NATURE OF THE POST-1995 CODE

Law Commission Report on Privity of Contract: Contracts for the Benefit of Third Parties 1996 (Law Com No 242 Cm 3329), para. 2.11

'The law on covenants relating to leasehold land has recently been reformed by the Landlord and Tenant (Covenants) Act 1995.[6] The effect of the 1995 Act can be briefly explained in the following four points:—

(i)   The benefit and burden of covenants in a lease granted prior to 1996 would pass on an assignment of the lease or reversion so as to benefit or bind the assignee of the lease or the reversion, provided that the covenant

---

[5]   Increase of Rent and Mortgage Interest (Restrictions) Act 1920, s. 15(1); now Rent Act 1977, s. 3(1).

[6]   Based on the recommendations made in Landlord and Tenant Law: Privity of Contract and Estate (1988) Law Com No 174.

"touched and concerned" the land.[7] As a result of the Landlord and Tenant (Covenants) Act 1995, in relation to leases granted after 1995, the benefit and burden of *all* covenants in a lease pass on an assignment of the lease or reversion unless the covenant is expressed to be personal.[8] It is now for the parties to decide whether a covenant is to be regarded as personal. It is no longer for the court to try to decide it objectively according to whether it is thought to "touch and concern" the land.

(ii) Where, prior to 1996, L granted a lease to T and T then sublet to S, the burden of the covenants in the headlease did *not* bind S, the sublessee, because there was no privity of estate[9] between L and S. This was subject to an exception. If the covenant was a restrictive covenant, it would bind S as an equitable property right, provided that, where the title was unregistered, he had notice of the covenant (as he would in practice)[10] or, where the title was registered, in any event.[11] In leases granted after 1995, this rule is codified. A restrictive covenant in the headlease binds any sublessee automatically.[12]

(iii) Where, prior to 1996, L granted a lease to T and T then sublet to S, S *could* enforce the benefit of any landlord covenants which touched and concerned the land against L, despite the absence of privity of contract. This is because the benefit of such covenants was annexed under section 78 of the Law of Property Act 1925 and could be enforced by a person with a derivative interest.[13] In a lease granted after 1995, this is no longer possible.[14] S cannot enforce any covenant in the headlease against L.

(iv) For leases granted prior to 1996, the original tenant and landlord remained liable for a breach of covenant in the lease despite assignment. For leases granted after 1995 the original tenant[15] will generally be released from covenants in the lease once the lease has been assigned.[16] This aspect of the reforms is concerned to cut back a normal feature of privity of contract rather than being concerned with the exception to privity of contract constituted by covenants running with land.'

---

[7] *Spencer's Case* (1583) 5 Co Rep 16a; 787 ER 72 (leases); LPA 1925, ss. 141–142 (reversions), p. 563, ante.

[8] Landlord and Tenant (Covenants) Act 1995, s. 3(6), p. 586, post.

[9] Which simply means the relationship of landlord and tenant.

[10] See LPA 1925, s. 44; *White v Bijou Mansions Ltd* [1937] Ch 610, p. 560, n. 14, ante.

[11] LRA 1925, s. 23(1)(a).

[12] Landlord and Tenant (Covenants) Act 1995, s. 3(5), p. 584, post.

[13] *Smith v River Douglas Catchment Board* [1949] 2 KB 500 (lessee able to enforce annexed freehold covenant on the wording of s. 78). As it is clear that s. 78 applies to leases as well as to freeholds: *Caerns Motor Services Ltd v Texaco Ltd* [1994] 1 WLR 1249, S must be able to enforce the covenant against L.

[14] LPA 1925, s 78 does not apply to such leases (Landlord and Tenant (Covenants) Act 1995, s. 30(4)) and this effect of that section is not replicated: cf Landlord and Tenant (Covenants) Act 1995, s. 15, p. 584, post.

[15] Somewhat different provisions apply in respect of an assignment of the reversion by the landlord. The landlord must apply to the tenant to be released from the landlord covenants. If the tenant refuses to do so, the court may release the landlord if it considers it reasonable to do so. See Landlord and Tenant (Covenants) Act 1995, ss. 6–8, pp. 586–587, post.

[16] Landlord and Tenant (Covenants) Act 1995, ss. 3 and 5, pp. 583, 585, post, although under s. 16, p. 590, post, a tenant may enter into an 'authorised guarantee agreement' to guarantee compliance with the covenants by the assignee.

LANDLORD AND TENANT (COVENANTS) ACT 1995 [17]

1. Tenancies to which the Act applies.—(1) Sections 3 to 16 and 21 apply only to new tenancies.

(2) Sections 17 to 20 apply to both new and other tenancies. [18]

(3) For the purposes of this section a tenancy is a new tenancy if it is granted on or after the date on which this Act comes into force [19] otherwise than in pursuance of—

(a) an agreement entered into before that date, or

(b) an order of a court made before that date.

(4) Subsection (3) has effect subject to section 20(1) in the case of overriding leases granted under section 19.

(5) Without prejudice to the generality of subsection (3), that subsection applies to the grant of a tenancy where by virtue of any variation of a tenancy there is deemed surrender and regrant as it applies to any other grant of a tenancy.

(6) Where a tenancy granted on or after the date on which this Act comes into force is so granted in pursuance of an option granted before that date, the tenancy shall be regarded for the purposes of subsection (3) as granted in pursuance of an agreement entered into before that date (and accordingly is not a new tenancy), whether or not the option was exercised before that date.

(7) In subsection (6) 'option' includes right of first refusal.

2. Covenants to which the Act applies.—(1) This Act applies to a landlord covenant or a tenant covenant of a tenancy—

(a) whether or not the covenant has reference to the subject matter of tenancy, and

(b) whether the covenant is express, implied or imposed by law, but does not apply to a covenant falling within subsection (2).

(2) Nothing in this Act affects any covenant imposed in pursuance of—

(a) section 35 or 155 of the Housing Act 1985 (covenants for repayment of discount on early disposals);

(b) paragraph 1 of Schedule 6A to that Act (covenants requiring redemption of landlord's share); or

(c) section 11 or 13 of the Housing Act 1996 or [20] paragraph 1 or 3 of Schedule 2 to the Housing Associations Act 1985 (covenants for repaying of discount on early disposals or for restricting disposals).

28. Interpretation.—(1) In this Act (unless the context otherwise requires)—

'assignment' includes equitable assignment, and in addition (subject to section 11) assignment in breach of a covenant of a tenancy or by operation of law;

'covenant' includes term, condition and obligation, and references to a covenant (or any description of covenant) of a tenancy include a covenant (or a covenant of that description) contained in a collateral agreement;

'landlord' and 'tenant', in relation to a tenancy, mean the person for the time being entitled to the reversion expectant on the term of the tenancy and the person so entitled to that term respectively;

'landlord covenant', in relation to a tenancy, means a covenant falling to be complied with the landlord of premises demised by the tenancy;

[17]   Landlord and Tenant (Covenants) Act 1995 (Notices) Regulations 1995 (SI 1995 No. 2964).
[18]   P. 573, ante.
[19]   1 January 1996.
[20]   As added by Housing Act 1996 (Consequential Provisions) Order 1996 art 5, Sch. 2, para. 22, (SI 1996 No. 2325).

'reversion' means the interest expectant on the termination of a tenancy;
'tenancy' means any lease or other tenancy and includes—
(a) a sub-tenancy, and
(b) an agreement for a tenancy,
but does not include a mortgage term;
'tenant covenant', in relation to a tenancy, means a covenant falling to be complied with by the tenant of premises demised by the tenancy.[21]

---

ii. TRANSMISSION OF COVENANTS

Under the Act the benefit and burden of all leasehold covenants automatically pass on an assignment of the lease or of the reversion. If a covenant is not to pass, it must be expressed to be personal. The effect of an equitable assignment (for example, where there is an agreement for a lease) is the same as that of a legal assignment.[1]

The Act also provides for covenants to be enforceable by and against persons other than the reversioner who are for the time being entitled to the rents and profits under the tenancy, and mortgagees in possession of the reversion who are similarly entitled.[2]

LANDLORD AND TENANT (COVENANTS) ACT 1995

3. Transmission of benefit and burden of covenants.—(1) The benefit and burden of all landlord and tenant covenants of a tenancy—
(a) shall be annexed and incident to the whole, and to each and every part, of the premises demised by the tenancy and of the reversion in them, and
(b) shall in accordance with this section pass on an assignment of the whole or any part of those premises or of the reversion in them.[3]
(2) Where the assignment is by the tenant under the tenancy, then as from the assignment the assignee—
(a) becomes bound by the tenant covenants of the tenancy except to the extent that—
(i) immediately before the assignment they did not bind the assignor, or
(ii) they fall to be complied with in relation to any demised premises not comprised in the assignment; and
(b) becomes entitled to the benefit of the landlord covenants of the tenancy except to the extent that they fall to be complied with in relation to any such premises.
(3) Where the assignment is by the landlord under the tenancy, then as from the assignment the assignee—
(a) becomes bound by the landlord covenants of the tenancy except to the extent that—

---

[21] *First Penthouse Ltd v Channel Hotels (UK) Ltd* [2004] 1 EGLR 16 (obligatons to grant sub-lease and pay commission held not to be tenant covenants).
[1] S. 28(1), supra (meanings of assignment and tenancy).
[2] S. 15, p. 584, post.
[3] For the non-applicability of LPA 1925, ss. 78, 79, 141 and 142 in the case of covenants in post-1995 leases, see s. 30(4).

(i) immediately before the assignment they did not bind the assignor, or

(ii) they fall to be complied with in relation to any demised premises[4] not comprised in the assignment; and

(b) becomes entitled to the benefit of the tenant covenants of the tenancy except to the extent that they fall to be complied with in relation to any such premises.

(4) In determining for the purposes of subsection (2) or (3) whether any covenant bound the assignor immediately before the assignment, any waiver or release of the covenant (in whatever terms) is expressed to be personal to the assignor shall be disregarded.

(5) Any landlord or tenant covenant of a tenancy which is restrictive of the user of land shall, as well as being capable of enforcement against an assignee, be capable of being enforced against any other person who is the owner or occupier of any demised premises to which the covenant relates, even though there is no express provision in the tenancy to that effect.[5]

(6) Nothing in this section shall operate—

(a) in the case of a covenant which (in whatever terms) is expressed to be personal to any person, to make the covenant enforceable by or (as the case may be) against any other person; or

(b) to make a covenant enforceable against any person if, apart from this section, it would not be enforceable against him by reason of its not having been registered under the Land Registration Act 2002[6] or the Land Charges Act 1972.

(7) To the extent that there remains in force any rule of law by virtue of which the burden of a covenant whose subject matter is not in existence at the time when it is made does not run with the land affected unless the covenantor covenants on behalf of himself and his assigns, that rule of law is hereby abolished in relation to tenancies.[7]

4. Transmission of rights of re-entry. —The benefit of a landlord's right of re-entry under a tenancy—

(a) shall be annexed and incident to the whole, and to each and every part of the reversion in the premises demised by the tenancy, and

(b) shall pass on an assignment of the whole or any part of the reversion in those premises.

15. Enforcement of covenants.—(1) Where any tenant covenant of a tenancy, or any right of re-entry contained in a tenancy, is enforceable by the reversioner in respect of any premises demised by the tenancy, it shall also be so enforceable by—

(a) any person (other than the reversioner) who, as the holder of the immediate reversion in those premises, is for the time being entitled to the rents and profits under the tenancy in respect of those premises, or

---

4   *Oceanic Village Ltd v United Attractions Ltd* [2000] Ch 234, [2000] 1 All ER 975 ('any demised premises' refers only to premises demised by the lease in question, and not to all premises demised by the landlord, if only to have conformity with s. 3(2) and (3) where 'any demised premises' can only refer to the premises comprised in the relevant lease).

5   This preserves the right to sue in equity in respect of restrictive covenants, p. 942, post. See *Hemingway Securities Ltd v Dunraven Ltd* [1995] 1 EGLR 61.

6   As substituted by LRA 2002, s. 133, Sch. 1, para. 33(2).

7   This abolishes the rule contained in *Spencer's Case* (1583) 3 Co Rep 16a, governing covenants made before 1926, p. 563, ante, to do some act relating to the use where the subject-matter is not in existence at the time the covenant was made (for example, to erect a new house).

(b) any mortgagee in possession of the reversion in those premises who is so entitled.

(2) Where any landlord covenant of a tenancy is enforceable against the reversioner in respect of any premises demised by the tenancy, it shall also be enforceable against any person falling within subsection (1)(a) or (b).

(3) Where any landlord covenant of a tenancy is enforceable by the tenant in respect of any premises demised by the tenancy, it shall also be so enforceable by any mortgagee in possession of those premises under a mortgage granted by the tenant.

(4) Where any tenant covenant of a tenancy, or any right of re-entry contained in a tenancy, is enforceable against the tenant in respect of any premises demised by the tenancy, it shall also be so enforceable against any such mortgagee. [8]

iii. RELEASE OF COVENANTS ON ASSIGNMENT

(a) Release of Tenant

Section 5 of the Act, under which a tenant is released from the tenant covenants (and also ceases to be entitled to enforce the landlord covenants) is the raison d'être of the legislation. At the same time, a guarantor of the tenant's liability is released to the same extent.

LANDLORD AND TENANT (COVENANTS) ACT 1995

5. Tenant released from covenants on assignment of tenancy.—(1) This section applies where a tenant assigns premises demised to him under a tenancy.

(2) If the tenant assigns the whole of the premises demised to him, he—
(a) is released from the tenant covenants of the tenancy, and
(b) ceases to be entitled to the benefit of the landlord covenants of the tenancy,
as from the assignment.

(3) If the tenant assigns part only of the premises demised to him, then as from the assignment he—
(a) is released from the tenant covenant of the tenancy, and
(b) ceases to be entitled to the benefit of the landlord covenants of the tenancy,
only to the extent that those covenants fall to be complied with in relation to that part of the demised premises. [9]

(b) Release of Landlord and Former Landlord

There is no automatic release for the landlord on his assignment of the reversion. He must apply to the tenant by serving a notice and requesting release within four weeks of the assignment. The reason for this difference is that a tenant cannot vet the landlord's assignee and prevent assignment to a nominee.

---

[8]   On covenants with management companies, see s. 12.
[9]   For joint and several liability on covenants binding two or more persons, see s. 13; and for apportionment of liability, see ss. 9 and 10.

LANDLORD AND TENANT (COVENANTS) ACT 1995

6. Landlord may be released from covenants on assignment of reversion.—
(1) This section applies where a landlord assigns the reversion in premises of which he is the landlord under a tenancy.

(2) If the landlord assigns the reversion in the whole of the premises of which he is the landlord—

(a) he may apply to be released from the landlord covenants of the tenancy in accordance with section 8; and

(b) if he is so released from all of those covenants, he ceases to be entitled to the benefit of the tenant covenants of the tenancy as from the assignment.

(3) If the landlord assigns the reversion in part only of the premises of which he is the landlord—

(a) he may apply to be so released from the landlord covenants of the tenancy to the extent that they fall to be complied with in relation to that part of those premises; and

(b) if he is, to that extent, so released from all of those covenants, then as from the assignment he ceases to be entitled to the benefit of the tenant covenants only to the extent that they fall to be complied with in relation to that part of those premises.

(4) This section applies as mentioned in subsection (1) whether or not the landlord is landlord of the whole of the premises comprised in the tenancy.

In **BHP Petroleum Great Britain Ltd v Chesterfield Properties Ltd** [2002] 2 EGLR 122, the question arose as to whether a landlord was entitled to be relieved from his liability for covenants which were expressed in the lease to be 'personal obligations of the landlord' by the service of a section 8 notice. In holding that he was not, JONATHAN PARKER LJ said at 127:

'The crux, as we see it, is the definition of "landlord" in section 28(1) (p. 582, post) as meaning "the person *for the time being* entitled to the reversion expectant on the term of the tenancy" (my emphasis). We find it impossible to read that definition as meaning only the original landlord. In agreement with the judge (see para. 22 of his judgment), we consider that those words clearly connote the person who may *from time to time* be entitled to the reversion on the tenancy. It follows that, transposing that definition into the definition of the expression "landlord covenant", what one has is an obligation "falling to be complied with by [the person who may from time to time be entitled to the reversion on the tenancy]". An obligation that (that is to say, the burden of which) is personal to the original landlord is, by definition, not such an obligation, since it does not fall to be performed by the person who may from time to time be entitled to the reversion on the tenancy.

It follows that, in our judgment, Chesterfield's obligations in clause 12 of the agreement, being expressed to be personal to Chesterfield, are not "landlord covenants" within the meaning of the 1995 Act, and that the notice was accordingly ineffective to release Chesterfield from such obligations.

With respect to Mr Lewison, Chesterfield's argument on the 1995 Act issue seems to us to be based upon the fallacy that there is a direct antithesis between a personal covenant (that is to say, a covenant that is personal in the sense that the burden of it is expressed to be personal to the covenantor), on the one hand, and a covenant that "touches and concerns", or that relates to, the land, on the other. As Mr Barnes correctly submits, there is no such direct antithesis. A covenant that relates to the land may nevertheless be expressed to be personal to one or other or both of the parties to it. That is a matter for the contracting parties.

Nor can we see anything in the 1995 Act to fetter the freedom of contracting parties to place a contractual limit on the transmissibility of the benefit or burden of obligations under a tenancy. On the contrary, that no such fetter was intended by parliament is clearly demonstrated, in our judgment, by section 3(6)(a) (p. 584, ante).

LANDLORD AND TENANT (COVENANTS) ACT 1995

The same would apply to personal covenants by a tenant; they would not automatically be released on a lawful assignment by section 5, p. 585, ante.

---

7. Former landlord may be released from covenants on assignment of reversion.—
(1) This section applies where—
    (a) a landlord assigns the reversion in premises of which he is the landlord under a tenancy, and
    (b) immediately before the assignment a former landlord of the premises remains bound by a landlord covenant of the tenancy ("the relevant covenant").

(2) If immediately before the assignment the former landlord does not remain the landlord of any other premises demised by the tenancy, he may apply to be released from the relevant covenant in accordance with section 8.

(3) In any other case the former landlord may apply to be so released from the relevant covenant to the extent that it falls to be complied with in relation to any premises comprised in the assignment.

(4) If the former landlord is so released from every landlord covenant by which he remained bound immediately before the assignment, he ceases to be entitled to the benefit of the tenant covenants of the tenancy.

(5) If the former landlord is so released from every such landlord covenant to the extent that it falls to be complied with in relation to any premises comprised in the assignment, he ceases to be entitled to the benefit of the tenant covenants of the tenancy to the extent that they fall to be so complied with.

(6) This section applies as mentioned in subsection (1)—
    (a) whether or not the landlord making the assignment is landlord of the whole of the premises comprised in the tenancy; and
    (b) whether or not the former landlord has previously applied (whether under section 6 or this section) to be released from the relevant covenant. [10]

(c) Effect of Release

LANDLORD AND TENANT (COVENANTS) ACT 1995

24. Effects of release from liability under, or loss of benefit of, covenant.—
(1) Any release of a person from a covenant by virtue of this Act does not affect

---

[10]   For the procedure for seeking release from a covenant under ss. 6 and 7, see s. 8.

any liability of his arising from a breach of the covenant occurring before the release.

(2) Where—

    (a) by virtue of this Act a tenant is released from a tenant covenant of a tenancy, and

    (b) immediately before the release another person is bound by a covenant of the tenancy imposing any liability or penalty in the event of a failure to comply with that tenant covenant,

then, as from the release of the tenant, that other person is released from the covenant mentioned in paragraph (b) to the same extent as the tenant is released from that tenant covenant.

(3) Where a person bound by a landlord or tenant covenant of a tenancy—

    (a) assigns the whole or part of his interest in the premises demised by the tenancy, but

    (b) is not released by virtue of this Act from the covenant (with the result that subsection (1) does not apply),

the assignment does not affect any liability of his arising from a breach of the covenant occurring before the assignment.

(4) Where by virtue of this Act a person ceases to be entitled to the benefit of a covenant, this does not affect any rights of his arising from a breach of the covenant occurring before he ceases to be so entitled. [11]

23. Effects of becoming subject to liability under, or entitled to benefit of, covenant etc—(1) Where as a result of an assignment a person becomes by virtue of this Act, bound by or entitled to the benefit of a covenant, he shall not by virtue of this Act have any liability or rights under the covenant in relation to any time falling before the assignment.

(2) Subsection (1) does not preclude any such rights being expressly assigned to the person in question. [12]

(d)   Excluded Assignments

LANDLORD AND TENANT (COVENANTS) ACT 1995

11. Assignments in breach of covenant or by operation of law—(1) This section provides for the operation of sections 5 to 10 in relation to assignments in breach of a covenant of a tenancy or assignments by operation of law. [13]

(2) In the case of an excluded assignment subsection (2) or (3) of section 5—

    (a) shall not have the effect mentioned in that subsection in relation to the tenant as from that assignment, but

    (b) shall have that effect as from the next assignment (if any) of the premises assigned by him which is not an excluded assignment.

(3) In the case of an excluded assignment subsection (2) or (3) of section 6 or 7—

    (a) shall not enable the landlord or former landlord to apply for such a release as is mentioned in that subsection as from that assignment, but

---

[11]   This represents a change from the pre-1996 law in *Re King* [1963] Ch 459, [1963] 1 All ER 781, p. 565, ante.

[12]   By LPA 1925, s. 136.

[13]   By devolution to a trustee in bankruptcy or on death to personal representatives.

(b) shall apply on the next assignment (if any) of the reversion assigned by the landlord which is not an excluded assignment so as to enable the landlord or former landlord to apply for any such release as from that subsequent assignment.

'Where the property is a lease which was granted after 1995, the registration of the squatter as the new proprietor will operate as an excluded agreement under section 11. This is one case under the Act where the former tenant will remain liable on the covenants of the lease': Law Commission Report on Land Registration for the Twenty-First Century 2001 (Law Com No. 271), para. 14.71, n. 242.

iv. ANTI-AVOIDANCE PROVISIONS

The court has wide powers to strike down any schemes to circumvent purposes of the Act.

LANDLORD AND TENANT (COVENANTS) ACT 1995

25. Agreement void if it restricts operation of the Act.—(1) Any agreement relating to a tenancy is void to the extent that—
   (a) it would apart from this section have effect to exclude, modify or otherwise frustrate the operation of any provision of this Act, or
   (b) it provides for—
   (i) the termination or surrender of the tenancy, or
   (ii) the imposition on the tenant of any penalty, disability or liability,
   in the event of the operation of any provision of this Act, or
   (c) it provides for any of the matters referred to in paragraph (b)(i) or (ii) and does so (whether expressly or otherwise) in connection with, or in consequence of, the operation of any provision of this Act.
   (2) To the extent that an agreement relating to a tenancy constitutes a covenant (whether absolute or qualified) against the assignment, or parting with the possession, of the premises demised by the tenancy or any part of them—
   (a) the agreement is not void by virtue of subsection (1) by reason only of the fact that as such the covenant prohibits or restricts any such assignment or parting with possession; but
   (b) paragraph (a) above does not otherwise affect the operation of that subsection in relation to the agreement (and in particular does not preclude its application to the agreement to the extent that it purports to regulate the giving of, or the making of any application for, consent to any such assignment or parting with possession).
   (3) In accordance with section 16(1) nothing in this section applies to any agreement to the extent that it is an authorised guarantee agreement; but (without prejudice to the generality of subsection (1) above) an agreement is void to the extent that it is one falling within section 16(4)(a) or (b).[14]
   (4) This section applies to an agreement relating to a tenancy whether or not the agreement is—
   (a) contained in the instrument creating the tenancy; or
   (b) made before the creation of the tenancy.

---

[14]   P. 590, post.

V. AUTHORISED GUARANTEE AGREEMENTS

"A landlord consenting to an assignment may impose a condition that the tenant guarantees the performance of the lease covenants by his successor, but only until the following assignment'. [15]

LANDLORD AND TENANT (COVENANTS) ACT 1995

16. Tenant guaranteeing performance of covenant by assignee [16].—(1) Where on an assignment a tenant is to any extent released from a tenant covenant of a tenancy by virtue of this Act ('the relevant covenant'), nothing in this Act (and in particular section 25) [17] shall preclude him from entering into an authorised guarantee agreement with respect to the performance of that covenant by the assignee.

(2) For the purposes of this section an agreement is an authorised guarantee agreement if—

(a) under it the tenant guarantees the performance of the relevant covenant to any extent by the assignee; and

(b) it is entered into in the circumstances set out in subsection (3); and

(c) its provisions conform with subsections (4) and (5).

(3) Those circumstances are as follows—

(a) by virtue of a covenant against assignment (whether absolute or qualified) the assignment cannot be effected without the consent of the landlord under the tenancy or some other person; [18]

(b) any such consent is given subject to a condition (lawfully imposed) that the tenant is to enter into an agreement guaranteeing the performance of the covenant by the assignee; and

(c) the agreement is entered into by the tenant in pursuance of that condition.

(4) An agreement is not an authorised guarantee agreement to the extent that it purports—

(a) to impose on the tenant any requirement to guarantee in any way the performance of the relevant covenant by any person other than the assignee; or

(b) to impose on the tenant any liability, restriction or other requirement (of whatever nature) in relation to any time after the assignee is released from that covenant by virtue of this Act.

(5) Subject to subsection (4), an authorised guarantee agreement may—

(a) impose on the tenant any liability as sole or principal debtor in respect of any obligation owed by the assignee under the relevant covenant;

---

[15] Law Committee Report on Privity of Contract and Estate (1988) Law Com No 174, para. 5(1),(2).

[16] See also s. 17 for the restriction on liability of former tenant or his guarantor for rent or service charge etc; *Cheverell Estates Ltd v Harris and Hadden* [1998] 02 EG 127 (service of notices by landlord); s. 19 for their right to an overriding lease; and s. 18 for the restriction on their liability for post-assignment variation, p. 573, ante. These sections apply to all tenancies whether created before or after the Act.

[17] P. 589, ante.

[18] *Wallis Fashion Group Ltd v CGU Life Assurance Ltd* [2000] 2 EGLR 49 (where an assignment of a lease requires the landlord's consent, and the alienation covenant is silent on the specific issue of whether or not he can demand an authorised guarantee agreement, then the landlord can only refuse consent if it is reasonable to do so; Landlord and Tenant Act 1927, s. 19(1), p. 592, post. Therefore a landlord can only impose a condition upon the grant of his consent if that condition is reasonable).

(b) impose on the tenant liabilities as guarantor in respect of the assignee's performance of that covenant which are no more onerous than those to which he would be subject in the event of his being liable as sole or principal debtor in respect of any obligation owed by the assignee under that covenant;

(c) require the tenant, in the event of the tenancy assigned by him being disclaimed, to enter into a new tenancy of the premises comprised in the assignment—

(i) whose term expires not later than the term of the tenancy assigned by the tenant, and

(ii) whose tenant covenants are no more onerous than those of that tenancy;

(d) make provision incidental or supplementary to any provision made by virtue of any of paragraphs (a) to (c).

(6) Where a person ('the former tenant') is to any extent released from a covenant of a tenancy by virtue of section 11(2) [19] as from an assignment and the assignor under the assignment enters into an authorised guarantee agreement with the landlord with respect to the performance of that covenant by the assignee under the assignment—

(a) the landlord may require the former tenant to enter into an agreement under which he guarantees, on terms corresponding to those of that authorised guarantee agreement, the performance of that covenant by the assignee under the assignment; and

(b) if its provisions conform with subsections (4) and (5), any such agreement shall be an authorised guarantee agreement for the purposes of this section; and

(c) in the application of this section in relation to any such agreement—

(i) subsections (2)(b) and (c) and (3) shall be omitted, and

(ii) any reference to the tenant or to the assignee shall be read as a reference to the former tenant or to the assignee under the assignment.

(7) For the purposes of subsection (1) it is immaterial that—

(a) the tenant has already made an authorised guarantee agreement in respect of a previous assignment by him of the tenancy referred to in that subsection, it having been subsequently revested in him following a disclaimer on behalf of the previous assignee, or

(b) the tenancy referred to in that subsection is a new tenancy entered into by the tenant in pursuance of an authorised guarantee agreement; and in any such case subsections (2) to (5) shall apply accordingly.

(8) It is hereby declared that the rules of law relating to guarantees (and in particular those relating to the release [20] of sureties) are, subject to its terms applicable in relation to any authorised guarantee agreement. [1]

vi. LANDLORD'S CONSENT TO ASSIGNMENT OF TENANCY

Section 22 amends the Landlord and Tenant Act 1927 by providing that where a post-1995 lease contains a qualified covenant against assignment (one which

---

[19] P. 588, ante.

[20] Subject to the terms of the guarantee, a release occurs where there has been a substantial variation of the tenancy after the date of the guarantee. See *Howard de Walden Estates v Pasta Place* [1995] 1 EGLR 79.

[1] Implied indemnity covenants under LPA 1925, s. 77(1)(c), (d) and 7(c) and LRA 1925, s. 24(1)(b) and (2), p. 571, n. 20 have been abolished in respect of post-1995 leases: s. 30(2), Sch. 2.

permits assignment with the landlord's licence or consent), the parties may agree what conditions shall govern the question of whether the landlord consents to an assignment. These conditions are not capable of being struck down by the court on the ground that they are unreasonable. The amendment only applies to non-agricultural business leases. It is a quid pro quo for the abolition of privity of contract liability. [2]

LANDLORD AND TENANT ACT 1927

19. Provisions as to covenants not to assign, etc, without licence or consent.— (1) In all leases whether made before or after the commencement of this Act containing a covenant condition or agreement against assigning, under-letting, charging or parting with the possession of demised premises or any part thereof without licence or consent, such covenant condition or agreement shall, notwithstanding any express provision to the contrary, be deemed to be subject—

(*a*) to a proviso to the effect that such licence or consent is not to be unreasonably withheld, but this proviso does not preclude the right of the landlord to require payment of a reasonable sum in respect of any legal or other expenses incurred in connection with such licence or consent; and

(*b*) (if the lease is for more than forty years, and is made in consideration wholly or partially of the erection, or the substantial improvement, addition or alteration of buildings, and the lessor is not a Government department or local or public authority, or a statutory or public utility company) to a proviso to the effect that in the case of any assignment, under-letting, charging or parting with the possession (whether by the holders of the lease or any under-tenant whether immediate or not) effected more than seven years before the end of the term no consent or licence shall be required, if notice in writing of the transaction is given to the lessor within six months after the transaction is effected.

(1A) Where the landlord and the tenant under a qualifying lease have entered into an agreement specifying for the purposes of this subsection—

(a) any circumstances in which the landlord may withhold his licence or consent to an assignment of the demised premises of any part of them, or

(b) any conditions subject to which any such licence or consent may be granted,

then the landlord—

(i) shall not be regarded as unreasonably withholding his licence or consent to any such assignment if he withholds it on the ground (and it is the case) that any such circumstances exist, and

(ii) if he gives such licence or consent subject to any such conditions, shall not be regarded as giving it subject to unreasonable conditions;

and section 1 of the Landlord and Tenant Act 1988 (qualified duty to consent to assignment etc.) shall have effect subject to the provisions of this subsection.

(1B) Subsection (1A) of this section applies to such an agreement as is mentioned in that subsection—

(a) whether it is contained in the lease or not, and

2   (1996) 59 MLR 78 at 89 (M. Davey).

(b) whether it is made at the time when the lease is granted or at any other time falling before the application for the landlord's licence or consent is made.

(1C) Subsection (1A) shall not, however, apply to any such agreement to the extent that any circumstances or conditions specified in it are framed by reference to any matter falling to be determined by the landlord or by any other person for the purposes of the agreement, unless under the terms of the agreement—

(a) that person's power to determine that matter is required to be exercised reasonably, or

(b) the tenant is given an unrestricted right to have any such determination reviewed by a person independent of both landlord and tenant whose identity is ascertainable by reference to the agreement,

and in the latter case the agreement provides for the determination made by any such independent person on the review to be conclusive as to the matter in question.

(1D) In its application to a qualifying lease, subsection (1)(b) of this section shall not have effect in relation to any assignment of the lease.

(1E) In subsections (1A) and (1D) of this section—

(a) 'qualifying lease' means any lease which is a new tenancy for the purposes of section 1 of the Landlord and Tenant (Covenants) Act 1995 other than a residential lease, namely a lease by which a building or part of a building is let wholly or mainly as a single private residence; and

(b) references to assignment include parting with possession on assignment. [3]

---

[3] Sub-sections (1A) to (1E) were added by Landlord and Tenant (Covenants) Act 1995, s. 22. Further duties were imposed on the landlord by Landlord and Tenant Act 1988 (to give consent within a reasonable time, and to prove that refusal of such consent was reasonable). See *International Drilling Fluids Ltd v Louisville Investments (Uxbridge) Ltd* [1986] Ch 513 at 519, [1986] 1 All ER 321 at 325, per BALCOMBE LJ.

For the award of exemplary damages where a landlord deliberately tried to prevent assignment in order to procure a surrender from the tenant so as to obtain value of the under-rented property for itself, see *Design Progression Ltd v Thurloe Property Ltd* [2004] EWHC 324 (Ch), [2004] 10 EG 184 (CS).

9. Licences [1]

I. Introduction [2]

In its simplest form, a licence is a permission to enter upon land. It makes lawful what would otherwise be a trespass; [3] and, in the absence of special circumstances, is revocable at the will of the licensor. It is not a proprietary interest, and is not the subject matter of a grant. But there are many ways in which a licence has progressed from this simplistic form. Since the Judicature Act 1873, equitable remedies became available to protect a licensee in suitable cases. The years since World War II have seen a rapid development of their use, and this development is not fully worked out. The earlier cases focused on the question whether the licensee was to be protected against the licensor, by an injunction restraining the licensor from revoking the licence. Protection of the licensee against the licensor inevitably gave rise to the next question; whether the licensee was also to be protected against third parties, who would usually be the successors in title of the licensor. Protection against third parties further gave rise to the question whether such a licence had acquired proprietary characteristics. It may be that a licence which protects the licensee against third parties should be regarded as

---

[1] C & B, chap. 19; Gray, pp. 138–187, 753–818; M & W, chap. 17; MM, pp. 475–489; Smith, chap. 19; H & M, chap. 27; Dawson and Pearce, *Licences Relating to the Occupation or Use of Land* (1979).

[2] (1954) 70 LQR 326 (Lord EVERSHED).

[3] VAUGHAN CJ in *Thomas v Sorrel* (1673) Vaugh 330 at 351.

'proprietary' in nature, or it may be that an interest should only be regarded as proprietary[4] if it is capable of being assigned, bought and sold, and of passing through the estate of a deceased person. There have not yet been cases in which a protected licensee has purported to 'sell' his licence. But there are cases in which licensees have been held to be entitled to an order transferring to them an easement, or a life interest, or a fee simple in the land;[5] or have been held, even in the absence of such order, to be entitled to compensation, in their capacity as licensees, under statutory provisions authorising the payment of compensation to persons having interests in the land.[6]

The facts of the cases will show in what a wide variety of circumstances questions of protection of licensees can arise. And it will not be a matter of surprise to recognise that a large percentage of current cases are dealing with arrangements for the occupation of family homes, using 'family' in a sense wide enough to include mistresses. This question is related to that discussed in the context of trusts of land.[7] Where a proprietary interest is found by the application of trust doctrines (usually resulting or constructive trust) in the party who is not the legal owner, a beneficial co-ownership is created; and various questions then arise as to the determination of the rights of the parties, as by sale of the premises, or by their retention as a home for (usually) the woman and children. Where a non-owner has no such proprietary interest, protection may be given, by restraining the legal owner from evicting the licensee.

The litigation on the protection of licensees has generally concerned licences of four main types: contractual licences; licences arising under a constructive trust; licences by estoppel; and, for the short period of their recognition, the deserted wife's licence.[8] Each of these will be looked at in turn; but it will be useful, first of all, to lay down some of the basic propositions of the common law. The modern development has been by way of the application of equitable principles and remedies to that situation.

II. The Common Law Rules[9]

A. A Bare and Gratuitous Licence is Revocable at the Will of the Licensor

The licensee here avoids being a trespasser only because of the licensor's permission to enter. Such is the position of a guest at dinner, or of a picnic party in a friend's garden. The licensor is free to withdraw his permission, as is a bailor in the case of gratuitous bailment. The licensee then becomes a trespasser, but

---

[4]　*National Provincial Bank Ltd v Ainsworth* [1965] AC 1175 at 1247–1248, [1965] 2 All ER 472 at 494–495.

[5]　P. 667, post.

[6]　P. 656, post.

[7]　P. 263, ante.

[8]　Dawson and Pearce use nine categories of licences: Bare Licences; Contractual Licences; Licences by Estoppel; Licences arising under the doctrine of benefit and burden; Licences arising under the doctrine against derogation from grant; Licences and s. 62 LPA 1925; Licences arising by operation of law; Licences coupled with an interest; Licences as interests under a constructive trust.

[9]　C & B, pp. 640–641; Gray, pp. 138–170; M & W, paras. 17.003–17.012; MM, pp. 427–429; Smith, pp. 461–462; Dawson and Pearce, pp. 22–24, 68–73.

is first allowed a reasonable time in which to collect his goods, if any, and to leave the land. [10]

B. Entry upon a Licence does not make it Irrevocable

There was also a doctrine [11] of long standing, little relied on, to the effect that, if a licence has been acted upon, it is not revocable. Such an argument would prove too much, for it disregards the many cases in which licensees are permitted to be evicted after entry; [12] and also disregards the reasoning in other cases in which the licensee has been protected on other grounds. *Tayler v Waters* (1816) 7 Taunt 374, one of the leading cases in support of this theory, was disapproved in *Wood v Leadbitter* and described as being 'to the last degree unsatisfactory' (1845) 13 M & W 838 at 852, p. 597, post. If the principle of *Tayler v Waters* had developed, it 'would go close to reversing the general rule of the revocability of licences'. [13] The cases have been explained as illustrations of the principle of estoppel, discussed below. [14] But there is no indication that the judges in the cases so thought, and no express reference to that principle. A related but distinct concept appears in modern law in the rule formulated by Lord EVERSHED in *Armstrong v Sheppard and Short Ltd* [1959] 2 QB 384 at 399, [1959] 2 All ER 651 at 658: 'If A gives authority to B for the doing of an act on A's land, and the act is done and completed, then, whatever be the strict description of the authority … it is, generally speaking at any rate, too late for A … to complain of it.' [15]

---

[10]   [2002] CLJ 89 (J. Hill); *Minister of Health v Bellotti* [1944] 1 All ER 238; *Canadian Pacific Rly Co v R* [1931] AC 414; *Australian Blue Metal Ltd v Hughes* [1963] AC 74, [1962] 3 All ER 335; *Wallshire Ltd v Advertising Sites Ltd* [1988] 2 EGLR 167; *Express Newspapers plc v Silverstone Circuits Ltd* (1989) Times, 20 June (right to place advertisements on bridge at Woodcote Corner); *Governing Body of Henrietta Barnett School v Hampstead Garden Suburb Institute* (1995) Times, 13 April (nine months' notice given to school 'for all purposes from four to four score' held to be inadequate 'by any standards of reasonableness'; public nature of licensee's function, known to the licensor, taken into account); [1996] CLJ 229 (T. Kerbal).

For a possession action under RSC Ord 113 by a licensee against a trespasser on the land which the licensee occupies, even though not in de facto occupation of it, see *Manchester Airport plc v Dutton* [2000] QB 133, [1999] 2 All ER 675; [1999] Conv. 535 (E. Paton and G. Seabourne) cf *Countryside Residential (North Thames) Ltd v Tugwell* [2000] 2 EGLR 59.

For the abandonment of a licence, see *Bone v Bone* [1992] EGCS 81 (no formalities are necessary: 'it is enough that the parties have so conducted themselves that it ought to be inferred that they have mutually agreed to bring the contract to an end').

[11]   *Webb v Paternoster* (1619) Palm 71; *Wood v Lake* (1751) Say 3; *Winter v Brockwell* (1807) 8 East 308; *Tayler v Waters* (1816) 7 Taunt 374; *Wallis v Harrison* (1838) 4 M & W 538 at 544; *Feltham v Cartwright* (1839) 5 Bing NC 569; *Wood v Manley* (1839) 11 Ad & El 34 where, however, the licence was coupled with an interest, for the licensee was the owner of the hay; *Bendall v McWhirter* [1952] 2 QB 466 at 479, [1952] 1 All ER 1307 at 1312, per DENNING LJ; *Armstrong v Sheppard and Short Ltd* [1959] 2 QB 384, [1959] 2 All ER 651; *Hounslow London Borough Council v Twickenham Garden Developments Ltd* [1971] Ch 233 at 255, [1970] 3 All ER 326 at 344; (1965) 29 Conv (NS) 19 (M. C. Cullity).

[12]   E.g. *Winter Garden Theatre (London) Ltd v Millennium Productions Ltd* [1948] AC 173, [1947] 2 All ER 331, p. 602, post.

[13]   (1965) 29 Conv (NS) 19 at p. 31.

[14]   P. 622, post. See Dawson and Pearce, p. 31.

[15]   See *Hounslow London Borough Council v Twickenham Garden Developments Ltd* [1971] Ch 233 at 255, [1970] 3 All ER 326 at 344.

C. A Licence is not the Subject Matter of a Grant

This and the following proposition are closely related, and are both based upon the elementary rule that a grant of property is not revocable. A conveyance transfers to the grantee the subject matter of the grant, and it is beyond the grantor's power to recall.

But, of course, to be effective, the conveyance must have concerned something which the law recognises as being the subject matter of a grant and capable of being conveyed. A licensee, as stated above, is merely 'not a trespasser'. A licence is not a piece of property. But a licence may be coupled with a grant of an interest in property, real or personal, and, as shown in D below, p. 549, post, it will then be irrevocable.

In **Wood v Leadbitter** (1845) 13 M & W 838,[16] the plaintiff bought a ticket entitling him to enter the grandstand at Doncaster racecourse. On account of alleged malpractices on a previous occasion, he was ordered by the defendant, who was the servant of Lord Eglintoun, the steward of the course, to leave the racecourse. On his refusal, he was physically removed, no more force being used than was reasonably necessary. His action for assault and false imprisonment failed. He was a licensee only; and not a grantee of an interest in land. ALDERSON B, delivering the judgment of the Court of Exchequer, said at 845:

'It may further be observed, that a license under seal (provided it be a mere license) is as revocable as a license by parol; and, on the other hand, a license by parol, coupled with a grant, is as irrevocable as a license by deed, provided only that the grant is of a nature capable of being made by parol. But where there is a license by parol, coupled with a parol grant, or pretended grant, of something which is incapable of being granted otherwise than by deed, there the license is a mere license; it is not an incident to a *valid* grant, and it is therefore revocable.'

This may be logical; but hardly satisfactory. Where a licensee has paid to enter premises for a period of time, and he observes the terms and conditions of the licence, is it right that the licensor should be allowed to break the contract and turn the licensee into a trespasser?

In **Hurst v Picture Theatres Ltd** [1915] 1 KB 1, the plaintiff bought a ticket for 6d. to watch a cinema show at a theatre of the defendants. During the performance, the plaintiff was requested to leave on the ground, as the defendants incorrectly believed, that he had not paid for his ticket. He refused, and was ejected forcibly, but without the use of unnecessary violence. His action for assault and false imprisonment succeeded by a majority of 2 to 1. The majority (BUCKLEY and KENNEDY LJJ) found that he had an interest in the land. Since the Judicature Act, an interest in land could be granted without a deed. A contract for valuable consideration of which equity would decree specific performance would suffice.

---

[16] On the background to the case, see (1993) 14 Journal of Legal History 28 (P. Polden).

The fallacy of this reasoning was shown by PHILLIMORE LJ, dissenting. The doctrine of *Walsh v Lonsdale* (1882) 21 Ch D 9, p. 84, ante, he said, is that a man 'has the estate which equity thinks he ought to have. That has no bearing on the question if there is no estate, and no interest in land given by the document relied on'.

In short, contractual licences are not grants. They are contracts, and should be treated as such.

In **Cowell v Rosehill Racecourse Co Ltd** (1937) 56 CLR 605, LATHAM CJ said at 616:

'The doctrine of *Wood v Leadbitter* is clear and coherent. If a man creates a proprietary right in another and gives him a licence to go upon certain land in order that he may use or enjoy that right, the grantor cannot divest the grantee of his proprietary right and revest it in the grantor, or simply determine it, by breaking the agreement under which the licence was given. The grantee owns the property to which the licence is incident, and this ownership, with its incidental licence, is unaffected by what purports to be a revocation of the licence. The revocation of the licence is ineffectual. Easements and *profits à prendre* supply examples of interests to which licences to enter and remain upon land may be incidental.

The majority judgment in *Hurst's* case modified, if it did not reject, the law of *Wood v Leadbitter* by holding that a "right to see" a spectacle was an interest which could be granted so that a licence to go into a theatre or a racecourse to see a play or to witness races was, when given for value, irrevocable because it was a licence coupled with an interest. Further, the majority judgment held that, in so far as *Wood v Leadbitter* rested upon the rule that no incorporeal hereditament affecting land can be created or transferred otherwise than by deed, the Judicature Act had radically changed the position. The court was now bound to give effect to equitable doctrines and would therefore ignore the absence of a seal and would (as in *Frogley v Earl of Lovelace* (1859) John 333) grant an injunction to protect the right granted.

The first ground of the decision, in my opinion, ignores the distinction between a proprietary right and a contractual right. In *Wood v Leadbitter* there was obviously a contractual "interest" in a sense quite different from that in which the word was used in *Wood v Leadbitter*. The learned judge said that there was a grant of a right to come to see a spectacle. The licence is described as "only something granted to him for the purpose of enabling him to have that which had been granted to him, namely, the right to see." The "right to see" is treated as the "interest" which has been "granted."

It is clear that the learned judge used the word "grant" in a sense very different from that in which it was used in *Wood v Leadbitter*. It was there used in relation to interests in land which were, if they existed at all, clearly proprietary interests. The right to see a spectacle cannot, in the ordinary sense of legal language, be regarded as a proprietary interest. Fifty thousand people who pay to see a football match do not obtain fifty thousand interests in the football ground.

The second ground of the decision in *Hurst's* case is based upon the opinion that the plaintiff in *Wood v Leadbitter* failed because he did not have a grant under seal of the right which he claimed. It is true that the absence of a seal was a complete reply, in an action at law, to the contention of the plaintiff that he had an interest in the land upon which a race meeting was being held. But in fact the presence of a seal would not have assisted the plaintiff to establish the impossible proposition that he had an easement in gross. It is true that, as the majority judgments in *Hurst's* case state, a grant of an interest in land need not, in order to be effective in a court of equity, be made by deed, and that, since the Judicature Act, this rule is enforced in all divisions of the High Court in England: *Walsh v Lonsdale* (1882) 21 ChD 9, p. 84, ante. But this proposition does not justify the assertion that interests in land can, since the Judicature Act, be created by simple contract even though, before that Act, they were of such a character that they could not be created by deed as interests in land. *Buckley* LJ applies to the facts of *Hurst's* case the statement of *Parker* J in *James Jones & Sons Ltd v Earl of Tankerville* [1909] 2 Ch 440 at 443 that an injunction restraining the revocation of a licence "merely prevents" the defendant "from breaking his contract, and protects a right in equity which but for the absence of a seal would be a right at law, and since the *Judicature Act* it may well be doubted whether the absence of a seal in such a case can be relied on in any court." This statement was made with respect to a proprietary right (a *profit à prendre*) and it is a begging of the question to apply it to a case in which the matter in dispute is whether the alleged interest is such that it can be an interest in land, whether created by deed or not. *Frogley v Earl of Lovelace*, which is relied upon in *Hurst's* case, was a case of an agreement for a *profit à prendre*, an incorporeal hereditament. Thus the second ground for the majority judgments in *Hurst's* case cannot, in my opinion, be supported. I regard the dissenting judgment of *Phillimore* LJ as a convincing statement of the true position both at law and in equity.'

D. A Licence Coupled with a Grant (or an Interest) is Irrevocable

It is an anciently established rule that a licence coupled with a proprietary interest (in land or in a chattel) is irrevocable.[17] The interest must, of course, have been correctly granted.[18] In the grant of incorporeal hereditaments in realty at common law, a seal was needed; but, since the Judicature Act, an agreement for valuable consideration suffices.[19] It is, indeed, somewhat artificial to speak of a licence coupled with an interest in realty; for if the interest is properly granted and is one which involves entry upon another's land, the grantee enters by force of the grant and does not need to rely on a licence.

In the case of licences coupled with a chattel interest, that interest must again be properly granted, usually by gift or sale. Thus, where the occupier gives or sells a stack of coal on the land to a purchaser, the donee or purchaser is entitled to enter the land to take away the coal, and the donor or seller cannot deny him the right.[20] And a contract to cut and carry away timber on the Earl of Tankerville's Estate[1] created a chattel interest in the cut timber and a realty interest in the growing trees.

---

[17]   *Webb v Paternoster* (1619) Palm 71; *Wood v Manley* (1839) 11 Ad & El 34; *James Jones & Sons Ltd v Earl of Tankerville* [1909] 2 Ch 440.

[18]   On the question whether certain interests need to be regarded as realty or personalty for the purpose of a grant or of compliance with LPA 1925, s. 40, see M & W, paras. 12.025–12.026; see also p. 65, ante.

[19]   *Walsh v Lonsdale* (1882) 21 ChD 9, p. 84, ante.

[20]   *Wood v Manley* (1839) 11 Ad & El 34.

[1]   *James Jones & Sons Ltd v Earl of Tankerville* [1909] 2 Ch 440.

III. Licences for Consideration: Contractual Licences[2]

A. Damages for Breach of Contract

It has been seen that much confusion has been caused by the inability of the common law to give protection to a contractual licensee unless he has a proprietary interest in the land or chattels upon it. This position, based upon *Wood v Leadbitter*, meant that the licensor could, without giving any reason, turn out at will any watchers of a cinema show, horse race or football match.[3] The only difference between a contractual and a gratuitous licence was that, in the former, the licensor must pay damages. These were commonly assumed to be the price which the licensee had paid to enter. But there seems to be no reason why the damages should not reflect the loss of the licensee's expectation under the contract.[4]

B. Restitution

An alternative basis for compensation is the licensor's obligation to restore to the licensee the unjust benefit which he has received as a result of his wrongful termination of the contract.

In **Tanner v Tanner** [1975] 1 WLR 1346, [1975] 3 All ER 776,[5] the plaintiff and defendant had baby daughters. They were not married. The plaintiff purchased a house for the defendant, and she accordingly left her rent-controlled flat. The time came when the plaintiff, having changed his affections, decided to turn out the defendant and the children. She stayed, claiming that she should be allowed to remain in the house with the children until they had finished school. In the county court, an order for possession was made, and the defendant was rehoused by the local authority.

The Court of Appeal held that she was a licensee entitled to protection. She should have been entitled to stay in the house with the children until they left school, if the house continued to be needed for that purpose. But, as they had left, damages were awarded, compensating her for her loss. Lord DENNING MR said at 1350, at 780:

'It seems to me that enables an inference to be drawn, namely that in all the circumstances it is to be implied that she had a licence — a contractual licence — to have accommodation in the house for herself and the children so long as they were of school age and the accommodation was reasonably required for her and the children. There was, it is true, no express contract to that effect, but the circumstances are such that the court should imply a contract by the plaintiff — or, if need be impose the equivalent of a contract by him — whereby they were

---

2   C & B, pp. 641–646; Gray, pp. 170–184; M & W, paras. 17.004, 17.016–17.020; MM, pp. 477–482; Smith, pp. 463–471; Dawson and Pearce, pp. 24–38, 73–97, 133–144, 153–161, 167. See MEGARRY J's summary in *Hounslow London Borough Council v Twickenham Garden Developments Ltd* [1971] Ch 233 at 254, [1970] 3 All ER 326 at 343; *Chandler v Kerley* [1978] 1 WLR 693, [1978] 2 All ER 942, p. 604, post.
3   Per PHILLIMORE LJ in *Hurst v Picture Theatres Ltd* [1915] 1 KB 1, p. 597, ante; *Cowell v Rosehill Racecourse Co Ltd* (1937) 56 CLR 605, p. 598, ante.
4   *Kerrison v Smith* [1897] 2 QB 445.
5   (1976) 92 LQR 168 (J. L. Barton).

entitled to have the use of the house as their home until the girls had finished school. ...

If therefore the defendant had sought an injunction restraining the plaintiff from determining the licence, it should have been granted. The order for possession ought not to have been made.

[But the order for possession had been made and the defendant had moved out. His Lordship continued at 1351, at 780:]

What is to be done? The judge ordered possession in six weeks. Thereupon the local housing authority (as they usually do when an order for possession is made) provided accommodation for the defendant and the children. She moved out in pursuance of the order and does not ask to be put back now. Seeing that the order ought not to have been made and we reverse it, what is to be done? It seems to me that this court has ample power, when it reverses an order of the court below, to do what is just and equitable to restore the position as fairly as it can in the circumstances. The plaintiff has obtained an unjust benefit and should make restitution. In the circumstances the court can and should assess compensation to be payable by him. ... It seems to me a reasonable sum for loss of this licence (which the defendant ought not to have lost) would be £2,000.'[6]

C. Injunction To Restrain Breach of Contract

The more realistic question, however, is whether a licensee may obtain a remedy to prevent the revocation of the licence; as the defendant in *Tanner v Tanner* would have done if she had not previously been rehoused. The plain fact is that the common law had no appropriate remedy; and this may explain the development of the tenuous and unsatisfactory common law doctrine that a licence, once entered upon, was irrevocable.[7]

After the Judicature Act, equitable remedies became available. We saw that, in *Hurst's Case*,[8] the Court of Appeal found that the licensee should be protected; but only by reasoning the weakness of which is shown in the dissenting judgment of PHILLIMORE LJ, and in the judgment of LATHAM CJ in *Cowell v Rosehill Racecourse Co Ltd* (1937) 56 CLR 605, p. 598, ante. The availability of equitable rights and remedies is vital in this situation. The normal way of protecting a contractual licensee against wrongful revocation is by issuing an injunction to restrain the breach by the licensor. And, as we shall see, the Court of Appeal has held that a contractual licence may also be enforceable by a decree of specific performance.[9]

The crucial question in considering the revocability of contractual licences is whether the licence is revocable according to the proper construction of the contract.[10] Express provision will often be made. In its absence, the right to revoke will depend upon the intention of the parties as gathered from all the

---

[6]   No contract was implied in similar circumstances in *Horrocks v Forray* [1976] 1 WLR 230, [1976] 1 All ER 737 (described in (1976) 40 Conv (NS) 362 (M. Richards) as '*Tanner v Tanner* in a middle class setting'); *Coombes v Smith* [1986] 1 WLR 808 (no contract implied that man would provide mistress with house for rest of her life).

[7]   P. 596, ante.

[8]   [1915] 1 KB 1, p. 597, ante. The plaintiff received £150 as damages for assault and false imprisonment.

[9]   *Verrall v Great Yarmouth Borough Council* [1981] QB 202, [1980] 1 All ER 839, p. 609, post.

[10]   *Winter Garden Theatre (London) Ltd v Millennium Productions Ltd* [1948] AC 173, [1947] 2 All ER 331.

surrounding circumstances. There is no presumption one way or the other; [11] but it will presumably be more difficult to establish the non-revocability of a licence unlimited in time than it would be in the case of a licence for a specific period. The court may find that the licensor has a right to revoke upon giving reasonable notice, and will determine what that period is. If the licensor has no right to revoke, the question is whether the case is one in which it is appropriate to protect the licensee by an injunction restraining the licensor from breaking the contract, or whether the licensee should be left to his remedy in damages.

A licensee who is himself in breach of the terms of the contractual licence will not be protected; [12] nor presumably if the effect of the injunction would be to compel people to live together in intolerable circumstances. [13] And it has been held that a licensee, whose occupation of premises was dependent upon his employment, was not protected where he was dismissed in breach of contract. [14]

In **Winter Garden Theatre (London) Ltd v Millennium Productions Ltd** [1948] AC 173, [1947] 2 All ER 331, the appellants granted to the respondents a licence to use and present plays in the Winter Garden Theatre in Drury Lane for a period of six months, from 6 July 1942, with an option to renew for a further six months at an increased payment. The licence provided that on the expiration of these periods the respondents should have the option to continue the licence for an unstated period, terminable by them at a month's notice. No provision was made for termination by the appellants. The options were duly exercised. The appellants retained possession of the bars and cloakrooms. After three years the appellants wished to terminate the licence, and on 11 September 1945 served a notice requiring the respondents to vacate the theatre on 13 October 1945. The respondents refused to leave and brought an action for a declaration that the licence was not revocable; or, alternatively, if it was, that a reasonable period after the service of the notice had not expired.

The House of Lords held that, on the proper construction of the contract, the licence was terminable on giving reasonable notice, and that the notice given was reasonable. The question of wrongful revocation did not arise. But, on that subject, Lord UTHWATT said at 202, at 343:

'My view as to the construction of the agreement renders it unnecessary to consider whether *Hurst v Picture Theatres Ltd* [1915] 1 KB 1, p. 597, ante was rightly decided, or to express any concluded opinion on the question of the remedies now open in every court to a bare licensee who claims that the licensor has in breach of his bargain affected to revoke it. I merely confess my present inability to see any answer to the propositions of law stated by the Master of the Rolls in

11   Ibid at 203, at 344, per Lord MACDERMOTT. Lord PORTER said at 195, at 339, that a licence was prima facie revocable. See also *Re Spenborough UDC's Agreement* [1968] Ch 139, [1967] 1 All ER 959; *Beverley Corpn v Richard Hodgson & Sons Ltd* (1972) 225 EG 799.

12   *Thompson v Park* [1944] KB 408, [1944] 2 All ER 477, where the defendant had 'been guilty at least of riot, affray, wilful damage, forcible entry, and, perhaps, conspiracy', per GODDARD LJ at 409. The defendant was a preparatory school master who had moved, with his pupils, to the plaintiff's school when the defendant's premises were unavailable because of the war.

13   Ibid, per GODDARD LJ at 409, at 478–479.

14   *Ivory v Palmer* [1975] ICR 340. For a consideration of the question of the circumstances in which misbehaviour by a licensee by estoppel will allow his licence to be terminated, see *Williams v Staite* [1979] Ch 291, [1978] 2 All ER 928; *Brynowen Estates Ltd v Bourne* (1981) 131 NLJ 1212; *Willis & Sons v Willis* (1985) 277 EG 1133; p. 687, post.

his judgment in the case under appeal. [15] The settled practice of the courts of equity is to do what they can by an injunction to preserve the sanctity of a bargain. To my mind, as at present advised, a licensee who has refused to accept the wrongful repudiation of the bargain which is involved in an unauthorised revocation of the licence is as much entitled to the protection of an injunction as a licensee who has not received any notice of revocation; and, if the remedy of injunction is properly available in the latter case against unauthorised interference by the licensor, it is also available in the former case. In a court of equity, wrongful acts are no passport to favour.'

The Court of Appeal in this case had been faced with the question of the proper solution to the problem of the protection of a contractual licensee under a contract which was construed as irrevocable; it had taken a different view from the House of Lords of the construction of the contract. The statement of the law by Lord GREENE MR, referred to by Lord UTHWATT is as follows [1946] 1 All ER 678 at 684:

'The next question which I must mention is this. The respondents [16] have purported to determine the licence. If I have correctly construed the contract their doing so was a breach of contract. It may well be that, in the old days, that would only have given rise to a right to sue for damages. The licence would have stood revoked, but after the expiration of what was the appropriate period of grace the licensees would have been trespassers and could have been expelled, and their right would have been to sue for damages for breach of contract, as was said in *Kerrison v Smith* [1897] 2 QB 445. But the matter requires to be considered further, because the power of equity to grant an injunction to restrain a breach of contract is, of course, a power exercisable in any court. The general rule is that, before equity will grant such an injunction, there must be, on the construction of the contract, a negative clause express or implied. In the present case it seems to me that the grant of an option which, if I am right, is an irrevocable option, must imply a negative undertaking by the licensor not to revoke it. That being so, in my opinion, such a contract could be enforced in equity by an injunction. Then the question would arise, at what time can equity interfere? If the licensor were threatening to revoke, equity, I apprehend, would grant an injunction to restrain him from carrying out that threat. But supposing he has in fact purported to revoke, is equity then to say: "We are now powerless. We cannot stop you from doing anything to carry into effect your wrongful revocation?" I apprehend not. I apprehend equity would say: "You have revoked and the licensee had no opportunity of stopping you doing so by an injunction; but what the court of equity can do is to prevent you from carrying that revocation into effect and restrain you from doing anything under it." In the present case, nothing has been done. The appellants are still there. I can see no reason at all why, on general principles, equity should not interfere to restrain the licensors from acting upon the purported revocation, that revocation being, as I consider, a breach of contract.

Looking at it in that rather simple way, one is not concerned with the difficulties which are suggested to arise from the decision of this court in *Hurst v Picture Theatres Ltd* [1915] 1 KB 1, p. 597, ante. Counsel for the respondents

------

[15] Infra.
[16] I.e., *Winter Garden Theatre (London) Ltd* who became the appellants in the House of Lords.

agreed that in this court he could not ask us to take a different view to the view there taken. It is a decision which has not satisfied everybody, but, quite apart from that decision, the simple propositions which I have just enunciated, which I cannot help thinking are right, would appear to me to get round any difficulties which might be felt as to the reasoning in *Hurst v Picture Theatres Ltd.* We are not concerned here with a licence coupled with a grant. Nothing of that kind is suggested. It is not suggested that that type of licence is in question here. It is a pure licence and nothing else, and the breach of the licence contract by the licensor could be restrained by a court of equity, and a court of equity would interfere to prevent the licensor taking steps pursuant to this wrongful revocation. That seems to me to put the matter right so far as this case is concerned.' [17]

CHANDLER v KERLEY
[1978] 1 WLR 693, [1978] 2 All ER 942 (CA, Lord SCARMAN, MEGAW and ROSKILL LJJ) [18]

LORD SCARMAN: This appeal is concerned with the right to occupy a dwelling-house, 30 Salisbury Road, Testwood, Totton, in Hampshire. The plaintiff owns it: the defendant, with her two children, occupies it. She will not leave, because she says the plaintiff has agreed that she may stay there as long as she pleases. The plaintiff went to the Southampton County Court with a claim for possession, alleging that the defendant was a trespasser, her licence having been terminated. The defendant not only resisted the claim, but also counterclaimed for a declaration that she is a tenant for life, alternatively that 'she is the beneficiary under a trust ... upon terms that she is entitled to remain therein with her children for as long as she wishes.' In this court the defendant was allowed, the plaintiff not opposing, to amend her counterclaim by adding in the further alternative that she is a licensee for life, or for so long as her children remain in her custody and the younger is of school age and so long as she does not remarry, or for a period terminable only by reasonable notice.

On 26 May 1977, Judge McCreery dismissed the plaintiff's claim and gave judgment for the defendant on the counterclaim, declaring that the defendant is a beneficiary under a trust upon terms that she is entitled to occupy the house for her life or for so long as she pleases. The plaintiff now appeals.

The facts are unusual. The plaintiff, Mr Chandler, acquired the house from the defendant, Mrs Kerley, and her husband in the following circumstances. In 1972 Mr and Mrs Kerley jointly bought the house for £11,000, intending it to be their family home. The purchase was partly financed by a building society mortgage for £5,800. Mr Kerley paid the mortgage instalments. They have two children, both of whom are now living with their mother. In 1974 the marriage broke down. In May of that year Mr Kerley left home, not to return. However, he continued to pay the building society instalments. The defendant and the children continued to live in the house.

---

[17]   See also *Hounslow London Borough Council v Twickenham Garden Developments Ltd* [1971] Ch 233 at 254, [1970] 3 All ER 326 at 343, where MEGARRY J summarises the law relating to contractual licences; (1971) 87 LQR 309; *Mayfield Holdings Ltd v Moana Reef Ltd* [1973] 1 NZLR 309.

[18]   *Roach v Johannes* [1976] CLY 1549 (licence of 'paying guest' terminable on giving reasonable notice, which in the circumstances was not less than 21 days); *Piguet v Tyler* [1978] CLY 119 (irrevocable licence for life of defendants, who had, by arrangement with plaintiff, surrendered protected tenancy to look after plaintiff's aged mother).

At about the time Mr Kerley left home, the defendant met the plaintiff. They became friends: sexual intercourse followed, and the defendant became the plaintiff's mistress. This relationship continued until January 1976, when it ended.

Early in 1975 Mr Kerley stopped paying the building society: he said he could not afford it. He and his wife put the house on the market for £14,950, but failed to find a buyer — even when in the autumn they reduced the asking price to £14,300. Meanwhile the building society was threatening to foreclose. The defendant naturally told the plaintiff of her anxieties. He wanted to help, and said he could afford £10,000, but no more. Finally, it was agreed that the Kerleys should sell the house to the plaintiff for that figure, and the house was sold to him in December 1975. The net proceeds of sale, after they had paid off the debt to the building society, were divided — £1,000 to the defendant and £1,800 to Mr Kerley. The defendant accepted less than her half-share because she understood that the plaintiff was going to let her live in the house.

The arrangement between the plaintiff and the defendant which made all this possible was, according to the judge's findings, the following. The plaintiff agreed to buy the house for £10,000 (a figure substantially less than the asking price) upon the understanding that the defendant would continue to live in it indefinitely till he moved in. For at this time, 1975, they contemplated living together in the house as man and wife once they were free to do so, that is to say, after a divorce between Mr and Mrs Kerley. The defendant, very sensibly, did ask the plaintiff what would happen if they parted: he replied that he could not put her out.

Within six weeks of the purchase of the house, the plaintiff had brought their relationship to an end. It was not suggested, however, that he did so in order to get the defendant out of the house. Nevertheless he did purport in 1976 to serve a notice terminating her licence. It was given by solicitors' letter dated April 29 requiring the lady to quit on May 28.

The judge found that the plaintiff had granted the defendant an express licence and that the notice was not effectual to terminate it. There is now no challenge to these findings. The defendant is, therefore, a licensee, whose right to occupy has not yet been terminated. In so far, therefore, as the appeal is against the dismissal of the plaintiff's claim for possession, it must fail. The true dispute, however, between the parties arises on the counterclaim. There are two substantial issues: (1) the terms of the licence; and (2) whether the defendant has an equitable interest arising under a constructive trust; and, if so, what is the extent of the interest.

The judge's findings as to the terms of the licence are obscure. He rejected the submission made on behalf of the defendant that she had an implied licence to remain in the house all her life: yet he also held (and I quote from the notes of judgment) 'that there was an express agreement between the two and, as a result, there was a constructive trust with Mr Chandler as trustee and Mrs Kerley being the beneficiary.' It is possible, though certainly not clear to me, that the judge is here finding an express agreement that she may remain for life: for he certainly granted her a declaration that she had an equity to that effect. But, whatever the finding as to the terms of the agreement, the reasoning of the judge in this passage is, in my judgment, unsound. If the defendant can establish a licence for life, there is neither room nor need for an equitable interest. Since the fusion of law and equity, such a legal right can be protected by injunction: see *Hurst v Picture Theatres Ltd* [1915] 1 KB 1, p. 597, ante, *Winter Garden Theatre (London) Ltd v Millennium Productions Ltd* [1948] AC 173, [1947] 2 All ER 331, p.

602, ante and *Foster v Robinson* [1951] 1 KB 149, [1950] 2 All ER 342, per Lord Evershed MR, at 156, at 346. If she cannot establish such a licence (express or implied), she cannot establish an equity: for no question of estoppel arises in this case. It is simply a case of what the parties envisaged by their arrangement: see *Dodsworth v Dodsworth* (1973) 228 EG 1115, p. 671, post, where the Court of Appeal considered it not right to confer upon the defendants a greater interest than was envisaged by the parties. In the present case the parties certainly intended that the arrangement between them should have legal consequences. If, therefore, they agreed upon a right of occupation for life, there is a binding contract to that effect: if they did not so agree, there is nothing to give rise to an equity to that effect.

In a case such as the present, the role of equity is supportive and supplementary. Where the parties have contracted for a licence, equity will today provide an equitable remedy to protect the legal right, for example by injunction, which may be by interlocutory order, if the court considers it just and convenient: see section 45, Supreme Court of Judicature (Consolidation) Act 1925.[19] If, however, the legal relationship between the parties is such that the true arrangement envisaged by the parties will be frustrated if the parties are left to their rights and duties at law, an equity will arise which the courts can satisfy by appropriate equitable relief. An old illustration of equity at work in this way was given by Parker J in *Jones v Earl of Tankerville* [1909] 2 Ch 440 at 443 (quoted in *Hurst's* case [1915] 1 KB 1 at 9). Likewise in another old case, *Frogley v Earl of Lovelace* (1859) John 333, Page Wood V-C granted an injunction to restrain the defendant from interfering with the plaintiff shooting over his land 'until the defendant shall have executed a proper legal grant of the right claimed by the plaintiff.'

The judge in the present case believed he was constrained by the decision in *Bannister v Bannister* [1948] 2 All ER 133, p. 615, post to declare the existence of a right of occupation for life, even though he had rejected an implied contractual right to that effect. But, when analysed, *Bannister v Bannister* is no more than an illustration of the supportive and supplementary role of equity. It was a case in which the plaintiff gave an oral undertaking that the defendant would be allowed to live in the cottage rent-free for as long as she desired. The defendant could not show a legal right: but she did establish the existence of an understanding or arrangement with the plaintiff which, though giving rise to no legal right, brought into existence an equity which the court thought it just to satisfy by declaring the defendant had an equitable life interest in the cottage with the plaintiff as her trustee. The court treated this life interest as the equivalent to a tenancy for life under the Settled Land Act 1925.[20]

Errington v Errington and Woods [1952] 1 KB 290, [1952] 1 All ER 149, p. 613, post is a decision which follows the same pattern. The arrangement in that case was oral. The father bought a house, put his son and daughter-in-law into occupation and promised them that if they paid the instalments on the mortgage the house would be theirs when the last instalment was paid. The Court of Appeal held that the arrangement conferred upon the daughter-in-law (father having died, son having left his wife and she continuing to pay the instalments) a contractual right of occupation which carried with it an equity which on payment of the last instalment would give her a good equitable title to the house. The case may be said to be a classic illustration of equity supplementing a contractual

[19]   Now Supreme Court Act 1981, s. 37.
[20]   See p.326, n. 6, ante.

right so as to give effect to the intention of the parties to the arrangement. *Binions v Evans* [1972] Ch 359, [1972] 2 All ER 70, p. 617, post, is to the same effect.

The defendant in this appeal, however, relied strongly on *Bannister v Bannister* to support a submission that she has a tenancy for life. Like Megaw LJ in *Binions v Evans* at 370, at 78, I find great difficulty in understanding how the court in *Bannister's* case came to conclude that there was in that case a tenancy for life under the Act. It was, however, a matter which depended upon the particular facts of the case.

As Russell LJ commented in *Dodsworth v Dodsworth* (1973) 228 EG 1115, there is a risk that such an inference may fall foul of the Settled Land Act 1925, which confers a power of sale and of leasing upon the tenant — powers which cannot, for instance, have been in the minds of the parties in the present case. The present is *not*, in my judgment, a case of life tenancy: and in this respect *Bannister v Bannister* is a decision to be treated as turning on the particular facts of that case.

The most recent case to which we were referred is the decision of the Court of Appeal in *Tanner v Tanner* [1975] 1 WLR 1346, [1975] 3 All ER 776, p. 600, ante. It is close on its facts to the present case, in that the defendant was found to have no proprietary interest in the house but did have a contractual right to live in it until her two children, of whom the plaintiff was the father, were no longer of school age. The defendant had been the mistress of the plaintiff, who had bought the house (when she had been a tenant protected by the Rent Act) to provide accommodation for her and their two children. The court held it to be a case of contractual licence, Lord Denning MR saying at 1350, at 780:

'It was a contractual licence of the kind which is specifically enforceable on her behalf: and which he can be restrained from breaking: and he could not sell the house over her head so as to get her out in that way.'

It is yet another case of a contractual licence supported by equity so far, and only so far, as is necessary to give effect to the expectations of the parties when making their arrangement

Accordingly, the task in this case is to determine what were the terms of the arrangement, express and implied, between the parties. I agree with the judge that it is not possible to imply a licence to the defendant to occupy the house for her life. The plaintiff had invested £10,000 in the house and, in the absence of express stipulation, cannot be supposed in the circumstances to have frozen his capital for as long as the defendant pleased or for the duration of her life. On the other hand, the plaintiff was well aware that the defendant wanted the house as a home for her children as well as for herself. It would be wrong, however, to infer, in the absence of an express promise, that the plaintiff was assuming the burden of housing another man's wife and children indefinitely, and long after his relationship with them had ended. The balance of these factors leads me to the conclusion that the defendant's contractual licence was terminable upon reasonable notice, and that the notice must be such as to give the defendant ample opportunity to re-house herself and her children without disruption. In my judgment 12 calendar months' notice is reasonable in the circumstances.

For these reasons I do not think this is a case in which it is necessary to invoke the support of any equitable doctrine. The defendant is entitled to 12 months' notice. It follows that the appeal against the dismissal of the claim to possession fails in my judgment, the licence not yet having been determined. The order upon the counterclaim should, in my judgment, be varied so as to substitute for the declaration granted by the judge a declaration that the defendant's licence is terminable upon reasonable notice and that reasonable notice is one of 12 calendar months from its service.

In **Hardwick v Johnson** [1978] 1 WLR 683, [1978] 2 All ER 935, a mother purchased a house for occupation by her son and daughter-in-law as their home. Rent of £7 per week was payable, but it ceased to be paid after a month or two, and the mother did not demand it. Within a year the marriage was collapsing, and the son was about to leave his wife. The mother sued for possession and arrears of rent. The daughter-in-law gave birth to a child, and claimed to be entitled to remain in possession on paying £7 a week. The Court of Appeal held that the licence was irrevocable. The daughter-in-law was not in breach in respect of the arrears because the mother had indicated no desire to claim the rent. ROSKILL LJ said at 690, at 940:

'When one looks at the correspondence before action brought and indeed at the pleadings, one sees an ever increasing number of legal arguments being found upon a perfectly simple family arrangement; but in my judgment this case can be decided upon one very short ground. It is plain, as the deputy judge said, that there was here never any tenancy. It is equally plain, in my judgment, that there was here a licence; and for my part, with respect to Lord Denning MR, I prefer to call it a contractual licence rather than an equitable licence.

The only question we have to decide is what was the nature of that contractual licence. Was it a licence to both the son and his future wife as joint licensees or was it a licence to the son alone? Nobody contemplated the possibility that this marriage would break down as soon as it did. Nobody contemplated that the son would within a couple of years or so go off and have an affair with another woman, abandoning his wife with the child of the marriage who remained in the house. What the parties would have agreed upon if they had thought of that possibility in March 1973 no one can tell; but the court, as Lord Denning MR has said and as has been said many times before (and Lord Diplock also said it in *Pettitt v Pettitt* [1970] AC 777 at 821–823, [1969] 2 All ER 385 at 413–414), has in those circumstances to impute to the parties a common intention to make some arrangement in the events which have occurred, albeit unexpectedly. I cannot, for my part, think that anybody would impute to these parties an intention that if the marriage broke down as soon as it did and the husband went off with another woman the wife would be liable to be ejected from the home together with the child of the marriage. It seems to me that the arrangement was perfectly straightforward: it was a joint contractual licence to the husband and wife to live there. It was not conditional upon the marriage succeeding. It was not conditional upon a number of other possibilities.

I am disinclined to express any opinion on what if any events that licence is now determinable. Suffice it to say that in my judgment it is not determinable in the event which has occurred, namely, that the husband has left the wife — no divorce proceedings are pending, as Lord Denning MR has said — since that licence was not given only to the husband. It seems to me that no event has yet taken place which justifies the bringing to an end of this contractual licence; and therefore, for that reason, I think the deputy circuit judge reached the right conclusion in a careful and closely reasoned judgment.'

Lord DENNING said that the licence was a personal equitable licence. BROWNE LJ delivered a judgment agreeing with ROSKILL LJ.

D. Specific Performance

VERRALL v GREAT YARMOUTH BOROUGH COUNCIL
[1981] QB 202, [1980] 1 All ER 839 (CA, Lord DENNING MR, ROSKILL and CUMMING-BRUCE LJJ)

The Conservative council of Great Yarmouth agreed in April 1979 to a two-day hiring of the Wellington Pier Pavilion by the National Front for its annual conference in October. In May 1979 the council, following a change in its political control to Labour, purported to repudiate the contract. An action was brought on behalf of the National Front for specific performance.

Held. Specific performance granted.

LORD DENNING MR: Since the *Winter Garden* case, it is clear that once a man has entered under his contract of licence, he cannot be turned out. An injunction can be obtained against the licensor to prevent his being turned out. On principle it is the same if it happens before he enters. If he has a contractual right to enter, and the licensor refuses to let him come in, then he can come to the court and in a proper case get an order for specific performance to allow him to come in. An illustration was taken in the course of the argument. Supposing one of the great political parties — say, the Conservative Party — had booked its hall at Brighton for its conference in September of this year: it had made all its arrangements accordingly: it had all its delegates coming: it had booked its hotels, and so on. Would it be open to the local council to repudiate that agreement, and say that the Conservative Party could not go there? Would the only remedy be damages? Clearly not. The court would order the council in such a case to perform its contracts. It would be the same in the case of the Labour Party, or whoever it may be. When arrangements are made for a licence of this kind of such importance and magnitude affecting many people, the licensors cannot be allowed to repudiate it and simply pay damages. It must be open to the court to grant specific performance in such cases. ... The newly constituted council is bound by what the old constituted council did. The newly constituted council must honour the contract. I see no sufficient reason for not holding the council to their contract. In the interests of our fundamental freedoms — freedom of speech, freedom of assembly, and the importance of holding people to their contracts — we ought to grant specific performance in this case, as the judge did.

E. Enforcement of Contractual Licences Against Third Parties [1]

The next question is whether a contractual licence, which is irrevocable by the licensor, is binding on a third party. On the one hand, it is well settled that, subject to exceptions, contractual rights are binding on, and enforceable by, the parties to the contract only. [2] On the other hand, the protection given to the

---

[1]   Dawson and Pearce, pp. 153–161.

[2]   *Tweddle v Atkinson* (1861) 1 B & S 393; *Dunlop Pneumatic Tyre Co Ltd v Selfridge & Co Ltd* [1915] AC 847; *Beswick v Beswick* [1968] AC 58, [1967] 2 All ER 1197; *Woodar Investment Development Ltd v Wimpey Construction (UK) Ltd* [1980] 1 WLR 277, [1980] 1 All ER 571; Cheshire, Fifoot and Furmston, *Law of Contract* (14th edn., 2001), chap. 14; Treitel, *Law of Contract* (11th edn.), chap. 15.

An important exception to the privity rule was made by the Contracts (Third Rights of Third Parties) Act 1999, p. 76, ante; C & B, p. 646, n. 8; Law Commission Report on Privity of Contract: Contracts for the Benefit of Third Parties 1996 (Law Com No. 242 Cm 3329).

licensee may be of little use if a transfer of the land to a third party leaves that third party free to claim possession, and leaves the licensee to his remedy in damages against the original licensor. Further, a licensee's right to protection by injunction against the licensor gives him some sort of equity, and it is arguable that such an equity should give him protection against all but bona fide purchasers for value without notice.

Whether or not contractual licences should be held to be binding on third parties is ultimately a policy question. So it has been in other areas of the law. Contractual restrictions on the use of chattels have been held not to be binding on third parties even though they have express notice of the restriction.[3] The great case of *Tulk v Moxhay*[4] decided that a covenant restricting the user of land was binding on successors in title of the covenantor taking with notice. It was soon found that so wide a doctrine would create burdens on land for which there was no justification, and the basis of the doctrine was later changed so as to limit the running of the burden to cases in which the continuation of the covenant was necessary to protect land capable of benefiting; more like a negative equitable easement.[5] The point is that the whole question whether an equity enforceable against one contracting party is enforceable against third parties is determined, not by a rule of thumb, but by an examination of the policy questions applicable to the particular situation.

On this basis, it would seem clear that contractual licences should not, in the ordinary case, be binding on third parties. Otherwise, thousands of minor personal arrangements, like hotel bookings, contracts for lodgings, car parking contracts, and a host of other minor non-proprietary arrangements would in effect come on to the title; with no effective way of determining the question whether or not the third party had notice. After all, the contractual licensee has his remedy in damages.

Authority is to the same effect.[6] In spite of the privity of contract rule, however, a contractual licensee may be able to enforce a right against a third party, if the facts give rise to some other legal relationship outside the sphere of contract, i.e. under the doctrine of proprietary estoppel or of the constructive trust. In both these spheres, which require different criteria of proof and give rise to different remedies, the licensee acquires an equitable interest, either as an estoppel licensee or as a beneficiary under a trust, which is enforceable against a third party with notice. *Errington v Errington and Woods* [1952] 1 KB 290, [1952] 1 All ER 149, p. 613, post is generally accepted as being a case of a contractual licence. But there is clearly an estoppel situation also. In *Binions v Evans* [1972] Ch 359, [1972] 2 All ER 70, p. 617, post, the conveyance was made expressly subject to the contractual right of the licensee; and this was held to create a constructive trust. In *Ashburn Anstalt v Arnold* [1989] Ch 1, [1988] 2 All ER 147,

---

[3]   *De Mattos v Gibson* (1858) 4 De G & J 276; *Lord Strathcona Steamship Co Ltd v Dominion Coal Ltd* [1926] AC 108; *Port Line Ltd v Ben Line Steamers Ltd* [1958] 2 QB 146, [1958] 1 All ER 787. See however, *Swiss Bank Corpn v Lloyds Bank Ltd* [1979] Ch 548 at 569–575, [1979] 2 All ER 853 at 869–874; revsd. on different grounds [1982] AC 584, [1981] 2 All ER 449; (1982) 98 LQR 279 (S. Gardner).

[4]   (1848) 2 Ph 774, p. 942, post.

[5]   P. 946, post.

[6]   *Clore v Theatrical Properties Ltd and Westby & Co Ltd* [1936] 3 All ER 483; *King v David Allen & Sons, Billposting Ltd* [1916] 2 AC 54, infra; *Ashburn Anstalt v Arnold* [1988] 2 All ER 147, p. 612, post. See also *Midland Bank Ltd v Farm Pride Hatcheries Ltd* (1980) 260 EG 493, p. 28, ante, where the issue of the binding effect of a contractual licence on a third party was not raised; *Lloyd v Dugdale* [2002] 2 P & CR 167, per. Sir Christopher SLADE, p. 621, post.

p. 612, post, however, the Court of Appeal took the view that the mere fact that land is expressed to be conveyed 'subject to' a contract does not necessarily imply that the grantee is to be under an obligation, not otherwise existing, to give effect to the provisions of the contract. In *DHN Food Distributors Ltd v Tower Hamlets London Borough Council* [1976] 1 WLR 852, [1976] 3 All ER 462,[7] an irrevocable contractual licence was said, as one of three rationes in the case, to give rise to a constructive trust, and to 'give to D.H.N. a sufficient interest in the land to qualify them for compensation for disturbance' upon compulsory purchase by the local authority. In *Re Sharpe* [1980] 1 WLR 219, [1980] 1 All ER 198, p. 681, post, an irrevocable licence to occupy a house until a loan was repaid, 'whether it be called a contractual licence or an equitable licence or an interest under a constructive trust', was held to be binding on the trustee in bankruptcy of the licensor.

It will be obvious that this possibility of the multiple characterisation of the right gives to the court the powers which it needs to reach a just solution.

KING v DAVID ALLEN AND SONS, BILLPOSTING LTD

[1916] 2 AC 54 (HL, LORD BUCKMASTER LC, Earl LOREBURN and Lord ATKINSON)

By an agreement of 1 July 1913, the appellant gave to the respondents an exclusive permission to affix advertisements for a stated period to the walls of a cinema which was to be built.

In September 1913 the appellant executed a lease of the property to the cinema company, but the lease, disregarding arrangements previously made, contained no reference to the agreement of 1 July. The company refused to allow the advertisement to be posted and the respondents brought an action against the appellant King, for breach of the agreement of 1 July.

Held. The appellant (the licensor) was liable in damages.

EARL LOREBURN: My Lords, I agree in the opinion expressed by the Lord Chancellor, and with him I greatly regret the position in which Mr King has been placed, which seems to me to be hard upon him. He has behaved perfectly honestly in the whole business, and one cannot help regretting the expense to which he has been put.

I have very little to add to what has been said, but I look at the case in this way. The plaintiffs say that Mr King promised them for four years the use of a certain wall for advertising purposes by the agreement of 1 July 1913, and they say that after that Mr King demised that land, and that Mr King's lessees refused to make good the promise in regard to advertisement. Well, if the agreement of 1 July, which purports to be on the face of it a licence, was equivalent to creating an incorporeal hereditament or a sufficient interest in land, Mr King did not break his contract in making the lease, and would not be responsible for any trespasses that were committed by his licensees. But we must look at the document itself, and it seems to me that it does not create any interest in land at all; it merely amounts to a promise on the part of Mr King that he would allow the other party to the contract to use the wall for advertising purposes, and there was an implied undertaking that he would not disable himself from carrying out his contract. Now Mr King has altered his legal position in respect of his control of this land. Those to whom he granted the lease have disregarded his wishes and refused to allow his bargain to be carried out, and they have been practically enabled to do

---

7   (1977) 93 LQR 170 (D. Sugarman and F. Webb); (1977) 41 Conv (NS) 73; p. 683, post.

so by reason of the demise that he executed. In these circumstances it seems to me that there has been a breach in law of the contract of 1 July, and Mr King has disabled himself from giving effect to it as intended by parting with his right to present possession. That is enough to establish a case for damages against Mr King. There may be a remedy over against the lessees. I say nothing of that, because they are not here, and I do not wish either to encourage or to discourage any further proceedings; but this I think is clear: that the existence of such a remedy, if remedy there be, does not release Mr King from his liability to answer for breaking the contract which he made.

In **Ashburn Anstalt v Arnold** [1989] Ch 1, [1988] 2 All ER 147, [9] prior to 28 February 1973, Mr Arnold held the head lease, and Arnold & Co the sublease of shop premises in Gloucester Road, Kensington, forming part of registered land owned by Cavendish Land Co Ltd. By agreements on 28 February, Mr Arnold sold the headlease to Matlodge Ltd and Arnold & Co the sublease also to Matlodge Ltd. On the same day the benefit of these agreements was assigned by Matlodge Ltd to Cavendish Land Co Ltd, the headlease and the sublease thereby merging with the freehold.

Clause 5 of the agreement between Arnold & Co and Matlodge Ltd provided that from the date of completion the vendors would 'be entitled as licensees to remain at the property and trade therefrom' until 29 September, without payment of rent, and from that date to remain there until it received notice from the purchaser that he was ready to demolish and redevelop the property, whereupon it would give up possession and in due course be granted a lease of shop premises on the redeveloped site.

Cavendish Land Co Ltd transferred the freehold to the Legal and General Assurance Society Ltd, who then sold it to Ashburn Anstalt, the plaintiff, subject to the 1973 agreement between Arnold & Co and Matlodge Ltd. The plaintiff claimed possession from the defendants who had been in actual occupation throughout.

In dismissing the plaintiff's claim, the Court of Appeal held (1) that Clause 5 of the agreement created a lease which was binding on the plaintiff as an overriding interest under section 70(1) (*g*) of the Land Registration Act 1925. [10]

(2) obiter, that, on the assumption that clause 5 created a contractual licence, it would not be enforceable against the plaintiff. It did not create an interest in land, nor did it give rise to a constructive trust. [11]

Fox LJ said at 13, at 157:

'If, as we have concluded, Arnold & Co. is a tenant, it follows that the plaintiff holds the land subject to the tenancy. That is sufficient to dispose of the claim, as the action is for possession. Since, however, we have heard full argument on the case, we will consider the position on the basis that we are wrong, and no tenancy was created.

It is Arnold & Co.'s case that even if the 1973 agreement created no tenancy after 28 February 1973, so that its occupancy thereafter is that of a contractual

---

[9]   The Appeal Committee dismissed a petition for leave to appeal [1989] Ch 32. [1988] CLJ 353 (A. J. Oakley); 104 LQR 175 (P. Sparkes); 51 MLR 226 (J. Hill); Conv 201 (M. P. Thompson); All ER Rev 176 (P. J. Clarke).
[10]   P, 150, ante.
[11]   P. 618, post.

licensee only, its rights are nevertheless binding upon a purchaser for value with notice of the licence. ...

Until comparatively recently it would, we think, have been rejected. As long ago as 1674, in *Thomas v Sorrell* (1674) Vaugh 330, 351, Vaughan CJ said:

"A dispensation or licence properly passeth no interest, nor alters or transfers property in any thing, but only makes an action lawful, which without it had been unlawful."

A number of cases in this century support that view. ...

[His Lordship referred to *Daly v Edwardes* (1900) 83 LT 548; affd sub nom *Edwardes v Barrington* (1901) 85 LT 650; *Frank Warr & Co Ltd v LCC* [1904] 1 KB 713; *King v David Allen & Sons (Billposting) Ltd* [1916] 2 AC 54, p. 611, ante; *Clore v Theatrical Properties Ltd* [1936] 3 All ER 483 and continued:]

Down to this point we do not think that there is any serious doubt as to the law. A mere contractual licence to occupy land is not binding on a purchaser of the land even though he has notice of the licence.

We come now to a case which is of central importance on the present issue. That is *Errington v Errington and Woods* [1952] 1 KB 290, [1952] 1 All ER 149. A father, wishing to provide a home for his son who had recently married, bought a house with the help of a building society mortgage. He paid a lump sum towards the purchase price, the remainder of which was provided by the building society's loan. The loan was repayable by instalments. He retained the conveyance in his own name and paid the rates, but he promised that if the son and daughter-in-law continued in occupation and duly paid all the instalments, he would then transfer the property to them. The father died and by his will left the house to his widow. Up to that time the son and his wife had lived in the house and paid the instalments. The son then separated from his wife and left the house. The daughter-in-law continued to pay the mortgage instalments. The widow then sought possession of the house from the daughter-in-law. The county court judge dismissed the action. He held that the daughter-in-law was a tenant at will and that the claim against her was statute-barred. That reasoning was rejected by the Court of Appeal, though the actual decision of the judge was upheld. Denning LJ, whose reasons for dismissing the appeal were concurred in by Somervell LJ, said, at 298–299, at 155:

"it seems to me that, although the couple had exclusive possession of the house, there was clearly no relationship of landlord and tenant. They were not tenants at will but licensees. They had a mere personal privilege to remain there, with no right to assign or sub-let. They were, however, not bare licensees. They were licensees with a contractual right to remain. As such they have no right at law to remain, but only in equity, and equitable rights now prevail. I confess, however, that it has taken the courts some time to reach this position. At common law a licence was always revocable at will, notwithstanding a contract to the contrary: *Wood v Leadbitter* (1845) 13 M & W 838. The remedy for a breach of the contract was only in damages. That was the view generally held until a few years ago: see, for instance, what was said in *Book v Palmer* [1942] 2 All ER 674, 677 and *Thompson v Park* [1944] KB 408, 410, [1944] 2 All ER 477, 479. The rule has, however, been altered owing to the interposition of equity. Law and equity have been fused for nearly 80 years, and since 1948 it has been clear that, as a result of the fusion, a licensor will not be permitted to eject a licensee in breach of a contract to allow him to remain: see *Winter Garden Theatre (London) Ltd v Millennium Productions Ltd* [1946] 1 All ER 678, 680, per Lord Greene, and in the House of Lords per Lord Simon, nor in breach of a promise on which the licensee has acted, even though he gave no value for it: see *Foster v Robinson* [1951] 1 KB 149, 156, where Sir

Raymond Evershed MR said that as a result of the oral arrangement to let the man stay, he was entitled as licensee to occupy the premises without any payment of rent for the rest of his days. This infusion of equity means that contractual licences now have a force and validity of their own and cannot be revoked in breach of the contract. Neither the licensor nor anyone who claims through him can disregard the contract except a purchaser for value, without notice."

It is not in doubt that the actual decision was correct. It could be justified on one of three grounds. (i) There was a contract to convey the house on completion of the payments giving rise to an equitable interest in the form of an estate contract which would be binding on the widow: see *Megarry & Wade, The Law of Real Property* 5th ed. (1984), p. 806. The widow was not a purchaser for value. (ii) The daughter-in-law had changed her position in reliance upon a representation binding on the widow as a privy of the representor: see *Spencer Bower and Turner, Estoppel by Representation*, 3rd ed. (1977), p. 123. (iii) The payment of the instalments by the son or the daughter-in-law gave rise to direct proprietary interests by way of constructive trust, though it is true that, until *Gissing v Gissing* [1971] AC 886, the law relating to constructive trusts in this field was not much considered.

Accordingly, it does not appear to have been necessary, in order to produce a just result, to have accepted the broad principle stated, at p. 299, in the passage which we have quoted, that "Neither the licensor nor anyone who claims through him can disregard the contract except a purchaser for value without notice." That statement itself is not supported by any citation of authority, and indeed we do not think it could have been supported on the authorities. None of the cases prior to *Errington v Errington and Woods* to which we have referred, except *Thomas v Sorrell*, is mentioned in the judgments and it does not appear that any was cited.

[His Lordship referred to *Winter Gardens Theatre (London) Ltd v Millennium Productions Ltd* [1948] AC 173, [1947] 2 All ER 331; *National Provincial Bank Ltd v Ainsworth* [1965] AC 1175, [1965] 2 All ER 472; *Re Solomon* [1967] Ch 573, [1966] 3 All ER 255 and continued:]

It must, we think, be very doubtful whether this court's decision in *Errington v Errington and Woods* is consistent with its earlier decisions in *Daly v Edwardes* 83 LT 548; *Frank Warr & Co v LCC* [1904] 1 KB 713 and *Clore v Theatrical Properties Ltd* [1936] 3 All ER 483. That decision cannot be said to be in conflict with any later decision of the House of Lords, because the House expressly left the effect of a contractual licence open in the *Hastings Car Mart* case. But there must be very real doubts whether *Errington* can be reconciled with the earlier decisions of the House of Lords in *Edwardes v Barrington* 85 LT 650, and *King v David Allen & Sons (Billposting) Ltd* [1916] 2 AC 54. It would seem that we must follow those cases or choose between the two lines of authority. It is not, however, necessary to consider those alternative courses in detail, since in our judgment the House of Lords cases, whether or not as a matter of strict precedent they conclude this question, state the correct principle which we should follow.

Our reasons for reaching this conclusion are based upon essentially the same reasons as those given by Russell LJ in the *Hastings Car Mart* case [1964] Ch 665, 697 [1964] 1 All ER 688, 701, 702, and by Professor Wade in the article, "Licences and Third Parties" (1952) 68 LQR 337, to which Russell LJ refers. Before *Errington* the law appears to have been clear and well understood. It rested on an important and intelligible distinction between contractual obligations which gave rise to no estate or interest in the land and proprietary rights which, by definition, did. The far-reaching statement of principle in *Errington* was not supported by authority, not necessary for the decision of the case and per incuriam in the sense that it was made without reference to authorities which, if they would not have compelled, would surely have persuaded the court to adopt a different ratio. Of course, the law must be free to develop. But as a response to problems which had arisen, the *Errington* rule (without more) was neither practically necessary nor theoretically convincing. By contrast, the finding on appropriate facts of a constructive trust may well be regarded as a beneficial adaptation of old rules to new situations.' [12]

QUESTIONS

Should contractual licences be interests in land? (1953) 16 MLR 1 (G. C. Cheshire); (1952) 16 Conv (NS) 323 (F. R. Crane); (1953) 17 Conv (NS) 440 (L. A. Sheridan); (1984) 100 LQR 376 (S. Moriarty) and articles on p. 612, n 9; Dawson and Pearce, chap. 11; Smith, pp. 468–471.

IV. Constructive Trusts [13]

Before dealing with the major topic of licences by estoppel, it will be useful to refer to the doctrine of the constructive trust in favour of the licensee. Equity finds a constructive trust, in various circumstances, on the principle of unjust enrichment. In the present context, the finding of a constructive trust in favour of the licensee creates an equitable interest in his favour. This solution has sometimes been too readily applied; without appreciating the conveyancing problems which follow. This development stems back to *Bannister v Bannister* [1948] 2 All ER 133, where the facts provided a compelling situation for the protection of an old lady who had no proprietary interest in the premises. This was before the doctrine of promissory estoppel in *Central London Property Trust Ltd v High Trees House Ltd* [1947] KB 130, [1956] 1 All ER 256n had been widely recognised, and before licensees were protected on the ground of estoppel. The advantage of an estoppel theory is that, as will be seen, the court has available to it a much wider choice of remedy. *Bannister v Bannister* would probably be so treated at the present day. [14]

A. Purchaser Taking Subject to Licensee's Right

BANNISTER v BANNISTER
[1948] 2 All ER 133 (CA, SCOTT and ASQUITH LJJ and JENKINS J)

The defendant was the owner of two cottages, Nos. 30 and 31. In 1943, she sold them to the plaintiff, her brother-in-law, for £250 (£150 below the market price) under an oral arrangement by which the brother-in-law would 'let you stay [in

---

[12] P. 618, post.
[13] C & B, pp. 647–649; Smith, pp. 471–473. On constructive trusts generally, see Gray, pp. 735–753; H & M, chap. 12; Underhill, chap. 7; M & B, *Trusts and Trustees* (6th edn., 2002), chap. 7; Oakley, *Constructive Trusts* (3rd edn., 1997), chap 11; Elias, *Explaining Constructive Trusts*.
[14] (1977) 93 LQR 561 (J. A. Hornby); [1980] Conv 250; *Binions v Evans* [1972] Ch 359, [1972] 2 All ER 70, p. 617, post; *DHN Food Distributors Ltd v Tower Hamlets London Borough Council* [1976] 1 WLR 852, [1976] 3 All ER 462, p. 683, post; *Re Sharpe* [1980] 1 WLR 219, [1980] 1 All ER 198, p. 681, post.

No. 30] as long as you like, rent free'. No mention of this arrangement was made in the conveyance. The defendant lived in the cottage until 1945 when she gave up possession of all except one downstairs room. In 1947, the plaintiff claimed possession of that, on the ground that she was a tenant at will only.

Held. The defendant was entitled to a life interest determinable upon her ceasing to reside in the cottage under a constructive trust created by the oral agreement.

SCOTT LJ: It is, we think, clearly a mistake to suppose that the equitable principle on which a constructive trust is raised against a person who insists on the absolute character of a conveyance to himself for the purpose of defeating a beneficial interest, which, according to the true bargain, was to belong to another, is confined to cases in which the conveyance itself was fraudulently obtained. The fraud which brings the principle into play arises as soon as the absolute character of the conveyance is set up for the purpose of defeating the beneficial interest, and that is the fraud to cover which the Statute of Frauds or the corresponding provisions of the Law of Property Act, 1925, cannot be called in aid in cases in which no written evidence of the real bargain is available. Nor is it, in our opinion, necessary that the bargain on which the absolute conveyance is made should include any express stipulation that the grantee is in so many words to hold as trustee. It is enough that the bargain should have included a stipulation under which some sufficiently defined beneficial interest in the property was to be taken by another. The above propositions are, we think, clearly borne out by the cases to which we were referred of *Booth v Turle* (1873) LR 16 Eq 182, *Chattock v Muller* (1878) 8 ChD 177, *Re Duke of Marlborough* [1894] 2 Ch 133, and *Rochefoucauld v Boustead* [1897] 1 Ch 196.

We see no distinction in principle between a case in which property is conveyed to a purchaser on terms that the entire beneficial interest in some part of it is to be retained by the vendor (as in *Booth v Turle*) and a case, like the present, in which property is conveyed to a purchaser on terms that a limited beneficial interest in some part of it is to be retained by the vendor. We are, accordingly, of opinion that the third ground of objection to the learned county court judge's conclusion also fails. His finding that there was no fraud in the case cannot be taken as meaning that it was not fraudulent in the plaintiff to insist on the absolute character of the conveyance for the purpose of defeating the beneficial interest which he had agreed the defendant should retain. The conclusion that the plaintiff was fraudulent, in this sense, necessarily follows from the facts found, and, as indicated above, the fact that he may have been innocent of any fraudulent intent in taking the conveyance in absolute form is for this purpose immaterial. ... The plaintiff holds No. 30 in trust during the life of the defendant to permit the defendant to occupy the same for so long as she may desire to do so, and subject thereto in trust for the plaintiff. A trust in this form has the effect of making the beneficiary a tenant for life within the meaning of the Settled Land Act, 1925. [15]

---

[15]   See now TLATA 1996, s. 2, p. 267, ante, p. 673, post.

B. Third Parties Taking Expressly Subject to Licensee's Right

BINIONS v EVANS [16]

[1972] Ch 359, [1972] 2 All ER 70 (CA, Lord DENNING MR, MEGAW and STEPHENSON LJJ)

The trustees of the Tredegar Estate in Monmouthshire and South Wales entered into an agreement with Mrs. Evans, the 79 year old widow of an employee of the Estate. The trustees agreed to permit her to reside in and occupy a cottage on the estate for the remainder of her life as tenant at will rent free. She agreed to keep it in a proper manner and 'personally occupy and live in it as a private residence only and not assign, sub-let or part with the possession' of it. Two years later the trustees sold the cottage to the plaintiffs expressly subject to Mrs. Evans's tenancy agreement, a copy of which was handed to the purchasers. Six months later the plaintiffs gave Mrs. Evans notice to quit as a mere tenant at will and claimed possession of the cottage.

Held. Order for possession refused. Per MEGAW and STEPHENSON LJJ: Mrs. Evans was tenant for life under the Settled Land Act 1925. [17]

LORD DENNING MR (having held that Mrs. Evans was not a tenant at will, nor a lessee nor a tenant for life under the Settled Land Act):

Suppose, however, that the defendant did not have an equitable interest at the outset, nevertheless it is quite plain that she obtained one afterwards when the Tredegar Estate sold the cottage. They stipulated with the plaintiffs that they were to take the house 'subject to' the defendant's rights under the agreement. They supplied the plaintiffs with a copy of the contract: and the plaintiffs paid less because of her right to stay there. In these circumstances, this court will impose on the plaintiffs a constructive trust for her benefit: for the simple reason that it would be utterly inequitable for the plaintiffs to turn the defendant out contrary to the stipulation subject to which they took the premises. That seems to me clear from the important decision of *Bannister v Bannister* [1948] 2 All ER 133, p. 615, ante, which was applied by the judge, and which I gladly follow.

The imposing of a constructive trust is entirely in accord with the precepts of equity. As Cardozo J once put it: 'A constructive trust is the formula through which the conscience of equity finds expression,' see *Beatty v Guggenheim Exploration Co* 225 NY 380, 386 (1919): or, as Lord Diplock put it quite recently in *Gissing v Gissing* [1971] AC 886 at 905, [1970] 2 All ER 780 at 790, a constructive trust is created 'whenever the trustee has so conducted himself that it would be inequitable to allow him to deny to the cestui que trust a beneficial interest in the land acquired'.

I know that there are some who have doubted whether a contractual licensee has any protection against a purchaser, even one who takes with full notice. We were referred in this connection to Professor Wade's article Licences and Third Parties in (1952) 68 LQR 337, and to the judgment of Goff J in *Re Solomon* [1967] Ch 573, [1966] 3 All ER 255. None of these doubts can prevail, however, when the situation gives rise to a constructive trust. Whenever the owner sells the land to a purchaser, and at the same time stipulates that he shall take it 'subject to' a contractual licence, I think it plain that a court of equity will impose on the purchaser a constructive trust in favour of the beneficiary. ...

---

[16]   (1972) 88 LQR 336 (P.V.B.); (1972) 36 Conv (NS) 266 (J. Martin); 277 (D. J. Hayton); [1973] CLJ 123 (R. J. Smith); (1973) 117 SJ 23 (B. W. Harvey); (1977) 93 LQR 561 (J. A. Hornby).

[17]   See p. 673, post.

In my opinion the defendant, by virtue of the agreement, had an equitable interest in the cottage which the court would protect by granting an injunction against the landlords restraining them from turning her out. When the landlords sold the cottage to a purchaser 'subject to' her rights under the agreement, the purchaser took the cottage on a constructive trust to permit the defendant to reside there during her life, or as long as she might desire. The courts will not allow the purchaser to go back on that trust. I entirely agree with the judgment of Judge Bulger. I would dismiss this appeal.

STEPHENSON LJ: Apart from authority, I would not have thought that such an interest could be understood to amount to a tenancy for life within the meaning of the Settled Land Act 1925, and I would have thought that the other terms of her tenancy (as I think it ought properly to be called) are inconsistent with a power to ask for the legal estate to be settled on her or to sell the cottage. But *Bannister v Bannister* is a clear decision of this court that such words as have been used in this agreement (excepting, I must concede, the words 'as tenant at will of them') create a life interest determinable (apart from the special considerations introduced by the Settled Land Act 1925) on the beneficiary ceasing to occupy the premises and the landlords hold the cottage on trust to permit her to occupy it 'during her life or as long as she lives,' as Judge Bulger held, and subject thereto in trust for them.

I therefore find it unnecessary to consider or decide the vexed questions (1) whether this agreement is or creates an irrevocable contractual licence to occupy, and (2) whether such a licence has been elevated to a status equivalent to an estate or interest in land by decisions of this court such as *Errington v Errington and Woods* [1952] 1 KB 290, [1952] 1 All ER 149 or *Foster v Robinson* [1951] 1 KB 149, [1950] 2 All ER 342 or still awaits legislation before it can so achieve transmissibility to subsequent purchasers with notice: see the rival views set out by Goff J in *Re Solomon* [1967] Ch 573 at 582–586, [1966] 3 All ER 255 at 259–262. [18]

In **Ashburn Anstalt v Arnold** [1989] Ch 1, [1988] 2 All ER 147, p. 612, ante. Fox LJ said at 22, at 164:

'The constructive trust principle, to which we now turn, has been long established and has proved to be highly flexible in practice. It covers a wide variety of cases from that of a trustee who makes a profit out of his trust or a stranger who knowingly deals with trust properties, to the many cases where the courts have held that a person who directly or indirectly contributes to the acquisition of a dwelling house purchased in the name of and conveyed to another has some beneficial interest in the property. The test, for the present purposes, is whether the owner of the property has so conducted himself that it would be inequitable to allow him to deny the claimant an interest in the property: see *Gissing v Gissing* [1971] AC 886, 905, [1970] 2 All ER 780, 790, per Lord Diplock.

[His Lordship referred to *Bannister v Bannister* [1948] 2 All ER 133, p. 560, ante; *Re Schebsman* [1944] Ch 83, [1943] 2 All ER 768 and *Binions v Evans* [1972] Ch 359, [1972] 2 All ER 70, p. 617, ante, and continued:]

---

[18]   MEGAW LJ also suggested at 371, at 78 that the plaintiffs would be guilty of the tort of interference with existing contractual rights if they were to evict the defendant; (1977) 41 Conv (NS) 318 (R. J. Smith).

[In *Binions v Evans* Lord Denning MR] held that the plaintiffs took the property subject to a constructive trust for the defendant's benefit. In our view that is a legitimate application of the doctrine of constructive trusts. The estate would certainly have allowed the defendant to live in the house during her life in accordance with their agreement with her. They provided the plaintiffs with a copy of the agreement they made. The agreement for sale was subject to the agreement, and they accepted a lower purchase price in consequence. In the circumstances it was a proper inference that on the sale to the plaintiffs, the intention of the estate and the plaintiffs was that the plaintiffs should give effect to the tenancy agreement. If they had failed to do so, the estate would have been liable in damages to the defendant.

[His Lordship referred to *DHN Food Distributors Ltd v Tower Hamlets Borough Council* [1976] 1 WLR 852, [1976] 3 All ER 462; *Re Sharpe* [1980] 1 WLR 219, [1980] 1 All ER 198, p. 611, post; *Lyus v Prowsa Developments Ltd* [1982] 1 WLR 1044, [1982] 2 All ER 952, p. 176, ante, and continued:]

We come to the present case. It is said that when a person sells land and stipulates that the sale should be "subject to" a contractual licence, the court will impose a constructive trust upon the purchaser to give effect to the licence: see *Binions v Evans* [1972] Ch 359, 368, [1972] 2 All ER 70, 76, per Lord Denning MR. We do not feel able to accept that as a general proposition. We agree with the observations of Dillon J in *Lyus v Prowsa Developments Ltd* [1982] 1 WLR 1044, 1051, [1982] 2 All ER 953, 960.

By contrast, there are many cases in which land is expressly conveyed subject to possible incumbrances when there is no thought at all of conferring any fresh rights on third parties who may be entitled to the benefit of the incumbrances. The land is expressed to be sold subject to incumbrances to satisfy the vendor's duty to disclose all possible incumbrances known to him, and to protect the vendor against any possible claim by the purchaser ... So, for instance, land may be contracted to be sold and may be expressed to be conveyed subject to the restrictive covenants contained in a conveyance some 60 or 90 years old. No one would suggest that by accepting such a form of contract or conveyance a purchaser is assuming a new liability in favour of third parties to observe the covenants if there was for any reason before the contract or conveyance no one who could make out a title as against the purchaser to the benefit of the covenants.

The court will not impose a constructive trust unless it is satisfied that the conscience of the estate owner is affected. The mere fact that that land is expressed to be conveyed "subject to" a contract does not necessarily imply that the grantee is to be under an obligation, not otherwise existing, to give effect to the provisions of the contract. The fact that the conveyance is expressed to be subject to the contract may often, for the reasons indicated by Dillon J, be at least as consistent with an intention merely to protect the grantor against claims by the grantee as an intention to impose an obligation on the grantee. The words "subject to"'will, of course, impose notice. But notice is not enough to impose on somebody an obligation to give effect to a contract into which he did not enter. Thus, mere notice of a restrictive covenant is not enough to impose upon the estate owner an obligation or equity to give effect to it: *LCC v Allen* [1914] 3 KB 642, p. 943, post.

The material facts in the present case are as follows. (i) There is no finding that the plaintiff paid a lower price in consequence of the provision that the sale was subject to the 1973 agreement. (ii) The 1973 agreement was not contractually enforceable against Legal & General, which was not, therefore, exposed to the risk of any contractual claim for damages if the agreement was not complied with.

The 1973 agreement was enforceable against Cavendish and it seems that in 1973 Cavendish was owned by Legal & General. There is no finding as to the relationship between Cavendish and Legal & General in August 1985, when Legal & General sold to the plaintiff. And there is no evidence before the deputy judge as to the circumstances or the arrangements attending the transfer by Cavendish to Legal & General. (iii) Whilst the letter of 7 February 1985 is not precisely worded, it seems that Legal & General was itself prepared to give effect to the 1973 agreement.

In matters relating to the title to land, certainty is of prime importance. We do not think it desirable that constructive trusts of land should be imposed in reliance on inferences from slender materials. In our opinion the available evidence in the present case is insufficient. The deputy judge, while he did not have to decide the matter, was not disposed to infer a constructive trust, and we agree with him.' [19]

In **IDC Group Ltd v Clark** [1992] 1 EGLR 187, [20] Sir Nicolas Browne-Wilkinson V-C, in holding that an agreement for the provision of a fire-escape route through a door in a party wall into the interior of an adjacent flat was not enforceable against a third party, said at 189:

'[In *Ashburn Anstalt v Arnold* [1989] Ch 1, [1988] 2 All ER 147, p. 612, ante] the Court of Appeal put what I hope is the *quietus* to the heresy that a mere licence creates an interest in land. They also put the *quietus* to the heresy that parties to a contractual licence necessarily become constructive trustees. They also held (at p. 25 D–E) that the mere fact that property is sold subject to a contractual licence is not sufficient to create a constructive trust. They held (at p. 26A) that the mere fact that somebody has purchased with notice of a claim does not give rise to a constructive trust. ...

The result, as it seems to me, is that in the normal case a conveyance of land subject to or with notice of prior incumbrances or prior interests will not operate so as to make enforceable under a constructive trust such prior incumbrances or interests which would otherwise be unenforceable. However, in certain circumstances equity raises a constructive trust because it is unconscionable for the person having received such property not to give effect to the terms on which he received it. As the Court of Appeal said, and with respect I would agree, at p. 26E:

'In matters relating to the title to land certainty is of prime importance. We do not think it desirable that constructive trusts of land should be imposed in reliance on inferences from slender materials.'

It is important always to bear in mind that it is of the greatest importance that the title to land should be capable of being ascertained in accordance with well-known procedures. To raise constructive trusts which do not fit into the conveyancing machinery currently operating, thereby giving rise to liabilities of which purchasers might otherwise not be aware, is a dangerous course to pursue.

In my judgment, the decision in *Ashburn Anstalt* does not warrant the creation of a constructive trust unless there are very special circumstances showing that the transferee of the property undertook a new liability to give effect to provisions

---

[19]   *Sparkes v Smart* [1990] 2 EGLR 245 (collusive transaction between purchaser of freehold farm and ageing tenant, purchaser's father-in-law, with object of destroying youngest son's tenancy; CA held obiter constructive trust in favour of the son).

[20]   The decision was upheld by CA [1992] 2 EGLR 184.

for the benefit of third parties. It is the conscience of the transferee which has to be affected and it has to be affected in a way which gives rise to an obligation to meet the legitimate expectations of the third party.'

In **Lloyd v Dugdale** [2002] 2 P & CR 167, Sir Christopher SLADE summarised the law at para. 52:

'The relevant principles to be extracted from the authorities may for present purposes be summarised as follows:

(1) Even in a case where, on a sale of land, the vendor has stipulated that the sale shall be subject to stated possible incumbrances or prior interests, there is no general rule that the court will impose a constructive trust on the purchaser to give effect to them. In *Ashburn and Anstalt v Arnold* at page 25E, Fox LJ, delivering the judgment of the Court, expressed agreement with the following observations of Dillon J in *Lyus v Prowsa Development Ltd* at page 1051:

"By contrast, there are many cases in which land is expressly conveyed subject to possible incumbrances when there is no thought at all of conferring any fresh rights on third parties who may be entitled to the benefit of the incumbrances. The land is expressed to be sold subject to incumbrances to satisfy the vendor's duty to disclose all possible incumbrances known to him, and to protect the vendor against any possible claim by the purchaser ... So, for instance, land may be contracted to be sold and may be expressed to be conveyed subject to the restrictive covenants contained in a conveyance some 60 or 90 years old. No one would suggest that by accepting such a form of contract or conveyance a purchaser is assuming a new liability in favour of third parties to observe the covenants if there was for any reason before the contract or conveyance no one who could make out a title as against the purchaser to the benefit of the covenants."

(2) The court will not impose a constructive trust in such circumstances unless it is satisfied that the conscience of the estate owner is affected so that it would be inequitable to allow him to deny the claimant an interest in the property: (see *Ashburn Anstalt v Arnold* at pages 22E–F and 25H).

(3) In deciding whether or not the conscience of the new estate owner is affected in such circumstances, the crucially important question is whether he has undertaken a new obligation, not otherwise existing, to give effect to the relevant incumbrance or prior interest. If, but only if, he has undertaken such a new obligation will a constructive trust be imposed. The importance of this point was repeatedly stressed in *Ashburn Anstalt v Arnold*: see, for example, at pages 23G, 25A–26A, and 27B. See also *Lyus v Prowsa Development Ltd* at page 1051; *IDC Group Ltd v Clark* (1992) 1 EGLR at page 190B–C; *Melbury Road Properties 1995 Ltd v Kreidi* [1999] 3 EGLR 108 at page 110G.

(4) Notwithstanding some previous authority suggesting the contrary, a contractual licence is not to be treated as creating a proprietary interest in land so as to bind third parties who acquire the land with notice of it, on this account alone: see *Ashburn Anstalt v Arnold (supra)* at pages 15H and 24D.

(5) Proof that the purchase price by a transferee has been reduced upon the footing that he would give effect to the relevant incumbrance or prior interest may provide some indication that the transferee has undertaken a new obligation to give effect to it: see *Ashburn Anstalt v Arnold (supra)* at page 23F–G. However, since in matters relating to the title to land certainty is of prime

importance, it is not desirable that constructive trusts of land should be imposed in reliance on inferences from "slender materials"; [1999] 2 EGLR 108, at page 26E.'

V. Licences by Estoppel [2]

The doctrine of estoppel, which is of general application at law and in equity, has played a significant part in the modern development of the law of licences. The basic principle of the doctrine is that a person who makes, by words or conduct, a representation to another, intending that other to act on it, and the other does so to his detriment, [3] will not be allowed subsequently to take a position inconsistently with the representation. At common law, the representation had to be one of existing fact. [4] The estoppel acted as a rule of evidence. The representor could not subsequently allege, in dealings with the representee, that the facts were different from those represented. The estoppel did not however give rise to any independent cause of action.

The doctrine widened in equity so as to cover a representation, not only of fact, but of intention, or a promise. This is promissory estoppel; which became well known through *Central London Property Trust Ltd v High Trees House Ltd* [1947] KB 130, [1956] 1 All ER 256n, and was firmly established in later years. Promissory estoppel also gives negative protection only, and is not a cause of action. [5]

The last half of the twentieth century saw a remarkable growth, in the context of licences, of a different, but related doctrine: called proprietary estoppel. The doctrine deals with the equities arising out of a situation in which one party (O) knowingly encourages another (A) to act, or acquiesces in his acting to his detriment and in infringement of O's rights, so that it would be unconscionable for O to insist on his strict legal rights. O will be unable to complain later of the infringement; and may indeed be required to make good A's expectations in respect of the rights exercised. Thus, unlike other estoppels, this doctrine may create a claim, and an entitlement to property rights in or over land. [6] Authoritative statements laying down the requirements for the operation of the doctrine appear below.

[2]   C & B, pp. 649–663; Gray, pp. 753–818; ;M & W, paras. 13.001–13.037; MM, pp. 69, 483–489; Smith, chap. 9; Cooke, *The Modern Law of Estoppel* (2000); Pawlowski, *The Doctrine of Proprietary Estoppel* (1996); Spencer Bower and Turner, *Estoppel by Representation* (4th edn., 2004) passim, and especially chap. 12; Wilken and Villiers, *The Law of Waiver, Variation and Estoppel* (2nd edn, 2002), chap. 11; Dawson and Pearce, pp. 29–36, 97–99, 144–145, 161–163; Snell, chap. 39; [1981] Conv 347 (P. N. Todd); [1981] Conv 118 at pp. 125–132 (A. R. Everton); (1984) 100 LQR 376 (S. Moriarty); [1983] CLJ 257 (M. P. Thompson); [1986] 49 MLR 741 (J. Dewar); [1988] Conv 346 (P. T. Evans); [1991] Conv 36 (G. Battersby); [1994] 14 LS 147 (S. Baughen); (1995) 58 MLR 637 (G. Battersby); (1997) 17 LS 258 (E. Cooke); Sir Christopher SLADE, *The Informal Creation of Interests in Land* (1984) Child & Co Oxford Lecture; Finn, *Essays in Equity* (1985), pp. 59–94; J. Cartwright in Getzler ed. Rationalizing Property, Equity and Trusts, chap. 3; (2003) 11 STEP Journal 2 (Lord WALKER of GESTINGHORPE).

On the relationship between contractual and estoppel licences, see the controversy between [1981] Conv 212; [1983] Conv 285 (A. Briggs) and [1983] Conv 50, 471 (M. P. Thompson).

[3]   As by expenditure of money, or giving up present accommodation.

[4]   *Jorden v Money* (1854) 5 HL Cas 185.

[5]   *Combe v Combe* [1951] 2 KB 215, [1951] 1 All ER 767; *A-G of Hong Kong v Humphreys Estate (Queen's Gardens) Ltd* [1987] AC 114 at 121, [1987] 2 All ER 387 at 390.

[6]   *Western Fish Products Ltd v Penwith District Council* [1981] 2 All ER 204, p. 626, *post.*

These estoppel doctrines have been applied to many cases involving licences. The licence may be gratuitous or contractual. The categories of licences may therefore overlap. [7] If the licence is contractual, the licensee may be protected under the doctrines relating to contractual licences, discussed above; and it may be unnecessary to invoke the doctrine of estoppel. [8] Where, however, the licensee is seeking protection against a third party, a licence by estoppel is more effective. It will be seen that the courts appear to have these factors in mind in categorising licences.

Decisions to protect licensees of all kinds raise a number of difficulties. Some of these have been seen in the context of contractual licences. With licences by estoppel, the courts recognise their power and duty in these cases as being to 'look at the circumstances in each case to decide in what way the equity can be satisfied.' [9] The court may decide to protect the licensee by means of an injunction restraining the licensor from interfering; and in cases of estoppel by representation, this may be the only choice. [10] Such a solution produces conveyancing difficulties; for it leaves the licensee in possession with no title. His equity is good, not only against the licensor, but also against third parties other than a bona fide purchaser for value without notice. [11] In such a situation, it seems that, in the case of unregistered land, the licence not being registrable, we are thrown back on the hazards of notice. [12] With registered land, a licensee in occupation has an overriding interest, and may be able to acquire protection by entering a notice. [13]

The negative protection under the classical estoppel principle has advantages in situations where the time is not yet ripe for a final settlement; as where a licensee is protected in occupation which may only be temporary and something less than a permanent solution is required; as where a son builds a bungalow on his father's land in the expectation of being allowed to stay there for the rest of his life; [14] or parents give up a home and move in to look after an aged grandparent; [15] or a mistress requires a home until the children are of school age; [16] or a garage is built which overlaps a neighbour's

---

[7]   In *Hardwick v Johnson* [1978] 1 WLR 683, [1978] 2 All ER 935, p. 608, ante, the Court of Appeal divided 2–1 on the question of the type of licence. But that made no difference to the result. See also *Re Sharpe* [1980] 1 WLR 219 , [1980] 1 All ER 198, p. 681, post.

[8]   *Tanner v Tanner* [1975] 1 WLR 1346, [1975] 3 All ER 776, p. 600, ante.

[9]   *Plimmer v Wellington Corpn* (1884) 9 App Cas 699 at 714; *Chalmers v Pardoe* [1963] 1 WLR 677 at 682, [1963] 3 All ER 552 at 555; *Inwards v Baker* [1965] 2 QB 29 at 37, [1965] 1 All ER 446 at 449; *ER Ives Investment Ltd v High* [1967] 2 QB 379 at 395, [1967] 1 All ER 504 at 507, p. 665, post; *Crabb v Arun District Council* [1976] Ch 179 at 188, [1975] 3 All ER 865 at 871, p. 659, post.

[10]   Unless a constructive trust is found: *Bannister v Bannister* [1948] 2 All ER 133, p. 615, ante; *Hussey v Palmer* [1972] 1 WLR 1286, [1972] 3 All ER 744; *Re Sharpe*, supra.

[11]   *Hopgood v Brown* [1955] 1 WLR 213, [1955] 1 All ER 550.

[12]   Which may not be a serious problem if the licensee is in occupation; but could be if the licensee's rights were only exercisable periodically: (1956) 20 Conv (NS) 281 (R. H. Maudsley); Dawson and Pearce, p. 162.

[13]   LRA 2002, ss. 32, 116, p. 686, post; C & B, p. 663; Dawson and Pearce, pp. 194–200; (1995) 58 MLR 637 at pp. 640–653 (G. Battersby).

[14]   *Hopgood v Brown*, supra.

[15]   *Piquet v Tyler* [1978] CLY 119; *Dodsworth v Dodsworth* (1973) 228 EG 1115, p. 671, post; *Williams v Staite* [1979] Ch 291, [1978] 2 All ER 928; *Griffiths v Williams* (1977) 248 EG 947, p. 673, post.

[16]   *Tanner v Tanner*, supra (a contractual licence also; damages were awarded because the licensee had already been rehoused).

boundary; [17] or a housekeeper remains in a house looking after a family in the expectation of being allowed to stay there rent free for the rest of her life. [18]

In several cases, the court, applying the doctrine of proprietary estoppel, has found it best to declare that some interest is to be vested in the licensee. If the proper documentation follows, the conveyancing difficulties are avoided; but until that time, they exist as before; perhaps more acutely; for it is one thing for a purchaser to buy land which is subject to a licensee's temporary rights of protection; and another to find that he has taken title from a non-owner, or has bought settled land from someone other than the tenant for life. Some of these difficulties were not foreseen in the earlier cases; but the courts, as will be seen from the cases, have been aware of the problems, especially that of the application of the Settled Land Act 1925 [19] and have attempted to avoid them. [20] Under the Trusts of Land and Appointment of Trustees Act 1996, however, no new strict settlements can be created or arise after 1996. [1] This removes the need for the court to avoid a settlement arising where a right to occupy land for life is characterised as a life interest. [2] But the possibility of a settlement remains where the right has been created before 1997.

The court exercises wide discretionary powers in seeking the just solution. Negative protection may be hazardous and inadequate. A positive solution, ordering a transfer of the land to the licensee, may do injustice to the legal owner; as where a prior owner promised a gift, failed to make it, and a conveyance was ordered, without payment, by the successor owner. [3] The court has power to order a transfer, subject to payment by the licensee of the value of the site; or to order compensation to the licensee for his expenditure; and it may in some circumstances be best to give to the licensee the choice. This situation indeed 'displays equity at its most flexible'. [4] The court has to bear in mind the equities between the parties involved in all the circumstances; and also the effect of its order upon the conveyancing system. The extent to which these principles have been observed should be considered in the cases which follow.

In **Ramsden v Dyson** (1866) LR 1 HL 129, Lord KINGSDOWN in a dissenting speech, where however the difference of opinion was on the application of the principle to the facts, and not on the statement of the principle, said at 170:

'If a man, under a verbal agreement with a landlord for a certain interest in land, or, what amounts to the same thing, under an expectation, created or encouraged by the landlord, that he shall have a certain interest, takes possession of such land, with the consent of the landlord, and upon the faith of such promise or expectation, with the knowledge of the landlord,

---

17   *Hopgood v Brown*, supra.
18   *Greasley v Cooke* [1980] 1 WLR 1306 , [1980] 3 All ER 710, p. 643, post.
19   See (1977) 93 LQR 561 (J. A. Hornby); [1978] Conv 250; p. 326, n. 6, ante.
20   *Griffiths v Williams* (1977) 248 EG 947, p. 673, post.
1   S. 2, p. 267, ante.
2   P. 326, n. 6, ante.
3   *Dillwyn v Llewelyn* (1862) 4 De GF & J 517; *Pascoe v Turner* [1979] 1 WLR 431, [1979] 2 All ER 945, p. 667, post; *Voyce v Voyce* (1991) 62 P & CR 290, p. 667, n. 9, post; *Gillett v Holt* [2001] Ch 210, p. 637, post. See also *Sledmore v Dalby* (1996) 72 P & CR 196, p. 650, post
4   Snell, para. 39.18.

and without objection by him, lays out money upon the land, a court of equity will compel the landlord to give effect to such promise or expectation.'

In **Willmott v Barber** (1880) 15 ChD 96 at 105, p. 630, post, FRY J specified the detailed requirements in what have come to be called 'the five probanda', and nearly a century later SCARMAN LJ was listing them in *Crabb v Arun District Council* [1976] Ch 179 at 194–195, [1975] 3 All ER 865 at 876–877, p. 659, post.[5] FRY J said:

'A man is not to be deprived of his legal rights unless he has acted in such a way as would make it fraudulent for him to set up those rights. What, then, are the elements or requisites necessary to constitute fraud of that description? In the first place the plaintiff must have made a mistake as to his legal rights. Secondly, the plaintiff must have expended some money or must have done some act (not necessarily upon the defendant's land) on the faith of his mistaken belief. Thirdly, the defendant, the possessor of the legal right, must know of the existence of his own right which is inconsistent with the right claimed by the plaintiff. If he does not know of it he is in the same position as the plaintiff, and the doctrine of acquiescence is founded upon conduct with a knowledge of your legal rights. Fourthly, the defendant, the possessor of the legal right, must know of the plaintiff's mistaken belief of his rights. If he does not, there is nothing which calls upon him to assert his own rights. Lastly, the defendant, the possessor of the legal right, must have encouraged the plaintiff in his expenditure of money or in the other acts which he has done, either directly or by abstaining from asserting his legal right. Where all these elements exist, there is fraud of such a nature as will entitle the court to restrain the possessor of the legal right from exercising it, but, in my judgment, nothing short of this will do.'

In more recent years, however, the principle in *Ramsden v Dyson* has been expressed in much broader terms. In *Taylors Fashions Ltd v Liverpool Victoria Trustees Co Ltd* (1979) [1982] QB 133n, [1981] 1 All ER 897, OLIVER J said at 151, at 915:

'The more recent cases indicate, in my judgment, that the application of the *Ramsden v Dyson* principle — whether you call it proprietary estoppel, estoppel by acquiescence or estoppel by encouragement is really immaterial — requires a very much broader approach which is directed rather at ascertaining whether, in particular individual circumstances, it would be unconscionable for a party to be permitted to deny that which, knowingly, or unknowingly, he has allowed or encouraged another to assume to his detriment than to inquiring whether the circumstances can be fitted within

---

[5]   *E. and L. Berg Homes Ltd v Grey* (1979) 253 EG 473 (where the plaintiff failed because he was unable to satisfy the first and fifth requirements); *Crabb v Arun District Council* [1976] Ch 179, [1975] 3 All ER 865. See also the approval of the probanda in *Kammins Ballrooms Co Ltd v Zenith Investments (Torquay) Ltd* [1971] AC 850 at 884, [1970] 2 All ER 871 at 895, per Lord DIPLOCK, and their application in detail by Jonathan Parker QC in *Combes v Smith* [1986] 1 WLR 808; *Matharu v Matharu* (1994) 68 P & CR 93. See also *Gloucestershire County Council v Farrow* [1984] 1 WLR 262, [1983] 2 All ER 1031.

the confines of some preconceived formula serving as a universal yardstick for every form of unconscionable behaviour.'[6]

The effect of this approach is that the court now regards the five probanda no longer as rigid criteria to be satisfied, but as being 'guidelines, which will probably prove to be the necessary and essential guidelines, to assist the court to decide the question whether it is unconscionable for the plaintiffs to assert their legal rights by taking advantage of the defendant'.[7] OLIVER J had suggested at 146, at 911, that the five probanda might be necessary where the defendant has done no positive act, and merely 'stands by without protest'.

In **Western Fish Products v Penwith District Council** [1981] 2 All ER 204,[8] where MEGAW LJ said at 218:

'We know of no case, and none has been cited to us, in which the principle set out in *Ramsden v Dyson* and *Crabb v Arun District Council* has been applied otherwise than to rights and interests created in and over land. It may extend to other forms of property.[9] See Lord Denning MR in *Moorgate Mercantile Co Ltd v Twitchings* [1976] QB 225 at 242, [1975] 3 All ER 314 at 323. In our judgment there is no good reason for extending the principle further.'

In **Gillett v Holt** [2001] Ch 210, p. 637, post, ROBERT WALKER LJ followed the approach of OLIVER J and emphasised that unconscionable conduct underpins

---

[6]   Approved by OLIVER LJ in *Habib Bank Ltd v Habib Bank AG Zurich* [1981] 1 WLR 1265 at 1285, [1981] 2 All ER 650 at 666; (1981) 97 LQR 513; *Pridean Ltd v Forest Taverns Ltd* (1998) 75 P & CR 447. See also SCARMAN LJ in *Crabb v Arun District Council* [1976] Ch 179 at 194, [1975] 3 All ER 865 at 876, p. 659, post; MEGARRY V-C in *Appleby v Cowley* (1982) Times, 14 April, p. 614, post; ROBERT GOFF J in *Amalgamated Investment and Property Co Ltd v Texas Commerce International Bank Ltd* [1982] QB 84 at 103, [1981] 1 All ER 923 at 935; affd [1982] QB 84, [1981] 3 All ER 577; (1982) 79 LSG 662 (P. Matthews); *Esso Petroleum Co Ltd v Anthony Gibbs Financial Services Ltd* (1981) 262 EG 661; *Pacol Ltd v Trade Lines Ltd and R/I Sif IV* [1982] 1 Lloyd's Rep 456; *Waltons Stores (Interstate) Ltd v Maher* (1988) 62 ALJR 110; (1988) 104 LQR 362 (A. Duthie).

For recent illustrations of this broader approach by PC, see *Lim Teng Huan v Ang Swee Chuan* [1992] 1 WLR 113, p. 671, post; *Lloyds Bank plc v Carrick* [1996] 4 All ER 630; *Elitestone Ltd v Morris* (1995) 73 P & CR 259; cf. *Matharu v Matharu* (1994) 68 P & CR 93, where majority of CA somewhat liberally applied the five probanda; (1995) 58 MLR 412 (P. Milne); *Jones v Stones* [1999] 1 WLR 1739 (no acquiesence where delay in complaining about acts of trespass in using wall to place flower pots thereon and to support an oil tank).

For the close relationship of proprietary estoppel to restitutionary principles, see *Sledmore v Dalby* (1996) 72 P & CR 196 at 208, p. 650, post, per HOBHOUSE LJ. And for the relationship of estoppel to change of position, see *Philip Collins Ltd v Davis* [2000] 3 All ER 808; [2000] Conv 548 (M. P. Thompson). And for the availability of estoppel and constructive trust where s. 2 of LP (Miscellaneous Provisions) Act 1989 has not been complied with, see p. 70, ante.

[7]   *Swallow Securities Ltd v Isenberg* (1985) 274 EG 1028 at 1030, per CUMMING-BRUCE LJ (no evidence to induce in the defendant an expectation that she had legal rights more extensive than was in fact the case).

[8]   It was held not to apply where an owner spent money on his own land in the expectation encouraged by a local authority that he would acquire a planning permission.

[9]   *Re Foster* [1938] 3 All ER 610 (life insurance policy); *Re Basham* [1986] 1 WLR 1498, [1987] 1 All ER 405 (future property; representor's residuary estate); [1987] Conv 211 (J. E. Martin); [1987] CLJ 215 (D. J. Hayton); [1987] All ER Rev 156 (P. J. Clarke), 260 (C. H. Sherrin); (1988) 8 LS 92 (M. Davey); cf *Layton v Martin* [1986] 2 FLR 227 (offer of 'financial security' too vague).

all the elements of the doctrine. He said, at 225, that 'the doctrine of proprietary estoppel cannot be treated as subdivided into three or four watertight compartments. The fundamental principle that equity is concerned to prevent unconscionable conduct permeates all the elements of the doctrine. In the end the court must look at the matter in the round.'

A. Establishment of the Equity

i. GENERAL PRINCIPLES

TAYLORS FASHIONS LTD v LIVERPOOL VICTORIA TRUSTEES CO LTD
OLD & CAMPBELL LTD v LIVERPOOL VICTORIA FRIENDLY SOCIETY
[1982] QB 133n, [1981] 1 All ER 897 (ChD, OLIVER J)

The first plaintiffs (Taylors) sought to exercise an option to renew a lease, granted in 1948, of commercial premises at No 22 Westover Road, Bournemouth. The option had not been registered as a Class C(iv) Land Charge under the Land Charges Act 1925, and, following *Beesly v Hallwood Estates Ltd* [1960] 1 WLR 549, [1960] 2 All ER 314, p. 32, n. 10, ante, was void as against the defendants. The question was whether the defendants were estopped from asserting their strict legal rights against Taylors, who had spent some £12,000 on improving the premises, including the installation of a lift, in the expectation that the option would be enforceable. The defendants acquiesced in the works carried out by Taylors, and at the time did not suspect that they might have any reason for challenging the validity of the option. The fourth of FRY J's five probanda (see p. 625, ante) was therefore not fulfilled.

The second plaintiffs (Olds) had been granted a lease in 1949 of No 21 (adjacent to Taylors' premises), and a further lease in 1963 of No 20. The 1949 lease contained a clause permitting the defendants to determine that lease, if Taylors did not exercise their option in regard to No 22. The 1963 lease contained in Clause 4 an option enabling Olds to renew, if Taylors in fact exercised their option.

Held. Taylors were not entitled to obtain a renewal of their lease, but the defendants were estopped from denying that Olds were entitled to exercise their option.

OLIVER J: The points which arise for decision, therefore, are these. (1) Is Taylors' option, as the defendants claim and as the plaintiffs contest, void against the defendants for want of registration? (2) If it is, are the defendants estopped as against Taylors from relying upon this ground of invalidity having regard to the expenditure by Taylors made with the defendants' concurrence in 1959 and 1960? (3) If the option is indeed unenforceable against the defendants, has it nevertheless been 'exercised' for the purposes of the break and renewal clauses in the lease to Olds? (4) If it has not, are the defendants estopped as against Olds from relying upon the invalidity of an option which their own grants assert to be subsisting?

[His Lordship considered the first point, concluded that he must follow the decision of BUCKLEY J in *Beesly v Hallwood Estates Ltd* [1960] 1 WLR 549, [1960] 2 All ER 314, [10] and continued:]

---

[10] Approved by CA in *Phillips v Mobil Oil Co Ltd* [1989] 1 WLR 888, [1989] 3 All ER 97.

I approach the case, therefore, on the footing that, whatever the parties may have thought, the option was in fact void as against the defendants (although of course still contractually binding as between the original parties) from the moment when they completed their purchase. This brings me to the second and fourth questions which I have postulated above. As regards the general principles applicable I can treat the two questions together, although there are certain circumstances peculiar to Olds and some additional arguments of law in their case to which I shall have to refer later on. The starting point of both Mr Scott's and Mr Essayan's arguments on estoppel is the same and was expressed by Mr Essayan in the following proposition: if A under an expectation created or encouraged by B that A shall have a certain interest in land, thereafter, on the faith of such expectation and with the knowledge of B and without objection by him, acts to his detriment in connection with such land, a Court of Equity will compel B to give effect to such expectation. This is a formulation which Mr Millett accepts but subject to one important qualification, namely that at the time when he created and encouraged the expectation and (I think that he would also say) at the time when he permitted the detriment to be incurred (if those two points of time are different) B not only knows of A's expectation but must be aware of his true rights and that he was under no existing obligation to grant the interest.

This is the principal point upon which the parties divide. Mr Scott and Mr Essayan contend that what the court has to look at in relation to the party alleged to be estopped is only his conduct and its result, and not — or, at any rate, not necessarily — his state of mind. It then has to ask whether what that party is now seeking to do is unconscionable. Mr Millett contends that it is an essential feature of this particular equitable doctrine that the party alleged to be estopped must, before the assertion of his strict rights can be considered unconscionable, be aware both of what his strict rights were and of the fact that the other party is acting in the belief that they will not be enforced against him.

The point is a critical one in the instant case and it is one upon which the authorities appear at first sight to be divided. The starting point is *Ramsden v Dyson* (1866) LR 1 HL 129 where a tenant under a tenancy at will had built upon the land in the belief that he would be entitled to demand a long lease. The majority in the House of Lords held that he would not, but Lord Kingsdown dissented on the facts. There was no — or certainly no overt — disagreement between their Lordships as to the applicable principle, but it was stated differently by Lord Cranworth LC and Lord Kingsdown and the real question is how far Lord Cranworth was purporting to make an exhaustive exposition of principle and how far what he stated as the appropriate conditions for its application are to be treated, as it were, as being subsumed sub silentio in the speech of Lord Kingsdown. Lord Cranworth expressed it thus, at 140–141:

'If a stranger begins to build on my land supposing it to be his own, and I, perceiving his mistake, abstain from setting him right, and leave him to persevere in his error, a court of equity will not allow me afterwards to assert my title to the land on which he had expended money on the supposition that the land was his own. It considers that, when I saw the mistake into which he had fallen, it was my duty to be active and to state my adverse title; and that it would be dishonest in me to remain wilfully passive on such an occasion, in order afterwards to profit by the mistake which I might have prevented. But it will be observed that to raise such an equity two things are required, first, that the person expending the money supposes himself to be building on his own land; and, secondly, that the real owner at the time of the expenditure knows that the land belongs to him and not to the person expending the money in the belief that he is the owner.

For if a stranger builds on my land knowing it to be mine, there is no principle of equity which would prevent my claiming the land with the benefit of all the expenditure made on it. There would be nothing in my conduct, active or passive, making it inequitable in me to assert my legal rights.'

So here, clearly stated, is the criterion upon which Mr Millett relies. Lord Kingsdown stated the matter differently and rather more broadly although in the narrower context of landlord and tenant. He says, at 170:

'The rule of law applicable to the case appears to me to be this: If a man, under a verbal agreement with a landlord for a certain interest in land, or, what amounts to the same thing, under an expectation, created or encouraged by the landlord, that he shall have a certain interest, takes possession of such land, with the consent of the landlord, and upon the faith of such promise or expectation, with the knowledge of the landlord, and without objection by him, lays out money upon the land, a court of equity will compel the landlord to give effect to such promise or expectation. This was the principle of the decision in *Gregory v Mighell* (1811) 18 Ves 328, and as I conceive, is open to no doubt.'

So here, there is no specific requirement, at any rate in terms, that the landlord should know or intend that the expectation which he has created or encouraged is one to which he is under no obligation to give effect.

Mr Millet does not — nor could he in the light of the authorities — dispute the principle. What he contends is that even if (which he contests) this is a case where the defendants could be said to have encouraged the plaintiffs' expectations — and that it is not necessarily the same as having encouraged or acquiesced in the expenditure — the principle has no application to a case where, at the time when the expectation was encouraged, both parties were acting under a mistake of law as to their rights.

There is, he submits, a clear distinction between cases of proprietary estoppel or estoppel by acquiescence on the one hand and promissory estoppel or estoppel by representation (whether express or by conduct) on the other. In the latter case, the court looks at the knowledge of the party who has acted and the effect upon him of his having acted. The state of mind of the promissor or representor (except to the extent of knowing, either actually or inferentially, that his promise or representation is likely to be acted upon) is largely irrelevant. In the former case, however, it is essential, Mr Millett submits, to show that the party alleged to have encouraged or acquiesced in the other party's belief himself knew the true position, for if he did not there can be nothing unconscionable in his subsequently seeking to rely upon it. Mr Millett concedes that there may be cases which straddle this convenient dichotomy — cases which can be put either as cases of encouragement or proprietary estoppel on Lord Kingsdown's principle or as estoppel by representation, express or implied. But, he submits, the party alleging the estoppel must, whichever way he elects to put his case or even if he runs them as alternatives, demonstrate the presence of all the essential ingredients of whatever type of estoppel he relies on. He cannot manufacture a third and new hybrid type of estoppel by an eclectic application of some of the ingredients of each. So, if he wishes to put his case as one of estoppel by representation, he must, for instance, show an unequivocal representation of existing fact. Equally, if he wants to rely upon the circumstances of the case as raising a proprietary estoppel arising from acquiescence in his having acted upon an erroneous supposition of his legal rights, then he must accept the burden of showing that the error was known to the other party.

So far as proprietary estoppel or estoppel by acquiescence is concerned, he supports his submission by reference to the frequently cited judgment of Fry J in *Willmott v Barber* (1880) 15 ChD 96 p. 625, ante, which contains what are described as the five 'probanda'. The actual case was one where what was alleged was a waiver by acquiescence. A lease contained a covenant against assigning, subletting or parting with possession without the lessor's consent and the lessee had let a sublessee into possession of part of the land under an agreement with him which entitled him to occupy that part for the whole term and conferred an option to purchase the remaining land for the balance of the term outstanding when the option was exercised. The sublessee built on the land and the head landlord was aware that he was in possession and was expending money. It was, however, proved that he did not then know that his consent was required to a sub-letting or assignment. The question arose between the sublessee and the head landlord when the sublessee tried to exercise his option over the remaining land and found himself met with the response that the head landlord refused consent to the assignment. The case was, on Fry J's finding of fact, one simply of acquiescence by standing by and what was being argued was that the landlord was estopped by his knowledge of the plaintiff's expenditure on the part of the land of which the plaintiff *was* in possession from withholding his consent to an assignment of that part of which he was not. It having been found as a fact that the landlord did not, at the time of the plaintiff's expenditure, know about the covenant against assignment and that there was nothing in what had passed between them to suggest either that the landlord was aware that the plaintiff was labouring under the belief that no consent was necessary or to encourage that belief, Fry J dismissed the plaintiff's claim. It has to be borne in mind, however, in reading the judgment, that this was a pure acquiescence case where what was relied on was a waiver of the landlord's rights by standing by without protest. It was a case of mere silence where what had to be established by the plaintiff was some duty in the landlord to speak. The passage from the judgment in *Willmott v Barber* most frequently cited is where Fry J says, at 105–106:

[His Lordship cited the passage set out at p. 625, ante, and continued:]

Mr Millett's submission is that when one applies these five probanda to the facts of the instant case it will readily be seen that they are not all complied with. In particular, Mr Millett submits, the fourth probandum involves two essential elements, viz., (i) knowledge by the possessor of the legal right of the other party's belief; and (ii) knowledge that that belief is mistaken. In the instant case the defendants were not aware of their inconsistent right to treat the option as void and equally they could not, thus, have been aware that the plaintiff's belief in the validity of the option was a mistaken belief. The alternative approach via estoppel by representation is not, he submits, open to the plaintiffs in this case because so far as Taylors were concerned the defendants made no representation to them at all and so far as Olds were concerned the representation of the continuing validity of the option, if there was one at all, was a representation of law.

Now, convenient and attractive as I find Mr Millett's submissions as a matter of argument. I am not at all sure that so orderly and tidy a theory is really deducible from the authorities — certainly from the more recent authorities, which seem to me to support a much wider equitable jurisdiction to interfere in cases where the assertion of strict legal rights is found by the court to be unconscionable. It may well be (although I think that this must now be considered open to doubt) that the strict *Willmott v Barber* probanda are applicable as necessary requirements in those cases where all that has happened is that the party alleged to be estopped has stood by without protest while his rights have been infringed. It is suggested in *Spencer Bower and Turner, Estoppel by Representation*, 3rd edn. (1977), para. 290 that acquiescence, in its strict sense, is merely an instance of estoppel by representation and this derives some support from the judgment of the Court of Appeal in *De Bussche v Alt* (1878) 8 ChD 286 at 314. If that is a correct analysis then, in a case of mere passivity, it is readily intelligible that there must be shown a duty to speak, protest or interfere which cannot normally arise in the absence of knowledge or at least a suspicion of the true position. Thus for a landowner to stand by while a neighbour lays drains in land which the landowner does not believe that he owns (*Armstrong v Sheppard & Short Ltd* [1959] 2 QB 384, [1959] 2 All ER 651) or for a remainderman not to protest at a lease by a tenant for life which he believes he has no right to challenge (*Svenson v Payne* (1945) 71 CLR 531) does not create an estoppel. Again, where what is relied on is a waiver by acquiescence, as in *Willmott v Barber* itself, the five probanda are no doubt appropriate. There is, however, no doubt that there are judicial pronouncements of high authority which appear to support as essential the application of all the five probanda over the broader field covering all cases generally classified as estoppel by 'encouragement' or 'acquiescence': see, for instance, the speech of Lord Diplock in *Kammins Ballrooms Co Ltd v Zenith Investments (Torquay) Ltd* [1971] AC 850 at 884, [1970] 2 All ER 871 at 875.

Mr Scott submits, however, that it is historically wrong to treat these probanda as holy writ and to restrict equitable interference only to those cases which can be confined within the strait-jacket of some fixed rule governing the circumstances in which, and in which alone, the court will find that a party is behaving unconscionably. Whilst accepting that the five probanda may form an appropriate test in cases of silent acquiescence, he submits that the authorities do not support the absolute necessity for compliance with all five probanda, and, in particular, the requirement of knowledge on the part of the party estopped that the other party's belief is a mistaken belief, in cases where the conduct relied on has gone beyond mere silence and amounts to active encouragement. In Lord Kingsdown's example in *Ramsden v Dyson*, for instance, there is no room for the literal application of the probanda, for the circumstances there postulated do not presuppose a 'mistake' on anybody's part, but merely the fostering of an expectation in the minds of *both* parties at the time but from which, once it has been acted upon, it would be unconscionable to permit the landlord to depart. As Scarman LJ pointed out in *Crabb v Arun District Council* [1976] Ch 179, [1975] 3 All ER 865, the 'fraud' in these cases is not to be found in the transaction itself but in the subsequent attempt to go back upon the basic assumptions which underlay it.

[His Lordship considered *Stiles v Cowper* (1748) 3 At 692; *Jackson v Cator* (1800) 5 Ves 688; *Gregory v Mighell* (1811) 18 Ves 328; *Plimmer v Wellington Corpn* (1884) 9 App Cas 699, p. 659, post; *Sarat Chunder Dey v Gopal Chunder Laha* (1892) 19 LR Ind App 203; *Craine v Colonial Mutual Fire Insurance Co Ltd* (1920) 28 CLR 305; *Re Eaves* [1940] Ch 109, [1939] 4 All ER 260; *Hopgood v Brown* [1955] 1 WLR 213, [1955] 1 All ER 550; *Electrolux Ltd v Electric Ltd* (1953) 71 RPC 23, and continued:]

Furthermore the more recent cases indicate, in my judgment, that the application of the *Ramsden v Dyson* principle — whether you call it proprietary estoppel, estoppel by acquiescence or estoppel by encouragement is really immaterial — requires a very much broader approach which is directed rather at ascertaining whether, in particular individual circumstances, it would be unconscionable for a party to be permitted to deny that which, knowingly, or unknowingly, he has allowed or encouraged another to assume to his detriment than to inquiring whether the circumstances can be fitted within the confines of some preconceived formula serving as a universal yardstick for every form of unconscionable behaviour.

So regarded, knowledge of the true position by the party alleged to be estopped, becomes merely one of the relevant factors — it may even be a determining factor in certain cases — in the overall inquiry. This approach, so it seems to me, appears very clearly from the authorities to which I am about to refer. In *Inwards v Baker* [1965] 2 QB 29, [1965] 1 All ER 446, p. 654, post, there was no mistaken belief on either side. Each knew the state of the title, but the defendant had been led to expect that he would get an interest in the land on which he had built and, indeed, the overwhelming probability is that that was indeed the father's intention at the time. But it was not mere promissory estoppel, which could merely be used as a defence, for, as Lord Denning MR said, at 37, at 449, 'it is for the court to say in what way the equity can be satisfied.' The principle was expressed very broadly both by Lord Denning MR and by Danckwerts LJ. Lord Denning said at 37, at 449:

'But it seems to me, from *Plimmer's* case, 9 App Cas 699, 713–714 in particular, that the equity arising from the expenditure on land need not fail "merely on the ground that the interest to be secured has not been expressly indicated … the court must look at the circumstances in each case to decide in what way the equity can be satisfied." '

And a little further down he said:

'All that is necessary is that the licensee should, at the request or with the encouragement of the landlord, have spent the money in the expectation of being allowed to stay there. If so, the court will not allow that expectation to be defeated where it would be inequitable so to do.'

And Danckwerts LJ said, at 38, at 449:

'It seems to me that this is one of the cases of an equity created by estoppel, or equitable estoppel, as it is sometimes called, by which the person who has made the expenditure is induced by the expectation of obtaining protection, and equity protects him so that an injustice may not be perpetrated.'

An even more striking example is *ER Ives Investment Ltd v High* [1967] 2 QB 379, [1967] 1 All ER 504, p. 665, post. Here again, there does not appear to have been any question of the persons who had acquiesced in the defendant's expenditure having known that his belief that he had an enforceable right of way was mistaken. Indeed, at the stage when the expenditure took place, both sides seem to have shared the belief that the agreement between them created effective rights. Nevertheless the successor in title to the acquiescing party was held to be estopped. Lord Denning MR said, at 394–395, 507:

'The right arises out of the expense incurred by Mr High in building his garage, as it is now, with access only over the yard: and the Wrights standing by and acquiescing in it, knowing that he believed he had a right of way over the yard. By so doing the Wrights created in Mr High's mind a reasonable expectation that his access over the yard would not be disturbed. That gives rise to an "equity arising out of acquiescence." It is available not only against the Wrights but also their successors in title. The court will not allow that expectation to be defeated when it would be inequitable to do so. It is for the court in each case to decide in what way the equity can be satisfied …'

It should be mentioned that the Wrights themselves clearly also believed that Mr High had a right of way, because when they came to sell, they sold expressly subject to it. So, once again, there is an example of the doctrine of estoppel by acquiescence being applied without regard to the question of whether the acquiescing party knew that the belief of the other party in his supposed rights was erroneous.

Mr Scott and Mr Essayan have also drawn my attention to the Privy Council decision in *Bank Negara Indonesia v Hoalim* (1973) 2 MLJ 3 where again, it seems that the misconception of the legal position which gave rise to the assurance creating the estoppel seems to have been shared by both parties. This is, however, rather a case of promissory estoppel than of the application of the *Ramsden v Dyson* principle. More nearly in point is *Crabb v Arun District Council* [1976] Ch 179, [1975] 3 All ER 865, p. 659, post, where the plaintiff had altered his legal position in the expectation, encouraged by the defendants, that he would have a certain access to a road. Now there was no mistake here. Each party knew that the road was vested in the defendants and each knew that no formal grant had been made. Indeed I cannot see why in considering whether the defendants were behaving unconscionably, it should have made the slightest difference to the result if, at the time when the plaintiff was encouraged to open his access to the road, the defendants had thought that they were bound to grant it. The fact was that he had been encouraged to alter his position irrevocably to his detriment on the faith of a belief, which was known to and encouraged by the defendants, that he was going to be given a particular right of access — a belief which, for all that appears, the defendants probably shared at that time.

The particularly interesting features of the case in the context of the present dispute are, first, the virtual equation of promissory estoppel and proprietary estoppel or estoppel by acquiescence as mere facets of the same principle and secondly the very broad approach of both Lord Denning MR and Scarman LJ, both of whom emphasised the flexibility of the equitable doctrine. It is, however, worth noting that Scarman LJ adopted and applied the five probanda in *Willmott v Barber*, which he described as 'a valuable guide.' He considered that those probanda were satisfied and it is particularly relevant here to note again the fourth one — namely that the defendant, the possessor of the legal right, must know of the plaintiff's mistaken belief. If Scarman LJ had interpreted this as meaning — as Mr Millett submits that it does mean — that the defendant must know not only of the plaintiff's belief but also that it was mistaken, then he could not, I think, have come to the conclusion that this probandum was satisfied, for it seems clear from Lord Denning's recital of the facts that, up to the critical moment when the plaintiff acted, *both* parties thought that there *was* a firm assurance of access. The defendants had, indeed, even erected a gate at their own expense to give effect to it. What gave rise to the necessity for the court to intervene was the defendant's attempt to go back on this subsequently when they fell out with the plaintiff. I infer therefore that Scarman LJ must have construed this probandum in the sense which Mr Scott and Mr Essayan urge upon me, namely that the defendant must know merely of the plaintiff's belief which, in the event, turns out to be mistaken.

Finally, there ought to be mentioned the most recent reference to the five probanda which is to be found in *Shaw v Applegate* [1977] 1 WLR 970, [1978] 1 All ER 123. That was a case where the plea of estoppel by acquiescence failed on appeal, but it is significant that two members of the court expressed serious doubt whether it was necessary in every case of acquiescence to satisfy the five probanda. Buckley LJ said at 977–978, at 130:

'As I understand that passage' and there he is referring to the passage from the judgment of Fry J in *Willmott v Barber* to which I have already referred, 'what the judge is there saying is that where a man has got a legal right — as the plaintiffs have in the present case, being legal assignees of the benefit of the convenant binding the defendant — acquiescence on their part will not deprive them of that legal right unless it is of such a nature and in such circumstances that it would really be dishonest or unconscionable of the plaintiffs to set up that right after what was occurred. Whether in order to reach that stage of affairs it is really necessary to comply strictly with all five tests there set out by Fry J may, I think, still be open to doubt, although no doubt if all those five tests were satisfied there would be shown to be a state of affairs in which it would be dishonest or unconscionable for the owner of the right to insist upon it. In *Electrolux Ltd v Electric Ltd* (1953) 71 RPC 23 Sir Raymond Evershed MR said, at 33: "I confess that I have found some difficulty — or should find some difficulty if it were necessary to make up my mind and express a view whether all five requisites which Fry J stated in *Willmott v Barber* must be present in every case in which it is said that the plaintiff will be deprived of his right to succeed in an action on the ground of acquiescence. All cases (and this is a trite but useful observation to repeat) must be read in the light of the facts of the particular case." So I do not, as at present advised, think it is clear that it is essential to find all the five tests set out by Fry J literally applicable and satisfied in any particular case. The real test, I think, must be whether upon the facts of the particular case the situation has become such that it would be dishonest or unconscionable for the plaintiff, or the person having the right sought to be enforced, to continue to seek to enforce it.'

And Goff LJ referred again to the judgment in *Willmott v Barber* and said, at 980, at 132:

'But for my part, I share the doubt entertained by Sir Raymond Evershed MR in the *Electrolux* case, whether it is necessary in all cases to establish the five tests which are laid down by Fry J, and I agree that the test is whether, in the circumstances, it has become unconscionable for the plaintiff to rely upon his legal right.'

So here, once again, is the Court of Appeal asserting the broad test of whether in the circumstances the conduct complained of is unconscionable without the necessity of forcing those incumbrances[11] into a Procrustean bed constructed from some unalterable criteria.

The matter was expressed by Lord Denning MR in *Moorgate Mercantile Co Ltd v Twitchings* [1976] QB 225 at 241, [1975] 3 All ER 314 at 323 as follows:

'Estoppel is not a rule of evidence. It is not a cause of action. It is a principle of justice and of equity. It comes to this: when a man, by his words or conduct, has led another to believe in a particular state of affairs, he will not be allowed to go back on it when it would be unjust or inequitable for him to do so. Dixon J put it in these words: "The principle upon which estoppel in pais is founded is that the law should not permit an unjust departure by a party from an assumption of fact which he has caused another party to adopt or accept for the purpose of their legal relations." Sir Owen said so in 1937 in *Grundt v Great Boulder Proprietary Gold Mines Ltd* (1937) 59 CLR 641 at 674. In 1947 after the *High Trees* case (*Central London Property Trust Ltd v High Trees House Ltd* [1947] KB 130, [1956] 1 All ER 256n), I had some correspondence with Sir Owen about it: and I think I may say that he would not limit the principle to an assumption of fact, but would extend it, as I would, to include an assumption of fact or law, present or future. At any rate, it applies to an assumption of ownership or absence of ownership. This gives rise to what may be called proprietary estoppel. There are many cases where the true owner of goods or of land had led another to believe that he is not the owner,

---

11   Presumably circumstances is intended.

or, at any rate, is not claiming an interest therein, or that there is no objection to what the other is doing. In such cases it has been held repeatedly that the owner is not to be allowed to go back on what he has led the other to believe. So much so that his own title to the property, be it land or goods, has been held to be limited or extinguished, and new rights and interests have been created therein. And this operates by reason of his conduct — what he has led the other to believe — even though he never intended it.'

The inquiry which I have to make therefore, as it seems to me, is simply whether, in all the circumstances of this case, it was unconscionable for the defendants to seek to take advantage of the mistake which, at the material time, everybody shared, and, in approaching that, I must consider the cases of the two plaintiffs separately because it may be that quite different considerations apply to each.

So far as Taylors are concerned there seem to me to be two difficulties in counsel's way. In the first place, whilst it is, no doubt, true that at that time when the work of putting in the lift was commenced with the defendants' knowledge and co-operation — co-operation at least, to the extent of entering into discussions with regard to the siting of the lift — all parties shared the common belief that there was a valid and enforceable option, it is difficult to see how that belief had been in any way created or encouraged by the defendants. ... So far as acquiescence pure and simple is concerned the defendants could not lawfully object to the work and could be under no duty to Taylors to communicate that which they did not know themselves, namely that the non-registration of the option rendered it unenforceable. So far as encouragement is concerned, it is not in my judgment possible fairly to say that the mere presence of the defendants' representative at a site meeting 'encouraged' Taylors in their belief that the option was valid. No doubt it did nothing to discourage such a belief, but their representative would, I venture to think, have been present even if Taylors had already made up their minds that the option was not going to be exercised. ...

The second difficulty in Mr Scott's way seems to me to be this. The work which was carried out was work which was referable to the unexpired term which Taylors then held and was no doubt undertaken with a view to making the premises more attractive and convenient for customers of the business which, after all, was going to be carried on for another 18 years before any question of exercising the option even arose. By that time, the initial expense would long since have been written off by normal depreciation. Taylors believed that the option was a valid option — that is to say that they had, potentially, a longer term than they had in fact. But what is there to indicate that the work was undertaken 'on the faith of' that belief rather than merely 'in' that belief?

[His Lordship referred to Lord Eldon LC in *Dann v Spurrier* (1802) 7 Ves 231 at 235–236; and Lord Hardwicke LC in *A-G v Balliol College, Oxford* (1744) 9 Mod Rep 407 at 411, and continued:]

It is conceivable that Taylors might not have done the work, although I find it difficult to believe that they would have contemplated operating a ladies' store on three floors in a fashionable Bournemouth shopping centre for 18 years without the convenience of a lift. It is conceivable that, if they had known the true position, they might have sought to re-negotiate a fresh option with the defendants rather than rely upon their rights under the Landlord and Tenant Act 1954. But what Mr Taylor was unable to say was that they would not have done the work if they had not thought that option was available, much less that the defendants were or must have been aware that they would not have done it.

Whilst, therefore, it may not seem very admirable for the defendants to avail themselves of a technicality which runs counter to the common assumption entertained by all the parties to the transaction, that is what the law permits them to do; and I cannot find, in the circumstances of this case, and even given the flexibility of the equitable principles, that Taylors have discharged the burden of showing that it is dishonest or unconscionable for them to do so. I must, therefore, dismiss Taylors' claim for specific performance of the option, although I do so with some regret.

Turning now to the case of Olds, the position appears to me to be very different. ...

Mr Essayan puts his case ... upon the *Ramsden v Dyson* principle. Here Olds were encouraged by the defendants to alter their legal position irrevocably upon the faith of the belief or expectation, of which the defendants knew and which they themselves fostered by the terms of the lease, that they would be getting a term which was to be cut down only upon a particular supposition, namely that Taylors would be either unwilling or would disentitle themselves from exercising their option.

But it is, I think, unnecessary for Mr Essayan to rely solely upon the transaction in 1949. The 1963 transaction presents an even clearer picture, because Olds were encouraged by the defendants to expend a very large sum on the premises and to take a lease of the adjoining premises, upon the faith of the expectation, encouraged by the defendants that they would be entitled to renew in a particular event which, whether it was probable or not, Olds were at least invited to believe was possible. That they acted upon that supposition cannot I think be doubted. One has only to refer to Mr Old's statement in the correspondence leading up to the lease that 'this is no 14-year project.' Nor, equally, can it be doubted that the defendants were aware of, and indeed, shared that supposition. Again, I do not think that it really matters whether the case is put as one of estoppel by acquiescence or of estoppel by representation. Clause 4 of the 1963 lease, in its entirety, is without sense except on the footing that the reference to the tenants of the neighbouring premises known as no. 22 Westover Road exercising 'their option to have granted to them by the landlords,' i.e., by the defendants, 'a further term' is construed as a reference to an option between those tenants and the defendants subsisting and still capable of being exercised at the date of the lease. On any other footing the clause never could have any sphere of operation at all. ...

It would, in my judgment, be most inequitable that the defendants, having put forward Taylors' option as a valid option in two documents, under each of which they are the grantors, and having encouraged Olds to incur expenditure and to alter their position irrevocably by taking additional premises on the faith of that supposition, should now be permitted to resile and to assert, as they do, that they are and were all along entitled to frustrate the expectation which they themselves created and that the right which they themselves stated to exist did not, at any material time, have any existence in fact. ...

In the result, therefore, the claim of Taylors for specific performance must be dismissed and there will be in favour of Olds a declaration as regards the non-operation of the break clause in the 1949 lease and a decree of specific performance of the renewal option in the 1963 lease.

GILLETT v HOLT

[2001] Ch 210, [2000] 2 All ER 289 (CA, BELDAM, WALLER and ROBERT WALKER LJJ) [12]

Holt, a wealthy landowner, farmed land near Horncastle in Lincolnshire. Gillett, whom he had persuaded to leave school and to farm instead, was Holt's friend and farm manager for some 40 years. Holt made repeated promises and assurances, usually on special family occasions, that Gillett and his family would inherit the farm business, including The Beeches, the house in which they had been living for the past 25 years. He made a will to that effect. After 1992 relations between Holt and Gillett deteriorated when Holt formed a friendship with Wood, a trainee solicitor. In 1995 Holt dismissed Gillett and changed his will in favour of Wood.

Held: Gillett granted equitable relief based on proprietary estoppel.

ROBERT WALKER LJ: This judgment considers the relevant principles of law, and the judge's application of them to the facts which he found, in much the same order as the appellant's notice of appeal and skeleton argument. But although the judgment is, for convenience, divided into several sections with headings which give a rough indication of the subject matter, it is important to note at the outset that the doctrine of proprietary estoppel cannot be treated as subdivided into three or four watertight compartments. Both sides are agreed on that, and in the course of the oral argument in this court it repeatedly became apparent that the quality of the relevant assurances may influence the issue of reliance, that reliance and detriment are often intertwined, and that whether there is a distinct need for a 'mutual understanding' may depend on how the other elements are formulated and understood. Moreover the fundamental principle that equity is concerned to prevent unconscionable conduct permeates all the elements of the doctrine. In the end the court must look at the matter in the round.

In his discussion of the law the judge took as his starting point the decision of Mr Edward Nugee QC in *Re Basham* [1986] 1 WLR 1498, [1987] 1 All ER 405. [13] In that case the claimant and her husband had helped her mother and her stepfather in all sorts of ways throughout the claimant's adult life. She received no remuneration but understood that she would inherit her stepfather's property when he died. After her mother's death in 1976, and until her stepfather's death in 1982, she and her husband lived near the cottage to which her stepfather had moved (but never lived in the cottage). The claimant was told by her stepfather that 'she would lose nothing' by her help and (a few days before his death) that she was to have the cottage. The deputy judge held that she was entitled, by proprietary estoppel, to the whole of the estate of her stepfather (who died intestate). He rejected the submission that the principle could not extend beyond cases where the claimant already had enjoyment of an identified item of property: see pp. 1509–1510. In that context he referred to the well known judgment of Oliver J in *Taylors Fashions Ltd v Liverpool Victoria Trustees Co Ltd (Note) (1979)* [1982] QB 133.

Re Basham has been referred to at least twice in this court without its correctness being challenged. In *Jones v Watkins* (unreported) 26 November 1987; Court of Appeal (Civil Division) Transcript No 1200 of 1987, Slade LJ referred to it as containing a helpful statement of the principle. Slade LJ's

---

[12]   [2000] CLJ 453 (M. Dixon), [2000] All ER Rev 244 (P. J. Clarke), 370 (C. H. Sherrin); [2001] Conv 78 (M. P. Thompson).
[13]   [1987] Conv 211 (J. E. Martin); [1987] CLJ 215 (D. Hayton). See also Sir Christopher SLADE's Child & Co Oxford Lecture 1984 on the *Informal Creation of Interests in Land* at p. 12.

judgment also contains some important observations about the possibility of proprietary estoppel (unlike promissory estoppel) arising even from an equivocal representation:

'At first sight, it may be surprising that a promise to confer an interest in property which is so equivocal in its terms that it would be incapable of giving rise to a binding contract may be capable of conferring on the promisee a right in equity to a transfer of the whole property. However, I think that [counsel] must be right in describing this as simply one instance of equity supplementing the law. The equivocal nature of the promises found by the judge is clearly one relevant factor when considering whether or not it would be unconscionable to permit the administrators to rely on their strict legal title, having regard to any detriment suffered by the plaintiff in reliance on them.'

The other case in which *Re Basham* has been referred to in this court is *Wayling v Jones* (1993) 69 P & CR 170. It concerned an assurance ('It'll all be yours one day') given by the elder partner in a male homosexual relationship to his younger partner. . . .

Irrevocability of assurances

The judge referred to these authorities and then to the decision of Judge Weeks QC in *Taylor v Dickens* [1998] 1 FLR 806 (which has since been compromised on appeal). That was the case of the elderly lady who said that she would leave her estate to the gardener and did so, but then changed her mind (without telling him) after he had stopped charging her for his help with gardening and odd jobs. Judge Weeks rejected the claim and, at p. 821, criticised *Re Basham* in two respects. The first criticism was that Mr Nugee's judgment omitted the requirement of unconscionability. That criticism seems misplaced: see [1986] 1 WLR 1498, 1504A–B and 1509A–C. The second criticism was [1998] 1 FLR 806, 821:

'It is not sufficient for A to believe that he is going to be given a right over B's property if he knows that B has reserved the right to change his mind. In that case, A must show that B created or encouraged a belief on A's part that B would not exercise that right.'

For that proposition Judge Weeks referred to the decision of the Privy Council in *Attorney General of Hong Kong v Humphreys Estate (Queen's Gardens) Ltd* [1987] AC 114, [1987] 2 All ER 387.

Taylor v Dickens has itself attracted a good deal of criticism: see, for instance, Professor M. P. Thompson, 'Emasculating Estoppel' [1998] Conv 210, and William Swadling [1998] RLR 220; but compare the contrary view in M. Dixon, 'Estoppel: A panacea for all wills?' [1999] Conv 39, 46. Mr Swadling's comment is short and pithy:

'This decision is clearly wrong, for the judge seems to have forgotten that the whole point of estoppel claims is that they concern promises which, since they are unsupported by consideration, are initially revocable. What later makes them binding, and therefore irrevocable, is the promisee's detrimental reliance on them. Once that occurs, there is simply no question of the promisor changing his or her mind.'

Mr McDonnell has added his voice to the criticism. In his skeleton argument he has submitted that *Taylor v Dickens* is 'simply wrong'. Mr Martin, while reminding the court that it is not hearing an appeal in *Taylor v Dickens*, has not given the case whole-hearted support. He has been inclined to concede that Judge Weeks should have focused on the promise which was made and whether it was of an irrevocable character, instead of looking for a second promise not to revoke a testamentary disposition.

In my judgment these criticisms of *Taylor v Dickens* are well founded. The actual result in the case may be justified on the other ground on which it was put (no unconscionability on the facts); or (as Mr Swadling suggests later in his note) the gardener's unremunerated services might have merited some modest restitutionary relief. But the inherent revocability of testamentary dispositions (even if well understood by the parties, as Mr Gillett candidly accepted that it was by him) is irrelevant to a promise or assurance that 'all this will be yours' (the sort of language used on the occasion of The Beeches incident in 1975). Even when the promise or assurance is in terms linked to the making of a will (as at the 1974 Golf Hotel dinner) the circumstances may make clear that the assurance is more than a mere statement of present (revocable) intention, and is tantamount to a promise. *Attorney General of Hong Kong v Humphreys Estate (Queen's Gardens) Ltd*, on which Judge Weeks relied, is essentially an example of a purchaser taking the risk, with his eyes open, of going into possession and spending money while his purchase remains expressly subject to contract. Carnwath J observed that the advice to the claimant in *Taylor v Dickens* 'not to count his chickens before they were hatched' is [1998] 3 All ER 917, 929:

'an apt statement of how, in normal circumstances, and in the absence of specific promise, any reasonable person would regard—and should be expected by the law to regard—a representation by a living person as to his intentions for his will.'

In the generality of cases that is no doubt correct, and it is notorious that some elderly persons of means derive enjoyment from the possession of testamentary power, and from dropping hints as to their intentions, without any question of an estoppel arising. But in this case Mr Holt's assurances were repeated over a long period, usually before the assembled company on special family occasions, and some of them (such as 'it was all going to be ours anyway' on the occasion of The Beeches incident) were completely unambiguous. With all respect to the judge, I cannot accept the conclusion which he reached on this point (at p. 932, a passage which I have already quoted). The judge attached weight to The Beeches incident in reaching his conclusion. To my mind it is highly significant, but its significance goes the other way. I find it wholly understandable that Mr and Mrs Gillett, then 10 years married and with two young sons, may have been worried about their home and their future depending on no more than oral assurances, however emphatic, from Mr Holt. The bitterly fought and ruinously expensive litigation which has ensued shows how right they would have been to be worried. But Mr Gillett, after discussing the matter with his wife and his parents, decided to rely on Mr Holt's assurances because 'Ken was a man of his word.' Plainly the assurances given on this occasion were intended to be relied on, and were in fact relied on. In any event reliance would be presumed: see *Greasley v Cooke*. Mr Martin accepted that, while challenging the suggestion that that case also supported any presumption of detriment.

It may be that the judge, having gone deeply and correctly into the law of mutual wills in *Re Goodchild* [1996] 1 WLR 694 [1996] 1 All ER 620 (affirmed by this court [1997] 1 WLR 1216, [1997] 3 All ER 63) went too far in seeking a parallel between those principles and those of proprietary estoppel. Mr Nugee also discerned a parallel in *Re Basham* [1986] 1 WLR 1498, 1504. But although both doctrines show equity intervening to prevent unconscionable conduct, the special feature of the mutual wills and secret trust cases is that they involve not two parties but three. In mutual wills cases they are (typically) a testator (A), a testatrix (B) and an intended beneficiary or class of beneficiaries (C). In secret trust cases they are the testator (A), the secret trustee (B) and the beneficiary (C). There must be an agreement between A and B as to conferring a benefit on C because it is the agreement (and not C's moral claims) which would make it unconscionable for B to resile from his agreement. The judge did make clear [1998] 3 All ER 917, 929, and again at p. 930, that he was well aware of the differences between mutual wills and proprietary estoppel as regards the need for a binding contract. But whether or not he was influenced in that way, I differ from his conclusion that Mr Holt's assurances were incapable of forming the foundation for an enforceable claim based on proprietary estoppel. In my judgment they were well capable of doing so. ...

Mutual understanding and reliance

The judge's approach seems also to have been influenced by the need to find what he called, at p. 929:

'a mutual understanding—which may be express or inferred from conduct—between promisor and promisee, both as to the content of the promise [15] and as to what the promisee is doing, or may be expected to do, in reliance on it.'

Similarly he set out his view that, at p. 932, 'the *Re Basham* principle requires some mutual "understanding" as to the quid pro quo'—ie the consideration—'for the promise ...'

Here again I think that the judge may have been too influenced by the cases on mutual wills in which a definite agreement is an essential part of the doctrine. There is of course a kernel of truth, indeed a considerable nugget of truth in this approach, because (as Balcombe LJ said in *Wayling v Jones* (1993) 69 P & CR 170, and other distinguished judges said in the earlier cases which he cited) there must be a sufficient link between the promises relied on and the conduct which constitutes the detriment. In cases where the detriment involves the claimant moving house (as in *Watts v Story* (unreported), 14 July 1983; Court of Appeal (Civil Division) Transcript No. 319 of 1983) p. 644, post, or otherwise taking some particular course of action at the other party's request, the link is, in the nature of things, going to have some resemblance to the process of offer and acceptance leading to a mutual understanding. But in other cases well within the mainstream of proprietary estoppel, such as *Inwards v Baker* [1965] 2 QB 29 [1965 1 All ER 446 and the 19th century decisions which this court applied in that case, there is nothing like a bargain as to what particular interest is to be granted, or when it is to be granted, or by what type of disposition it is to be granted. The link is provided by the bare fact of A encouraging B to incur expenditure on A's land.

Detriment

It is therefore necessary to go on to consider detriment. The judge would have decided the case against Mr Gillett on this point also, as he indicated at the end

---

[15]   On the content of the promise, see *Orgee v Orgee* [1997] EGCS 152 (claim to agricultural tenancy on basis of estoppel refused in the absence of details as to crucial terms on which tenancy was expected to be based, for example, provisions for repairs and rent and rent review regime); cf *JT Developments Ltd v Quinn* (1990) 62 P & CR 33; (1998) 114 LQR 351 (M. Pawlowski). See also *Earl of Macclesfield v The Beechwood Estates Co* [2003] EWHC 1846 (Ch) (expectation too vague and indefinite): [2004] Conv 516 (M. P. Thompson).

of his judgment in the main action [1998] 3 All ER 917, 932–936. The judge devoted almost all of this part of his judgment to an analysis of whether Mr Gillett was substantially underpaid between 1965 and 1995. He dealt with the other matters relied on as detriment in a manner which Mr McDonnell has described as perfunctory ...

Both sides agree that the element of detriment is an essential ingredient of proprietary estoppel.

[His Lordship referred to *Greasley v Cooke*, infra and *Watts v Story* and continued:]

The overwhelming weight of authority shows that detriment is required. But the authorities also show that it is not a narrow or technical concept. The detriment need not consist of the expenditure of money or other quantifiable financial detriment, so long as it is something substantial. The requirement must be approached as part of a broad inquiry as to whether repudiation of an assurance is or is not unconscionable in all the circumstances.

There are some helpful observations about the requirement for detriment in the judgment of Slade LJ in *Jones v Watkins* 26 November 1987. There must be sufficient causal link between the assurance relied on and the detriment asserted. The issue of detriment must be judged at the moment when the person who has given the assurance seeks to go back on it. Whether the detriment is sufficiently substantial is to be tested by whether it would be unjust or inequitable to allow the assurance to be disregarded—that is, again, the essential test of unconscionability. The detriment alleged must be pleaded and proved ...

The matters which Mr Gillett pleaded as detriment, and on which he adduced evidence of detriment, included, apart from the level of his remuneration, (i) his continuing in Mr Holt's employment (through KAHL) and not seeking or accepting offers of employment elsewhere, or going into business on his own account; (ii) carrying out tasks and spending time beyond the normal scope of an employee's duty; (iii) taking no substantial steps to secure his future wealth, either by larger pension contributions or otherwise; and (iv) expenditure on improving The Beeches farmhouse which was, Mr Gillett said, barely habitable when it was first acquired by KAHL in 1971. That company paid for some structural work, with a local authority improvement grant, but Mr Gillett paid for new fittings and materials and carried out a good deal of the work himself. The details are set out in part 3 and appendix 1 of Mr Gillett's witness statement.

I have to say that I see some force in Mr McDonnell's criticism of the judge's approach to this part of the evidence (although the judge, having decided the main action on the issue of assurances, was not obliged to cover the issue of detriment in great detail). After listening to lengthy submissions about the judgment, and after reading much of Mr Gillett's evidence both in his witness statement and under cross-examination, I am left with the feeling that the judge, despite his very clear and careful judgment, did not stand back and look at the matter in the round. Had he done so I think he would have recognised that Mr Gillett's case on detriment (on the facts found by the judge, and on Mr Gillett's uncontradicted evidence) was an unusually compelling one.

In my judgment the cumulative effect of the judge's findings and of the undisputed evidence is that by 1975 (the year of The Beeches incident) Mr Gillett had an exceptionally strong claim on Mr Holt's conscience. Mr Gillett was then 35. He had left school before he was 16, without taking any of the examinations which might otherwise have given him academic qualifications, against the advice of his headmaster and in the face of his parents' doubts, in order to work for and live with a 42 year-old bachelor who was socially superior to, and very much wealthier than, his own parents. Mr Holt seriously raised the possibility of adopting him. Mr Holt's influence extended to Mr Gillett's social and private life and it seems to have been only through the diplomacy of Miss Sally Wingate (as she then was) that Mr Holt came to tolerate, and then accept, the notion of Mr Gillett having a girlfriend. Mr Holt had said that he would arrange for Mr Gillett to go to agricultural college but then did not arrange it, and it was only through Mr Gillett's own hard work and determination that he learned additional skills at evening classes. He proved himself by getting in the harvest in 1964 when Mr Holt was away fishing. All these matters preceded the first of the seven assurances on which Mr Gillett relied, so they are in a sense no more than background. But they are very important background because they refute Mr Martin's suggestion (placed in the forefront of his skeleton argument) that Mr Gillett's claim should be regarded as a 'startling' claim by someone who was no more than an employee. On the contrary, Mr McDonnell was not putting it too high when he said that for 30 years Mr and Mrs Gillett and their sons provided Mr Holt with a sort of surrogate family.

However, a surrogate family of that sort is not the same as a birth family, and it is clear that Mr Gillett and his wife must often have been aware of the ambivalence of their position. Mr Holt was generous but it was the generosity of the patron; his will prevailed; Mr and Mrs Gillett were expected to, and did, subordinate their wishes to his: compare *Re Basham* at 1505, at 405–411. One telling example of this was over the education of their sons. Mr Holt decided that he would like to pay for the Gilletts' elder son, Robert, to go to Mr Holt's old school (Greshams in Norfolk). The offer did not extend to their younger son, Andrew, and the Gilletts not unnaturally felt that if one boy was to go to boarding school then both should go. In the end Robert went to Greshams and Andrew to a less well known boarding school at Grimsby, and Mr and Mrs Gillett used some maturing short-term endowment policies and increased their overdraft in order to bear half the combined cost of the school fees and extras.

Mr Gillett also incurred substantial expenditure on the farmhouse at The Beeches, most of it after the clear assurance which Mr Holt gave him when, in 1975, he ventured to ask for something in writing: 'that was not necessary as it was all going to be ours anyway'. This was after the Gilletts had sold their own small house at Thimbleby and so had stepped off the property-owning ladder which they had got on to in 1964.

It is entirely a matter of conjecture what the future might have held for the Gilletts if in 1975 Mr Holt had (instead of what he actually said) told the Gilletts frankly that his present intention was to make a will in their favour, but that he was not bound by that and that they should not count their chickens before they were hatched. Had they decided to move on, they might have done no better. They might, as Mr Martin urged on us, have found themselves working for a less generous employer. The fact is that they relied on Mr Holt's assurance, because they thought he was a man of his word, and so they deprived themselves of the opportunity of trying to better themselves in other ways. Although the judge's view, after seeing and hearing Mr and Mrs Gillett, was that detriment was not established, I find myself driven to the conclusion that it was amply established. I think that the judge must have taken too narrowly financial a view of the requirement for detriment, as his reference [1998] 3 All ER 917, 936 to 'the balance of advantage and disadvantage' suggests. Mr Gillett and his wife devoted the best years of their lives to working for Mr Holt and his company, showing loyalty and devotion to his business interests, his social life and his personal wishes, on the strength of clear and repeated assurances of testamentary benefits.

They received (in 1983) 20% of the shares in KAHL, which must be regarded as received in anticipation of, and on account of, such benefits. Then in 1995 they had the bitter humiliation of summary dismissal and a police investigation of alleged dishonesty which the defendants called no evidence to justify at trial. I do not find Mr Gillett's claim startling.

[His Lordship held that the minimum equity to do justice of Gillett was for Holt to convey to him the freehold of the Beeches together with a sufficient sum of money (£100,000) to compensate for exclusion from the rest of the farming business.]

II. DETRIMENTAL RELIANCE

In **Greasley v Cooke** [1980] 1 WLR 1306, [1980] 3 All ER 710, [16] Doris Cooke aged 16 went as a maid servant in 1938 to help in the house of a widower Arthur Greasley and was paid 10 shillings a week. From 1946 she cohabited with one of his sons until the son died in 1975. She was paid wages until Arthur's death in 1948, and thereafter continued, without wages, to live in the house and to look after it and the family, including a mentally ill daughter. After Arthur's death, members of the family led Doris to believe that she could regard the property as her home for the rest of her life and accordingly did not ask for any payment.

The Court of Appeal held that Doris was entitled to occupy the house rent-free so long as she wished to stay there. Lord DENNING MR said at 1311, at 713:

'The first point is on the burden of proof. Mr Weeks referred us to many cases, such as *Reynell v Sprye* (1852) 1 De GM & G 660 at 708; *Smith v Chadwick* (1882) 20 ChD 27 at 44 and *Brikom Investments Ltd v Carr* [1979] QB 467 at 481–483, [1978] 2 All ER 753 at 759, where I said that when a person makes a representation intending that another should act on it:

"It is no answer for the maker to say: 'You would have gone on with the transaction anyway.' That must be mere speculation. No one can be sure what he would, or would not, have done in a hypothetical state of affairs which never took place. ... Once it is shown that a representation was calculated to influence the judgment of a reasonable man, the presumption is that he was so influenced." [17]

So here. These statements to Miss Cooke were calculated to influence her — so as to put her mind at rest — so that she should not worry about being turned out. No one can say what she would have done if Kenneth and Hedley had not made those statements. It is quite possible that she would have said to herself: "I am not married to Kenneth. I am on my own. What will happen to me if anything happens to him? I had better look out for another job now: rather than stay here where I have no security".

So, instead of looking for another job, she stayed on in the house looking after Kenneth and Clarice. There is a presumption that she did so, relying on the assurances given to her by Kenneth and Hedley. The burden is not on her, but on them, to prove that she did not rely on their assurances. They did not

---

[16] [1981] Conv 154 (R. E. Annand); 44 MLR 461 (G. Woodman); 125 NLJ 539 (M. P. Thompson). Detriment was required by CA in *Christian v Christian* (1981) 131 NLJ 43. See also *Watkins v Emslie* (1981) 261 EG 1192; *Dann v Spurrier* (1802) 7 Ves 231 at 235–236, per Lord ELDON LC, cited in *Taylors Fashions Ltd v Liverpool Victoria Trustees Co Ltd* [1982] QB 133n at 156, [1981] 1 All ER 897 at 919; *Watts v Story* [1983] CA Transcript 319, p. 644, post; Pawlowski, *The Doctrine of Proprietary Estoppel*, pp. 43–71.

[17] Similarly for the requirement of reliance where there is a material representation to another to induce him to enter into a contract: *Redgrave v Hurd* (1881) 20 ChD 1 at 21, per JESSEL MR.

prove it, nor did their representatives. So she is presumed to have relied on them. So on the burden of proof it seems to me that the judge was in error.

The second point is about the need for some expenditure of money — some detriment — before a person can acquire any interest in a house or any right to stay in it as long as he wishes. It so happens that in many of these cases of proprietary estoppel there has been expenditure of money. But that is not a necessary element. I see that in *Snell's Principles of Equity*, 27th ed. (1973) p. 565, it is said: "A must have incurred expenditure or otherwise have prejudiced himself." But I do not think that that is necessary. It is sufficient if the party, to whom the assurance is given, acts on the faith of it — in such circumstances that it would be unjust and inequitable for the party making the assurance to go back on it: see *Moorgate Mercantile Co Ltd v Twitchings* [1976] QB 225, [1975] 3 All ER 314 and *Crabb v Arun District Council* [1976] Ch 179 at 188, [1976] 3 All ER 865 at 871. Applying those principles here it can be seen that the assurances given by Kenneth and Hedley to Doris Cooke — leading her to believe that she would be allowed to stay in the house as long as she wished — raised an equity in her favour. There was no need for her to prove that she acted on the faith of those assurances. It is to be presumed that she did so. There is no need for her to prove that she acted to her detriment or to her prejudice. Suffice it that she stayed on in the house — looking after Kenneth and Clarice — when otherwise she might have left and got a job elsewhere. The equity having thus been raised in her favour, it is for the courts of equity to decide in what way that equity should be satisfied. In this case it should be by allowing her to stay on in the house as long as she wishes.'

DUNN LJ said at 1313, at 715:

'There is no doubt that for proprietary estoppel to arise the person claiming must have incurred expenditure or otherwise have prejudiced himself or acted to his detriment. The only question before us is as to the burden of proof of the detriment. The judge thought that the onus lay on the claimant to prove it. I agree that in that he fell into error for the reasons given by Lord Denning MR, and I also would allow this appeal.'

In **Watts v Story** [1983] CA Transcript 319, the Court of Appeal (DUNN and SLADE LJJ) held that an action for possession succeeded against a grandson aged 30 who had not shown 'that when the benefits derived by him from his rent free occupation of Apple House, Woodborough, Nottingham (owned by his grandmother whose mind was "as sharp as a razor") are set against any detriments suffered by him as a result of making the move from his Rent Act protected flat in Leeds, he has on balance suffered any detriment in financial or material terms.'

DUNN LJ said:

'There was some discussion at the Bar as to what Lord Denning MR meant in the passage which I have cited from *Greasley v Cooke* [1980] 1 WLR 1306, [1980] 3 All ER 710. In that case there was no doubt on the evidence that Miss Cooke had been given assurances by the Greasley family that she could regard the property as her home for the rest of her life. Equally, there was no doubt on the facts that she had suffered a detriment, because she had devoted her life to looking after the Greasley family without payment instead of getting a paid job. The only question in the case was whether that admitted detriment was caused by the assurances, or whether she would have continued to look after the family anyway because she was fond of Kenneth Greasley. The judge held that the onus was on her to prove that the detriment was caused by the assurances and that she had failed to discharge the burden of proof. That is clear from, in particular, the judgment of Waller LJ at 1312, at 714. It is in that context that the words of Lord Denning cited by the judge in this case should be read. ...

Lord Denning was not saying that there was no need for detriment in order to establish proprietary estoppel. On the facts of the case detriment spoke for itself, and was admitted. All that Lord Denning was saying was that, the assurances having been established, there was no need for Doris Cooke to prove that the obvious detriment had resulted from them.

The law is well stated in Snell's Principles of Equity (28th Edition) at page 561 in the following passage: "Once it is shown that O gave assurances or other encouragement to A, and A suffers detriment, it will readily be inferred that the detriment was suffered as a result of the encouragement; the burden of proof is on O to show that A's conduct was not induced by the assurances."

Nor, if that passage from Lord Denning's judgment is read as a whole, was he stating any new proposition of law. As the judge said, it matters not whether one talks in terms of detriment or whether one talks in terms of it being unjust or inequitable for the party giving the assurance to go back on it. It is difficult to envisage circumstances in which it would be inequitable for the party giving an assurance alleged to give rise to a proprietary estoppel, i.e., an estoppel concerned with the positive acquisitions of rights and interests in the land of another, unless the person to whom the assurance was given had suffered some prejudice or detriment.'[18]

B. Discretionary Nature of Remedy. Proportionality

In **Gillett v Holt** [2001] Ch 210, [2000] 2 All ER 289, p. 637 ante, ROBERT WALKER LJ said at 235; at 311:

'Since Mr Gillett has established his claim to equitable relief, this court must decide what is the most appropriate form for the relief to take. The aim is, as Sir Arthur Hobhouse said in *Plimmer v Wellington Corporation* (1884) 9 App Cas 699, 714, to "look at the circumstances in each case to decide in what way the equity can be satisfied". The court approaches this task in a cautious way, in order to achieve what Scarman LJ, in *Crabb v Arun District Council* [1976] Ch 179, 198, [1975]

---

[18] *Coombes v Smith* [1986] 1 WLR 808 at 821 (no detriment where wife left husband and went to live with lover and their child); [1986] CLJ 394 (D. J. Hayton); *Hammersmith and Fulham London Borough Council v Top Shop Centres Ltd* [1990] Ch 237, [1989] 2 All ER 655 (failure to negotiate for grant of new lease or to apply for relief against forfeiture held to be detriment; reliance presumed); *Wayling v Jones* (1993) 69 P & CR 170; [1994] LS 15 (M. Halliwell) (requirement of promise and 'conduct of such a nature that inducement may be inferred' per BALCOMBE LJ at 175); (1995) 111 LQR 389 (E. Cooke); [1995] Conv 409 (C. J. Davis); [1996] 16 LS 218 (A. Lawson); *Walton v Bell* [1994] NPC 55A (working long hours for low wages held to give rise to inference that it was induced by the promise being made and reliance on it); *Matharu v Matharu* (1994) 68 P & CR 93 (son's expenditure in improving property held to be detrimental reliance on part of his wife); [1995] 7 CFLQ 59 (G. Battersby); [1995] Conv 61 (M. Welstead); *Durant v Heritage* [1994] EGCS 134 (legal owner must be unable to prove that claimant, in relying on the belief, did not rely on it to his prejudice or detriment); *Gan v Wood* [1998] EGCS 77 (expenditure amounting to minor detriment held not to suffice); *Brinnand v Ewens* [1987] 2 EGLR 67 (expenditure incurred on work done 'to make the home more comfortable'): 'The acting to the detriment must have taken place in the belief either that the claimant owned a sufficient interest in the property to justify the expenditure or that he would obtain such an interest' per NOURSE LJ at 68; *Downderry Construction Ltd v Secretary of State for Transport, Local Government and the Regions* [2002] EWHC 2 (Admin), (2002) 152 NLJ 108 (reliance need not be reasonable); *Keelwalk Properties Ltd v Waller* [2002] EWCA Civ 1076, [2002] 3 EGLR 79 (landlord's long practice of renewing leases did not found estoppel).

3 All ER 865, 880 called "the minimum equity to do justice to the plaintiff". The wide range of possible relief appears from *Snell's Equity*, 30th ed (2000), pp. 641–643, p. 652, post.'

And in **Jennings v Rice** [2003] 1 P & CR 100, infra. ALDOUS LJ said at para. 36: 'The value of that equity will depend upon all the circumstances including the expectation and the detriment. The task of the court is to do justice. The most essential requirement is that there must be proportionality between the expectation and the detriment.' [19]

JENNINGS v RICE
[2003] 1 P & CR 8 (CA, ALDOUS, MANTELL and ROBERT WALKER LJJ [20]

Mrs Royle, a childless widow, died in 1997 aged 93. She lived at Lawn House, Shapwick, Somerset. Her estate was valued at some £1.3 million net and her house and furniture at £435,000. Mr Jennings, who was born in 1939, was a self-employed bricklayer. In 1970 he began to work for Mrs Royle as a part-time gardener for 30 pence an hour. He gradually did more for her, including taking her shopping and running errands. In the late 1980s Mrs Royle stopped paying Mr Jennings but told him that he did not need to be worried about not being paid, since 'he would be alright' and she 'would see to it'.

At about the same time, Mrs Royle was keen that Mr Jennings would continue to live in the neighbourhood and provided the deposit of £2,000 which enabled him and his wife to buy a house locally. She became more dependent on him, especially after a burglary in 1993. From 1994 until she died in 1997 he spent almost every night on a sofa in a sitting room at Lawn House. He also collected her prescriptions, helped her to dress and go to the toilet, made sure that she had food and drink available and continued to work in the garden.

Mr Jennings claimed that under the doctrine of proprietary estoppel he should receive the whole of Mrs Royle's estate, or alternatively the value of her house and furniture, since that was his expectation. At first instance Mr Jennings was awarded £100,000 which represented the cost of full-time nursing care over the relevant period.

Held. Award affirmed.

ROBERT WALKER LJ:

42. This court was referred to two recent articles which contain a full and illuminating discussion of this area: *Estoppel and the Protection of Expectations* by Elizabeth Cooke [1997] 17 LS 258 and *The Remedial Discretion in Proprietary Estoppel* by Simon Gardner (1999) 115 LQR 438. Those articles could with advantage have been cited in *Gillett v Holt* [2001] Ch 210. Both are concerned with whether the fundamental aim of this form of estoppel is to fulfil the claimant's expectations, or to compensate him for his detrimental reliance on the defendant's non-contractual assurances, or is some intermediate objective; and (following on from the identification of the correct principle) the nature of the discretion which the court exercises in granting a remedy to the claimant. The

[19]   *Sledmore v Dalby* (1996) 72 P & CR 196, p. 650, post; *Campbell v Griffin* [2001] EWCA Civ 990, p. 650. n. 2, post.
[20]   [2003] Conv 225 (M. P. Thompson); (2002) 118 LQR 319 (M. Pawlowski).

articles amply demonstrate that the range of English authorities provides some support for both theories and for a variety of intermediate positions; and that recent Australian authority (especially the decision of the High Court in *Commonwealth v Verwayen* (1990) 160 CLR 394) has moved in favour of the reliance loss theory.

43. It cannot be doubted that in this as in every other area of the law, the court must take a principled approach, and cannot exercise a completely unfettered discretion according to the individual judge's notion of what is fair in any particular case. Dr Gardner's fourth hypothesis [1] ('the approach is for the court to adopt whatever style and measure of relief it thinks fit, for whatever reason it thinks fit') cannot be right. I do not think that the judgment of Hobhouse LJ in *Sledmore v Dalby* (1996) 72 P & CR 196 (to which I shall return) can possibly be regarded as adopting or advocating an unfettered judicial discretion.

44. The need to search for the right principles cannot be avoided. But it is unlikely to be a short or simple search, because (as appears from both the English and the Australian authorities) proprietary estoppel can apply in a wide variety of factual situations, and any summary formula is likely to prove to be an over-simplification. The cases show a wide range of variation in both of the main elements, that is the quality of the assurances which give rise to the claimant's expectations and the extent of the claimant's detrimental reliance on the assurances. The doctrine applies only if these elements, in combination, make it unconscionable for the person giving the assurances (whom I will call the benefactor, although that may not always be an appropriate label) to go back on them.

45. Sometimes the assurances, and the claimant's reliance on them, have a consensual character falling not far short of an enforceable contract (if the only bar to the formation of a contract is non-compliance with s. 2 of the Law of Property (Miscellaneous Provisions) Act 1989, the proprietary estoppel may become indistinguishable from a constructive trust: *Yaxley v Gotts* [2000] Ch 162, [2000] 1 All ER 711, p. 70, ante). In a case of that sort both the claimant's expectations and the element of detriment to the claimant will have been defined with reasonable clarity. A typical case would be an elderly benefactor who reaches a clear understanding with the claimant (who may be a relative, a friend, or a remunerated companion or carer) that if the claimant resides with and cares for the benefactor, the claimant will inherit the benefactor's house (or will have a home for life). In a case like that the consensual element of what has happened suggests that the claimant and the benefactor probably regarded the expected benefit and the accepted detriment as being (in a general, imprecise way) equivalent, or at any rate not obviously disproportionate. Cases of that sort, if free from other complications, fit fairly comfortably into Dr Gardner's first or second hypothesis (both of which aim to vindicate the claimant's expectations as far as possible, and if possible by providing the claimant with the specific property which the benefactor has promised).

46. However, the claimant's expectations may not be focused on any specific property. In *Re Basham* [1986] 1 WLR 1489, [1987] 1 All ER 405, p. 637, ante, the deputy judge (Mr Edward Nugee QC) rejected the submission that there must be some clearly identified piece of property, and that decision has been approved more than once in this court. Moreover (as the judge's findings in this case vividly illustrate), the claimant's expectations may have been formed on the basis of vague and inconsistent assurances. The judge said of Mrs Royle that she:

---

[1]   The hypotheses are set out at p. 652, post.

"... was prone to saying different things at different times and, perhaps deliberately, couched her promises in non-specific terms."

He made that observation in relation to the failure of the contract claim, but it is relevant to the estoppel claim also.

47. If the claimant's expectations are uncertain (as will be the case with many honest claimants) then their specific vindication cannot be the appropriate test. A similar problem arises if the court, although satisfied that the claimant has a genuine claim, is not satisfied that the high level of the claimant's expectations is fairly derived from his deceased patron's assurances, which may have justified only a lower level of expectation. In such cases the court may still take the claimant's expectations (or the upper end of any range of expectations) as a starting point, but unless constrained by authority I would regard it as no more than a starting point.

48. I do not see that approach as being inconsistent with authority. On the contrary, I think it is supported by a substantial body of English authority. Scarman LJ's well-known reference to 'the minimum equity to do justice to the plaintiff' (*Crabb v Arun District Council* [1976] Ch 179, 198, [1975] 3 All ER 865, 880, p. 659, post) must no doubt be read in the context of the rather unusual facts of that case, but it does not stand alone. As Scarman LJ recognised, the line of authority goes back to nineteenth-century cases such as *Duke of Beaufort v Patrick* (1853) 17 Beav 60 and *Plimmer v Wellington Corporation* (1884) 9 App Cas 699. A passage in the opinion of the Privy Council (delivered by Sir Arthur Hobhouse) in *Plimmer's* case at pp. 713–714 is particularly instructive. The conclusion of the passage is that:

'In fact the court must look at the circumstances in each case to decide in what way the equity can be satisfied.'

Scarman LJ's reference to the minimum does not require the court to be constitutionally parsimonious, but it does implicitly recognise that the court must also do justice to the defendant.

49. It is no coincidence that these statements of principle refer to satisfying the equity (rather than satisfying, or vindicating, the claimant's expectations). The equity arises not from the claimant's expectations alone, but from the combination of expectations, detrimental reliance, and the unconscionableness of allowing the benefactor (or the deceased benefactor's estate) to go back on the assurances. There is a faint parallel with the old equitable doctrine of part performance, of which Lord Selborne said in *Maddison v Alderson* (1883) 8 App Cas 467, 475.

'In a suit founded on such part performance, the defendant is really "charged" upon the equities resulting from the acts done in execution of the contract, and not (within the meaning of the statute) upon the contract itself.'

So with proprietary estoppel the defendant is charged with satisfying the equity which has arisen from the whole sequence of events. But the parallel is only faint since in the case of estoppel there is no contract and the nexus between the benefactor's assurances and the resulting equity is less direct; the assurances are only half the story. In *Dillwyn v Llewelyn* (1862) 4 De G. F. & J. 517, 522 Lord Westbury expressed the point in terms which anticipated Lord Selborne:

'The equity of the donee and the estate to be claimed by virtue of it depend on the transaction, that is, on the acts done, and not on the language of the memorandum [which amounted to an imperfect gift].'

50. To recapitulate: there is a category of case in which the benefactor and the claimant have reached a mutual understanding which is in reasonably clear terms but does not amount to a contract. I have already referred to the typical case of a carer who has the expectation of coming into the benefactor's house, either outright or for life. In such a case the court's natural response is to fulfil

the claimant's expectations. But if the claimant's expectations are uncertain, or extravagant, or out of all proportion to the detriment which the claimant has suffered, the court can and should recognise that the claimant's equity should be satisfied in another (and generally more limited) way.

51. But that does not mean that the court should in such a case abandon expectations completely, and look to the detriment suffered by the claimant as defining the appropriate measure of relief. Indeed in many cases the detriment may be even more difficult to quantify, in financial terms, than the claimant's expectations. Detriment can be quantified with reasonable precision if it consists solely of expenditure on improvements to another person's house, and in some cases of that sort an equitable charge for the expenditure may be sufficient to satisfy the equity (see *Snell's Equity*, 30th ed., para. 39–21 and the authorities mentioned in that paragraph). But the detriment of an ever-increasing burden of care for an elderly person, and of having to be subservient to his or her moods and wishes, is very difficult to quantify in money terms. Moreover the claimant may not be motivated solely by reliance on the benefactor's assurances, and may receive some countervailing benefits (such as free bed and board). In such circumstances the court has to exercise a wide judgmental discretion.

52. It would be unwise to attempt any comprehensive enumeration of the factors relevant to the exercise of the court's discretion, or to suggest any hierarchy of factors. In my view they include, but are not limited to, the factors mentioned in Dr Gardner's third hypothesis (misconduct of the claimant as in *J. Willis & Sons v Willis* [1979] Ch 261 or particularly oppressive conduct on the part of the defendant, as in *Crabb v Arun District Council* or *Pascoe v Turner* [1979] 1 WLR 421, [1979] 2 All ER 945). To these can safely be added the court's recognition that it cannot compel people who have fallen out to live peaceably together, so that there may be a need for a clean break; alterations in the benefactor's assets and circumstances, especially where the benefactor's assurances have been given, and the claimant's detriment has been suffered, over a long period of years; the likely effect of taxation; and (to a limited degree) the other claims (legal or moral) on the benefactor or his or her estate. No doubt there are many other factors which it may be right for the court to take into account in particular factual situations.

53. The judge did in this case consider, although not in detail, what Mr Jennings might reasonably have earned in the way of arm's length remuneration for his services. He also considered what professional nursing care might have cost during the last eight years of Mrs Royle's life. A detailed computational approach was adopted (but with a different outcome, limited to compensation of reliance loss) by the Supreme Court of Tasmania in *Public Trustee v Wadley* [1997] 7 Tas. LR 35, in which the court discussed the appropriate hourly rate and the total number of hours of housework undertaken by a daughter who (as it was put in the dissenting judgment of Wright J.):

'had subordinated her own life to that of her father and [whose] attentive and affectionate service, often no doubt at considerable inconvenience to herself, put her assistance on a higher plane than that of a domestic servant'.

54. That illustrates the Australian preference for compensating the reliance loss only. Under English law that approach may sometimes be appropriate (see paragraph 51 above) but only where, on the facts, a higher measure would amount to overcompensation. In my view it would rarely if ever be appropriate to go into detailed inquiries as to hours and hourly rates where the claim was based on proprietary estoppel (rather than a restitutionary claim for services which were not gratuitous). But the going rate for live-in carers can provide a useful cross-check in the exercise of the court's discretion.

55. I have made some references to the general trend of Australian jurisprudence in this area. It is unnecessary to attempt any detailed study of the different views expressed by the High Court in the *Verwayen* case (which was concerned with estoppel in the very different context of litigation arising out of personal injuries suffered in a collision between two warships) or of Australian cases since then.

56. However, I respectfully agree with the view expressed by Hobhouse LJ in *Sledmore v Dalby* (1996) 72 P & CR 196, infra, that the principle of proportionality (between remedy and detriment), emphasised by Mason CJ in *Verwayen*, is relevant in England also. As Hobhouse LJ observed at p. 209, to recognise the need for proportionality:

'… is to say little more than that the end result must be a just one having regard to the assumption made by the party asserting the estoppel and the detriment which he has experienced.'

The essence of the doctrine of proprietary estoppel is to do what is necessary to avoid an unconscionable result, and a disproportionate remedy cannot be the right way of going about that. Cases on interim injunctive relief have recognised the importance of proportionality in the granting of equitable remedies: see for instance *Lock International v Beswick* [1989] 1 WLR 1268, 1281. Where the court is granting final relief after investigating all the facts proportionality is even more important.

57. I do not consider that the judge made any error of law in his approach to the exercise of his discretion, or that it was otherwise flawed. He did make an error in his reference to the quantum of the relief granted in *Gillett v Holt* (the claimant was awarded a farmhouse and 42 hectares of land as well as £100,000). But every case depends on its own facts and that slip cannot in my view have played a significant part in the judge's disposal of the case.

58. I would therefore dismiss this appeal. [2]

In **Sledmore v Dalby** (1996) 72 P & CR 196, [3] Mr and Mrs Sledmore jointly purchased 15A, The Green, Acomb, York. In 1965 their daughter married Mr Dalby and they moved into the house as tenants of the Sledmores. In 1976, when the daughter became ill and Mr Dalby became unemployed, the Sledmores refused to accept any more rent, but the Dalbys continued to pay the rates and maintain the house.

Between 1976 and 1979 Dalby carried out substantial improvements to it, with the encouragement of Mr Sledmore. In 1979 Mr Sledmore conveyed his share to his wife, and she changed her will to ensure that her daughter inherited it to the exclusion of Dalby. Mr Sledmore died in 1980, Dalby's wife in 1983 and Dalby continued to occupy the house rent free. He spent only a few nights a week in it, and the rest of the week in his new partner's house. He was in employment. One of his two daughters still lived at the house and she was now aged 27 and in employment. Mrs Sledmore's house was in need of repair and she was in serious financial difficulty; she was on income support and her mortgage interest, which was in arrears, was being paid by the Department of Social Security.

---

[2]   *Campbell v Griffin* [2001] EWCA 990, a family carer in a similar situation was awarded £35,000 charged on the property, but had to give up vacant possession to enable the house to be sold. His rent-free occupation did not extinguish his equity; [2002] Conv 519 (M. Pawlowski); [2003] Conv 157 (M. P. Thompson).

[3]   [1997] CLJ 34 (P. Milne); [1997] Conv 458 (J. E. Adams); *Ottey v Grundy* [2003] EWCA Civ 1176 (lack of proportionality).

Mrs Sledmore sought possession of 15A. In rejecting Dalby's claim under proprietary estoppel, HOBHOUSE LJ said at 207:

'The judgment of Mason CJ in *Commonwealth of Australia v Verwayen* (1990) 95 ALR 321, at 331 contains a discussion of the law of estoppel which is of particular value. I will cite three passages which are relevant to what I have said and to the correct approach to the present case.

In conformity with the fundamental purpose of all estoppels to afford protection against the detriment which would flow from a party's change of position if the assumption that led to it were deserted, these developments have brought a grater underlying unity to the various categories of estoppel. Indeed, the consistent trend in the modern decisions points inexorably towards the emergence of one overarching doctrine of estoppel rather than a series of independent rules. The element which both attracts the jurisdiction of a Court of Equity and shapes the remedy to be given is unconscionable conduct on the part of the person bound by the equity, and the remedy required to satisfy an equity varies according to the circumstances of the case. As Robert Goff J said in *Amalgamated Property Co v Texas Bank* [1982] QB 84 at 103, [1981] 1 All ER 923 at 935 "Of all doctrines, equitable estoppel is surely one of the most flexible ... However, in moulding its decree, the court, as a court of conscience, goes no further than is necessary to prevent unconscionable conduct.

... it should be accepted that there is but one doctrine of estoppel, which provides that a court of Common Law or Equity may do what is required, but not more, to prevent a person who has relied upon an assumption as to a present, past or future state of affairs (including a legal state of affairs), which assumption the party estopped has induced him to hold, from suffering detriment in reliance upon the assumption as a result of the denial of its correctness. A central element of that doctrine is that there must be a proportionality between the remedy and the detriment which is its purpose to avoid. It would be wholly inequitable and unjust to insist upon a disproportionate making good of the relevant assumption."

There are similarly illuminating passages in the judgment of Deane J, at pp. 346 et seq.

It is thus always necessary to ask what is the assumption made by the party asserting the estoppel for which the party affected is to be treated as responsible. In the present case it was no more than the assumption that the mother, Mrs Sledmore, would leave number 15A to her daughter Jacqueline Dalby. That was the assumption which the defendant recognised was capable of encompassing and fulfilling his legitimate expectation. That assumption was never falsified. The disappointment of the defendant was that his wife sadly died and did so before his mother-in-law; further, 20 years later, his mother-in-law is still alive. Therefore there is no assumption in the relevant sense which was ever falsified. The assumption upon which the defendant was entitled to say that he incurred the expenditure was in fact fulfilled.

The other aspect clearly illustrated by the quotations which I have made from Mason CJ is the need for proportionality. This is to say little more than that the end result must be a just one having regard to the assumption made by the party asserting the estoppel and the detriment which he has experienced. Here is it unreal to suggest that the conclusion of the County Court judge is proportionate to what happened over 15 years earlier. Similarly, it is unreal to say that the Defendant has suffered any injustice. He expended money in 1976 to 1978 upon his then family home and he and his family fully enjoyed the benefits of such expenditure. He has also enjoyed within the same framework over a period of over 15 years the rent-free occupation of the property. By the same token it cannot be properly said that there was anything unconscionable in Mrs Sledmore seeking the possession of number 15A in 1990.

In my judgment there is no estoppel operating against the plaintiff. Her claim in this action falsifies no legitimate assumption or expectation. The effect of any equity that may at any earlier time have existed has long since been exhausted and no injustice has been done to the defendant. The plaintiff is entitled to an order for possession and the defendant's counter-claim must be dismissed. This appeal should be allowed accordingly.

(1999) 115 LQR 438 (S. Gardner) at pp. 442, 444, 446, 452, 461, 468.

'Below are set out four hypotheses. They identify a variety of ways in which the law may, in proprietary estoppel claims, make the issue of a certain remedy depend at least partly on the judge taking a certain view. They are arranged as a series, in ascending order of the extent to which they diverge from a simple proposition that the only possible remedy is expectation relief *in specie*.

Hypothesis 1. The approach is to vindicate the plaintiff's expectations in specie, *care being taken to achieve the best match between the details of the plaintiff's expectations and the possible legal responses*
Hypothesis 2. The approach is:
— *to vindicate the plaintiff's expectations (care being taken to achieve the best match between the details of the plaintiff's expectations and the possible legal responses);*
— *to vindicate those expectations* in specie *if practicable, but otherwise in a monetary form; but*
— *to resort to some other quantum, not more generous than the expectation measure, if it is impracticable to give relief in the expectation measure*
Hypothesis 3. The approach is:
— *to vindicate the plaintiff's expectations (care being taken to achieve the best match between the details of the plaintiff's expectations and the possible legal responses);*
— *to vindicate those expectations* in specie *if practicable, but otherwise in a monetary form; but*
— *to resort to some other quantum, not more generous than the expectation measure, if it is impracticable to give relief in the expectation measure; and*
— *to resort to some other quantum, with no ceiling at the expectation measure, in the presence of another factor from a limited range recognised as meriting a departure from expectation relief*
Hypothesis 4. The approach is for the court to adopt whatever style and measure of relief it thinks fit, for whatever reason it thinks fit

In the end hypothesis 3 probably offers the most accurate and supportable account of the law as it stands, but it is neither a perfect match for the material to be described nor likely to be immune from challenge.'

C. Satisfaction of the Equity [4]

Snell's Equity (20th edn., 2000), pp. 641–643

'If the equity is established, effect is given to it in whatever is the most appropriate way taking into account all relevant circumstances including the conduct of the

---

[4]   Pawlowski, *The Doctrine of Proprietary Estoppel*, pp. 43–71.

parties.[5] Often it suffices merely to dismiss an action brought by O to enforce his legal rights. Thus a claim for possession may be dismissed[6] or a claim to enforce a mortgage may be restrained.[7] Similarly, where O and A are trustees for sale, O's application to have the trust executed may be refused.[8] In such cases the equity is given effect as a defence like any other estoppel. Often, however, more positive action is required.[9]

(1) INJUNCTIONS. O may be restrained by injunction from interfering with possession of land,[10] or from exercising a right to cut down trees and so destroy the beauty of improvements made by A in which he has acquiesced,[11] or from obstructing ancient lights altered by A with O's acquiescence.[12] Further, the injunction may be granted subject to an undertaking by A, e.g. to exercise compulsory powers of acquisition.[13]

(2) CHARGE FOR EXPENDITURE. A may be given an equitable lien on the property for his expenditure,[14] or for the value of his improvements,[15] and in such a case he will be treated as a mortgagee in possession.[16] Alternatively, an order for possession against A may be made conditionally upon O repaying the cost of improvements effected by A.[17] Or it may appear that A has already had "sufficient satisfaction" for his expenditure, and so is entitled to no relief.[18]

(3) CONFERMENT OF TITLE. In many cases justice cannot be done by the mere use of the doctrine by way of defence, or by the recoupment of expenditure, even where this is small,[19] but A must be granted some right. Thus if O has made an imperfect gift of the land to A, as by merely signing an informal memorandum[20] or uttering words of abandonment,[1] the court will compel O to perfect the gift by conveying the land to A.[2] In such cases the court may act by analogy with the specific

---

[5]   *Burrows v Sharp* (1991) 23 HLR 82; and see *Lord Cawdor v Lewis* (1835) 1 Y & C Ex 427 at 433; *Plimmer v Wellington Corpn* (1884) 9 App Cas 699 at 713, 714. The assumption of a general discretion is criticised in a closely reasoned article by S. Moriarty (1984) 100 LQR 376 but defended by M. P. Thompson [1986] Conv 406.

[6]   *Forbes v Ralli* (1925) LR 52 Ind App 178; *Inwards v Baker* [1965] 2 QB 29, [1965] 1 All ER 446, p. 654, post; *Williams v Staite* [1979] Ch 291, [1978] 2 All ER 928; and see *Powell v Thomas* (1848) 6 Hare 300 (injunction restraining action for ejectment).

[7]   *Steed v Whitaker* (1740) Barn Ch 220.

[8]   *Jones (AE) v Jones (FW)* [1977] 1 WLR 438, [1977] 2 All ER 231.

[9]   *Quaere* why in *Cullen v Cullen* [1962] IR 268 the equity was held to give no more than a defence.

[10] *Duke of Devonshire v Eglin* (1851) 14 Beav 530 (obstruction of water course).

[11] *Jackson v Cator* (1800) 5 Ves 688.

[12] *Cotching v Bassett* (1862) 32 Beav 101.

[13] *Somersetshire Coal Canal Co v Harcourt* (1858) 2 De G & J 596.

[14] *Unity Joint Stock Mutual Banking Association v King* (1858) 25 Beav 72 (land); *Re Foster* [1938] 3 All ER 610 (life insurance policy): and see *Veitch v Caldicott* (1945) 173 LT 30; *Taylor v Taylor* [1956] NZLR 99; *Neesom v Clarkson* (1845) 4 Hare 97 (form of account); *Hussey v Palmer* [1972] 1 WLR 1286, [1972] 3 All ER 744 (trust interest proportionate to expenditure); *sed quaere:* see (1973) 89 LQR 2.

[15] *Raffaele v Raffaele* [1962] WAR 29, discussed by D. E. Allan (1963) 79 LQR 238.

[16] *Neesom v Clarkson* (1845) 4 Hare 97.

[17] *Dodsworth v Dodsworth* (1973) 228 EG 1115, p. 671, post; and see *Baker v Baker* (1993) 25 HLR 408.

[18] *A-G v Balliol College, Oxford* (1744) 9 Mod Rep 407 at 412, per Lord HARDWICKE LC (expenditure by lessee).

[19] See *Pascoe v Turner* [1979] 1 WLR 431 at 438, [1979] 2 All ER 945 at 951, p. 667, post.

[20] *Dillwyn v Llewelyn,* (1862) 4 De GF & J 517.

[1]   *Thomas v Thomas* [1956] NZLR 785 (husband and wife).

[2]   *Pascoe v Turner,* supra. [*Voyce v Voyce* (1991) 62 P & CR 290, p. 667, n. 9, post; *Lim Teng Huan v Ang Swee Chuan* [1992] 1 WLR 113.

performance of contracts: A's expenditure with O's knowledge plays the part both of valuable consideration and of part performance.[3] If the circumstances do not suggest a gift, O may be compelled to convey the land on being paid its unimproved value,[4] or to hold the land on trust for sale, and to hold the proceeds after discharge of the respective expenditure of A and O to divide the residue between them.[5] Or the circumstances may indicate that A is to have a lease,[6] a perpetual easement,[7] a life interest,[8] a perpetual licence[9] or a licence as long as he desires to use the premises as his home[10] or a licence to remain until a loan is repaid,[11] and a lessor may be compelled to grant a licence to assign.[12] Again, if O has encouraged A to move to other land, O may be compelled to purchase A's original land.[13] Interests created by the doctrine are not registrable as land charges.'[14]

i. NEGATIVE PROTECTION[15]

INWARDS v BAKER[16]
[1965] 2 QB 29, [1965] 1 All ER 446 (CA, Lord DENNING MR, DANCKWERTS and SALMON LJJ)

In 1931, the younger Mr Baker wished to build a bungalow for himself on land which he hoped to purchase, but the project was beyond his means. His father said 'Why not put the bungalow on my land and make the bungalow a little bigger?' The son did so, building the bungalow largely through his own labour and expense. He lived there continuously until his father's death in 1951, and also from his father's death until the proceedings began.

---

[3]   See *Dillwyn v Llewelyn*, supra, at 521, 522; and see Lord RUSSELL OF KILLOWEN's restrictive interpretation of *Ramsden v Dyson* (1866) LR 1 HL 129 in *Ariff v Jadunath Majundar* (1931) LR 58 Ind App 91 at 102, 103.

[4]   *Duke of Beaufort v Patrick* (1853) 17 Beav 60.

[5]   *Holiday Inns Inc v Broadhead* (1974) 232 EG 951 (proposed joint venture to build and operate hotel on O's land).

[6]   *Stiles v Cowper* (1748) 3 Atk 692; *Siew Soon Wah v Yong Tong Hong* [1973] AC 836; *Griffiths v Williams* (1977) 248 EG 947, p. 673, post, and see *Gregory v Mighell* (1811) 18 Ves 328; *Ramsden v Dyson*, supra; *Taylors Fashions Ltd v Liverpool Victoria Trustees Co Ltd* [1982] QB 133n, [1981] 1 All ER 897, p. 627, ante.

[7]   *Ward v Kirkland* [1967] Ch 194, [1966] 1 All ER 609; *ER Ives Investment Ltd v High* [1967] 2 QB 379, [1967] 1 All ER 504, p. 665, post; *Crabb v Arun District Council* [1976] Ch 179, [1975] 3 All ER 856, p. 659, post (where payment was considered but not imposed in the circumstances).

[8]   *Ungurian v Lesnoff* [1990] Ch 206.

[9]   *Plimmer v Wellington Corpn* (1884) 9 App Cas 699.

[10]   *Inwards v Baker* [1965] 2 QB 29, [1965] 1 All ER 446, infra (son builds a bungalow on father's land); *Matharu v Matharu* [1994] 2 FLR 597

[11]   *Re Sharpe* [1980] 1 WLR 219, [1980] 1 All ER 198, p. 681, ante.

[12]   *Willmott v Barber* (1880) 15 Ch D 96 (where the claim failed).

[13]   *Salvation Army Trustee Co Ltd v West Yorkshire Metropolitan County Council* (1980) 41 P & CR 179, p. 659, n. 20, post. [See also *Lim Teng Huan v Ang Swee Chuan* [1992] 1 WLR 113, p. 671, post (joint purchaser of land who built house for own use on it held to acquire interest in other's undivided share subject to payment of compensation.]

[14]   *ER Ives Investment Ltd v High*, supra; and see J. F Garner (1967) 31 Conv (NS) 332.

[15]   (1976) 40 Conv (NS) 416 (A. M. Everton). See also *Jones v Jones* [1977] 1 WLR 438, [1977] 2 All ER 231. It is not clear whether the case fits best into this category or the later one; *Matharu v Matharu* (1994) 68 P & CR 93.

[16]   (1965) 81 LQR (R. H. Maudsley); *Ward v Kirkland* [1967] Ch 194 at 235–243, [1966] 1 All ER 609 at 621–627; *ER Ives Investment Ltd v High* [1967] 2 QB 379, [1967] 1 All ER 504; *Siew Soon Wah v Yong Tong Hong* [1973] AC 836; *Maharaj v Chand*, supra.

The land was left elsewhere in a will dated 1922, and in 1963 the trustees for sale of the land brought proceedings for possession.

Held. The son could not be disturbed.

LORD DENNING MR: The trustees say that at the most Jack Baker had a licence to be in the bungalow but that it had been revoked and he had no right to stay. The judge has held in their favour. He was referred to *Errington v Errington and Woods* [1952] 1 KB 290, [1952] 1 All ER 149, p. 613, ante but the judge held that that decision only protected a contractual licensee. He thought that, in order to be protected, the licensee must have a contract or promise by which he is entitled to be there. The judge said: 'I can find no promise made by the father to the son that he should remain in the property at all — no contractual arrangement between them. True the father said that the son could live in the property, expressly or impliedly, but there is no evidence that this was arrived at as the result of a contract or promise — merely an arrangement made casually because of the relationship which existed and knowledge that the son wished to erect a bungalow for residence.' Thereupon, the judge, with much reluctance, thought the case was not within *Errington's* case, and said the son must go.

The son appeals to this court. We have had the advantage of cases which were not cited to the county court judge, — cases in the last century, notably *Dillwyn v Llewelyn* (1862) 4 De GF & J 517, p. 669, post, and *Plimmer v Wellington Corpn* (1884) 9 App Cas 699, p. 656, post. This latter was a decision of the Privy Council which expressly affirmed and approved the statement of the law made by Lord Kingsdown in *Ramsden v Dyson* (1866) LR 1 HL 129, 170, p. 624, ante. It is quite plain from those authorities that if the owner of land requests another, or indeed allows another, to expend money on the land under an expectation created or encouraged by the landlord that he will be able to remain there, that raises an equity in the licensee such as to entitle him to stay. He has a licence coupled with an equity. Mr Goodhart urged before us that the licensee could not stay indefinitely. The principle only applied, he said, when there was an expectation of some precise legal term. But it seems to me, from *Plimmer's* case in particular, that the equity arising from the expenditure on land need not fail 'merely on the ground that the interest to be secured has not been expressly indicated ... the court must look at the circumstances in each case to decide in what way the equity can be satisfied.'

So in this case, even though there is no binding contract to grant any particular interest to the licensee, nevertheless the court can look at the circumstances and see whether there is an equity arising out of the expenditure of money. All that is necessary is that the licensee should, at the request or with the encouragement of the landlord, have spent the money in the expectation of being allowed to stay there. If so, the court will not allow that expectation to be defeated where it would be inequitable so to do. In this case it is quite plain that the father allowed an expectation to be created in the son's mind that this bungalow was to be his home. It was to be his home for his life or, at all events, his home as long as he wished it to remain his home. It seems to me, in the light of that equity, that the father could not in 1932 have turned to his son and said: 'You are to go. It is my land and my house.' Nor could he at any time thereafter so long as the son wanted it as his home.

Mr Goodhart put the case of a purchaser. He suggested that the father could sell the land to a purchaser who could get the son out. But I think that any purchaser who took with notice would clearly be bound by the equity. So here, too, the present plaintiffs, the successors in title of the father, are clearly themselves bound by this equity. It is an equity well recognised in law. It arises from the expenditure of money by a person in actual occupation of land when he is led to believe that, as the result of that expenditure, he will be allowed to remain there. It is for the court to say in what way the equity can be satisfied. I am quite clear in this case it can be satisfied by holding that the defendant can remain there as long as he desires to as his home.

I would allow the appeal accordingly and enter judgment for the defendant.

DANCKWERTS LJ: I agree and I will add only a few words. It seems to me the claim of the defendant in respect of this property is amply covered by *Errington v Errington and Woods, Dillwyn v Llwelyn,* and *Plimmer v Wellington Corpn.* Further, it seems to me to be supported by the observations of Lord Kingsdown in *Ramsden v Dyson.* It is true that in that case Lord Kingsdown reached a result on the facts of the case which differed from that reached by the other members of the House of Lords, but Lord Kingsdown's observations which are relevant in the present case have received support since that case was decided; and, in particular, I would like to refer to the observations in the judgment of the Privy Council in *Plimmer v Wellington Corpn.* It is said there (1884) 9 App Cas 699 at 713: 'Their Lordships consider that this case falls within the principle stated by Lord Kingsdown as to expectations created or encouraged by the landlord, with the addition that in this case the landlord did more than encourage the expenditure, for he took the initiative in requesting it.'

There are similar circumstances in the present case. The defendant was induced to give up his project of building a bungalow on land belonging to somebody else other than his father, in which case he would have become the owner or tenant of the land in question and thus have his own home. His father induced him to build on his, the father's, land and expenditure was made by the defendant for the purpose of the creation of the bungalow.

In my view the case comes plainly within the proposition stated in the cases. It is not necessary, I think, to imply a promise. It seems to me that this is one of the cases of an equity created by estoppel, or equitable estoppel, as it is sometimes called, by which the person who has made the expenditure is induced by the expectation of obtaining protection, and equity protects him so that an injustice may not be perpetrated.

I am clearly of opinion that the appeal should be allowed and judgment should be entered for the defendant.

ii. ACQUISITION OF PROPRIETARY INTEREST

(a) Perpetual Licence

PLIMMER v WELLINGTON CORPORATION [17]
(1844) 9 App Cas 699 (PC, Lord WATSON, Sir Barnes PEACOCK, Sir Robert P. COLLIER, Sir Richard COUCH and Sir Arthur HOBHOUSE)

Plimmer moored an old hulk on the foreshore of Wellington Bay and used it as a wharf and store by permission of the Crown. An earthquake raised the level of the land and necessitated the building of a jetty, which Plimmer built. Between

---

[17]   Cf. *DHN Food Distributors Ltd v Tower Hamlets London Borough Council* [1976] 1 WLR 852, [1976] 3 All ER 462, p. 611, ante (a case of a contractual licence). See also *Pennine Raceway Ltd v Kirklees Metropolitan Council* [1983] QB 382, [1982] 3 All ER 628, where a licensee of land was held entitled to compensation under TPCA 1971, s. 164 as a person 'interested in the land' on withdrawal of planning permission; [1982] All ER Rev 173 (P. J. Clarke).

1856 and 1861, at the instance of the Provincial Government, Plimmer extended the jetty. Subsequently the Government took possession of the jetty under statutory powers, and Plimmer and another claimed compensation under the Public Works Loans Act 1882 under which any person who 'had any estate or interest in, to or out of the lands ... vested in the Corporation ... shall be entitled to ... compensation'.

Held. The equitable right so acquired is an 'estate or interest in, to or out of land' within the meaning of the Act of 1882.

SIR ARTHUR HOBHOUSE: The law relating to cases of this kind may be taken as stated by Lord Kingsdown in the case of *Ramsden v Dyson* (1866) LR 1 HL 129. The passage is at 170: 'If a man, under a verbal agreement with a landlord for a certain interest in land, or, what amounts to the same thing, under an expectation created or encouraged by the landlord that he shall have a certain interest, takes possession of such land with the consent of the landlord, and upon the faith of such promise or expectation, with the knowledge of the landlord and without objection by him, lays out money upon land, a Court of Equity will compel the landlord to give effect to such promise or expectation. This was the principle of the decision in *Gregory v Mighell* (1811) 18 Ves 328, and, as I conceive, is open to no doubt. If at the hearing of the cause there appears to be such uncertainty as to the particular terms of the contract as might prevent a Court of Equity from giving relief if the contract had been in writing but there had been no expenditure, a Court of Equity will nevertheless, in the case which is above stated, interfere in order to prevent fraud, though there has been a difference of opinion amongst great judges as to the nature of the relief to be granted. Lord Thurlow seems to have thought that the Court would ascertain the terms by reference to the Master, and if they could not be ascertained would itself fix reasonable terms. Lord Alvanley and Lord Redesdale, and perhaps Lord Eldon, thought this was going too far; but I do not understand any doubt to have been entertained by any of them that, either in the form of a specific interest in the land, or in the shape of compensation for the expenditure, a Court of Equity would give relief, and protect in the meantime the possession of the tenant. If, on the other hand, a tenant being in possession of land, and knowing the nature and extent of his interest, lays out money upon it in the hope or expectation of an extended term or an allowance for expenditure, then, if such hope or expectation had not been created or encouraged by the landlord, the tenant has no claim which any Court of Law or Equity can enforce. This was the principle of the decision in *Pilling v Armitage* (1805) 12 Ves 78, and, like the decision in *Gregory v Mighell*, seems founded on plain rules of reason and justice ...'

In the present case, the equity is not claimed because the landowner has stood by in silence while his tenant has spent money on his land. This is a case in which the landowner has, for his own purposes, requested the tenant to make the improvements. The Government were engaged in the important work of introducing immigrants into the colony. For some reason, not now apparent, they were not prepared to make landing-places of their own, and in fact they did not do so until the year 1863. So they applied to John Plimmer to make his landing-place more commodious by a substantial extension of his jetty and the erection of a warehouse for baggage. Is it to be said that, when he had incurred the expense of doing the work asked for, the Government could turn round and revoke his licence at their will? Could they in July, 1856, have deprived him summarily of the use of the jetty? It would be in a high degree injust that they should do so, and that the parties should have intended such a result is, in the absence of evidence, incredible. ...

Their Lordships will not be the first to hold, and no authority has been cited to them to shew that after such a landowner has requested such a tenant to incur expense on his land for his benefit, he can without more and at his own will take away the property so improved. Their Lordships consider that this case falls within the principle stated by Lord Kingsdown as to expectations created or encouraged by the landlord, with the addition that in this case the landlord did more than encourage the expenditure, for he took the initiative in requesting it. ...

The question still remains as to the extent of interest which Plimmer acquired by his expenditure in 1856. Referring again to the passage quoted from Lord Kingsdown's judgment, there is good authority for saying what appears to their Lordships to be quite sound in principle, that the equity arising from expenditure on land need not fail merely on the ground that the interest to be secured has not been expressly indicated.

In such a case as *Ramsden v Dyson* the evidence (according to Lord Kingsdown's view) shewed that the tenant expected a particular kind of lease, which Vice-Chancellor Stuart decreed to him, though it does not appear what form of relief Lord Kingsdown himself would have given. In such a case as the *Duke of Beaufort v Patrick* (1853) 17 Beav 60, nothing but perpetual retention of the land would satisfy the equity raised in favour of those who spent their money on it, and it was secured to them at a valuation. In such a case as *Dillwyn v Llewlyn* (1862) 4 De G F & J 517, nothing but a grant of the fee simple would satisfy the equity which the Lord Chancellor held to have been raised by the son's expenditure on his father's land. In such a case as that of the *Unity Joint-Stock Mutual Banking Association v King* (1858) 25 Beav 72, the Master of the Rolls, holding that the father did not intend to part with his land to his sons who built upon it, considered that their equity would be satisfied by recouping their expenditure to them. In fact, the Court must look at the circumstances in each case to decide in what way the equity can be satisfied.

In this case their Lordships feel no great difficulty. In their view, the licence given by the Government to John Plimmer, which was indefinite in point of duration but was revocable at will, became irrevocable by the transactions of 1856, because those transactions were sufficient to create in his mind a reasonable expectation that his occupation would not be disturbed, and because they and the subsequent dealings of the parties cannot be reasonably explained on any other supposition. Nothing was done to limit the use of the jetty in point of duration. The consequence is that Plimmer acquired an indefinite, that is practically a perpetual, right to the jetty for the purposes of the original licence, and if the ground was afterwards wanted for public purposes, it could only be taken from him by the legislature.

An analogy to this process may be found in such cases as *Winter v Brockwell* (1807) 8 East 308 and *Liggins v Inge* (1831) 7 Bing 682. These cases shew that where a landowner permits his neighbour to execute works on his (the neighbour's land), and the licence is executed, it cannot be revoked at will by the licensor. If indefinite duration, it becomes perpetual. Their Lordships think that the same consequence must follow where the licence is to execute works on the land of the licensor, and owing to some supervening equity the licence has become irrevocable.

There are perhaps purposes for which such a licence would not be held to be an interest in land. But their Lordships are construing a statute which takes away private property for compensation, and in such statutes the expression 'estate or interest in, to or out of land' should receive a wide meaning. Indeed the statute itself directs that, in ascertaining the title of anybody to compensation, the Court shall not be bound to regard strict legal rights only, but shall do what is reasonable and just. Their Lordships have no difficulty in deciding that the equitable right acquired by John Plimmer is an interest in land carrying compensation under the Acts of 1880 and 1882. [18]

(b) Acquisition of Incorporeal Interest

1. AS BETWEEN THE PARTIES

CRABB v ARUN DISTRICT COUNCIL
[1976] Ch 179, [1975] 3 All ER 865 [19] (CA, Lord DENNING MR, LAWTON and SCARMAN LJJ)

The plaintiff owned two acres of land. The outlet to the road was through a point of access (point A) to a lane owned by the defendants, and by a right of way over that lane in a northerly direction to the road.

He decided to divide his land into two parts, and to sell them separately. This would require another point of access to the South, together with an additional right of way over the lane, to serve the Southern part. This was negotiated with the defendants at a meeting in July 1967, at which there was an oral agreement in principle that the plaintiff should have another access at point B; but no formal agreement was signed. The defendants, in accordance with the terms of the informal agreement, fenced the boundary between their land and the plaintiff's, leaving gaps at A and B, and erected gates at these points, the gateposts being set in concrete.

The plaintiff sold the Northern part, together with the right of way and access from point A. Differences arose between the plaintiff and defendants. The defendants uprooted the gatepost at point B, continued the fence to cover the gateway, and left the Southern part of the plaintiff's land landlocked. They offered access at point B and right of way for £3,000. The action was for a declaration and injunction, claiming that the defendants were estopped by their conduct from denying the plaintiff a right of access at point B and a right of way.

Held. Rights of access and way awarded to the plaintiff without payment. [20]

SCARMAN LJ: I agree that the appeal should be allowed. The plaintiff and the defendants are adjoining landowners. The plaintiff asserts that he has a right of way over the defendant's land giving access from his land to the public highway. Without this access his land is in fact landlocked, but, for reasons which clearly appear from the narration of the facts already given by my Lords, the plaintiff cannot claim a right of way by necessity. The plaintiff has no grant. He has the benefit of no enforceable contract. He has no prescriptive right. His case has to be that the defendants are estopped by their conduct from denying him a right of access over their land to the public highway. If the plaintiff has any right, it is

[18]   Cf. *Canadian Pacific Rly Co v R* [1931] AC 414 at 428–429; *Lee-Parker v Izzet (No 2)* [1972] 1 WLR 775 at 780–781, [1972] 2 All ER 800 at 804–805.

[19]   (1976) 40 Conv (NS) 156 (F. R. Crane); (1976) 92 LQR 174 (P. S. Atiyah); 342 (P. J. Millett); (1995) 58 MLR 637 at p. 640 (G. Battersby).

[20]   See *Crabb v Arun District Council (No 2)* (1976) 121 SJ 86 where Crabb was refused an enquiry as to damages. See also *Salvation Army Trustee Co Ltd v West Yorkshire Metropolitan County Council* (1980) 41 P & CR 179 (where proprietary estoppel was extended to the *disposal* of an interest in land where the disposal was closely linked by an arrangement that also involved the acquisition of an interest in land); discussed in *A-G of Hong Kong v Humphreys Estate (Queen's Gardens) Ltd* [1987] AC 114 at 126, 127, [1987] 2 All ER 387 at 394.

an equity arising out of the conduct and relationship of the parties. In such a case I think it is now well settled law that the court, having analysed and assessed the conduct and relationship of the parties, has to answer three questions. First, is there an equity established? Secondly, what is the extent of the equity, if one is established? And, thirdly, what is the relief appropriate to satisfy the equity? See *Duke of Beaufort v Patrick* (1853) 17 Beav 60; *Plimmer v Wellington Corpn* (1884) 9 App Cas 699, p. 656, ante and *Inwards v Baker* [1965] 2 QB 29, [1965] 1 All ER 445, p. 654, ante, a decision of this court, and particularly the observations of Lord Denning MR at 37, at 448–449. Such therefore I believe to be the nature of the inquiry that the courts have to conduct in a case of this sort. In pursuit of that inquiry I do not find helpful the distinction between promissory and proprietary estoppel. This distinction may indeed be valuable to those who have to teach or expound the law; but I do not think that, in solving the particular problem raised by a particular case, putting the law into categories is of the slightest assistance.

Nor do I think it necessary in a case such as this to inquire minutely into the law of agency. These defendants could, of course, only act through agents; but, as I have already made clear, from the very nature of the case, there would be no question of grant, no question of legally enforceable contract. We are in the realm of equity; and within that realm we find that equity, to its eternal credit, has developed an immensely flexible, yet perfectly clear, doctrine: see *ER Ives Investment Ltd v High* [1967] 2 QB 379, [1967] 1 All ER 504, p. 665, post, per Danckwerts LJ at 399, at 510–511. The approach of equity, when there is a question of agency in a field such as this, must I think be a very simple one. It will merely be that, within reasonable limits, those to whom a defendant entrusts the conduct of negotiations must be treated as having the authority, which, within the course of the negotiations, they purport to exercise. I put it in that way in the light of the comments of Lord Denning MR in *Moorgate Mercantile Co Ltd v Twitchings* [1976] QB 225 at 243, [1975] 3 All ER 314 at 324, comments which were themselves made upon a judgment to the same effect in *Attorney-General to the Prince of Wales v Collom* [1916] 2 KB 193 at 203. I would add only one reservation to this broad proposition. The defendant, if he thinks that an agent has exceeded his instructions, can always so inform the plaintiff before the plaintiff acts to his detriment in reliance upon what the agent has said or done. If a defendant has done so, the plaintiff cannot then establish the equity: for the defendant will have intervened to prevent him acting to his detriment. Nothing of that sort happened in this case. After the meeting in July 1967, to which both my Lords have referred, the plaintiff was left to form his own conclusions as to the intentions of the defendants.

I come now to consider the first of the three questions which I think in a case such as this the court have to consider. What is needed to establish an equity? In the course of an interesting addition to his submissions this morning, Mr Lightman cited *Ramsden v Dyson* (1886) LR 1 HL 129, 142, to support his proposition that in order to establish an equity by estoppel there must be a belief by the plaintiff in the existence of a right created or encouraged by the words or actions of the defendant. With respect, I do not think that that is today a correct statement of the law. I think the law has developed so that today it is to be considered as correctly stated by Lord Kingsdown in his dissenting speech in *Ramsden v Dyson*. Like Lord Denning MR, I think that the point of dissent in *Ramsden v Dyson* was not on the law but on the facts. Lord Kingsdown's speech, in so far as it dealt with propositions of law, has been often considered, and recently followed by this court in *Inwards v Baker*. So what is the effect of looking to Lord

Kingsdown's speech for a statement of the law? Lord Kingsdown said, LR 1 HL 129, 170:

'The rule of law applicable to the case appears to me to be this: If a man, under a verbal agreement with a landlord for a certain interest in land, or, what amounts to the same thing, *under an expectation, created or encouraged by the landlord,*' — my italics — 'that he shall have a certain interest, takes possession of such land, with the consent of the landlord, and upon the faith of such promise or expectation, with the knowledge of the landlord, and without objection by him, lays out money upon the land, a court of equity will compel the landlord to give effect to such promise or expectation.'

That statement of the law is put into the language of landlord and tenant because it was a landlord and tenant situation with which Lord Kingsdown was concerned; but it has been accepted as of general application. While *Ramsden v Dyson* may properly be considered as the modern starting-point of the law of equitable estoppel, it was analysed and spelt out in a judgment of Fry J in 1880 in *Willmott v Barber* (1880) 15 ChD 96, a decision to which Pennycuick V-C referred in his judgment. I agree with Pennycuick V-C in thinking that the passage from Fry J's judgment, from p. 105, is a valuable guide as to the matters of fact which have to be established in order that a plaintiff may establish this particular equity. Moreover, Mr Lightman for the defendants sought to make a submission in reliance upon the judgment. Fry J said, at 105–106:

'It has been said that the acquiescence which will deprive a man of his legal rights must amount to fraud, and in my view that is an abbreviated statement of a very true proposition. A man is not to be deprived of his legal rights unless he has acted in such a way as would make it fraudulent for him to set up those rights. What, then, are the elements or requisites necessary to constitute fraud of that description? In the first place the plaintiff must have made a mistake as to his legal rights.[1] Secondly, the plaintiff must have expended some money or must have done some act (not necessarily upon the defendant's land) on the faith of his mistaken belief. Thirdly, the defendant, the possessor of the legal right, must know of the existence of his own right which is inconsistent with the right claimed by the plaintiff. If he does not know of it he is in the same position as the plaintiff, and the doctrine of acquiescence is founded upon conduct with a knowledge of your legal right. Fourthly, the defendant, the possessor of the legal rights, must know of the plaintiff's mistaken belief of his rights.[2] If he does not, there is nothing which calls upon him to assert his own rights. Lastly,' — If I may digress, this is the important element as far as this appeal is concerned — 'the defendant, the possessor of the legal right, must have encouraged the plaintiff in his expenditure of money or in the other acts which he has done, either directly or by abstaining from asserting his legal right.'

Mr Lightman, in the course of an interesting and vigorous submission, drew the attention of the court to the necessity of finding something akin to fraud before the equity sought by the plaintiff could be established. 'Fraud' was a word often in the mouths of those robust judges who adorned the bench in the 19th century. It is less often in the mouths of the more wary judicial spirits today who sit upon the bench. But it is clear that whether one uses the word 'fraud' or not,

---

[1]   In *E & L Berg Homes Ltd v Grey* (1979) 253 EG 473, the plaintiff failed because he was unable to satisfy this requirement. See also *Gloucestershire County Council v Farrow* [1983] 2 All ER 1031.

[2]   Though this was said not to be essential in *Taylor Fashions Ltd v Liverpool Victoria Friendly Society* [1982] QB 133n at 147–148; [1981] 1 All ER 897 at 911–912, pp. 630–632, ante.

the plaintiff has to establish as a fact that the defendant, by setting up his right, is taking advantage of him in a way which is unconscionable, inequitable or unjust. It is to be observed from the passage that I have quoted from the judgment of Fry J that the fraud or injustice alleged does not take place during the course of negotiation, but only when the defendant decides to refuse to allow the plaintiff to set up his claim against the defendants' undoubted right. The fraud, if it be such, arises after the event, when the defendant seeks by relying on his right to defeat the expectation which he by his conduct encouraged the plaintiff to have. There need not be anything fraudulent or unjust in the conduct of the actual negotiations — the conduct of the transaction by the defendants.

The court therefore cannot find an equity established unless it is prepared to go as far as to say that it would be unconscionable and unjust to allow the defendants to set up their undoubted rights against the claim being made by the plaintiff. In order to reach a conclusion upon that matter the court does have to consider the history of the negotiations under the five headings to which Fry J referred. I need not at this stage weary anyone with an elaborate statement of the facts. I have no doubt upon the facts of this case that the first four elements referred to by Fry J exist. The question before the judge and now in this court in whether the fifth element is present: have the defendants, as possessor of the legal right, encouraged the plaintiff in the expenditure of money or in the other acts which he has done, either directly or by abstaining from asserting their legal rights? The first matter to be considered is the meeting on site of 26 July 1967. Pennycuick V-C made a finding of fact about the meeting; and for myself I am not prepared to dissent from his finding. But the substance of the finding of fact has to be regarded; not its phrasing. One must not be misled by words or phrases into misconstruing the nature of the finding. Pennycuick V-C found there was no definite assurance given by the defendants' representative to the plaintiff and his architect.

[His Lordship summarised the evidence and continued:]

That was a finding that there was acceptance in principle that there should be access and a right of way over the defendants' land at point B; and I am content to go no further and to base my judgment on what I believe to be that finding of Pennycuick V-C. Clearly the plaintiff and Mr Alford came away from that meeting in the confident expectation that a right would in due course be accorded to the plaintiff. Mr Alford did foresee 'further processes.' Of course, there would be further processes. The nature of the legal right to be granted had to be determined. It might be given by way of licence. It might be granted by way of easement. Conditions might be imposed. Payment of a sum of money might be required. But those two men, the plaintiff and his architect, came away from the meeting in the confident expectation that such a right would be granted upon reasonable conditions. What happened? By August — a month or less, after the meeting — posts for a fence were already on the ground, though not erected. There was already an indication, at about that time, I think — if not then, certainly soon after — of the presence of a gap at point B, that being the point of access agreed in principle. During the later months of 1967 nothing relevant transpired in the conduct of the negotiations between the plaintiff and the defendants. I accept Mr Lightman's submission that relationship as well as conduct is relevant: but during this period their relationship did not develop at all. They remained adjoining landowners, one of whom had agreed in principle at a meeting upon the site that there should be a right of way from point B over his land to the public road. Yet, things were happening. In the later months of 1967 the defendants, who were the local authority, were busy developing on neighbouring land, which the plaintiff's predecessor in title had sold them, a council housing estate. Lorries were being used for carting building materials, removing debris and so forth; and these lorries were in fact going upon the land of the plaintiff. Unfortunately materials on the land, the property of the plaintiff, were being pilfered. And so there came a meeting in January 1968, the point of which was to draw the attention of the defendants' officers to the situation which was developing. By the time the meeting took place the fence, which the defendants were obliged under the conveyance of their estate to erect between their land and the plaintiff's land, was substantially in position with gaps at point A, the access to the northern land, and at point B, the access in dispute. Nobody on behalf of the defendants gave the slightest indication to the plaintiff and his representatives at that meeting that there was going to be any difficulty or was likely to be any difficulty about access at point B. The confident expectation with which the plaintiff and Mr Alford left the meeting in July remained remarkably undisturbed by the meeting of January 1968. Indeed it was reinforced because there on the ground, plain for all to see, was a fence with gaps which accorded exactly with the agreement in principle reached in the previous July. Ten days later the defendants ordered gates, and by March the gates were installed. I ask myself: as at March 1968 had these defendants encouraged the plaintiff to think that he had or was going to be given a right? To use the language of Fry J, had they done it directly or had they done it by abstaining from asserting a legal right? Their encouragement of the belief in the mind of the plaintiff and Mr Alford was both direct and indirect. It was direct because of what they had done on the ground. It was indirect because ever since the July meeting they had abstained from giving the plaintiff or his architect any indication that they were standing on their rights, or had it in mind to go back, as, of course, they were entitled at that stage to go back, upon the agreement in principle reached at that meeting. And so matters proceeded until September 1968. By now, be it observed, over a year had passed since that first meeting when there was agreement in principle. Nothing had been done to disabuse the minds of the plaintiff and Mr Alford of the expectation reasonably induced by what the defendants' engineer then said: and there had been the direct encouragement of the gates. In September 1968, without telling the defendants or giving them any notice, so far as I am aware, the plaintiff entered into a contract to sell the northern piece of land without reservation over that land of any right of way. This was the act which was detrimental to the interests of the plaintiff. He did it in the belief that he had or could enforce a right of way and access at point B in the southern land.

One of the points taken by Mr Lightman is that the defendants had no notice of the sale, and therefore no opportunity to correct what on his case was a false belief in the mind of the plaintiff. Mr Millett in the course of his submissions conceded that he had not found in the books any case in which the sort of estoppel which we are here considering had arisen when the fact known to the defendants was an intention and not the realisation of that intention. That is, of course, what differentiates this case from one such as *E R Ives Investment Ltd v High* [1967] 2 QB 379, [1967] 1 All ER 504, p. 665, post. There the party who was found to be estopped did have notice of what the other party was doing at the time he was doing it. Therefore I think Mr Lightman rightly invites us to face this question: Does the fact that the defendants had no notice of the sale of the northern land before it was completed destroy the equity? Mr Lightman will concede, as I understand this part of his argument, no more than this: that the plaintiff might have been able to establish an equity if he had referred to the defendants before binding himself to the purchaser of the northern land: for that would have given the defendants an opportunity of disabusing the mind of the plaintiff before he acted to his detriment. The point is worthy of careful consideration. I reject it because, in my judgment, in this sort of proceedings, the court must be careful to avoid generalisation. I can conceive of cases in which it would be absolutely appropriate for a defendant to say: 'But you should not have acted to your detriment until you had had a word with me and I could have put you right.' But there are cases in which it is far too late for a defendant to get himself out of his pickle by putting upon the plaintiff that sort of duty; and this, in my judgment, is one of those cases. If immediately following the July meeting the clerk to the defendant authority had written saying: 'I have had a report of the meeting with the assistant engineer and I must inform you that whether or not there is to be an easement or a licence is a matter which can only be decided by the council,' the plaintiff would not now establish his equity: in selling the northern land without reservation of a right of way, he would have acted at his own risk. But one has to look at the whole conduct of the parties and the developing relationship between them. By September 1968, 13½ months after the initial meeting, the plaintiff must really and reasonably have been attaching importance to the abstention of the defendants from declaring to him in correspondence, or by telephone to his agent, their true position, namely, that there would be no acceptance in principle of a right until the matter had been considered by the authority itself. By that time there had been, as well, the laying out of the fence and the installing of the gates. It is for those reasons — the passage of time, the abstention and the gates — that I think the defendants cannot rely upon the fact that the plaintiff acted, without referring to the defendants, on his intention — an intention of which they had had notice ever since their agent was informed of it at the meeting in July 1967. I think therefore an equity is established.

I turn now to the other two questions — the extent of the equity and the relief needed to satisfy it. There being no grant, no enforceable contract, no licence, I would analyse the minimum equity to do justice to the plaintiff as a right either to an easement or to a licence upon terms to be agreed. I do not think it is necessary to go further than that. Of course, going that far would support the equitable remedy of injunction which is sought in this action. If there is no agreement as to terms, if agreement fails to be obtained, the court can, in my judgment, and must, determine in these proceedings upon what terms the plaintiff should be put to enable him to have the benefit of the equitable right which he is held to have. It is interesting that there has been some doubt amongst distinguished lawyers in the past as to whether the court can so proceed. Lord Kingsdown refers in fact to those doubts in a passage, which I need not quote, in *Ramsden v Dyson* (1866) LR 1 HL 129 at 171. Lord Thurlow clearly thought that the court did have this power. Other lawyers of that time did not. But there can be no doubt that since *Ramsden v Dyson* the courts have acted upon the basis that they have to determine not only the extent of the equity, but also the conditions necessary to satisfy it, and they have done so in a great number and variety of cases, I need refer only to the interesting collection of cases enumerated in *Snell's Principles of Equity*, 27th edn. (1973), at pp. 567–568, para. 2(*b*).[3]

In the present case the court does have to consider what is necessary now in order to satisfy the plaintiff's equity. Had matters taken a different turn, I would without hesitation have said that the plaintiff should be put upon terms to be agreed if possible with the defendants, and, if not agreed, settled by the court.

---

[3]   See now 30th edn. (2000), pp. 641–643, p. 652, ante.

But, as already mentioned by Lord Denning MR and Lawton LJ, there has been a history of delay, and indeed high-handedness, which it is impossible to disregard. In January 1969 the defendants, for reasons which no doubt they thought good at the time, without consulting the plaintiff, locked up his land. They removed not only the padlocks which he had put on the gates at point B, but the gates themselves. In their place they put a fence — rendering access impossible save by breaking down the fence. I am not disposed to consider whether or not the defendants are to be blamed in moral terms for what they did. I just do not know. But the effect of their action has been to sterilise the plaintiff's land; and for the reasons which I have endeavoured to give, such action was an infringement of an equitable right possessed by the plaintiff. It has involved him in loss, which has not been measured; but, since it amounted to sterilisation of an industrial estate for a very considerable period of time, it must surpass any sort of sum of money which the plaintiff ought reasonably, before it was done, to have paid the defendants in order to obtain an enforceable legal right. I think therefore that nothing should now be paid by the plaintiff and that he should receive at the hands of the court the belated protection of the equity that he has established. Reasonable terms, other than money payment, should be agreed: or, if not agreed, determined by the court.

For those reasons I also would allow the appeal.

2. AS AGAINST A PURCHASER. THE PROBLEM OF NOTICE

E R IVES INVESTMENT LTD v HIGH [4]
[1967] 2 QB 379, [1967] 1 All ER 504 (CA, LORD DENNING MR, DANCKWERTS and WINN LJJ)

In 1946, the defendant, High, began to build a house on a plot of land. Soon after, Westgate, his neighbour, started to erect a block of flats in such a way that their foundations encroached by about one foot upon the defendant's land. The defendant and Westgate agreed that the foundation could remain, and that the defendant should have a right of way for his car across Westgate's yard. The agreement for the right of way was never registered.

Westgate sold the block to Flt.-Lt. and Mrs Wright who knew of the agreement, and also knew that in 1959 the defendant erected a garage so sited that it could only be approached across the yard. In 1960, the defendant contributed to the surfacing of the yard.

In 1962 the Wrights sold the flats to the plaintiffs, expressly subject to the right of way. The plaintiffs sued the defendant for trespass to the yard, claiming that the defendant had no legal right of way, and that if he was entitled to an equitable easement, it was void against them because it was not registered.

Held. The defendant was entitled to use the way across the yard.

LORD DENNING MR: One thing is quite clear. Apart from this point about the Land Charges Act 1925, Mr High would have in equity a good right of way across the yard. This right arises in two ways:

1. *Mutual benefit and burden.* The right arises out of the agreement of 2 November 1949, and the subsequent action taken on it: on the principle that 'he who takes the benefit must accept the burden.' When adjoining owners of land make an agreement to secure continuing rights and benefits for each of them in or over the land of the other, neither of them can take the benefit of the agreement and throw over the burden of it. This applies not only to the original

---

[4]   *Montague v Long* (1972) 24 P & CR 240.

parties, but also their successors. The successor who takes the continuing benefit must take it subject to the continuing burden. This principle has been applied to neighbours who send their water into a common drainage system: see *Hopgood v Brown* [1955] 1 WLR 213, [1955] 1 All ER 550, and to purchasers of houses on a building estate who had the benefit of using the roads and were subject to the burden of contributing to the upkeep: see *Halsall v Brizell* [1957] Ch 169, [1957] 1 All ER 371, p. 936, post. The principle clearly applies in the present case. The owners of the block of flats have the benefit of having their foundations in Mr High's land. So long as they take that benefit, they must shoulder the burden. They must observe the condition on which the benefit was granted, namely, they must allow Mr High and his successors to have access over their yard: cf. *May v Belleville* [1905] 2 Ch 605. Conversely, so long as Mr High takes the benefit of the access, he must permit the block of flats to keep their foundations in his land.

2. *Equity arising out of acquiescence.* The right arises out of the expense incurred by Mr High in building his garage, as it is now, with access only over the yard: and the Wrights standing by and acquiescing in it, knowing that he believed he had a right of way over the yard. By so doing the Wrights created in Mr High's mind reasonable expectation that his access over the yard would not be disturbed. That gives rise to an 'equity arising out of acquiescence.' It is available not only against the Wrights but also their successors in title. The court will not allow that expectation to be defeated when it would be inequitable so to do. It is for the court in each case to decide in what way the equity can be satisfied: see *Inwards v Baker* [1965] 2 QB 29, [1965] 1 All ER 446, p. 654, ante; *Ward v Kirkland* [1967] Ch 194, [1966] 1 All ER 609 and the cases cited therein. In this case it could only be satisfied by allowing Mr High and his successors to have access over the yard so long as the block of flats has its foundations in his land.

The next question is this: was that right a land charge such as to need registration under the Land Charges Act 1925? For if it was a land charge, it was never registered and would be void as against any purchaser: see section 13 of the Act.[5] It would, therefore, be void against the plaintiffs, even though they took with the most express knowledge and notice of the right.

It was suggested that the agreement of 2 November 1949, was 'an estate contract' within Class C(iv). I do not think so. There was no contract by Mr Westgate to convey a legal estate of any kind.

It was next suggested that the right was an 'equitable easement' within Class D(iii). This class is defined as 'any easement right or privilege over or affecting land created or arising after the commencement of this Act, and being merely an equitable interest'. Those words are almost identical with section 2(3)(iii) of the Law of Property Act 1925, and should be given the same meaning. They must be read in conjunction with sections 1(2)(*a*), 1(3) and 4(1) of the Law of Property Act 1925. It then appears that an 'equitable easement' is a proprietary interest in land such as would before 1926 have been recognised as capable of being conveyed or created *at law*, but which since 1926 only takes effect as an equitable interest. An instance of such a proprietary interest is a profit à prendre for life. It does not include a right to possession by a requisitioning authority: see *Lewisham Borough Council v Maloney* [1948] 1 KB 50, [1947] 2 All ER 36. Nor does it include a right, liberty or privilege arising in equity by reason of 'mutual benefit and burden,' or arising out of 'acquiescence,' or by reason of a contractual licence: because none of those before 1926 were proprietary interests such as were capable of being conveyed or created *at law*. They only subsisted *in equity*. They do not

---

5   Now LCA 1972, s. 2(6).

need to be registered as land charges, so as to bind successors, but take effect in equity without registration: see an article by Mr C. V. Davidge on 'Equitable Easements' in (1937) 53 Law Quarterly Review, p. 259 and by Professor H. W. R. Wade in [1956] Cambridge Law Journal, pp. 225–226.[6]

The right of Mr High to cross this yard was not a right such as could ever have been created or conveyed at law. It subsisted only in equity. It therefore still subsists in equity without being registered. Any other view would enable the owners of the flats to perpetrate the grossest injustice. They could block up Mr High's access to the garage, whilst keeping their foundations in his land. That cannot be right.

I am confirmed in this construction of the statute when I remember that there are many houses adjoining one another which have drainage systems in common, with mutual benefits and burdens. The statute cannot have required all these to be registered as land charges.

I know that this greatly restricts the scope of Class D(iii) but this is not disturbing.[7] A special committee has already suggested that Class D(iii) should be abolished altogether: see the report of the Committee on Land Charges ((1956) Command Paper 9825, para. 16).[8]

(c) Acquisition of Fee Simple Estate

1. WITHOUT COMPENSATION

PASCOE v TURNER[9]
[1979] 1 WLR 431, [1979] 2 All ER 945 (CA, ORR, LAWTON and CUMMING-BRUCE LJJ)

The plaintiff and defendant lived together in the plaintiff's home. Later, the plaintiff purchased another house and they moved in. He told the defendant that the house was hers, and everything in it. In reliance on this gratuitous promise, she expended, to the plaintiff's knowledge, her own money on repairs, improvements and redecoration; and also on furniture.

Later, when the relationship ended, the plaintiff gave to the defendant two months' notice to determine the licence.

Held. The defendant occupied the house as a licensee. There was a gift of the contents, but no valid gift or declaration of trust of the house. But an estoppel operated in her favour, and this could most properly be satisfied by a conveyance of the house to the defendant.

CUMMING-BRUCE LJ:

The issues

The appeal raises three issues about the house: (*a*) Did the defendant prove the trust found by the judge? (*b*) Did she prove such facts as prevented the plaintiff by estoppel from asserting his legal title? (*c*) If the answer to that

---

[6]   P. 32, ante; p. 711, post.
[7]   See *Shiloh Spinners Ltd v Harding* [1973] AC 691 at 719–721, [1973] 1 All ER 90 at 98–99, p. 36, ante.
[8]   P. 712, n. 7, post.
[9]   [1979] Conv 379 (F. R. Crane); (1979) 42 MLR 574 (B. Sufrin); (1995) 58 MLR 637 at p. 642 (G. Battersby). Cf. *Dillwyn v Llewelyn* (1862) 4 De GF & J 517; *Voyce v Voyce* (1991) 62 P & CR 290 (donee of farm and cottage from licensor ordered to convey fee simple to licensee); *Durant v Heritage* [1994] EGCS 134.

question is yes, what is the equitable relief to which she is entitled? In respect of the contents of the house, did the defendant prove that they were given to her by the plaintiff's voluntary gift? ...

The judge found that the plaintiff had made a gift to her of the contents of the house. I have no doubt that he was right about that. She was already in possession of them as a bailee when he declared the gift. Counsel for the plaintiff submitted that there was no gift because it was uncertain what he was giving her. He pointed to a safe and to the defendant's evidence that she had sent round an orange bedroom suite to the plaintiff so that he should have a bed to sleep on. The answer is that he gave her everything in the house, but later, recognising his need, she gave back some bits and pieces to him. So much for the contents.

Her rights in the realty are not quite so simply disposed of because of section 53 and section 54 of the Law of Property Act 1925. There was nothing in writing. The judge considered the plaintiff's declarations, and decided that they were not enough to found an express trust. We agree. But he went on to hold that the beneficial interest in the house had passed under a constructive trust inferred from words and conduct of the parties. He relied on the passage in *Snell's Principles of Equity*, 27th edn. (1973), p. 185, in which the editors suggest a possible definition of a constructive trust. But there are difficulties in the way. The long and short of events in 1973 is that the plaintiff made an imperfect gift of the house. There is nothing in the facts from which an inference of a constructive trust can be drawn. If it had not been for section 53 of the Law of Property Act 1925 the gift of the house would have been a perfect gift, just as the gift of the contents was a perfect gift. In the event it remained an imperfect gift and, as Turner LJ said in *Milroy v Lord* (1862) 4 De GF & J 264 at 274: 'there is no equity in this court to perfect an imperfect gift.' So matters stood in 1973, and if the facts had stopped there the defendant would have remained a licensee at will of the plaintiff.

But the facts did not stop there. On the judge's findings the defendant, having been told that the house was hers, set about improving it within and without. Outside she did not do much: a little work on the roof and an improvement which covered the way from the outside toilet to the rest of the house, putting in a new door there, and Snowcem to protect the toilet. Inside she did a good deal more. She installed gas in the kitchen with a cooker, improved the plumbing in the kitchen and put in a new sink. She got new gas fires, putting a gas fire in the lounge. She redecorated four rooms. The fitted carpets she put in the bedrooms, the stair carpeting, and the curtains and the furniture that she bought are not part of the realty, and it is not clear how much she spent for those items. But they are part of the whole circumstances. There she was, on her own after he left her in 1973. She had £1,000 left of her capital, and a pension of some kind. Having as she thought been given the house, she set about it as described. On the repairs and improvement to the realty and its fixtures she spent about £230. She had £300 of her capital left by the date of the trial, but she did not establish in evidence how much had been expended on refurbishing the house with carpets, curtains and furniture. We would describe the work done in and about the house as substantial in the sense that that adjective is used in the context of estoppel. All the while the plaintiff not only stood by and watched but encouraged and advised, without a word to suggest that she was putting her money and her personal labour into his house. What is the effect in equity?

The cases relied upon by the plaintiff are relevant for the purpose of showing that the judge fell into error in deciding that on the facts a constructive trust could be inferred. They are the cases which deal with the intention of the parties when a house is acquired. But of those cases only *Inwards v Baker* [1965] 2 QB 29, [1965] 1 All ER 446, p. 654, ante is in point here. For this is a case of estoppel arising from the encouragement and acquiescence of the plaintiff between 1973 and 1976 when, in reliance upon his declaration that he was giving and, later, that he had given the house to her, she spent a substantial part of her small capital upon repairs and improvements to the house. The relevant principle is expounded in *Snell's Principles of Equity*, 27th edn., p. 565 in the passage under the heading 'Proprietary Estoppel,' and is elaborated in *Spencer Bower and Turner, Estoppel by Representation*, 3rd edn. (1977), chapter 12 entitled 'Encouragement and Acquiescence.'

The cases in point illustrating that principle in relation to real property are *Dillwyn v Llewelyn* (1862) 4 De GF & J 517; *Ramsden v Dyson* (1866) LR 1 HL 129 and *Plimmer v Wellington Corpn* (1884) 9 App Cas 699. One distinction between this class of case and the doctrine which has come to be known as 'promissory estoppel' is that where estoppel by encouragement or acquiescence is found on the facts, those facts give rise to a cause of action. They may be relied upon as a sword, not merely as a shield. In *Ramsden v Dyson* the plaintiff failed on the facts, and the dissent of Lord Kingsdown was upon the inferences to be drawn from the facts. On the principle, however, the House was agreed, and it is stated by Lord Cranworth LC and by Lord Wensleydale as well as by Lord Kingsdown. Likewise in *Plimmer's* case the plaintiff was granted a declaration that he had a perpetual right of occupation.

The final question that arises is: to what relief is the defendant entitled upon her counterclaim? In *Dillwyn v Llewelyn* there was an imperfect gift of land by a father who encouraged his son to build a house on it for £14,000. Lord Westbury LC said, at 521:

'About the rules of the court there can be no controversy. A voluntary agreement will not be completed or assisted by a court of equity, in cases of mere gift. If anything be wanting to complete the title of the donee, a court of equity will not assist him in obtaining it; for a mere donee can have no right to claim more than he has received. But the subsequent acts of the donor may give the donee that right or ground of claim which he did not acquire from the original gift. Thus, if A gives a house to B, but makes no formal conveyance, and the house is afterwards, on the marriage of B, included, with the knowledge of A, in the marriage settlement of B, A would be bound to complete the title of the parties claiming under that settlement. So if A puts B in possession of a piece of land, and tells him, "I give it to you that you may build a house on it," and B on the strength of that promise, with the knowledge of A, expends a large sum of money in building a house accordingly, I cannot doubt that the donee acquires a right from the subsequent transaction to call on the donor to perform that contract and complete the imperfect donation which was made.'

In *Plimmer's* case the Privy Council pose the question, how should the equity be satisfied? (See pp. 713, 714). And the Board declare that on the facts a licence revocable at will became irrevocable as a consequence of the subsequent transactions. So in *Thomas v Thomas* [1956] NZLR 785 the Supreme Court of New Zealand ordered the defendant to execute a proper transfer of the property.

In *Crabb v Arun District Council* [1976] Ch 179, [1975] 3 All ER 865, p. 659, ante, this court had to consider the principles upon which the court should give effect to the equity: see Lord Denning MR at 189, at 872. Lawton and Scarman LJJ agreed with the remedy proposed by Lord Denning MR. On the facts of that case Scarman LJ expressed himself thus at 198–199, at 880:

[His Lordship quoted the paragraph set out on p. 664, ante, beginning 'I turn now to ...' and continued:]

So the principle to be applied is that the court should consider all the circumstances, and the counterclaimant having at law no perfected gift or licence other than a licence revocable at will, the court must decide what is the minimum equity to do justice to her having regard to the way in which she changed her position for the worse by reason of the acquiescence and encouragement of the legal owner. The defendant submits that the only appropriate way in which the equity can here be satisfied is by perfecting the imperfect gift as was done in *Dillwyn v Llewelyn.*

Counsel for the plaintiff on instructions has throughout submitted that the plaintiff is entitled to possession. The only concession that he made was that the period of notice given in the letter of 9 April 1976 was too short. He made no submission upon the way the equity, if there was an equity, should be satisfied save to submit that the court should not in any view grant a remedy more beneficial to the defendant than a licence to occupy the house for her lifetime.

We are satisfied that the problem of remedy on the facts resolves itself into a choice between two alternatives: should the equity be satisfied by a licence to the defendant to occupy the house for her lifetime, or should there be a transfer to her of the fee simple?

The main consideration pointing to a licence for her lifetime is that she did not by her case at the hearing seek to establish that she had spent more money or done more work on the house than she would have done had she believed that she had only a licence to live there for her lifetime. But the court must be cautious about drawing any inference from what she did not give in evidence as the hypothesis put is one that manifestly never occurred to her. Then it may reasonably be held that her expenditure and effort can hardly be regarded as comparable to the change of position of those who have constructed buildings on land over which they had no legal rights.

This court appreciates that the moneys laid out by the defendant were much less than in some of the cases in the books. But the court has to look at all the circumstances. When the plaintiff left her she was, we were told, a widow in her middle fifties. During the period that she lived with the plaintiff her capital was reduced from £4,500 to £1,000. Save for her invalidity pension that was all that she had in the world. In reliance upon the plaintiff's declaration of gift, encouragement and acquiescence she arranged her affairs on the basis that the house and contents belonged to her. So relying, she devoted a quarter of her remaining capital and her personal effort upon the house and its fixtures. In addition she bought carpets, curtains and furniture for it, with the result that by the date of the trial she had only £300 left. Compared to her, on the evidence the plaintiff is a rich man. He might not regard an expenditure of a few hundred pounds as a very grave loss. But the court has to regard her change of position over the years 1973 to 1976.

We take the view that the equity cannot here be satisfied without granting a remedy which assures to the defendant security of tenure, quiet enjoyment, and freedom of action in respect of repairs and improvements without interference from the plaintiff. The history of the conduct of the plaintiff since 9 April 1976 in relation to these proceedings leads to an irresistible inference that he is determined to pursue his purpose of evicting her from the house by any legal means at his disposal with a ruthless disregard of the obligations binding upon conscience. The court must grant a remedy effective to protect her against the future manifestations of his ruthlessness. It was conceded that if she is granted a licence, such a licence cannot be registered as a land change, so that she may find herself ousted by a purchaser for value without notice. If she has in the future to do further and more expensive repairs she may only be able to finance them by a loan, but as a licensee she cannot charge the house. The plaintiff as legal owner may well find excuses for entry in order to do what he may plausibly represent as necessary works and so contrive to derogate from her enjoyment of the licence in ways that make it difficult or impossible for the court to give her effective protection.

Weighing such considerations this court concludes that the equity to which the facts in this case give rise can only be satisfied by compelling the plaintiff to give effect to his promise and her expectations. He has so acted that he must now perfect the gift.

2. WITH COMPENSATION

In **Lim Teng Huan v Ang Swee Chuan**[10] [1992] 1 WLR 113, A built a house on land which he jointly owned with L. A and L entered into a contract, under which L acknowledged that he had no title to the house and agreed to exchange his half share in the land for unspecified land which he expected to obtain from the Government of Brunei. The contract was void for uncertainty. L claimed that he was the sole beneficial owner of A's share.

In rejecting L's claim, the Privy Council held that L was estopped from denying A's title to the whole of the land, and that he was entitled to compensation representing a half-share in the present value of the land without the house; on payment L should convey his half-share in the land to A. Lord BROWNE-WILKINSON said at 117:

'The decision in *Taylors Fashions* showed that, in order to found a proprietary estoppel, it is not essential that the representor should have been guilty of unconscionable conduct in permitting the representee to assume that he could act as he did: it is enough if, in all the circumstances, it is unconscionable for the representor to go back on the assumption which he permitted the representee to make.'

(d) Licence to Occupy until Expenditure Reimbursed

In **Dodsworth v Dodsworth** (1973) 228 EG 1115, giving the judgment of the court, RUSSELL LJ said:

'In this case the plaintiff, aged over 70, owned in 1967 a bungalow near Boston, Lincolnshire, and lived there alone. Her younger brother and his wife — the two defendants — returned to England from Australia and were looking for a house to acquire as their home. The plaintiff persuaded them to join her in her bungalow. The judge held on the evidence that the defendants spent a sum of over £700 on improvements to the plaintiff's bungalow in the expectation, encouraged and induced by the plaintiff, that the defendants and the survivor of them would be able to remain in the bungalow as their home — sharing of course with the plaintiff while she lived — for as long as they wished to do so, in circumstances that raised an equity in favour of the defendants on the footing of

---

[10]   [1993] Conv 173 (S. K. Goo); *Price v Hartwell* [1996] EGCS 98 (joint owner licensee permitted to remain on premises so long as she made mortgage repayments, but must refund payments made by licensor after his severance of joint tenancy).

principles exemplified in a passage from Lord Kingsdown's speech in *Ramsden v Dyson* (1866) LR 1 HL 129, and in other cases since then. The judge, however, held on the evidence that the parties did not intend to create a legal relationship. Not many months after the defendants moved into the bungalow, the plaintiff repented of her invitation for reasons, or alleged reasons, which need not be rehearsed. She started proceedings for possession: the defendants counterclaimed to assert an equity. The plaintiff did not appear at the hearing, and her claim for possession was non-suited. The question on the counterclaim was whether the proper way in which the equity should be satisfied would be to make some order which would assure the defendants in their occupation of the bungalow as their home for as long as they wished, or on the other hand to declare in effect that possession could only be obtained against them by the plaintiff if they were repaid their outlay on improvements to the bungalow.

The judge decided upon the latter as the appropriate course. His main ground was this. The plaintiff was anxious to sell the bungalow and buy a smaller and less expensive one for herself. She could not do this, having no other capital asset, if the defendants were entitled to stay rent free. She would therefore have to continue sharing her home for the rest of her life with the defendants, with whom she was, or thought she was, at loggerheads. Against this the defendants would, on leaving, recover and have available towards another home the expenditure which they laid out in the expectation, albeit encouraged by the plaintiff, of ability to stay there as their home. We think that the judge in balancing these considerations was entitled, and right, to come to that decision. We do not accept that the judge was wrong on the ground submitted to us that where the extent of the expectations was defined, though without intention to create a legal relationship, between the parties, compensation for outlay could not be an appropriate satisfaction of the equity. On the appeal, the plaintiff having died intestate after notice of appeal, leave was given to the respondents, who are her administrators under a grant of letters of administration, to be joined as parties to the appeal. They do not contend that there was not an equity. They support the view, in the changed circumstances, of the judge that it was proper to satisfy the defendants' equity by protecting their occupation unless and until their expenditure was reimbursed.

Now it is clear that the ground upon which the judge mainly decided upon the appropriate remedy has, by the plaintiff's death, disappeared. But what is the situation now? Apart from the equity, the situation is this. The estate vested in the legal personal representatives consists only of the bungalow. This is subject to a standing mortgage of some £200 to £300. Its value free of any occupation rights in the defendants might be £5,000. Under the Administration of Estates Act 1925 the administrators hold the bungalow on trust for sale and to pay out of the proceeds of sale debts, duties, if any, and administration expenses (which must include their costs of this appeal), and then to divide among ten stirpes of beneficiaries, the first defendant in fact being one stirps. The immediate problem seems to be this. If immediate and direct effect is given to the expectations of the defendants, to take effect in priority to the respondents' entitlement and statutory duties, we cannot see but that it will lead, by virtue of the provisions of the Settled Land Act, to a greater and more extensive interest than was ever contemplated by the plaintiff and the defendants. The defendants would necessarily become joint tenants for life. As such they could sell the property, or quit and let it. In the one case, they would be entitled to the income of the invested proceeds of sale for life and the life of the survivor: in the other, they would be entitled to the net rents. None of these possibilities could conceivably have been embodied in the expectations giving rise to the equity in question, and we do not think that it can be right to satisfy such an equity by conferring upon the defendants a greater interest in the property than was envisaged by the parties. This, we should say, is a point which appears to have been overlooked in *Inwards v Baker* [1965] 2 QB 29, [1965] 1 All ER 446, p. 654, ante.

Is it possible in the present case to give effect to the expectation without falling foul of the impact of the Settled Land Act? ... Yes it was. In short therefore we do not see how we can sensibly, and without awarding to the defendants a greater interest in law than was within the induced expectation, satisfy this equity save by securing their occupation until this expenditure has been reimbursed, which was the effect of the judge's order or declaration.' [11]

(e) *Grant of Lease*

GRIFFITHS v WILLIAMS
(1977) 248 EG 947 (CA, Megaw, Orr and Goff LJJ)

No. 1 Gordon Villa, in Hereford, was owned by Mrs Cole, who was the mother of Mrs Williams, who was the mother of Mrs Griffiths. Mrs Williams was a school teacher, who had lived most of her life at the house.

Mrs Cole had always indicated her intention of leaving Mrs Williams a life interest in the house, and made a will to that effect in 1971. But in 1974, she changed her will, and left the house absolutely to Mrs Griffiths.

Mrs Williams looked after Mrs Cole in her latter years, and expended her money on repairs and improvements to the house. She did so primarily for the care of her mother, but also in the belief that she would be entitled to live in the house for the rest of her life.

Held. Mrs Williams was protected under the doctrine of estoppel. The award of a life interest was not appropriate, because that might create a settlement under the Settled Land Act 1925. Mrs Williams should receive (with all the parties' agreement) a lease determinable upon death, with no power to assign, and at a nominal rent which did not exceed two thirds of the rateable value.

Goff LJ: [The] equity is said to arise because the grandmother had repeatedly assured Mrs Williams that she would be allowed to live in the house for the whole of her life, and because, on the faith of those assurances, Mrs Williams had expended money upon the property which otherwise she would not have done. It emerged at the trial that she had spent in all, out of her own moneys, a sum of £2,000. Part of that was spent upon improvements to the property which consisted of putting in a bathroom and an indoors toilet, rewiring for electricity, concreting the yard, and repairs to one of the walls; but part of it had been spent in paying outgoings. In so far as the expenditure was of the latter character, I doubt whether it would raise an equity in Mrs Williams' favour, because it could be regarded simply as current payment for the benefits which she was enjoying by being allowed to live in the house. But in so far as money was spent upon permanent improvements such as I have mentioned, it would be capable of creating what is known as promissory estoppel. [12] It seems that a grant in aid towards the improvements was obtained from the local authority; but, even so, as I read the

---

[11] *Burrows v Sharpe* (1991) 23 HLR 82 (clean break only proper and fair solution in view of breakdown between parties; compensation in return for loss of accommodation); [1992] Conv 54 (J. E. Martin); *Baker v Baker* (1993) 25 HLR 408 (granny flat).

[12] Presumably proprietary estoppel is intended.

evidence Mrs Williams did incur expenditure out of her own money on improvements. But the evidence does not show how the £2,000 should be broken down between expenditure of that character and expenditure on current repairs.

In these circumstances, in my judgment, we have to determine three questions, which were propounded by Scarman LJ in his judgment in the case of *Crabb v Arun District Council* [1976] Ch 179, [1975] 3 All ER 865, p. 659, ante the relevant passage being at 193, at 875. I will read them from another case where they were cited, namely, *Jones v Jones* [1977] 1 WLR 438, [1977] 2 All ER 231, because there Roskill LJ answered those questions — of course, on the facts of the case before him, but the answers I think throw light on the nature of the questions and what the approach to answering them should be. I cite from the judgment of Roskill LJ at 443, at 235, where his Lordship said:

'As for the rest, Lord Denning MR has referred to the decision of this court, consisting of himself and Lawton and Scarman LJJ, in *Crabb v Arun District Council*. I would refer to the three questions, posed by Scarman LJ at the beginning of his judgment, which the court has to ask in relation to the now well-settled law of estoppel, at 193, at 875. "First, is there an equity established?" The answer here is unquestionably Yes. "Secondly, what is the extent of the equity, if one is established?" — and the answer, shortly is that the equity is of a possessory nature entitling the defendant to remain in this house —'
and then (though not relevant for present purposes)
'but it would not, in my judgment, extend to the defendant's wife. "And, thirdly, what is the relief appropriate to satisfy the equity?"'

Then he went on to answer that question, saying:
'All the members of the court in *Crabb v Arun District Council* thought that in some circumstances a court might impose the making of payment of some form or another as a condition of giving effect to the equity, but in the present case it seems to me that it would be wrong to impose as a condition of protecting the equity that the defendant should pay rent to the plaintiff for the following reasons. ...'
which he then set out.

That indicates to my mind that the third question is one upon which the court has to exercise a discretion. If it finds that there is an equity, then it must determine the nature of it, and then, guided by that nature and exercising discretion in all the circumstances, it has to determine what is the fair order to make between the parties for the protection of the claimant.

So I direct my mind to the first question: Was there here an equity? Mr McCarthy says that there was not, because the defendant failed to prove, and the learned judge did not find, that the grandmother at the time the improvements were effected knew that Mrs Williams was making a mistake as to her position. He relied on the passage in *Snell's Equity*, 27th edn. at p. 566, where it is said:

'Knowledge of the mistake makes it dishonest for him to remain wilfully passive in order afterwards to profit by the mistake he might have prevented. The knowledge must accordingly be proved by "strong and cogent evidence."'

He also points to the learned judge's judgment, where he said:
'It was clear that Mrs Williams — and I think this would apply to most sensitive people in her position — was reluctant to admit, even to herself, that in spending her own money on housekeeping and house improvement, she was thinking predominantly of her own inheritance rather than the care and comfort of her mother. What she did say, however, was that had it occurred to her that her

enjoyment and benefit of these improvements, or rather of the house as improved (a house that she had always regarded as her home) would be limited to her mother's life span, she would have had to think whether she was not obliged to look more closely to her own future. … It was equally clear, however, that none of this occurred to her at the time, or perhaps even not until it was put to her in this court.'

In so far as it is necessary to prove that Mrs Williams made a mistake, I think the mistake is to be found in her belief that she would be allowed to live in the house for the whole of her life. But I do not myself think that it really depends upon mistake. The equity is based upon the fact that where one has made a representation on the faith of which another party has expended his money, then the man who made the representation will not, to the prejudice of the other, be allowed to go back on it and assert his strict legal rights if to do so would be unconscionable. I cite this passage from the judgment of Lord Denning MR in *Inwards v Baker* [1965] 2 QB 29 at 37, [1965] 1 All ER 446 at 448:

[His Lordship quoted the paragraph set out on p. 655, ante, beginning 'So in this case …', and continued:].

The facts in that case were different, but the principle appears to me to apply precisely to the facts of the present case. Mrs Williams' evidence, which the learned judge preferred to that of Mrs Griffiths, was as follows: 'Whenever the question arose in any discussion Mrs Williams had always been assured that the house was her home of life. That was always what was said and she never expected more than a life interest.' That does not read as if it was the lady giving evidence, but the notes of the evidence appear throughout in that form, and this was obviously a record which the learned judge was making of the evidence which had been given before him. Then Mr Hedley Williams, whose evidence the learned judge also accepted, said — or the effect of his evidence is recorded — as follows: 'He had always understood that the house was his mother's for life, and this had been said to, or in front of, him over many years by both his grandmother and his mother'; and, again, 'As to the improvements etc there was no objection by the grandmother and he had never heard any mention (prior to his grandmother's death) of his mother leaving, or being asked to leave.' So when the learned judge speaks of what Mrs Williams would have thought had it occurred to her, it is clear that it would have occurred to her but for the fact that Mrs Cole, the testatrix, was throughout repeatedly assuring Mrs Williams that she could live in the house for the rest of her life. It seems to me, on this evidence, clear that Mrs Williams expended her money on the faith of those repeated assurances, and it is, I think, an irresistible inference that Mrs Cole knew that Mrs Williams was relying on the assurances which she herself was repeatedly making to her daughter. In my judgment, therefore, there is no doubt at all in this case but that an equity is made out.

I therefore pass to the second question, and that is: What is the equity? That must be an equity to have made good, so far as may fairly be done between the parties, the representation that Mrs Williams should be entitled to live in the house rent-free for the rest of her life.

So I come to the third question, which is really the one which gives rise to such difficulties as there are in this case. In *Dodsworth v Dodsworth* (1973) 228 EG 1115, p. 671, ante this court unanimously decided that if an equity of this nature were implemented by giving the claimant the right to occupy the house (as it was in that case) for his life, the result would be to create a tenancy for life within the meaning of the Settled Land Act, and so the party setting up the equity would get more than it was ever represented that he should have, because he would get all the statutory powers of a tenant for life under the Act: he could sell the property and take the income of the proceeds for his life, or he could grant a long lease. In that case the court does not seem to have considered what may in such cases be a difficult problem, namely, what is the 'settlement?' I think there are many authorities which establish that a right to occupy property for one's life is the equivalent of a tenancy for life under the Act. But the Act defines 'settlement' in section 1 in these terms:

'Any deed, will, agreement for a settlement or other agreement, Act of Parliament, or other instrument, or any number of instruments, whether made or passed before or after, or partly before and partly after, the commencement of this Act, under or by virtue of which instrument or instruments any land, after the commencement of this Act, stands for the time being. ...'

and then follow the various limitations which make it settled land.

Where the interest arises under a contract or other agreement, of course, there is no difficulty, because that falls fairly and squarely within the words of subsection (1) of section 1. But where what is set up is an equity arising from acting upon a representation, it is not obvious how that can be brought within the terms of section 1(1). There are two other cases in which this type of problem was considered by this court, namely, *Binions v Evans* [1972] Ch 359, [1972] 2 All ER 70, p. 617, ante and *Bannister v Bannister* [1948] 2 All ER 133, p. 615, ante. In *Binions v Evans* the Master of the Rolls thought that such an equity would not in any event create a settlement; but, with all respect, I think his reasoning leads to difficulties, because at 367, at 75 he reached the conclusion that it created an equitable interest, and once that is established then the ground on which he said (at 366, at 74) there was no settlement appears to me to be undermined. The other two Lord Justices who heard that case, Megaw LJ and Stephenson LJ, felt that they were bound by the earlier decision in *Bannister v Bannister* to hold that there was a settlement; but they did not direct themselves to any question under section 1; nor, I think, need they have done so, because in *Binions v Evans* and the earlier case of *Bannister v Bannister* there was actually an agreement. So that the difficulty which in my view arises, on the case of *Dodsworth v Dodsworth* and upon the present case, of seeing whether there can be a settlement when you have an interest which appears to give you a tenancy for life but there does not obviously appear to be anything which is a 'settlement' within the Act, did not arise in those two earlier cases. If it were necessary, we would have to decide what is, I think, a serious problem — whether *Dodsworth v Dodsworth* is binding upon us or whether it was decided strictly *per incuriam* because the learned Lord Justices who heard it did not advert to section 1 of the Settled Land Act, and, if it be not binding upon us, whether in truth it be right, and if so, what is the answer to the conundrum posed by subsection (1) of section 1. It may be that in such a case there is a settlement, and it is the order of the court declaring the equity, which is an 'instrument' and, therefore, the 'settlement' within the meaning of that subsection.

Happily, by the good sense of the parties in accepting a solution of the problem which I propounded for their consideration, it is unnecessary for this court to resolve those problems. In *Dodsworth v Dodsworth*, having decided that a right of occupation for the whole life of the claimant would be a wrong way of giving effect to the equity because it would create a settlement under the Settled Land Act and give the claimant too much, the court then adopted an alternative suggestion of compensation by recouping the claimant his expenditure (I think with interest) and giving him possession until payment.

They recognised that that really went too far the other way; and certainly it would not be appropriate in this case — if for no other reason, because of the difficulty of quantification. But it seems to me that *Dodsworth v Dodsworth* proceeded upon the basis which I have spelt out of *Crabb's* case — that the third problem is one of discretion: the court ought to see, having regard to all the circumstances, what is the best and fairest way to secure protection for the person who has been misled by the representations made to him and subsequently repudiated.

In the present case, it seemed to me, and I suggested to the parties, that the fairest way of dealing with the matter would be to direct the plaintiffs to grant Mrs Williams a long lease, determinable upon her death, at a nominal rent, since that would give her the right of occupation for her whole life and could not in any event give her the statutory powers under the Settled Land Act. The nominal rent would be an obligation not contemplated when the representations were made to her, but perfect equity is seldom possible.

There appeared to be only two objections to this course. One was that she might assign the lease; but that can be dealt with by including in the lease an absolute covenant not to assign, and by her giving an undertaking to this court, which I understand she is prepared to do, not to assign. The other difficulty was that, if she were to marry again, her husband might be able to claim a protected tenancy under the Rent Acts. I know that to Mrs Williams that appears a flight of fantasy; but we have to take precautions to see that what we propose is something which will not go wrong in an event which is not impossible and could happen. Counsel have made inquiries and they assured us that the husband would not be entitled to protection under the Rent Acts if the rent did not exceed two-thirds of the rateable value at the relevant date; and they have ascertained that that rateable value is £46 per annum. Therefore, if we direct the lease to be at a rent of £30 per annum we will have served the two ends of keeping it below two-thirds of the rateable value and making it nominal; and that is what I would propose. I took the precaution of making it clear to counsel, and they have made it clear to the parties, that, while we might order that as a term after deciding whether or not a life interest would be a 'settlement' within the meaning of the Act, if we were to decide that it was not a settlement within the Act Mrs Williams would be entitled to claim a full life interest without reservation of any rent, and therefore we could only adopt this course of a long lease at this stage if the parties consented to it, otherwise we must first determine the problem which I have mentioned and then consider what it would be right to order in the light of that determination. Counsel, having withdrawn and consulted with their clients and taken instructions, say that they are content that we should adopt the solution proposed by me.

I would therefore allow the appeal, discharge the order of the learned deputy circuit judge, and direct the plaintiffs to grant to Mrs Williams the lease which I have indicated. [13]

The award of a life interest would now be an interest under a trust of land: Trusts of Land and Appointment of Trustees Act 1996, p. 267, ante. In *Campbell v Griffin* [2001] EWCA 990 at para. 34, ROBERT WALKER LJ said:

[13] For the effect of TLATA 1996, see p. 266, ante.

'This would be administratively inconvenient ... It would probably involve disproportionate legal expenses (including trustees' remuneration) and might well lead to further disputes (especially in relation to Mr Campbell's keeping the property in good repair and condition).'

(f) No Remedy

In **Appleby v Cowley** (1982) Times, 14 April, [14] a claim was based on proprietary estoppel, that the plaintiffs were entitled to occupy a building in Nottingham indefinitely and use it as barristers' chambers subject to indemnifying Mr Cowley the defendant for the costs of providing it. In holding that it failed, MEGARRY V-C said:

'That leaves the fourth head of expenditure, the repairs and renovations to the roof and exterior walls in 1973 at a cost of some £7,700. ... As the law has developed, it may be that in cases in which a claim based on proprietary estoppel is made, the real question comes down simply to whether or not the assertion of strict legal rights would be unconscionable, without any detailed conditions or criteria being specified: see *Taylors Fashions Ltd v Liverpool Victoria Trustees Co Ltd* [1982] QB 133n at 151–154, [1981] 1 All ER 897 at 915–918, and *Amalgamated Investment and Property Co Ltd v Texas Commerce International Bank Ltd* [1982] QB 84 at 103–104, [1981] 1 All ER 923 at 935–936. In the present case, would it be unconscionable for the company to take the benefit of these remedial works to its building?

I think that there are circumstances in which the answer would be Yes. If soon after the works had been done the company had evicted all the members of chambers, or had required them to make payments equal to the full rental value of the chambers, then the company might well be said to be reaping the fruits of the expenditure unfairly. However, that is not what has happened. When the work was being done the rental value of the premises for which some £1,500 a year had been paid for some 10 years was about £4,300; and as events have turned out, Mr Cowley is making no claim for use and occupation at a rate grater than £1,500 a year until 30th November 1976 onwards. In those circumstances I think Mr Cowley may echo the phrase of Lord Hardwicke LC in *A-G v Baliol College, Oxford* (1744) 9 Mod Rep 407 at 412, when directing an inquiry in chambers, and say that the plaintiffs have had "sufficient satisfaction" for their expenditure. Certainly I do not think that Mr Cowley is acting unconscionably. It may be a nice academic point whether the result is that no case of proprietary estoppel has been established, or whether it is that such a case has been established but no remedy should be granted. I shall not debate that. All I need do is to say that the claim on proprietary estoppel fails. Certainly I can see nothing which comes within measurable distance of establishing any sort of a case that because of the expenditure the plaintiffs are beneficially entitled to the building, subject to indemnifying Mr Cowley.'

In **Savva v Costa and Harymode Investments Ltd** [1980] CA Transcript 723 (BUCKLEY, SHAW and OLIVER LJJ), the plaintiff, a Cypriot seamstress, and the

---

[14]   The extract is taken from the Bar Library Transcript. A claim based on fiduciary or confidential relationship was also rejected. One reason was 'the nature of the alleged beneficiaries. I do not think that practising barristers are in consimili casu with children, wards, patients, clients and the like. As a class they are not immature, weak, credulous creatures, easily persuaded and ready to yield their powers of decision to others.'

defendant had lived together from 1967 to 1968. Thereafter the defendant assumed responsibility for the maintenance and education of their two children who lived with the plaintiff. In early 1977 the defendant suggested to the plaintiff that she should move with the children and live in a house which he owned. The plaintiff's expenditure on work carried out to the house was substantial; the defendant was aware that the work was going on, although he claimed that he had protested that some of it was extravagant and unnecessary.

In May 1977, the defendant indicated his intention to transfer the house to trustees for the two children, on terms that the plaintiff would be permitted to reside there with them. The plaintiff claimed a beneficial half share in the property, or, alternatively, a lien on the property for the amount which she had expended.

In rejecting both claims, OLIVER LJ said:

'Mr Goodenday has drawn our attention to a line of authorities, starting with the well-known dictum of Lord Kingsdown in *Ramsden v Dyson* and applied in *Plimmer v Wellington Corpn* (1884) 9 App Cas 699, p. 656, ante; *Inwards v Baker* [1965] 2 QB 29, [1965] 1 All ER 445, p. 654, ante; *Ward v Kirkland* [1967] Ch 194, [1966] 1 All ER 609 and other cases. These relate to what is known as a proprietary estoppel. The effect can be summarised by saying that where A under an expectation created or encouraged by B that A shall have a certain interest in land, expends money on B's land on the faith of such expectation and to the knowledge of B, a court of equity will not allow B to take the benefit of such expenditure without giving effect to the expectation so created or encouraged. The expenditure in such circumstances gives rise to an equity to which the court will give effect in such way as may be appropriate in the circumstances of the individual case. It may be by injunction, it may be by declaring a trust of the beneficial interest or it may be by a declaration of lien for monies expended. This line of cases Mr Goodenday has conveniently referred to as "the representation cases"; but he accepts that, in the light of the learned deputy judge's findings of fact in the instant case, he cannot bring himself directly within them. What he submits is that the representation cases do not exhaust the category of cases in which equities of this type can arise. There are, he suggests, two other categories of case, under either of which he is entitled to succeed in the claim which he makes for a beneficial interest in the property.

The first category of case represents, as he submits, an extension of the *Ramsden v Dyson* principle to a situation in which there is no representation or expectation, but merely an expenditure of money with the consent of the landowner. If I have his submission aright, Mr Goodenday expresses the principle thus: Where a person expends money on the land of another with the knowledge and consent of that other but without any sort of representation, this gives rise to an equity in the person making the expenditure to have either an interest in the land commensurate with his expenditure or at least a lien for the amount expended.

In support of this Mr Goodenday relies upon two authorities.

[His Lordship referred to *Unity Joint Stock Mutual Banking Association v King* (1858) 25 Beav 72, and *Hussey v Palmer* [1972] 1 WLR 1286, [1972] 3 All ER 744, and continued:]

Now these cases do not, in my judgment at any rate, support any such broad principle as that for which Mr Goodenday contends. Mr Reid submits, and for my part I accept the submission, that on analysis they are not extensions of the *Ramsden v Dyson* principle, but merely examples of its application, and they do not support the broad proposition relied upon by Mr Goodenday that mere expenditure with the consent of the landowner is sufficient to raise an equity without any representation or expectation created by the landowner. The *Unity Joint Stock Banking* case was so treated in *Chalmers v Pardoe* [1963] 1 WLR 677, [1963] 3 All ER 552, itself a representation case, and it is clear that in *Hussey v Palmer*, the common expectation was that the plaintiff would continue to live in the house, an expectation which was not realised in the event, but on the strength of which the expenditure was made.

In my judgment these cases cannot be prayed in aid to demonstrate that the mere expenditure by A on improvements to B's land with B's knowledge without more, gives rise to some equity in the payer. ...

In the instant case, on the facts as found by the learned deputy judge, there was no agreement and there was no request on the part of the defendant. The plaintiff was aware that the house belonged to the defendant and if she believed that she was to get any interest in it, there is nothing to indicate that the defendant knew that that was her belief. The most that can be inferred in these circumstances is that she expended monies in improvements in the expectation that, as in fact was and is the case, she would be permitted to live there with the children.

[His Lordship rejected a claim based on 'a resulting trust which arises by the establishment by evidence of conduct of a common intention on the acquisition of the property, that the beneficial interest shall be shared in some way': *Gissing v Gissing* [1971] AC 886, [1970] 2 All ER 780, and continued:]

I should perhaps add this. As the learned deputy judge pointed out, his decision in no way determined the question of the plaintiff's right to continue in occupation of the property. That was not in issue before him and it is not in issue before this court. It may very well be that, although Mr Goodenday has felt unable to rely upon the principle of *Ramsden v Dyson* to establish the equitable interest claimed by the plaintiff in this action, the plaintiff would be entitled, if her enjoyment of the property is terminated in the future, to invoke that principle in support of a claim to an irrevocable licence — an equity to which, if it is established, the court might then give effect by a declaration of lien as suggested in *Hussey v Palmer*, if the circumstances and the duration or terms of the licence were thought to render that course appropriate. That is something about which I think it safer and wiser to express no view. It was not argued below and, understandably, there are no findings by the learned deputy judge as to the terms or duration of any such licence — matters which it would be essential, as I see it, to determine before the court could give any relief. The plaintiff's occupation has not in fact been disturbed and Mr Reid, on instructions, disclaims any present intention on his client's part to disturb it. I agree with the learned deputy judge, therefore, that it would be premature for the court to intervene now, and indeed it does not, as I think, have before it the material to enable it to do so. I mention the matter only to make clear that the present appeal, which I would dismiss, is in no way determinative of such rights of occupation as the plaintiff may have, or be entitled to, or of the course which the court might think it appropriate to take if such occupation were to be disturbed in the future.'

SHAW LJ said:
'I only append a footnote. The questions raised and to be decided on this appeal are of course confined to the issues with which the learned deputy judge had to deal, and to his findings of fact in regard to them. It may be that there remain outside the context of the present proceedings, prospective potential

rights which will accrue to Miss Savva in certain eventualities; the existence and nature of those rights may have to be determined in the future; they are not within the ambit of this appeal.

I would therefore echo Lord Justice Oliver's indication as to what the position in law might be if Miss Savva were at any time to be denied the advantage of residing in No 6 Windermere Road, having regard to the considerable expenditure by her on the improvement of the property. ...

If at some time it should be sought to turn Miss Savva out, there would arise a serious question as to the protection of an interest in the property on her behalf commensurate with the money she has spent on improving its condition so as to provide a proper degree of amenity for the accommodation of the children, who are intended to be the ultimate proprietors of the property.'[15]

VI. Multiple Characterisation of Licensee's Right

In **Re Sharpe** [1980] 1 WLR 219, [1980] 1 All ER 198, [16] an aunt lent £12,000 to her nephew to enable him to purchase a property in Hampstead for £17,000. She also spent over £2,000 on its decorations and fittings, and paid off some of the nephew's debts in order to stave off his bankruptcy. The understanding was that the aunt should live there and be looked after by the nephew and his wife. The aunt moved in, the nephew finally went bankrupt, and his trustee in bankruptcy made a contract to sell the property with vacant possession for £17,000. In holding that the circumstances gave rise to a constructive trust in the aunt's favour, which conferred on her an interest binding on the trustee in bankruptcy, BROWNE-WILKINSON J said at 223, at 201:

'I turn then to the alternative claim that Mrs Johnson is entitled to something less than an aliquot share of the equity in the premises, namely, the right to stay on the premises until the money she provided indirectly to acquire them has been repaid. This right is based upon the line of recent Court of Appeal decisions which has spelt out irrevocable licences from informal family arrangements, and in some cases characterised such licences as conferring some equity or equitable interest under a constructive trust. I do not think that the principles lying behind these decisions have yet been fully explored and on occasion it seems that such rights are found to exist simply on the ground that to hold otherwise would be a hardship to the plaintiff. It appears that the principle is one akin to or an extension of a proprietary estoppel stemming from Lord Kingsdown's well-known statement of the law in *Ramsden v Dyson* (1866) LR 1 HL 129 at 170, p. 624, post. In a strict case of proprietary estoppel the plaintiff has expended his own money on the defendant's property in an expectation encouraged by or known to the defendant that the plaintiff either owns the property or is to have some interest conferred on him. Recent authorities have extended this doctrine and, in my judgment, it is now established that, if the parties have proceeded on a common assumption that the plaintiff is to enjoy a right to reside in a particular property and in reliance

---

[15] See also *Bristol and West Building Society v Henning* [1985] 1 WLR 778, [1985] 2 All ER 606, p. 144, n. 6, ante.

[16] [1980] Conv 207 (J. Martin), suggesting estoppel licence as a preferable basis for the decision; (1980) 96 LQR 336 (G. Woodman); Gray, pp. 686–687.

on that assumption the plaintiff has expended money or otherwise acted to his detriment, the defendant will not be allowed to go back on that common assumption and the court will imply an irrevocable licence or trust which will give effect to that common assumption. Thus in *Errington v Errington and Woods* [1952] 1 KB 290, [1952] 1 All ER 149, p. 613, ante, Denning LJ held that the son, who had paid the instalments under the mortgage in the expectation that the property would eventually become his, had an equitable right to stay in occupation until the mortgage was paid off. In *Tanner v Tanner* [1975] 1 WLR 1346, [1975] 3 All ER 776, p. 600, ante, the plaintiff was held entitled to a licence to occupy a house bought in contemplation of it being a home for herself and her children, there being no express contract to that effect. In *Hardwick v Johnson* [1978] 1 WLR 683, [1978] 2 All ER 935, p. 608, ante, where the plaintiff's house had been occupied by the plaintiff's son and his first wife under an informal family arrangement, the Court of Appeal imputed an intention to grant an irrevocable licence to the wife on payment by her of a weekly sum.

Applying those principles to the present case, I have little doubt that as between the debtor on the one hand and Mrs Johnston on the other, the circumstances in which she provided the money by way of loan in order to enable the premises to be bought do give rise to some right in Mrs Johnson. It is clear that she only loaned the money as part of a wider scheme, an essential feature of which was that she was to make her home in the property to be acquired with the money loaned. Say that immediately after the property had been bought the debtor had tried to evict Mrs Johnson without repaying the loan; can it be supposed that the court would have made an order for possession against her? In my judgment, whether it be called a contractual licence or an equitable licence or an interest under a constructive trust, Mrs Johnson would be entitled as against the debtor to stay in the house. *Dodsworth v Dodsworth* (1973) 228 EG 1115, p. 671, post shows that there are great practical difficulties in finding that she is entitled to a full life interest: but there is no reason why one should not imply an intention that she should have the right to live there until her loan is repaid, which was the result reached in *Dodsworth v Dodsworth*.

Unfortunately, this case does not arise for decision simply between Mrs Johnson on the one hand and the debtor on the other. She has to show some right good against the trustee in bankruptcy and the purchaser from the trustee in bankruptcy. Due to an unfortunate procedural position, the purchaser is not a party to this application and nothing I can say can, or is intended to, bind him. As an antidote to the over-indulgence of sympathy which everyone must feel for Mrs Johnson, I put on record that the purchaser's plight is little better. He apparently had no reason to suspect that there was any flaw in the trustee's right to sell with vacant possession. As a result of the trustee's inability to complete the sale he cannot open the business he intended and he and his wife and two children are being forced to live in a small motorised caravan parked in various places on or near Hampstead Heath.

Is then Mrs Johnson's right against the debtor binding on the trustee in bankruptcy? This is an important and difficult point and, were it not for the urgency of the matter and the late stage of the term, I would like to have given it longer consideration. In general the trustee in bankruptcy steps into the shoes of the debtor and takes the debtor's property subject to all rights and equities affecting it: see *Halsbury's Laws of England*, 4th edn., vol. 3 (1973), para. 594. However, the trustee in bankruptcy is free to break any merely contractual obligation of the debtor, leaving the other party to his remedy in damages, which damages will only give rise to a right to prove in the bankruptcy.

Are rights of the kind spelt out in the cases I have referred to merely contractual licences or do they fetter the property and create some right over it? On the authorities as they stand, I think I am bound to hold that the rights under such an irrevocable licence bind the property itself in the hands of the trustee in bankruptcy. Lord Denning MR has, on a number of occasions, said that these licences arise under a constructive trust and are binding on the third party's acquiring with notice. These statements are for the most part obiter dicta with which other members of the court have not associated themselves, preferring to rest their decision on there being a contractual licence. But in *Binions v Evans* [1972] Ch 359, [1972] 2 All ER 70, p. 617, ante, a third party taking with notice of, and expressly subject to, such a licence was held bound by it. In that case the liability could not have depended merely on contract. Closer to the present case is a decision which was not referred to in argument and therefore any comments on it must be treated with some reserve. In *DHN Food Distributors Ltd v Tower Hamlets London Borough Council* [1976] 1 WLR 852, [1976] 3 All ER 462, p. 611, ante, certain premises were legally owned by one company (Bronze) but occupied by an associated company (DHN) under an informal arrangement between them. The premises were compulsorily acquired and the question was whether any compensation for disturbance was payable, it being said that Bronze had not been disturbed. The Court of Appeal held that DHN had an irrevocable licence to remain in the premises indefinitely and this gave DHN a compensatable interest in the land. Lord Denning MR said, at 859, at 466–467.

"It was equivalent to a contract between the two companies whereby Bronze granted an irrevocable licence to DHN to carry on their business on the premises. In this situation Mr Dobry cited to us *Binions v Evans*, to which I would add *Bannister v Bannister* [1948] 2 All ER 133 and *Siew Soon Wah v Yong Tong Hong* [1973] AC 836, p. 654, n. 13, ante. Those cases show that a contractual licence (under which a person has the right to occupy premises indefinitely) gives rise to a constructive trust, under which the legal owner is not allowed to turn out the licensee. So, here. This irrevocable licence gave to DHN a sufficient interest in the land to qualify them for compensation for disturbance."

Goff LJ also made this a ground of his decision: see pp. 860–861, pp. 467–468.

It seems to me that this is a decision that such contractual or equitable licence does confer some interest in the property under a constructive trust. Accordingly, in my judgment, it follows that the trustee in bankruptcy takes the property subject to Mrs Johnson's right to live there until she is repaid the moneys she provided to acquire it.

Mr Moss, for the trustee in bankruptcy, argued that this was the wrong approach. He said that the species of constructive trust which Lord Denning MR was considering in the cases was different from the traditional constructive trust known to equity lawyers. It is not, Mr Moss says, a substantive right but an equitable remedy: see per Lord Denning MR in *Hussey v Palmer* [1972] 1 WLR 1286 at 1290, [1972] 3 All ER 744 at 747, and in *Binions v Evans* [1972] Ch 359 at 368, [1972] 2 All ER 70 at 76. Then, says Mr Moss, the time to decide whether to grant such a remedy is when the matter comes before the court in the light of the then known circumstances. In the present case those circumstances are that the debtor is a bankrupt and Mrs Johnson has failed to put forward her claim until after the trustee has contracted to sell the property to an innocent third party, notwithstanding two inquiries as to whether she had a claim. Accordingly, he says, it would not be equitable to grant her an interest under a constructive trust at this time.

I cannot accept that argument in that form. Even if it be right to say that the courts can impose a constructive trust as a remedy in certain cases — which to my mind is a novel concept in English law — in order to provide a remedy the court must first find a right which has been infringed. So far as land is concerned an oral agreement to create an interest in it must be evidenced in writing: see section 40 of the Law of Property Act 1925. Therefore if these irrevocable licences create an interest in land, the rights cannot rest simply on an oral contract. The introduction of an interest under a constructive trust is an essential ingredient if the plaintiff has any right at all. [17] Therefore in cases such as this, it cannot be that the interest in property arises for the first time when the court declares it to exist. The right must have arisen at the time of the transaction in order for the plaintiff to have any right the breach of which can be remedied. Again, I think the *DHN Food Distributors Ltd* case shows that the equity predates any order of the court. The right to compensation in that case depended on substantive rights at the date of compulsory acquisition, not on what remedy the court subsequently chose to grant in the subsequent litigation.

Accordingly, if I am right in holding that as between the debtor and Mrs Johnson she had an irrevocable licence to remain in the property, authority compels me to hold that that gave her an interest in the property before the bankruptcy and the trustee takes the property subject to that interest. In my judgment the mere intervention of the bankruptcy by itself cannot alter Mrs Johnson's property interest. If she is to be deprived of her interest as against the trustee in bankruptcy, it must be because of some conduct of hers which precludes her from enforcing her rights, that is to say, the ordinary principles of acquiescence and laches which apply to all beneficiaries seeking to enforce their rights apply to this case.

I am in no way criticising the trustee in bankruptcy's conduct; he tried to find out if she made any claim relating to the £12,000 before he contracted to sell the property. But I do not think that on ordinary equitable principles Mrs Johnson should be prevented from asserting her rights even at this late stage. She is very old and in bad health. No one had ever advised her that she might have rights to live in the property. As soon as she appreciated that she was to be evicted she at once took legal advice and asserted her claim. This, in my judgment, is far removed from conduct which precludes enforcement by a beneficiary of his rights due to his acquiescence, the first requirement of acquiescence being that the beneficiary knows his or her rights and does not assert them.

Accordingly, I hold that Mrs Johnson is entitled as against the trustee in bankruptcy to remain in the property until she is repaid the sums she advanced. I reach this conclusion with some hesitation since I find the present state of the law very confused and difficult to fit in with established equitable principles. I express the hope that in the near future the whole question can receive full consideration in the Court of Appeal, so that, in order to do justice to the many thousands of people who never come into court at all but who wish to know with certainty what their proprietary rights are, the extent to which these irrevocable licences bind third parties may be defined with certainty. Doing justice to the litigant who actually appears in the court by the invention of new principles of law ought not to involve injustice to the other persons who are not litigants before the court but whose rights are fundamentally affected by the new principles.

---

[17]   See Sir Christopher SLADE's Child & Co Oxford Lecture 1984 on *the Informal Creation of Interests in Land* at p. 12.

Finally, I must reiterate that I am in no way deciding what are the rights of the purchaser from the trustee as against Mrs Johnson. It may be that as a purchaser without express notice in an action for specific performance of the contract his rights will prevail over Mrs Johnson's. As to that, I have heard no argument and express no view. I do, however, express my sympathy for him in the predicament in which he finds himself.

I therefore dismiss the trustee's application for possession against Mrs Johnson.'[18]

VII. Nature of the Right Before Order of the Court

There is controversy as to whether the equity which arises from estoppel can bind third parties in its inchoate form; and also the effect on third parties when the right has crystallised into a choate judicial remedy.[19]

Law Commission Consultation Document: Land Registration for the Twenty-First Century 1998 (Law Com No. 254), para 3.35.

'3.35 It will be apparent from this that the doctrine of proprietary estoppel involves two stages. First, the circumstances must occur which generate the "equity" in B's favour. Secondly, the court may give effect to that equity in proceedings brought for that purpose or in which it is in issue. Clearly, once the court has declared how the equity should be satisfied there is little difficulty. If B is held entitled to a property right, that right can then be recorded in the usual manner on the register.[20] In such circumstances the register can be amended to give effect to the order of the court.[1] The difficulty arises in the interim period between the equity arising and effect being given to it. There is some controversy as to the status of the equity in this interim period. Because the court may not grant B any proprietary rights over A's land, but only, say, a sum of compensation, some commentators have tended to regard B's equity as a purely personal right.[2] If that is so, it cannot be protected against third parties either as a minor interest, or by B's actual occupation of the land affected, as an overriding interest.[3] Against this however, there are good reasons for regarding the inchoate equity as a property right.[4] There is indeed some authority that, where title to the land is unregistered, the equity is binding on both a purchaser of the land affected who

---

[18] See *Bristol & West Building Society v Henning* [1985] 1 WLR 778 at 783, [1985] 2 All ER 606 at 610, where BROWNE-WILKINSON LJ said: 'Nothing in this judgment should be taken as expressing any view on the questions … whether the decision in *Re Sharpe* was correct.'

[19] Pawlowski, *The Doctrine of Proprietary Estoppel*, chap. 7.

[20] See G. Battersby, 'Informal Transactions in Land, Estoppel and Registration' (1995) 58 MLR 637, 641, 642.

[1] See Land Registration Act 1925, s. 82(1)(a).

[2] See D. J. Hayton 'Developing the Law of Trusts for the Twenty-First Century' (1990) 106 LQR 87, 97, n. 26.

[3] Under the Land Registration Act 1925, s. 70(1)(g).

[4] See in particular G. Battersby, 'Contractual and Estoppel Licences as Proprietary Interests in Land' [1991] Conv 36, 45; S. Baughen, 'Estoppels Over Land and Third Parties: An Open Question' (1994) 14 LS 147, 154; G. Battersby, 'Informal Transactions in Land, Estoppel and Registration' (1995) 58 MLR 637, 642.

has notice of B's rights[5] and a donee regardless of notice.[6] Furthermore, where the title is registered, not only has it been accepted that an equity arising by estoppel coupled with actual occupation could be an overriding interest,[7] but it is already the practice of the Land Registry to allow such an equity to be registered as a minor interest.[8]

In view of the increasing importance of estoppel as a mechanism for the informal creation of rights over land, it is obviously desirable to clarify in relation to registered land the status of an equity arising by estoppel before effect has been given to it by a court order. We therefore provisionally recommend that an equity arising by estoppel or acquiescence in relation to registered land should be regarded as an interest from the time at which it arises.[9] This will make clear that such an equity is a minor interest and that it may also exist as an overriding interest where the person having the benefit of it is in actual occupation.'

This was recommended in the Law Commission Report on Land Registration for the Twenty-First Century 2001 (Law Com No. 271), paras. 5.29–5.31, and is now

LAND REGISTRATION ACT 2002

116 Proprietary estoppel and mere equities

It is hereby declared for the avoidance of doubt that, in relation to registered land, each of the following—

(a) an equity by estoppel, and

(b) a mere equity,

has effect from the time the equity arises as an interest capable of binding successors in title (subject to the rules about the effect of dispositions on priority).[10]

---

5   *Duke of Beaufort v Patrick* (1853) 17 Beav 60, 78; *Inwards v Baker* [1965] 2 QB 29, 37; *E R Ives Investment Ltd v High* [1967] 2 QB 379. In *Lloyds Bank Plc v Carrick* [1996] 4 All ER 630, 642, MORRITT LJ commented that '[i]n the circumstances it is unnecessary to consider further the submission ... to the effect that a proprietary estoppel cannot give rise to an interest in land capable of binding successors in title. This interesting argument will have to await another day, though it is hard to see how in this court it can surmount the hurdle constituted by the decision of this court in *Ives v High*'.

5   *Voyce v Voyce* (1991) 62 P & CR 290, 294, 296.

6   *Lee-Parker v Izzet (No 2)* [1972] 1 WLR 775, 780, obiter. Cf *Habermann v Koehler* (1996) 73 P & CR 515, where the Court of Appeal remitted a case for a retrial to determine *inter alia* whether an equity arising by estoppel could bind a purchaser as an overriding interest under Land Registration Act 1925, s. 70(1)(g).

7   Under the Land Registration Act 1925, ss. 49(1)(f) (notice); 54(1) (caution). See Ruoff & Roper, *Registered Conveyancing*, 8 – 02; 35 – 33; 36 – 13.

8   It has not been definitively settled when an equity arises. At the very latest it will be when the circumstances make it unconscionable for the land owner. A, to go back on the expectation which he has created by representation or conduct: *Lim v Ang* [1992] 1 WLR 113, 118. In most cases that will be when the other party, B, has acted to his detriment in reliance upon the expectation. That moment will not always be easy to define.

9   R & R, 15.028–15.030.

10   See *Brocket Hall (Jersey) Ltd v Clague* [1998] CLY 443; *Birmingham Midshires Mortgage Services Ltd v Saberwal* (1999) 80 P & CR 256; *Habermann v Koehler (No 2)* (2000) Times, 22 November; *Lloyd v Dugdale* [2002] 2 P & CR 167; (2002) 146 SJ 90 (M. Pawlowski); [2003] CLJ 661 (B. McFarlane).

Although there is no direct authority, more recent cases are favourable to the view that the equity does bind third parties.

QUESTIONS

1. How would you reformulate the principle of *Ramsden v Dyson*? Consider, in particular whether
   (a) there is any difference between estoppel by acquiescence or silence, estoppel by encouragement and promissory estoppel
   (b) the principle should be confined to land or other property.
2. Is the requirement of unconscionability referable to the establishment of the equity, or to its satisfaction, or to both?
3. Do the courts apply the same criteria when considering whether an equity is established in the case of
   (a) a claim by a licensee to a proprietary interest; and
   (b) a defence by a licensee to an action for possession by the licensor? *Pascoe v Turner* [1979] 1 WLR 431, [1979] 2 All ER 945, p. 667, ante; *Savva v Costa and Harymode Investments Ltd* [1980] CA Transcript 723, p. 678, ante; *Bristol and West Building Society v Henning* [1985] 1 WLR 778, [1985] 2 All ER 606, p. 144, n. 6, ante.
4. Is a licence by estoppel an interest in land? Can it be sold? Does it pass with the land? Is it assignable? *Hamilton v Geraghty* (1901) 1 SR NSW Eq 81; *Lands Comr v Hussein* [1968] EA 585; (1969) ASCL 354 (E. H. Burn); *ER Ives Ltd v High* [1967] 2 QB 379 at 395, [1967] 1 All ER 504 at 507; *Cameron v Murdoch* [1983] WAR 321 at 360; affd (1986) 63 ALR 575 at 595; C & B, p. 658.
5. Should proprietary estoppel be regarded as a species of constructive trust? *Re Basham* [1986] 1 WLR 1498 at 1503, [1987] 1 All ER 405 at 410; p. 637, n. 13, ante, and articles cited there.
6. (a) Do you think that an estoppel licence is a choate or an inchoate right? (1995) 58 MLR 640–643 (G. Battersby); Pawlowski, *The Doctrine of Proprietary Estoppel,* chap. 7; pp. 685–686, ante.
   (b) On 1 July 1996 X is given a right to occupy land for his life. All the indicia of an estoppel licence are in place, but by 1 July 1998 the court has not yet decreed how the equity is to be satisfied. The Trusts of Land and Appointment of Trustees Act 1996 came into force on 1 January 1997, under which no new strict settlements can be created under the Settled Land Act 1925. Is X a tenant for life of settled land?
7. Consider the position of the defendant in *Inwards v Baker* [1965] 2 QB 29, [1965] 1 All ER 446, p. 654, ante, if he had remained in possession for thirteen years: [1991] Conv 280 (M. Welstead).
8. Consider the solutions reached in the various cases in Section V, and compare them with those reached in sections III and IV.
9. What criteria have emerged to guide the courts in 'satisfying the equity' which arises for proprietary estoppel?
10. To what extent is a licensee's right to protection affected by his conduct (a) before and (b) after his licence is established? Why are contractual licences and licences by estoppel treated differently? *Thompson v Park* [1944] KB 408; *Ivory v Palmer* [1975] ICR 340; *Williams v Staite* [1979] Ch 291, [1978] 2 All ER 928; [1986] Conv 405 (M. P. Thompson); *Brynowen Estates Ltd v Bourne* (1981) 131 NLJ 1212; *Willis & Son v Willis* (1985) 277 EG 1133; Dawson and Pearce, pp. 223–224.
11. How would you solve (a) *Inwards v Baker* [1965] 2 QB 29, [1965] 1 All ER 446, p. 654, ante and (b) *E R Ives Investment Ltd v High* [1967] 2 QB 379, [1967]

1 All ER 504, p. 659, ante, if the title of the land of the licensor were registered.

12. Before the Trusts of Land and Appointment of Trustees Act 1996 the courts were reluctant to allow an estoppel licence to create a settlement: *Dodsworth v Dodsworth* (1973) 228 EG 1115, p. 671, ante; *Griffiths v Williams* (1997) 248 EG 947, p. 673, ante. Even though no new strict settlements can be created after 1996 (p. 267, ante), are there circumstances in which the courts might still be reluctant to satisfy an equity under an estoppel licence by granting a licence for life? *Matharu v Matharu* (1994) 68 P & CR 93; *Dent v Dent* [1996] 1 WLR 683, [1996] 1 All ER 659; [1996] All ER Rev 258 (P. J. Clarke).

13. Do you think that Parliament should intervene to give protection to a licensee for life? See the statutory protection given in Ireland: Republic of Ireland Registration of Title Act 1964, s. 81; Northern Ireland Land Registration Act 1970, s. 47; (1970) 21 NILQ 389 (B. W. Harvey); Wylie, *Irish Land Law* (2nd edn., 1986) paras. 20.15–20.19. Law Commission Working Paper No. 94 on Trusts of Land (1985), paras. 16.6–16.18.

14. An aged relative asks his adult child to move into his house and look after him for the rest of his days. In return the relative makes an oral promise to leave the house by will to the child or to the child and his or her spouse. The child moves in, but the aged relative fails to leave the house by will. Consider the possible legal analyses and solutions, and in particular:

   (*a*) in property, as a licence;

   (*b*) in trust, as an express or constructive trust (or a resulting trust if the child makes any financial contribution);

   (*c*) in succession, under the Inheritance (Provision for Family and Dependants) Act 1975;

   See generally [1982] CLJ 290 (S. J. Burridge).

VIII. Deserted Wives. An Historical Note

Brief mention should be made here of a body of doctrine which grew up in the nineteen-fifties, with the object of protecting a deserted wife in the occupation of the family home. If a husband owns the matrimonial home and deserts his wife, does the wife become a trespasser, liable to eviction by the husband; or by a third party, if the husband has transferred the title? In a number of cases, the deserted wife was protected on the theory that she was a licensee under a licence which was irrevocable by the husband, or by a transferee other than a bona fide purchaser of a legal estate for value without notice.[12] There is no need now to enter into the complexities and controversies which this situation created; for the House of Lords held in *National Provincial Bank Ltd v Ainsworth* [1965] AC 1175, [1965] 2 All ER 472 that she had no interest capable of enforcement against a third party; and the short but active career of 'the deserted wife's equity' came

---

[12]   *Bendall v McWhirter* [1952] 2 QB 466, [1952] 1 All ER 1307; *Ferris v Weaven* [1952] 2 All ER 233; *Street v Denham* [1954] 1 WLR 624, [1954] 1 All ER 532; *Lee v Lee* [1952] 2 QB 489n, [1952] 1 All ER 1299; *Jess B Woodcock & Sons Ltd v Hobbs* [1955] 1 WLR 152, [1955] 1 All ER 445; *Westminster Bank Ltd v Lee* [1956] Ch 7, [1955] 2 All ER 883; *Miles v Bull* [1969] 1 QB 258, [1968] 3 All ER 632.

to an end. [13] 'The deserted wife therefore', said Lord Wilberforce, 'cannot resist a claim from a "purchaser" from her husband whether the "purchase" takes place after or before the desertion. As regards transactions subsequent to the desertion this disability is somewhat mitigated by three factors. First, if it appears that the husband is threatening to dispose of the house in such a manner as to defeat her rights, she may be able to obtain an injunction to restrain him from doing so (*Lee v Lee* [1952] 2 QB 489n, [1952] 1 All ER 1299). An injunction is, of course, a discretionary remedy and it does not follow that the wife will be granted it in every case, but in suitable circumstances she has this protection. Secondly, the courts have ample powers to detect, and to refuse to give effect to, sham or fraudulent transactions — such as that which was attempted in *Ferris v Weaven* [1952] 2 All ER 233.'

A deserted wife (spouse) has, in recent years, earned protection under different theories. She is not merely a licensee of her husband in the family home. Her contributions to the establishment of the home have been more and more readily treated as an entitlement to a share in the ownership of the family home. Regardless of any property ownership, however, she has a right of occupation, and may protect this against third parties by registration, as has been seen, under the Family Law Act 1996. [14] Further, her shared ownership, together with her occupation of the home, along with her husband, has been held to be sufficient to entitle her to an overriding interest. [15] It remains to be seen whether occupation based upon a licence by estoppel would be similarly treated. And, where the wife has protection, the mistress does not follow far behind.

[13] See also *Hall v King* [1987] 2 EGLR 121 where Sir JOHN DONALDSON MR said at 212: 'A wife's right to occupy the matrimonial home is of a very special nature, depending upon her status as a wife and not upon any leave or licence of her husband ... This accords with common sense and experience. Whoever heard of a husband expressly or impliedly saying to his wife "Do come and stay with me in the matrimonial home, dear"'.

[14] P. 312, ante. The right of occupation was created in Matrimonial Homes Act 1967. On the matrimonial home in registered land. See R & R, chap. 45.

[15] *Williams & Glyn's Bank Ltd v Boland* [1981] AC 487, [1980] 2 All ER 408, p. 136, ante.

10. Easements and Profits à Prendre [1]

I. General

Easements and profits à prendre are interests entitling their owners to exercise certain rights over the land of another. They may be legal [2] or equitable. They are distinguishable in that a profit entitles its owner to take away something capable of ownership from the servient land, while an easement does not; and also in that a profit may exist 'in gross', while an easement must always be appurtenant to land. Little will be said of profits, owing to lack of available space; or, indeed, of commons. [3]

---

[1] C & B, chap. 18; Gray, pp. 419–537; M & W, paras. 18.040–18.228; MM, pp. 413–451; Smith, chap. 20; *Gale on Easements* (17th edn., 1997); Jackson, *Law of Easements and Profits* (1978); Sara, *Boundaries and Easements* (2nd edn., 2002); American Law Institute, *Restatement of the Law: Property Servitudes*.

[2] LPA 1925, ss. 1(2), 187.

[3] For registration of commons under Commons Registration Act 1965, see p. 60, ante.

II. Nature of Easements [4]

A. Introduction

The detailed characteristics of an easement are discussed in the text-books and need not be repeated here. In short, an easement is a right, appurtenant to one piece of land [5] and exercisable over another piece of land, and capable of forming the subject matter of a grant. Indeed, all easements, other than those created by statute, are either granted expressly or impliedly, or are presumed to have been granted. An easement must be distinguished from a licence in that it is a proprietary interest and must be appurtenant to land; from a lease in that it does not give the owner of the easement any possessory rights over the land of another; from local customary rights in that there cannot be a grant without a capable grantee; and from natural rights in that these need no grant; from a covenant in that it must be a right capable of being granted. Thus rights which are properly licences, leases, customary rights, natural rights or covenants may look very much like easements, but they may be very different. If X, the owner of Whiteacre, tells Y, the owner of Blackacre, that Y's son may enter Whiteacre to collect a lost ball, that is clearly a licence; but if X were to permit the owner of Blackacre to enter Whiteacre at any time for pleasure and recreation, it might create an easement. [6] Again, a letting of a garage on a weekly tenancy is clearly in no sense an easement; but a right to park vehicles on a neighbour's ground without interfering with his user of the land looks more like an easement, [7] and the right to fix a signboard on a neighbour's house can be an easement. [8] Again, local inhabitants of a particular area may have the right to pass across another's land on the way to church, [9] or to dry their nets on someone's land; [10] but these rights rely on custom and not on grant and cannot be easements. Again, every landowner has the right of support from his neighbour to his land in its natural state. [11] A right of support to buildings on land is, however, a right which must be claimed as the result of a grant. [12] A right in the nature of an easement may arise by estoppel, where it would be unconscionable to deny that such a right exists. [13] A covenant not to use land as a fish shop is clearly no easement; but an arrangement permitting the owner of neighbouring land to walk across it in perpetuity to the road is capable of being an

---

[4]   C & B, pp. 567–581; Gray, pp. 449–491; M & W, paras. 18.040–18.089; MM, pp. 413–424; Smith, pp. 484–500; Gale, paras. 1–01 to 1–133; Jackson, pp. 1–27, 39–49; (1964) 28 Conv (NS) 450 (M. A. Peel).

[5]   See (1980) 96 LQR 557 (M. F. Sturley) for criticism of the rule that an easement cannot exist in gross. See also (1982) 98 LQR 279 at p. 305 (S. Gardner).

[6]   *Horton v Tidd* (1965) 196 EG 697; *Re Ellenborough Park* [1956] Ch 131, [1955] 3 All ER 667, p. 694, post; *Miller v Jackson* [1977] QB 966, [1977] 3 All ER 338.

[7]   *Copeland v Greenhalf* [1952] Ch 488, [1952] 1 All ER 809, p. 700, post; *Newman v Jones* (22 March, 1982 unreported), p. 703, post; cf. (1977) 93 LQR 481.

[8]   *Re Webb's Lease* [1951] Ch 808, [1951] 2 All ER 131, p. 736, post.

[9]   *Brocklebank v Thompson* [1903] 2 Ch 344.

[10]   *Mercer v Denne* [1905] 2 Ch 538; *Alfred F Beckett Ltd v Lyons* [1967] Ch 449, [1967] 1 All ER 833.

[11]   *Hunt v Peake* (1860) John 705; *Backhouse v Bonomi* (1861) 9 HL Cas 503; *Midland Bank plc v Bardgrove Property Service Ltd* [1991] 2 EGLR 283; *Holbeck Hall Hotel Ltd v Scarborough Borough Council* [2000] QB 836; [2002] 2 All ER 705; [2001] Conv 177 (M. P. Thompson).

[12]   *Dalton v Angus* (1881) 6 App Cas 740; *Ray v Fairway Motors (Barnstaple) Ltd* (1968) 20 P & CR 261.

[13]   *ER Ives Investments Ltd v High* [1967] 2 QB 379, [1967] 1 All ER 504, p. 665, ante; *Soames-Forsythe Properties Ltd v Tesco Stores Ltd* [1991] EGCS 22 ('full and free right of way on foot only' from supermarket at St Ouen's Centre, Worsley, Manchester, to car park held to include right for customers to use a supermarket trolley on it; a right also arose by estoppel conferring on Tesco a right in the nature of an easement of stacking trolleys on the walkway).

easement. In connection with this comparison between easements and covenants, the anomalous position of the easement of light may be noted. [14] For this easement is more like a negative right; the grantor does not grant the light; he is rather under obligation not to obstruct it. One can only suppose that in the times of narrow streets, poor lighting and small windows, some way of protecting the access of light to houses in towns was necessary. Until 1848, [15] there was no way of providing that a negative covenant between freeholders could run with the land, and the only way in which a landowner could be protected was by regarding him as the owner of an easement. It seems, however, more natural to look upon that situation as one of covenant—one in which the neighbour is under an obligation not to build, rather than one in which he has granted the landowner a right 'not to have his light obstructed'. Nevertheless it is so treated historically. A similar situation arises in the case of an easement of support. [16] A further anomaly exists in the case of an easement to repair a fence. The general principle is that the servient owner is under no obligation to expend money on the maintenance of any property over which an easement is exercised. [17] The dominant owner may enter to effect the necessary repairs. [18] Thus the easement of fencing is unusual in that the servient owner is under a duty to take positive steps to maintain the fence, including the expenditure of money. [19] There may also be cases where the parties have expressly or impliedly agreed that the servient owner shall bear the burden; as where a local authority, which owned a high-rise block of flats, let them to tenants. Easements of access over the common parts of the building retained by the local authority were implied in favour of the tenants (the dominant owners). And the authority was held liable, on an implied term of the contract, to maintain those parts. [20]

[14]   See p. 775, post. Cf. *Hunter v Canary Wharf Ltd* [1997] AC 655, [1997] 2 All ER 426, at 708, p 708, post (no easement for reception of television waves from distant transmitter).

[15]   *Tulk v Moxhay* (1848) 2 Ph 774, p. 742, post.

[16]   *Dalton v Angus* (1881) 6 App Cas 740.

[17]   See *Holden v White* [1982] QB 679, [1982] 2 All ER 328 (servient owner owed no duty of care at common law to milkman injured by disintegrating manhole cover on private footpath giving access to terraced house, nor under Occupiers' Liability Act 1957. See now Occupiers' Liability Act 1984, in effect reversing the decision); *McGeown v Northern Ireland Housing Executive* [1995] 1 AC 233; *Vodden v Gayton* [2001] PIQR P4; Gale, paras. 1.91–1.97.

[18]   There is no *general* right. For a statutory right, see Access to Neighbouring Land Act 1992, p. 713, post.

[19]   *Lawrence v Jenkins* (1873) LR 8 QB 274 (a 'spurious easement'); *Jones v Price* [1965] 2 QB 618, [1965] 2 All ER 625; *Crow v Wood* [1971] 1 QB 77, [1970] 3 All ER 425, p. 710 post; other rights cannot be easements if they involve expenditure by the servient owner: *Regis Property Co Ltd v Redman* [1956] 2 QB 612, [1956] 2 All ER 335 (covenant to supply hot water held not to be an easement so as to pass under LPA 1925, s. 62 being a personal contract to perform services); *Rance v Elvin* (1983) 49 P & CR 65 (right to metered water supply paid for by servient owner held not to be an easement, even though dominant owner agreed to reimburse water charges); (1985) 50 P & CR 9 (CA held that the right was to the uninterrupted passage of water, and not to its supply; it was therefore an easement, and the servient owner was liable in quasi-contract to reimburse); [1985] CLJ 458 (A. J. Waite); *Palmer v Bowman* [2000] 1 WLR 842, [2000] 1 All ER 22 (no easement of right by owner of higher land to have water pass by natural flow onto neighbouring lower land); (2000) 150 NLJ 311 (H. W. Wilkinson); [2000] All ER Rev 237 (P. J. Clarke). *Coopind (UK) Ltd v Walton Commercial Group Ltd* [1989] 1 EGLR 241 ('a right to receive a supply of gas' held to extend to right to lay new gas main under service roads retained by lessors); *Duffy v Lamb* [1997] EGCS 50 (right to uninterrupted passage of electricity held to be easement).

[20]   *Liverpool City Council v Irwin* [1977] AC 239, [1976] 2 All ER 39; *King v South Northamptonshire District Council* [1992] 1 EGLR 53; cf. *Duke of Westminster v Guild* [1985] QB 688, [1984] 3 All ER 144 (tenant qua dominant owner of right of drainage held to be liable for repairs). See also *Stokes v Mixconcrete (Holdings) Ltd* (1978) 38 P & CR 488.

While the essential characteristics of an easement are reasonably clear, and no right which fails to comply with them can exist as an easement, it is not possible to say that the law will recognise as an easement every right that does comply. An easement can be described rather than defined, and lists of those judicially recognised are collected in the books. [1] New ones may arise: 'The category of servitudes and easements must alter and expand with the changes that take place in the circumstances of mankind.' [2] Whether or not a new right, complying with the accepted requirements of an easement, will be judicially recognised or not is difficult to forecast. [3] Inevitably the cases in this section are a random selection.

B. Capability of Existence as Easement

HILL v TUPPER

(1863) 2 H & C 121 (Exch, POLLOCK CB, MARTIN and BRAMWELL BB)

The Company of Proprietors of the Basingstoke Canal Navigation leased premises on the bank of the canal to the plaintiff, a boat proprietor. The lease to the plaintiff purported to give to him, inter alia, 'the sole and exclusive right or liberty to put or use boats on the said canal, and let the same for hire for the purpose of pleasure only'. It was alleged that the defendant, the landlord of an inn adjoining the canal, had interfered with the plaintiff's right by putting boats on the canal. The judge refused an application to nonsuit the plaintiff. A rule *nisi* was obtained to enter a nonsuit.

Held. Rule made absolute. The plaintiff was a licensee only and was not entitled to an easement.

POLLOCK CB. We are all of opinion that the rule must be absolute to enter the verdict for the defendant on the second plea. After the very full argument which has taken place, I do not think it necessary to assign any other reason for our decision, than that the case of *Ackroyd v Smith* (1850) 10 CB 164 expressly decided that it is not competent to create rights unconnected with the use and enjoyment of land, and annex them to it so as to constitute a property in the grantee. This grant merely operates as a licence or covenant on the part of the grantors, and is binding on them as between themselves and the grantee, but gives him no right of action in his own name for any infringement of the supposed exclusive right. It is argued that, as the owner of an estate may grant a right to cut turves, or to fish or hunt, there is no reason why he may not grant such a right as that now claimed by the plaintiff. The answer is, that the law will not allow it. So the law will not permit the owner of an estate to grant it alternately to his heirs male and heirs female. A new species of incorporeal hereditament cannot be created at the will and pleasure of the owner of property; but he must be content to accept the estate and the right to dispose of it subject to the law as settled by decisions or controlled by Act of Parliament. A grantor may bind himself by covenant to allow any right he pleases over this property, but he cannot annex to it a new incident, so as to

---

[1] C & B, pp. 574–577, M & W, paras. 18.043–18.059, 18.212; MM, pp. 443–449; Gale, paras. 1–64 to 1–68.

[2] *Dyce v Lady James Hay* (1852) 1 Macq 305 at 312–313, per Lord ST LEONARDS.

[3] *A-G of Southern Nigeria v John Holt & Co (Liverpool) Ltd* [1915] AC 599; *Miller v Emcer Products Ltd* [1956] Ch 304, [1956] 1 All ER 237; (1956) 72 LQR 172 (R.E.M.); *Phipps v Pears* [1965] 1 QB 76, [1964] 2 All ER 35; (1964) 80 LQR 318 (R.E.M.), p. 706, post; *Dowty Boulton Paul Ltd v Wolverhampton Corpn (No 2)* [1976] Ch 13, [1973] 2 All ER 491.

enable the grantee to sue in his own name for an infringement of such a limited
right as that now claimed.

i. ESSENTIAL CHARACTERISTICS

RE ELLENBOROUGH PARK
[1956] Ch 131, [1955] 3 All ER 667 (ChD, DANCKWERTS J and CA, EVERSHED MR,
BIRKETT and ROMER LJJ)

In 1855 the White Cross Estate, which included Ellenborough Park, was being
developed for building purposes. Purchasers of the several plots surrounding
the Park were given in their conveyances certain rights of user over the Park;
and for the purposes of the present action it was agreed to take as typical of all
these conveyances, one dated 1864 conveying a plot to John Porter. The material
part of this conveyance was as follows: 'Together with ... and also full enjoyment
at all times hereafter in common with the other persons to whom such easements
may be granted of the pleasure ground set out and made in front of the said plot
of land ... in the centre of the square called Ellenborough Park ... but subject to
the payment of a fair and just proportion of the costs charges and expenses of
keeping in good order and condition the said pleasure ground.' John Porter
covenanted to pay a fair proportion of the expenses of the upkeep of the Park,
and the vendors covenanted to keep the Park as an ornamental pleasure ground.
The Park became vested in the plaintiffs on statutory trusts for sale.

During the Second World War, the Park was requisitioned, and subsequently
the War Office paid sums of money in respect of compensation rental and on
account of dilapidations. Various questions arose, concerning the rights of the
original purchasers and their successors in title to use the Park, and concerning
the allocation of compensation money from the War Office. The question was
whether the surrounding owners had lost a legal right, for which they would be
entitled to be compensated.

Held (affirming DANCKWERTS J). The right of enjoyment was an easement
appurtenant to the plots bought by the original purchasers, and the plaintiffs
were therefore entitled to compensation.

EVERSHED MR: The substantial question in the case, which we have briefly
indicated, is one of considerable interest and importance. It is clear from our
brief recital of the facts that, if the house owners are now entitled to an
enforceable right in respect of the use and enjoyment of Ellenborough Park,
that right must have the character and quality of an easement as understood
by, and known to, our law. It has, therefore, been necessary for us to consider
carefully the qualities and characteristics of easements, and, for such purpose,
to look back into the history of that category of incorporeal rights in the
development of English real property law. It may be fairly assumed that, in the
case of *Duncan v Louch* (1845) 6 QB 904, the Court of Queen's Bench in the
year 1845, and particularly Lord Denman CJ, who delivered the first judgment
in the court, was of opinion that such a right as the respondent claims was
capable of fulfilling the qualifying conditions of an easement. And Buckley J,
in the case in 1904 of *Keith v Twentieth Century Club Ltd* (1904) 73 LJ Ch 545,
answered certain questions which Byrne J had ordered to be set down to be
argued before the court, themselves depending upon the assumption that such
a right could exist in law. On the other hand, Farwell J, a judge peculiarly
experienced and learned in real property law, on two occasions, namely, in
1903 in the case of *International Tea Stores Co v Hobbs* [1903] 2 Ch 165 at 172, and
in 1905 in *A-G v Antrobus* [1905] 2 Ch 188 at 198, used language appearing to

treat as axiomatic the proposition, that a right, which should properly be described as a jus spatiandi, was a right excluded by English law, as by Roman law, from the company of servitudes.

The four cases which we have mentioned must be considered hereafter at greater length. But it can be said at once that, with the possible exception of the first, none of them constitutes or involves a direct decision upon the question now before us: and although the existence of gardens surrounded by houses, the owners or occupiers of which enjoy in practice the amenities of the gardens, is a well-known feature of town development throughout the country, no other case appears to have come before the courts in which the validity of the rights in fact enjoyed in the gardens has ever been tested. ...[4]

For the purposes of the argument before us, Mr Cross and Mr Goff [counsel for each side] were content to adopt, as correct, the four characteristics formulated in Dr Cheshire's *Modern Real Property* 7th edn., pp. 465[5] et seq. They are (1) there must be a dominant and a servient tenement: (2) an easement must 'accommodate' the dominant tenement: (3) dominant and servient owners must be different persons,[6] and (4) a right over land cannot amount to an easement, unless it is capable of forming the subject-matter of a grant. ...

We pass, accordingly, to a consideration of the first of Dr Cheshire's conditions—that of the accommodation of the alleged dominant tenements by the rights as we have interpreted them. For it was one of the main submissions by Mr Cross on behalf of the appellant that the right of full enjoyment of the park, granted to the purchaser by the conveyance of 23 December 1864, was insufficiently connected with the enjoyment of the property conveyed, in that it did not subserve some use which was to be made of that property; and that such a right accordingly could not exist in law as an easement. In this part of this argument Mr Cross was invoking a principle which is, in our judgment, of unchallengeable authority, expounded, in somewhat varying language, in many judicial utterances, of which the judgments in *Ackroyd v Smith* (1850) 10 CB 164 are, perhaps, most commonly cited.[7] We think it unnecessary to review the authorities in which the principle has been applied; for the effect of the decisions is stated with accuracy in Dr Cheshire's *Modern Real Property* 7th edn., p. 457. After pointing out that 'one of the fundamental principles concerning easements is that they must be not only appurtenant to a dominant tenement, but also connected with the normal enjoyment of the dominant tenement' and referring to certain citations in support of that proposition the author proceeded: 'We may expand the statement of the principle thus: a right enjoyed by one over the

---

[4] Lord EVERSHED referred to Holdsworth, *Historical Introduction to Land Law* (1927), p. 265.

[5] 16th edn., pp. 570, et seq.

[6] This is not strictly true. A tenant may grant an easement, for a period not exceeding that of his lease, in favour of another tenant of the same landlord; and an easement of light may be so acquired by prescription: *Morgan v Fear* [1907] AC 425; (1949) 13 Conv (NS) 104 (A. K. R. Kiralfy); (1958) 74 LQR 82 (V. T. H. Delany); M & W, para. 18.049.

[7] *Weekly v Wildman* (1698) 1 Ld Raym 405, per TREBY CJ; *London & Blenheim Estates Ltd v Ladbroke Retail Parks Ltd* [1994] 1 WLR 31, [1993] 4 All ER 157 (right intended as easement and attached to servient tenement before dominant tenement identified held not to be an easement); *Voice v Bell* (1993) 68 P & CR 441. In the USA both easements and profits may be *in gross*. See American Law Institute *Restatement of the Law of Property* (1940), vol. 5, paras. 454, 489–96; and generally (1980) 96 LQR 557 (M. F. Sturley), criticising the rule; (1982) 98 LQR at p. 305 (S. Gardner); *Jobson v Record* (1997) 74 P & CR D16 ('a right of way granted for the benefit of a defined area of land may not be used in substance for accommodating another area of land' per MORRITT LJ).

land of another does not possess the status of an easement unless it accommodates and serves the dominant tenement, and is reasonably necessary for the better enjoyment of that tenement, for if it has no necessary connexion therewith, although it confers an advantage upon the owner and renders his ownership of the land more valuable, it is not an easement at all, but a mere contractual right personal to and only enforceable between the two contracting parties.'

[His Lordship rejected the argument, based on an observation of WILLES J in *Bailey v Stephens* (1862) 12 CB NS 91 to the effect that a right could only exist as an easement if it could benefit only the claimant to the easement and no other person, and continued:] Can it be said, then, of the right of full enjoyment of the park in question, which was granted by the conveyance of 23 December 1864, and which, for reasons already given, was, in our view, intended to be annexed to the property conveyed to Mr Porter, that it accommodated and served that property? It is clear that the right did, in some degree, enhance the value of the property, and this consideration cannot be dismissed as wholly irrelevant. It is, of course, a point to be noted; but we agree with Mr Cross's submission that it is in no way decisive of the problem; it is not sufficient to show that the right increased the value of the property conveyed, unless it is also shown that it was connected with the normal enjoyment of that property. It appears to us that the question whether or not this connexion exists is primarily one of fact, and depends largely on the nature of the alleged dominant tenement and the nature of the right granted. As to the former, it was in the contemplation of the parties to the conveyance of 1864 that the property conveyed should be used for residential and not commercial purposes. ... As to the nature of the right granted, the conveyance of 1864 shows that the park was to be kept and maintained as a pleasure ground or ornamental garden. ...

On these facts Mr Cross submitted that the requisite connexion between the right to use the park and the normal enjoyment of the houses which were built around it or near it had not been established. He likened the position to a right granted to the purchaser of a house to use the Zoological Gardens free of charge or to attend Lord's Cricket Ground without payment. Such a right would undoubtedly, he said, increase the value of the property conveyed but could not run with it at law as an easement, because there was no sufficient nexus between the enjoyment of the right and the use of the house. It is probably true, we think, that in neither of Mr Cross's illustrations would the supposed right constitute an easement, for it would be wholly extraneous to, and independent of, the use of a house as a house, namely, as a place in which the householder and his family live and make their home; and it is for this reason that the analogy which Mr Cross sought to establish between his illustrations and the present case cannot, in our opinion, be supported. A much closer analogy, as it seems to us, is the case of a man selling the freehold of part of his house and granting to the purchaser, his heirs and assigns, the right, appurtenant to such part, to use the garden in common with the vendor and his assigns. In such a case, the test of connexion, or accommodation, would be amply satisfied; for just as the use of a garden undoubtedly enhances, and is connected with, the normal enjoyment of the house to which it belongs, so also would the right granted, in the case supposed, be closely connected with the use and enjoyment of the part of the premises sold. Such, we think, is in substance the position in the present case. The park became a communal garden for the benefit and enjoyment of those whose houses adjoined it or were in its close proximity. Its flower beds, lawns and walks were calculated to afford all the amenities which it is the purpose of the garden of a house to provide; and, apart from the fact that these amenities extended to a number of householders, instead of being confined to one (which on this aspect of the case is immaterial), we can see no difference in principle between Ellenborough Park and a garden in the ordinary signification of that word. It is the collective garden of the neighbouring houses, to whose use it was dedicated by the owners of the estate and as such amply satisfied, in our judgment, the requirement of connexion with the dominant tenements to which it is appurtenant. The result is not affected by the circumstance that the right to the park is in this case enjoyed by some few houses which are not immediately fronting on the park. The test for present purposes, no doubt, is that the park should constitute in a real and intelligible sense the garden (albeit the communal garden) of the houses to which its enjoyment is annexed. But we think that the test is satisfied as regards these few neighbouring, though not adjacent, houses. We think that the extension of the right of enjoyment to these few houses does not negative the presence of the necessary 'nexus' between the subject-matter enjoyed and the premises to which the enjoyment is expressed to belong. [8]

Mr Cross referred us to, and to some extent relied upon, *Hill v Tupper*, but in our opinion there is nothing in that case contrary to the view which we have expressed. In that case, the owner of land adjoining a canal was granted the exclusive right to let boats out for hire on the canal. He did so and then sought to restrain a similar activity by a neighbouring landowner. He sought to establish that his grant constituted an easement but failed. Pollock CB said in his judgment: 'It is not competent to create rights unconnected with the use and enjoyment of land, and annex them to it so as to constitute a property in the grantee.' It is clear that what the plaintiff was trying to do was to set up, under the guise of an easement, a monopoly which had no normal connexion with the ordinary use of his land, but which was merely an independent business enterprise. So far from the right claimed subserving or accommodating the land, the land was but a convenient incident to the exercise of the right. ...

For the reasons which we have stated, we are unable to accept the contention that the right to the full enjoyment of Ellenborough Park fails in limine to qualify as a legal easement for want of the necessary connexion between its enjoyment and the use of the properties comprised in the conveyance of 1864, and in other relevant conveyances.

We turn next to Dr Cheshire's fourth condition for an easement—that the right must be capable of forming the subject-matter of a grant. As we have earlier stated, satisfaction of the condition in the present case depends on a consideration of the questions whether the right conferred is too wide and vague, whether it is inconsistent with the proprietorship or possession of the alleged servient owners, and whether it is a mere right of recreation without utility or benefit.

To the first of these questions the interpretation which we have given to the typical deed provides, in our judgment, the answer; for we have construed the right conferred as being both well defined and commonly understood. In these essential respects the right may be said to be distinct from the indefinite and

---

Todrick v Western National Omnibus Co Ltd [1934] Ch 561; *Birmingham, Dudley and District Banking Co v Ross* (1888) 38 ChD 295 at 314; *Pugh v Savage* [1970] 2 QB 373, [1970] 2 All ER 353 (intervening land between dominant and servient tenements).

unregulated privilege which, we think, would ordinarily be understood by the Latin term 'jus spatiandi', a privilege of wandering at will over all and every part of another's field or park, and which, though easily intelligible as the subject-matter of a personal licence, is something substantially different from the subject-matter of the grant in question, namely, the provision for a limited number of houses in a uniform crescent of one single large but private garden.

Our interpretation of the deed also provides, we think, the answer to the second question; for the right conferred no more amounts to a joint occupation of the park with its owners, no more excludes the proprietorship or possession of the latter, than a right of way granted through a passage, or than the use by the public of the gardens of Lincoln's Inn Fields (to take one of our former examples) amount to joint occupation of that garden with the London County Council, or involve an inconsistency with the possession or proprietorship of the council as lessees.

[His Lordship referred to *Copeland v Greenhalf* [1952] Ch 488, [1952] 1 All ER 809, p. 700, post, discussed the nature of the right claimed in the present case and continued:]

The right to full enjoyment of Ellenborough Park, which was granted by the 1864 and other relevant conveyances, was, in substance, no more than a right to use the park as a garden in the way in which gardens are commonly used. In a sense, no doubt, such a right includes something of a jus spatiandi, inasmuch as it involves the principle of wandering at will round each part of the garden, except of course, such parts as comprise flower beds, or are laid out for some other purpose, which renders walking impossible or unsuitable. We doubt, nevertheless, whether the right to use and enjoy a garden in this manner can with accuracy be said to constitute a mere jus spatiandi. Wandering at large is of the essence of such a right and constitutes the main purpose for which it exists. A private garden, on the other hand, is an attribute of the ordinary enjoyment of the residence to which it is attached, and the right of wandering in it is but one method of enjoying it. On the assumption, however, that the right now in question does constitute a jus spatiandi, or that it is analogous thereto, it becomes necessary to consider whether the right, which is in question in these proceedings, is, for that reason, incapable of ranking in law as an easement.

[His Lordship referred to dicta of Farwell J in *International Tea Stores Co v Hobbs* [1903] 2 Ch 165 at 171, and in *A-G v Antrobus* [1905] 2 Ch 188 at 198, 199, 205, which spoke of a jus spatiandi as being a right 'not known to our law'. These statements were obiter and 'cannot be regarded as authoritative'. His Lordship continued:]

Duncan v Louch (1845) 6 QB 904, on the other hand, decided more than 100 years ago but not, as we have observed, quoted to Farwell J in either of the two cases which we have cited, is authoritative in favour of the recognition by our law as an easement of a right closely comparable to that now in question which, if it involves in some sense a jus spatiandi, is nevertheless properly annexed and appurtenant to a defined hereditament. ...

We agree with Danckwerts J in regarding *Duncan v Louch* as being a direct authority in the defendant's favour. It has never, so far as we are aware, been since questioned, and we think it should, in the present case, be followed.

For the reasons which we have stated, Danckwerts J came, in our judgment, to a right conclusion in this case and, accordingly, the appeal must be dismissed.

In **Jackson v Mulvaney** [2003] 1 WLR 360[9] the question was whether a right in common with the owners of the freehold properties surrounding the freehold land shown edged in blue on the plan ('the blue land') to use the blue land as their communal garden was capable of existing as an easement and/or could be acquired by prescription or implied grant.

In holding that it could, LATHAM LJ said at 368:

'22. As to the fourth characteristic, the Court of Appeal in *Re Ellenborough Park* held that an easement to use land as a communal garden was capable of forming the subject matter of a grant. However, there is no doubt that there is a real difference between a case in which the easement claimed is said to have been the subject matter of an express grant, and one which is said to arise by reason of prescription or under section 62 of the Law of Property Act 1925. In the former case, the issue is simply one of construction of the grant. And the court will undoubtedly lean in favour of the creation of an easement if the intention of the parties was clearly to that end. In the latter case, the court has the more difficult task of assessing the evidence as to alleged use in order to determine whether the claimed right has been established. But if it is clear from that evidence that use has been made of the land for the requisite period which is capable of amounting to an easement, it seems to me that a court should not be deflected from declaring the existence of an easement which can sensibly be formulated by the fact that, of necessity, its parameters may not be so clearly defined as they could be in a deed.

24. In my judgment, the findings of fact by the district judge are conclusive of the matter in the claimant's favour. Even though the [servient owners] had not themselves created or maintained the communal garden, the blue land had been used as such ever since the sale of the properties. The fact that they had been content to allow the dominant owners over the years to determine the layout of the garden and to have maintained it themselves does not seem to me to derogate from the conclusion that they have been prepared to set aside this land for the use of the dominant owners as a communal garden. As the district judge himself recognised, this was a potential advantage to the [servient owners] and their predecessors in title at the time that the properties were originally sold.

25. I am therefore satisfied that the facts found by the district judge were sufficient to justify both his and the circuit judge's conclusions that the claimant was entitled to a right to use the blue land as a communal garden along with the other dominant owners.'

---

ii. BUSINESS ON DOMINANT TENEMENT

An easement may exist for the purpose of a business carried on on the dominant tenement.

In **Moody v Steggles** (1879) 12 Ch D 261, Harriet Moody, the plaintiff, owned the Grosvenor Arms in Newmarket, which was set back from the High Street down a narrow yard. The defendants' house projected in front of the Grosvenor Arms,

---

[9] [2003] CLJ 571 (M. P. Thompson).

making it invisible from the High Street. For some forty years a sign-board advertising the Grosvenor Arms had been affixed to the defendants' house. In granting an injunction to restrain the removal of the sign-board by the defendants, Fry J said at 266:

> 'The next point taken on behalf of the Defendants is this: It is said that the easement in question relates, not to the tenement, but to the business of the occupant of the tenement, and that therefore I cannot tie the easement to the house. It appears to me that the argument is of too refined a nature to prevail, and for this reason, that the house can only be used by an occupant, and that the occupant only uses the house for the business which he pursues, and therefore in some manner (direct or indirect) an easement is more or less connected with the mode in which the occupant of the house uses it.'[10]

iii. EXCLUSIVE OR JOINT USER

(a)   General Rule

COPELAND v GREENHALF[11]
[1952] Ch 488, [1952] 1 All ER 809 (ChD, UPJOHN J)

The plaintiff was the owner of an orchard and an adjoining house. Access to the orchard from the road was provided by a strip of land of varying width about 150 ft. long.

The defendant was a wheelwright whose premises were across the road from the plaintiff's land. The defendant proved that for 50 years he and his father before him had to the plaintiff's knowledge used one side of the plaintiff's strip of land to store and repair vehicles in connection with his business as wheelwright; leaving always room for the plaintiff to have access to the orchard. He claimed a prescriptive right to do so. The plaintiff brought this action to restrain him.

Held. Such a right was not an easement, and the claim amounted to one for beneficial user of the land.

UPJOHN J: Mr Horne [for the plaintiff] ... says that there are two reasons why this cannot be a valid easement. First, he says that it is uncertain. He says that the court is not in a position to control the exercise of this easement. He relied on *Hill v Tupper* (1863) 2 H & C 121, p. 693, ante, and he referred to the well-known passage in the judgment of Pollock CB, which says: 'A new series of incorporeal hereditament cannot be created at the will and pleasure of the owner of property; but he must be content to accept the estate and the right to dispose of it subject to the law as settled by decisions or controlled by Act of Parliament. A grantor may bind himself by covenant to allow any right he pleases over his property, but he cannot annex to it a new incident, so as to enable the grantee to sue in his own name for an infringement of such a limited right as that now claimed.'

---

10   *Copeland v Greenhalf*, infra; *Henry Ltd v M'Glade* [1926] NI 144 (stationary sandwich-man). See *Hill v Tupper* [1863] 2 H & C 121 at 175, p 693, ante. See also *Newton Abbot Co-operative Society v Williamson & Treadgold* [1952] Ch 286, [1952] 1 All ER 229, p 972, post.
11   Gale, paras. 1.52 to 1.62.

He pressed me, of course, very strongly with the well-known case of *Dyce v Lady James Hay* (1852) 1 Macq 305, in the House of Lords, in which the sidenote reads as follows: 'There can be no prescriptive right in the nature of a servitude or easement so large as to preclude the ordinary uses of property by the owner of the lands affected. *Semble*, that where a claim in the nature of a servitude or easement is incapable of judicial control and restriction it cannot be sustained by prescription. It does not follow the rights sustainable by grant are necessarily sustainable by prescription. The law of Scotland agrees with the law of England in holding that the right to village greens and playgrounds stands upon a principle of original dedication to the use of the public. Where new inventions come into use they may have the benefit of servitudes and easements, the law accommodating its practical operation to the varying circumstances of mankind.'
...

He contended that there is nothing novel in the business of a wheelwright, but that it is an entirely novel suggestion that a wheelright or anyone else carrying on trade can have such a right as this. He pointed out the great width of the right claimed: vehicles can be left there for an indefinite time, for years, if necessary; they can be left in a vague and undefined part of the strip, leaving an ill-defined gangway, as it has been called, for the owner of the strip to use in getting to his land. He further pointed out that the defendant is really doing much more than an ordinary wheelright's business; that he is doing repairs to every form of modern type of vehicle, such as motor lorries, and that that also makes the claim really too uncertain to be enforceable.

Mr Horne's second point is this, that an easement must be for the benefit of the land, and not for a business carried on in connexion with the land. ...

I think that ... the matter is concluded for me by the decision of Fry J in *Moody v Steggles* (1879) 12 ChD 261 in which he said: 'The next point taken on behalf of the defendants is this: It is said that the easement in question relates, not to the tenement, but to the business of the occupant of the tenement, and that therefore I cannot tie the easement to the house. It appears to me that that argument is of too refined a nature to prevail, and for this reason, that the house can only be used by an occupant, and that the occupant only uses the house for the business which he pursues, and therefore in some manner (direct or indirect) an easement is more or less connected with the mode in which the occupant of the house uses it.' Then he proceeds to illustrate that by reference to certain cases. I also have in mind that the Judicial Committee in the *Nigerian* case [1915] AC 599 felt no difficulty in principle in holding that there might be an easement in connexion with a right to deposit trade goods.

So far, therefore, as that point is concerned, I decide that it does not avail the plaintiff; but I must return to the point of uncertainty.

I think that the right claimed goes wholly outside any normal idea of an easement, that is, the right of the owner or the occupier of a dominant tenement over a servient tenement. This claim (to which no closely related authority has been referred to me) really amounts to a claim to a joint user of the land by the defendant. Practically, the defendant is claiming the whole beneficial user of the strip of land on the south-east side of the track there; he can leave as many or as few lorries there as he likes for as long as he likes; he may enter on it by himself, his servants and agents to do repair work thereon. In my judgment, that is not a claim which can be established as an easement. It is virtually a claim to possession of the servient tenement, if necessary to the exclusion of the owner; or, at any rate, to a joint user, and no authority has been cited to me which could justify the conclusion that a right of this wide and undefined nature can be the proper subject-matter of an easement. It seems to me that to succeed, this claim must amount to a successful claim of possession by reason of long adverse possession. [12] I say nothing, of course, as to the creation of such rights by deeds or by covenant; I am dealing solely with the question of a right arising by prescription.

In **Miller v Emcer Products Ltd** [1956] Ch 304, [1956] 1 All ER 237, [13] premises were demised to a tenant together with the right to use two lavatories on upper floors which were occupied by a third party. One question, inter alia, which arose was whether or not such a right could exist as an easement. As to this ROMER LJ, in a judgment with which Lord EVERSHED MR and BIRKETT LJ concurred, said at 316, at 240:

'In my judgment the right had all the requisite characteristics of an easement. There is no doubt as to what were intended to be the dominant and servient tenements respectively, and the right was appurtenant to the former and calculated to enhance its beneficial use and enjoyment. It is true that during the times when the dominant owner exercised the right, the owner of the servient tenement would be excluded, but this in greater or less degree is a common feature of many easements (for example, rights of way) and does not amount to such an ouster of the servient owner's rights as was held by Upjohn J to be incompatible with a legal easement in *Copeland v Greenhalf* [1952] Ch 488, [1952] 1 All ER 809, p. 700, ante. [14] No case precisely in point on this issue was brought to our attention, but the right to use a lavatory is not dissimilar, I think, to the right to use a neighbour's kitchen for washing, the validity of which as an easement was assumed without question in *Heywood v Mallalieu* (1883) 25 ChD 357. No objection can fairly be made based upon uncertainty, and it follows, in my judgment, that the right may properly be regarded as an easement which the lessors were professing to grant for a term of years; and such an easement would rank as an interest in or over land capable of being created at law by virtue of section 1(2) of the Law of Property Act 1925.'

In **Grigsby v Melville** [1972] 1 WLR 1355, [1973] 1 All ER 385, [15] the plaintiff and the defendants were neighbours. The defendants claimed the right to store articles in a cellar beneath the plaintiff's drawing room floor. BRIGHTMAN J, in rejecting the claim to an easement of storage, said at 1363, at 391:

'There are, I think, two issues here: first, whether an easement of unlimited storage within a confined or defined space is capable of existing as a matter of law. Secondly, if so, whether such an easement was reserved in the present case.

[His Lordship referred to *Copeland v Greenhalf* [1952] Ch 488, [1952] 1 All ER 809 and continued:]

---

[12]   (1968) 32 Conv (NS) 270 (M. J. Goodman).
[13]   (1956) 72 LQR 172 (R.E.M.).
[14]   In *Ward v Kirkland* [1967] Ch 194 at 222, [1966] 1 All ER 609 at 615, a right to enter and maintain a wall was held to be an easement and not to amount to 'the possession or joint possession of part of the servient property'.
[15]   Affd [1974] 1 WLR 81, [1973] 3 All ER 455, when CA held that there was no evidence to support the claim to an easement, and declined to 'embark upon an analysis of the cases'; (1973) 37 Conv (NS) 60 (D. J. Hayton).

Mr Ainger countered by observing that *Copeland v Greenhalf* was inconsistent with *Wright v Macadam* [1949] 2 KB 744, [1949] 2 All ER 565, p. 723, post, an earlier decision of the Court of Appeal in which it was held that the right of a tenant to store domestic coal in a shed on the landlord's land could exist as an easement for the benefit of the demised premises. I am not convinced that there is any real inconsistency between the two cases. The point of the decision in *Copeland v Greenhalf* was that the right asserted amounted in effect to a claim to the whole beneficial user of the servient tenement and for that reason could not exist as a mere easement. The precise facts in *Wright v Macadam* in this respect are not wholly clear from the report and it is a little difficult to know whether the tenant had exclusive use of the coal shed or of any defined portion of it. To some extent a problem of this sort may be one of degree.

In the case before me, it is, I think, clear that the defendant's claim to an easement would give, to all practical intents and purposes, an exclusive right of user over the whole of the confined space representing the servient tenement. I think I would be at liberty, if necessary, to follow *Copeland v Greenhalf*. I doubt, however, whether I need express any concluded view on this aspect of the case.'

[His Lordship then held that an easement was not reserved in the present case.] [16]

(b) Right to Park a Car

The question as to whether the right to park a car on the servient tenement can be an easement has arisen in recent years.

In **London & Blenheim Estates Ltd v Ladbroke Retail Parks Ltd** [1992] 1 WLR 1278, [1993] 1 All ER 307, [17] Judge Paul Baker QC said at 1287, at 316:

'The other unreported decision is that of Sir Robert Megarry V-C in *Newman v Jones* (unreported), 22 March 1982. One of the issues was whether the lessees of the flats in a block of 14 flats were entitled to park their cars in the grounds of the block. ... The importance of the case for present circumstances resides in the following dicta of Sir Robert Megarry V-C:

"In view of *Wright v Macadam* [1949] 2 KB 744 [1949] 2 All ER 565 (which was not cited in *Copeland v Greenhalf* [1952] Ch 488 [1952] 1 All ER 809) ... I feel no hesitation in holding that a right for a landowner to park a car anywhere in a defined area nearby is capable of existing as an easement. ... An easement may take effect subject to the right of others with a like right, without any guarantee that there will be no competition. In any case, I cannot see why the mere risk of there being not enough space for all to park simultaneously should be a reason for denying that any rights at all exist, though doubtless the limited space available confines the right to one car per flat—of course, referring to the particular flats in that case." ...

In the present case the right on its true construction is dependent on the continued existence of car parking facilities for other persons. That leaves the main point under this head, whether the right to park cars can exist at all as an

---

[16] *Hanina v Morland* (2000) 97 (47) LSG 41 (use of adjoining roof for entertaining, sunbathing and generally as an extension of living room held to be exclusive user and therefore no easement); *Jackson v Mulvaney* [2003] 1 WLR 360 at 365.

[17] Affd [1994] 1 WLR 31, [1993] 4 All ER 117; [1994] CLJ 229 (S. Bridge); *Handel v St Stephens Close Ltd* [1994] 1 EGLR 70; (1994) 144 NLJ 579 (H. W. Wilkinson); Gale, paras. 9.73–9.90; [1996] 16 LS 51 (P. Luther).

easement. I would not regard it as a valid objection that charges are made, whether for the parking itself or for the general upkeep of the park. The essential question is one of degree. If the right granted in relation to the area over which it is to be exercisable is such that it would leave the servient owner without any reasonable use of his land, whether for parking or anything else, it could not be an easement though it might be some larger or different grant. [18] The rights sought in the present case do not appear to approach anywhere near that degree of invasion of the servient land. If that is so—and I emphasise that I have not gone into the facts— I would regard the right claimed as a valid easement.'

(1973) 37 Conv (NS) 62 (D. J. Hayton)

'On this footing it would appear, for example, that a right to park a car in a particular defined space amounts to a claim to whole beneficial user of the servient space and so cannot rank as an easement, whilst a right to park a car anywhere in a large area does not amount to a claim to whole beneficial user of any servient area and so can rank as an easement. Lawyers advising companies allocating car spaces in basements of flats for flat owners should thus use leases or licences or merely grant a general easement of parking in the basement but ensure that a practical *modus vivendi* is arrived at between the car-owning flat-occupiers. However, the law would adapt itself much better to "the conditions of modern society and trade", to use Lord Shaw's words in the *Holt* case [1915] AC 599 at 617, if it were to treat as valid easements of parking or of storage in particular defined places, as held by Judge Block in the case of parking in *Sweet and Maxwell Ltd v Michael-Michaels Advertising Ltd* [1965] CLY 2192.' [19]

Gale on Easements (19th edn) 2002, paras. 9–73 to 9–76, 9–82

'9–73 There appears to be no reason in principle why a right to park a car somewhere in a defined area should not be capable of being an easement provided that (a) it is made appurtenant to a dominant tenement, and (b) the right is not so excessive as to exclude the servient owner and leave him without any use of the area in question for parking or anything else. Indeed, counsel have often accepted or assumed [20] and the courts have on a number of occasions now decided [1] that a right to park is capable of being an easement.

---

18 For example, a lease, for which exclusion possession would be necessary.
19 See also (1976) 40 Conv (NS) 317.
20 *Graham v Philcox* [1984] QB 747 [1984] 2 All ER 643; p. 762 post; *Patel v WH Smith (Eziot) Ltd* [1987] 1 WLR 853 at 859H; *Papworth v Lindhaven* [1988] EGCS 54; *Pavledes v Ryesbridge Properties Ltd* (1989) 58 P & CR 459; *Penn v Wilkins*, unreported, 15 February 1966, CA (Civil Division) Transcript No. 36 of 1966 referred to at [1992] 1 WLR 128H; *Bye v Marshall* [1993] CLY 1627; *Saeed v Plustrade Ltd* [2001] RTR 452 at [5], but in the Court of Appeal, Sir Christopher SLADE said that he would prefer to leave the point open, it not being necessary to the decision; [2002] 25 EG 154 [22].
1   *Bilkus v Redbridge LBC* (1968) 207 EG 803; *Newman v Jones*, unreported, 22 March 1982 cited in *Handel v St Stephens Close* [1994] 1 EGLR 70 at 71M; *London & Blenheim Estates Ltd v Ladbroke Retail Parks Ltd* [1992] 1 WLR 1278; [1993] 1 All ER 307, p. 703, ante; *Leon Asper Amusements Ltd v Northmain Carwash* (1966) 56 DLR (2d) 173. *Queanbeyan Leagues Club Ltd v Poldune Pty Ltd* (1996) 7 BPR 15,078; *Owners of Strataplan 42472 v Menala Pty Ltd* (1998) 9 BPR 97717; *Hair v Gillman* [2000] 3 EGLR 74.

9–74 It is, of course, essential that there must be a dominant tenement nearby to which the right is appurtenant. So in *Le Strange v Pettefar*, [2] a facility of parking cars on waste land which had been enjoyed by a tenant of the landowner not as such but as a member of the general public was held not to pass to the tenant under the statutory general words in the conveyance of the reversion to his property.

9–75 Secondly, if the right in question did amount to a right to use the whole of the area to the exclusion of the owner, it could not be an easement. [3] While there would appear to be no difficulty in a right to park at large anywhere in a defined area forming the subject-matter of the grant of an easement, a question might arise if the right were such as substantially to exclude the landowner from the area in question: for example, if the right were granted in respect of a single car space reserved for the grantee's sole use and protected by a chain or a lockable post. No doubt the question is one of degree. [4] It is thought that the above facts might well, at least if the right were granted in a lease, result in the space being regarded as part of the demise. [5] So where an exclusive right to park cars on a strip of land during normal business hours on weekdays was claimed, the Court of Appeal held that the right claimed was not capable of being an easement because the owner would not have had any reasonable use of the land for parking or any other purpose; the curtailment of his right to use the land for intermittent periods would make his ownership illusory. [6] A right to park a car on a forecourt capable of taking two or three other cars is, however, capable of being an easement and falls on the easement side of what has been called the "ill defined line" between rights in the nature of an easement and rights in the nature of an exclusive right to possess or use. [7]

It would not appear, however, to be any objection to the existence of an easement that charges are made, whether for the parking itself or for the upkeep of the parking area. [8]

If, of course, the grant is, on its true construction only intended to be personal to the parties, it will only amount to a licence, [9] though a licence may ripen into an easement upon a subsequent conveyance under the operation of section 62 of the Law of Property Act 1925. [10]

---

[2]   (1939) 161 LT 300.

[3]   *Copeland v Greenhalf* [1952] Ch. 488 [1952] 1 All ER 809, p. 700, ante; in which, however, *Wright v Macadam* was not referred to; *London & Blenheim Estates Ltd v Ladbroke Retail Parks Ltd* supra at 1288C.

[4]   As H. H. Judge Baker said in *London & Blenheim Estates Ltd v Ladbroke Retail Parks Ltd* supra at 1288C.

[5]   *Hilton v James Smith & Sons (Norwood) Ltd* [1979] 2 EGLR 44, where a tenant was given liberty to use a defined part of a private roadway as a parking area. ORMROD LJ regarded the tenant as being in possession of that area and entitled to sue in trespass and to place posts around the land (at 46G), but *cf. Simpson v Fergus* (2000) 79 P & CR 398, to the opposite effect.

[6]   *Batchelor v Marlow* (2001) 82 P & CR 459; reversing [2001] 1 EGLR 119, where the deputy judge had held that the right claimed, being limited in time, did not, as a matter of degree, amount to such exclusion of the owner as to preclude it subsisting as an easement (see at 125M).

[7]   *Hair v Gillman* [2000] 3 EGLR 74 at 75G, p. 726, n.9, post.

[8]   [2000] 3 EGLR 74 at 1288B.

[9]   Cf *IDC Group v Clark* [1992] 2 EGLR 184, p. 620, ante.

[10] As happened in *Sweet & Maxwell v Michael-Michaels (Advertising)* [1965] CLY 2192; and in *Hair v Gillman*, supra.

Right to vary, regulate or extinguish parking rights

9–82 Parking rights are often conferred in terms which give the grantor power to control, regulate or alter the parking arrangements. In *Saeed v Plustrade Limited*[11] the tenant of a flat was granted a right in common with 12 others to park on such part of the forecourt as might from time to time be specified by the landlord as reserved for parking when space was available and subject to such regulations as the landlord might make from time to time. There were 12 spaces originally and the landlords proposed to reduce them to four and charge for them. It was held that the power to specify spaces only entitled the landlord to change the location of spaces, not to extinguish the right; the power was conferred on him for the purpose of giving effect to that right, not extinguishing or reducing it. There is, however, no reason why a power to extinguish parking rights on notice cannot be reserved but this would have to be done clearly and expressly.'[12]

iv. NEGATIVITY

In **Phipps v Pears** [1965] 1 QB 76, [1964] 2 All ER 35,[13] the question was whether a right to make use of a neighbour's house as protection from the weather could exist as an easement.

Two houses, Nos. 14 and 16 Market St., Warwick, were owned by a single owner. No. 16 was rebuilt, 'with its flank wall flat up against the old wall of No. 14,' the two walls not being bonded together. No. 16 was sold and then No. 14. No. 14 was demolished, and the flank wall of No. 16 was exposed to the weather, and damage resulted.

The owner of No. 16 argued that a right to protection passed to him on the purchase of No. 16 by virtue of Law of Property Act 1925, section 62, p. 722, post.

On the question whether such a right could exist as an easement, Lord DENNING MR said at 82, at 37:

'There are two kinds of easements known to the law: positive easements, such as a right of way, which give the owner of land *a right himself to do something* on or to his neighbour's land: and negative easements, such as a right of light, which gives him *a right to stop his neighbour doing something* on his (the neighbour's) own land. The right of support does not fall neatly into either category. It seems in some way to partake of the nature of a positive easement rather than a negative easement. The one building, by its weight, exerts a thrust, not only downwards, but also sideways on to the adjoining building or the adjoining land, and is thus doing something to the neighbour's land, exerting a thrust on it, see *Dalton v Angus* (1881) 6 App Cas 740, 793, per Lord Selborne LC. But a right to protection from the weather (if it exists) is entirely negative. It is a right to stop your neighbour pulling down his own house. Seeing that it is a negative easement, it must be looked at with caution. Because the law has been very chary of creating any new negative easements.

---

[11]   [2001] RTR 452 at 18, approved by CA [2002] 25 EG 154 at 32.
[12]   See also *Liverpool & Lancashire Properties Ltd v B & Q plc* (2000) 28 June (unreported). A right to park can be created by implied grant; *Newman v Jones*, supra; and by prescription: *Bye v Marshall* [1993] CLY 1627; of *Pavledes v Ryesbridge Properties Ltd* (1989) 58 P & CR 459.

The grant of a right to pass and repass does not per se include a right to park: *Newman v Jones*, supra; *Buttle v Muddle* (1995) 6 BPR 77532; a right to use a way includes a right to stop to load and unload: *Snell & Prideaux Ltd v Dutton Mirrors Ltd* [1995] 1 EGLR 259 at 262M–263D.
[13]   Criticised (1964) 80 LQR 318 (R.E.M.); 27 MLR 614; (1965) 28 MLR 264 (H. W. Wilkinson); supported in (1964) 27 MLR 768 (J. F. Garner).

[His Lordship referred to the fact that the law recognised no easement to a view: *Bland v Mosely* (1587) cited in 9 Co Rep at 58a; nor to the passage of air through an undefined channel to the sails of a windmill[14] and continued:] The reason underlying these instances is that if such an easement were to be permitted, it would unduly restrict your neighbour in his enjoyment of his own land. It would hamper legitimate development, see *Dalton v Angus* per Lord Blackburn (1881) 6 App Cas at 824. Likewise here, if we were to stop a man pulling down his house, we would put a brake on desirable improvement. Every man is entitled to pull down his house if he likes. If it exposes your house to the weather, that is your misfortune. It is no wrong on his part. Likewise every man is entitled to cut down his trees if he likes, even if it leaves you without shelter from the wind or shade from the sun, see the decision of the Master of the Rolls in Ireland in *Cochrane v Verner* (1895) 29 ILT 571. There is no such easement known to the law as an easement to be protected from the weather. The only way for an owner to protect himself is by getting a covenant from his neighbour that he will not pull down his house or cut down his trees. Such a covenant would be binding on him in contract: and it would be enforceable on any successor who took with notice of it. But it would not be binding on one who took without notice.'[15]

(1964) 80 LQR 321 (R. E. Megarry)

'Finally, there seems to be at least one field in which the decision [*Phipps v Pears*] may cause difficulty, namely, that of freehold flats and maisonettes. If A sells the upper part of his house to B, the conveyance may well provide for the grant of easements of support by A to B, and for the reservation of easements of shelter and protection by A against B: see, e.g. George, *The Sale of Flats* (2nd edn., 1959), pp. 27, 128. *Phipps v Pears* now seems to mean that the reservation by A creates no easement, and that B's successors in title will not be bound by it. Yet it would be most unsatisfactory to be compelled to hold that although A's successors in title may not remove the support from B's flat, B's successors in title may freely remove

[14] *Webb v Bird* (1861) 10 CBNS 268; *Hunter v Canary Wharf Ltd* [1997] AC 655, [1997] 2 All ER 426, p. 708, post.
[15] Cf. *Rees v Skerrett* [2000] 1 WLR 1541 (where the adjacent buildings were *not* free-standing; on demolition right of support was infringed: para. 15; there was also breach of the duty of care to take steps to waterproof wall after demolition: para. 27). The case would now have been governed by the Party Wall etc Act 1996: para. 34; [2002] Conv 237 (T. H. Wu). In *Sedgwick Forbes Bland Payne Group Ltd v Regional Properties Ltd* (1979) 257 EG 64 at 70, it was suggested that a right to protection against the weather by a roof might be an easement, thereby limiting *Phipps v Pears* to an easement of protection against the weather in the vertical plane.
   On party walls generally, see C & B, p. 268; Gale, paras. 11.01 to 11.35; Beckford-Smith and Sydenham, *Party Walls Law and Practice* (2004). The Party Wall Etc Act 1996 which extends to England and Wales repealed London Building Acts (Amendment) Act 1939 as from 1 July 1997, which only applied to London; *Roadrunner Properties Ltd v Dean* [2003] EWCA Civ 1816, [2004] 1 EGLR 73. For liability for weather proofing of party walls where there is a right of support, see *Bradburn v Lindsay* [1983] 2 All ER 408 (servient owner held liable in negligence for infestation of dominant tenement by dry rot, and in nuisance for loss of support to, and consequent exposure of, the side of the dominant tenement to rot and decay); [1984] Conv 54 (P. Jackson). See also *Brace v South East Regional Housing Association Ltd* (1984) 270 EG 1286; [1987] Conv 47 (A. J. Waite), *Tollemache & Cobbold Breweries Ltd v Reynolds* (1983) 268 EG 52 (fire damage); (1984) 269 EG 200 (C. M. Brand and D. W. Williams).

any or all of their flat and leave A's flat at the mercy of the elements. Even though a right "to protection from the weather", *totidem verbis,* may well be too indefinite to be an easement, it is still questionable why such a right, if sufficiently and clearly defined in its ambit by the instrument granting it, should be refused recognition as an easement, and left to more complex and less potent means of enforcement such as covenants of indemnity and the doctrine of *Halsall v Brizell* [1957] Ch 169, [1957] 1 All ER 371. In recent years many new rights have been accepted as easements, not least the right to use a lavatory: see *Miller v Emcer Products Ltd* [1956] Ch 304, [1956] 1 All ER 237, p. 702, ante. Is the law of easements not ample enough to match bodily relief with protection from the elements?' [16]

HUNTER v CANARY WHARF LIMITED [17]
[1997] AC 655, [1997] 2 All ER 426 (HL, Lords GOFF OF CHIEVELEY, LLOYD OF BERWICK, HOFFMANN, COOKE OF THORNDON and HOPE OF CRAIGHEAD)

LORD HOFFMANN: Canary Wharf is part of the old West India Docks which straddle the neck of land formed where the Thames doubles back on itself between Limehouse Reach and Blackwall Reach. That part of the river used to be a thriving port. Thousands of people who worked in the docks or on the ships lived nearby in Limehouse and Poplar to the north and the Isle of Dogs to the south. But container transport and motorways made the London docks obsolete. By the mid-1970s they had largely been abandoned. The land along the river lay derelict.

[In 1981 the Secretary of State designated the London docklands as an urban development area, and planning permission was granted.]

The local residents complain that the construction of the Canary Wharf Tower and the Limehouse Link Road caused them serious disturbance and inconvenience. First, the construction of the road caused a great deal of dust in the air which settled upon their homes and gardens. If they opened their windows, everything in the room was soon covered in a layer of dust. If they hung out the washing in the garden it became dirty again. [18] Secondly, the Canary Wharf Tower interfered with television reception. The great metal-clad tower stood between the BBC transmitter at Crystal Palace in south London and a swathe of houses, mainly in Poplar to the north of Canary Wharf, which lay in the building's electromagnetic shadow. The effect was that many houses could not receive television at all. In others the quality of the signal was impaired. This state of affairs continued until April 1991, when the BBC brought a relay transmitter into service. Between July 1991 and August 1992 the residents had their aerials aligned to the new transmitter and the problem was thereby solved. ...

In the television action, the plaintiffs complain that Canary Wharf Tower has diminished the amenity of their houses by interfering with television reception. In *Bridlington Relay Ltd v Yorkshire Electricity Board* [1965] Ch 436, 447, [1965] 1 All ER 264, Buckley J said, tentatively and obiter:

"For myself, however, I do not think that it can at present be said that the ability to receive television free from occasional, even if recurrent and severe,

---

[16]   Many of the difficulties can be overcome by suitably drawn restrictive covenants. See p. 938, post.

[17]   (1997) 113 LQR 515 (P. Cane); [1997] CLJ 483 (J. O'Sullivan); [1997] Conv 145 (P. R. Ghandi).

[18]   HL held that an action in private nuisance can only be brought in respect of acts directed against the enjoyment of rights over land, so that, generally only a person with an interest in land can sue; 'Many of the plaintiffs [in the dust action] had no proprietary interests in land at all'.

electrical interference is so important a part of an ordinary householder's enjoyment of his property that such interference should be regarded as a legal nuisance, particularly, perhaps, if such interference affects only one of the available alternative programmes."

The judge was plainly not laying down a general rule that interference with television can never be an actionable nuisance. In principle I do not see why in an appropriate case it should not. *Bridlington Relay* was a case of alleged interference by electromagnetic radiation from high tension electric cables. The Court of Appeal left open the question of whether interference of such a kind could be actionable and so would I.

In this case, however, the defendants say that the type of interference alleged, namely by the erection of a building between the plaintiffs' homes and the Crystal Palace transmitter, cannot as a matter of law constitute an actionable nuisance. This is not by virtue of anything peculiar to television. It applies equally to interference with the passage of light or air or radio signals or to the obstruction of a view. The general principle is that at common law anyone may build whatever he likes upon his land. If the effect is to interfere with the light, air or view of his neighbour, that is his misfortune. The owner's right to build can be restrained only by covenant or the acquisition (by grant or prescription) of an easement of light or air for the benefit of windows or apertures on adjoining land.

That such has until now been the law of England seems to me indisputable. A right to an uninterrupted prospect cannot be acquired even by prescription: *Aldred's Case*, 9 Co Rep. 57b. The same is true of a right to the uninterrupted flow of undefined air to a chimney: *Bryant v Lefever* (1879) 4 CPD 172.[19] In the absence of an easement, there is no right to light. In *Bury v Pope* (1588) 1 Cro Eliz 118 the owner of land was held entitled to erect a house against his neighbour's windows even though they had enjoyed light for over 30 years. Reporting the case, Sir George Croke succinctly noted the ratio decidendi in terms which might have had in mind Canary Wharf: "Nota, Cujus est solum, ejus est summitas usque ad coelum. Temp. Ed. 1."

The circumstances in which this principle should be subject to limitations in favour of neighbours was considered by the House of Lords in *Dalton v Angus* (1881) 6 App Cas 740. By that time it was well established that a neighbour could prescribe for a right of light which would restrict his neighbour's freedom to build. The Prescription Act 1832 (p. 775, post) had fixed the period for the acquisition of such an easement at 20 years. As Willes J pointed out in *Webb v Bird* (1861) 10 CB (NS) 268, 285, prescription for an easement of light was anomalous. In the normal case of prescription, the dominant owner will have been doing something for the period of prescription (such as using a footpath) which the servient owner could have stopped. But one cannot stop a neighbour from erecting a building with windows. Nevertheless, they will after 20 years acquire an

---

[19] In *Cable v Bryant* [1908] 1 Ch 259, it was held that an easement could exist which entitled the dominant owner to the access of air through a defined aperture (a ventilator), although there was no defined channel across the servient tenement through which the air flowed. See also *Harris v De Pinna* (1886) 33 ChD 238. The right may arise under the doctrine of non-derogation from grant: *Aldin v Latimer, Clark, Muirhead & Co* [1894] 2 Ch 437; *Chartered Trust plc v Davies* [1997] 2 EGLR 83. On the doctrine generally, see C & B, pp. 423–424; Gale, paras. 1.79, 3–31 to 3–51; (1964) 80 LQR 244 (D. W. Elliott); (1965) 81 LQR 28 (M. A. Peel); *Johnston & Sons Ltd v Holland* [1988] 1 EGLR 264 at 267–268, per NICHOLLS LJ: 'The expression "derogation from grant" conjures up images of parchment and sealing wax, of copperplate handwriting and fusty title deeds. But the principle is not based on some ancient technicality of real property ... it is a principle which merely embodies in a legal maxim a rule of common honesty': *Romulus Trading Co Ltd v Comet Properties Ltd* [1996] 2 EGLR 70.

easement of light. In *Dalton v Angus* the House of Lords decided that, in like fashion, the owner of a building could prescribe for an easement of support from neighbouring land. On the other hand, it was well settled that one could not prescribe for a right to an uninterrupted view or to a flow of air otherwise through a defined aperture or channel. Lord Blackburn considered how these cases were to be distinguished. He said, at p. 824, that allowing the prescription of a right to a view would impose a burden 'on a very large and indefinite area.' Rights of light, air and support were strictly a matter between immediate neighbours. The building entitled to support, the windows entitled to light and the apertures entitled to air would be plain and obvious. The restrictions on the freedom of the person erecting the building would be limited and precise.

In the absence of agreement, therefore, the English common law allows the rights of a landowner to build as he pleases to be restricted only in carefully limited cases and then only after the period of prescription has elapsed. In this case there is no claim to an easement of television by prescription. And in any event, on the reasoning in *Dalton v Angus* I do not think that such an easement can exist. The extent to which a building may interfere with television reception is far from obvious. Nor is its potential effect limited to immediate neighbours. The number of plaintiffs in the television action [690] is itself enough to demonstrate how large a burden would be imposed on anyone wishing to erect a tall building.

Once again we must consider whether modern conditions require these well established principles to be modified. ...

On the one hand, therefore, we have a rule of common law which, absent easements, entitles an owner of land to build what he likes upon his land. It has stood for many centuries. If an exception were to be created for large buildings which interfere with television reception, the developers would be exposed to legal action by an indeterminate number of plaintiffs, each claiming compensation in a relatively modest amount. Defending such actions, whatever their merits or demerits, would hardly be cost-effective. The compensation and legal fees would form an unpredictable additional cost of the building. On the other hand, the plaintiffs will ordinarily have been able to make their complaints at the planning stage of the development and, if necessary, secure whatever conditions were necessary to prove them with an alternative source of television signals. The interference in such a case is not likely to last very long because there is no technical difficulty about the solution. In my view the case for a change in the law is not made out.

I would therefore agree with the Court of Appeal on this point and dismiss the plaintiffs' appeal in the television action.

V. EXPENDITURE BY SERVIENT OWNER

In **Crow v Wood** [1971] 1 QB 77, [1970] 3 All ER 425, [20] the parties farmed land adjoining a large sheep moor in the North Riding of Yorkshire. Each had the right to allow his sheep to stray on the moor. The defendant's sheep trespassed on the plaintiff's land by passing through the plaintiff's fence, which had not been repaired since 1966. There was no arrangement between the parties as to fencing, but the defendant claimed that he was entitled to an easement requiring the plaintiff to maintain the fence. Such an easement, if it existed, passed to the defendant under Law of Property Act 1925, section 62. LORD DENNING said at 84, at 428:

'The question is, therefore, whether a right to have a fence or wall kept in repair is a right which is capable of being granted by law. I think it is because it is in the nature of an easement. It is not an easement strictly so called because it involves the

---

[20]   *Liverpool City Council v Irwin* [1977] AC 239, [1976] 2 All ER 39, p. 692, ante.

servient owner in the expenditure of money. It was described by Gale [*Easements,* 11th edn. (1932), p. 432] as a "spurious kind of easement". But it has been treated in practice by the courts as being an easement. Professor Glanville Williams on *Liability for Animals* (1939), says, at p. 209: "If we put aside these questions of theory and turn to the practice of the courts, there seems to be little doubt that fencing is an easement." In *Jones v Price* [1965] 2 QB 618 at 633, [1965] 2 All ER 625 at 630, Willmer LJ said: "It is clear that a right to require the owner of adjoining land to keep the boundary fence in repair is a right which the law will recognise as a quasi-easement." Diplock LJ, at 639, at 634, points out that it is a right of such a nature that it can be acquired by prescription which imports that it lies in grant, for prescription rests on a presumed grant.

It seems to me that it is now sufficiently established—or at any rate, if not established hitherto, we should now declare—that a right to have your neighbour keep up the fences is a right in the nature of an easement which is capable of being granted by law so as to run with the land and to be binding on successors. It is a right which lies in grant and is of such a nature that it can pass under section 62 of the Law of Property Act 1925.'[1]

QUESTION

Having read the cases on the nature of easements, can you set out any guidelines to help a court decide whether or not a right which complies with the accepted requirements of an easement is to be recognised judicially? C & B, pp. 577–579; *Dowty Boulton Paul Ltd v Wolverhampton Corpn (No 2)* [1976] Ch 13 at 23, [1973] 2 All ER 491 at 495, per RUSSELL LJ: 'A tendency in the past to freeze the categories of easements has been overtaken by the defrosting operation in *Re Ellenborough Park* [1956] Ch 131, [1955] 3 All ER 667'.

C. Legal and Equitable Easements

LAW OF PROPERTY ACT 1925

1. Legal estates and equitable interests.
    (2) (*a*), p. 6, ante.
    (3), p. 7, ante.

2. Conveyances overreaching certain equitable interests and powers.
    (3) (iii), p. 295, ante.

4. Creation and disposition of equitable interests.
    (1), p. 12, ante.

LAND CHARGES ACT 1972

2. Register of land charges.
    (4) Class C (iv), p. 32, ante.
    (5) Class D (iii), p. 33, ante.

---

[1] An easement of fencing may also be acquired (i) as an easement by prescription: *Lawrence v Jenkins* (1873) LR 8 QB 274; *Jones v Price* [1965] 2 QB 618, [1965] 2 All ER 625 (ii) by custom: *Egerton v Harding* [1975] QB 62, [1974] 3 All ER 689.

An easement is capable of being a legal interest if it (a) complies with section 1(2)(a), Law of Property Act 1925 and is held for 'an interest equivalent to an estate in fee simple absolute in possession or a term of years absolute', (b) is created either by statute, deed or prescription, and (c) in registered land has not satisfied the requirements for registration.

An easement which fails to satisfy either (a) or (b) is not a legal, but an equitable, interest, e.g., if it is for the life of the grantee or created by an equitable owner. In unregistered land, an equitable easement is registrable, if created after 1925, as a Land Charge Class D(iii), or, if it is granted informally or is the subject of a contract to grant an easement, as an estate contract Class C(iv).[2] In registered land, an equitable easement must be protected by a notice or actual occupation under the Land Registration Act 2002.[3a]

In spite of some earlier views to the contrary,[3] it is now settled that the definition of an equitable easement (which is defined in section 2(3)(iii) of the Law of Property Act 1925 as 'any easement, liberty,[4] or privilege over or affecting land and being merely an equitable interest') is to be construed narrowly. This excludes such informal equitable rights as an equitable right of re-entry,[5] or any rights arising in equity by reason of an estoppel licence or the doctrine of mutual benefit and burden.[6] These rights are therefore not registrable as land charges, and their enforcement against third parties depends solely on the doctrine of notice.[7]

III. Acquisition [8]

Easements, like any other incorporeal hereditaments,[9] lie in grant at common law. They could not, like corporeal hereditaments, pass by 'livery of seisin', and, as an easement is real property, a deed of grant was required. Situations could arise, however, in which it was felt that the landowner should have an easement, but he could show no express grant. The common law, true to the basic rule that easements lie in grant, developed rules whereby the grant could be *implied* in a deed conveying land but making no mention of the easement, or could be *presumed*

---

2   *McManus v Cooke* (1887) 35 ChD 681 (easement); *Mason v Clarke* [1955] AC 778, [1955] 1 All ER 914 (profit à prendre); *Lowe v J W Ashmore Ltd* [1971] Ch 545 at 557–558, [1971] 1 All ER 1057 at 1068–1069 (profit à prendre).

3   (1935) 15 Bell Yard 18 (G. Cross); see also (1948) 12 Conv (NS) 202 (J. F. Garner).

3a   P. 717, post.

4   The definition in LCA 1972, s. 2(5) substitutes the word 'right' for 'liberty'.

5   *Shiloh Spinners Ltd v Harding* [1973] AC 691, [1973] 1 All ER 90, p. 34, ante.

6   *ER Ives Investment Ltd v High* [1967] 2 QB 379, [1967] 1 All ER 504, p. 665, ante; followed in *Poster v Slough Estates Ltd* [1969] 1 Ch 495, [1968] 3 All ER 257 (right of entry to remove fixtures at end of lease); (1937) 53 LQR 259 (C. V. Davidge); (1969) 33 Conv (NS) 135 (P. Jackson). See also *Lewisham Borough Council v Maloney* [1948] 1 KB 50, [1947] 2 All ER 36 (requisitioning authority's right to possession).

7   P. 26, ante. Report of the Committee on Land Charges 1956 (Cmnd 9825), para. 16 suggested that Class D (iii) might be abolished. Law Commission Report on Land Charges affecting Unregistered Land 1969 (Law Com No. 18, HC 125), para. 65, recommended its retention. Registrations in that class were then running at an annual rate of 2,500–3,500; there were 689 registrations during the year 1995–1996.

8   C & B, pp. 582–608; Gray, pp. 491–533; M & W, paras. 18.090–18.170; MM, pp. 424–441; Smith, pp. 501–521; Gale, Part II; Jackson, pp. 71–138, 189–194.

9   See *Willies-Williams v National Trust* (1993) 65 P & CR 359 at 361, per HOFFMANN LJ.

where there was no deed at all; this latter case deals with what is more commonly called prescription. As has been seen, an easement may be granted in equity. There are statutory provisions relating to various aspects of acquisition by grant. [10] And, on occasion, statutes have been passed specifically creating easements between adjoining owners; the common example of this type of statute is an Inclosure Act which distributes among individual owners land which had been subject to rights of common and created certain easements among these owners. [11] Modern examples of easements created by statute are to be found in local Acts of Parliament. Statutory rights similar to easements are also created by general Acts and are sometimes called statutory easements. [12]

A landowner may acquire an easement to enter upon his neighbour's land in order to carry out maintenance work to his own property. [13] The Access to Neighbouring Land Act 1992 [14] enables him to obtain an order of the court if the neighbour refuses access where an easement has not been acquired.

ACCESS TO NEIGHBOURING LAND ACT 1992

1. Access orders
(1)   A person—
     (*a*) who, for the purpose of carrying out works to any land [15] (the 'dominant land'), desires to enter upon any adjoining or adjacent land (the 'servient land'), and
     (*b*) who needs, but does not have, the consent of some other person to that entry,
may make an application to the court for an order under this section ('an access order') against that other person.
    (2) On an application under this section, the court shall make an access order if, and only if, it is satisfied—
     (*a*) that the works are reasonably necessary for the preservation of the whole or any part of the dominant land; and
     (*b*) that they cannot be carried out, or would be substantially more difficult to carry out, without entry upon the servient land;
but this subsection is subject to subsection (3) below.
    (3) The court shall not make an access order in any case where it is satisfied that, were it to make such an order—
     (*a*) the respondent or any other person would suffer interference with, or disturbance of, his use or enjoyment of the servient land, or

---

[10]   LPA 1925, s. 62, p. 722, post.
[11]   For example, *Adeane v Mortlock* (1839) 5 Bing NC 236.
[12]   Gale, paras. 1–110 to 1–118; Jackson, chap. 12; (1956) 20 Conv (NS) 208 (J. F. Garner).
[13]   *Ward v Kirkland* [1967] Ch 194, [1966] 1 All ER 609; p. 702, n. 14, ante.
[14]   The Act is based on the Law Commission Report on Rights of Access to Neighbouring Land 1985 (Law Com No. 151, Cmnd 9692). The Act had a chequered history: [1992] 26 EG 136 (J. Adams). It came into force on 31 January 1993. An access order is registrable as a writ or order under LCA 1972, s. 6(1)(*d*), and is regarded as a pending land action under s. 5(1). If the land is registered, the order is registrable by way of notice under LRA 2002, and cannot be an overriding interest: Access to Neighbouring Land Act 1992, s. 5. LRA 2002, s. 133, Sch. 11, para. 26(4). See Gale, paras. 11–41 to 11–69.
[15]   Land does not include a highway; s. 8(3); but does include a party wall; *Dean v Walker* (1996) 73 P & CR 366.

(*b*) the respondent, or any other person (whether of full age or capacity or not) in occupation of the whole or any part of the servient land, would suffer hardship,

to such a degree by reason of the entry (notwithstanding any requirement of this Act or any term or condition that may be imposed under it) that it would be unreasonable to make the order.

A. Acquisition by Express Grant or Reservation [16]

i. AT LAW

Coke (Co Litt 9a): 'And here is implyed a division of fee, or inheritance, *viz*, into corporeall, ... and incorporeall (which lie in grant, and cannot passe by livery, but by deede, as advowsons, commons &c., and of some is called haereditas incorporata, and, by the delivery of the deede, the freehold, and inheritance of such inheritance, as doth lie in grant, doth passe) comprehended in this word grant. And the deed of incorporeate inheritances doth equall the livery of corporeate.'

LAW OF PROPERTY ACT 1925

52. Conveyances to be by deed.—(1) p. 77, ante. [17]

65. Reservation of legal estates.—(1) A reservation of a legal estate shall operate at law without any execution of the conveyance by the grantee of the legal estate out of which the reservation is made, or any regrant by him, so as to create the legal estate reserved, and so as to vest the same in possession in the person (whether being the grantor or not) for whose benefit the reservation is made.

(2) A conveyance of a legal estate expressed to be made subject to another legal estate not in existence immediately before the date of the conveyance, shall operate as a reservation, unless a contrary intention appears. [18]

(3) This section applies only to reservations made after the commencement of this Act.

In **St Edmundsbury and Ipswich Diocesan Board of Finance v Clark (No 2)** [1975] 1 WLR 468, [1975] 1 All ER 772, the question arose whether on the reservation of an easement by a vendor the terms of the reservation were, in case of doubt, to be construed against the vendor or against the purchaser. The Court of Appeal held that it should be construed against the purchaser, as on a re-grant. Sir John PENNYCUICK said at 477, at 780:

'Second, is the maxim "omnia praesumuntur contra proferentem" applicable against the vendor or against the purchaser where there is a conveyance subject to the reservation of a new right of way? In view of the full discussion of this

---

[16] C & B, pp. 583–589; Gray, pp. 526–527; M & W, paras. 18.092–18.096; MM, pp. 425–427; Gale, paras. 3-02 to 3-04; Jackson, pp. 108–109.

[17] The creation of a licence by a deed does not convert it into an easement: *IDC Group Ltd v Clark* [1992] 1 EGLR 187 (deed purporting to 'grant licence and consent' to the use of a fire escape).

[18] *Wiles v Banks* (1983) 50 P & CR 80 (conveyance 'subject to a right of way').

question by Megarry J, and of the fact that we do not agree with his conclusion, we think it right to deal fairly fully with it. But it is necessary to make clear that this presumption can only come into play if the court finds itself unable on the material before it to reach a sure conclusion on the construction of a reservation. The presumption is not itself a factor to be taken into account in reaching the conclusion. In the present case we have indeed reached a sure conclusion, and on this footing the presumption never comes into play, so that the view which we are about to express upon it is not necessary to the decision of the present case.

The point turns upon the true construction of section 65(1) of the Law of Property Act 1925. [His Lordship read the section and continued:] Formerly, the law was that on a conveyance with words merely reserving an easement, the easement was held to be created, provided that the purchaser executed the conveyance, without the necessity for words of regrant. The law treated the language of the reservation as having the same effect as would the language of regrant though there was not in terms a regrant, and in those circumstances regarded the purchaser as the proferens for present purposes. This was a relaxation of the strict requirements for the creation of an easement. (An easement could be created without execution by the purchaser of a conveyance by reference to the Statute of Uses, once section 62 of the Conveyancing Act 1881 removed the technical objection that that statute could not operate to create an easement. This method disappeared with the repeal of the Statute of Uses in the 1925 property legislation.

Section 65 must be read in the light, therefore, of two aspects of the preceding law. First: that previously the law was sufficiently relaxed from its prima facie stringency to permit the language of mere reservation to have the effect of a regrant though it was not in truth a regrant by its language. Second: that for this purpose the purchaser must execute the conveyance if an easement was to be created; that is to say, although a regrant in terms was not required. Against that background, are the words in section 65 "without ... any regrant by" the purchaser to be regarded as altering the law so that the purchaser is no longer to be regarded as the relevant proferens? Or are they to be regarded as merely maintaining for the avoidance of doubt the situation that had been already reached by the development of the law, viz. that mere words of reservation could be regarded as having the same effect as would the language of regrant though without there being in terms any purported regrant by the purchaser? We would, apart from authority, construe the words in the latter sense, so that the only relevant change in the law is the absence of the requirement that the purchaser should execute the conveyance. We read the section as if it were in effect saying that whereas an easement could be created by mere words of reservation without any words of regrant by the purchaser, provided that the purchaser executes the conveyance, hereafter the easement can be created by mere words of reservation without any words of regrant by the purchaser even if he does not execute the conveyance: it is not to be said that in the latter event the previous relaxation of the strict law has disappeared, so that the language of the conveyance must be more than the mere language of reservation. It will be observed that that view keeps in line, on the relevant point, a post-1925 conveyance executed by the purchaser, which is apparently not touched by section 65, and one which is executed by him.

The above is our view apart from authority. What then of authority? We start with the fact that Sir Benjamin Cherry, architect of the 1925 property legislation, made no reference to this suggested change of principle in the law in the first edition of *Wolstenholme and Cherry's Conveyancing Statutes* after the 1925 property legislation. Further, in more than one case since 1925, judges of high authority took it for granted that the old principle still prevails: see *Bulstrode v Lambert* [1953] 1 WLR 1064, [1953] 2 All ER 728 per Upjohn J at 1068, at 731; *Mason v Clarke* [1954] 1 QB 460, [1954] 1 All ER 189, in the Court of Appeal, per Denning LJ at 467, at 192 and in the House of Lords per Lord Simmonds [1955] AC 778 at 786, [1955] 1 All ER 914 at 915. In these cases the contrary was not argued and the judicial statements are not of binding authority. But in *Johnstone v Holdway* [1963] 1 QB 601, [1963] 1 All ER 432 in the Court of Appeal, Upjohn LJ, giving the judgment of the court, not only in terms re-stated the old principle but made it part of the ratio decidendi of his judgment. He said, at 612, at 436:

"that the exception and reservation of the mines and minerals was to the vendor, that is the legal owner, but the exception and reservation of the right of way was to the company, the equitable owner. If the reservation of a right of way operated strictly as a reservation, then, as the company only had an equitable title, it would seem that only an equitable easement could have been reserved. But it is clear that an exception and reservation of a right of way in fact operates by way of regrant by the purchaser to his vendor and the question, therefore, is whether as a matter of construction the purchaser granted to the company a legal easement or an equitable easement."

The opposing view was expressed by Megarry J in *Cordell v Second Clanfield Properties Ltd* [1969] 2 Ch 9, [1968] 3 All ER 746 (upon motion and without being referred to *Johnstone v Holdway*) and in the present case (after a full review of the authorities, including *Johnstone v Holdway*). He distinguishes *Johnstone v Holdway* as a decision based on mistake and states his own conclusion in the following words [1973] 1 WLR 1572 at 1591, [1973] 3 All ER 902 at 921: "The fair and natural meaning of section 65(1) seems to me to be that if a vendor reserves an easement, the reservation is to be effective at law without any actual or notional regrant by the purchaser, and so without the consequences that flow from any regrant. At common law, the rule that a reservation of an easement was to be construed against the purchaser depended solely upon the notional regrant. Apart from that, the words of reservation, being the words of the vendor, would be construed against the vendor in accordance with the general principle stated in *Norton on Deeds*, 2nd edn. (1928), just as an exception or a reservation of a rent would; it was the fiction of a regrant which made reservations of easements stand out of line with exceptions and reservations in the strict sense. With the statutory abolition of the fictitious regrant, reservations of easements fall into line with the broad and sensible approach that it is for him who wishes to retain something for himself to see that there is an adequate statement of what it is that he seeks to retain; and if after considering all the circumstances of the case there remains any real doubt as to the ambit of the right reserved, then that doubt should be resolved against the vendor. Accordingly, in this case I hold that the words 'subject also to a right of way over the land coloured red on the said plan to and from St Botolph's Church' in the 1945 conveyance should, if their meaning is not otherwise resolved, be construed against the church authorities and so in favour of Mr Clark."

We see much force in this reasoning. But we find it impossible to accept Megarry J's analysis of the decision in *Johnstone v Holdway*. We are not prepared to infer from the report that experienced and responsible counsel misrepresented the terms of section 65 to the court and that the judge based his decision on the terms of the section as so misrepresented. It follows that the decision in *Johnstone v Holdway* is binding upon this court and that we ought to follow it.'

ii. IN EQUITY

An agreement for valuable consideration to grant an easement or a profit à prendre is a contract which equity will specifically enforce and is registrable as an estate contract. Equity looks on that as done which ought to be done and such an agreement operates as a grant in equity of an easement. Further, equity construes an informal (unsealed) grant as a contract to grant an easement. Such a contract, being an agreement for a disposition of an interest in land, is required to be in writing;[19] and, as in the case of an agreement for a lease, equity will construe a purported oral or written grant as an agreement to grant an easement.[20]

iii. REGISTRATION

Under the Land Registration Act 1925 easements and profits à prendre enjoyed a privileged position. Under section 70(1)(*a*), p. 148, ante, legal easements and profits à prendre were overriding interests, as were equitable easements and profits à prendre. Under the Land Registration Act 2002[1] equitable easements and profits à prendre are no longer interests which override either on first registration or on registered disposition. They must be protected by a notice or actual occupation.[21]

Legal easements and profits à prendre which are expressly granted or reserved are registrable dispositions and do not take effect at law until they are registered.[2] An easement or profit à prendre which arises as a result of the operation of section 62 of the Law of Property Act 1925 (p. 702, post) is not an express grant (section 27(7), p. 123, ante).

Implied easements and profits à prendre which arise by implied grant or by prescription are interests which override (paragraph 3 of Schedules 1 and 3).

Registration requirements are that a notice of the interest must be entered on the register of the servient land.[3] If the interest is for the benefit of a registered dominant tenement, the registered proprietor must be entered on the register as its proprietor.[4]

B. Acquisition by Implied Grant or Reservation[5]

When the owner of land grants part of it, or certain interests in part of it, to another person, there will be implied, in appropriate circumstances (i) certain rights in favour of the grantee exercisable over the land retained (implied grant), and (ii) certain rights in favour of the grantor over the land granted (implied reservation). These rights are rights in the nature of easements, but which could not be easements before the grant because all the land was under single

---

[19] LP (Miscellaneous Provisions) Act 1989, s. 2, p. 67, ante.

[20] See also *McManus v Cooke* (1887) 35 ChD 681; *May v Belleville* [1905] 2 Ch 605; *Mason v Clarke* [1955] AC 778, [1955] 1 All ER 914 (profit à prendre), p. 87, n. 9, ante.

[21] See p. 786, poast.

[1] R & R, chap. 33; H & B, paras. 3.18–3.19; Law Commission Report on Land Registration for the Twenty-First Century 2001 (Law Com No. 217), paras. 4.24–4.26. For a critical analysis, see [2002] Conv 304 (P. Kenny).

[2] Profits in gross (i.e. where there is no dominant land to which the profit is appurtenant) are registrable with a separate title (LRA 2002, s. 3(1)(a), p. 112, ante).

[3] In the case of first registration the registrar will enter a notice on the register of the servient land. See also LRA 2002, s. 13; LRR 2003, rr 73–76.

[4] LRA 2002, Sch. 2, para. 7: 'Obviously this cannot be done when the easement or profit is for the benefit of an estate in unregistered land. Nor can it be done in respect of an easement that is granted for the benefit of a lease that was not capable of registration when it was granted.' H & B para. 3.19, n. 1).

[5] C & B, pp. 589–594; Gray, pp. 496–514; M & W, paras. 18.097–18.120; MM, pp. 427–430; Smith, pp. 589–594; Gale, paras. 3-17 to 3-153; Jackson, pp. 70–109; Farrand (2nd edn.), pp. 377–392.

ownership. These two cases—implied grant and implied reservation—are treated differently and must be dealt with separately.

i. EASEMENTS IMPLIED IN FAVOUR OF THE GRANTEE

(a) The Common Law Rule

Consistently with the principle that a grantor must not derogate from his grant, [6] the law readily implies easements in favour of the grantee. The rule has been laid down in an obiter dictum in *Wheeldon v Burrows*, which has subsequently been accepted universally as a correct statement of the law, to the effect that in a grant of land there may be implied in favour of the grantee those rights in the nature of easements which (1) are 'continuous and apparent' or 'in other words all those easements which are necessary to the reasonable enjoyment of the property granted' and (2) have been and are, at the time of the grant, used by the grantor for the benefit of the part granted. Easements of necessity without which the property could not be enjoyed at all and easements which were clearly within the common intention of the parties [7] will also be implied in favour of the grantee; and sometimes in favour of the grantor also.

The doctrine of *Wheeldon v Burrows* has been shorn of much of its importance by section 62 of the Law of Property Act 1925. But it still remains available wherever, for one reason or another, a claimant cannot rely on section 62. [8] It always operates subject to the terms of the contract or conveyance, [9] and to the circumstances existing at the date of the grant.

WHEELDON v BURROWS
(1879) 12 ChD 31 (CA, THESIGER, JAMES and BAGGALLAY LJJ)

Of land owned in 1875 by one Tetley, part was sold in January 1876 to the plaintiff's husband, William Wheeldon. Another part was sold in February 1876

---

[6]   P. 209, n. 19, ante. *Ward v Kirkland* [1967] Ch 194 at 226–227, [1966] 1 All ER 609 at 617; *Sovmots Investments Ltd v Secretary of State for the Environment* [1979] AC 144 at 165, [1977] 2 All ER 385 at 391, per Lord WILBERFORCE, p. 731, post.

[7]   *Pwllbach Colliery Co Ltd v Woodman* [1915] AC 634; *Keewatin Water Power Co Ltd v Lake of the Woods Milling Co Ltd* [1930] AC 640; *Wong v Beaumont Trust Ltd* [1965] 1 QB 173, [1964] 2 All ER 119, p. 720, post; *Nickerson v Barraclough* [1981] Ch 426, [1981] 2 All ER 369, p. 734, n. 5, post; *Manjang v Drammeh* (1990) 61 P & CR 194 (PC held no easement of necessity where available access by water across the River Gambia 'albeit perhaps less convenient than access across *terra firma*'). [1992] CLJ 220 (C. Harpum); *Stafford v Lee* (1992) 65 P & CR 172 (common intention implied by reference to conveyancing plan); *Mobil Oil Co v Birmingham City Council* [2002] 2 P & CR 186.

[8]   See p. 722, post.

[9]   This may be expressed by a condition of sale; see *Standard Conditions of Sale*. See Standard Conditions of Sale (3rd edn, 1995), para. 3.4; *Selby District Council v Samuel Smith Old Brewery* (2000) 80 P & CR 466, where PETER GIBSON LJ said at 474: 'The rule in *Wheeldon v Burrows* only operates to the extent that it is not inconsistent with the intention of the parties which may be inferred from the circumstances.' For doubt as to whether the contrary intention should only be sought in the words used in the conveyancing documents, see *Emmet on Title*, para. 17.055, citing *Mllman v Ellis* (1995) 71 P & CR 158. *Squarey v Harris-Smith* (1981) 42 P & CR 118 (where a standard condition that the purchaser should not acquire any rights which would restrict the free use of the vendor's other land for building was held to negative the operation of s. 62); cf. *Lyme Valley Squash Club Ltd v Newcastle under Lyme Borough Council* [1985] 2 All ER 405, in which *Squarey v Harris-Smith* was not cited, and the opposite conclusion was reached; [1985] Conv 243. See also *William Hill (Southern) Ltd v Cabras Ltd* [1987] 1 EGLR 37; *Pretoria Warehousing Co Ltd v Shelton* [1993] EGCS 120; [1996] Conv 238 (A. Dowling); *Millman v Ellis*, supra (grant of narrower easement not necessarily a contrary intention); [1995] Conv 346 (J. West).

to the defendant; on this part there was a shed containing, and lighted by, three windows which overlooked the plaintiff's land. In 1878 the plaintiff, then the widow and devisee of William Wheeldon, erected hoardings near the edge of her land facing the defendant's shed for the purpose of ascertaining her right to exclude the light from the shed. The defendant, claiming an easement of light, knocked down the hoardings, and this action was brought for trespass.

Held. The defendant had no right to knock down the hoardings because no right to the access of light to the windows of the shed had been reserved by Tetley on the sale of the land to the plaintiff's husband.

THESIGER LJ: We have had a considerable number of cases cited to us, and out of them I think that two propositions may be stated as what I may call the general rules governing cases of this kind. The first of these rules is, that on the grant by the owner of a tenement of part of that tenement as it is then used and enjoyed, there will pass to the grantee all those continuous [10] and apparent easements (by which, of course, I mean *quasi* easements), or, in other words, all those easements which are necessary to the reasonable enjoyment of the property granted, and which have been and are at the time of the grant used by the owners of the entirety for the benefit of the part granted. The second proposition is that, if the grantor intends to reserve any right over the tenement granted, it is his duty to reserve it expressly in the grant. Those are the general rules governing cases of this kind, but the second of those rules is subject to certain exceptions. One of those exceptions is the well-known exception which attaches to cases of what are called ways of necessity; and I do not dispute for a moment that there may be, and probably are, certain other exceptions, to which I shall refer before I close my observations upon this case.

Both of the general rules which I have mentioned are founded upon a maxim which is as well established by authority as it is consonant to reason and common sense, viz., that a grantor shall not derogate from his grant. It has been argued before us that there is no distinction between what has been called an implied grant and what is attempted to be established under the name of an implied reservation; and that such a distinction between the implied grant and the implied reservation is a mere modern invention and one which runs contrary, not only to the general practice upon which land has been bought and sold for a considerable time, but also to authorities which are said to be clear and distinct upon the matter. So far, however, from that distinction being one which was laid down for the first time by and which is to be attributed to Lord Westbury in *Suffield v Brown* (1864) 4 De GJ & Sm 185, it appears to me that it has existed almost as far back as we can trace the law upon the subject; and I think it right, as the case is one of considerable importance, not merely as regards the parties, but as regards vendors and purchasers of land generally, that I should go with some little particularity into what I may term the leading cases upon the subject.

… These cases in no way support the proposition for which the appellant in this case contends; but, on the contrary, support the propositions that in the case of a grant you may imply a grant of such continuous and apparent easements or such easements as are necessary to the reasonable enjoyment of the property conveyed, and have in fact been enjoyed during the unity of ownership, but that, with the

---

[10]   C & B, pp. 592–593; M & W, para. 18.105; MM, pp. 428–430; Gale, paras. 3–52 to 3–53; Jackson, pp. 77–79; Farrand (2nd edn.), pp. 383–384; *Polden v Bastard* (1865) LR 1 QB 156; *Hansford v Jago* [1921] 1 Ch 322; *Millman v Ellis*, supra (driveway and lay-by both covered with unbroken and undivided layer of tarmac held to be continuous and apparent); cf. MAUGHAM J in *Borman v Griffith* [1930] 1 Ch 493, p. 524, ante; *Ward v Kirkland* [1967] Ch 194 at 224–225, [1966] 1 All ER 609 at 615, per UNGOED-THOMAS J, citing with approval Cheshire, *Modern Law of Real Property* (9th edn.), p. 468.

exception which I have referred to of easements of necessity, you cannot imply a similar reservation in favour of the grantor of land. [11]

In **Ward v Kirkland** [1967] Ch 194, [1966] 1 All ER 609, Ungoed-Thomas J referred to the discrepancy in the first and last paragraphs of Thesiger LJ's judgment.[12] Of the first paragraph he said at 224, at 615: 'There, it might appear that the words "in other words" in that passage would indicate that the requirement, "which are necessary to the reasonable enjoyment of the property granted", and the earlier words, "continuous and apparent easements", refer to the same easements.'

Of the last paragraph he said:

'Reading that passage on its own, on first impression, it would appear that the "easements which are necessary to the reasonable enjoyment of the property conveyed" might be a separate class from "continuous and apparent easements." … It has been suggested that perhaps the "easements necessary to the reasonable enjoyment of the property conveyed" might refer to negative easements. … I understand that there is no case in which positive easements which are not "continuous and apparent" have been held to come within the doctrine of *Wheeldon v Burrows*.' …

The words "continuous and apparent" seem to be directed to there being on the servient tenement a feature which would be seen on inspection and which is neither transitory nor intermittent, for example, drains, paths, as contrasted with the bowsprits of ships overhanging a piece of land. [13]

WONG v BEAUMONT PROPERTY TRUST LTD

[1965] 1 QB 173, [1964] 2 All ER 119 (CA, Lord Denning MR, Pearson and Salmon LJJ)

In 1957, three cellars in Exeter were let to one Blackaby who covenanted to use the premises as a popular restaurant and to control all smells and odours according to health regulations and so as not to become a nuisance. To comply with these undertakings, it was necessary to construct a ventilation duct fixed to the outside wall of the landlords' premises. This was not realised by the parties at the time, and no duct was built.

In 1961 the plaintiff bought the remainder of the lease and developed the premises into a highly successful Chinese restaurant. The smells and odours caused the Midland Bank, who occupied the floor above, to complain and the public health inspector required the duct to be built. The defendants, assignees in 1962 of the original landlords, refused to allow the work to be done, and the plaintiff asked for a declaration of entitlement and damages.

Held. Declaration that the plaintiff was entitled to an easement as an easement of necessity.

Lord Denning MR: The question is: Has the plaintiff a right to put up this duct without the landlords' consent? If he is to have any right at all, it must be by way of easement and not merely by way of implied contract. He is not the original lessee,

[11]   *Aldridge v Wright* [1929] 2 KB 117; *Suffield v Brown* (1864) 4 De GJ & Sm 185; *Borman v Griffith*, supra.

[12]   See also *Squarey v Harris-Smith* (1981) 42 P & CR 118 at 124, per Oliver LJ; *Wheeler v J J Saunders Ltd* [1996] Ch 19, at 30, [1995] 2 All ER 697 at 707, per Peter Gibson LJ; [1995] Conv 239 (M. P. Thompson); [1995] All ER Rev 311 (P. J. Clarke).

[13]   (1967) 83 LQR 240 (A. W. B. Simpson).

nor are the defendants the original lessors. Each is a successor in title. As between them, a right of this kind, if it exists at all, must be by way of an easement. In particular, an easement of necessity. The law on the matter was stated by Lord Parker of Waddington in *Pwllbach Colliery Co Ltd v Woodman* [1915] AC 634, where he said at 646, omitting immaterial words, 'The law will readily imply the grant or reservation of such easements as may be necessary to give effect to the common intention of the parties to a grant of real property, with reference to the manner or purposes in and for which the land granted ... is to be used. But it is essential for this purpose that the parties should intend that the subject of the grant ... should be used in some definite and particular manner. It is not enough that the subject of the grant ... should be intended to be used in a manner which may or may not involve this definite and particular use.' That is the principle which underlies all easements of necessity. If you go back to Rolle's Abridgment you will find it stated in this way: 'If I have a field inclosed by my own land on all sides, and I alien this close to another, he shall have a way to this close over my land, as incident to the grant; for otherwise he cannot have any benefit by the grant.'

I would apply those principles here. Here was the grant of a lease to the lessee for the very purpose of carrying on a restaurant business. It was to be a popular restaurant, and it was to be developed and extended. There was a covenant not to cause any nuisance; and to control and eliminate all smells; and to comply with the Food Hygiene Regulations. That was 'a definite and particular manner' in which the business had to be conducted. It could not be carried on in that manner at all unless a ventilation system was installed by a duct of this kind. In these circumstances it seems to me that, if the business is to be carried on at all—if, in the words of Rolle's Abridgment, the lessee is to 'have any benefit by the grant' at all—he must of necessity be able to put a ventilation duct up the wall. It may be that in Blackaby's time it would not have needed such a large duct as is now needed in the plaintiff's time. But nevertheless a duct of some kind would have had to be put up the wall. The plaintiff may need a bigger one. But that does not matter. A man who has a right to an easement can use it in any proper way, so long as he does not substantially increase the burden on the servient tenement. In this case a bigger duct will not substantially increase the burden.

There is one point in which this case goes further than the earlier cases which have been cited. It is this. It was not realised by the parties, at the time of the lease, that this duct would be necessary. But it was in fact necessary from the very beginning. That seems to me sufficient to bring the principle into play. In order to use this place as a restaurant, there must be implied an easement, by the necessity of the case, to carry a duct up this wall. The county court judge so held. He granted a declaration. I agree with him.[14]

In **Barry v Hasseldine** [1952] Ch 835, [1952] 2 All ER 317, DANCKWERTS J said at 839, at 319:

'In my opinion, however, if the grantee has no access to the property which is sold and conveyed to him except over the grantor's land or over the land of some person or persons whom he cannot compel to give him any legal right of way, common sense demands that a way of necessity should be implied, so as to confer on the grantee a right of way, for the purposes for which the land is

---

[14] *MRA Engineering Ltd v Trimster Co Ltd* (1987) 56 P& CR 1 (no easement of necessity because access on foot was 'merely difficult and inconvenient'; land was not inaccessible or useless without right of way claimed).

conveyed, over the land of the grantor; and it is no answer to say that a permissive method of approach was in fact enjoyed, at the time of the grant, over the land of some person other than the grantor because that permissive method of approach may be determined on the following day, thereby leaving the grantee with no lawful method of approaching the land which he has purchased.'

QUESTION

Is there a difference between an easement of necessity, and an easement which is 'necessary to give effect to the common intention of the parties?'

If there is a difference, is it relevant in either case that the parties did not realise that the necessity existed?

(1964) 80 LQR 322–323 (R. E. Megarry) and pp. 733–739; post; *Horn v Hiscock* (1972) 223 EG 1437 at 1441; *Nickerson v Barraclough* [1980] Ch 325 at 332, [1979] 3 All ER 312 at 320–321.

(b) Law of Property Act 1925, section 62

The Law of Property Act 1925, section 62 (replacing the Conveyancing Act 1881, section 6), has taken over much of the area formerly governed by the rule in *Wheeldon v Burrows*, p. 718, ante. Its application is wider, in that the right need not be 'continuous and apparent' [15] nor 'necessary for the reasonable enjoyment of the property granted'; [16] it also applies to profits à prendre. [17] On the other hand, it does not apply where the dominant owner obtains his interest without a conveyance under seal (as by will or under contract), [18] or where there was previously no diversity of occupation of the two tenements. [19]

LAW OF PROPERTY ACT 1925

62. General words implied in conveyances [20]—(1) A conveyance of land shall be deemed to include and shall by virtue of this Act operate to convey, with the land, all buildings, erections, fixtures, commons, hedges, ditches, fences, ways, waters, watercourses, liberties, privileges, easements, rights, and advantages whatsoever, appertaining or reputed to appertain to the land, or any part thereof, or, at the time of conveyance, [1] demised, occupied, or enjoyed

---

[15]   *Ward v Kirkland* [1967] Ch 194, [1966] 1 All ER 609 (right to enter farmyard to maintain a wall held to be not continuous and apparent, but to be an easement created under s. 62).

[16]   *Goldberg v Edwards* [1950] Ch 247, p. 726, post.

[17]   *Polden v Bastard* (1865) LR 1 QB 156; *White v Williams* [1922] 1 KB 727; *White v Taylor (No 2)* [1969] 1 Ch 160, [1968] 1 All ER 1015; *Anderson v Bostock* [1976] Ch 312, [1976] 1 All ER 560; *Re Yateley Common, Hampshire* [1977] 1 WLR 840 at 850, [1977] 1 All ER 505 at 514; *Re Broxhead Common, Whitehill, Hampshire* (1977) 33 P & CR 451.

[18]   *Borman v Griffith* [1930] 1 Ch 493, p. 524, ante; *Schwann v Cotton* [1916] 2 Ch 459; *Horn v Hiscock* (1972) 223 EG 1437.

[19]   *Long v Gowlett* [1923] 2 Ch 177, p. 729, post; *Ward v Kirkland* [1967] Ch 194, [1966] 1 All ER 609; *Sovmots Investments Ltd v Secretary of State for the Environment* [1979] AC 144, [1977] 2 All ER 385, p. 731, post.

[20]   (1966) 30 Conv (NS) 340 (P. Jackson); Jackson, pp. 92–108. See also LPA 1925, s. 63 (all estate clause implied), p. 564, n. 8a.

[1]   This section is not concerned with future rights: *Nickerson v Barraclough* [1981] Ch 426, [1981] 2 All ER 369; *Payne v Inwood* (1996) 74 P & CR 42 ('section 62 cannot create new rights where there has been no actual enjoyment of a facility by the owner or occupier of the dominant tenement over the servient tenement', at 47, per ROCH LJ); [1997] Conv 453 (M. P. Thompson). The right must be exercised at the date of the conveyance: *Penn v Wilkins* (1974) 236 EG 203 (passage of sewage, which ceased many years before conveyance, not covered by s. 62).

with [2] or reputed or known as part or parcel of or appurtenant to the land or any part thereof.

(2) A conveyance of land, having houses or other buildings thereon, shall be deemed to include and shall by virtue of this Act operate to convey, with the land, houses, or other buildings, all outhouses, erections, fixtures, cellars, areas, courts, courtyards, cisterns, sewers, gutters, drains, ways, passages, lights, watercourses, liberties, privileges, easements, rights, and advantages whatsoever, appertaining or reputed to appertain to the land, houses, or other buildings conveyed, or any of them, or any part thereof, or, at the time of conveyance, demised, occupied, or enjoyed with,[3] or reputed or known as part or parcel of or appurtenant to, the land, houses, or other buildings conveyed, or any of them, or any part thereof.

(4) This section applies only if and as far as a contrary intention is not expressed in the conveyance, and has effect subject to the terms of the conveyance and to the provisions therein contained. [4]

(6) This section applies to conveyances made after the thirty-first day of December, eighteen hundred and eighty-one.

1. LICENCE INTO EASEMENT

WRIGHT v MACADAM [5]
[1949] 2 KB 744, [1949] 2 All ER 565 (CA, Tucker, Jenkins and Singleton LJJ)

In 1940, the defendant let a top floor flat at 13 Mount Ararat Road, Richmond, to Mrs Wright for one week. After the expiration of that time Mrs Wright continued in occupation by virtue of the Rent Acts.

In 1941, the defendant gave Mrs Wright permission to use a shed in the garden for the storage of coal, and this permission was exercised.

In 1943, the defendant granted a new tenancy of the premises with an additional room to Mrs Wright and her daughter by an unsealed document which made no reference to the use of the shed. The Wrights enjoyed the use of the shed until 1947 when the defendant suggested that 1s. 6d. a week should be paid for its use. They refused, and were denied the use of the shed. This action was brought for an injunction to restrain interference with their use of it and for £10 in damages.

Held. The right to use the coalshed passed to the Wrights as an easement under section 62 of the Law of Property Act 1925 on the grant of the tenancy in 1943.

Jenkins LJ: The plaintiffs claimed an injunction to restrain the defendant from trespassing or otherwise interfering with their lawful use of the coal shed, a declaration that their tenancy of the flat included the right to use the coal shed, and damages limited to 10*l.* I may mention that, as matters stand at

---

[2] This is not synonymous with user: *Re Yateley Common, Hampshire,* supra; *MRA Engineering Ltd v Trimster Co Ltd* (1987) 56 P & CR 1, p. 721, n. 14, ante (rights of access granted to an existing tenant held not to pass under s. 62 on sale of freehold after surrender of the lease); *Re St. Clements, Leigh-on-Sea* [1988] 1 WLR 720.

[3] *Commission for New Towns v JJ Gallagher Ltd* [2003] 2 P & CR 24 ('enjoyed with' and 'appurtenant' refer to incorporeal hereditaments, such as easements, and not to physical property; land cannot be appurtenant to other land: citing *Lister v Pickford* (1865) 34 Beav 576 at 580).

[4] See p. 718, n. 9, ante.

[5] (1950) 66 LQR 302 (R. E. M.). Followed in *Graham v Philcox* [1984] QB 747, [1984] 2 All ER 643, p. 762, post; *P & S Platt Ltd v Crouch* [2002] 32 EG 67 (CS) (right to moor boats on land adjacent to the Norfolk Broads).

present, the last of those claims appears to be the only relevant one, inasmuch as we were informed in the course of the hearing that the defendant has in fact pulled down the coal shed. The question, therefore, is simply this: whether the plaintiffs, as tenants of the top floor flat at 13, Mount Ararat Road, were entitled to the use of the coal shed in question. It is argued for the plaintiffs that they were so entitled, by virtue of section 62 of the Law of Property Act, 1925, which is the section replacing the old section 6 of the Conveyancing Act 1881, and providing by statute the general words which it was formerly customary to insert in full in the parcels of conveyances and other dispositions of land. The plaintiffs claim that this section covers the case. The defendant, on the other hand, claims that, although the coal shed was admittedly used, it was used under no sufficiently definite arrangement; that it was used purely as a matter of personal licence and precariously; and that the arrangement under which it was used could not be said to confer a right in any way appurtenant to the flat, but was an arrangement of a kind to which section 62 of the Act had no application.

[His Lordship came to the conclusion that the tenancy agreement, being sufficient by virtue of the Law of Property Act 1925, section 52, 54, to pass a legal estate, was a 'conveyance' within the meaning given to that term in section 205(1)(ii). There was therefore a 'conveyance of land' within the meaning of section 62(1). He continued:]

The question in the present case, therefore, is whether the right to use the coal shed was at the date of the letting of 28 August 1943 a liberty, privilege, easement, right or advantage appertaining or reputed to appertain, to the land, or any part thereof, or, at the time of the conveyance, demised, occupied or enjoyed with the land—that is the flat—or any part thereof. It is enough for the plaintiffs' purposes if they can bring the right claimed within the widest part of the subsection—that is to say, if they can show that the right was at the time of the material letting demised, occupied or enjoyed with the flat or any part thereof.

The predecessor of section 62 of the Act of 1925, in the shape of section 6 of the Act of 1881 has been the subject of a good deal of judicial discussion, and I think the effect of the cases can be thus summarised. First, the section is not confined to rights which, as a matter of law, were so annexed or appurtenant to the property conveyed at the time of the conveyance as to make them actual legally enforceable rights. Thus, on the severance of a piece of land in common ownership, the quasi easements de facto enjoyed in respect of it by one part of the land over another will pass although, of course, as a matter of law, no man can have a right appendant or appurtenant to one part of his property exercisable by him over the other part of his property. [6] Secondly, the right, in order to pass, need not be one to which the owner or occupier for the time being of the land has had what may be described as a permanent title. A right enjoyed merely by permission is enough. The leading authority for that proposition is the case of *International Tea Stores Co v Hobbs* [1903] 2 Ch 165. [7] That was a decision of Sir George Farwell as a judge of first instance. It was a case in which the defendant, who owned two houses, let one of them for business purposes and there had been a practice of giving permission to the successive

---

6   Compare *Long v Gowlett* [1923] 2 Ch 177, p. 729, post.
7   See the remarks of Cross J in *Green v Ashco Horticulturist Ltd* [1966] 1 WLR 889 at 896–897, [1966] 2 All ER 232 at 238; *Ward v Kirkland* [1967] Ch 194, [1966] 1 All ER 609; [1998] Conv 115 (L. Tee).

managers of the property to let to pass and re-pass with their servants and so forth across a yard which was part of the property and remained in the defendant's occupation. The part of the property which had been let was later sold to the tenants, nothing being said in the conveyance about the right of way. The purchasers claimed to exercise the right of way by virtue of section 6 of the Act of 1881. That claim was disputed, and the point was taken that it could not be a right which would pass under the implied general words inasmuch as it was only precariously enjoyed. The learned judge held that the fact that the way was permissive only was irrelevant for this purpose, and that by virtue of section 6 of the Act of 1881 the grant included a corresponding right of way in fee simple. Dealing with the question of licence or permission, the learned judge said this: 'Unless I am prepared to say that in no case can a tenant obtain under the Conveyancing Act 1881 a right of way unless he has enjoyed it as of right, I must hold in this case that the fact of licence makes no difference. In all these cases the right of way must be either licensed or unlicensed. If it is unlicensed it would be at least as cogent an argument to say, "True you went there, but it was precarious, because I could have sent a man to stop you or stopped you myself any day." If it is by licence, it is precarious, of course, in the sense that the licence, being ex hypothesi revocable, might be revoked at any time; but if there be degrees of precariousness, the latter is less precarious than the former. But, in my opinion, precariousness has nothing to do with this sort of case, where a privilege which is by its nature known to the law—namely, a right of way—has been in fact enjoyed. Lord Coleridge's argument was founded upon a misconception of a judgment of mine in *Burrows v Lang* [1901] 2 Ch 502, where I was using the argument of precariousness to show that the right which was desired to be enjoyed there was one which was unknown to the law—namely, to take water if and whenever the defendant chose to put water into a particular pond; such a right does not exist at law; but a right of way is well known to the law.'

[His Lordship referred also to *Lewis v Meredith* [1913] 1 Ch 571 and *White v Williams* [1922] 1 KB 727 and continued:] There is, therefore, ample authority for the proposition that a right in fact enjoyed with property will pass on a conveyance of the property by virtue of the grant to be read into it under section 62, even although down to the date of the conveyance the right was exercised by permission only, and therefore was in that sense precarious.

The next proposition deducible from the cases is the one laid down in *Burrows v Lang*, which has been referred to in some of the passages I have already read. It is that the right in question must be a right known to the law. ... For the purposes of section 62, it is only necessary that the right should be one capable of being granted at law, or, in other words, a right known to the law. If it is a right of that description it matters not, as the *International Tea Stores* case [1903] 2 Ch 165 shows, that it has been in fact enjoyed by permission only. The reason for that is clear, for, on the assumption that the right is included or imported into the parcels of the conveyance by virtue of section 62, the grant under the conveyance supplies what one may call the defect in title, and substitutes a new title based on the grant.

[His Lordship also referred to *Birmingham, Dudley and District Banking Co v Ross* (1888) 38 ChD 295 and continued:] I think those are all the cases to which I can usefully refer, and applying the principles deducible from them to the present case one finds, I think, this. First of all, on the evidence the coal shed was used by Mrs Wright by the permission of Mr Macadam, but *International Tea Stores Co v Hobbs* shows that that does not prevent section 62 from applying, because permissive as the right may have been it was in fact enjoyed.

Next, the right was, as I understand it, a right to use the coal shed in question for the purpose of storing such coal as might be required for the domestic purposes of the flat. In my judgment that is a right or easement which the law will clearly recognise, [8] and it is a right or easement of a kind which could readily be included in a lease or conveyance by the insertion of appropriate words in the parcels. This, therefore, is not a case in which a title to a right unknown to the law is claimed by virtue of section 62. Nor is it a case in which it can be said to have been in the contemplation of the parties that the enjoyment of the right should be purely temporary. [9] No limit was set as to the time during which the coal shed could continue to be used. Mr Macadam simply gave his permission; that permission was acted on; and the use of the coal shed in fact went on down to 28 August 1943, and thereafter down to 1947. Therefore, applying to the facts of the present case the principles which seem to be deducible from the authorities, the conclusion to which I have come is that the right to use the coal shed was at the date of the letting of 28 August 1943 a right enjoyed with the top floor flat within the meaning of section 62 of the Law of Property Act 1925, with the result that (as no contrary intention was expressed in the document) the right in question must be regarded as having passed by virtue of that letting, just as it would have passed if it had been mentioned in express terms in cl. 1, which sets out the subject-matter of the lease. ...

For these reasons I would allow the appeal and direct that, inasmuch as the coal shed is now no longer in existence, judgment should be entered for the plaintiffs for the sum of damages claimed.

TUCKER LJ: The result is that the defendant, through his act of kindness in allowing this lady to use the coalshed, is probably now a wiser man, and I may perhaps regret that the decision in this case may tend to discourage landlords from acts of kindness to their tenants. But there it is: that is the law.

GOLDBERG v EDWARDS
[1950] Ch 247 (CA, EVERSHED MR, COHEN and ASQUITH LJJ)

The first defendant was the owner of a house at Salford and of an annexe consisting of two storeys at the rear. The annexe could be reached by an uncovered passage to the East of the house, and this approach had always been used by the tenants previous to the plaintiffs. During the course of the negotiations with the plaintiffs, Isadore Goldberg and Barnett Sewelson, for the letting of the annexe, the first defendant agreed to give a personal privilege to the plaintiffs to use another approach to the annexe which led through the front door of the house, and to use the letter box in that door.

On 13 January 1947, an oral agreement for a lease of the annexe to the plaintiffs was reached, and they went into possession on 18 January 1947. On 10 July 1947, the first defendant, pursuant to this agreement, demised the annexe

---

[8]   On easements of storage, cf. *Copeland v Greenhalf* [1952] Ch 488, [1952] 1 All ER 809, p. 700, ante; *Grigsby v Melville* [1972] 1 WLR 1355, [1973] 1 All ER 385, p. 702, ante.

[9]   In *Hair v Gillman* (2000) 80 P & CR 108 (right to park car which could be withdrawn at any time held to be within s. 62.) CHADWICK LJ identified at 114 'the distinction between a right that is temporary, in the sense that it is merely precarious, so that it can be withdrawn at any time, and a right that is temporary in the sense that, to the knowledge of the parties, it will only be capable of being enjoyed for some limited period because of the nature of the property over which it is to be enjoyed'. Only the former can become an easement under s. 62).

to the plaintiffs 'with the appurtenances' for two years from 18 January 1947 with an option to renew for a further two. From the time of taking possession the plaintiffs took privileges beyond those given to them, but the first defendant was held by the Vice-Chancellor of the County Palatine Court of Lancaster to have consented to such acts for the period of time during which she should be in possession of the house.

In January 1949, the first defendant agreed to let the house to the second defendant who went into possession and obstructed the plaintiffs in the enjoyment of these privileges. The action was to restrain interference with the use of the passage through the front door to the annexe by the plaintiffs, their servants and agents.

Held (reversing in part the Vice-Chancellor of the County Palatine). The plaintiffs were entitled to the right of way because it was a right appertaining to their premises on 10 July 1947, the date of the lease; but not to the other privileges.

EVERSHED MR: The substance of the judge's finding is clearly this: he found that there was a sharp and substantial distinction between the privilege to the two plaintiffs themselves to go to and from the annexe through the front door, on the one hand, and all the other privileges on the other. [His Lordship quoted from the judge's judgment and continued:] The passage just read seems to me consistent only with the view that in the Vice-Chancellor's opinion the privilege given to the plaintiff tenants was intended to be one which otherwise was capable of annexation to the demised property and therefore capable of being caught by section 62 of the Law of Property Act 1925.

The claim of the plaintiffs ... has been based on two grounds: first, implied grant, apart altogether from section 62 of the Law of Property Act 1925, and secondly section 62. In my judgment, the first ground cannot be sustained.

[His Lordship explained that the use of the front door and passage was not 'necessary for the reasonable or convenient enjoyment' of the annexe, and a grant could not therefore be implied, and continued:] I therefore reject the argument based on implied grant, and turn to section 62.

The various rights here claimed are these: first, a right for the plaintiffs personally to pass through the front door and along the passage of the house. ... Secondly, a right to maintain a signboard and an electric bell; thirdly, as a necessary corollary to that, a right for the plaintiff's customers to use the front door and passage; and, fourthly, a right to use it for the passage of goods. ... It is plain, in my view, that these rights, other than the plaintiffs' personal right of passage, were not within the language of section 62 so as to be covered by the demise to them.

That leaves only the personal right. ... Having regard to his judgment, I think that I am bound to regard the view of the judge as having been that, in contra-distinction to the other rights, it was intended to be something which the plaintiffs should enjoy qua lessees during the term of the demise, though it should not be enjoyed by their servants, workmen or any other persons with their authority. Therefore, I think, to quote Jenkins LJ, in the recent case of *Wright v Macadam* [1949] 2 KB 744 at 752, [1949] 2 All ER 565 at 572, p. 723, ante: 'It is a right or easement of a kind which could be readily included in a lease or conveyance by the insertion of appropriate words in the parcels.' What those would be I will state later, because, in the view which I take, it is necessary to see that the injunction or declaration to which the plaintiffs may be entitled is properly formulated.

Wright v Macadam was decided after the Vice-Chancellor gave judgment in this case. ... The present privilege is in some ways indeed not dissimilar to that which in *Wright v Macadam* was held to be covered by section 62, namely, a privilege for the tenant to use a shed for storing her coal. I therefore think that, if the right which I have defined was one which was being enjoyed at the time of the conveyance, it is covered by section 62.

That therefore leaves the final point: what is the 'time of conveyance' within the meaning of section 62, subsections 1 and 2? The arrangement about this use of the passage appears to have been made at various dates, the last of which was 13 January 1947. The plaintiffs went into occupation of the annexe on 18 January 1947. The fitting of the bell and signboard took place after that. Several months passed (why, I know not, and it is quite immaterial) before the lease was executed on 10 July 1947, though the term was expressed to run from 18 January. It is plain that before 10 July there was no written instrument whatever. Possession may no doubt have been attributable to an oral agreement of which, having regard to the position, specific performance might have been granted; but I fail to find any instrument in writing within the meaning of section 62 before the lease of 10 July. It seems to me, therefore, that the phrase 'at the time of conveyance' must mean in this case 10 July. I am unable to accept the view that one should construe that as meaning at the time when the terms granted by the lease is stated to have begun. On 10 July 1947, under the privilege granted, this right of ingress and egress was being enjoyed in fact. As I have held, though it is limited to the lessees themselves and does not extend to other persons, it would be capable of formulation and incorporation as a term of the lease, and it is, in my judgment, covered by section 62. To that extent, therefore, but to that limited extent only, the plaintiffs are entitled to succeed.

2. NATURE OF RIGHT

In **Phipps v Pears** [1965] 1 QB 76, [1964] 2 All ER 35, p. 706, ante, Lord DENNING MR, after holding that a right to protection from the weather could not exist as an easement, added at 84, at 38:

'There is a further point. It was said that when the owner … conveyed No. 16 to Helena Field, the plaintiff's predecessor, there was implied in the conveyance all the general words of section 62 of the Law of Property Act 1925. The conveyance included all "easements, rights and advantages whatsoever appertaining or reputed to appertain to the land". On the conveyance of No. 16, Market Street, to the plaintiff's predecessor, there passed to him all these "advantages" appertaining to No. 16. One of these advantages, it was said, was the benefit of having the old No. 14 there as a protection from the weather. I do not think this argument avails the plaintiff for the simple reason that, in order for section 62 to apply, the right or advantage must be one which is known to the law, in this sense, that it is capable of being granted at law so as to be binding on all successors in title, even those who take without notice, see *Wright v Macadam* [1949] 2 KB 744, [1949] 2 All ER 565, p. 723, ante. A fine view, or an expanse open to the winds, may be an "advantage" to a house but it would not pass under section 62. Whereas a right to use a coal shed or to go along a passage would pass under section 62. The reason being that these last are rights known to the law, whereas the others are not. A right to protection from the weather is not a right known to the law. It does not therefore pass under section 62.'

3. DIVERSITY OF OCCUPATION

Section 62 only applies, unlike the rule in *Wheeldon v Burrows*, if there has been a 'diversity of occupation' before the sale or lease; that is to say that the section does not apply where a person who has been both owner and occupier of adjoining premises sells or leases one of them.

A number of problems would arise if the exercise of general rights of ownership by the common owner and occupier over the part to be sold were treated as 'rights and advantages' so as to give the purchaser an easement in respect of such of them as were capable of existing as easements.

In **Long v Gowlett** [1923] 2 Ch 177,[10] Mrs Nichols, the owner of land adjoining the River Granta at Linton, Cambridgeshire, sold the land in two lots by contemporaneous sales to two purchasers; Lot 1 to Gowlett and Lot 2 to Long's predecessor in title. The common owner had been accustomed to go from Lot 1, on which Hadstock Mill stood, to Lot 2 higher up the river, to repair the river bank and cut weeds therefrom, so as to ensure a free flow of water downstream to the Mill. Gowlett, the owner of Lot 1, claimed that an easement to enter Lot 2 to repair and cut had been created in his favour by the conveyance of 1909 under section 6 Conveyancing Act 1881 (now section 62 Law of Property Act 1925). Long sought an injunction and damages for trespass. In rejecting Gowlett's claim, SARGANT J said at 199:

'And on these facts it is contended for the defendant that this constituted a "privilege easement right or advantage" over or in relation to Lot 2, which at the time of the conveyance was occupied or enjoyed with Lot 1, and accordingly, that this advantage passed to the defendant by virtue of the express words of the sub-section as included in the conveyance by virtue of the statute. The argument is not based in any way on the existence of any continuous and apparent easement existing over Lot 2 in favour of Lot 1; indeed, any such claim would be incompatible with the evidence, which clearly established that there was no defined way at all along the south bank. The claim is founded upon there having been a statutory introduction into the conveyance to the defendant of words equivalent to or identical with those either expressly contained or statutorily introduced in the corresponding conveyances in such cases as *James v Plant* (1836) 4 Ad & El 749; *Watts v Kelson* (1870) 6 Ch App 166; *Bayley v Great Western Rly Co* (1884) 26 ChD 434; and *White v Williams* [1922] 1 KB 727.

It is, therefore, necessary for the purpose of dealing with the matter on this footing to consider whether, during the common ownership and occupation of Lot 1 and Lot 2 by Mr Nichols and his widow, and therefore at the date of the conveyance, there was a "privilege, easement, right or advantage" of the kind now claimed, which can properly be said to have been "demised, occupied or enjoyed" with Lot 1 over Lot 2. It is very difficult to see how this can have been the case. No doubt the common owner and occupier did in fact repair the bank of Lot 2, and cut the weeds there; and no doubt also this repair and cutting would enure not solely for the benefit of Lot 2 (which comprised, amongst other things, a lawn tennis court), so as to prevent its being flooded, but also and very likely to a greater extent for the benefit of Lot 1. But there is nothing to indicate that the acts done on Lot 2 were done otherwise than in the course of the ownership and occupation of Lot 2, or that they were by way of using a "privilege, easement or advantage" over Lot 2 in connection with Lot 1. The common owner and occupier of Whiteacre and Blackacre may in fact use Blackacre as an alternative and more

---

[10] See also *Ward v Kirkland* [1967] Ch 194 at 227–231, [1966] 1 All ER 609 at 618–620, p. 722, n. 15, ante.

convenient method of communication between Whiteacre and a neighbouring village. But it has never been held, and would I think be contrary to principle to hold, that (in default of there being a made road over Blackacre forming a continuous and apparent means of communication) a sale and conveyance of Whiteacre alone would carry a right to pass over Blackacre in the same way in which the common owner had been accustomed to pass. As it seems to me, in order that there may be a "privilege, easement or advantage" enjoyed with Whiteacre over Blackacre so as to pass under the statute, there must be something done on Blackacre not due to or comprehended within the general rights of an occupying owner of Blackacre, but of such a nature that it is attributable to a privilege, easement, right or advantage, however precarious, which arises out of the ownership or occupation of Whiteacre, altogether apart from the ownership or occupation of Blackacre. And it is difficult to see how, when there is a common ownership of both Whiteacre and Blackacre, there can be any such relationship between the two closes as (apart from the case of continuous and apparent easements or that of a way of necessity) would be necessary to create a "privilege, easement, right or advantage" within the words of section 6, subsection 2, of the statute. For this purpose it would seem that there must be some diversity of ownership or occupation of the two closes sufficient to refer the act or acts relied on not to mere occupying ownership, but to some advantage or privilege (however far short of a legal right) attaching to the owner or occupier of Whiteacre as such and de facto exercised over Blackacre. Let me illustrate my meaning from the latest case on the subject—namely, *White v Williams* [1922] 1 KB 727. ...

Mr Greene for the defendant was challenged to produce from the very many cases in which, on a conveyance of Whiteacre, an easement over Blackacre has been held to pass under the statutory words or their equivalent, a single case in which both the closes in question had been in common ownership and occupation, or in which there had not been an actual enjoyment over Blackacre on the part of an owner or occupier of Whiteacre who was not the owner and occupier of Blackacre. And neither from among the cases cited to me, nor from any other case in the books, was he able (with one solitary exception) to produce such a case as required. The exception, however, is one of high authority—namely, that of *Broomfield v Williams* [1897] 1 Ch 602—and it is necessary to examine it with some attention.[10a]

In that case the common owner of a house and of adjoining land over which light had in fact been received through the windows of the house, sold and conveyed the house by a conveyance after the date of the Conveyancing Act 1881, but retained the adjoining land. It was held by the Court of Appeal that, although the retained land was marked on the plan on the conveyance as "building land", the vendor was not at liberty subsequently to build on the retained land so as to interfere substantially with the access of light to the windows of the house. A. L. Smith LJ, it is true, based his judgment solely on the principle that the grantor was not entitled to derogate from his grant; and this was quite sufficient to support the actual decision. But the other two members of the Court relied mainly, if not exclusively, on the express words of section 6, subsection 2, of the Act; and the decision is, therefore, undoubtedly binding on me with regard to the access of light, and also with regard to any other "privilege, easement, right or advantage" that is on the same footing as "light."

But such an easement or advantage as is now claimed is, in my judgment, very different from light, or a right to light. The access of light to a window over

---

[10a]   See *Payne v Inwood* (1996) 74 P & CR 42 at 48–51, per ROCH LJ.

adjoining land is a physical fact plainly visible to any one buying a house. It is extremely similar to a continuous and apparent easement. It is mentioned in the subsection in the midst of a number of physical features ending with the word "watercourses"; and the special position of light to an existing window as compared with other easements is fully recognised in the Prescription Act, which makes the acquisition of an easement of light depend on the enjoyment of the light simpliciter, and not, as in the case of other easements, on enjoyment as of right. The fact, therefore, that the inclusion of light in the subject matter of conveyance in section 6, subsection 2, has been held to entitle the grantee to the light coming to an existing window, does not necessarily involve the further inclusion of imperceptible rights or advantages, corresponding with intermittent practice or user as between two tenements of the common owner and occupier of both. Such an intermittent and non-apparent user or practice stands, in my judgment, on a completely different footing from the visible access of light to an existing window.

The importance of such a distinction is specially obvious in a case like the present, where there is a contemporaneous sale by a common owner to two separate purchasers of adjoining lots completely divided by a physical boundary. If the contention of the defendant is correct, it would be necessary in any such case for the purchaser to inquire how the common owner and occupier had been accustomed to make use of each close in connection with the other. Would the plaintiff, for instance, in this case be entitled, as against the defendant, to an alternative way over Lot 1 to reach Lot 2, because while both lots were in common ownership and occupation, it was the practice of Mr and Mrs Nichols by way of Lot 1 to repair the south bank of Lot 2? Any number of similar puzzles would arise, if the law were as the defendant would have it. The fact that the common owner and occupier sells two adjoining closes separately is, in my mind, a negation of the intention to preserve access between them: compare such a case as *Midland Rly Co v Gribble* [1895] 2 Ch 827.

The only two exceptions to this rule appear to be those of ways of necessity and of continuous and apparent easements. Had the general words of section 6, subsection 2, any such effect as is suggested by the defendant—and it must be remembered that these words were not new, but represented conveyancing practice for many years previously—it is difficult, if not impossible, to understand how there have not been numerous cases in which, on a severance of two closes, a subsisting practice by the common owner and occupier of both has not been given effect to by way of legal easement as a result of general words of this kind.'

In **Sovmots Investments Ltd v Secretary of State for the Environment** [1979] AC 144, [1977] 2 All ER 385,[11] the House of Lords considered both the rule in *Wheeldon v Burrows* and section 62. The London Borough of Camden made a compulsory purchase order to acquire 36 residential maisonettes in Centre Point. The question was whether certain rights over and in respect of other parts of Centre Point, without which the maisonettes could not be used as housing accommodation, passed on the conveyance; and whether, if they did not pass, the Borough had power to make a compulsory purchase order to acquire the

[11]   (1977) 41 Conv (NS) 415; [1979] Conv 113 (C. Harpum); [1978] Conv 449 (P. Smith); 127 NLJ 695 (H. W. Wilkinson); Jackson, pp. 100–103.

maisonettes which, without the additional rights, could not be used for housing purposes. In quashing the order, Lord WILBERFORCE said at 168, at 391: [12]

'The main argument before the inspector and in the courts below was that in this case and under the compulsory purchase order as made no specific power to require the creation of ancillary rights was necessary because these would pass to the acquiring authority under either, or both, of the first rule in *Wheeldon v Burrows* (1879) 12 ChD 31 ('the rule') or of section 62 of the Law of Property Act 1925. Under the rule (I apologise for the reminder but the expression of the rule is important)

"on the grant by the owner of a tenement of part of that tenement *as it is then used and enjoyed*, there will pass to the grantee all those continuous and apparent easements (by which, of course, I mean quasi-easements), or, in other words, all those easements which are necessary to the reasonable enjoyment of the property granted, and *which have been and are at the time of the grant used* by the owners of the entirety for the benefit of the part granted" (see per Thesiger LJ at 49, my emphasis).

Under section 62 a conveyance of land operates to convey with the land all ways, watercourses, liberties, privileges, easements, rights and advantages whatsoever, appertaining or reputed to appertain to the land, or any part thereof, or, at the time of conveyance, demised, occupied or enjoyed with, or reputed or known as part or parcel of or appurtenant to the land or any part thereof.

My Lords, there are very comprehensive expressions here, but it does not take much analysis to see that they have no relevance to the situation under consideration.

The rule is a rule of intention, based on the proposition that a man may not derogate from his grant. He cannot grant or agree to grant land and at the same time deny to his grantee what is at the time of the grant obviously necessary for its reasonable enjoyment. To apply this to a case where a public authority is taking from an owner his land without his will is to stand the rule on its head: it means substituting for the intention of a reasonable voluntary grantor the unilateral, opposed, intention of the acquirer.

Moreover, and this point is relevant to a later argument, the words I have underlined [13] show that for the rule to apply there must be actual, and apparent, use and enjoyment at the time of the grant. But no such use or enjoyment had, at Centre Point, taken place at all.

Equally, section 62 does not fit this case. The reason is that when land is under one ownership one cannot speak in any intelligible sense of rights, or privileges, or easements being exercised over one part for the benefit of another. Whatever the owner does, he does as owner and until a separation occurs, of ownership or at least of occupation, the condition for the existence of rights, etc., does not exist: see *Bolton v Bolton* (1879) 11 ChD 968, 970 per Fry J and *Long v Gowlett* [1923] 2 Ch 177, 189, 198, in my opinion a correct decision. [14]

A separation of ownership, in a case like the present, will arise on conveyance of one of the parts (e.g. the maisonettes), but this separation cannot be projected back to the stage of the compulsory purchase order so as, by anticipation to bring into existence rights not existing in fact.'

---

[12]   See also at 175–176 at 397–398, per Lord EDMUND-DAVIES.
[13]   As printed in italics.
[14]   See *Ward v Kirkland*, at 227–231, at 617–20; *Wright v Macadam* [1949] 2 KB 744 at 748; [1949] 2 All ER 565 at 569; *Squarey v Harris-Smith* (1981) 42 P & CR 118 at 129, per OLIVER LJ.

[1978] Conv 449, at pp. 454–455 (P. Smith)

'In fact there is a considerable body of authority against [*Long v Gowlett*], both academic and precedent based, none of which was seriously considered by the House of Lords. There is no need to consider it in any detail as most readers will be aware of it. [15] The first limitation namely that section 62 has no ambit where there is no diversity of occupation, does not stand up to precedent for a start. In *Broomfield v Williams* [16] the Court of Appeal made no such limitation as suggested by Sargant J in *Long v Gowlett* and Lord Wilberforce and Lord Edmund-Davies in the *Sovmots case*. With respect to Lord Edmund-Davies and to Mr Harpum, [17] merely to state easements of light are different from other easements does not explain why section 62, apparently very widely drawn, applies to those easements and not to others when there is no diversity of occupation. There is absolutely nothing in the section to justify such a limitation. Furthermore the objection that the rights etc. do not exist at the relevant time, ignores the substantial body of case law where section 62 has turned a precarious right into a full legal easement. ... [18]

The real problem now is what is left after *Sovmots*? It appears that one of the major opponents of the limitations imposed by the case is prepared to concede it now, [19] but is such resignation necessary? Only two of the five law lords considered the point, no argument was addressed to them on the point and no cases cited.'

QUESTIONS

1. Is there good reason in particular or authority for requiring a diversity of occupation for the operation of section 62? What bearing does the *Sovmots* case have on the matter? And is there justification for applying a different rule to easements of light?

    Jackson, pp. 9 et seq; [1978] Conv 449 (P. Smith); M & W, p. 865 n. 97; *Broomfield v Williams* [1897] 1 Ch 602.

2. Is there good reason for differentiating in this respect between the operation of the rule in *Wheeldon v Burrows* and the Law of Property Act 1925, section 62? See JENKINS LJ in *Wright v Macadam* [1949] 2 KB 744, [1949] 2 All ER 565, p. 723, ante; C & B, pp. 592–593; M & W, paras. 18.117–18.120; MM, pp, 429–430; Smith, pp. 512–513; Gale, paras. 3.122–3.126; Jackson, pp. 100–103.

ii. EASEMENTS IMPLIED IN FAVOUR OF THE GRANTOR

Generally, any rights which a grantor wishes to enjoy as easements in favour of the land he retains, and exercisable over the land sold, must be expressly

---

[15] For starters Jackson (1966) 30 Conv (NS) 342–348 and thence Jackson, *The Law of Easements and Profits*, pp. 97–103; Megarry and Wade, *The Law of Easements and Profits*, pp. 97–103; Megarry and Wade, *The Law of Real Property* (4th edn.), pp. 835, note 47 and 837–838; Farrand, *Contract and Conveyance* (2nd edn.), pp. 384–386; *Emmet*, p. 515; Barnsley, *Conveyancing Law and Practice*, pp. 484–485 (perhaps?); and *Gale on Easements* (14th edn.), pp. 125–126. The last book is particularly significant as the Thirteenth Edition of that book supported *Long v Gowlett* but was changed after Professor Jackson's article supra.

[16] [1897] 1 Ch 602.

[17] (1977) 41 Conv (NS) 415.

[18] See e.g. *Wright v Macadam* [1949] 2 KB 744, [1949] 2 All ER 565; *Goldberg v Edwards* [1950] Ch 247 and *International Tea Stores v Hobbs* [1903] 2 Ch 165. None of these cases featured in the *Sovmots* case.

[19] See Jackson, p. 100.

reserved [20] or regranted. Otherwise he may not derogate from his grant. [1] In exceptional cases, however, easements will be implied in his favour. These are easements of necessity, [2] and may be (a) 'an easement without which the property retained cannot be used at all, and not one merely necessary to the reasonable enjoyment of that property', [3] and (b) an easement which is required to carry out the common intention of the parties. [4] These are usually easements of support, and such easements can only be claimed when the intention is clear. [5] In each case the right which the grantor can claim is the minimum necessary to comply with the rule under which it is claimed.

CORPORATION OF LONDON v RIGGS
(1880) 13 ChD 798 (ChD, JESSEL MR)

In 1887, Heathcote, the owner of land in Essex, conveyed part of this land to London Corporation who declared that they would hold the land conveyed as an open space for ever. This land completely encircled a close of about two acres called Barn Hoppet which was owned also by Heathcote, and had been used up to that time for agricultural purposes only. No easements in favour of Barn Hoppet were reserved in the conveyance of the other land to London Corporation. In 1879 Riggs entered into possession of Barn Hoppet as tenant, and he made preparations for the erection of a house and of other buildings for the sale of refreshments to the public. The plaintiffs claimed a declaration that Riggs' right of way of necessity was limited to purposes sufficient to the use of Barn Hoppet for agricultural purposes only; and an injunction and damages. The action was tried on demurrer.

Held. The defendant's right of way was limited to the purposes for which it was used in 1877.

JESSEL MR: I am afraid that, whatever I may call my decision, it will, in effect, be making law, which I never have any desire to do; but I cannot find that the point is covered by any decided case, or even appears to have been discussed in any decided case. The only satisfaction I have in deciding the point is this, that it will in all probability be carried to a higher court, and it will be for that court to make the law, or, as we say, declare the law, and not for me.

The real question I have to decide is this—whether, on a grant of land wholly surrounding a close, the implied grant, or re-grant, of a right of way by the grantee to the grantor to enable him to get to the reserved, or excepted, or inclosed close, is a grant of a general right of way for all purposes, or only a grant of a right of way for the purpose of the enjoyment of the reserved or excepted close in its then state.

---

[20]   LPA 1925, s. 65, p. 714, ante.
[1]   (1964) 80 LQR 244 (D. W. Elliott).
[2]   See *Nickerson v Barraclough* [1980] Ch 325 at 332, [1979] 3 All ER 312 at 320–321.
[3]   *Union Lighterage Co v London Graving Dock Co* [1902] 2 Ch 557 at 573; *Pinnington v Galland* (1853) 9 Exch 1; *Deacon v South Eastern Rly Co* (1889) 61 LT 377; *Midland Rly Co v Miles* (1886) 33 ChD 632.
[4]   *Richards v Rose* (1853) 9 Exch 218; *Shubrook v Tufnell* (1882) 46 LT 886; *Re Webb's Lease* [1951] Ch 808, [1951] 2 All ER 131, p. 736, post.
[5]   See *Nickerson v Barraclough* [1981] Ch 426, [1981] 2 All ER 369 (where CA, reversing MEGARRY V-C, held that 'the doctrine of way of necessity is not founded upon public policy at all but upon an implication from the circumstances' (per BRIGHTMAN LJ at 440, at 379); and so if the grant implied by way of construction was negated by an express contrary provision in the conveyance, no grant could be implied by the court under a rule of public policy, for example, against land being rendered unusable by being landlocked); [1981] Conv 442 (L. Crabb).

There is, as I have said, no distinct authority on the question. It seems to me to have been laid down in very early times—and I have looked into a great number of cases, and among others several black-letter cases—that the right to a way of necessity is an exception to the ordinary rule that a man shall not derogate from his own grant, and that the man who grants the surrounding land is in very much the same position as regards the right of way to the reserved close as if he had granted the close, retaining the surrounding land. In both cases there is what is called a way of necessity; and the way of necessity, according to the old rules of pleading, must have been pleaded as a grant, or, where the close is reserved, as it is here, as a re-grant. ...

Well, now, if we try the case on principle—treating this right of way as an exception to the rule—ought it to be treated as a larger exception than the necessity of the case warrants? That of course brings us back to the question, What does the necessity of the case require? The object of implying the regrant, as stated by the older Judges, was that if you did not give the owner of the reserved close some right of way or other, he could neither use nor occupy the reserved close, nor derive any benefit from it. But what is the extent of the benefit he is to have? Is he entitled to say, I have reserved to myself more than that which enables me to enjoy it as it is as the time of the grant? And if that is the true rule, that he is not to have more than necessity requires, as distinguished from what convenience may require, it appears to me that the right of way must be limited to that which is necessary at the time of the grant; that is, he is supposed to take a re-grant to himself of such a right of way as will enable him to enjoy the reserved thing as it is.

That appears to me to be the meaning of a right of way of necessity. If you imply more, you reserve to him not only that which enables him to enjoy the thing he has reserved as it is, but that which enables him to enjoy it in the same way and to the same extent as if he reserved a general right of way for all purposes: that is—as in the case I have before me—a man who reserves two acres of arable land in the middle of a large piece of land is to be entitled to cover the reserved land with houses, and call on his grantee to allow him to make a wide metalled road up to it. I do not think that is a fair meaning of a way of necessity: I think it must be limited by the necessity at the time of the grant; and that the man who does not take the pains to secure an actual grant of a right of way for all purposes is not entitled to be put in a better position than to be able to enjoy that which he had at the time the grant was made. I am not aware of any other principle on which this case can be decided.

I may be met by the objection that a way of necessity must mean something more than what I have stated, because, where the grant is of the inclosed piece, the grantee is entitled to use the land for all purposes, and should therefore be entitled to a right of way commensurate with his right of enjoyment. But there again the grantee has not taken from the grantor any express grant of a right of way: and all he can be entitled to ask is a right to enable him to enjoy the property granted to him as it was granted to him. It does not appear to me that the grant of the property gives any greater right. But even if it did, the principle applicable to the grantee is not quite the same as the principle applicable to the grantor: and it might be that the grantee obtains a larger way of necessity—though I do not think he does—than the grantor does under the implied re-grant.

I am afraid that I am laying down the law for the first time—that I am for the first time declaring the law; but it is a matter of necessity from which I cannot escape.

The demurrer must, therefore, be overruled, with costs.

RE WEBBS'S LEASE
[1951] Ch 808, [1951] 2 All ER 131 (CA, EVERSHED MR, JENKINS and MORRIS LJJ)

The defendant (the landlord) was head lessee of a three storey building. He occupied the ground floor for his own business as a butcher, and leased the upper two storeys to the plaintiff (the tenant). The first letting was in 1939 for three years; the tenant remained in occupation until 1949 when he was granted a 21 year lease. Throughout all this time one side of the building contained an advertisement for the defendant's business, and another side (the west wall) one for Bryant and May's matches, both of which covered all or part of the external walls of the upper two storeys. None of the leases made any reservation of the right of the landlord to use the outer walls of the demised premises for this purpose. In 1950, the tenants began to make enquiries concerning the landlord's right so to use the walls and finally issued this summons to determine the question.

Held (reversing DANCKWERTS J). Without express reservation, the landlord had no right to claim the easement in question.

JENKINS LJ: The matter therefore stands thus: The landlord did not include in the provisions of the lease as executed any reservation of advertising rights over any part of the outer walls; but, at the date of the lease, the advertisements now in dispute were in their present positions on the walls and plainly to be seen. Moreover, they had existed in their present positions continuously since before the commencement of the tenant's original tenancy in 1939; and the tenant never objected to their presence at any time during his original tenancy, or at the time of the granting of the lease of 11 August 1949, or thereafter until January 1950. There is no evidence that either party ever even mentioned the subject of the advertisements to the other during the whole of this period of more than ten years.

This being in substance the whole of the available facts, the question is whether on those bare facts without more, the court can and ought as a matter of law to imply in favour of the landlord a reservation during the term of twenty-one years granted by the lease of 11 August 1949, of advertising rights over the outer walls demised, at all events to the extent required to enable him to maintain the existing advertisements and to retain for his own benefit any periodical payments receivable from the Borough Billposting Company in respect of the site of the 'Brymay' poster.

As to the law applicable to the case, it is not disputed that as a general rule a grantor, whether by way of conveyance or lease, of part of a hereditament in his ownership, cannot claim any easement over the part granted for the benefit of the part retained, unless it is expressly reserved out of the grant. See (for instance) *Suffield v Brown* (1864) 4 De GJ & Sm 185; *Crossley & Sons Ltd v Lightowler* (1867) 2 Ch App 478; *Wheeldon v Burrows* (1879) 12 ChD 31, p. 718, ante.

There are, however, certain exceptions to the general rule. Two well-established exceptions relate to easements of necessity and mutual easements such as rights of support between adjacent buildings. But it is recognised in the authorities that these two specific exceptions do not exhaust the list, which is indeed incapable of exhaustive statement, as the circumstances of any particular case may be such as to raise a necessary inference that the common intention of the parties must have been to reserve some easement to the grantor, or such as to preclude the grantee from denying the right consistently with good faith, and there appears to be no doubt that where circumstances such as these are clearly established the court will imply the appropriate reservation.

[His Lordship quoted from the judgment of THESIGER LJ, in *Wheeldon v Burrows*, p. 718, ante, referred to *Russell v Watts* (1885) 10 App Cas 590; *Aldridge v Wright* [1929] 2 KB 117; *Liddiard v Waldron* [1934] 1 KB 435, and continued:] The most comprehensive statement of the area of potential exceptions is probably that contained in the speech of Lord Parker in *Pwllbach Colliery Co Ltd v Woodman* [1915] AC 634, where his Lordship, after referring to the exception with respect to easements of necessity, said this: 'The second class of cases in which easements may impliedly be created depends not upon the terms of the grant itself, but upon the circumstances under which the grant was made. The law will readily imply the grant or reservation of such easements as may be necessary to give effect to the common intention of the parties to a grant of real property, with reference to the manner or purposes in and for which the land granted or some land retained by the grantor is to be used. See *Jones v Pritchard* [1908] 1 Ch 630, and *Lyttleton Times Co Ltd v Warners Ltd* [1907] AC 476. But it is essential for this purpose that the parties should intend that the subject of the grant or the land retained by the grantor should be used in some definite and particular manner. It is not enough that the subject of the grant or the land retained should be intended to be used in a manner which may or may not involve this definite and particular use.' ...

The question is whether the circumstances of the case as proved in evidence are such as to raise a necessary inference that the common intention of the parties was to reserve to the landlord during the twenty-one years' term some, and if so what, rights in regard to the display of advertisements over the outer walls of the demised premises, or such as to preclude the tenant from denying the implied reservation to the landlord of some such rights consistently with good faith.

That question must be approached with the following principles in mind: (i) If the landlord intended to reserve any such rights over the demised premises it was his duty to reserve them expressly in the lease of 11 August 1949: *Wheeldon v Burrows* (1879) 12 ChD 31; (ii) The landlord having failed in this duty, the onus was upon him to establish the facts to prove, and prove clearly, that his case was an exception to the rule: *Aldridge v Wright* [1929] 2 KB 117; (iii) The mere fact that the tenant knew at the date of the lease of 11 August 1949 that the landlord was using the outer walls of the demised premises for the display of the advertisements in question did not suffice to absolve the landlord from his duty of expressly reserving any rights in respect of them he intended to claim, or to take the case out of the general rule: see *Suffield v Brown* (1864) 4 De GJ & Sm 185; *Crossley & Sons Ltd v Lightowler* (1867) 2 Ch App 478.

Applying these principles to the present case, I ask myself whether the landlord has on the meagre facts proved discharged the onus which lies upon him of proving it an exception to the general rule. He can, so far as I can see, derive no assistance from the passage quoted above from Lord Parker's speech in the *Pwllbach Colliery Case* [1915] AC 634. It might, I suppose, be said to have been in the contemplation of the parties that the landlord would continue to use the ground floor of the premises for the purposes of his business as a butcher and provision merchant, but it cannot in my view be contended that the maintenance during the term of the lease of his advertisement over the door was a necessary incident of the user so contemplated. This applies a fortiori to the 'Brymay' advertisement, the display of which on the outer wall of the demised premises by the Borough Billposting Company as licensees of the landlord was so far as I can see not related in any way to the use or occupation of the ground floor for the existing or any other purpose. The transaction with the Borough Billposting Company was simply a hiring out for reward of part of an outer wall of the demised premises for use as an advertising or billposting site or station.

The mere fact that the tenant knew of the presence of the advertisements at the date when the lease of 11 August 1949 was granted being, as stated above, beside the point, nothing is left beyond the bare circumstance that the advertisements were not only present at the date of the grant but had been continuously present without objection by the tenant since the commencement of his original tenancy in 1939. Does this circumstance suffice to raise a necessary inference of an intention common to both parties at the date of the lease that the landlord should have reserved to him the right to maintain these advertisements throughout the twenty-one years' term thereby granted? I cannot see that it does. The most that can be said is that the facts are consistent with such a common intention. But that will not do. The landlord must surely show at least that the facts are not reasonably consistent with any other explanation. Here he manifestly fails. ...

In short, I can hold nothing more established by the facts proved than permissive user of the outer walls by the landlord for the display of the advertisements during the original tenancy and thereafter from the granting of the lease until the tenant's objection in January 1950; with nothing approaching grounds for inferring, as a matter of necessary inference, an intention common to both parties that such permissive user should be converted by the lease into a reservation to the landlord of equivalent rights throughout the twenty-one years' term thereby granted.

In **Peckham v Ellison** (2000) 79 P & CR 276, CAZALET J, in holding that there was an implied reservation of a right of way in favour of No. 16 Kirklands over No. 15, said at 278: [6]

'In the mid-1940s, Preston Council built a housing estate in Chipping, Preston, which included, at the end of a cul-de-sac, a row of four terraced houses—Nos 15, 16, 17 and 18 Kirklands. I shall refer to them by their numbers. Facing the front of the properties they are numbered consecutively from 15 on the right to 18 on the left. The defendants own and occupy No. 15, which is the end of terrace property. The plaintiffs own No. 16 which adjoins No. 15 on one side and No. 17 on the other. The plaintiffs claim a right of way ("the claimed right of way"), for all purposes around the side and across the rear of the defendants' house, that claimed right of way providing a means of access to the rear of the plaintiff's house. The four houses were occupied from the late 1940s by council tenants until the "right to buy" provisions of the Housing Act 1980 came into force. Subsequently each house was bought by its tenant. ...

I do not accept that the judge applied the wrong test. In my view, his findings demonstrated a necessary inference of an intention common to both parties that the council should have a right of way reserved to it over No. 15 for the benefit of

---

[6]   Citing with approval at 285 Cheshire and Burn: *Modern Law of Real Property* (15th edn) p. 538, para. (ii); (2000) 150 NLJ (H. W. Wilkinson); cf. *Chaffe v Kingsley* (1999) 79 P & CR 404; *Holaw (470) Ltd v Stockton Estates Ltd* (2001) 81 P & CR 404.

No. 16. Furthermore, although the judge indicated that the grounds for dismissing the appeal might constitute an extension to the exceptions to the rule in *Wheeldon v Burrows* I consider that the judge's decision came fully within the formula laid down by Jenkins LJ in *Re Webb's Lease*, and did not constitute a new exception to that rule.

I would also add, having considered the facts of the different cases in the line of authorities cited, that this case is clearly an exceptional one, not least (i) because of the grantees' acknowledged belief that the claimed right of way existed over the servient tenement, (ii) that such claims to the right of way had in fact been exercised for more than 30 years, (iii) that the vendor Miss Rich, of the servient tenement (No. 15) disclosed to the defendants in the pre-contract enquiries in regard to the sale in 1993 of No. 15 to the defendants the existence of the claimed right of way, (iv) that following the defendants moving into No. 15 the claimed right of way was used by the plaintiffs for more than 10 months, (v) that there was evidence that other properties on the estate enjoyed "mirror" rights and (vi) that the judge found that the grantor (the council) under the later conveyance of No. 16 had mistakenly omitted properly to deal with rights of way.'

HIRST LJ said at 298:

'I entirely agree and only wish to stress that, in my judgment the upholding of an implied reservation is, on the special facts of this case fully in line with the established authorities and is in no sense an extension let alone a relaxation, of the very stringent tests there laid down.'

C. Acquisition by Presumed Grant, or Prescription [7]

i. PRESCRIPTION AT COMMON LAW: TIME IMMEMORIAL

In **Bryant v Foot** (1867) LR 2 QB 161,[8] the question was whether the rector of Horton, Buckinghamshire, could establish a claim based on long user, to a fee of 13s. for marriages performed in the parish church. User was proved since 1808, but there was no evidence prior to that time.

COCKBURN CJ, MELLOR and LUSH (BLACKBURN J dissenting) held that the size of the fee made it impossible to believe that it existed in the time of Richard I. The presumption of immemorial legal existence which arose from user within living memory was rebutted. In discussing the methods of proof of immemorial user, COCKBURN CJ said at 179:

'The law of England ever has been and still is, in respect of prescriptive rights, in a most unsatisfactory state. The common law admitted of no prescription in the matter of real estate, or of any franchise which was matter of record, as not lying in grant. In respect of things incorporeal, lying in grant, it admitted of a species of prescription, not upon the ground that possession or enjoyment for a given period gave an indefeasible right, but on the assumption, when possession or enjoyment had been carried back as far as living memory would go, that a grant had once existed which had since been lost.

---

[7] C & B, pp. 594–608; Gray, pp. 514–526; M & W, paras. 18.121–18.170; MM, pp. 430–441; Smith, pp. 513–531; Gale, chap. 4, paras. 4.01–4.113; Jackson, pp. 110–138; (1975) 38 MLR 641 (S. Anderson).

[8] *Duke of Norfolk v Arbuthnot* (1880) 5 CPD 390 (no prescription in respect of church built about 1380).

Practically speaking, by means of this presumption prescriptive rights were established in respect of matters which lay in grant. Protection, in respect of real estates, after continued and peaceable enjoyment, was effected, not by the law being that after possession for a given number of years the right of property should be absolutely acquired, but by the indirect contrivance of debarring the adverse claimant from the benefit of the procedure by which alone his right could be established. And here again our ancestors, instead of fixing a given number of years as the period within which legal proceedings to recover real property must be resorted to, had recourse to the singular expedient of making the period of limitation run from particular events or dates. From the time of Henry I to that of Henry III, on a writ of right, the time within which a descent must be shewn was the time of King Henry I (Co Litt 114b). In the 20th year of Henry III, by the Statute of Merton (c. 8) the date was altered to the time of Henry II. Writs of mort d'ancestor were limited to the time of the last return of King John into England; writs of novel disseisin to the time of the King's first crossing the sea into Gascony. In the previous reign, according to Glanville (Lib 13, c. 33), the disseisin must have been since the last voyage of King Henry II into Normandy. So that the time necessary to bar a claim varied materially at different epochs. Thus matters remained till the 3 Edw I (Stat West 1 c. 39), when, as all lawyers are aware, the time within which a writ of right might be brought was limited to cases in which the seisin of the ancestor was since the time of King Richard I, which was construed to mean the beginning of that king's reign (2 Inst 238), a period of not less than eighty-six years. The legislature having thus adopted the reign of Richard I as the date from which the limitation in a real action was to run, the courts of law adopted it as the period to which, in all matters of prescription or custom, legal memory, which till then had been confined to the time to which living memory could go back, should thenceforth be required to extend. Thus the law remained for two centuries and a half, by which time the limitation imposed in respect of actions to recover real property having long become inoperative to bar claims which had their origin posterior to the time of Richard I, and having therefore ceased practically to afford any protection against antiquated claims, the legislature, in 32nd of Henry VIII (c. 2), again interfered, and on this occasion, instead of dating the period of limitation from some particular event or date, took the wiser course of prescribing a fixed number of years as the limit within which a suit should be entertained. The legislature having thus altered the period within which rights to real estate could be asserted by parties out of possession, the courts on this occasion omitted to follow the analogy of the recent statute as fixing the date from which legal memory was to commence, as they had done on the passing of the statute of the 3 Edw I, and adhered in all that related to prescription or custom to the previously established standard. It was of course impossible that as time went on the adoption of a fixed epoch, as the time from which legal memory was to run, should not be attended by grievous inconvenience and hardship. Possession, however long, enjoyment, however uninterrupted, afford no protection against stale and obsolete claims, or the assertion of long abandoned rights. And as parliament failed to intervene to amend the law, the judges set their ingenuity to work, by fictions and presumptions, to atone for the supineness of the legislature, and to amend, so far as in them lay, the law, which I cannot think they were bound to administer as they found it. They first laid down the somewhat startling rule that from the usage of a lifetime the presumption arose that a similar usage had existed from a remote antiquity. Next, as it could not but happen that, in the case of many private rights, especially in that of easements, which had a more recent origin, such a presumption was impossible, judicial astuteness to support possession and enjoyment, which the law ought to have invested with the character of rights, had recourse to the questionable theory of lost grants. Juries were first told that from user, during living memory, or even during twenty years, they might presume a lost grant or deed; next they were recommended to make such presumption; and lastly, as the final consummation of judicial legislation, it was held that a jury should be told, not only that they might, but also that they were bound to presume the existence of such a lost grant, although neither judge nor jury, nor any one else, had the shadow of a belief that any such instrument had ever really existed. In this manner the courts have endeavoured to supply the deficiency of the law in the matter of rights acquired by possession and enjoyment. When the doctrine of presumptions had proceeded far towards its development, the legislature at length interfered, and in respect of real property and of certain specified easements, fixed certain periods of possession or enjoyment as establishing presumptive rights. But with regard to all prescriptions or customs not provided for by statutory enactment the law remains as before.' [9]

In advising the House of Lords in **Dalton v Angus** (1881) 6 App Cas 740 at 773–774, where a claim to an easement of support for a building based upon 27 years' user was upheld, FRY J, in a famous passage, based the doctrine of prescription upon acquiescence.

'But leaving such technical questions aside, I prefer to observe that, in my opinion, the whole law of prescription and the whole law which governs the presumption or inference of a grant or covenant rest upon acquiescence. The Courts and the Judges have had recourse to various expedients for quieting the possession of persons in the exercise of rights which have not been resisted by the persons against whom they are exercised, but in all cases it appears to me that acquiescence and nothing else is the principle upon which these expedients rest. It becomes then of the highest importance to consider of what ingredients acquiescence consists. In many cases, as, for instance, in the case of that acquiescence which creates a right of way, it will be found to involve, 1st, the doing of some act by one man upon the land of another; 2ndly, the absence of right to do that act in the person doing it; 3rdly, the knowledge of the person affected by it that the act is done; 4thly, the power of the person affected by the act to prevent such act either by act on his part or by action in the Courts; and lastly, the abstinence by him from any such interference for such a length of time as renders it reasonable for the Courts to say that he shall not afterwards interfere to stop the act being done. In some other cases, as, for example, in the case of lights, some of these ingredients are wanting; but I cannot imagine any case of acquiescence in which there is not shewn to be in the servient owner: 1, a knowledge of the acts done; 2, a power in him to stop the acts or to sue in respect of them; and 3, an abstinence on his part from the exercise of such power. That such is the nature of acquiescence and that such is the ground upon which presumptions or inferences of grant or covenant may be made appears to me to be plain both from reason, from maxim, and from the cases.

As regards the reason of the case, it is plain good sense to hold that a man who can stop an asserted right, or a continued user, and does not do so for a long

---

[9]   See *R v Oxfordshire County Council, ex p Sunningwell Parish Council* [2000] 1 AC 335 at 349-353, [1999] 3 All ER 385 at 390-392, per Lord HOFFMANN.

time, may be told that he has lost his right by his delay and his negligence, and every presumption should therefore be made to quiet a possession thus acquired and enjoyed by the tacit consent of the sufferer. But there is no sense in binding a man by an enjoyment he cannot prevent, or quieting a possession which he could never disturb.'

ii. USER AS OF RIGHT [10]

GARDNER v HODGSONS'S KINGSTON BREWERY CO LTD
[1903] AC 229 (HL, Lords HALSBURY, ASHBOURNE, MACNAGHTEN, DAVEY, ROBERTSON and LINDLEY)

For some 70 or 80 years, the owners of the plaintiff's house had been accustomed to use a way from their stable across the yard of the defendant's inn to reach a road. The user was open and uninterrupted, but, for a long period, and certainly since 1855, an annual payment of 15s. had been made.

The plaintiff claimed a declaration that she was entitled to a right of way.

Held. No claim could be made under the Prescription Act or under the doctrine of lost modern grant because the user, being by permission, was not 'as of right'.

LORD LINDLEY: The plaintiff's statement of claim is so drawn as to entitle her to succeed if she can bring herself within the Prescription Act, or failing that, if the facts warrant the presumption of a lost grant. Cozens-Hardy J considered that she was entitled to succeed under the Prescription Act; but that if not, a lost grant in her favour ought to be presumed. It is necessary to consider both of these methods of establishing her right; for the Prescription Act has not taken away any of the modes of claiming easements which existed before that Act was passed: see *Aynsley v Glover* (1875) 10 Ch App 283.

I will take the Prescription Act first. Section 2 is the important section, and the last part of it is relied upon by the plaintiff. To bring herself within this enactment she must prove that she and her predecessors in title have enjoyed the way in question 'claiming right thereto' without interruption for forty years. The difficulty is raised by the words 'claiming right thereto', and by the payment of the 15s. a year. I understand the words 'claiming right thereto' and the equivalent words 'as of right', which occur in section 5, to have the same meaning as the older expression nec vi, nec clam, nec precario. A temporary permission, although often renewed, would prevent an enjoyment from being 'as of right'; but a permanent, irrevocable permission attributable to a lost grant would not have the same effect. The common law doctrine is that all prescription presupposes a grant. But if the grant is proved and its terms are known, prescription has no place.

---

[10]   M & W, para. 18.123, n. 2: '*Solomon v Mystery of Vintners* (1859) 4 H & N 585 at 602 (common law prescription); *Sturges v Bridgman* (1879) 11 ChD 852 at 863 (lost modern grant); *Tickle v Brown* (1836) 4 Ad & El 369 at 382 (prescription under the Prescription Act 1832; and see ss. 1, 2); [1998] Conv 442 at p. 448 (E. Simpson). Illegal user prevents prescription: *Neaverson v Peterborough Rural District Council* [1902] 1 Ch 557; *George Legge & Son Ltd v Wenlock Corporation* [1939] AC 204, 222: cf. where user would not have been illegal if the landowner had consented to it: *Bakewell Management Ltd v Brandwood* [2004] 2 WLR 955 (driving over common land without lawful authority under LPA 1925, s. 193(4)), thus rendering s. 68 of the Countryside and Rights of Way Act 2000 otiose: [2004] Conv 67 (C. McNall): (2004) 148 SJ 455 (S. Bickford-Smith and C. Lamont). 'It was the landowner's unfettered power of dispensing from criminal liability, exercisable at his own discretion and if though fit for his own private profit, that was the key to the disposal of the appeal', per Lord WALKER OF GESTINGHORPE.

A title by prescription can be established by long peaceable open enjoyment only; but in order that it may be so established the enjoyment must be inconsistent with any other reasonable inference than that it has been as of right in the sense above explained. This, I think, is the proper inference to be drawn from the authorities discussed in the court below. If the enjoyment is equally consistent with two reasonable inferences, enjoyment as of right is not established; and this, I think, is the real truth in the present case. [11]

The enjoyment is equally open to explanation in one of two ways, namely, by a lost grant of a right of way in consideration of a rent-charge on the plaintiff's land of 15s. a year, or by a succession of yearly licences not, perhaps, expressed every year, but implied and assumed and paid for. [12]

In **Mills v Silver** [1991] Ch 271, [1991] 1 All ER 449, [13] the defendants purchased in 1985 a hill farm in Herefordshire to which the only access was along a track on the plaintiff's adjoining land. A previous occupier of the hill farm had used the track sporadically between 1922 and 1981 when it was dry enough to be passable. No express grant or permission was ever given for the use although it was known to and acquiesced in by the then owners of the land. From 1981 until the defendants purchased the farm in 1985, very little use of the track occurred. In 1987 the defendants put down between 600 and 700 tons of stone along the length of the track in order to make it passable in all weathers.

The plaintiffs sought an injunction to restrain the defendants from using the track with vehicles and damages for trespass for the laying of the stone. The defendants claimed a prescriptive right of way over the track and the right to repair it. The Court of Appeal held (1) that a right of way for vehicles had been sufficiently continuous to warrant the implication of a lost modern grant; mere tolerance by the owners of the land over which the track passed would not defeat such a claim; and (2) that the defendants were entitled to repair but not to improve it. The laying of the stone road went far beyond repair and damages of £8,175 were awarded.

PARKER LJ said at 337, at 461:

'In *Sturges v Bridgman* (1879) 11 ChD 852, 863, Thesiger LJ giving the judgment of the court said:

"the law governing the acquisition of easements by user stands thus: Consent or acquiescence of the owner of the servient tenement lies at the root of prescription, and of the fiction of a lost grant, and hence the acts or user, which go to the proof of either the one or the other, must be, in the language of the civil law, nec vi, nec clam, nec precario; for a man cannot, as a general rule, be said to consent to or acquiesce in the acquisition by his neighbour of an easement through an enjoyment of which he has no knowledge, actual or constructive, or which he contests and endeavours to interrupt, or which he temporarily licenses."

This passage is in my judgment of prime importance in the determination of the present appeal for it makes plain (i) that consent or acquiescence to the user asserted as giving rise to the easement is an essential ingredient of the

---

[11]   *Smith v Brudenell-Bruce* [2002] 2 P & CR 2.
[12]   *Monmouth Canal Co v Harford* (1834) 1 Cr M & R 614; *Diment v NH Foot Ltd* [1974] 1 WLR 1427, [1974] 2 All ER 785 (agent's knowledge); *Patel v WH Smith (Eziot) Ltd* [1987] 1 WLR 853, [1987] 2 All ER 569.
[13]   [1992] CLJ 222 (C. Harpum).

acquisition of the easement and (ii) that it is the nature of the acts of user which has to be examined in order to see whether the easement is established.

Unless the acts of user are of the requisite character, consent or acquiescence is irrelevant. If they are then consent or acquiescence is essential.

In *Hollins v Verney* (1884) 13 QBD 304, 315, Lindley LJ giving the judgment of the court said:

"no actual user can be sufficient to satisfy the statute, unless during the whole of the statutory term ... the user is enough at any rate to carry to the mind of a reasonable person who is in possession of the servient tenement, the fact that a continuous right to enjoyment is being asserted, and ought to be resisted if such right is not recognised, and if resistance to it is intended."

This shows clearly that the crucial matter for consideration is whether for the necessary period the use is such as to bring home to the mind of a reasonable person that a continuous right of enjoyment is being asserted. If it is and the owner of the allegedly servient tenement knows or must be taken to know of it and does nothing about it the right is established. It is no answer for him to say, "I 'tolerated' it." If he does nothing he will be taken to have recognised the right and not intended to resist it. He will have consented to it or acquiesced in it.

For the plaintiffs it was submitted that this apparently simple position had been altered or modified by later cases. I do not consider that it has. Certainly there are statements in speeches in the House of Lords and the judgments of this court in later cases which might appear to suggest that a claim will be defeated if there are two possible explanations of the situation or if it is not shown that the user is against the will of the owner or if the user has been "tolerated." Such statements, however, were in my judgment not statements of principle but statements relating to the particular facts of the cases under consideration.

I instance but one of such cases by way of example, namely, *Gardner v Hodgson's Kingston Brewery Co Ltd* [1903] AC 229, supra. In that case the owner of a house had for more than 40 years used a cart way from his stables through the yard of an adjoining inn. He paid 15s. a year to the owners of the yard but there was no conclusive evidence as to the origin of this payment. The owners of the yard contended that the payment was for rent or for a series of annual licences. The owner of the house contended that it was more probably a perpetual payment attached to some original grant of the alleged right of way. The observations in their Lordship's speeches must therefore be considered in the light of these facts and contentions. ...

[His Lordship referred to the speech of Lord Lindley at 239, p. 742, ante, and continued:]

In my judgment that passage is of no assistance to the plaintiffs. There being one of two possible explanations of the annual payment of 15s. one of which would and the other of which would not establish the easement claimed and the plaintiff being unable to prove which was the correct one, she simply failed to make out the case.

The statement made must be related to the facts and cannot be regarded as a statement of principle for if it were no one could as it seems to me ever establish an easement by prescription or by the fiction of lost modern grant.

On examination none of the other cases cited, in my judgment, detract from the principles so clearly stated in *Sturges v Bridgman* and *Hollins v Verney*. The true approach is to determine the character of the acts of user or enjoyment relied on. If they are sufficient to amount to an assertion of a continuous right, continue for the requisite period, are actually or presumptively known to the owner of the servient tenement and such owner does nothing that is sufficient, as May LJ said in *Goldsmith v Burrow Construction Ltd* (1987) Times, 31 July:

"I agree with Mr Mowbray's submission that it is not merely a question of the servient owner saying 'I could have locked the gate and therefore there was no permission.' The fact in this case is that he did lock the gate."

Every servient owner can always say, until it is too late: "I could have stopped it." That is not enough.

I add only this, that any statement that the enjoyment must be against the will of the servient owner cannot mean more than "without objection by the servient owner." If it did, a claimant would have to prove that the right was contested and thereby defeat his own claim.'

Davies v Du Paver [1953] 1 QB 184, [1952] 2 All ER 991, p. 752, post.

In **Healey v Hawkins** [1968] 1 WLR 1967, [1968] 3 All ER 836, the question arose of the effect of initial oral permission on user for the 20 year period under the Prescription Act 1832. GOFF J held that the user which was permissive in origin did not so continue and thus prevent the defendant from acquiring an easement of way. He said at 1973, at 841:

'In principle it seems to me that once permission has been given, the user must remain permissive and not be capable of ripening into a right save where the permission is oral and the user has continued for 40 or 60 years, unless and until, having been given for a limited period only, it expires or, being general, it is revoked, or there is a change in circumstances from which revocation may fairly be implied. Moreover, *Gaved v Martyn* (1865) 19 CBNS 732 appears to me to be a decision expressly in point and in accordance with the conclusion in Megarry and Wade (p. 850, para. 4(iii)). In that case, oral permission had been given to use an artificial watercourse, and a successor who did not claim under the original licensee and who had no actual knowledge of permission having been given continued to exercise the privilege, but in circumstances which ought to, or might, have put him on inquiry, and the court held that there was evidence and, as Byles J at 747 thought, abundant evidence, on which the jury could find, as it had done, that the user even by the new occupier remained permissive.

Of course, when the user has continued for 40 or 60 years a prior parol consent affords no answer, because it is excluded by the express terms of section 2 of the Prescription Act, but, even so, permission given during the period will defeat the claimant because it negatives user as of right. That is, in my judgment, the explanation of the distinction drawn by the House of Lords in *Gardner v Hodgson's Kingston Brewery* [1903] AC 229, between antecedent and current parol consents.' [14]

iii. USER IN FEE SIMPLE [15]

In **Kilgour v Gaddes** [1904] 1 KB 457, a dispute arose between two neighbouring tenants of Sir James Graham in connection with the use of a pump which was situated

---

[14]   *Jones v Price and Morgan* (1992) 64 P & CR 404 (claim defeated by 40 year user which continued on common understanding that the user was, and continued, by permission).
[15]   *Pugh v Savage* [1970] 2 QB 373, [1970] 2 All ER 353; *Davis v Whitby* [1973] 1 WLR 629, [1973] 3 All ER 403; *Simmons v Dobson* [1991] 1 WLR 720, [1991] 4 All ER 25, p. 746, post (lost modern grant).

on the land occupied by the plaintiff. The defendant and his predecessors in title had used the pump for forty years before the action was brought.

The Court of Appeal held that there was no prescriptive right to use the pump, COLLINS MR saying at 460:

'The question in this case is whether, as between two persons who are termors of different tenements, a right of way to a pump has been acquired by prescription for the owner of one of the tenements over the other tenement under section 2 of the Prescription Act 1832. I say a right for the owner, for it appears to me clear that under the section the right cannot be acquired merely by a tenant as against a tenant, but must be acquired by the owner of the fee in one of the tenements as against the owner of the fee in the other. Here the respective tenants of the so-called dominant and servient tenements hold under the same landlord; and, if the proposition be correct that a prescriptive right of way under section 2 of the Act must be acquired by the owner of the fee in one of the tenements as against the owner of the fee in the other, then in this case the defendant's contention would involve the result that the tenant of one of the tenements has acquired for his landlord a right of way over the landlord's own land; which is impossible and inconsistent with the essential notion of a right by prescription, namely, that the right is acquired by the owner of land over land belonging to another owner. I limit what I am saying to such an easement as a right of way, because questions with regard to the easements of light stand on a different footing, and depend on the provisions of section 3 of the Act. [16] ... "If I am asked how it is consistent with the Prescription Act, I answer that such user and enjoyment is not as of right within the meaning of the 2nd section. It is a user by a termor, who, if he acquire the right, must acquire it as incident to the land of which he is termor, and thus for the benefit of his reversioner. Such user cannot be as of right, unless a reversioner can in law by user acquire a right against himself." [17] That reasoning appears to me conclusive of the present case. There was a long discussion in the course of the argument as to the possibility of a termor under one landlord acquiring for his landlord an easement by user over land in the occupation of a termor under another landlord, and as to whether an easement in such a case could be acquired, unless and until the user had continued for the period of three years after the determination of the term in the servient tenement without interference by the reversioner. [18] That no doubt raises an interesting question, which appears to have been decided in Ireland in the case of *Beggan v M'Donald* (1877) 2 LR IR 560, contrary to the view expressed in this country in *Bright v Walker* (1834) 1 Cr M & R 211 and also in *Wheaton v Maple & Co* [1893] 3 Ch 48, in neither of which cases, however, was it necessary actually to decide the point. That question, however, is not the question raised in the present case. ...

In the case of *Wheaton v Maple & Co* the view which I am expressing was very clearly stated by Lindley LJ in his judgment. He dealt first with the question of the possibility of acquiring an easement as against a tenant of land by a presumption of a lost grant as follows: "I am not aware of any authority for presuming, as a matter of law, a lost grant by a lessee for years in the case of ordinary easements, or a lost covenant by such a person not to interrupt in the case of light, and I am certainly not prepared to introduce another fiction to support a claim to a novel prescriptive right. The whole theory of prescription at common

---

[16]   P. 775, post.
[17]   Quoting PALLES CB, in *Timmons v Hewitt* (1888) 22 LR Ir 627.
[18]   Prescription Act 1832, s. 8, p. 751, post.

law is against presuming any grant or covenant not to interrupt, by or with any one except an owner in fee. A right claimed by prescription must be claimed as appendant or appurtenant to land, and not as annexed to it for a term of years. Although, therefore, a grant by a lessee of the Crown, commensurate with his lease, might be inferred as a fact, if there was evidence to justify the inference, there is no legal presumption, as distinguished from an inference in fact, in favour of such a grant. This view of the common law is in entire accordance with *Bright v Walker* where this doctrine of presumption is carefully examined." He was there dealing with the question of an implied grant.'

In **Simmons v Dobson** [1991] 1 WLR 720, [1991] 4 All ER 25, [19] the free-holder of two adjoining properties in Smallbrook Lane, Leigh, retained one and leased the other. Subsequently the lease was assigned to the plaintiff and the retained property leased to the defendants. At all material times the fee simple of both properties was vested in the same person. The defendants blocked a passageway along two sides of their land which the plaintiff used to reach the road from the rear of his garden. The plaintiff claimed a right of way under the doctrine of lost modern grant.

In rejecting the claim, Fox LJ said at 724, at 28:

'I take the view that, as a matter of authority, it is established that one tenant cannot acquire an easement by prescription at common law against another tenant holding under the same landlord. The position is, I think, the same in relation to section 2 of the Prescription Act 1832. The purpose of that section is to shorten the period required by common law prescription to 20 years prior to the bringing of the action. ...

What we are concerned with here is neither common law prescription strictly so called nor a claim under the Prescription Act 1832 but a claim based on the lost modern grant doctrine. The question is whether the restrictive rule as to prescription by and against leaseholders applies to cases of lost modern grant.

In terms of practicalities, it is difficult to see if one were starting from scratch that there is serious objection to leaseholders prescribing against each other for the duration of their limited interests (but it has to be said that to introduce such a rule retrospectively now could affect what were hitherto bought and sold as clear titles). And, as Mr Vickers says, in a modern, urban situation it is hard to see why two householders on one side of the street should be able to prescribe for easements against each other's land because each holds in fee simple while on the other side of the street one leaseholder under the residue of a 999-year lease can for 20 years or more walk along a path at the back of his neighbour's garden (also held on a long lease) without acquiring any rights in respect thereof. That, however, is the way the law has gone in England. The point about long leaseholds held of the same landlord was recognised by Scrutton LJ in the passage in *Derry v Sanders* [1919] 1 KB 223, 237, to which I have referred, where he regarded the law as clear.

[His Lordship referred to *Wheaton v Maple & Co* [1893] 3 Ch 48, 63 per Lindley LJ and *Kilgour v Gaddes* [1904] 1 KB 457, 465 per Collins MR, and continued:]

---

[19] Criticised [1992] Conv 167 (P. Sparkes); [1992] CLJ 222 (C. Harpum), following (1958) 74 LQR 82 (V. T. H. Delany).

While, therefore, there appears to be no case which directly decides that there can be no lost modern grant by or to a person who owns a lesser estate than the fee, the dicta are to the contrary and are very strong and of long standing. I take them to represent settled law. I should mention for completeness that the law in Ireland has gone the other way: *Flynn v Harte* [1913] 2 IR 322 and *Tallon v Ennis* [1937] IR 549.

As to any departure from that state of the law, there are, I think difficulties of principle. It is clear that common law prescription and prescription under the Act of 1832 are, as a matter of decision, not available by or to owners of less estates than the fee. Lost modern grant is merely a form of common law prescription. It is based upon a fiction which was designed to meet, and did meet, a particular problem. It would, I think, be anomalous to extend the fiction further by departure, in relation to lost modern grant, from the fundamental principle of common law prescription referred to by Lindley LJ.'

iv. THE DOCTRINE OF LOST MODERN GRANT [20]

HULBERT v DALE

[1909] 2 Ch 570 (ChD, JOYCE J; CA, COZENS-HARDY MR, FLETCHER MOULTON and FARWELL LJJ)

By an Inclosure Award of 1804, a 'private carriage road of the width of thirty feet' over Crown Farm (now owned by the plaintiff) was allotted to the predecessor in title of the defendant's lessor, owner of Fishmore Farm. The road was never made, and trees grew and buildings were built on the intended site. However, the defendant and his predecessor in title or occupation had, since 1804, uninterruptedly used a private road running across the plaintiff's farm, parallel to the site of the awarded road and some 100 yards from it.

There had been unity of possession of the two farms from 1889 to 1905, while they were in the occupation of the same tenant.

The plaintiff brought this action for an injunction to restrain the defendant from using the road.

Held (affirming JOYCE J). A lost grant of a right of way should be presumed.

JOYCE J: There was a considerable conflict of evidence in the case, but, upon the whole, the result to my mind is that I come to the conclusion, and find as a fact, that for a period as far back as living memory extends the owners and occupiers for the time being of Fishmore Farm have openly and without interruption had an unquestioned user until quite recently, when the dispute arose, of the now disputed road, and I should have held such user to have been as of right (or by persons claiming a right thereto) but for the circumstance that during the period between the years 1889 and 1905 there was unity of possession (not of ownership) of the two farms, Fishmore and Crown Farms, both being in the occupation of the same tenant or tenants.

---

[20]   Holdsworth, vol. vii, pp. 347–349; *Healey v Hawkins* [1968] 1 WLR 1967, [1968] 3 All ER 836, p. 745, ante (grant of right of way presumed); *Oakley v Boston* [1976] QB 270, [1975] 3 All ER 405 (incumbent of glebe land is capable grantor with consent of Ecclesiastical Commissioners); *Ward (Helston) Ltd v Kerrier District Council* (1981) 42 P & CR 412 (grant of right of way presumed); *Mills v Silver* [1991] Ch 271, [1991] 1 All ER 449, p. 743, ante; *Simmons v Dobson* [1991] 1 WLR 720, [1991] 4 All ER 25, p. 747, ante; *Bowring Services Ltd v Scottish Widows' Fund & Life Assurance Society* [1995] 1 EGLR 158 (presumption failed because of custom of City of London that a man may rebuild upon ancient foundations to what height he pleases); *Smith v Brudenell –Bruce* [2002] 2 P & CR 4.

This being so, the defendant could not make good any claim to a right of way along the disputed road by prescription under the 2nd section of the Prescription Act. Nor could he, I think, have succeeded upon a claim by prescription at common law, because I consider it to be tolerably plain, for various reasons, that the existence of the right of way claimed, if it does exist, originated and commenced at a date long subsequent to the reign of King Richard I—in fact very little more than one hundred years ago. The defendant, therefore, has to base his claim upon the existence of a grant not produced, and he contends that it is a case for presuming a grant, now lost, of the right to use the disputed road.

I must say that it seems to me that if ever there was a case in which some such presumption ought to be made, this is the case. For I am tolerably certain that the owners and occupiers of Fishmore Farm have had the use of the disputed road without interruption and with the full knowledge of the occupiers, and presumably of the owners, of Crown Farm, who have acquiesced in such use possibly because of the existence of the right of the awarded way, which right, if enforced, would have been much more disadvantageous to Crown Farm than the user of the disputed road by the owners and occupiers of Fishmore Farm.

In **Tehidy Minerals Ltd v Norman** [1971] 2 QB 528, [1971] 2 All ER 475, the defendants proved that they were accustomed to graze Tawna Down, Cardinham, Cornwall, from 19 January 1920 to 6 October 1941, a period of 21 years, eight and a half months. In holding that they had acquired a profit à prendre under the doctrine of lost modern grant, BUCKLEY LJ, in delivering the judgment of the Court of Appeal (SALMON, SACHS and BUCKLEY LJJ) said at 547, at 486:

'The question is whether on the facts of this case enjoyment of this grazing for a period of upwards of 20 years preceding 6 October 1941 permits or requires us to presume that such enjoyment was had by virtue of grants made after 19 January 1920, but before 6 October 1921 (being 20 years before 6 October 1941), and subsequently lost, and whether we ought to act on such a presumption. [1] [His Lordship then analysed the judgments in *Angus v Dalton* (1877) 3 QBD 85, (1878) 4 QBD 162, (1881) 6 App Cas 740 'which in the course of its history enjoyed the attention of no less than 18 judges and members of the House of Lords, perhaps embodying a greater variety of judicial opinion than any other leading case', and continued:] In our judgment *Angus v Dalton* decides that, where there has been upwards of 20 years' uninterrupted enjoyment of an easement, such enjoyment having the necessary qualities to fulfil the requirements of prescription, then unless, for some reason such as incapacity on the part of the person or persons who might at some time before the commencement of the 20-year period have made a grant, the existence of such a grant is impossible, the law will adopt a legal fiction that such a grant was made, in spite of any direct evidence that no such grant was in fact made.

If this legal fiction is not to be displaced by direct evidence that no grant was made, it would be strange if it could be displaced by circumstantial evidence leading to the same conclusion, and in our judgment it must follow that circumstantial evidence tending to negative the existence of a grant (other than

---

[1]　CA rejected an argument that, as the Prescription Act 1832 lays down longer periods for prescription in respect of profits than in respect of easements, so by analogy a longer period of enjoyment should be required in the case of a profit than in the case of an easement to support the prescription.

evidence establishing impossibility) should not be permitted to displace the fiction. Precisely the same reasoning must, we think, apply to a presumed lost grant of a profit à prendre as to an easement.

In the present case, if we are to presume lost grants, we must do so in respect of each of the four farms, Higher and Lower Hill, Cabilla and Pinsla Park. Each of the presumed grants must be supposed to have been made between 20 January 1920 and 5 October 1921, and to have been since lost in circumstances of which no one now has any recollection. This combination of circumstances seems to us to be exceedingly improbable, and we feel sympathy for the view expressed by Farwell J in *A-G v Simpson* [1901] 2 Ch 671 at 698: "It cannot be the duty of a judge to presume a grant of the non-existence of which he is convinced, nor can he be constrained to hold that such a grant is reasonably possible within the meaning of the authorities." In view, however, of the decision in *Angus v Dalton* we consider that it is not open to us in the present case to follow this line.' [2]

V. THE PRESCRIPTION ACT 1832 [3]

PRESCRIPTION ACT 1832

Whereas the expression 'time immemorial, or time whereof the memory of man runneth not to the contrary,' is now by the Law of England in many cases considered to include and denote the whole period of time from the Reign of King Richard the First, whereby the title to matters that have been long enjoyed is sometimes defeated by shewing the commencement of such enjoyment, which is in many cases productive of inconvenience and injustice;

1. Claims to right of common [4] and other profits à prendre, not to be defeated after thirty years enjoyment by shewing the commencement; after sixty years enjoyment the right to be absolute, unless had by consent or agreement.—No claim which may be lawfully made at the common law, by custom, prescription, or grant, to any right of common or other profit or benefit to be taken and enjoyed from or upon any land of our sovereign lord the King, or any land being parcel of the duchy of Lancaster or of the duchy of Cornwall, or of any ecclesiastical or lay person, or body corporate, except such matters and things as are herein specially provided for, and except tithes, rent, and services, shall, where such right, profit, or benefit shall have been actually taken and enjoyed by any person claiming right thereto without interruption for the full period of thirty years, be defeated or destroyed by showing only that such right, profit, or benefit was first taken or enjoyed at any time prior to such period of thirty years, but nevertheless such claim may be defeated in any other way by which the same is now liable to be defeated; and when such right, profit, or benefit shall have been so taken and

---

[2] *Bridle v Ruby* [1989] QB 169, [1988] 3 All ER 64 (mistaken belief of dominant owner and predecessors in title that a right of way had been reserved over servient tenement held not to rebut presumption of lost modern grant arising from 22 years' user). See too *Thomas W. Ward Ltd v Alexander Bruce (Grays) Ltd* [1959] 2 Lloyd's Rep 472, where HARMAN LJ also reviewed *Earl de la Warr v Miles* (1881) 17 ChD 535 and *Chamber Colliery Co v Hopwood* (1886) 32 ChD 549; *Hamilton v Joyce* [1984] 3 NSWLR 279; [1986] Conv 356 (A. H. Hudson).

[3] 'One of the worst drafted Acts on the Statute Book': Law Reform Committee Report on Acquisition of Easements and Profits by Prescription (1966) Cmnd 3100, p. 784, post. For the history of prescription, see Holdsworth, vol. vii, pp. 343 et seq.; Simpson, *A History of the Land Law* (2nd edn.), pp. 266–269; Underhill, *Century of Law Reform*, p. 308.

[4] P. 60, ante.

enjoyed as aforesaid for the full period of sixty years, the right thereto shall be deemed absolute and indefeasible, unless it shall appear that the same was taken and enjoyed by some consent or agreement expressly made or given for that purpose by deed or writing.

2. In claims of right of way or other easements the periods to be twenty years and forty years.—… No claim which may be lawfully made at the common law, by custom, prescription, or grant, to any way or other easement, or to any watercourse, or the use of any water, to be enjoyed or derived upon, over, or from any land or water of our said lord the King, or being parcel of the duchy of Lancaster or of the duchy of Cornwall, or being the property of any ecclesiastical or lay person, or body corporate, when such way or other matter as herein last before mentioned shall have been actually enjoyed by any person claiming right thereto without interruption for the full period of twenty years, shall be defeated or destroyed by showing only that such way or other matter was first enjoyed at any time prior to such period of twenty years, but nevertheless such claim may be defeated in any other way by which the same is now liable to be defeated; and where such way or other matter as herein last before mentioned shall have been so enjoyed as aforesaid for the full period of forty years, the right thereto shall be deemed absolute and indefeasible, unless it shall appear that the same was enjoyed by some consent or agreement expressly given or made for that purpose by deed or writing.

4. [5] Before mentioned periods to be deemed those next before suit.—Each of the respective periods of years herein-before mentioned shall be deemed and taken to be the period next before some suit or action wherein the claim or matter to which such period may relate shall have been or shall be brought into question; and no act or other matter shall be deemed to be an interruption, within the meaning of this statute, unless the same shall have been or shall be submitted to or acquiesced in for one year after the party interrupted shall have had or shall have notice thereof, and of the person making or authorising the same to be made. [6]

7. Proviso for infants, &c.—Provided also, that the time during which any person otherwise capable of resisting any claim to any of the matters before mentioned shall have been or shall be an infant, idiot, non compos mentis, feme covert, or tenant for life, or during which any action or suit shall have been pending, and which shall have been diligently prosecuted, until abated by the death of any party or parties thereto, shall be excluded in the computation of the periods hereinbefore mentioned, except only in cases where the right or claim is hereby declared to be absolute and indefeasible.

8. What time to be excluded in computing the term of forty years appointed by this Act.—Provided always, that when any land or water upon, over, or from

---

[5] Prescriptive claims to rights of common are not to be defeated by reason of interruptions due to requisition of the common land by a Government Department, or to inability to exercise a right to graze animals for reasons of animal health: Commons Registration Act 1965, s. 16. See Rights of Light Act 1959, s. 3(6), p. 780, post.

[6] *Newnham v Willison* (1987) 56 P & CR 8 (interruption lasting more than a year before action brought); [1989] Conv 357 (J. E. Martin).

which any such way or other convenient[7] watercourse or use of water shall have been or shall be enjoyed or derived hath been or shall be held under or by virtue of any term of life, or any term of years[8] exceeding three years from the granting thereof, the time of the enjoyment of any such way or other matter as herein last before mentioned, during the continuance of such term, shall be excluded in the computation of the said period of forty years, in case the claim shall within three years next after the end or sooner determination of such term be resisted by any person entitled to any reversion expectant on the determination thereof.

Lord MACNAGHTEN in **Gardner v Hodgson's Kingston Brewery Co Ltd** [1903] AC 229, p. 742, ante, said at 236:

'I rather doubt whether the scope and effect of the Prescription Act have been always rightly apprehended. The Act was passed, as its preamble declares, for the purposes of getting rid of the inconvenience and injustice arising from the meaning which the law of England attached to the expressions "time immemorial" and "time whereof the memory of man runneth not to the contrary". The law as it stood put an intolerable strain on the consciences of judges and jurymen. The Act was an Act "for shortening the time of prescription in certain cases". And really it did nothing more. A person who claims a right of way and invokes the protection of the Act must claim "as of right". But when the way in question has been used without interruption, as defined in the Act, for forty years "as of right"—whether the claimant is really entitled of right or not—the claim cannot be defeated except by shewing that the right claimed was enjoyed "by some consent or agreement expressly given or made for that purpose by deed or writing". No parol consent will do. I fail to understand how that provision helps the appellant. The respondents do not set up a parol consent given before the period of forty years. They rely on the acknowledgment and recognition of their dominion over the property—their right to grant or withhold the grant of the way in question—involved in and evidenced by the annual payment accompanying the use of the way, and they point out that no other reasonable explanation of that payment is forthcoming.'

(a) Interruption

In **Davies v Du Paver** [1953] 1 QB 184, [1952] 2 All ER 991, a dispute arose over the question whether the plaintiff had acquired a right (profit) by prescription based upon 60 years' user to pasture sheep upon the defendant's land. Two main questions arose:

i.   The defendant in August 1950 completed a fence which excluded the sheep in spite of the plaintiff's vigorous protests. No further action was taken until the writ was issued in September 1951, and the defendant argued that the user was interrupted for more than a year.

ii.   During the first 55 of the 60 years during which user was proved, the defendant's land (servient tenement) had been in the possession of lessees.

The Court of Appeal (BIRKETT and MORRIS LJJ, SINGLETON LJ, dissenting) held that:

---

[7]   Probably a misprint for 'easement': *Wright v Williams* (1836) Tyr & Gr 375 at 390; *Laird v Briggs* (1881) 19 ChD 22 at 33.

[8]   *Palk v Shinner* (1852) 18 QB 568.

i.   there was no interruption within the Act, but

ii. the plaintiff failed to show that the defendant had the knowledge or means of knowledge of the user and the power to object to it.

On the first point, Morris LJ said at 206, at 1000:

'The first point raised by the defendant is that there was a fatal interruption of the enjoyment by the plaintiff of his alleged rights of pasturage. In the notice of appeal this contention is formulated on the basis that there was no evidence that Mr Davies "had asserted his alleged rights or protested at the interruption of his alleged rights of pasturage" between 1 August 1950 and 28 September 1951, and "that accordingly the judge was wrong in law in holding that the plaintiff Davies did not acquiesce in, or submit to, any interruption which had continued for more than one year". This language raises the question as to the meaning of an "assertion of rights or of a protest". But the real question is not whether there was an assertion of rights or a protest during some period, but whether there was in this case a submission or an acquiescence. It is provided by the Prescription Act 1832, that no act or other matter is deemed to be an interruption within the meaning of the Act unless submitted to, or acquiesced in, for one year after the party interrupted has notice of the interruption and of the person making it or authorising it to be made.

There is no doubt that there was an actual interruption for more than a year before 27 September 1951. The question is whether there was acquiescence in such interruption or submission to it lasting for one year. This is, in my judgment, a question of fact. If a case were being tried with a jury it would be a question for the jury to determine: see *Bennison v Cartwright* (1864) 5 B & S 1. ...

The fence was completed on 9 August. Could it be said that the plaintiff had submitted to, or acquiesced in, the existence of the fence by that date? Having regard to the events that had happened, and to the correspondence, I would have thought, had it been for me to decide this question of fact, that the answer would be in the negative. The parties were breathing fury on each side of a newly erected fence. Could it be said that the challenging protests of the plaintiff must, as the August days passed, be deemed to have signified nothing, and that his former claims and assertions should be regarded as supplanted by submission and acquiescence? As time went by, it might well be that silence and inaction could be interpreted as submission or acquiescence. But the date when submission or acquiescence begins must be determined as a question of fact, having regard to all the circumstances. Had there been a beginning by 1 January 1951, or by 1 December 1950, or by 1 November 1950? These are all questions of fact. Unless it is held that there was submission or acquiescence by 27 September 1950, there would not be a period of one year. The judge referred to *Glover v Coleman* (1874) LR 10 CP 108, and stated: "On the evidence I hold that neither of the plaintiffs submitted to or acquiesced in the interruption." This was a finding of fact which the judge was, in my view, entitled to make, and accordingly I consider that the first submission fails.'[9]

On the second point, the court appears to have treated the question of the knowledge or means of knowledge of the user as being a matter related to user as of right. Birkett LJ said at 206, at 1000:

<hr/>

[9]   Cf. *Dance v Triplow* [1992] 1 EGLR 190 (where 'the plaintiffs failed to prove both their unwillingness to tolerate the interruption and some word or act making that clear to the defendant', per Glidewell LJ); [1992] Conv 197 (J. Martin).

'I see no evidence on which the judge could find that the common knowledge extended to the servient owner, or any evidence that the servient owner had the means of knowledge. It is on this ground that I would allow the appeal, for the claim "as of right" cannot in these circumstances be established.'

The user, as the judge found, was common knowledge; the defendant was unaware because he was the lessor, not in possession. The question should then be, it is submitted, not whether the user was as of right, but whether it was in fee simple. The answer to that question would be that, in the case of 40 years' user for easements under the Prescription Act (60 years for profits), the fact that the servient tenement was in the occupation of a tenant for years was immaterial— unless the period of user under the tenancy was excluded under the special defence provided by section 8. [10]

(b) User as of Right is Necessary for Prescription under Either Period

Gardner v Hodgson's Kingston Brewery Co Ltd [1903] AC 229, p. 742, ante.

Healey v Hawkins [1968] 1 WLR 1967, [1968] 3 All ER 836, p. 745, ante.

In **Union Lighterage Co v London Graving Dock Co** [1902] 2 Ch 557, one question was whether the defendants could prescribe for an easement in respect of underwater support of a wharf, none of the metal supports except two nuts showing above the surface. The Court of Appeal (ROMER and STIRLING LJJ, VAUGHAN WILLIAMS LJ dissenting) held that there could be no prescription as the user was secret. ROMER LJ said at 570:

'Now, on principle, it appears to me that a prescriptive right to an easement over a man's land should only be acquired when the enjoyment has been open— that is to say, of such a character that an ordinary owner of the land, diligent in the protection of his interests, would have, or must be taken to have, a reasonable opportunity of becoming aware of that enjoyment. And I think on the balance of authority that the principle has been recognised as the law, and ought to be followed by us.' [11]

(c) Next before Action Brought

HYMAN v VAN DEN BERGH
[1908] 1 Ch 167 (CA, COZENS-HARDY MR, FLETCHER MOULTON and FARWELL LJ)

In 1877, one Cox, a former tenant of the plaintiff, built a cowshed with eight windows overlooking land subsequently purchased by the defendant. In 1896 and 1898, the defendant obstructed the windows by boards but these were quickly removed by the plaintiff. On 18 January 1899, Cox wrote a letter agreeing to pay 1s. per annum for the use of the light. In 1906, Cox left, and a dispute arose between the parties as to the right to the light.

Held. The plaintiff was not entitled to an easement although 22 years' uninterrupted user had been enjoyed before the permission was given.

---

[10]   *Wright v Williams* (1836) 1 M & W 77 (not cited); (1956) 72 LQR 32 (R.E.M.). Compare *Kilgour v Gaddes* [1904] 1 KB 457, p. 745, ante, where both tenements were owned by the same landlord.
[11]   *Barney v BP Tuckshops Ltd* [1995] NPC 5.

COZENS-HARDY MR: It is often asserted that an absolute right is obtained to access of light by reason merely of twenty years' undisturbed enjoyment, but I think this statement is too wide. Lord Macnaghten in *Colls v Home and Colonial Stores* [1904] AC 179 at 189, after referring to certain 'expressions not perhaps sufficiently guarded' which are to be found in the judgment in the House of Lords in *Tapling v Jones* (1865) 11 HL Cas 290, said: 'In that case Lord Westbury, Lord Cranworth, and Lord Chelmsford all assumed that a period of twenty years' enjoyment of the access and use of light to a building creates an absolute and indefeasible right immediately on the expiration of the period of twenty years. No doubt section 3 says so in terms, but section 4 must be read in connection with section 3; and if the two sections are read together it will be seen that the period is not a period in gross, but a period next before some suit or action wherein the claim or matter to which such period may relate shall have been or shall be brought into question. Unless and until the claim or matter is thus brought into question, no absolute or indefeasible right can arise under the Act. There is what has been described as an inchoate right. The owner of the dominant tenement after twenty years' uninterrupted enjoyment is in a position to avail himself of the Act if his claim is brought into question. But in the meantime, however long the enjoyment may have been, his right is just the same, as the origin of his right is just the same, as if the Act had never been passed. No title is as yet acquired under the Act. This point seems to have been much discussed shortly after the Act was passed. It was finally settled in a series of cases at common law, beginning, I think, with *Wright v Williams* (1836) 1 M & W 77, and including *Richards v Fry* (1837) 7 Ad & El 698 and *Cooper v Hubbuck* (1862) 12 CB NS 456.' If this is to be regarded as a decision upon sections 3 and 4, it is of course binding upon us. If, however, it is to be regarded only as a dictum of Lord Macnaghten, I desire respectfully to say that I agree with it, and I accept it as an accurate statement of the law.

It only remains to apply the law to the facts of the present case. No action was brought by the plaintiff or any other person until the present action was commenced on 11 July 1906. The only material period to be considered is the period of twenty years prior to that date. No evidence as to what was the condition of the windows prior to that date can be regarded. Now during that period there was undoubtedly the actual enjoyment of light through the windows in question, but at the end of 1898 the windows were for a short time obstructed by the defendant. The then tenant in occupation having a doubt whether a right to light could be established, and being desirous of avoiding litigation, signed and addressed to the defendant the letter of 18 January 1899; thereupon the boards were removed, and the lights were thenceforth actually enjoyed. Under these circumstances I think it is clear that the light was enjoyed by 'consent or agreement' expressly made or given for that purpose by writing. It is true that it was made or given, not to or with the freeholder, but to or with the tenant in occupation. The tenant in occupation was the proper person to make such agreement or to obtain such consent as the section requires. In my view it is a fallacy to say that the freeholder had an absolute right which his lessee ought not to be permitted to defeat. In truth he had only an inchoate right which never became an absolute and indefeasible right. The judgment of Parker J so carefully deals with the law applicable to the case under the Prescription Act that I do not think I should be justified in saying anything more. In my opinion this appeal must be dismissed with costs.

Hulbert v Dale [1909] 2 Ch 570, p. 748, ante.

In **Reilly v Orange** [1955] 2 QB 112, [1955] 2 All ER 369, neighbouring owners in 1934 came to an agreement whereby the defendant could use a way over the plaintiff's land until the defendant should construct a way of his own; this he did in 1953. In December 1953 the plaintiff purported to terminate the defendant's right to use the way, and began proceedings for this purpose; the defendant counterclaimed for a declaration that, by reason of his user for over 19 years, he was entitled to an easement.

The Court of Appeal (SINGLETON, JENKINS and MORRIS LJJ) affirmed the county court judge in finding for the plaintiff, JENKINS LJ saying at 116, at 371:

'Mr Blease, for the defendant, very properly admits that for the purpose of this appeal he must accept the deputy judge's finding as to the nature and terms of the agreement, but he says that notwithstanding this he is entitled to succeed. He says that on two grounds: (1) that he has had 20 years' uninterrupted enjoyment of the right claimed, as required by the Prescription Act 1832; (2) that although the right he claims had its origin in the agreement of 1934, and although that agreement, as found by the deputy judge, would only give him a right to use the drive for domestic purposes, and only until such time as he made a drive of his own, that permission did not prevent the 20 years' user on which he relies from establishing his right under the Prescription Act 1832. The second of those points can only arise if Mr Blease is entitled to succeed on the first. ...

Mr Blease's argument on this part of the case is of this nature: he says that what must be shown is 20 years' uninterrupted user, and that, according to section 4, no act or matter counts as an interruption unless the same shall have been or shall be submitted to or acquiesced in for one year. It follows, says Mr Blease, that inasmuch as in this case over 19 years' user down to the commencement of the action is proved, the defendant's right is made good inasmuch as there could be no interruption acquiesced in for one year between the date of the commencement of the action and the completion of the full period of 20 years.

In support of that proposition he referred us to the well-known case of *Flight v Thomas* (1841) 8 Cll & Fin 231. In that case: "A. had the free access of light and air through a window of his house for nineteen years and 330 days, and B. then raised a wall which obstructed the light, and the obstruction was submitted to only for 35 days, when A. brought an action to remove it." It was held: "that the right of action was complete; that the twenty years' enjoyment was to be reckoned from the commencement of the enjoyment to the time of bringing the action; and that an interruption of the enjoyment, in whatever period of the twenty years it may happen, cannot be deemed an interruption within the meaning of the Act, unless it is acquiesced in for a whole year."

Mr Blease seeks to apply that to the present case in this way: he says that the commencement of the action constituted an interruption, and that, inasmuch as the action was not commenced until after the alleged easement had been enjoyed for more than 19 years, the interruption so constituted could not last for the required period of one year, so that his title was complete at the time of action brought. In my view that argument cannot prevail. What the Prescription Act requires, as appears from the combined effect of section 2 and section 4, is the full period of 20 years, being "the period next before some suit or action wherein the claim or matter to which such period may relate shall have been or shall be brought into question." The commencement of the suit or action in my view is clearly not an interruption within the meaning of section 4, but is the event marking the date down to which the requisite period of user must be shown. What must be shown is a full 20 years reckoned down to the date of action brought. That must be an uninterrupted period, but in considering whether it is an uninterrupted period or not, interruptions not acquiesced in for at least a year are not to be counted as interruptions.'

In **Davis v Whitby** [1974] Ch 186, [1974] 1 All ER 806 (CA, LORD DENNING MR, STAMP and ORR LJJ), STAMP LJ said at 192, at 810:
'As the point is a somewhat novel one, I will express my views in my own words. The basis of prescription, as Lord Denning MR has pointed out, is that if long enjoyment of a right is shown, the courts will strive to uphold the right by presuming that it had a lawful origin. Here, the owner of no. 51 (which, for the purpose of convenience, I will call "the dominant tenement") has for upwards of 30 years enjoyed access from the rear of his house over no. 49 (which I will call "the servient tenement"). During the first 15 years it was enjoyed over one path, and during the second period of over 15 years it was enjoyed partly over that path and partly over a substituted path. Viewed as the exercise of a right to pass and re-pass over the servient tenement, it has been enjoyed for upwards of 30 years, which is more than a sufficiently long period for it to be presumed that the right had a lawful origin. Viewed as a right so to pass and re-pass over a specified path, it has not. The question, as I see it, is which is the right way of looking at it. What happened was that in 1950 the new track or path over the back garden of the servient owner's house was established; but, using it, the dominant owner still used, as he had formerly done, the path at the side of the servient owner's house. Was the dominant owner then using the new way as of right and as of the same right as formerly? I think he was. In substance, what was enjoyed as well before as after 1950 was access by the dominant owner to the back of his little house from the road in front of the terrace along the side of the servient owner's premises and across his back garden.

On the facts of this case, the use of the substituted route is, in my judgment, to be considered as substantially an exercise of the right claimed and enjoyed for the whole period of 30 years. It is not as though the servient owner had said: "I will stop up the way you have been using over these last 15 years, but you may have a new defined way over a wholly different part of my land", a situation about which I will say nothing.

I had at one time thought that the point taken that the agreement of 1950 by the servient owner amounted to a consent by him which interrupted the enjoyment as of right and so made the user "precario" was a good point. [12] But I accept Mr Gidley Scott's submission that what was agreed in 1950 did not involve a simple consent to the user given by the owner of the dominant tenement, but is more consistent (as I think Burgess V-C thought) with the existence of a claim of right by the dominant owner settled by the servient owner affording a route less disadvantageous to him than a path crossing the middle of his garden; and I do not think that it was a case of consent, but rather of compromise.

I would, for these reasons, dismiss the appeal.'

---

[12]   *Rafique v Trustees of the Walton Estate* (1992) 65 P & CR 356; [1994] Conv 196 at pp. 207–210 (H. Wallace).

IV. Content of Easements [13]

After establishing that an easement has been created, questions can still arise as to its content and extent. Such questions often relate to changes in the neighbourhood and, in connection with rights of way, to changes in methods of transportation. The principles applicable vary with the mode of creation of the easement.

A. Easements Created by Express Grant

The extent of an easement is dependent upon the proper construction of the deed of grant. This is dependent upon the circumstances surrounding its execution, and they may be sufficient to restrict an apparently unlimited grant.

WILLES J, in **Williams v James** (1867) LR 2 CP 577, said at 581:
'The distinction between a grant and prescription is obvious. In the case of proving a right by prescription the user of the right is the only evidence. In the case of a grant the language of the instrument can be referred to, and it is of course for the court to construe that language; and in the absence of any clear indication of the intention of the parties, the maxim that a grant must be construed most strongly against the grantor must be applied.'

In **White v Grand Hotel Eastbourne Ltd** [1913] 1 Ch 113, [14] an unrestricted right of way to a public road granted to the owner of a private house was held not to be limited to the circumstances existing at the time of the grant. When the private house became the Grand Hotel, Eastbourne, the owners of the hotel were entitled to a right of way for the general purposes of the hotel.

In **Kain v Norfolk** [1949] Ch 163, [1949] 1 All ER 176, the rector of Bradwell had conveyed to a purchaser in 1919 land adjoining the rectory, together with a grant of the 'right at all times hereafter with or without horses carts and agricultural machines and implements to go pass and repass' over a strip of land within the rectory grounds.

A sand and gravel pit was later opened, and substantial traffic of lorries carrying sand developed. The question was whether such user was within the terms of the grant of the easement. JENKINS J, relying on *White v Grand Hotel Eastbourne Ltd*, held that it was.

---

13   C & B, pp. 608–610; Gray, pp. 482–491; Smith, pp. 521–524. As to easements of light, see p. 775, post. As to rights of way, see M & W, paras. 18.192–18.200; Gale, paras. 9-01 to 9-56; Jackson, pp. 139–155.
14   *United Land Co v Great Eastern Rly Co* (1875) 10 Ch App 586; *Robinson v Bailey* [1948] 2 All ER 791 (right of way to building plot held to include business user); *Jalnarne Ltd v Ridewood* (1989) 61 P & CR 143 (right of way held to permit its use by juggernaut lorries and customers in vans and cars for access to dominant tenements subsequently used for motorcar dealing, frozen food business and snooker club with bar); *Hamble Parish Council v Haggard* [1992] 1 WLR 122, [1992] 4 All ER 147.

In **Bulstrode v Lambert** [1953] 1 WLR 1064, [1953] 2 All ER 728,[15] a reservation in the conveyance by the plaintiff's predecessor in title to the defendant's predecessor in title in 1944 had been made of a right of way as follows—'reserving unto the vendor his tenants and workmen and others authorised by him the right to pass and repass with or without vehicles over and along the land coloured brown on the ... plan for the purpose of obtaining access to the building at the rear of the said premises and known as the auction mart.'

At the date of the conveyance the route to the auction mart (coloured brown) was obstructed and could not be used by large vans. The obstructions were removed, and, on occasions when a better route was too crowded, the plaintiff made use of the route with furniture vans and pantechnicons for bringing goods to the mart. The defendant objected on the ground that the parked pantechnicons interfered with his business as a café and car hire proprietor, but UPJOHN J held that the plaintiff could use the way with pantechnicons which could park as long as was necessary for loading and unloading, this being an incident of a right of way.[16]

KEEFE v AMOR
[1965] 1 QB 334, [1964] 2 All ER 517 (CA, SELLERS, RUSSELL and DAVIES L JJ)

The plaintiff was the owner of one (No. 1) of two semi-detached houses whose only outlet to the road was a strip of land to the rear. This land and the other house (No. 2) were owned by the defendant.

The plaintiff's parents had bought No. 1 in 1930 from the previous owner of both houses and the conveyance contained an express grant of a right of way in the following terms: 'Together also with a right of way over the land shown and coloured brown on the plan hereto annexed the purchasers paying a fair proportion in common with the adjoining owners of the cost of keeping the said way in good repair and condition subject to the liability of contributing (in common with the adjoining owners) to the upkeep and repair of the wall on the west side of the said right of way shown and marked with a T on the plan drawn hereon.'

At the date of the transfer there was at the frontage to the highway a continuous wall, except for a gap four feet six inches wide between two brick pillars. Inside, a gravelled strip eight feet wide led to a doorway three feet wide to the plaintiff's property and to a gap some seven feet wide leading to the remainder of the defendant's property. In 1962 the defendant widened the entrance from the highway to about seven feet six inches wide by rehanging the original gate and hanging another, three feet wide, alongside, which she kept locked, claiming the right so to do. The plaintiff sought a declaration that she was entitled to a right of way for all purposes, including vehicular traffic, over the whole of the strip of land coloured brown and an injunction to restrain the defendant from interfering with her reasonable enjoyment of this right.

---

[15] *McIlraith v Grady* [1968] 1 QB 468, [1967] 3 All ER 625 (a right 'to pass and repass through over and along' included a right for vehicles to stop for a reasonable time to load and unload).

[16] Cf. *London and Suburban Land and Building Co (Holdings) Ltd v Carey* (1991) 62 P & CR 480 (express grant of a right of way to commercial premises did not imply a right to unload from the access way onto the dominant tenement); *CP Holdings v Dugdale Real Property* [1998] NPC 97 (unrestricted right of way over disused railway line; servient owner reopening line held not able to lower level crossing thereby causing temporary but lengthy queues); *Nationwide Building Society v James Beauchamp* [2001] 3 EGLR 6 (grant of right of way includes ancillary rights to make grant effective).

The defendant contended that, in accordance with the circumstances existing at the time of the grant, the right of way was a footway only, or, at most, for such use as the four feet six inch gap permitted.

Held. On the proper construction of the grant, the right of way included user by vehicular traffic.

RUSSELL LJ: What were the circumstances and the condition of the property at the time of the grant? The inward end of the 'brown strip' abutted on the boundary wall of the plaintiff's property, No. 1—in which was a doorway about three feet wide. Down one side of the 'brown strip' was the wall referred to in the transfer. Down the other side was a hedge, which, at the inward end, left a gap of some seven feet or so, which afforded access between the 'brown strip' and No. 2. At the highway frontage of the 'brown strip' was a wall between the ends of the hedge and the other wall, continuous except for the gap of about four feet six inches between two 14-inch-square brick pillars suitable for a gateway; and from this gateway to the inward end of the 'brown strip' was a gravelled strip appreciably wider than the gateway, with some kind of edging of tiles, and on each side beyond that edging were garden beds and bushes, though apparently not much kept up. In appearance it looked like a footpath rather than a roadway. During the tenancy of the plaintiff's parents (which had lasted since 1903), there did not appear to have been any vehicular use of the 'brown strip' by them.

Bearing all those matters in mind, do they lead to the conclusion that the grant was of a footway only, or alternatively, if the grant was of a vehicular way, then that it was one limited as to the dimensions of the vehicle in the manner I have indicated? For myself, I think not. It is argued that that view, which I have just expressed, means that the plaintiff's parents could, had they been so minded, immediately after the transfer have insisted on the four feet six inch wide gap being widened, by pulling down a post and a part of the wall, if the vendor refused to do so, so as to enable a motor car, if they so wished, to come right up to their property, to enter and leave, and it is said that this surely would not have been a situation intended by the parties at the time of the grant. But there are several aspects of the transfer which I think lead to the conclusion that the greater right was intended.

First and foremost, the right of way was expressed to be over the strip whose whole 20-feet width was coloured brown. It would have been perfectly simple to define it more narrowly if that had been intended, or, of course, to define it as a footway, or as a right of way to and from the then existing gateway. Moreover, the fact that the whole 20-feet width was regarded as available if necessary for the exercise of the right is stressed by the reference to the wall marked with a 'T' as being 'on the west side of the said right of way', showing that the whole of the 20-feet strip was being referred to as the right of way. Why (I ask myself) should the whole width be regarded as being available, if necessary, for the use as a right of way, if all that was intended was the restricted right suggested by the defendant?

I further observe that there was no obligation imposed to contribute to the upkeep of the frontage wall and, further, that an express grant of the footway alone would have been quite superfluous in the circumstances. I refer, of course, to the history of previous user; and, whether one speaks of it as a way of necessity or whether one speaks of it, as I think more correctly, as a grant which would have been implied having regard to the pre-existing user, in either event an express grant in 1930 was technically a superfluity.

Finally I would add that an obligation to pay a fair proportion of the cost of keeping the way in good repair and condition is at least unusual if all that was envisaged was the impact of human feet.

The county court judge decided against the defendant because he felt himself bound so to do by the decision of Upjohn J in *Bulstrode v Lambert* [1953] 1 WLR 1064, [1953] 2 All ER 728, p. 759, ante. In that case there was at the time of the grant a gateway and an overhead bar which would have limited the size of vehicles having access to the auction room premises and prevented the entry of furniture vans or pantechnicons. Nevertheless, in the judge's view that did not restrict the scope of the grant. I do not myself think that that case is conclusive of the present case, because the terms of the grant in that case were very particular, though I think that it is of use in approaching the alternative contention (which, if I may say so, was certainly not Mr Poole's favourite of the two contentions), namely, the small-vehicle right.

Perhaps it would be desirable to stress what I have said by quoting from the judgment in that case where the judge says: 'I am unable to accept that submission. Here is a perfectly plain, unambiguous reservation for "the vendor, his tenants and workmen"—there is no limitation whatever upon the vehicles— "over and along the land coloured brown" on the plan. Pausing there, in my judgment the true effect of those words, that there is a right of way over and along the land coloured brown, cannot be affected by the circumstance that at the date of the grant there was this gate and bar across. The words of the grant are plain and unambiguous, and in my judgment the plaintiff plainly has a right over the whole of the yard coloured brown, and not merely a right to enter through the gates some six feet in width. Not only that: he has a right to enter it with vehicles. That must mean vehicles of any size appropriate to go down the yard, and as the yard is at no stage, until the garage is reached, less than eleven feet wide, there seems to be no reason why a pantechnicon should not use that yard.'

The part that I have quoted there shows that there were particular considerations in the language of the grant in the *Bulstrode* case which are absent from the present case; and for my part I would not have thought that the judge was necessarily bound, simply as a result of that decision, to conclude that in the present case there was more than a footpath. However, as I say, I differ in the end from the conclusion at which, but for the *Bulstrode* decision, the judge would have arrived. ...

I would remark that it is sometimes thought that the grant of a right of way in respect of every part of a defined area involves the proposition that the grantee can object to anything on any part of the area which would obstruct passage over that part. This is a wrong understanding of the law. Assuming a right of way of a particular quality over an area of land, it will extend to every part of that area, as a matter, at least, of theory. But a right of way is not a right absolutely to restrict user of the area by the owner thereof. The grantee of the right could only object to such activities of the owner of the land, including retention of obstruction, as substantially interfered with the use of the land in such exercise of the defined right as for the time being is reasonably required.[17] (I am, of course, talking now about private rights of way.)

This proposition is exemplified by the decision of this court in *Dyer v Mousley*, (1962) unreported Transcript No. 315, where the dominant owner asserted the

---

[17] See *Celsteel Ltd v Alton House Holdings Ltd* [1985] 1 WLR 204, [1985] 2 All ER 562, p. 148, post (interference with driving in forwards and reversing out of a garage held to be substantial); *West v Sharp* (1999) 79 P & CR 327; *B & Q Plc v Liverpool and Lancashire Properties Ltd* [2001] 1 EGLR 92 at 96G: 'the test of an actionable interference is not whether what the grantee is left with is reasonable, but whether his insistence upon being able to continue the use of the whole of what he contracted for is reasonable': (per BLACKBURNE J).

right to clear and level the whole of the strip dedicated to the right of way, at a time when there was no need to do so for the current requirement of the dominant tenant.

For those reasons, in my judgment, this appeal fails.

In **Jelbert v Davis** [1968] 1 WLR 589, [1968] 1 All ER 1182, [18] the plaintiff, in a conveyance of agricultural land to him in 1961, was granted 'a right of way at all times and for all purposes over the driveway retained by the vendor leading to the main road in common with all other persons having the like right'. In 1966 he obtained planning permission to use part of the land as a tourist and caravan site for up to 200 caravans or tents. The defendants, two neighbouring landowners, objected to the proposed use of the driveway for caravan traffic and put up notices warning off caravans and campers. The plaintiff sued for nuisance and slander of title, and the defendants counter-claimed for an injunction to restrain the plaintiff from using the driveway for access to the caravan site. The Court of Appeal held that the plaintiff was entitled to use the driveway for caravans, but not so as to cause substantial interference with its use by the defendants: the user by 200 caravans was excessive. DANCKWERTS LJ said at 597, at 1186:

'On the authorities, it is plain that the easement so granted is in such wide terms that the use by the plaintiff of it for caravans is permissible; but it is an easement which on its terms is a right which is to be used "in common with all other persons having the like right". That includes the defendants. A use of the right of way which is so excessive that it renders the rights of such other persons practically impossible, therefore, is not justified. The difficulty is to fix the limit in respect of such use. The test must be whether the interference is so substantial as to interfere with the rights of other persons in an unreasonable manner. It cannot be right that the others should be swamped by the traffic created by the plaintiff so as to amount to a legal nuisance. It is impossible to quantify this in figures, particularly as the problem relates to the future. These people are neighbours and share the right of way and there must be give and take and accommodation. Time will show what is practicable, and in the interests of both parties a practical solution must be found or a deadlock will result. [19]

In **Graham v Philcox** [1984] QB 747, [1984] 2 All ER 643, [20] M, who owned a large house and garden and a coach house at the rear in High Rocks Lane, Tunbridge Wells, let the first floor flat of the coach house in 1960 to B for five years together with a right of way for all purposes over the entrance drive to the house and thence along the side of the garden as far as the coach house. In 1963 B assigned his lease to D who later became a statutory tenant under the Rent

---

[18]   *Hanover Trust Co Ltd v Eastern Counties Leather Group Ltd* (2000) 25 July, CA, unreported (grant to purchase of rights to be excercisable over retained land of vendor 'in common with the vendor and all persons authorised by it' held expressly to contemplate that vendor might grant further rights over that land in favour of third parties.

[19]   *Rosling v Pinnegar* (1986) 54 P & CR 124 (access to Hammerwood Park, near East Grinstead, built by Latrobe, American architect of the White House); cf. *National Trust v White* [1987] 1 WLR 907 (access to Figsbury Ring, near Salisbury); *White v Richards* (1993) 68 P & CR 105 (track not intended to carry juggernauts); *Gardner v Davis* [1998] PLSCS 219 (extent ot sewage easement unreasonable).

[20]   [1985] Conv 60 (P. Todd); [1985] CLJ 15 (S. Tromans).

Act. In 1975 M's executors conveyed the freehold of the entire coach house to W, subject to D's tenancy of the first floor flat. Nothing was said in the conveyance about the means of access.

In June 1977 M's executors conveyed to the defendants, Mr and Mrs Philcox, the freehold of that part of the retained land over which the right of way had been granted in the lease of 1960. Finally in November 1970, W's interest in the coach house was conveyed to the plaintiffs, Mr and Mrs. Graham, subject to D's tenancy. D later surrendered his tenancy to the plaintiffs who then occupied the whole coach house as their residence. The defendants refused to allow the plaintiffs to continue to use the right of way.

The Court of Appeal, following *Wright v Macadam* [1949] 2 KB 744, [1949] 2 All ER 565, p. 723, ante, held that, when the coach house was conveyed in 1925, the right of way had passed under LPA 1925, s. 62(2) to the plaintiffs' predecessor in title. PURCHAS LJ said at 760, at 652:

'It was certainly an easement, right or advantage "*reputed to appertain to the first floor flat*" and was enjoyed with that part *of the* "land, houses or other buildings conveyed." I can find nothing in the wording of section 62(2) of the Act to indicate that the "land conveyed" cannot include land subject to a lease or an adverse right of occupation by a tenant protected by statute. The easement, right or advantage is enjoyed with and appertains to the land, not to the statutory right of occupation.'

The Court of Appeal further held that the alteration of the dominant tenement by the enlargement of the first floor flat of the coach house into one dwelling did not affect the existence of the right of way. MAY LJ said at 156, at 648:

'Mr Godfrey's principal submission was that as the dominant tenement for the benefit of which the way is now claimed, namely the coach house, is not the same as and is indeed greater than the dominant tenement for the benefit of which the way was originally granted, namely only the upper flat in the coach house, therefore the plaintiffs cannot use that way now when the coach house is now one dwelling and the original two flats which it comprised have been combined into one ... Mr Godfrey submitted further that if one substantially alters a dominant tenement, an easement therefore enjoyed with it can no longer be used, because by the alterations one has increased the burden of the use on the servient tenement. The easement is consequently lost, or at least suspended temporarily: thus in the present case the plaintiffs must accept that they cannot enforce their use of the disputed right of way for so long as the coach house remains one dwelling ...

In none of the judgments in any of the cases to which Mr Godfrey referred us is there suggestion that a mere alteration of a dominant tenement to which a right of way may be appurtenant is sufficient to extinguish it, or indeed to affect the entitlement to its use unless as the result of that alteration the extent of the user is thereby increased.

In my opinion, therefore, the mere alteration of the coach house into one dwelling cannot have had any effect upon the existence of the right of way. It should be borne in mind that there was no evidence whatever before the judge that the actual or anticipated user by the plaintiffs of the way was in any way excessive, either in quantity or quality.

Further, I do not think that on this issue any real distinction can be drawn between the instant case on the one hand and *Wright v Macadam*, on the other. In the latter case also the right for which the plaintiffs contended had, at the date of the conveyance relied on for the purposes of section 62(2), been enjoyed by the occupier of only part of the whole premises in respect of which the continued enjoyment of the right was claimed in the action.'[1]

In **St. Edmundsbury and Ipswich Diocesan Board of Finance v Clark (No 2)** [1975] 1 WLR 468, [1975] 1 All ER 772, land, including the former rectory of St. Botolph's Church, Iken, in Suffolk, was sold and conveyed in 1945 by the church authorities to the defendant. It then wholly surrounded the church and churchyard. Access from the village to the church porch was by Church Lane (a narrow public highway) which then became a path 100 yards long leading to the church porch. The first third of the path ('the disputed strip') crossed the rectory grounds, and the remainder ('the church path') was within the churchyard and church property. The first 7 yards of the disputed strip could be used by vehicles for access from the lane to a driveway, leading to the rectory. The remainder ('the chestnut path') was not wider than 4 feet 6 inches and was a derelict gravel and sandy path covered with leaves. At the end of the chestnut path on the defendant's land was a gate between two gateposts, standing no more than 4 feet apart. There was no evidence that the path was used by vehicles before 1946.

On 31 December 1945 the land was conveyed to the defendant 'subject to a right of way over the land coloured red on the said plan to and from St. Botolph's Church'. The question was whether the right of way reserved by the church authorities was a right exercisable on foot only, or with vehicles also.

The Court of Appeal, construing the language of the conveyance in the light of all the surrounding circumstances, decided that it was a right of footway only. In explaining the correct approach in these matters, Sir John PENNYCUICK said at 476, at 779:

'What is the proper approach upon the construction of a conveyance containing the reservation of a right of way? We feel no doubt that the proper approach is that upon which the court construes all documents; that is to say, one must construe the document according to the natural meaning of the words contained in the document as a whole, read in the light of surrounding circumstances.'

A similar approach is adopted in the identification of the dominant tenement. In **Johnstone v Holdway** [1963] 1 QB 601, [1963] 1 All ER 432, George Horace Johnstone agreed in 1936 to sell land to the Trewithin Estates Company, but no conveyance was executed. In 1948 Trewithin Estates Company sold part of the land to Henry Bosustow, whereupon Johnstone as trustee and the company as beneficial owner conveyed it to Bosustow. The conveyance excepted and reserved to the company and its successors in title 'a right of way at all times and for all purposes (including quarrying)' over the land conveyed from a point on its north-western boundary to a point on its south-eastern boundary. The conveyance failed to specify any dominant tenement for the right of way, but it was meant to be the quarry, retained as part of their land by the company. The plaintiffs, as successors in title of the company, claimed a right of way against the successors in title of Bosustow.

---

[1]   *Mills v Silver* [1991] Ch 271, [1991] 1 All ER 449, p. 743, ante (grantee of prescriptive right of way entitled to repair but not to improve it; improvement would increase burden on servient tenement).

In holding that the plaintiffs were entitled to a legal easement, UPJOHN LJ said at 609, at 434: 'Mr Seward, for the defendant ... submits that it is essential to the valid creation of every easement that the dominant tenement must be defined in the deed itself and that no extrinsic evidence is admissible to define it. ... But the question we have to determine is whether that is essential to the validity of the easement or whether it is permissible to identify the dominant tenement by inferences from facts and circumstances which must have been known to the parties at the time of the conveyance. ...

In our judgment, it is a question of the construction of the deed creating a right of way as to what is the dominant tenement for the benefit of which the right of way is granted and to which the right of way is appurtenant. In construing the deed the court is entitled to have evidence of all material facts at the time of the execution of the deed, so as to place the court in the situation of the parties. ... It seems to us perfectly plain that in this case the dominant tenement was the land and quarry.'[2]

B. Easements Created by Implied Grant

As explained above the rules for the creation of easements by implied grant vary with the question whether the easement is claimed by the grantor or grantee.

Easements implied in favour of the grantor are limited to cases of necessity or to cases where the intention of the parties is clear.[3] Easements of necessity are strictly limited to the circumstances of the necessity.

In the case of easements implied in favour of the grantee—where they are 'continuous and apparent', 'necessary for the reasonable enjoyment of the property granted', or where the common intention of the parties was clear—there seems to be little authority on the question of the extent of the easement. If tested at the time of the conveyance, no difficulty arises, for the same rules as govern implication will govern extent. But difficulties may arise if the matter is tested at a time when circumstances have changed. If, for example, a narrow track is sufficient to establish that a right of way is 'continuous and apparent' in a conveyance of 1880, will this cover travellers on foot, horseback, by car or by lorry? The cases on easements by express grant would suggest that the extent of the

---

[2] See p. 714, ante. (1963) 79 LQR 182 (R.E.M.); *Shannon Ltd v Venner Ltd* [1965] Ch 682, [1965] 1 All ER 590; *Bracewell v Appleby* [1975] 1 All ER 993 (right to pass over close A to reach close B held to be not usable as access to close C lying beyond close B), following *Harris v Flower* (1904) 74 LJ Ch 127; (1975) 39 Conv (NS) 277 (F. R. Crane); *Nickerson v Barraclough* [1980] Ch 325 at 336, [1979] 3 All ER 312 at 324 (such a right held to be usable as access where close B is itself used as access to close C at time of grant); *Jobson v Record* (1997) 75 P & CR 375; *Peacock v Custins* [2001] 1 WLR 1815; *Das v Linden Mews Ltd* (2003) 2 P & CR 58; [2003] Conv 127 (E. Paton and G. Seabourne); *Massey v Boulden* [2003] 1 WLR 1792; *Macepark (Whittlebury) Ltd v Sargeant* [2003] 1 WLR 2284; *Scott v Martin* [1987] 1 WLR 841, [1987] 2 All ER 813 (plan used to explain 'private road'); *Hamble Parish Council v Haggard* [1992] 1 WLR 122 ('I have to put myself into the shoes of the notional judge visiting the site with the conveyance in one hand and gazing about him to identify on the ground those features which would enable him to ascertain the extent of the dominant land', per MILLETT J at 130). See also *Minor v Groves* (1997) 80 P & CR 136 (dominant owner limited in user to extend with right of way; occasional technical trespasses caused by side of vehicles intruding into airspace of servient tenement did not give rise to a right over it).

[3] *London Corpn v Riggs* (1880) 13 ChD 798, p. 734, ante; *Nickerson v Barraclough* [1981] Ch 426, [1981] 2 All ER 369; *Re Webb's Lease* [1951] Ch 808, [1951] 2 All ER 131, p. 736, ante.

easement will develop as circumstances change and that limitations will only be imposed where such a restriction is clearly justified. [4]

C. Easements Acquired by Prescription

Easements acquired by prescription are dependent upon user and their content is limited by the user proved. Small adjustments are allowed. Whether a variation is a new form of user or an extended example of that proved may be a difficult question.

BRITISH RAILWAYS BOARD v GLASS
[1965] Ch 538, [1964] 3 All ER 418 (CA, Lord DENNING MR, HARMAN and DAVIES LJJ

In 1847 the Wilts, Somerset and Weymouth Railway, predecessors in title to the plaintiffs, constructed a railway line near a farm owned by X, the defendant's predecessor in title, and through a field owned by X, the defendant's predecessor in title, and through a field also owned by him but occupied by a tenant Y. They purchased part of this field, and the conveyance contained the following proviso (inter alia): 'Save and except that the ... company and their successors shall and will at all times hereafter allow unto ... my heirs and assigns at all times ... a right of crossing the ... railway to the extent of twelve feet in width on the level thereof with all manner of cattle to and from one part of the land ... to the other part ... severed by the ...railway.' To provide for this right of way, the company constructed a level crossing. For many years prior to 1942 one of the fields near the crossing, formerly owned by X and occupied by Z (called the 'blue land') was used for campers and caravanners and in 1942 there were six caravans established on the site. Since then the numbers had grown, and the traffic of vehicles and people over the crossing substantially increased. The plaintiffs brought this action to limit the user of the crossing.

It was conceded that (i) the right of way was not limited to linking the separated parts of the field previously occupied by Y, but linked the farm occupied by Z (which included the 'blue land') with the severed part of that field and with a highway beyond, and (iii) the way was not limited to foot passengers or cattle, but extended to vehicles.

Two main questions arose:
  (i) Whether the grant of the right of way covered the traffic of the caravanners;
  (ii) Whether, if not covered by the grant, there was a prescriptive right for all the caravanners, the defendant admitting a prescriptive right since 1942 for 6 caravanners.

Held (affirming UNGOED-THOMAS J; Lord DENNING MR dissenting).
  (i) The right of way was general and not limited to agricultural purposes in the contemplation of the parties to the conveyance;
  (ii) A prescriptive right had been acquired for the use of the crossing by the caravanners, the increase in number of caravanners since 1942 not being an excessive user.

The construction of the express grant of the right of way was influenced by the fact that the conveyance of 1847 was stated to be in compensation for, inter

---

[4]   See, however, *Milner's Safe Co Ltd v Great Northern and City Rly Co* [1907] 1 Ch 208; *Stafford v Lee* (1992) 65 P & CR 172.

alia, the right to have certain 'accommodation works' carried out by the railway company in pursuance of their duties under the Railways Clauses Consolidation Act 1845, section 68. It was argued that the right of way should not be more extensive than the company's duty in respect of the 'accommodation works', for it was an exception to them, and should therefore be limited to agricultural or domestic purposes and those in the contemplation of the parties in 1847. The Court of Appeal (LORD DENNING MR dissenting), as stated above, rejected this argument.[5] The present extracts from the judgments are limited to the issue of prescription.

LORD DENNING MR (dissenting): *The Prescriptive Right.* The defendant says that alternatively he obtained a right by prescription. The judge found that for 20 years before the action, from 1942 to 1962, there had been six caravans on the site permanently, but that there had been 10 or 11 there at times from 1942 to 1945 and thereafter, and increased to 28 or 29 immediately before the issue of the writ. It is clear that by prescription there is a right of way for six caravans. But is there a right for 28 or 29 caravans?

It is quite clear that, when you acquire a right of way by prescription, you are not entitled to change the character of your land so as substantially to increase or alter the burden upon the servient tenement. If you have a right of way for your pasture land, you cannot turn it into a manufactory and claim a right of way for the purposes of the factory. If you have a right of way by prescription for one house, you cannot build two more houses on the land and claim a right of way for the purposes of those houses also. I think this rule is not confined to the character of the property. It extends also to the intensity of the user. If you use your land for years as a caravan site for six caravans and thereby gain a prescriptive right over a level crossing, you are not thereby entitled to put 30 caravans on the site and claim a right for those 30. As Baggallay JA said in *Wimbledon and Putney Commons Conservators v Dixon* (1875) 1 ChD 362 at 374, 'You must neither increase the burden on the servient tenement nor substantially change the nature of the user.' This seems to me good sense. It would be very wrong that, because the plaintiffs have been so tolerant as to allow the occupants of six caravans to use the crossing, in consequence they are thereby to be saddled with the use of 30 caravans. Trains would be obstructed and delayed. Dangers would abound. After all, prescription is a presumed grant. No such grant for 30 caravans could ever be presumed from user for six.

On this part of the case, counsel for the defendant made a technical point. He said that the defendant had a prescriptive right to a 'caravan site' and so phrased it in his defence: and that in the reply the plaintiffs had admitted that the field had been used 'as a caravan site' since 1938. He says that, by this admission, the plaintiffs are debarred from saying that the defendant had a prescriptive right only for six caravans, and that the defendant has a right for as many caravans as the site will hold. I regard this as special pleading of the worst description. The facts and issues before the court are plain enough: and no one has been in the least misled by this verbal nicety. I would decide this case on the facts found, and I hold that the defendant had no prescriptive right to use the crossing for more than six caravans.

[5] For a similar construction of s. 68, see *TRH Sampson Associates Ltd v British Railway Board* [1983] 1 WLR 170, [1983] 1 All ER 257 (owner of dominant tenement held entitled to alter user of bridge provided no increased burden on servient tenement).

We were told that the local authority have taken steps to deal with this caravan site. They have exercised their statutory powers to see that it is gradually removed. All the caravans should be gone by 1966. That is satisfactory, in a way. But I do not see why the local authority should be forced to do this: or to pay compensation to the defendant. I think the plaintiffs are entitled to come to the court and ask for protection on their own account. I think they are entitled to restrain the defendant from putting this greatly increased burden on the crossing.

I would allow the appeal and grant a declaration and injunction as asked in the notice of appeal.

HARMAN LJ: It appeared from the evidence that before the last war there were three caravans and a tent dwelling permanently situated upon the 'blue land', and that this number increased after the war began, when the Admiralty moved some of its departments to Bath, to six permanent caravans and five more that came and went, and there was a further increase in the spring of 1942 after the first bombs fell on Bath, and that after the war there were further increases from time to time until shortly before the writ was issued the number of caravans had increased to 29 and it was of this burden that the plaintiffs not unnaturally complained. All the caravanners and those who visited them, and their suppliers, had no access to the blue land save over the level crossing.

This part of the case has become largely academic because the local planning authority has, by exercise of its statutory powers, ordered the gradual clearance of the site from caravans. At the date of the hearing in the court below the number had been reduced to 16 and will be reduced to none by the end of the year 1966 or thereabouts. Nevertheless the judge considered the state of things when the writ was issued, and rightly so, and he came to the conclusion that the plaintiffs could not complain of the state of things as it then existed. He reached this conclusion upon the admissions appearing upon the face of the pleadings. The plaintiffs admitted that the 'blue land' was used 'as a caravan site', that is to say, the whole of the 'blue land' was used 'as a caravan site', that is to say, the whole of the 'blue land' and not merely such portions of it as had in fact been the standings of caravans. I understand that in fact there were no such permanent standings, but that caravans coming and going occupied any part of the field they chose. The prescriptive claim was not made in the right of individual caravans, which would have been a claim by individual caravanners, but by the defendant as the owner of the whole of the 'blue land' and on the footing that it constituted 'the caravan site'. It may be regrettable that this part of the case should turn on a point of pleading, as this to some extent has, but I do not think the judge could have come to his conclusion upon any other footing. The fact is that this expression 'caravan site' has only recently come into prominence, and it was not perhaps fully appreciated until the recent decision of this court in *Biss v Smallburgh RDC* [1965] Ch 335, [1964] 2 All ER 543, that it ought not to be used in a loose way. In that case a large area, which varied at various stages of the action from 70-odd acres to three or four, was claimed as being a 'caravan site', but the court came to the conclusion that there was no caravan site at all within the meaning of that phrase in the Caravan Sites and Control of Development Act 1960, that the mere casual placing of caravans here and there on a large area did not constitute that area a 'caravan site'. So here, if the plaintiffs had not admitted that the 'blue land' constituted a 'caravan site', the defendant might have been in great difficulty in defining the area of the site. He was relieved of that difficulty by the pleadings and his case was that, admitting the whole 'blue land' to be 'a caravan site', the mere increase from, say, 10 to 29 caravans did not constitute such an increase in the burden of the prescriptive right as was a legitimate subject of complaint by the plaintiffs. The leading case on this subject is *Williams v James* (1867) LR 2 CP 577. The headnote reads: 'The defendant being entitled by immemorial user to a right of way over the plaintiff's land from field N, used the way for the purpose of carting from field N some hay stacked there, which had been grown partly there and partly on land adjoining. The jury found in effect that the defendant in so doing had used the way bona fide, and for the ordinary and reasonable use of field N as a field: *Held,* that the mere fact that some of the hay had not been grown on field N did not make the carrying of it over the plaintiff's land an excess in the user of the right of way.' Bovill CJ says this at 580: 'In all cases of this kind which depend upon user the right acquired must be measured by the extent of the enjoyment which is proved. When a right of way to a piece of land is proved, then that is, unless something appears to the contrary, a right of way for all purposes according to the ordinary and reasonable use to which that land might be applied at the time of the supposed grant. Such a right cannot be increased so as to affect the servient tenement by imposing upon it any additional burthen. It is also clear, according to the authorities, that where a person has a right of way over one piece of land to another piece of land, he can only use such right in order to reach the latter place. He cannot use it for the purpose of going elsewhere.' Willes J says this at 582: 'I agree with the argument of Mr Jelf that in cases like this, where a way has to be proved by user, you cannot extend the purposes for which the way may be used, or for which it might be reasonably inferred that parties would have intended it to be used. The land in this case was a field in the country, and apparently only used for rustic purposes. To be a legitimate user of the right of way, it must be used for the enjoyment of the nine acre field, and not colourably for other closes. I quite agree also with the argument that the right of way can only be used for the field in its ordinary use as a field. The right could not be used for a manufactory built upon the field. The use must be the reasonable use for the purposes of the land in the condition in which it was while the user took place.'

Applying that to the present case, you must do what the judge did, namely, base your conclusion on a consideration of what must have been the supposed contents of the lost grant on which the prescription rests. If this be supposed to be a grant of the right to use the 'blue land' as 'a caravan site', then it is clear that a mere increase in the numbers of the caravans using the site is not an excessive user of the right. A right to use a way for this purpose or that has never been to my knowledge limited to a right to use the way so many times a day or for such and such a number of vehicles so long as the dominant tenement does not change its identity. If there be a radical change in the character of the dominant tenement, then the prescriptive right will not extend to it in that condition. The obvious example is a change of a small dwelling-house to a large hotel, but there has been no change of that character according to the facts found in this case. The caravan site never became a highly organised town of caravans with fixed standings and roads and all the paraphernalia attendant on such a place and in my opinion the judge was right in holding that there had been so such increase in the burden of the easement as to justify the plaintiffs in seeking as they did by injunction to restrict the user to three caravans or six or to prevent its use as what in the statement of claim is called 'a caravan camp or site.'

I, accordingly, hold the judge was right in both branches of the case and that the appeal should be dismissed.

DAVIES LJ: If any prescriptive right has been acquired, it has been acquired not by any one or more caravans but by the 'blue land' as dominant tenement. And it is not easy to contemplate an express grant of a right of way in respect of a specified or limited number of caravans. The 'blue land' is still being used as a caravan site. Its use as such has been intensified. But there has been no alteration in the nature of its use ... So here, once it is admitted, as it has been admitted, that the 'blue land' as 'a caravan site' acquired by prescription a right of way, it does not seem to me that the plaintiffs can prevent a mere increase in the number of caravans upon the site and the consequent increase in the use of the right of way. An increase in the number of caravans on the site is quite a different thing from the erection of a number of new houses, though no doubt from the point of view of the servient tenement the effect is somewhat similar.

(1965) 81 LQR, at p. 18 (R. E. Megarry).

'Two cases that were not cited provide a little assistance on the point. First, in *Lock v Abercester Ltd* [1939] Ch 861, [1939] 3 All ER 562, the dominant owners had to rely on user for the prescriptive period mainly for horse-drawn vehicles delivering goods to the dominant tenement, a house previously used as a rectory. Within the last few years these owners had begun to keep cows, pigs and chickens on the land held with the house, and motor-vehicles brought the food stuffs for these animals as well as other goods. Despite this additional burden on the way, Bennett J held that the way established by prescription was wide enough to cover this user. The main point of the case was, of course, the question whether user by horse-drawn vehicles authorised enjoyment by horseless vehicles; but the element of the recent increase in agricultural user was mentioned in the judgment.

Secondly, there is *Cowling v Higginson* (1838) 4 M & W 245. This raised the question of the validity of a claim to a right of way for all purposes where the user proved was for a variety of purposes though not for every conceivable purpose. If the right were to be measured by the *de facto* user, then such a claim would fail; for the right would be "confined to the identical carriages that have previously been used upon the road, and would not warrant even the slightest alteration in the carriage or the loading, or the purpose for which it was used": *Cowling v Higginson* (1838) 4 M & W at 254, per Parke B. On this footing, there might be "a right to carry corn and manure, though not coals" (at 253). And so it was laid down that "If a way has been used for several purposes, there may be a ground for inferring that there is a right of way for all purposes" (at 256, per Lord Abinger CB). As Parke B said during the argument, if the dominant owners "shew that they have used [the way] time out of mind, for all the purposes that they wanted, it would seem to me to give them a general right" (at 252). If user for a limited number of purposes can be generalised into a right to use for all purposes, it would be remarkable if on a claim to use the way for one purpose only there were to be imposed a strict quantitative restriction to the amount of use for that purpose during the prescriptive period. In the end, the point seems to come down to the difference between quantity and quality. It may well be that a change in quantity may be so vast as to amount to a change in quality; but short of such extremities, the distinction seems valid.'

In **Woodhouse & Co Ltd v Kirkland (Derby) Ltd** [1970] 1 WLR 1185, [1970] 2 All ER 587, PLOWMAN J held that a considerable increase in the number of customers using a right of way was 'a mere increase in user and not a user of a different kind or for a different purpose'. [6]

In **Giles v County Building Contractors (Hertford) Ltd** (1971) 22 P & CR 978, BRIGHTMAN J referred to HARMAN LJ in *British Railways Board v Glass* [1965] Ch 583 at 562, [1964] 3 All ER 418 at 428, p. 766, ante and said at 987:

'The important expressions, to my mind, are "change of identity" and "radical change in character". In my view, the use of the convent site for the erection of seven modern dwelling units in place of the two existing houses, cannot properly be described as "changing the identity" or "radically changing the character" of the convent site. I think it is evolution rather than mutation.'

In **Atwood v Bovis Homes Ltd** [2001] Ch 379, [2002] 4 All ER 948, [7] the defendant was the registered proprietor of agricultural land in the Isle of Sheppey. It had a prescriptive right to drain surface water through the land of the plaintiffs. In 1998 the defendant began an extensive development on its land of 1,000 houses, a shopping centre, community facilities, hospital and school and associated infrastructure. The plaintiff sought a declaration that the easement of drainage was no longer exercisable, since the defendant's land had undergone a radical alteration irrespective of the fact that there would be no material increase in the volume of water discharged.

In holding that the easement of drainage remained enforceable, NEUBERGER J said at 381:

'The issue in the present proceedings is one of some potential general significance in relation to the law of easements, and in particular to the extent of an easement acquired by prescription ...

The issue

Is an easement of drainage acquired by prescription still exercisable over the servient tenement (ie the plaintiffs' land) following a radical alteration (ie from fields used for agricultural purposes to a substantial residential development with associated commercial, community and infrastructure aspects) to the dominant tenement (ie the defendant's land) even where the alterations will have no material effect on the volume or rate of discharge of water over the servient tenement?

At first sight, it may be thought that the question should be resolved in the defendant's favour, once it is accepted that the ditches on the plaintiffs' land, burdened with the defendant's right to discharge water from its land by virtue of use and enjoyment over a substantial period, will not have that burden in any way increased or altered because of the change, however radical it may be, to the

---

[6]   See also *Cargill v Gotts* [1981] 1 WLR 441, [1981] 1 All ER 682 (drawing of extra water from neighbour's millpond for agricultural purposes held to be mere increase in user, but not exercisable without licence under Water Resources Act 1963, s. 24(1)). Cf. *Ward (Helston) Ltd v Kerrier District Council* (1981) 42 P & CR 412 (right of way for use in connection with slaughter house not extended to cartage of materials for house building).

[7]   [2000] All ER Rev 238 (P. J. Clarke); (2001) 151 NLJ 1307 (H. W. Wilkinson).

nature and use of the defendant's land. After all, the plaintiffs are only concerned with the drainage of water over their land and, if the volume passing through the ditches in their land is unaffected by any change in the defendant's land, why should they have any cause for complaint? They may object to the development of, and consequent change of use to, the defendant's land. They may wish to cash in on the profit which the defendant may make from that development. However, such matters are extraneous to the question of drainage. The essential point is that neither the plaintiffs nor their land will be detrimentally affected by the change of use and development of the defendant's land so far as water drainage is concerned. That, in essence, is the argument of Mr Martin Rodger, who appears on behalf of the defendant.

However, Mr Rodney Stewart Smith, who represents the plaintiffs, contends that, as is frequently the case with easements, the law is not as simple or commonsensical as that. His case is that, on the basis of a number of authorities, it is clear that an easement of drainage which has been acquired by prescription will be lost, or at least incapable of lawful enjoyment, if and so long, as there is a radical change in the use or nature of the dominant tenement.

The authorities relied on by the plaintiffs

[His Lordship referred to *Williams v James* (1867) LR 2 CP 577; *Wimbledon and Putney Commons Conservators v Dixon* (1875) 1 ChD 362); *British Railways Board v Glass* [1965] Ch 538, [1964] 3 All ER 418, p. 766, ante; *Loder v Gaden* (unreported 28 July 1999); and *Cargill v Gotts* [1981] 1 WLR 441; [1981] 1 All ER 682, and continued:]

The principles derived from the cases

I would summarise the points to be derived from these cases as follows.

1 The only case where the question at issue was whether a change in the nature of use (as opposed to intensification of the existing use) of the dominant tenement could destroy or result in an impermissible enjoyment of a right of way obtained by prescription was *Wimbledon and Putney Commons Conservators v Dixon.*

2 Not only in the decision in the *Wimbledon* case (binding on me as a decision of the Court of Appeal) but in other cases, it has been stated or assumed to be right that a substantial change in the nature of the use of the dominant tenement will result in the right to use the way, obtained by prescription, being either destroyed or impermissible.

3 There is a dispute between the parties in relation to the observations of the Court of Appeal in the *Wimbledon* case, and indeed in the other cases, as to the proper analysis of those observations. Is the principle that a radical alteration in the use or nature of the dominant tenement of itself puts an end to, or renders impermissible any use of, the right of way? This is what I shall call the "strict rule". Alternatively, is the rule more flexible, namely, that a radical change in the use or nature of a dominant tenement will lead to such a conclusion, unless the change is such that it will not result in any significant increase in the quantum, or of any significant alteration in the nature, of the use of the way from that enjoyed in relation to the original use of the way. By "quantum" I mean frequency of usage, and by "nature" I mean, for instance, lorries, motor cars, pedestrians, bicycles and so on.

4 In that connection, observations which one sees in the cases, whether part of the ratio (as in the *Wimbledon* case) or included as the obiter observations (as

in *Williams v James* and *British Railways Board v Glass*), relating to a change from a field to a factory, from a house to a hotel or from a field to a house building site, do not seem to me to be decisive. They all carry with them the understandable assumption that the changes would involve an increase in the quantum of the user and/or a change in the nature of the user of the way resulting from the change in the use of the dominant tenement.

5 The advantage of the flexible rule is that it can be said to be in accordance with commercial common sense as discussed above. Why should the owner of the servient tenement, in that capacity, care about a change of use to the dominant tenement, however radical, if it can be shown that it makes no difference to the quantum or nature of the use of the way? It could be said to be contrary to common sense that, if a right of way has been obtained by prescription in favour of a building being used as a hotel, the right to use the way would be lost if the owner of the dominant tenement changed the use to a house and could demonstrate that it was inconceivable that anything other than a diminution in the quantum of the use will arise and that there will be no change in the nature of the use.

6 The advantage of the strict rule is that it leads to a relative degree of certainty. It might be asked how one could predict the extent of the future likely use of the way following a change of use of the dominant tenement. For instance, what would be the position if the radical change of use was itself changed or subsequently intensified? It might also be asked, is one to compare the projected use of the way following the change of use of the dominant tenement with the historic actual use of the way, or with what might have been the maximum permitted use of the way in relation to the original use of the dominant tenement?

7 I would tentatively suggest that the rule may be that, if there is a subsequent radical change in the use of the dominant tenement, a right of way acquired by prescription can only continue to be used in connection with the dominant tenement if the court can be satisfied that the change cannot result in the use of the way being greater in quantum or different in character from that which it was for any continuous period of 20 or 40 years during the period of use of the way in connection with the original use of the dominant tenement. (For completeness, I should explain that the periods of 20 or 40 years are selected on the basis of the periods necessary to obtain an easement, be it a right of way or other easement, by prescription.) The onus would be on the owner of the dominant tenement, and would, I suspect, normally be difficult to satisfy in relation to a right of way.

8 It should be added, however, that the strict rule can be justified on an additional ground to that of certainty. I have in mind the reasoning of Harman LJ in *British Railways Board v Glass*, to which I have not so far referred. This is to the effect that a prescriptive right of way involves a fictional grant, and one should presume that this fictional grant is related to, indeed limited to, the type of use to which the dominant tenement was put at the time the right was acquired.

9 Whichever of the two rules is correct, it is clear that a prescriptive right of way arises from a fictional grant. Whether the flexible rule or the strict rule applies, it is accepted by both parties that the general purpose of the rule is to ensure that the owner of the dominant tenement does not use the way for a purpose, or to a degree, not contemplated by the fictional grant.

Application of the principles in this case

I turn now to consideration of the application of these principles, so far as one can identify them, to the present case.

1 It is clear to my mind that there are principles to be derived from the right of way cases which apply equally to all easements. The law of easements relates to a particular category of rights, and there will be principles which apply to all types of rights within that category. That is demonstrated by the decision in *Cargill v Gotts*, where the principles in the right of way cases were applied to a different easement.

2 However, to my mind equally self-evidently, while there will be general principles applicable to all easements to be derived from the right of way cases, there will also be principles applicable more specifically to rights of way, which do not, at least necessarily, apply to all other types of easements.

3 Thus, on any view, a change of use of a building in the dominant tenement, however radical and far-reaching that change may be, cannot result in an easement of support acquired by prescription against an adjoining building being lost. A change from a house to a hotel, assuming that it will result, as it apparently will, in the loss of a right of way acquired by prescription in favour of the building, would not, at least in the absence of very special facts, result in the building losing its right of support acquired by prescription from the adjoining building. In such a case one would expect the right of support to continue and to be exercisable, at least unless there was a change in the structure or use of the building on the dominant tenement which substantially increased the burden on the servient tenement. That, indeed, appears to be the law: *Lloyds Bank Ltd v Dalton* [1942] Ch 466.

4 Although the easement in *Cargill v Gotts* had obvious similarities to the easement in the present case, in that it involved water, there are important differences. First, like a right of way, the easement in *Cargill's* case involved the owner of the dominant tenement going onto the servient tenement, and indeed stopping on the servient tenement with large vehicles: see the observations of Templeman LJ at p. 448E, at 687. Secondly, *Cargill's* case involved the abstraction of water from the servient tenement, not merely the running off of water over the servient tenement.

5 If what I have called the flexible rule in relation to rights of way is correct, then the defendant clearly succeeds here. There would be no change in the volume of the water discharging from the defendant's land over the plaintiffs' land, and, therefore, whether one looks at the quantum of water or the manner of its discharge, there is no change.

6 If, however, the strict rule applies to rights of way, then I accept that the position is more difficult, but in the end it does not cause me to reach a different conclusion.

It seems to me that, in relation to the point at issue between the parties, the easement in the present case is very different from a right of way. The change of use of the dominant tenement would not increase the quantum of water coming on to the dominant tenement. It would not therefore, by any means, automatically be expected to alter the quantum of water passing from the dominant tenement to the servient tenement, and would most certainly not alter the nature of what passes from the dominant tenement to the servient tenement. ...

Conclusion

In the event, therefore, I propose to determine this issue in favour of the defendant. In reaching this conclusion, I have not relied on cases which were referred to me involving express grants of easements. While nothing in those cases has caused me to doubt the conclusion that I have reached, I think it is safer to rest my reasoning on authorities dealing with easements acquired by prescription.[7a]

[7a]   For a similar approach where an easement of drainage was created by implied grant under LPA 1925, s. 62, see *McAdams Homes Ltd v Robinson* [2004] EWCA Civ 214, [2004] 2 P & CR D7.

QUESTION

A landlord granted to his tenant a right of way 'at all times and for all purposes' over a roadway leading to the tenant's factory. The landlord then started to build over the roadway and planned to construct a long bridge or tunnel through which the tenant could have access to the factory. Although this would not affect the roadway itself, the freedom of manoeuvre, during loading and unloading from the tenant's vehicles, would be restricted, both vertically and laterally. Is the tenant entitled to an injunction to restrain the landlord from building in such a way as to restrict his freedom to load and unload as he had been accustomed to do? See *VT Engineering Ltd v Richard Barland & Co Ltd* (1968) 19 P & CR 890; *Hayns v Secretary of State for the Environment* (1977) 36 P & CR 317.

V. Easement of Light [8]

A. Prescription Act 1832

PRESCRIPTION ACT 1832

3. Claim to the use of light enjoyed for 20 years.—When the access and use of light to and for any dwelling house, workshop, or other building[9] shall have been actually enjoyed therewith for the full period of twenty years without interruption, the right thereto shall be deemed absolute and indefeasible, any local usage or custom to the contrary notwithstanding,[10] unless it shall appear that the same was enjoyed by some consent or agreement expressly made or given for that purpose by deed or writing.

COLLS v HOME AND COLONIAL STORES LTD

[1904] AC 179 (HL, Earl of HALSBURY LC, Lords MACNAGHTEN, DAVEY, ROBERTSON and LINDLEY)

The Home and Colonial Stores were the lessees of a building in Shoreditch where they carried on their business. They brought an action for an injunction against Colls to restrain him from building on the opposite side of the road. JOYCE J found as a fact that, even after the erection of the building, the Home and Colonial Stores premises would be 'well and sufficiently lighted for all ordinary purposes of occupancy as a place of business'. JOYCE J refused an injunction and was reversed by the Court of Appeal.

Held (reversing the Court of Appeal). Injunction refused.

LORD LINDLEY: The language of section 3 of the Prescription Act shews that in order to acquire a right to a light there must be—(1) Access and use of light, not access alone. Access here is understood to refer to free passage of light over the

[8]   C & B, pp. 605–607; Gray, pp. 489–491; M & W, paras. 18.163–18.170, 18.201–18.207; MM, pp. 439–441, 445–446; Gale, paras. 4-21 to 4-34, 7-01 to 7-30; Jackson, pp. 133–137, 156–166; Bickford-Smith and Francis, *Rights of Light: The Modern* Law (2000); Ellis, *Rights to Light* (1989).

[9]   *Allen v Greenwood* [1980] Ch 119, [1979] 1 All ER 819, p. 778, post (greenhouse); *Carr-Saunders v Dick McNeil Associates Ltd* [1986] 1 WLR 922, [1988] 2 All ER 888 (dominant owner's right was for access of light to building as a whole and not to any particular room; therefore there was a right to light to windows of rooms produced by sub-division).

[10] *Bowring Services Ltd v Scottish Widows' Fund & Life Assurance* [1995] 1 EGLR 158 (custom of City of London).

servient tenement (see per Fry LJ, in *Scott v Pape* (1886) 31 ChD at 575, and per Kay J, in *Cooper v Straker* (1888) 40 ChD 21). (2) Such access and use must be to and for some dwelling-house, workshop, or other building (as to which see *Harris v De Pinna* (1886) 33 ChD 238). (3) Such access and use must be actually enjoyed therewith. (4) Such enjoyment must be without interruption for twenty years. (5) If all these are proved, the right to the access and use of light so enjoyed becomes absolute and indefeasible, unless it can be explained by some deed or writing.

Pausing here for a moment, it will be observed that the statute does not in terms confer a right to light, but rather assumes its acquisition by use and enjoyment, and declares it to be 'absolute and indefeasible'.

Again, your Lordships will observe that nothing is said about enjoyment as of right; and notwithstanding section 5 of the Act, which refers to enjoyment as of right, it was early decided that as regards light claimed under section 3 enjoyment as of right need not be alleged or proved, and that the right, whatever it may be, is acquired by twenty years' use and enjoyment without interruption and without written consent: see *Truscott v Merchant Taylors' Co* (1856) 11 Exch 855 and *Frewen v Phillips* (1861) 11 CBNS 449; *Simper v Foley* (1862) 2 John & H 555 and *Harbridge v Warwick* (1849) 3 Exch 557. This was not so under the old law.

As regards use and enjoyment, there are some instructive decisions on unfinished and uninhabited houses, and on windows kept closed by shutters. These decisions shew that a right to light may be acquired in respect of a house which has stood for twenty years without being occupied or even finished so as to be fit for occupation; and that the fact that shutters have been closed for some months at a time does not prevent the acquisition of a right to light through the windows: see *Courtauld v Legh* (1869) LR 4 Exch 126; *Cooper v Straker* (1888) 40 ChD 21; *Colls v Laugher* [1894] 3 Ch 659; *Smith v Baxter* [1900] 2 Ch 138.

These decisions did not, however, turn upon or settle with any precision the amount of light to which a right is acquired by twenty years' user. Nor is the statute clear upon this point. ...

The doctrine laid down in *Back v Stacey* (1826) 2 C & P 465, as I understand it, is the same as that laid down, although in somewhat different language, by the Court of Appeal in *Kelk v Pearson* (1871) 6 Ch App 809 and *City of London Brewery Co v Tennant* (1873) 9 Ch App 212, and must, I think, be taken as finally established and as good sound law, which your Lordships should adopt, notwithstanding the observations in the Irish case of *Mackey v Scottish Widows' Fund Assurance Society* (1877) IR 11 Eq 541. That doctrine, as stated in *City of London Brewery Co v Tennant*, is that generally speaking an owner of ancient lights is entitled to sufficient light according to the ordinary notions of mankind for the comfortable use and enjoyment of his house as a dwelling-house, if it is a dwelling-house, or for the beneficial use and occupation of the house if it is a warehouse, a shop, or other place of business (1873) 9 Ch App at 217. The expressions 'the ordinary notions of mankind', 'comfortable use and enjoyment', and 'beneficial use and occupation' introduce elements of uncertainty; but similar uncertainty has always existed and exists still in all cases of nuisance, and in this country an obstruction of light has commonly been regarded as a nuisance, although the right to light has been regarded as a peculiar kind of easement. ...

The expression 'right to light' is sanctioned by the Prescription Act, and is convenient; but its use is apt to lead to error and to forgetfulness of the burden thrown on the servient tenement. This burden, however, ought never to be lost sight of in considering the extent of the right claimed in respect of the dominant tenement.

But the adoption of the more flexible standard of comfort and convenience has introduced difficulties of a serious nature, especially when dealing with places of business, and it is not surprising that different views on this subject should have been taken, and that the decisions upon it should be inconsistent with each other. ...

There is no rule of law that if a person has 45 degrees of unobstructed light through a particular window left to him he cannot maintain an action for a nuisance caused by diminishing the light which formerly came through that window: *Theed v Debenham* (1876) 2 ChD 165. [11] But experience shews that it is, generally speaking, a fair working rule to consider that no substantial injury is done to him where an angle of 45 degrees is left to him, especially if there is good light from other directions as well. The late Lord Justice Cotton pointed this out in *Ecclesiastical Commissioners for England v Kino* (1880) 14 ChD 213 at 228; see also *Parker v First Avenue Hotel Co* (1883) 24 ChD 282.

As regards light from other quarters, such light cannot be disregarded; for, as pointed out by James V-C, in the *Dyers' Co v King* (1870) LR 9 Eq 438, the light from other quarters, and the light the obstruction of which is complained of, may be so much in excess of what is protected by law as to render the interference complained of non-actionable. I apprehend, however, that light to which a right has not been acquired by grant or prescription, and of which the plaintiff may be deprived at any time, ought not to be taken into account. (See the case just cited.)

The purpose for which a person may desire to use a particular room or building in future does not either enlarge or diminish the easement which he has acquired. If he chooses in future to use a well-lighted room or building for a lumber-room for which little light is required, he does not lose his right to use the same room or building for some other purpose for which more light is required. *Aynsley v Glover* (1875) 10 Ch App 283 is in accordance with this view. But if a room or building has been so built as to be badly lighted, the owner or occupier cannot by enlarging the windows or altering the purpose for which he uses it increase the burden on the servient tenement. *Martin v Goble* (1808) 1 Camp 320, where a malthouse was turned into a workhouse, may, I think, be upheld on this principle; and the observations of Wood V-C on *Martin v Goble* in *Dent v Auction Mart Co* (1866) LR 2 Eq 238 support this view. ...

Joyce J was asked for an injunction and he refused it, and, in my opinion, quite rightly. He came to the conclusion that although there would be a sensible diminution of light and some inconvenience to the plaintiffs, yet they had not established by twenty years' user a right to all the light which they had had, and that the obstruction complained of would not amount to an actionable nuisance, and so infringe the plaintiff's right. The Court of Appeal, taking a different view of the amount of light to which the plaintiffs were entitled, reversed this decision, and ordered a partial demolition of the buildings erected by the defendants. For the reasons already given, I have come to the conclusion that this was wrong. [12]

---

[11] Nor is there a rule of law that if half a room at table height is receiving one or more lumens the room as a whole is adequately lit: *Ough v King* [1967] 1 WLR 1547, [1967] 3 All ER 859; *Frogmore Developments Ltd v Shirayama Shokusan Ltd* [2000] 1 EGLR 121 (grant of right to 'the free and unobstructed passage of light and air to the premises at all times' held to entitle grantee only to a degree of light which satisfies the test in *Colls v Home and Colonial Stores*).

[12] See *Pugh v Howells* (1984) 48 P & CR 298, where a mandatory injunction was granted; *Blue Town Investments Ltd v Higgs and Hill plc* [1990] 1 WLR 696, [1990] 2 All ER 897; *Marine and General Mutual Life Assurance Society v St. James' Real Estate Co Ltd* [1991] 38 EG 230 (measure of damages); *Voyce v Voyce* (1991) 62 P & CR 290 (right of light enforceable against equitable owner); *Deakins v Hookings* [1994] 1 EGLR 190; (1994) 144 NLJ 875 (H. W. Wilkinson).

In **Allen v Greenwood** [1980] Ch 119, [1979] 1 All ER 819, [13] the plaintiffs were the owners of 13 Woodtop Avenue, Rochdale, in which there was a greenhouse. After the greenhouse had been in use as an ordinary domestic greenhouse for more than 20 years, the defendants erected a fence on their adjoining property. This left sufficient light in the greenhouse for working in it, but insufficient for growing plants ('tomatoes, geraniums, stocks, anti-rrhinums, marigolds, zinnias, violets, pansies, the red ones that are rather tender'). The plaintiffs brought an action for injunctions to restrain the defendants from causing a nuisance by diminution of the access of the light to the greenhouse.

In granting the injunctions, the Court of Appeal (BUCKLEY, ORR and GOFF LJJ) held that the light required for the normal use of a greenhouse is ordinary, and also that a right to a specially high degree of light may be acquired by prescription. The Court rejected 'an overriding argument' that 'in any event one can only prescribe a right to light, whether ordinary or special in degree, for purposes of illumination, not a right to the direct rays of the sun, or to heat, or to other beneficial properties from the sun's rays'. GOFF LJ said at 132, at 826:

'In my judgment, therefore, the crux of this case at the end of the day is the overriding argument, which I must now consider.

The defendants argue on this as follows. (1) In *Colls' Case* [1904] AC 179, p. 775, ante the House of Lords was seeking to limit, or restrict, the extent of the right to light, so as to prevent undue restrictions on the development or improvement of surrounding land or buildings, and the court should be very chary of any extension of the right. (2) Although the standards prescribed by the speeches in *Colls'* case are expressed in terms susceptible of a wider interpretation, in their context they must be taken as referring to illumination only. (3) In all cases, at least since *Colls*, the right to light has been tested or measured in terms of illumination only. They refer, for example, to Mr Waldram's calculations and the theory of the "grumble point:" see *Charles Semon & Co Ltd v Bradford Corpn* [1922] 2 Ch 737, 746–747, and to *Hortons' Estate Ltd v James Beattie Ltd* [1927] 1 Ch 75, where the question was whether the extent of the right to light should vary according to locality, and Russell J said, at 78: "The human eye requires as much light for comfortable reading and sewing in Darlington Street, Wolverhampton, as in Mayfair." Mr Maddocks on the defendants' behalf, in his supporting argument, referred also to *Warren v Brown* [1900] 2 QB 722, 725, where the test was stated to be "all ordinary purposes of inhabitancy or business," and to the test applied by the Court of Appeal in *Ough v King* [1967] 1 WLR 1657, [1967] 3 All ER 859, ordinary notions of contemporary mankind. These, however, I think, are at best neutral and possibly tell the other way, since a greenhouse is perfectly normal and ordinary in private gardens. ... (6) In reality or in substance the injury here is not deprivation of light, but of heat or other energising properties of the sun and it is the plant life and not the human beings who are deprived.

I do not think this last point is in any case wholly accurate, as plants need light as well as heat, but it seems to me, with all respect to Blackett-Ord V-C and to counsel, to lead to an absurd conclusion. It cannot, I think, be right to say that there is no nuisance because one can see to go in and out of a greenhouse and to pot plants which will not flourish, and to pick fruit which cannot properly be developed and ripened, still less because one can see to read a book.

[13]   [1979] Conv 298 (F. R. Crane); [1984] Conv 408 (A. H. Hudson); Conv Prec 19–32. See also *Carr-Saunders v Dick McNeil Associates Ltd* [1986] 1 WLR 922, [1986] 2 All ER 888, p. 715, n. 9, ante.

The plaintiffs answer all this simply by submitting that they are entitled, by virtue of their prescriptive right to light, to all the benefits of the light, including the rays of the sun. Warmth, they say, is an inseparable product of daylight, and they stress the absurd conclusion which I have already mentioned, to which the contrary argument inevitably leads. This reply commends itself to me, and I adopt it.

So the overriding argument, in my judgment, does not prevail, and for the reasons I have already given the plaintiffs are right, both on their primary and their alternative case, and I would allow this appeal.

I desire, however, to add one important safeguarding proviso to this judgment. On other facts, particularly where one has solar heating (although that may not arise for some years) it may be possible and right to separate the heat, or some other property of the sun, from its light, and in such a case a different result might be reached. I leave that entirely open for decision when it arises. My judgment in this case is based upon the fact that this was a perfectly ordinary greenhouse, being used in a perfectly normal and ordinary manner, which user has, by the defendants' acts, been rendered substantially less beneficial than it was throughout the period of upwards of 20 years before action brought, and if necessary upon the fact that all this was known to the defendants and their predecessors for the whole of the relevant time.'

In **Morgan v Fear** [1907] AC 425, it was held that a tenant could, by 20 years' enjoyment of access to light from neighbouring land in the occupation of another tenant of the same landlord, prescribe for an easement of light under section 3. The House of Lords relied upon established authority, Lord LOREBURN LC said at 428:

'The question ... is whether a right can be acquired by a termor over land held by another termor under the same reversion, by virtue of section 3 of the Prescription Act. This has been decided in the affirmative as long ago as 1861, in *Frewen v Phillips* (1861) 11 CB NS 449, and the same view was expressly indicated in *Mitchell v Cantrill* (1887) 37 ChD 56. I think it is accurate to say that that rule of law has been acted upon for forty-six years. I cannot advise your Lordships to disturb so well settled a rule.'

Prescription is in favour of the fee simple owner, and even in the case of an easement of light, there cannot be prescription in favour of a leaseholder. [14]

QUESTIONS

Why can prescription not operate in favour of a leasehold estate? Compare:
  Morgan v Fear [1907] AC 425;
  Kilgour v Gaddes [1904] 1 KB 457, p. 745, ante;
  Wheaton v Maple & Co [1893] 3 Ch 48, p. 746, ante.
  Simmons v Dobson [1991] 1 WLR 720, [1991] 4 All ER 25, p. 747, ante.

[14]   *Wheaton v Maple & Co* [1893] 3 Ch 48.

B. Rights of Light Act 1959

RIGHTS OF LIGHT ACT 1959 [15]

2. Registration of notice in lieu of obstruction of access of light.—(1) For the purpose of preventing the access and use of light from being taken to be enjoyed without interruption, any person who is an owner of land (in this and the next following section referred to as 'the servient land') over which light passes to a dwelling-house, workshop or other building (in this and the next following section referred to as 'the dominant building') may apply to the local authority in whose area the dominant building is situated for the registration of a notice under this section. [16]

3. Effect of registered notice and proceedings relating thereto.—(1) Where, in pursuance of an application made in accordance with the last preceding section, a notice is registered thereunder, then, for the purpose of determining whether any person is entitled (by virtue of the Prescription Act, 1832, or otherwise) to a right to the access of light to the dominant building across the servient land, the access of light to that building across that land shall be treated as obstructed to the same extent, and with the like consequences, as if an opaque structure, of the dimensions specified in the application. —

   (*a*) had, on the date of registration of the notice, been erected in the position on the servient land specified in the application, and had been so erected by the person who made the application, and

   (*b*) had remained in that position during the period for which the notice has effect and had been removed at the end of that period.

(2) For the purposes of this section a notice registered under the last preceding section shall be taken to have effect until either —

   (*a*) the registration is cancelled, or

   (*b*) the period of one year beginning with the date of registration of the notice expires, or

   (*c*) in the case of a notice registered in pursuance of an application accompanied by a certificate issued under paragraph (*b*) of subsection (3) of the last preceding section, the period specified in the certificate expires without such a further certificate as is mentioned in paragraph (*c*) of subsection (5) of that section having before the end of that period been lodged with the local authority, [17]

and shall cease to have effect on the occurrence of any of those events.

(3) Subject to the following provisions of this section, any person who, if such a structure as is mentioned in subsection (1) of this section had been erected as therein mentioned, would have had a right of action in any court in respect of that structure, on the grounds that he was entitled to a right to the access of light to the dominant building across the servient land, and that the

---

[15] This is based on recommendations in the Report of the Committee on Rights of Light (1958 Comnd 473); [1959] CLJ 182 (H. W. R. Wade). See *Hawker v Tomalin* (1969) 20 P & CR 550 at 551, per HARMAN LJ.

[16] Lands Tribunal Rules 1996 (SI 1996 No. 1002); Lands Tribunal Fees Rules 1996 (SI 1996 No. 1021); Part VI; Local Land Charges Rules 1977 (SI 1977 No. 985), r. 10. The application must be accompanied by a certificate from the Lands Tribunal, 938 definitive and 211 temporary certificates were issued between 1959 and 1980; see (1978) 122 SJ 515, 534; (1981) 259 EG 123 (W. A. Greene).

[17] *Bowring Services Ltd v Scottish Widows' Fund & Life Assurance Society* [1995] 1 EGLR 158 (calculation of date from which time runs).

said right was infringed by that structure, shall have the like right of action in that court in respect of the registration of a notice under the last preceding section:

Provided that an action shall not be begun by virtue of this subsection after the notice in question has ceased to have effect.

(4) Where, at any time during the period for which a notice registered under the last preceding section has effect, the circumstances are such that, if the access of light to the dominant building had been enjoyed continuously from a date one year earlier than the date on which the enjoyment thereof in fact began, a person would have had a right of action in any court by virtue of the last preceding subsection in respect of the registration of the notice, that person shall have the like right of action in that court by virtue of this subsection in respect of the registration of the notice.

(6) For the purposes of section four of the Prescription Act, 1832 (under which a period of enjoyment of any of the rights to which that Act applies is not to be treated as interrupted except by a matter submitted to or acquiesced in for one year after notice thereof) —

(*a*) as from the date of registration of a notice under the last preceding section, all persons interested in the dominant building or any part thereof shall be deemed to have notice of the registration thereof and of the person on whose application it was registered;

(*b*) until such time as an action is brought by virtue of subsection (3) or subsection (4) of this section in respect of the registration of a notice under the last preceding section, all persons interested in the dominant building or any part thereof shall be deemed to acquiesce in the obstruction which, in accordance with subsection (1) of this section, is to be treated as resulting from the registration of the notice;

(*c*) as from the date on which such an action is brought, no person shall be treated as submitting to or acquiescing in that obstruction:

Provided that if, in any such action, the court decides against the claim of the plaintiff, the court may direct that the preceding provisions of this subsection shall apply in relation to the notice as if that action had not been brought.

VI. Extinguishment [18]

Easements and profits may be extinguished by statute (e.g. under an Inclosure Act or the Town and Country Planning Act 1971, [19] or as a result of failure to register under the Commons Registration Act 1965 [20]), by release, express or implied, and by unity of both ownership and possession.

---

[18]   C & B, pp. 610–614; Gray, pp. 533–537; M & W, paras. 18.176–18.191; MM, pp. 441–443; Smith, pp. 524–526; Gale, paras. 12-01 to 12-82; Jackson, pp. 195–200.

[19]   Ss. 118, 127. See also Housing Act 1985, s. 295(1)–(3); New Towns Act 1981, s. 19, as amended by Telecommunications Act 1984, s. 109(1), Sch. 4, para. 79(3); TCPA 1990, ss. 236, 237(1); *R v City of London Council, ex p Mystery of the Barbers of London* (1996) 73 P & CR 59.

[20]   S. 1(2), p. 60, ante.

A. Implied Release Abandonment

In **Tehidy Minerals Ltd v Norman** [1971] 2 QB 528, [1971] 2 All ER 475,[1] BUCKLEY LJ said at 553, at 492:

'Abandonment of an easement or of a profit à prendre can only, we think, be treated as having taken place where the person entitled to it has demonstrated a fixed intention never at any time thereafter to assert the right himself or to attempt to transmit it to anyone else.'

The difficulty of proving that an easement or profit à prendre has been released by abandonment because it has not been exercised for many years has been lessened by LRA 2002, Schedule 3, paragraph 3, p. 163, ante.[2]

In **Huckvale v Aegean Hotels Ltd** (1989) 58 P & CR 163,[3] the Court of Appeal considered a novel claim that an easement can be extinguished by its ceasing to accommodate the dominant tenement. In granting an interlocutory injunction, SLADE J said at 173:

'In the absence of evidence of proof of abandonment, the court should be slow to hold that an easement has been extinguished by frustration, unless the evidence shows clearly that because of a change of circumstances since the date of the original grant there is no practical possibility of its ever again benefiting the dominant tenement in the matter contemplated by that grant.'[4]

MOORE v RAWSON[5]
(1824) 3 B & C 332 (Ct of KB, ABBOTT CJ, BAYLEY, HOLROYD and LITTLEDALE JJ)

The plaintiff's predecessor in title enjoyed easements of light and air in respect of certain windows in a wall of his house. He pulled down this wall and built another wall without any windows. Fourteen years later the defendant erected a building opposite to the plaintiff's blank wall. After another three years the plaintiff opened a window in the blank wall in the place of one of the old windows, and then brought an action for obstruction.

Held. The plaintiff failed, because he had abandoned his rights.

HOLROYD J: I am of the same opinion. It appears that the former owner of the plaintiff's premises at one time was entitled to the house with the windows, so that the light coming to those windows over the adjoining land could not be obstructed by the owner of that land. I think, however, that the right acquired by the enjoyment of the light, continued no longer than the existence of the thing itself in respect of which the party had the right of enjoyment; I mean the house

---

[1]   *Gotobed v Pridmore* (1971) 217 EG 759; *Benn v Hardinge* (1992) 66 P & CR 246 (no abandonment in spite of 175 years of non-user); *Bosomworth v Faber* (1995) 69 P & CR 288; *Snell & Prideaux Ltd v Dutton Mirrors Ltd* [1995] 1 EGLR 259; [1995] Conv 291 (C. J. Davis).

[2]   See H & B, para. 3.107; Law Commission Report on Land Registration for the Twenty-First Century (Law Com No. 271), paras. 8.65, 8.72.

[3]   [1990] Conv 292 (G. Kodilinye).

[4]   The onus of proof lies fairly and squarely on the person who alleges abandonment, and the onus is a very heavy one: *Re Yateley Common* [1977] 1 WLR 840 at 846, [1977] 1 All ER 505 at 511.

[5]   *Crossley & Sons Ltd v Lightowler* (1867) 2 Ch App 478; *Cook v Bath Corpn* (1868) LR 6 Eq 177; *Ecclesiastical Comrs for England v Kino* (1880) 14 ChD 213; *Swan v Sinclair* [1924] 1 Ch 254; affd [1925] AC 227; *Re Yateley Common, Hampshire*, supra.

with the windows; when the house and the windows were destroyed by his own act, the right which he had in respect of them was also extinguished. If, indeed, at the time when he pulled the house down, he had intimated his intention of rebuilding it, the right would not then have been destroyed with the house. If he had done some act to shew that he intended to build another in its place, then the new house, when built, would in effect have been a continuation of the old house, and the rights attached to the old house would have continued. If a man has a right of common attached to his mill, or right of turbary attached to his house, if he pulls down the mill or the house, the right of common or of turbary will prima facie cease. If he shew an intention to build another mill or another house, his right continues. But if he pulls down the house or the mill without shewing any intention to make a similar use of the land, and after a long period of time has elapsed, builds a house or mill corresponding to that which he pulls down, that is not the renovation of the old house or mill, but the creation of a new thing, and the rights which he had in respect of the old house or mill, do not in my opinion attach to the new one. In this case, I think, the building of a blank wall is a stronger circumstance to shew that he had no intention to continue the enjoyment of his light than if he had merely pulled down the house. In that case he might have intended to substitute something in its place. Here, he does in fact substitute quite a different thing, a wall without windows. There is not only nothing to shew that he meant to renovate the house so as to make it a continuance of the old house, but he actually builds a new house different from the old one, thereby shewing that he did not mean to renovate the old house. It seems to me, therefore, that the right is not renewed as it would have been, if, when he pulled down the old house, he had shewn an intention to rebuild it within a reasonable time, although he did not do so eo instanti. [6]

B. Unity of Ownership and Possession

Unity of both ownership and possession may cause extinguishment. [7] 'An unity of possession merely suspends; there must be an unity of ownership to destroy a prescriptive right'. [8] Similarly unity of ownership without unity of possession does not suffice; the easement continues until there is also unity of possession. [9] If an easement is extinguished, it may nevertheless be re-created under the doctrine of *Wheeldon v Burrows* [10] if the land is later severed into its original parts.

In **Richardson v Graham** [1908] 1 KB 39, BUCKLEY LJ said at 44. [11]

'On 29 March 1906, the plaintiffs were entitled to a leasehold interest for a term of years in the dominant tenement. The reversion in the dominant tenement was in one Eadie. The dominant tenement enjoyed over the servient

---

[6] On implied rules for alterations to the servient tenancies, see *Greenwich Healthcare National Health Service Trust v London and Quadrant Housing Trust* [1998] 1 WLR 1749.

[7] *Buckby v Coles* (1814) 5 Taunt 311 (easement); *Tyrringham's Case* (1584) 4 Co Rep 36b at 38a (profit à prendre).

[8] *Canham v Fisk* (1831) 2 Cr & J 126, per BAYLEY B.

[9] *Richardson v Graham* [1908] 1 KB 39.

[10] But not under LPA 1925, s. 62, since there would be no diversity of occupation; p. 728, ante.

[11] This was a case on the easement of light, but, in principle, the rule should apply generally. Cf. *Buckby v Coles*, supra, at 315, 316; M & W, para. 18.191, n. 32.

tenement which was vested in the defendant a prescriptive right to ancient light acquired by user for more than twenty years. On 29 March 1906, Eadie conveyed to the defendant the reversion in the dominant tenement. It is said that the effect of that conveyance was to destroy the easement of ancient light; that is to say, that by acts done by the plaintiffs' lessor and by the owner of the servient tenement the rights enjoyed by the plaintiffs were destroyed.

In my opinion that is not the law. ... So that it is perfectly plain on the authorities that if in this case the two tenements had belonged throughout, not to different owners, but to one owner, but the circumstances were such that a lessee of the dominant tenement had acquired a prescriptive right against the servient tenement, the right would have been good as against all the world. It is said, however, that this case is different because there was not a common owner of the dominant and servient tenement during the whole period, but common ownership of the two tenements arose after the right to light had been acquired. This seems to me an extravagant proposition.'

VII. Law Reform Committee Report on Acquisition of Easements and Profits by Prescription (1966 Cmnd 3100) [12]

There has been judicial criticism of the law relating to the acquisition of easements and profits by prescription. In *Tehidy Minerals Ltd v Norman* [1971] 2 QB 528, [1971] 2 All ER 475, BUCKLEY LJ said at 543, at 484: 'The co-existence of three separate methods of prescribing is, in our view, anomalous and undesirable, for it results in much unnecessary complication and confusion. We hope that it may be possible for the Legislature to effect a long-overdue simplification in this branch of the law.'

In 1966, the Law Reform Committee recommended the abolition of the prescriptive acquisition of easements (para. 32) and of profits à prendre (para. 98); in the former case by a majority of 8–6; in the latter unanimously.

The Committee, however, considered the ways in which prescriptive acquisition—if it should be retained for easements—should operate, and was unanimous on the new system which should be adopted.

The main recommendations, in brief outline, are:

(1) All existing methods of acquisition of easements and profits by prescription should be abolished. This recommendation includes the abolition of prescription at common law and under the doctrine of a lost modern grant, and the repeal of the Prescription Act 1832 (paras. 40, 98, 99(1)–(3)).

(2) Under the new system (for easements only) (para. 99(6)):

(*a*) The prescriptive period should be a period in gross of 12 years (i.e., it need not be 'next before action brought') (paras. 41–43: Prescription Act 1832, section 4; *Hyman v Van den Bergh* [1908] 1 Ch 167, p. 754, ante).

(*b*) There should be no 'disabilities' (para. 44; Prescription Act 1832, sections 7, 8; p. 751, ante).

(*c*) An easement should be capable of being acquired against the owner of a limited interest in the servient land so as to subsist as long as that servient owner's interest subsists (paras. 47–49; pp. 748, 779, ante). Prescription by the owner of a limited interest in the dominant land should continue, as at present, in favour of the freeholder (para. 50). A tenant should be able to prescribe against his landlord and vice-versa (para. 51).

[12]   (1967) 30 MLR 189 (H. W. Wilkinson); Jackson, chap. 15.

(*d*) Enjoyment:
  (i)   by force should not count in favour of the dominant owner (para. 57);
  (ii) must have been actually known to the servient owner or ought reasonably to have been known to him (para. 58);
  (iii) must be of such a kind and frequency as would only be justified by the existence of an easement (para. 59);
  (iv) by consent or agreement should not count. If so enjoyed for one year or more, the consent, like an interruption, would prevent earlier enjoyment being added to later enjoyment for the purpose of making up the required total of 12 years. A consent which is indefinite in duration should operate for one year (paras. 61–63).

(*e*) Notional interruption, on the lines of the Rights of Light Act 1959 (p. 780, ante), should be extended to easements generally: this should be by registration after notice given. Interruption, notional or actual, should endure for 12 months in order to be effective (as at present: Prescription Act 1832, section 4) (para. 75).

(*f*) An easement, acquired by prescription, should be lost by 12 years' continuous non-user (para. 81).

(3) The Committee is unanimous about provisions to facilitate, subject to compensation where appropriate, the acquisition of easements of support for buildings by land or for buildings by buildings (paras. 89–95, 99(8)–(11)).

(4) Shelter should be treated in the same way as support (paras. 96, 99(12): *Phipps v Pears* [1965] 1 QB 76, [1964] 2 All ER, 35, p. 706, ante).

(5) The Lands Tribunal should be empowered to discharge easements or substitute more convenient ones, subject to payment of compensation where appropriate (paras. 97, 99(13)).

Law Commission Annual Report 2002/03 (Law Com No. 280), paras. 7.6–7.7.

'Easements and Analogous Rights and Land Obligations
  7.6 This area of law affects many landowners. However, the law of easements has never been subject to a comprehensive review, and many aspects of the law are now outdated and a cause of difficulty. The most recent edition of the leading practitioners' work, Gale on Easements, supported the need for reform identified by the Law Commission:–

If one stands back from the detail, however, it cannot be denied that there is much that is unsatisfactory about the law of easements. In essence, easements can sometimes be acquired too easily (light and support by prescripton, any easement by mistake under section 62 of the Law of Property Act 1925), are too difficult to detect (because they are overriding interests and not required to be entered on the register) and are impossible to get rid of or to modify (there being in this jurisdiction no equivalent to section 84 of the Law of Property Act 1925 which enables the discharge or modification of restrictive covenants). And there is the Prescription Act.

  7.7 We have started conducting a full review of the current law. Consideration is being given to the Law Commission's earlier work in this[13] and related areas

---

[13] Law Commission Working Paper on Rights Appurtenant to Land 1971 (Law Com No. 36); For Law Commission Reports on Land Obligations, see pp. 1015, 1016, post.

with a view to producing a coherent scheme of land obligations. We hope to publish a consultation paper in the summer of 2004. [14]

QUESTIONS

1.   Consider the arguments for and against the abolition of the acquisition of easements and profits à prendre by prescription. How is the matter affected by the extension of the practice of Registration of Title to land? See the Report, paras. 30–38; Law Commission Consultation Document on Land Registration for the Twenty-First Century 1998 (Law Com No. 254) paras. 10.79–10.94, 10.108–10.112.

2.   'We do not consider that it is necessary or appropriate for the same legal rules to apply to the acquisition of easements by prolonged enjoyment as apply to the acquisition of title to land by adverse possession'. (Para. 36.)

'In spite of the differences between adverse possession and prescription, the same fundamental considerations apply to them.' (Para. 38(*d*).)

Law Reform Committee 14th Report (Acquisition of Easements and Profits by Prescription) 1966 (Cmnd 3100).

With which of these two views do you agree?

3.   How would the facts of *Copeland v Greenhalf* [1952] Ch 488, [1952] 1 All ER 809, p. 700, ante, have to be altered so as to establish a claim:
     (*a*)   to an easement over the plaintiff's land;
     (*b*)   to the plaintiff's land by adverse possession under the Limitation Act 1980?

(1968) 32 Conv (NS) 270 (M. J. Goodman); *Central Midlands Estates Ltd v Leicster Dyers Ltd* [2003] 2 P & CR D2.

4.   In what circumstances can equitable easement be protected under Land Registration Act 2002, paragraph 2 of Schedules 1 and 3 (interests of persons in actual occupation):

Consider (a) rights of way, and (b) rights of storage and parking: *Celsteel Ltd v Alton House Holdings Ltd* [1985] 1 WLR 204 at 219E -F; *Copeland v Greenhalf* [1952] Ch 458. [1952] 1 All ER 809, p. 700, ante; *Wright v Macadam* [1949] 2 KB 744, [1949] 2 All ER 565, p. 723, ante; *Atwood v Bovis Homes Ltd* [2001] Ch 379, [2002] 4 All ER 948, p. 711, ante.

---

[14]   New Zealand's New Property Act, proposed by its Law Commission Report No. 29, provides for the creation of an easement in gross, and for the abolition of the acquisition of easements and profits by prescription: [1994] Conv 428 (H. W. Wilkinson).

11. Mortgages [1]

[1] C & B, chap. 22; Gray, chap 12; M & W, chap 19; MM, chap 13; Smith, chap. 22. See generally Coote, *Law of Mortgages* (9th edn. 1927); Cousins, *Law of Mortgages* (2nd edn. 2001), chap. 22; Fisher and Lightwood, *Law of Mortgage* (11th edn. 2002); *Snell's Equity* (30th edn.), Part IV; Waldock, *Law of Mortgage* (2nd edn. 1950); (1978) 94 LQR 571 (P. Jackson); Code of Mortgage Lending Practice; *Council of Mortgage Lenders Handbook* (2nd edn, 2002); American Law Institute, *Restatement of the Law of Mortgages* (1997).

I. Introduction

The mortgage transaction has, throughout its history, been a collection of contradictions. Maitland described it as 'one long suppressio veri and suggestio falsi'. [2] Before 1926, the usual form of mortgage of a fee simple was by conveyance of that fee simple subject to an undertaking by the mortgagee to reconvey on payment, at a stated time in the future, of all moneys due; mortgages of leaseholds were by assignment or by sub-demise. In 1925, mortgages of freeholds could only be by way of demise and mortgages of leaseholds by sub-demise; or, in either case by charge by deed expressed to be by way of legal mortgage in accordance with section 87(1) of the Law of Property Act 1925. In 2003 the obsolescent demise and sub-demise became obsolete. [3] Statutory provision for the creation of charges by way of legal mortgage at last made it possible for a mortgage transaction to appear to be what it really is – the charging of property as security for the repayment of a loan. The historical practice of conveying an estate in land to the mortgagee had hidden the true nature of the transaction, and had made it necessary for Courts of Chancery to make great exertions to prevent the mortgagee from using the property as something more than a security for the debt.

The legal mortgage before 1926 and the mortgage by demise or sub-demise were drafted so as to appear to give the mortgagee something more than a security; they provided for reconveyance, or for cesser of the demise respectively, on repayment of all sums due at a time in the future. This was usually six months ahead, although in most cases there was no intention on the part of either party that the payment should be made by that date. The mortgagor's legal right was then lost and the only protection that he received was from equity; he was given an equitable right to redeem, and this right was held by a series of cases to be absolute and inviolable. [4]

In accordance with the proviso for redemption given by the mortgagee, the mortgagor has a legal, or contractual, right to redeem and to obtain a reconveyance of the property; and by virtue of his right to obtain specific performance of the mortgagee's covenant to reconvey, equity considered him to be the owner of the land subject to the mortgage. Equity's insistence upon the inviolability of the mortgagor's right to redeem, even after his contractual right had ended, led to the creation of an equitable right to redeem; and equity's willingness to enforce this right at any time on payment of all sums due meant that he continued to be the owner in equity subject to the mortgage. The equitable interest which he owns is called the Equity of Redemption; and just as, centuries earlier, equitable estates in land became proprietary by the protection given by equity to the cestui que use against everyone except the bona fide purchaser of the legal estate for value without notice, [5] so also the equity of redemption was regarded as a

---

On law reform, see the Law Commission Report on Land Mortgages 1991 (Law Com No. 204, HC 5), Part X, p. 920, post; and Unjust Credit Transactions: Report by the Director General of Fair Trading (1991), p. 850, post.

[2]   Maitland, p. 182; Simpson, *A History of the Land Law* (2nd edn. 1986), pp. 141–143, 242–247. In *Samuel v Jarrah & Wood Paving Corpn Ltd* [1904] AC 323 at 326, Lord MACNAGHTEN said: 'No one . . . by the light of nature ever understood an English mortgage of real estate.' See also *National Westminster Bank v Kitch* (1996) 74 P & CR 98 at 101 (writ issued for sums due on two overdrawn accounts secured by mortgage held not to be a 'mortgage action').

[3]   LRA 2002, s. 23(1), p. 785, post.

[4]   See pp. 801, et seq.

[5]   See p. 24, ante.

proprietary interest which could be bought, sold, mortgaged, and, if it were personalty, pass to the Crown as bona vacantia.[6]

Since the interest which the mortgagor retained after parting with the legal fee simple in a mortgage by conveyance before 1926 was merely equitable, all subsequent mortgages were of necessity equitable. In a mortgage by demise after 1925, the mortgagor retains an equitable interest in the term granted, the interest being the equity of redemption of the term; but he also retains the legal fee simple from which he can create subsequent legal mortgages taking effect subject to the prior mortgage and created either by legal charge or by demise for a period, usually a day longer than the first legal mortgage. The change introduced in 1925 was one of form rather than substance. For 'the equity of redemption has in no way lost its importance. A fee simple giving the right to possession of land only when a lease for 3,000 years has expired is of little value compared with the right to insist that the fee simple shall forthwith be freed from the term of 3,000 years on payment of the money due.'[7]

The interest which the mortgagee acquires is a real and not merely a personal security, which prevails against the general body of creditors in the event of the mortgagor's bankruptcy. He is not only a creditor of the mortgagor; he is a secured creditor. As long as the mortgaged property remains worth as much as the debt, the mortgagee will receive payment in full; but if it falls in value and becomes worth less than the debt, the mortgagee will only be a secured creditor to the extent of its value, and he must prove in the mortgagor's bankruptcy with the unsecured creditors for the remainder of the debt.

Courts of Equity have looked upon a mortgage transaction as one in which the terms were likely to be dictated by the mortgagee. In early days the mortgagor was at a disadvantage in that he was in need of money and must take it on the mortgagee's terms; it was a lender's market. And, while the law followed the maxim 'caveat emptor' in the affairs of merchants and trade, equity not surprisingly took a different view in the case of mortgages. The fact that mortgagors were, in the early days, often members of great families and mortgagees were professional money lenders no doubt contributed to some extent to the development. A consideration of the changed position of borrowers and lenders in the capitalist society of the present day will suggest that the old cases should be accepted with some reserve. The cases on this subject show a continual struggle between the principle of binding precedent and the requirements of a changing society; they can only be understood with this in mind. Those which were decided about the turn of the twentieth century do not create the principle they apply. That litigation was a challenge to the validity of the principle laid down in earlier centuries, but generally it succeeded only in re-affirming the old principles; it was not until 1914[8] that substantial progress was made.

The problem at the present day is the extent to which these old rules still hold good. A modern mortgage of land is usually a transaction between an individual house-buyer and a building society or other institutional lender,[9] or forms part of a development project embarked upon by property financiers. The

---

[6]   *Re Sir Thomas Spencer Wells* [1933] Ch 29, p. 801, post.
[7]   M & W, para. 19.022.
[8]   *Kreglinger v New Patagonia Meat and Cold Storage Co Ltd* [1914] AC 25, p. 816, post.
[9]   Lord DIPLOCK in *Pettitt v Pettitt* [1970] AC 777 at 824, [1969] 2 All ER 385 at 414 referred to 'a real-property-mortgaged-to-a-building-society-owning democracy'. For the two main types of mortgage, the endowment mortgage and the instalment or repayment mortgage, see p. 867, n. 11, post.

small man is protected from unfair pressure by the high standards set by building societies and also by statutory safeguards, [10] and the financiers must look after themselves.

The mortgage industry is big business. According to the Financial Services Authority the total assets of the 65 Building Societies [11] in 2001 were £171,375 million, the number of borrowers was 2,750,000 and of shareholders 20,310,000. In 2001 itself the societies made 509,000 advances, totalling £31,845 million. [12] In addition to Building Societies, there are three other substantial institutional lenders of money; Banks, Insurance Companies, and Local Authorities. The Consumer Credit Act 1974 [13] gives protection to individuals who borrow not more than £15,000, usually by way of second mortgage. The rate of interest charged is fixed by the individual lending institution and is related to interest rates applicable to the market generally. The average rate is currently 6.50 per cent.

When a borrower falls into arrears with his payments, a building society does all it can to avoid repossession, but if it has to take action to enforce the security, difficult social questions arise. The mortgagor has given as security, not an investment, but his home. And a mortgagor who has defaulted with one building society will have difficulty in borrowing money from another.

Most of the litigation is in respect of applications for possession. [14] The mortgagee is, in law, entitled to possession 'before the ink is dry on the mortgage.' [15] A building society will not go into possession without a court order; but it will go into possession before sale in order to be able to give vacant possession to a purchaser. Applications for possession are thus usually a preliminary to sale by the mortgagee. It is in this context that questions arise at the present day concerning the mortgagor's need for protection, and mortgagors of dwelling houses have had statutory protection since 1970. [16]

———————

Central Statistical Office Social Trends 27 (2004 edn.), pp. 162–164

'A feature of home ownership in the United Kingdom is the relatively large number of homes purchased with a mortgage. Approximately three quarters of house purchases are financed with a mortgage loan facility. In 2002, 76 per cent of loans for home purchase were obtained through banks and 17 per cent through building societies, with 7 per cent through other lenders.

Those buying a home can choose from a variety of different types of mortgage, the most common being repayment and interest-only. With repayment mortgages

———

[10]   Building Societies Act 1986, as amended by Building Societies Act 1997 which considerably extend the range of their activities. A society may now lend for all forms of housing, rented as well as owner occupied and, with a few exceptions may carry on any type of business within the terms of its memorandum. See generally Wurtzburg and Mills, *Building Society Law* ; Cousins, chap. 8; Fisher and Lightwood, paras. 12.73–12.79; the Annual Reports of the Building Societies Commission.

[11]   Reduced by mergers, conversions and takeovers.

[12]   Building Societies: Statistical Tables 2002.

[13]   See p, 846, post.

[14]   See p. 855, post.

[15]   Per HARMAN J, in *Four-Maids Ltd v Dudley Marshall (Properties) Ltd* [1957] Ch 317 at 320, [1957] 2 All ER 35 at 36, p. 855, post.

[16]   Administration of Justice Act 1970, s. 36. On mortgage fraud, see Clarke, *Mortgage Fraud* (1991); [1993] Conv 181 (H. W. Wilkinson); Theft (Amendment) Act 1996, creating two new offences by inserting s. 15 A (obtaining a money transfer by deception) and 24 A (dishonestly retaining a wrongful credit). See Law Commission Report Offences of Dishonesty: Money Transfers (1996) Law Com No 243.

the debt and the interest are both repaid during the life of the mortgage (usually 25 years). Around 81 per cent of all new mortgages were standard repayment mortgages in 2002. Interest-only mortgages, which include endowment policies, ISAs (individual savings accounts) and personal pensions, account for the bulk of other mortgages. Since the late 1980s there has been a decrease in the popularity of endowment mortgages because of the possibility that investments may not grow fast enough to repay the capital borrowed. In 1988, 83 per cent of new mortgages for house purchase were endowment mortgages but by 2002 this had fallen to 5 per cent. The proportion of fixed (as opposed to variable) rate mortgages is markedly lower in the United Kingdom than in many other countries. Research published by the Council of Mortgage Lenders in July 2002 suggested that flexible mortgages are accounting for a rapidly growing share of the mortgage market. Flexible mortgages allow people to pay off some of the loan early through overpayments and lump sum investments, and to borrow funds back by withdrawing lump sums.

Affordability is a concern to both first-time buyers and moving owner-occupiers. Although recent UK base interest rates have been at low levels compared with previously, repaying mortgages still often consumes a substantial proportion of people's income. In 1972, first-time buyers spent on average, 15 per cent of their household income on mortgage repayments and owner occupiers who moved and bought a new home, 14 per cent. The proportion of income paid as a mortgage in recent years is higher: in 2002 first-time buyers spent 18 per cent of their income on mortgage repayments and moving owner-occupiers, 17 per cent. These were not as high as during the last property boom when the proportion paid by first-time buyers in 1990 was 28 per cent and 26 per cent for moving owner-occupiers.

The warning given with every mortgage is that "your home is at risk if you do not keep up repayments on a mortgage or other loan secured on it" and the same is true of rented property. When people fall behind with rent or mortgage repayments and are unable to reach an alternative payment arrangement with their landlord or mortgage lender, a county court possession summons may be issued, with the view to obtaining a court order. Not all orders will result in repossession; it is not uncommon for courts to make suspended orders which provide for arrears to be paid off within a reasonable period. If the court decides not to adjourn the proceedings or suspend a possession order, the warrant will be executed and the home repossessed by the landlord or mortgagee. As base interest rates and mortgage interest rates rose during the late 1980s and early 1990s, repayments became increasingly difficult for some people, particularly those who had borrowed a high proportion of the value of their properties. Consequently arrears and repossessions increased during this time. However, largely owing to lower interest rates, arrears and repossessions have fallen over the last decade. At its peak in 1992, the number of loans in arrears by 6 to 12 months in the United Kingdom was 205,000. By 2002 this had fallen to 34,000 and the number of homes repossessed was 12,000. According to the Survey of English Housing, many people in England in 2001/02 cited more than one reason for their arrears but for the vast majority, the loss of income was the main contributor.

Regardless of whether the home is owned or rented, housing constitutes a significant proportion of a household's budget. These costs include, for example, structural insurance, council tax payments and repairs and maintenance, as well as mortgage interest payments or rent (net of housing benefit).

In 2002/03 the median weekly rent (before housing benefit) for those living in private accommodation in England was £121. Like house prices, rents vary according to location. Private rents, which are typically higher than social sector rents, ranged from £65 a week in the North to £162 a week in London. The cost of renting from the local authority ranged from £45 in the North to £64 in London.'

II. Methods of Creation

A. Legal Mortgages and Legal Charges [17]

i. UNREGISTERED LAND

LAW OF PROPERTY ACT 1925

85. Mode of mortgaging freeholds.—(1) A mortgage of an estate in fee simple shall only be capable of being effected at law either by a demise for a term of years absolute, subject to a provision for cesser on redemption, or by a charge by deed expressed to be by way of legal mortgage:

Provided that a first mortgagee shall have the same right to the possession of documents as if his security included the fee simple.

(2) Any purported conveyance of an estate in fee simple by way of mortgage made after the commencement of this Act shall (to the extent of estate of the mortgagor) operate as a demise of the land to the mortgagee for a term of years absolute, without impeachment for waste, but subject to cesser on redemption, in manner following, namely:—

   (*a*) A first or only mortgagee shall take a term of three thousand years from the date of the mortgage;

   (*b*) A second or subsequent mortgagee shall take a term (commencing from the date of the mortgage) one day longer than the term vested in the first or other mortgagee whose security ranks immediately before that of such second or subsequent mortgagee; . . .

(3) Subsection (2) does not apply to registered land, but, subject to that, this section applies whether or not the land is registered land and whether

---

17   C & B, pp. 723–732; Gray, pp. 541–549; M & W, paras. 19.006–19.041; MM, pp. 491–503; Smith, pp. 560–561; Waldock, pp. 19–43; Fisher and Lightwood, paras. 3.1–3.5, 3.17–3.53. For a mortgagor's action in negligence against (*a*) his solicitor where he enters into a mortgage as a result of the solicitor's failure to give proper advice, see *Forster v Outred & Co* [1982] 1 WLR 86, [1982] 2 All ER 753; *Mortgage Express v Bowerman* [1996] 2 All ER 836 (duty of solicitor acting for mortgagor and sub-purchaser to inform mortgagor of price increase); *National Home Loans Corpn plc v Giffen Couch & Archer* [1998] 1 WLR 207 (solicitor acting for both mortgagor and mortgagee under a duty to inform mortgagee of mortgagor's default in previous mortgage); (*b*) the mortgagee's surveyor on whose negligent report he relied, see *Smith v Eric S Bush* [1990] 1 AC 831, [1989] 2 All ER 514; [1989] Conv 359 (C. Francis); [1989] CLJ 306 (W. V. H. Rogers); (1989) 105 LQR 511 (D. Allen); (1989) 52 MLR 841 (T. Kaye); *Beaumont v Humberts* [1990] 2 EGLR 166; *Roberts v J Hampson & Co* [1990] 1 WLR 94, [1989] 2 All ER 504; and (*c*) a valuer: *Banque Bruxelles Lambert SA v Eagle Star Insurance Co* [1997] AC 191 (extent of liability of valuer who provided mortgagee with negligent overvaluation, where mortgagee would not have lent if it had received careful valuation); (1997) 113 LQR 1 (J. Stapleton); [1997] CLJ 19 (J. O'Sullivan); *Platform Homes Ltd v Oyston Shipways Ltd* [1996] 2 EGLR 110, per JACOB J ('valuation is an art not a science, but it is not astrology'); [2002] 2 AC 190, [1999] 1 All ER 833, [1998] EGCS 148 (imprudent lending policy can constitute contributory negligence under LR (Contributory Negligence) Act 1945, s. 1 when loan made in reliance on negligent valuation); *United Bank of Kuwait v Prudential Property Services Ltd* [1994] 30 EG 103 (criteria for valuation; contributory negligence of mortgagee in making advance); RICS Appraisal and Valuation Manual: Approved European Property Valuation Standards.

or not the mortgage is expressed to be made by way of trust for sale or otherwise. [18]

86. Mode of mortgaging leaseholds.—(1) A mortgage of a term of years absolute shall only be capable of being effected at law either by a subdemise for a term of years absolute, less by one day at least than the term vested in the mortgagor, and subject to a provision for cesser on redemption, or by a charge by deed expressed to be by way of legal mortgage; and where a licence to subdemise by way of mortgage is required, such licence shall not be unreasonably refused. [19]

Provided that a first mortgagee shall have the same right to the possession of documents as if his security had been effected by assignment.

(2) Any purported assignment of a term of years absolute by way of mortgage made after the commencement of this Act shall (to the extent of the estate of the mortgagor) operate as a subdemise of the leasehold land to the mortgagee for a term of years absolute, but subject to cesser on redemption, in manner following, namely:-

(*a*) The term to be taken by a first or only mortgagee shall be ten days less than the term expressed to be assigned;

(*b*) The term to be taken by a second or subsequent mortgagee shall be one day longer than the term vested in the first or other mortgagee whose security ranks immediately before that of the second or subsequent mortgagee, if the length of the last mentioned term permits, and in any case for a term less by one day at least than the term expressed to be assigned; . . .

(3) Subsection (2) does not apply to registered land, but, subject to that, this section applies whether or not the land is registered land and whether or not the mortgage is made by way of sub-mortgage of a term of years absolute, or is expressed to be by way of trust for sale or otherwise. [20]

87. Charges by way of legal mortgage.—(1) Where a legal mortgage of land is created by a charge by deed expressed[1] to be by way of legal mortgage, the mortgagee shall have the same protection, powers and remedies (including the right to take proceedings to obtain possession from the occupiers and the persons in receipt of rents and profits, or any of them) as if—

(*a*) where the mortgage is a mortgage of an estate in fee simple, a mortgage term of three thousand years without impeachment of waste had been thereby created in favour of the mortgagee; and

(*b*) where the mortgage is a mortgage of a term of years absolute, a sub-term less by one day than the term vested in the mortgagor had been thereby created in favour of the mortgagee. ...

(4) Subsection (1) of this section shall not be taken to be affected by section 23(1)(a) of the Land Registration Act 2002 (under which owner's powers in relation to a registered estate do not include power to mortgage by demise or sub-demise). [2]

---

[18]   As substituted by LRA 2002, s. 133, Sch 11, para. 2(1), (6).
[19]   A charge probably dispenses with the need for a licence: *Gentle v Faulkner* [1900] 2 QB 267; *Matthews v Smallwood* [1910] 1 Ch 777; *Grand Junction Co Ltd v Bates* [1954] 2 QB 160, [1954] 2 All ER 385, p. 795, n. 3, post; M & W, para. 19.034, n. 86.
[20]   As substituted by LRA 2002, s. 133, Sch 11, para. 2(1), (7).
[1]   Such a statement is not required in the case of registered land: *Cityland and Property (Holdings) Ltd v Dabrah* [1968] Ch 166, [1967] 2 All ER 639.
[2]   LRA 2002, s. 133, Sch. 11, para. 2(1), (8)

FIFTH SCHEDULE

Forms of Instruments

Section 206   Form No. 1

Charge by way of legal mortgage

This Legal Charge is made [&c.] between *A.* of [&c.] of the one part and *B.* of [&c.] of the other part.

[*Recite the title of A. to the freeholds or leaseholds in the Schedule and agreement for the loan by B.*]

Now in consideration of the sum of . . . pounds now paid by *B.* to *A.* (the receipt &c.) this Deed witnesseth as follows:-

1. *A.* hereby covenants with *B.* to pay [*Add the requisite covenant to pay principal and interest*].

2. *A.* as Beneficial Owner hereby charges by way of legal mortgage All and Singular the property mentioned in the Schedule hereto with the payment to *B.* of the principal money, interest, and other money hereby covenanted to be paid by *A.*

3. [*Add covenant to insure buildings and any other provisions desired.*]

In witness [&c.] [*Add Schedule*].

Note. – *B.* will be in the same position as if a mortgage had been effected by a demise of freeholds or a subdemise of leaseholds.

In **Regent Oil Co Ltd v JA Gregory (Hatch End) Ltd** [1966] Ch 402, [1965] 3 All ER 673, the Court of Appeal held that an attornment clause in a charge by way of legal mortgage enabled covenants in the charge to be enforced against successors in title of the mortgagor. HARMAN LJ said at 431, at 678:

'In my opinion, the new charge by way of legal mortgage created by section 87 was intended to be a substitute in all respects for a mortgage by demise, and anything which would be good in the one is good in the other. It would indeed be a trap if the rights of the mortgagee depended on whether his charge were created in one way or the other. Support for this view is to be found in *Grand Junction Co Ltd v Bates* [1954] 2 QB 160, [1954] 2 All ER 385; I read from the judgment of Upjohn J at 168, at 388: "My approach to the problem is this: A charge by way of legal mortgage, as I have already said, was introduced as a conveyancing device by the Law of Property Act 1925, with a view to simplifying conveyancing, and it would be pity to introduce subtle differences between one way of creating a charge and another way of creating a charge unless the words of the Act so required. It may be that there is a difference with regard to obtaining consent of the landlord to the charge, though that depends on the construction of the lease; but in any event that is no reason for making another difference between the two forms of creating a security, unless the Act so requires." It was there held that the chargee by way of legal mortgage had a right to claim relief against forfeiture just as if he had been a mortgagee by sub-demise.'

In **Weg Motors Ltd v Hales** [1962] Ch 49, [1961] 3 All ER 181, DONOVAN LJ said at 77, at 192:

'The section does not create even a notional term of years in the mortgagee but simply defines what protection, powers and remedies the mortgagee is to have.'[3]

ii. REGISTERED LAND

Under the Land Registration Act 2002[4] a registered proprietor may exercise owner's powers in relation to a registered charge. These are set out in section 23(1)–(3), infra. The main change is that in future it will no longer be possible to create a mortgage by demise or sub-demise.

Compulsory first registration was introduced by the Land Registration Act 1997 for the 'creation of a protected first legal mortgage': see now Land Registration Act 2002, section 4(1)(g) and (8), p. 113, ante. A charge of registered land is a disposition and must be completed by registration, but does not operate at law until the relevant registration requirements have been met: section 27(1), Schedule 2, paragraphs 8–11 (p. 125, ante). If the requirement of registration is not complied with, the creation becomes void as regards the creation of a legal estate, and has effect as 'a contract made for valuable consideration to create the legal estate': section 7(1)(2), p. 115, ante. This is an equitable interest and needs protection by a notice or actual occupation.

Land and charge certificates ceased to have any legal significance when the 2002 Act came into force. Instead, the Land Registry now issues an official copy showing the entries which exist on the register.

LAND REGISTRATION ACT 2002

23 Owner's powers

(1) Owner's powers in relation to a registered estate consist of—
  (a) power to make a disposition of any kind permitted by the general law in relation to an interest of that description, other than a mortgage by demise or sub-demise, and
  (b) power to charge the estate at law with the payment of money.
(2) Owner's powers in relation to a registered charge consist of—
  (a) power to make a disposition of any kind permitted by the general law in relation to an interest of that description, other than a legal sub-mortgage, and
  (b) power to charge at law with the payment of money indebtedness secured by the registered charge.
(3) In subsection (2)(a), 'legal sub-mortgage' means—
  (a) a transfer by way of mortgage,
  (b) a sub-mortgage by sub-demise, and

---

[3] See also *Grand Junction Co Ltd v Bates* [1954] 2 QB 160 at 168, [1954] 2 All ER 385 at 388, where it was said that a tenant who charges his lease is probably not in breach of a covenant against sub-letting without the landlord's consent. Nor does a chargee have a term so as to effect a transfer to him under LPA 1925, s. 115: *Cumberland Court (Brighton) Ltd v Taylor* [1964] Ch 29, [1963] 2 All ER 536; nor is it necessary to serve upon a chargee a notice under LPA 1925, s. 146, p. 531, ante; nor under Leasehold Property (Repairs) Act 1938, p. 546, ante; *Church Comrs for England v Ve-Ri-Best Manufacturing Ltd* [1957] 1 QB 238, [1956] 3 All ER 777; *Ushers Brewery v PS King & Co (Finance) Ltd* (1969) 212 EG 787; *Thompson v Salah* [1972] 1 All ER 530; *Edwards v Marshall-Lee* (1975) 235 EG 901; W & C, vol i., 177–178.
[4] LRR 2003, Part 9; R & R, chap. 25; H & B, chap. 4; Law Commission Report on Land Registration for the Twenty-First Century 2001 (Law Com No. 271) paras. 4.29–4.30, Part VII.

(c)   a charge by way of legal mortgage.

51 Effect of completion by registration

On completion of the relevant registration requirements, a charge created by means of a registrable disposition of a registered estate has effect, if it would not otherwise do so, as a charge by deed by way of legal mortgage.

52 Protection of disponees

(1) Subject to any entry in the register to the contrary, the proprietor of a registered charge is to be taken to have, in relation to the property subject to the charge, the powers of disposition conferred by law on the owner of a legal mortgage.

(2) Subsection (1) has effect only for the purpose of preventing the title of a disponee being questioned (and so does not affect the lawfulness of a disposition).

53 Powers as sub-chargee

The registered proprietor of a sub-charge has, in relation to the property subject to the principal charge or any intermediate charge, the same powers as a sub-chargor.

132 General interpretation

(1) In this Act
  'charge' means any mortgage, charge or lien for securing money or money's worth;
  'registered charge' means a charge the title to which is entered on the register;
  'sub-charge' means a change under section 23(2)(b).

LAND REGISTRATION RULES 2003

Form of charge of registered estate

103. A legal charge of a registered estate may be made in Form CH1 (see opposite).

B. Equitable Mortgages and Equitable Charges [5]

i. UNREGISTERED LAND

(a) Mortgage of an Equitable Interest

This is created by assigning the equitable interest to the mortgagee with a proviso for reassignment on redemption. The assignment, if not made by will, must satisfy the requirements of section 53(1)(c) of the Law of Property Act 1925. [6]

(b) Agreement to Create a Legal Mortgage

In accordance with the principle that Equity looks on that as done which ought to be done, an agreement to create a legal mortgage (or an imperfect legal

---

[5]   C & B, pp. 729–731; Gray, pp. 597–604; M & W, paras. 19.038–19.040; MM, pp. 499–501; Smith, pp. 559, 561; Cousins (2nd edn), chap. 5; Waldock, pp. 43–59, 136–139; Fisher and Lightwood, paras. 1.17–1.22.
[6]   See p. 84, ante.

Legal charge of a

registered estate

Land Registry CH1

This form should be accompanied by Form AP1 or Form FRI.

If you need more room than is provided for in a panel, use continuation sheet CS and attach to this form.

---

1. Title number(s) of the Property *Leave blank if not yet registered.*

---

2. Property

---

3. Date

---

4. Lender *Give full name(s) and company's registered number, if any.*

---

5. Borrower **for entry on the register** *Give full name(s) and company's registered number, if any. For scottish caompanies use an SC prefix and for limited liability partherships use an OC prefix before the registered number, if any. For foreign companies give territory in which incorporated.*

---

6. **The Borrower with** *(Delete as appropriate)* **[full title guarantee][limited title guarantee] charges the Property by way of legal mortgage as security for the payment of the sums detailed in panel 8**

---

7. *Place "X" in teh appropriate bo(es).*

❑   The Lender is under an obligation to make further advances and applies for the obligation to be entered in the register

❑   The Borrower applies to enter the following restriction in the charges register of the registered estate

---

8. Additional provisions Insert here details of the sums to be paid (amounts and dates), etc.

---

9. Execution *The Borrower must execute th is charge as a deed using the space below. If there is more than one Borrower, all must execute. Forms of execution are given in Schedule 9 to the Land Registration Rules 2003. If a note of an obligation to make further advances has been applied for in panel 7 this socument must be signed by the Lender or its conveyancer.*

mortgage) is treated as an actual mortgage,[7] if it satisfies section 2 of the Law of Property (Miscellaneous Provisions) Act 1989.[8]

(c) Deposit of Title Deeds

Since *Russel v Russel*[9] in 1783 a deposit of title deeds, with the intention that the depositee shall hold them as a security, creates an equitable mortgage of the land. This is because such a deposit is construed as a contract to create a mortgage. Before 1989 no formalities were necessary, because the deposit ranked as an act of part performance. Under section 2 of the Law of Property (Miscellaneous Provisions) Act 1989, however, that doctrine ceased to apply. Equitable mortgages by deposit survived the removal of their original basis and must now satisfy the requirements of the section.[10]

It is usual for a memorandum of the agreement to accompany the deposit, and, if it is desired to enable the mortgagee to pass a legal estate on sale, the mortgagor will execute a deed and insert in it a power of attorney or a declaration of trust, or both.[11]

(d) Equitable Charge

This arises where property is charged in equity with the payment of a debt or some other obligation. In **Matthews v Goodday** (1861) 31 LJ Ch 282, KINDERSLEY V-C said at 282:

'Suppose a man signed a written contract, by which he simply agreed that he thereby charged his real estate with 500*l* to A, what would be the effect of it? It would be no agreement to give a legal mortgage, but a security by which he equitably charged his land with the payment of a sum of money.'[12]

An equitable charge does not have to satisfy section 2 of the Law of Property (Miscellaneous Provisions) Act 1989. It involves the *creation* of a security rather than an *agreement to create* a legal charge. Its validity depends on section 53 (1) (*a*) of the Law of Property Act 1925, which requires the writing to be signed by the chargor only.[13]

---

[7] See p. 87, n. 8, ante.
[8] See p. 67, ante.
[9] (1783) 1 Bro CC 269; *Dixon v Muckleston* (1872) 8 Ch App 155; *Re Wallis and Simmonds (Builders) Ltd* [1974] 1 WLR 391, [1974] 1 All ER 561; *Thames Guaranty Ltd v Campbell* [1985] QB 210, [1984] 2 All ER 585 (deposit of title deeds (land certificate) to secure a debt by one joint tenant without consent of the other joint tenant not effective to create equitable charge of the jointly owned land; but it may create a charge of the equitable interest to the depositor, if the deposit amounts to an act of severance, p. 303, ante); *First National Securities Ltd v Hegerty* [1985] QB 850, [1984] 3 All ER 641, p. 304, n. 6, ante.
[10] *United Bank of Kuwait v Sahib* [1997] Ch 107, [1996] 3 All ER 215 ('The clear intention of section 2 . . . is to introduce certainty in relation to contracts for the disposition of interests in land where uncertainty existed before', per PHILLIPS LJ at 387), p. 67, n. 18, ante; (1997) 113 LQR 533 (M. Robinson).
[11] See p. 871, post. The right to create this kind of equitable mortgage was saved by LPA 1925, s. 13. The mortgagee could retain the deeds until he was paid, but had no separate legal lien: *Re Molton Finance Ltd* [1968] Ch 325, [1967] 3 All ER 843; see also *Capital Finance Co Ltd v Stokes* [1969] 1 Ch 261 at 278; [1968] 3 All ER 625 at 629.
[12] See *Swiss Bank Corpn v Lloyds Bank Ltd* [1982] AC 584 at 594–595, [1980] 2 All ER 419 at 425, per BUCKLEY LJ; *Thames Guaranty Ltd v Campbell*, supra; *First National Securities Ltd v Hegerty*, supra; *Re Cosslett (Contractors) Ltd* [1998] 2 WLR 131; [1997] 4 All ER 115. See *Kinane v MacKie-Conteh* [2004] 19 EG 164 (CS).
[13] *Emmet on Title*, paras. 25.116–25.118.

ii. REGISTERED LAND

Law Commission Report on Land Registration for the Twenty-First Century 2001 (Law Com No. 271), para. 7.9.

'Equitable charges

7.9 The Bill has nothing specific to say about equitable charges. A registered proprietor may create them to the extent permitted by the general law under his or her owner's powers. They may also arise in other ways, as where a creditor obtains a charging order over the land of a registered proprietor. [14]

The fact that the Bill says nothing about such charges is important for one specific reason. In the Consultative Document, [15] we recommended that the statutory power [16] to create a lien over registered land by depositing the land certificate as security should be abolished. Our reasoning was as follows. Such charges operated by analogy with the mortgage by deposit of title deeds in unregistered land. However, in *United Bank of Kuwait Plc v Sahib*, [17] the Court of Appeal held that the basis for mortgages by deposit of title deeds was the doctrine of part performance that had been abolished by the Law of Property (Miscellaneous Provisions) Act 1989. Such mortgages were only valid if they complied with the formal requirements for contracts laid down in that Act. The decision rendered obsolete the power to create a lien by the deposit of a land certificate. The Bill therefore contains nothing replicating the power. [18]

C. Charging Orders

The court has powers under the Charging Orders Act 1979 to impose a charge on the land of a judgment debtor to secure the payment of his judgment debt. Such a charge has the same effect as 'an equitable charge created by the debtor by writing under his hand.' [19]

CHARGING ORDERS ACT 1979

1. Charging orders. —(1) Where, under a judgment or order of the High court or a county court, a person (the 'debtor') is required to pay a sum of money to another person (the 'creditor') then, for the purpose of enforcing that judgment or order, the appropriate court may make an order in accordance with the provisions of this Act imposing on any such property of the debtor as may be specified in the order a charge for securing the payment of any money due or to become due under the judgment or order.

(5) In deciding whether to make a charging order the court shall consider all the circumstances of the case and, in particular, any evidence before it as to –

    (*a*) the personal circumstances of the debtor, and

    (*b*) whether any other creditor of the debtor would be likely to be unduly prejudiced by the making of the order.

---

[14] Such a charge takes effect as 'an equitable charge created by the debtor by writing under his hand': Charging Orders Act 1979, s. 3(4).

[15] Law Com No. 254, paras. 9.8–9.11.

[16] Found in Land Registration Act 1925, s. 66.

[17] [1997] Ch 107; explained in Law Com No. 254, para. 9.9.

[18] Furthermore, under LRA 2002, land certificates are no longer issued by the Land Registry, p. 795, ante.

[19] See Walker and Buckley, *Charging Orders against Land* (2nd edn).

2. Property which may be charged. —(1) Subject to subsection (3) below, a charge may be imposed by a charging order only on –
   (*a*) any interest held by the debtor beneficially –
      (i) in any asset of a kind mentioned in subsection (2) below, or
      (ii) under any trust;[20] or
   (*b*) any interest held by a person as trustee of a trust ('the trust'), if the interest is in such an asset or is an interest under another trust and –
      (i) the judgment or order in respect of which a charge is to be imposed was made against that person as trustee of the trust, or
      (ii) the whole beneficial interest under the trust is held by the debtor unencumbered and for his own benefit, or
      (iii) in a case where there are two or more debtors all of whom are liable to the creditor for the same debt, they together hold the whole beneficial interest under the trust unencumbered and for their own benefit.
   (2) The assets referred to in subsection (1) above are –
   (*a*) land
   (*b*) securities of any of the following kinds –
      (i) government stock,
      (ii) stock of any body (other than a building society) incorporated within England and Wales,
      (iii) stock of any body incorporated outside England and Wales or of any state or territory outside the United Kingdom, being stock registered in a register kept at any place within England and Wales,
      (iv) units of any unit trust in respect of which a register of the unit holders is kept at any place within England and Wales, or
   (*c*) funds in court.
   (3) In any case where a charge is imposed by a charging order on any interest in an asset of a kind mentioned in paragraph (*b*) or (*c*) of subsection (2) above, the court making the order may provide for the charge to extend to any interest or dividend payable in respect of the asset.

3. Provisions supplementing sections 1 and 2.—(2) The Land Charges Act 1972 and the Land Registration Act 2002[1] shall apply in relation to charging orders as they apply in relation to other orders or writs issued or made for the purpose of enforcing judgments.

---

[20]   *Ladup Ltd v Williams & Glyn's Bank plc* [1985] 1 WLR 851, [1985] 2 All ER 577; *Clark v Chief Land Registrar* [1994] Ch 370, [1994] 4 All ER 96.
   If a charging order is obtained, the judgment creditor may then apply to the court under TLATA 1996, s. 14, p. 282, ante, for an order for sale of the property: *Midland Bank plc v Pike* [1988] 2 All ER 434; [1988] All ER Rev 234 (A. A. S. Zuckerman). For the reluctance of the court to anticipate this application, see *First National Securities Ltd v Hegerty* [1985] QB 850, [1984] 3 All ER 641; cf. *Harman v Glencross* [1985] Fam 49, [1984] 2 All ER 577 (competition between one co-owning spouse and judgment creditors of the other); affd [1986] Fam 81 where Balcombe LJ sets out guidelines for the solution of this type of problem; [1985] Conv 129 (P. F. Smith); (1985) 5 OJLS 132 (N. P. Gravells); *Austin-Fell v Austin-Fell* [1990] Fam 172, [1990] 2 All ER 455; *Lloyds Bank plc v Byrne* (1993) 23 HLR 472; *Barclays Bank plc v Hendricks* [1996] 1 FLR 258; [1997] Conv 464 (N. S. Price).
[1]   As amended by LRA 2002, s. 133, Sch 11, para. 15.

There were difficulties over the registration of an order charging a debtor's beneficial interest under a trust for sale. If the order affected only part of the equitable interest, it was not registrable owing to the doctrine of conversion: *Perry v Phoenix Assurance plc* [1988] 1 WLR 940, [1988] 3 All ER 60. This difficulty has disappeared with the abolition of the doctrine by TLATA 1996, s. 3.

III. The Equity of Redemption [2]

A. The Equity of Redemption as a Proprietary Interest

In **Casborne v Scarfe** (1738) 1 Atk 603, Lord HARDWICKE LC said at 605:

'An equity of redemption has always been considered as an estate in the land, for it may be devised, granted, or entailed with remainders, and such cannot be considered as a mere right only, but such an estate whereof there may be a seisin; the person therefore entitled to the equity of redemption is considered as the owner of the land . . . . The interest of the land must be somewhere, and cannot be in abeyance, but it is not in the mortgagee, and therefore must remain in the mortgagor.'

In **Re Sir Thomas Spencer Wells** [1933] Ch 29, the question was whether the Crown could claim, as bona vacantia, the equity of redemption of property owned by a company on its dissolution and not disposed of in its winding up. The property was leasehold land, and at the time of the dissolution, the rents received from it were insufficient to cover the interest on the mortgage money. The liquidator concluded that the equity of redemption was of no value. After a considerable time, the rents increased and were greater than the interest due on the mortgage to which the plaintiffs, as mortgagees, were entitled. All arrears of interest were paid off; the equity of redemption thus became of value. It was claimed by the plaintiffs on the ground that they were the legal owners of the term of years and that, the mortgagor having ceased to exist, no-one was entitled to redeem. The Court of Appeal (Lord HANWORTH MR, LAWRENCE and ROMER LJJ) held (reversing FARWELL J) that the equity of redemption was a proprietary interest which had never passed to the mortgagees. The Crown was therefore entitled to claim the equity of redemption as bona vacantia. [3]

B. The Protection of the Mortgagor

Equity insists that unfair advantage shall not be taken of the mortgagor. It will be seen that mortgagors have been subjected to schemes which attempt to take away the right to redeem by providing that the mortgagee may purchase the mortgaged property, or that the mortgagor shall not be permitted to redeem it for a certain period of time, or that, even after redemption, certain advantages shall still be enjoyed by the mortgagee. The rules which equity has laid down have been

---

[2] C & B, pp. 720, 732–749; Gray, pp. 1365–1393; M & W, paras. 19.017–19.018, 19.022, 19.125–19.178; MM, pp. 520–526; Smith, pp. 571–581; Cousins (2nd edn), chap. 17; Waldock, pp. 170–223; Fisher and Lightwood, chap. 28.

[3] On bona vacantia, see Ing, *Bona Vacantia* (2nd edn).

developed during the centuries, and have been summarised in the words: 'Once a mortgage, always a mortgage.' [4]

i. ONCE A MORTGAGE ALWAYS A MORTGAGE

Where a transaction is, on its proper construction, a mortgage, any provisions inserted for the advantage of the mortgagee which are inconsistent with the nature of a mortgage are void.

SAMUEL v JARRAH TIMBER AND WOOD PAVING CORPORATION LTD[5]
[1904] AC 323 (HL, Earl of HALSBURY LC, Lords MACNAGHTEN and LINDLEY)

First mortgage debenture stock of £30,000 was mortgaged to Samuel to secure an advance of £5,000 at 6 per cent. The principal was to become payable with interest at thirty days' notice on either side; and the mortgagee, Samuel, was given 'the option to purchase the whole or any part of such stock at 40 per cent at any time within twelve months'. Within that period Samuel claimed to exercise this option in respect of the whole stock. The Company claimed to redeem and to have a declaration that the option was illegal and void.

Held (affirming the Court of Appeal [1903] 2 Ch 1). The option was void, and the Company was entitled to redeem.

EARL OF HALSBURY LC: My Lords, I regret that the state of the authorities leaves me no alternative other than to affirm the judgment of Kekewich J and the Court of Appeal. A perfectly fair bargain made between two parties to it, each of whom was quite sensible of what they were doing, is not to be performed because at the same time a mortgage arrangement was made between them. If a day had intervened between the two parts of the arrangement, the part of the bargain which the appellant claims to be performed would have been perfectly good and capable of being enforced; but a line of authorities going back for more than a century has decided that such an arrangement as that which was here arrived at is contrary to a principle of equity, the sense or reason of which I am not able to appreciate, and very reluctantly I am compelled to acquiesce in the judgments appealed from.

LORD MACNAGHTEN: In *Vernon v Bethell* (1762) 2 Eden 110, 113, however, Northington LC (then Lord Henley) laid down the law broadly in the following terms: 'This Court, as a Court of conscience, is very jealous of persons taking securities for a loan and converting such securities into purchases. And therefore I take it to be an established rule that a mortgagee can never provide at the time of making the loan for any event or condition on which the equity of redemption shall be discharged and the conveyance absolute. And there is great reason and justice in this rule, for necessitous men are not, truly speaking, free men, but to answer a present exigency will submit to any terms that the crafty may impose upon them.'

This doctrine, described by Lord Henley as an established rule nearly 150 years ago, has never, so far as I can discover, been departed from since or

---

[4]   *Seton v Slade* (1802) 7 Ves 265, 273, per Lord ELDON LC.
[5]   Followed in *Lewis v Frank Love Ltd* [1961] 1 WLR 261, [1961] 1 All ER 446; (1961) 77 LQR 163 (P. V. Baker); *Re Supreme Court Registrar to Alexander Dawson Inc* [1976] 1 NZLR 615; cf. *Pye v Ambrose* [1994] NPC 53 (obligation to repay only arose when option no longer exercisable); *Jones v Morgan* [2001] 1 EGLR 125, p. 484, post. See also *Salt v Marquess of Northampton* [1892] AC 1, discussed by Lord DAVEY in *Noakes & Co Ltd v Rice* [1902] AC 24, p. 813, post.

questioned in any reported case. It is, I believe, universally accepted by text-writers of authority. Speaking for myself, I should not be sorry if your Lordships could see your way to modify it so as to prevent its being used as a means of evading a fair bargain come to between persons dealing at arms' length and negotiating on equal terms. The directors of a trading company in search of financial assistance are certainly in a very different position from that of an impecunious landowner in the toils of a crafty money-lender. At the same time I quite feel the difficulty of interfering with any rule that has prevailed so long, and I am not prepared to differ from the conclusion at which the Court of Appeal has arrived.

In **Reeve v Lisle** [1902] AC 461 property was mortgaged to secure a loan of money. At a later date it was agreed between the parties to the mortgage that, if within five years the mortgagees should elect to enter into partnership with the mortgagors, they should be entitled to do so on the terms, inter alia, that the mortgagors should be relieved of the liability to repay the loan and that a ship (which was part of the security) should be transferred free from the mortgage for the purposes of the partnership. The House of Lords (Earl of HALSBURY LC, and Lords MACNAGHTEN, BRAMPTON and LINDLEY) construed these two transactions as being separate and independent, and held that the agreement was binding on the mortgagor. [6]

(1903) 13 LQR 359 (Sir Frederick Pollock)

'The doctrine of "clogging" threatens to become an intolerable nuisance – an interference with the freedom of the subject. It was a useful enough doctrine in a primitive and more technical age when ignorant people were often entrapped into oppressive bargains, but today it is an anachronism and might with advantage be jettisoned. Instead the Courts have taken to emphasizing the doctrine in all its original crudity. It was open to them a few years since to have moulded the doctrine to meet the changing conditions of modern life, and to have confined redress to cases where there was something oppressive or unconscionable in the bargain to make this the test, as it was the origin of the doctrine; but the Courts have preferred to adhere to technicality and an unprogressive judicial policy. The decision of the Court of Appeal in *Jarrah Timber and Wood Paving Corpn v Samuel* [1903] 2 Ch 1 was inevitable after *Noakes & Co Ltd v Rice* [1902] AC 24, p. 813, post; but see to what a conclusion it leads. A company with a board of directors composed of experienced men of business, advised by a competent solicitor, after it has invited a loan and settled considered terms is supposed to be the victim of some oppression at the hands of the mortgagee, because it has given the mortgagee an option of purchasing the mortgaged property at a certain price, and is permitted by the Court to repudiate its own bargain deliberately entered into in its own interests – surely a proceeding more unconscionable than anything involved in the so-called "clogging", if there is any such thing as sanctity in

---

[6] See *Alec Lobb (Garages) Ltd v Total Oil Great Britain Ltd* [1983] 1 WLR 87, [1983] 1 All ER 944 (sale and 51 year leaseback of part of property entered into between mortgagor and mortgagee after date of mortgage held valid under mortgage rules, but reversed in CA [1985] 1 WLR 173, [1985] 1 All ER 303 as being void for restraint of trade).

contracts. Alas! for the cobwebs of technicality which lawyers are so fond of spinning, and which so often shut out the daylight of common sense.' [7]

In **Jones v Morgan** [2001] 1 EGLR 125, [8] the Court of Appeal followed the House of Lords decision in *Samuel v Jarrah Timber and Wood Paving Corporation.*

Two brothers, William and John Morgan, owned Vauxhall Farm in the Vale of Glamorgan. In June 1994 they mortgaged it to Mr Jones, a retired investment broker for £105,000, in order to develop it as a nursing home. This was however insufficient to fund the development.

In June 1997 a new agreement was made between the broker and Mr Jones under which part of the land was to be sold to a neighbouring farmer. The proceeds of sale were to be used to discharge the mortgage loan, and by clause (2) the brothers were to transfer to Mr Jones 'a one half share or interest in the legal estate'. Mr Jones sought specific performance of the 1997 agreement.

The Court of Appeal, in refusing specific performance, held that:

   (i)   the bargain was neither unconscionable [9] nor procured by duress

   (ii) (by a majority: Lord PHILLIPS MR and CHADWICK LJ) the 1997 agreement was a clog on the equity of redemption.

Lord PHILLIPS MR said at 86:

'This appeal turns on the question of whether clause 2 of the 1997 agreement is unenforceable as a clog on the equity of redemption of a mortgage. That question I have found far from easy because (i) the doctrine of a clog on the equity of redemption is, so it seems to me, an appendix to our law that no longer serves a useful purpose and would be better excised; and (ii) the nature of the 1997 agreement and the circumstances in which it was concluded are neither clear nor satisfactory ... The 1997 agreement varied the loan and the mortgage that secured it, but did not alter the nature of the contract. Clause (2) was inserted as an integral part of the refinancing agreement. It was not part of a collateral contract.'

PILL LJ (dissenting) said at 80: 'The 1997 agreement was, in my judgment, neither in substance a rearrangement of the 1994 mortgage nor in substance a fresh mortgage loan. Being a commercial agreement made in the circumstances described, the doctrine of clog on the equity of redemption does not extend to render it unenforceable.'

---

[7]   See (1985) Real Property Probate and Trust Journal 821 (L. C. Prebble and D. W. Cartwright); (1986–86) 60 St John's Law Review 452 (J. L. Light).

    For legislation in the USA removing the mortgagee's option from the purview of the doctrine of clogs, see Uniform Land Security Interest Act 1986, para. 211; New York General Obligations Law 1986, para. 5.334; California Civil Code (1984), para. 2906; cited 60 St John's Law Review at pp. 492–497.

[8]   [2001] Conv 500 (M. P. Thompson).

[9]   'Mr Will Morgan is naïve, trusting and unbusinesslike and no match for an astute business man like Mr Tudor Jones. But it is for a solicitor to advise the naïve, trusting or the unbusinesslike in their dealings with the more astute. In such a case the client relies on the solicitor to protect his interests': per CHADWICK LJ at 40.

    See also *Warnborough Ltd v Garmite Ltd* [2003] EWCA Civ 1544, [2004] 1 P & CR D18 (contemporaneous option to purchase development site held valid where site sold by greantee of option as owner of site to grantor for a price to be left outstanding on mortgage: substance of transaction was sale and not mortgage, and therefore not a clog on the equity of redemption).

ii. CONTRACTUAL POSTPONEMENT OF THE RIGHT TO REDEEM

This section deals with cases in which the mortgagor covenants to postpone redemption for a substantial length of time. The situations cover a wide range between two extremes. On the one hand are cases in which the mortgagee, solely for his own benefit, insists on the postponement of redemption for so long a time that the security is virtually irredeemable. On the other hand are cases in which a fair business transaction includes, at the request of the mortgagor, a term postponing redemption for a certain period of time, and the mortgagor, finding that interest rates have gone down, makes use of these rules to escape from his bargain.

It used to be said that a postponement was valid if it were for a reasonable time. It is clear, however, since the *Knightsbridge* case, [10] that this is not the proper test, whether 'reasonableness' is judged in terms of mere length of time or in terms of all the circumstances of the case. Sir Wilfrid GREENE MR, laid down the test in that case as follows: [11] 'Equity is concerned to see two things – one that the essential requirements of a mortgage transaction are observed, and the other than oppressive and unconscionable terms are not enforced.' With the second requirement no-one could quarrel; it is possible, however, that the first one may some day be held to be too wide. In that case, the mortgagor covenanted not to redeem a mortgage of freehold land for 40 years, and the covenant was held valid. There was no suggestion of hardship or oppression. An interesting situation would have arisen if the property mortgaged had been a forty-one year lease; [12] assuming again that there was no hardship or oppression, the conflict between *Fairclough v Swan Brewery Co Ltd* [1912] AC 565, p. 807, post and *Santley v Wilde* [1899] 2 Ch 474 would then have to be resolved, and there is much to be said for the view that a business transaction of that nature ought to be upheld.

Cases falling within the present section should be distinguished from those dealt with in the next. The next section deals with cases where an advantage still remains to the mortgagee after redemption. Failure to appreciate this distinction has caused most of the misunderstanding of *Santley v Wilde*. The criticism which that case received in the House of Lords, [13] and particularly from Lord DAVEY, was directed against it on the assumption that it concerned a collateral advantage existing after redemption. It is clear, however, from the judgment of the case itself, that Lord LINDLEY treated it as a case of contractual postponement.

(a) Mortgage of Leasehold

SANTLEY v WILDE[13a]
[1899] 2 Ch 474 (CA, LINDLEY MR, Sir F. H. JEUNE AND ROMER LJ, reversing BYRNE J [1899] 1 Ch 747)

The plaintiff, as sub-lessee of a theatre, had the option to take over the head lease on payment of £2,000. She arranged to borrow this money from the defendant Wilde, and mortgaged to him her sub-lease as security. The mortgage provided that the mortgagor should repay the capital by instalments under an arrangement

---

[10] *Knightsbridge Estates Trust Ltd v Byrne* [1939] Ch 441, [1938] 4 All ER 618; affd. [1940] AC 613, [1940] 2 All ER 401, p. 816, post.
[11] [1939] Ch 441 at 457, [1938] 4 All ER 618 at 626.
[12] See the question on p. 811, post.
[13] Especially in *Noakes & Co Ltd v Rice* [1902] AC 24 at 33, p. 813, post.
[13a] C & B, p. 716. It was the view of Dr J. H. C. Morris that 'the transaction was not in essence one of mortgage, but a partnership agreement to share in the profits of the theatre', and therefore valid on that ground: Waldock, *Law of Mortgages* (2nd edn), p. 187.

which was not challenged, and that she should 'during the residue of the term . . . notwithstanding that all principal moneys and interest may have been paid . . . pay . . . a sum equal to one-third part of the clear net profit rent or rents to be derived' from the lease. The proviso for cesser provided that the mortgage should determine on payment of the principal sum and interest, 'and all other the moneys hereinbefore covenanted . . . to be paid . . . ' etc. After certain payments had fallen into arrear, the plaintiff, on payment of all arrears, and on tender of the outstanding principal, interest and costs, claimed a declaration that she was entitled to redeem on payment of principal, interest and costs and that so far as the mortgage deed provided for payment of a share of the rents and profits or precluded her from redeeming on payment of principal and interest, it was invalid.

Held. The plaintiff could not redeem except by observing all the covenants for which her property was given as security, including the covenant to pay the profits.

LINDLEY MR: The question raised on this appeal is extremely important: I do not profess to be able to decide it on any principle which will be in harmony with all the cases; but it appears to me that the true principle running through them is not very difficult to discover, and I think that it can be applied so as to do justice in this case and in all other cases on the subject that may arise. The principle is this: a mortgage is a conveyance of land or an assignment of chattels as a security for the payment of a debt or the discharge of some other obligation for which it is given. This is the idea of a mortgage: and the security is redeemable on the payment or discharge of such debt or obligation, any provision to the contrary notwithstanding. That, in my opinion, is the law. Any provision inserted to prevent redemption on payment or performance of the debt or obligation for which the security was given is what is meant by a clog or fetter on the equity of redemption and is therefore void. . . . A clog or fetter is something which is inconsistent with the idea of security: a clog or fetter is in the nature of a repugnant condition. If I convey land in fee subject to a condition forbidding alienation, that is a repugnant condition. If I give a mortgage on a condition that I shall not redeem, that is a repugnant condition. The Courts of Equity have fought for years to maintain the doctrine that a security is redeemable. But when and under what circumstances? On the performance of the obligation for which it was given. If the obligation is the payment of a debt, the security is redeemable on the payment of that debt. That, in my opinion, is the true principle applicable to the cases, and that is what is meant when it is said there must not be any clog or fetter on the equity of redemption. If so, this mortgage has no clog or fetter at all. Of course, the debt or obligation may be impeachable for fraud, oppression, or over-reaching: there the obligation is tainted to that extent and is invalid. But, putting such cases out of the question, when you get a security for a debt or obligation, that security can be redeemed the moment the debt or obligation is paid or performed, but on no other terms.

Now, let us see what the contract here is. It is not suggested that there has been fraud or undue influence of over-reaching or hard bargaining. Here is a lady who has a lease, of which there are ten years to run, subject to a rent and covenants. She wants to carry on a theatre, and she wants to borrow a sum of 2,000*l.* for the purpose. What is the security she offers? The security of the lease is probably absolutely insufficient. A security of that sort, unless it is kept up for the ten years, is very shaky. The lender took that view. He says, 'I will lend you the money, and you may have five years in which to pay it; and you shall pay me a sum equal to one-third part of the net profits to be derived from any underleases'. What is the lender's position? It is obvious that his security depends not only on the solvency of the lady, but also on the success of the theatre. This is the kind of security proposed, and the lender says he will lend upon that. Accordingly the 2,000*l.* is lent, and the mortgagor by her security covenants to repay the money by instalments; the deed then further goes on as follows: [His Lordship read the second testatum and covenant by the mortgagor for payment to the mortgagee of one-third of the net profit rents to be derived from any underleases or undertenancies, and also the provision for redemption: and continued:]

The means that this lease is granted or assigned by the mortgagor to the mortgagee as security not only for the payment of the 2,000*l.* and interest, but also for the payment of the one-third of the net profit rents to the end of the term. If I am right in the principle which I have laid down, that does not clog the right of redemption upon the performance of the obligation for which the security was given. That is the nature of the transaction, and the good sense of it.

But it is said that is not good law. Those, however, who say so lose sight of the true principle underlying the expression that there must be no clog or fetter on the equity of redemption. The plaintiff says, 'I will pay off the balance of the 2,000*l.* and interest, and you will give me back the lease, and this is the end of my obligation.' But the mortgagee says, 'No; that is not the bargain: you cannot redeem on those terms. On the contrary, you may pay me the 2,000*l.* and interest, but if you do, you must also pay the one-third profit rents'. On principle that is right: it follows from what I have said. That is the bargain, and there has been no oppression, and there is no reasonable legal ground for relieving this lady.

FAIRCLOUGH v SWAN BREWERY CO LTD
[1912] AC 565 (PC, Lords MACNAGHTEN, ATKINSON, SHAW OF DUNFERMLINE, and MERSEY)

The appellant was lessee for 17½ years of a hotel owned by the respondent brewery. He executed a mortgage of his lease for £500 which contained a clause precluding him from redeeming the mortgage during the remainder of his term less six weeks, and from purchasing beer from any person other than the respondent brewery during the continuance of the mortgage. On the appellant's offering to redeem and claiming to be free to purchase beer elsewhere, the respondent brewery brought this action in the Supreme Court of Western Australia for damages for breach of covenant and an injunction to restrain further breaches. The appellant argued that the covenant was void on the ground, inter alia, that it was a clog on his equity of redemption, and claimed that he was entitled to redeem.

Held. The covenant was void and the appellant was entitled to redeem.

LORD MACNAGHTEN: The arguments of counsel ranged over a very wide field. [14] But the real point is a narrow one. It depends upon a doctrine of equity, which is not open to question.

'There is', as Kindersley V-C said in *Gossip v Wright* (1863) 32 LJ Ch 648 at 653, 'no doubt that the broad rule is this: that the Court will not allow the right of redemption in any way to be hampered or crippled in that which the parties intended to be a security either by any contemporaneous instrument with the deed in question, or by anything which this Court would regard as a simultaneous arrangement or part of the same transaction.' The rule in comparatively recent times was unsettled by certain decisions in the Court of Chancery in England which seem to have misled the learned judges in the Full Court. But it is now firmly established by the House of Lords that the old rule still prevails and that

---

[14] Restraint of trade was also pleaded, at p. 566.

equity will not permit any device or contrivance being part of the mortgage transaction or contemporaneous with it to prevent or impede redemption. The learned counsel on behalf of the respondents admitted, as he was bound to admit, that a mortgage cannot be made irredeemable. That is plainly forbidden. Is there any difference between forbidding redemption and permitting it, if the permission be a mere pretence? Here the provision for redemption is nugatory. . . . For all practical purposes this mortgage is irredeemable. It was obviously meant to be irredeemable. It was made irredeemable in and by the mortgage itself.

(b) Mortgage of Freehold

KNIGHTSBRIDGE ESTATES TRUST LTD v BYRNE
[1939] Ch 441, [1938] 4 All ER 618 (CA, Sir Wilfrid GREENE MR, SCOTT and FARWELL LJJ)

The plaintiff company was the owner of certain freehold property in London which had been mortgaged at 6½ per cent. Wishing to pay off their mortgage, they asked the defendants for a loan of £310,000 at 5½ per cent repayable over forty years. The defendants agreed to make this loan, repayment to be made by half-yearly instalments over forty years. The deed so provided, and in it the defendant mortgagees undertook, if the instalments were promptly paid, not to require repayment in any other way.

The plaintiffs claimed, less than six years later, that they were entitled to redeem on payment of all principal, interest and costs, on the ground that, in so far as the term prevented them from redeeming on making such payments, it was illegal and void as a clog on their right to redeem and that it rendered the mortgage irredeemable for an undue length of time.

Held (reversing LUXMOORE J [1938] Ch 741, [1938] 2 All ER 444). The plaintiffs were bound by the agreement and could only redeem in accordance with its terms.

Sir WILFRID GREENE MR: We will deal first with the arguments originally presented on behalf of the respondents. The first argument was that the postponement of the contractual right to redeem for forty years was void in itself, in other words, that the making of such an agreement between mortgagor and mortgagee was prohibited by a rule of equity. It was not contended that a provision in a mortgage deed making the mortgage irredeemable for a period of years is necessarily void. The argument was that such a period must be a 'reasonable' one, and it was said that the period in the present case was an unreasonable one by reason merely of its length. This argument was not the one accepted by the learned judge.

Now an argument such as this requires the closest scrutiny, for, if it is correct, it means that an agreement made between two competent parties, acting under expert advice and presumably knowing their own business best, is one which the law forbids them to make upon the ground that it is not 'reasonable'. If we were satisfied that the rule of equity was what it is said to be, we should be bound to give effect to it. But in the absence of compelling authority we are not prepared to say that such an agreement cannot lawfully be made. A decision to that effect would, in our view, involve an unjustified interference with the freedom of business men to enter into agreements best suited to their interests and would impose upon them a test of 'reasonableness' laid down by the Courts without reference to the business realities of the case.

It is important to remember what those realities were. The respondents are a private company and do not enjoy the facilities for raising money by a public issue possessed by public companies. They were the owners of a large and valuable block of property, and so far as we know they had no other assets. The property was subject to a mortgage at a high rate of interest and this mortgage was liable to be called in at any time. In these circumstances the respondents were, when the negotiations began, desirous of obtaining for themselves two advantages: (1) a reduction in the rate of interest, (2) the right to repay the mortgage moneys by instalments spread over a long period of years. The desirability of obtaining these terms from a business point of view is manifest, and it is not to be assumed that these respondents were actuated by anything but pure considerations of business in seeking to obtain them. The sum involved was a very large one, and the length of the period over which the instalments were spread is to be considered with reference to this fact. In the circumstances it was the most natural thing in the world that the respondents should address themselves to a body desirous of obtaining a long term investment for its money. The resulting agreement was a commercial agreement between two important corporations experienced in such matters, and has none of the features of an oppressive bargain where the borrower is at the mercy of an unscrupulous lender. In transactions of this kind it is notorious that there is competition among the large insurance companies and other bodies having large funds to invest, and we are not prepared to view the agreement made as anything but a proper business transaction.

But it is said not only that the period of postponement must be a reasonable one, but that in judging the 'reasonableness' of the period the considerations which we have mentioned cannot be regarded; that the Court is bound to judge 'reasonableness' by a consideration of the terms of the mortgage deed itself and without regard to extraneous matters. In the absence of clear authority we emphatically decline to consider a question of 'reasonableness' from a standpoint so unreal. To hold that the law is to tell business men what is reasonable in such circumstances and to refuse to take into account the business considerations involved, would bring the law into disrepute. Fortunately we do not find ourselves forced to come to any such conclusion. . . .

Assuming therefore, without in any way deciding, that the period during which the contractual right of redemption is postponed must be a 'reasonable' one (a question which we will not proceed to examine), we are of the opinion that the respondents have failed to establish (and the burden is on them) that there is anything unreasonable in the mere extension of the period for forty years in the circumstances of the present case.

But in our opinion the proposition that a postponement of the contractual right of redemption is only permissible for a 'reasonable' time is not well-founded. Such a postponement is not properly described as a clog on the equity of redemption, since it is concerned with the contractual right to redeem. It is indisputable that any provision which hampers redemption after the contractual date for redemption has passed will not be permitted. Further, it is undoubtedly true to say that a right of redemption is a necessary element in a mortgage transaction, and consequently that, where the contractual right of redemption is illusory, equity will grant relief by allowing redemption. This was the point in the case of *Fairclough v Swan Brewery Co Ltd* [1912] AC 565. . . .

Moreover, equity may give relief against contractual terms in a mortgage transaction if they are oppressive or unconscionable, and in deciding whether or not a particular transaction falls within this category the length of time for which the contractual right to redeem is postponed may well be an important consideration. In the present case no question of this kind was or could have been raised.

But equity does not reform mortgage transactions because they are unreasonable. It is concerned to see two things – one that the essential requirements of a mortgage transaction are observed, and the other that oppressive or unconscionable terms are not enforced. Subject to this, it does not, in our opinion, interfere. The question therefore arises whether, in a case where the right of redemption is real and not illusory and there is nothing oppressive or unconscionable in the transaction, such as we have in the present case, that is inconsistent with the essential requirements of a mortgage transaction? Apart from authority the answer to this question would, in our opinion, be clearly in the negative. Any other answer would place an unfortunate restriction on the liberty of contract of competent parties who are at arm's length – in the present case it would have operated to prevent the respondents obtaining financial terms which for obvious reasons they themselves considered to be most desirable. It would, moreover, lead to highly inequitable results. The remedy sought by the respondents and the only remedy which is said to be open to them is the establishment of a right to redeem at any time on the ground that the postponement of the contractual right to redeem is void. They do not and could not suggest that the contract as a contract is affected, and the result would accordingly be that whereas the respondents would have had from the first the right to redeem at any time, the appellants would have had no right to require payment otherwise than by the specified instalments. Such an outcome to a bargain entered into by business people negotiating at arm's length would indeed be unfortunate, and we should require clear authority before coming to such a conclusion.

We will now turn to the relevant authorities cited in argument by counsel for the parties. The first in order of date is *Talbot v Braddill* (1683) 1 Vern 183. [His Lordship referred also to *Cowdry v Day* (1859) 1 Giff 316; *Teevan v Smith* (1882) 20 ChD 724; *Biggs v Hoddinott* [1898] 2 Ch 307 at 311, p. 812, post; *Bradley v Carritt* [1903] AC 253, p. 815, post; *Williams v Morgan* [1906] 1 Ch 804; *Morgan v Jeffreys* [1910] 1 Ch 620; and *Davis v Symons* [1934] Ch 442, and continued:]

The second ground upon which the respondents endeavoured to support the judgment of the Court below was that the postponement of the contractual right to redeem for a period of forty years offended the rule against perpetuities and was therefore invalid. The learned judge decided against the respondents on this question and in our judgment rightly.

This decision was affirmed on appeal to the House of Lords [1940] AC 613, [1940] 2 All ER 401, on the ground that the mortgage was a debenture within the meaning of the Companies Act 1929, section 380 [15] and, as such and by virtue of section 74 of that Act, not invalid by reason of postponement of the date for redemption. No views were expressed in the House of Lords on the reasoning of the Court of Appeal.

(c) Misleading Maxims

In **Kreglinger v New Patagonia Meat and Cold Storage Co Ltd** [1914] AC 25, Lord Parker said at 53:

---

[15]   Now Companies Act 1985, s. 193.

'My Lords, I desire, in connection with what I have just said, to add a few words on the maxims in which attempts have been made to sum up the equitable principles applicable to mortgage transactions. I refer to the maxims, "Once a mortgage, always a mortgage", or, "A mortgage cannot be made irredeemable". Such maxims, however convenient, afford little assistance where the Court has to deal with a new or doubtful case. They obviously beg the question, always of great importance, whether the particular transaction which the Court has to consider is, in fact, a mortgage or not, and if they be acted on without a careful consideration of the equitable considerations on which they are based, can only, like Bacon's idols of the market place, lead to misconception and error.

We will suppose that money is advanced to a company repayable at the expiration of fifteen years, not an unusual period, and that the company by way of security subdemises (as is often the case) to trustees for the lenders a number of leaseholds, some of which are held for terms less than fifteen years. It would, in my opinion, be a serious error to argue that this was an attempt to make an irredeemable mortgage. There would be the same error in objecting on the like ground to a mortgage of leaseholds to secure an annuity for a period exceeding the term of the lease. If the mortgage is irredeemable at all, this arises from the nature of the property mortgaged, and not from any penal or repugnant stipulation on the part of the mortgagee, and the maxim properly understood is in no way infringed.'

QUESTION

X owned a 99-year lease in Blackacre. He wished to raise £100,000 in order to develop the land. His calculations showed that once the buildings were erected – estimated at 5 years – the income from the land would allow him to pay interest on the loan at 8 per cent and repay £1,000 of the capital each year. As the capital outstanding and thus the interest payable each year was reduced, a sum, increasing annually, would be available for himself. His expectation was that interest rates would rise.

With this plan in mind, he suggested to Y that he borrow £100,000 at 8 per cent, the capital repayable at the rate of £1,000 per annum starting five years hence, and £2,000 per annum in the last six years of the lease. Y agreed, saying that the repayment of capital was longer delayed than he wished, but that he was happy to help X.

Interest rates then declined to 6½ per cent. X claimed to be entitled to pay off the capital forthwith, on the ground that the terms of the mortgage made it irredeemable and therefore void.

Will he succeed? What assistance could Y obtain from (*a*) *Knightsbridge Estates Trust Ltd v Byrne*, from (*b*) *Santley v Wilde*?

iii. COLLATERAL ADVANTAGES

The cases in this section show how modifications have been made in recent times to the strict rule that an advantage or benefit collateral to the mortgage and in favour of the mortgagee is void in so far as it is to continue after redemption. A covenant is collateral where an obligation is placed on the mortgagor which is independent of that for the performance of which the land is charged. *Biggs v Hoddinott* [1898] 2 Ch 307 held that such a collateral advantage was valid if it was to exist only until redemption; but covenants drafted so as to exist beyond redemption were struck down in *Noakes & Co Ltd v Rice* [1902] AC 24 and *Bradley v Carritt* [1903] AC 253, even though in the latter case the covenant was not of such a type that it could in any circumstances 'run with' the property mortgaged. Inevitably the situation arose in which the strict application of this rule was not consistent with contemporary business requirements; and the speeches of Lords HALDANE and PARKER in *Kreglinger v New Patagonia Meat and Cold Storage Co Ltd*[16] [1914] AC 25 show that the law has managed to conform both to the requirements of the day and to the precedents and rules of earlier times.

The most common method of reconciling the *Kreglinger* case with *Noakes & Co Ltd v Rice* and *Bradley v Carritt,* is to construe the covenant to sell the skins in the *Kreglinger* case as being a 'contract, contained in the same document as constituted the security, but in substance independent of it.'[17] Once it is so construed it must stand or fall on its own merits. It is difficult to see why a commercial contract, which is in itself valid, should become void because it is recorded in the same document as a mortgage. Where it can be construed as separate from the mortgage, the position is that if it were entered into on Monday and the mortgage on Tuesday,[18] the two are separate and incapable of affecting each other. It has already been seen that a covenant to do something other than repay principal, interest and costs may be part of the obligation for the performance of which the mortgage is given to secure; and a covenant of this type is not a 'collateral advantage' and cannot be affected by these rules.[19] Whether or not a contract is (i) part of the mortgage security, as in *Santley v Wilde,* (ii) entirely independent of the mortgage transaction, as in the *Kreglinger* case, or (iii) part of the mortgage transaction without being part of the security, as in *Noakes & Co Ltd v Rice* and *Bradley v Carritt,* is a question of construction in each particular case. If the contract is of types (i) or (ii), it is not affected by the rules relating to collateral advantages. If it is of type (iii), which is in its nature between types (i) and (ii), then it is subjected to the authority of the cases declaring collateral advantages to be void. The selection of the correct category for any particular contract is a question for the court in each particular case, but the way is at least open now to the courts to permit the enforcement of bona fide business deals by construing them as falling outside the authority of *Noakes & Co Ltd v Rice* and *Bradley v Carritt.*

(a) Ending With Redemption

BIGGS v HODDINOTT
[1898] 2 Ch 307 (CA, LINDLEY MR, CHITTY and COLLINS LJJ)

On 18 March 1896, the defendant Hoddinott, the owner of a public house, mortgaged it to Biggs, a brewer. The deed contained an undertaking by Hoddinott that during the continuance of the mortgage he would deal with only the plaintiff in his purchase of certain liquor; an undertaking by the plaintiff that during the continuance of the mortgage he would supply such liquor at the

---

[16]   See *Cityland and Property (Holdings) Ltd v Dabrah* [1968] Ch 166, [1967] 2 All ER 639, p. 821, post.

[17]   Per Lord HALDANE at 41; *Re Petrol Filling Station, Vauxhall Bridge Road, London* (1968) 20 P & CR 1, p. 824, post.

[18]   See Lord HALSBURY in *Samuel v Jarrah Timber and Wood Paving Corpn Ltd* [1904] AC 323, p. 802, ante.

[19]   Because it does not continue after redemption: *Santley v Wilde* [1899] 2 Ch 474, p. 805, ante.

scheduled prices; and a provision that redemption should not take place, nor should the money be called in, for five years. About two years later, the defendant ceased to purchase liquor from the plaintiff who brought this action for an injunction, and the defendant claimed to be entitled to redeem the mortgage. Romer J granted an injunction and refused to allow the defendant to redeem. On appeal on the question of the issue of the injunction.

Held. The covenant tying the public house during the continuance of the mortgage was valid.

LINDLEY MR: We have listened to a very ingenious and learned argument with the view of inducing us under pressure to lay down a proposition of law which would be very unfortunate for business men. The proposition contended for comes to this – that while two people are engaged in a mortgage transaction they cannot enter into any other transaction with each other which can possibly benefit the mortgagee, and that any such transaction must be before or after the mortgage and be independent of it, so that it cannot be said that the mortgagee got any additional benefit from the mortgage transaction. Mr Farwell did not attempt to uphold this on any rational principle, but relied on authority. Of course, we must follow settled authorities whether we like them or not; but do they support this proposition? *Jennings v Ward* (1705) 2 Vern 520 was the first case relied upon. That was a redemption suit, and the stipulation which was in question seriously interfered with the redemption of the mortgaged property, and the Master of the Rolls (Sir J Trevor) decreed redemption without regard to that stipulation. He is reported to have said: 'A man shall not have interest for his money, and a collateral advantage besides for the loan of it, or clog the redemption with any by-agreement.' That has been understood as meaning exactly what was said, without regard to the circumstances of the case, and has found its way into the text-books as establishing that a mortgagee cannot have principal, interests, and costs, and also some collateral advantage. But that supposed rule has been departed from again and again. Take the case of West India mortgages: it has been repeatedly decided that the mortgagee, if not in possession, may stipulate that he shall be appointed consignee. The proposition stated in *Jennings v Ward* is too wide. If properly guarded it is good law and good sense. A mortgage is regarded as a security for money, and the mortgagor can always redeem on payment of principal, interest, and costs; and no bargain preventing such redemption is valid, nor will unconscionable bargains be enforced. There is no case where collateral advantages have been disallowed which does not come under one of these two heads. To say that to require such a covenant as that now in question is unconscionable is asking us to lay down a proposition which would shock any business man, and we are not driven to it by authority. . . .

The appeal will be dismissed.

(b) Existing After Redemption

NOAKES & CO LTD v RICE
[1902] AC 24 (HL, Earl of HALSBURY LC, Lords MACNAGHTEN, SHAND, DAVEY, BRAMPTON, ROBERTSON and LINDLEY)

Rice, the plaintiff, purchased, in 1897, the lease of a public house; the lease was to expire in 1923. Before this purchase, Noakes and Co, brewers, were mortgagees of the house and advanced money to Rice to enable him to purchase the leasehold premises which were mortgaged to them as security for the loan. Both this and the prior mortgage included a covenant, 'so as to charge the premises

into whosesoever possession the same may come . . . and to the further intent
that the obligation of this covenant may run with the land' that the mortgagor
would not, during the continuance of the lease, 'whether any principal moneys
or interest shall or shall not be owning' under the mortgage, use any liquor that
had not been purchased from Noakes and Co. Provision was made for payment
of liquidated damages in case of breach.

Rice now wished to pay off the loan and claimed to redeem the property fee
from the covenant tying the house.

Held. On payment of all that was due, the plaintiff could recover the property
free from the tie.

LORD DAVEY: My Lords, there are three doctrines of the Courts of Equity in
this country which have been referred to in the course of the argument in this
case. The first doctrine to which I refer is expressed in the maxim, 'Once a
mortgage always a mortgage'. The second is that the mortgagee shall not reserve
to himself any collateral advantage outside the mortgage contract; and the third
is that a provision or stipulation which will have the effect of clogging or fettering
the equity of redemption is void.

My Lords, the first maxim presents no difficulty: it is only another way of saying
that a mortgage cannot be made irredeemable, and that a provision to that effect
is void. In the case of *Salt v Marquess of Northampton* [1892] AC 1 the question was
whether a certain life policy, the premiums on which were charged against the
mortgagor, was comprised in the mortgage security. That question having been
decided in the affirmative, it was declared to be redeemable, notwithstanding
an express provision to the contrary contained in the deed.

My Lords, the second doctrine to which I refer, namely that the mortgagee
shall not reserve to himself any collateral advantage outside the mortgage
contract, was established long ago when the usury laws were in force. The Court
of Equity went beyond the usury laws, and set its face against every transaction
which tended to usury. It therefore declared void every stipulation by a mortgagee
for a collateral advantage which made his total remuneration for the loan
indirectly exceed the legal interest. I think it will be found that every case under
this head of equity was decided either on this ground, or on the ground that the
bargain was oppressive and unconscionable. The abolition of the usury laws has
made an alteration in the view the Court should take on this subject, and I agree
that a collateral advantage may now be stipulated for by a mortgage, provided
that no unfair advantage be taken by the mortgagee which would render it void
or voidable, according to the general principles of equity, and provided that it
does not offend against the third doctrine. On these grounds I think the case of
Biggs v Hoddinott [1898] 2 Ch 307 in the Court of Appeal was rightly decided.

The third doctrine to which I have referred is really a corollary from the first,
and it might be expressed in this form: Once a mortgage always a mortgage and
nothing but a mortgage. The meaning of that is that the mortgagee shall not
make any stipulation which will prevent a mortgagor, who has paid principal,
interest, and costs, from getting back his mortgaged property in the condition
in which he parted with it. I do not dissent from the opinion expressed by my
noble and learned friend opposite (Lord Lindley), when Master of the Rolls, in
the case of *Santley v Wilde* [1899] 2 Ch 474. He says: 'A clog or fetter is something
which is inconsistent with the idea of security; a clog or fetter is in the nature of
a repugnant condition.' But I ask, 'security' for what? I think it must be security
for the principal, interest, and costs, and, I will add, for any advantages in the
nature of increased interest or remuneration for the loan which the mortgagee

has validly stipulated for during the continuance of the mortgage. There are two elements in the conception of a mortgage: first, security for the money advanced; and, secondly, remuneration for the use of the money. When the mortgage is paid off the security is at an end, and, as the mortgagee is no longer kept out of his money, the remuneration to him for the use of his money is also at an end. I confess I should have decided the case of *Santley v Wilde* differently from the way in which it was dealt with in the Court of Appeal. After the payment of principal and interest, and everything which had become payable up to the date of redemption, the property in that case remained charged with the payment to the mortgagee of one-third share of the profits, and the stipulation to that effect should, I think, have been held to be a clog or fetter on the right to redeem. The principle is this—that a mortgage must not be converted into something else; and when once you come to the conclusion that a stipulation for the benefit of the mortgagee is part of the mortgage transaction, it is but part of his security, and necessarily comes to an end on the payment off of the loan. In my opinion, every yearly or other recurring payment stipulated for by the mortgagee should be held to be in the nature of interest, and no more payable after the principal is paid off than interest would be. I apprehend a man could not stipulate for the continuance of payment of interest after the principal is paid, and I do not think he can stipulate for any other recurring payment such as a share of profits. Any stipulation to that effect, would, in my opinion be void as a clog or fetter on the equity of redemption.

LORD LINDLEY: The conclusion thus arrived at is not inconsistent with *Santley v Wilde* on which the appellants so strongly rely. Some of your Lordships think that case went too far. I do not think so myself; but I will not trouble your Lordships with its details, which were complicated. The principle on which the Court of Appeal decided the case was, I still think, sound. Whether it was properly applied in that case is now of no importance. I believe the true principle applicable to these cases to be that expounded by the Court of Appeal in *Biggs v Hoddinott* and *Santley v Wilde*. That principle is perfectly consistent with a real pledge and with the maxim 'Once a mortgage always a mortgage'; but it will not render valid the covenant which your Lordships have to consider in the present case.

In **Bradley v Carritt** [1903] AC 253, one Bradley, who was the owner of a controlling number of shares in the Sephinjuri Bheel Tea Company, mortgaged them to Carritt, a tea broker, who wished to become the sole broker for the sale of the company's teas. By a written agreement, Bradley undertook, in clause 4, to use his 'best endeavours to secure that [Carritt, the plaintiff] shall always hereafter have the sale of all the company's teas as broker; and, in the event of any of the company's teas being sold otherwise than through' Carritt, to pay to him the commission which he would have earned if they had been sold through him. After the mortgage was paid off, the shares were again mortgaged to a different mortgagee, who took advantage of his voting-power to oust the plaintiff from his position as broker of the company. Carritt sued to recover, as damages for breach of contract, the amount of the commission.

By a bare majority, Lords MACNAGHTEN, DAVEY and ROBERTSON, with Lords SHAND and LINDLEY dissenting, the House of Lords reversed BIGHAM J and the Court of Appeal and held that the covenant was void as a clog on the equity of redemption, and that no action therefore lay.

The covenant was one that on its terms continued after redemption. The main question was whether or not it was a clog on the equity of redemption. It differed in this respect from the covenant in *Noakes v Rice* [1902] AC 24, for the covenant in that case was one that directly affected the property mortgaged; the mortgagor, having mortgaged a free house, would on redemption have received back a tied house. In this case, however, the covenant did not run with the tea shares; as Lord LINDLEY said at 276: 'Clause 4 in no way fetters the right to redeem, nor obstructs the mortgagor in the practical exercise of that right, or of the use or enjoyment of his shares when he gets them back. He can then do what he likes with them, free from all control by the mortgagee.' Lord DAVEY said at 268:'. . .Can it be said that the mortgagee does not retain a hold upon the shares which form the mortgaged property, or that the mortgagor has full redemption of it, when the latter is not free to exercise an important right in such manner as he may think most conducive to his own interests? . . . . Again, the appellant could not part with or otherwise deal with his shares without losing the influence in the company's counsels which might enable him to secure the performance of the first part of the agreement, or running a serious risk of liability under the second part.'

The speeches show again the different views of Lords LINDLEY and DAVEY upon the principles involved in the question of collateral advantages in particular and of the protection of the mortgagor in general.

KREGLINGER v NEW PATAGONIA MEAT AND COLD STORAGE CO LTD

[1914] AC 25 (HL, Viscount HALDANE LC, EARL OF HALSBURY, Lords ATKINSON, MERSEY and PARKER OF WADDINGTON)

The appellants, a firm of woolbrokers agreed to lend £10,000 to the respondents, a firm of meat packers. Provided all interest was paid punctually and all the terms of the agreement observed, the appellants agreed not to call in the principal for five years, but the respondents were at liberty to pay off the loan whenever they wished. The loan was secured by a floating charge [20] on the respondents' undertaking. Clause 8 of the agreement provided in sub-clause (A) that the respondents would not, for a period of five years, 'sell any sheepskins to any person . . . other than the lenders so long as the lenders are willing to purchase the same at a price equal to the best price . . . offered . . . by any . . . other person . . .'. Sub-clause (C) provided that the respondent company 'will pay to the lenders a commission of 1 per cent upon the sale price of all sheepskins sold by the company' to anyone other than the lenders.

After a few months over two years the respondents paid off the loan in accordance with the terms of the agreement, and disputed the right of the appellants to exercise their option to purchase the sheepskins. The appellants

[20] This, though a charge upon the assets for the time being, does not prevent a company from dealing with its property in the ordinary course of business, but it does so when the chargee takes steps, such as by the appointment of a receiver, to crystallise the security. For the characteristics of the charge, see *Re Yorkshire Woolcombers Association Ltd* [1903] 2 Ch 284 at 295, per ROMER J: and for crystallisation of a charge: see *Re Woodroffes (Musical Instruments) Ltd* [1986] Ch 366, [1985] 2 All ER 908; *Re Brightlife Ltd* [1987] Ch 200, [1986] 3 All ER 673; (1976) 40 Conv (NS) 397 (J. H. Farrar); [1988] CLJ 213 (E. Ferran); *William Gaskell Group v Highley* [1993] BCC 200. See generally [1994] CLJ 81 (S. Worthington); *Re Cosslett (Contractors) Ltd* [1998] Ch 495, [1997] 4 All ER 115; *Agnew v IRC* [2001] BCC 252; [2001] CLJ 472 (P. R. Wood); *Re Spectrum Plus Ltd* [2004] EWCA Civ 670, [2004] 2 WLR 783; (2004) 120 LQR 108 (R. C. Nolan).

brought an action for an injunction to restrain the sale of sheepskins to other persons.

Held (reversing SWINFEN EADY J and the Court of Appeal (COZENS-HARDY MR, BUCKLEY and KENNEDY LJJ) (1913) 29 TLR 393; 464). Appellants entitled to an injunction.

VISCOUNT HALDANE LC: My Lords, the respondents have now, as they were entitled to do under the agreement, paid off the loan. They claim that such payment has put an end to the option of the appellants to buy the respondents' sheepskins. Under the terms of the agreement this option, as I have already stated, will, if it is valid, continue operative until 24 August 1915. What the respondents say is that the stipulation is one that restricts their freedom in conducting the undertaking or business which is the subject of the floating charge; that it was consequently of the nature of a clog on their right to redeem and invalid; and that, whether it clogged the right to redeem or was in the nature of a collateral advantage, it was not intended and could not be made to endure after redemption. The appellants, on the other hand, say that the stipulation in question was one of a kind usual in business, and that it was in the nature not of a clog but of a collateral bargain outside the actual loan, which they only agreed to make in order to obtain the option itself. They further say that even if the option could be regarded as within the doctrine of equity which forbids the clogging of the right to redeem, that doctrine does not in a case such as this extend to a floating charge. . . .

My Lords, before I refer to the decisions of this House which the Courts below have considered to cover the case, I will state what I conceive to be the broad principles which must govern it.

The reason for which a Court of Equity will set aside the legal title of a mortgagee and compel him to reconvey the land on being paid principal, interest and costs is a very old one. . . .

The principle was . . . in the early days limited in its application to the accomplishment of the end which was held to justify interference of equity with freedom of contract. It did not go further. As established it was expressed in three ways. The most general of these was that if the transaction was once found to be a mortgage, it must be treated as always remaining a mortgage and nothing but a mortgage. That the substance of the transaction must be looked to in applying this doctrine and that it did not apply to cases which were only apparently or technically within it but were in reality something more than cases of mortgage, *Howard v Harris* (1683) 1 Vern 190 and other authorities shew. It was only a different application of the paramount doctrine to lay it down in the form of a second rule that a mortgagee should not stipulate for a collateral advantage which would make his remuneration for the loan exceed a proper rate of interest. The Legislature during a long period placed restrictions on the rate of interest which could legally be exacted. But equity went beyond the limits of the statutes which limited the interest, and was ready to interfere with any usurious stipulation in a mortgage. In so doing it was influenced by the public policy of the time. That policy has now changed, and the Acts which limited the rate of interest have been repealed. The result is that a collateral advantage may now be stipulated for by the mortgagee provided that he has not acted unfairly or oppressively, and provided that the bargain does not conflict with the third form of the principle. That is that a mortgage . . . cannot be made irredeemable, and that any stipulation which restricts or clogs the equity of redemption is void. It is obvious that the reason for the doctrine in this form is the same as that which gave rise to the other forms. It is simply an assertion in a different way of the principle that once a mortgage always a mortgage and nothing else.

My Lords, the rules I have stated have now been applied by Courts of Equity for nearly three centuries, and the books are full of illustrations of their application. But what I have pointed out shews that it is inconsistent with the objects for which they were established that these rules should crystallize into technical language so rigid that the letter can defeat the underlying spirit and purpose. Their application must correspond with the practical necessities of the time. The rule as to collateral advantages, for example, has been much modified by the repeal of the usury laws and by the recognition of modern varieties of commercial bargaining . . . .

[His Lordship referred to *Biggs v Hoddinott* [1899] 2 Ch 307 and to the dictum of Trevor MR in *Jennings v Ward* (1705) 2 Vern 520 and continued:]

Unless such a bargain is unconscionable it is now good. But none the less the other and wider principle remains unshaken, that it is the essence of a mortgage that in the eye of a Court of Equity it should be a mere security for money, and that no bargain can be validly made which will prevent the mortgagor from redeeming on payment of what is due including principal, interest, and costs. He may stipulate that he will not pay off his debt, and so redeem the mortgage, for a fixed period. But whenever a right to redeem arises out of the doctrine of equity, he is precluded from fettering it. This principle has become an integral part of our system of jurisprudence and must be faithfully adhered to.

My Lords, the question in the present case is whether the right to redeem has been interfered with. And this must, for the reasons to which I have adverted in considering the history of the doctrine of equity, depend on the answer to a question which is primarily one of fact. What was the true character of the transaction? Did the appellants make a bargain such that the right to redeem was cut down, or did they simply stipulate for a collateral undertaking, outside and clear of the mortgage, which would give them an exclusive option of purchase of the sheepskins of the respondents? The question is in my opinion not whether the two contracts were made at the same moment and evidenced by the same instrument, but whether they were in substance a single and undivided contract or two distinct contracts. Putting aside for the moment considerations turning on the character of the floating charge, such an option no doubt affects the freedom of the respondents in carrying on their business even after the mortgage has been paid off. But so might other arrangements which would be plainly collateral, an agreement, for example, to take permanently into the firm a new partner as a condition of obtaining fresh capital in the form of a loan. The question is one not of form but of substance, and it can be answered in each case by looking at all the circumstances, and not by mere reliance on some abstract principle, or upon the dicta which have fallen obiter from judges in other and different cases. . . .

My Lords, if in the case before the House your Lordships arrive at the conclusion that the agreement for an option to purchase the respondents' sheepskins was not in substance a fetter on the exercise of their right to redeem, but was in the nature of a collateral bargain the entering into which was a preliminary and separable condition of the loan, the decided cases cease to present any great difficulty. In questions of this kind the binding force of previous decisions, unless the facts are indistinguishable, depends on whether they establish a principle. To follow previous authorities, so far as they lay down principles, is essential if the law is to be preserved from becoming unsettled and vague. In this respect the previous decisions of a Court of co-ordinate jurisdiction are more binding in a system of jurisprudence such as ours than in systems where the paramount authority is that of a code. But when a previous case has not laid down any new principle but has merely decided that a particular set of facts illustrates an existing rule, there are few more fertile sources of fallacy than to search in it for what is simply resemblance in circumstances, and to erect a previous decision into a governing precedent merely on this account. To look for anything except the principle established or recognised by previous decisions is really to weaken and not to strengthen the importance of precedent. . . .

It is not, in my opinion, conclusive in favour of the appellants that the security assumed the form of a floating charge. A floating charge is not the less a pledge because of its floating character, and a contract which fetters the right to redeem on which equity insists as regards all contracts of loan and security ought on principle to be set aside as readily in the case of a floating security as in any other case. But it is material that such a floating charge, in the absence of bargain to the contrary effect, permits the assets to be dealt with freely by the mortgagor until the charge becomes enforceable. . . . No doubt it is the fact that on redemption the respondents will not get back their business as free from obligation as it was before the date of the security. But that may well be because outside the security and consistently with its terms there was a contemporaneous but collateral contract, contained in the same document as constituted the security, but in substance independent of it. If it was the intention of the parties, as I think it was, to enter into this contract as a condition of the respondents getting their advance, I know no reason either in morals or in equity which ought to prevent this intention from being left to have its effect. What was to be capable of redemption was an undertaking which was deliberately left to be freely changed in its details by ordinary business transactions with which the mortgage was not to interfere. Had the charge not been a floating one, it might have been more difficult to give effect to this intention.

[His Lordship referred to *Noakes & Co Ltd v Rice* [1902] AC 24, p. 813, ante, where 'this difficulty is illustrated' and to *Bradley v Carritt* [1903] AC 253, p. 815, ante, and continued:]

[The decision in *Bradley v Carritt*] certainly cannot, in my opinion, be taken as authoritatively laying down that the mere circumstances that after redemption the property redeemed may not, as the result of some bargain made at the time of the mortgage, be in the same condition as it was before that time, is conclusive against the validity of that bargain. To render it invalid the bargain must, when its substance is examined, turn out to have formed part of the terms of the mortgage and to have really cut down a true right of redemption. I think that the tendency of recent decisions has been to lay undue stress on the letter of the principle which limits the jurisdiction of equity in setting aside contracts. The origin and reason of the principle ought, as I have already said, to be kept steadily in view in applying it to fresh cases. There appears to me to have grown up a tendency to look at the letter rather than the spirit of the doctrine. The true view is, I think, that judges ought in this kind of jurisdiction to proceed cautiously, and to bear in mind the real reasons which have led Courts of Equity to insist on the free right to redeem and the limits within which the purpose of the rule ought to confine its scope. I cannot but think that the validity of the bargain in such cases as *Bradley v Carritt* and *Santley v Wilde* [1899] 2 Ch 474, p. 804, ante, might have been made free from serious question if the parties had chosen to seek what would have been substantially the same result in a different form. . . .

LORD PARKER OF WADDINGTON: My Lords, the defendants in this case are appealing to the equitable jurisdiction of the Court for relief from a contract which they admit to be fair and reasonable and of which they have already enjoyed the full advantage. Their title to relief is based on some equity which they say is inherent in all transactions in the nature of a mortgage. They can state no intelligible principle underlying this alleged equity, but contend that your Lordships are bound by authority. That the Court should be asked in the exercise of its equitable jurisdiction to assist in so inequitable a proceeding as the repudiation of a fair and reasonable bargain is somewhat startling, and makes it necessary to examine the point of view from which Courts of Equity have always regarded mortgage transactions. . . .

My Lords, after the most careful consideration of the authorities I think it is open to this House to hold, and I invite your Lordships to hold, that there is now no rule in equity which precludes a mortgagee, whether the mortgage be made upon the occasion of a loan or otherwise, from stipulating for any collateral advantage, provided such collateral advantage is not either (1) unfair and unconscionable, or (2) in the nature of a penalty clogging the equity of redemption, or (3) inconsistent with or repugnant to the contractual and equitable right to redeem.

In the present case it is clear from the evidence, if not from the agreement of 24 August 1910 itself, that the nature of the transaction was as follows: The defendant company wanted to borrow 10,000*l*, and the plaintiffs desired to obtain an option of purchase over any sheepskins the defendants might have for sale during a period of five years. The plaintiffs agreed to lend the money in consideration of obtaining this option, and the defendant company agreed to give the option in consideration of obtaining the loan. The loan was to carry interest at 6 per cent per annum, and was not to be called in by the plaintiffs for a specified period. The defendant company, however, might pay it off at any time. It was to be secured by a floating charge over the defendant company's undertaking. The option was to continue for five years, whether the loan was paid off or otherwise, and if the plaintiffs did not exercise their option as to any of the defendant company's skins, a commission on the sale of such skins was in certain events payable to the plaintiffs.

I doubt whether, even before the repeal of the usury laws, this perfectly fair and businesslike transaction would have been considered a mortgage within any equitable rule or maxim relating to mortgages. The only possible way of deciding whether a transaction is a mortgage within any such rule or maxim is by reference to the intention of the parties. It never was intended by the parties that if the defendant company exercised their right to pay off the loan they should get rid of the option. The option was not in the nature of a penalty, nor was it nor could it ever become inconsistent with or repugnant to any other part of the real bargain within any such rule or maxim. The same is true of the commission payable on the sale of skins as to which the option was not exercised. Under these circumstances it seems to me that the bargain must stand and that the plaintiffs are entitled to the relief they claim.[1]

In **Multiservice Bookbinding Ltd v Marden** [1979] Ch 84, [1978] 2 All ER 489,[2] the plaintiffs in September 1966 charged their business premises to the

[1]   (1944) 60 LQR 191 (G. L. Williams).
[2]   [1978] Conv 346 (H. W. Wilkinson); 432 (D. W. Williams); and for an economist's view (1981) 131 NLJ 4 (R. A. Bowles). The Consumer Credit Act 1974, p. 846, post, was not applicable because the mortgagor was a body corporate.

defendant as security for a loan of £36,000, in order to purchase new premises in North London. The defendant was only willing to lend the money if he could be safeguarded against a decline in the purchasing power of sterling. The terms of the mortgage, which was created with solicitors' advice, were that (i) interest be payable at 2 per cent above bank rate on the full capital sum for the duration of the mortgage (ii) arrears of interest be capitalised after 21 days (thus providing for interest on interest) (iii) the loan be neither called in nor redeemed for 10 years, and (iv) the value of the capital and interest be index-linked to the Swiss franc ('the Swiss franc uplift' clause 6).

In September 1966 the Swiss franc was just over 12 to the pound but in October 1976, when a redemption statement was prepared, it had fallen to just over 4. The total capital repayment was £87,588, as against £36,000 lent, and the total interest due was £45,380 (£31,051 basic plus £14,329 uplift). The average rate of interest over the ten years would have been 16.01 per cent. On the other hand, the book value of the mortgaged property had more than doubled, and the plaintiff company's 'growth had been considerable.'

The plaintiffs took out a summons to determine how far the terms of the mortgage were enforceable. BROWNE-WILKINSON J held that all terms were valid. Having decided that an index-linked money obligation is not contrary to public policy, his Lordship continued at 109, at 501:

'I have dealt with these authorities [*Kreglinger v New Patagonia Meat and Cold Storage Co Ltd* [1914] AC 25, p. 816, ante; *Knightsbridge Estates Trust Ltd v Byrne* [1939] Ch 441, [1938] 4 All ER 618, p. 808, ante; *Biggs v Hoddinott* [1898] 2 Ch 307, p. 812, ante; *Davis v Symons* [1934] Ch 442] at some length because the sheet anchor of Mr Nugee's argument, that mere unreasonableness is sufficient to invalidate a stipulation, is the use of the word "unreasonable" by Goff J in *Cityland and Property (Holdings) Ltd v Dabrah* [1968] Ch 166, [1967] 2 All ER 639. In that case the plaintiff company was the freehold owner of a house of which the defendant had been the tenant for 11 years. His lease expired and the plaintiff company sold the freehold to him for £3,500, of which the defendant paid £600 in cash and the balance of £2,900 was left by the plaintiff company on mortgage. The mortgage was in unusual terms in that it contained simply a covenant to pay, by instalments, the sum of £4,553, that is to say, a premium of 57 per cent over the sum advanced. No explanation was given as to what this premium represented. The defendant defaulted in paying his instalments after only one year, and the plaintiff was seeking to enforce his security for the full sum of £4,553 less payments actually made. Not surprisingly Goff J refused to permit this on the grounds that the excess over £2,900 was an unlawful premium. Bearing in mind the relative strength of lender and borrower, the size of the premium and the lack of any explanation or justification for it, the premium in that case was unconscionable and oppressive. . . .

I therefore approach the second point on the basis that, in order to be freed from the necessity to comply with all the terms of the mortgage, the plaintiffs must show that the bargain, or some of its terms, was unfair and unconscionable: it is not enough to show that, in the eyes of the court, it was unreasonable. In my judgment a bargain cannot be unfair and unconscionable unless one of the parties to it has imposed the objectionable terms in a morally reprehensible manner, that is to say, in a way which affects his conscience.

The classic example of an unconscionable bargain is where advantage has been taken of a young, inexperienced or ignorant person to introduce a term which no sensible well-advised person or party would have accepted. But I do not think the categories of unconscionable bargains are limited: the court can and should intervene where a bargain has been procured by unfair means.

Mr Nugee submitted that a borrower was, in the normal case, in an unequal bargaining position vis-à-vis the lender and that the care taken by the courts of equity to protect borrowers – to which Lord Parker referred in the passage I have quoted [3] – was reflected in a general rule that, except in the case of two large equally powerful institutions, any unreasonable term would be "unconscionable" within Lord Parker's test. I cannot accept this. In my judgment there is no such special rule applicable to contracts of loan which requires one to treat a bargain as having been unfairly made even where it is demonstrated that no unfair advantage has been taken of the borrower. No decision illustrating Mr Nugee's principle was cited. However, if, as in the *Cityland* case, there is an unusual or unreasonable stipulation the reason for which is not explained, it may well be that in the absence of any explanation, the court will assume that unfair advantage has been taken of the borrower.

In considering all the facts, it will often be the case that the borrower's need for the money was far more pressing than the lender's need to lend: if this proves to be the case, then circumstances exist in which an unfair advantage could have been taken. It does not necessarily follow that what could have been done has been done: whether or not an unfair advantage has in fact been taken depends on the facts of each case.

Applying those principles to this case, first I do not think it is right to treat the "Swiss franc uplift" element in the capital-repayments as being in any sense a premium or collateral advantage. In my judgment a lender of money is entitled to insure that he is repaid the real value of his loan and if he introduces a term which so provides, he is not stipulating for anything beyond the repayment of principal. I do not think equity would have struck down clause 6 as a collateral advantage even before the repeal of the usury laws. . . .

Secondly, considering the mortgage bargain as a whole, in my judgment there was no great inequality of bargaining power as between the plaintiffs and the defendant. The plaintiff company was a small but prosperous company in need of cash to enable it to expand: if it did not like the terms offered it could have refused them without being made insolvent or, as in the *Cityland* case, losing its home. The defendant had £40,000 to lend, but only, as he explained to the plaintiffs, if its real value was preserved. The defendant is not a professional moneylender and there is no evidence of any sharp practice of any kind by him. The borrowers were represented by independent solicitors of repute. Therefore the background does not give rise to any presupposition that the defendant took an unfair advantage of the plaintiffs.

Mr Nugee's main case is based on the terms of the mortgage itself. He points to the facts that (1) the defendant's principal and interest is fully inflation proofed (2) that interest is payable at two per cent above minimum lending rate and (3) that interest is payable on the whole £36,000 throughout the term of the loan. He says that although any one of these provisions by itself might not be objectionable, when all these are joint in one mortgage they are together "unfair and unconscionable". He adds further subsidiary points, amongst them that it is impossible to know the sum required for redemption when notice to redeem has to be given; that interest is payable in advance; that no days of grace were allowed for paying the instalments of capital and any expenses incurred by the lender are

---

[3]   *Kreglinger v New Patagonia Meat and Cold Storage Co Ltd* [1914] AC 25 at 49–50, 54–56.

charged on the property and therefore under clause 6 subject to the Swiss franc uplift even though incurred long after 1966. He also contends that if there were capitalised arrears of interest, the Swiss franc uplift would be applied twice: once when the arrears are capitalised and again when the capitalised sum is paid: in my opinion this is not the true construction of the mortgage.

However, Mr Nugee's other points amount to a formidable list and if it were relevant I would be of the view that the terms were unreasonable judged by the standards which the court would adopt if it had to settle the terms of a mortgage. In particular I consider that it was unreasonable both for the debt to be inflation proofed by reference to the Swiss franc and at the same time to provide for a rate of interest two per cent above bank rate – a rate which reflects at least in part the unstable state of the pound sterling. On top of this interest on the whole sum advanced was to be paid throughout the term. The defendant made a hard bargain. But the test is not reasonableness. The parties made a bargain which the plaintiffs, who are businessmen, went into with their eyes open, with the benefit of independent advice, without any compelling necessity to accept a loan on these terms and without any sharp practice by the defendant. I cannot see that there was anything unfair or oppressive or morally reprehensible in such a bargain entered into in such circumstances. The need for the defendant to invest his money in a way which preserved its real purchasing power provides an adequate explanation of all the terms of the mortgage.[4]

In **De Beers Consolidated Mines Ltd v British South Africa Co** [1912] AC 52, a company agreed to grant a perpetual licence for mining diamonds on its land, and later mortgaged the land to the licensee. The House of Lords held that after redemption the agreement to grant the licence still bound the company. This was so even though the agreement for the licence expressly contemplated the later mortgage, since the two transactions were substantially independent of each other. When the property was mortgaged, 'it had already been burdened and encumbered with the prior obligation, superior to the mortgage security, to grant the licence' (at 66, per Lord ATKINSON). The licence was not a clog on the equity of redemption, 'because when the redemption took place everything which had been charged was restored to the mortgagor' (at 73, per Earl LOREBURN LC).

The problem has also arisen in connection with the distribution of petroleum products through tied garages. In general terms, the garage proprietor undertakes to deal only in the products of a particular oil company. The oil company undertakes to supply the products and to allow a special rebate. Sometimes the oil company advances money to the garage proprietor, and in such a case the mortgage of the garage will include an undertaking to observe the terms of the agreement during the continuance of the mortgage.

A garage proprietor who wishes to pay off the mortgage before the due date and to be free of its provisions may attack its validity on two grounds. First, on the

---

[4] A building society has power to make an index-linked mortgage: *Nationwide Building Society v Registry of Friendly Societies* [1983] 1 WLR 1226, [1983] 3 All ER 296. See *Boustany v Piggott* (1995) 69 P & CR 288, where PC set aside a lease on the grounds that it was an unconscionable bargain; *Commercial Bank of Australia Ltd v Amadio* (1983) 46 ALR 402; [1996] Conv 454 (M. Pawlowski).

ground of the doctrine, previously discussed, which protects a mortgagor against oppression. Secondly, on the ground that the agreement is void as being in restraint of trade. This second ground is a matter for the law of contract and its details must be sought elsewhere. [5] We should, however, note here an argument that the doctrine of restraint of trade has no application to mortgages; that the mortgagor, being especially protected by equity, has equity's protection but no other. As would be expected, this argument has not been accepted. [6]

Thus a mortgage is open to attack on both grounds. The two grounds must be kept distinct, for different evidence is relevant to each, and different rules are applicable; and, following the doctrine of the *Kreglinger* case, the court may consider whether an operation is properly construed as a single transaction or as two separate transactions; one being a mortgage which is governed by the doctrine here discussed, and the other being a commercial agreement which is dealt with under the doctrine of restraint of trade.

RE PETROL FILLING STATION, VAUXHALL BRIDGE ROAD LONDON
(1968) 20 P & CR 1 (ChD, Ungoed-Thomas J)

The plaintiffs were owners of a petrol filling station, and entered into a twenty-year contract on 9 April 1956 with the defendants, whereby the plaintiffs agreed to sell only the defendants' products, and were entitled to a rebate on the price in addition to the usual commission.

On 1 November 1956 the plaintiffs mortgaged their garage to the defendants in consideration of a loan which was required for the modernisation of the premises. The mortgage deed:

(1) provided for the repayment of the loan over nineteen years;
(2) gave the defendants (the mortgagees) a right of pre-emption over the premises during the continuance of the mortgage;
(3) provided that the term of the contract of 9 April 1956 tying the petrol station should remain in force during the continuance of the mortgage.

The question was whether the plaintiffs were entitled to redeem, and to be free of the restrictions contained in the contract and the mortgage.

Held. The plaintiffs were bound by the terms of the mortgage.

Ungoed-Thomas J: It is common ground that the ties in the November agreement are, in accordance with its express provisions, limited to the continuance of the security and that, therefore, on redemption they cease to operate and no question of clog can arise with regard to them. It is also common ground that the ties contained in the sales agreement are capable of constituting a clog on an equity of redemption if they are (and I purposely use vague words) sufficiently connected with it. Therefore, the only question for my decision becomes whether the ties imposed by the sales agreement of April are sufficiently

---

5   Cheshire, Fifoot and Furmston, *Law of Contract* (14th edn, 1996), pp. 449–467; Treitel, *Law of Contract* (11th edn), pp. 453–477; (1969) 85 LQR 229 (J. D. Heydon); Heydon, *Restraint of Trade Doctrine* (1971), chaps. 3, 9; Jefferson, *Restraint of Trade* (1997).

As to the possible impact of Article 85 (now Article 81) of the European Community Treaty on solus agreements, see *Delimitis v Henninger Brau A-G*, [1991] ECR 1–935; *Courage Ltd v Crehan* [1999] 2 EGLR 145; *Crehani v Interpreneur Pubs Co (CPC)* [2004] EWCA Civ 317.

6   *Esso Petroleum Co Ltd v Harper's Garage (Stourport) Ltd* [1968] AC 269, [1967] 1 All ER 699, per Lord Wilberforce at 342, at 735; *Alec Lobb (Garages) Ltd v Total Oil Great Britain Ltd* [1985] 1 WLR 173, [1985] 1 All ER 303, p. 803, n. 6, ante; [1985] Conv 141 (P. Todd); *Plummer v Tibsco Ltd* [2002] 1 EGLR 29 (option to renew lease of public house subject to purchase of minimum quantity of liquor from landlord held void).

connected with the equity of redemption of the legal charge of November as to constitute a clog upon it. . . .

If, in accordance with my view, the plaintiffs executed the sales agreement without there being any contract with regard to the loan, then it seems to me to follow that the sales agreement and the legal charge were what they appear on their face to be, namely, two separate contracts. Such a conclusion would be in line with the reliance, based on *De Beer's Consolidated Mines Ltd v British South Africa Co* [1912] AC 52, p. 832, ante, on the British South Africa Company's obligation to grant the licence being absolute and immediate and their granting of the mortgage being optional. This distinction in that case was relied on as itself establishing that there were two contracts, one with regard to the licence and one with regard to the mortgage, and not one contract comprehending them both.

Secondly, even if there were, contrary to my view, a binding contract with regard to the loan and with regard to the sales agreement before or at the time of the sales agreement, the question would still remain whether they constituted one or two contracts. Having regard to authorities and the evidence, which I have already considered, including the commercial nature of the ties in the sales agreement, it seems to me that at its highest the defendants' agreement to lend 'in return for the plaintiffs' agreeing to enter into a petrol sales agreement' as stated by Mr Pugh, was, in the words of Lord Haldane in the *Kreglinger* case [1914] AC 25 'in consideration of being given' a petrol sales agreement, which was 'a collateral bargain the entering into which was a preliminary and separable condition of the loan.'

Thirdly, even if there were one contract, as the plaintiffs contend, I, for my part, if I were driven to it, would conclude that that contract comprehending the sales agreement and the agreement to lend on the legal charge was not in its 'real nature and substance', as a whole, a mortgage transaction, nor, to use Lord Haldane's words, 'a mere mortgage', and so falls outside the doctrine of once a mortgage always a mortgage, of which the clog on the equity of redemption is an emanation. I again quote Lord Haldane, where he said, at 37:

'That the substance of the transaction must be looked to in applying this doctrine and that it did not apply to cases which were only apparently or technically within it but were in reality something more than cases of mortgage'.

If there were the one contract, as the plaintiffs say, then it was 'something more than' a mortgage – it was a commercial transaction, of which the mortgage formed part, leaving at any rate the sales agreement part of the transaction with the sales agreement ties outside the ambit of the other part of the transaction, namely, the mortgage, altogether. As I have indicated, the effect on the ties specified in the document of legal charge if those ties were expressed to endure beyond redemption, does not arise.

My conclusion, therefore, is that the defendants succeed on the issue before me.

iv. UNDUE INFLUENCE, MISREPRESENTATION AND THIRD PARTIES

(a) The O'Brien Rule

A mortgage may be set aside for undue influence, not only where the mortgagee himself exerts it on the mortgagor, but also where the mortgagee is in some way responsible for undue influence exerted on a third party by the mortgagor. It may also be set aside for misrepresentation.

In **Barclays Bank plc v O'Brien** [1994] 1 AC 180, [1993] 4 All ER 417, the House of Lords considered whether a bank was entitled to enforce against a wife an obligation to secure a debt owed by her husband to the bank, where the wife had been induced to stand as surety for her husband's debt by his undue influence or misrepresentation. Lord BROWNE-WILKINSON said at 191, at 424:

'Up to this point I have been considering the right of a claimant wife to set aside a transaction as against the wrongdoing husband when the transaction has been procured by his undue influence. But in surety cases the decisive question is whether the claimant wife can set aside the transaction, not against the wrongdoing husband, but against the creditor bank. Of course, if the wrongdoing husband is acting as agent for the creditor bank in obtaining the surety from the wife, the creditor will be fixed with the wrongdoing of its own agent and the surety contract can be set aside as against the creditor. Apart from this, if the creditor bank has notice, actual or constructive, of the undue influence exercised by the husband (and consequentially of the wife's equity to set aside the transaction) the creditor will take subject to that equity and the wife can set aside the transaction against the creditor (albeit a purchaser for value) as well as against the husband: see *Bainbrigge v Browne* (1881) 18 Ch D 188 and *Bank of Credit and Commerce International SA v Aboody* [1990] 1 QB 923, 973, [1992] 4 All ER 955, 980.

A wife who has been induced to stand as a surety for her husband's debts by his undue influence, misrepresentation or some other legal wrong has an equity as against him to set aside that transaction. Under the ordinary principles of equity, her right to set aside that transaction will be enforceable against third parties (e.g. against a creditor) if either the husband was acting as the third party's agent or the third party had actual or constructive notice of the facts giving rise to her equity. Although there may be cases where, without artificiality, it can properly be held that the husband was acting as the agent of the creditor in procuring the wife to stand as surety, such cases will be of very rare occurrence. The key to the problem is to identify the circumstances in which the creditor will be taken to have had notice of the wife's equity to set aside the transaction.

The doctrine of notice lies at the heart of equity. Given that there are two innocent parties, each enjoying rights, the earlier right prevails against the later right if the acquirer of the later right knows of the earlier right (actual notice) or would have discovered it had he taken proper steps (constructive notice). In particular, if the party asserting that he takes fee of the earlier rights of another knows of certain facts which put him on inquiry as to the possible existence of the rights of that other and he fails to make such inquiry or take such other steps as are reasonable to verify whether such earlier right does or does not exist, he will have constructive notice of the earlier right and take subject to it. Therefore where a wife has agreed to stand surety for her husband's debts as a result of undue influence or misrepresentation, the creditor will take subject to the wife's equity to set aside the transaction if the circumstances are such as to put the creditor on inquiry as to the circumstances in which she agreed to stand surety. ...

Therefore in my judgment a creditor is put on inquiry when a wife offers to stand surety for her husband's debts by the combination of two factors: (a) the transaction is on its face not to the financial advantage of the wife; and (b) there is a substantial risk in transactions of that kind that, in procuring the wife to act as surety, the husband has committed a legal or equitable wrong that entitles the wife to set aside the transaction.

It follows that unless the creditor who is put on inquiry takes reasonable steps to satisfy himself that the wife's agreement to stand surety has been properly obtained, the creditor will have constructive notice of the wife's rights.'

[His Lordship then set out the guide lines to what reasonable steps a bank has to take in order to avoid being fixed by constructive notice. These principles are not limited to transactions involving husband and wife, but apply to all other cases where there is an emotional relationship between co-habitees.

Royal Bank of Scotland v Etridge (No 2) has refined the approach to this problem and has set new detailed guidelines for its solution.

ROYAL BANK OF SCOTLAND PLC v ETRIDGE (NO 2) [7] [2002] 2 AC 73, [2001] 4 All ER 449 (HL, Lords BINGHAM OF CORNHILL, NICHOLLS OF BIRKENHEAD, CLYDE, HOBHOUSE OF WOODBOROUGH and SCOTT OF FOSCOTE).

LORD BINGHAM OF CORNHILL:

2 The transactions which give rise to these appeals are commonplace but of great social and economic importance. It is important that a wife (or anyone in a like position) should not charge her interest in the matrimonial home to secure the borrowing of her husband (or anyone in a like position) without fully understanding the nature and effect of the proposed transaction and that the decision is hers, to agree or not to agree. It is important that lenders should feel able to advance money, in run-of-the-mill cases with no abnormal features, on the security of the wife's interest in the matrimonial home in reasonable confidence that, if appropriate procedures have been followed in obtaining the security, it will be enforceable if the need for enforcement arises. The law must afford both parties a measure of protection. It cannot prescribe a code which will be proof against error, misunderstanding or mishap. But it can indicate minimum requirements which, if met, will reduce the risk of error, misunderstanding or mishap to an acceptable level. The paramount need in this important field is that these minimum requirements should be clear, simple and practically operable.

LORD NICHOLLS OF BIRKENHEAD:

5 My Lords, before your Lordships' House are appeals in eight cases. Each case arises out of a transaction in which a wife charged her interest in her home in favour of a bank as security for her husband's indebtedness or the indebtedness of a company through which he carried on business. The wife later asserted she signed the charge under the undue influence of her husband. In *Barclays Bank plc v O'Brien* [1994] 1 AC 180 your Lordship enunciated the principles applicable in this type of case. Since then, many cases have come before the courts, testing the implications of the *O'Brien* decision in a variety of different factual situations. Seven of the present appeals are of this character. In each case the bank sought to enforce the charge signed by the wife. The bank claimed an order for possession of the matrimonial home. The wife raised a defence that the bank was on notice that her concurrence in the transaction had been procured by her husband's undue influence. The eighth appeal concerns a claim by a wife for damages from a solicitor who advised her before she entered into a guarantee obligation of this character.

---

[7]   [2002] Conv 174 (M. P. Thompson); [2002] CLJ 229 (M. Oldham); (2002) 65 MLR 435 (R. Bigwood); (2002) 118 LQR 337 (D. O'Sullivan); [2001] All ER Rev 254 (P. J. Clarke). For a useful comparison between *O'Brien* and *Etridge (No. 2)* see *Emmet on Title*, para. 25.040–25.040D9.

Undue influence

6 The issues raised by these appeals make it necessary to go back to first principles. Undue influence is one of the grounds of relief developed by the courts of equity as a court of conscience. The objective is to ensure that the influence of one person over another is not abused. ...

8 Equity identified broadly two forms of unacceptable conduct. The first comprises overt acts of improper pressure or coercion such as unlawful threats. Today there is much overlap with the principle of duress as this principle has subsequently developed. The second form arises out of a relationship between two persons where one has acquired over another a measure of influence, or ascendancy, of which the ascendant person then takes unfair advantage. An example from the 19th century, when much of this law developed, is a case where an impoverished father prevailed upon his inexperienced children to charge their reversionary interests under their parents' marriage settlement with payment of his mortgage debts: see *Bainbrigge v Browne* (1881) 18 Ch D 188.

9 In cases of this latter nature the influence one person has over another provides scope for misuse without any specific overt acts of persuasion. The relationship between two individuals may be such that, without more, one of them is disposed to agree a course of action proposed by the other. Typically this occurs when one person places trust in another to look after his affairs and interests, and the latter betrays this trust by preferring his own interests. He abuses the influence he has acquired.

[His Lordship referred to *Allcard v Skinner* (1882) 36 Ch D 145, 181 and *Zamet v Hyman* [1961] 1 WLR 1442, 1444–1445, [1961] 3 All ER 993, 936 and continued:]

10 The law has long recognised the need to prevent abuse of influence in these 'relationship' cases despite the absence of evidence of overt acts of persuasive conduct. The types of relationship, such as parent and child, in which this principle falls to be applied cannot be listed exhaustively. Relationships are infinitely various. Sir Guenter Treitel QC has rightly noted that the question is whether one party has reposed sufficient trust and confidence in the other, rather than whether the relationship between the parties belong to a particular type: see *Treitel, The Law of Contract*, 10 ed (1999), pp. 380–381. For example, the relation of banker and customer will not normally meet this criterion, but exceptionally it may: see *National Westminster Bank plc v Morgan* [1985] AC 686, 707–709, [1983] 3 All ER 821, 829–831.

11 Even this test is not comprehensive. The principle is not confined to cases of abuse of trust and confidence. It also includes, for instance, cases where a vulnerable person has been exploited. Indeed, there is no single touchstone for determining whether the principle is applicable. Several expressions have been used to an endeavour to encapsulate the essence: trust and confidence, reliance, dependence or vulnerability on the one hand and ascendancy, domination or control on the other. None of these descriptions is perfect. None is all embracing. Each has its proper place.

12 In *CIBC Mortgages plc v Pitt* [1994] 1 AC 200, [1993] 4 All ER 433 your Lordships' House decided that in cases of undue influence disadvantage is not a necessary ingredient of the cause of action. It is not essential that the transaction should be disadvantageous to the pressurised or influenced person, either in financial terms or in any other way. ...

Burden of proof and presumptions

13 Whether a transaction was brought about by the exercise of undue influence is a question of fact. Here, as elsewhere, the general principle is that

he who asserts a wrong has been committed must prove it. The burden of proving an allegation of undue influence rests upon the person who claims to have been wronged. This is the general rule. The evidence required to discharge the burden of proof depends on the nature of the alleged undue influence, the personality of the parties, their relationship, the extent to which the transaction cannot readily be accounted for by the ordinary motives of ordinary persons in that relationship, and all the circumstances of the case.

14 Proof that the complainant placed trust and confidence in the other party in relation to the management of the complainant's financial affairs, coupled with a transaction which calls for explanation, will normally be sufficient, failing satisfactory evidence to the contrary, to discharge the burden of proof. On proof of these two matters the stage is set for the court to infer that, in the absence of a satisfactory explanation, the transaction can only have been procured by undue influence.

[His Lordship referred to *Bainbrigge v Browne*, and *National Westminster Bank plc v Morgan*, and continued:] ...

16 Generations of equity lawyers have conventionally described this situation as one in which a presumption of undue influence arises. This use of the term 'presumption' is descriptive of a shift in the evidential onus on a question of fact. When a plaintiff succeeds by this route he does so because he has succeeded in establishing a case of undue influence. The court has drawn appropriate inferences of fact upon a balanced consideration of the whole of the evidence at the end of a trial in which the burden of proof rested upon the plaintiff. The use, in the course of the trial, of the forensic tool of a shift in the evidential burden of proof should not be permitted to obscure the overall position. These cases are the equitable counterpart of common law cases where the principle of res ipsa loquitur is invoked. There is a rebuttable evidential presumption of undue influence. ...

18 The evidential presumption discussed above is to be distinguished sharply from a different form of presumption which arises in some cases. The law has adopted a sternly protective attitude towards certain types of relationship in which one party acquires influence over another who is vulnerable and dependent and where, moreover, substantial gifts by the influenced or vulnerable person are not normally to be expected. Examples of relationships within this special class are parent and child, guardian and ward, trustee and beneficiary, solicitor and client, and medical adviser and patient. In these cases the law presumes, irrebuttably, that one party had influence over the other. The complainant need not prove he actually reposed trust and confidence in the other party. It is sufficient for him to prove the existence of the type of relationship.

19 It is now well established that husband and wife is not one of the relationships to which this latter principle applies. In *Yerkey v Jones* (1939) 63 CLR 649, 675 Dixon J explained the reason, ...

Independent advice

20 Proof that the complainant received advice from a third party before entering into the impugned transaction is one of the matters a court takes into account when weighing all the evidence. The weight, or importance, to be attached to such advice depends on all the circumstances. In the normal course advice from a solicitor or other outside adviser can be expected to bring home to a complainant a proper understanding of what he or she is about to do. But a person may understand fully the implications of a proposed transaction, for instance, a substantial gift, and yet still be acting under the undue influence of another. Proof of outside advice does not, of itself, necessarily show that the subsequent completion

of the transaction was free from the exercise of undue influence. Whether it will be proper to infer that outside advice had an emancipating effect, so that the transaction was not brought about by the exercise of undue influence, is a question of fact to be decided having regard to all the evidence in the case.

Manifest disadvantage

21 As already noted, there are two prerequisites to the evidential shift in the burden of proof from the complainant to the other party. First, that the complainant reposed trust and confidence in the other party, or the other party acquired ascendancy over the complainant. Second, that the transaction is not readily explicable by the relationship of the parties.

22 Lindley LJ summarised this second prerequisite in the leading authority of *Allcard v Skinner* (1882) 36 Ch D 145, where the donor parted with almost all her property. Lindley LJ pointed out that where a gift of a small amount is made to a person standing in a confidential relationship to the donor, some proof of the exercise of the influence of the donee must be given. The mere existence of the influence is not enough. He continued, at p. 185, 'But if the gift is so large as not to be reasonably accounted for on the ground of friendship, relationship, charity, or other ordinary motives on which ordinary men act, the burden is upon the donee to support the gift.' In *Bank of Montreal v Stuart* [1911] AC 120, 137 Lord Macnaghten used the phrase 'immoderate and irrational' to describe this concept. ...

26 [In *National Westminster Bank plc v Morgan* at 703–707, at 826–829

Lord Scarman attached the label 'manifest disadvantage' to this second ingredient necessary to raise the presumption. This label has been causing difficulty. It may be apt enough when applied to straightforward transactions such as a substantial gift or a sale at an undervalue. But experience has now shown that this expression can give rise to misunderstanding. The label is being understood and applied in a way which does not accord with the meaning intended by Lord Scarman, its originator.

27 The problem has arisen in the context of wives guaranteeing payment of their husband's business debts. In recent years judge after judge has grappled with the baffling question whether a wife's guarantee of her husband's bank overdraft, together with a charge on her share of the matrimonial home, was a transaction manifestly to her disadvantage.

28 In a narrow sense, such a transaction plainly ('manifestly') is disadvantageous to the wife. She undertakes a serious financial obligation, and in return she personally receives nothing. But that would be to take an unrealistically blinkered view of such a transaction. Unlike the relationship of solicitor and client or medical adviser and patient, in the case of husband and wife there are inherent reasons why such a transaction may well be for her benefit. Ordinarily, the fortunes of husband and wife are bound up together. If the husband's business is the source of the family income, the wife has a lively interest in doing what she can to support the business. A wife's affection and self-interest run hand-in-hand in inclining her to join with her husband in charging the matrimonial home, usually a jointly-owned asset, to obtain the financial facilities needed by the business. The finance may be needed to start a new business, or expand a promising business, or rescue an ailing business.

29 Which, then, is the correct approach to adopt in deciding whether a transaction is disadvantageous to the wife: the narrow approach, or the wider approach? The answer is neither. The answer lies in discarding a label which gives rise to this sort of ambiguity. The better approach is to adhere more directly to the test outlined by Lindley LJ in *Allcard v Skinner*, and adopted by Lord

Scarman in *National Westminster Bank plc v Morgan*, in the passages I have cited.

30 I return to husband and wife cases. I do not think that, in the ordinary course, a guarantee of the character I have mentioned is to be regarded as a transaction which, failing proof to the contrary, is explicable only on the basis that it has been procured by the exercise of undue influence by the husband. Wives frequently enter into such transactions. There are good and sufficient reasons why they are willing to do so, despite the risks involved for them and their families. They may be enthusiastic. They may not. They may be less optimistic than their husbands about the prospects of the husbands' businesses. They may be anxious, perhaps exceedingly so. But this is a far cry from saying that such transactions as a class are to be regarded as prima facie evidence of the exercise of undue influence by husbands.

31 I have emphasised the phrase 'in the ordinary course'. There will be cases where a wife's signature of a guarantee or a charge of her share in the matrimonial home does call for explanation. Nothing I have said above is directed at such a case.

A cautionary note

32 I add a cautionary note, prompted by some of the first instance judgments in the cases currently being considered by the House. It concerns the general approach to be adopted by a court when considering whether a wife's guarantee of her husband's bank overdraft was procured by her husband's due influence. Undue influence has a connotation of impropriety. In the eye of the law, undue influence means that influence has been misused. Statements or conduct by a husband which do not pass beyond the bounds of what may be expected of a reasonable husband in the circumstances should not, without more, be castigated as undue influence. Similarly, when a husband is forecasting the future of his business, and expressing his hopes or fears, a degree of hyperbole may be only natural. Courts should not too readily treat such exaggerations as misstatements.

33 Inaccurate explanations of a proposed transaction are a different matter. So are cases where a husband, in whom a wife has reposed trust and confidence for the management of their financial affairs, prefers his interests to hers and makes a choice for both of them on that footing. Such a husband abuses the influence he has. He fails to discharge the obligation of candour and fairness he owes a wife who is looking to him to make the major financial decisions.

The complainant and third parties: suretyship transactions

34 The problem considered in *O'Brien's* case and raised by the present appeals is of comparatively recent origin. It arises out of the substantial growth in home ownership over the last 30 or 40 years and, as part of that development, the great increase in the number of homes owned jointly by husbands and wives. More than two-thirds of householders in the United Kingdom now own their own homes. For most home-owning couples, their homes are their most valuable asset. They must surely be free, if they so wish, to use this asset as a means of raising money, whether for the purpose of the husband's business, or for any other purpose. Their home is their property. The law should not restrict them in the use they may make of it. Bank finance is in fact by far the most important source of external capital for small businesses with fewer than ten employees. These businesses comprise about 95% of all businesses in the country, responsible for nearly one-third of all employment. Finance raised by second mortgages on the principal's home is a significant source of capital for the start-up of small businesses.

35 If the freedom of home-owners to make economic use of their homes is not to be frustrated, a bank must be able to have confidence that a wife's signature of the necessary guarantee and charge will be as binding upon her as is the signature of anyone else on documents which he or she may sign. Otherwise banks will not be willing to lend money on the security of a jointly owned house or flat.

36 At the same time, the high degree of trust and confidence and emotional interdependence which normally characterises a marriage relationship provides scope for abuse. One party may take advantage of the other's vulnerability. Unhappily, such abuse does occur. Further, it is all too easy for a husband, anxious or even desperate for bank finance, to misstate the position in some particular or to mislead the wife, wittingly or unwittingly, in some other way. The law would be seriously defective if it did not recognise these realities.

37 In *O'Brien's* case this House decided where the balance should be held between these competing interests. On the one side, there is the need to protect a wife against a husband's undue influence. On the other side, there is the need for the bank to be able to have reasonable confidence in the strength of its security. Otherwise it would not provide the required money. The problem lies in finding the course best designed to protect wives in a minority of cases without unreasonably hampering the giving and taking of security. The House produced a practical solution. The House decided what are the steps a bank should take to ensure it is not affected by any claim the wife may have that her signature of the documents was procured by the undue influence or other wrong of her husband. Like every compromise, the outcome falls short of achieving in full the objectives of either of the two competing interests. In particular, the steps required of banks will not guarantee that, in future, wives will not be subjected to undue influence or misled when standing as sureties. Short of prohibiting this type of suretyship transaction altogether, there is no way of achieving that result, desirable although it is. What passes between a husband and wife in this regard in the privacy of their own home is not capable of regulation or investigation as a prelude to the wife entering into a suretyship transaction.

38 The jurisprudential route by which the House reached its conclusion in *O'Brien's* case has attracted criticism from some commentators. It has been said to involve artificiality and thereby create uncertainty in the law. I must first consider this criticism. In the ordinary course a bank which takes a guarantee security from the wife of its customer will be altogether ignorant of any undue influence the customer may have exercised in order to secure the wife's concurrence. In *O'Brien* Lord Browne-Wilkinson prayed in aid the doctrine of constructive notice (p. 28, ante). In circumstances he identified, a creditor is put on inquiry. When that is so, the creditor 'will have constructive notice of the wife's rights' unless the creditor takes reasonable steps to satisfy himself that the wife's agreement to stand surety has been properly obtained: see [1994] 1 AC 180, 196, [1993] 4 All ER 417, 429.

39 Lord Browne-Wilkinson would be the first to recognise this is not a conventional use of the equitable concept of constructive notice. The traditional use of this concept concerns the circumstances in which a transferee of property who acquires a legal estate from a transferor with a defective title may nonetheless obtain a good title, that is, a better title than the transferor had. That is not the present case. The bank acquires its charge from the wife, and there is nothing wrong with her title to her share of the matrimonial home. The transferor wife is seeking to resile from the very transaction she entered into with the bank, on the ground that her apparent consent was procured by the undue influence or other misconduct, such as misrepresentation, of a third party (her husband). She is seeking to set aside her contract of guarantee and, with it, the charge she gave to the bank.

40 The traditional view of equity in this tripartite situation seems to be that a person in the position of the wife will only be relieved of her bargain if the other party to the transaction (the bank, in the present instance) was privy to the conduct which led to the wife's entry into the transaction. Knowledge is required: see *Cobbett v Brock* (1855) 20 Beav 524, 528, 531, per Sir John Romilly MR, *Kempson v Ashbee* (1874) LR 10 Ch App 15, 21, per James LJ, and *Bainbrigge v Browne* 18 Ch D 188, 197, per Fry J. The law imposes no obligation on one party to a transaction to check whether the other party's concurrence was obtained by undue influence. But *O'Brien* has introduced into the law the concept that, in certain circumstances, a party to a contract may lose the benefit of his contract, entered into in good faith, if he ought to have known that the other's concurrence had been procured by the misconduct of a third party.

41 There is a further respect in which *O'Brien* departed from conventional concepts. Traditionally, a person is deemed to have notice (that is, he has 'constructive' notice) of a prior right when he does not actually know of it but would have learned of it had he made the requisite inquiries. A purchaser will be treated as having constructive notice of all that a reasonably prudent purchaser would have discovered. In the present type of case, the steps a bank is required to take, lest it have constructive notice that the wife's concurrence was procured improperly by her husband, do not consist of making inquiries. Rather, *O'Brien* envisages that the steps taken by the bank will reduce, or even eliminate, the risk of the wife entering into the transaction under any misapprehension or as a result of undue influence by her husband. The steps are not concerned to discover whether the wife has been wronged by her husband in this way. The steps are concerned to minimise the risk that such a wrong may be committed.

42 These novelties do not point to the conclusion that the decision of this House in *O'Brien* is leading the law astray. Lord Browne-Wilkinson acknowledged he might be extending the law: see at 197, at 428; Some development was sorely needed. The law had to find a way of giving wives a reasonable measure of protection, without adding unreasonably to the expense involved in entering into guarantee transactions of the type under consideration. The protection had to extend also to any misrepresentations made by a husband to his wife. In a situation where there is a substantial risk the husband may exercise his influence improperly regarding the provision of security for his business debts, there is an increased risk that explanations of the transaction given by him to his wife may be misleadingly incomplete or even inaccurate.

43 The route selected in *O'Brien* ought not to have an unsettling effect on established principles of contract. *O'Brien* concerned suretyship transactions. These are tripartite transactions. They involve the debtor as well as the creditor and the guarantor. The guarantor enters into the transaction at the request of the debtor. The guarantor assumes obligations. On the face of the transaction the guarantor usually receives no benefit in return, unless the guarantee is being given on a commercial basis. Leaving aside cases where the relationship between the surety and the debtor is commercial, a guarantee transaction is one-sided so far as the guarantor is concerned. The creditor knows this. Thus the decision in *O'Brien* is directed at a class of contracts which has special features of its own. That said, I must at a later stage in this speech return to the question of the wider implications of the *O'Brien* decision.

The threshold: when the bank is put on inquiry

44 In *O'Brien* the House considered the circumstances in which a bank, or other creditor, is 'put on inquiry'. Strictly this is a misnomer. As already noted, a

bank is not required to make inquiries. But it will be convenient to use the terminology which has now become accepted in this context. The House set a low level for the threshold which must be crossed before a bank is put on inquiry. For practical reasons the level is set much lower than is required to satisfy a court that, failing contrary evidence, the court may infer that the transaction was procured by undue influence. Lord Browne-Wilkinson said at 796, at 429:

'Therefore in my judgment a creditor is put on inquiry when a wife offers to stand surety for her husband's debts by the combination of two factors: (a) the transaction is on its face not to the financial advantage of the wife; and (b) there is a substantial risk in transactions of that kind that, in procuring the wife to act as surety, the husband has committed a legal or equitable wrong that entitles the wife to set aside the transaction.'

In my view, this passage, read in context, is to be taken to mean, quite simply, that a bank is put on inquiry whenever a wife offers to stand surety for her husband's debts.

45 The Court of Appeal, comprising Stuart-Smith, Millett and Morritt LJJ, interpreted this passage more restrictively. The threshold, the court said, is somewhat higher. Where condition (a) is satisfied, the bank is put on inquiry if, but only if, the bank is aware that the parties are cohabiting or that the particular surety places implicit trust and confidence in the principal debtor in relation to her financial affairs: see *Royal Bank of Scotland plc v Etridge (No 2)* [1998] 4 All ER 705, 719.

46 I respectfully disagree. I do not read (a) and (b) as factual conditions which must be proved in each case before a bank is put on inquiry. I do not understand Lord Browne-Wilkinson to have been saying that, in husband and wife cases, whether the bank is put on inquiry depends on its state of knowledge of the parties' marriage, or of the degree of trust and confidence the particular wife places in her husband in relation to her financial affairs. That would leave banks in a state of considerable uncertainty in a situation where it is important they should know clearly where they stand. The test should be simple and clear and easy to apply in a wide range of circumstances. I read (a) and (b) as Lord Browne-Wilkinson's broad explanation of the reason why a creditor is put on inquiry when a wife offers to stand surety for her husband's debts. These are the two factors which, taken together, constitute the underlying rationale.

47 The position is likewise if the husband stands surety for his wife's debts. Similarly, in the case of unmarried couples, whether heterosexual or homosexual, where the bank is aware of the relationship: see Lord Browne-Wilkinson in *O'Brien's* case, at p. 198 at p. 431. Cohabitation is not essential. The Court of Appeal rightly so decided in *Massey v Midland Bank plc* [1995] 1 All ER 929: see Steyn LJ, at p. 933.

48 As to the type of transactions where a bank is put on inquiry, the case where a wife becomes surety for her husband's debts is, in this context, a straightforward case. The bank is put on inquiry. On the other side of the line is the case where money is being advanced, or has been advanced, to husband and wife jointly. In such a case the bank is not put on inquiry, unless the bank is aware the loan is being made for the husband's purposes, as distinct from their joint purposes. That was decided in *CIBC Mortgages plc v Pitt* [1994] 1 AC 200, [1993] 4 All ER 433.[7a]

[7a]   *Chater v Mortgage Agency Services Number Two Ltd* [2004] 1 P & CR 28 (the bank was not put on inquiry as to any equitable wrong. The transaction would have appeared to the bank as perfectly ordinary: it was a joint application for a joint loan by a mother and son living in the same house. The mere fact that the application was by a mother and son, and that is was the mother's house that was to be the security for the loan, was not enough.

49 Less clear cut is the case where the wife becomes surety for the debts of a company whose shares are held by her and her husband. Her shareholding may be nominal, or she may have a minority shareholding or an equal shareholding with her husband. In my view the bank is put on inquiry in such cases, even when the wife is a director or secretary of the company. Such cases cannot be equated with joint loans. The shareholding interests, and the identity of the directors, are not a reliable guide to the identity of the persons who actually have the conduct of the company's business.

The steps a bank should take

50 The principal area of controversy on these appeals concerns the steps a bank should take when it has been put on inquiry. In *O'Brien* [1994], at 196–197, at 429–430 Lord Browne-Wilkinson said that a bank can reasonably be expected to take steps to bring home to the wife the risk she is running by standing as surety and to advise her to take independent advice. That test is applicable to past transactions. All the cases now before your Lordships' House fall into this category. For the future a bank satisfies these requirements if it insists that the wife attend a private meeting with a representative of the bank at which she is told of the extent of her liability as surety, warned of the risk she is running and urged to take independent legal advice. In exceptional cases the bank, to be safe, has to insist that the wife is separately advised.

51 The practice of the banks involved in the present cases, and it seems reasonable to assume this is the practice of banks generally, is not to have a private meeting with the wife. Nor do the banks themselves take any other steps to bring home to the wife the risk she is running. This has continued to be the practice since the decision in *O'Brien's* case. Banks consider they would stand to lose more than they would gain by holding a private meeting with the wife. They are, apparently, unwilling to assume the responsibility of advising the wife at such a meeting. Instead, the banking practice remains, as before, that in general the bank requires a wife to seek legal advice. The bank seeks written confirmation from a solicitor that he has explained the nature and effect of the documents to the wife. [8]

52 Many of the difficulties which have arisen in the present cases stem from serious deficiencies, or alleged deficiencies, in the quality of the legal advice given to the wives. I say 'alleged', because three of the appeals before your Lordships' House have not proceeded beyond the interlocutory stage. The banks successfully applied for summary judgment. In these cases the wife's allegations, made in affidavit form, have not been tested by cross-examination. On behalf of the wives it has been submitted that under the current practice the legal advice is often perfunctory in the extreme and, further, that everyone, including the banks, knows this. Independent legal advice is a fiction. The system is a charade. In practice it provides little or no protection for a wife who is under a misapprehension about the risks involved or who is being coerced into signing. She may not even know the present state of her husband's indebtedness.

53 My Lords, it is plainly neither desirable nor practicable that banks should be required to attempt to discover for themselves whether a wife's consent is

---

There was nothing to indicate the loan was solely for the purposes of the son's business. The bank did not know the true purpose of the loan, and was under no obligation to discover that. Even if the bank had known that the advance was for the son alone, there were many reasons why a mother might justifiably wish to help her son financially, without there being any unfair pressure on her to do so.)

[8]   See [2001] Conv 229 at 237–238, 241–243 (M. Pawlowski and S. Greer).

being procured by the exercise of undue influence of her husband. This is not a step the banks should be expected to take. Nor, further, is it desirable or practicable that banks should be expected to insist on confirmation from a solicitor that the solicitor has satisfied himself that the wife's consent has not been procured by undue influence. As already noted, the circumstances in which banks are put on inquiry are extremely wide. They embrace every case where a wife is entering into a suretyship transaction in respect of her husband's debts. Many, if not most, wives would be understandably outraged by having to respond to the sort of questioning which would be appropriate before a responsible solicitor could give such a confirmation. In any event, solicitors are not equipped to carry out such an exercise in any really worthwhile way, and they will usually lack the necessary materials. Moreover, the legal costs involved, which would inevitably fall on the husband who is seeking financial assistance from the bank, would be substantial. To require such an intrusive, inconclusive and expensive exercise in every case would be an altogether disproportionate response to the need to protect those cases, presumably a small minority, where a wife is being wronged.

54 The furthest a bank can be expected to go is to take reasonable steps to satisfy itself that the wife has had brought home to her, in a meaningful way, the practical implications of the proposed transaction. This does not wholly eliminate the risk of undue influence or misrepresentation. But it does mean that a wife enters into a transaction with her eyes open so far as the basic elements of the transaction are concerned.

55 This is the point at which, in the *O'Brien* case, the House decided that the balance between the competing interests should be held. A bank may itself provide the necessary information directly to the wife. Indeed, it is best equipped to do so. But banks are not following that course. Ought they to be obliged to do so in every case? I do not think Lord Browne-Wilkinson so stated in *O'Brien.* I do not understand him to have said that a personal meeting was the only way a bank could discharge its obligation to bring home to the wife the risks she is running. It seems to me that, provided a suitable alternative is available, banks ought not to be compelled to take this course. Their reasons for not wishing to hold a personal meeting are understandable. Commonly, when a bank seeks to enforce a security provided by a customer, it is met with a defence based on assurances alleged to have been given orally by a branch manager at an earlier stage: that the bank would continue to support the business, that the bank would not call in its loan, and so forth. Lengthy litigation ensues. Sometimes the allegations prove to be well founded, sometimes not. Banks are concerned to avoid the prospect of similar litigation which would arise in guarantee cases if they were to adopt a practice of holding a meeting with a wife at which the bank's representative would explain the proposed guarantee transaction. It is not unreasonable for the banks to prefer that this task should be undertaken by an independent legal adviser.

56 I shall return later to the steps a bank should take when it follows this course. Suffice to say, these steps, together with advice from a solicitor acting for the wife, ought to provide the substance of the protection which *O'Brien* intended a wife should have. Ordinarily it will be reasonable that a bank should be able to rely upon confirmation from a solicitor, acting for the wife, that he has advised the wife appropriately.

57 The position will be otherwise if the bank knows that the solicitor has not duly advised the wife or, I would add, if the bank knows facts from which it ought to have realised that the wife has not received the appropriate advice. In such circumstances the bank will proceed at its own risk.

The content of the legal advice

58 In *Royal Bank of Scotland plc v Etridge (No 2)* [1998] 4 All ER 705, 715, para. 19, the Court of Appeal set out its views of the duties of a solicitor in this context: [9]

'A solicitor who is instructed to advise a person who may be subject to the undue influence of another must bear in mind that it is not sufficient that she understands the nature and effect of the transaction if she is so affected by the influence of the other that she cannot make an independent decision of her own. It is not sufficient to explain the documentation and ensure she understands the nature of the transaction and wishes to carry it out: see *Powell v Powell* [1900] 1 Ch 243, 247, approved in *Wright v Carter* [1903] 1 Ch 27. His duty is to satisfy himself that his client is free from improper influence, and the first step must be to ascertain whether it is one into which she could sensibly be advised to enter if free from such influence. If he is not so satisfied it is his duty to advise her not to enter into it, and to refuse to act further for her in the implementation of the transaction if she persists. In this event, while the contents of his advice must remain confidential, he should inform the other parties (including the bank) that he has seen his client and given her certain advice, and that as a result he has declined to act for her any further. He must in any event advise her that she is under no obligation to enter into the transaction at all and, if she still wishes to do so, that she is not bound to accept the terms of any document which has been put before her: see *Credit Lyonnais Bank Nederland NV v Burch* [1997] 1 All ER 144.'

59 I am unable to accept this as an accurate formulation of a solicitor's duties in cases such as those now under consideration. In some respects it goes much too far. The observations of Farwell J in *Powell v Powell* [1900] 1 Ch 243, 247, should not be pressed unduly widely. *Powell v Powell* was a case where strong moral pressure was applied by a stepmother to a girl who was only just 21. She was regarded as not really capable of dealing irrevocably with her parent or guardian in the matter of a substantial settlement. Farwell J's observations cannot be regarded as of general application in all cases where a solicitor is giving advice to a person who may have been subject to undue influence.

60 More pertinently, in *Re Coomber* [1911] 1 Ch 723, 730, Fletcher Moulton LJ summarised the general rules applicable to cases of persons who are competent to form an opinion of their own:

'All that is necessary is that some independent person, free from any taint of the relationship, or of the consideration of interest which would affect the act, should put clearly before the person what are the nature and the consequences of the act. It is for adult persons of competent mind to decide whether they will do an act, and I do not think that independent and competent advice means independent and competent approval. It simply means that the advice shall be removed entirely from the suspected atmosphere; and that from the clear language of an independent mind, they should know precisely what they are doing.'

61 Thus, in the present type of case it is not for the solicitor to veto the transaction by declining to confirm to the bank that he has explained the documents to the wife and the risks she is taking upon herself. If the solicitor considers the transaction is not in the wife's best interests, he will give reasoned advice to the wife to that effect. But at the end of the day the decision on whether to proceed is the decision of the client, nor the solicitor. A wife is not to be

---

[9]   'An experienced legal executive in a firm with a conveyancing practice is well able to give full and adequate advice as to the contents and effect of a straightforward legal charge': per Lord SCOTT OF FOSCOTE at para. 292.

precluded from entering into a financially unwise transaction if, for her own reasons, she wishes to do so.

62 That is the general rule. There may, of course, be exceptional circumstances where it is glaringly obvious that the wife is being grievously wronged. In such a case the solicitor should decline to act further. In *Wright v Carter* [1903] 1 Ch 27, 57–58, Stirling LJ approved Farwell J's observations in *Powell v Powell* [1900] 1 Ch 243, 247. But he did so by reference to the extreme example of a poor man divesting himself of all his property in favour of his solicitor.

63 In *Royal Bank of Scotland plc v Etridge (No 2)* [1998] 4 All ER 705, 722, para 49, the Court of Appeal said that if the transaction is 'one into which no competent solicitor could properly advise the wife to enter', the availability of legal advice is insufficient to avoid the bank being fixed with constructive notice. It follows from the views expressed above that I am unable to agree with the Court of Appeal on this point.

64 I turn to consider the scope of the responsibilities of a solicitor who is advising the wife. In identifying what are the solicitor's responsibilities the starting point must always be the solicitor's retainer. What has he been retained to do? As a general proposition, the scope of a solicitor's duties is dictated by the terms, whether express or implied, of his retainer. In the type of case now under consideration the relevant retainer stems from the bank's concern to receive confirmation from the solicitor that, in short, the solicitor has brought home to the wife the risks involved in the proposed transaction. As a first step the solicitor will need to explain to the wife the purpose for which he has become involved at all. He should explain that, should it ever become necessary, the bank will rely upon his involvement to counter any suggestion that the wife was overborne by her husband or that she did not properly understand the implications of the transaction. The solicitor will need to obtain confirmation from the wife that she wishes him to act for her in the matter and to advise her on the legal and practical implications of the proposed transaction. [10]

65 When an instruction to this effect is forthcoming, the content of the advice required from a solicitor before giving the confirmation sought by the bank will, inevitably, depend upon the circumstances of the case. Typically, the advice a solicitor can be expected to give should cover the following matters as the core minimum. (1) He will need to explain the nature of the documents and the practical consequences these will have for the wife if she signs them. She could lose her home if her husband's business does not prosper. Her home may be her only substantial asset, as well as the family's home. She could be made bankrupt. (2) He will need to point out the seriousness of the risks involved. The wife should be told the purpose of the proposed new facility, the amount and principal terms of the new facility, and that the bank might increase the amount of the facility, or change its terms, or grant a new facility, without reference to her. She should be told the amount of her liability under her guarantee. The solicitor should discuss the wife's financial means, including her understanding of the value of the property being charged. The solicitor should discuss whether the wife or her husband has any other assets out of which repayment could be made if the husband's business should fail. These matters are relevant to the seriousness of the risks involved. (3) The solicitor will need to state clearly that the wife has a choice. The decision is

[10]   Lord SCOTT said at para. 168: 'Knowledge by a bank that a solicitor is acting for a surety wife does not, without more, justify the bank in assuming that the solicitor's instructions extend to advising her about the nature and effect of the transaction'. See *UCB Corporate Services Ltd v Williams* [2003] 1 P & CR 168.

hers and hers alone. Explanation of the choice facing the wife will call for some discussion of the present financial position, including the amount of the husband's present indebtedness, and the amount of his current overdraft facility. (4) The solicitor should check whether the wife wishes to proceed. She should be asked whether she is content that the solicitor should write to the bank confirming he has explained to her the nature of the documents and the practical implications they may have for her, or whether, for instance, she would prefer him to negotiate with the bank on the terms of the transaction. Matters for negotiation could include the sequence in which the various securities will be called upon or a specific or lower limit to her liabilities. The solicitor should not give any confirmation to the bank without the wife's authority.

66 The solicitor's discussion with the wife should take place at a face-to-face meeting, in the absence of the husband. It goes without saying that the solicitor's explanations should be couched in suitably non-technical language. It also goes without saying that the solicitor's task is an important one. It is not a formality.

67 The solicitor should obtain from the bank any information he needs. If the bank fails for any reason to provide information requested by the solicitor, the solicitor should decline to provide the confirmation sought by the bank.

68 As already noted, the advice which a solicitor can be expected to give must depend on the particular facts of the case. But I have set out this 'core minimum' in some detail, because the quality of the legal advice is the most disturbing feature of some of the present appeals. The perfunctory nature of the advice may well be largely due to a failure by some solicitors to understand what is required in these cases.

Independent advice

69 I turn next to the much-vexed question whether the solicitor advising the wife must act for the wife alone. Or, at the very least, the solicitor must not act for the husband or the bank in the current transaction save in a wholly ministerial capacity, such as carrying out conveyancing formalities or supervising the execution of documents and witnessing signatures. Commonly, in practice, the solicitor advising the wife will be the solicitor acting also for her husband either in the particular transaction or generally.

70 The first point to note is that this question cannot be answered by reference to reported decisions. The steps a bank must take once it is put on inquiry, if it is to avoid having constructive notice of the wife's rights, are not the subject of exposition in earlier authority. This is a novel situation, created by the *O'Brien* decision.

71 Next, a simple and clear rule is needed, preferably of well nigh universal application. In some cases a bank deals directly with a husband and wife and has to take the initiative in requiring the wife to obtain legal advice. In other cases, a bank may deal throughout with solicitors already acting for the husband and wife. *Bank of Baroda v Rayarel* [1995] 2 FLR 376 is an example of the latter type of case. It would not be satisfactory to attempt to draw a distinction along these lines. Any such distinction would lack a principled base. Inevitably, in practice, the distinction would disintegrate in confusion.

72 Thirdly, here again, a balancing exercise is called for. Some features point in one direction, others in the opposite direction. Factors favouring the need for the solicitor to act for the wife alone include the following. Sometimes a wife may be inhibited in discussion with a solicitor who is also acting for the husband or whose main client is the husband. This occurred in *Banco Exterior Internacional v Mann* [1995] 1 All ER 936: see the finding of the judge, at p. 941F–G. Sometimes a solicitor whose main client is the husband may not, in practice, give the same

single-minded attention to the wife's position as would a solicitor acting solely for the wife. Her interests may rank lower in the solicitor's scale of priorities, perhaps unconsciously, than the interests of the husband. Instances of incompetent advice, or worse, which have come before the court might perhaps be less likely to recur if a solicitor were instructed to act for the wife alone and gave advice solely to her. As a matter of general understanding, independent advice would suggest that the solicitor should not be acting in the same transaction for the person who, if there is any undue influence, is the source of that influence.

73 The contrary view is that the solicitor may also act for the husband or the bank, provided the solicitor is satisfied that this is in the wife's best interests and satisfied also that this will not give rise to any conflicts of duty or interest. The principal factors favouring this approach are as follows. A requirement that a wife should receive advice from a solicitor acting solely for her will frequently add significantly to the legal costs. Sometimes a wife will be happier to be advised by a family solicitor known to her than by a complete stranger. Sometimes a solicitor who knows both husband and wife and their histories will be better placed to advise than a solicitor who is a complete stranger.

74 In my view, overall the latter factors are more weighty than the former. The advantages attendant upon the employment of a solicitor acting solely for the wife do not justify the additional expense this would involve for the husband. When accepting instructions to advise the wife the solicitor assumes responsibilities directly to her, both at law and professionally. These duties, and this is central to the reasoning on this point, are owed to the wife alone. In advising the wife the solicitor is acting for the wife alone. He is concerned only with her interests. I emphasise, therefore, that in every case the solicitor must consider carefully whether there is any conflict of duty or interest and, more widely, whether it would be in the best interests of the wife for him to accept instructions from her. If he decides to accept instructions, his assumption of legal and professional responsibilities to her ought, in the ordinary course of things, to provide sufficient assurance that he will give the requisite advice fully, carefully and conscientiously. Especially so, now that the nature of the advice called for has been clarified. If at any stage the solicitor becomes concerned that there is a real risk that other interests or duties may inhibit his advice to the wife he must cease to act for her.

Agency

75 No system ever works perfectly. There will always be cases where things go wrong, sometimes seriously wrong. The next question concerns the position when a solicitor has accepted instructions to advise a wife but he fails to do so properly. He fails to give her the advice needed to bring home to her the practical implications of her standing as surety. What then? The wife has a remedy in damages against the negligent solicitor. But what is the position of the bank who proceeded in the belief that the wife had been given the necessary advice?

76 Mr Sher contended that, depending on the facts, the solicitor should be regarded as the agent of the bank. Commonly, what happens is that the bank asks the solicitor acting for the husband to undertake the conveyancing formalities on behalf of the bank. The bank also asks the solicitor to undertake the further task of explaining the nature and effect of the documents to the wife, and then confirming to the bank that he has done so. In carrying out these requested tasks, it was submitted, the solicitor is acting for the bank. The bank requires the solicitor to advise the wife, not for her benefit, but for the benefit and protection of the bank. Any deficiencies in the advice given to the wife should be attributed to the bank. In this regard, it was submitted, the solicitor's

knowledge is to be imputed to the bank. A certificate furnished by the solicitor to the bank should not prejudice the position of the wife when, as happened in several cases, the contents of the certificate are untrue. If the solicitor has not given the wife any advice, her rights should not be diminished by the solicitor telling the bank that she has been fully advised.

77 I cannot accept this analysis. Confirmation from the solicitor that he has advised the wife is one of the bank's preconditions for completion of the transaction. But it is central to this arrangement that in advising the wife the solicitor is acting for the wife and no one else. The bank does not have, and is intended not to have, any knowledge of or control over the advice the solicitor gives the wife. The solicitor is not accountable to the bank for the advice he gives to the wife. To impute to the bank knowledge of what passed between the solicitor and the wife would contradict this essential feature of the arrangement. The mere fact that, for its own purposes, the bank asked the solicitor to advise the wife does not make the solicitor the bank's agent in giving that advice.

78 In the ordinary case, therefore, deficiencies in the advice given are a matter between the wife and her solicitor. The bank is entitled to proceed on the assumption that a solicitor advising the wife has done his job properly. I have already mentioned what is the bank's position if it knows this is not so, or if it knows facts from which it ought to have realised this is not so.

Obtaining the solicitor's confirmation

79 I now return to the steps a bank should take when it has been put on inquiry and for its protection is looking to the fact that the wife has been advised independently by a solicitor.

(1) One of the unsatisfactory features in some of the cases is the late stage at which the wife first became involved in the transaction. In practice she had no opportunity to express a view on the identity of the solicitor who advised her. She did not even know that the purpose for which the solicitor was giving her advice was to enable him to send, on her behalf, the protective confirmation sought by the bank. Usually the solicitor acted for both husband and wife.

Since the bank is looking for its protection to legal advice given to the wife by a solicitor who, in this respect, is acting solely for her, I consider the bank should take steps to check *directly with the wife* the name of the solicitor she wishes to act for her. To this end, in future the bank should communicate directly with the wife, informing her that for its own protection it will require written confirmation from a solicitor, acting for her, to the effect that the solicitor has fully explained to her the nature of the documents and the practical implications they will have for her. She should be told that the purpose of this requirement is that thereafter she should not be able to dispute she is legally bound by the documents once she has signed them. She should be asked to nominate a solicitor whom she is willing to instruct to advise her, separately from her husband, and act for her in giving the necessary confirmation to the bank. She should be told that, if she wishes, the solicitor may be the same solicitor as is acting for her husband in the transaction. If a solicitor is already acting for the husband and the wife, she should be asked whether she would prefer that a different solicitor should act for her regarding the bank's requirement for confirmation from a solicitor.

The bank should not proceed with the transaction until it has received an appropriate response directly from the wife.

(2) Representatives of the bank are likely to have a much better picture of the husband's financial affairs than the solicitor. If the bank is not willing to undertake the task of explanation itself, the bank must provide the solicitor with

the financial information he needs for this purpose. Accordingly it should become routine practice for banks, if relying on confirmation from a solicitor for their protection, to send to the solicitor the necessary financial information. What is required must depend on the facts of the case. Ordinarily this will include information on the purpose for which the proposed new facility has been requested, the current amount of the husband's indebtedness, the amount of his current overdraft facility, and the amount and terms of any new facility. If the bank's request for security arose from a written application by the husband for a facility, a copy of the application should be sent to the solicitor. The bank will, of course, need first to obtain the consent of its customer to this circulation of confidential information. If this consent is not forthcoming the transaction will not be able to proceed.

(3) Exceptionally there may be a case where the bank believes or suspects that the wife has been misled by her husband or is not entering into the transaction of her own free will. If such a case occurs the bank must inform the wife's solicitors of the facts giving rise to its belief or suspicion.

(4) The bank should in every case obtain from the wife's solicitor a written confirmation to the effect mentioned above.

80 These steps will be applicable to future transactions. In respect of past transactions, the bank will ordinarily be regarded as having discharged its obligations if a solicitor who was acting for the wife in the transaction gave the bank confirmation to the effect that he had brought home to the wife the risks she was running by standing as surety. [11]

The creditor's disclosure obligation

81 It is a well-established principle that, stated shortly, a creditor is obliged to disclose to a guarantor any unusual feature of the contract between the creditor and the debtor which makes it materially different in a potentially disadvantageous respect from what the guarantor might naturally expect. The precise ambit of this disclosure obligation remains unclear. A useful summary of the authorities appears in *O'Donovan & Phillips, The Modern Contract of Guarantee,* 3rd ed (1996), pp. 122–130. It is not necessary to pursue these difficult matters in this case. It is sufficient for me to say that, contrary to submissions made, the need to provide protection for wives who are standing as sureties does not point to a need to re-visit the scope of this disclosure principle. Wives require a different form of protection. They need a full and clear explanation of the risks involved. Typically, the risks will be risks any surety would expect. The protection needed by wives differs from, and goes beyond, the disclosure of information. The *O'Brien* principle is intended to provide this protection.

A wider principle

82 Before turning to the particular cases I must make a general comment on the *O'Brien* principle. As noted by Professor Peter Birks QC, the decision in *O'Brien* has to be seen as the progenitor of a wider principle: see 'The Burden on the Bank', in *Restitution and Banking Law,* edited by Francis Rose (1998), at p. 195. This calls for explanation. In the *O'Brien* case the House was concerned with formulating a fair and practical solution to problems occurring when a creditor obtains a security

---

[11]   *Royal Bank of Scotland v Hill* [2002] EWCA Civ 101; *National Westminster Bank plc v Amin* [2002] 1 FLR 735; [2002] Conv 499 (M. Haley); *First National Bank plc v Achampong* [2004] 1 FCR 18; [2003] Conv 314 (M. P. Thompson). On prospective overruling, see (2004) 120 LQR 7 (ARDEN LJ).

from a guarantor whose sexual relationship with the debtor gives rise to a heightened risk of undue influence. But the law does not regard sexual relationships as standing in some special category of their own so far as undue influence is concerned. Sexual relationships are no more than one type of relationship in which an individual may acquire influence over another individual. The *O'Brien* decision cannot sensibly be regarded as confined to sexual relationships, although these are likely to be its main field of application at present. What is appropriate for sexual relationships ought, in principle, to be appropriate also for other relationships where trust and confidence are likely to exist.

83 The courts have already recognised this. Further application, or development, of the *O'Brien* principle has already taken place. In *Credit Lyonnais Bank Nederland NV v Burch* [1997] 1 All ER 144 the same principle was applied where the relationship was employer and employee. Miss Burch was a junior employee in a company. She was neither a shareholder nor a director. She provided security to the bank for the company's overdraft. She entered into a guarantee of unlimited amount, and gave the bank a second charge over her flat. Nourse LJ, at p. 146, said the relationship 'may broadly be said to fall under [*O'Brien*]'. The Court of Appeal held that the bank was put on inquiry. It knew the facts from which the existence of a relationship of trust and confidence between Miss Burch and Mr Pelosi, the owner of the company, could be inferred.

84 The crucially important question raised by this wider application of the *O'Brien* principle concerns the circumstances which will put a bank on inquiry. A bank is put on inquiry whenever a wife stands as surety for her husband's debts. It is sufficient that the bank knows of the husband-wife relationship. That bare fact is enough. The bank must then take reasonable steps to bring home to the wife the risks involved. What, then, of other relationships where there is an increased risk of undue influence, such as parent and child? It is enough that the bank knows of the relationship? For reasons already discussed in relation to husbands and wives, a bank cannot be expected to probe the emotional relationship between two individuals, whoever they may be. Nor is it desirable that a bank should attempt this. Take the case where a father puts forward his daughter as a surety for his business overdraft. A bank should not be called upon to evaluate highly personal matters such as the degree of trust and confidence existing between the father and his daughter, with the bank put on inquiry in one case and not in another. As with wives, so with daughters, whether a bank is put on inquiry should not depend on the degree of trust and confidence the particular daughter places in her father in relation to financial matters. Moreover, as with wives, so with other relationships, the test of what puts a bank on inquiry should be simple, clear and easy to apply in wifely varying circumstances. This suggests that, in the case of a father and daughter, knowledge by the bank of the relationship of father and daughter should suffice to put the bank on inquiry. When the bank knows of the relationship, it must then take reasonable steps to ensure the daughter knows what she is letting herself into.

85 The relationship of parent and child is one of the relationships where the law irrebuttably presumes the existence of trust and confidence. Rightly, this has already been rejected as the boundary of the *O'Brien* principle. *O'Brien* was a husband-wife case. The responsibilities of creditors were enunciated in a case where the law makes no presumption of the existence of trust and confidence.

86 But the law cannot stop at this point, with banks on inquiry only in cases where the debtor and guarantor have a sexual relationship or the relationship is one where the law presumes the existence of trust and confidence. That would

be an arbitrary boundary, and the law has already moved beyond this, in the decision in *Burch*. As noted earlier, the reality of life is that relationships in which undue influence can be exercised are infinitely various. They cannot be exhaustively defined. Nor is it possible to produce a comprehensive list of relationships where there is a substantial risk of the exercise of undue influence, all others being excluded from the ambit of the *O'Brien* principle. Human affairs do not lend themselves to categorisations of this sort. The older generation of a family may exercise undue influence over a younger member, as in parent-child cases such as *Bainbrigge v Browne* 18 ChD 188 and *Powell v Powell* [1900] 1 Ch 243. Sometimes it is the other way round, as with a nephew and his elderly aunt in *Inche Noriah v Shaik Allie Bin Omar* [1929] AC 127. An employer may take advantage of his employee, as in *Credit Lyonnais Bank Nederland NV v Burch* [1997] 1 All ER 144. But it may be the other way round, with an employee taking advantage of her employer, as happened with the secretary-companion and her elderly employer in *Re Craig* [1971] Ch 95. The list could go on.

87 These considerations point forcibly to the conclusion that there is no rational cut-off point, with certain types of relationship being susceptible to the *O'Brien* principle and others not. Further, if a bank is not to be required to evaluate the extent to which its customer has influence over a proposed guarantor, the only practical way forward is to regard banks as 'put on inquiry' in every case where the relationship between the surety and the debtor is non-commercial. the creditor must always take reasonable steps to bring home to the individual guarantor the risks he is running by standing as surety. As a measure of protection, this is valuable. But, in all conscience, it is a modest burden for banks and other lenders. It is no more than is reasonably to be expected of a creditor who is taking a guarantee from an individual. If the bank or other creditor does not take these steps, it is deemed to have notice of any claim the guarantor may have that the transaction was procured by undue influence or misrepresentation on the part of the debtor.

88 Different considerations apply where the relationship between the debtor and guarantor is commercial, as where a guarantor is being paid a fee, or a company is guaranteeing the debts of another company in the same group. Those engaged in business can be regarded as capable of looking after themselves and understanding the risks involved in the giving of guarantees.

89 By the decisions of this House in *O'Brien* and the Court of Appeal in *Credit Lyonnais Bank Nederland NV v Burch* [1997] 1 All ER 144, English law has taken its first strides in the development of some such general principle. It is a workable principle. It is also simple, coherent and eminently desirable. I venture to think this is the way the law is moving, and should continue to move. Equity, it is said, is not past the age of child-bearing. In the present context the equitable concept of being 'put on inquiry' is the parent of a principle of general application, a principle which imposes no more than a modest obligation on banks and other creditors. The existence of this obligation in all non-commercial cases does not go beyond the reasonable requirements of the present times. In future, banks and other creditors should regulate their affairs accordingly.

LORD SCOTT OF FOSCOTE:

Summary

191 My Lords I think, given the regrettable length of this opinion, I should try and summarise my views about the principles that apply and the practice that should be followed in surety wife cases.

(1) The issue as between the surety wife and the lender bank is whether the bank may rely on the apparent consent of the wife to the suretyship transaction.

(2) If the bank knows that the surety wife's consent to the transaction has been procured by undue influence or misrepresentation, or if it has shut its eyes to the likelihood that that was so, it may not rely on her apparent consent.

(3) If the wife's consent has in fact been procured by undue influence or misrepresentation, the bank may not rely on her apparent consent unless it has good reason to believe that she understands the nature and effect of the transaction.

(4) Unless the case has some special feature, the bank's knowledge that a solicitor is acting for the wife and has advised her about the nature and effect of the transaction will provide a good reason for the purposes of (3) above. That will also be so if the bank has a reasonable belief that a solicitor is acting for her and has so advised her. Written confirmation by a solicitor acting for the wife that he has so advised her will entitle the bank to hold that reasonable belief.

(5) So, too, a sufficient explanation of the nature and effect of the transaction given by a senior bank official would constitute good reason for the purposes of (3) above.

(6) If there are any facts known to the bank which increase the inherent risk that the wife's consent to the transaction may have been procured by the husband's undue influence or misrepresentation, it may be necessary for the bank to be satisfied that the wife has received advice about the transaction from a solicitor independent of the husband before the bank can reasonably rely on the wife's apparent consent.

(7) If the bank has not taken reasonable steps to satisfy itself that the wife understands the nature and effect of the transaction, the wife will, subject to such matters as delay, acquiescence, change of position etc, be able to set aside the transaction if her consent was in fact procured by undue influence or misrepresentation.

(8) Subject to special instructions or special circumstances, the duty of a solicitor instructed to act for a wife proposing to stand as surety, or to give security, for her husband's debts is to try and make sure that she understands the nature and effect of the transaction.

(9) In all surety wife cases the bank should disclose to the surety wife, or to the solicitor acting for her, the amount of the existing indebtedness of the principal debtor to the bank and the amount of the proposed new loan or drawing facility.

(10) Subject to (9) above, a creditor has no greater duty of disclosure to a surety wife than to any other intending surety.

192 I am in full agreement with the analysis of the applicable principles of law and with the conclusions expressed in the opinion of my noble and learned friend, Lord Nicholls of Birkenhead. I believe the analysis I have sought to give in this opinion and my conclusions are consistent with them. [12]

[12] On relief for the surety, see *TSB Bank plc v Camfield* [1995] 1 WLR 430, [1995] 1 All ER 951 (wife entitled to have charge set aside in toto; bank can be in no better position than husband); (1995) 111 LQR 555 (P. Ferguson); [1996] RLR 21 (L. Proksch); followed in *Bank Melli Iran v Samadi-Rad* [1995] 2 FLR 367; *Castle Phillips Finance v Piddington* [1995] 1 FLR 783 (subrogation). Cf. *Midland Bank plc v Greene* (1995) 27 HLR 350 (set aside on terms); *Dunbar Bank plc v Nadeem* [1997] 2 All ER 253 (set aside on condition that wife repaid to bank half of amount of loan used to purchase property in joint names of wife and husband); *Barclays Bank plc v Caplan* [1997] EGCS 165 (wife succeeds in transaction in respect of which bank failed to see that she had independent advice, but bank held able to sever transactions in respect of which she did receive such advice).

(b) The Rule in Scotland

In **Smith v Governor and Company of the Bank of Scotland** [1997] NPC 94, the House of Lords (Lords GOFF OF CHIEVELEY, JAUNCEY OF TULLICHETTLE, LLOYD OF BERWICK, HOFFMANN and CLYDE), reversing the Court of Session in *Mumford v Bank of Scotland* (1995) Times 29 September, held that 'the development of the law which was achieved in *Barclays Bank plc v O'Brien* should be extended to Scotland'. Lord CLYDE said: 'It was not disputed that effect could be given in Scotland to the decision in *O'Brien* by the use of the concept of constructive notice. . . But it seems to me preferable to recognise the element of good faith which is required of the creditor on the constitution of a contract of cautionary and find there a proper basis for decision. The law already recognises, as I have sought to explain, that there may arise a duty of disclosure to a potential cautioner in certain circumstances. As a part of that same good faith which lies behind that duty it seems to me reasonable to accept that there should also be a duty in particular circumstances to give the potential cautioner certain advice. Thus in circumstances where the creditor should reasonably suspect that there may be factors bearing on the participation of the cautioner which might undermine the validity of the contract through his or her intimate relationship with the debtor the duty would arise and would have to be fulfilled if the creditor is not to be prevented from later enforcing the contract. Such a duty does not alter the existing law regarding the duty, or the absence of a duty, to make representations. Nor does it carry with it a duty of investigation. This is simply a duty arising out of the good faith of the contract to give advice'. [13]

QUESTION

How has *Royal Bank of Scotland v Etridge (No. 2)* changed the positions of
(a) The mortgagor husband?
(b) The mortgagor's surety wife?
(c) The Bank?
(d) The solicitor acting for the wife?
Are their positions better or worse?

V. EXTORTIONATE CREDIT BARGAINS

(a) Mortgages and the Consumer Credit Act 1974

Cheshire and Burn: *Modern Law of Real Property* (16th edn, 2000), pp. 741–743.

'The Consumer Credit Act 1974 [14] establishes a comprehensive code which regulates the supply of credit not exceeding £25,000 [15] to an individual. [16] It

---

[13]   Lord JAUNCEY concurred with reservations; (1998) 114 LQR 17 (C. E. F. Rickett).
[14]   See Bennion and Dobson, *Consumer Credit Control*; Guest and Lloyd, *Encyclopedia of Consumer Credit Law*; Goode, *Consumer Credit Law and Practice Handbook*; Cousins (2nd edn), chap. 11; Fisher and Lightwood, chap. 10; Gray, pp. 1380–1383; (1975) 34 CLJ 79 (R. M. Goode); (1975) 39 Conv (NS) 94 (J. E. Adams).
　　　　See also Unfair Terms in Consumer Contracts Regs 1999 (SI 1999 No. 3159), p. 436, n. 19, ante; *Emmet on Title*, paras. 25.143–25.148; (1999) 115 LQR 360; (2000) 20 LS 31 (S. Bright). The Law Commission is revising the law and intends to publish a Report in 2004; Law Commission Annual Report 2002/03 (Law Com No. 280) paras. 4.4–4.5.
[15]   Consumer Credit (Increase of Monetary Limits) Order 1998 (SI 1998 No. 996), increasing the amount from £5,000.
[16]   This includes sole traders and partnerships: s. 189(1).

includes provisions on advertising and canvassing; the licensing of credit and hire businesses; all aspects of the agreement; and judicial control over its enforcement.

To come within the Act, a mortgage must constitute a regulated consumer agreement, that is to say, a personal credit agreement by which a creditor provides a debtor with credit not exceeding £25,000.[17] There are, however, exempt agreements,[18] of which the most important are loans made by a building society or local authority for house purchase. Banks are not exempt.

Owing to the financial limit of £25,000, only second mortgages are likely to come within the definition of a regulated consumer agreement. As the Crowther Report, on which the Act is based, said:[19]

"Much of the money borrowed on second mortgage is spent on improvements of various kinds to houses that are used as security. But there is no necessary tie, in most cases, between the loan and the purpose for which it is used – indeed, many of the advertisements emphasise the borrower's freedom to spend it on anything he chooses. Undoubtedly, there are people who have been led by this sort of advertising to endanger the security of their homes for the sake of some unnecessary extravagance."

We can only notice in very general terms the main areas where the law of mortgage is affected.

1. CREATION

If the formalities prescribed by the Act are not complied with,[20] section 65 provides that an agreement which is "improperly-executed" can be enforced against the debtor on an order of the court only.[1]

2. RIGHTS OF MORTGAGOR

The most far-reaching provision for the protection of the mortgagor is the power given to the court to "re-open" a credit agreement if the credit bargain is extortionate.[2] This power extends to *all* credit bargains, whether regulated,

---

[17] S. 8.
[18] S. 16; as amended.
[19] (1971) Cmnd 4596, para. 2.4.52.
[20] Part V of the Act. See also s. 105.
[1] The County Court has exclusive jurisdiction: s. 141(1). See also s. 127; *R v Modupe* (1991) Times, 27 February; *Nissan Finance UK v Lockhart* [1993] CCLR 39; *Dimond v Lovell* [2002] 1 AC 384, [2002] 2 All ER 897. In certain cases the Court is precluded from making an enforcement order where there is improper execution; s. 127(3), (4); in which case the creditor has no claim in restitution; *Wilson v First County Trust Ltd (No 2)* [2003] 3 WLR 568 (s. 127(3) is not incompatible with Human Rights Act 1998).
[2] Ss. 137–140. These sections 'apply to agreements and transactions whenever made': s. 192(1), Sch. 3, para. 42. [1989] Conv 164 (L. Bently and G. G. Howells). The County Court has exclusive jurisdiction whatever the amount involved in the proceedings; s. 139(5)(*b*); High Court and County Courts Jurisdiction Order 1991 (SI 1991 No. 724), art. 3(1)(*h*). For orders which the court can make, see Part IX of the Act; *First National Bank plc v Syed* [1991] 2 All ER 250, *Cedar Holdings Ltd v Thompson* [1993] CCLR 7 (extension time). For making an order to reschedule mortgage agreements made under the Act; see ss. 129 and 136; *Southern and District Finance plc v Barnes* (1995) Times, 19 April; [1996] Conv 209 (A. Dunn). On the application of the Limitation Act 1980 to extortionate bargain claims, see *Rahman v Sterling Credit Ltd* [2001] 1 WLR 496; (2000) 150 NLJ 1307 (S. Neville).

exempt or above the £25,000 limit, other than those in which the debtor is a body corporate.[3]

Under section 138(1), a credit bargain is extortionate either if the payments to be made under it are grossly exorbitant or if it otherwise grossly contravenes ordinary principles of fair dealing. The court is required to take into account

(i) interest rates prevailing when the bargain was made,

(ii) factors in relation to the debtor, such as his age, experience, business capacity and state of health, and the degree to which he was under financial pressure when he made the bargain,

(iii) the creditor's relationship to the debtor and the degree of risk accepted by him, having regard to the value of the security provided, and

(iv) any other relevant considerations.

The test of extortionate is similar but not identical to that of unconscionability which is the basis of the equitable protection of the mortgagor. There is overlap, and it has been said:

"Under the Act the test is not whether the creditor has acted in a morally reprehensible manner, but whether one or other of the conditions of section 138(1) is fulfilled, and although it may be thought that if either condition is fulfilled there is likely to be something morally reprehensible about the creditor's conduct, the starting and ending point in determining whether a credit bargain is extortionate must be the words of section 138(1)."[4]

All these matters were considered in *A Ketley Ltd v Scott*,[5] where the court refused an application to re-open a credit agreement involving a loan of £24,500, secured by a legal charge on a flat, at 12 per cent for three months; this was equal to a rate of interest of 48 per cent per annum. The mortgagor had been advised by his own solicitor, and judging by his earnings and business experience knew exactly what he was doing.[6]

---

3   Where the mortgagor is a company, the court has power to set aside or vary the terms of any extortionate credit transaction entered into within three years before the day on which the company goes into liquidation or an administration order is made: Insolvency Act 1986, s. 244.

4   *Davies v Direct Loans Ltd* [1986] 1 WLR 823 at 831, per Edward Nugee QC. It is for the creditor to prove that a bargain is not extortionate: s. 171(7); *Coldunell Ltd v Gallon* [1986] QB 1184, [1986] 1 All ER 429; *Broadwick Financial Services Ltd v Spencer* [2002] All ER (Comm) 446.

5   [1981] ICR 241; 130 NLJ 749; (1979) 8 Anglo-Am 240; (1986) 136 NLJ 796 (H. W. Wilkinson). See also *Castle Phillips v Khan* [1980] CCLR 1; *First National Securities v Bertrand* [1980] CCLR 5, discussed in (1982) 132 NLJ 1041 (R. G. Lawson); *Wills v Wood* (1984) Times, 24 March, where Sir John DONALDSON MR said: 'The word is "extortionate" not "unwise". The jurisdiction seems to me to contemplate at least a substantial imbalance in bargaining power of which one party has taken advantage.' *Woodstead Finance Ltd v Petrou* [1986] NLJ Rep 188 (interest of 42.5 per cent per annum for short term loan of £25,000 for six months held to be the normal rate, and therefore not extortionate); *Shahabinia v Gyachi* (1989) unreported (debtor took three loans from creditor for business purposes with flat rates of interest at 78 per cent, 104 per cent and 156 per cent. CA reopened bargain and substituted flat rate of 30 per cent on each loan. 'It seems that the word "extortionate" is to be equated with the words "harsh and unconscionable",' per RUSSELL LJ); *Castle Phillips Co Ltd v Wilkinson* [1992] CCLR 83 (rate of interest 3¼ times rate charged by a building society; debtor was person of little financial understanding; rate of 20 per cent substituted). *Batooneh v Asombang* [2003] EWHC 2111 (QB), [2004] BPIR 1 (continuing interest rate of 100% exorbitant and reduced to 25%).

6   See *Castle Phillips Finance Co Ltd v Williams* [1986] BT CL 186, where interest was charged on a short term loan at the rate of 48 per cent per annum; CA, instead of staying an order for possession and remitting the case to the county court to consider whether the bargain was extortionate, referred it to the Director General of Fair Trading to consider the revocation of the lender's licence or any other action under the 1974 Act.

There are also provisions which protect a debtor under a regulated agreement. These include section 93 which prohibits any term requiring the rate of interest to be increased on default; and section 94 under which the debtor has the right, on giving notice to the creditor, to repay prematurely at any time. Any provision in the agreement which limits his rights in this respect is void. It would seem that if a provision to postpone the contractual right to redeem were included in a regulated agreement it would be void. [7]

3. RIGHTS OF THE MORTGAGEE

Consonant with the object of the Act, these are curtailed. A security cannot be enforced by reason of any breach of a regulated agreement by the debtor, until the creditor has served a notice under section 87. This is similar to, but not identical with, the notice required by section 146 of the Law of Property Act 1925 in the case of forfeiture of a lease. [8] Further, a land mortgage securing a regulated agreement is enforceable by an order of the court only. [9] This is a most important provision, since a mortgagee cannot exercise his rights of taking possession and of sale without such an order. If, however, he sells without an order, it would seem that he can pass a good title to the purchaser. [10]

Finally, under section 113, a creditor shall not derive from the enforcement of the security any greater benefit than he would obtain from enforcement of a regulated agreement, if the security were not provided. This would seem to deny the mortgagee the full benefit of foreclosure.' [11]

CONSUMER CREDIT ACT 1974

137. Extortionate credit bargains. – (1) If the court finds a credit bargain extortionate it may reopen the credit agreement [12] so as to do justice between the parties.

(2) In this section and sections 138–140—

  (*a*) 'credit agreement' means any agreement between an individual (the 'debtor') and any other person (the 'creditor') by which the creditor provides the debtor with credit of any amount, and

  (*b*) 'credit bargain' –

  (i) where no transaction other than the credit agreement is to be taken into account in computing the total charge for credit, means the credit agreement, or

  (ii) where one or more other transactions are to be so taken into account, means the credit agreement and those other transactions, taken together.

138. When bargains are extortionate. – (1) A credit bargain is extortionate if it –

  (*a*) requires the debtor or a relative of his to make payments (whether unconditionally, or on certain contingencies) which are grossly exorbitant, or

  (*b*) otherwise grossly contravenes ordinary principles of fair dealing.

---

[7]   *Knightsbridge Estates Trust Ltd v Byrne* [1939] Ch 441, [1938] 4 All ER 618, p. 888, ante.
[8]   P. 531, ante.
[9]   S. 126.
[10]   S. 177(2).
[11]   P. 895, post; (1975) 39 Conv (NS) 94 at p. 108.
[12]   S. 126.

(2) In determining whether a credit bargain is extortionate, regard shall be had to such evidence as is adduced concerning –
   (*a*) interest rates prevailing at the time it was made,
   (*b*) the factors mentioned in subsections (3) to (5), and
   (*c*) any other relevant considerations.
(3) Factors applicable under subsection (2) in relation to the debtor include –
   (*a*) his age, experience, business capacity and state of health; and
   (*b*) the degree to which, at the time of making the credit bargain, he was under financial pressure, and the nature of that pressure.
(4) Factors applicable under subsection (2) in relation to the creditor include –
   (*a*) the degree of risk accepted by him, having regard to the value of any security provided;
   (*b*) his relationship to the debtor; and
   (*c*) whether or not a colourable cash price was quoted for any goods or services included in the credit bargain. [13]
(5) Factors applicable under subsection (2) in relation to a linked transaction include the question how far the transaction was reasonably required for the protection of debtor or creditor, or was in the interest of the debtor.

(b) Law Reform

Unjust Credit Transactions: Report by the Director General of Fair Trading (1991), paras. 1.7, 1.9 and 3.9. [14]

'*1.7* The extortionate credit bargain provisions of the Act have not effectively dealt with the problems to which they were addressed. There have been very few cases in the courts indeed and, in most of those cases which have reached the courts, a restrictive interpretation of the provisions has been adopted. The provisions are not aligned with the consumer credit licensing regime. It is not certain whether the power to reopen a credit bargain extends to various abuses which are to be found on the margins of the market, so that there may be no relief for the borrower. In any event the courts and commentators have tended to focus on the first leg of the statutory definition of an extortionate credit bargain (grossly exorbitant payments), rather than the second leg – the untested concept of "grossly contravenes the ordinary principles of fair dealing."

1.9 Recommendations The Government should introduce legislation to reform and develop sections 137 – 140 of the Consumer Credit Act, re-casting them with a view to making them work as originally intended. The concept of an "unjust credit transaction" should replace that of an "extortionate credit bargain". In such cases the court would, as now, have the power to reopen an agreement, on application by the debtor (or surety), so as to do justice between the parties.

A finding that a transaction involved excessive – not grossly exorbitant – payments should be a factor in determining whether the transaction was unjust.

---

[13]   All these matters must be considered as at the date when the credit bargain is made; *Paragon Finance plc v Nash* [2002] 1 WLR 685.
[14]   See also Law Commission Report on Land Mortgages 1991 (Law Com. No 204, HC 5), Part VIII.

A new test of whether the transaction involved business activity which was deceitful or oppressive or otherwise unfair or improper (whether unlawful or not) – using the same statutory wording as is used to assess the fitness of a trader to hold a credit licence – should be a further factor in determining whether a transaction was unjust.

The other factors to be taken into account should remain as they are, but with one addition – "the lender's care and responsibility in making the loan, including steps taken to find out and check the borrower's credit-worthiness and ability to meet the full terms of the agreement".

The court should be empowered to re-open a credit transaction of its own motion. It should also be stated explicitly that this would apply to defended and undefended cases.

The court should be required to notify the Director General of each case where a credit transaction has been found to be unjust.

The Director General and local authority trading standards departments should be empowered to initiate proceedings for a declaration that a particular credit transaction or any particular aspect of it shall be deemed unjust. Such power should be exercisable only in the public interest.

Tougher penalties should be introduced for the unlicensed (ie illegal) provision of credit.

Experience in the courts

3.9   The Office is aware of only 23 court cases in which the above provisions have been used or mentioned since 1977. The analysis in Annex A shows that in only 15 cases was the issue of whether or not a credit bargain was extortionate actually decided. Only one case involved proceedings initiated by the debtor, and in only four cases [15] was the debtor successful in having the credit transaction ruled extortionate by the court.'

QUESTIONS

1.   X Co wishes to lend money on mortgage to Y Co to enable Y Co to acquire land and to develop it. X Co requires interest on the loan and an option to purchase the developed site within the next ten years. Advise X Co on the difficulties which arise from the cases on
    (*a*) option to purchase (*b*) collateral advantages.
    See articles on p. 804, n. 7, ante.
2.   A mortgagee wishes to ensure prompt payment of interest by the mortgagor. How would you draft the clause in the mortgage deed?
    Dunlop Pneumatic Tyre Co Ltd v New Garage and Motor Co Ltd [1915] AC 79; *Wallingford v Mutual Society and Official Liquidator* (1880) 5 App Cas 685; *Union Bank of London v Ingram* (1880) 16 Ch D 53; *Swingcastle Ltd v Alastair Gibson* [1991] 2 AC 223, [1991] 2 All ER 353.

---

[15]   *Barcabe v Edwards* [1983] CCLR 11; *Devogate v Jarvis* (16 November 1987, unreported); *Prestonwell Ltd v Capon* (1988) unreported; and *Shahabinia v Gyachi* (1989) unreported, details of which are in Annex A to the Report.

IV. Statutory Provisions Affecting the Rights of the Mortgagor [16]

LAW OF PROPERTY ACT 1925

91. Sale of mortgaged property in action for redemption or foreclosure. – (1) Any person entitled to redeem mortgaged property may have a judgment or order for sale instead of for redemption in an action brought by him either for redemption alone, or for sale alone, or for sale or redemption in the alternative. [17]

(2) In any action, whether for foreclosure, or for redemption, or for sale, or for the raising and payment in any manner of mortgage money, the court, on the request of the mortgagee, or of any person interested either in the mortgage money or in the right of redemption, [18] and, notwithstanding that –

(*a*) any other person dissents; or

(*b*) the mortgagee or any person so interested does not appear in the action;

and without allowing any time for redemption or for payment of any mortgage money, may direct a sale of the mortgaged property, on such terms as it thinks fit, including the deposit in court of a reasonable sum fixed by the court to meet the expenses of sale and to secure performance of the terms. [19]

95. Obligation to transfer instead of reconveying, and as to right to take possession. – (1) Where a mortgagor is entitled to redeem, then subject to compliance with the terms on compliance with which he would be entitled to require a reconveyance or surrender, he shall be entitled to require the mortgagee, instead of re-conveying or surrendering, to assign the mortgage debt and convey the mortgaged property to any third person, as the mortgagor directs; and the mortgagee shall be bound to assign and convey accordingly.

(2) The rights conferred by this section belong to and are capable of being enforced by each incumbrancer, or by the mortgagor, notwithstanding any intermediate incumbrance; but a requisition of an incumbrancer prevails over a requisition of the mortgagor, and, as between incumbrancers, a requisition of a prior incumbrancer prevails over a requisition of a subsequent incumbrancer.

(3) The foregoing provisions of this section do not apply in the case of a mortgagee being or having been in possession.

(4) Nothing in this Act affects prejudicially the right of a mortgagee of land whether or not his charge is secured by a legal term of years absolute to take possession of the land, but the taking of possession by the mortgagee does not convert any legal estate of the mortgagor into an equitable interest.

(5) This section applies to mortgages made either before or after the commencement of this Act, and takes effect notwithstanding any stipulation to the contrary.

96. Regulations respecting inspection, production and delivery of documents, and priorities. – (1) A mortgagor, as long as his right to redeem subsists, shall be entitled from time to time, at reasonable times, on his request, and at his own cost, and on payment of the mortgagee's costs and expenses in this behalf, to inspect and make copies or abstracts of or extracts from the documents of title relating to the mortgaged property in the custody or power of the mortgagee.

---

[16]   C & B, pp. 752–755; M & W, paras. 19.141–19.157; MM, pp. 520–526.

[17]   He is apparently entitled to such an order as of right: *Clarke v Pannell* (1884) 29 SJ 147.

[18]   *Palk v Mortgage Services Funding plc* [1993] Ch 330, [1993] 2 All ER 481, p. 886, post (mortgagor).

[19]   *Twentieth Century Banking Corpn Ltd v Wilkinson* [1977] Ch 99, [1976] 3 All ER 361; *Arab Bank plc v Mercantile Holdings Ltd* [1994] Ch 71, [1994] 2 All ER 74.

This subsection applies to mortgages made after the thirty-first day of December, eighteen hundred and eighty-one, and takes effect notwithstanding any stipulation to the contrary.

98. Actions for possession by mortgagors. – (1) A mortgagor for the time being entitled to the possession or receipt of the rents and profits of any land, as to which the mortgagee has not given notice of his intention to take possession or to enter into the receipt of the rents and profits thereof, may sue for such possession, or for the recovery of such rents or profits, or to prevent or recover damages in respect of any trespass or other wrong relative thereto, in his own name only, unless the cause of action arises upon a lease or other contract made by him jointly with any other person.

(2) This section does not prejudice the power of a mortgagor independently of this section to take proceedings in his own name only, either in right of any legal estate vested in him or otherwise.

(3) This section applies whether the mortgage was made before or after the commencement of this Act.

V. Rights Common to Mortgagor and Mortgagee [20]

LAW OF PROPERTY ACT 1925

91. Sale of mortgaged property in action for redemption or foreclosure. – p. 852, ante.

99. Leasing powers of mortgagor and mortgagee in possession. – (1) A mortgagor of land while in possession shall, as against every incumbrancer, have power to make from time to time any such lease of the mortgaged land, or any part thereof, as is by this section authorised.

(2) A mortgagee of land while in possession shall, as against all prior incumbrancers, if any, and as against the mortgagor, have power to make from time to time any such lease as aforesaid.

(3) The leases which this section authorises are –
  (i) agricultural or occupation leases for any term not exceeding twenty-one years, or, in the case of a mortgage made after the commencement of this Act, fifty years; and
  (ii) building leases for any term not exceeding ninety-nine years, or, in the case of a mortgage made after the commencement of this Act, nine hundred and ninety-nine years. [1]

(5) Every lease shall be made to take effect in possession not later than twelve months after its date.

(6) Every such lease shall reserve the best rent that can reasonably be obtained; regard being had to the circumstances of the case, but without any fine being taken.

(7) Every such lease shall contain a covenant by the lessee for payment of the rent, and a condition of re-entry on the rent not being paid within a time therein specified not exceeding thirty days.

---

[20] C & B, pp. 752–755; M & W, paras. 19.112–19.124; MM, pp. 518–520.
[1] For further details, see sub-ss. 9, 10.

(8) A counterpart of every such lease shall be executed by the lessee and delivered to the lessor, of which execution and delivery the execution of the lease by the lessor shall, in favour of the lessee and all persons deriving title under him, be sufficient evidence.

(11) In case of a lease by the mortgagor, he shall, within one month after making the lease, deliver to the mortgagee, or, where there are more than one, to the mortgagee first in priority, a counterpart of the lease duly executed by the lessee, but the lessee shall not be concerned to see that this provision is complied with.

(13) This section applies only if and as far as a contrary intention is not expressed by the mortgagor and mortgagee in the mortgage deed, or otherwise in writing, and has effect subject to the terms of the mortgage deed or of any such writing and to the provisions therein contained. [2]

(14) The mortgagor and mortgagee may, by agreement in writing, whether or not contained in the mortgage deed, reserve to or confer on the mortgagor or the mortgagee, or both, any further or other powers of leasing or having reference to leasing; and any further or other powers so reserved or conferred shall be exercisable, as far as may be, as if they were conferred by this Act, and with all the like incidents, effects, and consequences:. . .

100. Powers of mortgagor and mortgagee in possession to accept surrenders of leases. – (1) For the purpose only of enabling a lease authorised under the last preceding section, or under any agreement made pursuant to that section, or by the mortgage deed (in this section referred to as an authorised lease) to be granted, a mortgagor of land while in possession shall, as against every incumbrancer, have, by virtue of this Act, power to accept from time to time a surrender of any lease of the mortgaged land or any part thereof comprised in the lease, with or without an exception of or in respect of all or any of the mines and minerals therein, and, on a surrender of the lease so far as it comprises part only of the land or mines and minerals leased, the rent may be apportioned.

(2) For the same purpose, a mortgagee of land while in possession shall, as against all prior or other incumbrancers, if any, and as against the mortgagor, have, by virtue of this Act, power to accept from time to time any such surrender as aforesaid.

(5) No surrender shall, by virtue of this section, be rendered valid unless: –

   (a)   An authorised lease is granted of the whole of the land or mines and minerals comprised in the surrender to take effect in possession immediately or within one month after the date of the surrender; and

   (b)   The term certain or other interest granted by the new lease is not less in duration than the unexpired term or interest which would have been subsisting under the original lease if that lease had not been surrendered; and

   (c)   where the whole of the land mines and minerals originally leased has been surrendered, the rent reserved by the new lease is not less than the rent which would have been payable under the original lease if it

---

[2]   There is no implied term that the mortgagee must act reasonably in considering an application to let; nor that consent should not be unreasonably withheld; *Citibank International plc v Kessler* [1999] Lloyd's Bank LR 123; Cf. LTA 1927, s. 19(1), p. 592, ante; nor is the mortgagee under a duty in equity properly to consider any request for permission: *Starling v Lloyds TSB Bank Ltd* [2000] 1 EGLR 101 (in extreme circumstances there might be scope for a complaint of bad faith).

had not been surrendered; or where part only of the land or mines and minerals has been surrendered, the aggregate rents respectively remaining payable or reserved under the original lease and new lease are not less than the rent which would have been payable under the original lease if no partial surrender had been accepted.

(7) This section applies only if and as far as a contrary intention is not expressed by the mortgagor and mortgagee in the mortgage deed, or otherwise in writing, and shall have effect subject to the terms of the mortgage deed or of any such writing and to the provisions therein contained.

VI.   Rights and Remedies of the Mortgagee[3]

A. Possession of the Mortgaged Premises[4]

I. RIGHT TO ENTER

LAW OF PROPERTY ACT 1925

95. Obligation to transfer instead of reconveying, and as to right to take possession.

(4), p. 852, ante.

FOUR-MAIDS LTD v DUDLEY MARSHALL (PROPERTIES) LTD
[1957] Ch 317, [1957] 2 All ER 35 (ChD, HARMAN J)[5]

The legal charge provided that, if the interest payments were made punctually, the principal would not be called in for some 2 years 10 months. Six months after the loan was made interest was late and the lender called in the principal. Arrears of interest were then paid, but the lender claimed the whole sums due and took out an originating summons asking for possession.

---

[3]   C & B, pp. 755–777; Gray, pp. 1410–1455; M & W, paras. 19.044–19.111; MM, pp. 501–518; Smith, pp. 556–602; Cousins, chap. 16; Waldock, pp. 224–295; Fisher and Lightwood, Part V. The mortgagee's remedies are cumulative: *Rudge v Richens* (1873) LR 8 CP 358 (mortgagee, after exercising power of sale, may sue for balance on personal covenant); *Gordon Grant & Co Ltd v FL Boos* [1926] AC 781 (purchase of land (by leave) at auction and re-sale at a large profit still leaves personal action for balance not found at the auction sale); *Refuge Assurance Co Ltd v Pearlberg* [1938] Ch 687, [1938] 3 All ER 231 (a mortgagee in possession is not prevented from appointing a receiver). See also *Alliance and Leicester plc v Slayford* [2001] 1 All ER (Comm) 1; [2002] Conv 53 (M. P. Thompson). Foreclosure however puts an end to other remedies.

Where there are successive mortgages on the same property, the mortgagor is not entitled to require the satisfaction of the debts in the original order, if both mortgagees agree to vary the priority of the mortgages without the mortgagor's consent: *Cheah Theam Swee v Equiticorp Finance Group Ltd* [1992] 1 AC 472, [1991] 4 All ER 989.

[4]   C & B, pp. 757–760; Gray, pp. 1414–1426; M & W, paras. 19.067–19.078; MM, pp. 506–511; Smith, pp. 583–593; Cousins (2nd edn), paras. 16.22–16.40; Fisher and Lightwood, chap. 19; [1979] Conv (NS) 266 (R. J. Smith); [1983] Conv 293 (A. Clarke); [1997] LS 483 (M. Haley); [1998] LS 279 (M. Dixon). Report of the Committee on the Enforcement of Judgment Debts 1969 (Cmnd. 3909), paras. 1363–1427. As to the rights of an equitable mortgagee to possession, see M & W, paras. 19.083–19.091; (1955) 71 LQR 204 (H. W. R. Wade).

[5]   (1957) 73 LQR 300 (R.E.M.); *Birmingham Citizens' Permanent Building Society v Caunt* [1962] Ch 883, [1962] 1 All ER 163, p. 858, post; *Alnwick RDC v Taylor* [1966] Ch 355, [1966] 1 All ER 899.

Held. The mortgagee was entitled to possession.

HARMAN J: This is an originating summons for possession. . . . This subject is one which is constantly being agitated in this court. I have had my attention called to some observations I made on it recently in *Hughes v Waite* [1957] 1 WLR 713, [1957] 1 All ER 603, and even more recently in *Alliance Perpetual Building Society v Belrum Investments Ltd* [1957] 1 WLR 720, [1957] 1 All ER 635, which came before me on an application to commit the editor of the 'Daily Mail' for comments on a mortgagee's action for possession of a sort exactly similar to the present. The comments and, indeed, the arguments of counsel for the newspaper showed an entire misapprehension of what an originating summons for possession is about. They all assumed that it involved some kind of default on the part of the mortgagor, but I said there, and I repeat now, that the right of the mortgagee to possession in the absence of some contract has nothing to do with default on the part of the mortgagor. The mortgagee may go into possession before the ink is dry on the mortgage unless there is something in the contract, express or by implication, [6] where he has contracted himself out of that right. He has the right because he has a legal term of years in the property or its statutory equivalent. If there is an attornment clause, he must give notice. If there is a provision that, so long as certain payments are made, he will not go into possession, then he has contracted himself out of his rights. Apart from that, possession is a matter of course.

[An application for possession] has become a very fashionable form of relief because, owing to the conditions now prevailing, if it is desired to realise a security by sale, vacant possession is almost essential. Where, therefore, the mortgagor is in occupation, a summons for possession is taken out, and no other relief is sought, and where the mortgagee is in a position to exercise his power of sale, that is all the help he requires from the court. . . .

The mortgagor said here that his default was of a very small order. So it was. If this were a case where there was discretion in the matter, I should feel that it was a hard case. But the mortgagor has entered into a contract with the mortgagee, and the mortgagee asks for his rights under the contract, and this court, in my judgment, has no power to refuse him those rights.

ii. LIABILITY OF MORTGAGEE IN POSSESSION

WHITE v CITY OF LONDON BREWERY CO
(1889) 42 ChD 237 (CA, Lord ESHER MR, COTTON and FRY LJJ)

In 1868, the plaintiff, a publican, mortgaged his public house to the defendants in return for a loan. In 1869, when the plaintiff's financial affairs were in a serious condition, the defendants exercised their right to take possession, and leased the premises to a tenant who covenanted to purchase his ale, beer and porter from the defendants.

In 1879, the defendants sold the property, took what they claimed was due to them under the mortgage debt and paid the surplus to second mortgagees. The plaintiff, acting in the interests of the second mortgagees, brought this action for an account of what was due to the defendants. One question which arose was whether the defendants were chargeable, not merely with the rent which they received from their tenants, but with the rent which they would have obtained if

---

[6]   See *Esso Petroleum Co Ltd v Alstonbridge Properties Ltd* [1975] 1 WLR 1474, [1975] 3 All ER 358; *Western Bank Ltd v Schindler* [1977] Ch 1, [1976] 2 All ER 393.

the premises had been let free from the covenant to purchase ale, etc., from the defendants.

Held. The defendants were chargeable with the rent which they would have obtained if the tenant had not been so restricted.

COTTON LJ: There is then another point to be considered. A mortgagee in possession must account for the rents, which, but for his wilful default, he would have received. The plaintiff says that if he fails as to the brewers' profits yet he ought to have a larger sum in respect of the rents which the mortgagees would, but for their wilful default, have received. . . .The learned Judge has allowed an addition of £20 a year from 19 August 1874, down to the date of the sale, in addition to the rent obtained by the mortgagees. [His Lordship considered the evidence relating to the rent for which the public house could have been let, and continued:] The evidence on that question is of a somewhat doubtful character, but I think the plaintiff has not established that more should be given him than what the learned Judge has allowed, *viz.* £20 a year, which comes altogether, as the Master of the Rolls has said, to £100.[7]

It is possible also to take possession for the purpose of receiving the income of the property. It is more usual, however, to appoint a receiver[8] if the object is to make up income in arrear, for a mortgagee in possession is made to account not only for what he received, but also for what he could, by prudent management, have received.

iii. RELIEF OF MORTGAGOR

Contract and statute apart, a legal mortgagee's right to possession of the mortgaged property cannot be defeated by a cross-claim on the part of the mortgagor, even if it is both liquidated and admitted, and even if it exceeds the amount of the mortgage arrears.[9]

(a) At Common Law

In **Mobil Oil Co Ltd v Rawlinson** (1981) 43 P & CR 221, Rawlinson was the owner of the equity of redemption in respect of Heathfield Garage, North Petherton in Somerset. The mortgage on the petrol station secured a loan from, and also all sums due to, the defendants under a supply agreement. When Rawlinson fell into arrears, the plaintiffs sought possession of the filling station. Rawlinson sought to counterclaim and set off against the arrears sums alleged to be due to him from the defendants under the supply agreement. The Master made an order for possession, subject to a proviso that it was not to be enforced, if Rawlinson paid £8,000 into court within 14 days. In holding that the proviso should be deleted, NOURSE J said at 224:

'Before 1936 a mortgagee who was only asking for possession had to commence his proceedings in the Queen's Bench Division. That was because possession alone could not be sought by summons in the Chancery Division. But in 1936,

---

[7] See also *Hughes v Williams* (1806) 12 Ves 493; *Nelson v Booth* (1858) 3 De G & J 119; *Wrigley v Gill* [1905] 1 Ch 241; (1979) 129 NLJ 334 (H. E. Markson); [1982] Conv 345 at pp. 346–348 (J. E. Stannard).

[8] See p. 893, post.

[9] *Midland Bank plc v McGrath* [1996] EGCS 61.

R.S.C., Ord. 55, r. 5A was amended so as to make that possible. The Chancery judges of the time issued a practice direction which said, amongst other things, that when possession was sought and the defendant was in arrear with any instalments due under the mortgage or charge and the master was of the opinion that the defendant ought to be given an opportunity to pay off the arrears, the master might adjourn the summons on such terms as he thought fit. The direction caused confusion. It led to a general view among the Chancery masters, no doubt assisted by the benevolent attitude which the legislature had by then assumed towards tenants faced with eviction by their landlords, that they had a discretion to adjourn a legal mortgagee's application for possession, at any rate in instalment cases, against the wishes of the mortgagee in order to enable the mortgagor to catch up on instalment arrears; and, inferentially, a right, if he did so, to continue to deny the mortgagee possession notwithstanding that on the default the whole of the mortgage money had become and thereafter remained repayable. By the end of the 1950s it had become necessary for the Chancery judges of a later generation to reassert the legal mortgagee's right to possession. In the van of the movement was Harman J, although even he subscribed to the view that the practice direction had qualified the right in the case of an instalment mortgage: see *Four-Maids Ltd v Dudley Marshall (Properties) Ltd* [1957] Ch 317 at 321, [1957] 2 All ER 35 at 36, p. 855, ante.

In 1961 the whole question was fully argued and considered in *Birmingham Citizens Permanent Building Society v Caunt* [1962] Ch 883, [1962] 1 All ER 163, and it is on Russell J's judgment in that case that the foregoing summary of the earlier history is based. I well remember that decision and the general view of the profession that it had settled once and for all the limited extent of the court's power to adjourn a legal mortgagee's application for possession. The rule in regard to instalment mortgages, and a fortiori in regard to ordinary mortgages, was stated by Russell J at the end of his judgment, in the following terms at 912, at 182:

"Accordingly, in my judgment, where (as here) the legal mortgagee under an instalment mortgage under which by reason of default the whole money has become payable, is entitled to possession, the court has no jurisdiction to decline the order or to adjourn the hearing whether on terms of keeping up payments or paying arrears, if the mortgagee cannot be persuaded to agree to this course. To this the *sole exception* is that the application may be adjourned for a short time to afford to the mortgagor a chance of paying off the mortgagee in full or otherwise satisfying him; but this should not be done if there is no reasonable prospect of this occurring. When I say the sole exception, I do not, of course, intend to exclude adjournments which in the ordinary course of procedure may be desirable in circumstances such as temporary inability of a party to attend, and so forth."

The reason for the exception is that the court has never allowed a mortgagee to enforce his rights under the mortgage in the face of a concrete offer by the mortgagor to redeem.

Since then the court has twice been given additional powers of adjournment in cases where the mortgaged property consists of or includes a dwellinghouse: see section 36 of the Administration of Justice Act 1970 and section 8 of the Administration of Justice Act 1973. But the general rule continues to apply to other types of property, for example commercial premises of the kind with which the present case is concerned. . . .[10]

---

[10]   *Cheltenham and Gloucester plc v Krausz* [1997] 1 WLR 1558 at 1561, [1997] 1 All ER 21 at 24, p. 887, post.

I am prepared to assume in the defendant's favour that the amount of his cross-claims exceeds the amount of the mortgage debt. I say at once that I regard that as an assumption of extremely doubtful validity – on the Master's estimate there is a shortfall of about £8,000 – but I will make it nonetheless. However, I find it impossible to make any distinction between this case and *Samuel Keller (Holdings) Ltd v Martins Bank Ltd* [1971] 1 WLR 43 at 47–48, [1970] 3 All ER 950 at 953. Megarry J's statement of the principle which was expressly approved by the Court of Appeal, is in entirely general terms. The principle is that a mortgagor cannot unilaterally appropriate the amount of a cross-claim, even if it is both liquidated and admitted, and *a fortiori* if it is unliquidated or not admitted, in discharge of the mortgage debt. On that footing the origin and nature of the cross-claim and its relationship to the mortgage debt are wholly irrelevant.

In the circumstances this case must be approached on the footing that when the matter came before the Master there were substantial arrears outstanding. Consistently with the general rule established in *Birmingham Citizens Permanent Building Society v Caunt* he ought then to have made an unconditional order for possession, unless of course he was satisfied that there was a reasonable prospect of the defendant's paying the arrears in full, not into court but to the plaintiffs, or otherwise satisfying the plaintiffs, in which case he should have adjourned the application for a short time.

I do not intend to suggest that there may not be other circumstances in which the court will refuse a mortgagee possession on terms that the mortgagor pays the full amount of the mortgage debt into court. A number of other possibilities are mentioned in the passage in Fisher and Lightwood's *Law of Mortgage* (9th edn. 1977) p. 325 which I have already read. Without attempting to decide any point which does not arise for decision in the present case, I will only say that it seems to me that that course could only be adopted in the case where there was a substantial question as to the existence or enforceability of the right to possession, for example where it was claimed that the mortgage was void for illegality or that the mortgagee was in some way estopped from asserting his right. It appears probable that *Lido Investments Ltd v Hale* (1971) 219 EG 715 is a case which falls within the former category.' [11]

(b) In Equity

QUENNELL v MALTBY
[1979] 1 WLR 318, [1979] 1 All ER 568 (CA, Lord DENNING MR, BRIDGE and TEMPLEMAN LJJ) [12]

Quennell, who owned a large house in Lewes, Sussex, worth more than £30,000, mortgaged it to Barclays Bank Ltd to secure a loan of £2,500. The mortgage deed prohibited the creation of a tenancy without the bank's consent. In breach of that covenant Quennell let the house to the defendants who became statutory

---

[11] *Citibank Trust Ltd v Ayivor* [1987] 1 WLR 1157, [1987] 3 All ER 241 (right to possession not affected where mortgagor's counterclaim for damages greater than arrears due under mortgage); *First National Bank plc v Syed* [1991] 2 All ER 250; (1991) 141 NLJ 793 (H. W. Wilkinson); (1994) 110 LQR 221 (N. Hickman); *National Westminster Bank plc v Skelton* [1993] 1 WLR 72n, [1993] 1 All ER 242; *Ashley Guarantee plc v Zacaria* [1993] 1 WLR 62, [1993] 1 All ER 254 (no distinction in principle where mortgagor is principal debtor and where he is only guarantor); [1993] All ER Rev 253 (P. J. Clarke); *Midland Bank Co plc v McGrath* [1996] EGCS 61. See Derham, *Set-Off* (3rd edn. 2003), para. 4.93.

[12] (1979) 129 NLJ 624 (H. W. Wilkinson); 38 CLJ 257 (R. A. Pearce).

tenants protected by the Rent Act 1977. This tenancy was binding on Quennell but not on the bank. [13]

Quennell, who wanted to sell the house with vacant possession, asked the bank to bring an action for possession against the defendants. On the bank's refusal, Quennell's wife then paid off the mortgage debt, took a transfer of the mortgage from the bank and claimed possession against the defendants as mortgagee.

Held (reversing the County Court judge). The wife was not entitled to an order for possession.

LORD DENNING MR: [The decision of the judge], if right, opens the way to widespread evasion of the Rent Acts. If the owner of a house wishes to obtain vacant possession, all he has to do is charge it to the bank for a small sum. Then grant a new tenancy without telling the bank. Then get his wife to pay off the bank and take a transfer. Then get the wife to sue for possession.

That indeed was what happened here. In October 1977, when Mr Quennell went to the bank, he told them about the tenancies. They said that they did not intend to take proceedings. So he got Mrs Quennell to do it. In evidence, she said:

'I paid £2,500. This was for my husband. I took the charge to make the debt to his bank less onerous. I was aware he wanted to obtain possession of the house to sell it. I merely paid off the charge. These proceedings have been brought to get possession to sell.'

So the objective is plain. It was not to enforce the security or to obtain repayment or anything of that kind. It was in order to get possession of the house and to overcome the protection of the Rent Acts.

Is that permissible? It seems to me that this is one of those cases where equity steps in to mitigate the rigour of the law. Long years ago it did the same when it invented the equity of redemption. As is said in *Snell's Principles of Equity*, 27th edn. (1973), p. 376:

'The courts of equity left the legal effect of the transaction unaltered but declared it to be unreasonable and against conscience that the mortgagee should retain as owner for his own benefit what was intended as a mere security.'

So here in modern times equity can step in so as to prevent a mortgagee, or a transferee from him, from getting possession of a house contrary to the justice of the case. A mortgagee will be restrained from getting possession except when it is sought bona fide and reasonably for the purpose of enforcing the security and then only subject to such conditions as the court thinks fit to impose. When the bank itself or a building society lends the money, then it may well be right to allow the mortgagee to obtain possession when the borrower is in default. But so long as the interest is paid and there is nothing outstanding, equity has ample power to restrain any unjust use of the right to possession.

---

[13]   *Dudley and District Benefit Building Society v Emerson* [1949] Ch 707, [1949] 2 All ER 469; *Sadiq v Hussain* (1997) 73 P & CR D44.

Section 98 of the Rent Act 1977 prohibits the court from ordering possession of a dwelling house subject to a statutory tenancy unless certain criteria are met: it does not prohibit a prior mortgagee with title paramount from recovering possession (i) from a protected contractual tenant: *Dudley and District Benefit Building Society v Emerson*, supra; (ii) from a statutory tenant: *Britannia Building Society v Earl* [1990] 1 WLR 422, [1990] 2 All ER 469; [1990] Conv 450 (S. Bridge); but it does prohibit a mortgagee in all cases where the tenancy pre-dates the mortgagee's mortgage: *Woolwich Building Society v Dickman* [1996] 3 All ER 204; [1996] All ER Rev 254 (P. J. Clarke); 279 (P.H. Pettit); cf. *Barclays Bank plc v Zaroovabli* [1997] Ch 321 (tenancy predated registration but not grant of bank's charge); (1997) 113 LQR 390 (M. Robinson).

It is plain that in this transaction Mr and Mrs Quennell had an ulterior motive. It was not done to enforce the security or due payment of the principal or interest. It was done for the purpose of getting possession of the house in order to resell it at a profit. It was done so as to avoid the protection which the Rent Acts afford to tenants in their occupation. If Mr Quennell himself had sought to evict the tenants, he would not be allowed to do so. He could not say the tenancies were void. He would be estopped from saying so. They certainly would be protected against him. Are they protected against his wife now that she is the transferee of the charge? In my opinion they are protected. For this simple reason, she is not seeking possession for the purpose of enforcing the loan or the interest or anything of that kind. She is doing it simply for an ulterior purpose of getting possession of the house, contrary to the intention of Parliament as expressed in the Rent Acts.

On that simple ground it seems to me that this action fails and it should be dismissed. The legal right to possession is not to be enforced when it is sought for an ulterior motive. I would on this account allow the appeal and dismiss the action for possession. [14]

BRIDGE LJ: I entirely agree. The situation arising in this case is one, it seems to me, in which the court is not only entitled but bound to look behind the formal legal relationship between the parties to see what is the true substance of the matter. Once one does that, on the facts of this case it is as plain as a pikestaff that the purpose of the bringing of these proceedings via Mrs Quennell is not for her own benefit to protect or enforce the security which she holds as the transferee of the legal charge but for the benefit of her husband as mortgagor to enable him to sell the property with the benefit of vacant possession. In substance she is suing as his agent. That being so, it seems to me inevitably to follow that she can be in no better position in these proceedings than her husband would be if they had been brought in his name. If they had been brought in his name, it is clear that the defendants would have had an unanswerable defence under the Rent Acts.

I agree that the appeal should be allowed. [15]

(c) By Statute

Since 1970 there has been a statutory exception to the Draconian rule in *Four-Maids Ltd v Dudley Marshall Properties Ltd* [1957] Ch 317, [1957] 2 All ER 35, p. 855, ante in favour of the mortgagor. [16] The additional powers can be exercised by the court whether or not the mortgagor is in default [17] and whether the loan is by way of an instalment or endowment mortgage. [18]

1. ADMINISTRATION OF JUSTICE ACT 1970, S. 36

ADMINISTRATION OF JUSTICE ACT 1970

36. Additional powers of court in action by mortgagee for possession of dwelling-house.—(1) Where the mortgagee under a mortgage of land which consists of

---

[14] Followed in *Albany Home Loans Ltd v Massey* [1997] 2 All ER 609; *Abbey National v Tufts* [1999] 2 FLR 399.

[15] TEMPLEMAN LJ delivered a judgment concurring with BRIDGE LJ.

[16] For a similar system of protection for mortgages in Scotland, see Mortgage Rights (Scotland) Act 2001.

[17] *Western Bank Ltd v Schindler* [1977] Ch 1, [1976] 2 All ER 393.

[18] *Governor and Co of the Bank of Scotland v Grimes* [1985] QB 1179, [1985] 2 All ER 254, p. 867, post.

or includes a dwelling-house [19] brings an action in which he claims possession
of the mortgaged property, not being an action for foreclosure in which a claim
for possession of the mortgaged property is also made, the court [20] may exercise
any of the powers conferred on it by subsection (2) below if it appears to the
court that in the event of its exercising the power the mortgagor [1] is likely to be
able within a reasonable period [2] to pay any sums due under the mortgage or to
remedy a default consisting of a breach of any other obligation arising under or
by virtue of the mortgage.

(2) The court –
   (*a*) may adjourn the proceedings, [3] or
   (*b*) on giving judgment, or making an order, for delivery of possession of
          the mortgaged property, or at any time before the execution of such
          judgment or order, may –
   (i)   stay or suspend execution of the judgment or order, [4] or
   (ii) postpone the date for delivery of possession,
for such period or periods as the court thinks reasonable. [5]

(3) Any such adjournment, stay, suspension or postponement as is referred
to in subsection (2) above may be made subject to such conditions with regard to

---

[19]   The fact that part is used as a shop or office or for business, trade or professional purposes
       does not prevent a house from being a dwelling-house: s. 39(2). The relevant date for
       determining whether premises consist of a dwelling-house is the date when the mortgagee
       brings an action for possession: *Royal Bank of Scotland v Miller* [2002] QB 255.
[20]   RSC Ord. 88: CPR 1998, Sch. 1 (SI 1998 No. 3132); County Courts Act 1984, s. 21(1)
       gives jurisdiction to the County Court when the net annual value for rating does not
       exceed the county court limit: *P B Frost Ltd v Green* [1978] 1 WLR 949, [1978] 2 All ER
       206; *Universal Showcards and Display Manufacturing Ltd v Brunt* (1984) Times, 26 March;
       County Court (Amendment No. 3) Rules 1993 (SI 1993 No. 2175); (1993) 143 NLJ 1762
       (R. C. M. Jones). See also Consumer Credit Act 1974, s. 126, p. 847, n. 2, ante, post. On
       the procedures for personal claims, see (1999) 143 SJ 1134 (County Court) and 1160
       (High Court) (G. Webber). If the land is outside Greater London or the County Palatine
       of Lancaster, and, if a County Court has jurisdiction, the action must be brought in the
       County Court: ss. 37–38.
[1]   Mortgagor and mortgagee includes any person deriving title under the original mortgagor
       or mortgagee: s. 39(1); *Britannia Building Society v Earl* [1990] 1 WLR 422, [1990] 2 All
       ER 469 (statutory tenant of mortgagor whose tenancy was not binding on mortgagee, p.
       860, n. 14, ante, was not such a person and court had no jurisdiction to adjourn
       proceedings); (1990) 140 NLJ 823 (H. W. Wilkinson).
[2]   *Royal Trust Co of Canada v Markham* [1975] 1 WLR 1416, [1975] 3 All ER 433 (an order
       for suspension must be for a fixed 'period'; and the mortgagor must provide evidence
       that he is 'likely to be able to pay'); *Cheltenham and Gloucester Building Society v Norgan*
       [1996] 1 WLR 343, [1996] 1 All ER 449, p. 868, post; *Bristol and West Building Society v
       Ellis* (1996) 73 P & CR 158, p. 870, post.
[3]   *Albany Homes Ltd v Massey* (1997) 73 P & CR 509 (joint mortgagors in default; order for
       possession made against husband alone; in absence of undertaking by mortgagee not to
       enforce the order, proceedings should be adjourned with liberty to restore if wife was
       ordered out or left).
[4]   *Target Homes Loans Ltd v Clothier* (1992) 25 HLR 48 (3 months' postponement; mortgagor
       had better prospect of achieving earlier sale if in possession); [1993] Conv 62 (J. Martin).
[5]   *National Provincial Building Society v Ahmed* [1995] 2 EGLR 127 at 129; *Cheltenham and
       Gloucester Building Society v Obi* (1994) 28 HLR 22 (after mortgagee has obtained possession
       order, court cannot suspend effect of order unless the order itself can be set aside);
       Cheltenham and Gloucester Building Society v Grattidge (1993) 25 HLR 454; *Cheltenham and
       Gloucester Building Society v Johnson* (1996) 73 P & CR 293 (when a mortgagee is entitled
       to a money judgment, this may be suspended on same terms as, and in line with, the
       possession order itself). For the inter-relation between s. 36(1) and LPA 1925, s. 91(2),
       p. 852, ante, see *Cheltenham and Gloucester plc v Krausz* [1997] 1 WLR 1558, [1997] 1 All
       ER 21, p. 887, post.

payment by the mortgagor of any sum secured by the mortgage or the remedying of any default as the court thinks fit.

(4) The court may from time to time vary or revoke any condition imposed by virtue of this section.

38A. [6] This part of this Act shall not apply to a mortgage securing an agreement which is a regulated agreement within the meaning of the Consumer Credit Act 1974. [7]

In **Ropaigealach v Barclays Bank plc** [2000] QB 263 [1999] 4 All ER 235, [8] the question arose whether the common law right of a mortgagee to take possession of the premises without a court order had been abrogated by section 36 of the Administration of Justice Act 1970. In holding that it had not, Chadwick LJ said at 271:

'The section is expressed to apply where a mortgagee brings an action in which he claims possession of the mortgaged property. Where the conditions in subsection (1) are satisfied the court is given powers, by subsection (2), which may fairly be described as procedural—in the sense that they are only capable of being exercised in the context of existing proceedings in which a claim for possession is made. But, it is said, Parliament could not have intended that the protection against ejectment which the section was plainly intended to give to mortgagors in respect of their homes should be capable of being circumvented by a mortgagee who resorted to self-help; that is to say, by a mortgagee who obtained possession by entry without the assistance of the court. Accordingly, so it is contended, the section must be construed in such a way as to make it unlawful for a mortgagee to take possession of a dwelling house except under an order of the court. It never became clear in argument how, by any interpretation of the words actually used, that result could be achieved; but that objection was brushed aside as unduly technical. What mattered, it was said, was that the court should give effect to the purpose of which the section was plainly enacted.

I find it impossible to be satisfied that Parliament must have intended, when enacting section 36 of the Act of 1970, that the mortgagee's common law right to take possession by virtue of his estate should only be exercisable with the assistance of the court. In my view, the only conclusion as to parliamentary intention that this court can properly reach is that which can be derived from the circumstances in which the section was enacted, the statutory context in which it appears and the language which was used. All point in the same direction. Parliament was concerned with the problem which had arisen following *Birmingham Citizens Permanent Building Society v Caunt* [1962] Ch. 883, [1962] 1 All ER 163; it intended to restore the position to what it had been thought to be before that decision; and it did not address its mind to the question whether the mortgagor required protection against the mortgagee who took possession without the assistance of the court. It is impossible to be sure what course

---

[6] Added by Consumer Credit Act 1974, s. 192, Sch. 4, para. 30; p. 765, ante.

[7] Where one spouse has defaulted on the mortgage of a dwelling-house, and the mortgagee brings an action for possession, the other spouse may be entitled to be made a party to the action: Family Law Act 1996, s. 54, p. 315, ante; LRA 1925, s. 112 B.

[8] Leave to appeal to HL was refused: [2000] 1 WLR 1034 [1999] Conv 263 (A. Dunn); [1999] CLJ 281 (M. Dixon); [1999] All ER Rev 226 (P. J. Clarke). As to the compatibility of this right to peaceable re-entry and its exclusion from AJA 1970, s. 36, with the Human Rights Act 1998. See Rook, *Property Law and Human Rights*, pp. 199–203.

Parliament would have thought it appropriate to adopt, in 1970, if it had identified and addressed that question. It is impossible to be sure that Parliament did not intend (or would not have intended, if it had addressed its mind to the question) to leave the position as it was in that regard. It is not irrelevant that, at the date at which the Act of 1970 was enacted, the mortgagor who was in occupation had the protection—subsequently replaced in a different and, perhaps, more limited form by section 6 of the Criminal Law Act 1977—afforded by the Forcible Entry Acts 1381–1623 (p. 526, ante). It is because it is impossible to be sure that Parliament cannot have intended to leave the position as it was— but must have intended that the mortgagee should only be entitled to exercise his common law right to possession with the assistance of the court—that it cannot be appropriate to embark on an investigation whether the words which have been used are capable of some other construction than that which they naturally bear.'

2. ADMINISTRATION OF JUSTICE ACT 1973, S. 8

ADMINISTRATION OF JUSTICE ACT 1973

8. Extension of powers of court in action by mortgagee of dwelling-house.— (1) Where by a mortgage of land which consists of or includes a dwelling-house, or by any agreement between the mortgagee under such a mortgage and the mortgagor, the mortgagor is entitled or is to be permitted to pay the principal sum secured by instalments or otherwise to defer payment of it in whole or in part, but provision is also made for earlier payment in the event of any default by the mortgagor or of a demand by the mortgagee or otherwise, then for purposes of section 36 of the Administration of Justice Act 1970 (under which a court has power to delay giving a mortgagee possession of the mortgaged property so as to allow the mortgagor a reasonable time to pay any sums due under the mortgage) a court may treat as due under the mortgage on account of the principal sum secured and of interest on it only such amounts as the mortgagor would have expected to be required to pay if there had been no such provision for earlier payment.[9]

(2) A court shall not exercise by virtue of subsection (1) above the powers conferred by section 36 of the Administration of Justice Act 1970 unless it appears to the court not only that the mortgagor is likely to be able within a reasonable period to pay any amounts regarded (in accordance with subsection (1) above) as due on account of the principal sum secured, together with the interest on those amounts, but also that he is likely to be able by the end of that period to pay any further amounts that he would have expected to be required to pay by then on account of that sum and of interest on it if there had been no such provision as is referred to in subsection (1) above for earlier payment.

(3) Where subsection (1) above would apply to an action in which a mortgagee only claimed possession of the mortgaged property, and the mortgagee brings an action for foreclosure (with or without also claiming possession of the property), then section 36 of the Administration of Justice Act 1970 together

---

[9]   Reversing the effect of *Halifax Building Society v Clark* [1973] Ch 307, [1973] 2 All ER 33; but the grant of the statutory concession was unnecessary: *First Middlesbrough Trading and Mortgage Co Ltd v Cunningham* (1974) 28 P & CR 69; (1973) 37 Conv (NS) 213; (1974) 38 Conv (NS) 309. See *Centrax Trustees Ltd v Ross* [1979] 2 All ER 952; [1979] Conv 371 (F. R. Crane); *Habib Bank Ltd v Tailor* [1982] 1 WLR 1218, [1982] 3 All ER 561; *Governor and Co of the Bank of Scotland v Grimes* [1985] QB 1179, [1985] 2 All ER 254, p. 867, post; *Royal Bank of Scotland v Miller* [2002] QB 257.

with subsections (1) and (2) above shall apply as they would apply if it were an action in which the mortgagee only claimed possession of the mortgaged property, except that –

(*a*) section 36(2) (*b*) shall apply only in relation to any claim for possession.

HABIB BANK LTD v TAILOR
[1982] 1 WLR 1218, [1982] 3 All ER 561 (CA, CUMMING-BRUCE, DUNN and OLIVER LJJ) [10]

Tailor mortgaged his dwelling-house, 142 Walton Avenue, Harlow, to Habib Bank Ltd to secure an overdraft of up to £6,000. He covenanted to pay, on demand in writing, all moneys which might become owing to the bank. When Tailor exceeded the overdraft limit, the bank made a written demand for the whole sum owing for principal, interest and bank charges, and later began proceedings for possession. The sum owing was £7,212, and there was no likelihood of Tailor being able to repay the whole sum within a reasonable period.

The question was whether Administration of Justice Act 1973, s. 8 applied, so as to bring into operation Administration of Justice Act 1970, s. 36.

Held (reversing the County Court judge). The Acts did not apply.

OLIVER LJ: The reasoning by which the judge arrived at his conclusion that the section applied was that he was referred to a decision of Goulding J in *Centrax Trustees Ltd v Ross* [1979] 2 All ER 952. It was a case in which there was a mortgage with a fixed date for repayment six months ahead of the date of the mortgage, the classic case in effect of the old type of fixed mortgage where the legal date for redemption is fixed at six months after the date of the execution of the mortgage, but there was a clear intention from other provisions in the mortgage, notably the provision for the payment of interest (which was clearly envisaged as extending beyond the period of six months limited for the repayment of the principal) which indicated that the common intention of the parties was that the mortgage would be allowed to stay out indefinitely and that the mortgagor would be entitled to defer payment of the principal sum beyond the date fixed so long as he paid interest on that principal sum. ...

[His Lordship quoted from the judgment of GOULDING J at 955 and continued:]

He goes on to hold that the section applied in that case.

That of course was a very different case from the instant case. It was a case where there was a fixed date for repayment of the principal sum and it was a case where it was quite clearly intended that the actual payment of the principal sum should be deferred beyond that fixed date. And it was a case also where, if default was made in payment of interest, the mortgage contained a provision for calling in the whole sum.

Mr Wilmers, who appears for the bank in this case, has forcibly submitted that the reasoning of that case cannot apply here. In my judgment he is right in making that submission. I say nothing about the correctness of the decision in the *Centrax Trustees* case on the construction of the section. It is indeed difficult, I think, to escape from the conclusion that the section did apply to that case, even though I, for myself, rather question whether it was intended by the legislature to do so. But the instant case is really quite a different case. As

---

[10]   [1983] Conv 80 (P. H. Kenny); [1982] All ER Rev 177 (P. J. Clarke); [1984] Conv 91 (S. Tromans).

Mr Wilmers pointed out, and indeed as was pointed out by Goulding J in the *Centrax Trustees* case, there are two necessary conditions for the application of the section: first, either the mortgage itself or some agreement made under it must have the effect that—I will quote only the relevant words—'the mortgagor ... is to be permitted ... otherwise to defer payment of' the principal sum 'in whole or in part'; secondly, provision must be made in the mortgage or agreement 'for earlier payment in the event of any default by the mortgagor or of a demand by the mortgagee or otherwise.' Mr Wilmers's first submission is that there is no permission to defer payment. As he points out, this is a simple case of a bank mortgage to secure an overdraft. It is quite clear on the authorities that in these circumstances the money is not capable of being sued for by the bank until demand has been made. Indeed, the mortgage itself so provides, because it is to secure the moneys covenanted to be paid and the moneys are covenanted to be paid on demand having been made in writing. This nowhere more clearly appears than from *Lloyds Bank Ltd v Margolis* [1954] 1 WLR 644, [1954] 1 All ER 734. I think it is only necessary to read briefly from the judgment of Upjohn J at 649, at 738. ...

When one looks at the charge in the instant case, one asks immediately: 'Where is the agreement to be found that the mortgagor is to be permitted otherwise to defer payment of the principal?' because, by definition, the principal does not become due, and cannot be sued for by the bank, until a written demand has been made. Deferment, I think, involves the deferment of payment after it has become due, and quite clearly in this case there appears to me to be no provision, either in the agreement between the parties or in the mortgage itself, by which, on any realistic construction, it can be said that payment by the customer was to be 'deferred,' or that the customer was permitted to 'defer' payment. Mr Cutting has in fact submitted that every case where the principal money does not become payable immediately the mortgage is executed is a case where the mortgagor is entitled to defer payment. That is a submission which I find is impossible to accept.

It seems to me that the defendant's case on the application of section 8 fails at that point, but it also fails, I think, on the other condition, too, because, as Mr Wilmers pointed out, the section requires that provision must be made for earlier payment, and one has to ask oneself: 'Earlier than what?' In the instant case the payment was not due until the demand was made, and there is no provision for any payment earlier than that. It is the demand itself which makes the payment due.

For both those reasons, it seems to me that this is clearly a case where section 8 cannot apply to this mortgage, and that really concludes the case. I think it unnecessary to elaborate the matter further. If there had been some reasonable prospect of the defendant repaying the whole of the principal sum, then no doubt it would have been appropriate for the judge to have remitted the matter back to the registrar for a determination of whether he should exercise his power under section 36(2) of the Act of 1970 to adjourn the proceedings or to postpone the date for the delivery of possession, but that, as Mr Cutting accepts, does not arise. Section 8 does not apply. There is then no further room for the operation of the discretion under section 36, and accordingly in my judgment the decision of the judge must be reversed and the decision of the deputy registrar restored. I would therefore allow the appeal.

In **Governor and Company of the Bank of Scotland v Grimes** [1985] QB 1179, [1985] 2 All ER 254, the defendants borrowed from the plaintiffs £15,015 in order to purchase 26 Guppy Street, Swindon. The loan was secured by an endowment mortgage[11] which provided for repayment of the principal sum at the end of 25 years, with interest payable by monthly instalments, and for the principal sum and accrued interest to be payable immediately in the case of default.

The defendants defaulted on the payments of interest, and the endowment policy lapsed. On the bank's summons for the payment of interest due and an order for possession, the County Court judge held that there was no deferred repayment of capital within section 8 of the Administration of Justice Act 1973, and that he could not exercise his discretion to postpone possession under section 36 of the 1970 Act.

In allowing the appeal, Sir John ARNOLD P said at 1187, at 257:

'In certain circumstances the provisions of section 36 are amended and controlled by section 8 of the Administration of Justice Act 1973, and the principal issue in this case is whether that amendment and control extends to the present case.

[His Lordship read s. 8 and continued:]

What that effects in substance is an omission of the obligation for expedited payment which is to be found in the default clause for the purpose of the application of section 36 as a matter of the discretion of the court.

We have considered, and have been assisted by counsel, in the task of giving some meaning to the words "or is to be permitted" following the word "entitled" in that subsection, but we have been wholly unable to come to any conclusion as to any possible meaning of that phrase. It must have been included for some purpose, but what that purpose is, for my part at least, I find myself wholly unable to determine. If it is something which is short of a contractual obligation or a contractual right which is there intended to be referred to, the words "is to be" are peculiarly unsuitable. If it is something distinct from being entitled, then what it is, is wholly obscure. But I do not think much turns on that in the present case; it is the presence of so impenetrable a phrase which makes one think that one has to be very careful in construing this section to feel oneself free to give effect to the general tenor of the language in a purposive way so as to make it fit in with the general intention which is evidently exhibited and the context of section 36 in the Administration of Justice Act 1970 in which it has to be read rather than to be bound by a literal meaning of the language used which would not have the purposive effect which seems to be desired. There is no doubt whatever that section 36 of the Act of 1970 applies to such a case as this. It is not made any the less to apply because this is a case in which there is a fixed period for payment of the mortgage principal as a whole rather than an instalment arrangement. One might expect that in a suitable case in which that was the situation, for the purpose of effecting the mitigation which was evidently intended by section 8 of the Administration of Justice Act 1973, the two situations would be equated.

---

[11] In an endowment mortgage, an endowment assurance policy is taken out at the same time as the money is borrowed; only interest payments are made by the mortgagor during the life of the mortgage, the outstanding debt being repaid when the policy matures. Cf. an instalment or repayment mortgage, where the debt is paid off by monthly instalments at a rate which covers payment of interest and repayment of capital, so that the capital is paid off over an agreed period of time, for example 25 years.

The construction which appealed to the judge was that a deferred payment was a payment which the payer was required to make under one provision of the bargain, but which he was entitled to have deferred under another provision of the bargain, so that, unless there was to be found an obligation to make the payment in question at some time earlier than the date of postponement of that obligation to be found in the relevant other provisions, section 8 of the Administration of Justice 1973 could not be made to apply. ...

Habib Bank Ltd v Tailor [1982] 1 WLR 1218, [1982] 3 All ER 561, p. 865, ante was a case in which what was before the court was a charge to secure an ordinary banking overdraft so that the subject matter of the debt was one which was due immediately upon the making of an unconditional demand. That is a rather different case, at least socially, in regard to the purpose of this legislation, from the present case where what is primarily in question is a mortgage of a fixed sum for a fixed term. I do not find anything in *Habib Bank Ltd v Tailor* which prevents this court giving to the conception of "deferred payment" a definition which includes any case in which there is a stated period before the end of which payment does not require to be made which extends into a defined future, and it seems to me that that condition is satisfied by the language of the agreement which, in its extended interpretation, which is not in dispute, is imported by the language "period of loan 25 years." It seems to be, therefore, that it can without doing violence to the language of the section and by way of giving effect and purpose to this section, be construed in that way so that there is, thus looked at, a provision here for deferred payment to be found in the agreement. There is no question but that there is also a provision for earlier payment in the event of any default, because that is to be found in clause 4 of the agreement. It seems to me, therefore, that this is a case in which section 8 of the Administration of Justice Act 1973 applies to modify and control the language of section 36 of the Administration of Justice Act 1970 and for that reason I would allow the appeal.'

GRIFFITHS LJ said at 301, at 259: 'It seems to me that it would be highly improbable that Parliament would intend such relief to apply only to instalment mortgages taken out with a building society and not to apply to the alternative and increasingly popular form of finance by loan from a bank, backed by an endowment policy. I am satisfied, for the reasons given by Sir John Arnold P that the wording "or otherwise to defer payment of it in whole or in part" are deliberately inserted to cover this second type of mortgage transaction where there is no obligation to repay the capital until the end of the term of the loan.' [12]

---

3. REASONABLE PERIOD

In **Cheltenham and Gloucester Building Society v Norgan** [1996] 1 WLR 343, [1996] 1 All ER 449, [13] the Court of Appeal set out the considerations which are likely to be relevant when a reasonable period has to be established for the purposes of section 36 of the Administration of Justice Act 1970. WAITE LJ said at 345, at 450:

[12]   *Royal Bank of Scotland plc v Miller* [2002] QB 255 (mortgage repayable at end of fixed period was a provision for deferred payment).

[13]   (1996) 146 NLJ 252 (H. W. Wilkinson); [1996] Conv 118 (M. P. Thompson); (1996) 112 LQR 553 (J. Morgan); [1996] All ER Rev 260 (P. J. Clarke); *Household Mortgage Corporation plc v Pringle* [1998] 30 HLR 250 (duration of mortgage 25 years with 17 years outstanding).

'The rights of mortgagees to take possession of a dwelling house, whether by virtue of their legal estate in the land or in fulfilment of some express term of the mortgage operating in the event of default or arrears, have for many years been moderated by statutory powers giving the court discretion to suspend possession orders on appropriate terms. The mortgage to which this appeal relates is a term mortgage – that is to say a charge under which no instalments of capital are repayable and the whole principal debt remains outstanding until a specified date in the future, with the mortgagor being liable in the meantime for instalments of interest only. The appellant mortgagor fell into arrear with her interest payments. Thereupon, under the terms of the mortgage, the whole mortgage debt became immediately repayable. The mortgagee sought and obtained a possession order, execution of which was suspended by a series of orders on terms as to payment of current interest instalments and payment-off of arrears with which the mortgagor made strenuous efforts to comply, but without success, so that she remained in default, both under the terms of the mortgage and the terms of the suspension. . . . In the present plight of the housing market possession cases play a major part in the case-load for the county courts. That is particularly true of the district judges, who deal with those cases in such numbers that they develop a "feel" for them and have achieved an excellent disposal record. It is not surprising that they have found it convenient to adopt a relatively short period of years as the rough rule of thumb which aids a just determination of the "reasonable period" for the purposes of section 36 of the Act of 1970 and section 8 of the Act of 1973. Nevertheless, although I would not go quite so far with Mr Croally as to say it should be an "assumption," it does seem to me that the logic and spirit of the legislation require, especially in cases where the parties are proceeding under arrangements such as those reflection in the CML statement, [14] that the court should take as its starting point the full term of the mortgage and pose at the outset the question: "Would it be possible for the mortgagor to maintain payment-off of the arrears by instalments over that period?"'

Evans LJ said at 357, at 463: 'In conclusion, a practical summary of our judgments may be helpful in future cases. Drawing on the above and on the judgment of Waite LJ, the following considerations are likely to be relevant when a "reasonable period" has to be established for the purposes of section 36 of the Act of 1970. (a) How much can the borrower reasonably afford to pay, both now and in the future? (b) If the borrower has a temporary difficulty in meeting his obligations, how long is the difficulty likely to last? (c) What was the reason for the arrears which have accumulated? (d) How much remains of the original term? (e) What are the relevant contractual terms, and what type of mortgage is it, i.e. when is the principal due to be repaid? (f) Is it a case where the court should exercise its power to disregard accelerated payment provisions (section 8 of the Act of 1973)? (g) Is it reasonable to expect the lender, in the circumstances of the particular case, to recoup the arrears of interest (1) over the whole of the original term, or (2) within a shorter period, or even (3) within a longer period, i.e. by extending the repayment period? Is it reasonable to expect the lender to capitalise the interest or not? (h) Are there any reasons

---

[14] Council of Mortgage Lenders Statement of Current Practice (February 1995) dealing with 'Alleviating Arrears Problems'. Under this lenders can help borrowers by lengthening the term of a repayment loan; changing from an endowment mortgage to a repayment or interest-only mortgage; deferment of part of the interest where there is a temporary shortfall of income; capitalisation of interest; and ensuring that borrowers are aware of social security benefits.

affecting the security which should influence the length of the period for payment? In the light of the answers to the above, the court can proceed to exercise its overall discretion, taking account also of any further factors which may arise in the particular case.'

In **Bristol and West Building Society v Ellis** (1996) 73 P & CR 158, [15] AULD LJ said at 161:

'In the absence of unusual circumstances and where discharge of all arrears by periodic payments is proposed, the outstanding period of the mortgage, whether term or repayment, is the starting point in determining the reasonableness of the period for payment of sums due under a mortgage. See *Cheltenham & Gloucester Building Society v Norgan.*

However, that convenient starting point is not available to a mortgagor who cannot discharge the arrears by periodic payments and whose only prospect of repaying the entire mortgage loan and accrued and accruing interest is from the sale of the property. In such a case the only general guidance is that the reasonableness of the period is a matter for the court in the circumstances of the case. See *Royal Trust Co of Canada v Markham* [1975] 1 WLR 1416, [1975] 3 All ER 433 and *National & Provincial Building Society v Lloyd* [1996] 1 All ER 630.

The prospect of settling the mortgage debt, including arrears of principal and/or interest, by sale of the property raises a number of questions on the reasonableness of any period which a court may consider allowing for the purpose.

The critical matters are, of course, the adequacy of the property as a security for the debt and the length of the period necessary to achieve a sale. There should be evidence, or at least some informal material (see *Cheltenham & Gloucester Building Society v Grant* [1994] 26 HLR 703), before the court of the likelihood of a sale the proceeds of which will be discharge of the debt and of the period within which such a sale is likely to be achieved. If the court is satisfied on both counts and that the necessary period for sale is reasonable, it should, if it decides to suspend the order for possession, identify the period in its order.

The instinct of the courts in determining a reasonable period for this purpose seems to have been to adopt the common law approach before the 1970 Act, see *Birmingham Citizens Permanent Building Society v Caunt* [1962] Ch 883, [1962] 1 All ER 163, p. 858, ante, of fixing on a "short period". See *Target Home Loans Ltd v Clothier*, (1992) 25 HLR 48. However, in *Markham* neither the county court judge nor the Court of Appeal considered what, in the circumstances of that case, might have been a reasonable period. The defendants had called no evidence and the judge had not fixed any period in his order. The Court of Appeal contented itself with ruling that he should have fixed a period, but only after hearing evidence on the matter. In *Clothier*, the Court of Appeal, on the strength of evidence before it, but not before the county court judge, made an order for possession, suspending it for three months.

In *Lloyd*, Neill LJ, with whom Bennet J agreed, after reviewing the above authorities, held that the word "reasonable" in the statute should not necessarily be equated with "short"; what was a reasonable period was "a question for the court in the individual case". He said:

"if there were, in a hypothetical case, clear evidence that the completion of the sale of a property, perhaps by piecemeal disposal, could take place in six or

---

[15]   [1998] Conv 125 (M. P. Thompson).

nine months or even a year, I see no reason why a court could not come to the conclusion in the exercise of its discretion under the two sections that, to use the words of the section 'the mortgagor [was] likely to be able within a reasonable period to pay any sums due under the mortgage'. The question of a 'reasonable period' would be a question for the court in the individual case".' [16]

QUESTION

How would you have decided *Quennell v Maltby* [1979] 1 WLR 318, [1979] 1 All ER 568, p. 859, ante?

B. Powers to Grant and Accept Surrenders of Leases

LAW OF PROPERTY ACT 1925

99. Leasing powers of mortgagor and mortgagee in possession.—p. 853, ante.

100. Powers of mortgagor and mortgagee in possession to accept surrenders of leases.—p. 854, ante.

C. Sale, Insurance, Appointment of Receiver, Cutting and Selling of Timber [17]

LAW OF PROPERTY ACT 1925

101. Powers incident to estate or interest of mortgagee.—(1) A mortgagee, where the mortgage is made by deed, shall, by virtue of this Act, have the following powers, to the like extent as if they had been in terms conferred by the mortgage deed, but not further (namely): —

    (i) A power, when the mortgage money has become due, [18] to sell, or to concur with any other person in selling, the mortgaged property, or any part thereof, either subject to prior charges or not, [19] and either

---

[16]   *National Home Loans Corpn plc v Yaxley* (1997) 73 P & CR D41 (hope of successful litigation by mortgagor against mortgagee for breach of duty not relevant to discharge of liability to pay); (1997) 147 NLJ 459 (N. Madge).
    For postponement to enable sale to take place, see *National & Provincial Building Society v Lloyd* [1996] 1 All ER 630 (sale by part disposals). For retention by mortgagor while mortgagee sells, see *Target Homes Loans Ltd v Clothier* [1994] 1 All ER 439 (three months postponement; mortgagor had better prospect of achieving earlier sale if in possession); [1993] Conv 62 (J. Martin); *Cheltenham & Gloucester plc v Booker* (1996) 73 P & CR 412 at 415 per MILLET LJ (possible if mortgagor's presence will not depress sale price, and mortgagor will complete sale and give up possession to purchaser on completion).

[17]   In unregistered land, the first mortgagee is entitled also to the custody of the title deeds: LPA 1925, ss. 85(1), 86(1), p. 792, ante; on redemption by the mortgagor, the mortgagee must deliver the deeds to him, unless he has notice of a later mortgage, when he must deliver them to the mortgagee next in order of priority of whom he has notice. In this context, registration is not notice: LPA 1925, s. 96(2) as amended by LP(A) A 1926, Sch.

[18]   I.e., as soon as the contractual date for redemption has passed. If the mortgage money is payable by instalments the power of sale arises as soon as any instalment is in arrear: *Payne v Cardiff RDC* [1932] 1 KB 241; cf. *Twentieth Century Banking Corpn Ltd v Wilkinson* [1977] Ch 99, [1976] 3 All ER 361 (where interest was in arrear but capital not yet due: held no power of sale). See also AJA 1973, s. 8, p. 864, ante.

[19]   See *Kaolim Private Ltd v United Overseas Land Ltd* [1983] 1 WLR 472 at 476, per Lord BRIGHTMAN.

together or in lots, by public auction or by private contract, subject to such conditions respecting title, or evidence of title, or other matter, as the mortgagee thinks fit, with power to vary any contract for sale, and to buy in at an auction, or to rescind any contract for sale, and to re-sell, without being answerable for any loss occasioned thereby; and

(ii) A power, at any time after the date of the mortgage deed, to insure [1] and keep insured against loss or damage by fire any building, or any effects or property of an insurable nature, whether affixed to the freehold or not, being or forming part of the property which or an estate or interest wherein is mortgaged, and the premiums paid for any such insurance shall be a charge on the mortgaged property or estate or interest, in addition to the mortgage money, and with the same priority, and with interest at the same rate, as the mortgage money; and

(iii) A power, when the mortgage money has become due, to appoint a receiver of the income of the mortgaged property, or any part thereof; or, if the mortgaged property consists of an interest in income, or of a rentcharge or an annual or other periodical sum, a receiver of that property or any part thereof; and

(iv) A power, while the mortgagee is in possession, to cut and sell timber and other trees ripe for cutting, and not planted or left standing for shelter or ornament, or to contract for any such cutting and sale, to be completed within any time not exceeding twelve months from the making of the contract.

(3) The provisions of this Act relating to the foregoing powers, comprised either in this section, or in any other section regulating the exercise of those powers, may be varied or extended by the mortgage deed, and, as so varied and extended, shall, as far as may be, operate in the like manner and with all the like incidents, effects, and consequences, as if such variations or extensions were contained in this Act.

(4) This section applies only if and as far as a contrary intention is not expressed in the mortgage deed, and has effect subject to the terms of the mortgage deed and to the provisions therein contained.

i. SALE [2]

(a) Legal Mortgagee

LAW OF PROPERTY ACT 1925

101. Powers incident to estate or interest of mortgage.—(1) (i) p. 871, ante.

103. Regulation of exercise of power of sale.—A mortgagee shall not exercise the power of sale conferred by this Act unless and until —
(i)   Notice requiring payment of the mortgage money has been served on the mortgagor or one of two or more mortgagors, and default has been

---

[1]   See *Colonial Mutual General Insurance Co Ltd v ANZ Banking Group (New Zealand) Ltd* [1995] 1 WLR 1140, [1995] 3 All ER 987. For amount and application of insurance money, see LPA 1925, s. 108.

[2]   C & B, pp. 762–768; Gray, pp. 1427–1451, M & W paras. 19.056–19.067; MM, pp. 504–506; Smith, pp. 593–601; Cousins (2nd edn), paras. 16.53–16.80; Fisher and Lightwood, chap. 20; (1976) 73 LSG 92, 654; (1977) 74 LSG 493 (H. E. Markson). For a detailed analysis of the mortgagee's power of sale, see (1995) 46 NILQ 182 (P. Devonshire); and *Silven Properties v Royal Bank of Scotland plc* [2004] 1 WLR 997, at paras. 13–20, per LIGHTMAN J.

made in payment of the mortgage money, or of part thereof, for three months after such service; or

(ii) Some interest under the mortgage is in arrear and unpaid for two months after becoming due; or

(iii) There has been a breach of some provision contained in the mortgage deed or in this Act, or in an enactment replaced by this Act, and on the part of the mortgagor, or of some person concurring in making the mortgage, to be observed or performed, other than and besides a covenant for payment of the mortgage money or interest thereon.

104. Conveyance on sale.—(1) A mortgagee exercising the power of sale conferred by this Act shall have power, by deed, to convey the property sold, for such estate and interest therein as he is by this Act authorised to sell or convey or may be the subject of the mortgage, freed from all estates, interests, and rights to which the mortgage has priority, but subject to all estates, interests, and rights which have priority to the mortgage.[3]

(2) Where a conveyance is made in exercise of the power of sale conferred by this Act, or any enactment replaced by this Act, the title of the purchaser shall not be impeachable on the ground —

(a) that no case had arisen to authorise the sale; or

(b) that due notice was not given; or

(c) where the mortgage is made after the commencement of this Act, that leave of the court, when so required, was not obtained,[4] or

(d) whether the mortgage was made before or after such commencement, that the power was otherwise improperly or irregularly exercised; and a purchaser is not, either before or on conveyance, concerned to see or inquire whether a case has arisen to authorise the sale, or due notice has been given, or the power is otherwise properly and regularly exercised;[5] but any person damnified by an unauthorised, or improper, or irregular exercise of the power shall have his remedy in damages against the person exercising the power.

(3) A conveyance on sale by a mortgagee, made after the commencement of this Act, shall be deemed to have been made in exercise of the power of sale conferred by this Act unless a contrary intention appears.

105. Application of proceeds of sale.—The money which is received by the mortgagee, arising from the sale, after discharge of prior incumbrances to which the sale is not made subject, if any, or after payment into court under this Act of a sum to meet any prior incumbrance, shall be held by him in trust to be applied

---

[3] Compare LPA 1925, s. 2(1)(iii), p. 294, ante.

[4] See LPA 1925, s. 110, as amended by Insolvency Act 1985, s. 222, Sch 10, Part III (mortgagor a bankrupt and mortgage executed after 1925); (1944) 5 Conv YB, pp. 70–71.

[5] See *Bailey v Barnes* [1894] 1 Ch 25 at 30, per STIRLING J. If, however, he 'becomes aware … of any facts showing that the power of sale is not exercisable, or that there is some impropriety in the sale, then, in my judgment, he gets no good title on taking the conveyance'; *Lord Waring v London and Manchester Assurance Co Ltd* [1935] Ch 310 at 318, per CROSSMAN J; *Jenkins v Jones* (1860) 2 Giff 99; *Selwyn v Garfit* (1888) 38 ChD 273; *Price Bros (Somerford) Ltd v J Kelly Homes (Stoke-on-Trent) Ltd* [1975] 1 WLR 1512, [1975] 3 All ER 369; *Northern Developments (Holdings) Ltd v UDT Securities Ltd* [1976] 1 WLR 1230, [1977] 1 All ER 747; *Forsyth v Blundell* (1973) 129 CLR 477; *Pasquarella v National Australia Finance Ltd* [1987] 1 NZLR 312 and generally Emmet, para. 25.048; [1988] Conv 317; [1989] Conv 412 (S. Robinson); *Corbett v Halifax Building Society* [2003] 1 WLR 964, [2003] 4 All ER 180.

by him, first, in payment of all costs, charges, and expenses properly incurred by him as incident to the sale or any attempted sale, or otherwise; and secondly, in discharge of the mortgage money, interest, and costs, and other money, if any, due under the mortgage; and the residue of the money so received shall be paid to the person entitled to the mortgaged property,[6] or authorised to give receipts for the proceeds of the sale thereof.

106. Provisions as to exercise of power of sale.—(1) The power of sale conferred by this Act may be exercised by any person for the time being entitled to receive and give a discharge for the mortgage money.

(2) The power of sale conferred by this Act does not affect the right of foreclosure.

88. Realisation of freehold mortgages.—(1) Where an estate in fee simple has been mortgaged by the creation of a term of years absolute limited thereout or by a charge by way of legal mortgage and the mortgagee sells under his statutory or express power of sale —

(*a*)   the conveyance by him shall operate to vest in the purchaser the fee simple in the land conveyed subject to any legal mortgage having priority to the mortgage in right of which the sale is made and to any money thereby secured, and thereupon;

(*b*)   the mortgage term or the charge by way of legal mortgage and any subsequent mortgage term or charges shall merge or be extinguished as respects the land conveyed;

and such conveyance may, as respects the fee simple, be made in the name of the estate owner in whom it is vested.

89. Realisation of leasehold mortgages.—(1) Where a term of years absolute has been mortgaged by the creation of another term of years absolute limited thereout or by a charge by way of legal mortgage and the mortgagee sells under his statutory or express power of sale, —

(*a*)   the conveyance by him shall operate to convey to the purchaser not only the mortgage term, if any, but also (unless expressly excepted with the leave of the court)[7] the leasehold reversion affected by the mortgage, subject to any legal mortgage having priority to the mortgage in right of which the sale is made and to any money thereby secured, and thereupon;

(*b*)   the mortgage term, or the charge by way of legal mortgage and any subsequent mortgage term or charge, shall merge in such leasehold reversion or be extinguished unless excepted as aforesaid;

---

[6]   M & W point out (para. 1197, n. 49) that these words literally refer to the purchaser; 'but plainly the phrase must be read as "to the person who *immediately before the sale* was entitled to the mortgaged property"' and this of course includes other mortgagees. But if the rights of the mortgagor and other encumbrances have become extinguished by lapse of time (Limitation Act 1980, s. 16, p. 233, ante) the mortgagee may keep all the purchase money himself: *Young v Clarey* [1948], Ch 191, [1948] 1 All ER 197. See also *Halifax Building Society v Thomas* [1996] Ch 217, [1995] 4 All ER 673 (mortgagee to pay surplus proceeds of sale to Crown Prosecution Service which had obtained a confiscation order in respect of fraudulent mortgagor's interest in sale proceeds).

[7]   This may be done to prevent the purchaser becoming liable upon the covenants in the lease.

and such conveyance may, as respects the leasehold reversion, be made in the name of the estate owner in whom it is vested.

Where a licence to assign is required on a sale by a mortgagee, such licence shall not be unreasonably refused.

2. Conveyances overreaching certain equitable interests and powers. (1) (iii) p. 294, ante.

1. EFFECT OF MORTGAGEE'S CONTRACT TO SELL

In **Lord Waring v London and Manchester Assurance Co Ltd** [1935] Ch 310, the mortgagee had contracted to sell the property for £186,000. The mortgagor, who was negotiating elsewhere for a loan (on a mortgage of the property) of £200,000, sought an injunction to stop the sale.

CROSSMAN J refused, and said at 317:

'After a contract has been entered into, however, it is, in my judgment, perfectly clear (subject to what has been said to me to-day) that the mortgagee (in the present case, the company) can be restrained from completing only on the ground that he has not acted in good faith and that the sale is therefore liable to be set aside. Counsel for the plaintiff, who has argued the case most excellently, submitted that, notwithstanding that the company exercised its power of sale by entering into the contract, the plaintiff's equity of redemption has not been extinguished, as there has been no completion by conveyance, and that, pending completion, the plaintiff is still entitled to redeem, that is, to have the property reconveyed to him on payment of principal, interest, and costs. Counsel is relying, to some extent, on the provisions of the Law of Property Act 1925, which creates a statutory power of sale. In my judgment, section 101 of that Act, which gives to a mortgagee power to sell the mortgaged property, is perfectly clear, and means that the mortgagee has power to sell out and out, by private contract or by auction, and subsequently to complete by conveyance; and the power to sell is, I think, a power by selling to bind the mortgagor. If that were not so, the extraordinary result would follow that every purchaser from a mortgagee would, in effect, be getting a conditional contract liable at any time to be set aside by the mortgagor's coming in and paying the principal, interest and costs. Such a result would make it impossible for a mortgagee, in the ordinary course of events, to sell unless he was in a position to promise that completion should take place immediately or on the day after the contract, and there would have to be a rush for completion in order to defeat a possible claim by the mortgagor.'[8]

2. DUTY OF MORTGAGEE TO OBTAIN THE TRUE MARKET VALUE

PARKER-TWEEDALE v DUNBAR BANK PLC[9]
[1991] Ch 12, [1990] 2 All ER 577 (CA, PURCHAS and NOURSE LJJ and Sir Michael KERR)

The plaintiff and his wife purchased Ditchford Hill Farm, Fosseway, Moreton-in-Marsh, with the aid of a mortgage from Dunbar Bank Plc. The wife was sole

---

8   Followed in *Property and Bloodstock Ltd v Emerton* [1968] Ch 94, [1967] 3 All ER 321; *National and Provincial Building Society v Ahmed* [1995] 2 EGLR 127; *Corbett v Halifax Building Society* [2003] 1 WLR 964. For the effect of a contract of sale by the mortgagor upon the mortgagee's powers, see *Duke v Robson* [1973] 1 WLR 267, [1973] 1 All ER 481, p. 892, post.

9   [1990] Conv 431 (L. Bentley). HL Appellate Committee refused leave to appeal: [1990] 3 WLR 767 at 779. In *Bishop v Bonham* [1988] 1 WLR 742, SLADE LJ said at 752: 'The duty

legal owner and mortgagor; the plaintiff had a beneficial interest in the farm and occupied it as a licensee. In 1988 the mortgagee, in the exercise of its power of sale under the mortgage, sold the farm, with the wife's consent, for £575,000. It had been valued by estate agents at between £380,000 and £450,000. A week later it was resold to another developer for £700,000.

The plaintiff brought an action against the Bank claiming that it was in breach of a duty to take reasonable care to obtain a proper price.

Held. The plaintiff failed:

(i) The Bank did not owe him a duty of care.

(ii) On the evidence £575,000 was a proper price.

NOURSE LJ: In this case a husband claims that a mortgagee, in exercising its power of sale over joint property of which his wife was the sole legal owner and mortgagor, owed him an independent duty to take reasonable care to obtain a proper price. He also claims that the mortgagee did not take reasonable care and did not obtain a proper price. Peter Gibson J decided both issues in favour of the mortgagee and the husband has now appealed to this court.

It was settled by the decision of this court in *Cuckmere Brick Co Ltd v Mutual Finance Ltd* [1971] Ch 949, [1971] 2 All ER 633, that a mortgagee, although he may exercise his power of sale at any time of his own choice, owes the mortgagor a duty to take reasonable care to obtain a proper price for the mortgaged property at that time.[10] But there is no support, either in the authorities or on principle, for the proposition that where the mortgagor is a trustee, even a bare trustee, of the mortgaged property, a like duty is owed to a beneficiary under the trust of whose interest the mortgagee has notice.

In seeking to support that proposition the plaintiff relied on the decision of this court in *Jarrett v Barclays Bank Ltd* [1947] Ch 187, [1947] 1 All ER 72. For reasons which were stated by Peter Gibson J and need not be repeated here, that case does not assist him. He also relied on the following passage in the judgment of Salmon LJ in *Cuckmere Brick Co Ltd v Mutual Finance Ltd* [1971] Ch 949, 966, [1971] 2 All ER, 633.

'Approaching the matter first of all on principle, it is to be observed that if the sale yields a surplus over the amount owed under the mortgage, the mortgagee holds this surplus in trust for the mortgagor. If the sale shows a deficiency, the mortgagor has to make it good out of his own pocket. The mortgagor is vitally affected by the result of the sale but its preparation and conduct is left entirely in the hands of the mortgagee. The proximity between them could scarcely be closer. Surely they are "neighbours." Given that the power of sale is for the benefit of the mortgagee and that he is entitled to choose the

---

of care imposed on a selling mortgagee, by what I may call the *Cuckmere* principle, is essentially in the nature of an obligation implied by law, and as such is, in my judgment, undoubtedly capable of being excluded by agreement. The exclusion clause must be construed strictly.'; *Mercantile Credit Co v Clarke* (1995) 71 P & CR D18 (agreement of mortgagor to a lower sale price); *Raja Lloyds v TSB Bank plc* (2001) 82 P & CR 191 (the duty being in equity, mortgagor's claim statute barred after six years under Limitation Act 1980, s. 8); [2001] Conv 421 (L. McMurtry).

10 A building society must take reasonable care to obtain a proper price or true market value; Building Societies Act 1997, s. 12(2). *Reliance Permanent Building Society v Harwood-Stamport* [1944] Ch 362, [1944] 2 All ER 76; *Adamson v Halifax plc* [2003] 1 WLR 60 (measure of damages for breach of a statutory duty is reduction in value of equity of redemption).

moment to sell which suits him[11] it would be strange indeed if he were under no legal obligation to take reasonable care to obtain what I call the true market value at the date of the sale.'

This reference to 'neighbours' has enabled the plaintiff to argue that the duty is owed to all those who are within the neighbourhood principle; i.e., to adapt the words of Lord Atkin, to all persons who are so closely and directly affected by the sale that the mortgagee ought reasonably to have them in contemplation as being so affected when he is directing his mind to the sale. Further support for the application of the neighbourhood principle in this context can be gained from the judgment of Lord Denning MR in *Standard Chartered Bank Ltd v Walker* [1982] 1 WLR 1410, 1415, [1982] 3 All ER 938, 942 where it was held that the duty to take reasonable care to obtain a proper price was owed to a surety for the mortgage debt as well as to the mortgagor himself.

In my respectful opinion it is both unnecessary and confusing for the duties owed by a mortgagee to the mortgagor and the surety, if there is one, to be expressed in terms of the tort of negligence. The authorities which were considered in the careful judgments of this court in *Cuckmere Brick Co Ltd v Mutual Finance Ltd* [1971] Ch 949, [1971] 2 All ER 633 demonstrate that the duty owed by the mortgagee to the mortgagor was recognised by equity as arising out of the particular relationship between them. Thus Salmon LJ himself said, at 967, at 644:

'It would seem, therefore, that many years before the modern development of the law of negligence, the courts of equity had laid down a doctrine in relation to mortgages which is entirely consonant with the general principles later evolved by the common law.'

The duty owed to the surety arises in the same way. In *China and South Sea Bank Ltd v Tan Soon Gin (alias George Tan)* [1990] 1 AC 536, [1989] 3 All ER 839, pp. 878, post. Lord Templeman, in delivering the judgment of the Privy Council, having pointed out that the surety in that case admitted that the moneys secured by the guarantee were due, continued at 543, at 841:

'But the surety claims that the creditor owed the surety a duty to exercise the power of sale conferred by the mortgage and in that case the liability of the surety under the guarantee would either have been eliminated or very much reduced. The Court of Appeal [in Hong Kong] sought to find such a duty in the tort of

---

[11]   *China and South Sea Bank Ltd v Tan Soon Gin (alias George Tan)* [1990] 1 AC 536 at 545, [1989] 3 All ER 839 at 842, p. 878, post, per Lord TEMPLEMAN; *Countrywide Banking Corpn v Robinson* [1991] 1 NZLR 75; *Tse Kwong Lam v Wong Chit Sen* [1983] 1 WLR 1349, [1983] 3 All ER 54, p. 881, post. Cf. *Standard Chartered Bank Ltd v Walker* [1982] 1 WLR 1410, [1982] 3 All ER 938 where Lord DENNING MR said at 1415, at 942: 'There are several dicta to the effect that the mortgagee can choose his own time for the sale, but I do not think this means that he can sell at the worst possible time. It is at least arguable that, in choosing the time, he must exercise a reasonable degree of care'. See also *Predeth v Castle Phillips Finance Co Ltd* [1986] 2 EGLR 144 (where CA accepted the judge's finding that the exercise of reasonable care required mortgagee to expose uninhabitable bungalow at Alton in Hampshire to the market for approximately three months); *Palk v Mortgage Services Funding plc* [1993] Ch 330, [1993] 2 All ER 481, p. 886, post, where Sir Donald NICHOLLS V-C said at 338, at 486: 'If the mortgagee sells the property, he cannot sell hastily at a knock-down price sufficient to pay off his debt'; *Downsview Nominees Ltd v First City Corpn Ltd* [1993] AC 295, [1993] 3 All ER 626; [1993] Conv 401 (R. Grantham); *Meftah v Lloyds TSB Bank plc* [2001] 2 All ER (Comm) 741 (timing of sale is for mortgagee; if there is urgency 'the necessity of exposure to the market must be evaluated in the light of the circumstances', per LAWRENCE COLLINS J at 745); *Silven Properties v Royal Bank of Scotland plc* [2004] 1 WLR 997, p. 883, post (mortgagee under no duty to postpone sale until after further pursuit of application for planning permission or grant of a lease, even though outcome of either course might increase value of property. See *Emmet on Title*, para. 25.043.

negligence but the tort of negligence has not yet subsumed all torts and does not supplant the principles of equity or contradict contractual promises ... Equity intervenes to protect a surety.'

Once it is recognised that the duty owed by the mortgagee to the mortgagor arises out of the particular relationship between them, it is readily apparent that there is no warrant for extending its scope so as to include a beneficiary or beneficiaries under a trust of which the mortgagor is the trustee. The correctness of that view was fully established in the clear and compelling argument of Mr Lloyd, who drew particular attention to the rights and duties of the trustee to protect the trust property against dissipation or depreciation in value and the impracticabilities and potential rights of double recovery inherent in giving the beneficiary an additional right to sue the mortgagee, a right which is in any event unnecessary.

The only exception for which Mr Lloyd allowed was the special case where the trustee has unreasonably refused to sue on behalf of the trust or has committed some other breach of his duties to the beneficiaries, e.g., by consenting to an improvident sale, which disables or disqualifies him from acting on behalf of the trust. In such a case the beneficiary is permitted to sue on behalf of the trust. This exception is established by a series of authorities, some of which were recently considered by the Privy Council in *Hayim v Citibank NA* [1987] AC 730. In delivering the judgment of their Lordships, Lord Templeman said, at 748:

'These authorities demonstrate that a beneficiary has no cause of action against a third party save in special circumstances which embrace a failure, excusable or inexcusable, by the trustees in the performance of the duty owed by the trustees to the beneficiary in the trust estate.'

It is important to emphasise that when a beneficiary sues under the exception he does so in right of the trust and in the room of the trustee. He does not enforce a right reciprocal to some duty owed directly to him by the third party.[12]

In **China and South Sea Bank Ltd v Tan Soon Gin (alias George Tan)** [1990] 1 AC 536, [1989] 3 All ER 839, the appellant creditor advanced $30,000,000 to Carrian Holdings Ltd. The loan was secured by a mortgage of shares in Carrian Holdings Ltd and by a guarantee by the respondent. At the time of the loan the shares were worth $60,000,000, at the time of default $30,000,000, and at the

---

[12]   See also *Palmer v Barclays Bank Ltd* (1971) 23 P & CR 30; *Johnson v Ribbins* (1975) 235 EG 757; *Waltham Forest London Borough v Webb* (1974) 232 EG 461; *Bank of Cyprus (London) Ltd v Gill* [1979] 2 Lloyd's Rep 508; affd [1980] 2 Lloyd's Rep 51; (1981) 25 NLJ 249 (H. E. Markson); *Norwich General Trust v Grierson* [1984] CLY 2306 (mortgagee held liable for diminution of purchase price due to his negligence in allowing premises to deteriorate between date of taking possession and date of sale); *Garland v Ralph Ray & Ransom* (1984) 271 EG 106, 197 (action by mortgagor against mortgagee's valuer for negligent marketing technique and valuation); *Predeth v Castle Phillips Finance Co Ltd* [1986] 2 EGLR 144 (action by mortgagee against surveyor instructed to provide 'crash-sale' valuation); [1986] Conv 442 (M. P. Thompson); *AIB Finance Co Ltd v Debtors* [1997] 4 All ER 677 (security included good will of business carried on on mortgaged property; held duty on mortgage to ensure that on sale value of the combined asset was maximised); *Struggles v Lloyds TSB plc* [2000] EGCS 17 (for a quarry to be sold for the best possible price, it should be exposed to the market for 6 to 12 months to enable investigations to be made of both mineral and waste-fill potential).; *Skipton Building Society v Stott* [2000] 2 All ER 779 (guarantor liable for difference between amount owed under guarantee and market value of premises at date of sale); *Michael v Miller* [2004] EWCA Civ 282, [2004] 2 P & CR D12 ('bracket' or margin of error approach for assessing whether mortgagee in breach of duty).

time of the action nothing. The respondent claimed that he was not liable because of the appellant's negligence in not selling the shares. The Privy Council rejected this view, and Lord TEMPLEMAN said at 543, at 841:

'The surety does not and cannot impugn the validity of the provisions of the guarantee and admits that the moneys claimed by the creditor are due in accordance with the express terms of the guarantee. But the surety claims that the creditor owed the surety a duty to exercise the power of sale conferred by the mortgage and in that case the liability of the surety under the guarantee would either have been eliminated or very much reduced. The Court of Appeal sought to find such a duty in the tort of negligence but the tort of negligence has not yet subsumed all torts and does not supplant the principles of equity or contradict contractual promises or complement the remedy of judicial review or supplement statutory rights.[13]

Equity intervenes to protect a surety. In *Watts v Shuttleworth* (1860) 5 H & N 235 the creditor had covenanted to insure mortgaged goods and failed to insure. A surety was released. Pollock CB said, at 247–248:

"The substantial question in the case is, whether the omission to insure discharges the defendant, the surety. The rule upon the subject seems to be that if the person guaranteed does any act injurious to the surety, or inconsistent with his rights, or if he omits to do any act which his duty enjoins him to do, and the omission proves injurious to the surety, the latter will be discharged ... the rights of a surety depend rather on principles of equity than upon the actual contract."

[His Lordship referred to *Wulff v Jay* (1872) LR 7 QB 756, and continued:]

The creditor had three sources of repayment. The creditor could sue the debtor, sell the mortgage securities or sue the surety. All these remedies could be exercised at any time or times simultaneously or contemporaneously or successively or not at all. If the creditor chose to sue the surety and not pursue any other remedy, the creditor on being paid in full was bound to assign the mortgaged securities to the surety. If the creditor chose to exercise his power of sale over the mortgaged security he must sell for the current market value but the creditor must decide in his own interest if and when he should sell. The creditor does not become a trustee of the mortgaged securities and the power of sale for the surety unless and until the creditor is paid in full and the surety, having paid the whole of the debt is entitled to a transfer of the mortgaged securities to procure recovery of the whole or part of the sum he has paid to the creditor.

The creditor is not obliged to do anything. If the creditor does nothing and the debtor declines into bankruptcy the mortgaged securities become valueless and the surety decamps abroad, the creditor loses his money. If disaster strikes the debtor and the mortgaged securities but the surety remains capable of repaying the debt then the creditor loses nothing. The surety contracts to pay if the debtor does not pay and the surety is bound by his contract. If the surety, perhaps less indolent or less well protected than the creditor, is worried that the mortgaged securities may decline in value then the surety may request the creditor to sell and if the creditor remains idle then the surety may bustle about, pay off the debt, take over the benefit of the securities and sell them. No creditor could carry on the business of lending if he could become liable to a mortgagor and to a surety or to either of them for a decline in value of mortgaged property,

---

[13] See *Murphy v Brentwood District Council* [1991] 1 AC 398, [1990] 2 All ER 269 for the restrictive approach of HL to a remedy in negligence for economic loss. See generally Winfield and Jolowicz on *Tort* (16th edn), pp. 328 et seq, 381 et seq.

unless the creditor was personally responsible for the decline. Applying the rule as specified by Pollock CB in *Watts v Shuttleworth* at 247, it appears to their Lordships that in the present case the creditor did not act injurious to the surety, did not act inconsistent with the rights of the surety and the creditor did not omit any act which his duty enjoined him to do. The creditor was not under a duty to exercise his power of sale over the mortgaged securities at any particular time or at all.

Their Lordships will humbly advise Her Majesty that this appeal should be allowed.'

[1990] Conv 431 (L. Bently), at p. 439.

'At first glance *Parker-Tweedale* looks very much as if it is a backward step in terms of protection for borrowers. Such a view fits well with arguments about the decline of the courts' willingness to grant protection to individuals (at the expense of lenders) from that seen in the 1970s and early 1980s.[14] However, in terms of changing developments in legal doctrine it places the mortgagor's rights on much safer ground than they would be if based on the shifting sands of liability in negligence. It is important to remember that recent developments have revealed that the role of tort is not quite as all-encompassing as it at one time seemed. In particular it is now clear that tortious duties will rarely be held to exist with respect to economic loss. The *Parker-Tweedale* approach is solid because it rests on principle—namely that prior to the Judicature Acts all mortgage actions would have taken place in Chancery, and that to apply tort principles to any of these relationships represents a "fusion fallacy."[15] It also has the advantage of simplicity and avoids difficult questions concerning the overlapping of tort and equity. In the current climate this is the most solid basis for the duty—that is until the Law Commission makes its final recommendations.[16] It would be useful if the Commission recommended an exhaustive list of the parties covered by any such duty.'

3. SALE BY MORTGAGEE TO SELF

It has long been the rule that in exercising the power of sale a 'mortgagee cannot sell to himself, either alone or with others, nor to a trustee for himself, nor to anyone employed by him to conduct the sale. A sale by a person to himself is no sale at all.[17] But there is no hard and fast rule that a mortgagee may not sell to a company in which he is interested.[18]

---

[14]   Particularly, the retreat from *William & Glyn's Bank v Boland* [1981] AC 487, [1980] 2 All ER 408, evidenced in cases such as *City of London Building Society v Flegg* [1988] AC 54, [1987] 3 All ER 435 and *Abbey National Building Society v Cann* [1991] 1 AC 56, [1990] 1 All ER 1085.

[15]   *E.g.* Meagher, Gummow & Lehane, *Equity: Doctrine and Remedies* (3rd edn. 1992) para. 230, at p. 51; Hayton & Marshall, *Cases and Commentary on the Law of Trusts* (11th ed.), para. 1.20; Tyler (1981) 55 ALJ at p. 568.

[16]   See Law Commission Report on Land Mortgages 1991 (Law Com. No. 204, HC 5), para. 7.23, p. 920, post.

[17]   *Farrar v Farrars Ltd* (1888) 40 ChD 395 at 409, per LINDLEY LJ; *Martinson v Clowes* (1882) 21 ChD 857 (purchase by secretary of building society mortgage); *Williams v Wellingborough Borough Council* [1975] 1 WLR 1327, [1975] 3 All ER 462 ('a see-through dress of a sale', at 1329, at 463, per RUSSELL LJ: the decision itself was reversed by Housing Act 1980, s. 112 for the benefit of existing local authority mortgagees).

[18]   *Tse Kwong Lam v Wong Chit Sen*, infra.

TSE KWONG LAM v WONG CHIT SEN

[1983] 1 WLR 1349, [1983] 3 All ER 54 (PC, Lords FRASER of TULLYBELTON, BRANDON of OAKBROOK, BRIGHTMAN and TEMPLEMAN and Sir John MEGAW). [19]

In 1963 the appellant mortgagor constructed a large building, containing shops, offices and flats at Kowloon in Hong Kong. He financed it by a loan from the respondent to whom he mortgaged the building.

In 1966 the appellant fell into arrears and the outstanding mortgage debt was $HK 1.4 m. The respondent arranged for the building to be sold at public auction on 24 June. A few days before the auction, the respondent and his wife, as directors of a company, of which they and their children were the sole shareholders, held a directors' meeting at which they resolved that the wife should bid for the property on behalf of the company up to a price of $HK 1.2 m. At the auction, which was attended by some 30–40 people, the respondent informed the auctioneer that $HK 1.2 m. was the reserve price; and at that price the wife, who was the sole bidder, purchased the property for the company.

In an action by the respondent in 1966, the appellant counter-claimed that the sale should be set aside on the ground that it had been improper and at an undervalue. This counter-claim was not pursued to judgment until 1979.

Held.

(1) The respondent had failed to show that he had taken reasonable steps to obtain the best price reasonably obtainable.

(2) By reason of his inexcusable delay, the appellant was not entitled to have the sale set aside but only to damages.

LORD TEMPLEMAN: In the view of this Board on authority and on principle there is no hard and fast rule that a mortgagee may not sell to a company in which he is interested. The mortgagee and the company seeking to uphold the transaction must show that the sale was in good faith and that the mortgagee took reasonable precautions to obtain the best price reasonably obtainable at the time. [20] The mortgagee is not however bound to postpone the sale in the hope of obtaining a better price or to adopt a piecemeal method of sale which could only be carried out over a substantial period or at some risk of loss. This view of the matter is consistent with the decision of the House of Lords in *York Buildings Co v Mackenzie* (1795) 3 Pat 378. ...

In the present case in which the mortgagee held a large beneficial interest in the shares of the purchasing company, was a director of the company, and was entirely responsible for financing the company, the other shareholders being his wife and children, the sale must be closely examined and a heavy onus lies on the mortgagee to show that in all respects he acted fairly to the borrower and used his best endeavours to obtain the best price reasonably obtainable for the mortgaged property.

[His Lordship referred to *Hodson v Deans* [1903] 2 Ch 647; *Kennedy v De Trafford* [1897] AC 180; *McHugh v Union Bank of Canada* [1913] AC 299; and *Cuckmere Brick Co Ltd v Mutual Finance Ltd* [1971] Ch 949, [1971] 2 All ER 633, and continued:]

In the result their Lordships consider that in the present case the company was not debarred from purchasing the mortgaged property but, in view of the

[19] [1984] Conv 143 (P. Jackson); [1983] All ER Rev 57 (D. D. Prentice).
[20] *Downsview Nominees Ltd v First City Corpn Ltd* [1993] AC 295, [1993] 3 All ER 626, where Lord TEMPLEMAN said at 312, at 635, 'Powers must be exercised in good faith for the purpose of obtaining repayment'; *Caricom Cinemas Ltd v Republic Bank Ltd* [2003] UKPC 2.

close relationship between the company and the mortgagee and in view in particular of the conflict of duty and interest to which the mortgagee was subject, the sale to the company for $1.2 m. can only be supported if the mortgagee proves that he took reasonable precautions to obtain the best price reasonably obtainable at the time of sale.

On behalf of the mortgagee it was submitted that all reasonable steps were taken when the mortgagee, with adequate advertisement, sold the property at a properly conducted auction to the highest bidder. The submission assumes that such an auction must produce the best price reasonably obtainable or, as Salmon LJ expressed the test, the true market value. But the price obtained at any particular auction may be less than the price obtainable by private treaty and may depend on the steps taken to encourage bidders to attend. An auction which only produces one bid is not necessarily an indication that the true market value has been achieved. ...

The mortgagee could have consulted estate agents about the method of sale and about the method of securing the best price. At the very least he could have consulted an estate agent about the level of the reserve price. The auctioneer was not informed of the reserve price until immediately before the auction and in evidence he very properly declined to comment on the reserve because he had not valued the property. This confirms the impression that the auctioneers were not instructed to do more than put the property under the hammer, a procedure which may be appropriate to the sale of second-hand furniture but is not necessarily conducive to the attainment of the best price for freehold or leasehold property. It was not of course in the interests of the company that enthusiasm for the sale should be stimulated or that the reserve should be settled by anyone other than the mortgagee. The reserve of $1.2 m. was fixed by the mortgagee and was the price at which he advised and intended that the company should purchase. The mortgagee was a property investor and speculator. The company was his family company and he held shares in and financed the company. The mortgagee would not have advised the company to bid $1.2 m. for the property unless he thought that was an advantageous price for the company to pay. ...

At the trial and on this appeal the mortgagee adopted the attitude that a mortgagee exercising his power of sale is entitled to secure the mortgaged property for a company in which he is interested at a price advised by the mortgagee provided that the property is properly advertised and sold by auction. A decision to this effect would expose borrowers to greater perils than those to which they are now subject as a result of decisions which enable a mortgagee to choose the date of the exercise of his powers. A mortgagee who wishes to secure the mortgaged property for a company in which he is interested ought to show that he protected the interests of the borrower by taking expert advice as to the method of sale, as to the steps which ought reasonably to be taken to make the sale a success and as to the amount of the reserve. There was no difficulty in obtaining such advice orally and in writing and no good reason why a mortgagee, concerned to act fairly towards his borrower, should fail or neglect to obtain or act upon such advice in all respects as if the mortgagee were desirous of realising the best price reasonably obtainable at the date of the sale for property belonging to the mortgagee himself.

Where a mortgagee fails to satisfy the court that he took all reasonable steps to obtain the best price reasonably obtainable and that his company bought at the best price, the court will, as a general rule, set aside the sale and restore to the borrower the equity of redemption of which he has been unjustly deprived.

But the borrower will be left to his remedy in damages against the mortgagee for the failure of the mortgagee to secure the best price if it will be inequitable as between the borrower and the purchaser for the sale to be set aside. In the present case. … the mortgagee and the company submit that the delay on the part of the borrower in pursuing his counter-claim has rendered it unjust for the building to be restored to the borrower. …

The borrower has been guilty of inexcusable delay in prosecuting his counterclaim.

[His Lordship reviewed the evidence, and continued:]

The borrower by his delay achieved a favourable position; if the property decreased in value he could either abandon his action or seek damages in setting aside the sale. If the property increased in value he could persist with his claim to set aside the sale. In the circumstances the Board consider that the borrower is not[1] entitled to the alternative remedy of damages. That was the view taken by the trial judge.

The measure of damages must be the difference between the best price reasonably obtainable on June 24, 1966, and the price of $1.2 m. paid by the company.'

4. SUMMARY

In **Silven Properties Ltd v Royal Bank of Scotland** [2004] 1 WLR 997, the appellants brought a claim for damages, contending that the respondents had sold the properties at an undervalue in breach of their duties to the appellants. They did not dispute that the prices obtained had been the best reasonably obtainable for the properties in their then current condition. Instead, they agued that the properties should not have been sold in that state, but had been under a duty to pursue planning applications for development of the properties and to proceed with the grant of leases, deferring sale until these goals had been achieved. In holding that the appellants failed, LIGHTMAN J said at 1003:

'13. A mortgagee has no duty at any time to exercise his powers as mortgagee to sell, to take possession or to appoint a receiver and preserve the security or its value or to realise his security. He is entitled to remain totally passive. If the mortgagee takes possession, he becomes the manager of the charged property: see *Kendle v Melsom* (1998) 93 CLR 46, at p. 64 (High Court of Australia). He thereby assumes a duty to take reasonable care of the property secured (see *Downsview Nominees Ltd v First City Corporation Ltd (No 1)* [1993] AC 295, [1993] 3 All ER 626 at p. 315A, at p. 637, per Lord Templeman) and this requires him to be active in protecting and exploiting the security, maximising the return, but without taking undue risks: see *Palk v Mortgage Services Funding plc* [1993] Ch 330, at p. 338A, [1993] 2 All ER 481, at p. 486, per Nicholls V-C.

14. A mortgagee is not a trustee of the power of sale for the mortgagor. This time-honoured expression can be traced back at least as far as Sir George Jessel MR in *Nash v Eads* (1880) 25 Sol J 95. In default of provision to the contrary in the mortgage, the power is conferred upon the mortgagee by way of bargain by the mortgagor for his own benefit and he has an unfettered discretion to sell when he likes to achieve repayment of the debt that he is owed: see *Cuckmere Brick Co v Mutual Finance Ltd* [1971] Ch 949 at p. 969G, [1971] 2 All ER 633, p. 646, p. 876, ante. A mortgagee is at all times free to consult his own interests alone as to whether and when to exercise his power of sale. The most recent authoritative restatement of this principle is to be found in *Raja v Austin Gray*

---

[1]   The word 'not' is correctly omitted in [1983] 3 All ER 54 and 64.

[2002] EWCA Civ 1965 at 95 per Peter Gibson LJ. The mortgagee's decision is not constrained by reason of the fact that the exercise or non-exercise of the power will occasion loss or damage to the mortgagor: see *China & South Sea Bank Ltd v Tan Soon Gin* [1990] 1 AC 536 [1989] 3 All ER 839, p. 878 ante. It does not matter that the time may be unpropitious and that, by waiting, a higher price could be obtained: he is not bound to postpone in the hope of obtaining a better price: see *Tse Kwong Lam v Wong Chit Sen* [1983] 1 WLR 1349, at p. 1355B [1983] 3 All ER 54, at p. 59.

15. The claimants contend that a mortgagee is not entitled to ignore the fact that a short delay might result in a higher price. For this purpose, they rely upon certain obiter dicta of Lord Denning MR in *Standard Chartered Bank Ltd v Walker* [1982]1 WLR 1410, at pp. 1415G–H and 1416A, [1982] 3 All ER 938 at p. 942. The mortgagee in that case, having obtained insufficient funds on the sale at auction of the property charged to recover the sum secured, applied for summary judgment against the mortgagor for that sum. The mortgagor resisted the application, alleging that the mortgagee had sold at an undervalue on a variety of grounds, one of which was that the sale took place at the wrong time of year. The Court of Appeal gave the mortgagor leave to defend on the ground that there was an arguable case that the sale had been negligently handled. It was common ground in that case that a mortgagee can choose his own time for sale: see Fox LJ at p. 1418F–G, at p. 944. Lord Denning accepted that there were dicta to this effect, but added that he did not think that this meant that the mortgagee could sell at the worst possible moment and that it was at least arguable that in choosing the time he must exercise a reasonable degree of care. The view expressed by Lord Denning cannot stand with the later authorities to which we have referred and which state quite categorically that the mortgagee is under no such duty of care to the mortgagor in respect of the timing of a sale and can act in his own interests in deciding whether and when he should exercise his power of sale.

16. The mortgagee is entitled to sell the mortgaged property as it is. He is under no obligation to improve it or to increase its value. There is no obligation to take any such pre-marketing steps to increase the value of the property, as is suggested by the claimants. [His Lordship referred to *McHugh v Union Bank of Canada* [1913] AC 299 and continued:]

17. The mortgagee is free (in his own interest as well as that of the mortgagor) to investigate whether and how he can "unlock"; the potential for an increase in value of the property mortgaged (eg by an application for planning permission or the grant of a lease), and, indeed, (going further) he can proceed with such an application or grant. But he is likewise free, at any time, to halt his efforts and proceed instead immediately with a sale. By commencing on this path, the mortgagee does not, in any way, preclude himself from calling a halt at will: he does not assume any such obligation of care to the mortgagor in respect of its continuance, as the claimants contend. If, however, the mortgagee is to seek to charge to the mortgagor the costs of the exercise that he has undertaken of obtaining planning permission or a lessee, subject to any applicable terms of the mortgage, the mortgagee may be entitled to do so only if he acted reasonably in incurring those costs and fairly balanced the costs of the exercise against the potential benefits taking fully into account the possibility that he might, at any moment, "pull the plug" on these efforts and the consequences for the mortgagor if he did so.

18. If the mortgagor requires protection in any of these respects, whether by imposing further duties on the mortgagee or limitations on his rights and

powers, he must insist upon them when the bargain is made and upon the inclusion of protective provisions in the mortgage. In the absence of such protective provisions, the mortgagee is entitled to rest on the terms of the mortgage and (save where statute otherwise requires) the court must give effect to them. The one method available to the mortgagor to prevent the mortgagee exercising the rights conferred upon him by the mortgage is to redeem the mortgage. If he redeems, there can be no need or justification for recourse by the mortgagee to the power of sale to achieve repayment of the debt due to him secured by the mortgage.

19. When and if the mortgagee does exercise the power of sale, he comes under a duty in equity (and not tort) to the mortgagor (and all others interested in the equity of redemption) to take reasonable precautions to obtain "the fair" or "the true market" value of, or the "proper price" for, the mortgaged property at the date of the sale, and not (as the claimants submitted) the date of the decision to sell. If the period of time between the dates of the decision to sell and of the sale is short, there may be no difference in value between the two dates and, indeed, in many, if not most, cases, this may be readily assumed. But where there is a period of delay, the difference in date could prove significant.

The mortgagee is not entitled to act in a way that unfairly prejudices the mortgagor by selling hastily at a knock-down price sufficient to pay off his debt: *Palk* at p. 337–338, [1993] 2 All ER 481 at pp. 486–487, per Nicholls V-C. He must take proper care, whether by fairly and properly exposing the property to the market or otherwise, to obtain the best price reasonably obtainable at the date of sale. The remedy for breach of this equitable duty is not common law damages, but an order that the mortgagee account to the mortgagor and all others interested in the equity of redemption, not just for what he actually received, but for what he should have received: see *Standard Chartered*, at p. 1416B, at p. 942.

20. In our judgment, there can, accordingly, be no duty on the part of a mortgagee, as suggested by the claimants, to postpone exercising the power of sale until after the further pursuit (let alone the outcome) of an application for planning permission or the grant of a lease of the mortgaged property, though the outcome of the application and the effect of the grant of the lease may be to increase the market value of the mortgaged property and price obtained on sale. A mortgagee is entitled to sell the property in the condition in which it stands, without investing money or time in increasing its likely sale value. He is entitled to discontinue efforts already undertaken to increase the likely sale value in favour of such a sale. A mortgagee is under a duty to take reasonable care to obtain a sale price that reflects the added value available on the grant of planning permission and the grant of a lease of a vacant property and (as a means of achieving this end) to ensure that the potential is brought to the notice of prospective purchasers and, accordingly, taken into account in their offers: see *Cuckmere*. But that is the limit of his duty.'

5. DISCRETION OF COURT TO ORDER SALE AT REQUEST OF MORTGAGOR

Under section 91(2) of the Law of Property Act 1925 the court has discretion to order a sale at the request of the mortgagor. This may be of significant help to a mortgagor with negative equity, but the court will only order a sale where an application has been made by the mortgagor before the mortgagee has obtained a warrant for possession.

LAW OF PROPERTY ACT 1925

91. Sale of mortgaged property in action for redemption or foreclosure. — (2) p. 852, ante.

In **Palk v Mortgage Services Funding plc** [1993] Ch 330, [1993] 2 All ER 481,[2] Mr and Mrs Palk borrowed £300,000 from Mortgage Services Funding plc on a joint mortgage in 1990. Mr Palk's business failed and he went bankrupt; Mrs Palk remained liable. In 1991 when £360,000 was needed for redemption, the Palks negotiated a sale for £283,000. They wished to sell the house in order to stop interest continuing to accrue on the debt, but the mortgagees wished to take possession of the house and to let it on a short-term lease and then sell when the market improved.

In holding that the court had a discretion under section 91 (2) of the Law of Property Act 1925 to order a sale at a depressed market price, even against the wishes of the mortgagor, Sir Donald NICHOLLS V-C said at 340, at 488:

'Section 91 (2) gives the court a discretion in wide terms. The discretion is unfettered. It can be exercised at any time. Self-evidently, in exercising that power the court will have due regard to the interests of all concerned. The court will act judicially. But it cannot be right that the court should decline to exercise the power if the consequence will be manifest unfairness.

In my view this is a case in which a sale should be directed even though there will be a deficiency. It is just and equitable to order a sale because otherwise unfairness and injustice will follow. I can summarise the four factors which combine to produce this result. First, there is a substantial income shortfall: the rental under the proposed letting would fall significantly short of the interest Mrs Palk would save if the house were sold. Second, the only prospect of recoupment of the shortfall lies in the hope that there will be a substantial rise in house prices generally. This is not a case where sale is being postponed for a reason specific to this property: for example, pending the outcome of an application for planning permission for development. Following on from this, third, on the scanty evidence before the court the likelihood of Mrs Palk suffering increased loss if the company's plan proceeds is so high as to make the plan oppressive to her. Her liability is open-ended and will increase indefinitely. This risk of increased loss to her under her repayment obligation far outweighs the prospect of any gain the company may make from its proposed realisation scheme for the house. The one is unacceptably disproportionate to the other. Fourth, directing a sale will not preclude the mortgagee from having the opportunity to wait and see what happens to house prices. The mortgagee can buy the property. A mortgagee cannot buy property from itself, but here the sale is directed by the court; it is not a sale by a mortgagee in exercise of its own power of sale.'

---

[2]   [1993] Conv 59 (J. Martin); (1993) 143 NLJ 448 (H. W. Wilkinson); *Barrett v Halifax Building Society* (1985) 28 HLR 634; *Polonski v Lloyds Bank Mortgages Ltd* (1999) 31 HLR 721; *Emmet on Title*, para. 25.063

In **Cheltenham and Gloucester plc v Krausz** [1997] 1 WLR 1558, [1997] 1 All ER 21 [3] the mortgagors of 8 Springhill, Clapton, London E5, had fallen into arrears with their mortgage. The mortgagee obtained an order for possession of the property and on four occasions warrants for possession were issued. Each time the warrant was discharged after agreement between the parties and on each occasion the mortgagors defaulted on the agreement. A fifth warrant was issued and had fallen due for execution when the mortgagors arranged a sale of the property to the M. Y. A. Charitable Trust. They applied to the County Court for an order suspending the warrant for possession pending an application to the High Court for an order that the property be sold under section 91(2) of the Law of Property Act 1925. The mortgagees resisted the application because the mortgage debt, which had increased from £58,300 in January 1987 to some £83,000 in 1995, far exceeded the sale price of £65,000, which the mortgagees believed to be based on an underestimation of the value of the property. The judge granted the order.

In allowing the appeal, PHILLIPS LJ said at 1561, at 24:

'The law

This appeal requires consideration of the interrelationship of two areas of the law relating to the mortgage of a dwelling-house: (1) the circumstances in which the mortgagor is entitled to an order for the sale of the mortgaged property: (2) the circumstances in which the court has jurisdiction to suspend entry into possession of the dwelling-house by the mortgagee.

Mortgagor's right of sale

[His Lordship read section 91 of the Law of Property Act 1925, p. 886, *ante*, and continued:]

The origin and history of these provisions are described by Sir Donald Nicholls V-C in *Palk v Mortgage Services Funding plc* [1993] Ch 330, 335, [1993] 2 All ER 481, 484, p. 886, *ante*. Sir Donald Nicholls V-C also cited the statement of Jessel MR in *Union Bank of London v Ingram* (1882) 20 Ch D 463, 464 about the essentially identical provisions of section 25(2) of the Conveyancing Act 1881;

"The Act is a remedial act, one effect of it being to allow a mortgagor whose property is worth more than the mortgage-money, but who cannot raise it, to obtain a sale and get the benefit of the surplus."

Until *Palk's* case it was the practice of the Chancery court only to entertain an application for sale by the mortgagor if the proceeds of sale were expected to be sufficient to discharge the entirety of the mortgage debt. In such circumstances the mortgagor might initiate proceedings by bringing an action for sale under section 91(1), or, if the mortgagee sought to foreclose, the mortgagor could apply for an order for sale in place of foreclosure. The practice thus reflected the heading to section 91: "Sale of mortgaged property in action for redemption or foreclosure".

Palk's case established, for the first time, that the court has power under section 91(2) to make an order for sale on the application of a mortgagor, notwithstanding that the proceeds of sale will be insufficient to discharge the

---

[3]   [1998] Conv 223 (A. Kenny); [1998] LS 279 (M. Dixon); approved in *Albany Home Loans v Massey* (1997) 73 P & CR 509 at 513, per SCHLIEMANN LJ, referring to a similar requirement by Lord TEMPLEMAN in *Downsview Nominees Ltd v First City Corpn Ltd* [1993] AC 295 at 312; and to European Convention on Human Rights, art. 8.

mortgage debt. In *Palk's* case the mortgagees had obtained an order for possession with the intention, not of proceeding to sell the property but of waiting in the hope that the market might improve. The mortgagor was anxious that the property should be sold so that the proceeds would reduce the mortgage debt, on which interest was accruing at an alarming rate. The Court of Appeal held that, as the mortgagees could buy the property themselves if they wished to speculate on an increase in the value, in the interests of fairness the property should be sold.

In *Palk's* case the mortgagor had initially applied for an order for sale to the Eastbourne County Court. It is not clear on what basis that court entertained the claim, for the jurisdiction of the county court to make an order for sale is limited to cases where the value of the property does not exceed £30,000. It also appears from the judgment in the Court of Appeal that the mortgagees obtained an order for possession which was suspended pending the result of their application. It is not clear which court made the order for possession, or which court suspended that order. What does seem clear is that no challenge was made of the jurisdiction to suspend the possession order.

In *Palk's* case the issue was simply whether or not the property should be sold. No issue arose as to the terms on which it should be sold. As to that matter, section 91 (2) empowers the court to direct a sale 'on such terms as it thinks fit'. In cases before *Palk's* case, where the proceeds of sale were likely to exceed the mortgage debt, the court was prepared to entrust the sale to the mortgagor on the basis that the mortgagor had a keener interest than the mortgagee in obtaining the best price. We have not been referred to any case, however, where there was a contest between the mortgagee and the mortgagor as to who should have conduct of the sale.

Barrett v Halifax Building Society (1995) 28 HLR 634 marks the next development in this area of the law, and one which demonstrates the importance of the present appeal. In that case the plaintiffs had mortgaged their home and then defaulted on their repayment obligations. The situation was one of negative equity—the mortgage debt substantially exceeded the value of their home. On 6 August 1992 the mortgagees obtained a possession order, with a view to exercising their power of sale. There were numerous suspensions of this order to give the plaintiffs a chance to discharge the instalment arrears. What then occurred was explained by the judge, at p. 636:

"On 6 March 1995 there was a further suspension of the order for the purpose of leaving [the] mortgagors in possession of the property themselves to find a buyer notwithstanding that there was a deficit over the sum secured so that the property would be on the market, lived in and without it becoming known to the market that it was subject to a forced sale, thereby increasing the realisations available to discharge at least part of the amount due."

The plaintiffs then applied to the Chancery court for an order for sale pursuant to section 91 of the Law of Property Act 1925. By the time that their action came on for hearing they had negotiated a sale of the property, subject to contract. They sought an order that they be permitted to proceed with that sale and to remain in possession until completion. The judge summarised the evidence on which they relied, at p. 637:

"The evidence of the plaintiffs, including the expert evidence of a valuer, is that it is a recognised feature of today's property market that where a mortgagee obtains possession of property and sells in the exercise of its power of sale it is able to obtain a price which is usually not as good as the price which might have been obtained by the mortgagor had the mortgagor remained in possession and the fact of the forced sale not become apparent. It is also the plaintiffs' evidence that if the mortgagee building society were to take over the sale or were now to obtain possession and proceed to sell itself there would be likely to be a delay of some months at least before a fresh purchaser could be found and a sale completed."

The mortgagees resisted the order sought. They did not contend that they would be able to obtain a better price but urged that if the sale went ahead it would break their established policy not to permit borrowers with negative equity themselves to conduct the sale of their property without also at the same time making proposals for the repayment of any resulting deficit. The judge held that this was not a material circumstance which he ought to take into account when exercising his discretion. He held, at p. 640:

"I am left, therefore, with a case [in] which, on the evidence before me, there is no discernible advantage to the building society in refusing to allow this sale to complete, whereas there is an obvious advantage to the mortgagors to complete their proposed sale at what is accepted as the best price that is likely to be obtainable in the current market."

He proceeded to grant the plaintiffs the order that they sought. Just as in *Palk*'s case the report does not suggest that in *Barrett*'s case any challenge was made by the mortgagees to the order suspending possession pending the plaintiff's action to the Chancery court.

The consequences of the procedure followed in *Barrett*'s case appear to me to be far reaching. In any case in which there is negative equity it will be open to the mortgagor to resist an order for possession on the ground that he wishes to obtain a better price by remaining in possession and selling the property himself. In not every case will the primary motive for such an application be the wish to obtain a better price than that which the mortgagee is likely to obtain on a forced sale. Often the mortgagor will be anxious to postpone for as long as possible the evil day when he has to leave his home. This court has ample experience of hopeless applications for leave to appeal against possession orders designed to achieve just that end. There will be a danger, if the mortgagee does not obtain possession, that the mortgagor will delay the realisation of the property by seeking too high a price, or deliberately procrastinating on completion. At present there is a simple procedure for seeking possession in the county court and the issue tends to be whether there are arrears and whether the mortgagor is likely to be able to discharge these in a reasonable time. If possession is to be suspended whenever this appears reasonable in order to give mortgagors the opportunity to sell the property themselves, the courts are going to have to enter into an area of difficult factual inquiry in order to decide in the individual case whether or not this course will be to the common benefit of mortgagor and mortgagee. Furthermore there will be obvious practical difficulties for mortgagees in monitoring the negotiations of mortgagors who are permitted time to market their properties. For these reasons it seems to me that the procedure followed and the decision reached in the *Barrett* case tend fundamentally to undermine the value of the mortgagee's entitlement to possession. Having touched on the implications of the issue raised in this case I turn to consider whether, in law, the county court has jurisdiction to suspend possession in such circumstances.

Suspension of possession

The right of the mortgagee to enter into possession of the mortgaged property was one which the common law protected strictly. The position was accurately stated by RUSSELL J in *Birmingham Citizens Permanent Building Society v Caunt* [1962] Ch 883, 912, [1962] 1 All ER 163, 182:

"Accordingly, in my judgment, where (as here) the legal mortgagee under an instalment mortgage under which by reason of default the whole money has become payable, is entitled to possession, the court has no jurisdiction to decline the order or to adjourn the hearing whether on terms of keeping up payments or paying arrears, if the mortgagee cannot be persuaded to agree to this course. To this the *sole exception* is that the application may be adjourned for a short time to afford to the mortgagor a chance of paying off the mortgagee in full or otherwise satisfying him; but this should not be done if there is no reasonable prospect of this occurring. When I say the sole exception, I do not, of course, intend to exclude adjournments which in the ordinary course of procedure may be desirable in circumstances such as a temporary inability of a party to attend, and so forth."

The rigours of the common law in this respect were mitigated by section 36 of the Administration of Justice Act 1970, p. 861, ante.

[His Lordship read the section and continued:]

It seems likely that the draftsman of this section intended to confer on the court power to suspend possession where the mortgagor was in a position to pay arrears of instalments within a reasonable period. He overlooked the fact that most mortgages provide for the principal to become immediately payable if instalments are in arrears. It was held in *Halifax Building Society v Clark* [1973] Ch 307 that in that event, the court was only given power to suspend if it appeared that the mortgagor would be able within a reasonable time to repay the total mortgage debt. To reverse the effect of this decision section 36 was amended by section 8(1) of the Administration of Justice 1973, p. 864, ante.

[His Lordship read section 8(1) and continued:]

The effect of section 36, as amended, on the power to suspend possession is as follows. (1) The power can be exercised to enable the mortgagor to pay off instalment arrears due under the mortgage agreement from sources other than the sale of the mortgaged property, but (2) if the mortgagor intends to sell the mortgaged property to provide the source of payment, the court must be satisfied that the proceeds will be sufficient to discharge the entirety of the mortgage debt: see *Royal Trust Co of Canada v Markham* [1975] 1 WLR 1416, [1975] 3 All ER 433; *National and Provincial Building Society v Lloyd* [1996] 1 All ER 630.

Before the decision in *Palk*'s case it seemed that section 36 of the Act of 1970 and section 91 of the Act of 1925 were complementary. An application under section 91 of the Act of 1925 would only be contemplated where the proceeds of the sale were expected to exceed the mortgage debt. In these circumstances section 36 gave the court the power to suspend possession in order to enable an application for sale under section 91 to be made. It is, however, quite clear that section 36 does not empower the court to suspend possession in order to permit the mortgagor to sell the mortgaged premises where the proceeds of sale will not suffice to discharge the mortgage debt, unless of course, other funds will be available to the mortgagor to make up the shortfall. A mortgagor seeking relief in the circumstances of *Palk*'s case is thus unable to invoke any statutory power to suspend the mortgagee's right to possession...

In *Royal Trust Co of Canada v Markham* Sir John Pennycuick, when delivering the leading judgment of this court, cited with approval the passage from the judgment of Russell J in *Birmingham Citizens Permanent Building Society v Caunt* which I myself have cited above. He then said, at p. 1420, at p. 436:

"A characteristic instance in which that sole exception is applicable is where the mortgagor has entered or is about to enter into a contract for the sale of the property at a price which will enable the mortgage to be paid off in full ... So, as the law stood before 1970, the mortgagee had a right, subject only to that one exception mentioned by Russell J, to possession, and it was not in the power of the court to refuse him possession."

Megaw LJ added, at pp. 1423–1424, at p. 440:

"There was, as I think is clear, no power, before the enactment of section 36 of the Administration of Justice Act 1970, for a court to grant a stay or suspension of execution of an order for possession in a mortgagee's action, such as the present one, based on default in payment or breach of other obligations. Therefore, if there be such power to suspend or stay the execution of the order for possession, it can come only from the provisions of section 36 of the Act of 1970 as amended by section 8 of the Administration of Justice Act 1973."

In my judgment the very specific delimitation of the power given by section 36 makes it clear that the legislature did not intend that the court should have any wider jurisdiction to curtail the mortgagee's right to possession. That right enables the mortgagee to exercise his power of sale in the manner he chooses and in the confidence that he can offer a purchaser vacant possession. Section 36 circumscribes that right where the proceeds of the sale are likely to discharge the mortgage debt. It does not do so where the mortgage debt will not be fully discharged, and it is in those circumstances that the mortgagee's rights are of particular importance.

I recognise the principle of the inherent jurisdiction of the court, as explained by Lord Morris in *Connelly v Director of Public Prosecutions* [1964] AC 1254, but I question whether that principle can justify the court in exercising its power to order a sale of mortgaged property under section 91 in circumstances where the mortgagee is seeking to enter into possession in order to sell property in which there is negative equity and where the sole object with which the mortgagor seeks that order is to prevent the mortgagee exercising his right to possession so that the mortgagor can negotiate his own sale while in possession. Even if one assumes that the Chancery court has power to order sale of mortgaged property on terms that displace the mortgagee's right to possession, I do not consider that it follows from this that the county court, as part of its inherent jurisdiction, can properly suspend an order or warrant for posession in order to enable a mortgagor to apply to the High Court for an order under section 91. It seems to me incumbent on the mortgagor to seek from the High Court any relief which that court is empowered to give before the possession warrant takes place.

In the present case the judge purported in 1995 to suspend a warrant for possession that was properly issued pursuant to an order for possession made in 1991. For the reasons I have given I consider that he had no jurisdiction to make such an order and this appeal should be allowed.

MILLETT J: I have had the advantage of reading in draft the judgment of Phillips LJ with which I am in full agreement. *Palk v Mortgage Services Funding plc* was a case in which the mortgagee had no wish to realise its security in the foreseeable future, whether by sale or foreclosure. It established that in such a case the mortgagor might obtain an order for sale even though the proceeds of sale would be insufficient to discharge the mortgage debt. It does not support the making of such an order where the mortgagee is taking active steps to obtain possession and enforce its security by sale. Still less does it support the giving of the conduct of the sale to the mortgagor in a case where there is negative equity, so that it is the mortgagee who is likely to have the greater incentive to obtain the best price and the quickest sale. Both these steps were taken in *Barrett v Halifax Building Society*. I have serious doubt whether that case was rightly decided. In fairness to the judge it should be said that it does not appear to have been argued as a matter of principle; the mortgagor's application was resisted on purely pragmatic grounds, and somewhat feeble ones at that. For the reasons given by Phillips LJ I agree that this appeal should be allowed.'

QUESTIONS

1.   What restrictions, if any, should be placed on the time at which the mortgagee exercises his power of sale?
2.   A mortgagor defaults and then contracts to sell the mortgaged property to X. The contract is registered as an estate contract under the Land Charges Act 1972, section 2(4), Class C(iv). The mortgagee, under the statutory power of sale, contracts to sell the property to Y. Can X succeed in a claim for specific performance against the mortgagor and for an injunction against the mortgagee? *Duke v Robson* [1973] 1 WLR 267, [1973] 1 All ER 481; (1973) 27 Conv (NS) 210 (F. R. Crane); Law Commission Report on Land Mortgages 1991 (Law Com. No. 204, HC 5), paras. 7.16–7.19, p. 920, post.

(b) Equitable Mortgagee

LAW OF PROPERTY ACT 1925

90. Realisation of equitable charges by the court.—(1) Where an order for sale is made by the court in reference to an equitable mortgage on land (not secured by a legal term of years absolute or by a charge by way of legal mortgage) the court may, in favour of a purchaser, make a vesting order conveying the land or may appoint a person to convey the land or create and vest in the mortgagee a legal term of years absolute to enable him to carry out the sale, as the case may require, in like manner as if the mortgage had been created by deed by way of legal mortgage pursuant to this Act, but without prejudice to any incumbrance having priority to the equitable mortgage unless the incumbrancer consents to the sale.

(2) This section applies to equitable mortgages made or arising before or after the commencement of this Act, but not to a mortgage which has been over-reached under the powers conferred by this Act or otherwise.

In the case of an equitable mortgage by deposit of title deeds, the mortgagee has no power of sale. [4] If he wishes to sell, he must apply to the court under Law of Property Act 1925, section 91(2), p. 852, ante. The mortgagee's statutory power of sale becomes available if the mortgage is made by deed, and equitable mortgages are commonly accompanied by a memorandum under seal. Such a power, however, covers only 'the mortgaged property' [5]—that is the equitable interest. In order to give the mortgagee power to sell the legal estate, the deed often includes a power of attorney, [6] or a declaration of trust, or both.

---

[4]   C & B, pp. 775–777; Gray, pp. 1454–1455; M & W, paras. 19.084–19.086; MM, p. 513.
[5]   LPA 1925, s. 101(1)(i).
[6]   Powers of Attorney Act 1971, ss. 4(1), 5(3).

In **Re White Rose Cottage** [1965] Ch 940, [1965] 1 All ER 11, one question was whether a sale by the mortgagor (the Kamerun company) and the bank (an equitable mortgagee) gave a title free from or subject to an equitable charge in favour of a later equitable charge. The Court of Appeal construed the sale as one by the mortgagor with the concurrence of the mortgagee, and the title which passed was therefore that held by the mortgagor and the purchaser took subject to the later charge.

A different construction had been placed upon the sale by WILBERFORCE J at first instance [1964] Ch 483, [1964] 1 All ER 169; he treated it as being a sale by an equitable mortgagee.

The mortgagor had executed a memorandum under seal 'in the usual form for effecting a charge to secure [an] advance. It was stated that the documents of title had been deposited as security for the money due. The liability under the charge was not to exceed £50,000. The Kamerun company gave an undertaking to execute a legal charge or mortgage on request and agreed to hold the property as trustee for executing such a charge, the bank having power to appoint a new trustee in the place of the … company at any time. An irrevocable power of attorney was given to the bank so that the bank, in the name and on behalf of the … company, could vest the legal estate in the property in any purchaser or other person in exercise of the statutory powers conferred on mortgagees free and discharged from all rights of redemption'.

Both judgments of the Court of Appeal (Lord DENNING MR and HARMAN LJ, with SALMON LJ agreeing with both) expressed the view that, if they had construed the sale, as WILBERFORCE J did, as being a sale by an equitable mortgagee under a power of sale, the legal estate would have passed; and by virtue of Law of Property Act 1925, section 104(1), would have passed to the purchaser free from the subsequent charge.

HARMAN LJ said at 955, at 18: 'In other words, I think that an equitable mortgagee under a deed in the terms of the memorandum … can by virtue of the power of attorney contained in it convey to a purchaser the legal estate in the mortgaged property without first going through the form of calling for the execution by the mortgagor of a legal mortgage.'

Lord DENNING MR said at 951, at 15: 'Wilberforce J has held that that conveyance was an exercise by the bank of their statutory power of sale as mortgagees; and that selling as mortgagees they were entitled to sell the property freed from all charges subsequent to their own. If this be the correct construction of the conveyance, I would agree with him. [His Lordship referred to Law of Property Act 1925, section 104(1) and continued:] The subject of the mortgage here was the property itself, both the legal and equitable estate in it: and I see no reason why an equitable mortgagee, exercising his power of sale, should not be able to convey the legal estate.'[7]

ii. APPOINTMENT OF RECEIVER[8]

LAW OF PROPERTY ACT 1925

101. Powers incident to estate or interest of mortgagee.—(1) (iii), p. 872, ante.

109. Appointment, powers, remuneration and duties of receiver.—(1) A mortgagee entitled to appoint a receiver under the power in that behalf

---

[7]   See W & C, vol. i., 212, where this view is doubted.

[8]   C & B, pp. 761–762; Gray, pp. 1412–1414; M & W, paras. 19.079–19.083; MM, pp. 511–513; Smith, p. 602; Fisher & Lightwood, chap. 18.

conferred by this Act shall not appoint a receiver until he has become entitled to exercise the power of sale conferred by this Act, but may then, by writing under his hand, appoint such person as he thinks fit to be receiver.

(2) A receiver appointed under the powers conferred by this Act, or any enactment replaced by this Act, shall be deemed to be the agent of the mortgagor;[9] and the mortgagor shall be solely responsible for the receiver's acts or defaults unless the mortgage deed otherwise provides.[10]

(4) A person paying money to the receiver shall not be concerned to inquire whether any case has happened to authorise the receiver to act.

(8) Subject to the provisions of this Act as to the application of insurance money,[11] the receiver shall apply all money received by him as follows, namely:

    (i)   In discharge of all rents, taxes,[12] rates, and outgoings whatever affecting the mortgaged property; and

    (ii) In keeping down all annual sums or other payments, and the interest on all principal sums, having priority to the mortgage in right whereof he is receiver; and

    (iii) In payment of his commission,[13] and of the premiums on fire, life or other insurances, if any, properly payable under the mortgage deed or under this Act, and the cost of executing necessary or proper repairs directed in writing by the mortgagee; and

    (iv) In payment of the interest accruing due in respect of any principal money due under the mortgage; and

    (v) In or towards discharge of the principal money if so directed in writing by the mortgagee;

and shall pay the residue, if any, of the money received by him to the person who, but for the possession of the receiver, would have been entitled to receive the income of which he is appointed receiver, or who is otherwise entitled to the mortgaged property.[14]

D. Restitution

The law of restitution may provide a remedy for the mortgagee. In **Goss v Chilcott** [1996] AC 788, [1997] 2 All ER 110, Lord GOFF OF CHIEVELEY said at 792, at 112:

[9]   For the peculiar incidents of the agency, see *Silven Properties Ltd v Royal Bank of Scotland plc* [2004] 1 WLR 997, at paras. 21–29, per LIGHTMAN J.

[10] See *Chatsworth Properties Ltd v Effiom* [1971] 1 WLR 144, [1971] 1 All ER 604; *Standard Chartered Bank Ltd v Walker* [1982] 1 WLR 1410, [1982] 3 All ER 938; *American Express International Banking Corpn v Hurley* [1985] 3 All ER 564 (mortgagee responsible for what receiver does as his agent, but not responsible for what he does as mortgagor's agent, unless the mortgagee directs or interferes with receiver's activities); *Shamji v Johnson Matthey* [1991] BCLC 36 (mortgagee owes no duty of care to mortgagor or guarantor in deciding whether or not to appoint a receiver); *Lever Finance Ltd v Trustee of the Property of Needleman and Krentzer* [1956] Ch 375, [1956] 2 All ER 378 (receipt by receiver as agent of mortgagor does not create tenancy by estoppel binding on mortgagee): *Mann v Nijar* [1998] EGCS 188.

[11] LPA 1925, s. 108.

[12] *Sargent v Customs & Excise Comrs* [1993] EGCS 182 (V.A.T.).

[13] *Marshall v Cottingham* [1982] Ch 82, [1981] 3 All ER 8.

[14] A receiver, when managing the mortgaged property owes not only a duty of good faith to the mortgagor and anyone else with an interest in the equity of redemption, but also a duty to manage the property with due diligence; [2000] Ch 86; [1999] 3 All ER 97; [1999] Conv 434 (A. Kenny); [2000] CLJ 31 (L. S. Sealy); [1999] All ER Rev 227 (P. J. Clarke); *Medforth v Blake* [2000] Ch 86, [1999] 3 All ER 97.

'This appeal is concerned with an action brought by the plaintiff (as liquidator of a finance company, Central Acceptance Ltd) to recover from the defendants, Mr and Mrs Goss, the amount of an advance made by the company to the defendants which was secured by a mortgage over their property. (For the purposes of this appeal, their Lordships will for convenience treat the action as having been brought by the company itself.) The mortgage instrument was subsequently altered by a solicitor, Mr Haddon, in circumstances in which, on the authority of a line of cases stretching back to *Pigot's Case* (1614) 11 Co. Rep. 26b, the effect was that (as is now accepted) the defendants were discharged from liability under the instrument from the date of the alteration; and the central question in the case has been on what basis, if any, in these circumstances the company is entitled to recover the amount of the advance from the defendants. ...

From the beginning, the defendants were under an obligation to repay the advance once it had been paid to them or to their order; and this obligation was of course unaffected by the fact that they had allowed the money to be paid over to Mr Haddon. The effect of the alteration of the mortgage instrument was that their contractual obligation to repay the money was discharged; but they had nevertheless been enriched by the receipt of the money, and prima facie were liable in restitution to restore it. They had however allowed the money to be paid over to Mr Haddon in circumstances in which, as they well knew, the money would nevertheless have to be repaid to the company. They had, therefore, in allowing the money to be paid to Mr Haddon, deliberately taken the risk that he would be unable to repay the money, in which event they themselves would have to repay it without recourse to him. Since any action by them against Mr Haddon would now be fruitless they are seeking, by invoking the defence of change of position, to shift that loss onto the company. This, in their Lordships' opinion, they cannot do. The fact that they cannot now obtain reimbursement from Mr Haddon does not, in the circumstances of the present case, render it inequitable for them to be required to make restitution to the company in respect of the enrichment which they have received at the company's expense.'[15]

E. Foreclosure[16]

LAW OF PROPERTY ACT 1925

88. Realisation of freehold mortgages.—(2) Where any such mortgagee obtains an order for foreclosure absolute, the order shall operate to vest the fee simple in him (subject to any legal mortgage having priority to the mortgage in right of which the foreclosure is obtained and to any money thereby secured), and thereupon the mortgage term, if any, shall thereby be merged in the fee simple,

---

[15] The defence of change of position on the basis that the defendants had allowed the money to be paid to the solicitor was rejected; Goff and Jones, *The Law of Restitution* (6th edn), paras. 19.007–19.008. See also *Portman Building Society v Harmyn Taylor Neck* (1998) 76 P & CR D16 (mortgagee's loss arising from mistake induced by solicitor).

[16] C & B, pp. 768–770; Gray, pp. 1451–1454; M & W, paras. 19.049–19.055; MM, pp. 502–504; Smith, p. 581; Cousins (2nd edn), paras. 16.89–16.106; Fisher & Lightwood, chaps. 21, 22; (1978) LS Gaz 447; (1979) 129 NLJ 33 (H. E. Markson), 225 (C. M. Pepper); (1981) 260 EG 899 (D. Brahams). On a revival in its popularity as a remedy, see Report of Committee on Enforcement of Judgment Debts 1969 (Cmnd 1309), para. 1360; on its rarity, see *Palk v Mortgage Services Funding plc* [1993] Ch 330 at 336, [1993] 2 All ER 481 at 485; and on its commercial use, see *Lloyds and Scottish Trusts Ltd v Britten* (1982) 44 P & CR 249.

For registration requirements for foreclosure in registered land, see LRR 2003, para. 112.

and any subsequent mortgage term or charge by way of legal mortgage bound by the order shall thereupon be extinguished.

89. Realisation of leasehold mortgages.—(2) Where any such mortgagee obtains an order for foreclosure absolute, the order shall, unless it otherwise provides, operate (without giving rise to a forfeiture for want of a licence to assign) to vest the leasehold reversion affected by the mortgage and any subsequent mortgage term in him, subject to any legal mortgage having priority to the mortgage in right of which the foreclosure is obtained and to any money thereby secured, and thereupon the mortgage term and any subsequent mortgage term or charge by way of legal mortgage bound by the order shall, subject to any express provision to the contrary contained in the order, merge in such leasehold reversion or be extinguished.

The mortgagee or any person interested may ask the court to order a sale instead of foreclosure: Law of Property Act 1925, section 91 (2).[17]

In **Campbell v Holyland** (1877) 7 ChD 166, Blakely mortgaged a reversionary interest in a trust fund to Campbell and died insolvent. A foreclosure decree was made in 1876 ordering payment of the money by 4 January 1877. Blakely's administrator, Holyland, transferred the equity of redemption to X and Y who negotiated for the purchase of the interest of the mortgagee, Campbell; and failed to pay on 4 January 1877 because they thought, incorrectly, that they had purchased the interest. They discovered subsequently that Campbell had sold his interest on 3 January, to Ford, who was aware of the negotiations to sell to X and Y. The foreclosure decree was made absolute.

In March 1877, X and Y's executors moved to reopen the foreclosure decree, and JESSEL MR allowed them to do so. He said at 171:

'I have no doubt that I ought to make the order asked for.

The question in dispute is really whether a mortgagor can be allowed to redeem after an order of foreclosure absolute, and I think, on looking at the authorities, that no Chancellor or Vice-Chancellor has ever laid down that any special circumstances are essential to enable a mortgagor to redeem in such a case.

Now what is the principle? The principle in a Court of Equity has always been that, though a mortgage is in form an absolute conveyance when the condition is broken, in equity it is always security; and it must be remembered that the doctrine arose at the time when mortgages were made in the form of conditional conveyance, the condition being that if the money was not paid at the day, the estate should become the estate of the mortgagee; that was the contract between the parties; yet Courts of Equity interfered with actual contract to this extent, by saying there was a paramount intention that the estate should be security, and that the mortgage money should be debt; and they gave relief in the shape of redemption on that principle. Of course that would lead, and did lead, to this inconvenience, that even when the mortgagor was not willing to redeem, the mortgagee could not sell or deal with the estate as his own, and to remedy that

---

[17]   P. 852, ante. For the inter-relation between the two remedies, see *Twentieth Century Banking Corpn Ltd v Wilkinson* [1977] Ch 99, [1976] 3 All ER 361.

inconvenience the practice of bringing a foreclosure suit was adopted, by which a mortgagee was entitled to call on the mortgagor to redeem within a certain time, under penalty of losing the right of redemption. In that foreclosure suit the Court made various orders—interim orders fixing a time for payment of the money—and at last there came the final order which was called foreclosure absolute, that is, in form, that the mortgagor should not be allowed to redeem at all; but it was form only, just as the original deed was form only; for the Courts of Equity soon decided that, notwithstanding the form of that order, they would after that order allow the mortgagor to redeem. That is, although the order of foreclosure absolute appeared to be a final order of the Court, it was not so, but the mortgagee still remained liable to be treated as mortgagee and the mortgagor still retained a claim to be treated as mortgagor, subject to the discretion of the Court. Therefore everybody who took an order for foreclosure absolute knew that there was still a discretion in the Court to allow the mortgagor to redeem.

Under what circumstances that discretion should be exercised is quite another matter. The mortgagee had a right to deal with an estate acquired under foreclosure absolute the day after he acquired it; but he knew perfectly well that there might be circumstances to entitle the mortgagor to redeem, and everybody buying the estate from a mortgagee who merely acquired a title under such an order was considered to have the same knowledge, namely, that the estate might be taken away from him by the exercise, not of a capricious discretion, but of a judicial discretion by the Court of Equity which had made the order.

That being so, on what terms is that judicial discretion to be exercised? It has been said by the highest authority that it is impossible to say a priori what are the terms. They must depend upon the circumstances of each case. ... In the first place the mortgagor must come, as it is said, promptly; that is, within a reasonable time. He is not to let the mortgagee deal with the estate as his own—if it is a landed estate, the mortgagee being in possession of it and using it—and then without any special reason come and say, "Now I will redeem". He cannot do that; he must come within a reasonable time. What is a reasonable time? You must have regard to the nature of the property. As has been stated in more than one of the cases, where the estate is an estate in land in possession—where the mortgagee takes it in possession and deals with it and alters the property, and so on—the mortgagor must come more quickly than where it is an estate in reversion, as to which the mortgagee can do nothing except sell it. So that you must have regard to the nature of the estate in ascertaining what is to be considered reasonable time.

Then, again, was the mortgagee[18] entitled to redeem, but by some accident unable to redeem? Did he expect to get the money from a quarter from which he might reasonably hope to obtain it, and was he disappointed at the last moment? Was it a very large sum, and did he require a considerable time to raise it elsewhere? All those things must be considered in determining what is a reasonable time.

Then an element for consideration has always been the nature of the property as regards value.[19] For instance, if an estate were worth £50,000, and had been foreclosed for a mortgage debt of £5,000, the man who came to redeem that estate

---

[18]   Presumably 'mortgagor' was intended here.

[19]   *Lancashire and Yorkshire Reversionary Interest Co v Crowe* (1970) 114 SJ 435 (foreclosure decree made absolute in respect of mortgage of reversionary interest; and re-opened after the interest fell into possession on life tenant's death. The sum due was £3,000 and the fund £6,100).

would have a longer time than where the estate was worth £5,100, and he was foreclosed for £5,000. But not only is there money value, but there may be other considerations. It may be an old family estate or a chattel, or picture, which possesses a special value for the mortgagor, but which possesses not the same value for other people; or it may be, as has happened in this instance, that the property, though a reversionary interest in the funds, is of special value to both the litigants: it may possess not merely a positive money value, but a peculiar value having regard to the nature of the title and other incidents, so that you cannot set an actual money value upon it. In fact, that is the real history of this contest, for the property does not appear to be of much more money value— though it is of some more—than the original amount of the mortgage. All this must be taken into consideration.

Then it is said you must not interfere against purchasers. As I have already explained, there are purchasers and purchasers. If the purchaser buys a freehold estate in possession after the lapse of a considerable time from the order of foreclosure absolute, with no notice of any extraneous circumstances which would induce the Court to interfere, I for one should decline to interfere with such a title as that; but if the purchaser bought the estate within twenty-four hours after the foreclosure absolute, and with notice of the fact that it was of much greater value than the amount of the mortgage debt, is it to be supposed that a Court of Equity would listen to the contention of such a purchaser that he ought not to be interfered with? He must be taken to know the general law that an order for foreclosure may be opened under proper circumstances and under a proper exercise of discretion by the Court; and if the mortgagor in that case came the week after, is it to be supposed a Court of Equity would so stultify itself as to say that a title so acquired would stand in the way? I am of opinion it would not.

Now I come to the circumstances of this case, and I must say they are very strong in favour of opening the foreclosure. ...

The present purchaser, Mr Ford, being very desirous to acquire the property for a collateral object[20]—I am not saying a wrong object, but a collateral object— had, before the time for foreclosure absolute had arrived, entered into a contract with the mortgagee to buy it. He was not a purchaser coming in even the day after foreclosure, but a purchaser coming in before foreclosure, and at that time of course he knew the property was redeemable. He bought a property certainly redeemable, for the day for redemption had not even arrived. That is the kind of purchase I am dealing with. He was aware on the day of redemption that it was not from unwillingness to redeem that the mortgagor failed to pay the money, but because the mortgagor was under the belief that he had acquired a right to take the property on paying less than the mortgage money, by reason of a contract of purchase with the mortgagee. ...

I am of opinion, however, that such a sale as this ought to have no weight whatever, and that under the circumstances the mortgagor is entitled to open the foreclosure on the usual terms, that is, on payment of principal, interest, and costs.'

———————

In **Kinnaird v Trollope** (1888) 39 ChD 636, STIRLING J said at 642:
'Where a mortgagee has obtained a decree for foreclosure absolute he may still sue the mortgagor on the covenant for payment of the mortgage debt

———————

20   To obtain the property for Blakely's widow.

provided he retains the mortgaged property in his possession, but (as is laid down by Lord Langdale in *Lockhart v Hardy* (1846) 9 Beav 349 at 355) by so suing he gives the mortgagor a new right of redemption, notwithstanding the foreclosure, and the mortgagor may file a bill to redeem. If, however, the mortgagee has sold the mortgaged property, a Court of Equity will interfere to restrain an action on the covenant.'[1]

F. Consolidation[2]

If the same mortgagor has mortgaged more than one property to the same mortgagee, and if one of the properties so mortgaged is worth less than the debt for the repayment of which it has been charged as security, it is in the mortgagor's interest to redeem the other properties but not that one. The mortgagor is, however, asking a favour of equity in being allowed to redeem any property after the contractual date for redemption has passed, and, in accordance with the maxim: 'He who comes to Equity must do Equity', the mortgagor may be prevented from redeeming one mortgage without redeeming others. In other words, the mortgagee has a right in certain circumstances to consolidate the various mortgages against the mortgagor.

LAW OF PROPERTY ACT 1925

93. Restriction on consolidation of mortgages.—(1) A mortgagor seeking to redeem any one mortgage is entitled to do so without paying any money due under any separate mortgage made by him, or by any person through whom he claims, solely on property other than that comprised in the mortgage which he seeks to redeem.

This subsection applies only if and as far as a contrary intention is not expressed in the mortgage deeds or one of them.

(2) This section does not apply where all the mortgages were made before the first day of January, eighteen hundred and eighty two.

(3) Save as aforesaid, nothing in this Act, in reference to mortgages, affects any right of consolidation or renders inoperative a stipulation in relation to any mortgage made before or after the commencement of this Act reserving a right to consolidate.

PLEDGE v WHITE
[1896] AC 187 (HL, LORDS HALSBURY LC, WATSON and DAVEY)

There were mortgages on seven different properties; the properties will be referred to as Nos. 1–7. They were mortgaged by James Banks to various mortgagees between 1863 and 1866.

In 1866 James Banks the mortgagor made a second mortgage of Nos. 4–7 to Brockman: and in 1868 a third mortgage of these properties and a second mortgage of Nos. 1–3 to Brockman and Harrison. In 1885, Brockman and

---

[1] Followed in *Lloyds and Scottish Trust Ltd v Britten* (1982) 44 P & CR 249 (guarantor of mortgagor likewise held not suable).

[2] C & B, pp. 772–775; M & W, paras. 19.096–19.111; MM, pp. 515–518; Waldock, pp. 284–295; Cousins (2nd edn), chap. 24; Fisher and Lightwood, chap. 27. As to whether the right amounts to a general equitable charge within LCA 1972, s. 2(4), Class C(iii), see (1948) 92 SJ 736; W & C, vol. 1, 189. For registered land, see LRA 2002, r. 57; LRR 2003, r. 110, under which a right of consideration may be entered on the register.

Harrison assigned their equities of redemption in all 7 properties to Pledge, the appellant.

Between 1871 and 1890, Brockman became the transferee of all the first mortgages except that on No. 3.[3] He died in 1877, and in 1890 his executors, the respondents, took an assignment of the first mortgage on No. 3.

In 1890 the appellant claimed to redeem No. 2 alone. The respondents refused to allow him to do so without redeeming the other six.

Held. The mortgagee was entitled to consolidate.

LORD HALSBURY LC: My Lords, I have had an opportunity of considering the judgment prepared by my noble and learned friend (Lord Davey) and I am not prepared to dissent from it. I use that form of expression because I confess I lament the conclusion to which it has been found necessary to come, although I believe the strict principle upon which it rests is founded in our law at present, and in dealing with a technical system it is better to adhere to a principle when once established, than to create greater confusion by dissenting from it. I think the principle laid down in *Vint v Padget* (1858) 2 De G & J 611 has been so firmly established now by authority in our technical system, that I feel more mischief would be done by dissenting from it, than by acquiescing in it. ...

LORD DAVEY: The question for your Lordships' decision is whether the respondents have the right of consolidation which they claim, notwithstanding that the mortgages which it is sought to consolidate were not united in title with the mortgage sought to be redeemed until after the assignment of the equity of redemption to the present appellant's predecessors in title. ...

The equitable rule as to the consolidation of mortgages is not one of those doctrines of the Court of Chancery which has met with general approbation—at any rate as regards its later development. Originally it may have been a right of a mortgagee holding two separate mortgages on estates of the same mortgagor which have become absolute estates at law against the mortgagor and debtor personally to refuse to be redeemed as regards one estate without having his other debt also paid. But it has long been settled that the right of consolidation may be exercised by the transferee of the mortgages as well as by the original mortgagee, and may be exercised in respect of equitable mortgages as well as by a mortgagee holding the legal estate absolute at law; and on the other hand, that it may be asserted against the assignee of an equity of redemption from the mortgagor as well as against the mortgagor himself ...

The case of *Vint v Padget* came before Stuart V-C in the first instance, whose judgment may be referred to as shewing how entirely that experienced judge considered the point to be settled. 'In accepting', he says, 'by way of security the equity of redemption of two separate estates, Mr Lee deliberately incurred the risk of their uniting in one hand, and when that union has taken place there is only one single debt, and in order to redeem he must pay off both mortgages, each of which affects the entirety of both estates.'

[His Lordship referred to: *Bovey v Skipwich* (1671) 1 Cas in Ch 201; *Titley v Davies* (1743) 2 Y & C Ch Cas 399; *Selby v Pomfret* (1861) 3 De G F & J 595; *Beevor v Luck* (1867) LR 4 Eq 537; *White v Hillacre* (1839) 3 Y & C Ex 597; *Harter v Colman* (1882) 19 ChD 630; *Jennings v Jordan* (1881) 6 App Cas 698, and continued:]

---

[3]   The facts as given by Lord DAVEY do not explain how Brockman obtained the mortgages on Nos. 6 and 7.

It appears to me, my Lords, that an assignee of two or more equities of redemption from one mortgagor stands in a widely different position from the assignee of one equity only. He knows, or has the opportunity of knowing, what are the mortgages subject to which he has purchased the property, and he knows that they may become united by transfer in one hand. If the doctrine of consolidation be once admitted it appears to me not unreasonable to hold that a person in such a position occupies the place of the mortgagor or assignor to him towards the holders of the mortgages, subject to which he has purchased, although it may be unreasonable to hold that he can be affected by the transfer to such holders of mortgages to other persons by the same mortgagor on property which he has not purchased, and with the equity of redemption of which he has no concern. He does not investigate the title to such other property and cannot know in the latter case to what mortgages the property is subject. If your Lordships affirm the decree now under appeal, the doctrine of consolidation will be confined within at least intelligible limits. It will be applicable where at the date when redemption is sought all the mortgages are united in one hand and redeemable by the same person, or where after that state of things has once existed the equities of redemption have become separated.[4] If the purchaser of two or more equities of redemption desires to prevent consolidation, he has it in his power to redeem any one mortgage before consolidation takes place; but if for his own convenience he delays doing so, he runs the same risk as his assignor ran of the mortgages becoming united by transfer in one hand.

I am of opinion that the application of the doctrine of consolidation to a case like the present has been too long considered part of the equitable jurisprudence of this country to be altered at the present time, and it is not so unreasonable as to demand a reversal of it by this House.

I move, therefore, that this appeal be dismissed with costs.

In **Cummins v Fletcher** (1880) 14 Ch D 699, the trustees of a building society, who were mortgagees of two properties, refused to allow a bank, the second mortgagee of one of the properties, to redeem it, without also redeeming the other. All payments due under the first mortgage were up to date, but those on the second were in arrears.

The Court of Appeal (JAMES, COTTON and THESIGER LJJ, reversing HALL V-C) refused to allow the building society to consolidate, on the ground that consolidation arose only where the mortgagor was in default and was asking a favour of the Court of Equity. JAMES LJ said at 708:

'The whole doctrine of consolidation, whatever may have been the particular circumstances under which it has been applied to different cases, arises from the power of the Court of Equity to put its own price upon its own interference as a matter of equitable consideration in favour of any suitor.'

A further reason, mentioned by the court, was that the mortgagors were not the same in the two mortgages. In the first mortgage, the mortgagor was Vaugham and in the second Vaugham and Neesham, partners. This point was not necessary for the decision.

---

[4]   It will not apply where the equities of redemption separated before the mortgages became united in one hand: *Harter v Colman* (1882) 19 ChD 630.

In **Hughes v Britannia Permanent Building Society** [1906] 2 Ch 607, A in 1894 mortgaged Blackacre to the defendants, the mortgage providing that A should not be entitled to redeem without paying all the moneys due by A to the defendants under any other mortgage.

A then mortgaged Whiteacre to the defendants, and gave a second mortgage to the plaintiffs, the defendants having notice of this mortgage; A subsequently mortgaged two separate properties to the defendants.

The plaintiffs claimed to redeem Whiteacre, and the question was whether the defendants could consolidate against the plaintiffs all their mortgages or only those made before the second mortgage of Whiteacre to the plaintiffs.

KEKEWICH J held that the defendants could consolidate against the plaintiffs the mortgages on Blackacre and Whiteacre, but not those on the other properties. The mortgagor, by his express contract, would have been compelled to submit to consolidation of all the properties; and the plaintiffs would have been in the same position if the defendants, at the time of the later mortgages, had not had notice of the second mortgage on Whiteacre to the plaintiffs. [5]

VII. Discharge of Mortgages [6]

A. Unregistered Land

LAW OF PROPERTY ACT 1925

115. Reconveyances of mortgages by endorsed receipts.—(1) A receipt endorsed on, written at the foot of, or annexed to, a mortgage for all money thereby secured, which states the name of the person who pays the money and is executed by the chargee by way of legal mortgage or the person in whom the mortgaged property is vested and who is legally entitled to give a receipt for the mortgage money shall operate, without any reconveyance, surrender, or release —

(*a*) Where a mortgage takes effect by demise or subdemise, as a surrender of the term, so as to determine the term or merge the same in the reversion immediately expectant thereon;

(*b*) Where the mortgage does not take effect by demise or subdemise, as a reconveyance thereof to the extent of the interest which is the subject matter of the mortgage, to the person who immediately before the execution of the receipt was entitled to the equity of redemption;

and in either case, as a discharge of the mortgaged property from all principal money and interest secured by, and from all claims under the mortgage, but without prejudice to any term or other interests which is paramount to the estate or interest of the mortgagee or other person in whom the mortgaged property was vested. [7]

(2) Provided that, where by the receipt the money appears to have been paid by a person who is not entitled to the immediate equity of redemption, the receipt

---

[5]   See also *Andrews v City Permanent Benefit Building Society* (1881) 44 LT 641.
[6]   C & B, pp. 749–752; Gray, pp. 552–553; M & W, paras. 19.189–19.193; MM, pp. 529–530; Cousins, Part VIII; Fisher and Lightwood, chap. 20.
[7]   A building society may use either a reconveyance or a special statutory receipt: Building Societies Act 1986, Sch 4, para. 2.

shall operate as if the benefit of the mortgage had by deed been transferred to him; unless —

    (*a*) it is otherwise expressly provided; or

    (*b*) the mortgage is paid off out of capital money, or other money in the hands of a personal representative or trustee properly applicable for the discharge of the mortgage, and it is not expressly provided that the receipt is to operate as a transfer.

(3) Nothing in this section confers on a mortgagor a right to keep alive a mortgage paid off by him, so as to affect prejudicially any subsequent incumbrancer; and where there is no right to keep the mortgage alive, the receipt does not operate as a transfer. [8]

(4) This section does not affect the right of any person to require a reassignment, surrender, release, or transfer to be executed in lieu of a receipt.

(8) This section applies to the discharge of a charge by way of legal mortgage, and to the discharge of a mortgage, whether made by way of statutory mortgage or not, executed before or after the commencement of this Act, but only as respects discharges effected after such commencement.

(10) This section does not apply to the discharge of a registered charge within the meaning of the Land Registration Act 2002. [9]

116. Cesser of mortgage terms. —Without prejudice to the right of a tenant for life or other person having only a limited interest in the equity of redemption to require a mortgage to be kept alive by transfer or otherwise, a mortgage term shall, when the money secured by the mortgage has been discharged, become a satisfied term and shall cease. [10]

B. Registered Land

LAND REGISTRATION RULES 2003

Discharges and releases of registered charges

B114.—(1) Subject to rule 115, a discharge of a registered charge must be in Form DS1.

(2) Subject to rule 115, a release of part of the registered estate in a registered title from a registered charge must be in Form DS3.

(3) Any discharge or release in Form DS1 or DS3 must be executed as a deed or authenticated in such other manner as the registrar may approve.

(4) Notwithstanding paragraphs (1) and (2) and rule 115, the registrar is entitled to accept and act upon any other proof of satisfaction of a charge that he may regard as sufficient.

Discharges and releases of registered charges in electronic form

115.—(1) During the currency of a notice given under Schedule 2 and subject to and in accordance with the limitations contained in such notice, notification of—

    (a) the discharge of, or

---

[8]   *Otter v Lord Vaux* (1856) 6 De GM & G 638; *Parkash v Irani Finance Ltd* [1970] Ch 101, [1969] 1 All ER 930.

[9]   As amended by LRA 2002, s. 133, Sch. 11, para. 2(1), (11).

[10] *Edwards v Marshall-Lee* (1975) 235 EG 901 (vacating receipt on a legal charge not complying with s. 115 held a valid discharge); (1976) 40 Conv (NS) 102.

(b) the release of part of a registered estate in a registered title from a registered charge may be delivered to the registrar in electronic form.

(2) Notification of discharge or release of part given in accordance with paragraph (1) shall be regarded as having the same effect as a discharge in Form DS1, or a release of part in Form DS3, as appropriate, executed in accordance with rule 114 by or on behalf the person who has delivered it to the registrar.

VIII. Priority of Mortgages[11]

Very substantial alterations were made by the legislation of 1925 to the rules concerning the priority of mortgages. The rules which were in force before 1926 are of importance as there are still circumstances in which they may apply. The two systems for unregistered land will be considered separately, followed by the systems for registered land.

A. Before 1926

i. MORTGAGES OF INTERESTS IN LAND

The basic rule was that priority depended on the time of creation. '*Qui prior est tempore, potior est jure.*' This rule could, however, be made inapplicable by the other principle that 'Where the equities are equal, the law prevails'. Where, for example, a legal mortgagee has no notice, actual or constructive, of a prior equitable mortgage, the equities are equal and the legal mortgagee will take priority. However, wrongful conduct (fraud, misrepresentation or gross negligence) may deprive the earlier mortgagee, even the holder of the legal estate, of his normal priority.

These rules give rise to certain difficulties; inevitably, as they are conflicting. To decide which rule to apply is to determine the priority of the mortgages. And there is little guidance in the cases on the question of the tests to be applied in deciding whether the 'equities are equal' or in defining how serious must be the conduct of the mortgagee before he will be postponed. A number of questions are not made clear.

Firstly, it is not clear to what extent different rules for the displacement of the natural order of priority apply to the case of a prior equitable followed by a later legal mortgage from those applicable to a prior legal followed by a later equitable mortgage. Certainly the issues are different. The problem in the one case is to determine when the first rule is to be displaced by the second; in the other case both rules may be upset and the legal mortgagee who is first in time may be postponed.[12]

In the latter type of case, the reason for the postponement of the legal mortgagee is usually fraud or estoppel; but gross negligence by the legal mortgagee in respect of the title deeds is usually said to be sufficient.[13] The

---

[11]   C & B, pp. 777–800; Gray, pp. 1455–1462; M & W, paras. 19.194–19.264; MM, pp. 530–546; Cousins, chap. 18; Waldock, pp. 381–435; Fisher & Lightwood, chap. 24; (1949) 7 CLJ 243 (R. E. Megarry).

[12]   *Perry Herrick v Attwood* (1857) 2 De G & J 21, p. 908, post.

[13]   *Colyer v Finch* (1856) 5 HL Cas 905; *Perry Herrick v Attwood*, supra; *Clarke v Palmer* (1882) 21 Ch D 124; *Walker v Linom* [1907] 2 Ch 104, p. 910, post.

addition of adjectives to negligence always causes difficulty, and there is no precise test to show what is signified by the adjective 'gross'.

Secondly, the requirement of negligence in the case of a later legal following a prior equitable mortgage is not clear. The position is sometimes said to be that the later legal mortgagee will take priority over a prior equitable unless he was grossly negligent. Sometimes it is said that he will do so if he enquires for the deeds (deposited with the equitable mortgagee) and receives a reasonable excuse for non-production.[14] The obvious way to treat the question, one would have thought, would be to apply the ordinary rule relating to the bona fide purchaser for value and to postpone the later legal mortgagee unless he can pass that test.[15] But he has been more greatly favoured.

(a) The Superiority of the Legal Estate[16]

HEWITT v LOOSEMORE
(1851) 9 Hare 449 (TURNER V-C)

Robert Loosemore, the mortgagor, was a solicitor; in 1834, he deposited his lease with the plaintiff as an equitable mortgage to secure the repayment of a sum of money. In 1838, he assigned the lease by way of legal mortgage to the defendant John Loosemore, who was a farmer, unacquainted with legal forms; John asked Robert whether the lease ought not to be delivered to him, and Robert said that it should, but that, as he was rather busy then, he would give it to John when he next came to market. The plaintiff brought this bill praying, inter alia, for a declaration that he was entitled to priority over the defendant.

Held. The defendant as legal mortgagee was entitled to priority.

TURNER V-C: [The question in this case is] whether an equitable mortgagee by deposit of title deeds is entitled to priority over a subsequent legal mortgagee of the property comprised in the deeds, who has not made all the inquiries after the deeds which could or might have been made. ...

The law, ... as I collect it from the authorities, stands thus:—That a legal mortgagee is not to be postponed to a prior equitable one upon the ground of his not having got in the title-deeds, unless there be fraud or gross and wilful negligence on his part. That the court will not impute fraud, or gross or wilful negligence to the mortgagee if he has bona fide inquired for the deeds, and a reasonable excuse has been given for the non-delivery of them; but that the court will impute fraud, or gross and wilful negligence to the mortgagee if he omits all inquiry as to the deeds. And I think there is much principle both in the rule and the distinctions upon it.

When this court is called upon to postpone a legal mortgagee its powers are invoked to take away a legal right; and I see no ground which can justify it in doing so except fraud, or gross and wilful negligence, which, in the eyes of this court, amounts to fraud, and I think that in transactions of sale and mortgage of estates, if there be no inquiry as to the title-deeds, which constitute the sole evidence of the title to such property, the court is justified in assuming that the purchaser or mortgagee has abstained from making the inquiry, from a suspicion that his title would be affected if it was made, and is therefore bound to impute to

---

[14]   *Hewitt v Loosemore* (1851) 9 Hare 449; *Agra Bank Ltd v Barry* (1874) LR 7 HL 135; *Oliver v Hinton* [1899] 2 Ch 264, p. 906, post.
[15]   See p. 24, ante; *Pilcher v Rawlins* (1872) 7 Ch App 259.
[16]   *Barnett v Weston* (1806) 12 Ves 130; *Agra Bank Ltd v Barry*, supra; *Hewitt v Loosemore*, supra; *Walker v Linom*, supra; *Hudston v Viney* [1921] 1 Ch 98.

him the knowledge which the inquiry, if made, would have imparted. But I think that where bona fide inquiry, is made, and a reasonable excuse given, there is no ground for imputing the suspicion, or the notice which is consequent upon it.

Applying these principles to the present case, I am of opinion that the plaintiff has failed in making out a sufficient case for postponing the defendant, and that the only decree which I can make is the usual decree for redemption; but the plaintiff must pay the costs up to and including the decree.

OLIVER v HINTON
[1899] 2 Ch 264 (ChD, ROMER J, and CA, LINDLEY MR, Sir F. H. JEUNE and RIGBY LJ)

The plaintiff, Mrs Oliver, brought this action for a declaration that she was entitled to certain premises as equitable mortgagee as against the defendant Mrs Hinton, who had purchased them. The circumstances were that in 1888, Hill, a solicitor, had deposited the deeds of the premises with the plaintiff under an equitable mortgage. In 1890, Hill conveyed the property to the defendant, who was represented by an agent who was not a solicitor. This agent asked Hill to see the deeds, but Hill replied that they could not be seen as they related also to other property.

Held. The plaintiff was entitled to priority over the defendant, the purchaser of the legal estate.

LINDLEY MR: In my opinion this case does not present any serious difficulty when once the facts are understood. The defendant has been cheated by Hill, but she has not been in any way cheated by the plaintiff. In 1888, Hill gave the plaintiff a mortgage of the three houses in question and two others. It was not a legal mortgage, but an equitable mortgage by deposit of title-deeds, accompanied by a memorandum of deposit, by which Hill agreed to execute a legal mortgage when requested by the plaintiff to do so. The plaintiff had a good equitable mortgage, and she cannot be charged with any neglect or breach of duty in not obtaining a legal mortgage. She ran, however, the risk of losing her priority in case the legal estate should be conveyed to a subsequent purchaser for value without notice of her charge. Who is it that now claims to override her charge? The only person who can do so, if he has acquired his title subsequently to hers, is a bona fide purchaser for value without notice of her charge. But this does not include a purchaser for value who is so grossly negligent as to take none of the ordinary precautions which ought to be taken in such a matter—who, in fact, takes no precautions whatever. He may be a bona fide purchaser for value without notice of a prior charge, but he is not entitled to the protection of the Court. I do not base my judgment upon constructive notice of the plaintiff's charge, nor do I mean to suggest that there was any fraud or complicity in fraud on the part of either the defendant or her agent, Price. Price gave his evidence with perfect candour. The defendant left the arrangement of the purchase entirely to him. He inquired about the title-deeds, and was told by Hill that they were in his possession, but that they would not be delivered up to the purchaser because they related also to other property. No abstract of title was asked for or delivered, and no further inquiry was made. Price in his evidence admitted that he made a mistake in not asking to see the deeds, but said that he relied upon Hill. Can a person whose agent acted in this way be regarded as a bona fide purchaser for value without notice who is entitled to the protection of the legal estate? To allow a purchaser who acts with such gross carelessness to deprive a prior innocent mortgagee of her priority would be the greatest injustice. ...

In [*Hunt v Elmes* (1860) 2 De GF & J 578] and also in *Hewitt v Loosemore* (1857) 9 Hare 449, p. 905, ante, it was said that to deprive a man of the protection of the legal estate he must have been guilty of either fraud or gross and wilful negligence. To deprive a purchaser for value without notice of a prior incumbrance of the protection of the legal estate it is not, in my opinion, essential that he should have been guilty of fraud; it is sufficient that he has been guilty of such gross negligence as would render it unjust to deprive the prior incumbrancer of his priority.

The appeal must be dismissed.

(b) The Effect of Fraud, Misrepresentation, Gross Negligence

1. FRAUD[17]

NORTHERN COUNTIES OF ENGLAND FIRE INSURANCE CO v WHIPP
(1884) 26 ChD 482 (CA, COTTON, BOWEN and FRY LJJ)

On two occasions in 1878, Crabtree, the manager of the plaintiff company, executed legal mortgages of freehold properties to the company and delivered to the company the title deeds which were locked in the safe. Crabtree was entrusted by the company with one of the two sets of keys to the safe, and, later in 1878, extracted the deeds, and, suppressing the mortgages, deposited them with the defendant, Mrs Whipp, as security for a loan.

In an action by the company for foreclosure, Mrs Whipp claimed that her security should take priority over that of the company.

Held (reversing the Vice-Chancellor of the Court of the County Palatine of Lancaster). The mortgage to the company took priority.

FRY LJ: The question which has thus to be investigated is—What conduct in relation to the title deeds on the part of a mortgagee who has the legal estate, is sufficient to postpone such mortgagee in favour of a subsequent equitable mortgagee who has obtained the title deeds without knowledge of the legal mortgage? The question is not what circumstances may as between two equities give priority to the one over the other, but what circumstances justify the Court in depriving a legal mortgagee of the benefit of the legal estate. It has been contended on the part of the Plaintiffs that nothing short of fraud will justify the Court in postponing the legal estate. It has been contended by the Defendant that gross negligence is enough. ...

The authorities which we have reviewed appear to us to justify the following conclusions: —

(1) That the court will postpone the prior legal estate to a subsequent equitable estate: (*a*), where the owner of the legal estate has assisted in or connived at the fraud which has led to the creation of a subsequent equitable estate, without notice of the prior legal estate; of which assistance or connivance, the omission to use ordinary care in inquiry after or keeping title deeds may be, and in some cases has been, held to be sufficient evidence, where such conduct cannot otherwise be explained; (*b*), where the owner of the legal estate has constituted the mortgagor his agent with authority to raise money, and the estate thus created has by the fraud or misconduct of the agent been represented as being the first estate.

---

[17]   *Thatched House Case* (1716) 1 Eq Cas Abr 321.

But (2) that the Court will not postpone the prior legal estate to the subsequent equitable estate on the ground of any mere carelessness or want of prudence on the part of the legal owner.

Now to apply the conclusions thus arrived at to the facts of the present case. That there was great carelessness in the manner in which the Plaintiff company through its directors dealt with their securities seems to us to admit of no doubt. But is that carelessness evidence of any fraud? We think that it is not. Of what fraud is it evidence? The Plaintiffs never combined with *Crabtree* to induce the Defendant to lend her money. They never knew that she was lending it, and stood by. They can have had no motive to desire that their deeds should be abstracted and their own title clouded. Their carelessness may be called gross, but in our judgment it was carelessness likely to injure and not to benefit the Plaintiff company, and accordingly has no tendency to convict them of fraud.

The rule, referred to in this case, which lays down that an earlier legal mortgagee may be postponed on the ground of fraud is undoubted. The rule however that an earlier legal mortgagee will never be postponed on the grounds of negligence (not amounting to fraud) is questioned by many writers and is inconsistent with some cases (p. 909, post). Much reconciliation can be effected by limiting the decision in *Whipp's* case to a situation where the negligence was in failure to *retain* the deeds. It is difficult however to justify in principle a distinction between a failure to obtain and a failure to retain the deeds.

2. MISREPRESENTATION[18]

PERRY HERRICK v ATTWOOD
(1857) 2 De G & J 21 (Lord CRANWORTH LC)

In 1848 John Attwood was substantially indebted to the trustees of a family marriage settlement, and also to three of his sisters, the defendants. While he was being pressed for payment by the trustees, he executed a legal mortgage for the amount due to his sisters. The deeds, other than the mortgage, were, however, retained by the sisters' solicitor in order to enable John Attwood to execute a mortgage to secure his debts to the trustees. In April 1848, Attwood deposited the deeds with the solicitors for the trustees. Later, by employing those same solicitors, Attwood made several legal mortgages of the same property to various persons including the plaintiffs; the plaintiffs were also transferees of some of those mortgages.

The plaintiffs filed a bill to establish their mortgages as having priority over the mortgage to the Misses Attwood.

Held (affirming Sir John ROMILLY MR). The plaintiffs were entitled to priority.

LORD CRANWORTH LC: This case has occupied a long time in argument, and has given rise to the agitation of questions of great importance. It has been discussed how far a mortgagee, taking a mortgage without taking the title deeds, does or does not postpone himself to persons who take a subsequent conveyance for value without notice of the mortgage, and obtain possession of the title deeds, and the cases on that subject have been referred to, the last being *Colyer v Finch* (1856) 5 HL Cas 905, in the House of Lords.

---

[18]   *Briggs v Jones* (1870) LR 10 Eq 92; *Dixon v Muckleston* (1872) 8 Ch App 155 at 160; *Brocklesby v Temperance Permanent Building Society* [1895] AC 173; *Rimmer v Webster* [1902] 2 Ch 163; *Abigail v Lapin* [1934] AC 491.

I should think it very inexpedient now to treat it as a question open to discussion whether the law has or has not been correctly laid down on this subject, for I consider it to have been established beyond doubt that the law is, that the person having the legal estate without the title deeds is not to be postponed to a subsequent incumbrancer having the title deeds, unless he has been guilty of something which the law calls fraud or gross negligence. I agree that this rule may very often lead to great hardships on persons who have taken conveyances relying on the possession of the title deeds as evidence of unincumbered ownership in the conveying party. Such, however, is the law, and I must act upon it until it is otherwise settled. Still, if the present case had involved that principle, I should have taken time to consider my judgment, for it is difficult in each particular case to say what amounts to negligence, and still more is it difficult to say what constitutes negligence with the epithet of gross connected with it.

In my opinion no such question arises in the present case. I do not think there was here any fraud or any negligence, for I do not believe that any of the parties to the transaction of January 1848 intended that the mortgage then taken should interfere with any subsequent dealings for value which *Attwood* might have with his estate. If the parties did so intend, the transaction was a gross fraud on the part of *Attwood* and his solicitor, and of the ladies also, if they understood it.

The case is that: Mr *Attwood* was a single man advanced in life, and living with two of his sisters, who were not young. He managed all their affairs. He was indebted to each of his three sisters, the two who lived with him and another who was married, in the sum of 10,000*l* each. At the end of 1847 and the beginning of 1848 he was pressed by creditors who were insisting on payment of large sums of money, amounting altogether to above 15,000*l*. He proposed to give them a mortgage, they refused it, and insisted on having payment of the money. That took place in the early part of *January* 1848. I do not go into the details of the evidence, but there were angry discussions going on and actions brought; and pending these proceedings, after issue of the writs and the delivery of pleas in the actions, Mr *Attwood* executed the deed in question, for giving a security to his three sisters for the 30,000*l* that he owed to them, but intentionally did not give them the title deeds. ... What does that prove the purport of the transaction to have been? That this security was given either with the intention (to put the worse construction on the conduct of the parties) that the ladies should have a pocket security of which they could avail themselves afterwards, when those who were to claim under subsequent conveyances by Mr *Attwood* should assert their rights, or (to adopt a more favourable, and I hope and believe the true construction) that the deed was never intended to be set up against any subsequent dealing with the property by Mr *Attwood* by way of mortgage, the title deeds being returned to him to be dealt with as he thought fit. I think it is clear. ... that at this time it was contemplated by all parties that Mr *Attwood* should raise money to pay off the creditors by whom he was then being sued. Taking that to be the intention, I agree with the view of the Master of the Rolls, in every part of whose judgment in this cause I entirely concur, that if a person taking a legal mortgage chooses to leave the deeds with the mortgagor, not through negligence or through fraud, but with the intention of enabling him to raise a sum of 15,000*l*, which is to take precedence of the legal mortgage, the mortgagee cannot, as against subsequent mortgagees, complain if, instead of 15,000*l* the mortgagor raises 50,000*l*, because he has himself put it into his power to raise any sum of money he pleases. That is the true nature of this transaction. It is not a case in which there was any negligence. It is not a case, as I am willing to believe, in which there was any fraud, but it is a case in which the mortgagees did deliberately and intentionally leave the deeds in the hands of the mortgagor, in order that he might raise money. To hold that a person who advances money on an estate, the title deeds of which are under such circumstances left in the hands of the mortgagor, is not to have preference, would be to shut our eyes to the plainest equity.

In **Clarke v Palmer** (1882) 21 ChD 124, the first mortgagee X failed to obtain possession of the deeds. Part of the property was then mortgaged to Y who believed that he was the first mortgagee, and the whole of the property to Z, who knew of Y, but not of X. HALL V-C held that both Y and Z took priority over X; X's negligence had brought the principle of *Perry Herrick v Attwood* into play.

3. GROSS NEGLIGENCE

WALKER v LINOM
[1907] 2 Ch 104 (ChD, PARKER J)

In 1896 Walker conveyed land to trustees to be held on the trusts of his marriage settlement. The title deeds, with the exception of the conveyance to Walker, were handed over to the trustees, who were solicitors and who negligently failed to discover the omission.

Walker subsequently mortgaged the land to X, who sold it to Y. On the question (inter alia) of the competing claims of the trustees and the purchaser.

Held. The trustees by their negligence were postponed to the equitable interest of the purchaser.

PARKER J reviewed in detail the judgment of FRY LJ in *Northern Counties of England Fire Insurance Co v Whipp* (1884) 26 ChD 482, and continued:

The conclusion he ultimately arrives at is that in order to postpone a prior legal to a subsequent equitable estate there must be fraud as apart from negligence, and this conclusion is stated in language wide enough to cover cases of postponement based upon the conduct of the holder of the legal estate in not getting possession of the title deeds as well as cases of postponement based upon the conduct of such holder in dealing with the title deeds after he has got them. It would seem at first sight that the Lord Justice uses the word 'fraud' throughout this judgment as connoting a dishonest intent, notwithstanding that in the case of fraud to be gathered from conduct in relation to not getting in the title deeds he refers to such cases as *Le Neve v Le Neve* (1747) Amb 436 and *Ratcliffe v Barnard* (1871) 6 Ch App 652.

Now, as I have already said, I cannot under the circumstances of this case find that anyone concerned in the 1896 settlement, with the exception of George Church Walker, acted otherwise than honestly, and, if I treat Fry LJ's judgment as meaning that in no case can a prior legal estate be postponed to a subsequent equitable estate without the existence of fraud in its ordinary common law sense as necessarily connoting a dishonest intention, I must hold that the trustees are not postponed. There are, however, subsequent cases which suggest that at any rate in cases of postponement, based on no inquiry having been made for the deeds, fraud is not necessary. It is, for example, clear from the case of *Oliver v Hinton* [1899] 2 Ch 264, p. 906, ante that a purchaser obtaining the legal estate, but making no inquiry for the deeds, or making inquiry and failing to take reasonable means to verify the truth of the excuse made for not producing them or handing them over, is, although perfectly honest, guilty of such negligence as to make it inequitable for him to rely on his legal estate so as to deprive a prior incumbrancer of his priority. In this case Lindley MR disapproves of the passage in the judgment of James LJ, in *Ratcliffe v Barnard*, quoted by Fry LJ in *Northern*

Counties of England Fire Insurance Co v Whipp, and distinctly says that to deprive a purchaser for value without notice of a prior equitable incumbrance of the benefit of the legal estate it is not essential that he should have been guilty of fraud. And Sir F. H. Jeune, referring also to the judgment of James LJ in *Ratcliffe v Barnard*, comes to the conclusion that the word 'fraud', as there used, did not mean such conduct as would justify a jury or judge in finding that there had been actual fraud, but such conduct as would justify the Court of Chancery in concluding that there had been fraud in some artificial sense. Similarly in *Berwick & Co v Price* [1905] 1 Ch 632 at 640, Joyce J says: 'The omission by a purchaser to investigate the title or to require delivery or production of the title-deeds is not to my mind either fraudulent or culpable, nor does it, since the judgment of Lindley MR in *Oliver v Hinton*, seem necessary to characterize it by any such epithet; but the consequence of such omission or wilful ignorance is that it is held to be unjust to prefer the purchaser to the previous mortgagee who has the deeds although such mortgage be equitable and the purchaser have the legal estate.'

In both the cases last referred to the question was between a prior equitable and a subsequent legal estate, and I think the later case was actually decided on constructive or imputed notice. But the Master of the Rolls expressly refused to decide *Oliver v Hinton* on any such ground. The question, however, arises whether the principle laid down in *Oliver v Hinton* is equally applicable between the holder of the legal estate who has omitted to make inquiry for the title deeds and a subsequent equitable estate the creation of which has been rendered possible by such omission. In my opinion any conduct on the part of the holder of the legal estate in relation to the deeds which would make it inequitable for him to rely on his legal estate against a prior equitable estate of which he had no notice ought also to be sufficient to postpone him to a subsequent equitable estate the creation of which has only been rendered possible by the possession of deeds which but for such conduct would have passed into the possession of the owner of the legal estate. This must, I think, have been the opinion of Fry LJ in *Northern Counties of England Fire Insurance Co v Whipp* (1884) 26 Ch D 482; for he explains both *Worthington v Morgan* (1849) 16 Sim 547 and *Clarke v Palmer* (1882) 21 Ch D 124, as based upon the same sort of fraud. I do not think, therefore, that there is anything in the authorities to preclude me from holding, and I accordingly hold, that the trustees, although they have the legal estate, are postponed to the defendant.

———

In **Grierson v National Provincial Bank** [1913] 2 Ch 18, George Franklin, a leaseholder, deposited his lease with Grant and Maddison's Bank as security for a loan. Later, he granted a legal mortgage to Grierson which was expressly stated to be subject to the prior equitable mortgage.

Franklin then redeemed the equitable mortgage, recovered the lease, and deposited it with the defendant bank as security for a further loan. The defendant Bank knew nothing of the legal mortgage.

JOYCE J held that Grierson, the legal mortgagee, retained his priority.

ii. MORTGAGES OF EQUITABLE INTERESTS IN PURE PERSONALTY

The priority of mortgages and assignments of interests in pure personalty (including interests under a trust for sale)[19] depended before 1926 upon the

---

[19]   *Lee v Howlett* (1856) 2 K & J 531.

order in which notice was received by the legal owner of the personalty (i.e. usually by the trustees); however, a mortgagee who had actual or constructive notice of a prior mortgage when he lent his money could not gain priority by giving his notice first. The rule in *Dearle v Hall* was made applicable in 1925 to mortgages of all equitable interests, in land as well as pure personalty.

(a) The Rule in Dearle v Hall

DEARLE v HALL[20]
(1823) 3 Russ 1 (Sir Thomas PLUMER MR), affirmed (1827) 3 Russ 48 (Lord LYNDHURST LC)

Zachariah Brown was entitled under his father's will to a life interest in a fund which produced £93 per annum. In 1808, he sold to William Dearle an annuity of £37 to be paid out of this life interest, and charged upon it. In 1809, he assigned in a similar manner an annuity of £27 to Sherring. In 1812, he sold his life interest in the whole £93 to Hall. Hall's solicitors made all proper enquiries about Brown's title, and obtained no information concerning the prior assignments. Hall gave notice to the executors of the assignment to him. Later the executors of Brown's father's will learned of the assignments and refused to pay interest until the claimants' rights should be ascertained.

Held. The assignment to Hall took priority.

SIR THOMAS PLUMER MR: It is observable, in the first place, that the right which *Zachariah Brown* had under the will of his father was simply a right to a chose in action. The legal interest in the residue was vested in the executrix and executors. … Wherever it is intended to complete the transfer of a chose in action, there is a mode of dealing with it which a court of equity considers tantamount to possession, namely, notice given to the legal depository of the fund. Where a contract, respecting property in the hands of other persons, who have a legal right to the possession, is made behind the back of those in whom the legal interest is thus vested, it is necessary, if the security is intended to attach on the thing itself, to lay hold of that thing in the manner in which its nature permits it to be laid hold of—that is, by giving notice of the contract to those in whom the legal interest is. By such notice, the legal holders are converted into trustees for the new purchaser, and are charged with responsibility towards him; and the *cestui que trust* is deprived of the power of carrying the same security repeatedly into the market, and of inducing third persons to advance money upon it, under the erroneous belief that it continues to belong to him absolutely, free from incumbrance, and that the trustees are still trustees for him, and for no one else. That precaution is always taken by diligent purchasers and incumbrancers: if it is not taken, there is neglect; and it is fit that it should be understood that the solicitor, who conducts the business for the party advancing the money, is responsible for that neglect. The consequence of such neglect is, that the trustee of the fund remains ignorant of any alteration having taken place in the equitable

---

[20]   For comment on the rule (mostly adverse), see *Ward v Duncombe* [1893] AC 369; *Lyle v Rosher* [1959] 1 WLR 8, [1958] 3 All ER 597; *E Pfeiffer Weinkellerei-Weineinkauf GmbH & Co v Arbuthnot Factors Ltd* [1988] 1 WLR 150; *Rhodes v Allied Dunbar Pension Services Ltd* [1987] 1 WLR 1703, [1988] 1 All ER 524; (1989) 9 OJLS 513 (F. Oditah); *Compaq Computer Ltd v Abercorn Group Ltd* [1991] BCC 484, [1992] CLJ 19 (L. S. Sealy); *Australian Guaranteed Corpn (NZ) v CFC Commercial Finance* [1995] 1 NZLR 129; (1996) 112 LQR 215 (A. J. Oakley). For an analysis of the rule, see [1999] Conv 311 (J. de Lacey).

rights affecting it: he considers himself to be a trustee for the same individual as before, and no other person is known to him as his *cestui que trust*. The original *cestui que trust*, though he has in fact parted with his interest, appears to the world to be the complete equitable owner, and remains in the order, management and disposition of the property as absolutely as ever; so that he has it in his power to obtain, by means of it, a false and delusive credit. He may come into the market to dispose of that which he has previously sold; and how can those, who may chance to deal with him, protect themselves from his fraud? Whatever diligence may be used by a *puisne* incumbrancer or purchaser—whatever inquiries he may make in order to investigate the title, and to ascertain the exact state of the original right of the vendor, and his continuing right,—the trustees, who are the persons to whom application for information would naturally be made, will truly and unhesitatingly represent to all who put questions to them that the fund remains the sole absolute property of the proposed vendor. These inconveniences and mischiefs are the natural consequences of omitting to give notice to trustees; and they must be considered as foreseen by those who, in transactions of that kind, omit to give notice; for they are the consequences which in the experience of mankind usually follow such omissions. To give notice is a matter of no difficulty: and whenever persons, treating for a chose in action, do not give notice to the trustee or executor, who is the legal holder of the fund, they do not perfect their title; they do not do all that is necessary in order to make the thing belong to them in preference to all other persons; and they become responsible, in some respects, for the easily foreseen consequences of their negligence. …

The ground of this claim is priority of time. They rely upon the known maxim, borrowed from the civil law, which in many cases regulates equities—'*qui prior est in tempore, potior est in jure*'. If, by the first contract, all the thing is given, their remains nothing to be the subject of the second contract, and priority must decide. But it cannot be contended that priority in time must decide, where the legal estate is outstanding. For the maxim, as an equitable rule, admits of exception and gives way, when the question does not lie between bare and equal equities. If there appears to be, in respect of any circumstances independent of priority of time, a better title in the *puisne* purchaser to call for the legal estate, than in the purchaser who precedes him in date, the case ceases to be a balance of equal equities, and the preference, which priority of date might otherwise have given, is done away with and counteracted. The question here is,—not which assignment is first in date,—but whether there is not, on the part of *Hall*, a better title to call for the legal estate than *Dearle* or *Sherring* can set up? Or rather, the question is, Shall these Plaintiffs now have equitable relief to the injury of *Hall*?

What title have they shown to call on a court of justice to interpose on their behalf, in order to obviate the consequence of their own misconduct? All that has happened is owing to their negligence (a negligence not accounted for) in forbearing to do what they ought to have done, what would have been attended with no difficulty, and what would have effectually prevented all the mischief which has followed. Is the Plaintiff to be heard in a court of equity, who asks its interposition in his behoof, to indemnify him against the effects of his own negligence at the expense of another who had used all due diligence, and who, if he is to suffer loss, will suffer it by reason of the negligence of the very person who prays relief against him? The question here is not, as in *Evans v Bicknell* (1801) 6 Ves 174, whether a court of equity is to deprive the Plaintiffs of any right—whether it is to take from them, for instance, a legal estate, or to impose any charge upon them. It is simply, whether they are entitled to relief against their own negligence. They did not perfect their securities; a third party has innocently advanced his money, and has perfected his security as far as the nature of the subject permitted him: is this Court to interfere to postpone him to them?

They say, that they were not bound to give notice to the trustees; for that notice does not form part of the necessary conveyance of an equitable interest. I admit, that, if you mean to rely on contract with the individual, you do not need to give notice; from the moment of the contract, he, with whom you are dealing, is personally bound. But if you mean to go further, and to make your right attach upon the thing which is the subject of the contract, it is necessary to give notice; and, unless notice is given, you do not do that which is essential in all cases of transfer of personal property. The law of *England* has always been, that personal property passes by delivery of possession; and it is possession which determines the apparent ownership. If, therefore, an individual, who in the way of purchase or mortgage contracts with another for the transfer of his interest, does not divest the vendor or mortgagor of possession, but admits him to remain the ostensible owner as before, he must take the consequences which may ensue from such a mode of dealing. That doctrine was explained in *Ryall v Rowles* (1749) 1 Ves Sen 348 before Lord *Hardwicke* and three of the Judges. If you, having the right of possession, do not exercise that right, but leave another in actual possession, you enable that person to gain a false and delusive credit, and put it in his power to obtain money from innocent parties on the hypothesis of his being the owner of that which in fact belongs to you. The principle has been long recognised, even in courts of law. In *Twyne's* case (1602) 3 Co Rep 80b, one of the badges of fraud was, that the possession had remained in the vendor. Possession must follow right; and if you, who have the right, do not take possession, you do not follow up the title, and are responsible for the consequences.

(b) Circulus Inextricabilis

In **Re Wyatt** [1892] 1 Ch 188, the question arose whether notice to one of several trustees was a valid notice or not. The Court of Appeal established the rule that notice to one of several trustees was valid against incumbrancers who advanced money during the period of office of such trustee. This was held in spite of the argument of E. S. Ford, counsel for such an incumbrancer: 'Now take this case: A first mortgage is made, of which notice is given to A but not to B. Then a second mortgage is made, of which notice is given to both. A then dies, and a third mortgage is made, of which notice is given to B. The respondents say, that 1 has priority over 2. But unquestionably 2 is prior to 3, for in each case complete notice was given, and priority of dates much settle the matter. Now, according to *Re Hall* (1880) 7 LR Ir 180, 3 has priority over 1. If, therefore, the respondents are right, we get this circle: 1 prior to 2, 2 prior to 3, 3 prior to 1, which is a *reductio ad absurdum*; and this absurdity appears still more clearly where 1 is an absolute assignment, 2 is a mortgage, and 3 is an absolute assignment. If an assignee gives notice to all, he makes all his trustees. If he gives notice to one only, he makes only that one his trustee, and on his death the assignee has no longer a trustee and loses his priority.'

As to this, LINDLEY LJ, delivering the judgment of the Court (drawn up by FRY LJ), said at 209:

'The solution of the difficulty is probably to be found in the view that the third incumbrancer is subrogated to the rights of the first to the extent of his charge, and to that extent, and that extent only, can take in priority of the second incumbrancer, by which the latter sustains no injury, but that as to any excess of the amount claimed by the third incumbrancer, he comes in after the second, so that the fund would be distributed as follows. First, to the third incumbrancer to the extent of the claim of the first. Secondly, to the second incumbrancer. Thirdly, to the third incumbrancer to the extent to which he might remain unpaid after the money he had received whilst standing in the shoes of the first incumbrancer: see *Benham v Keane* (1861) 3 De GF & J 318 where a similar problem was similarly solved.'

Re Wyatt was affirmed by the House of Lords sub nom *Ward v Duncombe* [1893] AC 369 but there was no discussion of the solution of counsel's hypothetical case.[1]

B. After 1925

I. UNREGISTERED LAND

(a) Mortgages of Legal Estates

The system of priority of mortgages which is in operation at the present day is the creation of the legislation of 1925. The paucity of litigation on the subject suggests that the system has, on the whole, worked reasonably well; though it may be due more to the considerable rise in land prices than to the merits of the system. It is however open to certain theoretical objections which are fully explained elsewhere. No more will be attempted here than to give the statutory enactments on which the system is based.

LAW OF PROPERTY ACT 1925

13. Effect of possession of documents.—This Act shall not prejudicially affect the right or interest of any person arising out of or consequent on the possession by him of any documents relating to a legal estate in land, nor affect any question arising out of or consequent upon any omission to obtain or any other absence of possession by any person of any documents relating to a legal estate in land.

97. Priorities as between puisne mortgages.—Every mortgage affecting a legal estate in land made after the commencement of this Act, whether legal or equitable (not being a mortgage protected by the deposit of documents relating to the legal estate affected) shall rank according to its date of registration as a land charge pursuant to the Land Charges Act 1925.[2]

This section does not apply to mortgages or charges to which the Land Charges Act 1972 does not apply by virtue of section 14(3) of that Act (which excludes certain land charges created by instruments necessitating registration under the Land Registration Act 2002),[3] or to mortgages or charges of registered land[4] ...

---

[1] *Re Woodroffes (Musical Instruments) Ltd* [1986] Ch 366, [1985] 2 All ER 908; [1986] CLJ 25 (L. S. Sealy). See generally (1968) 32 Conv (NS) 325 (W. A. Lee); 71 Yale LJ 53 (G. Gilmore).

[2] Now LCA 1972.

[3] As substituted by LRA 2002, s. 133, Sch. 11, para. 2(1), (10).

[4] As amended by LCA 1972, s. 18(1), Sch. 3, para. 1, as substituted by LRA 1997, s. 4(1), Sch. 1, para. 3.

199. Restrictions on constructive notice.
   (1) (i) p. 45, ante.

LAND CHARGES ACT 1972

2. The register of land charges.
   (4) Class C, p. 32, ante.[5]

4. Effect of land charges and protection of purchasers.
   (5) p. 37, ante.

17. Interpretation.
   (1) p. 37, ante.

(b) Mortgages by companies

LAND CHARGES ACT 1972

3. Registration of land charges.—(7) and (8), p. 56, ante.

COMPANIES ACT 1985

396. Charges which have to be registered.—p. 57, ante.

(c) Mortgages of equitable interests

LAW OF PROPERTY ACT 1925

137. Dealings with life interests, reversions and other equitable interests.—
(1) The law applicable to dealings with equitable things in action which regulates the priority of competing interests therein, shall, as respects dealings with equitable interests in land, capital money, and securities representing capital money effected after the commencement of this Act, apply to and regulate the priority of competing interests therein.[6]
   This subsection applies whether or not the money or securities are in court.
   (2) (i) In the case of a dealing with an equitable interest in settled land, capital money or securities representing capital money, the persons to be served with notice of the dealing shall be the trustees of the settlement; and where the equitable interest is created by a derivative or subsidiary settlement, the persons to be served with notice shall be the trustees of that settlement.
   (ii) In the case of a dealing with an equitable interest in land subject to a trust of land, or the proceeds of the sale of such land, the persons to be served with notice shall be the trustees.[7]
   (iii) In any other case the person to be served with notice of a dealing with an equitable interest in land shall be the estate owner of the land affected.
   The persons on whom notice is served pursuant to this subsection shall be affected thereby in the same manner as if they had been trustees of personal property out of which the equitable interest was created or arose.

---

[5]   As to whether a protected equitable mortgage is registrable as an estate contract (Class C (iv)), see C & B, pp. 789–790; M & W, para. 19.129; Waldock, pp. 425–428; (1940) CLJ pp. 250–251 (R. E. Megarry); (1962) 26 Conv (NS), pp. 446–449 (R. G. Rowley); Williams, *Contract of Sale of Land*, p. 247; Fairest, *Mortgages* (2nd edn.), pp. 133–136; Fisher and Lightwood, para. 3.106.
[6]   For an analysis of the section, see [1993] Conv 22 (J. Howell).
[7]   As amended by TLATA 1996, s. 25(1), Sch. 3, para. 4(15).

This subsection does not apply where the money or securities are in court.

(3) A notice, otherwise than in writing, given to, or received by, a trustee after the commencement of this Act as respects any dealing with an equitable interest in real or personal property, shall not affect the priority of competing claims of purchasers in that equitable interest.

(4) Where, as respects any dealing with an equitable interest in real or personal property —

 (*a*) the trustees are not persons to whom a valid notice of the dealing can be given; or

 (*b*) there are no trustees to whom a notice can be given; or

 (*c*) for any other reason a valid notice cannot be served, or cannot be served without unreasonable cost or delay;

a purchaser may at his own cost require that —

 (i) a memorandum of the dealing be endorsed, written on or permanently annexed to the instrument creating the trust;

 (ii) the instrument be produced to him by the person having the possession or custody thereof to prove that a sufficient memorandum has been placed thereon or annexed thereto.

Such memorandum shall, as respects priorities, operate in like manner as if notice in writing of the dealing had been given to trustees duly qualified to receive the notice at the time when the memorandum is placed on or annexed to the instrument creating the trust.

(5) Where the property affected is settled land, the memorandum shall be placed on or annexed to the trust instrument and not the vesting instrument.

Where the property affected is land held subject to a trust of land,[8] the memorandum shall be placed on or annexed to the instrument whereby the equitable interest is created.

(6) Where the trust is created by statute or by operation of law, or in any other case where there is no instrument whereby the trusts are declared, the instrument under which the equitable interest is acquired or which is evidence of the devolution thereof shall, for the purposes of this section, be deemed the instrument creating the trust.

In particular, where the trust arises by reason of an intestacy, the letters of administration or probate in force when the dealing was effected shall be deemed such instrument.

(7) Nothing in this section affects any priority acquired before the commencement of this Act.

(8) Where a notice in writing of a dealing with an equitable interest in real or personal property has been served on a trustee under this section, the trustees from time to time of the property affected shall be entitled to the custody of the notice, and the notice shall be delivered to them by any person who for the time being may have the custody thereof; and subject to the payment of costs, any person interested in the equitable interest may require production of the notice.

(9) The liability of the estate owner of the legal estate affected to produce documents and furnish information to persons entitled to equitable interests therein shall correspond to the liability of a trustee for sale to produce documents and furnish information to persons entitled to equitable interests in the proceeds of sale of the land.[9]

---

8 As amended by TLATA 1996, s. 25(1), Sch. 3, para. 15.

9 This undermines *Low v Bouverie* [1891] 3 Ch 82. For the power to nominate a trust corporation to receive notices, see LPA 1925, s. 138: Law Reform Committee 23rd Report (The Powers and Duties of Trustees) 1982 (Cmnd 8733), paras. 2.17–2.24.

ii. REGISTERED LAND

Where there are registered charges on the same registered estate, they rank in priority as between themselves in the order shown on the register. [10] This was provided both by the Land Registration Act 1925 in section 29, and now by the Land Registration Act 2002 in section 48 (infra) and by the Land Registration Rules 2003, rules 101–103. The priority of equitable charges, however, depends upon the general rules of priority under sections 28–30 of the Land Registration Act 2002, p. 127 ante, where the order of priority is determined by the order in which the charges are created. [11]

LAND REGISTRATION ACT 2002

48 Registered charges

(1) Registered charges on the same registered estate, or on the same registered charge, are to be taken to rank as between themselves in the order shown in the register.

(2) Rules may make provision about—

(a) how the priority of registered charges as between themselves it to be shown in the register, and

(b) applications for registration of the priority of registered charges as between themselves.

LAND REGISTRATION RULES 2003

How ranking of registered charges as between themselves to be shown on register

101. Subject to any entry in the individual register to the contrary, for the purpose of section 48(1) of the Act the order in which registered charges are entered in an individual register shows the order in which the registered charges rank as between themselves.

Alteration of priority of registered charges

102.—(1) An application to alter the priority of registered charges, as between themselves, must be made by or with the consent of the proprietor or a person entitled to be registered as the proprietor of any registered charge whose priority is adversely affected by the alteration, but no such consent is required from a person who has executed the instrument which alters the priority of the charges.

(2) The registrar may accept a conveyancer's certificate confirming that the conveyancer holds any necessary consents.

(3) The registrar must make an entry in the register in such terms as the registrar considers appropriate to give effect to the application.

---

[10]   R & R, paras. 27.008–27.009. Law Commission Report on Land Registration in the Twenty-First Century 2001 (Law Com No 271); para 7.13–7.17; H & B, para, 103.

For the priority of overriding statutory charges, such as the legal aid charge under Legal Aid Act 1988, s. 16(b), see LRA 2002, s. 50; LRR 2003, rr. 105–106.

[11]   For priority involving liens by deposit of the land certificate under LRA 1925, see *Re White Rose Cottage* [1965] Ch 940, [1965] 1 All ER 11, p. 893, ante; (1966) 19 CLP 26 (E. C. Ryder); *Barclays Bank Ltd v Taylor* [1974] Ch 137, [1973] 1 All ER 752; (1973) 89 LQR 70 (P.V.B.); (1974) 124 NLJ 634 (S. Robinson) (1977) 93 LQR 541 (R. J. Smith) *Thames Guaranty Ltd v Campbell* [1985] QB 210; [1984] 2 All ER 585, p. 798, n. 4, ante.

C. Tacking and Further Advances[12]

I. UNREGISTERED LAND

LAW OF PROPERTY ACT 1925

94. Tacking and further advances.—(1) After the commencement of this Act, a prior mortgagee shall have a right to make further advances to rank in priority to subsequent mortgages (whether legal or equitable) —

(*a*) if an arrangement has been made to that effect with the subsequent mortgagees; or

(*b*) if he had no notice of such subsequent mortgages at the time when the further advance was made by him; or

(*c*) whether or not he had such notice as aforesaid, where the mortgage imposes an obligation on him to make such further advances.

This subsection applies whether or not the prior mortgage was made expressly for securing further advances.

(2) In relating to the making of further advances after the commencement of this Act a mortgagee shall not be deemed to have notice of a mortgage merely by reason that it was registered as a land charge ... if it was not so registered at the time when the original mortgage was created[13] or when the last search (if any) by or on behalf of the mortgagee was made, whichever last happened.

This subsection only applies where the prior mortgage was made expressly for securing a current account or other further advances.[14]

(3) Save in regard to the making of further advances as aforesaid, the right to tack is hereby abolished:

Provided that nothing in this Act shall affect any priority acquired before the commencement of this Act by tacking, or in respect of further advances made without notice of a subsequent incumbrance or by arrangement with the subsequent incumbrancer.

(4) This section applies to mortgages of land made before or after the commencement of this Act, but not to charges on registered land[15]

ii. REGISTERED LAND

There was no equivalent statutory code under the Land Registration Act 1925 which applied to tacking and further advances in relation to charges over registered land. 'The applicable law comprised the old common law rules of tacking that had been abolished in relation to unregistered land with a partial statutory gloss'.[16]

A statutory code is now set out in section 49 of the Land Registration Act 2002.[17] This contains a new provision in subsection (4) under which an agreement may be registered for the maximum amount secured by a charge. This will give the chargee priority over any later registered charges for the original loan and any further advances up to the maximum amount specified.

---

[12]   C & B, pp. 783–784, 795–797, 801; M & W, paras. 19.243–19.262; MM, pp. 530, 542–544. On tacking generally see *MacMillan Inc v Bishopsgate Trust (No. 3)* [1995] 1 WLR 978 at 1002–1005, [1995] 3 All ER 747, at 768–772, per MILLETT J. The doctrine is of reduced importance after 1925.

[13]   As substituted by LP(A) A 1926, s. 7 and Sch.

[14]   (1958) 22 Conv (NS) 44 (R. G. Rowley).

[15]   As amended by LRA 2002, s. 133, Sch. 11, para. 2(1), (9).

[16]   H & B, para. 4.12; R & R, paras. 27.014–27.015. See LRA 1925, s. 3.

[17]   H & B paras. 4.12–4.16; LRR 2002, rr. 107, 108, 109. Law Com Report on Land Registration for the Twenty-First Century 2001 (No 271), paras. 7.18–7.41

LAND REGISTRATION ACT 2002

49 Tacking and further advances

(1) The proprietor of a registered charge may make a further advance on the security of the charge ranking in priority to a subsequent charge if he has not received from the subsequent chargee notice of the creation of the subsequent charge.

(2) Notice given for the purposes of subsection (1) shall be treated as received at the time when, in accordance with rules, it ought to have been received.

(3) The proprietor of a registered charge may also make a further advance on the security of the charge ranking in priority to a subsequent charge if—

(a) the advance is made in pursuance of an obligation, and

(b) at the time of the creation of the subsequent charge the obligation was entered in the register in accordance with rules.

(4) The proprietor of a registered charge may also make a further advance on the security of the charge ranking in priority to a subsequent charge if—

(a) the parties to the prior charge have agreed a maximum amount for which the charge is security, and

(b) at the time of the creation of the subsequent charge the agreement was entered in the register in accordance with rules.

(5) Rules may—

(a) disapply subsection (4) in relation to charges of a description specified in the rules, or

(b) provide for the application of that subsection to be subject, in the case of charges of a description so specified, to compliance with such conditions as may be so specified.

(6) Except as provided by this section, tacking in relation to a charge over registered land is only possible with the agreement of the subsequent chargee.

QUESTIONS

1. Is it possible to postulate a principle governing the system of priority of mortgages after 1925?

2. To what extent do the pre-1926 rules of priorities of mortgages still apply? In particular:

(i) On what basis is priority calculated in the case of two mortgagees both claiming to be protected by deposit, and each having some of the deeds?

(ii) Is any significance now attached, in the issue of priority (whether in (i) above or otherwise) to the question whether a mortgage is legal or equitable?

(iii) Is a first mortgagee, legal or equitable, whose mortgage is protected by deposit of the title deeds and is unregistered, liable to be defeated by a later mortgagee who is given a 'reasonable' excuse for non-production of the title deeds?

3. Is it possible to find a satisfactory solution of the problem of the three mortgagees, each of whom has priority over the others? *Re Wyatt* [1892] 1 Ch 188, p. 914, ante; (1968) 32 Conv (NS) 325 (W. A. Lee); (1961) 71 Yale LJ 53 (G. Gilmore).

IX. Law Reform

Law Commission Report on Land Mortgages 1991 (Law Com. No. 204, HC 5).[18]

'The new mortgages

10.2 All existing methods of consensually mortgaging or charging interests in land should be abolished and replaced by new forms of mortgage (the formal land mortgage and the informal land mortgage) the attributes of which would be expressly defined by statute, and which would be the only permissible methods of mortgaging any interest in land, whether legal or equitable. (Paras. 2.20 to 2.30)

10.3 In principle, the rights, powers, duties and obligations of mortgagor and mortgagee under a land mortgage should be such as are appropriate for making the mortgaged property security for the performance of the mortgagor's obligations. (Paras. 3.2 and 6.1 to 6.3)

Variable and overriding provisions

10.4 The statutory provisions defining the rights, powers, duties and obligations of the parties to a land mortgage should be categorised as either "variable" or "overriding". Variable provisions should be variable or excludable, either directly by an express term of the mortgage or indirectly by necessary implication from any express term. Overriding provisions should apply notwithstanding any provision to the contrary contained in the mortgage or in any other instrument.[19] Any provision of a mortgagee or any other instrument should be void to the extent that it (i) purports to impose a liability which has the effect of allowing the mortgagee to escape or mitigate the consequences of an overriding provision, or to be reimbursed the consequences of complying with it or (ii) has the effect of preventing or discouraging the mortgagor or any other person from enforcing or taking advantage of an overriding provision. (Para. 3.3)

Requirement of good faith

10.5 The rights, remedies and powers of a mortgagee under a land mortgage should be expressly stated to be exercisable only in good faith and for the purposes of protecting or enforcing the security. This should apply to all the mortgagee's rights, remedies and powers, whether derived from statute, contract, or elsewhere. (Para. 3.4)

Creation of formal land mortgage

10.6 A formal land mortgage should not be valid unless made by deed, whether the property mortgaged is a legal estate or an equitable interest. No particular

---

[18] Appendix A of the Report contains a draft Bill. See [1992] Conv 69 (H. W. Wilkinson); (1992) 136 SJ 267, 292 (G. Frost). In March 1989 the Law Commission's Conveyancing Standing Committee published a consultation document suggesting the use of a new form of mortgage called a flexi-mortgage as a means of avoiding chains, cutting out delays and defeating gazumping. Its unique feature is that for a limited time it gives the borrower the right to extend the period of the mortgage on a property he is buying and increase the amount he borrows to cover the cost of an over-lapping sale and purchase. Payments under his old mortgage are suspended. This allows the house-owner to agree to buy a new property before selling his own by incurring only a small increase in mortgage interest and without increasing his capital repayments (Law Com. No. 190), para. 2.2. See also American Law Institute, *Restatement of the Law of Mortgages* (1996).

[19] For a summary of the overriding provisions, see para 5.8.

form of words should be necessary in order for it to be a valid formal land mortgage, provided the words used demonstrate an intention to make the mortgaged property security for performance of the mortgagor's obligations. As an additional requirement where the mortgagor's title to all or part of the mortgaged property is registered at H. M. Land Registry, the mortgage should not qualify as a formal land mortgage unless it is substantively registered against that title. (Paras. 3.5 to 3.8)

Informal land mortgage

10.7 Informal mortgages should be recognised, to the extent that any purported consensual security over an interest in land that does not constitute a formal land mortgage but would, in the present law, give rise to an equitable mortgage or charge, should take effect as an informal land mortgage, provided the formal requirements for the creation of an informal land mortgage (para. 10.9 below) are satisfied. (Paras. 3.6, 3.9, and 3.10)

10.8 A mortgagee under an informal land mortgage should have no right to enforce the security, nor to take any other action in relation to the mortgaged property, but should have a right to have the mortgage perfected by having a formal land mortgage granted to it. In the case of a protected mortgage (para. 10.16 below) the mortgagee should not be allowed to have the mortgage perfected without a court order; in all other cases a mortgagee who was able to procure perfection of the mortgage without recourse to the court (for example, by use of a power of attorney) should be entitled to do so. (Paras. 3.11 to 3.13 and 5.12)

10.9 An informal land mortgage should not be valid unless it is made by deed or it satisfies requirements equivalent to those set out in section 2 of the Law of Property (Miscellaneous Provisions) Act 1989, that is unless it is in writing signed by or on behalf of the parties to it and incorporating (either directly, or indirectly by reference to another document) all the terms expressly agreed between the parties. (Paras. 3.14 to 3.17, p. 67, ante)

All other consensual securities void

10.10 Any purported security interest that does not constitute a formal land mortgage or an informal land mortgage should be void (in the sense that, whilst the purported mortgagor remains personally liable to pay the debt or discharge the liabilities incurred, the purported mortgagee acquires no interest in the property and no right of recourse to it). This should not apply to non-consensual charges (that is, equitable charges arising by operation of law, statutory charges and liens): these are not affected by our recommendations. (Para. 2.6)

Protection and Priority

10.11 Where the mortgagor's title to the mortgaged property is registered at H. M. Land Registry, a formal land mortgage of that property should be substantively registrable. Unless and until registered it should take effect as an informal land mortgage. Once registered, it would constitute a registered charge for the purposes of the Land Registration Acts 1925 to 1988. As such, its priority would depend on the date of its registration. (Paras. 3.18 to 3.19; Schedule 1, paras. 9–15)

10.12 An informal land mortgage of a legal estate in registered land should be protectable by notice where the informal land mortgage is acknowledged by the registered proprietor. Otherwise, it should be protectable by caution. Protection by notice of deposit and notice of intended deposit should be abolished. The priority of informal land mortgages protected by notice or caution should, for the present, continue to be governed by the rules applicable to the priority of minor interests in the present law. (Paras. 3.20 and 3.21)

10.13 Formal and informal land mortgages of commercial equitable interests in registered land should be protectable by entry of notice or caution, but for the present, protection and priority of trust equitable interests should continue to be governed by the rule in *Dearle v Hall.* (Paras. 3.22 to 3.29, p. 912, ante)

10.14 In unregistered land all formal land mortgages of a legal estate or a commercial equitable interest should be registrable as Class C(i) land charges, and all informal land mortgages of a legal estate or a commercial equitable interest should be registrable as Class C(iii) land charges. Formal and informal mortgages of trust equitable interests should continue to be governed by the rule in *Dearle v Hall.* (Paras. 3.30 to 3.33, p. 32, ante)

10.15 Section 4(5) of the Land Charges Act 1972 should be amended to remove the possibility of insoluble priority circles arising where there are successive mortgages of the same property. (Para. 3.34, pp. 37, 914, ante)

Protected mortgages

10.16 There should be a class of protected mortgage consisting of all formal and informal land mortgages of any interest in land which includes a dwelling-house except those where either (*a*) the mortgagor is a body corporate, or (*b*) enforcement of the mortgage would not affect the occupation of the dwelling-house or (*c*) the dwelling-house is occupied under a service tenancy. (Part IV)

Standardisation

10.17 The front page of a protected mortgage should be in a form to be prescribed by regulations. ... (Paras. 5.1 to 5.11)

Rights and duties during the security

Interest rates

10.28 In all protected mortgages, a provision that purports to increase the rate of interest payable on default should be void. In all other mortgages, such a provision should be challengeable only under the general law relating to penalties or under the new general statutory jurisdiction to set aside or vary mortgage terms described in Part VIII of this Report. (Paras. 6.33 and 6.34)

10.29 In the case of all mortgages, the court should have jurisdiction to vary interest rates under the new general statutory jurisdiction described in Part VIII of this Report if the mortgage has become challengeable as a result of a variation of or failure to vary the rate of interest payable, even if under the mortgage the mortgagee is fully entitled to vary or not vary interest rates as it chooses. (Para. 6.36)

10.30 In the case of protected mortgages, the court should also be entitled to alter the interest rate payable, if satisfied by the mortgagor that the mortgagee has unreasonably varied or failed to vary the interest rate payable under the mortgage. In order to assess whether a variation or failure to vary is unreasonable, the court should be required to have particular regard to whether the difference between the rate complained of and the current market rate charged for loans made in equivalent circumstances is substantially greater than the difference between the rate originally charged and the then market rate. The Office of Fair Trading should have power to exempt specified lenders from these provisions. (Paras. 6.35 to 6.41)

Redemption

10.31 The equitable right to redeem the property free from the mortgage after the contractual redemption date by paying and discharging all obligations under it should apply to formal and informal mortgages as it applies to all other mortgages and charges. (para. 6.42, p. 803, ante)

10.32 In protected mortgages, any term of the mortgage which postpones the mortgagor's right to redeem should be void, unless the property includes non-residential premises. If it includes non-residential property, or the mortgage is not protected, then a postponement of the right to redeem should be challengeable only under the new general statutory jurisdiction described in Part VIII of this Report. (Para. 6.43(*a*))

Consolidation

10.35 In relation to all land mortgages the right to consolidate should be abolished. (Para. 6.44, p. 899, ante)

Enforcement of the Security

Sale

10.37 It should be a variable implied term of all formal land mortgages that the mortgagee has power to sell the mortgagor's interest in the mortgaged property, free from the mortgagee's own mortgage and from subsequent mortgages and other interests to which the mortgage has priority, but subject to all prior mortgages and interests taking priority over the mortgage. The power should not be exercisable unless a specified "enforceable event" has occurred and is still operative. This restriction on the exercise of the power of sale should be overriding and should also apply to the statutory power of sale varied or replaced by any contractual provisions. (Paras. 7.5 to 7.10, p. 872, ante)

10.38 If the mortgage is a protected mortgage, the mortgagee should not be entitled to exercise the power of sale without leave of the court. (Paras. 7.14 to 7.15)

10.39 In addition in the case of protected mortgages, before exercising the power of sale the mortgagee should first have served on the mortgagor an enforcement notice in prescribed form specifying the enforceable event on which the mortgagee relies and the action (if any) to be taken by the mortgagor to remedy any default. The enforcement notice should also explain the consequences of default and how to obtain help and advice. Once the mortgagor has taken the action required by the notice, or the enforceable event is no longer operative for some other reason, the power of sale should not be exercisable. (Paras. 7.11 to 7.13)

10.40 If the mortgagee exercises the power of sale after having been notified that the mortgagor has contracted to sell to someone else, the mortgagee should be liable to indemnify the mortgagor for any sum the mortgagor becomes liable to pay to a third party by reason of being unable to complete his sale contract. This should not apply if the mortgagee contracted to sell before receiving notice of the mortgagor's sale contract, or if it was reasonable for the mortgagee to sell, either because the mortgagor's contract was for sale at a price insufficient to pay off the mortgagee in full, and the mortgagee was able to sell at a higher price than the mortgagor's price, or because the mortgagor's sale was not completed within a reasonable time or because of some other reason. (Paras. 7.16 to 7.19)

10.41 A purchaser from a mortgagee purporting to sell in exercise of the power of sale should get a good title, provided there is a valid formal land mortgage and the purchaser is in good faith, unless the purchaser has notice that the power of sale is not exercisable or that the exercise is improper for some other reason. Notice should include constructive notice. (Paras. 7.20 and 7.21)

10.42 A mortgagee under a formal land mortgage should be entitled to exercise the power of sale by selling the property to itself, provided leave of the court is first obtained. The court should not grant leave unless satisfied that sale to the mortgagee is the most advantageous method of realising the security. (Paras. 7.22 and 7.27, p. 880, ante)

10.43 A mortgagee and a receiver appointed under a formal land mortgage should have an overriding duty (owed to the mortgagor, to any guarantors of the mortgagor, and to any subsequent mortgagees) to take reasonable care to ensure that on a sale the price is the best price that can reasonably be obtained. (Para. 7.23, p. 875, ante)

10.44 After paying off prior encumbrances, the mortgagee should hold the proceeds of sale on trust to be applied first in payment of the costs of sale, secondly in paying off everything due under the mortgage, and thirdly to be paid to the person next entitled (that is the subsequent encumbrancers or, if none, the mortgagor). (Para. 7.25)

Foreclosure

10.45 The remedy of foreclosure should be abolished. (Paras. 7.26 and 7.27, p. 895, ante)

Possession

10.46 In all formal land mortgages there should be an implied overriding provision that the mortgagee is entitled to take possession of the mortgaged property when it is reasonably necessary to do so to enable the property to be sold pursuant to the mortgagee's power of sale. Once in possession the mortgagee should be under an overriding duty to sell as quickly as is consonant with the duty to take reasonable care to ensure that on sale the price is the best price that can reasonably be obtained. (Paras. 7.28 to 7.30, p. 835, ante)

10.47 In protected mortgages the mortgagee should not be entitled to possession without serving an enforcement notice and obtaining a court order. The court making an order for possession should have discretion to order that interest payable under the mortgage should cease to accrue twelve weeks (or such other period as the court thinks fit) after the execution of the order for possession. Similar provisions should apply if the mortgagor leaves voluntarily in response to a demand for possession from the mortgagee. In both cases the mortgagee should be free to apply to the court for an extension of time at any stage. The Secretary of State should have power by order to vary the period of twelve weeks. (Paras. 7.31 to 7.35)

10.48 In formal land mortgages which are not protected, the mortgagee should also have a right to take possession of the property when it is reasonably necessary to do so in order to preserve its value. Once in possession, the mortgagee should be entitled to remain there only for so long as is reasonable, given that the purpose of being there is to preserve the value of the property. (Para. 7.36(*a*) and (*b*))

10.49 A mortgagee under a protected mortgage should have no right to take possession of the property for the purpose of preserving its value unless the property includes non-residential property. If non-residential property is included the mortgagee should be entitled to apply to the court for possession for this purpose: the court should be entitled to make an order affecting the non-residential part only on the same grounds as if it were a non-protected mortgage, but should not be entitled to make an order affecting the residential part unless satisfied that it would not otherwise be possible to preserve the value of the property. The court making an order for possession for this purpose should have the same discretion to order that interest should cease to accrue as if possession was for sale, and the same should apply if the mortgagor leaves voluntarily in response to a demand for possession from the mortgagee. (Para. 7.36(*c*), (*d*) and (*e*))

10.50 A mortgagee who is in possession, for whatever purpose, should have a duty to repair (para. 10.22 above) and a liability to account. The liability to account should not apply during a period when interest has ceased to accrue. (Paras. 6.14 and 7.37 to 7.38)

Appointment of a receiver

10.51 It should be a variable implied term of a formal land mortgage that the mortgagee should have power to appoint a receiver of the income of the property who should be the agent of the mortgagor. (Paras. 7.39 to 7.41, p. 893, ante)

10.52 The power should be exercisable only in circumstances in which the power of sale would be exercisable. ... (Para. 7.42)

Jurisdiction of the court on enforcement

10.55 In the case of a formal land mortgage which is not protected if a mortgagee applies to the court for an order to enforce or protect the security, the court should have no specific powers to delay or withhold the remedy requested once the mortgagee has established that the right to take the appropriate action is available and has become exercisable. (Paras. 7.48 and 7.49)

10.56 On an application by a mortgagee to protect or enforce a protected mortgage, or for payment of sums due under a protected mortgage, the court should have powers equivalent to those currently applicable to residential mortgages by virtue of Part IV of the Administration of Justice Act 1970, p. 861, ante, and the Consumer Credit Act 1974, p. 846, ante. In addition, it should have power to order the mortgagee to accept re-scheduled payments in some circumstances, and it should be allowed to consider whether any of the terms of the mortgage ought to be set aside or varied. It should not have power to refuse or delay an enforcement order on the ground that a tenant of the mortgagor whose tenancy is not binding on the mortgagee has offered to pay all sums due under the mortgage, nor should it have power to order that the mortgagor's interest should be transferred to such a tenant. (Paras. 7.48 to 7.59, p. 846, ante)

Jurisdiction to set aside or vary terms of the mortgage

10.57 There should be a new statutory jurisdiction for the court to set aside or vary terms of a land mortgage. The new jurisdiction should be in addition to the court's general law powers to set aside terms or bargains on grounds such as fraud, mistake, rectification, estoppel, undue influence, or restraint of trade. The equitable jurisdiction to set aside a term of a land mortgage which constitutes a clog or fetter on the equity of redemption should be abolished in so far as it relates to land mortgages, and the extortionate credit bargain provisions of the Consumer Credit Act 1974 should be amended so that they no longer apply to credit bargains secured by a land mortgage. (Paras. 8.1 to 8.4 and 8.8)

10.58 Under the new jurisdiction the court should have power to set aside or vary any term of a mortgage with a view to doing justice between the parties if (*a*) principles of fair dealing were contravened when the mortgage was granted, or (*b*) the effect of the terms of the mortgage is that the mortgagee now has rights substantially greater than or different from those necessary to make the property adequate security for the liabilities secured by the mortgage, or (*c*) the mortgage requires payments to be made which are exorbitant, or (*d*) the mortgage includes a postponement of the right to redeem. (Paras. 8.4 and 8.5)

10.59 In deciding whether to exercise its powers on grounds (*b*) or (*d*) the court should discount the fact that the terms were freely negotiated between the parties, but in such circumstances should have a discretion to order the mortgagor to compensate the mortgagee. Otherwise, the powers the court should have under the new jurisdiction, and the factors it ought to take into account should be analogous to those now contained in the extortionate credit bargain provisions of the Consumer Credit Act 1974. (Paras. 8.6 to 8.8)

Miscellaneous matters

Tacking of further advances

10.60 Section 94 of the Law of Property Act 1925 should be amended to make it clear (*a*) that registration of a later mortgage under the Companies Act 1989 does not constitute notice of it to an earlier mortgagee seeking to tack advances made after the creation of the later mortgage, and (*b*) that a mortgagee who is under an obligation to make further advances remains entitled to rely on section 94 despite any default by the mortgagor releasing the mortgagee from the obligation. (Paras. 9.3 to 9.4, p. 918, ante)

10.61 It should be made clear in section 30 of the Land Registration Act 1925 that where it is noted on the register that a charge contains an obligation to make further advances, subsequent charges that are unregistered, as well as those that are registered, will take subject to any such further advances made. (Para. 9.5)

Land mortgages and the Consumer Credit Act 1974

10.62 The Consumer Credit Act 1974 should continue to apply to land mortgages in so far as it regulates the carrying on of mortgage lending business, but no longer apply in so far as it regulates form and content of mortgages and their enforcement. (Para. 9.6, p. 846, ante)'

In 1998 the Government decided not to implement the Report due to lack of support, and invited the Law Commission to reconsider its proposals: Law Commission Thirty-Third Annual Report (Law Com No. 258), para. 1.10.

The Law Commission Report on Limitation of Actions 2001 (Law Com No. 270) makes recommendations on limitation and claims relating to mortgages and other charges in paras. 4.158–4.196. These are summarised at pp. 244, ante.

Part Four. Control of Land

12. Covenants Between Freeholders [1]

I. Introduction

In considering to what extent covenants between freeholders may be enforced between persons who were not original parties to the covenant, two main distinctions must be made. First, different rules apply to the 'running' of the benefit and the 'running' of the burden. And, secondly, in connection both with the burden and the benefit, the rules of common law are different from those of equity. This is most marked in connection with the running of the burden, where the decision in equity of *Tulk v Moxhay* in 1848 [2] provided the basis of the modern doctrine. The common law rules for the running of the benefit are still applicable, but they have been further developed in equity [3] and by statute. [4] The burden and the benefit will be considered separately.

The common law rules for the running of the benefit are ancient. As with every case of a covenant running at common law, the covenant ran with the estate of the covenantee and not with the land, [5] and it was necessary for the assignee of the covenantee to show that he had the same legal estate as the original

---

[1]   C & B, chap. 20; Gray, pp. 1133–1198; M & W, chap. 16; MM, pp. 453–473; Smith, chap. 21; Preston and Newsom, *Restrictive Covenants Affecting Freehold Land* (8th edn. 1999) Scamell, *Land Covenants* (1996); Francis, *Restrictive Covenants and Freehold Land: A Practical Guide* (1999); Elphinstone, *Covenants Affecting Land* (1946); Farrand (2nd edn. 1973), pp. 404–429; Maitland, pp. 162–178. For a historical account, see Simpson, *History of the Land Law* (2nd edn. 1986), pp. 116–118, 140–141, 256–259.

[2]   (1848) 2 Ph 774, p. 942, post.

[3]   See p. 959, post.

[4]   LPA 1925, s. 78, p. 959, post. See also Contracts (Rights of Third Parties) Act 1999, p. 76, ante.

[5]   For covenants in leases, see pp. 560 et seq., ante.

covenantee. [6] Equity, both with the benefit and the burden, developed a different concept of a covenant running with the land, and avoided the requirement that the assignee of the covenantee or convenantor should hold the same estate as his assignor. [7]

These factors have to be considered when the question is whether or not an assignee of the covenantee can sue. He may be able to do so under the common law rules alone, as where there is no servient land; [8] or he may have to rely on the further developments in equity and under statute. [9]

As indicated, the rules relating to the running of the burden of a covenant between freeholders are almost exclusively equitable. The origin of the rule is the equitable principle that a person cannot come to property with knowledge that a contract affecting the property is in existence and then ignore it. But there has been much development from the general principle in the case of restrictive covenants affecting land. [10] It is not in the general interest to allow burdens to be attached to land unless there is some corresponding benefit to be protected. And a covenant enforceable between adjoining freeholders is now looked upon as an interest which imposes a burden on one piece of land and confers a benefit on another; as something in the nature of an equitable negative easement. [11]

This branch of equity grew with the great era of suburban development in the 19th century; control was in the hands of individual landowners. But, since the 1930s, this type of control has been largely superseded by public control in the hands of planning authorities exercised in the public interest. [12] The development or change of user of land may now only be carried out after planning permission has been obtained. Public planning control has thus overtaken the earlier method, both in influence and complexity. But the law relating to covenants between freeholders is still operative. The two methods of control are sometimes complementary, sometimes contrary. They are cumulative, and a purchaser must satisfy himself in respect of both forms of restriction. [13]

It has always been clear that no covenant will run with the land unless it touches and concerns the land. This requirement exists also in connection with covenants between landlord and tenant, and has been discussed in that connection. [14] An additional point of importance here is the view current before 1926 that Real Property

---

[6]   See p. 866, post; *Smith and Snipes Hall Farm Ltd v River Douglas Catchment Board* [1949] 2 KB 500, [1949] 2 All ER 179.

[7]   See p. 867, post; *Tichbone v Weir* (1892) 67 LT 735; *Re Nisbet and Potts' Contract* [1906] 1 Ch 386.

[8]   *The Prior's Case* (1368) YB 42 Edw 3, fo 3A, pl. 14, discussed under *Spencer's Case* (1583) 5 Co Rep 16a; Smith's *Leading Cases* (13th edn. 1929), vol. I, pp. 51, 65, 73; *Smith and Snipes Hall Farm Ltd v River Douglas Catchment Board*, supra, per TUCKER: LJ at 506, at 183.

[9]   LPA 1925, s. 78(1); *Federated Homes Ltd v Mill Lodge Properties Ltd* [1980] 1 WLR 594, [1980] 1 All ER 371, p. 959, post; *Roake v Chadha* [1984] 1 WLR 40, [1983] 3 All ER 503, p. 963, post.

[10]   For the operation of this principle in the case of chattels, see Cheshire, Fifoot and Furmston *Law of Contract* (14th edn.) pp. 516–579; Treitel, *Law of Contract* (11th edn.), pp. 619–625.

[11]   *London and South Western Rly Co v Gomm* (1882) 20 ChD 562, p. 946, post; *LCC v Allen* [1914] 3 KB 642, p. 943, post; *Formby v Barker* [1903] 2 Ch 539, p. 944, post; *Re Nisbet and Potts' Contract* [1906] 1 Ch 386, p. 947, post.

[12]   Town and Country Planning Act 1990; Planning (Listed Buildings and Conservation Areas) Act 1990; Planning (Hazardous Substances) Act 1990; Planning (Consequential Provisions) Act 1990; Land Compensation Acts 1961, 1973; Compulsory Purchase Act 1965; Planning and Compensation Act 1991; Acquisition of Land Act 1981; Planning and Compulsory Purchase Act 2004; C & B, chaps. 30, 31; M & W, paras. 22.009–22.061; MM, pp. 1012–1014, post.

[13]   (1964) 28 Conv (NS) 190 (A. R. Mellows).

[14]   See p. 561, ante. The position in connection with covenants between freeholders is not exactly the same, for in this situation there are two pieces of land involved. Preston and Newsom, paras. 2.30 to 2.38; *Rogers v Hosegood* [1900] 2 Ch 388, p. 957, post; *Formby v*

Act 1845 section 5 (under which the benefit of a covenant in an indenture may be given to a person who was not a party to the indenture) applied only to cases of covenants which ran with the land. [15] This section is now repealed and replaced by Law of Property Act 1925, section 56, which has been said to be free from such restriction. The question whether a particular covenant touches and concerns the land is, therefore, not material in deciding whether the benefit of it can be given to a person not a party to it; it is material in deciding whether the benefit of the covenant so given will run with the land of the person to whom it was given.

This branch of the law is particularly concerned with covenants between freeholders. Covenants between landlord and tenant have already been discussed, and are governed by rules of their own. Where, however, a covenant between landlord and tenant is not enforceable under those special rules, it may, nevertheless, be enforceable under the rules discussed in this section where they are applicable. [16]

Finally, it will be seen that the law relating to the passing of the benefit of restrictive covenants has become difficult and technical. But there is a tendency now to escape from many of the technicalities. This is shown by recent decisions in the context of annexation of the benefit of a covenant to the land of the covenantee, [17] and also in connection with schemes of development. [18] 'The tendency is ... to assimilate the law of covenants to the law of easements, where no formalities are required for establishing the right as appurtenant to the dominant tenement'. [19] This policy, as will be seen, is a feature of the Law Commission Report in 1984 on the Law of Positive and Restrictive Covenants. [20]

II. The Burden [1]

A. Common Law

i. THE GENERAL RULE

The general rule is that the burden of a covenant affecting land does not run with the land at common law. This is a basic principle, the existence of which

---

Barker [1903] 2 Ch 539 at 554; *Dyson v Forster* [1909] AC 98; *Smith and Snipes Hall Farm Ltd v River Douglas Catchment Board* [1949] 2 KB 500 at 506, [1949] 2 All ER 179 at 193, p. 951, post; *Newton Abbot Co-operative Society Ltd v Williamson and Treadgold Ltd* [1952] Ch 286, [1952] 1 All ER 279, p. 972, post; *Federated Homes Ltd v Mill Lodge Properties Ltd* [1980] 1 WLR 594, [1980] 1 All ER 371, p. 959, post. The distinction is not kept clear by LINDLEY LJ in *Austerberry v Oldham Corpn* (1885) 29 ChD 750 at 781.

[15] *Kelsey v Dodd* (1881) 52 LJ Ch 34 at 39; *Forster v Elvet Colliery Co Ltd* [1908] 1 KB 629; affd sub nom *Dyson v Foster* [1909] AC 98; *Westhoughton UDC v Wigan Coal and Iron Co Ltd* [1919] 1 Ch 159; *Re Ecclesiastical Comrs for England's Conveyance* [1936] Ch 430, p. 994, post; *Amsprop Trading Ltd v Harris Distribution Ltd* [1997] 1 WLR 1025, [1997] 2 All ER 990, p. 998, post.

[16] *Hall v Ewin* (1887) 37 ChD 74, p. 939, n. 15, post; *Patman v Harland* (1881) 17 ChD 353, p. 559, ante.

[17] *Federated Homes Ltd v Mill Lodge Properties Ltd*, supra; *Roake v Chadha* supra.

[18] *Re Dolphin's Conveyance* [1970] Ch 654, [1970] 2 All ER 664, p. 984, post. The enforceability of obligations in respect of freehold flats is now possible under the Commonhold and Leasehold Reform Act 2002, p. 938, post.

[19] (1972 B) 31 CLJ 157 at 163 (H. W. R. Wade).

[20] Law Commission Report on the Law of Positive and Restrictive Covenants 1984 (Law Com No. 127, HC 201), p. 1015, post.

[1] C & B, pp. 667–678; Gray, pp. 1153–1161; M & W, paras. 16.017–16.029; MM, pp. 462–471; Smith, pp. 527–530, 538–542.

has necessitated the development in equity of the doctrine of restrictive covenants. The rule is one of the many results of the wider principle of privity of contract, that a person may neither sue upon nor be made liable upon a contract unless he is a party to it. If, for instance, A sold Whiteacre, part of his land, to B who covenanted with A to lay out pleasure gardens on Whiteacre, A could sue B at law for damages if B refused to perform the covenant; but if B sold or gave the land to C, C could not be made liable on the covenant, because he was not a party to it. This is a matter of the greatest importance because, apart from cases in which specific performance will be decreed, equity only interferes, as will be seen, where the covenant is 'restrictive'. Positive covenants are therefore not enforceable by an action for damages against an assignee of the covenantor.

It is questionable whether the policy behind such a rule is satisfactory, for it often has the effect of leaving a covenantee without a remedy. The matter was considered in 1965 by the Wilberforce Committee which recommended that, subject to certain conditions, the burden of positive covenants should run, and again in 1984 by the Law Commission on the wider topic of both Positive and Restrictive Covenants. [2] The rule does not exist in such absolute form in most of the United States. [3] It is, however, possible in England to effect the observance of a positive covenant in other ways. [4] And, under the Commonhold and Leasehold Reform Act 2002, the burden of a positive covenant may run by statute. [5]

RHONE v STEPHENS
[1994] 2 AC 310, [1994] 2 All ER 65 (HL, Lords TEMPLEMAN, OLIVER OF AYLMERTON, WOOLF, LLOYD OF BERWICK and NOLAN) [6]

Walford House and Walford Cottage were in common ownership until 1990 when Walford Cottage was sold. The vendor covenanted to keep the common roof which covered part of Walford Cottage in wind and water tight condition. The question arose whether the covenant was enforceable against the owners of Walford House.

Held. The covenant was not enforceable

LORD TEMPLEMAN: In the *Austerberry* case (1885) 29 ChD 750 the owners of a site of a road covenanted that they and their successors in title would make the road and keep it in repair. The road was sold to the defendants and it was held that the repair covenant could not be enforced against them ...

For over 100 years it has been clear and accepted law that equity will enforce negative covenants against freehold land but has no power to enforce positive covenants against successors in title of the land. To enforce a positive covenant would be to enforce a personal obligation against a person who has not

---

[2]   Report of the Committee on Positive Covenants Affecting Land (1965) Cmnd 2719; Law Commission Report on Restrictive Covenants 1967 (Law Com No. 11); Law Commission Report on Positive and Restrictive Covenants 1984 (Law Com No. 127, HC 201). See also (1972 B) 31 CLJ 157 (H. W. R. Wade).

[3]   Clark, *Real Covenants* (2nd edn. 1947), pp. 231–232; (1943) 52 Yale LJ 699; (1945) 30 Cornell LQ 378; American Restatement (1944) Property: vol. 5, Servitudes, chap. 45.

[4]   *Brewster v Kitchell* (1698) 12 Mod Rep 166 at 169; *Morland v Cook* (1868) LR 6 Eq 252; *Aspden v Seddon* (1876) 1 Ex D 496; *Austerberry v Oldham Corpn* (1885) 29 ChD 750 per LINDLEY LJ at 781; *South Eastern Rly Co v Associated Portland Cement Manufacturers (1900) Ltd* [1910] 1 Ch 12; *Westhoughton UDC v Wigan Coal and Iron Co Ltd* [1919] 1 Ch 159; *Halsall v Brizell* [1957] Ch 169, [1957] 1 All ER 371, p. 936, n. 12, post; (1954) 18 Conv (NS) 558–564 (E. H. Scamell); Preston and Newsom, paras. 3.01–3.04.

[5]   P. 938, post.

[6]   [1994] Conv 477 (J. Snape); (1994) 110 LQR 346 (N. P. Gravels); [1994] All ER Rev (P. J. Clarke); [1995] CLJ 60 (S. Gardner).

covenanted. To enforce negative covenants is only to treat the land as subject to a restriction.

Mr Munby, who argued the appeal persuasively on behalf of the plaintiffs, referred to an article by Professor Sir William Wade [1972 B] CLJ 157 and other articles in which the present state of the law is subjected to severe criticism. In 1965 a report by a committee appointed by the Lord Chancellor and under the chairmanship of Lord Wilberforce, the Report of the Committee on Positive Covenants Affecting Land (1965) (Cmnd. 2719), referred to difficulties caused by the decision in the *Austerberry* case and recommended legislation to provide that positive covenants which relate to the use of land and are intended to benefit specified other land should run with the land. The Law Commission published on 5 July 1971 Working Paper No. 36 in which the present law on positive rights was described as being illogical, uncertain, incomplete and inflexible. The Law Commission Report on Transfer of Land (1984) (Law Com 127) (HC 201) laid before Parliament in 1965 made recommendations for the reform of the law relating to positive and restrictive obligations and submitted a draft Bill for that purpose. Nothing has been done.

In these circumstances your Lordships were invited to overrule the decision of the Court of Appeal in the *Austerberry* case. To do so would destroy the distinction between law and equity and to convert the rule of equity into a rule of notice. It is plain from the articles, reports and papers to which we were referred that judicial legislation to overrule the *Austerberry* case would create a number of difficulties, anomalies and uncertainties and affect the rights and liabilities of people who have for over 100 years bought and sold land in the knowledge, imparted at an elementary stage to every student of the law of real property, that positive covenants, affecting freehold land are not directly enforceable except against the original covenantor. Parliamentary legislation to deal with the decision in the *Austerberry* case would require careful consideration of the consequences. Moreover, experience with leasehold tenure where positive covenants are enforceable by virtue of privity of estate has demonstrated that social injustice can be caused by logic. Parliament was obliged to intervene to prevent tenants losing their homes and being saddled with the costs of restoring to their original glory buildings which had languished through wars and economic depression for exactly 99 years.[7]

ii. METHODS OF CIRCUMVENTION

A number of current techniques and devices by which lawyers attempt to surmount or circumvent the difficulties of enforcing positive covenants are listed in the Report of the Committee on Positive Covenants Affecting Land.[8] They are:

(i) To lease land instead of selling it and to rely upon the enforceability of covenants between landlord and tenant.[9]

---

[7] The burden of a positive covenant was held by MACNAGHTEN J (following the dicta in *Austerberry v Oldham Corpn*) not to run at law with the land of the covenantor in *E and G C Ltd v Bate* (1935) 79 LJ 203.

[8] (1965) Cmd 2719. The quotations in (ii) and (iv) are from para. 8 of the report. See also Law Commission Report on Positive and Restrictive Covenants 1984 (Law Com No. 127, HC 201), paras. 3.19–3.42; Farrand (2nd edn.), pp. 422–427; George and George, *The Sale of Flats* (5th edn. 1984), pp. 76–89; (1973) 37 Conv (NS) 194 (A. M. Prichard).

[9] See p. 560, ante.

(ii) Chains of Indemnity Covenants. A covenant could be taken by each successive purchaser and liability on the covenant will exist down the line of purchasers. 'But in practice this device sooner or later becomes ineffective, either in consequence of the death or disappearance of the original convenantor, or because a break occurs in the chain of indemnities.'[10]

(iii) Covenants against sale of registered land without the developer's consent.[11] 'Where the title to plots on a newly developed estate is going to be registered and the developer is interested in the continuing observance of the covenants, he can insert a covenant in the original conveyances that the plot shall not be sold without his consent. He can then enter a restriction in the register to ensure compliance with the covenant and can refuse to give his consent to any sale under which the purchaser does not assume the appropriate positive obligations.'

(iv) The doctrine of *Halsall v Brizell*. 'In some cases a positive covenant can be enforced in practice by the operation of the maxim *qui sentit commodum sentire debet et onus*. This obliges a person who wishes to take advantage of a service or facility (e.g. a road or drains) to comply with any corresponding obligation to contribute to the cost of providing or maintaining it (*Halsall v Brizell* [1957] Ch 169, [1957] 1 All ER 371). The maxim cannot, however, be invoked where the burdened owner does not enjoy any service or facility to which his obligations attach or has no sufficient interest in the continuance of these benefits'.[12]

In **Thamesmead Town Ltd v Allotey** [1998] 3 EGLR 970 PETER GIBSON LJ explained the limits of the doctrine at 99:

'The reasoning of Lord Templeman [in *Rhone v Stephens*] suggests that there are two requirements for the enforceability of a positive covenant against a successor in title to the covenantor. The first is that the condition of discharging the burden must be relevant to the exercise of the rights that enable the benefit to be obtained. In *Rhone v Stephens* the mutual obligation of support was unrelated to and independent of the covenant to maintain the roof. The second is that the successors in title must have the opportunity to choose whether to take the benefit or, having taken it, to renounce it, even if only in theory, and thereby to escape

---

10   See *Radford v De Froberville* [1977] 1 WLR 1262, [1978] 1 All ER 33; *TRW Steering Systems Ltd v North Properties Ltd* (1993) 69 P & CR 265.

11   LRA 1925, s. 58; LRA 2002, s. 40, p. 172, ante.

12   (1957) 73 LQR 154 (R.E.M.); [1957] CLJ 35 (H. W. R. Wade); (1957) 21 Conv (NS) 160 (F. R. Crane); *E R Ives Investment Ltd v High* [1967] 2 QB 379, [1967] 1 All ER 504, p. 665, ante; *Montague v Long* (1972) 24 P & CR 240; *Four Oakes Estate Ltd v Hadley* [1986] LS Gaz R 2326 (no benefit to which burden could be attached); *Law Debenture Trust Corporation plc v Urial Caspian Oil Corporation Ltd* [1993] 1 WLR 148; *Rhone v Stephens* (1993) 67 P & CR 9 (CA) (doctrine not invoked where benefit technical or minimal). For a detailed discussion of the doctrine, see *Tito v Waddell (No 2)* [1977] Ch 106 at 289–311, [1977] 3 All ER 129 at 280–298, where MEGARRY V-C held at 303, at 292 that it covered not merely successors in title but also 'anybody whose connection with the transaction creating the benefit and burden is sufficient to show that he has some claim to the benefit whether or not he has a valid title to it'. See also (1977) 41 Conv (NS) 432–435 (F. R. Crane); [1985] Conv 12 (E. P. Aughterson); [1998] CLJ 523 (C. J. David); *Emmet on Title*, para. 19.020.

In *Rhone v Stephens* [1994] 2 AC 310, [1994] 2 All ER 65, p. 955, ante, LORD TEMPLEMAN said at 322, at 72: 'The condition must be relevant to the exercise of the right ... The owners of Walford House could not in theory or practice be deprived of the benefit of the mutual rights of support if they failed to repair the roof'.

the burden and that the successors in title can be deprived of the benefit if they fail to assume the burden.'
(v) Easement of fencing. [13]
(vi) On some occasions on which a long leasehold is converted into a freehold. Two statutes give such a right to a tenant:
  (a) The Law of Property Act 1925, section 153, [14] which provides for certain long leases [15] to be enlarged into freeholds, and for the freehold to be subject 'to all the same covenants ... as the term would have been subject to if it had not been so enlarged'.
  (b) The Leasehold Reform Act 1967 permits the tenant of a leasehold house [16] held on a long tenancy at a low rent, which he has occupied as his residence for three years, to acquire the freehold on fair terms and free from incumbrances, but 'Burdens ... in respect of the upkeep or regulation for the benefit of any locality of any land, building, structure, works, ways or watercourse [17] shall not be treated as incumbrances for purposes of this Part of this Act, but any conveyance executed to give effect to this section shall be made subject thereto ...'. [18]
(vii) Certain statutory powers which entitle Local Authorities to impose positive obligations on land and to enforce them upon successive owners. [19]
There are other possibilities.
(viii) Rentcharge. The creation of a rentcharge to secure the payment of money or contribution to the maintenance of property. [20] This method of enforcing a positive covenant was preserved by the Rentcharges Act 1977. [1]
(ix) Right of re-entry. A right of re-entry may be reserved exercisable on events which amount to the breach of a positive covenant. [2] This right of re-entry runs with the land, but is subject to the rule against perpetuities. [3]

---

[13] *Jones v Price* [1965] 2 QB 618, [1965] 2 All ER 625; *Crow v Wood* [1971] 1 QB 77, [1970] 3 All ER 425, p. 710, ante.
[14] As amended by TLATA 1996, s. 25(1), Sch. 3, para. 16.
[15] Restricted to those: (i) which were originally created for at least 300 years of which not less than 200 years is unexpired; (ii) in which no rent or money value is payable; (iii) which are not liable to be determined by re-entry for condition broken; (1958) 22 Conv (NS) 101 (T. P. D. Taylor).
[16] See C & B, pp. 534–543.
[17] This clearly includes provisions of the type found in *Halsall v Brizell* [1957] Ch 169, [1957] 1 All ER 371.
[18] Section 8(3). There is an exception in the case of rentcharges: s. 11. For restrictive covenants, see s. 10(4)(a).
[19] TCPA 1990, ss. 71–72, and 106; Highways Act 1980, s. 35; Local Government (Miscellaneous Provisions) Act 1982, s. 33, and various Private Acts.
[20] *Morland v Cook* (1868) LR 6 Eq 252; *Austerberry v Oldham Corpn* (1885) 29 ChD 750 at 782.
[1] Ss. 2(3)(c), (4), (5) (creation of 'estate rentcharges'); *Orchard Trading Estate Management Ltd v Johnson Security Ltd* [2002] 2 EGLR 1. See C & B, pp. 706–707; M & W, para. 18.017; George and George, pp. 82–89.
[2] *Shiloh Spinners Ltd v Harding* [1973] AC 691, [1973] 1 All ER 90, p. 34, ante. The possibility of relief against forfeiture reduces its effectiveness as a device.
[3] (1950) 14 Conv (NS) 350 at pp. 354–357 (S. M. Tolson). Legal rentcharges and rights of entry are registrable dispositions: LRA 2002, s. 27 (2)(c), Sch. 2, para. 6. Law Commission Report on Land Registration for the Twenty First Century (Law Com No. 271), paras. 3.18, 4.27. H & B, paras. 3.12, 3.20–3.21.

B. Commonhold

Under the Commonhold and Leasehold Reform Act 2002 [4] the burden of a positive covenant may run by statute. A commonhold [5] is a means of providing for the registered freehold ownership of two or more units of land, for example, in a block of flats or offices. Each unit is owned freehold by the registered proprietor; the remainder of the commonhold consists of the common parts which are vested freehold in a commonhold association. The association is a company limited by guarantee; and only members of the association are the owners of the individual units. Their rights and duties, as between themselves and as between themselves and the commonhold association, are specified in a Commonhold Community Statement. By section 16(1) a right or duty conferred or imposed by a commonhold community statement 'shall affect a new unit-holder in the same way as it affected the former unit-holder'. [6] This at a stroke does away with the problem of the enforceability of obligations in respect of freehold flats. 'That is a lacuna which has bedevilled conveyancing law and led to the ugly and varied leasehold structures which are a feature of our conveyancing landscape.' [7] The difficulty of enforcing the burden of a positive freehold covenant outside a commonhold scheme against a transferee from the covenantor remains. [8]

C. Equity

It was held in the leading case of *Tulk v Moxhay* in 1848 [9] that the purchaser of land with notice of a restrictive covenant affecting it would be restrained from using the land in a way inconsistent with that covenant. The vendor, who takes from a purchaser a covenant which restricts the way in which the land can be used, is entitled in appropriate circumstances to an injunction restraining improper use of the land, not only against the original covenantor, but also against other parties coming to the land. [10] This right to an injunction is of course an equitable right, and is never

---

4   Commonhold (Land Registration) Rules 2004 (SI 2004 No. 1830). Part I of the Act (Commonhold) comes into force on 27 September 2004. On commonhold generally, see Aldridge, *Commonhold Law* (2002); Clarke on *Commonhold: The New Law* (2002); Fetherstonhaugh, Peters and Sefton, *Commonhold* (2003); Woodfall, *Landlord and Tenant*, chap. 30; R & R, chap. 22. See also Aldridge Working Group on Freehold Flats and Freehold Ownership of Other Interdependent Buildings 1987 (Cmnd 79); Commonhold—A Consultation Paper 1990 (Cm 1345); [1991] Conv 170 (H. W. Wilkinson). In 1996 the Lord Chancellor's Department issued a further Consultation paper, [1997] Conv 6; (1996) IL & T Rev 3 (J. C. Williams). See also Blundell Memorial Lecture 1991: *Commonhold— Can we make it work* (J. Wylie and E. Nugee QC); [1997] Conv 169 (L. Charlebois); [1998] Conv 283 (L. Crabb); [2002] Conv 349 (D. N. Clarke).

5   Commonhold is similar to Condominium legislation in Canada, the United States and America and, under the name of strata titles, in Australia and New Zealand. Similar legislation has been in force in Europe since the 1930s, and it has been introduced in many other parts of the world. On strata titles in Australia, see (1991) 9107 EG 92 (N. Carter).

6   'Former unit-holder' means a person from whom a commonhold unit has been transferred'; and 'new unit-holder' means a person to whom a commonhold unit is transferred' (s. 16(4)).

7   Current Law Statutes 2002, chap. 15; commentary by P. H. Kenny on s. 16.

8   P. 933, ante.

9   (1848) 2 Ph 774; following Lord COTTENHAM's earlier decision in *Mann v Stephens* (1846) 15 Sim 377.

10   The court has power to grant damages in lieu of an injunction under Supreme Court Act 1981, s. 50 (formerly Chancery Amendment Act 1858, s. 2). See *Sefton v Tophams Ltd* [1965] Ch 1140, [1965] 3 All ER 1; *Baxter v Four Oaks Properties Ltd* [1965] Ch 816, [1965] 1 All ER 906; *Wrotham Park Estate Co v Parkside Homes Ltd* [1974] 1 WLR 798, [1974] 2 All ER 321; *Surrey County Council v Bredero Homes Ltd* [1993] 1 WLR 1361, [1993] 3 All ER 705; [1996] Conv 457 (N. S. Price); [1994] Conv 110 (T. Ingram); *Jaggard v*

enforceable against bona fide purchasers of the legal estate in the land for value without notice of the covenant,[11] but it can be enforced against all other persons. The burden of such a covenant is then said to run with the land in equity.

The conditions on which the burden of a covenant will so run are established in the cases leading from *Tulk v Moxhay*, and these cases show that the basic principle on which such covenants are enforced has changed since 1848. *Tulk v Moxhay* was decided on the general equitable ground that it was contrary to conscience that a person should come to land with notice of a covenant affecting it, and act in a way inconsistent with the covenant. And this principle was applied in a number of subsequent cases.[12] It soon became clear, however, that such a policy would result in the imposition of burdens on land without there being any corresponding interest in the plaintiff which required protection. The end of the 19th century saw the change of emphasis.[13] There must be an intent that the burden of the covenant should run with the land.[14] There must also be land benefited by the covenant, and the plaintiff must show that he has an interest in that land[15] the

---

Sawyer [1995] 1 WLR 269, [1995] 2 All ER 189; [1995] Conv 141 (T. Ingram); *Amec Developments Ltd v Jury's Hotel Management (UK) Ltd* (2001) 82 P & CR 286. On remedies for breach of restrictive covenants generally, see [1996] Conv 329 (J. Martin). Preston and Newsom, paras. 8–11 to 8–19.

On the jurisdiction of the Court of Chancery to award damages before the 1858 Act, see (1992) 108 LQR 652 (P. M. McDermott).

11   *Pilcher v Rawlins* (1872) 7 Ch App 259, p. 26, ante.

12   *Luker v Dennis* (1877) 7 ChD 227; *Catt v Tourle* (1869) 4 Ch App 654; *Millbourn v Lyons* [1914] 2 Ch 231; *Clegg v Hands* (1890) 44 ChD 503; *De Mattos v Gibson* (1859) 4 De G & J 276; *Western v MacDermott* (1866) 2 Ch App 72; *Lord Strathcona Ss Co Ltd v Dominion Coal Co Ltd* [1926] AC 108.

13   *London and South Western Rly Co v Gomm* (1882) 20 Ch D 562.

14   This intent may be clear from the nature of the covenant or by virtue of LPA 1925, s. 79, which will apply unless a contrary intention is shown: *Re Royal Victoria Pavilion (Ramsgate)* [1961] Ch 581, [1961] 3 All ER 83; *Tophams Ltd v Earl of Sefton* [1967] 1 AC 50 at 73, 81, [1966] 1 All ER 1039, at 1048, 1053, p 948, post; *Morrells of Oxford Ltd v Oxford United Football Club* [2001] Ch 459.

15   *Formby v Barker* [1903] 2 Ch 539, p. 944, post; *LCC v Allen* [1914] 3 KB 642, p. 943, post; *Millbourn v Lyons* [1914] 2 Ch 231; *Kelly v Barrett* [1924] 2 Ch 379; *Re Ballard's Conveyance* [1937] Ch 473, [1937] 2 All ER 691; *Tophams Ltd v Earl of Sefton* [1967] 1 AC 50 at 81, [1966] 1 All ER 1039 at 1053, per Lord WILBERFORCE ('under what I am content for present purposes to take as accepted doctrine'). There are exceptions to this rule in National Trust Act 1937, s. 8; *Gee v National Trust* [1966] 1 WLR 170 at 174, [1966] 1 All ER 954 at 957; Green Belt (London and Home Counties) Act 1938, s. 22; Water Act 1945, s. 15; Water Industry Act 1991, s. 164(3); National Parks and Access to the Countryside Act 1949, s. 16(4); Forestry Act 1967, s. 5(2); Town and Country Planning Act 1990, s. 106, as amended by Planning and Compensation Act 1991, s. 12 (see Francis, *Restrictive Covenants and Freehold Land*, chap. 10); *Re Martin's Application* (1988) 57 P & CR 119; Endowments and Glebe Measure 1976 s. 22; Ancient Monuments and Archaeological Areas Act 1979, s. 17(5); Wildlife and Countryside Act 1981, s. 39(3); Local Government (Miscellaneous Provisions) Act 1982, s. 33; Housing Act 1985, s. 609; and a number of local authorities have power under local Acts. See also *Governors of the Peabody Donation Fund v London Residuary Body* (1987) 55 P & CR 355 (Artisans and Labourers Dwellings Improvements Act 1875, s. 9 ('a valuable site in Covent Garden'). There are further exceptions in the cases of (i) schemes of development, p. 982, post' (ii) the landlord's reversion on a tenancy; *Hall v Ewin* (1887) 37 ChD 74; *Teape v Douse* (1905) 92 LT 319; (iii) the mortgagee's interest in the land: *Regent Oil Co Ltd v J A Gregory (Hatch End) Ltd* [1966] Ch 402, [1965] 3 All ER 673; following *John Bros Abergarw Brewery Co v Holmes* [1900] 1 Ch 188. On the question whether a covenant to restrain the pursuance of a non-noxious trade so as to avoid competition with the plaintiff can benefit the plaintiff's land, see *Wilkes v Spooner* [1911] 2 KB 473 at 485; *Newton Abbot Co-operative Society Ltd v Williamson and Treadgold Ltd* [1952] Ch 286, [1952] 1 All ER 279, p. 972, post; *Re Royal Victoria Pavilion (Ramsgate)* [1961] Ch 581, [1961] 3 All ER 83.

identity of which is 'easily ascertainable' from the instrument containing the covenant.[15a] On the question of benefit, the court does not apply its own standard, but takes a decision on expert evidence presented to it.[16] The onus is on the defendant to show that a covenant does not benefit the land,[17] either originally, or at the date of the action. 'This means that if there were possible opinions either way, the defendant will still fail unless he can show that the opinion that the covenant benefits the land could not reasonably be held.'[18] The benefit of such a covenant then becomes associated with a piece of land in the way that an easement is appurtenant to the dominant tenement; and the phraseology of the law of easements is introduced into the law of restrictive covenants.[19]

The doctrine of *Tulk v Moxhay* is applicable only to restrictive covenants; covenants, that is, which are negative in substance, even though positive in form: indeed, the covenant in *Tulk v Moxhay* itself was positive in form. But the boundary between those that are, and those that are not, negative in substance is not always easy to draw,[20] for almost every positive covenant can, in some sense, be regarded negatively. Moreover, it is difficult to see any inherent distinction between negative and positive covenants so far as enforceability is concerned.[1] In some situations, such as a covenant to supply water to land in a waterless area, the economic and moral reasons for enforcing positive covenants are just as strong as in the case of negative covenants. The jurisdiction, however, is exclusively equitable, and is limited to the situations which are susceptible to equitable remedies. The Report on Positive Covenants Affecting Land emphasised the inconvenience of the present law (under which the burden of positive covenants does not run) to adjoining owners of land and especially to owners of divided buildings and blocks of flats.[2] This has been remedied by the Commonhold and Leasehold Reform Act 2002 where there is freehold ownership of buildings divided into flats or other units.[3]

The positive remedy of specific performance and the doctrine of estate contracts are not indeed aspects of the doctrine of *Tulk v Moxhay*, but they provide an interesting analogy. An option in a lease to purchase the freehold has been held to be one which does not touch and concern the land and therefore does not run with the estate upon assignment by the tenant.[4] But the option to

---

[15a]   *Marquess of Zetland v Driver* [1939] Ch 1, at 8; *Crest Nicholson Residential (South) Ltd v McAllister* [2004] EWCA Civ 410, [2004] 2 All ER 991, [2004] 15 EG 105, at para. 33.

[16]   *Marten v Flight Refuelling Ltd* [1962] Ch 115 at 137, [1961] 2 All ER 696 at 706; *Earl of Leicester v Wells-next-the-Sea UDC* [1973] Ch 110, [1972] 3 All ER 77; *Wrotham Park Estate Co Ltd v Parkside Homes Ltd* [1974] 1 WLR 798, [1974] 2 All ER 321.

[17]   *Wrotham Park Estate Co Ltd v Parkside Homes Ltd*, supra, at 808, at 335; *Dano Ltd v Earl Cadogan* [2003] 12 EG 128 (CS); affd. [2004] 1 P & CR 169.

[18]   (1974) JPL at p. 133 (G. H. Newsom).

[19]   Per JESSEL MR in *London and South Western Rly Co v Gomm*, quoted at p. 946, post.

[20]   *Bridges v Harrow London Borough Council* (1981) 260 EG 284 at 288 (covenant to retain trees in hedgerow held to be probably negative in substance); *Bedwell Park Land Quarry Company v Hertfordshire County Council* [1993] JPL 349 ('It is hard to think of an obligation which was more positive in substance as well as in form').

[1]   Positive and negative undertakings may be contained in a single covenant, but 'there cannot be any doctrine of contagious proximity whereby the presence of the positive inhibits the enforcement of the neighbouring negative'; *Shepherd Homes Ltd v Sandham (No. 2)* [1971] 1 WLR 1062 at 1067, [1971] 2 All ER 1267 at 1272, per MEGARRY J; Preston and Newsom, paras. 3–06 to 3–11.

[2]   See Law Commission Report on Restrictive Covenants 1961 (Law Com No. 11); Law Commission Report on Positive and Restrictive Covenants 1984 (Law Com No. 127, HC 201), paras. 4.3–4.6.

[3.]   P. 938, ante.

[4]   *Woodall v Clifton* [1905] 2 Ch 257, p. 409, ante; *Worthing Corpn v Heather* [1906] 2 Ch 532.

purchase, if specifically enforceable, creates a proprietary interest in the grantee which is good against everyone coming to the land other than a bona fide purchaser of the legal estate for value without notice:[5] registration constituting notice in unregistered land; in registered law an option to purchase may be protected by a notice[6] or by actual occupation under the Land Registration Acts. An assignee of the covenantor will therefore take subject to the option.[7]

However, the burden of a positive covenant does not run in equity any more than it runs at law. Such covenants may, as we have seen,[8] be enforceable on other grounds, and will, if the Law Commission Report on Positive and Restrictive Covenants is adopted, be enforceable subject to certain conditions. In the early days of the *Tulk v Moxhay* doctrine, equity made gallant attempts to enforce some positive covenants by issuing an injunction restraining the defendant from omitting to perform the undertaking.[9] This development, not surprisingly, was brought to an abrupt halt five years later in *Haywood v Brunswick Permanent Benefit Building Society* (1881) 8 QBD 403. It is, however, of interest in demonstrating the crucial importance of the scope of equitable remedies in the development of the doctrine of *Tulk v Moxhay*.[10]

The burden of a covenant enforceable in equity under this doctrine is, unlike covenants between landlord and tenant, a burden on the land, and not on the estate held by the defendant.[11] Thus it is not necessary to show that the defendant holds the estate which the covenantor held; for the defendant is bound merely by coming to the land, whether as squatter, tenant at will, underlessee—as anyone indeed, other than bona fide purchaser of the legal estate for value without notice.[12]

In unregistered land, provision is made in section 2(5) of the Land Charges Act 1972 for the registration, as a land charge Class D(ii), of a restrictive covenant made after 1925 otherwise than between lessor and lessee;[13]

---

5 See p. 24, ante.
6 Or by a caution under LRA 1925.
7 LCA 1972, s. 2(4) Class C(iv); *London and South Western Rly Co v Gomm* (1882) 20 ChD 562; *Hutton v Watling* [1948] Ch 26, [1947] 2 All ER 641. The option, unless it be an option for a lessee or his successors in title to acquire an interest reversionary on the term of a lease and which ceases to be exercisable at or before the expiration of one year from the determination of the lease, must comply with the perpetuity rule, and the period, whether the issue is between the original contracting parties or not, is 21 years: Perpetuities and Accumulations Act 1964, ss. 9, 10, p. 410, ante.
8 See p. 935, ante.
9 *Morland v Cook* (1868) LR 6 Eq 252; *Cook v Chilcott* (1876) 3 ChD 694, which was expressly disapproved in *Haywood v Brunswick Permanent Benefit Building Society* (1881) 8 QBD 403; *Hall v Ewin* (1887) 37 ChD 74. In *Andrew v Aitken* (1882) 22 ChD 218 at 220 FRY J suggested that, in the case of a covenant to build, the covenantor and his assigns might be called upon to allow the covenantee to enter and carry out the work.
10 [1981] Conv 55 (C. D. Bell); [1983] Conv 29 (R. Griffith); 327 (C. D. Bell).
11 *Tichborne v Weir* (1892) 67 LT 735; *Re Nisbet and Potts' Contract* [1905] 1 Ch 391; affd [1906] 1 Ch 386, p. 946, post; *Mander v Falcke* [1891] 2 Ch 554.
12 *Pilcher v Rawlins* (1872) 7 Ch App 259; *Wilkes v Spooner* [1911] 2 KB 473.
13 This exception has been interpreted widely in both LCA 1925 and the LRA 1925 so as to exclude the protection of a restrictive covenant relating to *other* land of the lessor. LRA 2002 has changed this by excepting a restrictive covenant between lessor and lessee so far as relating to the demised premises; s. 33(c). The result is that a restrictive covenant relating to other land of the lessor can now be protected by the entry of a notice; *Oceanic Village Ltd v United Attractions Ltd* [2000] Ch 234, [2000] 1 All ER 875 (registered land); [2000] CLJ 451 (S. Bridges); [2001] All ER Rev 240 (P. J. Clarke). See also *Newman v Real Estate Debenture Corpn Ltd and Flower Decorations Ltd* [1940] 1 All ER 131 at 149–150; *Dartstone Ltd v Cleveland Petroleum Co Ltd* [1969] 1 WLR 1807, [1969] 3 All ER 668; (1956) 20 Conv (NS) 370 (R. G. Rowley).

and such registration, in accordance with the usual rules, is notice to all the world. [14] In registered land a restrictive covenant may be protected by the entry of a notice or caution under the Land Registration Act 1925 (s. 50(1)) and by the entry of a notice under Land Registration Act 2002 (s. 33(c), p. 169 ante).[15] The entry merely gives notice and does not mean that the covenant is necessarily enforceable against the servient land. [16] It cannot be an overriding interest. [17]

i. THE DOCTRINE OF *TULK v MOXHAY*

TULK v MOXHAY
(1848) 2 Ph 774 (Lord COTTENHAM LC)

In 1808, the plaintiff sold a vacant piece of land in Leicester Square to Elms, who covenanted for himself his heirs and assigns with the plaintiff his heirs and assigns that the purchaser would 'at all times thereafter at his ... own costs ... keep and maintain the said piece of ground ... in an open state, uncovered with any buildings, in neat and ornamental order ...' The piece of land passed by 'divers mesne conveyances into the hands of the defendant' whose conveyance did not contain any such covenant, but who admitted that he had notice of the covenant in the deed of 1808. The defendant threatened to build on the land in contravention of the covenant. An injunction was granted by Lord Langdale, the Master of the Rolls. On a motion to discharge that order.

Held. The plaintiff was entitled to an injunction to restrain a breach of the covenant by the defendant. [18]

LORD COTTENHAM: That this Court has jurisdiction to enforce a contract between the owner of land and his neighbour purchasing a part of it, that the latter shall either use or abstain from using the land purchased in a particular way, is what I never knew disputed. Here there is no question about the contract: the owner of certain houses in the Square sells the land adjoining, with a covenant from the purchaser not to use it for any other purpose than as a Square Garden. And it is now contended, not that the vendee could violate that contract, but that he might sell the piece of land, and that the purchaser from him may violate it without this Court having any power to interfere. If that were so, it would be impossible for an owner of land to sell part of it without incurring the risk of rendering what he retains worthless. It is said that, the covenant being one which does not run with the land, this Court cannot enforce it; but the question is, not whether the covenant runs with the land, but whether a party shall be permitted

---

[14]   LPA 1925, s. 198(1), p. 29, ante; positive and negative covenants entered into with a local authority, a Minister of the Crown or Government Department (otherwise than as between landlord and tenant) are registrable as local land charges: LLCA 1975, ss. 1, 2, p. 52, ante.
        For the duty of a solicitor to advise a purchaser on the nature and effect of a restrictive covenant, see *Bittlestone v Keegan Williams* [1997] EGCS 8.

[15]   R & R, paras. 9.018–9.021.

[16]   *Hodges v Jones* [1935] Ch 657 at 571, per LUXMOORE J.

[17]   *Cator v Newman and Bates* [1940] 1 KB 415. If the restrictive covenant was protected under LCA 1972 before first registration, it will become unenforceable if no notice is entered on first registration: *Freer v Unwins Ltd* [1976] Ch 288, [1976] 1 All ER 634; (1976) 40 Conv (NS) 304 (F. R. Crane); (1977) 41 Conv (NS) 1; (1976) 35 CLJ 211 (D. Hayton); (1976) 92 LQR 338 (R. J. Smith); (1976) 126 NLJ 523 (S. M. Cretney). See (1984) 81 LSG 1723, where Chief Land Registrar states that on first registration he does not normally inquire whether a covenant has become void for non-registration under LCA 1925; R & R, para. 9.020.

[18]   For the continued enforceability of the covenant, see *R v Westminster City Council and London Electricity Board* (1989) 59 P & CR 51, where SIMON BROWN J describes Leicester Square as 'one of London's ornaments'.

to use the land in a manner inconsistent with the contract entered into by his vendor, and with notice of which he purchased. Of course, the price would be affected by the covenant, and nothing could be more inequitable than that the original purchaser should be able to sell the property the next day for a greater price, in consideration of the assignee being allowed to escape from the liability which he had himself undertaken.

That the question does not depend upon whether the covenant runs with the land is evident from this, that if there was a mere agreement and no covenant, this Court would enforce it against a party purchasing with notice of it; for if an equity is attached to the property by the owner, no one purchasing with notice of that equity can stand in a different situation from the party from whom he purchased. ...

I think the cases cited before the Vice-Chancellor and this decision of the Master of the Rolls perfectly right, and, therefore, that this injunction [9] must be refused with costs.

ii. THE NECESSITY FOR BENEFITED LAND

LONDON COUNTY COUNCIL v ALLEN
[1914] 3 KB 642 (CA, BUCKLEY and KENNEDY LJJ and SCUTTON J)

In 1906, the defendant, M. J. Allen, a builder, applied to the L.C.C. for their permission to lay out certain land of which Allen was in possession under an option to purchase. He was treated in the Court of Appeal as if he were the owner. The L.C.C. gave permission subject to a condition that Allen would enter into a covenant not to build upon part of the land which was needed for the continuation of certain proposed streets. By a deed of 1907, Allen covenanted 'for himself, his heirs and assigns, and other the persons claiming under him, and so far as practicable to bind the land and hereditaments herein mentioned into whosesoever hands the same may come' that he would not place any erection on the land, and that he would give notice of this covenant in every document dealing with the land.

The land was conveyed to Allen in 1908; and part mortgaged to Willcocks who, in 1911, conveyed it on redemption, with M. J. Allen's concurrence, to Emily Allen, M. J. Allen's wife. Emily Allen built three houses on the plot, and mortgaged it to Norris.

The question was whether the covenant was binding on Emily Allen and Norris.

Held. Not binding, because the plaintiffs held no land for the benefit of which the covenant was taken.

SCRUTTON J: The question then is whether it is essential to the doctrine of *Tulk v Moxhay* that the covenantee should have at the time of the creation of the covenant, and afterwards, land for the benefit of which the covenant is created, in order that the burden of the covenant may bind assigns of the land to which it relates.

[His Lordship then reviewed the authorities, and referred to *Haywood v Brunswick Permanent Benefit Building Society* (1881) 8 QBD 403, *De Mattos v Gibson* (1858) 4 De G & J 276; *Luker v Dennis* (1877) 7 ChD 227; *London and South Western*

---

[19] Presumably 'motion' was intended here, and not 'injunction'. It is correct in (1848) 1 H & Tw 105 at 117.

Rly Co v Gomm (1882) 20 ChD 562; *Clegg v Hands* (1890) 44 ChD 503, and *Catt v Tourle* (1869) 4 Ch App 654, and continued:]

I think the result of this long chain of authorities is that, whereas in my view, at the time of *Tulk v Moxhay* and for at least twenty years afterwards, the plaintiffs in this case would have succeeded against an assign on the ground that the assign had notice of the covenant, since *Formby v Barker* [1903] 2 Ch 539; *Re Nisbet and Potts' Contract* [1905] 1 Ch 391; *affd.* [1906] 1 Ch 386 and *Milbourn v Lyons* [1914] 1 Ch 34; *affd.* [1914] 2 Ch 231, three decisions of the Court of Appeal, the plaintiffs must fail on the ground that they have never had any land for the benefit of which this 'equitable interest analogous to a negative easement' could be created, and therefore cannot sue a person who bought the land with knowledge that there was a restrictive covenant as to its use, which he proceeds to disregard, because he is not privy to the contract. I think the learned editors of Dart on Vendors and Purchasers (7th edn.), vol. ii, p. 769, are justified by the present state of the authorities in saying that 'the question of notice to the purchaser has nothing whatever to do with the question whether the covenant binds him, except in so far as the absence of notice may enable him to raise the plea of purchaser for valuable consideration without notice'. If the covenant does not run with the land in law, its benefit can only be asserted against an assign of the land burdened, if the covenant was made for the benefit of certain land, all or some of which remains in the possession of the covenantee or his assign, suing to enforce the covenant ... I regard it as very regrettable that a public body should be prevented from enforcing a restriction on the use of property imposed for the public benefit against persons who bought the property knowing of the restriction, by the apparently immaterial circumstance that the public body does not own any land in the immediate neighbourhood. But, after a careful consideration of the authorities, I am forced to the view that the later decisions of this court compel me so to hold. [20] In my opinion, therefore, the demurrer of Mr Norris and of Mrs Allen succeeds. This action against Mr Norris must be dismissed with costs. I regret that I do not see my way to depriving Mrs Allen of her costs, as, whatever may be her equitable rights, I am not at all favourably impressed with her conduct as a good citizen.

FORMBY v BARKER
[1903] 2 Ch 539 (CA, VAUGHAN WILLIAMS, ROMER and STIRLING LJJ)

In 1868, R. H. Formby sold all the land owned by him in Formby, Lancashire, to the Mutual Land Company Ltd, subject to various covenants restricting the user of the land. The defendant was an assignee of the company of part of the land, and took with notice of the covenants. R. H. Formby died in 1884, and letters of administration with the will annexed were granted to his widow, the plaintiff, to whom he had given all his property by his will. In 1902, the defendant began to erect certain shops which were alleged to be in breach of the covenant.

Held (affirming HALL V-C of the County Palatine of Lancaster).

(i) The building of the shops was not a breach of the covenant.

(ii) Even if it were, the plaintiff, having no land capable of benefiting, was unable to maintain the action.

VAUGHAN WILLIAMS LJ: The plaintiff sues in her individual capacity and also as administratrix with the will annexed of R. H. Formby deceased.

---

[20]   For exceptions to this rule, see p. 939, n. 15, ante, especially the statutory exceptions in favour of local authorities; Francis, *Restrictive Covenants and Freehold Land*, chap. 10.

[His Lordship held that, on its proper construction, the covenant had not been broken by the defendant, and continued:]

This view really puts an end to the plaintiff's case. But, as another defence was raised and was discussed by the learned Vice-Chancellor, I think it right to deal with that point also.

The learned Vice-Chancellor expressed an opinion that, even if the plaintiff's construction of the covenant was right, and there had been a breach of the covenant, nevertheless the plaintiff was not entitled to sue—that is, was not entitled to sue either as personal representative of R. H. Formby or as residuary devisee under his will. ...

Before dealing with the question of the plaintiff's right to sue, I wish to point out that that which R. H. Formby conveyed was his whole estate, and that he had no contiguous estate which would be benefited by the covenant in question. Moreover, there is in the deed no re-entry clause under which the vendor could go in as of his old estate, or, indeed, as of any estate. ...

It becomes necessary, therefore, to ascertain whether the principle of *Tulk v Moxhay* applies to a case in which the vendor sells his whole estate. I have not been able to find any case in which, after the sale of the whole of an estate in land, the benefit of a restrictive covenant has been enforced by injunction against an assignee of the purchaser at the instance of a plaintiff having no land retained by the vendor, although there are cases in which restrictive covenants seem to have been enforced at the instance of plaintiffs, other than the vendor, for the benefit of whose land it appears from the terms of the covenant, or can be inferred from surrounding circumstances, that the covenant was intended to operate. In all other cases the restrictive covenant would seem to be a mere personal covenant collateral to the conveyance. It is a covenant which cannot run with the land, either at law or in equity, and therefore the burden of the covenant cannot be enforced against an assignee of the purchaser.

In **Re Gadd's Land Transfer** [1966] Ch 56, [1965] 2 All ER 800, BUCKLEY J held that the retention only of a road to the land burdened by the covenant was sufficient to enable the covenantee to enforce a restrictive covenant.

BUCKLEY J said at 67, at 809: 'The question must, I think, be what is the impact of the covenants on the owner of Bridle Lane in respect of its occupation or enjoyment of that property. ...

If the use of the pink land is to be changed from agricultural use to use as a building estate of that kind, there will be a great increase in the traffic over the right-of-way. Now the increase in the traffic over the right-of-way must inevitably mean that the maintenance of the roadway will become a more burdensome expense than otherwise it would be. ...

If the cost of maintaining Bridle Lane became very much heavier than at present because of a great increase in the traffic over the road, it seems to me that there would be a risk that cannot be regarded as non-existent that the frontagers may not all be able to honour their obligations to contribute towards the cost of maintenance. I cannot suppose that that risk is negligible. ...

Moreover, I think there is substance in the suggestion that if the lane is not kept in a proper state of repair there will be a risk that the road will be taken over by the local authority and the defendant company would thereby be deprived of some element of its ownership in the road.

Now it may be that this road is not a readily saleable asset, but it is not, I think, inconceivable that the residents in the road under certain circumstances would want themselves to acquire the road from the defendant company with a view to preserving it as their private road. If the burden of maintaining the road were to be made substantially more onerous than it is at present owing to an increase of traffic, the likelihood of the defendant company being able to dispose of this asset in any such way as that would, I think, decrease. These may not be very substantial interests or benefits which result to the defendant company from possible enforcement of the restrictive covenants, but nevertheless I do not think they are wholly negligible; I do not think they are matters that the court ought to disregard and I think they are matters of sufficient significance to justify the view that the capacity to enforce the covenants is a matter which does affect the defendant company in its position as owner of Bridle Lane.'

iii. THE NATURE OF A RESTRICTIVE COVENANT

In **London and South Western Rly Company v Gomm** (1882) 20 ChD 562,[1] Sir George JESSEL MR described the doctrine of *Tulk v Moxhay* as follows, at p. 583:

'The doctrine of that case, rightly considered, appears to me to be either an extension in equity of the doctrine of *Spencer's Case* to another line of cases, or else an extension in equity of the doctrine of negative easements; such, for instance, as a right to the access of light, which prevents the owner of the servient tenement from building so as to obstruct the light. The covenant in *Tulk v Moxhay* was affirmative in its terms, but was held by the Court to imply a negative. Where there is a negative covenant expressed or implied, as, for instance, not to build so as to obstruct a view, or not to use a piece of land otherwise than as a garden, the Court interferes on one or other of the above grounds. This is an equitable doctrine, establishing an exception to the rules of Common Law which did not treat such a covenant as running with the land, and it does not matter whether it proceeds on analogy to a covenant running with the land or on analogy to an easement.'

In other words, the doctrine of *Spencer's Case* was to apply so as to impose liability between parties, between whom there was no privity of estate; or the concept of a negative easement was to be extended in equity to cover the burden imposed, not by grant but by covenant, upon one piece of land for the benefit of another piece of land. The latter is the better analogy; for, under *Spencer's Case*, as with all covenants running with land at common law, the covenant ran with the estate and not with the land. A restrictive covenant under the doctrine of *Tulk v Moxhay*, like an easement, runs with the land, and not with the estate.

TICHBORNE v WEIR
(1892) 67 LT 735 (CA, Lord ESHER MR, BOWEN and KAY LJJ)

The plaintiff's predecessor in title was seised of a house in fee simple. In 1802 she leased it to Baxter for eighty-nine years. The lease contained a covenant to repair. Baxter made an equitable mortgage of the premises to Giraud, and Giraud entered on the premises in 1836. In 1836 Baxter disappeared, and Giraud remained in occupation of the premises till 1876. During that period he paid the rent reserved in Baxter's lease to the lessor. In 1876 Giraud purported to

---

1   (1971) 87 LQR 539 (D. J. Hayton). See *Spencer's Case* (1583) 5 Co Rep 16a, p. 563, ante.

assign the lease to the defendant. The defendant entered and paid the rent till the term ended in 1891. He then delivered up possession to the plaintiff. The plaintiff sought to make him liable on the covenant to repair, but the Court of Appeal held that he was not liable.

The Real Property Limitation Act 1833 had barred the action and extinguished the right of Baxter; but it had not vested Baxter's lease in Giraud. The covenant to repair would run with the lease on an assignment; but neither Giraud nor the defendant had taken Baxter's lease and the defendant was not bound by the covenant to repair. [2]

To the argument that he was estopped by the payment of rent from denying that he had taken Baxter's estate, it was said that such payment estopped him from disputing the title of the plaintiff, but it did not estop him from denying that he was bound by the terms of the lease. It estopped him from denying that he was a lessee: it did not estop him from denying that he was the holder of Baxter's lease. [3]

RE NISBET AND POTTS' CONTRACT
[1905] 1 Ch 391 (Ch D, FARWELL J); [1906] 1 Ch 386 (CA, Sir RICHARD HENN COLLINS MR, ROMER and COZENS-HARDY LJJ)

A summons was taken out by Potts asking for a declaration that Nisbet, the vendor under a contract of sale, failed to produce a good title.

Nisbet had purchased in 1901 from X and Y who had themselves purchased in 1890 from Headde, whose title was based upon occupation since 1878. Nisbet agreed to accept a title commencing at that date. Restrictive covenants had been imposed on the land in 1867 and 1872; Nisbet knew nothing of these but would have discovered them if he had insisted on a forty years' title. [4]

On Potts' complaint that Nisbet was unable to produce a good title because of the restrictive covenants, Nisbet replied:

   (i) that he had purchased without notice; and
   (ii) that, in any case, covenants would not be binding upon a title acquired by adverse possession.

FARWELL J, affirmed by the Court of Appeal, held that a party had constructive notice of all that he would have ascertained if he had made proper enquiries and searched back for forty years; and also that the restrictive covenants were an equitable burden on the land, and were not terminated by the adverse possession. He said at 396:

'But if the covenant be negative, so as to restrict the mode of use and enjoyment of the land, then there is called into existence an equity attached to the property of such a nature that it is annexed to and runs with it in equity ... This equity, although created by covenant or contract, cannot be sued on as such, but stands on the same footing with, and is completely analogous to, an equitable charge on real estate created by some predecessor in title of the present owner of the land charged.'

---

[2]   See especially KAY LJ at 737, p. 241, ante.
[3]   Much of this account of *Tichborne v Weir* is taken from Holdsworth, *Historical Introduction to the Land Law* (1927), pp. 286–287.
[4]   The period of commencement of title which a purchaser could then require; see LPA 1925, s. 44(1), and LPA 1969, s. 23, p. 80, ante.

QUESTIONS

K Ltd., a garage company, owning the site of a garage, mortgaged it to E, and entered into a 'solus' agreement, under which they undertook to sell E's petrol only; and to extract similar undertakings from any person to whom they might sell the garage.

I H purchased all the sharers in K Ltd., and took a conveyance of the site of the garage, with the intention of breaking the provision relating to the sale of the petrol. They did so. E owned no land capable of benefiting. E sues for an injunction, joining K Ltd and I H as defendants. What result?

Esso Petroleum Co Ltd v Kingswood Motors (Addlestone) Ltd [1974] QB 142, [1973] 3 All ER 1057.

D. Law of Property Act 1925, Section 79[5]

In **Rhone v Stephens** [1994] 2 AC 310, [1994] 2 All ER 65, p. 934, ante, Lord TEMPLEMAN said at 322, at 72:

'Mr Munby submitted that the decision in the *Austerberry* case (1885) 29 Ch D 750 had been reversed remarkably but unremarked by section 79 of the Law of Property Act 1925 which, so far as material, provides:

"(1) A covenant relating to any land of a covenantor or capable of being bound by him, shall unless a contrary intention is expressed, be deemed to be made by the covenantor on behalf of himself, his successors in title and the persons deriving title under him or them, and, subject as aforesaid, shall have effect as if such successors and other persons were expressed …"

This provision has always been regarded as intended to remove conveyancing difficulties with regard to the form of covenants and to make it unnecessary to refer to successors in title. A similar provision relating to the benefit of covenants is to be found in section 78 of the Act of 1925. In *Smith and Snipes Hall Farm Ltd v River Douglas Catchment Board* [1949] 2 KB 500, [1949] 2 All ER 179, p. 951, post, followed in *Williams v Unit Construction Co Ltd* (1951) 19 Conv (NS) 262 p. 953, post, it was held by the Court of Appeal that section 78 of the Act of 1925 had the effect of making the benefit of positive covenants run with the land. Without casting any doubt on those long standing decisions I do not consider that it follows that section 79 of the Act of 1925 had the corresponding effect of making the burden of positive covenants run with the land. In *Jones v Price* [1965] 2 QB 618, 633, [1965] 2 All ER 625, 630 Willmer LJ repeated that: 'a covenant to perform positive acts … is not one the burden of which runs with the land so as to bind the successors in title of the conventor: see *Austerberry v Oldham Corporation*.' (1885) 29 ChD 750, p. 935, ante.

In *Sefton v Tophams Ltd* [1967] 1 AC 50, 73, 81, [1966] 1 All ER 1039, 1048, 1053, Lord Upjohn and Lord Wilberforce stated that section 79 of the Law of Property Act 1925 does not have the effect of causing covenants to run with the land. Finally, in *Federated Homes Ltd v Mill Lodge Properties Ltd* [1980] 1 WLR 594, 605–606, [1980] 1 All ER 371, 380, p. 959, post. Brightman J referred to the authorities on section 78 of the Act of 1925 and said that: "Section 79, in my view, involves quite different considerations and I do not think that it provides a helpful analogy."'[6]

---

5   P. 564, ante; [2000] Conv 377 (L. Tee).
6   See the laconic 'No' given as an answer by Sir Benjamin Cherry in his *Lectures on the New Property Acts* (1926), p. 131, to the question 'Is the case of *Austerberry v Corporation of Oldham* overruled by s. 79 of the Law of Property Act?'

Unlike section 78,[7] section 79 contains the words 'unless a contrary intention is expressed'. In **Re Royal Victoria Pavilion, Ramsgate** [1961] Ch 581, [1961] 3 All ER 83, PENNYCUICK J considered a covenant which began 'The vendors hereby covenant with the purchasers that they the vendors will ...'. He said at 589, at 87:

'Here it is contended that no contrary intention is expressed in the conveyance, ... and that, therefore, the covenant in clause 5 must be deemed to be made by Thanet Theatrical on behalf of itself and its successors in title. If the words 'unless the contrary intention is expressed' in section 79 mean: unless the instrument contains express provision to the contrary, this contention would, I think, be unanswerable. But it seems to me the words "unless a contrary intention is expressed" mean rather: unless an indication to the contrary is to be found in the instrument, and that such an indication may be sufficiently contained in the wording and context of the instrument even though the instrument contains no provision expressly excluding successors in title from its operation. It can hardly be the intention of the section that a covenant which, on its natural construction, is manifestly intended to be personal only, must be construed as running with the land merely because the contrary is not expressly provided. ...

So here, although the covenant contains no express provision to the effect that it is not made on behalf of successors in title, it does, as it seems to me, contain sufficient indication to this effect.'[8]

In **Lynnthorpe Enterprises Ltd v Sidney Smith (Chelsea) Ltd** [1990] 1 EGLR 148,[9] WARNER J said at 152:

'Mr Fenwick's main submission on this part of the case was that section 79 did not apply because at the time when the deed of 1986 was entered into the assignment to Lynnthorpe had not taken place, and indeed might never take place, so that Lynnthorpe had no land and was capable of binding no land to which the covenant related. ...

It seems to me that, in truth, I am faced here with a simple question of construction of section 79 itself. It is plain from the terms of the deed of 1986 that, at the time it was executed, the parties to it contemplated that the lease would be assigned to Lynnthorpe, though it might not be. Lynnthorpe thereby entered into a covenant that was to take effect if and when the lease was assigned to it. Is it to be held that the land comprised in the lease was not "capable of being bound" by Lynnthorpe in that event? To answer that question in the affirmative would, to my mind, be to place an unwarrantable restriction on the meaning of those words in the section. Parliament, by referring in the section to "any land of a covenantor or capable of being bound by him" has evinced an intention that the land need not belong to the covenantor at the time of the covenant. Otherwise, the words "or capable of being bound by him" add nothing. I therefore hold that section 79 does apply here.'

---

[7] P. 564, ante. See however, *Roake v Chadha* [1984] 1 WLR 40, [1983] 3 All ER 503, p. 963, post.

[8] Followed in *Morrells of Oxford Ltd v Oxford United Football Club* [2001] Ch 459 (covenant not to permit sale or consumption either on or off the premises of intoxicating liquors contained no reference to successors in title, whereas another covenant did: held that the first covenant was intended to be personal and s. 79 did not apply).

[9] Upheld by CA [1990] 2 EGLR 131; see STAUGHTON LJ at 134. See *Crest Nicholson Residential (South) Ltd v McAllister* [2004] EWCA Civ 410, [2004] 2 All ER 991, [2004] 15 EG 105, at paras. 41–44, where CHADWICK LJ expressed the view that s. 78 did not contain the words 'unless a contrary intention is expressed' because 'it did not need to'.

III. The Benefit[10]

A. Common Law

It has long been held that the benefit of a covenant will run with the land at law in certain circumstances. [11] The rule is thought to have its origin in the old warranties for title which were enforceable not only by the covenantee, but also by his heirs, and, later, by assigns; if the warranty were broken, the warrantor would be liable in some cases to provide lands of equal value, in other cases to pay damages. [12] The conditions which are necessary for the benefit of a covenant to run with the land at law are a matter of some doubt, owing to the paucity of modern authority; it is clear however that the covenant will run if the following conditions are complied with. [13]

(i)   The covenant must touch and concern the land. [14] It may do this even though the covenantor is a stranger to the land, and there is no servient tenement to be bound by the covenant. [15]

(ii) The land to be benefited must be expressly identified by the deed containing the covenant. There appears to be no authority for this; if it is a requirement, it is weakened by the operation of the maxim '*id certum est quod certum reddi potest.*' [16]

(iii)   There must be an intention that the benefit should run with the land owned by the covenantee at the date of the covenant. [17]

(iv) The covenant must have been entered into with the owner of the legal estate in the land to be benefited. [18]

(v) Before 1926, it was necessary for a person seeking to enforce the covenant to have the same legal estate in the land as the original covenantee. [19] It has been held that section 78(1) of the Law of Property Act 1925 excludes this last requirement. [20] It may be that the wide interpretation given to that section in *Federated Homes Ltd v Mill Lodge Properties Ltd* [1] will have the effect of excluding some of the others as well. This was a case dealing with the running of the benefit in equity, which is the context in which the question

---

[10]   C & B, pp. 655–667, 678–689; Gray, pp. 1144–1151, 1161–1178; M & W, paras. 16.004–16.016, 16.056–16.080; MM, pp. 454–461; Smith, pp. 531–532, 543–551; [1938] CLJ 339 (S. J. Bailey); (1971) 82 LQR 539 (D. J. Hayton); (1982) 2 LS 53 (D. J. Hurst); (1982) 98 LQR 279 (S. Gardner).

[11]   *The Prior's Case* (1368) YB 42 Edw 3, fo 3A pl 14; Smith's *Leading Cases* (13th edn. 1929), vol. i, pp. 51, 65, 73.

[12]   Simpson, *A History of the Land Law,* (2nd edn 1986), pp. 140–141.

[13]   Much of this section is based on (1954) 18 Conv (NS) 546 (E. H. Scamell).

[14]   See p. 932, n. 14, ante.

[15]   *The Prior's Case*, see p. 932, n. 8, ante; *Smith and Snipes Hall Farm Ltd v River Douglas Catchment Board* [1949] 2 KB 500, [1949] 2 All ER 179; and for cases where there is a servient tenement which would not be bound by the covenant, see *Sharp v Waterhouse* (1857) 7 E & B 816; *Shayler v Woolf* [1946] Ch 320, [1946] 2 All ER 54.

[16]   *Smith and Snipes Hall Farm Ltd v River Douglas Catchment Board* [1949] 2 KB 500, [1949] 2 All ER 179, at 508, 517, at 184, 189, infra.

[17]   *Rogers v Hosegood* [1900] 2 Ch 388 at 396; *Shayler v Woolf* [1946] Ch 320, [1946] 2 All ER 54; *Smith and Snipes Hall Farm Ltd v River Douglas Catchment Board*, supra at 506, at 183.

[18]   Co Litt 385a; *Webb v Russell* (1789) 3 Term Rep 393; cf. *Rogers v Hosegood* [1900] 2 Ch 388.

[19]   *Westhoughton UDC v Wigan Coal and Iron Co Ltd* [1919] 1 Ch 159; *Smith and Snipes Hall Farm Ltd v River Douglas Catchment Board*, supra.

[20]   *Smith and Snipes Hall Farm Ltd v River Douglas Catchment Board*, supra.

[1]   [1980] 1 WLR 594, [1980] 1 All ER 371, where the plaintiff took an assignment of part only of the land from the original covenantee; see pp. 959, 969, post.

usually arises; because the burdened land will commonly have also been assigned.

The common law rules continue to apply in cases not covered by equity, as, for example, where there is no land upon which the burden of the covenant is imposed. [2]

SMITH AND SNIPES HALL FARM LTD v RIVER DOUGLAS CATCHMENT BOARD [3]

[1949] 2 KB 500, [1949] 2 All ER 179 (CA, Tucker, Somervell and Denning LJJ)

The defendant Board was the Drainage Authority for a part of Lancashire. In 1938 the Board covenanted under seal with the freehold owners of land within that area that in consideration of the Board's widening, deepening and making good the banks of the Eller Brook, taking control thereof and maintaining for all time the work when it was completed, the landowners would contribute to the cost.

In 1940, Mrs Ellen Smith, one of the owners, sold her land, expressly with the benefit of the covenant, to the first plaintiff, John Bruce Smith, who leased it to the second plaintiff under a yearly tenancy. Owing to the faulty work of the defendants, the brook broke its banks, and flooded the land of the plaintiffs. They brought this action in tort and for breach of contract.

Held (reversing Morris J [1948] WN 414). Both plaintiffs could succeed under the contract.

The action in tort did not therefore arise for decision and no decision was reached on that point. The plaintiffs would have found it necessary to distinguish the House of Lords case of *East Suffolk Rivers Catchment Board v Kent* [1941] AC 74, [1940] 4 All ER 527.

Tucker LJ [having held that the defendants were in breach of the contract and that such breach caused the damage]: … It remains to consider whether, in these circumstances, the plaintiffs, or either of them, can sue in respect of this breach. It is said for the defendants that the benefit of the covenant does not run with the land so as to bind a stranger who has not and never had an interest in the land to be benefited and there being no servient tenement to bear the burden. Further, it is contended that such a covenant must by the terms of the deed in which it is contained relate to some specific parcel of land, the precise extent and situation of which can be identified by reference to the deed alone. It is first necessary to ascertain from the deed that the covenant is one which 'touches or concerns' the land, that is, it must either affect the land as regards mode of occupation, or it must be such as per se, and not merely from collateral circumstances, affects the value of the land, and it must then be shewn that it was the intention of the parties that the benefit thereof should run with the land. In this case the deed shews that its object was to improve the drainage of land liable to flooding and prevent future flooding. The location of the land is described as situate between the Leeds and Liverpool Canal and the River Douglas and adjoining the Eller Brook. In return for lump sum payments the board covenants to do certain work to the banks of the Eller Brook, one of such banks being in fact situate upon and forming part of the plaintiff's lands, and to maintain for all time the work when completed. In my view the language of the deed satisfies both tests. It affects the value of the land per se and converts it from flooded

---

[2] See p. 955, n. 15, ante.
[3] See (1981) 97 LQR 32, at pp. 43–47 (G. H. Newsom).

meadows to land suitable for agriculture, and shows an intention that the benefit of the obligation to maintain shall attach thereto into whosesoever hands the lands shall come.

With regard to the covenantor being a stranger, the case of *The Prior* is referred to in *Spencer's* case, in these words: 'In the case of a grandfather, father and two sons, the grandfather being seised of the manor of D, whereof a chapel was parcel: a prior with the assent of his convent, by deed covenanted for him and his successors, with the grandfather and his heirs that he and his convent would sing all the week in his chapel, parcel of the said manor, for the lord of the said manor and his servants, etc.; the grandfather did enfeoff one of the manor in fee, who gave it to the younger son and his wife in tail; and it was adjudged that the tenants in tail, as terre-tenants (for the elder brother was heir), should have an action of covenant against the prior, for the covenant is to do a thing which is annexed to the chapel, which is within the manor, and so annexed to the manor, as it is there said.' ...

In Rogers v Hosegood [1900] 2 Ch at 395, Farwell J, in a passage where he refers, amongst others, to *The Prior's* case—and I quote from Farwell J's judgment because, although this case went to the Court of Appeal, his judgment was approved, and the Court of Appeal had to deal with a rather different point— after stating what are the requirements in order that the covenant may run with the land, proceeds: 'It is not contended that the covenants in question in this case have not the first characteristic, but it is said that they fail in the second. I am of opinion that they possess both. Adopting the definition of Bayley J in *Congleton Corpn v Pattison* (1808) 10 East at 135, the covenant must either affect the land as regards mode of occupation, or it must be such as per se, and not merely from collateral circumstances, affects the value of the land. It is to my mind obvious that the value of Sir J Millais's land is directly increased by the covenants in question. If authority is needed, I would refer to *Mann v Stephens* (1846) 15 Sim 377, a case very similar to the present; *Vyvyan v Arthur* (1823) 1 B & C 410, *The Prior's* case, *Fleetwood v Hull* (1889) 23 QBD 35, *White v Southend Hotel Co* [1897] 1 Ch 767. I see no difficulty in holding that the benefit of a covenant runs with the land of the covenantee, while the burden of the same covenant does not run with the land of the covenantor..'

In this state of the authorities it seems clear, despite some dicta tending to the contrary view, that such a covenant if it runs with the land is binding on the covenantor though a mere stranger, and that this point will not avail the defendant board. As to the requirement that the deed containing the covenant must expressly identify the particular land to be benefited, no authority was cited to us and in the absence of such authority I can see no valid reason why the maxim 'Id certum est quod certum reddi potest' should not apply, so as to make admissible extrinsic evidence to prove the extent and situation of the lands of the respective land owners adjoining the Eller Brook situate between the Leeds and Liverpool Canal and the River Douglas.

... I have accordingly arrived at the conclusion that the covenant by the board in the agreement of 25 April 1938 is one which runs with the land referred to therein, which land is capable of identification, and that it is binding on the defendant board; and, further, that by virtue of section 78 of the Law of Property Act 1925, it can be enforced at the suit of the covenantee and her successors in title and the persons deriving title under her or them, so that both the plaintiff Smith and the plaintiff company can sue in respect of the damage resulting to their respective interests therein by reason of the defendants' breach of covenant.

DENNING LJ: The law on this subject was fully expounded by Mr Smith in his note in *Spencer's* case which has always been regarded as authoritative. Such covenants [relating to land] are clearly intended, and usually expressed, to be for the benefit of whomsoever should be the owner of the land for the time being; and at common law each successive owner has a sufficient interest to sue because he holds the same estate as the original owner. The reason which Lord Coke gave for this rule is the reason which underlies the whole of the principle now under consideration. He said in his work upon Littleton that it was 'to give damages to the party grieved'. If a successor in title were not allowed to sue it would mean that the covenantor could break his contract with impunity, for it is clear that the original owner, after he has parted with the land, could recover no more than nominal damages for any breach that occurred thereafter. It was always held, however, at common law that, in order that a successor in title should be entitled to sue, he must be of the same estate as the original owner. That alone was a sufficient interest to entitle him to enforce the contract. The covenant was supposed to be made for the benefit of the owner and his successors in title, and not for the benefit of anyone else. This limitation, however, was, as is pointed out in *Smith's* Leading Cases, capable of being 'productive of very serious and disagreeable consequences', and it has been removed by section 78 of the Law of Property Act 1925, which provides that a covenant relating to any land of the covenantee shall be deemed to be made with the covenantee and his successors in title, 'and the persons deriving title under him or them' and shall have effect as if such successors 'and other persons' were expressed.

The covenant of the catchment board in this case clearly relates to the land of the covenantees. It was a covenant to do work on the land for the benefit of the land. By the statute, therefore, it is to be deemed to be made, not only with the original owner, but also with the purchasers of the land and their tenants as if they were expressed. Now if they were expressed, it would be clear that the covenant was made for their benefit; and they clearly have sufficient interest to entitle them to enforce it because they have suffered the damage. The result is that the plaintiffs come within the principle whereby a person interested can sue on a contract expressly made for his benefit.

In **Williams v Unit Construction Co Ltd**[4] the question again arose whether section 78 of the Law of Property Act 1925[5] allowed the benefit of a restrictive covenant to pass at law in favour of persons who did not hold the same legal estate as the original covenantee. Counsel argued that a decision to that effect could only be taken by a court which was prepared also to hold that section 79 would have the same effect upon the burden; in other words, to hold that, since 1925, 'successors in title and persons deriving title under him or them' would be bound by the burden of the covenant. The Court of Appeal declined to express a view on the effect of section 79[6] upon the burden—the point not being before the court—and followed *Smith and Snipes Hall Farm Ltd v River Douglas Catchment Board.*

---

[4]   Unreported, but discussed in (1955) 19 Conv (NS) 262 (W. L. Blease).
[5]   See p. 564, ante.
[6]   On the application of s. 79, see p. 564, ante, p. 948, ante.

Similarly, in **Federated Homes Ltd v Mill Lodge Properties Ltd** [1980] 1 WLR 594, [1980] 1 All ER 371, BRIGHTMAN LJ said at 606, at 380:

'We were referred to observations in the speeches of Lord Upjohn and Lord Wilberforce in *Tophams Ltd v Earl of Sefton* [1967] 1 AC 50 at 73 and 81, [1967] 1 All ER 1039 at 1048, 1053, to the effect that section 79 ... achieved no more than the introduction of statutory shorthand into the drafting of covenants. Section 79, in my view, involves quite different considerations and I do not think that it provides a helpful analogy.'[7]

B. Contract. Statute

There are two ways in which a successor in title may be able to sue the original covenantor in contract

i. EXPRESS ASSIGNMENT

LAW OF PROPERTY ACT 1925
136. Legal assignments of things in action.—(1) Any absolute assignment by writing under the hand of the assignor (not purporting to be by way of charge only) of any debt or other legal thing in action, of which express notice in writing has been given to the debtor ... is effectual in law (subject to equities having priority over the right of the assignee) to pass and transfer from the date of such notice—

    (a) the legal right to such debt or thing in action;
    (b) all legal and other remedies for the same; and
    (c) the power to give a good discharge for the same without the concurrence of the assignor ...

ii. CONTRACTS (RIGHTS OF THIRD PARTIES) ACT 1999

This Act[8] applies to all contracts (including leases and land contracts) entered into on or after 11 May 2000.

In so far as the Act applies to the enforcement of a freehold covenant at common law, there are three observations to make. First, such phrases as successors in title bring the covenant within section 1(3), enabling them to sue directly the original covenantor on the covenant. Secondly, being a contractual and not a land law right, there is no need to satisfy the common law requirement of touching and concerning the land and of a legal estate to be benefited. And thirdly, it will only be rarely necessary to invoke the Act, since in most cases the width of section 78(1) of the Law of Property Act 1925 will suffice.

C. Equity

Where a person other than the original covenantee desires to enforce a covenant, he must show that he is the person entitled to the benefit of the covenant. He may do this by showing either that the benefit of the covenant has passed to him,

---

[7]   The case held that s. 78 effected an annexation of the benefit of the covenant in equity; p. 959, post. See also M & W, para. 16.013; W & C vol. i, 162–163; (1956) 20 Conv (NS) 43, 52 (D. W. Elliott); [1972 B] CLJ 157 at pp. 171–175 (H. W. R. Wade); *Emmet on Title*, para. 17.005–17.007.

[8]   P. 76, ante. It was possible for parties to contract into it six months before 11 May 2000. The Act does not affect the running of the burden of a covenant.

or that he was made an original covenantee by section 56 of the Law of Property Act 1925. As has been seen, the benefit of a covenant would run at law in certain circumstances. But there are some situations outside the limits of the common law where the benefit would run in equity. Generally, equity follows the law, and this development is probably an elucidation of the rules of common law, rather than a separate contribution of equity.[9]

The situations in which the equitable rules must be observed are these:

(i)   where the plaintiff or the covenantee was an equitable owner,[10]
(ii) (subject to section 78 of the Law of Property Act 1925) where the plaintiff does not have the same legal estate as the covenantee,[11]
(iii) where the servient land has been assigned, and enforcement depends on the doctrine of *Tulk v Moxhay*,[12]
(iv) where the plaintiff relies upon an express assignment of the benefit of the covenant without compliance with section 136 of the Law of Property Act 1925,[13]
(v)   where the plaintiff takes an assignment of part of the land only, for 'at law, the benefit could not be assigned in pieces. It would have to be assigned as a whole or not at all',[14]
(vi) where the plaintiff relies upon his land being part of a scheme of development.

A purchaser of land may show that the benefit of a restrictive covenant has passed to him in one of three ways.

In **Re Pinewood Estate** [1958] Ch 280, [1957] 2 All ER 517,[15] WYNN-PARRY J, said at 284, at 519:

'I propose first to consider whether there is in existence what is known as a building scheme affecting this area of land which is clearly ascertained; because, if there is an existing building scheme, fulfilling the conditions laid down by Parker J in *Elliston v Reacher* [1908] 2 Ch 374; affd. [1908] 2 Ch 665, p. 982, post, then the respondent and the other persons interested will have the benefit of the covenants in the deed ... It is admitted by Mr Newsom that she could claim the benefit of the restrictive covenants if it could be shown either that the benefit had been annexed by proper words of annexation, or that there was a complete chain of assignments of the benefit of the covenants; but it is conceded on behalf of the respondent that there are no words of annexation, and it is conceded that the chain is not complete. In those circumstances, what the respondent says is

---

[9]   (1938) 6 CLJ 339 (S. J. Bailey).
[10] *Fairclough v Marshall* (1878) 4 Ex D 37; *Rogers v Hosegood* [1900] 2 Ch 388 (a mortgagor before 1926), p. 957, post.
[11] *The Prior's Case* (1368) YB 42 Edw 3, fo 3A pl 14; Smith's *Leading Cases* (13th edn. 1929), vol. i, pp. 51, 65, 73.
[12] *Renals v Cowlishaw* (1878) 9 ChD 125, p. 959, post; *Re Union of London and Smith's Bank Ltd's Conveyance, Miles v Easter* [1933] Ch 611, per ROMER J at 630, p. 971, post; *Marten v Flight Refuelling Ltd* [1962] Ch 115, [1961] 2 All ER 696, p. 976, post.
[13] See p. 954, ante; *Re Union of London and Smith's Bank Ltd's Conveyance, Miles v Easter supra; Newton Abbot Co-operative Society Ltd v Williamson and Treadgold Ltd* [1952] Ch 286, [1952] 1 All ER 279, p. 972, post; *Stilwell v Blackman* [1968] Ch 508, [1967] 3 All ER 514.
[14] *Re Union of London and Smith's Bank Ltd's Conveyance*, supra, at 630 per ROMER LJ; *Federated Homes Ltd v Mill Lodge Properties Ltd* [1980] 1 WLR 594, [1980] 1 All ER 371, p. 959, post.
[15] [1957] CLJ 146 (H. W. R. Wade).

that she is entitled to the benefit of the restrictive provisions because it is a deed which shows clearly by its language an intention that the parties should be mutually bound by the restrictions, and that that element of mutuality is enough to carry the benefit of the restrictive stipulations. That means that they are endeavouring to set up a further method by which the benefit of restrictive stipulations can be transferred. ...

The real question is: Is there a fourth class at all? The first class is the *Elliston v Reacher* type of case; the second consists of cases where there are proper words of annexation; the third consists of cases where there is a continuous chain of express assignments. But is there a fourth class? ...

But I can find no authority, certainly none was cited to me, which establishes the fourth class suggested. In my opinion, therefore, it is not open either to the respondent or to anybody else upon this line of reasoning to rely on these restrictive covenants.'

i. BY ANNEXATION

Whether or not the benefit of a restrictive covenant has been annexed to the land of the covenantee depends upon the intention of the parties, as construed from the language of the conveyance.[16] If such an intention is manifested, the benefit of the covenant is notionally annexed to the land to be benefited; and the benefit of the covenant then passes automatically on an assignment of the covenantee's land.

This situation was contrasted with a covenant whose terms failed to manifest such an intention. The benefit of such a covenant was available, by the contract, to the covenantee; but was only available to successors in title of the covenantee if the benefit of the covenant was expressly assigned at the time of the conveyance; and, in the case of a series of assignments of the land, it was necessary to show that there was a similar 'chain of assignments' of the benefit of the covenant.

The leading cases illustrating these rules were *Rogers v Hosegood* [1900] 2 Ch 388, where annexation was achieved; and *Renals v Cowlishaw* [1878] 9 ChD 125, where it failed. Describing the methods of annexation, GREENE LJ said in *Drake v Gray* [1936] Ch 451 at 466:

'There are two familiar methods of indicating in a covenant of this kind the land in respect of which the benefit is to enure. One is to describe the character in which the covenantee receives the covenant. That is the form which is adopted here, a covenant with so and so, owners or owner for the time being of whatever the land may be. Another method is to state by means of an appropriate declaration that the covenant is taken "for the benefit of" whatever the lands may be.'[17]

The language which succeeded in effecting an annexation in *Rogers v Hosegood* was in this form: 'with intent that the covenants ... might enure for the benefit of the [vendors] ... their heirs and assigns and others claiming under them to all or any of their lands adjoining or near to the said premises.' It has never been suggested that that form of words was necessary; what was needed was a manifestation of an intention to annex. Would annexation be effected if the

---

[16]   See *Re MCA East Ltd* [2003] 1 P & CR 118.
[17]   The relevant date for identifying the benefited land is that of transfer not registration: *Mellon v Sinclair* [1996] CL January 560.

covenant were made in the following form? 'With the covenantee and his successors in title (including the owners and occupiers for the time being of the land of the covenantee intended to be benefited) and the persons deriving title under him or them.' If such a covenant would be effective to annex the benefit of the covenant, annexation would appear to be effected in every case; for, by section 78 of the Law of Property Act 1925, every covenant 'relating to the land of the covenantee' shall be deemed to be made in that form. And the problem of determining whether the language of the conveyance is sufficient to manifest an intention to annex would disappear. That is the decision in *Federated Homes Ltd v Mill Lodge Properties Ltd* [1980] 1 WLR 594, [1980] 1 All ER 371, p. 959, post.

(a) Construction of the Instrument
ROGERS v HOSEGOOD
[1900] 2 Ch 388 (Ch D, FARWELL J; affd, CA, Lord ALVERSTONE MR, RIGBY and COLLINS LJJ)

Four partners, carrying on business as builders, were the owners in fee simple, subject to a mortgage, of land at Palace Gate, Kensington. One plot was sold in 1869 to the Duke of Bedford who entered into a covenant 'with intent that the covenants ... might so far as possible bind the premises thereby conveyed and every part thereof and might enure to the benefit of [the vendors] ... their heirs and assigns and others claiming under them to all or any of their lands adjoining or near to the said premises' ... that 'no more than one messuage or dwelling house ... should at any one time be erected or be standing on the ... plot ...'. In 1872, a nearby plot was sold, and in 1873 conveyed to Sir John Millais, who had no knowledge of the covenant given by the Duke. Successors in title of the Duke by purchase proposed, in breach of the restrictive covenant, to erect, on this and adjoining plots, a large building which was to be occupied as residential flats. Among various actions, the trustees of the will of Sir John Millais claimed an injunction to restrain the defendants from erecting the block of flats.

Held. The plaintiffs were entitled to enforce the covenant.

COLLINS LJ (reading the judgment of the court): This case raises questions of some difficulty, but we are of opinion that the decision of Farwell J is right, and ought to be affirmed. ... The real and only difficulty arises on the question— whether the benefit of the covenants has passed to the assigns of Sir John Millais as owners of the plot purchased by him on 25 March 1873, there being no evidence that he knew of these covenants when he bought. [18] Here, again, the difficulty is narrowed, because by express declaration on the face of the conveyances of 1869 the benefit of the two covenants in question was intended for all or any of the vendor's lands near to or adjoining the plot sold, and therefore for (among others) the plot of land acquired by Sir John Millais, and that they 'touched and concerned' that land within the meaning of those words so as to run with the land at law we do not doubt. Therefore, but for a technical difficulty which was not raised before Farwell J, we should agree with him that the benefit of the covenants in question was annexed to and passed to Sir John Millais by the conveyance of the land which he bought in 1873. A difficulty, however, in giving effect to this view arises from the fact that the covenants in question in the deeds

---

[18] See *R v Westminster City Council and London Electricity Board* (1989) 59 P & CR 51 (benefit described as 'a hidden treasure in the hands of the present owner (whoever he may be) of Tulk's retained land').

of May and July 1869 were made with the mortgagors only, and therefore in contemplation of law were made with strangers to the land: *Webb v Russell* [1789] 3 Term Rep 393, to which, therefore, the benefit did not become annexed. That a court of equity, however, would not regard such an objection as defeating the intention of the parties to the covenant is clear; and, therefore, when the covenant was clearly made for the benefit of certain land with a person who, in the contemplation of such a court was the true owner of it, it would be regarded as annexed to and running with that land, just as it would have been at law but for the technical difficulty. ...

These observations [referring to observations of Jessel MR in *London and South Western Rly Co v Gomm* (1882) 20 ChD at p. 583] which are just as applicable to the benefit reserved as to the burden imposed, shew that in equity, just as at law, the first point to be determined is whether the covenant or contract in its inception binds the land. If it does, it is then capable of passing with the land to subsequent assignees ... of the land. The benefit may be annexed to one plot and the burden to another, and when this has been once clearly done, the benefit and the burden pass to the respective assignees, subject, in the case of the burden, to proof that the legal estate, if acquired, has been acquired with notice of the covenant. ...

[His Lordship then referred to *Renals v Cowlishaw* (1878) 9 ChD 125, infra and *Child v Douglas* (1854) Kay 560.]

These authorities establish the proposition that, when the benefit has been once clearly annexed to one piece of land, it passes by assignment of that land, and may be said to run with it, in contemplation as well of equity as of law, without proof of special bargain or representation on the assignment. In such a case it runs, not because the conscience of either party is affected, but because the purchaser has bought something which inhered in or was annexed to the land bought. This is the reason why, in dealing with the burden, the purchaser's conscience is not affected by notice of covenants which were part of the original bargain or on the first sale, but were merely personal and collateral, while it is affected by notice of those which touch and concern the land. The covenant must be one that is capable of running with the land before the question of the purchaser's conscience and the equity affecting it can come into discussion. When, as in *Renals v Cowlishaw*, there is no indication in the original conveyance, or in the circumstances attending it, that the burden of the restrictive covenant is imposed for the benefit of the land reserved, or any particular part of it, then it becomes necessary to examine the circumstances under which any part of the land reserved is sold, in order to see whether a benefit, not originally annexed to it, has become annexed to it on the sale, so that the purchaser is deemed to have bought it with the land, and this can hardly be the case when the purchaser did not know of the existence of the restrictive covenant. But when, as here, it has been once annexed to the land reserved, then it is not necessary to spell an intention out of surrounding facts, such as the existence of a building scheme, statements at auctions, and such like circumstances, and the presumption must be that it passes on a sale of that land, unless there is something to rebut it, and the purchaser's ignorance of the existence of the covenant does not defeat the presumption. We can find nothing in the conveyance to Sir John Millais in any degree inconsistent with the intention to pass to him the benefit already annexed to the land sold to him. We are of opinion, therefore, that Sir John Millais's assigns are entitled to enforce the restrictive covenant against the defendant, and that his appeal must be dismissed.

In **J Sainsbury plc v Enfield London Borough Council** [1989] 1 WLR 590, [1989] 2 All ER 817,[19] where there was no reference in the covenant either to the covenantee's land or to his successors in title other than his assigns, MORRITT J held that 'the intention must be manifested in the conveyance in which the covenant was contained when construed in the light of the surrounding circumstances, including any necessary implication in the conveyance from those surrounding circumstances.' He rejected a claim that 'such intention may be inferred from surrounding circumstances which fall short of those which necessitate an implication in the conveyance itself.'

Rogers v Hosegood is to be contrasted with **Renals v Cowlishaw** (1878) 9 ChD 125, the difference turning on the language of the covenant. In *Renals v Cowlishaw* trustees sold lands to a purchaser who covenanted 'for himself, his heirs, executors and administrators' with the trustees 'their heirs, executors, administrators and assigns' that he would not use the lands in certain ways. The lands purchased were later sold to other purchasers who took with notice of the covenant. And the trustees later sold their retained land to the plaintiffs, no mention being made of the covenant in this conveyance.

The question was whether the benefit of the covenant had passed to the plaintiffs. HALL V-C (affirmed by the Court of Appeal (1879) 11 ChD 866) held that it had not. There was no building scheme, no express assignment of the benefit of the covenant; and the language of the covenant was inadequate to annex the benefit of the covenant to the plaintiffs' land.

The modern practice is to draft the covenant so as to manifest an intention to annex the benefit of the covenant to the land retained by the vendor; unless the vendor wishes to retain the power to choose which of his later purchasers shall be given the benefit (by expressly assigning it[20]). Correct drafting may no longer be important, because it has been held that section 78 of the Law of Property Act 1925 supplies the words necessary to effect annexation.[1]

(b) Law of Property Act 1925, Section 78

LAW OF PROPERTY ACT 1925

78. Benefit of covenants relating to land.—p. 564, ante.

FEDERATED HOMES LTD v MILL LODGE PROPERTIES LTD

[1980] 1 WLR 594, [1980] 1 All ER 371 (CA, MEGAW, BROWNE and BRIGHTMAN LJJ)[2]

Mackenzie Hill Ltd owned land which was to be the subject of a large development in Newport Pagnell in Buckinghamshire. Planning permission was

---

[19]   P. 962, n. 5, post. [1991] Conv 52 (S. Goulding). See also *Shropshire County Council v Edwards* (1982) 46 P & CR 270, where Judge Rubin held that, on the construction of a covenant made in 1908, the benefit had been annexed: *R v Westminster City Council and London Electricity Board* (1989) 59 P & CR 51, p. 942, n. 18, p. 957, n. 18, ante.

[20]   *Marquess of Zetland v Driver* [1937] Ch 651; [1939] Ch 1; *Federated Homes Ltd v Mill Lodge Properties Ltd* [1980] 1 WLR 594 at 606, [1980] 1 All ER 371 at 380, per BRIGHTMAN LJ; *Roake v Chadha* [1984] 1 WLR 40, [1983] 3 All ER 503, p. 963, post; *Crest Nicholson Residential (South) Ltd v McAllister* [2004] EWCA Civ 410, [2004] 2 All ER 991, [2004] 15 EG 105.

[1]   *Federated Homes Ltd v Mill Lodge Properties Ltd*, infra.

[2]   [1980] JPL 371; (1981) 97 LQR 32; JPL 149; (1982) 98 LQR 202 (G. H. Newsom); (1980) 43 MLR 445 (D. J. Hayton); 130 NLJ 531 (T. Bailey); (1982) 2 LS (D. J. Hurst); C & B, pp. 680–682, esp. n. 2; M & W, paras. 16.063–16.064; *Robins v Berkeley Homes (Kent) Ltd* [1996] EGCS 75.

obtained in 1970, and was valid for 3 years. The building programme was phased, and was subject to restrictions upon the overall density of the number of houses to be built on the area. The present litigation arises out of sales by Mackenzie Hill Ltd of three parts of the land; the blue, the red and the green.

The blue land was sold to Mill Lodge Properties Ltd, the defendant company, subject to various conditions, the one relevant for present purposes being the following covenant:

'The Purchaser hereby covenants with the Vendor that ... (iv) in carrying out the development of the "blue" land the Purchaser shall not build at a greater density than a total of 300 dwellings so as not to reduce the number of units which the Vendor might eventually erect on the retained land under the existing Planning Consent.'

The red and green lands were also sold, and the plaintiff company eventually became the owner of each. It will be seen that the terms of the covenant were not such as, from the express language of the covenant, to annex the benefit of the covenant to the land of the covenantee under the rule in *Rogers v Hosegood*. There was, however, a complete chain of assignments of the benefit of the covenant, through the various purchasers to the plaintiff, in the case of the *green* land. But not in the case of the red.

The question was whether the plaintiffs could sue to restrain the breach of the defendants' covenant relating to building density.

Held. The plaintiff company was entitled to the benefit of the covenant in respect of the *green* land by reason of the completed chain of assignments; in respect of the *red* land, because section 78(1) had the effect of annexing the benefit of the covenant to all or any part of the land of the covenantee.

BRIGHTMAN LJ: In September 1978, after much prevarication on the part of Mill Lodge, the plaintiff issued a writ to restrain Mill Lodge from building on the blue land at a greater density than a total of 300 dwellings in breach, it was alleged, of clause 5(iv) of the Mill Lodge conveyance. The defences raised by Mill Lodge so far as relied upon in this appeal were as follows: (1) the covenant in clause 5(iv) was said to be personal to Mackenzie Hill so that the benefit thereof was incapable of assignment to the plaintiff; (2) alternatively, it was said that the covenant became spent when the 1970 planning permission became void at the end of the three-year period; and (3) it was said that, if the covenant was assignable and was not spent, then the benefit had not become vested in the plaintiff by assignment or otherwise.

That, in broad effect, was now the defence was pleaded so far as relevant for present purposes. In a reserved judgment Mr Mills held that the covenant was not personal to Mackenzie Hill and was not spent when the original planning permission lapsed. As regards the transmission of the benefit of the covenant, he held that the benefit was not annexed to the red and the green land, so that it did not automatically pass upon conveyances of the red and the green land. However, he found, as was clearly the fact, that there was an unbroken chain of assignments between transferor and transferee of the green land, so that the benefit of the covenant was now vested, by reason of such assignments, in the plaintiff as the present owner of the green land. There was no such unbroken chain of assignments in the case of the red land; but the judge considered that section 62 of the Law of Property Act 1925, which implies general words into a conveyance of land, was apt to carry the benefit of the covenant from U.D.T. Properties Ltd., the previous assignee of such benefit, to the plaintiff when the registered transfer in its favour was made. [3] The defence, therefore, failed. The

---

[3]   See *Roake v Chadha* [1984] 1 WLR 40 at 47, [1983] 3 All ER 503 at 509, p. 963, post.

judge rejected a submission that damages would be the proper remedy. He granted an injunction against building in excess of the permitted density and gave liberty to apply for a mandatory injunction.

I deal first with the question of construction, upon which two issues arise: whether the covenant was personal to Mackenzie Hill, and whether it is spent.

[His Lordship decided that the covenant was not personal to Mackenzie Hill; nor was the covenant 'spent' by the lapse of the planning permission in 1973].

Having reached the conclusion that the restrictive covenant was capable of assignment and is not spent, I turn to the question whether the benefit has safely reached the hands of the plaintiff. The green land has no problem, owing to the unbroken chain of assignments. I am disposed to think that is sufficient to entitle the plaintiff to relief, and that the plaintiff's right to relief would be no greater at the present time if it were held that it also had the benefit of the covenant in its capacity as owner of the red land. However, the judge dealt with both areas of land and I propose to do the same.

An express assignment of the benefit of a covenant is not necessary if the benefit of the covenant is annexed to the land. In that event, the benefit will pass automatically on a conveyance of the land, without express mention, because it is annexed to the land and runs with it. So the issue of annexation is logically the next to be considered. ...

In my judgment the benefit of this covenant was annexed to the retained land, and I think that this is a consequence of section 78 of the Act of 1925. ...

[His Lordship read this section and continued:]

Mr Price submitted that there were three possible views about section 78. One view, which he described as 'the orthodox view' hitherto held, is that it is merely a statutory shorthand for reducing the length of legal documents. A second view, which was the one that Mr Price was inclined to place in the forefront of his argument, is that the section only applies, or at any rate only achieves annexation, when the land intended to be benefited is signified in the document by express words or necessary implication as the intended beneficiary of the covenant. [4] A third view is that the section applies if the covenant in fact touches and concerns the land of the covenantee, whether that be gleaned from the document itself or from evidence outside the document.

For myself, I reject the narrowest interpretation of section 78, the supposed orthodox view, which seems to me to fly in the face of the wording of the section. Before I express my reasons I will say that I do not find it necessary to choose between the second and third views because, in my opinion, this covenant relates to land of the covenantee on either interpretation of section 78. Clause 5(iv) shows clearly that the covenant is for the protection of the retained land and that land is described in clause 2 as 'any adjoining or adjacent property retained by the vendor.' This formulation is sufficient for annexation purposes: see *Rogers v Hosegood* [1900] 2 Ch 388, p. 957, ante.

There is in my judgment no doubt that this covenant 'related to the land of the covenantee,' or, to use the old-fashioned expression, that it touched and concerned the land, even if Mr Price is correct in his submission that the document must show an intention to benefit identified land. The result of such

---

[4]   See *Bridges v Harrow London Borough Council* (1981) 260 EG 284, where STUART-SMITH J held that, even if this second and stricter view were preferable, the plaintiff failed as there was no such signification in the document; [1982] Conv 313 (F. Webb). In *Crest Nicholson Residential (South) Ltd v McAllister* [2004] EWCA Civ 410, [2004] 2 All ER 991, [2004] 15 EG 105, paras. 43–44, per CHADWICK LJ, where CA applied the second view.

application is that one must read clause 5(iv) as if it were written: 'The purchaser hereby covenants with the vendor and its successors in title and the persons deriving title under it or them, including the owners and occupiers for the time being of the retained land, that in carrying out the development of the blue land the purchaser shall not build at a greater density than a total 300 dwellings so as not to reduce, etc.' I leave out of consideration section 79 as unnecessary to be considered in this context, since Mill Lodge is the original covenantor.

The first point to notice about section 78(1) is that the wording is significantly different from the wording of its predecessor section 58(1) of the Conveyancing Act 1881. The distinction is underlined by section 78(2), which applies section 78(1) only to covenants made after the commencement of the Act. Section 58(1) of the Act of 1881 did not include the covenantee's successors in title or persons deriving title under him or them, or the owner or occupiers for the time being of the land of the covenantee intended to be benefited. The section was confined, in relation to realty, to the covenantee, his heirs and assigns, words which suggest a more limited scope of operation than is found in section 78. [5]

If, as the language of section 78 implies a covenant relating to land which is restrictive of the user thereof is enforceable at the suit of (1) a successor in title of the covenantee, (2) a person deriving title under the covenantee or under his successors in title, and (3) the owner or occupier of the land intended to be benefited by the covenant, it must, in my view, follow that the covenant runs with the land, because ex hypothesi every successor in title to the land, every derivative proprietor of the land and every other owner and occupier has a right by statute to the covenant. In other words, if the condition precedent of section 78 is satisfied— that is to say, there existed a covenant which touches and concerns the land of the covenantee—that covenant runs with the land for the benefit of his successors in title, persons deriving title under him or them and other owners and occupiers.

This approach to section 78 has been advocated by distinguished textbook writers; see Dr Radcliffe's article 'Some Problems of the Law Relating to Restrictive Covenants' (1941) 57 LQR 203, Professor Wade's article, 'Covenants—A Broad and Reasonable View' and the apt cross-heading 'what is wrong with section 78?' [1972B] CLJ 151, 171, and *Megarry and Wade, The Law of Real Property*, 4th edn. (1975), p. 764. Counsel pointed out to us that the fourth edition of *Megarry and Wade* indicates a change of mind on this topic since the third edition.

Although the section does not seem to have been extensively used in the course of argument in this type of case, the construction of section 78 which appeals to me appears to be consistent with at least two cases decided in this court. The first is *Smith and Snipes Hall Farm Ltd v River Douglas Catchment Board* [1949] 2 KB 500, [1949] 2 All ER 179, p. 951, ante. In that case an agreement was made in April 1938 between certain landowners and the catchment board under which the catchment board undertook to make good the banks of a certain brook and to maintain the same, and the landowners undertook to contribute towards the cost. In 1940 the first plaintiff took a conveyance from one of the landowners of a part of the land together with an express assignment of the benefit of the agreement. In 1944 the second plaintiff took a tenancy of that land without any express assignment of the benefit of the agreement. In 1946 the brook burst its banks and the land owned by the first plaintiff and tenanted by the second plaintiff was inundated. The two important points are that the

---

[5]   In *J Sainsbury plc v Enfield London Borough Council* [1989] 1 WLR 590, [1989] 2 All ER 817, MORRITT J held that the benefit of a covenant made in 1894 was not annexed by s. 58 of the Conveyancing and Law of Property Act 1881.

agreement was not expressed to be for the benefit of the landowner's successors in title; and there was no assignment of the benefit of the agreement in favour of the second plaintiff, the tenant. In reliance, as I understand the case, upon section 78 of the Act of 1925, it was held that the second plaintiff was entitled to sue the catchment board for damages for breach of the agreement. It seems to me that that conclusion can only have been reached on the basis that section 78 had the effect of causing the benefit of the agreement to run with the land so as to be capable of being sued upon by the tenant.

The other case, *Williams v Unit Construction Co Ltd* (unreported in the usual series of law reports but fully set out in 19 Conveyancer 262, p. 953, ante), was decided by this court in 1951. There a company had acquired a building estate and had underleased four plots to Cubbin for 999 years. The underlessors arranged for the defendant company to build houses on the four plots. The defendant covenanted with Cubbin to keep the adjacent road in repair until adopted. Cubbin granted a weekly tenancy of one house to the plaintiff without any express assignment of the benefit of the covenant. The plaintiff was injured owing to the disrepair of the road. She was held entitled to recover damages from the defendant for breach of the covenant.

We were referred to observations in the speeches of Lord Upjohn and Lord Wilberforce in *Tophams Ltd v Earl of Sefton* [1967] 1 AC 50 at 73 and 81, [1966] 1 All ER 1039 at 1048 and 1053, p. 954, ante, to the effect that section 79 of the Act of 1925, relating to the burden of covenants, achieved no more than the introduction of statutory shorthand into the drafting of covenants. Section 79, in my view, involves quite different considerations and I do not think that it provides a helpful analogy.

It was suggested by Mr Price that, if this covenant ought to be read as enuring for the benefit of the retained land, it should be read as enuring only for the benefit of the retained land as a whole and not for the benefit of every part of it; with the apparent result that there is no annexation of the benefit to a part of the retained land when any severance takes place. He referred us to a passage in *Re Union of London and Smith's Bank Ltd's Conveyance* [1933] Ch 611 at 628, p. 971, post, which I do not think it is necessary for me to read. ...

I find the idea of the annexation of a covenant to the whole of the land but not to a part of it a difficult conception fully to grasp. ... [The discussion of this question is postponed to section (*d*) p. 967, post].

In the end, I come to the conclusion that section 78 of the Law of Property Act 1925 caused the benefit of the restrictive covenant in question to run with the red land and therefore to be annexed to it, with the result that the plaintiff is able to enforce the covenant against Mill Lodge, not only in its capacity as owner of the green land, but also in its capacity as owner of the red land.

For these reasons I think that the judge reached the correct view on the right of the plaintiff to enforce the covenant, although in part he arrived there by a different route.

In **Roake v Chadha** [1984] 1 WLR 40, [1983] 3 All ER 503,[6] a part of the Sudbury Court Estate in North Wembley was sold and conveyed to Wembley (C and W) Land Co Ltd, who then proceeded to lay out the land in lots and sell them off,

---

[6]   [1984] Conv 68 (P. N. Todd); [1983] All ER Rev 231 (P. J. Clarke). The decision was approved by CA in *Crest Nicholson Residential (South) Ltd v McAllister* [2004] EWCA Civ 410, [2004] 2 All ER 991, [2004] 15 EG 105, at paras. 37–42.

using a standard form of transfer. In April 1934 William Lambert purchased one plot, No 4, Audrey Gardens, and covenanted not to erect any building on the plot apart from one private dwelling-house. The covenant contained the words 'so as to bind (so far as practicable) the land hereby transferred into whosesoever hands the same may come ... but so that this covenant shall not enure for the benefit of any owner or subsequent purchaser of any part of the estate unless the benefit of this covenant shall be expressly assigned.'

The defendant was the successor in title to William Lambert, and was proposing to erect an additional house on his plot. The plaintiffs were successors in title to Wembley (C & W) Land Co Ltd; they had subsequently purchased neighbouring plots, but had not had the benefit of the covenant expressly assigned to them.

In holding that the plaintiffs were not entitled to an injunction restraining the defendant from building the additional house, Judge Paul Baker QC said at 43, at 506:

'From these facts, which are not in dispute the plaintiffs contend that the benefit of the covenant of No 4, Audrey Gardens has become annexed to each of the plots respectively owned by them. Alternatively, it is contended that the benefit has passed under the general words of section 62 of the Law of Property Act 1925.

As to annexation, Mr Walter, appearing for the plaintiffs, conceded that the express terms of the covenant appeared to exclude annexation, and there was no suggestion that the case fell within the category known as building schemes. Mr Walter, however, in an interesting argument submitted that annexation had come about through the operation of section 78 of the Law of Property Act, as interpreted in *Federated Homes Ltd v Mill Lodge Properties Ltd* [1980] 1 WLR 594, [1980] 1 All ER 371, p. 959, ante, a Court of Appeal decision. I can summarise his argument by the following four points.

(1) The covenant was a covenant relating to the land of the covenantee.

(2) Section 78(1) of the Law of Property Act 1925 provides, as regards such covenants relating to land that they are deemed:

"to be made with the covenantee and his successors in title and the persons deriving title under him or them, and shall have effect as if such successors and other persons were expressed. For the purposes of this subsection in connection with covenants restrictive of the user of land "successors in title" shall be deemed to include the owners and occupiers for the time being of the land of the covenantee intended to be benefited."

(3) In the *Federated Homes* case it was held that by virtue of section 78(1) the benefit of a covenant relating to land retained by the covenantee ran with that land and was annexed to it and to every part of it.

(4) The provisions of section 78, unlike those of section 79 relating to the burden of the covenant, cannot be excluded by the expression of a contrary intention. Section 79 reads:

[His Honour read the section, and continued:]

Unlike section 78, which had a counterpart in section 58 of the Conveyancing Act 1881, section 79 was a new section in 1925. The important point to which attention is called is 'unless a contrary intention is expressed,' in section 79. There is no corresponding expression in section 78. Those are the main points of the argument.

I have no difficulty in accepting that the covenant in the standard form of the 1934 transfer is a covenant relating to the retained land of the convenantee, that is to say, Wembley (C & W) Land Co Ltd, and that therefore section 78 comes into play. It is the third and fourth points which have given rise to the argument in this case.

I must begin, therefore, by examining the *Federated Homes* case. …. The plaintiff became clearly entitled to the relief sought in right of the green land.

Mr Henty, for the defendant in the present case, has argued that accordingly the Court of Appeal's judgments in relation to the red land were obiter. I am unable to accept this view of the effect of the judgments. As it seems to me, the status of the covenant in relation to both pieces of land—the red and the green—was in issue in the case. If the defendant in subsequent proceedings had sought to challenge the validity of the covenant in relation to the red land, he could, as I would see it, be met by a plea of issue estoppel and consequently the principle underlying the court's conclusion cannot be regarded as obiter. [7] That principle I take from the following passage in the judgment of Brightman LJ, at 605, at 379:

"If, as the language of section 78 implies, a covenant relating to land which is restrictive of the user thereof is enforceable at the suit of (1) a successor in title of the covenantee, (2) a person deriving title under the covenantee or under his successors in title, and (3) the owner or occupier of the land intended to be benefited by the covenant, it must, in my view, follow that the covenant runs with the land, because ex hypothesi every successor in title to the land, every derivative proprietor of the land and every other owner and occupier has a right by statute to the covenant. In other words, if the condition precedent of section 78 is satisfied—that is to say, there exists a covenant which touches and concerns the land of the covenantee—that covenant runs with the land for the benefit of his successors in title, persons deriving title under him or them and other owners and occupiers."

That seems to be the essential point of the decision. Mr Henty made a frontal attack on this use of section 78, which he reinforced by reference to an article by Mr G. H. Newsom QC in (1981) 97 LQR 32 which is critical of the decision. The main lines of attack are (1) that the conclusion overlooks the legislative history of section 78 which it is said shows that it has a narrower purpose than is claimed and does not in itself bring about annexation; (2) this narrower purpose has been accepted in relation to the corresponding section 79 (relation to burden) by Lord Upjohn and Lord Wilberforce in *Tophams Ltd v Earl of Sefton* [1967] 1 AC 50 at 73, 81, [1966] 1 All ER 1039 at 1048, 1053. Further, it is said by way of argument sub silentio that in a number of cases, notably *Marquess of Zetland v Driver* [1939] Ch 1, [1938] 2 All ER 158 and *Re Jeff's Transfer (No. 2)* [1966] 1 WLR 841, [1966] 1 All ER 934, that the argument could have been used to good effect but was not deployed.

Now, all this is very interesting, and the views of Mr Newsom are entitled to very great respect seeing that until his recent retirement he was a practitioner of long experience who had made a special study of this branch of the law. He has written a valuable monograph on it. All the same, despite Mr Henty's blandishments, I am not going to succumb to the temptation of joining in any such discussion. Sitting here as a judge of the Chancery Division, I do not consider it to be my place either to criticise or to defend the decisions of the Court of Appeal. I conceive it my clear duty to accept the decision of the Court of Appeal as binding on me and apply it as best I can to the facts I find here.

---

[7]   In *Allen v Veranne Builders Ltd* [1988] EGCS 2 BROWNE-WILKINSON V-C also held that it was the ratio of the CA's decision.

Mr Walter's method of applying it is simplicity itself. The *Federated Homes* case shows that section 78 of the Act of 1925 brings about annexation, and that the operation of the section cannot be excluded by a contrary intention. As I have indicated, he supports this last point by reference to section 79, which is expressed to operate "unless a contrary intention is expressed," a qualification which, as we have already noticed, is absent from section 78. Mr Walter could not suggest any reason of policy why section 78 should be mandatory, unlike, for example, section 146 of the Act of 1925, which deals with restrictions on the right to forfeiture of leases and which, by an express provision "has effect notwithstanding any stipulation to the contrary."

I am thus far from satisfied that section 78 has the mandatory operation which Mr Walter claimed for it. But if one accepts that it is not subject to a contrary intention, I do not consider that it has the effect of annexing the benefit of the covenant in each and every case irrespective of the other express terms of the covenant. I notice that Brightman LJ in the *Federated Homes* case did not go so far as that, for he said, at 606, at 381:

"I find the idea of the annexation of a covenant to the whole of the land but not to a part of it a difficult conception fully to grasp. I can understand that a covenantee may expressly or by necessary implication retain the benefit of a covenant wholly under his own control, so that the benefit will not pass unless the covenantee chooses to assign; but I would have thought, if the benefit of a covenant is, on a proper construction of a document, annexed to the land, prima facie it is annexed to every part thereof, unless the contrary clearly appears".

So at least in some circumstances Brightman LJ is considering that despite section 78 the benefit may be retained and not pass or be annexed to and run with land. In this connection, I was also referred by Mr Henty to *Elphinstone's Covenants Affecting Land* (1946), p. 17, where it is said in a footnote:

"but it is thought that, as a covenant must be construed as a whole, the court would give due effect to words excluding or modifying the operation of the section ..."

The true position as I see it is that even where a covenant is deemed to be made with successors in title as section 78 requires, one still has to construe the covenant as a whole to see whether the benefit of the covenant is annexed. Where one finds, as in the *Federated Homes* case, the covenant is not qualified in any way, annexation may be readily inferred; but where, as in the present case, it is expressly provided:

"this covenant shall not enure for the benefit of any owner or subsequent purchaser of any part of the vendor's Sudbury Court Estate at Wembley unless the benefit of this covenant shall be expressly assigned ..."

One cannot just ignore these words. One may not be able to exclude the operation of the section in widening the range of the covenantees, but one has to consider the covenant as a whole to determine its true effect. When one does that, then it seems to me that the answer is plain and in my judgment the benefit was not annexed. That is giving full weight to both the statute in force and also what is already there in the covenant.

[His Honour then considered the alternative claim based on LPA 1925, s. 62; see p. 980, post) and concluded:]

I thus conclude overall that the plaintiffs have failed to show that they are entitled to the benefit of the covenant in relation to their respective properties.'

(c) Annexation to the Whole of the Covenantee's Land

The covenantee may enforce the covenant against the covenantor or his assigns, so long as the covenantee has some land capable of benefiting. But, when the question concerns the annexation of the benefit of the covenant to the dominant land, so as to make the benefit run with the land on a conveyance, it has been held that this can only be done at law or in equity, if substantially the whole of the 'dominant' land is capable of benefiting; it is not possible for the court to effect a severance and allow the covenant to be annexed to such land as is capable of benefiting.[8]

The difficulty, however, disappears if the covenant is correctly drafted, so as to show an intention to annex the benefit to the whole or *any part or parts of* the estate, for the benefit will then be annexed to such parts as are in fact benefited.[9] It has been held that the court will hear evidence as to the capability of the land to be benefited by the covenant,[10] and that the burden of proof is on the defendant to show that it does not do so, either originally, or at the date of the action.'[11]

(d) Annexation to Part of the Covenantee's Land

Even if the whole of the dominant land is capable of benefiting, and if the benefit of the covenant is annexed to the whole, it has usually been held that the benefit of the covenant will only run in favour of the purchaser of a *part* of the land, if he can show that the benefit was annexed to the part which he purchased, or to each portion of the whole.

'For instance, A, the owner of a large property, sells part of it to Y and takes a covenant that no public house shall be opened on it. This covenant is annexed to A's land. Later A sells part of the dominant land to B. If B seeks to enforce the covenant by virtue of its annexation to A's land, he must prove that its benefit was annexed to each and every part of those lands or to the very part bought by him.'[12]

In **Drake v Gray** [1936] Ch 451, [1936] 1 All ER 363,[13] the Court of Appeal (SLESSER, ROMER and GREENE LJJ) held that a covenant taken with the other parties to the deed ... 'and other the owners or owner for the time being of the remaining hereditaments so agreed to be partitioned' operated to annex the covenant to each portion of the land, so as to allow the benefit of the covenant to run with each portion of the partitioned land.

SLESSER LJ said at 461, at 372:

'I recognize, and I accept entirely, what was said by this Court in *Re Union of London and Smith's Bank Ltd's Conveyance, Miles v Easter* [1933] Ch 611, p. 971, post, that it must be shown that the benefit was intended to enure to each portion of

----

[8]   *Re Ballard's Conveyance* [1937] Ch 473, [1937] 2 All ER 691; 57 LQR at p. 210 (G. R. Y. Radcliffe); Elphinstone, *Covenants Affecting Land* (1946) p. 60; *Marten v Flight Refuelling Ltd* [1962] Ch 115 at 137, [1961] 2 All ER 696 at 706, p. 976, post.

[9]   *Marquess of Zetland v Driver* [1937] Ch 651, [1939] Ch 1; (1941) 57 LQR 203 (G. R. Y. Radcliffe).

[10] *Marten v Flight Refuelling Ltd*, supra; *Earl of Leicester v Wells-next-the Sea UDC* [1973] Ch 110, [1972] 3 All ER 77 (expert evidence admitted to show that a covenant restricting 19 acres afforded 'great benefit and much needed protection to the Holkham Estate as a whole' i.e. to 32,000 acres). In *Re Ballard's Conveyance*, supra, no evidence was offered to show benefit to the dominant land as a whole.

[11] *Wrotham Park Estate Co Ltd v Parkside Homes Ltd* [1974] 1 WLR 798, [1974] 2 All ER 321; *Cryer v Scott Bros (Sunbury) Ltd* (1986) 55 P & CR 183.

[12] C & B, p. 683; Preston & Newsom, paras. 2–20 to 2–29. In *Griffiths v Band* (1974) 29 P & CR 243 at 246, GOULDING J referred to 'this somewhat muddy corner of legal history.'

[13] *Reid v Bickerstaff* [1909] 2 Ch 305.

the land, and it is true that it has been held that the use of the words "or any part thereof" may be apt for that purpose; but I cannot read that case as meaning that those words, and those words only, are the sole means by which a conveyance may show that the benefit was intended to enure to each portion. In this case, the intention, as gathered from the documents and the recital of the whole history of the case, is clear that the benefit of the covenant was to enure to the owner of any part of the remaining hereditaments, and as the plaintiff was such an owner, the learned judge was right in the conclusion to which he came.'

In **Re Selwyn's Conveyance** [1967] Ch 674, [1967] 1 All ER 339, GOFF J held that a covenant 'for the protection of the adjoining or neighbouring land part of or lately part of the Selwyn Estate' was sufficient to annex the benefit to separate parts of the land.

In **Russell v Archdale** [1964] Ch 38, [1962] 2 All ER 305, [14] BUCKLEY J held that a restrictive covenant 'to benefit and protect the vendor's adjoining and neighbouring land' was annexed to that land as a whole, but that the plaintiff, a subsequent purchaser of only part of that land, was not entitled to rely on the annexation. He said at 45, at 311:

'The next question which was debated was whether this annexation was an annexation to the whole of the land referred to by the words "adjoining and neighbouring land" or to each and every part of it, and in that connection I was referred by Mr Arnold to the decision of the Court of Appeal in *Drake v Gray*. That was relied upon as authority for the proposition that where one finds annexation by general words such as "for the benefit of the vendor's remaining land" or, such as we have in the present case, "adjoining and neighbouring land", the proper interpretation is to construe that as a reference to each and every part of the land which falls within the description. ...

In the course of his judgment, Romer LJ said at 465, at 376: "Most of the cases that have come before the court have been cases where a covenant has been entered into by a vendor for the benefit of, say, the AB estate for the time being. There, of course, no intention is shown that the benefit should enure for any particular part of the estate; but where one finds not 'the land coloured yellow' or 'the estate' or 'the field named so-and-so' or anything of that kind, but 'the lands retained by the vendor', it appears to me that there is a sufficient indication that the benefit of the covenant enures to every one of the lands retained by the vendor, and if a plaintiff in a subsequent action to enforce a covenant can say: 'I am the owner of a piece of land that belonged to the vendor at the time of the conveyance', he is entitled to enforce the covenant. ..."

No doubt every case of this kind, being one of construction, must be determined on the facts and the actual language used, but with the utmost respect to Romer LJ, I cannot see that the mere fact that the land intended to be benefited was described by such an expression as "the land retained by the vendor" is sufficient to enable the court to come to the conclusion that the covenant is intended to benefit each and every part of that land. This observation of Romer

---

[14]   (1962) 78 LQR 334, 482 (R.E.M.); affd. CA (Lord DENNING MR, dissenting) (1962) Times, 1 December, where only the issue of acquiescence is discussed.

LJ was, I think, clearly obiter dictum, … and in my judgment that authority does not assist the plaintiffs to say that the benefit of the covenant is annexed to each and every part of what is described by the conveyance as "the adjoining and neighbouring land of the vendor". That being so, I think it must follow that the plaintiffs cannot, merely by reason of annexation of this covenant to the "adjoining and neighbouring land of the vendor" in the conveyance of 1938 and the fact that they have acquired part only of that land, enforce the covenant.' [15]

In **Federated Homes v Mill Lodge Properties Ltd** [1980] 1 WLR 594, [1980] 1 All ER 371 p. 959, ante, BRIGHTMAN LJ said at 606, at 380:

'It was suggested by Mr Price that, if this covenant ought to be read as enuring for the benefit of the retained land, it should be read as enuring only for the benefit of the retained land as a whole and not for the benefit of every part of it; with the apparent result that there is no annexation of the benefit to a part of the retained land when any severance takes place. He referred us to a passage in *Re Union of London and Smith's Bank Ltd's Conveyance* [1933] Ch 611 at 628, which I do not think it is necessary for me to read.

The problem is alluded to in *Megarry and Wade, The Law of Real Property*, 4th edn., p. 763.

"In drafting restrictive covenants it is therefore desirable to annex them to the covenantee's land 'or any part or parts thereof'. An additional reason for using this form of words is that, if there is no indication to the contrary, the benefit may be held to be annexed only to the whole of the covenantee's land, so that it will not pass with portions of it disposed of separately. But even without such words the court may find that the covenant is intended to benefit any part of the retained land; and small indications may suffice, since the rule that presumes annexation to the whole only is arbitrary and inconvenient. In principle it conflicts with the rule for assignments, which allows a benefit annexed to the whole to be assigned with part, and it also conflicts with the corresponding rule for easements."

I find the idea of the annexation of a covenant to the whole of the land but not to a part of it a difficult conception fully to grasp. I can understand that a covenantee may expressly or by necessary implication retain the benefit of a covenant wholly under his own control, so that the benefit will not pass unless the covenantee chooses to assign; but I would have thought, if the benefit of a covenant is, on a proper construction of a document, annexed to the land, prima facie it is annexed to every part thereof, unless the contrary clearly appears. It is difficult to see how this court can have reached its decision in *Williams v Unit Construction Co Ltd*, 19 Conveyancer 262, unless this is right. The covenant was, by inference, annexed to every part of the land and not merely to the whole, because it will be recalled that the plaintiff was a tenant of only one of the four houses which had the benefit of the covenant.

---

[15]   Similarly in *Re Jeff's Transfer (No 2)* [1966] 1 WLR 841, [1966] 1 All ER 837 ('for the benefit of the remainder of the Chorleywood Estate (Loudwater) belonging to the vendor'); *Stilwell v Blackman* [1968] Ch 508, [1967] 3 All ER 514 ('to benefit and protect the adjoining property of the vendor'). The Law Commission Report on Restrictive Covenants (1967 Law Com No. 11), p. 15 recommended that the benefit of a land obligation should be annexed to each and every part unless a contrary intention is expressed. See also Victoria Property Law Act 1958, s. 79A.

There is also this observation by Romer LJ in *Drake v Gray* [1936] Ch 451, 465. He was dealing with the enuring of the benefit of a restrictive covenant and he said:

[His Lordship quoted Romer LJ's dictum set out at p. 968, ante, and continued:]

In the instant case the judge in the course of his judgment appears to have dismissed the notion that any individual plot-holder would be entitled, even by assignment, to have the benefit of the covenant that I have been considering. I express no view about that. I only say this, that I am not convinced that his conclusion on the point is correct. I say no more about it.' [16]

ii. BY EXPRESS ASSIGNMENT

If the benefit of a restrictive covenant is not annexed to the land of the covenantee, an assignee must show that the benefit passed to him by express assignment of the benefit at the time of the conveyance. Such express assignment will be necessary in fewer cases in the future if, on the authority of *Federated Homes Ltd v Mill Lodge Properties Ltd* [1980] 1 WLR 594, [1980] 1 All ER 371, p. 959, ante, annexation is held to be effected by section 78 of the Law of Property Act 1925. Cases requiring express assignment can, however still arise; as where there is express provision to the effect that express assignment of the benefit of the covenant shall be required, [17] or where there is no identification in the conveyance of the land to be benefited. [18] Further, the benefit of a covenant passes under the 'general words' of section 62 of the Law of Property Act 1925, but only if there has already been annexation or assignment. [19]

Preston and Newsom, *Restrictive Covenants Affecting Freehold Land* (8th edn. 1991), para. 2.40.

'Where the defendant is the original covenantor, he is liable at law. Against him the original covenantee can succeed at common law in an ordinary action on the covenant. Further, a plaintiff who is the express assignee of the benefit of the covenant can succeed against the original covenantor in an action at law governed by the ordinary action rules as to the assignment of a chose in action. But "at law the benefit could not be assigned in pieces. It would have to be assigned as a whole or not at all." [20] The plaintiff must therefore rely upon an equitable title even as against the original covenantor if the benefit of the

---

[16]   See *Allen v Veranne Builders Ltd* [1988] EGCS 2, where Sir Nicolas BROWNE-WILKINSON V-C said: 'To my mind there is everything to suggest an intention to annex it to each and every part. We are not here dealing with an old-fashioned country gentleman's landed estate, where it might well be that there would be an intention to annex the benefit to the whole of the estate. In the present case we are dealing with a development estate, the whole of which was intended to be disposed of. I can see nothing in the case to suggest that one should depart from the general presumption as laid down by the Court of Appeal.'

[17]   *Marquess of Zetland v Driver* [1937] Ch 651; *Roake v Chadha* [1984] 1 WLR 40, [1983] 3 All ER 503, p. 963, ante.

[18]   *Newton Abbot Co-operative Society v Williamson and Treadgold Ltd* [1952] Ch 286, [1952] 1 All ER 279, p. 972, post. But see *Federated Homes Ltd v Mill Lodge Properties Ltd*, supra, at 604, at 379 per BRIGHTMAN LJ.

[19]   P. 981, n. 3, post; *Federated Homes Ltd v Mill Lodge Properties Ltd*, supra, at 601, at 376.

[20]   *Miles v Easter* [1933] Ch 611 at 630, per ROMER LJ.

covenant has been assigned "in pieces." And, more importantly, he must always rely on an equitable title against a defendant who is not the original covenantor (or his personal representative). For the burden of a covenant never runs at law and a successor of the covenantor is liable in equity, under the rule in *Tulk v Moxhay*. Requiring the assistance of equity, against a defendant who is liable in equity only or because his own title depends upon equity, a plaintiff must therefore show that he is within the special rules laid down by equity for establishing whether a title by express assignment can be relied upon.'

(a) Contemporaneous with Conveyance

It has long been clear that it was possible in equity to assign expressly the benefit of a restrictive covenant on the sale of the land of the covenantee. [1] Such assignment must be contemporaneous with the conveyance; if once the covenant becomes separated from the land to be benefited, it ceases to be operative. [2] It was not, however, until 1952 that it was authoritatively held that the benefit would pass in this way. [3] And this decision has been criticised. [4]

In **Re Union of London and Smith's Bank Ltd's Conveyance, Miles v Easter** [1933] Ch 611, [5] ROMER LJ referred to *Renals v Cowlishaw* (1878) 9 ChD 125 and *Rogers v Hosegood* [1900] 2 Ch 388, p. 957, ante and said at 629:

'In neither of these cases, therefore, did it become necessary for the court to inquire into the circumstances in which an express assignee of the benefit of a covenant that does not run with the land is entitled to enforce it. In the present case, however, it is necessary to do so, inasmuch as the defendants claim to be the express assignees of the benefit of the restrictive covenants contained in the deeds of 23 October 1908 and 11 May 1909.

Now it may be conceded that the benefit of a covenant entered into with the covenantee or his assigns is assignable. The use of the word "assigns" indicates this: see Williams on Personal Property, 18th edn. p. 33. But it by no means follows that the assignee of a restrictive covenant affecting land of the covenantor is entitled to enforce it against an assign of that land. For the burden of the covenant did not run with the land at law, and is only enforceable against a purchaser with notice by reason of the equitable doctrine that is usually referred to as the rule in *Tulk v Moxhay*. It was open, therefore, to the Courts of Equity to prescribe the particular class of assignees of the covenant to whom they should concede the benefit of the rule. This they have done, and in doing so have included within the class persons to whom the benefit of the covenant could not have been assigned at law. For at law the benefit could not be assigned in pieces. It would

---

[1]   *Renals v Cowlishaw* (1878) 9 ChD 125; *Ives v Brown* [1919] 2 Ch 314; *Lord Northbourne v Johnston & Son* [1922] 2 Ch 309; *Chambers v Randall* [1923] 1 Ch 149; *Re Union of London and Smith's Bank Ltd's Conveyance, Miles v Easter* [1933] Ch 611; *Re Rutherford's Conveyance* [1938] Ch 396, [1938] 1 All ER 495; (1948) 6 CLJ 339 (S. J. Bailey); (1952) 68 LQR 353 (Sir Lancelot Elphinstone). The assignment may be to a lessee; *South Eastern Rly Co v Associated Portland Cement Manufacturers (1900) Ltd* [1910] 1 Ch 12.

[2]   *Chambers v Randall*, supra; *Re Union of London and Smith's Bank Ltd's Conveyance, Miles v Easter*, supra; cf. *Lord Northbourne v Johnston*, supra; *Newton Abbot Co-operative Society Ltd v Williamson and Treadgold Ltd* [1952] Ch 286, [1952] 1 All ER 279, p. 972, post.

[3]   *Newton Abbot Co-operative Society Ltd v Williamson and Treadgold Ltd*, supra.

[4]   (1952) 68 LQR 353 (Sir Lancelot Elphinstone).

[5]   (1933) 49 LQR 483 (H. A. Hollond).

have to be assigned as a whole or not at all. And yet in equity the right to enforce the covenant can in certain circumstances be assigned by the covenantee from time to time to one person after another. Who then are the assignees of the covenant that are entitled to enforce it? The answer to this question is to be found in several authorities which it now becomes necessary to consider.

[His Lordship referred to *Formby v Barker* [1903] 2 Ch 539, p. 943, ante and *LCC v Allen* [1914] 3 KB 642, p. 944, ante, and continued:]

It is plain, however, from these and other cases, and notably that of *Renals v Cowlishaw*, that if the restrictive covenant be taken not merely for some personal purpose or object of the vendor, but for the benefit of some other land of his in the sense that it would enable him to dispose of that land to greater advantage, the covenant, though not annexed to such land so as to run with any part of it, may be enforced against an assignee of the covenantor taking with notice, both by the covenantee and by persons to whom the benefit of such covenant has been assigned, subject however to certain conditions. In the first place, the "other land" must be land that is capable of being benefited by the covenant—otherwise it would be impossible to infer that the object of the covenant was to enable the vendor to dispose of his land to greater advantage. In the next place, this land must be "ascertainable" or "certain", to use the words of Romer and Scrutton LJJ, respectively. For, although the Court will readily infer the intention to benefit the other land of the vendor where the existence and situation of such land are indicated in the conveyance or have been otherwise shown with reasonable certainty, it is impossible to do so from vague references in the conveyance or in other documents laid before the Court as to the existence of other lands of the vendor, the extent and situation of which are undefined. In the third place, the covenant cannot be enforced by the covenantee against an assign of the purchaser after the covenantee has parted with the whole of his land. ...'

NEWTON ABBOT CO-OPERATIVE SOCIETY LTD v WILLIAMSON AND TREADGOLD LTD
[1952] Ch 286, [1952] 1 All ER 279[6] (ChD, Upjohn J)

In 1923, Mrs Mardon, who was owner of premises known as Devonia, in Fore St., Bovey Tracey, on which she carried on business as an ironmonger, conveyed property on the other side of the street to a purchaser who covenanted not to use if for the business of an ironmonger. There was no indication in the conveyance of the land to be benefited, but Mrs Mardon's address was given as Devonia.

In 1941, Mrs Mardon died, having left Devonia in her will to her son Leonard Soper Mardon.

In 1947, the purchasers of the property opposite Devonia sold it to the defendants.

In 1948, Leonard Soper Mardon assigned the ironmongery business to Bovey Tracey Co-operative Society (which later amalgamated with the plaintiffs) together with the benefit of the restrictive covenant, and granted them a lease of Devonia for 21 years.

In 1950, the defendants began to expose articles of ironmongery for sale in breach of the restrictive covenant.

Held. The plaintiffs were entitled to an injunction. The covenant touched and concerned the land and had been validly assigned.

---

[6]   (1952) 68 LQR 353 (Sir Lancelot Elphinstone).

UPJOHN J: The sole issue before me is whether the plaintiffs are entitled to the benefit of the restrictive covenant, and, if so, whether they are entitled to enforce it against the defendants.

I will deal with the first point first. Mr Binney on behalf of the plaintiffs submitted first that the benefit of the restrictive covenant was annexed to Devonia so as to pass with the assignment of Devonia in equity without any express mention in that subsequent assignment; in other words, that the covenant runs with the land. Alternatively, he said that the plaintiffs are the express assigns of the benefit of the covenant, and as such are entitled to enforce it. In this difficult branch of the law one thing in my judgment is clear, namely, that in order to annex the benefit of a restrictive covenant to land, so that it runs with the land without express assignment on a subsequent assignment of the land, the land for the benefit of which it is taken must be clearly identified in the conveyance creating the covenant.

[His Lordship referred on this point to *Renals v Cowlishaw* (1878) 9 ChD 125, p. 959, ante, *Re Union of London and Smith's Bank Ltd's Conveyance, Miles v Easter* (1933) Ch 611, p. 971, ante, and came to the conclusion that the land for the benefit of which the covenant was taken was not sufficiently identified by the conveyance to annex the benefit of it to the land.]

I turn then to his second submission, namely, that the plaintiffs are express assigns of the benefit of the restrictive covenant. Mr Bowles, on behalf of the defendants, contends that, even if it be assumed that his submission (with which I shall deal later) that the covenant was not taken for the benefit of Devonia, but of the business carried on thereat, is wrong, and the covenant was taken by Mrs Mardon for the benefit of Devonia to enable her to dispose of it to better advantage, yet there is no complete chain of assignments vesting the benefit in the plaintiffs. He says that there was never any assignment of the benefit of the covenant by the executors of Mrs Mardon to Leonard Soper Mardon and therefore he was not in a position to assign the benefit of the covenant to the plaintiffs' predecessors in title. He relied on *Ives v Brown* [1919] 2 Ch 314 and *Lord Northbourne v Johnston & Son* [1922] 2 Ch 309.

In my judgment those authorities do not support his contention. The position as I see it was this: On the footing that the restrictive covenant was not annexed to the land so as to run with it, the benefit of the covenant is capable of passing by operation of law as well as by express assignment and formed part of Mrs Mardon's personal estate on her death: see *Ives v Brown*.

It was not suggested that there was any implied assent to the assignment of the benefit of the covenant to the residuary legatee, but in my judgment, when her estate was duly wound up and administered, and this case has been argued before me on the footing that that happened many years ago, the benefit of the covenant was held by the executors as bare trustees for the residuary legatee, Leonard Soper Mardon, who was himself one of the executors. He therefore became entitled to the benefit of this restrictive covenant in equity and, in my judgment, he was entitled to assign the benefit in equity on an assignment of Devonia. No doubt had the covenant been assigned to him by the executors, he could also have assigned it at law. That this is the position is, in my judgment, made clear by the ... judgment of Sargant J in *Lord Northbourne v Johnston & Son*. ...[7]

---

[7] See *Marten v Flight Refuelling Ltd* [1962] Ch 115 at 140, [1961] 2 All ER 696 at 976, where WILBERFORCE J relied upon SARGANT J's reasoning; *Earl of Leicester v Wells-next-the-Sea UDC* [1973] Ch 110, [1972] 3 All ER 77 (special executors of settled land held to be bare trustees of benefit of restrictive covenant for beneficiary under SLA 1925, s. 7(1), p. 359, ante).

The second main question was whether the defendants are liable to have the covenant enforced against them. This was Mr Bowles' main defence in this action and he says that the restrictive covenant was not taken for the benefit of Devonia, and he puts his case in this way: First, he says that in any event this was not taken for the benefit of any land, but was a covenant with Mrs Mardon personally, solely for the benefit of her business. Secondly, he says that in order that an express assign of the benefit may sue an assignee of the burden of the covenant there must be some reference in the conveyance creating that covenant to the land for the benefit of which it was taken. ...

[His Lordship came to the conclusion that the covenant was taken for the benefit of Devonia, and continued:]

Mr Bowles' second point was that, in order that the benefit of the covenant may be assignable, the land for which the benefit of the covenant is taken must in some way be referred to in the conveyance creating the covenant, and I was naturally pressed with the headnote in *Re Union of London and Smith's Bank Ltd's Conveyance, Miles v Easter* [1933] Ch 611, which reads as follows: 'Where on a sale otherwise than under a building scheme a restrictive covenant is taken, the benefit of which is not on the sale annexed to the land retained by the covenantee so as to run with it, an assign of the covenantee's retained land cannot enforce the covenant against an assign (taking with notice) of the covenantor unless he can show (i) that the covenant was taken for the benefit of ascertainable land of the covenantee capable of being benefited by the covenant, and (ii) that he (the covenantee's assign) is an express assign of the benefit of the covenant', and with the following passage in the judgment of Bennett J at 625: 'In my judgment, in order that an express assignee of a covenant restricting the user of land may be able to enforce that covenant against the owner of the land burdened with the covenant, he must be able to satisfy the court of two things. The first is that it was a covenant entered into for the benefit or protection of land owned by the covenantee at the date of the covenant. Otherwise it is a covenant in gross, and unenforceable except as between the parties to the covenant; see *Formby v Barker* [1903] 2 Ch 539, p. 944, ante. Secondly, the assignee must be able to satisfy the court that the deed containing the covenant defines or contains something to define the property for the benefit of which the covenant was entered into: see James LJ in *Renals v Cowlishaw* (1879) 11 ChD at 866.'

With all respect to the statement of the judge, I am unable to agree that where a person is suing as an assign of the benefit of the covenant there must necessarily be something in the deed containing the covenant to define the land for the benefit of which the covenant was entered into. In the first place, the passage in the judgment of James LJ in *Renals v Cowlishaw*, which I have already read, on which the judge relied, does not in my judgment support the statement of the law for which it was cited. In *Renals v Cowlishaw* there was no express assignment of the benefit of the restrictive covenant (see the statement of fact in the report in the court below); and when James LJ says that to enable an assign to take the benefit of restrictive covenants there must be something in the deed to define the property for the benefit of which they were entered into, he is, I think, dealing with the case where it is contended that the benefit of the covenant has been annexed to the land so as to run with the land. When he uses the word 'assign' he is using the word as meaning an assign of the land and not an assign of the benefit of the covenant. Secondly, the views expressed by Bennett J appear to me to be inconsistent with the views expressed in some of the earlier decisions. I do not propose to cite them, but I refer to the following observations on the law on this point, namely, the observations of Collins LJ, delivering the judgment of the Court of Appeal in *Rogers v Hosegood* [1900] 2 Ch at 407, those of Vaughan Williams LJ in *Formby v Barker* [1903] 2 Ch at 551; and to the observations of Cozens-Hardy MR in *Reid v Bickerstaff* [1909] 2 Ch at 319, 325; and to the words of Buckley LJ in the same case. Finally, in *Re Union of London and Smith's Bank Ltd's Conveyance, Miles v Easter* [1933] Ch at 628, 631, Romer LJ, reading the judgment of the Court of Appeal, having considered the cases where the benefit of the covenant is annexed to land so as to run without express mention, says: 'In all other cases the purchaser will not acquire the benefit of the covenant unless that benefit be expressly assigned to him—or to use the words of the Vice-Chancellor, "it must appear that the benefit of the covenant was part of the subject-matter of the purchase".'

[His Lordship then cited the paragraph from Romer LJ's judgment set out on p. 972, ante, and continued:]

In my judgment, therefore, the problem which I have to consider is this: First, when Mrs Mardon took the covenant in 1923, did she retain other lands capable of being benefited by the covenant? The answer is plainly yes. Secondly, was such land 'ascertainable' or 'certain' in this sense that the existence and situation of the land must be indicated in the conveyance or otherwise shown with reasonable certainty?

Apart from the fact that Mrs Mardon is described as of Devonia, there is nothing in the conveyance of 1923 to define the land for the benefit of which the restrictive covenant was taken, and I do not think that carries one very far; but, for the reasons I have given, I am, in my judgment, entitled to look at the attendant circumstances to see if the land to be benefited is shown 'otherwise' with reasonable certainty. That is a question of fact and, on the admitted facts, bearing in mind the close juxtaposition of Devonia and the defendants' premises, in my view the only reasonable inference to draw from the circumstances at the time of the conveyance of 1923 was that Mrs Mardon took the covenant restrictive of the user of the defendants' premises for the benefit of her own business of ironmonger and of her property Devonia where at all material times she was carrying on that business, which last-mentioned fact must have been apparent to the purchasers in 1923.

I should perhaps mention that at the date of her death, Mrs Mardon owned other property in Fore Street, but counsel on neither side founded any argument on that circumstance.

It follows, therefore, in my judgment, that Mrs Mardon could on any subsequent sale of her land Devonia, if she chose, as part of the transaction of sale, assign the benefit of the covenant so as to enable the purchaser from her and his assignees of the land and covenant to enforce it against an owner of the defendants' premises taking with notice, and her legatee, Leonard Soper Mardon, was in no worse position. I do not regard the fact that he assigned the covenant in the deed containing the assignment of the business as affecting the matter. I say nothing as to the position when the plaintiffs' lease expires so that their estate in Devonia comes to an end, nor whether Leonard Soper Mardon, having apparently assigned away the entire benefit of the covenant, will then be in any position further to enforce it.

Mr Bowles took one further point. He submitted that a covenant restrictive of business could not be annexed to land, unless it was a covenant not to carry on a business so as to be a nuisance or annoyance to an adjoining occupier, but he cited no authority for that proposition and, in my judgment, it cannot be maintained: see *Nicoll v Fenning* (1881) 19 ChD 258.

Accordingly, in my judgment, the plaintiffs are entitled to succeed in this action and to an injunction.

Marten v Flight Refuelling Ltd [1962] Ch 115, [1961] 2 All ER 696,[8] raised again, inter alia, the questions (*a*) of the enforceability of the benefit of a covenant when the identity of the land to be benefited could be shown by the use of extrinsic evidence but was not defined in the conveyance itself; and (*b*) of the devolution of the benefit of a covenant through personal representatives.

In 1943 Mrs Marten, the first plaintiff, was an infant tenant in tail of the Crichel estate, a large agricultural estate in Dorset of about 7,500 acres. In that year, the second plaintiffs, who were then holding the estate in trust for Mrs Marten as special executors under the Settled Land Act 1925, conveyed to Harding in fee simple Crook Farm of some 562 acres of which 200 acres had been requisitioned by the Air Ministry for the establishment of an aerodrome. Harding covenanted with the vendors and their successors in title that no part of the land conveyed nor any building thereon should thereafter be used for any purposes other than agricultural purposes. This covenant was registered in 1943 under Land Charges Act 1925, section 10(1),[9] as a land charge Class D(ii).

In 1947 the Air Ministry permitted the first defendants, Flight Refuelling Ltd, to occupy the aerodrome. In 1950 Mrs Marten attained her majority and disentailed; the second plaintiffs assented to the vesting in her of the fee simple, but the assent did not mention the covenant. In 1958 the Air Ministry compulsorily purchased most of the land still occupied by Flight Refuelling Ltd from Harding's executors. The plaintiffs claimed a declaration that they were entitled to the benefit of the covenant and an injunction to restrain Flight Refuelling Ltd from using the land for industrial purposes.

WILBERFORCE J held, inter alia, that the plaintiffs were entitled to the benefit of the covenant and to an injunction to restrain the company from undertaking industrial activities beyond those necessary for Air Ministry purposes. He said at 129, at 701:

'First, are the plaintiffs, or is one of them, entitled to the benefit of the restrictive covenant? This involves several subsidiary questions, namely (*a*) whether the covenant was entered into for the benefit of any land of the covenantee; (*b*) whether that land is sufficiently defined or ascertainable by permissible inference or evidence; (*c*) whether that land is, or was, capable of being benefited by the covenant; (*d*) whether, since the first plaintiff is not the express assignee of the covenant, the action can be brought by the second plaintiff or by the two plaintiffs jointly.

(*a*) and (*b*) … An elaborate argument was addressed to me by the defendants to support a contention that the benefit of the covenant was not available to the plaintiffs. The conveyance, it was said, does not "annex" the benefit of the covenant to any land so that it would pass automatically on a conveyance of the land to a purchaser. Further, it does not indicate that it was made for the benefit of any land, and even supposing that it was so made, it does not identify or provide any material upon which to identify what that land is.

It is, however, well established by the authorities that the benefit of restrictive covenants can pass to persons other than the original covenantee, even in the

---

8   This is not a case involving annexation or express assignment: (1972) 36 Conv (NS) 20 (E. C. Ryder).
9   Now LCA 1972, s. 2(5).

absence of annexation, provided that certain conditions are fulfilled. There is, however, dispute as to the nature of these conditions.

The defendants' contentions are, first, that there must appear from the terms of the deed itself an intention to benefit some land, and, secondly, that the precise land to be benefited must also be stated in the deed, or at least must be capable of ascertainment from the terms of the deed by evidence which is admissible in accordance with the normal rules of interpretation of documents. They rely principally on *Re Union of London and Smith's Bank Ltd's Conveyance, Miles v Easter* [1933] Ch 611, and submit that the decision of Upjohn J in *Newton Abbot Co-operative Society Ltd v Williamson and Treadgold Ltd* [1952] Ch 286, [1952] 1 All ER 279, p. 972, ante, which appears to admit parol evidence for the purpose of identifying the land to be benefited, goes too far.

[His Lordship then referred to *Re Union of London and Smith's Bank Ltd's Conveyance, Miles v Easter; Formby v Barker* [1903] 2 Ch 539, p. 971, ante; *Lord Northbourne v Johnston & Son* [1922] 2 Ch 309, and *Newton Abbot Co-operative Society Ltd v Williamson and Treadgold Ltd*, and, referring to the last, continued:]

This decision was attacked by the Attorney-General in a lively argument, and I was invited not to follow it. Of course, it relates to its own special facts, and no doubt I could leave it on one side. But I see nothing in it contrary to the principles which appear to be securely laid down. Here were two shops in common ownership facing each other in the same street, one of them, Devonia, an ironmonger's shop. The shops opposite are sold with a covenant against carrying on an ironmonger's business. What could be more obvious than that the covenant was intended for the protection or benefit of the vendor's property Devonia? To have rejected such a conclusion would, I venture to think, have involved not only an injustice, but a departure from common sense. So far from declining the authority of his case, I welcome it as a useful guide. But it is only a guide, and I must ultimately reach my conclusion on the facts of the present case. ...

On these facts I consider that I should come to the conclusion that the covenant was taken for the benefit of land of the vendors, that land being the Crichel estate. In doing so I do not, so it seems to me, go outside such surrounding or attendant circumstances as in accordance with the authorities, it is legitimate for the court to take into account. A decision based on the mere wording of cl. 2 of the conveyance would, in my judgment be unduly narrow and indeed technical, and would go far to undermine the usefulness of the rule which equity courts have evolved that the benefit of restrictive covenants may be capable of passing to assigns of the "dominant" land or of the covenant in cases other than those of annexation. I would add two observations: first, the rules in *Miles v Easter* properly relate to cases where the covenant is sought to be enforced by an assign from the original covenantee. In this case, however, the second plaintiff is the original covenantee and the first plaintiff is the person for whose benefit in equity the covenant was taken. To that important extent the plaintiffs' case is stronger than that of the defendant in *Miles v Easter*. Secondly, in holding that the covenant was for the benefit of the Crichel estate, I mean the Crichel estate as a whole, as a single agricultural estate which it was and is, and I express no opinion whether it enures for the benefit of each and every part, for example, if parts are separately sold off. That is not a question which arises in this case.

There remain certain specific arguments which were put forward, and I must shortly deal with them. ...

It was said that unless the identity of the land to be benefited was clearly stated in, or directly ascertainable from, the conveyance, a purchaser would be placed in an impossible position: he would never know by whom the covenant could be enforced, or whether it was enforceable at all.[10] I am not impressed by this objection: the original covenantee is ascertainable from the document—and moreover appears on or can be ascertained from the land charges register.[11] In a case where the covenant is sought to be enforced by an assign from him, such assign must always prove his right to sue, whether by virtue of annexation, by devolution, by assignment of the benefit of the covenant. The plaintiff may also (as in *Tulk v Moxhay*) have to show that he retains property for whose benefit the covenant was imposed. These are matters which arise in all cases where restrictive covenants are sought to be enforced otherwise than as between the original parties, and I see no greater difficulty in dealing with them in cases such as the present. ...

Question (*c*): Was the land capable of being benefited by the covenant? On this point, as on those last dealt with, the answer would appear to be simple. If an owner of land, on selling part of it, thinks fit to impose a restriction on user, and the restriction was imposed for the purpose of benefiting the land retained, the court would normally assume that it is capable of doing so. There might, of course, be exceptional cases where the covenant was on the face of it taken capriciously or not bona fide, but a covenant taken by the owner of an agricultural estate not to use a sold-off portion for other than agricultural purposes could hardly fall within either of these categories. As Sargant J said in *Lord Northbourne v Johnston & Son* [1922] 2 Ch at 319: "Benefit or detriment is often a question of opinion on which there may be the greatest divergence of view, and the greatest difficulty in arriving at a clear conclusion." Why, indeed, should the court seek to substitute its own standard for those of the parties—and on what basis can it do so? However, much argument was devoted to this point, and evidence was called as to it. These I must consider.

First it was said that a mere examination of the figures showed that the covenant could not benefit the estate: the Crichel estate extends in some 7,500 acres, and it was asked how such a covenant could benefit the estate as a whole. In my view, there is no such manifest impossibility about this. I have already referred to the character of the estate, and I can well imagine that, for the owner of it, whether he wished to retain it in his family or to sell it as a whole, it might be of very real benefit to be able to preserve a former outlying portion from development. This seems to me to be a question of fact to be determined on the evidence: and I note that when a similar argument was placed before the court in *Re Ballard's Conveyance* [1937] Ch 473, [1937] 2 All ER 691, Clauson J, while accepting it in the absence of evidence, showed it to be his opinion that evidence could have been called. ...

Question (*d*): Can the action be brought by the first plaintiffs or by the two plaintiffs jointly? I can deal with this point quite shortly. The second plaintiff is the original covenantee, and the first plaintiff is the person for whose benefit in equity the covenant was made. Taken together, the plaintiffs represent the whole legal and equitable interest in the covenant. The matter appears, therefore, to

[10]   (1952) 68 LQR 353, 361.
[11]   The position is rather more complex. Land charges are registered against the name of the estate owner whose estate is to be affected: that is against the name of the covenantor. A search will not reveal the name of the covenantee, nor a description of the land. The name and address of the original covenantee will be known to the Land Registry, for they would have been stated on the original application to register, and they may be ascertained by an application for an office copy of an entry in the register on Form K19, Land Charges Rules 1974. That will in most cases be sufficient to identify the benefited land; but often only with the assistance of extrinsic evidence.

be completely covered by the judgment of Sargant J in *Lord Northbourne v Johnston & Son* the reasoning of which I adopt. So much was not really contested by the Attorney-General, who, however, reserved the right to challenge that judgment should this case go to a higher court.'

(1968) 84 LQR at p. 29 (P. V. Baker)

'From the principles outlined above, and especially from the analogy of easements, we should expect the right to go along automatically with the benefited or dominant land, and, indeed, this happens where the benefit has been annexed by the original covenant. [12] There is, however, a complicating factor as not every restrictive covenant is initially annexed, and in these cases the covenantee has the option of annexing it to the land or allowing it to lapse. As it cannot exist as a separate piece of property like a profit in gross, there seems to be no justification in principle for requiring it to be passed by a succession of assignments parallel with the assignment of the benefited land, for this is still treating it as either a covenant which is only enforceable as such against the covenantor, or as existing in gross. If the original express covenantor is still the owner of the burdened land, the benefit of the covenant could be assigned separately and then ultimately annexed, but if the burdened land has passed it is annexation or nothing, for it is a piece of property which is an adjunct of the benefited land. In other words, express assignment is delayed annexation. One puts together the deed containing the original covenant and the subsequent conveyance of the benefited land. The original covenant in these cases does not have to indicate the benefited land, [13] but that deficiency is naturally supplied by the subsequent conveyance of it. Building schemes go still further since the annexation is effected by facts which are not necessarily or wholly indicated in the conveyance. ...

The proposition that an express assignment of the benefit of covenant annexes it to the land so that it will thereafter pass to future owners without express assignment is supported by dicta in older cases [14] and by some writers. [15] It is, however, repudiated by others, expressly [16] or by implication, [17] and in one recent case it was assumed, though not decided, that a chain of assignments was necessary. [18] Until *Stilwell v Blackman* [19] there was no decision which was

---

[12]   *Rogers v Hosegood* [1900] 2 Ch 388; and see *Lawrence v South County Freeholds Ltd* [1939] Ch 656 at 680, [1939] 2 All ER 503 at 523 ('a hidden treasure').
[13]   *Newton Abbot Co-operative Society Ltd v Williamson and Treadgold Ltd* [1952] Ch 286, [1952] 1 All ER 279.
[14]   *Renals v Cowlishaw* (1878) 9 ChD 125 at 131; affd (1879) 11 ChD 866; *Rogers v Hosegood* [1900] 2 Ch 388 at 408; *Reid v Bickerstaff* [1909] 2 Ch 305 at 320.
[15]   M & W (3rd edn. 1966), p. 771; M. Bowles [1962] JPL 234; S. J. Bailey (1938) 6 CLJ 339 at 360, 361.
[16]   Preston and Newsom, p. 45, n. 74, relying on a dictum of ROMER LJ in *Re Union of London and Smiths' Bank Ltd's Conveyance* [1933] Ch 611 at 631.
[17]   Cheshire (10th edn. 1967) p. 546, relying on another dictum of ROMER LJ at 630 of the case last cited, but this was dealing with concurrent assignments of different parts of the benefited land by the original covenantee.
[18]   *Re Pinewood Estate, Farnborough* [1958] Ch 280, [1957] 2 All ER 517, criticised H. W. R. Wade [1957] CLJ 146. [See also *Federated Homes Ltd v Mill Lodge Properties Ltd* [1980] 1 WLR 594 at 603, [1980] 1 All ER 371 at 378, where John Mills QC said: 'I am not satisfied or prepared to hold that there is any such thing as "delayed annexation by assignment" to which the covenantor is not party or privy.']
[19]   [1968] Ch 508, [1967] 3 All ER 514.

inconsistent with the proposition, but it must follow that if express assignment operates as a mode of annexation, it is necessarily excluded where annexation has already occurred. Nevertheless, as we have seen, it was decided that annexation did not preclude the passing of the benefit by express assignment.

To the learned judge it was "a question of construction whether or not express assignment is excluded by annexation". There was, he said, nothing to interfere with the ordinary principles of contract so that, for example, the covenant could in express terms provide that either annexation or express assignment should be the only method of passing the benefit, or "since they do not operate against each other, and if there were any advantage in so doing, by both methods simultaneously". [20] Reference was then made to the dicta in *Renals v Cowlishaw*[1] which supported the proposition that on express assignment the benefit became automatically annexed, but it was thought that these words were not directed to the question of the simultaneous application of both methods of passing the benefit, "or, indeed, even to the recognition that this question arose". Nor was it clear "whether, if there were such automatic annexation, it is suggested that the annexation would be merely to the whole, or also to each and every part of the land passing to the assignee of the covenant". Ungoed-Thomas J expressed his final conclusion that "there is no reason either in contract or in the relevant principles of equity why an express assignment of the benefit of a covenant with the passing of land should automatically operate exclusively, as an annexation of the covenant to the land (whether to the whole or to any part of it)." [2]

The reason, it is respectfully suggested, for such automatic annexation, is that when the burdened land passes from the covenantor, one leaves the realm of contract and enters that of property. The question then ceases to be exclusively a matter of what the original parties may or may not have agreed, but what incidents the law will allow. When one finds that the benefit of the covenant cannot exist by itself but only alongside the ownership of the benefited land, convenience suggests that it should be annexed to that land and not require a chain of assignments parallel with the conveyances of the land. Further, if the arguments in the earlier part of this article are accepted, the assignment of the benefit of the covenant by the covenantee would prima facie annex that benefit to each and every part of the land comprised in that benefit.'

(b) Law of Property Act 1925, Section 62

In **Roake v Chadha** [1984] 1 WLR 40, [1983] 3 All ER 503, p. 963, ante, Judge Paul Baker QC said at 46, at 508:

'I must now turn to the alternative argument of the plaintiffs based on section 62 of the Law of Property Act 1925. This argument is directed to the conveyances or transfers conveying the alleged benefited land to the predecessors of the plaintiffs, and ultimately to the respective plaintiffs themselves. In each of these transfers, so I am prepared to assume, there is to be implied the general words of section 62 of the Act of 1925:

---

[20]   [1968] Ch 508 at 525, [1967] 3 All ER 514 at 520.
[1]   See p. 980, n. 14, ante.
[2]   At 526, at 520.

[His Honour read sub-s. (1), p. 564, ante, and continued:]

I do not think I need read subsection (2) which deals with the conveyance of land having houses and buildings and various corresponding rights in relation to buildings.

The argument is that the benefit of the covenant contained in the original transfer to the predecessor of the defendants, William Lambert, was carried by the words "rights and advantages whatsoever appertaining or reputed to appertain to the land, or any part thereof." It seems an argument on these lines was accepted by Mr John Mills QC, the deputy judge who gave the decision at first instance in the *Federated Homes* case [1980] 1 WLR 594, [1980] 1 All ER 371, p. 959, ante, but I have not seen it, and so cannot comment on it. The proposition now contended for is not a new one. In *Rogers v Hosegood* [1900] 2 Ch 388, it was similarly put forward as an alternative argument to an argument based on annexation. In that case however it was decided that the benefit of the covenant was annexed so that the point on section 6 of the Conveyancing Act 1881, the forerunner of section 62 of the Law of Property Act 1925, did not have to be decided. Nevertheless, Farwell J, sitting in the Chancery Division, said, at 398:

"It is not necessary for me to determine whether the benefit of the covenants would pass under the general words to which I have referred above, if such covenants did not run with the land. If they are not in fact annexed to the land, it may well be that the right to sue thereon cannot be said to belong, or be reputed to belong, thereto; but I express no final opinion on this point."

In the Court of Appeal the point was canvassed in argument but not referred to in the judgment of the court, which was given by Collins LJ.

In the present case, the covenant in terms precludes the benefit passing unless it is expressly assigned. That being so, as it seems to me, it is not a right "appertaining or reputed to appertain" to land within the meaning of section 62 of the Law of Property Act 1925. As to whether the benefit of a covenant not annexed can ever pass under section 62, I share the doubts of Farwell J. Mr Henty suggested—and there may well be something in this— that the rights referred to in section 62 are confined to legal rights rather than equitable rights which the benefit of restrictive covenants is. But again I place it on construction. It cannot be described as a right appertaining or reputed to appertain to land when the terms of the covenant itself would seem to indicate, or indicates, to be the opposite.

I thus conclude overall that the plaintiffs have failed to show that they are entitled to the benefit of the covenant in relation to their respective properties.'[3]

---

[3] See also (1971) 87 LQR 539 at p. 570 (D. J. Hayton); *Shropshire County Council v Edwards* (1982) 46 P & CR 270 at 279, where Judge Rubin 'decided to remain silent on this highly debatable point under section 62, since a determination was not necessary.' See also *Kumar v Dunning* [1989] QB 193, [1987] 2 All ER 801, where Sir Nicolas BROWNE-WILKINSON V-C said at 198, at 805: 'A right under covenant cannot appertain to the land unless the benefit is in some way annexed to the land. If the benefit of a covenant passes under s. 62 even if not annexed to the land, the whole modern law of restrictive covenants would have been established on an erroneous basis.'

iii. SCHEME OF DEVELOPMENT [4]

The necessity to show either express annexation or express assignment of the benefit of a restrictive covenant is avoided if the circumstances surrounding a series of sales indicate an intention that all the purchasers should be bound by restrictive covenants, and that each should be able to enforce them against the others. In such circumstances there is a scheme of development. There is created a sort of 'local law'[5] among the purchasers, disregarding the ordinary rules of contract and covenants and permitting mutual enforcement. 'The major theoretical difficulties', says MEGARRY J, [6] 'based on the law of covenant seem to me to disappear when instead there is an equity created by circumstances which is independent of contractual obligation'. The same principle applies where there is a letting scheme for individual flats in a single building under which the intention is that each lessee should have the benefit of restrictive covenants relating to the common user of the property. [7]

The test for the existence of a scheme of development has been modified in the past 40 years; the emphasis has changed from a position in which specific requirements need to be observed to one in which there must be a defined area and 'the existence of the common interest and the common intention actually expressed in the conveyances themselves.' [8]

In **Elliston v Reacher** [1908] 2 Ch 374, PARKER J said at 384:

'I pass, therefore, to the consideration of the question whether the plaintiffs can enforce these restrictive covenants. In my judgment, in order to bring the principles of *Renals v Cowlishaw* (1878) 9 ChD 125 and *Spicer v Martin* (1888) 14 App Cas 12 into operation it must be proved (1) that both the plaintiffs and defendants derive title under a common vendor: (2) that previously to selling the lands to which the plaintiffs and defendants are respectively entitled, the vendor laid out his estate, or a defined portion thereof (including the lands purchased by the plaintiffs and defendants respectively), for sale in lots subject

---

4   For the history of the development of the present doctrine, see *Whatman v Gibson* (1838) 9 Sim 196; *Coles v Sims* (1854) 5 De GM & G 1; *Sidney v Clarkson* (1865) 35 Beav 118; *Western v MacDermott* (1866) 2 Ch App 72; *Renals v Cowlishaw* (1878) 9 ChD 125; *Gaskin v Balls* (1879) 13 ChD 324; *Nottingham Patent Brick and Tile Co v Butler* (1885) 15 QBD 261; on appeal (1886) 16 QBD 778; *Collins v Castle* (1887) 36 ChD 243; *Spicer v Martin* (1888) 14 App Cas 12; *Mackenzie v Childers* (1889) 43 ChD 265; *White v Bijou Mansions Ltd* [1938] Ch 351, [1938] 1 All ER 546. For successful schemes, see *Baxter v Four Oaks Properties Ltd* [1965] Ch 816, [1965] 1 All ER 906, p. 984, post; *Re Dolphin's Conveyance* [1970] Ch 654, [1970] 2 All ER 664, p. 984, post; *Eagling v Gardner* [1970] 2 All ER 838; *Brunner v Greenslade* [1971] Ch 993, [1970] 2 All ER 833; *Texaco Antilles Ltd v Kernochan* [1973] AC 609, [1973] 2 All ER 118; *Re 6, 8, 10 and 12 Elm Avenue, New Milton* [1984] 1 WLR 1398, [1984] 3 All ER 632; cf. *Lund v Taylor* (1975) 31 P & CR 167, p. 987, post, especially STAMP LJ at 176; *Kingsbury v LW Anderson Ltd* (1979) 40 P & CR 136, p. 988, n. 19, post; *Allen v Veranne Builders Ltd* [1988] EGCS 2; *Emile Elias & Co Ltd v Pine Groves Ltd* [1993] 1 WLR 305. This is in marked contrast to the usual fate of schemes during the previous four decades; Preston and Newsom, paras. 2–53 to 2–83.

On schemes of development in registered land, see R & R, chap. 21.

5   *Reid v Bickerstaff* [1909] 2 Ch 305 at 319; *Re Dolphin's Conveyance* [1970] Ch 654 at 663, [1970] 2 All ER 664 at 670, per STAMP J.

6   *Brunner v Greenslade* [1971] Ch 993 at 1005, [1970] 3 All ER 833 at 842.

7   *Spicer v Martin* (1888) 14 App Cas 13; extended in *Williams v Kiley* (2002) Times 5 Dec. to competing traders holding leases within a single development.

8   *Re Dolphin's Conveyance*, supra at 664, at 671; *Lund v Taylor*, supra, at 178.

to restrictions intended to be imposed on all the lots, and which, though varying in details as to particular lots, are consistent and consistent only with some general scheme of development;[9] (3) that these restrictions were intended by the common vendor to be and were for the benefit of all the lots intended to be sold,[10] whether or not they were also intended to be and were for the benefit of other land retained by the vendor,[11] and (4) that both the plaintiffs and the defendants, or their predecessors in title, purchased their lots from the common vendor upon the footing that the restrictions subject to which the purchases were made were to enure for the benefit of the other lots included in the general scheme whether or not they were also to enure for the benefit of other lands retained by the vendors. If these four points[12] be established, I think that the plaintiffs would in equity be entitled to enforce the restrictive covenants entered into by the defendants or their predecessors with the common vendor irrespective of the dates of the respective purchases. I may observe, with reference to the third point, that the vendor's object in imposing the restrictions must in general be gathered from all the circumstances of the case, including in particular the nature of the restrictions. If a general observance of the restrictions is in fact calculated to enhance the values[13] of the several lots offered for sale, it is an easy inference that the vendor intended the restrictions to be for the benefit of all the lots, even though he might retain other land the value of which might be similarly enhanced, for a vendor may naturally be expected to aim at obtaining the highest possible price for his land. Further, if the first three points be established, the fourth point may readily be inferred, provided the purchasers have notice of the facts involved in the three first points, but if the purchaser purchases in ignorance of any material part of those facts, it would be difficult, if not impossible, to establish the fourth point. ...

It is, I think, enough to say, using Lord Macnaghten's words in *Spicer v Martin* (1888) 14 App Cas 12, that where the four points I have mentioned are established, the community of interest imports in equity the reciprocity of obligation which is in fact contemplated by each at the time of his own purchase.'

A further requirement was added in **Reid v Bickerstaff** [1909] 2 Ch 305, where Cozens-Hardy MR said at 319:

---

[9] See *Jackson v Bishop* (1979) 48 P & CR 57 (developer held liable for breach of covenant of title and negligence where there was a double conveyance due to inaccurate plans of neighbouring plots).

[10] 'The mere fact that the covenant is not expressly stated to be for the benefit of the plot holders is in no sense decisive. ... I do not think that it is inconsistent with the existence of a scheme of development that the vendor retains his right to exempt part of the [Wildernesse] Estate from stipulations': *Allen v Veranne Builders Ltd*, supra, per Sir Nicolas Browne-Wilkinson V-C.

[11] The reservation to the vendor of the right to sell land free from the restriction is of little force either for or against the existence of a building scheme: *Re Wembley Park Estate Co Ltd's Transfer* [1968] Ch 491 at 498, [1968] 1 All ER 457 at 460; *Eagling v Gardner* [1970] 2 All ER 838.

[12] 'They are in summary, first, common title, second, setting out of lots, third, an intention to be for the benefit of all lots, and, fourth, purchase by the parties or their predecessors upon that footing': *Briggs v McCusker* [1996] 2 EGLR 197 at 199, per Judge Rich QC.

[13] 'Enhancement in value ... does not mean merely monetary enhancement, but also enhancement of the ambiance in which the residents live': *Allen v Veranne Builders Ltd*, supra.

'In my opinion there must be a defined area within which the scheme is operative. Reciprocity is the foundation of the idea of a scheme. A purchaser of one parcel cannot be subject to an implied obligation to purchasers of an undefined and unknown area. He must know both the extent of his burden and the extent of his benefit. Not only must the area be defined, but the obligations to be imposed within that area must be defined. [14] Those obligations need not be identical. For example, there may be houses of a certain value in one part and houses of a different value in another part. A building scheme is not created by the mere fact that the owner of an estate sells it in lots and takes varying covenants from various purchasers. There must be notice to the various purchasers of what I may venture to call the local law imposed by the vendors upon a definite area.' [15]

In **Baxter v Four Oaks Properties Ltd** [1965] Ch 816, [1965] 1 All ER 906, there was no evidence that the common vendor 'laid out the part of his estate ... in plots before beginning to sell it off. He appeared to have sold plots, of the size which purchasers wished to take, to purchasers as they came along'. Cross J held that there was a scheme, having found sufficient evidence of an intention to create mutually binding covenants, although Parker J's second requirement was not observed.

RE DOLPHIN'S CONVEYANCE
[1970] Ch 654, [1970] 2 All ER 664 (ChD, Stamp J) [16]

The Selly Hill Estate, of some 30 acres near Birmingham, became vested in fee simple in Ann and Mary Dolphin as tenants in common. In 1871 they sold off four parcels, and each purchaser entered into a restrictive covenant with them that only detached dwelling houses, each of at least one-quarter acre, should be built on the land. The vendors covenanted to procure similar covenants from subsequent purchasers of any other part of the estate. Ann Dolphin died in 1873, leaving by will her interest in the unsold part of the estate to her nephew, John Watts. In 1876 John became owner in fee simple in possession when Mary Dolphin made a deed of gift to him of her share. He then sold off the remainder of the estate in six parcels, in each case taking a restrictive covenant, and, except for the last parcel, giving a covenant to procure similar covenants from subsequent purchasers.

In 1969 part of the estate was purchased by Birmingham Corporation, whose predecessor in title had purchased part in 1871 from Ann and Mary, and part in 1877 from John. The Corporation wished to build in breach of the covenants, of which it had notice. It sought a declaration that the land was no longer subject to

---

14   'It is not necessary that the covenants entered into should benefit only the defined area: *Allen v Veranne Builders Ltd*, supra.

15   See also Buckley LJ at 323; cited with approval by PC in *Jamaica Mutual Life Assurance Society v Hillsborough Ltd* [1989] 1 WLR 1101 (no reciprocity: no building scheme); *Torbay Hotel Ltd v Jenkins* [1927] 2 Ch 225 at 240, per Clauson J; *Emile Elias & Co Ltd v Pine Groves Ltd* [1993] 1 WLR 305 at 310, per Lord Browne-Wilkinson; *Stocks v Whitgift Homes* [2001] EWCA (Civ) 1732, [2001] 48 EGCS 130 (no defined area within which scheme intended to operate; but land sufficiently identified for the purposes of annexatoin under LPA 1925, s. 78).

16   (1970) 86 LQR 445 (P. V. B.); 117 SJ 798 (G. H. Newsom). For the modification of these covenants under LPA 1925, s. 84, see *Re Farmiloe's Application* (1983) 48 P & CR 317, p. 1008, n. 15, post.

them, and argued that there was no building scheme, since there was no common vendor, and no lotted plan prior to the sales.

Held. There was a scheme, and the covenants were binding.

STAMP J: As Cross J pointed out in the course of the judgment in *Baxter v Four Oaks Properties Ltd* [1965] Ch 816, [1965] 1 All ER 906, ... the intention that the several purchasers from a common vendor shall have the benefit of the restrictive covenants imposed on each of them, may be evidenced by the existence of a deed of mutual covenant to which all the several purchasers are to be parties. [17] That common intention may also be evidenced by, or inferred from, the circumstances attending the sales: the existence of what has often been referred to in the authorities as a building scheme. I have been referred to a considerable number of authorities where the court has had to consider whether there were, or were not, present in the particular case those facts from which a building scheme— and, therefore, the common intention to lay down a local law involving reciprocal rights and obligations between the several purchasers—could properly be inferred. In *Elliston v Reacher* [1908] 2 Ch 374, 384, Parker J laid down the necessary concomitants of such a scheme.

What has been argued before me is that here there is neither a deed of mutual covenant nor a building scheme. In the latter connection, it is pointed out that there was not a common vendor, for the parcels were sold off, first by the Dolphins and then by Watts. Nor, prior to the sales, had the vendor laid out the estate, or a defined portion of it, for sale in lots. Therefore, so it is urged, there were not present the factors which, on the authority of *Elliston v Reacher* [1908] 2 Ch 374, p. 982, ante, are necessary before one can find the existence of a building scheme.

In my judgment, these submissions are not well-founded. To hold that only where you find the necessary concomitants of a building scheme or a deed of mutual covenant can you give effect to the common intention found in the conveyances themselves, would, in my judgment, be to ignore the wider principle on which the building scheme cases are founded and to fly in the face of other authority of which the clearest and most recent is *Baxter v Four Oaks Properties Ltd* [1965] Ch 816, [1965] 1 All ER 906. The building scheme cases stem, as I understand the law, from the wider rule that if there be found the common intention and the common interest referred to by Cross J at 825, at 913 in *Baxter v Four Oaks Properties Ltd* the court will give effect to it, and are but an extension and example of that rule. Hall V-C remarked in his judgment in *Renals v Cowlishaw* (1878) 9 ChD 125 at 129:

'This right exists not only where the several parties execute a mutual deed of covenant, but wherever a mutual contract can be sufficiently established. A purchaser may also be entitled to the benefit of a restrictive covenant entered into with his vendor by another or others where his vendor has contracted with him that he shall be the assign of it, that is, have the benefit of the covenant. And such contract need not be express, but may be collected from the transaction of sale and purchase.'

That passage was quoted, with approval, by Lord Macnaghten in *Spicer Martin* (1889) 14 App Cas 12, 24. (I ought perhaps to mention that the word 'contract' in the last sentence I have quoted was substituted for the word 'covenant' in the errata in the volume of the reports in which *Renals v Cowlishaw* is reported.) Moreover, where deeds of mutual covenant have fallen to be considered, effect

---

[17] See, for example, *Price v Bouch* (1986) 53 P & CR 257 (co-operative scheme on part of 53 Victorian tradesmen in Northumberland).

has been given not to the deed of mutual covenant itself as such but to the intention evidenced by its existence. *Baxter v Four Oaks Properties Ltd* is such a case. As Parker J in *Elliston v Reacher* [1908] 2 Ch 374 at 384 pointed out in a passage quoted by Cross J in *Baxter v Four Oaks Properties Ltd* the equity arising out of the establishment of the four points which he mentioned as the necessary concomitants of a building scheme has been sometimes explained by the implication of mutual contracts between the various purchasers and sometimes by the implication of a contract between each purchaser and the common vendor, that each purchaser is to have the benefit of all the covenants by the other purchasers, so that each purchaser is in equity an assign of the benefit of those covenants; but the implication of mutual contracts is not always a satisfactory explanation. Parker J in *Elliston v Reacher* … points out that a prior purchaser may be dead or incapable of contracting at the time of a subsequent purchase, and that in any event it is unlikely that the prior and subsequent purchasers are ever brought into personal relationship, and yet the equity may exist between them.

There is not, therefore, in my judgment, a dichotomy between the cases where effect has been given to the common intention inferred from the existence of the concomitants of a building scheme and those where effect has been given to the intention evidenced by the existence of a deed of covenant. Each class of case, in my judgment, depends upon a wider principle. Here the equity, in my judgment, arises not by the effect of an implication derived from the existence of the four points specified by Parker J in *Elliston v Reacher*, or by the implication derived from the existence of a deed of mutual covenant, but by the existence of the common interest and the common intention actually expressed in the conveyances themselves.

In *Nottingham Patent Brick and Tile Co v Butler* (1885) 15 QBD 261 at 268, Wills J, in a passage which I find illuminating and which was referred to with approval in the Court of Appeal (1886) 16 QBD 778, put the matter thus: 'The principle which appears to me to be deducible from the cases is that where the same vendor selling to several persons plots of land, parts of a larger property, exacts from each of them covenants imposing restrictions on the use of the plots sold without putting himself under any corresponding obligation, it is a question of fact whether the restrictions are merely matters of agreement between the vendor himself and his vendees, imposed for his own benefit and protection, or are meant by him and understood by the buyers to be for the common advantage of the several purchasers. If the restrictive covenants are simply for the benefit of the vendor, purchasers of other plots of land from the vendor cannot claim to take advantage of them. If they are meant for the common advantage of a set of purchasers, such purchasers and their assigns may enforce them inter se for their own benefit. Where, for instance, the purchasers from the common vendor have not known of the existence of the covenants, that is a strong, if not a conclusive, circumstance to shew that there was no intention that they should enure to their benefit. Such was the case in *Keates v Lyon* (1869) 4 Ch App 218; *Master v Hansard* (1876) 4 ChD 718; and *Renals v Cowlishaw* (1879) 11 ChD 886. But it is in all cases a question of intention at the time when the partition of the land took place, to be gathered, as every other question of fact, from any circumstances which can throw light upon what the intention was: *Renals v Cowlishaw*. One circumstance which has always been held to be cogent evidence of an intention that the covenants shall be for the common benefit of the purchasers is that the several lots have been laid out for sale as building lots, as in *Mann v Stephens* (1846) 15 Sim 377; *Western v MacDermott* (1866) 2 Ch App 72; *Coles v Sims* (1853) Kay 56, 5

De GM & G 1; or, as it has been sometimes said, that there has been "a building scheme": *Renals v Cowlishaw* (1879) 11 ChD 866 at 867.'

I can approach the matter in another way. The conveyances of the several parts of the estate taking the form they do, and evidencing the same intention as is found in a deed of mutual covenant, I equate those conveyances with the deed of mutual covenant considered by Cross J in *Baxter v Four Oaks Properties Ltd* [1965] Ch 816, [1965] 1 All ER 906—the deed which he did not treat for the purposes of his judgment as itself bringing all the successive purchasers and persons claiming through them into contractual relations one with the other, but as showing the common intention. So equating them, I follow what I conceive to be the ratio decidendi of *Baxter v Four Oaks Properties Ltd* and give effect to that intention by holding that the restrictive covenants are enforceable by the successors in title of each of the original covenantors against any of them who purchased with notice of those restrictions.

In **Lund v Taylor** (1975) 31 P & CR 167, [18] the Court of Appeal (RUSSELL and STAMP LJJ and Sir John PENNYCUICK) held that no scheme of development could be inferred. STAMP LJ (delivering the judgment of the Court) said at 176:

'Because there was no extrinsic evidence, nor anything in his own conveyance to show a purchaser that there was a scheme relating to a defined area or that Tellings [the vendors], if they did, intended that stipulations should be imposed in respect of each part of that area, he could not on the authority of *Reid v Bickerstaff* [1909] 2 Ch 305 be subject to an implied obligation to the other purchasers. On this ground alone the action must in our opinion fail. Whatever scheme involving reciprocal rights and obligations Tellings may have sought to establish, the necessary evidence that the several purchasers intended to be bound by a scheme or local law under which they were to have reciprocal rights and obligations is lacking. The difficulties of the plaintiffs in this regard are perhaps emphasised when one observes that whatever inference you may draw from the conveyances there is nothing in them from which a purchaser could draw the inference that Tellings intended to confer on a purchaser a right to prevent Tellings from dealing as they thought fit—e.g. by the erection of a block of flats—with the unplotted part of the estate. ...

Because it was submitted that in recent times the courts, in determining whether the necessary ingredients of a building scheme or local law are shown to have existed, have adopted what was called a more liberal approach than was formerly the case it is right that we should refer to the two cases relied upon in support of that submission. They are *Baxter v Four Oaks Properties Ltd* [1965] Ch 816, [1965] 1 All ER 906 and *Re Dolphin's Conveyance* [1970] Ch 654, [1970] 2 All ER 664. In both those cases it had been submitted that in order to establish a building scheme the requirements laid down by Parker J in *Elliston v Reacher* [1908] 2 Ch 374 must be satisfied. One of those requirements was, and we quote Parker J's judgment, that "in order to bring the principles of *Renals v Cowlishaw* and *Spicer v Martin* into operation it must be proved ... (2) that previously to selling the lands to which the plaintiffs and defendants are respectively entitled the vendor laid out his estate or a defined portion thereof (including the land purchased by the plaintiffs and defendants respectively) for sale in lots subject to restrictions intended to be imposed on all the lots. ..."

---

[18]   *Harlow v Hartog* (1977) 245 EG 140 (no scheme of development due to no estate plan).

In his judgment in *Baxter v Four Oaks Properties Ltd* Cross J rejected the condition that the defined estate should have been laid out for sale in lots. He pointed out that *Elliston v Reacher* was not a case in which there was direct evidence afforded by the execution of a deed of mutual covenant that the parties intended a building scheme but *whether one could properly infer that intention in all the circumstances.* Cross J took the view, also adopted in *Re Dolphin's Conveyance,* that Mr Justice Parker was not intending to lay down that the fact that the common vendor did not bind himself to sell off the defined area to which the local law was to apply in lots of any particular size but proposed to sell off parcels of various sizes according to the requirements of the various purchasers must, as a matter of law, preclude the court from giving effect to a clearly proved intention that the purchasers were to have rights *inter se* to enforce the provisions of the local law over the area.

In *Re Dolphin's Conveyance,* in which the *Baxter v Four Oaks* case was followed, the area over which the scheme or local law was to extend was specified and the intention that the purchasers were to have rights *inter se* to enforce the stipulations of the local law was, so the judge thought, expressed clearly in every conveyance. The stipulations which each purchaser covenanted to observe in the several conveyances were identical [19] and the first and every subsequent conveyance by the vendor contained a covenant by him, in effect, to obtain a covenant from every other purchaser to observe them; a useless series of covenants except upon the basis that all could enforce them. It would, no doubt, have been better if the draftsman of the conveyances in that case had added the words "to the intent that the covenants by the purchasers shall be mutually enforceable" and if a plan had been attached showing the area affected by the scheme; but the judge found a sufficient indication of that intention and a sufficient identification of that area.

No doubt the last mentioned two cases are authorities for the proposition that Mr Justice Parker, in the well known passage of his judgment in *Elliston v Reacher,* did not intend to lay down that the fact that the common vendor did not bind himself to sell off the defined area to which the local law was to apply in lots of any particular size was fatal to the creation of a local law over that area, but rather that if the vendor has done so you have one of the necessary ingredients from which the creation of the local law may be inferred. And where you find that all those concerned—the vendor and the several purchasers—have by the effect of the documents they have executed evidenced the intention to create such a local law over a defined area those cases are authority for saying that the court may give effect to that intention. But we find nothing in those cases indicating that the conditions from which a "building scheme" may be inferred from the facts are any different than was formerly the case.

In the instant case the creation of a building scheme cannot for the reasons we have given be inferred; and there is absent from the deeds themselves that clear evidence of intention to create reciprocal rights and obligations over a defined area which was found in *Baxter v Four Oaks Properties Ltd* and in the *Dolphin's Conveyance* cases.

We allow the appeal.'

---

[19]   In *Kingsbury v L W Anderson Ltd* (1979) 40 P & CR 136, the scheme failed where covenants imposed on some plots were expressed to be by way of indemnity only, and on others by way of absolute covenant.

Preston and Newsom: *Restrictive Covenants Affecting Freehold Land* (8th edn. 1991), paras. 2.71–2.73, 2.75.

'The final requirement is, as we have seen, that there shall be sufficient evidence to establish the intention that the purchasers of the lots shall have mutual rights and obligations. Or, as it was put by Stamp J. in *Dolphin's* case [20] there must be shown to be "common intention to lay down a local law involving reciprocal rights and obligations." Where that is so the purchasers and their successors "all have a common interest in maintaining the restriction. This community of interest necessarily … requires and imports reciprocity of obligation." [1] This requirement is undoubtedly essential. [2]

The intention can be found in the deed, but extrinsic evidence is admissible and is frequently relied upon

If the scheme of local law is modern, the common vendor may be called to give evidence of his own intention. [3] Evidence may also be given by someone who was closely involved with the transactions of the common vendor. [4] In the Lands Tribunal a common vendor has given evidence himself on at least one occasion. [5] Where a scheme is old, there may well be no documents at all except the formal conveyancing instruments, and often only a few of them. The proportion of conveyancing documents that survive varies enormously. In *Dolphin's* case [1970] Ch 654, [1970] 2 All ER 664, almost all of them had been found, though nothing else survived. In the *Wembley Park* case [1968] Ch 491, [1968] 1 All ER 457, a great many conveyancing instruments were in evidence. In the *Texaco* case [1973] AC 609, [1973] All ER 118, where the estate was of some 500 lots, only four conveyances were put in and one of them was of about 300 lots expressed to be subject to no restrictions at all. Nevertheless the scheme was upheld. On the other hand in *White v Bijou Mansions Ltd* [1938] Ch 351, [1938] 1 All ER 546, Lord Greene MR commented adversely on the fact that only two conveyances were available, and the scheme was not upheld. In *Baxter's* case [1965] Ch 816, [1965] 1 All ER 906, the intention of mutuality was evidenced by a deed of mutual covenant.

In regard to the extrinsic evidence, where it survives, a lotted plan is one of the ingredients from which the creation of a local law may be inferred, [6] as would auction particulars specifying a scheme. [7] The same would no doubt be true of a set of particulars and conditions of sale showing that all the lots were to be taken subject to the relevant paragraphs of a set of standard stipulations. A print of a common form of contract or of conveyance would point in the same direction, though the mere fact that the conveyances are broadly in a common form is not by itself enough. [8] The actual evidence in *Elliston v Reacher* itself is always worth study, if one has to consider a case in which extrinsic evidence is going to be

[20] [1970] Ch 654, 662, 663, [1970] 2 All ER 664, 670.
[1] *Spicer v Martin* (1888) 14 App. Cas. 12, 25, per Lord MACNAGHTEN.
[2] *Jamaica Life Mutual Assurance Society v Hillsborough* [1989] 1 WLR 1101.
[3] *Kelly v Battershell* [1949] 2 All ER 830, per COHEN LJ at 839.
[4] *Page v Kings Parade Properties Ltd* [1967] 20 P & CR 710; evidence was given by the conveyancing managing clerk of the solicitors for the alleged common vendor.
[5] *Re Emery's Application* (1956) 8 P & CR 113; this evidence was accepted as a substitute for a lotted plan.
[6] *Lund v Taylor* (1975) 31 P & CR 167, p. 987, ante.
[7] See *Re Birmingham & District Land Co. and Allday* [1893] Ch 342.
[8] *Re Wembley Park Estate Co Ltd's Transfer* [1968] Ch 491, [1968] 1 All ER 457; *Jamaica Mutual Life Assurance Society v Hillsborough Ltd* [1989] 1 WLR 1101.

important. In that case Parker J said "If a general observance of the restrictions is in fact calculated to enhance the value of the several lots offered for sale, it is an easy *inference* that the vendor intended the restrictions to be for the benefit of all."[9] Likewise, in *White v Bijou Mansions Ltd* Lord Greene MR said that "an auction sale with provisions for each purchaser to give the same covenants is strong evidence of the intention". Such contemporaneous, extrinsic evidence is essential where the deeds merely prove the existence of a common vendor and the existence of common covenants. These alone are not enough to prove the requisite intention. [10]

To conclude this review of the principles underlying the doctrine of schemes, two requirements are essential and are universally insisted upon, namely (i) that the area shall be defined; (ii) that the purchasers from the person who creates the scheme shall purchase on the footing that all purchasers shall be mutually bound by, and mutually entitled to enforce, a defined set of restrictions (varying no doubt to some extent as between lots). A common vendor is usual, but there may be cases in which the purpose of this requirement can be met by some other state of the title. A covenant is probably necessary and a lotted map probably is a great help; but again the purposes which these requirements serve can perhaps be fulfilled in other ways. None of these elements is necessarily decisive in itself or even in combination if the scheme fails for want of either of the two essentials. ...

Elliston v Reacher appeared to have put the doctrine into something like a final shape, and during the next 60 years schemes were always discussed in terms of the judgment of Parker J in that case. But in retrospect it now seems clear that that judgment was treated too narrowly as defining what came to be known as the rule in *Elliston v Reacher*. This rule was applied with great precision. Thus in *Lawrence v South County Freeholds Ltd* [1939] Ch 656, [1939] 2 All ER 503, Simonds J at 674, at 519 described the doctrine as "this very artificial branch of the law," and alleged schemes were held to fail in a remarkable number of cases. [11] Some of these decisions were indeed highly artificial and at least two of the cases (*Re Pinewood Estate, Farnborough* and *Page v Kings Parade Properties Ltd*) might very well be decided otherwise today. Between *Elliston v Reacher* in 1908 and *Baxter v Four Oaks Properties Ltd* in 1965 there appear to be only two reported cases in which schemes were upheld. One of them was *Bell v Norman C Ashton Ltd* (1956) 7 P & CR 359 in 1956, a freehold case noted above, and the other was a leasehold scheme in *Newman v Real Estate Debenture Corpn* [1940] 1 All ER 131. Of this last case Cohen LJ said in *Kelly v Battershell* [1949] 2 All ER 830 at 842 that it is "the high water mark of cases where a scheme can be inferred."

Since *Baxter's* case, the courts have been prepared to approach the question of a scheme more broadly [12] appealing to *Renals v Cowlishaw* and *Spicer v Martin* rather than to *Elliston v Reacher*. Although the alleged schemes failed to be upheld

---

9   Such value is not confined to monetary enhancement: per BROWNE-WILKINSON V-C, *Allen v Veranne Builders Ltd* [1988] EGCS 2.

10   *Re Wembley Park Estate Co Ltd's Transfer*, supra; *Jamaica Mutual Life Assurance Society v Hillsborough Ltd*, supra.

11   See *Reid v Bickerstaff* [1909] 2 Ch 305; *Willé v St. John* [1910] 1 Ch 84, 325; *Browne v Flower* [1911] 1 Ch 219; *Torbay Hotel Ltd v Jenkins* [1927] 2 Ch 225; *Ridley v Lee* [1935] Ch 591; *White v Bijou Mansions Ltd* [1938] Ch 351, [1938] 1 All ER 546; *Lawrence v South County Freeholds Ltd* [1939] Ch 656, [1939] 2 All ER 503; *Re Pinewood Estate, Farnborough* [1958] Ch 280, [1957] 2 All ER 517; *Page v Kings Parade Properties Ltd* (1967) 20 P & CR 710; *Re Wembley Park Estate Co Ltd's Transfer* [1968] Ch 491, [1968] 1 All ER 475.

12   But, curiously, in *Eagling v Gardner* (1970) 21 P & CR 723, decided six weeks after *Dolphin's* case, neither that case nor *Baxter's* case seems to have been cited, and the decision of the learned judge was founded entirely upon *Elliston v Reacher*.

in the *Wembley Park* case,[13] and in *Lund v Taylor* (1975) 31 P & CR 167 these decisions were based on the fundamental ground that there was no defined area.[14] In *Baxter's* case itself and also in *Dolphin's* case schemes were upheld notwithstanding the absence of lotting, and in the *Texaco* case notwithstanding a considerable scarcity of evidence. The doctrine of schemes, which had become very fragile through excessive reliance on *Elliston v Reacher*, has been given new vitality by the appeal to the principles of the earlier decisions. Nevertheless the limits to what can be enforced as a scheme are set by the two fundamental requirements upon which the court always insists.'

QUESTIONS

1. Why have the strict technicalities which grew up in relation to restrictive covenants been relaxed in favour of a general rule based on the intention of the parties? *Re Dolphin's Conveyance* [1970] Ch 654, [1970] 2 All ER 664, p. 984, ante; *Brunner v Greenslade* [1971] Ch 993, [1970] 3 All ER 833; *Lund v Taylor* (1975) 31 P & CR 167, p. 987, ante; [1972B] CLJ 157 (H. W. R. Wade).
2. Are restrictive covenants in schemes of development registrable? (1928) 78 LJ 39 (J.M.L.); (1933) 77 SJ 550; (1950) 20 Conv (NS) 370 (R. G. Rowley); *Emmet on Title*, para. 19.043; Farrand, *Contract and Conveyance* (2nd edn.), pp. 420–421; Barnsley, *Conveyancing Law and Practice* (4th edn. 1996), pp. 388–389; Preston & Newsom, paras. 2–80 to 2–83; *Freer v Unwins Ltd* [1976] Ch 288, [1976] 1 All ER 634, p. 942, n. 1, ante.
3. Which of the three views of the construction of LPA 1925, s. 78, as set out in the *Federated Homes* case [1980] 1 WLR 594 at 604, [1980] 1 All ER 371 at 378 (p. 961, ante) do you prefer? See *Crest Nicholson Residential (South) Ltd v McAllister* [2004] 15 EG 105, paras. 43–44, p. 961, n. 4, ante the articles at p. 959, n. 2, and [1972 B] CLJ 151 (H. W. R. Wade).

D. Third Party as Covenantee

LAW OF PROPERTY ACT 1925

56. Persons taking who are not parties and as to indentures.—(1) A person may take an immediate or other interest in land or other property, or the benefit of any condition, right of entry, covenant or agreement over or respecting land or other property, although he may not be named as a party to the conveyance or other instrument.

The effect of this section, when it applies, is to make into a covenantee a person claiming the benefit of the covenant, even though he was not a party to the

---

[13] If *Federated Homes Ltd v Mill Lodge Properties Ltd* [1980] 1 WLR 594, [1980] 1 All ER 371, was correctly decided the *Wembley Park* case must have been decided wrongly. For, though there was no scheme, the covenants must have been annexed to the land which the common vendor retained at the date of his conveyance to the applicants' predecessor in title. Thus an order under LPA 1925, s. 84(2) declaring the covenants unenforceable cannot have been right.

[14] In the latter case an indication against a scheme was found in the fact that these were provisions requiring the common vendor's consent for such things as lopping trees after the estate was fully developed.

instrument in which the covenant was contained. The situation here is therefore different from those discussed under the previous heading. They dealt with situations in which the benefit of a covenant could pass on a conveyance to a purchaser of the land. Once, however, the benefit of a covenant is given to a person by section 56(1), the benefit can then pass to his successors in title by annexation or assignment under the rules described above.

In **Beswick v Beswick** [1968] AC 58, [1967] 2 All ER 1197, Lord UPJOHN said at 102, at 1221:

'Section 56 of the Law of Property Act 1925 has a long history behind it. Section 56 replaced section 5 of the Real Property Act 1845, which amended some very ancient law relating to indentures inter partes, so I shall start by stating the common law on the subject.

The rule was that a grantee or covenantee, though named as such in an indenture under seal expressed to be made inter partes, could not take an *immediate* interest as grantee nor the benefit of a covenant as covenantee unless named as a party to the indenture. This rule, as the authorities I shall quote show, applied not only to real estate but to personal grants and covenants.

But how narrow this rule was, but equally, how well understood, will also be shown by those authorities.

[His Lordship referred to *Scudamore v Vandenstene* (1587) 2 Co Inst 673; *Cooker v Child* (1673) 2 Lev 74; *Berkeley v Hardy* (1826) 5 B & C 355 and continued:]

In *Forster v Elvet Colliery Co Ltd* [1908] 1 KB 629 at 639, Farwell LJ pointed out that the old rule of law still holds good that no one can sue on a covenant in an indenture who is not mentioned as a party to it, except so far as it had been altered by the Real Property Act 1845. Substituting a reference to section 56 for the Act of 1845 that statement, I suppose, is still true.

In 1844 Parliament abrogated this rule by section 11 of the Transfer of Property Act 1844, which enacted:

"That it shall not be necessary in any case to have a deed indented; and that any person, not being a party to any deed, may take an immediate benefit under it in the same manner as he might under a deed poll."

For whatever reason, this short workmanlike section, which plainly applied to all covenants whether relating to realty or personal grants or covenants, never had any operation, for it was repealed by the Real Property Act 1845, and replaced by section 5 of that Act in these terms:

"That, under an indenture, executed after 1 October 1845, an immediate estate or interest, in any tenements or hereditaments, and the benefit of a condition or covenant, respecting any tenements or hereditaments, may be taken, although the taker thereof be not named a party to the same indenture; ..."

No one has ever suggested that that section was intended to do more than supplant the old common law rule relating to indentures inter partes in relation to realty.

Then came the great changes in the law of real property; the Law of Property Act 1922, and the Law of Property (Amendment) Act 1924. The researches of counsel have not revealed any amendment in those Acts to section 5 of the Act of 1845. The Law of Property Act 1925 was a consolidation Act consolidating those and many earlier Acts. It repealed section 5 of the Act of 1845 and replaced it by section 56(1).'

Since a person who takes advantage of section 56 is treated as an original covenantee, it is essential that he should be in existence and identifiable at the time when the covenant was made; the section cannot be used to give the benefit of a covenant to future purchasers, for they could not be made covenantees. [15] Indeed, no enactment is needed to guard the interests of future purchasers, for they can obtain the benefit of existing covenants by virtue of the rules of annexation, or express assignment of the benefit of the covenant. The person who would suffer, apart from section 56 or the existence of a scheme of development, is the owner of adjoining land which needs protection from the covenant and which may have been sold to an earlier purchaser of the land sold off in plots by a common vendor.

Assume that X owns a piece of land, Blackacre, which he is selling off in plots, in circumstances which do not give rise to the existence of a scheme of development. Plot 1 is bought by A, who covenants, in terms appropriate to annex the benefit of the covenant to each and every part of the land retained by X, not to use the premises as a fish shop; plot 2 is bought by B who gives a similar covenant, and similarly plot 3 by C. B opens a fish shop. X of course can sue as covenantee; C will be able to sue as being the purchaser of land to which the benefit of the covenant is annexed; but A will not, for the benefit of B's covenant, being given later, was not annexed to the piece of land which he bought. Later purchasers, in other words, can sue earlier purchasers; earlier purchasers cannot sue later. Earlier purchasers can be given the right to sue by section 56. The safe way to do so is to draft the later covenants in such a way as to purport expressly to covenant with 'A, his heirs and assigns, successors in title, owners for the time being of (plot 1) land adjoining the premises now sold.' Some cases require that the benefit could only be taken by a person 'to whom that … instrument purports to grant something or with whom some agreement or covenant is purported to be made'. [16] This view that the covenant must purport to be made with A and not merely for the benefit of A, has been followed by NEUBERGER J in *Amsprop Trading Ltd v Harris Distribution Ltd.* [17] Further A may be able to enforce the covenant in his own right under the Contracts (Rights of Third Parties) Act 1999, if there is either a term to that effect or if the contract purports to confer a benefit on him. [18]

---

[15]   *Smith and Snipes Hall Farm Ltd v River Douglas Catchment Board* [1949] 2 KB 500, [1949] 2 All ER 179. See also *Pinemain Ltd v Welbeck International Ltd* (1984) 272 EG 1166 (benefit of covenant to sue surety on contract of guarantee not within s. 56, since plaintiffs were not identifiable when covenant was made); *Re Distributors and Warehousing Ltd* [1986] 1 EGLR 90, per WALTON J; cf. *Wiles v Banks* (1983) 50 P & CR 80 (plaintiff identifiable).

[16]   *White v Bijou Mansions Ltd* [1937] Ch 610 at 625, [1937] 3 All ER 269 at 277; affd [1938] Ch 351, [1938] 1 All ER 546, p. 995, post; *Re Ecclesiastical Comrs for England's Conveyance* [1936] Ch 430, infra.

[17]   [1997] 1 WLR 1025, [1997] 2 All ER 990 (covenant between tenant and sub-tenant that 'it shall be lawful for the superior landlords and the landlords' … to enter and to repair at the cost of the sub-tenant, held not to purport to be made with them, even though they were named as persons for whose benefit the covenant was made); rejecting a wider view in *Drive Yourself Hire Co (London) Ltd v Strutt* [1954] 1 QB 250, [1953] 2 All ER 1475; and *Stromdale & Ball Ltd v Burden* [1952] Ch 223, [1952] 1 All ER 59.

[18]   P. 76, ante.

RE ECCLESIASTICAL COMMISSIONERS FOR ENGLAND'S CONVEYANCE
[1936] Ch 430 (ChD, Luxmoore J)

An originating summons was brought under section 84(2) Law of Property Act 1925, [19] to decide whether West Heath House, in the ownership of the applicants, was bound by any, and if so, what, restrictive covenants. The applicants were successors in title of one Gotto who purchased in 1887 from the Ecclesiastical Commissioners giving the following covenant:

'The said Henry Gainsford Gotto doth hereby ... covenant with the said Ecclesiastical Commissioners and their successors' (in such a way as to annex the benefit of the covenant to the land retained by the vendor) 'and also as a separate covenant with their assigns owners for the time being of land adjoining or adjacent to the said land hereby conveyed in manner following, that is to say:' A number of covenants followed.

Some of the defendants were successors in title to land adjoining or adjacent to the applicants' house and which had been bought from the Ecclesiastical Commissioners before the conveyance of 1887. It was as to the position of these defendants that the main issue in the case arose.

Held. The owners of adjacent and adjoining lands and their successors in title were able to enforce the covenants although they or their predecessors in title were not parties to the conveyance of 1887.

Luxmoore J: The questions to be determined are: (1) were any restrictions imposed on West Heath House before or by the conveyance of 21 April 1887; (2) were such restrictions imposed for the benefit of any, and what other hereditaments; and (3) who are the persons, if any, now entitled to the benefit of such restrictive covenants? It is not contended by any of the parties that West Heath House forms part of a larger estate which has been subjected to what is usually referred to as a building scheme, and it is quite plain that there is not sufficient evidence on which it could be argued with any hope of success that such a scheme existed. ...

Having ascertained that restrictive covenants were imposed in respect of the West Heath House property and that the form of the covenants is such as to make the burden of them run with the land, it is necessary to consider whether they were imposed for the benefit of any and what other hereditaments. For it is well settled that, apart from any building scheme, restrictive covenants may be enforced if they are expressed in the original deed to be for the benefit of a particular parcel or particular parcels of land, either expressly mentioned or clearly identified in the deed containing the original covenants. It was argued on behalf of the applicants that the right to enforce such covenants is limited to the original covenantees and their successors in title—the right in the case of the successors in title being limited to those whose land was the property of the original covenantees at the date when the covenants were imposed. It was also argued that the right to enforce the covenants did not extend to any owners of land who were neither express assignees of the benefit of the covenants, nor successors in title of the original covenantees in respect to land acquired by such successors from the Ecclesiastical Commissioners subsequent to the date of the deed by which the covenants were imposed. I think these arguments failed to give due consideration to the provisions of section 5 of the Real Property Act, 1845, as

---

[19]   See p. 1003, post.

repealed and re-enacted by section 56 of the Law of Property Act, 1925. Section 5 of the Act of 1845 provides that under an indenture, executed after 1 October 1845, the benefit of a condition or covenant respecting any tenements or hereditaments may be taken, although the taker thereof be not named as a party to the indenture. In the case of *Forster v Elvet Colliery Co Ltd* [1908] 1 KB 629, it was held that the condition or covenant referred to in the section must, in order to be enforceable by a person not a party to the deed, be one the benefit of which runs with the land of the person seeking to enforce it. The actual decision was upheld in the House of Lords under the name *Dyson v Forster* [1909] AC 98, but Lord Macnaghten expressed doubt whether the section ought to be so restricted. He refrained however from resolving the doubt, because he agreed with the view that the covenants in the particular case ran with the land and it was therefore unnecessary to do so.

The alteration which has been made in the verbiage of section 5 of the 1845 Act by section 56 of the 1925 Act, has not in my opinion affected the position so as to limit the right of a person not a party to the deed to enforce covenants affecting land to those which run with the land. The material words are as follows: 'A person may take ... the benefit of any condition ... covenant or agreement ... respecting land or other property, although he may not be named as a party to the conveyance or other instrument.' It seems to me that the effect of these words is to enlarge the scope of the earlier words, for it extends the rights of a person not a party to a deed to covenants affecting every kind of property personal as well as real. So far as every species of personal property other than leasehold is concerned it is obvious that the covenants to be enforced cannot be restricted to those running with the property, for there are no such covenants. What it is necessary to consider is the true construction of the conveyance of 21 April 1887, in order to ascertain whether any persons, not parties thereto, are described therein as the covenantees, and whether such covenants are expressed to affect any and what hereditaments. To determine what is the true construction of that document it is necessary to consider the surrounding circumstances as they existed at the date when it was executed.

[His Lordship then examined the circumstances existing at the date of execution of the deed and concluded that the covenants were enforceable by the original covenantees, and persons deriving title under them; that the original covenantees need not have been parties to the conveyance of 1887; but that such persons could only enforce the covenant if they held land adjoining or adjacent to the applicants' house.] [20]

WHITE v BIJOU MANSIONS LTD
[1937] Ch 610, [1937] 3 All ER 269, affd [1938] Ch 351, [1938] 1 All ER 546 (SIMONDS J, ChD) (CA, Sir Wilfrid GREENE MR, LUXMOORE and FARWELL JJ)

The owners of the Shaftesbury House Estate conveyed part of it in 1887 to James Israel Fellows. Fellows covenanted that he would build a dwelling house for a certain sum and would use it only as a private dwelling house or as a residence and place of practice of a medical man. The vendors covenanted that every building lease or future sale should include covenants from the lessee or purchaser with the builders imposing similar restrictions on the use of the land, though certain parts were to be permitted to be used as shops. The plaintiff was

---

[20] Followed in *Re Shaw's Application* (1994) 68 P & CR 591 (purchaser covenanted '*with* the vendor').

the successor in title to Fellows.

In 1890, a nearby plot was conveyed to Nicholson, who covenanted for himself, his heirs, executors, administrators and assigns with the intent to bind himself and his successors in title and the owner for the time being of the property thereby conveyed with the vendors, their heirs and assigns, that the piece of land thereby conveyed should be used for the purpose of a private dwelling house only. This plot was later conveyed to Miss Plumbly who, in 1935, leased it to two ladies for a term of 28 years; the lease contained a covenant that no part of the demised premises would be used for any purpose other than a private dwelling house or for private suites or flats. The lease was in due course assigned to the defendants who used the house for flatlets. The action was for an injunction to restrain a breach of covenant.

Held (by SIMONDS J and the Court of Appeal). The plaintiff was not entitled to the benefit of the covenant given by Nicholson in the conveyance of 1890.

SIMONDS J (in the court of first instance): ... Then the question arises: Can the plaintiff here enforce that covenant? I turn to look at it once more. There are covenants entered into in the year 1890, the first with the Davidsons, the second with the Daws, and they are covenants which are not annexed to any particular parcel of land. They are covenants entered into four years after the plaintiff acquired the title to his land. They are covenants the benefit of which has not expressly or by implication, or in any manner whatsoever, been assigned to the plaintiff, and it appears to me to be quite impossible, apart from any building scheme or from the special statutory provision to which I shall presently refer, that the plaintiff can avail himself of this covenant and enforce it. There is here no question of a building scheme. ...

It remains to consider the only other ground on which, as it appears to me, Mr Grant can possibly rest his case. He claims that he is entitled to enforce this covenant, entered into on 2 May 1890, on the ground that either under section 5 of the Real Property Act 1845, or under section 56 of the Law of Property Act 1925, that right is conferred on him. In the view which I take of both these sections it is unnecessary for me to consider whether he is in any way entitled to call in aid section 56 of the Act of 1925, with regard to covenants or agreements contained in a deed executed in 1890. It is necessary for me to say something about the earlier section before I come to consider the later section.

Section 5 of the Real Property Act 1845, which was, as its title suggests, an Act to amend the law of real property, was aimed at remedying certain mischiefs in the state of the common law as it then was. There was a highly technical and artificial rule that by an indenture, as distinguished from a deed poll, an immediate interest in land could not be granted in favour of a grantee unless that grantee was a party to the deed. That mischief this section was designed to remedy. Further, there was the defect, as it was supposed, in the common law, that a person could not take advantage of a covenant in a deed unless he was a party to the deed. Be it observed that the Act of 1845 dealt with real property. This section was confined to the case of an indenture, and of an immediate interest created by that indenture, for it was never the law that an estate in remainder could not be validly granted in favour of a grantee if he were not a party. Indeed the common form of settlement then for centuries in vogue had limited estates in remainder not only to persons not parties to the deed but to persons not yet in existence.

[His Lordship read section 5 and continued:] I think the important aspect of that section for my present purpose is this. It appears to me to be quite plain that the section has a limited operation. It is intended to confer a benefit only on those persons to whom the deed purports to grant an estate or interest or those persons with whom there purports to be a covenant or agreement. It is impossible, in my view, to regard this section as creating a benefit in favour of any persons who may like to avail themselves of it and say: 'It we can take advantage of this it will be for our benefit.' It seems to me clear that this section was intended merely to provide that A.B., the grantee under a deed, might take an immediate interest although he was not a party, and similarly that A.B., with whom the covenant was purported to be made by the deed, should be able to avail himself of it although he was not a party to the deed, and in the few cases which have arisen under this section since 1845—and there appear to be very few—it will be found in every case where it has been applied that it has been in favour of a person who although not a party to the deed was a person to or with whom a grant or covenant purported to be made. That was the position under the Act of 1845.

I now turn to consider section 56 of the Act of 1925, which, it is said, however inaptly, takes the place of the earlier section. [His Lordship read subsection 1 and continued:] I think many difficulties may well arise on that section which do not fall to me to-day to solve. It appears to one at once that, so far as any other than an immediate interest in land is concerned the section is superfluous, because a person always could take another interest in land though not a party. It is at least a question how far such a provision is necessary at all in the case of personalty. Without deciding it, I should be disposed to think that equitable estates even in land were not subject to the old artificial rule and it is very doubtful if an interest in personalty was ever so subject. However that may be, for the purposes of the present case I think I am only concerned with one aspect of this question. Just as under section 5 of the Act of 1845 only that person could call it in aid who, although not a party, yet was a grantee or covenantee, so under section 56 of this Act only that person can call it in aid who, although not named as a party to the conveyance or other instrument, is yet a person to whom that conveyance or other instrument purports to grant some thing or with whom some agreement or covenant is purported to be made. To give it any other meaning appears to me to open the door to claims or assertion of rights which cannot have been contemplated by the Legislature, for if that be not the limitation which must be imposed on this section, it appears to me that there is no limit and it will be open to anybody to come into court and say: 'Here is a covenant which if enforced will redound to my advantage, therefore I claim the benefit of the section. I claim that this covenant or condition is one which should be enforced in my favour because it is for my benefit, whether intended for my benefit or not intended for my benefit would not appear to matter.' I cannot give to the section any such meaning as that. I interpret it as a section which can be called in aid only by a person in whose favour the grant purports to be made or with whom the covenant or agreement purports to be made. [1] If that is so, whether the plaintiff's claim arises under the earlier or the later Act, he cannot sue on it in this Court because he is not a person who, under the deed of 1890, can point to any grant or any covenant purported to be made to or with him. That is the construction which I place on section 56, with the result that the plaintiff's claim must fail.

---

[1] Similarly per Crossman J in *Re Foster* [1938] 3 All ER 357 at 365; per Dillon J in *Lyus v Prowsa Developments Ltd* [1982] 1 WLR 1044 at 1049, [1982] 2 All ER 953 at 958.

In the Court of Appeal, where Simonds J's decision was upheld, Sir Wilfrid Greene MR said at 365, at 554:

'Whatever else section 56 may mean, it is, I think, confined to cases where the person seeking to take advantage of it is a person within the benefit of the covenant in question, if I may use that phrase. The mere fact that somebody comes along and says: "It would be useful to me if I could enforce that covenant" does not make him a person entitled to enforce it under section 56. Before he can enforce it he must be a person who falls within the scope and benefit of the covenant according to the true construction of the document in question.'[2]

IV. Declaration, Discharge and Modification[3]

A. The Position Apart from Statute

I. CHANGE IN CHARACTER OF NEIGHBOURHOOD. NON-ENFORCEMENT

CHATSWORTH ESTATES CO v FEWELL[4]
[1931] 1 Ch 224 (ChD, Farwell J)

The predecessors in title of the plaintiffs, owners of Compton Place, Eastbourne, had sold land to the predecessors in title of the defendant subject to various covenants, of which the defendant had notice when he purchased, one of which was that he would not use the land 'otherwise than as a private dwelling house'. The land was on the sea front at Eastbourne, and various owners of adjoining land, which had also been purchased subject to the same covenant from the predecessors in title of the plaintiffs, had, with their consent, used the land for a school, for flats, and in three cases where the circumstances were exceptional for boarding houses. The defendant opened a guest house called Bella Vista; his attention was drawn to the covenant, and he was given an opportunity to apply under section 84 of the Law of Property Act 1925 for the modification of the covenant. He did nothing and this action was for an injunction and damages. The defendant admitted the breach and contended that the covenants were not enforceable for two reasons:

  (i) by reason of the change in the general character of the neighbourhood, whereby the object of those covenants had completely disappeared.
  (ii) by reason of the fact that this change had been brought about by the acts and omissions of the plaintiffs and their predecessors in title.

Held. The plaintiffs were entitled to an injunction.

---

[2] In *Amsprop Trading Ltd v Harris Distribution Ltd*, supra, Neuberger J said at 1032, at 997: 'In my opinion, the observations of Sir Wilfrid Greene MR were intended to have the same effect as the observations of Simonds J., and that view is supported by the fact that they are both cited as having the same effect by Lord Reid and Lord Guest and, inferentially Lord Pearce in *Beswick v Beswick* [1968] AC 58, 75A–D, 86B–C, 94B [1967] 2 All ER 1197, 1205, 1210–1211, 1216'.
[3] C & B, pp. 691–699; Gray, p. 1184–1195; M & W, paras. 16.083–16.093; MM, pp. 472–473; Preston and Newsom, chap. 12. Francis, *Restrictive Covenants and Freehold Land*, chap. 16; Scarmell, *Land Covenants*, chaps. 11–21; (1986) 48 MLR 195 (P. Polden).
[4] (1948) 92 SJ 570.

FARWELL J: Nothing can be said against the defendant's conduct of his establishment except that it is a breach of covenant. That being so ought I to refuse the plaintiffs relief?

The defendant's first ground of defence is that there has been such a complete change in the character of the neighbourhood, apart from the plaintiff's acts or omissions, that the covenants are now unenforceable. But to succeed on that ground the defendant must show that there has been so complete a change in the character of the neighbourhood that there is no longer any value left in the covenants at all. A man who has covenants for the protection of his property cannot be deprived of his rights thereunder merely by the acts or omissions of other persons unless those acts or omissions bring about such a state of affairs as to render the covenants valueless, so that an action to enforce them would be unmeritorious, not bona fide at all, and merely brought for some ulterior purposes. It is quite impossible here to say that there has been so complete a change in the character of this neighbourhood as to render the covenants valueless to the plaintiffs. Whether right or wrong the plaintiffs are bringing this action bona fide to protect their property, and it is hopeless to say that the change in the character of the neighbourhood is so complete that it would be useless for me to give them any relief.

The defendant really relied on the acts and omissions of the plaintiffs and their predecessors as a bar to equitable relief. Now the plaintiffs are not unduly insistent on the observance of these covenants in this sense, that they do not conduct inquisitorial examinations into their neighbours' lives, and do not make it their business to find out very carefully exactly what is being done, unless the matter is brought to their notice, either by complaints of other inhabitants, or by seeing some board or advertisement. I cannot think that plaintiffs lose their rights merely because they treat their neighbours with consideration. They are doing what they think sufficient to preserve the character of the neighbourhood. Whether they do enough is another matter, but I am quite satisfied that they are not intending, by their acts or omissions, to permit this area to be turned into anything other than a mainly residential area. There is no doubt however that they have permitted breaches of covenant in several cases where houses have been turned into flats, they have permitted at least four houses to be carried on as boarding houses or hotels, and they have not prevented—in some cases because they did not know of them—some half a dozen other houses being used as boarding houses or guest houses.

There are still however a very large number of private dwelling houses in the area, and I am satisfied that while the use of Bella Vista as a guest house or boarding house may not at the moment cause any actual damage to Compton Place or its owners, there is a prospect of damage in the future if the defendant is allowed to continue to use Bella Vista in that way, because it might well lead to many other houses being so used which would undoubtedly damnify the owners of Compton Place, especially if they develop the park and grounds as intended. In that way it will certainly be detrimental to the plaintiffs to permit Bella Vista to be used as a guest house. But whether they are entitled to relief depends on the exact effect of their past acts and omissions.

Now, as stated in many authorities, the principle upon which this equitable doctrine rests is that the plaintiffs are not entitled to relief if it would be inequitable to the defendant to grant it. In some of the cases it is said that the plaintiffs by their acts and omissions have impliedly waived performance of the covenants. In other cases it is said that the plaintiffs, having acquiesced in past breaches, cannot now enforce the covenants. It is in all cases a question of degree. It is in many ways analogous to the doctrine of estoppel, and I think it is a fair test to treat it in that way and ask, 'Have the plaintiffs by their acts and omissions represented to the defendant that the covenants are no longer enforceable and that he is therefore entitled to use his house as a guest house?' [5]

ii. UNITY OF SEISIN

In **Texaco Antilles Ltd v Kernochan** [1973] AC 609, [1973] 2 All ER 118, Lord CROSS OF CHELSEA said at 624 at 125:

'Their Lordships now turn to the "unity of seisin" point which was the main ground upon which the appellants founded their contention that the restrictions were not binding on them. As stated above from 12 January 1942 until 12 November 1951, Chapmans Ltd owned both the lots now owned by the respondents and also the lots now owned by the appellants. As soon as the two sets of lots came into the same hands it became impossible for any action to enforce the covenants to be brought by the owner of one set against the owner of the other since he was the same person and that fact, so the argument runs, put an end to the restrictions so far as concerned the relations of the two sets of lots inter se. …

The point of law which arises for consideration is therefore whether in a case where there is nothing in the conveyance putting an end to the unity of seisin or in the surrounding circumstances to indicate that the restrictions in the scheme are no longer to apply as between the owners of the lots previously in common ownership the fact that they have been in common ownership puts an end to the restrictions so far as concerns the relations of subsequent owners for the time being of that part of the estate inter se so that if the common owner of those lots wished them to apply after the severance he would have to reimpose them as fresh restrictions under a sub-scheme relating to them. It would their Lordships think be somewhat unfortunate if this was the law. … It is no doubt true that if the restrictions in question exist simply for the mutual benefit of two adjoining properties and both those properties are bought by one man the restrictions will automatically come to an end [6] and will not revive on a subsequent severance unless the common owner then recreates them. But their Lordships cannot see that it follows from this that if a number of people agree that the area covered by all their properties shall be subject to a "local law" the provisions of which shall be enforceable by any owner for the time being of any part against any other owner and the whole area has never at any time come into common ownership an action by one owner of a part against another owner of a part must fail if it can be shown that both parts were either at the inception of the scheme or at any time subsequently in common ownership. The view which their Lordships favour is

---

[5] See also *Westripp v Baldock* [1939] 1 All ER 279; *Shaw v Applegate* [1977] 1 WLR 970, [1978] 1 All ER 123, where an injunction was refused against the original covenantor on grounds of acquiescence, but damages were awarded. BUCKLEY LJ said at 978, at 131: 'The real test, I think, must be whether upon the facts of the particular case, the situation has become such that it would be dishonest or unconscionable for the plaintiff, or the person having the right sought to be enforced, to continue to seek to enforce it'; *Gafford v Graham* (1998) 77 P & CR 73; *A-G of Hong Kong v Fairfax Ltd* [1997] 1 WLR 149 (covenant in 999 year Crown lease abandoned).

[6] *Re Tiltwood, Sussex* [1978] Ch 269, [1978] 2 All ER 1091; (1980) 54 ALJ 156 (G. M. Bates); (1982) 56 ALJ 587 (A. A. Preece); *Re Victoria Recreation Ground, Portslade's Application* (1979) 41 P & CR 119. *Re MCA East Ltd* [2003] 1 P & CR 118.

supported by dicta of Sir H. H. Cozens-Hardy MR in *Elliston v Reacher* [1908] 2 Ch 665 at 673 and of Simonds J in *Lawrence v South County Freeholds Ltd* [1939] Ch 656 at 677, 683, [1939] 2 All ER 503, at 520, 524, but at the time when this case was heard by the Court of Appeal there was no decision on the point. Subsequently, however, in *Brunner v Greenslade* [1971] Ch 993, [1970] 3 All ER 833 which raised the point, Megarry J followed those dicta. The appellants submitted that his decision was wrong but in their Lordships' view it was right.'

B. Law of Property Act 1925, Section 84 [7]

Under section 84(2) the court may be asked to declare whether land is affected by a restrictive covenant, and, under section 84(1) the Lands Tribunal [8] has power in its discretion to modify or discharge such a covenant. Section 84 was substantially amended by Law of Property Act 1969, section 28, extending the powers of the Lands Tribunal to cover a situation where a restrictive covenant which prevents some reasonable use of land confers no substantial benefit on anyone or is contrary to the public interest. Compensation may be ordered in some cases. [9]

LAW OF PROPERTY ACT 1925

84. Power to discharge or modify restrictive covenants affecting land.—(1) The Lands Tribunal shall (without prejudice to any concurrent jurisdiction of the court) have power from time to time, on the application of any person interested in any freehold land affected by any restriction arising under covenant [10] or otherwise as to the user thereof or the building thereon, [11] by order wholly or partially to discharge or modify any such restriction [12] on being satisfied [13]

    (*a*)   that by reason of changes in the character of the property or the neighbourhood [14] or other circumstances of the case [15] which the Lands

---

[7]   See also Housing Act 1985, s. 610(1), (2); *Josephine Trust Ltd v Champagne* [1963] 2 QB 160, [1962] 3 All ER 136; TCPA 1990 ss. 106, 237; Local Government Act 1972, ss. 120(3), 124(2); *R v City of London Council, ex p Master Governors and Commonality of the Mystery of the Barbers of London* [1996] 2 EGLR 128.

[8]   On the Lands Tribunal generally, see Jones, *The Lands Tribunal* (1982); its address is 48/49 Chancery Lane, London WC2. See Law Commission Report on Land, Valuation and Housing Tribunals 2003 (Law Com No. 281).

[9]   For an unsuccessful application to the European Commission of Human Rights (No 1074/84) on the ground that the Northern Ireland equivalent of section 84 violated the European Convention for the Protection of Human Rights and Fundamental Freedoms, see [1986] Conv 124 (N. Dawson). As to whether s. 84 is incompatible with the Human Rights Act 1998, see Rook, *Property Law and Human Rights*, pp. 208–211.

[10]   The covenant may be personal only: *Shepherd Homes Ltd v Sandham (No 2)* [1971] 1 WLR 1062, [1971] 2 All ER 1267; *Gilbert v Spoor* [1983] Ch 27, [1982] 2 All ER 576.

[11]   *Re Milius's Application* (1995) 70 P & CR 427 (restriction on disposal may not be a restriction on user or building).

[12]   *Re Kentwood Properties Ltd's Application* [1987] JPL 137 (discretion to modify not exercised where there had been a 'flagrant, cynical and continuing breach of covenant').

[13]   There is a greater presumption that a restriction under a building scheme will be upheld; and a greater burden of proof on the applicant: *Re Lee's Application* (1996) 72 P & CR 439.

[14]   *Keith v Texaco Ltd* (1977) 34 P & CR 249 (coming of oil industry to Aberdeenshire); *Re Bradley Clare Estates Ltd's Application* (1987) 55 P & CR 126; *Re Quaffers Ltd's Application* (1988) 56 P & CR 142 (advent of motorway network); *Re North's Application* (1997) 75 P & CR 117 (change in neighbourhood not material; house in Winkfield, Berkshire, retained attractive semi-rural character despite infilling).

[15]   *Re Cox's Application* [1985] JPL 564 (covenant requiring occupiers of extension of house in East Sussex to be domestic staff employed for service in the house held obsolete); *Re*

Tribunal may deem material, the restriction ought to be deemed obsolete; or

(*aa*) that (in a case falling within subsection (1A) below) the continued existence thereof would impede some reasonable user of the land for public or private purposes[16] or, as the case may be, would unless modified so impede such user; or

(*b*) that the persons of full age and capacity for the time being or from time to time entitled to the benefit of the restriction, whether in respect of estates in fee simple or any lesser estates or interests in the property to which the benefit of the restriction is annexed, have agreed, either expressly or by implication,[17] by their acts or omissions, to the same being discharged or modified; or

(*c*) that the proposed discharge or modification will not injure the persons entitled to the benefit of the restriction,[18]

and an order discharging or modifying a restriction under this subsection may direct the applicant to pay to any person entitled to the benefit of the restriction such sum by way of consideration[19] as the Tribunal may think it just to award under one, but not both, of the following heads, that is to say, either —

(i) a sum to make up for any loss or disadvantage suffered by that person in consequence of the discharge or modification; or

(ii) a sum to make up for any effect which the restriction had, at the time when it was imposed, in reducing the consideration then received for the land affected by it.

(1A) Subsection (1)(aa) above authorises the discharge or modification of a restriction by reference to its impeding some reasonable user of land in any case in which the Lands Tribunal is satisfied that the restriction, in impeding that user, either —

(*a*) does not secure to persons entitled to the benefit of it any practical benefits of substantial value or advantage to them; or

(*b*) is contrary to the public interest;

and that money will be an adequate compensation for the loss or disadvantage

---

Beechwood Homes Ltd's Application [1994] 2 EGLR 178 (covenant requiring any building to be approved by vendors held not obsolete, even though vendors had altered pattern of development and had disappeared from the scene); *Re Kalsi's Application* (1993) 66 P & CR 313; *Re Wards Construction (Medway) Ltd's Application* (1994) 67 P & CR 379 (green field area now an infill site); *Re Kennet Properties Application* [1996] 1 EGLR 163 (original purpose of unimpeded views across each neighbour's land no longer possible due to housing development), *Re Nichols' Application* [1997] 1 EGLR 144; *Re Marcello Developments Ltd's Application* [2002] RVR 146 (frontage and building line restrictions obsolete); *Re Davies' Application* [2001] 1 EGLR 111; *Re Broomhead's Application* [2003] 2 EGLR 157 (purpose of covenant to control development and extract premium on release held not to be obsolete).

16   See *Stannard v Issa* [1987] AC 175, where PC construed a similar but not identical paragraph under the Restrictive Covenants (Discharge and Modification) Act (No. 2 of 1960) of Jamaica, s. 3(1).

17   *Re Memvale Securities Ltd's Application* (1975) 233 EG 689; *Re Fettishaw's Application (No. 2)* (1973) 27 P & CR 292; *In University of Westminster Application* (1999) 78 P & CR 82.

18   *Re Forestmere Properties Ltd's Application* (1980) 41 P & CR 390 ('replacement of one eyesore (Odeon cinema) by another could hardly be said to be an improvement'); *Re Bailey's Application* (1981) 42 P & CR 108 ('quaint rural backwater' not to be changed into riding school with attendant manure and noise including sound of human voice); *Re Livingstones' Application* (1982) 47 P & CR 462 ('eyesore' carport). *Re Severn Trent Water Ltd's Application* (1993) 67 P & CR 236 (site for sewage disposal works to become leisure centre).

19   In *SJC Construction Co Ltd v Sutton London Borough Council* (1975) 29 P & CR 322, STEPHENSON LJ said, arguendo, that 'consideration' was probably a mis-print for 'compensation'.

(if any) which any such person will suffer from the discharge or modification.

(1B) In determining whether a case is one falling within subsection (1A) above, and in determining whether (in any such case or otherwise) a restriction ought to be discharged or modified, the Lands Tribunal shall take into account the development plan [20] and any declared or ascertainable pattern for the grant or refusal of planning permission in the relevant areas, as well as the period at which and context in which the restriction was created or imposed and any other material circumstances.

(1C) It is hereby declared that the power conferred by this section to modify a restriction includes power to add such further provisions restricting the user of or the building on the land affected as appear to the Lands Tribunal to be reasonable in view of the relaxation of the existing provisions, and as may be accepted by the applicant; and the Lands Tribunal may accordingly refuse to modify a restriction without some such addition. [1]

(2) The court shall have power on the application of any person interested —

  (*a*) to declare whether or not in any particular case any freehold land is, or would in any given event be, affected by a restriction imposed by any instrument; or

  (*b*) to declare what, upon the true construction of any instrument purporting to impose a restriction, is the nature and extent of the restriction thereby imposed and whether the same is, or would in any given event be, enforceable and if so by whom. [2]

(3) The Lands Tribunal shall, before making any order under this section, direct such enquiries, if any, to be made of any government department or local authority, and such notices, if any, whether by way of advertisement or otherwise, to be given to such of the persons who appear to be entitled to the benefit of the restriction intended to be discharged, modified, or dealt with as, having regard to any enquiries, notices, or other proceedings previously made, given or taken, the Lands Tribunal may think fit.

(3A) On an application to the Lands Tribunal under this section the Lands Tribunal shall give any necessary directions as to the persons who are or are not to be admitted (as appearing to be entitled to the benefit of the restriction) to oppose the application, and no appeal shall lie against any such direction; but rules under the Lands Tribunal Act 1949 shall make provision [3] whereby, in cases in which there arises on such an application (whether or not in connection with the admission of persons to oppose) any such question as is referred to in subsection (2) (a) or (b) of this section, the proceedings on the application can and, if the rules so provide, shall be suspended to enable the decision of the court to be obtained on that question by an application under that subsection, or by means of a case stated by the Lands Tribunal, or otherwise, as may be provided by those rules or by rules of court.

[20] *Re Kennet Properties' Application* [1996] 1 EGLR 163.

[1] *Re Patten Ltd's Application* (1975) 31 P & CR 180; *Re Dransfield's Application* (1975) 31 P & CR 192; *Re Kershaw's Application* (1975) 31 P & CR 187; *Re Banks Application* (1976) 33 P & CR 138; *Re Forestmere Properties Ltd's Application* (1980) 41 P & CR 390; *Re Austin's Application* (1980) 42 P & CR 102; *Re Shah and Shah's Application* (1991) 62 P & CR 450.

[2] Lands Tribunal Rules 1996, r. 16; *In The Girls' Day School Trust (1872) Application* [2002] 2 EGLR 89.

[3] Lands Tribunal Rules 1996 (SI 1996 No. 1002); Lands Tribunal Practice Directions 1/1997 to 8/1997, reproduced in [1997] JPL 256; Lands Tribunal (Fees) Rules 1996 (SI 1996 No. 1021); Lands Tribunal (Amendment) Rules 1997 (SI 1997 No. 1965); Lands Tribunal Fees (Amendment) Rules 2002 (SI 2002 No 770); Lands Tribunal (Amendment) Rules 2003 (SI 2003 No. 2945). Scamell, chap. 21.

(5) Any order made under this section shall be binding on all persons, whether ascertained or of full age or capacity or not, then entitled or thereafter capable of becoming entitled to the benefit of any restriction, which is thereby discharged, modified or dealt with, and whether such persons are parties to the proceedings or have been served with notice or not.

(8) This section applies whether the land affected by the restrictions is registered or not. [4]

(9) Where any proceedings by action or otherwise are taken to enforce a restrictive covenant, any person against whom the proceedings are taken, may in such proceedings apply to the court for an order giving leave to apply to the Lands Tribunal under this section, and staying the proceedings in the meantime.[4a]

(12) Where a term of more than forty years is created in land (whether before or after the commencement of this Act) this section shall, after the expiration of twenty-five years of the term, apply to restrictions affecting such leasehold land in like manner as it would have applied had the land been freehold:

Provided that this subsection shall not apply to mining leases.

In **Ridley v Taylor** [1965] 1 WLR 611, [1965] 2 All ER 51, HARMAN LJ said at 617, at 55:

'Section 84(1) of the Law of Property Act, 1925, primarily applies to restrictions on freehold land, but by subsection (12), as amended by the Landlord and Tenant Act, 1954, is made applicable to restrictions affecting leasehold land where a term of more than 40 years is created by the lease of which more than 25 years have expired. It seems to me that it should be more difficult to persuade the court to exercise its disertation in leasehold than in freehold cases. [5] In the latter the court is relaxing in favour of a freeholder's own land restrictions entered into for the benefit of persons owning other land. In the former the land in question is the property of the covenantee who is prima facie entitled to preserve the character of his reversion. Section 84 cases usually arise between the assigns of both the benefit and the burden of the covenant, and one may suppose that the section was designed with a view to cases within the doctrine of *Tulk v Moxhay*, but there is nothing in the language of the section to limit the power of the court to a case where the lessee is not himself bound by contract, and I do not feel able to say that such a covenant cannot be modified under the section, although it seems to me that the court should be slow to relieve an applicant of covenants which he himself has entered into. Were it otherwise, it would be easy to avoid the effect of the section by an assignment. It is to be observed that what is to be discharged or modified is not the covenant, but any restriction under the covenant, and it was suggested that this would leave direct contractual liability untouched. This would produce an extraordinary result in a case where the restriction was modified in favour of an assign if the covenantee could still sue the original covenantor in damages on his contractual liability

---

4   As amended by LRA 2002, ss. 133, Sch. 11, para. 2(1), (5), Sch. 13.
4a   *Luckies v Simons* [2003] 2 P &CR 30.
5   'Since 1950, something over a dozen of cases under s. 84(12) have appeared in P & CR and in about two-thirds of them the lessee has succeeded': Preston & Newsom, para. 10–21. See, e.g., *Re Briarwoods Estates Ltd* (1979) 39 P & CR 419; *Re EMI (Social Centres) Ltd's Application* (1979) 39 P & CR 421; *Re Forestmere Properties Ltd's Application* (1980) 41 P & CR 390.

although he had parted with all interest in the property. I cannot but think that the covenant must, where an order is made, be treated in all respects as modified or discharged.'

(1979) 129 NLJ 523 (H. W. Wilkinson) [6]

'In *Re Bass Ltd's Application* (1973) 26 P & CR 156, the Tribunal (J. S. Daniel QC) accepted the submission of counsel, Graham Eyre QC, that the questions which properly arose [under subsection (1) (*aa*)] were:

1 Is the proposed user reasonable?
2 Do the covenants impede that user?
3 Does impeding the proposed user secure practical benefits to the objectors?
4 If yes, are those benefits of substantial value or advantage?
5 Is impeding the proposed user contrary to the public interest?
6 If no, would money be an adequate compensation?
7 If yes, would money be an adequate compensation?

In considering questions 3 to 7 inclusive, regard must be had to the planning context, by subsection (1B).

The questions will be discussed in the order of formulation.

1. IS THE PROPOSED USER REASONABLE?

In the *Bass* case (1973) the applicants sought the modification of a covenant in order to allow them to use some of their land for the loading and unloading of 228 articulated lorries daily—a "trunker park". There had been objections from over 200 nearby house owners. The Tribunal considered that the purpose of the restriction was to make a "*cordon sanitaire* of residential buildings masking any new industrial development". The applicants already had planning permission for the development and the Tribunal said that "planning permissions are very persuasive in this connection" though it must not be thought that the question of reasonable user "could always be concluded in the affirmative by the production of a planning permission". Partly because of the need for businesses in the area to be provided with communications it was held that the proposed user was reasonable.

The first hurdle is not usually difficult for an applicant to surmount. It is not easy for an objector to establish that there is anything unreasonable about a wish to build houses or flats or to extend a legitimate business enterprise. The requirement of reasonableness was satisfied in all the following cases (though not all the applications eventually succeeded):

Re John Twiname Ltd's Application (1971) 23 P & CR 413; covenant imposed in 1924 not to build within 200 feet of a mansion house, The Towers, which was now four habitations and had two pairs of semi-detached houses in its grounds. A proposal to build three pairs of semis and three detached houses within 200 feet of the house was held to be reasonable.

Re Beardsley's Application (1972) 25 P & CR 233; covenant imposed in 1922 forbade the building of more than two private residences on the site. A proposed development of 12 flats, each with a garage, was held to be reasonable.

---

[6] See further (2000) 150 NLJ 1525, 1623 (H. W. Wilkinson).

Re Carter's Application (1973) 25 P & CR 542; infilling with a second house of conventional design in keeping with the other houses on the site held to be reasonable although there was a covenant against putting more than one dwelling house on the plot.

Re Osborn's and Easton's Application (1978) 38 P & CR 251; restrictions were imposed on two sites in 1913 to ensure that not more than one house was put on to each plot. A proposal to erect two blocks of flats to make 20 flats on one and 12 on the other was held reasonable.[7]

2. DO THE COVENANTS IMPEDE THAT USER?

If the applicant did not consider that the covenant impeded or was likely to impede his proposed development he would not make the application under section 84(1) and if the objector did not feel that the covenant impeded the user he would not object. An affirmative answer to question 2 will almost invariably follow an affirmative answer to question 1. If there is doubt about whether any land is affected by a restriction, or about the nature and extent of the restriction the appropriate procedure is to apply for construction of the restriction, under section 84(2).

3. DOES IMPEDING THE PROPOSED USER SECURE PRACTICAL BENEFITS TO THE OBJECTORS?

The following decisions may help to give meaning to the phrase "practical benefits". The statute is silent on the matter.

(a) Loss of privacy and view

A proposed block of flats would have had a "devastating effect" on the amenities and value of a house as the house's principal rooms would face it and be overlooked by it, *Re Mercian Housing Society's Application* (1971) 23 P & CR 116.

Gardens of existing houses would be overlooked by two proposed houses. One garden could be screened to some extent by a hawthorn hedge but as the Tribunal said, a hawthorn is a poor substitute for a covenant, *Re Gossip's Application* (1972) 25 P & CR 215.[8]

---

[7]   See also *Re Manxguard Ltd's Application* [1982] JPL 521 (restriction imposed in 1862 on use of building in Saltburn-by-the-Sea as a public house modified to convert it into Victorian style inn); *Re Hextall's Application* (2000) 79 P & CR 82 (development for social housing and open space purposes held to be reasonable user).

[8]   See also *Re Banks Application* (1976) 33 P & CR 138 ('direct view of the sea is of immense value'); *Re Bovis Homes Southern Ltd's Application* [1981] JPL 368 (beauty and aesthetic and historic interest of National Trust house and its setting); *Gilbert v Spoor* [1983] Ch 27, [1982] 2 All ER 576 (resplendent view over Tyne valley from road *adjacent to* objector's land); [1984] Conv 429 (P. Polden); *Re Burr's Application* [1987] JPL 137 (amenities of a high class development); *Stannard v Issa* [1987] AC 175 ('the privacy and quietude of an enclave of single dwellings in large gardens is going to be adversely affected by the introduction on adjoining lands of no less than 40 additional families', per Lord OLIVER OF AYLMERTON at 196); *Re Bushell's Application* (1987) 54 P & CR 386 (particularly fine landscape view at Wimbledon 'very unusual so near the centre of London'); *Re Purnell's Application* (1987) 55 P & CR 133 (large garden providing privacy in Orpington, Kent); *Re William's Application* (1987) 55 P & CR 400 (sense of spaciousness; preventing nuisance of building works); *Re Whiting's Application* (1988) 58 P & CR 321 (natural beauty of Howley, Gloucestershire); *Re Tarhale Ltd's Application* (1990) 60 P & CR 368 (preventing intolerable nuisance during construction work); *Re Hopcraft's Application* (1993) 66 P & CR 475 (pleasant open area to remain open); *Re Heydeshire's Application* (1993) 67 P & CR 93.

(b) Increase in density

Covenants allowed one house per acre, the proposal was to put 32 houses into four acres. It was held that this would be alien to the character of the area, "it is not merely the arithmetic of the density which matters, but the general effect on the amenity of the area", *Re Collins' Application* (1974) 30 P & CR 527.[9]

A proposal to build ten houses on backland where covenants would allow none was refused. It would otherwise result in objectors finding "dumped virtually on their back doors a group of houses with no apparent visual relationship with their own properties", *Re Patten Ltd's Application* (1975) 31 P & CR 180.

(c) Other loss of amenity

A proposed block of 12 flats would deprive the objectors of space, quiet, light and some sunlight, *Re Ward's Construction (Medway) Ltd's Application* (1973) 25 P & CR 223; another proposal would deprive objectors of "peace and quiet and the feeling of openness which the restriction gave them", *Re Davies' Application* (1971) 25 P & CR 115. Both applications failed.[10]

A local authority which had granted planning permission for six flats in a two-storey block objected validly that the block would injure the view from an old people's dwelling which they proposed to erect on the dominant land, *Re SJC Construction Co Ltd's Application* (1974) 28 P & CR 200.

Increased traffic, noise, fumes, vibration, dirt and the risk of accidents were important factors against the applicants in *Re Bass* (1973).[11]

(d) Loss of value

Loss of amenity will often cause loss of value but the fact that it does not is not a reason for holding that the covenant does not secure a practical advantage. In *Re Collins* (1974) it was not disputed that the proposed development would not reduce the market value of existing houses. Nevertheless it was accepted as important that the objectors regarded the restrictions as having substantial advantage, some having bought their houses in reliance on them. Indeed in *Re Munday's Application* (1954) 7 P & CR 130 (a claim to declare a covenant obsolete) it was likely that a successful application would increase the value of the objectors' property by giving it a potential commercial user. The claim failed however as it was clear that the personal tastes of the objectors would be adversely affected if the covenant was lifted.[12]

---

[9] *Re Diggens Application* [2001] 2 EGLR 163 (practical benefits secured by density restriction were preservation of view, privacy, seclusion and sense of spaciousness and tranquility in semi-rural atmosphere).

[10] *Re Ballamy's Application* [1977] JPL 456 ('enjoyment of evening sunshine in the sun-lounge').

[11] See also *Re Crest Homes plc's Application* (1983) 48 P & CR 309 (proposal to build twelve houses to replace neglected Edgware Lawn Tennis Club would cause undesirable increase in housing density and change area from semi-rural to urban); *Re Lake's Application* [1984] JPL 887 (proposal to erect split-level house in Lyme Regis would be design out of character with surroundings); *Re Sheehy's Application* (1992) 63 P & CR 95 (moral obligation undertaken by the St. Aubyn Discretionary Trustees to maintain a scheme of covenants within the Devonport Estate, where cost of administration exceeded total rental income, held to be of practical benefit); *Re Azfar's Application* [2002] 1 P & CR 215 (adverse impact from traffic, parking, access to neighbouring properties and unsightliness of large extension).

[12] *Re H and H Ltd's Application* [1987] JPL 452 (10% reduction in value of objectors' properties).

(e) 'Thin end of the wedge' argument

It can be a relevant consideration that the proposal, though not particularly harmful in itself, must be rejected in case it gives rise to similar proposals which would succeed because the first had done so, and which would cumulatively be disadvantageous. In *Re Gossip* (1972) the applicant had converted two houses into flats in breach of covenant and now wished to build two further houses in their gardens. He argued that there had already been some breaches of covenant by other house-owners by conversions of single houses into flats but the Tribunal considered that these breaches had been minimal whereas a modification might be the 'thin end of the wedge' for a considerable change in the amenities and character of the neighbourhood. The recent case of *Re Osborn* (1979) illustrates this consideration along with several others. The applicants wished to erect two three-storey blocks of flats on a large estate of eight-bedroomed houses. Sixty-three owners of such houses objected. It was held that if the applications were granted it would set an undesirable precedent for other developments on the estate, particularly as there was much profit in such developments. Other important considerations were that the building would be out of place in a high value, low density, single house estate; that the flats would be visually injurious there; and that the traffic noise generated by the greater numbers of people would be injurious.

The validity of the 'thin end of the wedge' argument is not universally accepted. In *Re Forgacs' Application* (1976) 32 P & CR 464, Mr J. H. Emlyn-Jones FRICS in his judgment quoted what he said in *Re Gaffney's Application* (1974) 35 P & CR 440 to the effect that if a modification is in itself unlikely to cause injury it should not be refused on the ground that later applications might do so. They should each be looked at on the merits when they arise and should then be rejected if need be. [13]

4. ARE THE BENEFITS SECURED BY THE RESTRICTIONS OF SUBSTANTIAL VALUE OR ADVANTAGE TO THE OBJECTORS?

The use of the words 'value or advantage' in harness was said by the Tribunal in *Re Bass* (1973) to indicate that pecuniary values are not the only things to be considered in this context and *Re Collins* (1974) and *Re Munday* (1954) support this. [14] However, the benefits secured must be substantial. In *Re Dransfield's Application* (1975) 31 P & CR 192 the objector, in seeking to uphold a covenant made by the applicant himself only 20 years earlier, claimed that the proposed house would obstruct the view from the rear windows of his house and from the

---

[13]   See also *Re Chapman's Application* (1980) 42 P & CR 114; *Re Farmiloe's Application* (1983) 48 P & CR 317; *Re Love's and Love's Application* (1993) 67 P & CR 101; *Re Solarfilms (Sales) Ltd's Application* (1993) 67 P & CR 110; *Re Page's Application* (1995) 71 P & CR 440; *Re Snaith and Dolding's Application* (1995) 71 P & CR 104 ('erection of this house could materially alter the context in which further applications would be considered'). *Re Churchill's Application* (1994) LP/45/94; *Re Hunt's Application* (1996) 73 P & CR 126. *McMorris v Brown* [1998] 3 WLR 971, especially at 978, per Lord COOKE of THORNDON, citing this note.

[14]   *Re Matcham's Application* [1981] JPL 431 (house built on tranquil site because of wife's severe migraine); *Re Heydeshire's Application* (1993) 67 P & CR 93 (right to build within set limit, provided no one else had done so, held not a practical benefit); *Re Willis' Application* [1997] 2 EGLR 185 (bed and breakfast accommodation wholly compatible with surrounding residential area): cf. *Re Pennington's Application* [2002] RVR 271 (bed and breakfast accommodation would result in reduction of value of adjoining properties and loss of privacy).

first floor terrace where he frequently entertained guests. It was held that the restriction which prevented building did not secure a substantial benefit to him and that £1,000 was adequate compensation in money terms. [15]

5. IS IT CONTRARY TO THE PUBLIC INTEREST TO IMPEDE THE PROPOSED USER?

In *Re Collins* (1974) the Tribunal said that for an application to succeed on the ground of public interest "it must be shown that that interest is so important and immediate as to justify the serious interference with private rights and the sanctity of contract." Applications based on this ground seem to have a high rate of failure. We will examine three of the lines of approach which have been used. [16]

(a) Shortage of accommodation

In *Re New Ideal Homes Ltd's Application* [1978] JPL 632 a covenant linked with planning permission allowed 79 houses to be build on a plot of land. The applicants asked for the covenant to be modified only four years after they had entered into it, to permit 150 houses to be built there. They claimed that the 1973/4 property collapse has made it uneconomic to build at such a low density and that the covenant was against the public interest in preventing them from satisfying the great need for housing locally. The Tribunal held that the restriction was not against the public interest merely because there was a housing need but modified it, on payment of compensation, because it did not secure practical benefits of substantial value to the objecting local authority.

Similarly in *Re Osborn* (1979) the Tribunal held that although it was government policy to encourage high density development, that did not mean that all low density development was against the public interest and that it ought to be replaced by high density development. In *Re Beardsley* (1972) an acute shortage of building land in a given area was held not of itself to prove that a restriction was contrary to the public interest; the question was to be considered in a wider context, having regard especially to the planning considerations mentioned in section 84(1B). [17]

(b) Existence of planning permission

It has been argued in several cases that where the local planning authority has granted planning permission a restriction which prevents the development from proceeding must be contrary to the public interest. That argument was firmly dealt with in *Re Bass* (1973) where the Tribunal said, "a planning permission only says, in effect, that a proposal will be allowed; it implies perhaps that such

[15] On the meaning of 'substantial' see *Re Gaffney's Application* (1974) 35 P & CR 440.
[16] *Re Lloyd's and Lloyd's Application* (1993) 66 P & CR 112 (covenant modified to permit house to be used as community care home for ten psychiatric patients: government policy favoured their rehabilitation in the community); *Re Fisher of Gimson (Builders) Ltd's Application* (1992) 65 P & CR 312 (risk of demolition of important housing accommodation against public interest; £6,000 compensation); cf. *O'Reilly's Application* (1993) 66 P & CR 485; *Re Hounslow and Ealing London Borough Council's Application* (1995) 71 P & CR 100 (part of ground floor of mansion to be used as horticultural training centre); *Re Bromor Properties Ltd's Application* (1995) 70 P & CR 569; *Re Milius's Application* (1995) 70 P & CR 427 (restriction adopted by local authority pursuant to lawful policy approved by Parliament held not contrary to public interest).
[17] *Re Beech's Application* (1990) 59 P & CR 502 (residential enclave in predominantly commercial setting).

a proposal will not be a bad thing but it does not necessarily imply that it will be positively a good thing and in the public interest, and that failure of the proposal to materialise would be positively bad. Many planning permissions have got through by the skin of their teeth".

The Tribunal will resist attempts to turn the proceedings into a planning enquiry, by the introduction of miscellaneous documents concerning the planning of the vicinity or of wider areas. In *Re Collins* (1974) it refused to consider any documents save those which had been published, subjected to public enquiry and approved by the Minister, such as the approved town map or development plan.[18]

(c) Economic advantages

In *Re Bass* (1973) it was said that the company had a need to expand its trunker park because mergers and rationalisations within the company required it to reorganise its distribution system. The Tribunal said that this was not an irrelevant factor but that it must be set against other questions, such as amenity; "the proposition that this operation is in the public interest is strange indeed unless the public interest is to be equated to the economic benefits to this particular part of the beer trade".

A case where the public interest argument succeeded was *Re SJC Construction Co Ltd* (1975). Here £47,000 worth of building work on flats had been done with planning permission from the local authority when the same authority issued a writ to enforce restrictive covenants which would have prevented the building of the flats. Modification of the covenant to permit them to be built

---

[18]   See also *Re Beecham Group Ltd's Application* (1980) 41 P & CR 369 (refusal to differ from 'very carefully reasoned decision' of Secretary of State granting planning permission on appeal from inspector); *Gilbert v Spoor* [1983] Ch 27, [1982] 2 All ER 576 ('The subsection does not make planning decisions decisive', per EVELEIGH LJ at 34, at 581). *Re Hextall's Application* (2000) 79 P & CR 382 (planning permission is strongly persuasive); *Re Diggens Application (No 2)* [2001] 2 EGLR 163.

Under TCPA 1990, s. 106 (replacing TCPA 1971, s. 52, a local authority has power to regulate land use by agreement. Such an agreement is within LP (Miscellaneous Provisions Act 1989, s. 2; p. 67, ante. *Jelson Ltd v Derby County Council* [1999] 3 EGLR 91; [1999] Conv 379 (J.E.A.). See Current Law Statutes TCPA 1990, s. 106, annotated by M. Grant, paras. 8.299 to 8.302.

The authority is said to hold the benefit of the covenant as 'custodian of the public interest': *Re Abbey Homesteads (Developments) Ltd's Application* [1986] 1 EGLR 24; *Re Martin's Application* (1988) 57 P & CR 119, especially at 125, p. 1012, post, per FOX LJ; *Re Houdret & Co Ltd's Application* (1989) 58 P & CR 310; *Re Jones' and White & Co's Application* (1989) 58 P & CR 512; *Re Quartley's Application* (1989) 58 P & CR 518; *Re Beech's Application* (1989), supra; [1990] Conv 455 (N. D. M. Parry); *Re Wallace's Application* (1993) 66 P & CR 124; *Re Hopcraft's Application* (1993) 66 P & CR 475 (storage of touring caravans refused); *Re Bromor Properties Ltd's Application* (1995) 70 P & CR 569. *J. A. Pye (Oxford) Ltd v South Gloucestershire District Council* [2001] EGCS 47. For successful modifications, see *Re Cox's Application* (1985) 51 P & CR 335; *Re Towner's and Goddard's Application* (1989) 58 P & CR 316 (tennis-court with chain link fencing); *Re Barclays Bank plc's Application* (1990) 60 P & CR 354 (discharge in favour of mortgagee); *Re Poulton's Application* (1992) 65 P & CR 319 (extension of bungalow in Metropolitan Green Belt); *Re O'Reilly's Application* (1993) 66 P & CR 485 (user for car parking modified only to allow erection of six houses on payment of £11,000 compensation); *Re Williamson's Application* (1994) 68 P & CR 384 (granny annexe as a separate dwelling); *Re Bewick's Application* (1996) 73 P & CR 240; *Re Caton's Application* [1999] 3 EGLR 121 (change in planning policy did not render restriction obsolete).

was allowed because: planning permission existed, the adverse effect on the dominant land would not be serious, there was a scarcity of building land in the area, the work already done would otherwise have been wasted, the applicants had gone ahead in good faith, and substantial compensation would be paid by them.

6 AND 7. WOULD MONEY BE AN ADEQUATE COMPENSATION TO THE OBJECTOR?

It was emphasised by Lord Evershed MR in *Ghey and Galton's Application* [1957] 2 QB 650 that section 84 does not enable the court to expropriate objectors merely because an applicant may have put forward a worthy enterprise (in that case a proposal to turn a large house into a convalescent home). When modification is allowed money, in some cases coupled with a restriction on the development, must be capable of being an adequate compensation.

In *Re Carter* (1973) views of the sea from four dominant houses would have been impaired by a proposed bungalow. Sums of £200, £200 and £100 were awarded to three owners but nothing to the fourth as his loss was too small to be compensated. In addition an offer by the applicant to excavate so as to make the bungalow roof 2½ feet lower than originally intended was accepted and was made a condition of the modification order. *Re Banks Application* (1976) 33 P & CR 138 is a similar case but there compensation of £2,000 was ordered to be paid to each objector before the development was begun. In *Re Patten Ltd's Application* (1975) 31 P & CR 180 a proposed development of ten houses which would have caused overcrowding was allowed on payment of up to £750 compensation to objectors and the reduction of the number of houses to seven. [19]

It might be thought that all compensation payments must in the nature of things be modest because large awards would indicate that the application should have been refused. This is not necessarily so. In *Re New Ideal Homes* (1978) an agreed sum of £51,000 was awarded, representing the reduction in purchase money which had been allowed because of the covenant when it was imposed. By section 84(1) the Tribunal can award compensation either (*a*) for the loss or disadvantage suffered from the discharge or modification or (*b*) for making up for any effect the restriction had when it was imposed in reducing the consideration then received for the burdened land. In the *SJC Construction* case (1975) compensation was awarded so as to share the development value of the burdened land equally between the applicant and the objector. This decision purported to follow in principle *Wrotham Park Estate Co v Parkside Homes Ltd* (1973) 27 P & CR 296 where the compensation was calculated by taking 5 per cent of the profit made by the developer who had broken a layout covenant.

---

[19]   See also *Re Edwards' Application* (1983) 47 P & CR 458 (restriction modified to enable house in Mold, North Wales, to be used as a general village store, for 'groceries, sweets, tobacco, cigarettes, cigars, soft drinks, ice cream, newspapers, trinkets, haberdashery, gardening utensils and supplies, tools, nuts and bolts', subject to payment of £500 as compensation to objector for loss of amenity); *Re Shah and Shah's Application* (1991) 62 P & CR 450 (restriction impeding nursing home user so small as to warrant monetary compensation only of £23,000); *Re Cornick's Application* (1994) 69 P & CR 726 (jam factory).

The basis of the award in the *SJC* case was upheld on appeal at (1975) 29 P & CR 322.' [20]

In **Re Martin's Application** (1988) 57 P & CR 119, Fox LJ said at 125:

'In my view, the applicants' contention is wrong in so far as it suggests that the granting of planning permission by the Secretary of State necessarily involves the result that the Lands Tribunal must discharge the covenant. The granting of planning permission is, it seems to me, merely a circumstance which the Lands Tribunal can and should take into account when exercising its jurisdiction under section 84. To give the grant of planning permission a wider effect is, I think, destructive of the express statutory jurisdiction conferred by section 84. It is for the Tribunal to make up its own mind whether the requirements of section 84 are satisfied. All the facts of the case have to be examined by the Lands Tribunal. There is nothing in the Town and Country Planning Acts 1962 or 1971 [1] which suggests that these are intended to interfere in any way with the jurisdiction of the Lands Tribunal under section 84.'

V. Public Planning Control [2]

Tulk v Moxhay was decided in 1848 and the doctrine to which it gave rise was one of the bases for control of land use by private landowners during the suburban expansion of the 19th century. Together with leasehold and reciprocal positive freehold covenants (and, to a lesser extent, easements), it is fundamental to all private planning. Such private control can however only have a limited effect. It can only be effective where a landowner is in control of a considerable area of undeveloped land, and has the foresight to devise a suitable system of obligations at a time when demand for the development of that land is beginning to be felt—when that land is 'ripe for development'. It also requires constant vigilance and determination to enforce the covenants over an indefinite period of time at the discretion of a succession of private owners who are not in any way responsible to the public, legally or politically, for ensuring that the policy is carried out or even that the controls actually imposed are desirable. And so, in spite of the many excellent schemes of residential development carried out under freehold and leasehold covenants in the more spacious suburbs of many large and small towns,

---

[20]   *Re London Borough of Islington's Application* [1986] JPL 214 (covenant forbidding use of land in Islington 'except for open space', purchased from Greater London Council who remitted half of the purchase price, discharged on repayment of that half with adjustments for inflation).

Loss of bargaining power is not a proper head of compensation: *Stockport Metropolitan Borough Council Alwiyah Developments* (1986) 52 P & CR 278; *Re Bennett's and Tamarlin Ltd's Application* (1987) 54 P & CR 378 (loss of ability to extract money for agreeing to modification of restriction not a benefit); cf *Re Quaffers Ltd's Application* (1988) 56 P & CR 142 (loss of competition advantage). *Re Jillas' Application* [2000] 23 EG 147; (covenant modified to allow for extension of house; £10,000 compensation with adjustment for inflation); (2000) 150 NLJ 1523 (H. W. Wilkinson; *Re Davies' Application* [2001] 1 EGLR 111 (£2,000).

[1]   Or 1990.

[2]   C & B, pp. 1021–1066; M & W, paras. 22.009–22.061; MM, pp. 569–580.

including seaside resorts, spas and 'garden cities,'[3] a system of public control of the use and development of land had to be introduced.

The principal planning statute, which consolidates the previous statutes from the Town and Country Planning Acts of 1947 onwards, is the Town and Country Planning Act 1990. Under it planning control is administered by a system of central and local authorities. The central authority is now the Department of the Environment, Food and Rural Affairs. The Secretary of State for that Department does not usually administer planning control directly; but appeals are made to him from decisions of local planning authorities and he has the power to 'call in' applications from them for decision at first instance. Detailed administration is in the hands of the local planning authorities, which are county and district councils. The former are 'county planning authorities', concerned chiefly with strategic matters; the latter are 'district planning authorities', concerned normally with the routine business of planning control. In Greater London; the Metropolitan Counties and unitary council areas, there is a one-tier system i.e., a single local planning authority for each

Private planning thus co-exists side by side with the public control of the use and development of land. A purchaser of land must not only satisfy himself about the existence of private covenants that may bind the land which he is buying, but he must also investigate its planning aspect.

In 1979 the Royal Commission on Legal Services put forward the idea that all, or nearly all, existing and future restrictive covenants should become totally unenforceable except as between the original parties. In 1984 the Law Commission rejected this view.

Law Commission Report on The Law of Positive and Restrictive Covenants 1984 (Law Com No 127, HC 201), paras. 2.5–2.7.

'2.5 Planning law may overlap to some extent with restrictive covenants, but we do not believe that it has removed the need for them. Perhaps especially in residential property developments, restrictive covenants commonly regulate many things for which planning law would not cater—and do so for the mutual benefit of the residents and with the aim of preserving the character and standard of the development as a whole. Nor does it seem to us that these things are confined, as the Royal Commission suggested they might be, to matters affecting privacy. Powerful support for this view is to be found in this extract from the preface to the sixth edition of *Preston & Newsom's Restrictive Covenants Affecting Freehold Land*:

"One thing that is abundantly plain is that there is no prospect whatever that restrictive covenants will become unnecessary and that their place will be taken by the planning laws. For planning standards are still too often below the standards imposed by restrictive covenants. Thus in *Re Bass Ltd's Application*[4] the Lands Tribunal held that the suggested modification would inflict upon the persons

---

[3]   See Burke, *Towns in the Making* (1971).
[4]   (1973) 26 P & CR 156. There have been other cases in which the Lands Tribunal has refused to modify covenants so as to allow development for which planning permission has already been obtained – e.g., *Re M Howard (Mitcham) Ltd's Application* (1956) 7 P & CR 219; *Re Sloggetts (Properties) Ltd's Application* (1952) 7 P & CR 78. See pp. 1009, 1012, ante.

entitled to the benefit of the restriction noise, fumes, vibrations, dirt and the risk of accidents: these proposals had received planning permission. Again, in the *Wrotham Park* case [1974] 1 WLR 798, [1974] 2 All ER 321 it was the local authority itself which, having bought the land for a very small sum, put it up for sale and received £90,000 on the basis that it was to be built upon, thereby destroying an open space which the owners of surrounding houses valued and which had been deliberately created by the original covenantee."

It is also true that certain changes of use and building operations to which an adjoining resident might reasonably and justifiably object do not require planning permission at all.

2.6 It might perhaps be argued that the answer lies not in preserving the power to impose private restrictions but in extending the ambit of planning law. We think it unrealistic, however, to expect planning authorities to concern themselves with all the detailed matters for which restrictive covenants now commonly make provision. Indeed a Past President of the Royal Town Planning Institute[5] has expressed the view that: "It puts planning authorities under unreasonable pressure if they are expected to safeguard the interests of adjoining owners." It must also be remembered that restrictive covenants may be used to serve purposes which are private and individual and for which planning law would not cater however far it was extended.

2.7 It must also be remembered that planning restrictions, even if they are wholly adequate to the needs of adjoining owners, are enforceable only by the planning authorities. Most owners would wish to have the power of enforcement in their own hands.'

The statutes on Town and Country Planning[6] and Compulsory Purchase and Compensation of Land[7] and books dealing with them must be consulted before a working knowledge of the law of control of land can be obtained; but lack of space forbids their treatment here.[8]

---

[5]   Sir John Boynton, in an address in 1978 to a joint conference of The Law Society, the Bar Council and the Royal Institution of Chartered Surveyors.

[6]   Town and Country Planning Act 1990; Planning (Listed Buildings and Conservation Areas) Act 1990; Planning (Hazardous Substances) Act 1990; Planning (Consequential Provisions) Act 1990; Planning and Compensation Act 1991, Part I; Planning and Compulsory Purchase Act 2004. P(Parts 1 to 7). *Butterworths Planning Law Handbook*; *Encyclopedia of Planning Law and Practice*; McAuslan, *Land, Law and Planning* (1975); Telling and Duxbury, *Planning Law and Procedure* (12th edn. 2002).

[7]   Compulsory Purchase Act 1965; Acquisition of Land Act 1981; Compulsory Purchase (Vesting Declarations) Act 1980; Land Compensation Acts 1961 and 1973; Planning and Compensation Act 1991, Part III; Planning and Compulsory Purchase Act 2004 (Part 8). On the compatibility of planning law and compulsory purchase with the Human Rights Act 1998, see Rook, *Property Law and Human Rights*, pp. 233–246; *Encyclopedia of Compulsory Purchase and Compensation*; Davies, *Law of Compulsory Purchase and Compensation* (5th edn.); Denyer-Green, *Law of Compulsory Purchase and Compensation* (4th edn). The most recent legislation, the Act of 2004, supra, is largely concerned with regional planning and special strategy, with a variety of statutory amendments on detailed matters.

For proposed reform of compulsory purchase, see Law Commission Consultation Papers in 2002: Towards a Compulsory Purchase Code: (1) Compensation (Law Com No. 165); (2) Procedure (Law Com No. 169), which are the bases for Law Commission Reports on Towards a Compulsory Purchase Code (1) (2003) (Law Com No. 286) and (2), which is to be published in 2004.

[8]   See C & B, chaps. 29 and 30.

VI. Law Reform

A. Land Obligations

The Law Commission Report on the Law of Positive and Restrictive Covenants 1984 (Law Com No. 127) recommends a comprehensive reform of the law relating to covenants affecting freehold land.[9] It takes as its model the existing law of easements (paras. 4.21–4.36; 37.1 (1)).

The reforms proposed should enable obligations, whether restrictive or positive in nature, to run with the benefited and the burdened land so as to be directly enforceable by and against the current owners of each. They should also be such as to cater not only for the simple case of an obligation created between two neighbouring landowners, but also for the more complex needs of property developments (including those involving freehold flats).

In outline the main recommendations are:

(1) There should be a new interest in land, to be known as a Land Obligation (paras. 5.2; 27.1(2)).

The Land Obligation should be one of two types.

(a) The neighbour obligation (paras. 6.2–6.16; 27.1(3)–(6)) This is to be used where the obligation is imposed on one plot for the benefit of another plot. It can take one of three forms: a restrictive obligation; a positive obligation, which requires either the carrying out of works or the provision of services for the dominant land; and a reciprocal payment obligation, which requires the making of payments for expenditure incurred by a person who carries out a positive covenant, e.g. paying half the cost when the neighbour is under a covenant to repair the boundary fence.

(b) The development obligation (paras. 4.29–4.36; 27.1(7)–(11)) This is to be used where an area of land is to be divided into separately owned but inter-dependent units, such as a housing development or a block of flats. This obligation is to be of a necessarily wider scope than the neighbour obligation and it is to be capable of enforcement not only by owners of other parts of the development but also by a manager acting on their behalf, such as an estate agent, a management company or a residents' association.

(2) The development obligation can take the form of a restrictive or of a positive or of a reciprocal payment obligation. It can also require the servient land to be used in a particular way which benefits the whole or part of the development (such as to provide shopping facilities there), and to require payment to a manager for expenditure incurred in performing his functions under the development scheme.

(3) The Land Obligation may be either legal or equitable. To be legal, it must be created by deed, and be equivalent to an estate in fee simple absolute in

---

[9] For earlier Reports, see Wilberforce Committee on Positive Covenants 1965 (Cmnd 2719); Law Commission on Restrictive Covenants 1967 (Law Com No. 11) and its Working Paper on Rights Appurtenant to Land 1971 (No. 36); Benson Committee on Legal Services 1979 (Cmnd 7648); Second Report of the Conveyancing Committee: Conveyancing Simplifications 1985, paras. 4.52–4.57, 7.21–7.22. See also [1984] JPL 222, 317, 401, 485 (S. B. Odell); 134 NLJ 459, 481 (H. W. Wilkinson); (1984) 47 MLR 566 (P. Polden).

See A New Property Law Act, drafted by the Law Commission of New Zealand (Law Com Report No. 29) which proposes that the burden of both negative and positive covenants should run with the land if they relate to the subject matter of the land and are noted on the register; [1994] Conv 428 (H. W. Wilkinson).

possession or to a term of years absolute. If it is created in writing or if it is created for any other interest, such as for life, it will be equitable.

In either case, the obligation must be stated to be a Land Obligation, in order to distinguish it from an easement or similar right. The rule against perpetuities will not apply. (paras 27.1(12)–(20).)

(4) The person who enters into the Land Obligation will cease to be subject to it when he has disposed of the land. His liability under the doctrine of privity of contract to the covenantee will end and there will thus be no point in the creation of a chain of indemnity covenants. (paras. 11.32–11.34.)

(5) Land Obligations, whether legal or equitable, will be registrable as a new type of Class C land charge under the Land Charges Act 1972, in the case of unregistered land. In the case of registered land, they will be noted in the dominant and servient titles, and will not be overriding interests under section 70 of the Land Registration Act 1925. (Part IX; paras. 27.1.(21)–(23).)

(6) The new scheme will only apply to Land Obligations created after it comes into force. There will thus be three different schemes for covenants affecting freehold land; those created before 1926; those created after 1925 and those under the new scheme. (Part XXIV; paras. 27.1.(93)–(101).)

B. Obsolete Restrictive Covenants

The Law Commission, in its Report on Obsolete Restrictive Covenants in 1991, (Law Com No. 201) makes proposals to phase out most existing restrictive covenants after the introduction of the Land Obligations scheme envisaged in its Report on the Law of Positive and Restrictive Covenants.

The main proposal is that all restrictive covenants should automatically lapse 80 years after they were first created, but anyone entitled to the benefit of a covenant which was not then obsolete would have the right to replace it with a Land Obligation to the like effect. It would be up to him to take positive action to replace it; failure to do so would involve the automatic lapse of the covenant. A five year period of grace would be allowed for assessing restrictions which are already more than 80 years old.

The recommendations on the Development Obligation are otiose as a result of the Commonhold and Leasehold Reform Act 2002, p. 938, ante.

The Law Commission is conducting a full review of the law of easements, analogous rights and land obligations and hopes to publish a consultation paper during 2005.

'The object is to produce a coherent scheme of land obligations and easements that is compatible with the Land Registration Act 2002 and the commonhold system.': Law Commission Annual Report 2003/04 (Law Com No. 289), paras. 7.5–7.8.

Index

1017